Fromm

D0181394

New Zealand
4th Edition

by Adrienne Rewi

Here's what the critics say about Frommer's:

"Amazingly easy to use. Very portable, very complete."

—*Booklist*

"Detailed, accurate, and easy-to-read information for all price ranges."
—*Glamour Magazine*

"Hotel information is close to encyclopedic."

—*Des Moines Sunday Register*

"Frommer's Guides have a way of giving you a real feel for a place."
—*Knight Ridder Newspapers*

WILEY
Wiley Publishing, Inc.

About the Author

Adrienne Rewi is a Christchurch-based freelance photojournalist who writes regularly for more than 20 New Zealand and overseas publications, covering most subject areas. She is the author of three nonfiction book titles: *Architects at Home: 30 New Zealand Architects in Their Own Homes; Fine Cheese: Gourmet Cheesemaking in New Zealand;* and *Private Views: Interviews with 20 New Zealand Gardeners.* Adrienne has also worked as a photojournalist in several Asian countries and also writes fiction.

Published by:

Wiley Publishing, Inc.

111 River St.
Hoboken, NJ 07030-5774

ISBN-13: 978-0-471-74700-0
ISBN-10: 0-471-74700-9

Editor: Jennifer Anmuth
Production Editor: Katie Robinson
Cartographer: Elizabeth Puhl
Photo Editor: Richard Fox
Production by Wiley Indianapolis Composition Services
Front cover photo: Fiordland National Park: Giant's Gate Falls, Milford Track, people on bridge admiring view.
Back cover photo: Otago: Moeraki Boulders.

For information on our other products and services or to obtain technical support, please contact our Customer Care Department within the U.S. at 800/762-2974, outside the U.S. at 317/572-3993 or fax 317/572-4002.

Wiley also publishes its books in a variety of electronic formats. Some content that appears in print may not be available in electronic formats.

Manufactured in the United States of America

5   4   3   2   1

Contents

List of Maps

An Invitation to the Reader

In researching this book, we discovered many wonderful places—hotels, restaurants, shops, and more. We're sure you'll find others. Please tell us about them, so we can share the information with your fellow travelers in upcoming editions. If you were disappointed with a recommendation, we'd love to know that, too. Please write to:

Frommer's New Zealand, 4th Edition
Wiley Publishing, Inc. • 111 River St. • Hoboken, NJ 07030-5774

An Additional Note

Please be advised that travel information is subject to change at any time—and this is especially true of prices. We therefore suggest that you write or call ahead for confirmation when making your travel plans. The authors, editors, and publisher cannot be held responsible for the experiences of readers while traveling. Your safety is important to us, however, so we encourage you to stay alert and be aware of your surroundings. Keep a close eye on cameras, purses, and wallets, all favorite targets of thieves and pickpockets.

Other Great Guides for Your Trip:

Frommer's Adventure Guide to Australia & New Zealand
Frommer's Australia
Frommer's Portable Australia's Great Barrier Reef
Frommer's Southeast Asia
Frommer's South Pacific

Frommer's Star Ratings, Icons & Abbreviations

Every hotel, restaurant, and attraction listing in this guide has been ranked for quality, value, service, amenities, and special features using a **star-rating system.** In country, state, and regional guides, we also rate towns and regions to help you narrow down your choices and budget your time accordingly. Hotels and restaurants are rated on a scale of zero (recommended) to three stars (exceptional). Attractions, shopping, nightlife, towns, and regions are rated according to the following scale: zero stars (recommended), one star (highly recommended), two stars (very highly recommended), and three stars (must-see).

In addition to the star-rating system, we also use **seven feature icons** that point you to the great deals, in-the-know advice, and unique experiences that separate travelers from tourists. Throughout the book, look for:

Finds	Special finds—those places only insiders know about
Fun Fact	Fun facts—details that make travelers more informed and their trips more fun
Kids	Best bets for kids and advice for the whole family
Moments	Special moments—those experiences that memories are made of
Overrated	Places or experiences not worth your time or money
Tips	Insider tips—great ways to save time and money
Value	Great values—where to get the best deals

The following **abbreviations** are used for credit cards:

AE	American Express	DISC	Discover	V	Visa
DC	Diners Club	MC	MasterCard		

Frommers.com

Now that you have the guidebook to a great trip, visit our website at **www.frommers.com** for travel information on more than 3,000 destinations. With features updated regularly, we give you instant access to the most current trip-planning information available. At Frommers.com, you'll also find the best prices on airfares, accommodations, and car rentals—and you can even book travel online through our travel booking partners. At Frommers.com, you'll also find the following:

- Online updates to our most popular guidebooks
- Vacation sweepstakes and contest giveaways
- Newsletter highlighting the hottest travel trends
- Online travel message boards with featured travel discussions

What's New in New Zealand

New Zealand has had a booming 2 years in tourism. Overseas visitors continue to arrive in droves, emptying their wallets along the way—spending by tourists in 2003 grew to a record NZ$7.4 billion (US$5.2 billion), with those in the industry shrugging off threats of an overvalued Kiwi dollar, terrorism, and SARS. That said, my travels for this edition revealed a huge number of accommodations up for sale, so don't be surprised if you arrive at one of the recommended places to stay and find that "Bob and Sue" have changed into "Tom and Betty." Here's what else is new in New Zealand.

AUCKLAND The Sheraton Hotel has rebranded under new ownership and is now **Langham Hotel Auckland,** 83 Symonds St. (© **09/379-5132).** Across town, look out for the classy environs of the brand-new **SKYCITY Grand Hotel,** 90 Federal St. (© **09/363-7000),** which is linked to the greater SKYCITY complex by an overbridge. The hotel features one of Auckland's poshest new restaurants, **DINE,** and the new **East West Day Spa.**

New attractions have sprung up in the Auckland area, including **Snowplanet,** 91 Small Rd., Silverdale (© **09/427-0044),** an all-year indoor snow resort; and **Butterfly Creek,** Tom Pearce Drive (© **09/275-8880),** which features large butterfly houses, a train ride, and farm animals. **Tamaki Hikoi** (© **0800/282-5526** in NZ) is a new 4-hour walking tour across Auckland City that includes Maori stories and legends. **Kelly Tarlton's Antarctic**

Encounter & Underwater World, 23 Tamaki Dr. (© **09/528-0603),** is undergoing a NZ$12-million (US$8.4-million) refurbishment over the next 4 years. Stage 2 includes the newly opened Stingray Bay, which lets you get up close and personal with these large, winged marine creatures. See chapter 5 for complete details.

ROTORUA, TAUPO & TONGARIRO NATIONAL PARK Classy new accommodations are popping up all around Rotorua, led by the sublime **Okareka Lake House** (© **07/349-8123),** billed as one of the top five luxury lodges in New Zealand. **Lodge @ 199,** 199 Spencer Rd., Lake Tarawera (© **07/362-8122),** is another luxury stay; and **Duxton Hotel,** 366 St. Hwy. 33, Okawa Bay (© **07/362-4599),** has swept a classy broom across the former Okawa Bay Resort.

At **Rainbow Springs,** Fairy Springs Road (© **07/350-0440),** you'll find the new Kiwi Encounter attraction, celebrating the conservation of our rare iconic bird; **Realm of Tane,** 1220 Hinemaru St. (© **07/346-2823),** is a new Tamaki Heritage experience. One of New Zealand's top tourism icons took on a new name when the **New Zealand Maori Arts & Crafts Institute** (© **07/348-9047)** rebranded as **Te Puia.**

In Taupo, **Taupo Hot Springs Spa,** 102 Napier-Taupo Hwy. (© **07/377-6502),** continues with its ongoing refurbishments; while on the hilltop above, **Outrigger Terraces Resort** (© **07/378-7080)** has undergone a major overhaul and with the development of 80 new suites to be completed by late 2006, it will provide some of Taupo's top hotel accommodations. **Acacia Point Lodge,** 11 Sylvia Place, Acacia Bay, meanwhile, has closed down.

At Whakapapa in Tongariro National Park, millions have been spent at **The Grand Chateau,** Whakapapa Village (© **07/892-3809**), on a massive refurbishment of the existing hotel, including the development of a new 40-room wing and an atrium restaurant. With the final stages to be completed in the next 2 years, it's looking much better already.

See chapter 8 for complete details.

WELLINGTON The **Interislander** (© **0800/802-802** in NZ), has commissioned its new ferry, *Kaitaki,* giving them a fleet of three interisland ferries running between Picton and Wellington. But **The Lynx** fast ferry has ceased operation altogether.

Wellington Zoo, 200 Daniell St., Newton (© **04/381-6755**), has introduced new Red Panda Encounters, plus other interactive zookeeping activities for visitors. **Zest Food Tours** (© **04/801-9198**) is a new walking gourmet food experience in central city, and **Café Bastille,** 16 Majoribanks St. (© **04/382-9559**), is a new restaurant that has scooped national restaurant awards. Also look out for the very classy wine room, **Arbitrageur,** 125 Featherston St. (© **04/499-5530**).

The brand-new **Bolton Hotel,** at the corner of Bolton and Mowbray streets (© **04/472-9966**), features classy apartment-style accommodations. I've found some good new B&Bs in the capital as well: **Gardens Homestay,** 11 St. Mary St., Thorndon (© **04/499-1212**); **Rawhiti,** 40 Rawhiti Terrace, Kelburn (© **04/934-4859**); and **Mount Victoria Homestay,** 11 Lipman St., Mount Victoria (© **04/802-4886**).

See chapter 11 for complete details.

MARLBOROUGH & NELSON In Nelson, the **Monaco Hotel,** 6 Point Rd. (© **03/547-8233**), has opened its cool, English country village–style hotel, offering a wide range of room styles; **Angela's Little Retreat,** 22 Nile St. (© **03/545-1411**), is the modern sister of the highly sought-after Little Manor a few doors away. Also look out for the classic style of the new **Consulate Apartments,** 353 Trafalgar Sq. (© **03/545-8200**). A new attraction getting lots of attention is **Exhilarator,** Wakefield Quay, Nelson (© **03/548-8066**), now the fastest boat ride across the bay to Abel Tasman National Park.

See chapter 12 for complete details.

CHRISTCHURCH & CANTERBURY **Huntley House,** 67 Yaldhurst Rd., Upper Riccarton (© **03/348-8435**), is the newest upmarket addition to Christchurch's accommodations scene. Talk of several proposed new hotels—expected to open in the next 2 to 3 years—includes a NZ\$20-million (US\$14-million) luxury hotel, **Mercure Grand by Accor** at 152 Oxford Terrace; a new **Accor Ibis Hotel** in Cathedral Square; and an **Accor Novotel** in central city. Russley Golf Course, near the airport, is also planning construction of the **Russley International Colosseum.**

There's an exciting new inner city development happening in an old lane and first to open is the swanky restaurant, **Minx Dining Room and Rootes Bar,** 96 Lichfield St. (© **03/374-9944**). In another year, the lane will feature several other restaurants, bars, cafes, and boutique stores.

See chapter 13 for complete details.

QUEENSTOWN & ENVIRONS Additions to Queenstown accommodations include the brand-new luxurious **Sofitel,** 8 Duke St. (© **03/450-0045**), which opened in September 2005, and the very classy, small boutique hotel, **The Spire,** 3–5 Church Lane (© **03/441-0004**), which combines a Zen essence with high-tech convenience. And look out for the newly refurbished rooms of one of the town's old favorite small, midrange boutique properties, **The Dairy,** 10 Isle St. (© **03/442-5164**).

Getting to Queenstown from Australia is now even easier, due to **Qantas's** announcement of an extension to its Queenstown services. It now offers year-round service for the first time, with a weekly flight from Sydney.

See chapter 15 for complete details.

1

The Best of New Zealand

Back in 1979, New Zealand cartoonist and satirist Tom Scott, writing in *NZ Listener* magazine, had this to say about New Zealand: "Terrible tragedy in the South Seas. Three million people trapped alive."

The big news in 2003 was that we hit the four million population mark, and more than half of that increase was due to immigration. Given that we have around 44 million sheep, one New Zealander still equates to a whole lot of fresh lamb. Look beyond the farm gate, though, and you'll find we've caught up with the rest of the world. We may bob about at the bottom of the Southern Hemisphere, but it would be unfair to consider the country a backwater.

New Zealand has notched up a record year in tourism, welcoming more than two million visitors a year for the first time, despite international upheavals like terrorist attacks and SARS. Visitors contributed more than NZ$5 billion to the country's economy, making tourism one of New Zealand's biggest overseas income earners. And we're better equipped for tourists. Efficient visitor centers abound, and accommodations range from budget to exclusive. You can shop 7 days a week, whoop it up at clubs and bars 24 hours a day, or savor a glass of internationally recognized New Zealand wine in an inexpensive cafe. You can get real coffee in as many variations as you can imagine, and New Zealand's fresh, innovative cuisine will leave you breathless and begging for more.

Even provincial New Zealand has pulled up its socks without losing its heart. Small-town pride is beaming, and farmers are turning their hands to boutique tour operations and gorgeous restored B&Bs to supplement farm incomes, changing the whole nature of many backwater rural districts. Yet you'll still find, at its core, the very Kiwi hospitality that has made this country famous.

You may have heard that New Zealanders are born wearing wet suits and carrying paddles, such is their appetite for the outdoors and adventure. No part of the country is more than 128km (79 miles) from the sea, and a coastline spread with splendid beaches dishes up thousands of beautiful coastal walks and chances to surf and soak in the sun.

New Zealand is also a winter magnet for international skiers and is the white-knuckle capital of the world. This is where you can push it to the limits, pit yourself against your fears and limitations, take risk by the throat, and go for it—leaping off bridges into surging river gorges attached to a giant rubber band, or taking a stab at luging, zorbing, sky diving, paragliding, kayaking, white-water rafting, and jet-boating. There's no lack of invention when it comes to adrenaline-pumping activities in this country.

But you don't have to be an extreme athlete to enjoy New Zealand. There are just as many ways to be laid-back and indulgent—tour wineries that have stampeded their way to the top of world ratings in record time; take in the wealth of Polynesian and Maori culture that forms the backbone of an increasingly multicultural society; or check out the strong historic and architectural reminders of a colonial past. There are lush gardens, art galleries, museums, and plenty of one-off reminders that New Zealand is like no other place.

I was born in New Zealand and despite frequent trips overseas, I can't shake off the inherent sense of belonging here. This book presents "my" New Zealand. After many months traveling thousands of miles, testing mattresses, comparing prices, leaping off cliff tops (well, almost), speeding up rivers, and eating and drinking in far too many restaurants, I am more convinced than ever that New Zealand is one of the quirkiest, quaintest, craziest places on earth. It's one of the most favored destinations of the new millennium, and before you've even left here, you'll want to come back. Dip into these pages, and you'll see why.

1 The Best Beaches

- **Waiheke Island's Onetangi Bay:** Stand on the bay's wide stretch of golden sand, and you can see for miles. On a clear day, throw yourself down into the sand and gaze at the steep pinnacles of Great Barrier Island and Little Barrier, off in the hazy distance. There might even be a few glimpses of the Coromandel in between deliciously warm swims. See "A Side Trip to Waiheke Island" in chapter 5.

- **Karikari Peninsula's Beaches:** This is the Far North at its subtropical best—endless sweeps of sparkling white sand lapped by crystal-clear, azure-blue waters. And from Tokerau Beach to Rangiputa to Matai Bay, you could have miles of it to yourself for beach-combing, sunbathing, and swimming (with care). See "Bay of Islands & the Far North" in chapter 6.

- **Coopers Beach:** Partly shaded by a bank of red-emblazoned pohutukawa trees, how could you not be content to stretch out here? Exercise? A walk to the water should do it! See "Bay of Islands & the Far North" in chapter 6.

- **Hot Water Beach:** Don't ask me why, or how, but if you get here 2 hours before or after low tide, you can hollow out a spot on the beach for yourself, then wait for natural hot water to seep up through the sand. A natural spa experience without paying a cent!

See "The Coromandel Peninsula" in chapter 6.

- **Mount Maunganui's Ocean Beach:** Surf, sand, and sun—some people never want more than that. Throw on a bit of suntan lotion, a pair of sunglasses, and a skimpy swimsuit, and you'll be able to mix it with the best of the bronzed bodies that make an annual pilgrimage to this perennial beach and surf favorite. See "Tauranga & Bay of Plenty" in chapter 7.

- **Kaiteriteri Beach:** Half of Canterbury makes a beeline for these blissful shores every summer. It's not expansive—in fact it's quite small, but perfectly formed nonetheless, and there's a busy vacation atmosphere with packed campgrounds and holiday houses. And with Nelson's endless hours of sunshine, who could complain about size? See "Nelson, Richmond & Motueka" in chapter 12.

- **Abel Tasman National Park's Beaches:** Bush-wrapped and locked between rocky headlands, these idyllic golden patches from Marahau north to Totaranui are accessible by sea only. That's what makes them so special. Gliding through the turquoise waters in your sea kayak, with curious seals to keep you company, you can take your pick of isolated havens. See "Abel Tasman National Park & Golden Bay" in chapter 12.

2 The Best Active Vacations

- **Scuba Diving in the Poor Knights:** Jacques Yves Cousteau rated this among the best diving spots in the world. This unique marine reserve has the best of tropical currents sweeping in to make it warm and inviting for a wide variety of tropical species that aren't found anywhere else in New Zealand's waters. See "Into the Deep Blue Sea" on p. 173.

- **Blackwater Rafting in the Waitomo Glowworm Caves:** Daredevils can now go underground to leap off waterfalls; slink through dark, damp, underground waterways; abseil off Lost World rock faces; and do other things in the dark. See "Hamilton & the Waikato" in chapter 7.

- **Trout Fishing in Taupo:** They say the fish in Lake Taupo are so big that when you catch one, the lake level drops. The dozens of other rivers (especially world-renowned Tongariro) and streams in the region also have rich pickings for the fisherman. See "Taupo" in chapter 8.

- **Sea Kayaking in Abel Tasman National Park:** It takes a lot to beat this balmy little paddle into the best-preserved and most beautiful coastline of New Zealand. Keep company with nosy seal pups and dolphins; call into pristine, deserted beaches; and explore rocky headlands. See "Abel Tasman National Park & Golden Bay" in chapter 12.

- **Walking the Glaciers:** Dig out those snow boots and walking poles, add a dash of nerve and daring, and take the walk of a lifetime down Fox or Franz Josef glaciers in the deep south. And don't forget your camera so you can bring home those unforgettable views into the snow caves. See "Franz Josef & Fox Glaciers" in chapter 14.

- **Getting Wild in Queenstown:** This is New Zealand's adrenaline capital, where you get more than one chance to show how crazy you really are. There are more daredevil stunts per square inch here than anywhere else in the country. An international skiing mecca in winter, it readily transforms itself into summer madness as well. See "Queenstown" in chapter 15.

- **Walking the Fiordland Tracks:** If you fancy yourself as a multiday tramper, there's plenty to keep you out of mischief in Fiordland. This is where you get some of the best walks in the world—the Milford, the Hollyford, the Kepler, and the Routeburn tracks. See "Tramping" in chapter 3 and "Te Anau" in chapter 15.

3 The Best of Natural New Zealand

- **Ninety Mile Beach and Cape Reinga:** From the spiritual tip of the North Island where, Maori say, the souls of the dead depart, to mountainous sand dunes, quicksand, and the broad flat stretch of Ninety Mile Beach, this is a must-see area filled with the unexpected. See "Bay of Islands & the Far North" in chapter 6.

- **Waiotapu Thermal Wonderland:** The earth's molten core hints at its artistic potential in a veritable rainbow of color and steamy chaos manifested in geysers, mud pools, hot bubbling lakes, steamy terraces, and more. A photographer's paradise, but tread carefully. See "Bubble, Bubble, Toil & Trouble: The Geothermal Attractions" on p. 210.

- **Tongariro National Park:** Three major volcanoes dominate a rugged central plateau landscape: Ruapehu, Tongariro, and Ngauruhoe. An indomitable threesome, they're rife with

Maori legend and rich in a few modern stories as well. Great for skiers, trampers, and anyone wanting a physical challenge. See "Tongariro National Park" in chapter 8.

- **Fox and Franz Josef Glaciers:** This is one of the very few places on earth where you'll find full-fledged glaciers this close to the ocean. In a slow, ever-onward creep, they make their way from the heights of the Southern Alps down into untouched rainforest. See "Franz Josef & Fox Glaciers" in chapter 14.

- **Fiordland:** Come here on a wet day (and that's easy because this place gets the most rainfall in New Zealand), and you'll think you've stepped into the living set of *Lord of the Rings*. This place defies all superlatives. It is the ultimate must-see. See "Te Anau" in chapter 15.

- **The Catlins Coast:** This is wild, natural New Zealand at its unspoiled best. From unique fossil forests to all manner of seabirds and mammals, native bush, waterfalls, wild beaches, unforgettable tangles of driftwood, and a frustratingly changeable climate—the area takes a lot of beating, but the resulting dramatic impact is unforgettable. See "Dunedin" in chapter 16.

- **Ulva Island:** Tucked into Stewart Island's Paterson Inlet, tiny Ulva Island will leave you speechless with its incredible native bird life. It's wall-to-wall feathers here—and what's more, they're not afraid of humans. Don't go without your camera; you'll need evidence once you start telling friends back home about it. See "Stewart Island" in chapter 16.

4 The Best Tramps

For details, see "Tramping" in chapter 3.

- **Tongariro Crossing:** Often described as one of the best 1-day walks in New Zealand, this high-altitude hike across volcanic terrain will give you cold mountain springs, lava flows, an active crater, emerald-colored crater lakes, and unforgettable views. Be fit and enthusiastic. See "Tongariro National Park" in 8.

- **The Abel Tasman Coastal Track:** This is an easy 3- to 5-day walk where the guided option gives you the choice of ditching those hefty packs. From start to finish, 51km (32 miles) later, it winds in and out of gorgeous sheltered coves, golden beaches, rocky headlands, and natural unspoiled bush. See "Abel Tasman National Park & Golden Bay" in chapter 12.

- **The Heaphy Track:** No softy-guided options here: You go it alone for 4 to 6 days from the junction of the Brown and Aorere rivers, across tussock-covered flats to the wild seas of Karamea on the West Coast. See "Westport & Karamea" in chapter 14.

- **The Milford Track:** The mother of them all, the Milford is one of the world's best and most loved multiday tramps. Stretching through the best of Fiordland, this 54km (33-mile) trail follows the Clinton and Arthur valleys and crosses McKinnon Pass with views you'll never forget. See "Te Anau" in chapter 15.

- **The Routeburn Track:** Like the Milford and the Hollyford before it, this track makes its way into virgin rainforest and the sort of wild fairyland scenery where you'd expect to see elves and gnomes prancing around. See "Queenstown" in chapter 15.

- **The North West Circuit:** This is a real test for experienced trampers who think they can face 10 to 12 days walking 125km (78 miles) through bird-filled native bush, big beaches, and long stretches knee-deep in mud. I'm told the rewards are plenty. See "Stewart Island" in chapter 16.

5 The Best Offbeat Travel Experiences

- **Visit the World's Biggest Polynesian Market:** Why go all around the Pacific Islands when you can get the best of it in the comfort of an Otara parking lot? Go hungry and feast on island goodies, smell the smells, and buy beautiful tapa cloth and top-notch Polynesian weaving. See "The Markets" in chapter 5.

- **Swim with Sharks:** You've got to be keen, I admit, but this can be done in perfect safety. Along with those charming, perfectly harmless tropical fish in the Poor Knights Maritime Reserve, you can come face to face with *Jaws's* South Seas cousins in a tough metal cage. Gisborne offers a similar knuckle-biting thrill. See "Into the Deep Blue Sea" on p. 173 and "Gisborne & the East Cape" in chapter 9.

- **Visit a Maori Marae:** Experience the *hongi* (the formal nose-to-nose Maori greeting), see deeply moving song and dance performances, and eat from a traditional underground *hangi* (oven). Do this in Rotorua as part of an organized tour experience, or seek permission to visit one of the dozens of East Cape *marae* (village common). See "Rotorua" in chapter 8 and "Gisborne & the East Cape" in chapter 9.

- **Take the East Cape Road:** Journey back in time as you travel the last remote outreaches of the Pacific Coast Highway. It's a feast of living Maori culture, stunning coastline, empty beaches, stockmen herding sheep on horseback, wild horses, and roaming stock (drive carefully)—and it's the first place in the world to see the morning sun. See "Gisborne & the East Cape" in chapter 9.

- **Do the Eastern Bays Scenic Mail Run:** Get a feel for real rural New Zealand as you whiz around lonely, unpaved roads delivering mail to far-flung farming families. Hear all the latest community news firsthand and see some stunning landscapes in the bargain. See "On the Run" on p. 385.

- **Whale-Watch in Kaikoura:** When a mighty sperm whale flaps its tail at you, you won't forget it in a hurry. These big sea monsters come to this particular stretch of water for a marine habitat rich in their kind of plankton. Don't be surprised to see dolphins aplenty, too. See "Marine Experiences in Kaikoura" on p. 391.

- **Eat Bugs and Beetles at the Wildfoods Festival:** Prime yourself! You'll need culinary fortitude for this mind-boggling event—you could be served up anything from wriggling grubs to the unmentionable body parts of a number of wild and not-so-wild animals. The West Coast at its most rugged best. See "Hokitika: Greenstone, Glowworms & Gold" in chapter 14.

- **Drive into Skippers Canyon:** Relive the pioneer days as you make your way into one of the hottest old gold-mining areas via a treacherous road guaranteed to take your mind off any other troubles you thought you had! Take a bungy jump while you're here—if you dare. One thing's for sure—it couldn't be any worse than the road. See "Queenstown" in chapter 15.

- **Stalk Kiwis at Night:** And I mean the birds! Get ready for surprises on this little southern adventure. It's the only place in the country where you can creep about lonely beaches at night with flashlights and stealth and not get arrested! At the same time, you'll be one of the lucky few who get to see a wild kiwi foraging for its supper among the seaweed. See "Making a Date with a Kiwi" on p. 500.

6 The Best Views

- **Sky Tower:** The paramount city view in not only New Zealand, but also the entire Southern Hemisphere. Once you get out of that glass-faced lift, 328m (over 1,000 ft.) above the city, you'll know just what I mean. Fabulous 360-degree views of Auckland unfold below, and you can test your courage by walking over glass floors! See p. 125.

- **Hicks Bay:** Stop at the high point above Hicks Bay before you descend into Te Araroa to see New Zealand's largest pohutukawa tree and the East Cape Lighthouse. Resting awhile, high up between the two bays, see if you can imagine Captain Cook's expression when he first sighted the area, and his relief to be leaving again after a tragic Maori massacre in which one European was killed and eaten on his wedding night. See "Gisborne & the East Cape" in chapter 9.

- **Hastings's Te Mata Peak:** A big "sleeping giant" of a hill, 393m (1,289-ft.) Te Mata affords big views of endless green and brown undulations, reaching all the way to the coast. Havelock North, Hastings, and Napier all blend together below. See "Hawkes Bay" in chapter 9.

- **Wellington's Kelburn Cable Car:** Not so far above the capital's busy shopping streets, you'll be rewarded with postcard-perfect vistas of glass-faced high-rises silhouetted against the harbor. Step off the cute red cable car into the verdant acres of the Botanical Gardens and look seaward. No matter what the weather, the view is always memorable. See p. 295.

- **Queenstown's Skyline Gondola:** It's everybody's aim to get high in Queenstown one way or another. Make yours by way of a smooth gondola ride to the top of Bob's Peak. Step out into the cool, crisp, exceedingly fresh air with New Zealand's playground spread out at your feet. The Remarkables will keep the view in check, and Lake Wakatipu will be a big blue basin below. See "Queenstown" in chapter 15.

- **Nugget Point:** You may not have seen another human being for hours by the time you make your way to the lookout above Nugget Point. And once you've experienced the blissful solitude of standing on this wild, windswept Catlins promontory, you probably won't care if you don't see anyone for several more. Thick, swirling masses of kelp, seals, penguins, and seabirds galore—they're all here by the hundreds. See "Dunedin" in chapter 16.

7 The Best Drives

- **Auckland City to Mission Bay:** This is the stuff of a weekend afternoon spin to see how the other half lives. Best done in a Ferrari, a BMW, an Audi, or an equally cool classic if you want to leave a lasting impression. Tight shorts and in-line skates do the trick just as well if you want a cheaper set of wheels. Do the cafe crawl; join the walkers, the runners, and the dog strollers; or just drool over million-dollar real estate. See "Orientation" in chapter 5.

- **Rotorua's Blue and Green Lakes:** From the stately redwood forest on the edge of town, all the way past the Blue and Green lakes to the Buried Village and Lake Tarawera and back again, you'll squeal with delight at a dozen different things. There are lots of picnic spots on the way, but the Landing Café at Lake Tarawera is a good bet if you forget the hamper. See "Rotorua" in chapter 8.
- **The Capital to Mellow Martinborough:** Once you've left the motorways behind, you'll be up and over the winding Rimutaka Hill Road in little more than 40 minutes. Then it's downhill all the way to Martinborough's enchanting pocket of prize-winning wineries. Surrender to hedonism and squander time in idyllic vineyard settings. Make the only exercise you do raising your glass, or at most a wee stroll through pretty little Martinborough Village, where cute shops await. See "A Side Trip to Wairarapa" in chapter 11.
- **Queen Charlotte Sound:** Take the scenic loop from Picton to the little fishing village of Havelock and back to Picton on the main highway. Stop and admire the bush-clad sounds and the boats, and indulge in fresh green-lipped mussels grown in these very waters at The Mussel Boys restaurant, in Havelock. It's a narrow winding road around the Sounds, so take it quietly. See "Picton & Blenheim" in chapter 12.
- **Greymouth to Westport:** Pretty, pretty, pretty! Nikau palms, native bush, tree ferns, jagged rocks, roaring surf, and the big blue Tasman Sea combine to make this a lovely half-day outing. Be sure to stop at the famous Punakaiki Pancake Rocks, where blowholes have a spectacular hissy fit as the ocean roars into, under, and around rocky caverns on the coast. See "Westport & Karamea" in chapter 14.
- **The Famous Milford Road:** Even the Wanaka-Haast road can't match the splendor of this one. It's been called one of the best drives in the world, and no amount of raving can do it justice. You really have to experience it. Virgin rainforest, mirrorlike lakes, astounding waterfalls (especially during rain), beech forest, mountains of moss, bright orange lichens, and sheer mountain faces thousands of feet high contribute to the overall picture—not to mention the slightly daunting Homer Tunnel. See "Milford Sound" in chapter 15.

8 The Best Gardens

- **Hamilton Gardens:** Stretched along the banks of the Waikato River, this blissful, relatively new 58-hectare (143-acre) reserve is a lovely place to wander and picnic. Development began around 30 years ago; there's now a well-established Asian garden, English garden, herb and scented gardens, and lavish stands of trees. See "Hamilton & the Waikato" in chapter 7.
- **Eastwoodhill Arboretum:** One of the most magical places in the country, hardly a garden by normal standards, this astounding collection—the best in New Zealand—is one man's life's work and presents over 3,500 species often studied by international scientists. Go in autumn for unforgettable color displays—and bring a camera. See "Gisborne & the East Cape" in chapter 9.
- **Pukeiti Rhododendron Trust:** Here you get a world-class collection of rhododendrons, viraya, and azaleas

set in a centuries-old forest near Mount Egmont—our little Mount Fuji. The gardens spread over many acres in a lovely rural setting 30 minutes from New Plymouth. See "New Plymouth: Gateway to Egmont National Park" in chapter 10.

- **Christchurch's Botanic Gardens:** Regardless of the season, this central-city acreage has plenty to offer, but it's quintessentially Christchurch when the daffodils and bluebells bloom under the huge oak trees along the Avon River and avenues of weeping cherries burst into color. This is when people think of England. See p. 366.
- **Mona Vale:** This little beauty is often overlooked in favor of the city's Botanical Gardens, but it has an intimate charm all its own. Spreading out around a stately Victorian home, these public gardens have myriad lovely features, including iris collections along stream banks, fountains,

hostas by the yard, and that old favorite, the rose, which does so well in Canterbury. See "Exploring Christchurch" in chapter 13.

- **Ohinetahi:** If you're a garden fan, this is a must. Formal, architectural, and stately are all words that instantly spring to mind. Definitely English-inspired and modeled after the best of England's stately gardens, with quirky New Zealand modifications. See "Exploring Christchurch" in chapter 13.
- **Taunton Gardens:** Another Canterbury treat near Ohinetahi. This one is the result of Barry Sligh's ceaseless passion for plants, in particular hostas and rhododendrons. He collects, he breeds, he grows, he tends, he rakes, he weeds, and he still has time to talk gardening. You'll love the lush valley he has developed. See "Exploring Christchurch" in chapter 13.

9 The Best Museums

- **Auckland Museum:** After a very significant internal revamp, this museum is everything you'd want in a city's storehouse of treasures: fun, interactive, attractive, informative, and filled with interesting collections. Its Maori and Polynesian section, the biggest in the world, sends shivers down your spine; if you've got kids, let them loose in the Discovery Centre, where they can legally stick their fingers into just about anything. See p. 125.
- **New Zealand National Maritime Museum:** At the pinnacle of New Zealand's boating history—with the America's Cup Challenge right in our backyard—the Maritime Museum is booming. Look for *KZ1* outside, and inside discover 1,000 years of the country's maritime history. See sail makers, boat builders, and wood-turners at

work and take a cruise on one of the vessels. See p. 128.

- **Museum of New Zealand–Te Papa Tongarewa:** One of the largest national museums in the world, this giant new edifice on Wellington's waterfront is said to be 5 years ahead of anything else like it. Truly bicultural, it's a magical place where art and artifacts meet technological brilliance, creating riveting displays and interactive playthings for all ages. You'll find everything from a whale skeleton and a working Maori marae to art collections and virtual-reality diversions. See p. 294.
- **Canterbury Museum and the International Antarctic Centre:** Although these two museums are completely separate entities located miles apart, together they present a terrific

overview of life and history in Antarctica. Nowhere else in the world will you find this much gathered information about the great icy continent. There's everything from wildlife displays to human exploration accounts and a real ice chamber so you can get the feel of life in subzero temperatures. See p. 365 and p. 366.

10 The Best Maori Experiences

- **Auckland Museum:** This is the perfect place for an early lesson in things Maori. The recently revamped museum has the largest collection of Maori artifacts in the world. Large war canoes, meetinghouses, greenstone weapons, and feather cloaks are here. On top of that, the Manaia Maori Performance Group puts on a stunning show three times a day. See p. 125.
- **Te Puia's Whakarewarewa Thermal Reserve and New Zealand Maori Arts & Crafts Institute:** Maori guides will lead you through the thermal reserve, explaining the significance of the area to the Maori people. There's also a live song-and-dance performance, a tour of a replica Maori village, and the chance to watch working weavers and carvers in the Arts & Crafts Institute, which was set up in 1963 to foster traditional craft skills. See p. 204.
- **Tamaki Maori Village:** This re-created ancient Maori village was the New Zealand Tourism Awards Supreme winner in 1998. It presents Maori life as it used to be pre-European settlement. You'll tour the village with a Maori elder, learn the ancient myths, watch a traditional performance, and eat from a traditional hangi. See "Rotorua" in chapter 8.
- **Royal Lakeside Novotel:** Here you'll find the best Maori hangi and performance in Rotorua. It includes a steam-cooked hangi, *poi* dance, *haka* dance, traditional songs and games, and an excellent audiovisual presentation spanning 150 years of Rotorua's history. See "Rotorua" in chapter 8.
- **East Cape:** This is a remote enclave of Maori culture—one of the last places in New Zealand where the Maori language is part of everyday life. You'll find more than 100 marae scattered along the length of the East Cape Road, and if you ask permission, in most cases you'll be allowed to enter. There are numerous Maori settlements and highly decorative Maori churches. See "Gisborne & the East Cape" in chapter 9.

11 The Best B&Bs

- **Peace & Plenty Inn** (Devonport; ✆ 09/445-2925): Judy Machin's floral-themed home is an extravagant, romantic, and peaceful haven that will soothe all of your senses. English style meets Kiwi hospitality in a grand way here. See p. 116.
- **Villa Toscana** (Whitianga; ✆ 07/866-2293): Sit yourself high on a hill, on Giorgio and Margherita Allemano's stone terraces overlooking one of the finest beaches in New Zealand and try to tell me that you haven't landed in paradise. You'll be seduced with fine food, wine, humor, and hospitality, and you won't want to leave. See p. 183.
- **298 Oriental Bay** (Wellington; ✆ 04/384-4990): Nothing, and I mean nothing, is too much trouble for Susan

Bilbie when it comes to ensuring her guests are happy. Factor in a home on prime capital real estate, and you have a real winner. This is an exquisite property that deserves all the superlatives. See p. 287.

- **Grampian Villa** (Nelson; ℰ 03/545-8209): John and Jo Fitzwater are first-rate hosts and their grand old villa entices with big rooms and luscious finishes. As owners of a national motorcycle tour company, they know just what their guests are looking for and they deliver. See p. 333.
- **Teichelmann's** (Hokitika; ℰ 03/755-8232): Owners have come and gone at this well-established West Coaster, but Brian Ward and Frances Flanagan have really stamped it with the style it deserves. What's more, they've kept their prices at a sane level, ensuring value for money. It's an historic gem in the center of town. See p. 409.
- **Mahara** (Dunedin; ℰ 03/467-5811): As pretty as an iced wedding cake, Mahara sits high above Dunedin ready to indulge your every whim. Graham and Rosie are great hosts and their rooms will win you over in a second—especially the Annie Lees. See p. 482.
- **Maison de la Mer** (Akaroa; ℰ 03/304-8907): If you want to know how a top B&B should be run, visit the experts. Bruce and Carol Hyland have hosted over 12,000 guests during their tenure in the hospitality industry, and their new Akaroa venture is as luscious as their last. You'd be silly to miss it. See p. 384.

12 The Best Luxury Accommodations

- **Kauri Cliffs** (Kerikeri; ℰ 09/405-1900): I could find no fault whatsoever with this sublime northern retreat. It is, as the saying goes, "heaven on a stick," and I'm not even a golfer! The staff here were some of the friendliest in the country and the rooms—especially the bathrooms—are my idea of true luxury. See p. 168.
- **Eagles Nest** (Russell; ℰ 09/403-8333): Combine the very best of international taste with the magic of Northland's subtropical environment and a rich vein of natural energy, and you get a luxury retreat quite unlike any other in New Zealand. Daniel and Sandie Biskind have created a world-class retreat worthy of anyone's prolonged attention. See p. 167.
- **Huka Lodge** (Taupo; ℰ 07/378-5791): Exclusivity reigns supreme at this Small Luxury Hotels of the World member. International awards bounce off the walls, and guests invariably comment on rooms fit for kings. It has a supreme location beside the Waikato River just above the Huka Falls and a reputation for quality and service that seems impossible to shake. See p. 226.
- **Treetops Lodge** (Rotorua; ℰ 07/333-2066): My expectations may never be the same again after staying at Treetops. Being spoiled with one of the most gorgeous suites in the country tends to have that effect. Set in a unique native bush environment, it's a true sanctuary that will lower your heart rate within minutes of arriving. See p. 214.
- **Paratiho Farms** (Motueka; ℰ 03/528-2100): Americans Robert and Sally Hunt found their slice of paradise in an archetypal New Zealand setting—rolling green hills, big clear skies, balmy climate, endless peace and quiet. Now they're sharing the sublimely luxurious lodge they have created here. The attention to detail surpasses almost everything else in New Zealand. Don't miss it. See p. 334.

- **Eichardt's Private Hotel** (Queenstown; ℂ **03/441-0450**): This new Small Luxury Hotels of the World member has received glowing accolades in Andrew Harper's *Hideaway Report*, and it's becoming the hotel of choice for discerning, upscale travelers. In a remodeled historic building in central Queenstown, it oozes first-class style and understated glamour. It remains one of my favorites. See p. 445.

- **Blanket Bay** (Queenstown; ℂ **03/442-9442**): If you want luxury on a grand scale in a majestic setting to match, look no further than Blanket Bay. These gorgeous stone buildings marry so completely with the awesome landscape, it seems as if they were always here. Inside, you'll find an outstanding level of service and comfort. What more could you want? See p. 452.

13 The Best Boutique Hotels & Small Lodges

- **Te Whau Lodge** (Waiheke Island; ℂ **09/372-2288**): Every time I visit Te Whau I'm convinced all over again that Gene O'Neill and Liz Eglinton give you the best of everything—winning personalities, fabulous food, great rooms, and views you won't believe. There's something quintessentially Kiwi about the whole experience that I'm proud to recommend. See p. 149.

- **Ridge Country Retreat** (Tauranga; ℂ **07/542-1301**): The generosity and style of rooms here leave many more expensive stays in the shade. Joanne O'Keeffe and Penny Oxnam were some of the best (and funniest) hosts on my latest road trip, and I'm confident your expectations will be exceeded at every level. The food is divine! See p. 198.

- **White Swan Country Hotel** (Greytown; ℂ **06/304-8894**): Every room here is a delicious surprise—from an exotic touch of India and the restrained elegance of the Chinese boudoir to classic romance and contemporary coolness. I love them all. It's a classy, unexpected gem in rural Wairarapa with an excellent restaurant to boot. See p. 310.

- **Hapuku Lodge** (Kaikoura; ℂ **03/319-6559**): This has got to be *the* best-value, classy lodge in New Zealand. American Tony Wilson has poured good taste and top comfort into big rooms filled with exquisite handcrafted furniture and art. It's an unbeatable value and one of my top picks for something unique and memorable. See p. 390.

- **Huntley House** (Christchurch; ℂ **03/348-8435**): This brand-new boutique hotel has its toes firmly cemented in one of Christchurch's grand old homes, with new apartments built to look as if they've always been there. It's uncompromisingly extravagant and a masterful blend of old-world charm with modern conveniences. See p. 357.

- **The Spire** (Queenstown; ℂ **03/441-0004**): The brochure says it all: "an inspirationally urbane hotel where style, design, and technology blend seamlessly." This new boutique hotel is seriously gorgeous—contemporary without being clinical; luxurious without being over the top. Indulge yourself in its intimate cocoon. See p. 446.

- **Fiordland Lodge** (Te Anau; ℂ **03/249-7832**): Ron and Robynne Peacock have taken a mix of native timbers and Oregon pine, added local river boulders, and created a lodge that will knock your socks off. The internal architecture is of a *huge* scale—which, I suppose, is only fair when you have to compete with some of the most impressive landscapes in the country—and rooms are filled with lovely creative touches. See p. 462.

14 The Best Restaurants

- **White** (Auckland; ✆ **09/978-2000**): Named for its stunning minimal all-white interior, White is the handiwork of celebrated consulting chef Luke Mangan, who owns the award-winning restaurant Salt in Sydney. Its best feature is The Table, a big informal table for diners who like the idea of mixing with others over an outstanding meal. See "Where to Dine" in chapter 5.

- **Otto's** (Auckland; ✆ **09/300-9595**): This is posh-plush, professionalism-plus. Located in the delicious Ascott Metropolis Hotel, Otto's emphasizes the "fine" in fine dining and has staff that delivers the goods in terms of service and style. Just make sure you've swallowed your last mouthful before you catch your breath at the bill. See "Where to Dine" in chapter 5.

- **Dine by Peter Gordon** (Auckland; ✆ **09/363-7030**): The latest rave on the Auckland culinary scene, this lush little spot is the new playground of London/NZ celebrity chef Peter Gordon. Set in the new SKYCITY Grand Hotel, it's bound to stimulate every taste bud you own. See p. 119.

- **Café Bastille** (Wellington; ✆ **04/382-9559**): This cute little French bistro-style den is a winner if you're after a smart but casual ambience with terrific food. A winner in the Best Restaurant of New Zealand stakes, it shouldn't be bypassed. See p. 293.

- **Herzog** (Blenheim; ✆ **03/572-8770**): Expect the very best from this winery and restaurant that has been held up by New York's *Wine Spectator* for its impressive stock of around 3,200 of the world's best wines. It's a fine dining experience you won't forget in a hurry. See p. 321.

- **Rotherams** (Christchurch; ✆ **03/341-5142**): Swiss-born chef Martin Weiss has mastered the art of stunning his hungry patrons. In an interior that's all about romance and special occasions, he presents meals that excel in both presentation and taste. Not to be missed—likewise the extensive wine list. See p. 362.

- **The Bunker** (Queenstown; ✆ **03/441-8030**): Don't start celebrating until you've actually found it and are sitting at one of its tables! Notoriously hard to find (that's part of its charm), and expensive when you get there, this hidden culinary jewel delivers on all the superlatives it receives. Make sure you hunt it down. See p. 454.

15 The Best Shopping

- **Auckland:** The whole city is a treasure trove of shops. Try the chic fashion and design shops of High Street; international designer duty-free at DFS Galleria Customhouse; upmarket boutiques in Parnell; antiques on Manukau Road; mainstream fashion in Newmarket; big mall shopping at St. Luke's Shopping Centre; and fabulous specialty shops on K'Road and Ponsonby Road. See "Shopping" in chapter 5.

- **Rotorua:** A rich vein of New Zealand souvenirs runs right through the whole city, but for the best Maori arts and crafts, look to Tamaki Maori Village. See "Rotorua" in chapter 8.

- **Wellington:** The Old Bank Building on Lambton Quay has only added to the electric atmosphere of this capital shopping area. Wander the length of the Quay for fashion, books, shoes, and more; move up through Willis Street for more of the same, and into Cuba Mall for edgy design stores and off-the-wall retail surprises. Check out Tinakori Road for a handsome cluster of boutiques. See "Shopping" in chapter 11.

- **Nelson:** Long recognized as the best region for leisure crafts shopping, greater Nelson is dotted with hundreds of pottery studios. Find international-quality art glass at Höglund Art Glass Studio and a mixed complex of crafts at Craft Habitat. See "Nelson, Richmond & Motueka" in chapter 12.

- **Christchurch:** The Arts Centre Galleria is home to about 40 crafts stores selling a wide range of goods, from sheepskin products and leather to wood-turned bowls and ceramics.

More turn up for the weekend Arts Centre Market. Also in Christchurch, check out High Street for an eclectic mix of antiques, secondhand stores, cafes, and new and old clothing boutiques; Cashel Mall for fashion and design stores; Victoria Street for a whole host of new boutique stores; and Merivale Mall for upmarket fashion and specialty shops. See "Shopping" in chapter 13.

- **Hokitika and Greymouth:** Jade/greenstone/*pounamu* and gold are found in abundance in these two West Coast towns. Stores specializing in both are found side by side in both Hokitika and Greymouth. See "Greymouth & Lake Brunner" and "Hokitika: Greenstone, Glowworms & Gold" in chapter 14.

- **Queenstown:** This is the home of expensive shopping. You'll find that most things have big price tags, but the quality is invariably tops. There are leading New Zealand and international clothing labels, sheepskin products, souvenirs, leather, original arts and crafts, and masses of jewelry. See "Queenstown" in chapter 15.

2

Planning Your Trip
to New Zealand

With so much to see and do, it's easy to feel overwhelmed and unsure about where to start your New Zealand holiday. I'm here to help—in the pages that follow, you'll find a comprehensive appraisal of each of the regions, designed to help you isolate areas of interest. Hot on the tail of that, you'll find all the nitty-gritty for organizing your big South Seas excursion.

1 The Regions in Brief

THE NORTH ISLAND

AUCKLAND ✺✺✺ Far too often overlooked as little more than a landing port, Auckland has first-rate attractions, quality accommodations, and diverse leisure opportunities. It is without doubt the most cosmopolitan of the cities, and its balmy climate has a special appeal. Waitemata Harbour and Hauraki Gulf offer some of the world's finest sailing, boating, and fishing, and in the aftermath of the 2002–03 America's Cup yachting challenge, many quality hotels, bars, and restaurants are thriving. Cultural offerings abound in museums, galleries, and performing-arts centers; and shopping is the most diverse in the country. There are more than 900 restaurants and a wild nightlife scene, and if you're into a beach lifestyle, there are numerous choices within easy reach. You may think it's just another big city, but Auckland has a Polynesian backbone that makes it quite unique. If you're touring only the North Island, Auckland is a perfect base.

NORTHLAND ✺✺✺ **& COROMAN-DEL** ✺✺ Both are within easy reach of Auckland and can be tackled as a day trip if you're short on time. However, each warrants at least a couple of days' exploration; if you have to choose between the two, I'd definitely swing up to the far north.

Northland is served by a far better infrastructure in terms of transportation, hotels, and restaurants, and its beach attractions (on the east coast) are too numerous to itemize. That said, you'll find far more tourists here, too, at least in the Bay of Islands area. Head north, though, and a whole world of unpopulated beaches awaits. Fishing, diving, boating, and camping are all big draws. The area's rich Maori culture is also an excellent introduction to New Zealand's history.

The Coromandel Peninsula is a slightly more rugged version of Northland. It has a craggier coastline, a more remote landscape, and sections with very poor roads. Accommodations are middling to say the least (with a few exceptions). Still, there's color and character here, and it's long been a favorite with New Zealand campers and beach bunnies—especially the eastern side of the peninsula, where you'll find some top surf beaches.

WAIKATO ✈ & BAY OF PLENTY ✈✈
I spent my childhood in the Waikato, but I find little to recommend for the visitor. Hamilton is trying its hardest, and it would be fair to say that it suffers from being in Auckland's shadow. The Waitomo Caves have traditionally been the area's biggest attraction, and although their natural splendor is undeniable, I find Waitomo a rather depressing place—a strange hive of tourist buses, darting in and out of otherwise undisturbed farmland.

The Bay of Plenty, on the other hand, has come of age. Tauranga and Mount Maunganui have always been hot spots. Again, the emphasis is on a beach lifestyle—boating, fishing, surfing, sunbathing, and golf are the main attractions— and some stunning accommodations are available. If you've been to Australia's Gold Coast, you'll sense a hint of that style here.

ROTORUA ✈✈✈, TAUPO ✈ & TONGARIRO NATIONAL PARK ✈✈
Rotorua is on almost every visitor's hit list. Some would say that makes the area objectionably touristy. I don't agree. Rotorua has spent millions refining its attractions and accommodations, of which there are many, and it offers a unique geographic and Maori cultural slice of New Zealand life. In terms of adventure tourism, it is biting at the heels of Queenstown.

Taupo and Tongariro National Park, in combination with Rotorua, make the whole central region an unbeatable value in terms of volcanic landscape and adventure variety. And the area is plenty big enough to avoid being bothered by others. (It's away from key attractions.) Come here for volcanic and Maori attractions, the world's best trout fishing, mountaineering, skiing (water and snow), mountain biking, and tramping.

GISBORNE ✈✈ & HAWKES BAY ✈✈✈
This is one of the most underrated areas of the country. East Cape and Gisborne offer a rare insight into Maori culture, free of tourist hype. The area has amazing beaches and world-class surfing conditions, and, in combination with Hawkes Bay, is probably the country's most important wine-producing region. In terms of accommodations, Gisborne is definitely lacking, and its laid-back rural approach doesn't always find favor with visitors. Hawkes Bay, on the other hand, has the best range of boutique B&Bs and cottages in the country. Napier's Art Deco charms are legendary and definitely worthy of inspection.

TARANAKI ✈ & WANGANUI ✈   Let's put it this way—if you want the best of small-town, provincial New Zealand, this is it. I'm most drawn to Taranaki. New Plymouth is surprisingly vibrant in its own right, and you can't help but feel that, stuck out here on its own western limb, it couldn't care less about the rest of the country. Mount Egmont and the sea are big attractions for trampers and surfers, and the region's gardens are stunning. And Tom Cruise seemed to like the area when he was filming *The Last Samurai*. Wanganui has a major asset in its river, but it needs to spruce up accommodations.

WELLINGTON ✈✈✈   The capital has come alive in almost every aspect. The Museum of New Zealand–Te Papa Tongarewa is, of course, a major attraction and has been built with style and flair. Once you have explored it, you will understand more clearly much of what you have seen, or are about to see, throughout the country. Wellington is also home to several national cultural companies, so you'll find a rich performing arts program. In addition, its restaurant, nightlife, and shopping opportunities are many and varied.

And don't overlook the vineyard and craft delights of the **Wairarapa ✈✈✈**, where you'll find the biggest selection of stunning rural cottages in New Zealand.

North Island at a Glance

THE SOUTH ISLAND

NELSON ✹✹✹ & MARLBOROUGH ✹✹

The best year-round climate in New Zealand can be found here. Characterized by three stunning national parks and gorgeous beaches, Nelson is often talked about with a mix of derision and envy for its alternative, slightly hippie/artsy communities. A top region to visit if you're into arts and crafts and outdoor pursuits. And for oenophiles, there's a growing pocket of wineries that, in combination with the Marlborough wine region, make it a must-see destination. Both areas have some superb B&Bs, homestays, and backpacker accommodations.

CHRISTCHURCH & CANTERBURY ✹✹✹

After Auckland, Christchurch is the second major destination for overseas tourists. Quite apart from the fact that it's the primary starting point for South Island exploration, Christchurch is loved for its fine Victorian-Gothic architecture, its hints of old England, and its increasingly vibrant city lifestyle. It has several ski fields within a 2-hour drive, good surfing beaches, and over 35 wineries. Day trips to Hanmer, Kaikoura, Akaroa, and Methven are all popular, but each of them warrants a longer stay.

WEST COAST ✹✹ & THE GLACIERS ✹✹✹

The top of the West Coast, from Westport north to Karamea, and the south, from Haast to the glaciers, are quite remarkable. It's just a pity about the middle bit. Apart from greenstone shopping and the crazy Hokitika Wildfoods Festival, I can never find much to recommend in the central part of the West Coast. But I will concede that it has played a vigorous and important role in shaping New Zealand's history and economy, and you certainly won't find anything quite like it elsewhere.

QUEENSTOWN & ENVIRONS ✹✹✹

For sheer physical impact, this southwestern portion of New Zealand is utterly unbeatable. It's easy to understand why everyone flocks here at least once. Don't be put off by this nonsense about Queenstown being "too touristy." It's a recognized international tourist resort, for goodness sake, so of course there will be lots of tourists! It has a long-standing reputation for being a work-hard, play-hard, party-hard sort of a place, and as far as I'm concerned, the more the merrier.

Milford Sound ✹✹✹ is another matter entirely. It is simply stunning, but the excessive number of buses (over 50 a day) is quite disgusting and should be reduced to make it a better experience for everyone. It is a remote wilderness area, but it's hard to sense that with 3,000 other people standing around looking at the same mountain peak!

Wanaka ✹✹ has a much more low-key personality than Queenstown. It makes a beautiful stopover between Queenstown and the West Coast. You'll find some stunning lodges and B&Bs here.

DUNEDIN ✹✹, SOUTHLAND ✹ & STEWART ISLAND ✹✹

Invercargill and Southland are sleepy, slow, incredibly friendly, and very, very green, but not that well prepared for the visitor. Dunedin is simply gorgeous, very Gothic, and in winter, very grim. But as a summer destination, it's lovely and has lots to offer the wildlife lover. Get out onto Otago Peninsula and be prepared to have your breath taken away. It also has some handsome B&B and lodge-style accommodations in the most amazing old houses.

Farther south, the Catlins Coast and Stewart Island are remarkably unspoiled by anything—especially tourism. I'm almost loath to mention either for fear of instigating a mass influx of visitors, but good old Kiwi pride gets in the way, and I can't help boasting about these two truly magical destinations.

South Island at a Glance

Area of detail

Auckland

NORTH ISLAND

SOUTH ISLAND

Wellington

Christchurch

Dunedin

New Plymouth

Cape Egmont   45   Mt. Egmont 2518 m

Egmont National Park

Wanganui

NORTH ISLAND

40° S

Abel Tasman Nat'l Park

Tasman Bay   Marlborough Sounds

Kahurangi National Park   Motueka

Nelson

Picton

Karamea   61   WELLINGTON

Blenheim

Cook Strait

T a s m a n

S e a

Westport   69   63

Nelson Lakes National Park   65

KAIKOURA MTS.   1

Paparoa Nat'l Park   Reefton

Hanmer Forest Park

SOUTH ISLAND

Greymouth   7

Hokitika

Hanmer Springs   1

Arthur's Pass National Park

72   Kaiapoi

Christchurch

Franz Josef Glacier

Fox Glacier   Mt. Cook Nat'l Park   Methven   75   Akaroa

Westland National Park   Mt. Cook 3754 m

Lake Tekapo

6   Lake Pukaki   8   Lake Tekapo   Ashburton

Haast

Mount Aspiring National Park   Twizel   Timaru

Lake Wanaka   *Canterbury Bight*

Milford Sound   Lake Wanaka   83   45° S

Wanaka

Doubtful Sound   89   Cromwell   Oamaru

Queenstown   85

Fiordland   Lake Te Anau   Alexandra   1

National   Lake Wakatipu   Palmerston

Park   Te Anau   8

GARVIE MTNS.   Dunedin

Lake Manapouri   Roxburgh   Milton

94   PACIFIC

96   Gore   1   OCEAN

99   1

Invercargill

Foveaux Strait

Oban

Stewart Island

0   100 mi

0   100 km

N

2 Visitor Information

To get started, contact the nearest **New Zealand Tourism Board** for a complimentary copy of its *New Zealand Vacation Planner.*

New Zealand Tourism Board offices can be found in the **United States** at 501 Santa Monica Blvd., Suite 300, Santa Monica, CA 90401 (© **866/639-9325** in the U.S., or 310/395-7480; fax 310/395-5453); in **Canada** at 888 Dunsmuir St., Suite 1200, Vancouver, BC V6C 3K4 (© **800/888-5494** in Canada, or 604/684-2117); in **Australia** at Level 8, 35 Pitt St., Sydney, NSW 2000 (© **02/9247-5222**); in **England** at New Zealand House, Haymarket, SW1Y 4TQ, London (© **020/7930-1662**); in **Germany** at Rossmarkt 11, 60311 Frankfurt am Main (© **069/9712-1110;** fax 069/9712-1113); and in **Hong Kong** at Unit 1601 Vicwood Plaza, 199 Des Voeux Rd. (© **852/2526-0141**).

The official Tourism Board website is **www.purenz.com**. Click on your home country to see the latest deals, with contact information for travel agents. The site provides comprehensive details for every aspect of your trip and is a must visit. Other useful sites include **New Zealand on the Web** (www.nz.com), which offers hundreds of excellent links; and you'll find many more interesting New Zealand contacts at www.albatrosses.com. For up-to-the-minute ski information, click on to **NZSKI.COM** (www.nzski.com).

When you arrive in New Zealand, you'll find 90 official **i–Site Visitor Centres** scattered around the country. Friendly staff members can book accommodations, activities, and tours; provide maps; and sell stamps and phone cards. Each chapter in this book lists the particular district/city information centers, and you can pick up a list of i-Site locations at Auckland and Christchurch international airports.

3 Entry Requirements & Customs

ENTRY REQUIREMENTS

A **passport** is required for all entering visitors, and it must be valid for at least 3 months beyond your departure date from New Zealand. If you lose yours, visit the nearest consulate of your native country as soon as possible for a replacement. See "Embassies & Consulates" and "Passports" in "Fast Facts: New Zealand" at the end of this chapter.

Visas are not required for stays shorter than 3 months (as long as you don't plan to study, work, or undergo medical treatment) if you're a citizen of one of the following countries: Argentina, Austria, Bahrain, Belgium, Brazil, Brunei, Canada, Chile, Czech Republic, Denmark, Finland, France, Germany, Greece, Hong Kong (if you're traveling with a Special Administrative passport or if you hold a British

national passport), Iceland, Ireland, Israel, Italy, Japan, Kiribati, Kuwait, Liechtenstein, Luxembourg, Malaysia, Malta, Monaco, Nauru, the Netherlands, Norway, Oman, Portugal (Portuguese passport holders must have the right to live permanently in Portugal), Qatar, Saudi Arabia, Singapore, South Africa, South Korea, Spain, Sweden, Switzerland, Thailand, Tuvalu, United Arab Emirates, United States, and Uruguay. British citizens are allowed a 6-month stay without a visa.

If you're planning to visit for longer than is stated above, or if your country of origin is not listed, contact the nearest New Zealand embassy, consulate, or High Commission for information on the appropriate visa and an application. If you'd like to work or live in New Zealand, you can inquire at an embassy or consulate, or write to the **New Zealand Immigration Service**, P.O. Box 27-149, Wellington, NZ (www.immigration.govt.nz).

You must also have the following items before entering New Zealand: a confirmed round-trip or outward-bound ticket; enough money for your designated stay (NZ$1,000/US$700 per person per month; credit cards are accepted); and the necessary documents to enter the country from which you came or the next country on your itinerary.

CUSTOMS

WHAT YOU CAN BRING INTO NEW ZEALAND
Do not bring any fruit or plants into New Zealand. Because of the importance of agriculture and horticulture to the economy, animal products, fruit, plant material, and foodstuffs that may contain plant or animal pests and diseases will not be allowed into the country. Heavy fines may be imposed on people caught carrying these prohibited materials. If in doubt, place all questionable items, especially fruit, into the marked bins before approaching the immigration area upon arrival at a New Zealand airport.

Firearms and weapons, unless a permit is obtained from the New Zealand police upon arrival at the airport, are not allowed. *Note:* This includes firearms intended for sporting purposes. Other prohibited items include ivory, in any form; tortoise- or turtle-shell jewelry and ornaments; medicines that incorporate musk, rhinoceros, or tiger derivatives; carvings or anything made from whale bone or bone from any other marine animal; and cat skins or coats. Certain drugs (diuretics, tranquilizers, depressants, stimulants, cardiac drugs, and sleeping pills) may not be allowed unless they are covered by a doctor's prescription.

Customs duties are not assessed on personal items you bring into the country and plan to take with you. New Zealand's duty-free allowances are 200 cigarettes or 250 grams (about 8 oz.) of tobacco or 50 cigars; 4.5 liters of wine or beer (equivalent to six 750ml bottles); one bottle of spirits or liqueur (up to 1,125ml/about 2½ pints); and goods totaling NZ$700 (US$490) that were purchased for your own use or for a gift. If you plan to take in anything beyond those limits, contact the embassy or consulate office nearest you *before* you arrive or check **www.customs. govt.nz**.

WHAT YOU CAN BRING HOME
Returning **United States** citizens who have been away for 48 hours or more are allowed to bring back, once every 30 days, $800 worth of merchandise duty-free. You'll be charged a flat rate of 4% duty on the next $1,000 worth of purchases. Be sure to have your receipts handy. On mailed gifts, the duty-free limit is $200. You cannot bring fresh foodstuffs into the United States; tinned foods, however, are allowed. For more information, contact the **U.S. Customs Service**, 1300 Pennsylvania Ave., NW, Washington, DC 20229 (© **877/287-8867**), and request the free pamphlet *Know Before You Go*. It's also available online at www.customs.gov.

Canada allows its citizens a C$750 exemption, and you're allowed to bring back duty-free one carton of cigarettes, one can of tobacco, 40 imperial ounces of liquor, and 50 cigars. In addition, you're allowed to mail gifts to Canada valued at less than C$60 a day, provided they're unsolicited and don't contain alcohol or tobacco (write on the package "Unsolicited gift, under $60 value"). All valuables should be declared on the Y-38 form before departure from Canada, including serial numbers of valuables you already own, such as expensive foreign cameras. *Note:* The C$750 exemption can only be used once a year and only after an absence of 7 days. For a clear summary of Canadian rules, write for the booklet *I Declare,* issued by the **Canada Customs and Revenue Agency** (© **800/461-9999** in Canada, or 204/983-3500; www.ccra-adrc.gc.ca).

U.K. citizens returning from **a non-E.U. country** have a customs allowance of: 200 cigarettes, *or* 50 cigars, *or* 250 g of smoking tobacco; 2 liters of still table wine; 1 liter of spirits or strong liqueurs (over 22% volume); 2 liters of fortified wine, sparkling wine, or other liqueurs; 60cc (ml) perfume; 250cc (ml) of toilet water; and £145 worth of all other goods, including gifts and souvenirs. People under 17 cannot have the tobacco or alcohol allowance. For more information, contact HM Customs & Excise at © **0845/** 010-9000 (from outside the U.K., 020/ 8929-0152), or consult their website at www.hmce.gov.uk.

The duty-free allowance in **Australia** is A$400 or, for those under 18, A$200. Citizens age 18 and older can bring in 250 cigarettes or 250 grams of loose tobacco, and 1,125 milliliters of alcohol. If you're returning with valuables you already own, such as foreign-made cameras, you should file form B263. A helpful brochure available from Australian consulates or Customs offices is *Know Before You Go.* For more information, call the **Australian Customs Service** at © **1300/363-263,** or log on to www.customs.gov.au.

4 Money

The **New Zealand dollar** (NZ$) is based on the decimal system, and there are 100 cents in the dollar. There are coin denominations of 5, 10, 20, and 50 cents and $1 and $2, as well as banknotes in $5, $10, $20, $50, and $100 amounts.

Traveler's checks are easily converted to cash at banks, many hotels, some restaurants, duty-free stores, and currency converters, but they're less necessary now that most towns and cities have ATMs that allow you to withdraw small amounts of cash as needed. You can get traveler's checks at almost any bank, or by calling **American Express** (© **800/807-6233** or 800/221-7282 for American Express credit cardholders; www.americanexpress. com), **Visa** (© **800/732-1322,** or 866/ 339-3378 for AAA members), or **Master-Card** (© **800/223-9920**). *Note:* American Express now charges a $15 order fee, plus additional shipping costs, for traveler's checks and foreign currency exchanges.

If you choose to carry traveler's checks, be sure to keep a record of their serial numbers separate from your checks in the event that they are stolen or lost.

Most **ATM cards** are compatible with New Zealand systems. The Bank of New Zealand accepts ATM cards in the **Cirrus** system (© **800/424-7787;** www.master card.com); other banks accept cards in the **PLUS** system (© **800/843-7587;** www.visa.com). Look at the back of your bank card to see which network you're on, then call or check online for ATM locations in New Zealand. Be sure to find out your daily withdrawal limit before you depart, and remember that many banks impose a fee every time a card is used at a different bank's ATM (this fee can be higher for international transactions).

The most convenient, of course, are your **credit cards.** Most New Zealand businesses take MasterCard and Visa. American Express, Diners Club, Bankcard, and Japan Credit Bank are also widely accepted in major tourist centers, but less so in smaller towns. Notify your credit card company of your impending trip abroad so that they don't become suspicious when the card is used numerous times in a foreign destination. You can also get cash advances on your credit card at an ATM. Keep in mind that credit card companies try to protect themselves from theft by limiting the funds someone can withdraw outside their home country, so

The New Zealand Dollar, the U.S. Dollar & the British Pound

For U.S. readers: At this writing, US$1 = approximately NZ$1.43, and this was the rate of exchange used to calculate the dollar values given in this book (rounded up to the nearest nickel).

For British readers: At this writing, £1 = approximately NZ$2.60, and this was the rate of exchange used to calculate the pound values below.

Note: International exchange rates fluctuate depending on economic and political factors. Thus, the rates given in this table may not be the same when you travel to New Zealand.

NZ$	US$	UK£	NZ$	US$	UK£
0.25	0.18	0.10	50.00	35.00	19.00
0.50	0.35	0.19	75.00	52.50	28.50
1.00	0.70	0.38	100.00	70.00	38.00
2.00	1.40	0.76	200.00	140.00	76.00
5.00	3.50	1.90	250.00	175.00	95.00
10.00	7.00	3.80	500.00	193.00	190.00
15.00	10.50	5.70	750.00	525.00	285.00
20.00	14.00	7.60	1,000.00	700.00	380.00
25.00	17.50	9.50	5,000.00	3,500.00	1,900.00

call your credit card company before you leave home. Also be sure that you know your PIN (call your company to request yours, allowing at least a week for it to arrive by mail).

5 When to Go

New Zealand is in the Southern Hemisphere; therefore, all seasons are the opposite of those in North America, Europe, and other Northern Hemisphere locations.

There really isn't a bad time to travel to New Zealand. Keep in mind, though, that most Kiwi families take their main annual holidays between mid-December and the end of January, which puts enormous pressure on accommodations in major summer beach destinations. During the Easter break and school holidays in April, June to July, and September to October (see "Holidays," below, for exact dates), it also pays to reserve well in advance.

Remember, too, that accommodations at ski destinations, especially Queenstown, fill up quickly—reserve early and be prepared to pay higher winter rates. In most other areas, though, you'll be paying lower rates during the winter months (Apr–Aug). In some summer-peak areas, the winter also means that tour, lodge, and adventure operators may take advantage of lower tourist numbers and take their own holiday breaks, closing their businesses for 1- to 3-month periods.

THE WEATHER

New Zealand's climate, especially by Northern Hemisphere standards, is pretty mellow for much of the year. You'll find a far greater seasonal difference in the

> **Tips   Dialing the Weather**
>
> In New Zealand, call **Metfax** at ☎ **0900/77-999** to hear the current and expected weather conditions in all major towns and cities. Calls cost NZ$5.40 (US$3.78) for the first minute and NZ99¢ (US69¢) per minute thereafter. For further information, call **Metservice** toll-free at ☎ **0800/932-843**.

South Island than in the subtropical North, and don't believe anyone who says it never gets cold here or that there are no extremes. In Central Otago, winter temperatures are often 14°F (–10°C) and sometimes as low as –4°F (–20°C), with summers up to 100°F to 104°F (38°C–40°C). By comparison, the northern part of the North Island is subtropical. That means *lots* of winter/spring rain, often daily light showers.

The west coast of the South Island can get up to 100 inches or more of rain a year on its side of the Southern Alps, while just over the mountains to the east, rainfall is a moderate 20 to 30 inches annually. Rain is also heavier on the west coast of the North Island, averaging 40 to 70 inches annually. Milford Sound, though, beats the lot; it's the wettest place in the country, with a phenomenal 365 inches of rain a year.

THE SEASONS

SPRING (Sept, Oct, Nov) This is a beautiful time to visit—the countryside is flush with new green grass, baby lambs, and blooming trees. Christchurch in the spring means blossoms, bluebells, and daffodils in abundance; Dunedin is a splurge of rhododendron color. The weather can still be very changeable right up to mid-October, so come prepared with light rain gear. In the South Island, it's still perfectly normal to get late snowfalls in September.

New Zealand's Average Temperature & Rainfall

Temperatures reflected are daily averages (°C/°F). Rainfall reflects the daily average in millimeters/inches (mm/in.) and is accurate within 1mm.

	Summer	Fall	Winter	Spring		Summer	Fall	Winter	Spring
Bay of Islands					**Westport**				
Max. Temp	25/77	21/70	16/61	19/66	Max. Temp	22/72	17/63	13/55	15/59
Min. Temp	14/57	11/52	7/45	9/48	Min. Temp	12/54	10/50	5/41	8/46
Rainfall	7/0.28	1/0.44	16/0.64	11/0.44	Rainfall	12/0.48	14/0.56	15/0.6	16/0.64
Auckland					**Christchurch**				
Max. Temp	24/75	20/68	15/59	18/65	Max. Temp	22/72	18/65	12/54	17/63
Min. Temp	12/54	13/55	9/48	11/52	Min. Temp	12/54	8/46	3/37	7/45
Rainfall	8/0.32	11/0.44	15/0.6	12/0.48	Rainfall	7/0.28	7/0.28	7/0.28	7/0.28
Rotorua					**Mount Cook**				
Max. Temp	24/75	18/65	13/55	17/63	Max. Temp	20/68	14/57	8/46	14/57
Min. Temp	12/54	9/48	4/39	7/45	Min. Temp	9/48	4/39	-1/30	4/39
Rainfall	9/0.36	9/0.36	13/0.52	11/0.44	Rainfall	12/0.48	13/0.52	13/0.52	14/0.56
Wellington					**Queenstown**				
Max. Temp	20/68	17/63	12/54	15/59	Max. Temp	22/72	16/61	10/50	16/61
Min. Temp	13/55	11/52	6/43	9/48	Min. Temp	10/50	6/43	1/34	5/41
Rainfall	7/0.28	10/0.4	13/0.52	11/0.44	Rainfall	8/0.32	8/0.32	7/0.28	9/0.36

Nelson	Summer	Fall	Winter	Spring		Invercargill	Summer	Fall	Winter	Spring
Max. Temp	22/72	18/65	13/55	17/63		Max. Temp	18/65	15/59	11/52	15/59
Min. Temp	13/55	8/46	3/37	7/45		Min. Temp	9/48	6/43	1/34	5/41
Rainfall	6/0.24	8/0.32	10/0.4	10/0.4		Rainfall	13/0.52	14/0.56	12/0.48	13/0.52

SUMMER (Dec, Jan, Feb) This is peak tourist season, so you'll pay top dollar for accommodations and airfares. Book early to avoid disappointment—this also applies to the major walking tracks, such as Milford, for which you should make bookings 6 months ahead. Beaches all over the country come alive, and boaties flock to the water. Fresh fruits are falling off the trees. (You must try Central Otago cherries and apricots; the apple district is Hawkes Bay.) And everyone should see Central Otago when the lupines are flowering, with brilliant colors etched against blue skies and golden tussock.

AUTUMN (Mar, Apr, May) Personally, I think the best time to visit is February through April. The temperatures are pleasant (still hot in Feb in most parts), and even in April you'll be wearing summer clothes in the upper North Island. The most spectacular autumn colors are found in Queenstown, Central Otago, and Christchurch. Keep Easter and April school holidays in mind, though, when accommodations may be tight in some areas.

WINTER (June, July, Aug) If you're a skier, you'll be heading to Queenstown, Mount Hutt, Canterbury, or the Central Plateau in the North Island—and paying top dollar for the privilege. Otherwise, if you travel elsewhere during this period, you won't need to prebook much at all (except during the July school holidays). You'll find some excellent rates—just don't expect great things from the weather.

HOLIDAYS

National public holidays include New Year's Day (Jan 1), New Year's Holiday (Jan 2), Waitangi Day (Feb 6), Good Friday (varies), Easter and Easter Monday (varies), ANZAC Day (Apr 25), Queen's Birthday (first Mon in June), Labour Day (last Mon in Oct), Christmas Day (Dec 25), and Boxing Day (Dec 26).

Regional holidays include Wellington (Jan 22), Auckland (Jan 29), Northland (Jan 29), Nelson Region (Feb 1), Otago (Mar 23), Southland (Mar 23), Taranaki (Mar 31), Hawkes Bay (Nov 1), Marlborough (Nov 1), Westland (Dec 1), and Canterbury (Dec 16). Regional holidays are always observed on a Monday. If the date lands on a Friday or weekend, the holiday is observed on the following Monday. If it falls earlier in the week, it is observed on the preceding Monday.

School holidays consist of three midterm breaks—in April, June to July, and September to October—that last for 2 weeks each, plus 6 weeks for the December holidays. Kiwi families do much of their traveling during these periods, so be sure to reserve early.

NEW ZEALAND CALENDAR OF EVENTS

More information can be found in the regional chapters that follow and by going to the New Zealand Tourism Board website at **www.pure nz.com**.

January

ASB Bank Tennis Classic, Auckland. International women's tennis tour event preceding the Australian Open. Attracts leading overseas players. Call ✆ **09/ 373-3625,** or check **www.auckland tennis.co.nz.** First week of January.

Heineken Open, Auckland. International Men's ATP tennis tour event for leading international players. Call ☏ **09/373-3625,** or check www. heinekenopen.co.nz. Early January.

Auckland Anniversary Day Regatta, Auckland. "The City of Sails" hosts this colorful annual sailing event, which attracts both local and international competitors and spectators. Call ☏ **09/828-4009.** Last Monday in January.

World Buskers Festival, Christchurch. A week of zany street entertainment provided by leading international entertainers. Call ☏ **03/377-2365,** or check www.worldbuskersfestival.com. Mid- to late January.

Summer City Festival, Wellington. A range of daily entertainment and cultural and recreational events in the capital city, including a Mardi Gras and Summer City Valentine's Night. Call ☏ **04/801-3222.** January and February.

Wellington Cup Race Meeting, Wellington. Leading horse-racing event (galloping), held in conjunction with the National Yearling Sales. Call ☏ **04/801-4000.** Late January.

February

Hawkes Bay Wine and Food Festival, Hawkes Bay. A showcase of the region's world-class wines and good food. Call ☏ **06/834-1919,** or check www.harvesthawkesbay.co.nz. First week of February.

Speights Coast to Coast, South Island. A major multisport endurance race from Kumara on the West Coast to Sumner, Christchurch, featuring a 33km (20-mile) mountain run followed by a 67km (42-mile) kayak race and a 142km (88-mile) cycle dash. Call ☏ **03/326-7493,** or check www.coasttocoast.co.nz. February 5 to February 6.

Waitangi Day Celebrations, Bay of Islands. New Zealand's national day celebrating the signing of the Treaty of Waitangi. Call ☏ **09/402-7308.** February 6.

Wairarapa Wine and Food Festival, Masterton. Top-class entertainment and a showcase of local wines and cuisine. For details, fax **06/378-7042.** Mid-February.

Garden City Festival of Flowers, Christchurch. Garden visits, floating gardens, and floral carpets in the "Garden City" of the South Island. Call ☏ **03/365-5403.** Mid-February for 10 days.

Brebner Art Deco Weekend, Napier. A fun celebration of the city's Art Deco heritage that includes dancing, jazz, vintage cars, walks, and tours. Most participants dress in 1920s and 1930s fashions. Call ☏ **06/835-1191,** or check www.artdeconapier.com. Third weekend in February.

Devonport Food and Wine Festival, Devonport. Held near the Ferry Wharf in Auckland's picturesque North Shore village of Devonport, this weekend event includes jazz, classical, and opera performances. Call ☏ **09/445-3011,** or log on to www.devonportwinefestival. co.nz. Late February.

Auckland Arts Festival. An extravaganza of national and international dance, music, theater, and visual arts talent every 2 years. The next festival will be staged in 2007. Call ☏ **09/309-0101.** www.aucklandfestival.co.nz. Late February to March.

March

Pasifika Festival, Auckland. Auckland's Pacific Island communities celebrate the largest 1-day cultural festival in the South Pacific. Not to be missed. For details, fax **09/09/379-2020,** or check www.aucklandcity.govt.nz/pasifika. First week of March.

New Zealand International Festival of Arts, Wellington. The largest and most prestigious event on the New Zealand arts calendar features top overseas and national artists and entertainers. A vibrant mix of all art forms, from contemporary dance to fine music and theater. Call ☏ **04/473-0149,** or visit www.nzfestival.telecom. co.nz. Beginning of March.

Hokitika Wildfoods Festival, Hokitika. A culinary adventure for the brave and curious, this 1-day event presents the weird and wonderful of New Zealand's wild foods, including wild pig, possum pâté, goat, various bugs and insects, honey, fish, and venison. Call ☏ **03/755-8321,** or check www. wildfoods.co.nz. Mid-March.

Arrowtown Autumn Festival, Arrowtown. A week of market days, music, and street entertainment celebrating the gold-mining era. Call ☏ **03/442-1570.** The week after Easter.

April

Warbirds Over Wanaka, Wanaka. Now classified as one of the best Warbirds air shows in the world, it combines classic vintage and veteran aircraft, machinery, fire engines, and tractors with dynamic Air Force displays and aerobatic teams in the natural amphitheater of the Upper Clutha Basin. Call ☏ **03/356-0297,** or visit www.warbirdsoverwanaka.co.nz. Easter weekend (in even-numbered years only).

Fletcher Challenge Forest Marathon, Rotorua. A full marathon around Lake Rotorua for serious competitors. Attracts over 500 runners. Call ☏ **07/348-8448,** or check www.rotorua marathon.co.nz. Late April to early May.

May

Bay of Islands Country Music Festival, Bay of Islands. This festival draws musicians from all around New Zealand, and there's at least one international act each year. Call ☏ **09/404-1063.** Second weekend in May.

June

National Agricultural Fieldays, Hamilton. One of the largest agricultural shows in the world, exhibiting the best of New Zealand agriculture, horticulture, floriculture, and forestry products. Call ☏ **07/843-4499** or visit www.fieldays.co.nz. Mid-June.

July

Queenstown Winter Festival, Queenstown. Every year in July, Queenstown officially goes mad with a host of zany mountain events and street entertainment. Call ☏ **03/442-7440,** or check www.winterfestival.co.nz. Mid-July.

Christchurch Arts Festival. Every 2 years from in July to August, this festival showcases the best of national and international dance, music, theater, and visual arts. For more information, visit www.artsfestival.co.nz. The next festival will be in 2007.

August

Bay of Islands Jazz and Blues Festival, Bay of Islands. More than 50 jazz bands from New Zealand and overseas provide live entertainment at various places around Paihia and Russell, night and day. Call ☏ **09/402-7345,** or go to www.jazz-blues.co.nz. Early to mid-August.

September

The **Montana World of Wearable Art Awards** is a creative extravaganza not to be missed. Now based in Wellington, it's scheduled for September 22 to October 1 in 2006. Call ☏ **03/547-4573** or go to www.worldofwearable art.com. Mid- to late September.

Alexandra Blossom Festival, Alexandra. An annual parade of floats and entertainment celebrating the onset of spring. Call ☏ **03/448-9515** or check www.blossom.co.nz. Late September to early October.

Gay Ski Week. A week of celebrations on and around the slopes. See www. gayskiweeknz.com for more information. First week of September.

October

Kaikoura Seafest, Kaikoura. An annual celebration of the best seafood and Marlborough and Canterbury wines, plus fun and entertainment for the entire family. Call ℂ **0800/473-2337** in NZ or visit www.seafest.co.nz. Early October.

Gardenz, Christchurch. A 3-day garden extravaganza staged in Hagley Park, featuring garden displays and products. For more information, fax **03/348-4835.** Labour Day weekend.

Dunedin Rhododendron Festival, Dunedin. Fun-filled days highlighted by garden tours and cultural events to celebrate the city's magnificent displays of rhododendron blooms. Call ℂ **03/474-3300,** or check www.rhodo dunedin.com. Mid- to late October.

Queenstown Jazz Festival, Queenstown. Over 200 musicians attend and play in bars and restaurants in a nonstop jam session with food and dancing. Call ℂ **03/442-1211.** Late October.

November

Toast Martinborough, Martinborough. An annual wine and food festival. Call ℂ **06/306-9183,** or go to www.toastmartinborough.co.nz. Mid- to late November.

Canterbury A&P Show, Christchurch. The South Island's largest agricultural and pastoral event, which includes thoroughbred and standard-bred racing and the New Zealand Cup. Call ℂ **0800/800-970,** or go to www.theshow.co.nz. Second week of November.

Southern Traverse, South Island. An adventure race for teams of three to five serious competitors through New Zealand's toughest terrain. The endurance events cover high ridges, lakes, and river crossings throughout Otago. Call ℂ **03/442-3630** or check out www.southerntraverse.com. Late November.

Ellerslie Flower Show, Auckland. New Zealand's premier garden and outdoor living event, which includes display gardens and the latest in outdoor furniture. Call ℂ **09/309-7875.** Late November.

December

Sealord Summer Festival, Nelson. Six weeks of free street entertainment, children's events, concerts, and activities. Call ℂ **03/546-0254,** or check www. nelsonfestivals.co.nz. Late December to mid-February.

Nelson Jazz Festival, Nelson. A wide variety of local and national jazz bands perform in a weekend event, culminating in a special New Year's Eve concert. Call ℂ **03/548-9303,** or visit www. nelsonjazz.co.nz. Late December to early January.

6 Travel Insurance

Check your existing insurance policies and credit card coverage before you buy travel insurance. You may already be covered for lost luggage, canceled tickets, or medical expenses. The cost of travel insurance varies widely, depending on the cost and length of your trip, your age and health, and the type of trip you're taking, but expect to pay between 5% and 8% of the vacation itself. You can get estimates from various providers through **Insure-MyTrip.com.** Enter your trip cost and dates, your age, and other information, for prices from more than a dozen companies.

TRIP-CANCELLATION INSURANCE

Trip-cancellation insurance helps you get your money back if you have to back out of a trip, if you have to go home early, or if your travel supplier goes bankrupt. Allowed reasons for cancellation can range from sickness to natural disasters to the State Department declaring your destination unsafe for travel. (Insurers usually won't cover vague fears, though, as many travelers discovered who tried to cancel their trips in Oct 2001 because they were wary of flying.) In this unstable world, trip-cancellation insurance is a good buy if you're getting tickets well in advance—who knows what the state of the world, or of your airline, will be in 9 months? Insurance policy details vary, so read the fine print—and especially make sure that your airline or cruise line is on the list of carriers covered in case of bankruptcy. For information, contact one of the following insurers: **Access America** (℃ 866/807-3982; www.accessamerica.com); **Travel Guard International** (℃ 800/826-4919; www.travelguard.com); **Travel Insured International** (℃ 800/243-3174; www.travelinsured.com); and **Travelex Insurance Services** (℃ 888/457-4602; www.travelex-insurance.com).

MEDICAL INSURANCE

Most visitors are not entitled to publicly funded health services while in New Zealand unless they are residents, citizens of Australia, nationals of the United Kingdom in New Zealand, or hold a temporary permit that is valid for 2 years or more. If you do not belong to one of these special categories and you receive medical treatment during your visit, you will be responsible for the full cost of the treatment, so be sure to get that medical insurance before you arrive.

Most health insurance policies cover you if you get sick away from home—but

check, particularly if you're insured by an HMO. With the exception of certain HMOs and Medicare/Medicaid, your medical insurance should cover medical treatment—even hospital care—overseas. However, some make you pay the bills upfront at the time of care, and you get a refund only after you've returned and filed all the paperwork. And in a worst-case scenario, there's the high cost of emergency evacuation. If you require additional medical insurance, try **MEDEX International** (℃ **800/527-0218** or 410/453-6300; www.medexassist.com) or **Travel Assistance International** (℃ **800/821-2828;** www.travelassistance.com; for general information on services, call the company's Worldwide Assistance Services, Inc., at ℃ **800/777-8710**).

LOST-LUGGAGE INSURANCE

On international flights (including U.S. portions of international trips), baggage coverage is limited to approximately US$9.07 per pound, up to approximately US$635 per checked bag. If you plan to check items more valuable than the standard liability, see if your valuables are covered by your homeowner's policy, get baggage insurance as part of your comprehensive travel-insurance package, or buy Travel Guard's "Bag-Trak" product. Don't buy insurance at the airport, as it's usually overpriced. Be sure to take any valuables or irreplaceable items with you in your carry-on luggage, as many valuables (including books, money, and electronics) aren't covered by airline policies.

If your luggage is lost, immediately file a lost-luggage claim at the airport, detailing the luggage contents. For most airlines, you must report delayed, damaged, or lost baggage within 4 hours of arrival. The airlines are required to deliver luggage, once found, directly to your house or destination free of charge.

7 Health & Safety

For additional health and safety tips, see "Safety in the Great Outdoors" on p. 64.

STAYING HEALTHY
BEFORE YOU GO

Vaccinations are not required to enter New Zealand. **Health insurance** is strongly advised because New Zealand's public and private medical/hospital facilities are not free to visitors, except as a result of accident. Make sure your health insurance covers you when you're out of the country; if it doesn't, get temporary medical coverage for the duration of your trip (see "Travel Insurance," above). Be sure to carry your identification card in your wallet.

If you suffer from a chronic illness, consult your doctor before your departure. For conditions like epilepsy, diabetes, or heart problems, wear a **MedicAlert Identification Tag** (✆ **800/825-3785;** www.medicalert.org), which will immediately alert doctors to your condition and give them access to your records through MedicAlert's 24-hour hot line.

Pack **prescription medications** in your carry-on luggage, and carry prescription medications in their original containers, with pharmacy labels—otherwise they won't make it through airport security. Bring along your prescriptions (written in the generic name, not using brand names) from your doctor in case you need refills. Also note that you may not be allowed to bring in certain medications unless you have a doctor's prescription (see "Customs," earlier in this chapter, for a list of drugs that may be prohibited). Don't forget an extra pair of contact lenses or prescription glasses.

Contact the **International Association for Medical Assistance to Travelers (IAMAT)** (✆ **716/754-4883** or, in Canada, 416/652-0137; www.iamat.org) for tips on travel and health concerns in the countries you're visiting. The United States **Centers for Disease Control and Prevention** (✆ **800/311-3435;** www.cdc.gov) provides up-to-date information on necessary vaccines and health hazards by region or country.

If you have concerns about accessing New Zealand health services once you are here, call **Accident Info Services** at ✆ **0800/263-345** or 09/529-0488. They offer a 24-hour advisory service.

COMMON AILMENTS

BUGS & BITES You've heard that New Zealand is a relatively safe place? Believe it! We have no snakes, no alligators or crocodiles, no wild animals of note, no scorpions. The worst we can offer you is our poisonous **katipo spider,** but as you're about as likely to see one of those, much less be bitten, as you are encountering a bison in the main street of Auckland, I wouldn't start panicking just yet.

But knowledge is power, so here are the spidery details. The New Zealand katipo—*Latrodectus katipo* and *L.atritus* (yes, there are two species)—favors sparsely vegetated sand dunes and driftwood above the high-tide mark on sandy beaches. *L. katipo* is distinguished by the coloration of the adult female: black with a red stripe on the abdomen. The mature male is about one-sixth the size of the female and is predominantly white with a series of orange-red triangles and black lines on the abdomen. *L.atritus* is completely black.

Both species are poisonous, but they are rarely seen. And given that New Zealand is a nation of beach-lovers, it is comforting to know that there have only been two recorded fatalities, both in the 1800s—largely unconvincing evidence of toxic spiders. If, in the unlikely event that you are bitten by something black while on the beach, try to have the presence of mind to capture the offender and then take yourself off to the nearest hospital.

Heading inland, especially in the deep south around Fiordland, Te Anau, and up the South Island's West Coast, the biggest irritation will be **sand flies.** They may be tiny, but they have the power to drive you absolutely crazy. Take gallons of strong insect repellent, and keep dousing yourself in it. If you still get bitten, try not to scratch and ladle on plenty of antihistamine to prevent swelling. The good news is that not everybody suffers. I'm one of the lucky ones—sand flies don't seem to like my blood. You'll just have to hope you're as unattractive to them as I am.

ENVIRONMENTAL HAZARDS The ocean holds its fair share of dangers. Most popular New Zealand beaches are patrolled by lifeguards, and you should always swim between the flags. Ask if you're unsure, because many beaches have **dangerous currents and holes.** In more remote areas, beaches are not patrolled, and you should exercise common sense before entering the waves. This particularly applies to the hazardous west coast beaches of the whole country. Never swim alone anywhere.

On the subject of beaches, it's important to point out the danger of **sharks.** *Always* check with the locals as to the possibility of sharks in the ocean. As we all know, the threat of being attacked can never be underestimated.

As with beaches, **mountain and bush safety** *should* be a matter of common sense, but you would be amazed at how many people think they know better than the locals, setting off on a bush walk with no warm clothing (just because the sun is shining at the beginning is no guarantee that it will be further on), no extra water, and no precautionary measures taken whatsoever. Hypothermia, exposure, and excessive sunburn are very real dangers in New Zealand, and you take your life in your hands if you ignore warnings.

DIETARY DISTRESS The only thing to look out for in the bush is the possibility of *Giardia,* a waterborne parasite that causes diarrhea. Always boil water when you're hiking.

STAYING SAFE

New Zealand is generally a very safe destination, one of the safest in the world. Still, exercise the same care that you would in any major city. People-oriented dangers—theft, assault, murder—should be mentioned, but it's important to remember that violent crimes in most countries, especially in New Zealand, occur between acquaintances. As a traveler, it's unlikely you'll be a victim. If you're hitchhiking, however, that may be another matter; women should never hitchhike alone or at night.

On the subject of theft, it should be noted that many travelers are lulled into a false sense of security, leaving cars unlocked and valuables clearly visible. Always park your car in a well-populated area whenever possible; lock it and cover your luggage with a blanket or a coat. *Never* leave handbags or cameras in cars. The simple rule should be, if you can't do without it, don't leave it in the car, locked or otherwise.

ECOTOURISM

The International Ecotourism Society (TIES) defines ecotourism as "responsible travel to natural areas that conserves the environment and improves the well-being of local people." You can find ecofriendly travel tips, statistics, and touring companies and associations—listed by destination under "Travel Choice"—at the TIES website, www.ecotourism.org. **Ecotravel.com** is part online magazine and part ecodirectory that lets you search for touring companies in several categories (water-based, land-based, spiritually oriented, and so on). Also check out **Conservation International** (www.conservation.org)—which, with *National Geographic Traveler,* annually presents **World Legacy Awards** (www.wl award.org) to those travel tour operators, businesses, organizations, and places that have made a significant contribution to sustainable tourism.

For information about the ethics of swimming with dolphins and other outdoor activities, visit the **Whale and Dolphin Conservation Society** (www. wdcs.org) and **Tread Lightly** (www.tread lightly.org).

8 Specialized Travel Resources

FOR TRAVELERS WITH DISABILITIES

New Zealand is a relatively good destination for visitors with disabilities. Since 1975, every public building and every major renovated structure in the country has been required to provide reasonable and adequate access for those with disabilities. In addition, accommodations with five or more units are required to provide at least one room for guests with disabilities. For general information, contact the **New Zealand Disability Resource Centre,** 840 Tremaine Ave., Palmerston North, NZ (© **06/356-5459**).

Other organizations that offer assistance to travelers with disabilities include **MossRehab** (www.mossresourcenet.org), which provides a library of accessible-travel resources online; the **Society for Accessible Travel and Hospitality**, or SATH (© **212/447-7284;** www.sath.org; annual membership fees: $45 adults, $30 seniors and students), which offers a wealth of travel resources for all types of disabilities and informed recommendations on destinations, access guides, travel agents, tour operators, vehicle rentals, and companion services; and the **American Foundation for the Blind** (© **800/232-5463;** www.afb.org), which provides information on traveling with Seeing Eye dogs.

Budget (www.budget.com) offers specially equipped vehicles for travelers with physical disabilities. For details, contact the New Zealand Tourism Board (see "Visitor Information," earlier in this chapter).

Many travel agencies offer customized tours and itineraries for travelers with disabilities. **Flying Wheels Travel** (© **507/** **451-5005;** www.flyingwheelstravel.com) offers escorted tours and cruises that emphasize sports and private tours in minivans with lifts. **Accessible Journeys** (© **800/846-4537** or 610/521-0339; www.disabilitytravel.com) caters specifically to slow walkers and wheelchair travelers and their families and friends.

For more information specifically targeted to travelers with disabilities, the community website **iCan** (www.ican online.net/channels/travel) has destination guides and several regular columns on accessible travel. Also check out the quarterly magazine *Emerging Horizons* (www.emerginghorizons.com; $14.95 per year, $19.95 outside the U.S.); and *Open World* magazine, published by SATH (see above; subscription: $13 per year, $21 outside the U.S.).

FOR GAY & LESBIAN TRAVELERS

Gay and lesbian travelers will feel at ease in New Zealand, especially in Auckland and Wellington. For information, go to the **New Zealand Gay and Lesbian Tourism Association** website at www.iglta.org, or write to them at P.O. Box 24-558, Wellington 6015, NZ (© **04/917-9184;** fax 04/917-9176). Other New Zealand gay and lesbian websites include www.gay nz.com. **Pink Pages New Zealand** (www. pinkpagesnewzealand.com), **Queer Resources Aotearoa** (www.gaynz.net.nz), and **Gay Queenstown** (www.gayqueenstown. com).

The **International Gay & Lesbian Travel Association (IGLTA)** (© **800/ 448-8550** or 954/776-2626; www.iglta. org) is the trade association for the gay and lesbian travel industry, and offers an online directory of gay- and lesbian-friendly travel businesses; go to the website and click on "Members."

Many agencies offer tours and travel itineraries specifically for gay and lesbian travelers. **Above and Beyond Tours** (*©* 800/397-2681; www.abovebeyond tours.com) is the exclusive gay and lesbian tour operator for United Airlines. **Now, Voyager** (*©* 800/255-6951; www. nowvoyager.com) is a well-known San Francisco–based gay-owned and operated travel service. **Olivia Cruises & Resorts** (*©* 800/631-6277 or 510/655-0364; www. olivia.com) charters entire resorts and ships for exclusive lesbian vacations and offers smaller group experiences for both gay and lesbian travelers.

FOR SENIOR TRAVELERS

Discounts for those over 60 are increasingly available in New Zealand, so be sure to inquire when making reservations for accommodations and attractions. Don't forget to carry photo identification. Those over 60 are entitled to a 20% discount on InterCity coaches and Tranz Scenic trains. Newmans Coaches offers a 20% discount to anyone over 60.

Members of **AARP,** 601 E St. NW, Washington, DC 20049 (*©* 800/424-3410 or 202/434-2277; www.aarp.org), get discounts on hotels, airfares, and car rentals. AARP offers members a wide range of benefits, including *AARP The Magazine* and a monthly newsletter. Anyone over 50 can join.

Many reliable agencies and organizations target the 50-plus market. **Elderhostel** (*©* 877/426-8056; www.elder hostel.org) arranges study programs for those age 55 and over (and a spouse or companion of any age) in the U.S. and in more than 80 countries around the world, including New Zealand. Most courses last 5 to 7 days in the U.S. (2–4 weeks abroad), and many include airfare, accommodations in university dormitories or

modest inns, meals, and tuition. **ElderTreks** (*©* 800/741-7956; www. eldertreks.com) offers small-group tours to off-the-beaten-path or adventure-travel locations, restricted to travelers 50 and older.

Recommended publications offering travel resources and discounts for seniors include: the quarterly magazine *Travel 50 & Beyond* (www.travel50andbeyond. com); *Travel Unlimited: Uncommon Adventures for the Mature Traveler* (Avalon); *101 Tips for Mature Travelers,* available from Grand Circle Travel (*©* 800/221-2610 or 617/350-7500; www.gct. com); and *The 50+ Traveler's Guidebook* (St. Martin's Press).

FOR FAMILIES

New Zealand offers some of the most exciting vacation opportunities for families with kids. Hiking, swimming, sailing, and whale-watching are only a few of the activities children of all ages can enjoy. Older, more adventurous kids will no doubt love caving, rafting, kayaking, and bungy jumping. Most sightseeing attractions admit children at half price, and family prices are often available.

Although many of the better B&Bs do not accommodate children, motels and farmstays are ideal for families. Both are usually cheaper, motel rooms are regularly equipped with cooking facilities, and children will enjoy roaming the fields and helping out on a working farm.

Familyhostel (*©* 800/733-9753; www. learn.unh.edu/familyhostel) takes the whole family, including kids ages 8 to 15, on moderately priced domestic and international learning vacations (including a "Middle Earth" tour of New Zealand). Lectures, field trips, and sightseeing are guided by a team of academics.

You can find good family-oriented vacation advice on the Internet from sites like the **Family Travel Network** (www.familytravelnetwork.com); **Traveling Internationally with Your Kids** (www.travelwithyourkids.com), a comprehensive site offering sound advice for long-distance and international travel with children; and **Family Travel Files** (www.thefamilytravelfiles.com), which offers an online magazine and a directory of off-the-beaten-path tours and tour operators for families. *How to Take Great Trips with Your Kids* (The Harvard Common Press) is full of good general advice that can apply to travel anywhere.

FOR SOLO TRAVELERS

New Zealand is a perfectly safe place for traveling solo, although we assume that everyone will act with common sense in terms of personal safety and late-night wanderings. (And of course, you won't want to take off on a long trek into the mountains on your own.)

You'll find that people here are friendly and often go out of their way to make solo travelers feel welcome. It's likely that you'll go home with a book filled with the addresses of new friends. Some accommodations charge significantly less for one person than for two. All rates listed in this book are for doubles, so be sure to ask about single rates if you intend to travel alone.

Many reputable tour companies offer singles-only trips. For example, **Backroads** (© **800/462-2848;** www.backroads.com) offers more than 160 active trips to 30 destinations worldwide, including New Zealand, Bali, Morocco, and Costa Rica.

For more information, check out Eleanor Berman's *Traveling Solo: Advice and Ideas for More Than 250 Great Vacations* (Globe Pequot), a guide with advice on traveling alone, whether on your own or on a group tour. Or turn to the **Travel Alone and Love It** website (www.travelaloneandloveit.com), designed by former flight attendant Sharon Wingler, the author of the book of the same name. Her site is full of tips for solo travelers.

FOR STUDENTS

STA Travel (© **800/781-4040;** www.statravel.com) has offices around the world and offers discounts primarily to students, individuals under 26, and teachers. You can get discounted airfares, rail passes, and travel insurance; book tours and car rentals; and get an **International Student Identity Card** ($22). The New Zealand headquarters is at 10 High St., Auckland (© **09/309-0458**). (*Note:* In 2002, STA Travel bought competitors Council Travel and USIT Campus after they went bankrupt. It's still operating some offices under the Council name, but it's owned by STA.) **Travel CUTS** (© **800/667-2887** or 416/614-2887; www.travelcuts.com) offers similar services for both Canadians and U.S. residents.

9 Planning Your Trip Online

SURFING FOR AIRFARES

The "big three" online travel agencies, **Expedia.com, Travelocity,** and **Orbitz** sell most of the air tickets bought on the Internet. (Canadian travelers should try Expedia.ca and Travelocity.ca; U.K. residents can go for Expedia.co.uk and Opodo.co.uk.) Each has different business deals with the airlines and may offer different fares on the same flights, so it's wise to shop around. Expedia.com and Travelocity will also send you **e-mail** notification when a cheap fare becomes available to your favorite destination. Of the smaller travel agency websites, **SideStep** (www.sidestep.com) has gotten the best reviews from Frommer's authors. It's a browser add-on that purports to "search 140 sites at once," but in reality only beats competitors' fares as often as other sites do.

Also remember to check **airline websites.** You can often shave a few bucks from a fare by booking directly through

Frommers.com: The Complete Travel Resource

For an excellent travel-planning resource, we highly recommend **Frommers. com** (www.frommers.com). We're a little biased, of course, but we guarantee that you'll find the travel tips, reviews, monthly vacation giveaways, and online-booking capabilities thoroughly indispensable. Among the special features are our popular **Message Boards,** where Frommer's readers post queries and share advice (sometimes even our authors show up to answer questions); **Frommers.com Newsletter,** for the latest travel bargains and insider travel secrets; and **Frommer's Destinations Section,** where you'll get expert travel tips, hotel and dining recommendations, and advice on the sights to see for more than 3,000 destinations around the globe. When your research is done, the **Online Reservations System** (www.frommers.com/book_a_trip) takes you to Frommer's preferred online partners for booking your vacation at affordable prices.

the airline and avoiding a travel agency's transaction fee. But you'll get these discounts only by **booking online:** Most airlines now offer online-only fares that even their phone agents know nothing about. For the websites of airlines that fly to and from New Zealand, go to "Getting There," later in this chapter.

Great **last-minute deals** are available through free weekly e-mail services provided directly by the airlines. Most of these are announced on Tuesday or Wednesday and must be purchased online. Most are only valid for travel that weekend, but some can be booked weeks or months in advance. Sign up for weekly e-mail alerts at airline websites or check mega-sites that compile comprehensive lists of last-minute specials, such as **Smarter Travel** (www.smartertravel.com). For last-minute trips, **site59.com** in the U.S. and **lastminute.com** in Europe often have better deals than the major-label sites.

If you're willing to give up some control over your flight details, use an **opaque fare service** like **Priceline** (www. priceline.com; www.priceline.co.uk for Europeans) or **Hotwire** (www.hotwire.

com). Both offer rock-bottom prices in exchange for travel on a "mystery airline" at a mysterious time of day, often with a mysterious change of planes en route. The mystery airlines are all major, well-known carriers, and the airlines' routing computers have gotten a lot better than they used to be. But your chances of getting a 6am or 11pm flight are pretty high. Hotwire tells you flight prices before you buy; Priceline usually has better deals than Hotwire, but you have to play their "name our price" game. If you're new at this, the helpful folks at **BiddingForTravel** (www.biddingfortravel.com) do a good job of demystifying Priceline's prices. Priceline and Hotwire are great for flights within North America and between the U.S. and Europe. But for flights to other parts of the world, consolidators will almost always beat their fares.

SURFING FOR HOTELS

Shopping online for hotels is much easier in the U.S., Canada, and certain parts of Europe than it is in the rest of the world. Also, many smaller hotels and B&Bs—especially outside the U.S.—don't show up on websites at all. Of the "big three" sites, **Expedia.com** may be the best choice, thanks to its long list of special deals. **Travelocity** runs a close second. Hotel specialist sites **hotels.com** and **hoteldiscounts.com** are also reliable. An excellent free program, **TravelAxe** (www.travelaxe.net), can help you search multiple hotel sites at once, even ones you may never have heard of.

Priceline and Hotwire are even better for hotels than for airfares; with both, you're allowed to pick the neighborhood and quality level of your hotel before offering up your money. Priceline's hotel product even covers Europe and Asia, though it's much better at getting five-star lodging for three-star prices than at

finding anything at the bottom of the scale. *Note:* Hotwire overrates its hotels by one star—what Hotwire calls a four-star is a three-star anywhere else.

SURFING FOR RENTAL CARS

For booking rental cars online, the best deals are usually found at rental-car company websites, although all the major online travel agencies also offer rental-car reservations services. Priceline and Hotwire work well for rental cars, too; the only "mystery" is which major rental company you get, and for most travelers the difference between Hertz, Avis, and Budget is negligible.

10 The 21st-Century Traveler

INTERNET ACCESS AWAY FROM HOME

Travelers have any number of ways to check their e-mail and access the Internet on the road. Of course, using your own laptop—or even a PDA or electronic organizer with a modem—gives you the most flexibility. But even if you don't have a computer, you can still access your e-mail and even your office computer from cybercafes.

WITHOUT YOUR OWN COMPUTER

It's hard nowadays to find a city that *doesn't* have a few cybercafes. Although there's no definitive directory for cybercafes—these are independent businesses, after all—three places to start looking are at **www.cybercaptive.com**, **www.netcafe guide.com**, and **www.cybercafe.com**.

Aside from formal cybercafes, most **youth hostels** nowadays have at least one computer you can get to the Internet on. And most **public libraries** across the world offer Internet access free or for a small charge. Avoid **hotel business centers,** which often charge exorbitant rates.

Most major airports now have **Internet kiosks** scattered throughout their gates. These kiosks, which you'll also see in shopping malls, hotel lobbies, and tourist information offices around the world, give you basic Web access for a per-minute fee that's usually higher than cybercafe prices. The kiosks' clunkiness and high price means they should be avoided whenever possible.

To retrieve your e-mail, ask your **Internet Service Provider (ISP)** if it has a Web-based interface tied to your existing e-mail account. If your ISP doesn't have such an interface, you can use the free **mail2web** service (www.mail2web.com) to view and reply to your home e-mail. For more flexibility, you may want to open a free, Web-based e-mail account with **Yahoo! Mail** (http://mail.yahoo.com) or Fastmail (www.fastmail.fm). (Microsoft's Hotmail is another popular option, but Hotmail has severe spam problems.) Your home ISP may be able to forward your e-mail to the Web-based account automatically.

If you need to access files on your office computer, look into a service called

GoToMyPC (www.gotomypc.com). The service provides a Web-based interface for you to access and manipulate a distant PC from anywhere—even a cybercafe—provided your "target" PC is on and has an always-on connection to the Internet (such as with Road Runner cable). The service offers top-quality security, but if you're worried about hackers, use your own laptop rather than a cybercafe to access the GoToMyPC system.

WITH YOUR OWN COMPUTER

Major Internet Service Providers (ISP) have **local access numbers** around the world, allowing you to go online by simply placing a local call. Check your ISP's website or call its toll-free number and ask how you can use your current account away from home, and how much it will cost.

If you're traveling outside the reach of your ISP, the **iPass** network has dial-up numbers in most of the world's countries. You'll have to sign up with an iPass provider, who will then tell you how to set up your computer for your destination(s). For a list of iPass providers, go to www.ipass.com and click on "Reseller Locator." Under "Select a Country" pick the country that you're coming from, and under "Who is this service for?" pick "Individual." One solid provider is **i2roam** (www.i2roam.com; © **866/811-6209** or 920/235-0475).

Wherever you go, bring a **connection kit** of the right power and phone adapters (the voltage is 230 volts in New Zealand, and plugs are the three-prong type), a spare phone cord, and a spare Ethernet network cable.

If you have an 802.11b/**Wi-Fi** card for your computer, several commercial companies have made wireless service available in airports, hotel lobbies, and coffee shops, primarily in the U.S. **T-Mobile Hotspot** (www.t-mobile.com/hotspot) serves up wireless connections at more than 1,000 Starbucks coffee shops nationwide. **Boingo**

(www.boingo.com) and **Wayport** (www.wayport.com) have set up networks in airports and high-class hotel lobbies. iPass providers (see above) also give you access to a few hundred wireless hotel lobby setups. Best of all, you don't need to be staying at the Four Seasons to use the hotel's network; just set yourself up on a nice couch in the lobby. Unfortunately, the companies' pricing policies are byzantine, with a variety of monthly, per-connection, and per-minute plans.

Community-minded individuals have also set up **free wireless networks** in major cities around the world. These networks are spotty, but you get what you (don't) pay for. Each network has a home page explaining how to set up your computer for their particular system; start your explorations at www.personaltelco.net/index.cgi/WirelessCommunities.

USING A CELLPHONE

The three letters that define much of the world's **wireless capabilities** are GSM (Global System for Mobiles), a big, seamless network that makes for easy cross-border cellphone use throughout Europe and dozens of other countries worldwide. In the U.S., T-Mobile, AT&T Wireless, and Cingular use this quasi-universal system; in Canada, Microcell and some Rogers customers are GSM; and all Europeans and most Australians and New Zealanders use GSM.

If your cellphone is on a GSM system, and you have a world-capable phone such as many (but not all) Sony Ericsson, Motorola, or Samsung models, you can make and receive calls across civilized areas on much of the globe, from Andorra to Uganda. Just call your wireless operator and ask for "international roaming" to be activated on your account. Unfortunately, per-minute charges can be high—usually $1 to $1.50 in Western Europe and up to $5 in places like Russia and Indonesia.

Online Traveler's Toolbox

- **Visa ATM Locator** (www.visa.com), for locations of PLUS ATMs worldwide, or **MasterCard ATM Locator** (www.mastercard.com), for locations of Cirrus ATMs worldwide.
- **Intellicast** (www.intellicast.com) and **Weather.com** (www.weather.com). Gives weather forecasts for all 50 states and for cities around the world.
- **Universal Currency Converter** (www.xe.com/ucc). See what your dollar or pound is worth in more than 100 other countries.
- **Travel Warnings** (http://travel.state.gov, www.fco.gov.uk/travel, www.voyage.gc.ca, www.dfat.gov.au/consular/advice). These sites report on places where health concerns or unrest might threaten American, British, Canadian, and Australian travelers. Generally, U.S. warnings are the most paranoid; Australian warnings are the most relaxed.
- The **New Zealand Tourism Board** (www.purenz.com) lists suppliers of adventure, boat, cultural, educational, farm, fly/drive, motorcycle, hunting, nature, scenic, sporting, and wedding tours.

World-phone owners can bring down their per-minute charges with a bit of trickery. Call up your cellular operator and say you'll be going abroad for several months and want to "unlock" your phone to use it with a local provider. Usually, they'll oblige. Then, in your destination country, pick up a cheap, prepaid phone chip at a mobile phone store and slip it into your phone. (Show your phone to the salesperson, as not all phones work on all networks.) You'll get a local phone number in your destination country—and much, much lower calling rates.

Otherwise, **renting** a phone is a good idea. While you can rent a phone from any number of overseas sites, including kiosks at airports and at car-rental agencies, we suggest renting the phone before you leave home. That way you can give loved ones your new number, make sure the phone works, and take the phone wherever you go—especially helpful when you rent overseas, where phone-rental agencies bill in local currency and may not let you take the phone to another country.

Phone rental isn't cheap. You'll usually pay $40 to $50 per week, plus airtime fees of at least a dollar a minute. The bottom line: Shop around.

Two good wireless rental companies are **InTouch USA** (© 800/872-7626; www.intouchglobal.com) and **RoadPost** (© 888/290-1606 or 905/272-5665; www.roadpost.com). Give them your itinerary, and they'll tell you what wireless products you need. InTouch will also, for free, advise you on whether your existing phone will work overseas; simply call © 703/222-7161 between 9am and 4pm EST, or go to http://intouchglobal.com/travel.htm.

True wilderness adventurers should consider renting a **satellite phone.** Per-minute call charges can be even cheaper than roaming charges with a regular cellphone, but the phone itself is more expensive (up to $150 a week), and depending on the service you choose, people calling you may incur high long-distance charges.

11 Getting There

The cost of getting to New Zealand is likely to be your single biggest cash outlay, so it makes sense to shop around. Remember to check out those recommended agents and hot travel offers listed for your country of origin on the New Zealand Tourism Board website, **www.purenz.com**. Also go to Air New Zealand's website at **www.airnewzealand.com** for special deals.

BY PLANE

From the West Coast of the United States, you can fly to New Zealand nonstop overnight; a direct flight from Singapore takes 10 hours; and a flight from eastern Australia is around 3 hours.

There are at least 20 foreign airlines flying into Auckland. The main ones providing service from the **United States** are Air New Zealand, Qantas, and British Airways. United Airlines no longer flies into New Zealand, although it does fly to Sydney, a 3-hour flight from Auckland. To and from **Canada,** you can choose from Air New Zealand and Air Pacific; to and from **Europe** and the United Kingdom, Air New Zealand, British Airways, and Qantas. From **Asia,** options include Singapore Airlines, Korean Air, Japan Airlines, Malaysian Airlines, Cathay Pacific, Garuda Indonesia, and Thai Airways. Dubai-based Emirates Airline now flies into New Zealand as well. There are also code-sharing arrangements with Lufthansa, American Airlines, United Airlines, and several others.

Consolidators are wholesale agencies that buy seats from the airlines and sell them back to consumers at lower fees. Try **Discover Wholesale Travel, Inc.** (*© **800/576-7770** in California, 800/759-7330 elsewhere in the U.S.), **Pacific Destination Center** (*© **800/227-5317** in the U.S., or 714/960-4011), **1-800/FLY-CHEAP** (www.1800flycheap.com), or **TFI Tours International** (*© **800/745-8000** or 212/736-1140).

The timing of your trip can have a tremendous impact on your airline costs. New Zealand's **peak season** is December through February; the **shoulder season** includes March and September through November; and the **low season** begins in April and runs through August.

GETTING THROUGH THE AIRPORT

With the federalization of airport security, security procedures at U.S. airports are more stable and consistent than ever. Generally, you'll be fine if you arrive at the airport **2 hours** before an international flight; if you show up late, tell an airline employee and he or she will probably whisk you to the front of the line.

Bring a **current, government-issued photo ID** such as a driver's license or passport. Keep your ID at the ready to show at check-in, the security checkpoint, and

---

Tips **Principal Airlines with Service to New Zealand**

- **Air New Zealand** (*© **800/262-1234** in the U.S. and Canada; www.airnz.com)
- **Air Pacific** (*© **800/227-4446** in Canada)
- **British Airways** (*© **800/247-9297** in the U.S. and Canada; www.britishairways.com)
- **Canadian International Airlines** (*© **800/665-1177** in Canada)
- **Qantas** (*© **800/227-4500** in the U.S. and Canada; www.qantas.com.au)

sometimes even the gate. (Children under 18 do not need photo IDs for domestic flights, but the adults checking in with them should have them.)

In 2003, the TSA phased out **gate check-in** at all U.S. airports. Passengers with e-tickets can still beat the ticket-counter lines by using **electronic kiosks** or even **online check-in.** Ask your airline which alternatives are available, and if you're using a kiosk, bring the credit card you used to book the ticket or your frequent-flier card. If you're checking bags or looking to snag an exit-row seat, you will be able to do so using most airlines' kiosks; again, call your airline for up-to-date information. **Curbside check-in** is also a good way to avoid lines, although a few airlines still ban curbside check-in; call before you go.

Security checkpoint lines are getting shorter, but some doozies remain. If you have trouble standing for long periods of time, tell an airline employee; the airline will provide a wheelchair. Speed up security by **not wearing metal objects** such as big belt buckles. If you've got metallic body parts, a note from your doctor can prevent a long chat with the security screeners. Keep in mind that only **ticketed passengers** are allowed past security, except for folks escorting passengers with disabilities or children.

Federalization has stabilized **what you can carry on** and **what you can't.** The general rule is that sharp things are out, nail clippers are okay, and food and beverages must be passed through the X-ray machine—but that security screeners can't make you drink from your coffee cup. Bring food in your carry-on rather than checking it, as explosive-detection machines used on checked luggage have been known to mistake food (especially chocolate, for some reason) for bombs. Travelers in the U.S. are allowed one carry-on bag, plus a "personal item" such as a purse, briefcase, or laptop bag.

Carry-on hoarders can stuff all sorts of things into a laptop bag; as long as it has a laptop in it, it's still considered a personal item. The Transportation Security Administration (TSA) has issued a list of restricted items; check its website (www.tsa.gov) for details.

Airport screeners may decide that your checked luggage warrants a hand search. You can now purchase luggage locks that allow screeners to open and relock a checked bag if hand searching is necessary. Look for Travel Sentry certified locks at luggage or travel shops and Brookstone stores (you can buy them online at www.brookstone.com). Luggage inspectors can open these TSA-approved locks with a special code or key—rather than having to cut them off the suitcase, as they normally do to conduct a hand search. For more information on the locks, visit www.travelsentry.org.

FLYING FOR LESS: TIPS FOR GETTING THE BEST AIRFARE

Passengers sharing the same airplane cabin rarely pay the same fare. Travelers who need to purchase tickets at the last minute, change their itinerary at a moment's notice, or fly one-way often get stuck paying the premium rate. Here are some ways to keep your airfare costs down.

- Passengers who can book their ticket **long in advance,** who can **stay over Saturday night,** or who **fly midweek** or **at less-trafficked hours** will pay a fraction of the full fare. If your schedule is flexible, say so, and ask if you can secure a cheaper fare by changing your flight plans.

- You can also save on airfares by keeping an eye out in local newspapers for **promotional specials** or **fare wars,** when airlines lower prices on their most popular routes. You rarely see fare wars offered for peak travel times, but if you can travel in the off-months, you may snag a bargain.

Tips Travel in the Age of Bankruptcy

Airlines go bankrupt, so protect yourself by **buying your tickets with a credit card,** as the Fair Credit Billing Act guarantees that you can get your money back from the credit card company if a travel supplier goes under (and if you request the refund within 60 days of the bankruptcy). **Travel insurance** can also help, but make sure it covers against "carrier default" for your specific travel provider. And be aware that if a U.S. airline goes bust midtrip, a 2001 federal law requires other carriers to take you to your destination (albeit on a space-available basis) for a fee of no more than $25, provided you rebook within 60 days of the cancellation.

- Search **the Internet** for cheap fares (see "Planning Your Trip Online," earlier in this chapter).
- Try to book a ticket **in its country of origin.** For multileg trips, book in the country of the first leg; for example, book New York–London–Amsterdam–Rome–New York in the U.S.
- **Consolidators,** also known as bucket shops, are great sources for international tickets, although they usually can't beat the Internet on fares within North America. Start by looking in Sunday newspaper travel sections; U.S. travelers should focus on the *New York Times, Los Angeles Times,* and *Miami Herald.* For less-developed destinations, small travel agents who cater to immigrant communities in large cities often have the best deals. *Beware:* Bucket shop tickets are usually nonrefundable or rigged with stiff cancellation penalties, often as high as 50% to 75% of the ticket price, and some put you on charter airlines with questionable safety records.

  Several reliable consolidators are worldwide and available on the Net. **STA Travel** (© **800/781-4040;** www.statravel.com) is now the world's leader in student travel, thanks to their purchase of Council Travel. It also offers good fares for travelers of all ages. **Flights.com** (© **800/TRAV-800;** www.flights.com) started in Europe and has excellent fares worldwide, but particularly to that continent. **FlyCheap** (© **800/FLY-CHEAP;** www.1800flycheap.com) is owned by package-holiday megalith MyTravel and so has especially good access to fares for sunny destinations.
- Join **frequent-flier clubs.** Accrue enough miles, and you'll be rewarded with free flights and elite status. It's free, and you'll get the best choice of seats, faster response to phone inquiries, and prompter service if your luggage is stolen, your flight is canceled or delayed, or if you want to change your seat. You don't need to fly to build frequent-flier miles— **frequent-flier credit cards** can provide thousands of miles for doing your everyday shopping.

LONG-HAUL FLIGHTS: HOW TO STAY COMFORTABLE

Long flights can be trying; stuffy air and cramped seats can make you feel as if you're being sent parcel post in a small box. But with a little advance planning, you can make an otherwise unpleasant experience almost bearable.

- Your choice of airline and airplane will definitely affect your legroom. Among U.S. airlines, American Airlines has the best average seat pitch (the distance between a seat and the row in front of it). Find more details at **www.seatguru.com**, which has extensive details about almost every seat on six major U.S. airlines. For international airlines, research firm Skytrax has posted a list of average seat pitches at **www.airlinequality.com**.

- Emergency exit seats and bulkhead seats typically have the most legroom. Emergency exit seats are usually held back to be assigned the day of a flight (to ensure that the seat is filled by someone able-bodied); it's worth getting to the ticket counter early to snag one of these spots for a long flight. Keep in mind that bulkheads are where airlines often put baby bassinets, so you may be sitting next to an infant.

- To have two seats for yourself, try for an aisle seat in a center section toward the back of coach. If you're traveling with a companion, book an aisle and a window seat. Middle seats are usually booked last, so chances are good you'll end up with three seats to yourselves. And in the event that a third passenger is assigned the middle seat, he or she will probably be more than happy to trade for a window or an aisle.

- Ask about entertainment options. Many airlines offer seatback video systems where you get to choose your movies or play video games—but only on some of their planes. (Boeing 777s are your best bet.)

- To sleep, avoid the last row of any section or a row in front of an emergency exit, as these seats are the least likely to recline. Avoid seats near highly trafficked toilet areas. You also may want to reserve a window seat so

---

Tips **Coping with Jet Lag**

Jet lag is a pitfall of traveling across time zones. If you're flying north-south and you feel sluggish when you touch down, your symptoms will be caused by dehydration and the general stress of air travel. When you travel east to west or vice versa, however, your body becomes thoroughly confused about what time it is, and everything from your digestion to your brain gets knocked for a loop. Traveling east, say, from Chicago to Paris, is more difficult on your internal clock than traveling west, say, from Atlanta to Hawaii, as most peoples' bodies find it more acceptable to stay up late than to fall asleep early.

Here are some tips for combating jet lag:

- **Reset your watch** to your destination time before you board the plane.
- **Drink lots of water** before, during, and after your flight. Avoid alcohol.
- **Exercise and sleep well** for a few days before your trip.
- If you have trouble sleeping on planes, **fly eastward on morning flights.**
- **Daylight** is the key to resetting your body clock. At the website for **Outside In** (www.bodyclock.com), you can get a customized plan of when to seek and avoid light.
- If you need help getting to sleep earlier than you usually would, doctors recommend taking either the hormone **melatonin** or the sleeping pill **Ambien**—but not together. Some suggest that you take 2 to 5 milligrams of melatonin about 2 hours before your planned bedtime—but again, always check with your doctor on the best course of action for you.

that you can rest your head and avoid being bumped in the aisle.

- Get up, walk around, and stretch every 60 to 90 minutes to keep your blood flowing. This helps avoid deep vein thrombosis, or "economy-class syndrome," a rare and deadly condition that can be caused by sitting in cramped conditions for too long.
- Drink water before, during, and after your flight to combat the lack of humidity in airplane cabins—which can be drier than the Sahara. Bring a bottle of water on board. Avoid alcohol, which will dehydrate you.
- If you're flying with kids, don't forget to carry on toys, books, pacifiers, and chewing gum to help them relieve ear pressure buildup during ascent and descent. Let each child pack his or her own backpack with favorite toys.

12 Package Deals & Escorted Tours

PACKAGES FOR THE INDEPENDENT TRAVELER

Before you start your search for the lowest airfare, you may want to consider booking your flight as part of a travel package. Package tours are not the same thing as escorted tours. Package tours are simply a way to buy the airfare, accommodations, and other elements of your trip (such as car rentals, airport transfers, and sometimes even activities) at the same time and often at discounted prices—kind of like one-stop shopping. Packages are sold in bulk to tour operators—who resell them to the public at a cost that usually undercuts standard rates.

One good source of package deals is the airlines themselves. Most major airlines offer air/land packages, including **American Airlines Vacations** (© 800/321-2121; www.aavacations.com), **Delta Vacations** (© 800/221-6666; www.deltavacations.com), **Continental Airlines Vacations** (© 800/301-3800; www.coolvacations.com), and **United Vacations** (© 888/854-3899; www.unitedvacations.com). Several big **online travel agencies**—Expedia.com, Travelocity, Orbitz, Site59, and Lastminute.com—also do a brisk business in packages. If you're unsure about the pedigree of a smaller packager, check with the Better Business Bureau in the city where the company is based, or go online at www.bbb.org. If a packager won't tell you where it's based, don't fly with them.

Qantas Vacations USA (© 800/641-8772 in the U.S., or 310/322-6359; fax 310/535-1057) and **Qantas Vacations Canada** (© 800/268-7525 in Canada; fax 416/234-8569) offer good deals. Travel packages are also listed in the travel section of your local Sunday newspaper. Or check ads in the national travel magazines such as *Arthur Frommer's Budget Travel Magazine, Travel & Leisure, National Geographic Traveler,* and *Condé Nast Traveler.*

Package tours can vary by leaps and bounds. Some offer a better class of hotels than others. Some offer the same hotels for lower prices. Some offer flights on scheduled airlines, while others book charters. Some limit your choice of accommodations and travel days. You are often required to make a large payment upfront. On the plus side, packages can save you money, offering group prices but allowing for independent travel. Some even let you add on a few guided excursions or escorted day trips (also at prices lower than if you booked them yourself) without booking an entirely escorted tour. Be sure to shop around and watch out for hidden expenses. Ask whether airport departure fees and taxes, for example, are included in the total cost.

ESCORTED TOURS

Escorted tours are structured group tours, with a group leader. The price usually includes everything from airfare to hotels, meals, tours, admission costs, and local transportation.

Many people derive a certain ease and security from escorted trips. Escorted tours—whether by bus, motorcoach, train, or boat—let travelers sit back and enjoy their trip without having to spend lots of time behind the wheel. All the little details are taken care of; you know your costs upfront; and there are few surprises. Escorted tours can take you to the maximum number of sights in the minimum amount of time with the least amount of hassle—you don't have to sweat over the plotting and planning of a vacation schedule. Escorted tours are particularly convenient for people with limited mobility.

On the downside, an escorted tour often requires a big deposit upfront, and lodging and dining choices are predetermined. As part of a cloud of tourists, you'll get little opportunity for serendipitous interactions with locals. The tours can be jam-packed with activities, leaving little room for individual sightseeing, whim, or adventure—plus they also often focus only on the heavily touristed sites, so you miss out on the lesser-known gems.

Before you invest in an escorted tour, ask about the cancellation policy, the schedule, and the size and demographics of the group. Discuss what is included in the price, and find out if you'll be charged if you decide to opt out of certain activities or meals. *Note:* If you choose an escorted tour, think strongly about purchasing trip-cancellation insurance, especially if the tour operator asks you to pay upfront. See the section on "Travel Insurance," earlier in this chapter.

Mount Cook Tours (© 800/468-2665) offers escorted tour options. Other reputable tour companies include:

- **Contiki Holidays,** P.O. Box 6774, Wellesley St., Auckland (© **09/309-8824;** www.contiki.com), offering 3- to 15-day coach tours for 18- to 35-year-olds throughout New Zealand.
- **Thrifty Tours,** P.O. Box 31257, Milford, Auckland (© **0800/803-550** in NZ, or 09/359-8380; www.thrifty tours.co.nz), with well-planned 2- to 16-day tours.
- **Britz New Zealand,** 5 Aintree Ave., Auckland (© **09/275-9090;** www. britz.com), providing tours throughout New Zealand in modern coaches with multilingual guides.
- **Discover New Zealand,** Private Bag 92-637, Auckland (© **0800/330-188** in NZ, or 03/306-7670; www. discovernewzealand.com), which offers a range of 3- to 8-day tours designed for travelers who want the value and security of prebooked arrangements combined with the freedom and independence of doing their own thing.
- **Scenic Pacific Tours,** P.O. Box 14037, Christchurch (© **0800/500-388** in NZ, or 03/359-9133; www. scenicpacific.co.nz), which offers a large range of day excursions, short tours, and independent holidays.
- **Sheppard Touring,** P.O. Box 60097, Titirangi, Auckland (© **09/817-0044;** www.touring.co.nz), tours throughout New Zealand in two- to five-star coaches. It also operates as an inbound wholesaler and can package all of your travel arrangements at competitive rates.

13 Getting Around

BY PLANE

A year seldom passes without some slight upheaval in New Zealand's domestic air scene. **Air New Zealand** (© **0800/737-000** in NZ, or 03/479-6594; www.airnz.co.nz), with Air New Zealand Link, now dominates the airways, with **Qantas New Zealand** (© **0800/808-767** in NZ, or 09/357-8900; www.qantas.co.nz) servicing the main centers and **Freedom Air** (© **0800/600-500** in NZ, or 09/523-8686; www.freedomair.com) offering cheaper internal flights to major cities. **Origin Pacific** (© **0800/302-302** in NZ, or 03/547-2020; www.originpacific.co.nz) has scheduled air services to 14 internal destinations; and British-owned **Virgin Blue** recently was granted access to New Zealand and its trans-Tasman operations, as **Pacific Blue** (© **0800/670-000;** www.flypacificblue.com), began with Brisbane-to-Christchurch flights in late 2003. Several other smaller airlines fly internal routes, and you'll come across other aircraft willing to fly chartered routes.

If your time is limited, the **South Pacific Airpass** offered by Air New Zealand (© **800/262-1234** in the U.S.) is a good deal. It allows travel domestically within New Zealand, and also trans-Tasman from New Zealand and the Pacific Islands. The fare is broken into four zones, and each zone has a list of cities you can fly between. A New Zealand Zone One fare would be NZ$120 to NZ$144 (US$84–US$101); a Zone Four fare costs NZ$340 to NZ$408 (US$238–US$286). Stopovers are not permitted, and *fares must be purchased before you reach New Zealand, or any of the destinations included in the fares.* Refunds of unused coupons are possible if minimum conditions have been met. The **Star South Pacific** Airpass has all the same rules as the South Pacific Airpass

except that passengers must travel internationally on a Star Alliance carrier. By doing so, they get an even lower fare.

Air New Zealand Shortbreaks (© **0800/737-000** in NZ), available in New Zealand, are short packages for 2 to 4 nights. They offer an affordable way of seeing New Zealand and include airfare and accommodations.

BY COACH (BUS)

Coaches offer a cost-effective way of getting around New Zealand; as a bonus, you don't have to worry about driving on the left and studying maps. Most give excellent commentaries and stop frequently for refreshments en route, but smoking is not permitted. The two major services in New Zealand (both owned by the same company) are **InterCity,** operating three-star coaches on New Zealand's most comprehensive coach network, visiting 600 towns and cities daily; and **Newmans,** which operates a premier sightseeing service with five-star coaches on selected routes. *Reminder:* Book coach journeys in advance during peak travel periods (summer and holidays).

INTERCITY InterCity (© **09/913-6100** in Auckland and 03/379-9020 in Christchurch; www.intercitycoach.co.nz) offers discounts to students, seniors over 60, and YHA members and VIP (Backpackers) cardholders. Check out their **Flexi-Pass,** which allows travelers to buy blocks of travel time, up to 40% cheaper than standard fares on all InterCity and Newmans journeys. You can purchase anything from 5 hours of travel time for NZ$52 (US$36) to 60 hours for NZ$557 (US$390). For more information, check out www.flexipass.co.nz. InterCity also has a number of regional passes. For instance, the **West Coast Passport** costs from around NZ$110 to NZ$170 (US$77–US$119) depending on departure point and is good for 3 months on the route from Nelson to Queenstown. The **North Island Value Pass** costs around NZ$160 (US$112) and is also good for 3 months. You can also pay a one-off joining fee of NZ$15 (US$11) for **Club Free-Way** and for every dollar you spend with either InterCity or Newmans, you earn points, which entitle you to further free travel. Simply telephone to join.

InterCity and Newmans coaches are also included in the **Travelpass New Zealand** deal, which allows you to travel with New Zealand's largest coach, train, air, and ferry network. The **"3 in 1" Travelpass** gives you access to Tranz Scenic's four long-distance trains, the InterCity, Newmans and private coach companies' national networks, the Interislander ferry service, a sightseeing discount book, and more. The Travelpass with 5 days' travel over a 10-day period costs approximately NZ$460 (US$322); 22 days' travel within 8 weeks costs NZ$950 (US$665).

A **"4 in 1" Travelpass** is also available, and it includes one short or long domestic flight sector; up to three additional sectors can also be purchased. The "4 in 1" Travelpass with 5 days' travel over 10 days (long flight) costs approximately NZ$820 (US$574); 22 days' travel over 8 weeks, NZ$1,320 (US$924). For information, contact **Travelpass New Zealand** (© **0800/339-966** in NZ, or 09/638-5780; fax 09/638-5774; www.travelpass.co.nz).

NEWMANS COACH LINES   Newmans (© **09/913-6200** in Auckland; www.newmanscoach.co.nz) has added the lower half of the South Island to its extensive North Island coverage. In 2005, it also added new service between Rotorua and Wellington, with stops at the sights and attractions between. It offers discounts to anyone over 60, students, and holders of YHA cards, New Zealand Backpackers Passes, or Independent Traveller Discount Cards. Their five-star coaches are video- and restroom-equipped and they offer comprehensive multilingual commentaries in German, Japanese, Spanish, and Mandarin.

ALTERNATIVE BUSES & SHUTTLES

Great Sights, Private Bag 92637, Auckland (© **09/375-4700;** www.greatsights.co.nz), offers a wide range of day, overnight, and multiday tours throughout New Zealand, utilizing a modern fleet of luxury coaches with multilingual commentary and complimentary hotel pickups. For the young and/or adventurous, **Kiwi Experience,** 195–197 Parnell Rd., Parnell, Auckland (© **09/366-9830;** www.kiwiexperience.com), and the **Magic Travellers Network,** 120 Albert St., Auckland (© **09/358-5600;** www.magicbus.co.nz), provide something that's between a standard coach and a tour. Popular with backpackers, they travel over a half dozen pre-established routes, and passengers can get off whenever they like and pick up the next coach days or weeks later. The coaches make stops at scenic points along the way for bush walking, swimming, and sometimes even a barbecue. Prices vary according to the route, but typically are from around NZ$700 (US$490) to cover both islands in 14 days. Passes are valid for 12 months with Magic Travellers and 12 months with Kiwi Experience. **Flying Kiwi Expeditions,** 4B Forests Rd., Stoke, Nelson (© **03/547-0171;** www.flyingkiwi.com), is another fun-packed flexible alternative to the well-beaten tourist trail. They have 10 offers that combine travel and outdoor activities, priced according to the number of activities included. For other zany southern alternatives try **Bottom Bus,** P.O. Box 434, Dunedin (© **03/442-9708;** www.bottombus.co.nz), which offers fully guided bus tours exploring the very south of New Zealand.

Shuttle transport is another alternative. Numerous companies on both islands run minibus shuttles between cities. Some of them are listed in the regional chapters, and you can also get details from area information centers. **Atomic Shuttles** (© **03/322-8883;** www.atomic-travel.co.nz) in Christchurch offers service between 30 South Island destinations.

BY TRAIN

Tranz Scenic (© **0800/872-467** in NZ; www.tranzscenic.co.nz) now operates three long-distance train routes through rugged landscapes—the Overlander, which runs Auckland to Wellington; the TranzCoastal, Christchurch to Picton; and the TranzAlpine, Christchurch to Greymouth. The trains, under new ownership since 2001, are modern and comfortable, heated or air-conditioned, carpeted, and ventilated. Service has greatly improved under new management, and views of spectacular landscapes are assured. Tranz Scenic offers discounts for students, YHA members, Backpackers cardholders, and those over 55. It also has a limited number of Saver Fares and Super Saver Fares during off-peak times. Also inquire about the **Scenic Rail Pass** (© **0800/872-467** in NZ; www.tranz scenic.co.nz), which enables you to discover New Zealand by train at your own pace and includes one ferry crossing. A 7-day pass costs around NZ$300–NZ$350 (US$210–US$245).

The train routes and their fares are as follows:

- **Auckland-Wellington:** The Overlander has reclining seats and a licensed buffet car that serves drinks and food. The standard one-way fare is around NZ$150 (US$105) but look out for Super Saver fares.

  You get informative commentary as you pass through many scenic highlights. Hostesses and stewards supply newspapers, magazines, and drinks service.

- **Christchurch-Picton:** The Tranz-Coastal passes through dramatic landscapes for 5½ hours; the standard one-way fare is around NZ$130 (US$91) and you can choose to stop off in Kaikoura for a spot of whale-watching.
- **Christchurch-Greymouth:** The TranzAlpine is the best of the lot. It goes through the unforgettable landscape of Arthur's Pass National Park, depositing you 4½ hours later in Greymouth. The return fare is around NZ$162 (US$113). Day excursions are also available on these routes.

BY CAR

I think roads in New Zealand are pretty good, but I've heard many Americans say they're terrible and that New Zealanders are aggressive drivers. I do know that traffic on New Zealand roads, especially in the South Island, is minimal compared to that found in Northern Hemisphere cities. Unfortunately, I do have to agree with the bit about aggressive drivers. The biggest dangers are excessive speed and foolhardy overtaking, so be careful of both. It is also important that visitors do not underestimate travel times. Distances may seem short in kilometer terms but roads are very often winding and sometimes narrow. Progress can be slower than you expect. There are multilane motorways approaching most larger cities, and most roads are dual carriageways. There are some single lane and unsealed roads in remote areas, and these should be approached cautiously—as should all roads during the winter months when rain and ice can create treacherous surfaces. Statistics show that in 2003, 632 drivers in New Zealand with foreign licenses were involved in nonfatal road smashes and 23 in fatal crashes. Police at the scene of 85 of the nonfatal and 3 of the fatal crashes believed that the fact the driver was foreign was a factor in the accident. So, the message is: Keep your wits

---

Tips **Mapping a Path**

You'll receive a set of maps when you collect your rental car; if you're a member of the Automobile Association in the United States, Australia, Britain, or other European countries, you'll have reciprocal privileges with the New Zealand AA. One of the best maps of the country is issued by the **New Zealand Automobile Association**, 99 Albert St., Auckland (© **09/377-4660**); 343 Lambton Quay, Wellington (© **04/473-8738**); or 210 Hereford St., Christchurch (© **03/379-1280**). AA sells other detailed maps as well, plus "strip maps" of your itinerary and comprehensive guidebooks of accommodations (some of which give discounts to AA members). Be sure to bring your membership card from home. **Wises Mapping**, 360 Dominion Rd., Mount Eden, Auckland (© **09/638-7146**), also produces an excellent map, available at newsstands and bookshops throughout New Zealand.

---

about you and don't underestimate the danger just because fewer cars are on the roads.

If you plan to drive, consider joining the **Automobile Association (AA)** while you're here. In New Zealand, call © **0800/500-213;** there are also AA offices in most towns. AA offers excellent breakdown services and advice to drivers. If you belong to a similar organization in your home country, membership is free, so don't forget to bring along your membership card.

DRIVING RULES & REQUIREMENTS You must be at least 21 to 25 years old to rent a car in New Zealand, and you must have a driver's license that you've held for at least 1 year from the United States, Australia, Canada, or the United Kingdom (or an international driving permit). Recent law changes mean all drivers, including visitors, must carry their license or permit at all times.

Remember to drive on the left and wear seat belts at all times. The open-road speed limit is 100kmph (62 mph); in towns and built-up areas, 50kmph (31 mph). Rigid speeding laws are now in place and you face heavy fines if you exceed limits. New Zealand has also tightened up its drunk-driving laws, and if you are stopped in a random police

check for compulsory breath testing for alcohol, you must take the test.

CAR RENTALS Every major city has numerous rental-car companies and international companies like Avis, Budget, and Hertz hire a wide range of vehicles. Most offer good deals that can be prebooked before you leave home. However, it pays to shop around and compare not only the prices, but also the cars. Some companies offer cheap deals, but their cars may be well over 10 years old. Most companies also require that you take out accident insurance with an insurance company authorized by them, and you generally need to be 25 to be able to rent a car in New Zealand.

Maui Rentals (© **800/351-2323** in the U.S.; www.maui-rentals.com) has vehicles that are either brand-new or less than a year old. Daily rates range from NZ$75 to NZ$155 (US$53–US$109), depending on the size of the car and the time of year. The price includes GST and unlimited mileage, but insurance runs about NZ$20 (US$14) extra per day. Because Maui has offices in Auckland and Christchurch, there's no extra charge for one-way trips. Contact the local offices at 36 Richard Pearce Dr., Mangere, Auckland (© **09/275-3013;** fax 09/275-9690), or 530–544 Memorial Ave.,

Christchurch (℗ **0800/651-080** in NZ, or 03/358-4159). Both provide courtesy airport shuttle service.

Auto Rentals NZ Wide (℗ **0800/736-893** in NZ, or 800/905-8071 in U.S.; www.autorentals.co.nz) is an established chain offering a modern fleet of cars for budget-minded travelers. They offer sedans, station wagons, and minibuses at competitive rates. They are also an accredited TranzRail booking agency and can help with interisland ferry and train bookings, accommodations, and further vehicle rentals.

Affordable Rental Cars, 48 Carr Rd., Mount Roskill, Auckland (℗ **0800/454-443** in NZ, or 09/630-1567; fax 09/630-3692), has daily rates on unlimited-mileage vehicles from around NZ$35 to NZ$95 (US$25–US$67), depending on the vehicle and time of travel. Prices include GST and insurance.

If you want to spoil yourself, try **Classic Car Touring New Zealand,** 181 Hobson St., Auckland (℗ **021/702-623** in NZ; www.classiccartouring.co.nz), specializing in self-drive classic cars; or **Smartcars Luxury Car Hire,** 110 Nelson St., Auckland (℗ **0800/458-987** in NZ, or 09/307-3553; www.smartcars.co.nz), offering the very latest convertibles and 4×4s from Europe.

You can also rent in advance from the following: **Avis** (℗ **800/230-4898** in the U.S.; www.avis.com), **Budget** (℗ **800/527-0700** in the U.S.; www.budget.

com), **Hertz** (℗ **800/654-3131** in the U.S.; www.hertz.com), and **Thrifty** (℗ **800/847-4389** in the U.S.; www.thrifty.com). Daily costs average about NZ$100 to NZ$150 (US$70–US$105).

ALTERNATIVES TO RENTING A CAR   If you'll be in New Zealand for an extended period of time, it may be worthwhile to investigate the guaranteed tourist buyback plan offered by **North Harbour Hyundai,** 175 Wairau Rd., Takapuna (℗ **09/444-7795;** fax 09/444-7099). This Auckland dealership sells used Toyotas, Nissans, Hondas, and similar cars to visitors with a written agreement to purchase them back after a stipulated time period. Cars come with a nationwide warranty; the owner pays for the insurance. For an example of what to expect, **Wheels,** 179 Moorhouse Ave., Christchurch (℗ **03/366-4855**), has sold buyback vehicles for NZ$5,000 (US$3,500) and bought them back for approximately NZ$3,000 (US$2,100) after 3 months of use. (*Note:* This is only an example of a possible scenario.)

If you're staying in hostels, you'll often find car-share schemes advertised on notice boards. If you want to arrange a carpool officially, contact **Travelpool** (℗ **09/307-0001**). It puts people who need a ride in touch with those willing to give them one. The system operates throughout the country, and the person getting the ride pays a small commission

---

⟨Tips⟩ Taking to the Highways

Some kind and ever-so-thoughtful person—and I think it might be someone at **Jasons Publishing** (www.jasons.com)—had the frightfully good sense to create seven marvelous highway route planners. They include *The Twin Coast Discovery Highway,* covering Northland and Auckland, and *The Pacific Coast Highway,* covering Auckland, Coromandel, coastal Bay of Plenty, Eastland, and Hawkes Bay. These free maps detail the best features of each trip, places to stay and eat, and adventures to sample along the way. They're available at visitor centers throughout the country.

and something toward gas costs, which usually works out to be about half the cost of a bus ticket.

BY RV OR MOTOR HOME

If you want ultimate freedom, consider renting what we call a campervan. Both **Maui Rentals** (© **800/351-2323** in the U.S., or 0800/651-080 in NZ) and **Newmans** (© **09/302-1582** in Auckland) offer minivans and motor homes. Maui rents a two-berth vehicle (per day) from around NZ$70 to NZ$195 (US$49–US$137), a four-berth from NZ$115 to NZ$285 (US$81–US$200), and a six-berth from around NZ$124 to NZ$307 (US$87–US$215). Insurance will cost an extra NZ$20 to NZ$38 (US$14–US$27) per day. **Britz New Zealand** (© **0800/831-900** in NZ; www.britz.com) also has excellent rates.

If you fancy yourself in something super-funky, opt for New Zealand's most distinctive campervans, individually painted by top new Zealand artists. You can get these from **Escape Rentals** (© **0800/216-171;** www.escaperentals.co.nz), which has depots in Auckland, Wellington, and Christchurch. They offer competitive rates and unlimited free kilometers, but don't for one minute think you'll escape attention.

BY MOTORCYCLE

If you enjoy the thrill of speed and the wind in your hair, you can rent motorcycles or purchase tour packages with or without guides. Just bring your full motorcycle license or international driving permit and call **New Zealand Motorcycle Rentals and Tours,** 35 Crummer Rd., Ponsonby, Auckland (© **09/360-7940**), or 166 Gloucester St., Christchurch (© **03/377-0663;** www.nzbike.com), which has a wide range of BMW, Honda, Harley, and Yamaha bikes. They're official NZ Tourism Award winners and all their gear is in top condition. **Adventure New Zealand Motorcycle**

Tours & Rentals, 29 Bolt Rd., Nelson (© **021/969-071;** www.gotournz.com), offers a range of deluxe tours with top-class bikes and upmarket accommodation for the 35-to-65 age bracket. **Towanda Women,** 2 Scott St., Rangiora, Christchurch (© **03/313-2342;** www.towanda.org), specializes in guided New Zealand–wide motorcycle tours for women only.

BY BICYCLE

New Zealand's mild summer climate and varied landscape make it an ideal cycling destination. Many companies run tours or rent bicycles. Start with **Bicycle Rentals.co.nz,** 52 Rutherford St., Nelson (© **03/546-6936;** www.bicyclerentals.co.nz), which offers a range of cycles for rental, plus a buy-back option that allows you to sell your bike for 50% of its cost at the end of your tour. **City Cycle Hire,** 73 Wrights Rd., Christchurch (© **0800/343-848** in NZ, or 03/339-4020; www.cyclehire-tours.co.nz), has a 12-day South Island Explorer Tour, plus a 5-day adventure on the Central Otago Rail Trail. **Adventure South,** P.O. Box 33–153, Christchurch (© **03/942-1222;** www.advsouth.co.nz or www.remarkableadventures nz.co.nz), has a wide range of guided cycle tours in the South Island.

BY TAXI

Taxi stands are located at all airport and transport terminals and on major shopping streets of cities and towns. You cannot hail a taxi on the street within a quarter-mile of a stand. Taxis are on call 24 hours a day, although there's an additional charge if you call for one. Drivers don't expect a tip just to transport you, but if they handle a lot of luggage or perform other special services, it's perfectly acceptable to add a little extra. Be aware that many taxi drivers in Auckland, Wellington, and Christchurch are new immigrants and don't always have a comprehensive grasp of English. See regional chapters for specific taxi companies throughout New Zealand.

BY INTERISLAND FERRY

Crossing Cook Strait on one of the ferry services will give you a chance to see both islands from the water, as well as the serene Marlborough Sounds. There are two ferry companies operating on the Strait, which can be boarded in either Wellington or Picton.

The **Interislander** ferry system (© 0800/ 802-802 in NZ; www.interislander.co. nz) operates every day year-round with three vessels—*Arahura, Kaitaki,* and *Aratere*—that offer a tourism experience in their own right, not just a practical means of getting across the water. You can choose from six daily departure times; the crossing takes 3 hours. The ferries have licensed bar and cafe areas, TV lounges, shops, and play areas, and the new *Kaitaki,* the biggest ferry in New Zealand, has two movie theaters and room for 1,600 passengers. These three ferries have three fare types: Easy Change, Saver Change, and Ultra Saver. **Easy Change** are the most flexible fares and can be canceled right up to check-in without cancellation fees. **Saver Change** are the midrange fares that incur a 50% fee if canceled. **Ultra Saver** fares are the cheapest way to travel, but once booked they're nonrefundable. They are available all year but numbers are limited, so book early. **Overseas bookings** can be made by international customers online, or by calling © 64/4-498-3302, but from outside of New Zealand you can only book Easy Change fares. Ultra Saver and Saver Change fares can only be booked within New Zealand and they sell out quickly during peak season.

If you're traveling by train or InterCity Coach, ask about the cost-effective through-fares, which are subject to availability.

Bicycles and sports gear can be taken on the ferry for a small additional cost, as well as campervans or motor homes—though these travel at a premium fare. *Note:* If you plan to transport a vehicle by ferry, you need a confirmed reservation.

Bluebridge Cook Strait Ferry (© 0800/ 844-844 in NZ; www.bluebridge.co.nz) sails twice daily between Wellington and Picton. The vessel features lounges, cafe and bar facilities, outdoor decks, free big-screen movies, and a shop. Fare bookings are transferable until 24 hours before travel subject to availability, but they're nonrefundable.

Regardless of which ferry you select, keep in mind that Cook Strait is a notoriously changeable stretch of water, and high swells can affect those prone to seasickness. Bad weather may also affect scheduled departures.

14 Tips on Accommodations

Unfortunately, there's nothing standard about accommodations rates here, and what you get for NZ$150 (US$105) can be much better than something for two or three times the price. My words of advice are: Ask around, visit websites for photographs, and don't just assume that all places in the same price range offer the same standard of accommodations. (They probably do in the Expensive range, but certainly not in the Moderate and Inexpensive categories.) The big news is that New Zealand tourism's official mark of quality, **Qualmark** (www. qualmark.co.nz), has now been applied to all accommodations types and tourism businesses. This means they have been independently assessed as professional and trustworthy and graded one star (acceptable), two stars (good), three stars (very good), four stars (excellent), and five stars (exceptional, among the best in New Zealand). Each business has undergone a rigorous assessment and licensing process to become part of the Qualmark licensing system.

However, you should realize that—according to this Qualmark system—a three-star hotel is not the same as a three-star B&B or a three-star lodge; or that a five-star B&B is not the same as a five-star hotel. Each category of accommodations is assessed on different criteria.

It is also worth noting that many accommodations operators have little faith in this new rating system because it's voluntary and not all properties have been assessed. There is particular discontent at the top end of the market, where operators are disillusioned that star ratings are being applied to businesses that are already self-regulatory.

If you would like more information when you arrive in New Zealand, pick up the free **Qualmark Accommodation Guide** from information centers (or order it at www.qualmark.co.nz); it lists all participating hotels, motels, B&Bs, backpackers, campgrounds, and tourism businesses.

There is a multitude of lodging options available in New Zealand—here's a rundown on what you'll find.

HOTELS   A hotel generally provides a licensed bar and restaurant, and guest rooms do not usually have cooking facilities. In New Zealand, "hotel" refers to modern tourist hotels, including the big international chains and older public-licensed hotels generally found in provincial areas. The latter are completely different from the former.

The country hotel, or pub, offers inexpensive to moderate accommodations of a modest nature. It's often noisy and old-fashioned with shared bathrooms down the hall. There are definitely exceptions, with upgrading a big trend in popular tourist areas. One way or another, they're usually rich in character.

Modern hotels come in all price levels. Several big international chains have two

or three grades of hotels, and you can get exceptionally good deals if you book with the same chain throughout the country. In major tourist centers such as Queenstown, competition is fierce and good prices can be found. In major corporate destinations such as Auckland and Wellington, rates will be considerably higher during the week, with weekends bringing superb specials.

MOTELS & MOTOR INNS   A motel unit is self-contained and usually has cooking facilities, a bathroom, and one or two bedrooms. A motor inn often has a restaurant on the premises.

Don't assume that New Zealand motels are the same as those you find in, say, the United States. There has been a major shakeup of standards in the motel industry, and many motels and motor inns are superior to some hotels. Look for the Qualmark sign of quality, which is prominently displayed on signs and promotional material.

BED & BREAKFASTS   As the name suggests, B&B rates include bed and breakfast, but it's often difficult to tell the difference between a bed-and-breakfast, a homestay, a farmstay, a guesthouse, a lodge, and a boutique hotel. B&B operators seem to be using a plethora of terms to describe much the same thing. Suffice it to say, in all of the above, that the key advantage is interaction with New Zealanders.

Homestays and bed-and-breakfasts are pretty much the same thing when it comes to terminology, but the variation in quality within both can be disconcerting—you'll find both the ludicrously cheap and the ludicrously expensive, and price is not necessarily an indicator of what you'll get. **Homestays** tend to be more family oriented and modest, especially in rural areas and provincial towns. Be prepared to simply get a bed in a family home. **B&Bs,** on the other hand, can be as downmarket or as upmarket as

⌒Tips En Suites

In New Zealand, the term "en-suite bathroom" refers to a bathroom incorporated within the bedroom. A private bathroom refers to a bathroom outside the bedroom, which is used exclusively by the guests of one room. A shared bathroom is a communal bathroom used by all guests in the establishment. Many accommodations within New Zealand have en-suite bathrooms, but it still pays to request them in B&Bs and backpacker establishments, many of which still have shared or private bathrooms.

---

you're prepared to pay; some rival the best hotels for quality.

I strongly advise you to check websites, or wait until you're in New Zealand to purchase one of the numerous B&B guides. Look for *The New Zealand Bed & Breakfast Book,* which illustrates every property in full color. Another reliable source is *Heritage & Character Inns of New Zealand* (www.heritageinns.co.nz), which details about 90 of the country's best B&B lodgings in heritage homes. Ask for brochures at visitor centers.

We can safely assume that **farmstays** are located on farms. They present an ideal opportunity to get a feel for New Zealand's rural life. There are several organizations that will put you in touch with a reliable farmstay: **New Zealand Farm Holidays** (✆ **09/412-9649;** fax 09/412-9651; **www.accommodation-new-zealand.co.nz**), and **Hospitality Plus, The New Zealand Home & Farmstay Company** (✆ **03/693-7463;** fax 03/693-7462; www.hospitalityplus.co.nz).

Guesthouses generally offer good value: modest rooms at modest prices. You can check out a selection of them with **New Zealand's Federation of Bed & Breakfast Hotels Inc.,** 52 Armagh St., Christchurch (✆ **03/358-6928;** fax 03/355-0291; www.nzbnbhotels.com).

COUNTRY LODGES There are many establishments calling themselves "lodges" when, strictly speaking, they don't meet lodge criteria as defined by the New Zealand Lodge Association. In the truest sense, country lodges in New Zealand are small and highly individual, with 4 to 20 bedrooms. They're fully licensed and have an all-inclusive tariff. They generally offer the very best of everything, including fine dining (three-to five-course dinners). The unspoken factors are the degree of exclusivity that exceeds B&Bs and the degree of personalized service and pampering that exceeds most hotels. For information, go to **www.lodgesofnz.co.nz**. A new luxury accommodations category was also added to the Qualmark program in 2003.

HOLIDAY HOMES When they're not being used by their owners, holiday homes can be rented by the night or for longer periods. Known as **baches** in the North Island and **cribs** in the South Island, they are a good value for independent travelers. You can buy *Baches & Holiday Homes to Rent,* which details over 500 properties, from bookstores or the **Automobile Association,** 99 Albert St., Auckland (✆ **09/377-4660**); 343 Lambton Quay, Wellington (✆ **04/473-8738**); or 210 Hereford St., Christchurch (✆ **03/379-1280**). For a wider variety—from cozy cottages to super-luxury homes—contact **New Zealand Vacation Homes** (www.nzvacationhomes.co.nz), which lists self-catering properties throughout the country.

HOSTELS Hostels are generally frequented by backpackers, but most welcome people of all ages and have single and double rooms as well as dorms. They have shared facilities (some have en-suite bathrooms) and communal lounges and kitchens; some have cafes and/or bars.

Further information can be found by contacting the following: **YHA New Zealand National Reservations Centre** (② **03/379-9808;** fax 03/379-4415; www. yha.co.nz) has hostels open 24 hours a day that do not impose curfews or duties. **Budget Backpacker Hostels New Zealand** (②/fax **07/377-1568;** www.backpack.co. nz) lists over 300 hostels around the country; and **VIP Backpacker Resorts of New Zealand** (② **09/827-6016;** fax 09/827-6013; www.vip.co.nz) is supported by over 60 hostels. **Nomads** (② **0800/666-237;** www.nomadsworld.com) offers hostel accommodations at 16 sites.

MOTOR CAMPS & HOLIDAY PARKS

These properties have communal kitchens, toilets, showers, and laundries, and a variety of accommodations from campsites and cabins to flats and backpacker-style lodges. They are very popular with New Zealand holidaymakers during the summer months, so make sure you book ahead. They make an ideal base if you are traveling by motor home. Two contacts for holiday parks are **Top 10 Holiday Parks** (② **0800/867-836** in NZ; fax 03/377-9950; www.topparks.co.nz) and **Holiday Accommodation Parks New Zealand** (② **04/298-3283;** www.holiday parks.co.nz).

15 Tips on Dining

My best advice to anyone coming to New Zealand is to plan plenty of exercise so that you'll be perpetually hungry and therefore well able to justify every single overindulgence that you're likely to be faced with. Forget restraint and prepare to be surprised by the level of sophistication of the New Zealand dining experience. This is a land of edible bounty—Canterbury lamb, Central Otago pinot noir, Bluff and Nelson oysters, Nelson scallops, Kaikoura crayfish (lobster), West Coast whitebait, South Island venison, Waiheke cabernet sauvignon, Marlborough green-lipped mussels, Gisborne chardonnay, Akaroa salmon, Stewart Island blue cod, Central Otago cherries and apricots—and you shouldn't miss any of it.

On top of the usual restaurant and cafe experiences, you'd be doing yourself a disservice if you miss special events like the traditional Maori hangi, where food is cooked underground; the sheer craziness of the annual Hokitika Wildfoods Festival, where the policy is "If it's not moving, it's edible"; and the numerous annual wine and food festivals held in individual provinces and always well-publicized at information centers.

Within the restaurant scene itself, there has been a revolution in the last decade. Fine dining (silver service) still lingers in a few city pockets, but the upmarket trend is predominantly toward fine gourmet food in more relaxed, contemporary settings. You'll be spoiled with all the choices in this category, especially in Auckland, Wellington, Christchurch, and Queenstown (in that order).

For moderately priced, casual meals, including lunches, there are now so many cafes, restaurants, and bars it seems silly to try to define what each delivers. In short, you will seldom be without a choice. Just be aware that many cafe/bar establishments offer lighter meals and by 11pm often turn into rowdy drinking holes.

A word on service: New Zealand has not "grown up" with a long tradition of service in restaurants, so there will be times when you wonder if we even know what the word "service" means. For many young people, being a waitress or waiter is a reluctantly sought holiday job to earn money for university studies—and sadly, it often shows. However, the competitive market is forcing restaurant owners to wake up to the importance of good, friendly, smiling service, and many polytechnics now offer proper training. It is heartening to see a gradual swing towards a belief that restaurant service can be a career option, not just a long-suffering ordeal.

Service glitches are more noticeable in smaller provincial centers, and some of that can be attributed to a lack of suitable employees in the district. Areas such as the West Coast face the reality of young people moving out to the cities; and major tourist centers like Queenstown tend to have a very transient population of restaurant employees.

New Zealand restaurants are either licensed to serve alcohol or BYO (bring your own), and some are both. BYO of course is cheaper, as you don't have to pay the restaurant's surcharge on the wine. Some BYO establishments do charge a corkage fee (usually NZ$2–NZ$5/US$1.40–US$3.50) for opening the wine bottle. *Note:* BYO means wine only, not beer or any other alcoholic beverages.

New Zealand restaurants and cafes do not apply any sort of surcharge to simply sitting at a restaurant table. You are only charged for what you purchase. However, where there are outdoor cafe tables, you must purchase from the restaurant/cafe they're owned by. You cannot use this seating as a casual resting place when you get sore feet.

Most cafes and restaurants now have table service, but some smaller cafes still operate on a counter service policy, where you place your order at the counter and pay before receiving your meal.

Important note: All cateries are now smoke-free. This is a government edict, with smoking banned across the board in all restaurants, nightclubs, and public buildings.

Tipping is not customary in New Zealand, although I've never met a New Zealander who doesn't like a show of appreciation for good service and value. But that's relative. My policy is *don't tip for the sake of it.* You may be used to that in your own country, but I maintain that that does nothing to foster an improvement in New Zealand serving standards, which, let's face it, still need work. If you feel you've had a special dining experience and would like to reward the staff, then do so by all means, but be aware that many restaurants operate a shared tipping system, so your favorite waitress or waiter may not be the only recipient of your good will. She/he may have to share the goodies with others who may not deserve it—something I personally would like to see changed.

Dining hours vary from one eatery to another. Many cafes and restaurants open for coffee from around 9 to 10am and serve lunch between noon and 2 or 3pm, reverting to coffee and snack service only after that, then serving dinner from 6pm on. Others open for dinner only and that is almost always from 6pm onward.

Other than that, it's all pretty straight-forward—eat and enjoy! Oh, and don't forget New Zealand wine. With the many international award-winners to our credit, I can assure you, you *will* be tempted!

For more details about food and wine in New Zealand, see "A Taste of New Zealand" and "Wine, Wine & More Wine" in appendix A.

16 Recommended Books & Films

Katherine Mansfield (1888–1923) put us on the map with her still-admired short stories set in New Zealand (though she spent most of her adult life in Europe). Among contemporary fiction writers, Keri Hulme won the prestigious Booker McConnell Prize for *The Bone People* in 1985; Janet Frame is famous for *Owls Do Cry, An Angel at My Table,* and several others; Owen Marshall is perhaps our finest living short-story writer; and the late Barry Crump is a legend of a completely unique, raw, backcountry style, having produced books like *A Good Keen Man* and *Hang On a Minute Mate.*

Top Maori writers include Witi Ihimaera, Patricia Grace, and Alan Duff. In addition, Maurice Gee, Maurice Shadbolt, Fiona Kidman, and Lauris Edmond all warrant attention.

Jane Campion attracted world attention with *The Piano,* which was nominated for nine categories at the Academy Awards. (Anna Paquin of Wellington won best supporting actress.) Director Peter Jackson grabbed headlines when he secured Hollywood funding for *Lord of the Rings,* which was filmed in 2000 with the biggest film budget ever. His *Heavenly Creatures* (1994) was winner of the Silver Lion at the Venice Film Festival. Two of Maori author Alan Duff's novels have been made into films; *Once Were Warriors* and *What Becomes of the Broken Hearted* have shocked audiences with their true-to-life violent portrayal of Maori gang society. More recently, *Whalerider* has won international acclaim from movie audiences.

FAST FACTS: New Zealand

American Express The office is at 105 Queen St., Auckland (℡ 09/367-4422). Other offices are located in Christchurch, Hamilton, Nelson, Porirua, Pukekohe, Queenstown, Rotorua, Wellington, and Whangarei. They accept mail for clients, forward mail for a small fee, issue and change traveler's checks, and replace lost or stolen traveler's checks and American Express cards.

Business Hours Banks are open from 9am to 4:30pm Monday through Friday. Shops are usually open from 9am (sometimes 8am) to 5:30pm Monday through Thursday, and until 9pm on either Thursday or Friday. Increasingly, shops are open all day Saturday; many shops are also open all day Sunday, with others closing between noon and 4pm.

Drugstores Pharmacies observe regular shop hours, but most localities have an Urgent Pharmacy, which remains open until about 11pm every day except Sunday, when there are two periods during the day when it's open, usually one in the morning and one in the afternoon.

Electricity The voltage is 230 volts in New Zealand, and plugs are the three-prong type. If you bring a hair dryer, it should be a dual-voltage one, and you'll need an adapter plug. Most motels and some B&Bs have built-in wall transformers for 110-volt, two-prong razors, but if you're going to be staying in hostels, cabins, homestays, or guesthouses, bring dual-voltage appliances.

Embassies & Consulates In Wellington, the capital city, you'll find the United States Embassy, the Canadian High Commission, and the British High Commission (see "Fast Facts: Wellington," in chapter 11). In Auckland, you'll find consulates for the United States, Canada, and Ireland (see "Fast Facts: Auckland," in chapter 5).

Emergencies Dial © **111** to contact the police, call an ambulance, or report a fire.

Film Film is expensive in New Zealand, so try to carry as many rolls as you can. Most brands are available in larger cities.

Internet Access Internet facilities are available in all major cities and in many smaller towns. Consult visitor centers for specifics, or go to www.cybercafes.com. Many establishments now offer broadband and wireless connections.

Language English is spoken by all New Zealanders. You'll hear Maori spoken on some TV and radio programs and in some Maori settlements.

Liquor Laws The minimum drinking age is 18 in pubs. Children are allowed in pubs with their parents.

Lost & Found Be sure to tell all of your credit card companies the minute you discover your wallet has been lost or stolen and file a report at the nearest police precinct. Your credit card company or insurer may require a police report number or record of the loss. Most credit card companies have an emergency toll-free number to call if your card is lost or stolen; they may be able to wire you a cash advance immediately or deliver an emergency credit card in a day or two. Visa's emergency number is © **0508/600-300** in NZ. American Express cardholders and traveler's check holders should call collect to the U.S. at © **715/343-7977**. MasterCard holders should call © **0800/44-9140** in NZ.

If you need emergency cash over the weekend when all banks and American Express offices are closed, you can have money wired to you via **Western Union** (© **0800/005-253** in NZ; www.westernunion.com).

Identity theft or fraud are potential complications of losing your wallet, especially if you've lost your driver's license along with your cash and credit cards. Notify the major credit-reporting bureaus immediately; placing a fraud alert on your records may protect you against liability for criminal activity. The three major U.S. credit-reporting agencies are **Equifax** (© **800/766-0008**; www.equifax.com), **Experian** (© **888/397-3742**; www.experian.com), and **TransUnion** (© **800/680-7289**; www.transunion.com). Finally, if you've lost all forms of photo ID, call your airline and explain the situation; they might allow you to board the plane if you have a copy of your passport or birth certificate and a copy of the police report you've filed.

Mail New Zealand post offices will receive mail and hold it for you for 1 month. Have the parcel addressed to you c/o Poste Restante at the Chief Post Office of the town you'll be visiting. It costs NZ$2 (US$1.40) to send an airmail letter to the United States or Canada and NZ$2 (US$1.40) to the United Kingdom or Europe. Overseas postcards cost NZ$1.50 (US$1.05).

Maps Get free maps from AA offices around the country by showing your home-country membership card. Rental-car firms also furnish maps with rentals.

Passports **For Residents of the United States:** Whether you're applying in person or by mail, you can download passport applications from the U.S. State Department website at **http://travel.state.gov**. For general information, call the **National Passport Agency** (© **202/647-0518**). To find your regional passport office, either check the U.S. State Department website or call the **National Passport Information Center** (© **900/225-5674**); the fee is 55¢ per minute for automated information and $1.50 per minute for operator-assisted calls.

For Residents of Canada: Passport applications are available at travel agencies throughout Canada or from the central **Passport Office,** Department of Foreign Affairs and International Trade, Ottawa, ON K1A 0G3 (© **800/567-6868;** www.ppt.gc.ca).

For Residents of the United Kingdom: To pick up an application for a standard 10-year passport (5-year passport for children under 16), visit your nearest passport office, major post office, or travel agency or contact the **United Kingdom Passport Service** at © **0870/521-0410** or search its website at www.ukpa.gov.uk.

For Residents of Ireland: You can apply for a 10-year passport at the **Passport Office,** Setanta Centre, Molesworth Street, Dublin 2 (© **01/671-1633;** www.irl gov.ie/iveagh). Those under age 18 and over 65 must apply for a €12 3-year passport. You can also apply at 1A South Mall, Cork (© **021/272-525**) or at most main post offices.

For Residents of Australia: You can pick up an application from your local post office or any branch of Passports Australia, but you must schedule an interview at the passport office to present your application materials. Call the **Australian Passport Information Service** at © **131-232,** or visit the government website at www.passports.gov.au.

Pets New Zealand has strict restrictions on the importation of animals. If you must bring a pet, check first with any New Zealand embassy or consulate. Be prepared to quarantine pets in Hawaii for several months.

Restrooms There are "public conveniences" strategically located in all cities and many towns. Local **Plunket Rooms** come with a "Mother's Room," where you can change your child's diapers. The Plunket Society is a state-subsidized organization that provides free baby care to all New Zealand families.

Taxes There is a national 12.5% **Goods and Services Tax (GST)** that's applicable to everything. A **departure tax** of NZ$25 (US$18) is assessed and can be paid by credit card or in cash in New Zealand currency.

Telephone The country code for New Zealand is **64.** When calling New Zealand from outside the country, you must first dial the country code, then the city code (for example, 03, 09, or 06), but without the zero. The telephone area code in New Zealand is known as the **STD (subscriber toll dialing).** To call long distance within New Zealand, dial the STD—**09** for Auckland and Northland, **07** for the Thames Valley, **06** for the east coast and Wanganui, **04** for Wellington, or **03** for the South Island—and then the local number. (If you're calling from outside New Zealand, omit the zero.) For operator assistance within New Zealand, dial **010;** for directory assistance, **018.** There are three main kinds of public telephones in New Zealand: card phones, credit card phones, and coin phones. Magnetic strip **phone cards** for public phones can be purchased from supermarkets, post offices, dairies, and service stations.

The most economical way to make international phone calls from New Zealand is to charge them to an international calling card (available free from your long-distance company at home). All calls, even international ones, can be made from public phone booths. (Long-distance calls made from your hotel or motel often have hefty surcharges added.) To reach an international operator, dial **0170**; for directory assistance for an international call, dial **0172**. You can also call home using **Country Direct** numbers. They are **000-911** for the U.S.; **000-944** for British Telecom (operator); **000-912** for British Telecom (automatic); **000-940** for UK Mercury; **000-919** for Canada; **000-996** for Australia-Optus; and **000-961** for Australia-Telstra.

Time Zone New Zealand is located just west of the international dateline, and its standard time is 12 hours ahead of Greenwich Mean Time. Thus, when it's noon in New Zealand, it's 7:30am in Singapore, 9am in Tokyo, 10am in Sydney; and—all the previous day—4pm in San Francisco, 7pm in New York, and midnight in London. In New Zealand, daylight saving time starts the first weekend in October and ends in mid-March.

Tipping Most New Zealanders don't tip waitstaff unless they've received extraordinary service—and then only 5% to 10%. Give taxi drivers about 10% and porters NZ$1 to $2 (US70¢–US $1.40), depending on how much luggage you have.

Water New Zealand tap water is pollution free and safe to drink. In the bush, you should boil, filter, or chemically treat water from rivers and lakes to avoid contracting *Giardia* (a waterborne parasite that causes diarrhea).

3

The Active Vacation Planner

From the northernmost tip to the last speck of land in the south, New Zealanders have found ways to tackle the great outdoors, and their enthusiasm for the whole adventure game has drawn millions of curious people to see just what it's all about.

Regardless of your fitness level, you'll find something to suit you. You can do almost anything in New Zealand—rock climbing, caving, horse trekking, paragliding, and much more. Below are details on the major activities, such as tramping, skiing, and biking; look to the regional chapters for additional information.

The **New Zealand Tourism Board** website (www.purenz.com) will key you into wilderness and big thrills. Ask for the excellent *Naturally New Zealand Holidays* guide at an NZTB office near you (see "Visitor Information" in chapter 2) or from **Naturally New Zealand Holidays** (✆ **03/318-7540;** fax 03/318-7590; www.nzholidays.co.nz).

1 Tramping

Tramping (also known as hiking) is one of the best ways to explore the pristine forests, clear blue lakes, sparkling rivers, fern-filled valleys, and snow-capped peaks of New Zealand. The **Department of Conservation (DOC),** P.O. Box 10-420, Wellington (✆ **04/471-0726;** fax 04/471-1082; www.doc.govt.nz), maintains more than 8,000km (about 5,000 miles) of tracks (trails) and 900 backcountry huts throughout New Zealand's 13 national parks and numerous scenic reserves.

A series of short walks or one big multiday hike? Both are available, but much will depend on your fitness level and the amount of time you have. Consider whether you want to be a **freedom walker** (independent) or a **guided walker.** Independent walkers can sleep in huts with bunk beds, cooking facilities, and toilets, but they must carry their own food, bedding, and cooking utensils. These overnight huts are sometimes staffed, should you need any assistance or advice along the way.

Tramping in New Zealand is best tackled from late November to April, when temperatures are the most moderate. From May to October, alpine tracks can be difficult and often dangerous once snow falls. (See the weather and temperature information in chapter 2 before planning a hiking vacation.) Don't forget to bring broken-in boots, a daypack, water bottles, sunglasses, sunscreen, a flashlight (known as a "torch" in New Zealand), and a hat. *Remember:* You should never attempt any multiday hikes without first checking in, paying your fees, and giving DOC staff an idea of your plans; and always be aware of changeable weather conditions and the very real potential for hypothermia—even in summer.

SHORT WALKS There are literally hundreds of fabulous short walks through all sorts of landscapes. From a leisurely stroll along a city promenade to deserted beaches, fern-lined bush walks, forest trails, volcanic wanders—you name it, and you can probably have it. Every region has its hidden treats. Look in the regional chapters that follow for some of the most popular choices and seek advice from any visitor center or Department of Conservation office, most of which have an extensive array of walking brochures.

Short walks tend to range from 45 minutes to a full day. Depending on your interests, don't forget to bring along binoculars, a camera, and a sketchpad or journal. If you're in doubt about the difficulty of a trail, always ask the visitor center staff, or be prepared to turn back if the going gets too tough. Hiking trails in New Zealand are generally very well maintained.

HIKING SAFARIS Many companies offer combinations of hiking, kayaking, and other adventures in one or more areas. The **New Zealand Walks Network** (www.walknewzealand.com) was set up in conjunction with Tourism New Zealand to raise the profile of high-quality guided walking experiences available in New Zealand. The Walks Network is a group of independent companies that operate guided walks in our national parks, wilderness areas, and special reserves, providing the best available accommodations with meals, comfortable bedding, and bathroom facilities. Qualified guides provide comprehensive interpretation of natural and cultural history; walkers need only carry personal items—not including food or bedding.

  New Zealand Nature Safaris ✿✿, in Christchurch (© **025/360-268;** fax 03/ 328-8173; www.hikingnewzealand.com) offers small group hiking/camping tours of 3 to 10 days throughout the national parks. **Bush and Beyond** (©/fax **03/ 528-9054;** www.naturetreks.co.nz) offers guided 1- to 8-day tramps in Kahurangi National Park; you can also add in photography and wildlife excursions. **Kahurangi Guided Walks** (© **03/525-7177;** www.kahurangiwalks.co.nz), also operates in this area, offering year-round small-group guided walks in the Abel Tasman and Kahurangi national parks. **Absolutely Angling** (formerly Wilderness Adventures), in Taupo (©/fax **07/378-4514;** www.wilderness.co.nz), is where you'll find highly qualified guide Ian Ruthven, who can organize multiday adventures that include tramping, kayaking, canoeing, abseiling, climbing, fishing, and more. **Canterbury Trails,** in Christchurch (© **03/337-1185;** fax 03/337-5085; www.canterburytrails.co.nz), offers easy to moderate 9-day Wilderness South Expeditions via minivan, which include guided walks and heritage and ecology experiences. It also offers 14-day Natural North'South New Zealand tours in conjunction with Kiwi Dundee Adventures in the Coromandel (see chapter 6). And in the far south, **Kiwi Wilderness Walks** (© **0800/733-549** in NZ; fax 03/442-8342; www.nzwalk.com) offers 3- to 5-day tramping, kayaking, and wildlife experiences in remote areas of Stewart Island, the Waitutu Track, and Dusky Sound.

MULTIDAY WALKS New Zealand has some of the best multiday walks in the world. The trails are well maintained and take you through unforgettable scenery. Several can also be done as guided walks, which makes them accessible to people of all fitness levels.

  Not everyone can agree on which one is the *best* walk, but the Department of Conservation (www.doc.govt.nz/index.html) has identified these tramping tracks as the "Great Walks" in New Zealand: the **Waikaremoana,** the **Tongariro Crossing,** and the **Ruapehu Circuit** on the North Island; the **Abel Tasman Coastal Track** and the **Heaphy, Routeburn, Milford,** and **Kepler tracks** on the South Island; and the **Rakiura Track** on Stewart Island.

Safety in the Great Outdoors

You won't find snakes and predatory animals here (at least not the four-legged kind), but anyone venturing out into wilderness areas ought to be prepared with a few common-sense safety hints.

- **Emergencies:** For emergencies anywhere in the country, dial ✆ **111.**
- **Getting lost:** Trampers must register their intended route and estimated time and date of return with the Department of Conservation (DOC) office closest to where they plan to trek. This is vitally important because, if no one knows you're out there, they're not going to start looking for you if you get lost or injured. Likewise, let DOC know as soon as you're finished so search parties are not set into action—and be aware that you can now be billed hundreds of thousands of dollars for an unnecessary search brought about by your actions and lack of consideration.
- **Weather:** Although New Zealand has a mild climate, the weather can change rapidly at any time of year, especially in the high country. *Always* tell people where you are going and when you are due back, and always go prepared with the right all-weather gear (at all times of the year), a sensible survival kit, and a good topographical map *that you can read!*
- **Hypothermia:** Hypothermia can kill, and its signs and symptoms should never be ignored. Watch for early warning signs: feeling cold, shivering, tiredness or exhaustion, anxiety, lethargy, lack of interest, clumsiness, slurred speech, difficulty in seeing, a sense of unreality, and irrational behavior. The later signs indicating a serious medical emergency are obvious distress, the cessation of shivering despite the cold, collapse and unconsciousness, and coma. The progress of hypothermia can be very fast, with as little as 30 minutes from the first symptoms to unconsciousness. It is imperative that you stop and find shelter, prevent further heat

If you'd like to strike out on your own, contact the **Department of Conservation,** P.O. Box 10-420, Wellington (✆ **04/471-0726;** fax 04/471-1082; www.doc.govt. nz). It maintains visitor centers throughout the country. Freedom walkers (independent hikers) need to get hut passes or tickets and register their hiking plans (known as "intentions") before setting out. The Milford and the Routeburn are generally the only two tracks where freedom walkers need to make advance reservations. Facilities along other trails are on a first-come, first-served basis. The DOC advises against children under 10 attempting any of the serious multiday hikes.

See the individual walks below for information on **guided walks.** Outfitters will arrange a guide, accommodations, meals, and the carrying of all gear except daypacks, which individual walkers carry themselves.

NEW ZEALAND'S BEST TRAMPS
MARLBOROUGH, NELSON & BEYOND
See the map "Marlborough, Nelson & Beyond," on p. 314, for the tramps in this area.

loss, assist in rewarming, get the victim into dry clothes, and seek help as quickly as possible.

Hypothermia is caused by cold, wind, wet clothing, lack of food, fatigue, injury and anxiety, and recent illness, especially the flu. Everyone is at risk, even the fit and healthy. It is always best to have four or more people in your party so one can stay with the victim and two can go for help.

- **Avalanches:** Skiers and snowboarders often start the avalanche that catches them. Most avalanches occur during and immediately after storms, and they are common on slopes steeper than 20 degrees.
- **Sun:** New Zealand's clear, unpolluted atmosphere produces strong sunlight and high ultraviolet levels. Wear brimmed hats, sunglasses, and lots of SPF 15+ sunscreen if you plan to be outdoors for longer than 15 minutes.
- **River levels:** Plan your trip around the use of bridges. Avoid river crossings and be aware of rising water levels during heavy rain.
- *Giardia:* In the bush, you should boil, filter, or chemically treat all water from lakes and rivers to avoid contracting this waterborne parasite, which causes diarrhea.
- **Sand flies:** Small in size, but big in nuisance value, sand flies are found in wet bush areas around rivers, lakes, and streams. They can be effectively controlled with regular use of strong insect repellents. If you get bitten, topical application of hydrocortisone ointment or tea-tree lotion should ease itching.
- **Safety brochures:** All of the above issues are dealt with in detail in a range of excellent free brochures produced by the **New Zealand Mountain Safety Council,** P.O. Box 6027, Te Aro, Wellington (© 04/385-7162; fax 04/385-7366; www.mountainsafety.org.nz), and are available at visitor Information and DOC centers.

QUEEN CHARLOTTE WALKWAY This 71km (44-mile) track passes through lush coastal forest, around coves and inlets, and along ridges offering spectacular views of the Queen Charlotte and Kenepuru sounds. (Boating is also popular here.) Stretching from historic Ship Cove to Anakiwa, the track can be walked in 3 to 5 days, and if you want a richer experience, you can add kayaking, mountain biking, diving, fishing, and bird-watching along the way. If you take a guided walk, you'll stay in cabins, rustic lodges, and homestays, and your pack will be carried by boat, meeting you at each overnight stop. If you'd rather not complete the whole 5-day venture, you can take a guided 1-day walk. Access to Ship Cove is by boat or floatplane, and you can start or finish the walk at any point.

Duration/Distance: 5 days/71km (44 miles)
Start: Ship Cove, Marlborough Sounds
End: Anakiwa, Marlborough Sounds
Open: Year-round; guided walks conducted November through May only
Contact Information: For an independent walk, contact the **Department of Conservation,** Picton Field Centre, Picton (© **03/575-7582;** fax 03/573-8262;

www.qctrack.co.nz). Camping costs NZ$5 (US$3.50) per night; lodging is available at various price levels. Transfers are available with the **Cougar Line** (© **0800/ 504-090;** fax 03/573-7926; www.queencharlottetrack.co.nz), which will drop you off, transfer your pack, and pick you up. Similar services are offered by **Endeavour Express** (© **03/573-5456;** fax 03/573-5434; www.boatrides.co.nz).

You can arrange a guided walk with the **Marlborough Sounds Adventure Company** (© **0800/283-283** in NZ, or 03/573-6078; fax 03/573-8827; www. marlboroughsounds.co.nz). Its 4- to 5-day walks include boat transfers, a guide, meals, hot showers, and accommodations in three lodges for around NZ$1,120 (US$784). The Ultimate Sounds Adventure (3 days/2 nights) starts at NZ$495 (US$347) with bunkroom accommodations, or NZ$655 (US$459) twin-share en suite. There's also a paddle-and-walk option that includes 2 days of sea kayaking and dolphin-watching. **Southern Wilderness NZ** (© **0800/266-266** in NZ, or 03/578-4531; fax 03/578-4533; www.southernwilderness.com) organizes 1- to 5-day guided or independent walks including luggage transfers and hotel-style accommodations from NZ$130 to NZ$1,690 (US$91–US$1,183). **Tramp The Track Boat** (© **0800/287-267** in NZ; www. charterguide.co.nz) allows you to live aboard boat and tramp or cycle the track for 3 days and 2 nights with a maximum of 10 guests.

ABEL TASMAN COASTAL TRACK Because of the enormous popularity of this stunning walkway through coastal forest and gorgeous beaches, the Department of Conservation has introduced a booking system for overnight huts that is in effect from October 1 to April 30 each year. The four huts have bunks, heat, and water, but no cooking facilities. Access to Marahau, where you begin, is by road or boat. Water taxis make it convenient to do just 1 day of the walk if your time is short. Buses pick you up at the end of the trail.

Duration/Distance: 3 to 5 days/52km (32 miles)
Start: Marahau, Abel Tasman National Park
End: Wainui Bay, Abel Tasman National Park
Open: Year-round; guided walks available year-round
Contact Information: Independent walkers can contact the **Department of Conservation,** King Edward and High streets, P.O. Box 97, Motueka (© **03/528-1810;** fax 03/528-1811). Hut fees are about NZ$15 (US$11) per night; camp fees are NZ$7 (US$4.90) per person per night; transfers are extra.

For guided walks, contact **Abel Tasman Wilson's Experiences** (© **0800/ 221-888** in NZ, or 03/528-7801; fax 03/528-6087; www.abeltasman.co.nz). Its 3-day kayak-and-walk package costs about NZ$988 (US$697) for adults and NZ$798 (US$559) for children. **Kahurangi Guided Walks** (© **03/525-7177;** www.kahurangi walks.co.nz), has 1-, 2-, and 3-day walks in the Abel Tasman and customizes trips to meet customer needs.

HEAPHY TRACK This track is known for its beauty and diversity. It crosses a range of landscapes, from the junction of the Brown and Aorere rivers over expansive tussock downs to the lush forests and roaring sea of the West Coast. The seven huts on the track have bunks, heat, water, and cooking facilities (except at two huts), and although you need a hut and camp pass, this does not guarantee a bunk. There are accommodations and transport at each end of the track, but be sure to arrange this before setting out. For transport to the beginning of Heaphy Track, contact **Kahurangi Bus Services** (© **03/525-9434;** fax 03/525-9430; www.kahurangi.co.nz). It has scheduled service between Nelson, Abel Tasman National Park, Golden Bay, and

Heaphy Track for approximately NZ$30 (US$21). If you're planning to travel to Westport or return to Nelson at the end of the track, make your transport reservations before you leave through the **Golden Bay Visitor Information Centre,** Willow Street, Takaka (*©* **03/525-9136;** gb.vin@nelsonnz.com).

Duration/Distance: 4 to 6 days/77km (48 miles)

Start: Brown Hut, Kahurangi National Park

End: Kohaihai River Mouth, north of Karamea, Kahurangi National Park

Open: Year-round; guided walks available year-round

Contact Information: For an independent walk, contact the **Department of Conservation,** 1 Commercial St., P.O. Box 53, Takaka (*©* **03/525-8026**). Hut fees are around NZ$15 (US$11) per night; camping fees are about NZ$10 (US$7) per night; transfers are extra.

For guided walks, call **Kahurangi Guided Walks** (*©*/fax **03/525-7177;** www.kahurangiwalks.co.nz); **Bush and Beyond** (*©*/fax **03/528-9054;** www.naturetreks.co.nz); or **Southern Wilderness NZ** (*©* **03/578-4531;** fax 03/578-4533; www.southernwilderness.com).

CANTERBURY

KAIKOURA COAST TRACK   This popular, dramatic coastal walk takes you through the best of New Zealand's high-country farming territory, with cottage accommodations at three farms along the way. You'll need a reasonable degree of fitness, as the track climbs from the sea to a height of 600m (1,968 ft.), with wonderful views over the Kaikoura Mountains. The track is also suitable for mountain biking. It's located a 1½-hour drive north of Christchurch and 45 minutes south of Kaikoura.

Duration/Distance: 3 days/43km (27 miles)

Start & End: "Hawkswood" historic sheep station, Kaikoura

Open: October through April

Contact Information: Contact Sally and David Handyside (*©* **03/319-2715;** fax 03/319-2724; www.kaikouratrack.co.nz). The track costs about NZ$135 (US$95) per person; groups are limited to 10 people. A 2-day mountain-bike option is available for NZ$70 (US$49) per person. Public transport is available in the form of shuttle buses and the InterCity coach service, both of which run between Christchurch, Kaikoura, and Blenheim. Shuttles leave from the Christchurch visitor center, which can provide details on the service. The cost of a shuttle to the track beginning at The Staging Post (on St. Hwy. 1) is around NZ$25 (US$18).

BANKS PENINSULA TRACK   This private Canterbury track crosses farmland, Hinewai Reserve, and volcanic coastline. You'll experience sandy beaches, safe swimming, waterfalls, cliff faces, beech forest, penguins, seals, dolphins, and rich birdlife. The track twice rises to over 600m (1,968 ft.) and features rugged exposed headlands, requiring a reasonable level of fitness. Children must be accompanied at all times. Accommodations are supplied in four farm cottages, two of which have a small shop for purchasing basics.

Duration/Distance: 4 days/35km (22 miles)

Start & End: Akaroa Village, 80km (50 miles) from Christchurch

Open: October 1 to April 30

Contact Information: Call **Banks Peninsula Track Ltd.** (*©* **03/304-7612;** fax 03/304-7738; www.bankstrack.co.nz). The 4-day tramp costs NZ$200 (US$140) per person; the 2-day tramps costs NZ$125 (US$88).

QUEENSTOWN & FIORDLAND

Independent walkers must have a reservation for walking the Milford and Routeburn tracks discussed below. Contact the **Department of Conservation,** Great Walks Booking Desk, Fiordland National Park Visitor Centre, P.O. Box 29, Te Anau (© **03/249-8514** or fax 03/249-8515 outside NZ; 03/249-7924 or fax 03/249-7613 inside NZ; www.doc.govt.nz). The number of people allowed on the tracks is limited and the demand great, especially from mid-December through January, so reserve as early as possible—6 months ahead is sometimes necessary. Remember those safety rules and warnings about hypothermia (see "Safety in the Great Outdoors," above)— they hold particularly true here. In this region, unpredictable weather can occur at any time, in any season, and you should always carry appropriate clothing for the worst weather conditions.

ROUTEBURN TRACK The Routeburn is a moderate track that links Mount Aspiring and Fiordland national parks via the Harris Saddle. In summer, it is one of the most popular tracks, but in winter, it's extremely hazardous and impassable with high avalanche danger. It takes you into the heart of unspoiled forests, along river valleys, and across mountain passes, and requires a good level of fitness. Bus transfers are available to the start of the track and from the finish for about NZ$50 (US$35) one-way; the DOC can furnish you with a list of all transport options. Remember that the Routeburn is not a circuit track and there are over 350km (217 miles) of road transport required between both ends of the track. Transport may cost you up to NZ$120 (US$84) if you need to return to your starting point.

Duration/Distance: 2 to 3 days/39km (24 miles)
Start & End: The Routeburn Shelter, 75km (47 miles) from Queenstown via Glenorchy, or The Divide Shelter, 80km (50 miles) from Te Anau on the Milford Road. The Routeburn can be walked in either direction.
Open: Late October to mid-April
Contact Information: For independent walks, contact the **Department of Conservation,** Great Walks Booking Desk, Fiordland National Park Visitor Centre, P.O. Box 29, Te Anau (© **03/249-8514;** fax 03/249-8515; greatwalksbooking@ doc.govt.nz). Hut fees are about NZ$45 (US$32) per night, camping fees NZ$15 (US$11) per night. Transfer costs are extra; advance track reservations are required.

For guided walks, call **Routeburn Walk Limited** (© **0800/768-832** in NZ, or 03/442-8200; fax 03/442-6072; www.routeburn.co.nz). It offers a 3-day package that begins in Queenstown. A coach will take you to "The Divide" (on Milford Rd.); you'll walk to Lake McKenzie, across the Harris Saddle, and past the Routeburn Falls. A coach will return you to Queenstown. Comfortable lodges are provided. The cost is from NZ$1,090 (US$763) for adults and NZ$850 (US$595) for children ages 10 to 15. Rates include transport, meals, and accommodations. Tours depart regularly from November through April, but you should reserve as far in advance as possible. Richard Bryant of **Guided Walks New Zealand** (© **03/442-7126;** fax 03/442-7128; www.nzwalks.com) also offers a 1-day option on the Routeburn.

For a 6-day excursion, called **The Grand Traverse,** combine the Routeburn and Greenstone Valley (see below) tracks. With Routeburn Walks Limited, this will cost from NZ$1,475 (US$1,033) per adult and includes transport, meals, and accommodations.

GREENSTONE VALLEY TRACK This walk follows an ancient Maori trail used by tribes to access the rich greenstone lodes near Lake Wakatipu. The trail you'll walk, however, was cut in the late 1800s by Europeans, who created a route between Lake Wakatipu and Martins Bay on the Fiordland coast. You'll pass Lake Howden and Lake McKellar, and follow the Greenstone River through deep gorges and open valley to Lake Wakatipu. Boat transfers are available to and from Elfin Bay. The Greenstone track can be walked in either direction, or can be linked to the Routeburn or Caples tracks for a 4- to 5-day round-trip (see "The Grand Traverse," below).

Duration/Distance: 2 days/40km (25 miles)

Start & End: Elfin Bay, Lake Wakatipu, 86km (53 miles) from Queenstown via Glenorchy

Alternative Start & End: Lake Howden near The Divide Shelter, 80km (50 miles) from Te Anau on the Milford Road

Open: November through April

Contact Information: For independent walks, contact the **Department of Conservation,** Fiordland National Park Visitor Centre, Lakefront Drive, P.O. Box 29, Te Anau (℅ **03/249-7924;** fax 03/249-7613). The hut fee is about NZ$15 (US$11) per night, plus transfers.

For guided walks, call **Routeburn Walk Limited** (℅ **0800/768-832** in NZ, or 03/442-8200; fax 03/442-6072; www.routeburn.co.nz), which provides accommodations and knowledgeable guides. The 3-day walk costs from NZ$1,200 (US$840) for adults, NZ$850 (US$595) for children ages 10 to 15. (Children under 10 are not allowed.)

THE GRAND TRAVERSE   This is a 6-day excursion that follows the Routeburn Track northbound for 3 days and then crosses into the Greenstone Valley Track for 3 days; available between November and April each year. The guided walk costs around NZ$1,700 (US$1,190) for adults and NZ$1,300 (US$910) for children ages 10 to 15. Make arrangements through **Routeburn Walk Limited** (℅ **0800/768-832** in NZ, or 03/442-8200; fax 03/442-6072; www.routeburn.co.nz).

HOLLYFORD TRACK   This relatively flat track follows the Hollyford River out to the coast at Martins Bay. You can walk it as a round trip or as a one-way with a fly-out from Martins Bay. You can also jet-boat the Demon Trail section of the track. Because there are no alpine crossings, this is one of the few Fiordland tracks that can be done year-round.

Duration/Distance: 4 days/56km (35 miles) one-way

Start: Hollyford Camp, 9km (5.6 miles) off Milford Road

End: Martins Bay (walk back or fly out)

Open: Year-round; guided walks available October through April only

Contact Information: For independent walks, contact the **Department of Conservation,** Fiordland National Park Visitor Centre, P.O. Box 29, Te Anau (℅ **03/249-7924;** fax 03/249-7613). There is a hut fee of about NZ$12 (US$8.40) per night. The jet boat, flight out, and bus transfer are extra.

For guided walks, contact **Hollyford Valley Guided Walk** (℅ **0800/832-226** in NZ, or 03/442-3760; fax 03/442-3761; www.hollyfordtrack.com). It offers stays in a comfortable lodge with hot showers. The 3- to 4-day package costs from NZ$1,550 (US$1,085), including pretour accommodations in Te Anau.

KEPLER TRACK   This 4-day tramp starts and ends at the Lake Te Anau outlet control gates. You'll pass through beech forests and a U-shaped glacial valley, and walk along the edges of Lakes Te Anau and Manapouri. This is a challenging hike with a lot of altitude variations. The track zigzags up 800m (2,624 ft.) and drops 1,000m

(3,280 ft.)—the single most useful thing you can take is a walking pole. Access is provided by shuttle bus and boat transfer.

Duration/Distance: 3 to 4 days/67km (42 miles)

Start & End: Te Anau Control Gates

Open: Late October to mid-April

Contact Information: For independent walks, contact the **Department of Conservation,** Fiordland National Park Visitor Centre, P.O. Box 29, Te Anau (✆ **03/ 249-7924;** fax 03/249-7613). Hut fees are about NZ$25 (US$18) per night, or NZ$40 (US$28) if you don't reserve in advance; the night camping fee is NZ$15 (US$11). Transfers are extra. Early bookings are essential.

MILFORD TRACK 🐾 Many consider the famous Milford Track the finest anywhere in the world. Known for its glacially carved valleys, alpine flowers, and waterfalls, the 4-day walk is closely regulated by DOC staff, both for the safety of hikers and for the preservation of the wilderness region. You'll walk from Glade Jetty at Lake Te Anau's northern end to Sandfly Point on the western bank of Milford Sound. The track follows the Clinton and Arthur valleys and crosses MacKinnon Pass, the one steep and more difficult stretch that takes about 2 hours to ascend. From here, at 1,073m (3,519 ft.), it's all downhill to Sandfly Point, where you'll be ferried across Milford Sound. You can spend the night at Milford or return to Te Anau, but reservations must be made for either option.

Duration/Distance: 4 days/54km (34 miles)

Start: Lake Te Anau (Te Anau Downs)

End: Sandfly Point near Milford Sound

Open: Late October to mid-April

Contact Information: For independent walks, contact the **Department of Conservation,** Great Walks Booking Desk, Fiordland National Park Visitor Centre, P.O. Box 29, Te Anau (✆ **03/249-8514;** fax 03/249-8515; greatwalksbooking@ doc.govt.nz). Reservations are accepted from early November to mid-April for the following tramping season, which runs from mid-October to mid-April. No more than 24 people can start the walk on any given day. The cost is around NZ$250 (US$175), which includes huts and transportation.

Milford Track Guided Walk (✆ **0800/659-255** in NZ, or 03/441-1138; fax 03/ 441-1124; www.milfordtrack.co.nz) provides coach transport to Te Anau via Queenstown and allows walkers greater flexibility in making international flight connections. It also has a Te Anau office (✆ **03/249-7411,** ext. 8063; fax 03/249-7590). Prices include guides, meals at overnight lodges, and accommodations at each end of the trek. Walkers carry their own daypacks. From December 1 to March 13, fees run from around NZ$1,800 (US$1,260) for adults and NZ$1,050 (US$735) for children ages 10 to 15 for a 6-day package (beginning and ending in Te Anau). From November 1 to November 30 and from March 14 to April 4 (dates vary slightly each year), the package costs slightly less.

The highly rated **Trips 'n' Tramps** (✆ **03/249-7081;** fax 03/249-7089; www. milfordtourswalks.co.nz) offers a 1-day option, with one guide for a maximum of 12 people. The package includes a scenic Lake Te Anau cruise, up to 5 hours on the Milford Track, easy walking (no hills), and a lunch stop (bring your own) at Clinton Hut. The cost is around NZ$155 (US$109); it's available November through March.

STEWART ISLAND

This is New Zealand's third-biggest island and a veritable nature paradise overlooked by most of the world—including the rest of New Zealand. But it is a spot for some astounding multiday treks and hundreds of delightful short walks. For information on the island, see chapter 16.

RAKIURA TRACK This is one of New Zealand's Great Walks and is suitable for anyone of moderate fitness. It takes trampers through bush and along beaches and open coast, and much of it is boardwalked. There are two huts and three designated campsites.

Duration/Distance: 3 days/36km (22 miles)
Start & End: Half Moon Bay, Oban
Open: Year-round
Contact Information: For independent walks, contact the **Department of Conservation,** P.O. Box 3, Stewart Island (© **03/219-0002;** fax 03/219-0003; stewart islandfc@doc.govt.nz). You must purchase a date-stamped Great Walks Pass or campsite pass (NZ$10/US$7 per-night hut fee) before taking this walk. Conservation staff may be on the track, and they will impose a surcharge on trampers using accommodations facilities without a pass, which must be displayed on packs at all times. Nightly campsite fees are NZ$6 (US$4.20) per adult, NZ$3 (US$2.10) per student.

NORTH WEST CIRCUIT ⚐ This track is designed for well-equipped, experienced trampers who will take 10 to 12 days working their way around the island's northwest arm. Nature is at its best in clean beaches, birds, and bush, but mud is widespread and often knee-deep on the track. You'll get great views and complete solitude.

Duration/Distance: 8 to 12 days/125km (78 miles)
Start & End: Half Moon Bay, Oban
Open: Year-round
Contact Information: For independent walks, contact the **Department of Conservation,** P.O. Box 3, Stewart Island (© **03/219-1130;** fax 03/219-1555; stewart islandfc@doc.govt.nz). The North West Circuit Pass costs NZ$38 (US$27). A Great Walks Pass (NZ$10/US$7 per night) is required for Port William and North Arm huts, which are part of the Rakiura Track. This also applies to campgrounds at Port William, Maori Beach, and Sawdust Bay. All other huts require hut tickets. A NZ$90 (US$63) Backcountry Pass may be used on the North West Circuit or Southern Circuit tracks. Huts are equipped with running water, mattresses, toilets, and wood-fired stoves. Before undertaking this walk, it might be a good idea to watch the excellent video of the track at the Department of Conservation office in Oban village, Half Moon Bay.

Kiwi Wilderness Walks, 90 Fitzpatrick Rd., Queenstown (© **0800/733-549** in NZ, or 021/359-592; fax 03/442-8342; www.nzwalk.com), offers a 5-day tour in Stewart Island National Park, which includes kiwi spotting at Mason Bay, a visit to Ulva Island, and sea kayaking in Paterson Inlet for around NZ$1,550 (US$1,085) per adult, NZ$1,300 (US$910) per child ages 10 to 15.

2 Fishing

Any prospective fisherman in New Zealand should get a copy of *Sports Fishing Guide,* a free booklet produced by the **New Zealand Fish and Game Council** (© **04/499-4767;** fax 04/499-4768; www.fishandgame.org.nz). This guide supplies you with the myriad rules and regulations you need to know. It also gives details on major fresh-water fishing spots. The **New Zealand Professional Fishing Guides Association** (© **06/863-5822;** fax 06/863-5844; www.nzpfga.com) may also be helpful. Another worthwhile website is **FishingHunting** (www.fishing.net.nz), which details news, weather, advice, charters, clubs, and fishing organizations. Go to www.newzealand fishing.com for **New Zealand Fishing Magazine** online. For assistance in planning a New Zealand fishing holiday from North America, contact **The Best of New Zealand Adventure Travel,** 2817 Wilshire Blvd., Santa Monica, CA 90403 (© **800/528-6129** in the U.S., or 310/998-5880; fax 310/829-9221). This agency specializes in angler activities and has a 48-page brochure called *The Best of New Zealand Fly Fishing* (which also includes information on saltwater fishing). More information can also be found at www.bestofnzflyfishing.com.

FRESHWATER FISHING

New Zealand's reputation as a trout fisherman's paradise is well established interna-tionally. It is the world's best place to fish for wild **brown trout** during the season, which lasts from the first Saturday in October to the end of April. During this time, all rivers and streams are open for brown and **rainbow trout,** but local restrictions may apply. There are several areas where you can fish year-round: the **Rotorua District** and **Lake Taupo** on the North Island, and **Lake Te Anau, Lake Brunner,** and **Lake Wakatipu** on the South Island.

The **Tongariro River,** near Turangi, is one of the prime trout-fishing rivers in the world. May through October are the best months to snag rainbow and brown trout, which average nearly 2 kilograms (4 lb.)! This period is also good for fishing in Lakes Taupo and Rotorua. Lake Rotorua is not stocked, but it has one of the highest catch rates in the district.

The Eastern Fish and Game region is also an angler's land of opportunity, with a huge range of fishing opportunities and diversity in both lake and river fishing. The bush-clad **lakes Waikaremoana** and **Waikareiti** provide spectacular boat and shore-line fishing for both brown and rainbow trout in untouched Te Urewera National Park.

Fishing is good in almost all areas of the South Island. In **Nelson,** you'll get rain-bow trout and also Quinnat salmon in many places, but it's the brown trout that's king of these mixed waters. **Canterbury** is best known for its prolific salmon runs that enter the large braided rivers such as the **Rakaia** and **Waimakariri,** and high-country rivers are known for small numbers of big fish.

In the West Coast region, **Lake Brunner** has brown trout averaging 1.1 kilograms (2½ lb.), and is the most popular angling water in the region. Farther south, the **Waitaki** and **Rangitata rivers** have been known to land trophy chinook salmon of 15 kilograms (33 lb.).

Fish and Game Otago has an excellent book, *Guide to Trout Fishing in Otago,* which covers 140 waters and gives information on access and methods. In **Southland,** dozens of rivers, streams, and lakes hold brown and rainbow trout, plus quinnat salmon. The waters of this region are widely known throughout New Zealand, but you have to be a competent fisherman and know your way around to be successful. **Southland Fish and Game,** P.O. Box 159, Invercargill (© **03/214-4501;** fishgame@southnet.co.nz), will be happy to supply maps, advice, information, and guides.

FISHING GUIDES   If fishing is your passion, consider investing some cash in a good guide. Be warned, however, that freshwater fishing guides in New Zealand are not cheap; some run as high as NZ$1,200 to NZ$1,500 (US$840–US$1,050) per day for one or two people. If you shop around, cheaper deals can be found. I've listed a few outfitters in the regional chapters where fishing is popular.

If you'd like to organize a fishing holiday, contact **South Island Fishing Tours** (©/fax **03/755-8032**; www.flyfishingnewzealand.co.nz). Tony and Marj Allan of Kawhaka Lodge in Hokitika offer 2- to 14-day fishing tours for one to two people, starting and finishing in Christchurch. **Chris Jolly Outdoors** (© **07/378-0623**; fax 07/378-9458; www.chrisjolly.co.nz) specializes in trout fishing on Lake Taupo (among other things) and can take you to the best trout rivers that flow into the lake. In Wanaka, **Gerald Telford** (©/fax **03/443-9257**; www.flyfishhunt.co.nz) charges about NZ$500 (US$350) for a day's fishing with equipment supplied.

SALTWATER & BIG-GAME FISHING

Deep-sea fishing is at its best along the magnificent 500km (310 miles) of Northland's coastline, slipping down into the Bay of Plenty. Waters less than an hour out from shore can yield **marlin, shark** (mako, thresher, hammerhead, tiger), five species of **tuna, broadbill,** and **yellowtail.** The season runs from mid-January to April, and you'll find well-equipped bases at the Bay of Islands in Northland, Whitianga on the Coromandel, and Tauranga and Whakatane in the Bay of Plenty. You can also fish for **kahawai, snapper,** and more anywhere along the New Zealand coast. Licenses are not required. You'll find more information about fishing charters in chapter 6.

3 Boating & Other Watersports

BOATING

Whether it's cruising a secluded bay or inlet, exploring uninhabited islands, or sailing in harbors and on lakes, New Zealanders have got boating down to a fine art. Of course, Auckland is famous for its excessive boat tally, but you'll find this passion reflected everywhere (except perhaps on the South Island's West Coast). The Marlborough Sounds are another big boating haven, as are the Bay of Plenty and Northland. Anytime between December and April, you'll find Kiwis taking to the water in some kind of seaworthy vehicle.

CANOEING & KAYAKING   The prime kayaking spot is Abel Tasman National Park, where boats appear to float in midair because the water is so clear. Sea kayaking is also popular in the Bay of Islands, in Hauraki Gulf, around Coromandel Peninsula, in Marlborough Sounds, in Milford Sound, and around Banks Peninsula and Otago Peninsula.

Try to book your adventures with members of **SKOANZ,** the **Sea Kayak Operators Association of New Zealand** (© **09/630-7768**; fax 09/630-7768; www.sea kayak.org.nz), who must adhere to a code of practice covering safety, service, guides, and environment.

In Northland, you'll find reliable operators at **Coastal Kayakers,** Paihia (© **09/402-8105**; fax 09/403-8550; www.coastalkayakers.co.nz), which explores the outer islands with lagoons, rock caves, and sandy beaches. You can have canoe adventures with **Canoe Safaris,** Ohakune (© **06/385-9237**; fax 06/385-8758; www.canoe safaris.co.nz). It has 5-day expeditions in rugged Whanganui National Park from late October to mid-April.

In Abel Tasman National Park, **Ocean River Adventure Company** (© 0800/ 732-529 in NZ; fax 03/527-8006; www.seakayaking.co.nz) offers guided tours of 1 to 3 days, and **Abel Tasman Kayaks** (© 0800/527-8022 in NZ; fax 03/527- 8032; www.kayaktours.co.nz) has 13 years of experience with guided trips.

JET-BOATING   For an adrenaline rush, try jet-boating—which is possible along most major rivers throughout the country. See regional chapters for more information.

SAILING   Given the running of the 1999–2000 and the 2002–03 America's Cup Challenge in Auckland, it's a bit of an understatement to say that sailing is popular. For the warmest, balmiest, most subtropical experiences, head for Northland, Auckland, and the Bay of Plenty; there's plenty of excellent sailing farther south, too.

For bareboat and skippered charters, contact **Moorings Rainbow Yacht Charters,** Bay of Islands (© 09/377-4840; fax 09/377-4820; moorings@onenz.co.nz), or **Royal Akarana Yacht Club,** Auckland (© 09/524-9945; fax 09/520-1380; www.rayc.org. nz), which charges from NZ$75 (US$53) per hour, from NZ$395 (US$277) for an 8-hour sailing day with hands-on experience for everyone. In Marlborough Sounds, try **Compass Charters,** 20 Beach Rd., Waikawa (© 03/573-8332; fax 03/573-8587; www.compass-charters.co.nz), offering budget to luxury yacht and launch charters.

Pride of Auckland (© 09/373-4557; fax 09/377-0459; www.prideofauckland. com) has four 50-foot yachts available for daily scheduled and charter cruises for all ages and abilities (see chapter 5); and **tall ship *Soren Larsen*** (© 09/411-8755; fax 09/411-8484; www.sorenlarsen.co.nz) is the tall ship that starred in the BBC's *The Onedin Line* television series in the late 1970s. It has a rich history and is available for day sailings and holiday cruises in New Zealand and the South Pacific (see chapter 5).

For general information on sailing, contact **Yachting New Zealand** (© 09/488- 9325; fax 09/488-9326; www.yachtingnz.org.nz).

WHITE-WATER RAFTING   The challenging Wairoa, Mohaka, and Kaituna rivers are popular on the North Island; in the south, you'll find action on the Shotover, Kawarau, and Rangitata rivers. You can do this year-round—wet suits and warm clothing are required in winter, though. Operators give instruction, supply equipment, and arrange transfers to and from launch points.

Rock 'n' River Adventures, Southern Lake Taupo (© 0800/865-226 in NZ; fax 07/386-0352; rock.n.river@xtra.co.nz), offers 1- to 2-day rafting expeditions, and **Rapid Sensations,** Taupo (© 0800/227-238 in NZ; fax 07/378-7904; www.rapids. co.nz), takes 3-day trips on the upper Mohaka River. If you want an all-out 9 days of crazy fun, contact **Ultimate Descents,** Motueka (© 0800/748-377 in NZ; fax 03/523-9811; www.rivers.co.nz), which exposes you to the serious thrills of the Buller, Karamea, and Clarence rivers on the top of the South Island.

OTHER WATERSPORTS: SCUBA DIVING & SURFING

SCUBA DIVING   With over 32,000km (19,840 miles) of coastline, New Zealand has no shortage of diving opportunities. The best diving seas in the land are around the **Poor Knights Islands** in Northland. This is where you'll find the wreck of the *Rainbow Warrior,* which is now covered quite nicely with reef formations. Visibility ranges from 20 to 69m (66–226 ft.) in the best months (Feb–June). Another excellent dive spot, renowned for its crystal-clear waters, is the much chillier **Stewart Island.** Brave divers can also immerse themselves in the murky, tannin-stained waters of **Milford Sound** for a truly unique experience.

No matter where you take the plunge, you must have evidence of your diving certification with you. For details, contact the **Dive Industry of New Zealand** (© 09/849-5896; fax 09/849-3526). Good resources include *Dive New Zealand* magazine online (www.divenewzealand.com); the internationally renowned **Waikato Dive Centre** (© 07/849-1922; fax 07/849-1942), which offers courses and dive trips; and Napier-based **Adventure Dive** (© 06/843-5148; fax 06/843-5149) for courses and dive tours.

SURFING & WINDSURFING   "Surf" is an interesting four-letter word that brings to mind a whole culture—not to mention big waves, big breaks, and big parties. When asked, every surfer will, of course, tell you his or her favorite beach is best, although it does seem unanimous that **Eastland** and **Gisborne** reliably turn out some of the best waves in the country. **Raglan,** west of Hamilton, is also popular; **Whangamata** and **Mount Maunganui,** in Bay of Plenty, and **Taylors Mistake,** near Christchurch, are others to consider. For surfing tours contact **New Zealand Surf Tours** (©/fax **09/832-9622;** www.newzealandsurftours.com), offering 1- to 5-day tours of the Auckland-Northland region.

Windsurfing is popular in many areas around Auckland: at Ferrymead in Christchurch; on Lyttelton Harbour, Christchurch; on Otago Peninsula; at Oakura near New Plymouth; and on Wellington Harbour.

4 Golf

New Zealand is a nation of golfers. There are approximately 400 private and public courses that offer myriad opportunities. And we're lucky to have some of the best, yet cheapest, golfing facilities you'll find anywhere. Greens fees are well below the world's average—you'll pay anything from NZ$10 to NZ$90 (US$7–US$63) for 18 holes on a good course, and up to NZ$150–NZ$200 (US$105–US$140) for the country's top links. Clubs, equipment, and a motorized cart (trundler) can be rented.

Diehards hit the courses year-round, but the best time to golf is from October to April, when temperatures range from 60°F to 70°F (16°C–21°C). Courses tend to be crowded on weekends, less so during the week.

There are 40 golf courses in the Auckland area alone. The **Gulf Harbour** and **Formosa Country Clubs** are the newest on the scene, and the former hosted the 1998 World Cup of Golf. In Rotorua, the **Arikikapakapa** course is dotted with geothermal activity, which makes the course tricky to play; near Taupo, you'll find one of the country's finest, the **Wairakei International Golf Course.** Wellington's **Paraparaumu Beach Golf Club** was rated one of the world's top 50 courses by *Golf Digest.* In Christchurch, both **Russley** and **Shirley** are well rated, along with **Balmacewan** and **St. Clair** in Dunedin.

For more information, contact the **New Zealand Golf Association** (© 04/385-4330; fax 04/385-4331; www.nzga.co.nz).

For golf packages, contact **New Zealand Golf Excursions USA, Inc.,** 2141 Rosecrans Ave., no. 1199, El Segundo, CA 90245 (© **800/622-6606** in the U.S.; fax 310/322-4972), or **Kiwi Golf Tours** (© **800/873-6360**).

In New Zealand, try **Golf NZ** (© **06/870-8740;** fax 06/870-8749; www.golf newzealand.co.nz), which offers tours for 12 to 36 golfers and partners from NZ$200 (US$140) per day including accommodations, travel, and golf; or **Big Boys Golf**

Tours (☎ 025/512-020; fax 07/843-9677; www.bigboysgolf.co.nz), which offers tours of top golf courses in the Auckland region.

5 Skiing & Snowboarding

When the sun warms up in the Northern Hemisphere, skiers and snowboarders come down to the Southern Hemisphere. The ski season generally runs from late June to September. The country has 13 conventional ski areas; as an added bonus at Mount Cook, you can fly by ski plane or helicopter to the 2,400m (7,872-ft.) head of the Tasman Glacier and ski down the 14km (8¾-mile) run. For up-to-the-minute South Island ski details, check out www.nzski.com.

SKIING

The two major ski fields on the North Island are Whakapapa and Turoa, on the slopes of **Mount Ruapehu** in Tongariro National Park, now both owned by a single company, Ruapehu Alpine Lifts. Ruapehu, with a simmering crater lake, is an active volcano and extends up some 2,760m (9,053 ft.), making it the North Island's highest peak. It erupted in 1995 and again in 1996, effectively ending all skiing activity for about 2 years. **Whakapapa** (☎ 07/892-3738; fax 03/892-3732; www.mtruapehu.com) offers challenges for intermediate skiers and snowboarders and has good beginners' packages. **Turoa** (☎ 06/385-8456; fax 06/385-8992; info.turoa@mtruapehu.com) has great terrain for all levels of skiing, with good half-pipes for snowboarders. It also has good "Learn to Ski" and "Learn to Snowboard" packages.

On the South Island, **Mount Hutt Ski Field** (☎ 03/302-8811; fax 03/302-8697; www.nzski.com) is 1¾ hours from Christchurch, with a good shuttle service operating from the city. There are numerous club fields close to Christchurch, especially in the Porters Pass region. You'll find information on some of these fields at www.snow.co.nz, www.dobson.co.nz, www.porterheights.co.nz, or www.mtlyford.co.nz.

> *Tips* **Sloping Off to Ski School**
>
> The **Mount Hutt Ski School** (☎ 03/308-5074; fax 03/308-5076) was the 1997 winner of the New Zealand Tourism Board Awards Training & Education Programme. It has an extensive training program that caters to everyone from rank beginners all the way through to Advanced Level 6 skiers. It also offers extensive snowboarding instruction. **Whakapapa Ski & Snowboard School** (☎ 07/892-3738; fax 07/892-3732) makes it easy for everyone, with special learning packages and beginners-only slopes. Intermediate or advanced skiers can also improve their skills with group or private lessons. **Cardrona Development Centre** (☎ 03/443-7341; fax 03/443-8818) has an extensive program of beginners' lessons, private and group lessons, specialist improvement workshops, ski board instruction, plus an instructor-training program. **Treble Cone Ski School** (☎ 03/443-7456; fax 03/443-8401) has everything from the TC Cat Club Junior Ski School, for kids 3 to 12, to middle-range instruction and workshops to women's workshops, carving clinics, snowboard holiday camps, and a Masters program for competitive skiers over 30.

Farther south are the ski areas that lure New Zealanders and international skiers to the Southern Lakes Ski Region between Queenstown and Wanaka—the **Remarkables, Cardrona, Treble Cone,** and **Coronet Peak.** Among them, you can do downhill, cross-country, or heli-skiing and snowboarding; all have good trails for all skill levels.

Coronet Peak (© **03/442-4620;** fax 03/442-4624; www.nzski.com) is 18km (11 miles) from Queenstown with moderate to challenging fields. It's the oldest commercial field in the South Island and has three chairlifts, beginners' facilities, and good variety for experienced skiers. The **Remarkables** (© **03/442-4615**), 23km (14 miles) from Queenstown, has more diversity for experienced skiers. It's a smaller field with three chairlifts and is good for middle-ability skiers. It gets the afternoon sun, so it's slightly warmer in winter. There's a lot of heli-skiing on virgin snow in this area and an incredibly steep access road. **Cardrona** (© **03/443-7411;** fax 03/443-8818; www.cardrona.com) is a middle-range field with good family facilities, including brand-new social facilities, but it's a bit tame for experienced skiers. It lies 57km (35 miles) from Queenstown and 33km (20 miles) from Wanaka. **Treble Cone** (© **03/443-7443;** fax 03/443-8401; www.treblecone.co.nz) has the newest and biggest express chairlift in the country, which has improved the flow of skiers on the field. It's one of the more challenging fields and has a lot of variety, with very steep areas and narrow valleys. It also has a good base lodge and the best food facilities of all the southern ski areas. There's also heli-skiing in the Harris Mountains.

Lift ticket prices in New Zealand range from NZ$60 to NZ$90 (US$42–US$63); ski, boot, and pole rentals run from NZ$35 to NZ$55 (US$25–US$39); and lessons are from NZ$60 (US$42) for a half-day group class. Costs are lower for children.

For cross-country skiing, head for **Waiorau Nordic Ski Field,** located in the Pisa Range, near Wanaka (© **03/443-7542;** fax 03/443-9717; www.snowfarmnz.com), which is the only field of its kind in New Zealand. The area has ideal terrain for first-time cross-country skiers as well as good conditions for advanced skiers.

SKI PACKAGES & OUTFITTERS In winter, you'll always find good ski deals from the three major cities—Auckland, Wellington, and Christchurch—that usually include cheap transport, accommodations, and a specified number of ski days. Check with the visitor centers in each city for the latest ski-package brochures.

Pipers Ski Tours (© **09/415-5593;** fax 09/415-5594; www.pipersskitours.co. nz) has a range of tours via Auckland that include coach transport and guides, accommodations, mountain transfers, meals at Pipers Ski Lodge, and ski hire and lift passes. Check out the highly recommended **Snowco** (www.snowco.co.nz), which features online ski and snowboarding packages, and **Ski New Zealand Online** (www.ski-new zealand.co.nz), which offers 7-day ski package holidays from around NZ$800 (US$560) per person.

The **NZ Super Pass** can be used at any time on any of the following South Island ski fields: Treble Cone, Mount Dobson, Mount Lyford, Ohau, Broken River, Mount Olympus, Craigeburn, and Temple Basin, or you can choose a day's skiing or snowboarding at Coronet Peak, the Remarkables, or Mount Hutt. You can also swap a day on the mountains with one of a huge range of other activities, including heli-skiing, ballooning, jet-boating, and many more. Coupons for the NZ Super Pass start from around NZ$75 (US$53) per day. For information, contact **Coronet Peak** (© **03/372-1519;** fax 03/372-1499; www.nzski.com).

> **⟮Tips⟯ Sorry, Guys—Girls Only**
>
> If you're in the mood for a girls-only experience, contact **Bushwise Women** in Christchurch (**ⓒ/fax 03/332-4952;** www.bushwise.co.nz). They offer a wide range of outdoor adventures, from tramping and kayaking to Nordic skiing and ecotouring. **Wanderwomen,** in Auckland (**ⓒ 09/360-7330;** fax 09/360-7332; www.wanderwomen.co.nz), is where you'll find Lizzie Baker, who organizes abseiling, rock climbing, sea kayaking, and multiactivity weekends for women.

For heli-skiing in the Queenstown area, contact **HeliSki** (**ⓒ 03/442-7733;** fax 03/442-3299; www.flynz.co.nz). Members of the Gardner family are all expert skiers, with one or two pilots among them, too. They have access to some of the most fantastic heli-ski terrain in New Zealand. Another contact is **Harris Mountain Heli-Skiing** (**ⓒ 03/442-6722;** fax 03/442-2983; www.heliski.co.nz).

For more information on New Zealand skiing, check out the **New Zealand Snowsports Council** (**ⓒ 04/499-8135;** fax 04/499-8136; www.snow.co.nz), or the websites www.goski.com and www.onthesnow.com.

SNOWBOARDING

Treble Cone is "home to some of the best gully runs in New Zealand, which form into awesome quarter pipes, hips, and spines." So says one of the experts on www.boardtheworld.com, who rates Treble Cone eighth in the world for freeriding. Treble Cone is rated the top freeriding resort in Australasia and is best for experienced boarders. It has an active training program.

Cardona is better for beginner and intermediate boarders. It has undulating terrain, lots of gullies, and four half-pipes, and it offers a whole heap of support for snowboarders in general. It also has half-pipe camps throughout the season for all levels. **Coronet Peak** has lots of long groomed runs to tabletops, with quarter-pipes, kickers, and rollers. It's essentially a tourist field and is more expensive. The **Remarkables** offers pretty ho-hum snowboarding on the field itself, but the out-of-bounds territory offers extreme boarding for the daring. There's good stuff up in the backcountry if you're prepared to hike. Generally, though, the Remarkables is not a destination of choice for boarders.

Farther north, there's good snowboarding at **Temple Basin Ski Area,** in Arthurs Pass (**ⓒ 03/377-7788**), and at **Turoa Ski Resort,** in Tongariro National Park (**ⓒ 06/385-8456**).

SNOWBOARDING DEALS & TOURS   Steep & Cheap Snowboard Shop, 45 Camp St., Queenstown (**ⓒ 03/442-9330;** fax 03/442-9879), has good deals on equipment, servicing, and daily packages with discounted prices on rentals, transport, and lift passes. **Edgewater Adventures,** 59a Brownston St., Wanaka (**ⓒ/fax 03/443-8422;** www.adventure.net.nz), will organize your complete snowboarding holiday. Its packages include Auckland/Queenstown flights, transfers to Wanaka, mountain transfers, lift passes to either Treble Cone or Cardrona, daily ski-area guiding, and credit on nonski days when the mountain is closed.

Mount Aspiring Guides, in Wanaka (**ⓒ 03/443-9422;** fax 03/443-9540; www.mtaspiringguides.co.nz), offers a 5-day snowboarding tour in alpine wilderness areas, but snowboarders must be set up for backcountry travel. This is boarding in untracked areas, and you'll need an adventurous spirit and the proper gear.

Accommodations are in high mountain huts. (You get flown in.) This little venture will cost you in the vicinity of NZ$1,500 (US$1,050) per person.

6 Bicycling

Bicycle touring is a breathtakingly fresh way of seeing New Zealand, and it's quite popular, especially on the South Island.

SAFETY TIPS   Regardless of where you bike, always wear your helmet—they are mandatory in New Zealand, and you will be fined for not wearing one. Also, remember the following: Cyclists are not permitted on motorways (freeways); they must always ride on the left side of the road; and all traffic turning left gives way to everything on the right. At night, make sure you have a working white front light and a red rear light and reflector. It doesn't hurt to have pedal and jacket reflectors.

RENTALS   If you're not interested in an organized tour and want to rent a bike when you get here, **Adventure Cycles,** in Auckland (✆ **0800/335-566** in NZ, or 09/309-5566; fax 09/309-5564; www.adventure-auckland.co.nz), offers rentals throughout New Zealand and sales with a guaranteed buyback plan. It is also part of an association of 24 operators that can arrange organized activities.

TOURS   There's an increasing number of organized bike-tour companies in New Zealand. **New Zealand Pedaltours,** in Parnell, Auckland (✆ **09/302-0968;** fax 09/302/0967; www.pedaltours.co.nz), offers both North and South Island trips on 12 routes lasting from 3 to 19 days, on- and off-road. It creates customized tours of moderate exertion level, and a support van is always around to take the load off your pedals. **Adventure South** (✆ **03/942-1222;** fax 03/942-4030; www.advsouth.co.nz) offers a range of 6- to 21-day cycle tours of the South Island that may also include some walking excursions.

7 Other Guided Tours, Outfitters & Package Deals

In addition to all of the above, you can trust New Zealanders to come up with a tour for just about every specialty. Here are a few of them—if you still haven't found what you're looking for after this, well, I just don't know what to do with you! For more than 400 tours listed in alphabetical order, check out **www.piperpat.com**. Among the listings you'll find several for privately guided tours.

- **Agritour,** Hamilton (✆ **06/354-9063;** fax 06/354-9064; www.agritour.co.nz), arranges technical study tours visiting agribusinesses, research stations, orchards, and forests to suit your needs.

- **American Wilderness Experience,** a member of the **GORPtravel** family, 10055 Westmoor Dr., Suite 215, Westminster, CO 80021 (✆ **800/444-0099** in the U.S., or 720/887-8500; www.gorptravel.com), arranges trips to the national parks and the World Heritage Area; they include walking, rafting, and wildlife observation.

- **Aoraki Naturally,** Lake Tekapo (✆ **03/680-6549;** fax 03/680-6202; www.naturist.co.nz), is not so much a tour as a chance to get your clothes off and paddle a canoe, or swim in a spring-fed creek amid stunning mountain scenery. Kay Hannam and Brian Williams have a clothes-free homestay and camping facility where you can relax completely.

- **Backcountry Concepts,** Christchurch (✆ **03/302-8403;** fax 03/302-8701; www.backcountry-nz.com), offers a wide range of fishing tours with stays in luxury accommodations, several raft-based options, and custom tours that include time with local artists, wine-tasting tours, shopping tours, and garden tours.

- **Clean Green Photo Tours,** Wanaka (www.cleangreen.co.nz), can arrange anything from a 2-hour instructional course to multiday excursions to Stewart Island, Fiordland, and even the unforgettable Sub-Antarctic Islands onboard the 18m (59-ft.) ketch *Talisker*. Photographer Gilbery van Reenan shares his most beautiful, off-the-beaten-track locations.

- **Fiordland Ecology Holidays,** Manapouri (ⓒ/fax **03/249-6600;** www.fiordland.gen.nz), will take you away on its oceangoing yacht for 3 to 7 days of low-impact natural-history adventure in the remote areas of Fiordland. A maximum of 12 people can swim with seals and dolphins, go snorkeling and diving, and set out on bush walks. There are also berths available on scientific research trips.

- **Hiking New Zealand,** Christchurch (ⓒ **0800/697-232** in NZ, or 025/360-268; fax 03/328-8173; www.hikingnewzealand.com), and its superbly qualified guides offer a fabulous range of 5- to 10-day New Zealand–wide hiking tours.

- **Mid-Life Adventures,** Mount Roskill, Auckland (ⓒ **09/627-9683;** fax 09/626-3607; midlifeadventures@xtra.co.nz), has 13-day North or South Island adventures ready and waiting for those over 35.

- **Nimbus Paragliding Adventure Tours,** Christchurch (ⓒ **0800/111-611** in NZ; www.nimbusparagliding.co.nz), is just the ticket for you addicts who want to stay airborne. Grey Hamilton and his crew have three campervans, all the paragliding equipment, and the local knowledge. They'll personalize an itinerary that will take you to as many of the country's best paragliding sites as you can afford to visit.

- **Red Carpet Tours,** Auckland (ⓒ **09/410-6561;** fax 09/410-6591; www.redcarpet-tours.com), takes *Lord of the Rings* fans to Middle Earth and the sites of Peter Jackson's famous film trilogy.

- **Southern Discovery Holidays,** Greymouth (ⓒ **03/768-6649;** fax 03/768-9149; www.nzholidayheaven.com), offers a 12-day Millionaires Tour, visiting the South Island's gold fields in search of gold; 14-day School Geography Study Tours on the South Island, which include adventure activities; Golden Age Holidays, which offer small groups of retired people a new approach to vacationing; plus a wide range of special-interest holidays, including photography, painting, gardens, farms, ornithology—you name it, the staff will prepare it for you.

- **Te Urewera Adventures of New Zealand,** Rotorua (ⓒ **07/366-3969;** fax 07/366-3333; makere.biddle@xtra.co.nz), offers you a chance to get into the nitty-gritty of living Maori culture in the remote wilderness areas of Te Urewera National Park. It will take you horse trekking and fishing and to a Maori marae; 1- to 5-day treks go for about NZ$120 to NZ$1,000 (US$84–US$700).

- **Unimog 4WD Adventure Tours,** Greymouth (offered by Southern Discovery Holidays; for contact information, see above), has serious 17-seat, 4WD vehicles that go places most people only dream about (or dread). It has great 5- and 14-day tours that take you into back areas around the South Island, throwing in other delights, such as guided walks, seal colonies, and mountain biking.

- **Untapped Potential,** P.O. Box 128–231, Remuera, Auckland (fax **09/524-0567;** www.utp.co.nz), which is especially geared towards visiting sporting teams, takes you into the heart of new Zealand sporting culture by introducing you to grassroots rugby.

4

Suggested New Zealand Itineraries

Making your way around New Zealand is simple, and many tourists find renting a car the cheapest and most flexible option. But if you're short on time, fly between major destinations and pick up a rental car for short journeys.

Many of you will find the roads "virtually empty" compared to those in your own countries. That said, don't be misled by the seemingly short distances between places. Most roads are only two lanes—except near bigger cities, where they become four-lane highways—and in some places they're steep, winding, and narrow as they negotiate river gorges and mountain tracts. Allow much more time than you would for a similar length journey at home.

1 New Zealand in 1 Week

I hear it all the time: "This is such a small country, but we never realized there would be so much to see; we wish we'd allowed more time." Seeing New Zealand in 1 week is possible, but it will require early starts and long days. Personally, I'd ditch the car idea and fly between four major stops—Auckland, Wellington, Christchurch, and Queenstown—to save time. There are regular internal flights between all major towns and cities, and if you shop around some of the smaller airlines, you can get good deals. Otherwise, you'll spend 90% of your time in a vehicle suffering from jet lag, with little left over for the sights.

Day ❶: Arrive in Auckland ✸✸✸

Try to arrive early and focus your attention on **Viaduct Basin** (p. 127), a great introduction to New Zealand's passion for boats. Go for a sail on *NZL 40* (p. 127), which is moored here. The **New Zealand National Maritime Museum** (p. 128) is also here and gives a great overview of our maritime history and short cruises on the historic scow *Ted Ashby*. In between, join the crowds lazing about over good coffee and fine food. There are at least a dozen restaurants to choose from. Stay at **Hilton Auckland** (p. 107), perched on the end of the wharf.

Day ❷: Waiheke Island ✸✸✸

Catch a ferry across to Waiheke Island for a day of laid-back wine tasting and beach walking. Factor in lunch at **Te Whau Vineyard** (p. 148), where you can gaze over staggering views and one of the best wine cellars in the country. Visit **Connells Bay Waiheke Sculpture Park** (p. 147) with work by leading NZ artists and swim in the clear warm waters of **Onetangi Bay** (p. 147). Return to Auckland late afternoon, visit **Auckland Museum** (p. 125), and eat at **The French Café** (p. 119).

Day ❸: Wellington ✸✸✸

Get up early and fly to Wellington. For the definitive overview of New Zealand, go straight to **Te Papa** (p. 294). Don't miss the Passports and Manu Whenua displays. Walk along the waterfront, down the Lambton Quay shopping precinct and catch the **cable car** (p. 295) up to the **Botanic Gardens** (p. 295). Go down the other side to Tinakori Village for lunch. Walk back down Bowen Street, past the **Beehive and Parliament** (p. 296). After unwinding at **Caffe Astoria** (p. 290), enjoy dinner at **Café Bastille** (p. 293).

Day ❹: Christchurch ✸✸✸

Take an early flight to Christchurch, hire a car at the airport, skip the city, and drive 1 hour to pretty Akaroa, admiring rural landscapes along the way. For interesting art and great coffee, stop at **Little River Gallery** (p. 383). Take another break at the hilltop for great camera shots. Over the hills, try tasty **Barry's Bay Cheese** (p. 384) or divert to the right for lunch at **French Farm Winery**. In Akaroa, take a nature cruise with dolphin-watching, or saunter along the promenade taking in quaint architecture and dinky shops. When you return to Christchurch, stay at **Clearwater Resort** (p. 357), which is close to the airport.

Day ❺: Queenstown ✸✸✸

Sleep in and wake up to ducks floating on the lake outside your window. Ease yourself into a late breakfast before flying to Queenstown. Once there, at the airport, take a memorable helicopter ride with **Over The Top** (p. 440) and land high on a mountain peak for lunch in total solitude. You'll remember this forever. Back on the ground, spoil yourself at the new **Sofitel** (p. 446).

Day ❻: Queenstown

Rise early, meet the locals for breakfast at **Joe's Garage** (p. 454), and then have the quintessential adventure experience on **Shotover Jet** (p. 441). Move on to Arrowtown, explore the quaint old Chinese gold mining area, and have lunch at **Saffron** (p. 456). If you're ready for more action, do the **Kawarau Bungy** (p. 440) (or watch others) and then visit **Gibbston Valley Wines** (p. 438). Alternatively, use this day to enjoy **a scenic flight to Milford Sound,** a cruise, and return flight (p. 439).

Day ❼: Back to Christchurch

Fly back to Christchurch to connect with your international flight. If you have time between flights, visit the nearby **International Antarctic Centre** (p. 366), **Orana Park** (p. 367), or **Willowbank Wildlife Reserve** (p. 368)—where you're sure to see a kiwi. Alternatively, unwind with a round of golf at **Clearwater Resort** (p. 375). If you decide you were silly to try and cram it all into a week, see the next itinerary.

2 New Zealand in 2 Weeks

Two weeks in New Zealand gives you more opportunities to drive between destinations and take in the color of the provinces. Still, don't underestimate the time your journey will take. New Zealand has good roads, but 20km (12 miles) in some parts of the country could be narrow, steep, and winding—which means it might take you twice as long to negotiate them as it would 20km back home. In general, roads are well maintained and all major roads are sealed. Drive with care on narrow, unsealed roads if you venture in to more remote areas. What I've suggested here gives you a taste of both main islands, sticking to main centers with the greatest concentration of activities.

New Zealand 1- and 2-Week Itineraries

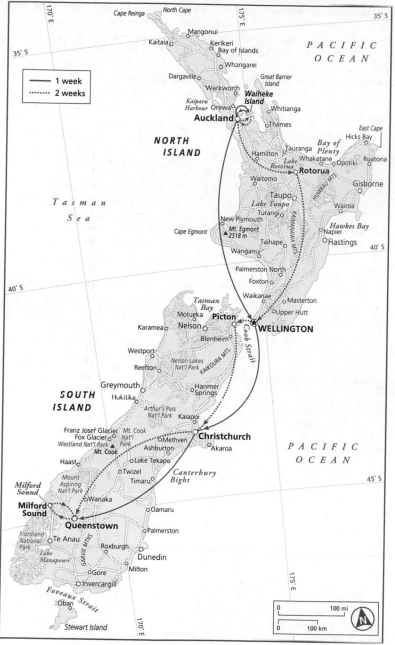

Day ❶: Arrive in Auckland 🐾🐾🐾

Arrive in Auckland and rest for a whole day, doing nothing more taxing than eating and drinking at **Viaduct Basin** (p. 127). At night, go to the top of **Sky Tower** (p. 125) for the big daddy of views and a meal in the revolving restaurant.

Day ❷: Auckland's Major Sights

Prepare to sightsee until you drop. Get on the **Explorer Bus** (p. 103)—the cheapest and easiest way to see as much as possible in 1 day. You'll set eyes on Mission Bay's pretty beach promenade, visit **Kelly Tarlton's Underwater World** (p. 126), and get a taste of Maori culture at **Auckland Museum** (p. 125). The bus drives through the leafy **Botanic Gardens** (p. 132) and through Parnell village. It stops at the **SKYCITY** complex (p. 110), the **Victoria Park Market** (p. 141), and much more.

Day ❸: Waiheke Island 🐾🐾🐾

Rise early and catch a ferry to **Waiheke Island** (p. 145). Hire a car and drive around the island, visiting wineries, olive groves, artists' studios, and unspoilt beaches. Some of the best surprises are in the little bays away from Oneroa township. Following visits to **Whittakers Musical Museum** (p. 147) and **Te Whau Garden** (p. 147), have lunch at **Mudbrick Vineyard** (p. 150). Later in the day, sit in Onetangi Beach and watch the sunset. Stay at **The Boatshed** (p. 149).

Day ❹: Rotorua 🐾🐾🐾

Arrive back in Auckland by midday and fly to Rotorua. Hire a car. If you want a day of complete rest and solitude in unabashed luxury, head for **Treetops Lodge** (p. 214). If you want to see the sights, go straight to **Rotorua Museum** (p. 203) for an excellent overview of geothermal and volcanic history. Spend the rest of the afternoon at **Te Puia** (p. 204) to see bubbling mud and Maori cultural performances. Watch the sun set over the lake and relax in a hot rock pool at **Polynesian Spa** (p. 204).

Day ❺: The Thermal Attractions 🐾🐾🐾

Drive 30 minutes south to see the wonders of **Waimangu** and **Waiotapu** (p. 210). Waimangu has more spectacular sights in a shorter walk. If you're back in town by early afternoon you could take a guided tour of **Ohinemutu** (p. 208), the original Maori village on the lakefront, followed by a walk among the **Whakarewarewa Forest** redwoods (p. 213). Finish the night with a tour and cultural performance at **Tamaki Maori Village** (p. 208).

Day ❻: Drive to Wellington

Rise early for a day of driving, but *be careful*, as roads in the Rotorua region are busy with huge logging trucks. A 5-hour journey will take you around **Lake Taupo** (p. 224) (where there are plenty of lake-edge stops for photographs), through the stark beauty of **Tongariro National Park** (p. 230), and through heartland farming provinces. You could stop off for a night in the **Wairarapa** (p. 306) (or at least stop to eat in one of **Greytown's cute cafes;** p. 311), or drive the last taxing, winding, uphill leg over the Rimutaka Hills to Wellington.

Day ❼: Wellington 🐾🐾🐾

Te Papa (p. 294) is a must-visit. Spend 2 to 3 hours there and don't miss the gift shop for top-quality crafts. And you can't visit the capital without a ride up the **cable car** (p. 295), a wander through the **Botanic Gardens** (p. 295) at the top, and a sit-in at a session of **Parliament** (p. 296). Art lovers should see **City Gallery Wellington** (p. 296) and if you like the funky side of life, wander up **Cuba Street** (p. 302). Late afternoon, amble around the waterfront to **Oriental Parade.** Have dinner at **Logan Brown** (p. 289) or **Café Bastille** (p. 293).

Day ❽: A Ferry Crossing

Rise early and catch one of the first ferries to **Picton** (p. 312) on the **Interislander** (p. 275). The 3-hour trip is an experience in its own right and if the weather's good you'll have a picturesque passage through **Queen Charlotte Sound.** Catch the 1:40pm **TranzCoastal** (p. 313). This rail journey is a scenic feast through vineyards and along a rugged coastline hugged by steep mountains. You might want to get out at **Kaikoura** (p. 387) and go **whale-watching** (p. 391), or continue on to Christchurch, arriving around 7pm.

Day ❾: Christchurch ✶✶✶

Get up early and head up Dyers Pass Road (in a hired car) to the top of the **Port Hills.** My favorite drive is along the top, heading east, stopping for the fabulous views down into **Lyttelton Harbour** (p. 348) on your right. Drop down into the trendy seaside village of **Sumner** (p. 348), have coffee at **Coffee Culture** (p. 364), and walk along the white sands of Sumner Beach. Back in town, the swanky new architectural wonder that is **Christchurch Art Gallery** (p. 366) is bound to impress—don't leave without visiting their shop and Form Gallery. Wander down the boulevard to **Canterbury Museum** (p. 365), the **Arts Centre** (p. 365), and the **Botanic Gardens** (p. 366).

Day ❿: Drive to Queenstown

Prepare to be impressed by the landscapes on this 5- to 6-hour journey. You'll pass by the unbelievably turquoise Lake Tekapo—look out for the stop at the south end of the lake, which affords picture-perfect views of Mount Cook—and through the grand beauty of Lindis Pass. The lupins will be flowering along the summer roadsides of the Mackenzie Country and you won't be able to resist pulling out your camera. Stop on the Queenstown side of Cromwell at **The Big Picture** (p. 430) for refreshments, wine tastings, and an overview of the region's vineyards and wineries. Don't miss stops at the fresh summer fruit stalls along the way. Apricots are near perfect here.

Day ⓫: Queenstown ✶✶✶

Sleep in and breakfast late at **Joe's Garage** (p. 454) before taking an early cruise across Lake Wakatipu on the vintage steamship **TSS *Earnslaw*** (p. 437). You'll be back in plenty of time to take the **gondola** (p. 434) up to Bob's Peak for breathtaking views over Queenstown. Leap off the **bungy** (p. 440) if you dare, or descend on the gondola and wander into the **Kiwi & Birdlife Park** (p. 434). Dine on seafood at **Boardwalk** (p. 452).

Day ⓬: The Wineries

Hire a car (or take a guided tour) and drive yourself around the best of Central Otago's wineries. The top four closest to Queenstown are **Gibbston Valley Wines** (p. 438), **Peregrine** (p. 438), **Amisfield** (p. 438), and **Chard Farm** (p. 438). Don't miss Gibbston's wine cave, its cheesery, and its excellent lunches under a canopy of vines. Alternatively, wander around central Queenstown stores for excellent duty-free shopping and have lunch at **Eichardt's** (p. 453), or take in a round of golf at **Millbrook Resort** (p. 441) and eat in one of its restaurants, finishing off with a soothing massage in the splendid spa. Have dinner at **The Bunker** (p. 454).

Day ⓭: Fly to Milford Sound ✶✶✶

Be up early for a memorable scenic flight or helicopter ride to **Milford Sound** (p. 439). Take a **boat cruise** (p. 465) and make sure you include the **Underwater Observatory** (p. 466). Flying is by far the best option if you're short on time, although it is weather dependent. Bus trips can take around 12 hours—including the return. When you're back in Queenstown at the end of the day, take a drive through **Deer Park Heights** (p. 434) and watch the sun set over the lake. Dine at **Saffron** (p. 456) in **Arrowtown** (p. 436).

Day ⓮: Back to Christchurch

Enjoy a lazy morning in Queenstown before flying to Christchurch to connect with your international flight. If you have time between the two flights, go to the **International Antarctic Centre** (p. 366) near the airport, or, if you've yet to see a live kiwi, check out the nearby **Willowbank Wildlife Reserve** (p. 368). If you fancy big cats, visit the cheetahs at **Orana Park** (p. 367).

3 New Zealand for Families

Kids will love New Zealand. There are enough weird, wonderful, curious, funny, and interesting things on these islands to amuse the most inquiring child's mind. I'd recommend 3 weeks if you're traveling with a family (you can stretch out the 2-week itinerary below), so it's less taxing on everyone. And I'd either go "bush and beach" with a tent at a northern beach camping ground so the kids can run wild and free; or I'd stick to three major centers—Auckland, Rotorua, and Nelson—for the best concentration of kid-related activities. Much of the gut-busting excitement of Queenstown has age limits, but if your kids are old enough and you want a longer trip, tack on the "Ten Action-Packed Days in the South Island" tour, later in this chapter.

Day ❶: Arrive in Auckland ✪✪✪

Start slowly with an easy day, checking out combo deals and family passes at the Visitor Centre at **Viaduct Basin** (p. 127), where the kids can watch the boats and visit the **New Zealand Maritime Museum** (p. 128). Boys, especially, seem to get a real kick out of a ride on the historic scow, *Ted Ashby*. Give them a bird's-eye view of the city from the **Sky Tower** (p. 125), taking them up in the exterior glass lift and letting them walk over the glass floor. Dine in the revolving restaurant at the top.

Day ❷: Auckland sights

Impress the kids right from the start with **Kelly Tarlton's Antarctic Encounter & Underwater World** (p. 126)—where else can they see an underground colony of penguins? Drive around to **Mission Bay** (p. 103), rent roller blades, swim at the beach, have a picnic lunch, and feed the seagulls. Spend the afternoon at **Auckland Museum** (p. 125) and make sure you let them loose in the superb Discovery Centre, where they can open drawers and touch exhibits. The Wild Child display and the Maori Treasures are also good value.

Day ❸: More of Auckland

Get off to an early start at **Auckland Zoo** (p. 129), which has heaps of great stuff for kids. Check out the daily animal encounters and view sea lions through underwater viewing windows. Or consider their Safari Night Sleepovers and guided night walks instead of a day outing. Drive to **Butterfly Creek** (p. 129), flirt with winged beauties, ride on the Red Admiral Express, and see animals at Buttermilk Farm. Drive north to **Snowplanet** (p. 129), where you have the unlikely pleasure of a midwinter snow experience in the midst of a subtropical summer.

Day ❹: Drive to Rotorua

Hire a car and start the 3-hour drive to Rotorua early. Stop at **Hamilton** (p. 186) along the way and take a ride down the river on the paddle steamer, **MV *Waipa Delta*** (p. 188), or stop and feed the ducks at **Hamilton Lake** (p. 188). In the afternoon, visit **Rotorua Museum** (p. 203) and "experience" a volcanic eruption in the theater there. Follow this with a leisurely drive around the Blue and Green Lakes to the **Buried Village** (p. 207), to see the remains of Te Wairoa village, which was buried by the eruption of Mount Tarawera in 1886.

Day ❺: Rotorua 🌟🌟🌟

The kids will be screwing their noses up at the smell of sulphur in the air, so get out there and show them what it's all about. Drive down to **Waimangu** and **Waiotapu** (p. 210). Allow half a day for both, or, if you have to choose, 2 hours for Waiotapu. Back in town, feed the kids from one of the takeaway stands at the lakefront and then let them loose at **Skyline Skyrides** (p. 206 on a luge, or better still, have an adventure in the **Zorb** (p. 213). The **Agrodome Leisure Park** (p. 206) is a hive of kids' activities—I'd plan to spend the afternoon here. Finish with a relaxing dip at **Polynesian Spa** (p. 204).

Day ❻: Maori Experiences

Spend the morning investigating the wonders of **Te Puia** (p. 204), which includes the Whakarewarewa Thermal Reserve and the New Zealand Maori Arts & Crafts Institute. Stay and watch Pohutu Geyser blow its top. In the afternoon take a guided tour of **Ohinemutu Maori Village** on the lakefront and a boat cruise over to **Mokoia Island** (p. 209) and hear about Maori legends. Set the evening aside for a hangi meal and a Maori experience at **Tamaki Maori Village** (p. 208).

Day ❼: Drive to Wellington

The drive south normally takes about 5 hours but allow a day. Stop at **Lake Taupo** (p. 224) for a go at the **Hole in One Challenge** (p. 226). And visit **Huka Falls** (p. 222), just off the main highway north of Taupo. Have a picnic at one of the little beaches around the lake and then head into **Tongariro National Park** (p. 230), for beautiful mountain landscapes. The kids will be ready for another stop at **Pukaha Mount Bruce National Wildlife Centre** (p. 306)—keep your eyes open to spot a kiwi; and maybe there'll be time to squeeze in a snack stop at **Greytown**

(p. 311) before you wind your way across the Rimutaka Ranges and down into Wellington by late afternoon.

Day ❽: Wellington 🌟🌟🌟

Spend your first 3 hours exploring the **Museum of New Zealand–Te Papa Tongarewa** (p. 294) and allow extra time for the kids to experience the interactive displays on the ground floor. Let them run free along the waterfront after that—there'll be boats and people aplenty for them to watch. Head up the **cable car** (p. 295) next to the **Botanic Gardens** (p. 295), where you should take them to the **Carter Observatory** (p. 295) for a bit of stargazing. If you never got to the zoo in Auckland, don't miss the **Wellington Zoo** (p. 296) interactive animal experiences. Wander down **Cuba Mall** late afternoon and let the kids get wet in the **Bucket Fountain** (p. 297).

Day ❾: Ferry Ride to Picton

Catch the early **Interislander** (p. 275) across to Picton. The ferry has movie theaters and play areas for kids. Hire a car and drive to Nelson. Stop 10 minutes short of Nelson at **Happy Valley Adventures** (p. 330) for 4WD bike adventures and the sky swing. In Nelson, hunt out **Penguino** (p. 336) for a well-deserved specialty ice cream. After settling into your stay, dine at **Ma Fish** (p. 337), which has a great kids' menu.

Day ❿: Nelson 🌟🌟🌟

Start at the **World of Wearable Art & Collectible Car Complex** (p. 325) where everyone's eyes will pop out on stalks. Let them loose next at **Nelson Fun Park** and **Natureland Zoological Park** (p. 328). Enjoy a picnic at nearby **Tahunanui Beach** and then spend the afternoon swimming, making sandcastles, and generally relaxing on one of the most popular beaches in the area. You'll probably want to visit Penguino again after that.

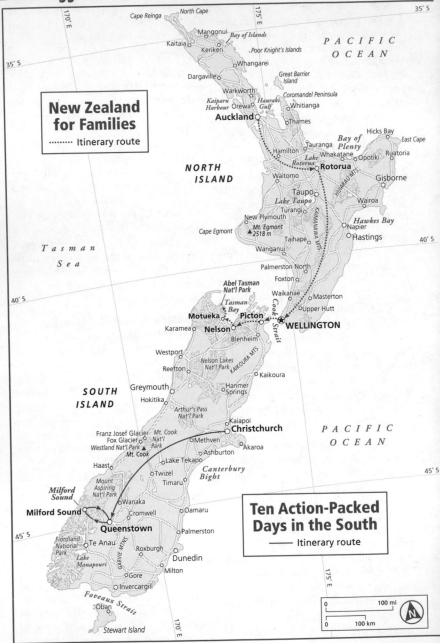

New Zealand for Families
········· Itinerary route

PACIFIC OCEAN

Cape Reinga
North Cape
Mangonui
Bay of Islands
Kaitaia
Kerikeri
Poor Knight's Islands
Whangarei
Dargaville
Great Barrier Island
Warkworth
Coromandel Peninsula
Kaiparu Harbour
Orewa
Hauraki Gulf
Whitianga
Auckland
Thames
Hicks Bay
Bay of Plenty
East Cape
Hamilton
Tauranga
Whakatane
Opotiki
Ruatoria
Lake Rotorua
Rotorua
Gisborne
Waitomo
Taupo
Lake Taupo
Wairoa
Turangi
Hawkes Bay
New Plymouth
Mt. Egmont 2518 m
Napier
Cape Egmont
Taihape
Hastings
Wanganui

NORTH ISLAND

Tasman Sea

Palmerston North
Foxton
Abel Tasman Nat'l Park
Waikanae
Tasman Bay
Masterton
Motueka
Picton
Upper Hutt
Karamea
Nelson
Cook Strait
WELLINGTON
Blenheim
Westport
Nelson Lakes Nat'l Park
Reefton
Kaikoura
Greymouth
Hanmer Springs
Hokitika
Arthur's Pass Nat'l Park
Kaiapoi
Franz Josef Glacier
Mt. Cook Nat'l Park
Christchurch
Fox Glacier
Methven
Akaroa
Westland Nat'l Park
Mt. Cook
Ashburton
Haast
Lake Tekapo
Canterbury Bight
Mount Aspiring Nat'l Park
Twizel
Timaru
Milford Sound
Wanaka
Milford Sound
Cromwell
Oamaru
Queenstown
Palmerston
Fiordland National Park
Te Anau
Roxburgh
Lake Manapouri
Dunedin
Gore
Milton
Invercargill
Foveaux Strait
Oban
Stewart Island

SOUTH ISLAND

PACIFIC OCEAN

Ten Action-Packed Days in the South
——— Itinerary route

0   100 mi
0   100 km

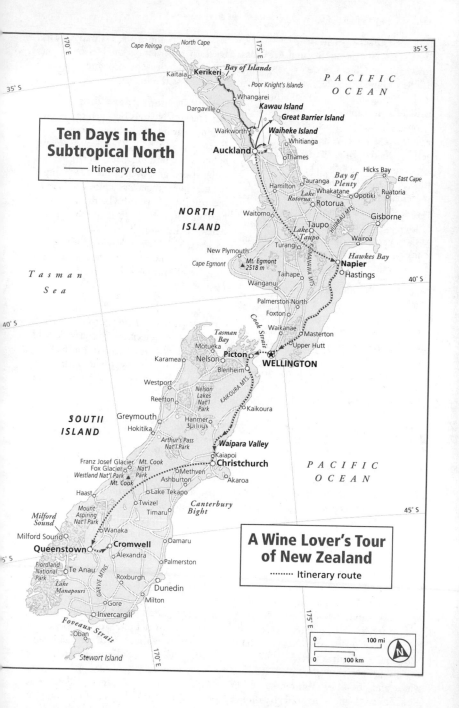

Ten Days in the Subtropical North
—— Itinerary route

A Wine Lover's Tour of New Zealand
········ Itinerary route

Cape Reinga
North Cape
PACIFIC OCEAN
35° S
Kaitaia
Kerikeri
Bay of Islands
Poor Knight's Islands
Whangarei
Dargaville
Kawau Island
Great Barrier Island
Warkworth
Waiheke Island
Whitianga
Auckland
Thames
Hicks Bay
East Cape
Hamilton
Tauranga
Bay of Plenty
Whakatane
Opotiki
Ruatoria
Lake Rotorua
Rotorua
Waitomo
Gisborne
Taupo
Lake Taupo
Wairoa
Turangi
Hawkes Bay
New Plymouth
Cape Egmont
▲ *Mt. Egmont 2518 m*
Napier
Taihape
Hastings
40° S
Wanganui
Tasman Sea
Palmerston North
Foxton
Waikanae
Masterton
Cook Strait
Upper Hutt
40° S
Tasman Bay
Motueka
Picton
★ **WELLINGTON**
Karamea
Nelson
Blenheim
Westport
Nelson Lakes Nat'l Park
Reefton
Kaikoura
SOUTH ISLAND
Greymouth
Hanmer Springs
Hokitika
Arthur's Pass Nat'l Park
Waipara Valley
Kaiapoi
Franz Josef Glacier
Mt. Cook Nat'l Park
Christchurch
Fox Glacier
Westland Nat'l Park
Methven
PACIFIC OCEAN
▲ *Mt. Cook*
Ashburton
Akaroa
Haast
Lake Tekapo
Canterbury Bight
Mount Aspiring Nat'l Park
Twizel
Timaru
45° S
Milford Sound
Wanaka
Milford Sound
Oamaru
Queenstown
Cromwell
Alexandra
Palmerston
Fiordland National Park
Te Anau
Roxburgh
Dunedin
Lake Manapouri
Milton
Gore
Invercargill
Foveaux Strait
Oban
Stewart Island

NORTH ISLAND

PACIFIC OCEAN

89

Day ⑪: Exploring the Area

Watch glass blowing at **Höglund Art Glass International Glass Centre** (p. 328), then drive to **Mapua** (p. 327), visiting pottery studios along the way. Stop at orchards stalls for a crisp apple snack. Dabble fingers in open displays at **Touch the Sea Aquarium** (p. 329) and have a yummy late lunch at **The Naked Bun Patisserie** (p. 338). Drive on through **Motueka** (p. 322) and turn right to **Kaiteriteri** (p. 329), one of the prettiest golden-sand beaches you'll ever see. Spend the afternoon playing and swimming, or take a water taxi around the gorgeous coast of **Abel Tasman National Park** (p. 338). Stay at Kaiteriteri or Motueka for the night.

Day ⑫: Abel Tasman National Park 🐸🐸🐸

Drive through Kaiteriteri and around to **Marahau** to get yourselves aboard one of the Abel Tasman kayaks (p. 339). This unbeatable experience amid clear waters will amaze you. Watch for seals and penguins and don't forget to take your swimming togs. Alternatively, take a guided day walk on the **Abel Tasman Coastal Track** (p. 66). Get back to Nelson in time for dinner—perhaps fish and chips on the beach as the sun sets.

Day ⑬: Outdoor Adventures

Get a feel for Nelson's big open spaces on a 4-hour outing with **Stonehurst Farm Horse Treks** (p. 330). They'll take you over hill-country farming land, down valleys, along rivers, and over plains. Don't forget to take your camera and a picnic to have in the country afterwards. In the afternoon hire bikes (p. 330), go swimming at the beach, or fish off the end of the Nelson wharves. Visit **Rosy Glow** (p. 336) for the ultimate afternoon treat (chocolates!) and then visit **Founder's Historic Park and Historic Village** (p. 326).

Day ⑭: Return to Wellington

Rise early for the 2-hour drive to Picton. Allow time to check out **Seahorse World** (p. 316), before getting back on the ferry to Wellington. Connect with your international flight home in the afternoon, or early evening.

4 A Wine Lover's Tour of New Zealand

New Zealand has come of age as a producer of internationally acclaimed wines and the great thing about the country's six major grape-growing regions is that they're packed into some of the most stunning landscapes. They're often close to gourmet food producers, many have terrific restaurants, some offer boutique lodgings, and impressive architecture is to the fore. In an ideal world, you could easily spend 2 to 3 weeks "soaking" in a New Zealand wine tour because it offers so much more than just wine and vineyards, but the following itinerary outlines a more realistic (for most travelers) 10-day tour of highlights.

Day ❶: Arrive in Auckland 🐸🐸🐸

The greater Auckland region (including Waiheke Island) has over 80 vineyards and wineries. In the interests of early research, head for the **New Zealand Winemakers Centre** (p. 133) in central city to sample your first New Zealand wines and to pick up information on New Zealand wine tourism. Have dinner at **Vinnies Restaurant** (p. 121).

Day ❷: Henderson Valley

Drive 30 minutes from the city to New Zealand's oldest grape-growing region, where there are a bundle of wineries along Henderson Valley Road and Lincoln Road. Seek out **Soljans Estate's new winery and café** (p. 133) for lunch and then drive on to **Kumeu River and Nobilo** (p. 133). If you don't want to drive yourself, contact Phil Parker's **Fine**

Wine Tours (p. 135) to get a comprehensive overview in a short time. Stay at Vineyard Cottages (p. 117), which are surrounded by Matua Valley Wines vineyards (p. 133). If you return to the city, dine at The French Café (p. 119).

Day ❸: Waiheke Island ✾✾✾

Catch the ferry to Waiheke Island (p. 145). Pick up a rental and visit some of the 45 vineyards on the island. Fullers (p. 145) and Ananda Tours (p. 147) both offer wine tours. If you'd rather be independent, make sure you visit Te Whau Vineyard (p. 148), which has more than 500 cellared wines. It's highly rated by Wine Spectator and has a impressive menu. You can't really get lost on this little paradise, and if you did, would you care? Splurge on a stay at Te Whau Lodge (p. 149), where you'll wine and dine in style overlooking vineyards.

Day ❹: Fly to Hawke's Bay ✾✾✾

Head back to the mainland (reluctantly, I'd guess) and fly to Napier (p. 245)—a twin heaven of endless grapes and oh-so-pretty Art Deco architecture (p. 249), not to mention gorgeous boutique vineyard accommodations, a dazzling array of restaurants, and some of the best wines in the country. Spend the afternoon at The National Aquarium of New Zealand (p. 247) for a change of pace and drink afternoon champagne at The County Hotel's bar (p. 254).

Day ❺: The Wine Trail

Do a fun bicycle tour of a handful of vineyards with On Yer Bike Winery Tours (p. 251), passing olive groves, orchards, wineries, and ostrich farms. Take your camera, as well as bottled water, a hat, sunscreen, and sunglasses to protect against the hot sun. Switch back to your car in the evening and splash out on dinner at the unforgettable Terroir (p. 258) at Craggy Range Winery (p. 250) in the Havelock North area. Get there in

daylight so you can look through the fabulous winery and tasting gallery. Try their classy vineyard stay, or plant yourself at nearby Mangapapa Lodge (p. 256).

Day ❻: More Tasting at Maraekakaho Road

If you haven't been there yet, head for the vineyards in the Maraekakaho Road area, finishing up at Sileni Estates Winery & Epicurean Centre (p. 251) in time for a drawn-out lunch at their classy restaurant. Head back into Napier for a 2-hour, self-guided afternoon Art Deco Walk (✆ 06/835-0022; www.artdeconapier.com; p. 249). Make sure you stop at Ujazi (p. 256) for coffee and cake, and right next door, loosen your purse strings on fabulous New Zealand arts and crafts at Statements Gallery (p. 248).

Day ❼: The Marlborough Wine Region ✾✾✾

Rise early and drive the 4 hours to Wellington, where you'll catch the Interislander (p. 275) to Picton. You'll find world-class vineyards here as far as the eye can see. Take plenty of film and stamina, along with a wine map from the Visitor Centre (p. 313), which lists all the wineries open for meals and tastings, plus the wines they produce. There are over 50 cellar doors open to you, so make a day of it. Splurge on dinner at Herzog (p. 321), an Epicurean and wine lovers' heaven with top European chefs, and stay in the heart of the Renwick wine area at Vintners Retreat (p. 317).

Day ❽: Waipara Valley ✾✾✾

Hire a car and drive the 4 hours south to Waipara Valley. Look out for Omihi School on your left, just north of Waipara (about 1 hr. south of Kaikoura) and turn there for Daniel Schuster Wines (p. 371). Danny is an internationally recognized wine consultant with a boundless knowledge and one of the prettiest vineyards and tasting rooms around. Call in at

Waipara Springs Winery (p. 372) for coffee and save yourself for lunch at award-winning **Pegasus Bay** (p. 371) just down the road. Visit other local wineries and call in at **Athena Olive Groves** (p. 370) for a different taste sensation. Drive 45 minutes south to Christchurch and catch a flight to Queenstown.

Day ❾: Queenstown ✸✸✸

Hire a car and call first on Johann Small-Smith at **Wine Deli** (p. 455) for all the advice you'll need on local wines—and to send some wine home via his international packing service. Pick up a wine map from the visitor center and head out to **Amisfield Winery** (p. 438) overlooking Lake Hayes. Be impressed by **Peregrine Wines'** (p. 438) unique architecture and make an extended stop at **Gibbston Valley Wines** (p. 438). Explore their wine tunnel, the great gift shop, and the cheesery. When you get back, hunt down **The Bunker** (p. 454) for perfectly matched wine and gourmet food.

Day ❿: Cromwell & Bannockburn

Take a scenic drive through Kawarau Gorge. Near Cromwell stop at fruit stalls and **The Big Picture** (p. 430) for an excellent film, a tasting auditorium, a selection of wines and gourmet foods, and a cafe. Set your sights on **Felton Road,** the **Mt. Difficulty Wines cafe,** and **Olssen's Garden Vineyard.** If you'd rather take a tour of this area contact **Queenstown Wine Trail** or **Appellation Central Wine Tours** (p. 439). Try the degustation menu at **The Spire** dining room (p. 446) for dinner if you have time, or catch a late flight to Christchurch to meet your international connection.

5 Ten Action-Packed Days in the South Island

The title of this itinerary assumes you're a fun-loving, adventure-seeking, fear-proof adrenalin addict with tons of stamina. If that's the case, you might want to head straight for Queenstown and stay there. It has more crazy, pulse-quickening activities per square inch than anywhere else and most are easily accessed without a vehicle. There's also an active hotel pick-up plan at work. Make sure you check out the many money-saving combo deals available. I haven't listed late-night fun here because that's a whole other story; chapter 15 gives you the pointers you'll need to ensure your nights are as vigorous as your days.

Day ❶: Arrive in Queenstown ✸✸✸

Spend the day regaining preflight energy with a leisurely amble around the town's adventure suppliers. Get social at **Joe's Garage** (p. 454), the preferred hangout of local adventure types, and soak up the energetic hum of hundreds of fellow international adventure seekers. Do some research at the **i-Site Visitor Centre** (p. 433) and have a few drinks at **Tatler** (p. 453) or **Old Man Rock** (p. 454), where local bar staff will fill you in on all the best night spots.

Day ❷: Up & About

Start with a gobsmackingly daring burst of speed through high rock canyons on the **Shotover Jet** (p. 441). Pick up your stomach and head back into town and take the **gondola** (p. 434) to the top of Bob's Peak. Pick up speed with a few **luge rides** (p. 441), scare yourself with a **bungy** (p. 440) overlooking the town, and float back down to Queenstown park via a **tandem parapente** (p. 441).

Day ❸: The Ultimate Jump

Be the ultimate daredevil and tackle the full bungy package—yes, that means all four of them! Start with 43m (141 ft.) at the "original" **Kawarau Suspension Bridge** and work your way up (and down) from there. If you've already done

The **Ledge** at the top of Bob's Peak, do the **Ledge Swing** instead—or try the bungy here again at night. Forget being squeamish, and take your camera because all four bungys are located in stunning landscapes. Make sure you get the T-shirt that attests to your courage!

Day ❹: The Dart River 🐸🐸🐸

Imagine rivers wild and calm overhung with lush green ferns, the sound of native bird call, and nothing else—except the excited squeals of your fellow adventurers. The Dart River deserves all the superlatives. Start with a 5-hour jet boat and a walk through unspoiled native bush with **Dart River Safaris** (p. 444). If you're short on daredevil confidence after all the bungy jumps, float the river with **Funyaks** (p. 443). A day to remember!

Day ❺: Taking to the Air

Push your budget to the limits with a helicopter ride into the mountains and have the highest altitude picnic you're ever likely to enjoy. Choppy Paterson of **Over The Top** (p. 440) knows how to impress with remote mountaintop lake settings. In the afternoon, do the **Fly By Wire** (p. 441), an adventure that will push you through the air at speeds of around 170kmph (105 mph) just for the hell of it.

Day ❻: Watersports

Fast-paced watersports are today's test. Start with **12 Mile Delta Canyoning** (p. 440), and find yourself slipping down river canyons in a wetsuit and a helmet. **Serious Fun River Surfing** (p. 442) brings a new twist to an old sport—it's all washing-machine rapids and rapid slithering down rocky river gorges. In the afternoon, go **white-water rafting** (p. 443). There are several operators to choose from and river grades to suit your nerves, physical prowess, and stamina. The Shotover River is generally viewed as more challenging than the Kawarau.

Day ❼: Milford Sound 🐸🐸🐸

Your toughest choice will be "fixed wing" or helicopter. Whichever you choose, be prepared to be impressed by jagged mountain peaks, lush green bush, unbelievably blue lakes, golden tussock, and azure blue skies. If a **Milford boat cruise** (p. 465) is not energetic enough for you, team up with **Rosco's Milford Sound Sea Kayaks** (p. 466) for a surreal paddling adventure. Take your camera and stay overnight at **Milford Sound Lodge** (p. 466).

Day ❽: Milford Track 🐸🐸🐸

Join a 1-day guided walk on **Milford Track** (p. 461) with **Trips 'n' Tramps** (p. 466)—just 12 people getting a taste of this world-famous mountain route. Enjoy total silence, majestic mountain landscapes, remote passes, a wilderness tea break, photography stops, waterfalls, and rainforest glades. This may be the quietest of your adventures, but it may be the *pièce de résistance*.

Day ❾: Back to Queenstown

Before you fly out of Milford, visit the **Underwater Observatory** (p. 466) for a unique glimpse of rare underwater life forms. Return to Queenstown by helicopter or plane (the 5- to 6-hour bus trip is dead time) and spend the afternoon doing a mountain bike tour with **Gravity Action** (p. 440), who will give you an up-close and personal look at the landscapes you've just flown over. Alternatively, challenge yourself with a bit of rock climbing on the **Via Ferrata climbing trail** (p. 442).

Day ❿: Back to Christchurch

Rise before dawn and join **Sunrise Balloons** (p. 441) for a last magical overview of this splendid place where mountains and lakes rise out of the early morning mists. It's the perfect memory to take away before you fly home.

6 Ten Days in the Subtropical North

It always astounds me that so many overseas visitors arrive in Auckland and immediately drive or fly south—or that they avoid the North Island altogether in favor of the south. Sure, the South Island landscapes are more dramatic, but the top of the North, especially in summer, is a quintessential Kiwi experience: white-sand beaches, warm oceans, endless days of swimming and sunbathing, barbecues at the beach, campfires, parties, boats, surf, and sun. I've mapped out 10 days to include three of Auckland's nearby islands to give you a feel for the more laid-back side of New Zealand life. Waiheke Island is the most populated and the most popular and heaven for wine drinkers, while the much less-visited Great Barrier Island (many New Zealanders have never even been there) is an unspoiled treasure that operates on its own clock.

Day ❶: Arrive in Auckland ☆☆☆
Rest for a while before heading off to **Viaduct Basin** (p. 127), which will give you an instant appreciation of New Zealanders' obsessions with boats. Sit in one of the stylish cafes and restaurants, and watch the boats come and go. Visit the **New Zealand National Maritime Museum** (p. 128) for an insight into what the ocean really means to northerners. In the afternoon, take the **Explorer Bus** (p. 103) to **Auckland Museum** (p. 125), where you can admire the views and the grassy green swathe of the **Botanic Gardens** (p. 132). Drive around to **Mission Bay's seaside promenade** (p. 103) and have a picnic dinner as you watch people swim at sunset.

Day ❷: Taking to the Water
Have a rare sailing experience on America's Cup yacht, *NZL 40* (p. 127), or join **Fullers Auckland** (p. 136) for an invigorating cruise of Waitemata Harbour. It's all sea spray, sunshine, and flapping sails out there, plus you'll have great views of the city skyline. Enjoy lunch wharf side at **Cin Cin** or **Harbourside** (p. 118) and then go up the **Sky Tower** (p. 125) for the best views in New Zealand.

Day ❸: Waiheke Island ☆☆☆
Rise early and take the ferry to **Waiheke Island** (p. 145). Save time and go straight into a guided tour of the island, or hire a car and drive around the beaches, wineries, and pretty, unpopulated bays. There's something intangible at work here and you'll quickly be seduced into the relaxed pace of island life. Have lunch at **Te Whau Vineyard** (p. 148) and dinner at **Mudbrick Vineyard** (p. 150), or eat fish and chips on **Onetangi Beach** after a late-afternoon swim.

Day ❹: Matakana & Kawau Island
Head back to Auckland and then drive north to Warkworth and the **Matakana/Sandspit** (p. 171) area. Take the **Kawau Kat's Royal Mail Run Cruise** (p. 174) to Kawau Island for a fun day out. New Zealand's early governor, Sir George Grey, built the historic Mansion House on the island and you'll find unexpected Australian "natives" here—eucalyptus trees, wallabies, kookaburras, and rosella parrots.

Day ❺: The Bay of Islands ☆☆☆
Back on the mainland, drive north to **Paihia** (p. 155). Base yourself here if you want to try all the attractions, or go to **Russell** (p. 159) if you're after a peaceful retreat. Visit **Waitangi Treaty Grounds** (p. 158) for a dose of Maori culture and some lovely boardwalks through native bush and mangrove swamps. Wander through the cool, green leafy grounds to find **Waikokopu Café** (p. 170) and the massive Maori *waka* (canoe) on display

by the beach. Sit on the beach and enjoy the sun.

Day ❻: Kerikeri

This is our northern fruit capital. Enjoy citrus, persimmons, kiwifruit, and macadamia nuts. Stop at **Makana Confections** (p. 161) for mouthwatering chocolates and at **Kerikeri Bakehouse** (p. 171) for picture-perfect picnic food. Take your bounty down to the **Kerikeri Basin** (p. 160) and eat by the river before exploring the local sights. Spend the afternoon at **Marsden Estate Winery** (p. 170) or drive to a local beach and swim until the sun goes down.

Day ❼: Drive to Auckland

Drive back to Auckland Airport and catch a plane to **Great Barrier Island** (p. 150). It's a 35-minute flight in a small plane, so don't go taking everything but the kitchen sink. Your fellow passengers are likely to be dogs, surfers with their boards, and other eccentric sorts who have made this charming island home. The flight is a worthwhile experience in its own right. Fly in over the beach and drop down onto the grass runway. Grab a hire car and make your way to **Foromor Lodge** (p. 153) on the sand hills of Medlands Beach.

Day ❽: The North of the Island

Drive north to **Glenfern Sanctuary** (p. 152) and take Tony Bouzaid's guided walk through native bush. Watch for dolphins leaping about in the deep green waters of Fitzroy Harbour. Drive farther north along unsealed roads to **Whangapoua Beach** (p. 152) and don't be surprised if you're the only person there. It's a surreal experience to feel like the last person left on earth as you stand on this perfect horseshoe of pristine white sand. Walk along the beach to the **S.S. Wairarapa** (p. 152) shipwreck graves.

Day ❾: Tryphena & Okupu

Spend the morning at **Tryphena** (p. 151). Take a kayak trip and watch for the friendly dolphins that swim here. Drive back to **Claris** (p. 151) for lunch at **Claris Texas Café** (p. 153) and ask about the historic pigeon post at the postal agency next door. Follow the road over to Okupu, calling at **Christine Young's unique little museum** (p. 152). Drop down to the beach, park your car, and walk to the south end of Okupu Beach to meet with the little track that takes you around the headland and into Blind Bay. This is where you'll find **John Mellars vineyard,** which you'll talk about for days afterwards.

Day ❿: Fly Back to Auckland

You'll have fallen love with "the Barrier" by now, so have a lazy morning on the beach, go for a swim, watch the surfers, or take a boat ride with Richard Lintott to see the **gannet colony** (p. 152). Fly back to **Auckland** in the late afternoon to connect with your ongoing flights.

5

Auckland

Auckland, known as the City of Sails, is as big, as cosmopolitan, as hedonistic, as subtropical, and as congested as any New Zealand city gets. If you're starting here, you're starting at the top. And if you haven't visited Auckland in the last 5 years, you're in for a major surprise—it has slipped into a new stylish skin that is leaving the rest of New Zealand in its wake.

Along with its much-touted 48 dead volcanoes, Auckland is home to more than 1.3 million people. It has the largest Polynesian population in the world; more boats per capita than any other city; 22 regional parks covering 37,038 hectares (91,484 acres); 50 islands; and more than 500km (310 miles) of walking and hiking tracks. It also has the tallest tower in the Southern Hemisphere, which attracts the most lightning, and if a daily shower is no longer enough, Auckland, surrounded on all sides by water, offers more ways of getting wet than just about anywhere.

This is our baby Sydney, and most of us are proud of it. It's a luscious, leafy city, and there's a contagious energy about this sprawling, show-off place. The injection of billions of dollars into the 1999–2000 and the 2002–03 America's Cup preparations and other international events polished Auckland's public face to gleaming.

Europeans arrived in Auckland in 1839, and the thriving area served as the nation's first capital until 1864, when the seat of government was transferred to Wellington because of its central location. Auckland, though, is still a capital place to visit. It isn't typical of New Zealand any more than New York and Los Angeles are typical of the United States, or Sydney is typical of Australia, but it does have a huge amount to offer.

1 Orientation

ARRIVING
BY PLANE

The **Auckland International Airport** (© **0800/247-767** toll-free in NZ; www.auckland-airport.co.nz) is 21km (13 miles) south of the city, behind Manukau Harbour; a new motorway makes it a swift 30- to 35-minute car trip into town. More than 25 international airlines serve the airport. The **Jean Batten International Terminal** opened in 1998; the first thing to greet you is "A World of Shopping," 56 retail outlets *before* you even hit Customs and Immigration. Auckland is the only airport in the world with two competing duty-free agencies (DFS and Regency), so you'll get great deals on fashion, souvenirs, accessories, and New Zealand art and crafts.

From the terminal, proceed down the escalator to Customs and Immigration. If you're connecting to a domestic flight, before entering the arrivals hall, turn left into the Independent Travelers' Area, where you'll find Air New Zealand transfer desks. This area also contains the **International Visitor Centre** (© **09/256-8535;** reservations@aucklandnz.com), rental-car companies, and currency exchange. For luggage storage, ask at the information center. A children's play area is on the second floor. If you want to rest between flights, take an airport dayroom, which includes a bed, shower, and desk and may be rented "airside" (after you pass through Immigration) between 5am and 11pm for NZ$45 to NZ$65 (US$32–US$46); for information, visit **The Collection Point** (✆ **09/256-8845**). If you feel like pampering yourself after a long flight, call in to the **Traveller's Oasis** (✆ **09/256-6167**; www.travellersoasis.com), between Oceanic and Art Port near the departure gates. It offers specialized treatments to prevent deep-vein thrombosis, plus therapeutic massage for face, body, and feet.

The **Domestic Terminal** is a 10-minute walk from the International Terminal. Simply follow the blue-and-white lines painted on the pavement. Alternatively, catch the free interterminal bus, which departs every 20 minutes between 6am and 10:30pm. Another **Visitor Information Centre** is in the Air New Zealand Terminal (✆ **09/256-8480**). It's open daily 7am to 5pm.

The **Airbus** (✆ **09/303-0309**; www.airbus.co.nz) is the best value for transport between the airport and the Downtown Airline Terminal. It runs every 20 minutes between 6:20am and 10pm. The fare is around NZ$15 (US$11) one-way, NZ$25 (US$18) round-trip. If you're staying in a city hotel on the direct route, the driver will drop you off.

Taxis wait outside the airport terminal; the fare between the airport and city center is about NZ$45 to NZ$50 (US$32–US$35) on weekdays, more on weekends and at night. **Auckland Co-op Taxi** (✆ **09/300-3000**) is a reliable company.

Numerous shuttle companies will take you from the airport to your lodging for around NZ$25 (US$18). **Super Shuttle** (✆ **0800/748-885** or 09/306-3960; www.tourismtransport.co.nz) and **Auckland Airport Shuttle** (✆ **09/576-8904**) both offer reliable service.

BY TRAIN & COACH (BUS)

The big news on the Auckland city transport scene is the opening of the **Britomart Transport Exchange** (Rideline ✆ **09/366-6400**; www.rideline.co.nz or www.auckland rail.com). Near the central business district, ferry terminals, and central city bus stops, it has streamlined all transport services. It features a new underground transport center where intercity and commuter rail, buses, taxis, light rail, and ferry services all connect. The train system has undergone major changes, with the old Railway at Beach Street closing and services relocating to Britomart (with one exception—The Strand, which remains functional for certain trains). There are five train platforms within Britomart, and trains depart from the same platform each day.

Most city buses have relocated to Britomart Bus Precinct, with a few exceptions. The Rideline website remains the best source of current information about these changes, and information centers also provide up-to-the-minute information. Most airport shuttles include Britomart in their circuits; and inner city bus services like The Link and the free City Circuit (see below) also travel via Britomart. For more detailed information about current fares, see "Getting Around," below.

The new center is open daily. It has storage lockers, electronic visual displays of departure and arrival times, top camera security, and ATMs.

For information on the Tranz Scenic trains that serve Auckland, contact **TranzRail** (✆ **0800/802-802** in NZ, or 09/366-6400). **InterCity** (✆ **09/913-6100**) and **Newmans** (✆ **09/913-6200**; www.newmanscoach.co.nz) buses arrive and depart from the SKYCITY Travel Centre Coach Terminal, 102 Hobson St. (✆ **09/913-6100**).

Greater Auckland

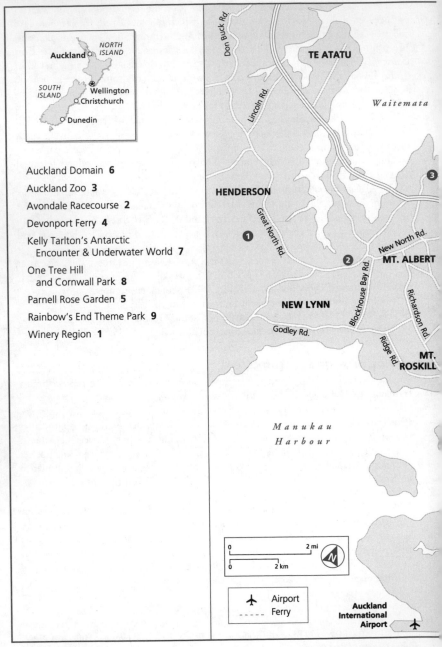

NORTH
ISLAND

Auckland

SOUTH
ISLAND

Wellington

Christchurch

Dunedin

Don Buck Rd.

TE ATATU

Waitemata

Lincoln Rd.

HENDERSON

Great North Rd.

❶

New North Rd.

❷

MT. ALBERT

Blockhouse Bay Rd.

❸

NEW LYNN

Godley Rd.

Richardson Rd.

Ridge Rd.

**MT.
ROSKILL**

*Manukau
Harbour*

0   2 mi

0   2 km

N

✈ Airport

----- Ferry

**Auckland
International
Airport** ✈

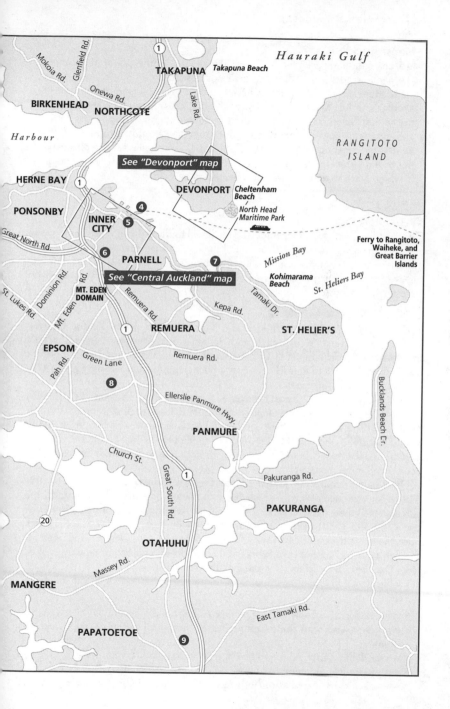

Haraki Gulf

RANGITOTO ISLAND

TAKAPUNA   Takapuna Beach

Mokoia Rd.
Glenfield Rd.
Onewa Rd.

BIRKENHEAD   NORTHCOTE

Lake Rd.

Harbour

See "Devonport" map

HERNE BAY   ①

DEVONPORT   Cheltenham Beach
                 North Head Maritime Park

PONSONBY

INNER CITY   ④
                  ⑤

Great North Rd.

⑥   PARNELL   ⑦   Mission Bay

See "Central Auckland" map

Kohimarama Beach   St. Heliers Bay

MT. EDEN DOMAIN

St. Lukes Rd.
Dominion Rd.
Mt. Eden Rd.

Remuera Rd.

Ferry to Rangitoto, Waiheke, and Great Barrier Islands

Tamaki Dr.

Kepa Rd.

①   REMUERA   ST. HELIER'S

EPSOM   Green Lane   Remuera Rd.

Pah Rd.

⑧

Ellerslie Panmure Hwy.

Bucklands Beach Dr.

PANMURE

Church St.

Great South Rd.

①   Pakuranga Rd.

⑳   PAKURANGA

OTAHUHU

MANGERE   Massey Rd.

East Tamaki Rd.

PAPATOETOE   ⑨

Maori Auckland

In Maori, Auckland is known as Tamaki-Makau-Rau—"the city of 100 lovers." The name is appropriate, for the area was desired by all and conquered by many. More than 18 Maori tribes have had claims to Auckland at one time or another. The first Maori settlers arrived in Hauraki Gulf about 1,000 years ago; the earliest Maori settlement, a site at Motutapu Island dating to the 1100s, was apparently buried under volcanic dust from the Rangitoto eruption. Of the 48 volcanic cones dotting Auckland's landscape, almost all wear the distinctive horizontal terracing that denotes a Maori *pa* site. A *pa* is essentially a fort built in a high place to defend the Maori people.

BY CAR

If you're driving, you will enter Auckland on **State Highway 1** from the south, on the major motorway system. I advise you to call ahead to your hotel and ask which motorway exit to take. Traffic congestion is an issue in Auckland, especially during morning and evening rush hours. If you don't have to drive in the city, avoid it. Parking is also increasingly expensive.

VISITOR INFORMATION

There are two centrally located Auckland Visitor Centres: **i-Site Visitor Centre–Viaduct Basin,** Princes Wharf, Quay and Hobson streets, downtown; and **i-Site Visitor Centre** at The Atrium, SKYCITY Auckland, Victoria and Federal streets. Both are open daily from 8am to 8pm. They share a phone number and website (© **09/979-2333;** www.aucklandnz.com).

The **Takapuna i-Site Visitor Centre,** 49 Hurstmere Rd., Takapuna (© **09/486-8670;** visitorinfo@nthshore.govt.nz), is open from 8:30am to 5pm Monday through Friday and 10am to 3pm Saturday, Sunday, and public holidays. The **Devonport i-Site Visitor Centre,** 3 Victoria Rd., Devonport (© **09/446-0677;** visitorinfo@nthshore.govt.nz), is open from 8am to 5pm Monday through Friday, 8:30am to 5pm Saturday, Sunday, and public holidays.

Other useful resources include the **Department of Conservation Centre** (© **09/379-6476;** www.doc.govt.nz), which has information on walks, campgrounds, the gulf islands, and the national parks. DOC and the **Regional Parks Information Centre** (© **09/303-1530**) share an office in the Ferry Building on Quay Street. They're open Monday through Friday from 9:30am to 5pm March to October, and Monday through Saturday November to February. They're closed Sunday and January 1, Waitangi Day (Feb 6), December 25, and Boxing Day (Dec 26).

Online, you'll find endless amounts of information on Auckland at the following websites:

- **www.aucklandnz.com:** The home page of Tourism Auckland.
- **www.eventsauckland.com:** Comprehensive listings of events in the Auckland region.
- **www.rideline.co.nz:** Auckland bus, ferry, and train information.
- **www.kidsauckland.com:** Information for parents and families.
- **www.akcity.govt.nz/whatson/index.asp:** The Auckland City Council's guide to events in the city.

- **www.aucklandtourism.co.nz**: An A-to-Z of Auckland.
- **www.tourismnorthshore.org.nz**: Information on the North Shore.
- **www.destination-waitakere.com**: A source of information about the primary wine region of Auckland.
- **www.manukau.govt.nz**: Information on Manukau City.
- **www.greatbarrier.co.nz**: Information on Great Barrier Island.
- **www.doc.govt.nz**: The Department of Conservation's information on the national parks and marine reserves.
- **www.gotowaiheke.com**: Information on Waiheke Island.

SPECIAL EVENTS

The annual **Auckland Anniversary Day Regatta** (© 09/534-8186) attracts local and international entrants on the last Monday in January. Held in Windsor Reserve in late February, the **Devonport Food & Wine Festival** ✵ (© 09/446-0688 or 09/445-3011; www.devonportwinefestival.co.nz) offers nonstop entertainment, samples from 20 wineries, and food galore. Jazz, classical music, and opera play a part. The **Auckland Festival** (© 09/309-0117; www.aucklandfestival.co.nz), a premier arts and cultural event held in the last week of September, celebrates Auckland's distinct characteristics—especially its Pacific style. The next festival, AK07, will be staged in 2007. **New Zealand Fashion Week** ✵✵, held in October, presents over 60 New Zealand designers to the world. International buyers and media arrive to check out fashion that is rapidly becoming a "must-see" on the global fashion map; visit www.nzfashionweek.com for details.

The fun **Round the Bays Run** ✵✵ (© 09/525-2166), held in late March, attracts runners from around the South Pacific, who participate in the 8km (5-mile) run around the central bays. It ends with a barbecue in one of the city's parks. The **Royal Easter Show** ✵✵ (© 09/638-9969; www.aucklandshowgrounds.co.nz), held at the Epsom Showgrounds, focuses on excellence in agriculture and animal husbandry with fresh produce stalls and the biggest carnival in New Zealand. November brings New Zealand's premier garden and outdoor-living event, the **Ellerslie Flower Show** ✵✵ (© 09/309-7875; www.ellerslieflowershow.co.nz), at the Auckland Regional Botanic Garden. It's the largest garden exhibition in the Southern Hemisphere.

CITY LAYOUT

Greater Auckland is actually a fusion of four cities—Auckland, Manukau, North Shore, and Waitakere. Each is on a motorway network, which crosses the harbor, rivers, creeks, and bays and carries the thousands who commute into the inner city to work. You can pick up a city map at the visitor center, but the Automobile Association has a better one.

MAIN ARTERIES & STREETS   The main street is **Queen Street,** which ends in Queen Elizabeth Square at **Customs Street. Quay Street** runs along the Waitemata Harbour. At the top end of Queen Street is **Karangahape Road** (usually called "K'Road"), a mere 2km (1¼ miles) from Quay Street. Within that area you'll find most of the city's shops, restaurants, nightspots, major hotels, and bus, rail, and air terminals. The most popular inner city suburbs with the best restaurants are **Parnell** and **Ponsonby. Newmarket** is favored for clothes and shoe shopping.

THE NEIGHBORHOODS IN BRIEF

First, let's get a feel for the four cities. **North Shore City** is contemporary, casual, and cool with, I'm told, a hint of California; **central city** and East Auckland are much more cosmopolitan, with a growing Asian community in the wealthy eastern areas. To the west, **Waitakere City** is the principal wine-growing region; it retains strong evidence of early Eastern European settlement from the 1900s. To the south, **Manukau City** is a melting pot of Polynesian, Maori, and European lifestyles. Now on to the main areas:

Inner City It's hard to decide where the inner city begins and ends, but let's say it's the central business district. This is where you'll find the major hotels and many attractions, including the boisterous and exciting Viaduct Basin, home of the former America's Cup Village. It's also where you'll see the clearest evidence of New Zealand's increasingly multicultural society. The High Street/Vulcan Lane area is an "edgy" part of town if you're looking for a good time. Most water-based tours leave from the downtown Quay Street area. This is a great place to base yourself if you don't want to bother with a vehicle; everything is in walking distance.

Ponsonby/Herne Bay This is quintessential Auckland—bold, brazen, bohemian. It's where most of the best restaurants, bars, and cafes are; it's where the nouveau riche and the almost famous hang out; and you'll find some exquisite specialty shops and lots of divine old wooden houses. Some lovely B&Bs are here, and you won't need a car to have fun. Just off Ponsonby Road is **Karangahape Road,** famous for everything from off-the-wall nightclubs and sassy restaurants to ethnic stores and the whole gamut of sex shops, massage parlors, tattoo and body-piercing studios, and strip joints.

Mount Eden/Epsom These leafy, green hillside suburbs reek of old money. You'll find stunning mansions and villas aplenty—not all peopled by resident bluebloods, though, because the area has a good number of student flats. Both Mount Eden and Epsom have trendy little villages, where old shops and restaurants have been tarted up so the resident folk can feel they're living on the edge. There are some lovely B&Bs in the area, which is a very pretty place to base yourself, close to One Tree Hill, Cornwall Park, and the inner city.

Parnell/Newmarket I refuse to write any Parnell jokes; suffice it to say that if you want plush, trendy, and sophisticated with an undercurrent of hedonism and excess, this is the suburb for you. Parnell Village is perfectly charming, with lots of super (and expensive) shops and restaurants (with nighttime bar action). It's close to the inner city, the Auckland Museum, and the beauteous Auckland Domain park. Lots of good B&Bs are in this area, and in Newmarket, the fashion shopper's Saturday-morning paradise, you'll find heaps of good motels.

Remuera Known locally as "Remmers," this is Auckland's most affluent suburb. Stunning mansions, new highrise apartments, some great upmarket

---

Tips Staying Safe

Personal safety is always a matter of common sense. Police cameras have been installed in several city areas to reduce crime, but it still pays to be vigilant. Much like public parks anywhere, the Auckland Domain is a place to avoid after dark. And it pays to take care at night in Albert Park and the Aotea Square area.

B&Bs, and an easily accessed village full of specialty shops make it a good base. It's also close to the inner city.

Mission Bay/St. Heliers Wealthy seaside suburbs with big real-estate price tags—if you have a Porsche or Ferrari, this is where you bring it to show off on a sunny weekend. Not such a good place to stay if you want to be within walking distance of the city, but it makes a delightful half-day outing. There are lots of excellent restaurants and cafes, and the place really buzzes on weekends, with people walking, running, and in-line skating along the waterfront.

Devonport/Takapuna These two lie over the Harbour Bridge, which can be a nightmarish drive in rush-hour traffic, but if you stay in Devonport you won't need a car at all. Simply lock it up, wander the cute village, and catch a ferry to the inner city when you want a faster pace. There are lots of excellent B&Bs here. Takapuna is the main shopping area of the North Shore, but it doesn't have as much character as Devonport.

The Eastern Suburbs Pretty to visit, all very well kept, but too far from inner city action—if that's what you're after. **Pakuranga, Howick,** and **Panmure** do, however, have a quiet beachside charm and are popular with boaties. To the south is **Otara,** home to Auckland's ever-growing Polynesian community.

2 Getting Around

BY BUS

The Link bus service runs both ways in a circuit around the attractions of the inner city rim. These distinctive white buses charge a NZ$1.30 (US90¢) fare. The whole circuit takes an hour and includes QEII Square, the Britomart Transport Exchange, Parnell, Newmarket, Karangahape Road, Ponsonby, SKYCITY, Queen Street, the University, Domain, Museum, and more. It operates every 10 minutes from 6am to 11:30pm Monday through Friday, every 15 minutes from 7am to 11:30pm Saturday and Sunday. Stagecoach Day and Group Passes (see below) are good on The Link. For more information, call **Stagecoach** (see below).

Stagecoach Auckland (© 09/366-6400; www.stagecoach.co.nz), the intracity bus system, offers good service to most city highlights. You can pick up timetables from **The Bus Place,** Victoria Street West; at Britomart; and at the visitor centers listed above. For schedules, fares, and routes, call the company or pick up the free brochure *Auckland's Top Spots by Public Transport* from a visitor center. Fares depend on zones, running from NZ$1.20 to NZ$8 (US70¢–US$5.60). Children 4 to 15 pay half price; those under 4 ride free. Exact change is not required. If you intend to ride the bus frequently, spend NZ$9 (US$6.30) and get a 1-day **Auckland Day Pass** for unlimited travel. The pass is good on The Link and on the ferry services to Devonport, Bayswater, and Birkenhead. There's also a NZ$18 (US$13) **Group Pass.** Buy passes from the driver or at the terminals.

A word of warning: Auckland buses stop running around 11:30pm (earlier on some routes) Monday through Saturday, and 8pm on Sunday. If you're planning a night of revelry, count on taking a taxi home.

The double-decker **Explorer Bus** ✺✺✺ (© 0800/439-756 or 09/571-3119; www.explorerbus.co.nz) departs from the Ferry Building on Quay Street every half-hour from 9am to 5pm daily in summer and 10am to 5pm in winter. It visits 14 major

> **Tips Lost?**
>
> If you need help finding your way around the city, keep an eye out for the **Auckland City Ambassadors** (© 09/379-2020; www.aucklandcity.govt.nz). They're decked out in bright yellow jackets and are on the streets in the downtown area daily from 9am to 6pm.

Auckland attractions; for NZ$30 (US$21) adult, NZ$15 (US$11) child 4 to 16, and NZ$70 (US$49) family, you can hop on and off as many times as you want in a day.

Look out for the **City Circuit** (© 09/366-6400), a free inner city bus loop operated by Stagecoach Auckland. It runs daily every 10 minutes between 8am and 6pm, connecting the waterfront and Viaduct Basin to Queen Street, the central universities, Civic Theatre, The Edge, and Sky Tower.

BY TAXI
Typical rates start at NZ$3 (US$2.10) and go up NZ$1.50 (US$1.05) per kilometer. Cabs can be flagged down, ordered by phone, or picked up at taxi stands. Stands are at all terminals and on the corner of Customs Street West at Queen Street. Call **Auckland Taxi Co-Op** (© 09/300-3000) or **Corporate Cabs** (© 09/631-1111).

BY TRAIN
Tranz Metro runs between Auckland, Newmarket, Waitakere, Papakura, and Orakei, stopping at Remuera, Mount Eden, Mount Albert, and many other suburbs along the way. Fares range from NZ$1.10 to NZ$8 (US80¢–US$5.60). You can buy 10-trip passes, a **Day Rover Pass** (about NZ$12/US$8.40 for adults, NZ$6/US$4.20 for children), or a **Family Pass** (about NZ$25/US$18). Contact **Rideline** (© 09/366-6400; www.rideline.co.nz) for details and schedules.

BY FERRY
The **Devonport Ferry** departs regularly daily from Queen's Wharf, Quay Street (© 09/367-9111; www.fullers.co.nz). The fare is about NZ$10 (US$7). Fullers and Subritzky ferries serve Waiheke Island; for details, see "A Side Trip to Waiheke Island" (p. 145).

BY CAR
Driving in downtown Auckland can be problematic. Finding parking is difficult. Given the efficiency of the Explorer, The Link, and the City Circuit buses, it's a much better idea to explore the town without a car. However, if you insist, there are parking buildings operated by the City Council on Beresford Street just off Karangahape Road; near the waterfront on Albert Street, west of Queen Street; on Victoria Street, slightly east of Queen Street; at Britomart off Customs Street, east of Queen Street; downtown to the east of Queen Street; downtown to the west of Queen Street, with an entrance from Customs Street West; Civic Underground on Mayoral Drive; and Victoria Street East. They're all open 24 hours daily; rates can be expensive.

BY BICYCLE
You can rent a bike from **Adventure Cycles,** 36 Customs St. E. (© 09/309-5566; www.adventure-auckland.co.nz). It's open daily from 7am to 7pm. Rates start at NZ$12 (US$8.40) for a half-day and include the mandatory helmet.

FAST FACTS: Auckland

American Express Offices are at 105 Queen St. ((C) **09/379-8286**) and 67–69 Symonds St. ((C) **09/367-4422**). For credit card queries, call (C) **0800/263-936**; for traveler's check queries, (C) **0800/263-982**.

Area Code Auckland's area code (STD) is **09**.

Babysitters Most major hotels can furnish babysitters. **Freemans Bay Child Care** on Pratt Street ((C) **09/376-7282**) will provide daytime child care and help in arranging babysitters for evenings.

Currency Exchange Go to city center banks and most neighborhood branches for your banking needs. Banks are open Monday through Friday from 9am to 4:30pm. Hotels and restaurants usually convert traveler's checks, but you'll get a much better rate at banks. Dedicated currency exchange outlets are at **Thomas Cook,** 159 Queen St., and at **TravelEx NZ,** 32 Queen St. (open normal business hours); and at SKYCITY and Auckland International Airport (both open daily during normal business hours; www.bnz.co.nz/currencyexchange).

Dentists For emergency and after-hours dental service, call **Auckland Accident & Emergency Clinic** ((C) **09/520-6609**). It's open Monday through Saturday from 8am to 11pm, Sunday until 10pm.

Doctors For emergency medical services, call (C) **09/524-5943** or 09/579-9909; for emergency ambulance service, dial (C) **111. The CityMed Medical Centre** is on the corner of Mills Lane and Albert Street, in the inner city ((C) **09/377-5525**).

Embassies & Consulates Embassies are in Wellington (see "Fast Facts: Wellington" in chapter 11). For additional information on embassies in New Zealand, contact the **Ministry of Foreign Affairs & Trade** in Wellington ((C) **04/494-8500;** www.mft.govt.nz; enquiries@mft.govt.nz).

Auckland has consulates of the **United States,** Level 3, 23 Customs St. E. ((C) **09/303-2724;** fax 09/366-0870); **Canada,** 48 Emily Pl. ((C) **09/309-8516**); **Ireland,** Dingwall Building, 87 Queen St. ((C) **09/302-2867**); and the **United Kingdom,** IAG House, 151 Queen St. ((C) **09/303-2973**).

Emergencies Dial (C) **111** to call the police, report a fire, or request an ambulance.

Hospitals Area hospitals include **Auckland Hospital,** Park Road, Grafton ((C) **09/367-7000**), which incorporates the National Women's Hospital and the Starship Children's Hospital; and **Greenlane Hospital,** Greenlane Road, Epsom ((C) **09/638-9909**).

Internet Access Give any of these a go: **Cyber Max,** 291 Queen St. ((C) 09/979-2468); **Citinet Cybercafe,** 115 Queen St. ((C) 09/377-3674); **Cyber City Internet Café,** 29 Victoria St. E. ((C) 09/303-3009); **Net Central Internet Café,** 5 Lorne St. ((C) 09/373-5186); and **Net Zone,** 4 Fort St. ((C) 09/377-3906).

Laundromat There is a 24-hour laundromat at 511 Great North Rd., Grey Lynn ((C) **09/376-6062**).

Lost Property Call the Central Police Station ((C) **09/379-4240**) or any local police station.

Luggage Storage & Lockers "Left luggage" facilities are at the Visitor Information Centre in the International Airport. The fee for 24 hours is about NZ$6

(US$4.20) for hand luggage, NZ$12 (US$8.40) for large items, and NZ$10 (US$7) per suitcase. For more information, call © **09/256-8845.**

Maps **Specialty Maps,** 46 Albert St. (© **09/307-2217**), is open Monday through Friday from 8:30am to 4:30pm and Saturday from 10am to 1pm. It sells maps, guidebooks, and topographical and park maps.

Newspapers & Magazines The *New Zealand Herald* is the daily paper. The *Sunday Star Times* and *Sunday News* are Sunday-morning publications.

Police For emergencies, dial © **111.** For other matters, call the Central Police Station (© **09/379-4240**).

Post Office Most post offices are open Monday through Friday from 9am to 5pm. The Chief Post Office (CPO), CML Mall, Queen Street at Wyndham Street, is open Monday through Thursday from 8:30am to 5pm, Friday from 8:30am to 6pm, and Saturday from 9am to noon. For poste restante pickup, go to the Post Shop in the Bledisloe Building on Wellesley Street. There is a conveniently located Post Shop in the Downtown Shopping Centre on Quay Street at QEII Square. For post office questions, call © **0800/501-501.**

Services for Travelers with Disabilities For information on ramps, toilets, parking lots, and telephones, and an equipment showroom, contact the **Disability Resource Centre,** 14 Erson Ave. (P.O. Box 24-042), Royal Oak, Auckland (© **09/625-8069;** www.disabilityresource.org.nz).

3 Where to Stay

If your idea of a holiday is the best views, the best beds, the best food, and the last word in service, Auckland's luxury hotels won't disappoint. As well as those listed below, the **Stamford Plaza** 🏵🏵🏵 , Albert Street, in the heart of the city (© **0508/658-888** in NZ, or 09/309-8888; www.stamford.com.au), offers superlative service. Various U.S. magazines have included it in the top 10 Asia-Pacific hotels. Also at the top of the heap is **Carlton Hotel** 🏵🏵🏵 , Mayoral Drive and Vincent Street (© **0800/666-777** in NZ, or 09/366-3000; www.carlton-auckland.co.nz), which is a favorite with the rich, the famous, and the corporately inclined.

For long stays, you might opt for a fully serviced apartment. Among the best options is **CityLife Auckland** 🏵🏵, 171 Queen St. (© **0800/368-888** in NZ, or 09/379-9222; www.heritagehotels.co.nz), with 253 suites and hotel rooms from around NZ$350 (US$245).

If you want home comforts, bed-and-breakfasts abound, many in homes of fine character. Pick up the free booklet *Auckland Home, Farmstay and Bed & Breakfast Accommodation* from the visitor center.

Rates include 12.5% GST (goods and services tax) and parking, unless stated otherwise.

IN INNER CITY
VERY EXPENSIVE

Ascott Metropolis Auckland 🏵🏵🏵   The stature of the Empire State Building, the luxury of the finest New York hotels, the convenience of High Street, the beauty of Albert Park—this complex right in the heart of downtown is worth your attention. Towering 40 stories over the city, the landmark development offers accommodations with luxurious earth-toned interiors. Suites are rich, with king-size beds, full designer kitchens, and even a telephone in the bathroom. All units open onto balconies. Harborview rooms cost a little extra; get one of these as high up as you can—the view is definitely worth it. The former Magistrates' Courthouse has been fully restored to provide a grand entrance to the complex. It's grand and elegant, and is injecting international style into the New Zealand hotel industry.

1 Courthouse Lane (enter from Kitchener St.). ℂ 0800/202-828 in NZ, or 09/300-8800. Fax 09/300-8899. www.the-ascott.com. 160 units. NZ$450 (US$315) studio; NZ$562–NZ$583 (US$393–US$408) deluxe studio; NZ$674–NZ$720 (US$471–US$504) premier 1-bedroom; NZ$899 (US$629) executive 1-bedroom; NZ$1,079–NZ$1,146 (US$755–US$799) premier 2-bedroom; NZ$1,688 (US$1,180) penthouse. Extra person NZ$56 (US$39). Long-stay and special deals available. AE, DC, MC, V. Valet parking NZ$25 (US$18). **Amenities:** 2 restaurants (Otto's [fine dining], Bistro Deux [a la carte]); bar; heated indoor pool; fully equipped gym; spa; 2 indoor/outdoor Jacuzzis; sauna; men's steam room; concierge; car rentals; business center; salon (next door); 24-hr. room service; massage; babysitting; laundry service; same-day dry cleaning; on-call doctor/dentist. *In room:* A/C, TV, dataport, kitchen, minibar, fridge, coffeemaker, hair dryer, iron, safe.

Hilton Auckland 🌸🌸🌸   There's no other Hilton in the world like the boutique-style Hilton Auckland, a NZ$50-million (US$27-million) development that opened in 2001. It's almost surrounded by water, perched on the end of Princes Wharf like the giant ship that inspired it and like those that tie up alongside it. Rooms are modern, sophisticated, stylish—not overly large in some cases, but always exquisitely furnished, with fabulous bathrooms and amazing sea views. If you want "super views," take 1 of the 12 deluxe corner rooms that feature two whole walls of glass. The suites are shaped like the bow of a ship and boast vast decks. The hotel is right in the heart of Viaduct Basin, amid the best restaurants and bars in Auckland.

Princes Wharf, 137–147 Quay St. ℂ 0800/448-002 in NZ, or 09/978-2000. Fax 09/978-2001. www.hilton.com. 166 units. NZ$585 (US$409) King Hilton room; NZ$645 (US$451) King Hilton deluxe; NZ$770 (US$539) deluxe plus; NZ$1,086 (US$759) Bow suite; NZ$1,467 (US$1,027) Premier suite. Off-season and special deals available. AE, DC, MC, V. Valet parking NZ$25 (US$18). **Amenities:** Restaurant (White); bar; glass-fronted heated outdoor pool suspended from 4th-floor bridge; gym w/trainer; concierge; tour bookings; car rentals; secretarial services; 24-hr. room service; massages and beauty therapy at adjacent Spa de Seville; babysitting; laundry service; same-day dry cleaning; on-call doctor/dentist. *In room:* A/C, TV, dataport, minibar, fridge, coffeemaker, hair dryer, iron, safe.

Langham Hotel Auckland 🌸🌸🌸   Formerly the Sheraton, this business favorite is reinventing itself under new ownership. A NZ$12-million (US$8.4-million) refurbishment in 2005 is stage one of a massive upgrade that will continue through 2006. The three floors of Club Rooms were the first to benefit, and they provide every comfort: king-size beds, robes, slippers, and lovely marble bathrooms, plus Club Lounge access and business facilities. There are also 12 elegant one-bedroom suites with connecting rooms. Overall, the Langham is plusher than the understated Carlton and more traditional than the Hilton or the Ascott Metropolis.

83 Symonds St. ℂ 0800/616-261 in NZ, or 09/379-5132. Fax 09/377-9367. www.langhamhotels.com. 410 units. NZ$618 (US$432) Superior; NZ$675 (US$472) Executive; NZ$844 (US$590) Club; NZ$1,125 (US$787) Executive suite; NZ$1,682 (US$1,176) Governor suite; NZ$2,340 (US$1,636) Royal suite. Leisure packages and long-stay rates available. AE, DC, MC, V. Valet parking NZ$20 (US$14). **Amenities:** 2 restaurants (Partingtons [fine dining], SBF Brasserie); 2 bars; heated rooftop lap pool; health club w/fully equipped gym and trainer; Jacuzzi; 2 saunas; concierge; tour bookings; car rentals; courtesy car to city; business center; secretarial services; shopping arcade; salon; 24-hr. room service; massage; babysitting; laundry service; same-day dry cleaning; concierge-level rooms; on-call doctor/dentist. *In room:* A/C, TV, VCR, dataport, minibar, fridge, coffeemaker, hair dryer, iron, safe.

Central Auckland

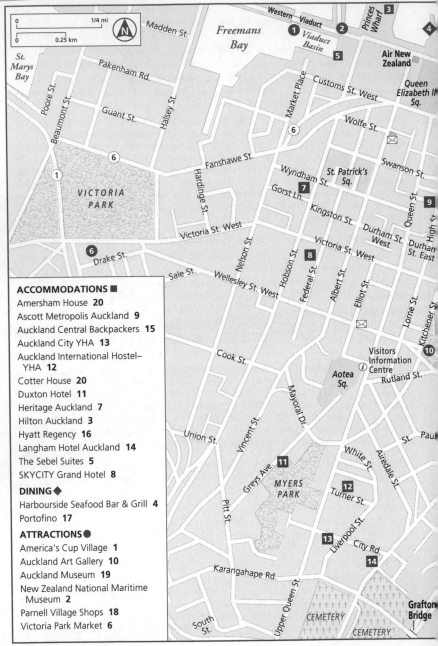

St. Marys Bay

Freemans Bay

St. Patrick's Sq.

Victoria Park

Myers Park

Aotea Sq.

Queen Elizabeth II Sq.

Air New Zealand

Visitors Information Centre

Grafton Bridge

CEMETERY

ACCOMMODATIONS ■
Amersham House **20**
Ascott Metropolis Auckland **9**
Auckland Central Backpackers **15**
Auckland City YHA **13**
Auckland International Hostel–
 YHA **12**
Cotter House **20**
Duxton Hotel **11**
Heritage Auckland **7**
Hilton Auckland **3**
Hyatt Regency **16**
Langham Hotel Auckland **14**
The Sebel Suites **5**
SKYCITY Grand Hotel **8**

DINING ◆
Harbourside Seafood Bar & Grill **4**
Portofino **17**

ATTRACTIONS ●
America's Cup Village **1**
Auckland Art Gallery **10**
Auckland Museum **19**
New Zealand National Maritime
 Museum **2**
Parnell Village Shops **18**
Victoria Park Market **6**

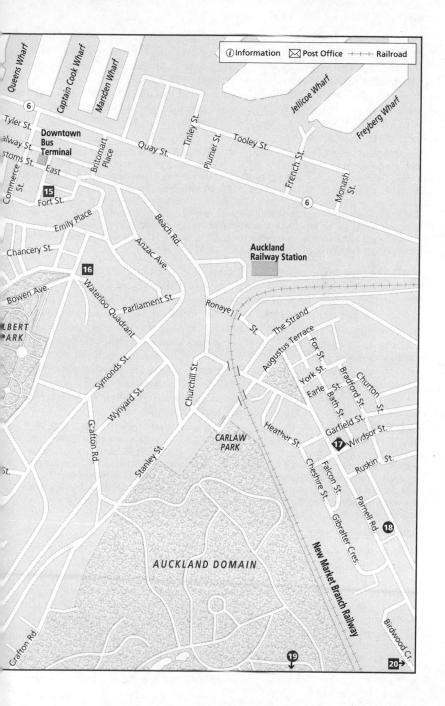

Information ⊠ **Post Office** ┼┼┼┼ **Railroad**

Queens Wharf
Captain Cook Wharf
Marsden Wharf
Jellicoe Wharf
Freyberg Wharf

6

Tyler St.
alway St.
stoms St.
Commerce St.

Downtown Bus Terminal

East

Britomart Place

Quay St.

Tinley St.
Plumer St.
Tooley St.
French St.
Monash St.

6

15

Fort St.

Emily Place

Beach Rd.

Auckland Railway Station

Chancery St.

Anzac Ave.

16

Bowen Ave.

Waterloo Quadrant

Parliament St.

Ronaye St.

The Strand

Augustus Terrace

Fox St.

Church St.

Bradford St.

Churton St.

York St.

ALBERT PARK

Symonds St.

Wynyard St.

Churchill St.

Earle

Bath St.

Windsor St.

Heather St.

Garfield St.

17

Ruskin St.

Grafton Rd.

Stanley St.

CARLAW PARK

Cheshire St.

Falcon St.

Parnell Rd.

18

St.

Gibralter Cres.

AUCKLAND DOMAIN

New Market Branch Railway

Birdwood Cr.

Grafton Rd.

19

20

109

EXPENSIVE

Heritage Auckland ⭐   With two distinct parts—the Hotel wing in a restored, landmark Art Deco building; and the purpose-built contemporary Tower wing—completed in 1998 and 1999 respectively, this property offers a choice of two of everything. All rooms are generous suite-style units with good-size bathrooms. A slight premium applies on the self-contained Tower suites, many of which boast great harbor views. The Hotel wing received a soft refurbishment of 160 rooms in 2005 and looks all the better for it.

Hotel Wing, 35 Hobson St; Tower Wing, 22 Nelson St. ℂ **0800/368-888** in NZ, or 09/379-8553. Fax 09/379-8554. www.heritagehotels.co.nz. 330 units. NZ$365 (US$255) Hotel superior; NZ$392 (US$274) Tower superior; NZ$418 (US$292) 1-bedroom deluxe Hotel suite; NZ$444 (US$311) 1-bedroom deluxe Tower suite. Long-stay, off-peak, and special deals available. AE, DC, MC, V. Valet parking NZ$20 (US$14). **Amenities:** 2 restaurants (Hectors in Hotel wing; Azure in Tower wing); 2 bars; rooftop heated outdoor pool, heated indoor lap pool; all-weather outdoor lit tennis court; 2 gyms; 2 Jacuzzis; sauna; concierge; tour bookings; car rentals; 2 business centers; salon; gift shop; 24-hr. room service; massage; babysitting; coin-op laundry; laundry service; same-day dry cleaning; nonsmoking rooms; currency exchange; on-call doctor/dentist; access for travelers w/disabilities. *In room:* A/C, TV, dataport, kitchenettes and full kitchens, minibar, fridge, coffeemaker, hair dryer, iron, safe, laundry facilities.

Hyatt Regency ⭐⭐⭐   The Hyatt Regency's 120 smart new apartment suites and a gymnasium and health spa facility to die for should make you sit up and take notice. The new suites contain kitchenettes, balconies, and swanky bathrooms; the 20 roomy corner suites with wraparound balconies are the pick of the bunch. Connecting rooms make them perfect for families or couples traveling together. Residence rooms have kitchens. By the end of 2006, 274 of the original hotel rooms will have been refurbished and upgraded. The original Hyatt is the oldest central city hotel, but it has stood the test of time. It has more of a boutiquey, personalized style than some of the other inner city biggies—an unassuming elegance that's very easy to feel comfortable in. Like most of its competitors, it offers enticing extras in club-level rooms, but even standard rooms are a rich reward after a hard day of sightseeing.

Waterloo Quadrant and Princes St. ℂ **0800/441-234** in NZ, or 09/355-1234. Fax 09/303-2932. www.auckland. regency.hyatt.com. 394 units. NZ$427 (US$299) view queen; NZ$444 (US$311) residence king; NZ$484 (US$339) club king, regency suite, residence deluxe, or 2-room deluxe; NZ$512 (US$358) regency executive; NZ$523–NZ$545 (US$366–US$381) residence suite; NZ$636 (US$445) residence 2-bedroom suite; NZ$1,018 (US$712) residence penthouse suite. Long-stay and special deals available. AE, DC, MC, V. Valet parking NZ$25 (US$18). **Amenities:** 2 restaurants; bar; heated indoor pool; gym; Jacuzzi; 2 saunas; concierge; tour bookings; car rentals; business center; secretarial services; 24-hr. room service; massage; babysitting; laundry service; same-day dry cleaning; on-call doctor/dentist. *In room:* A/C, TV, dataport, minibar, fridge, coffeemaker, hair dryer, iron.

SKYCITY Grand Hotel ⭐⭐⭐   This is the brand-new five-star baby in the SKYCITY stable. Linked to the SKYCITY hotel and casino complex by a bridge, it offers the best of everything: smart rooms with good bathrooms, one of the best restaurants in Auckland, and a gorgeous lap pool and spa facility. It's a centrally located oasis of luxury offering very good deals and a wow-factor New Zealand contemporary art collection.

90 Federal St. ℂ **0800/759-2489** in NZ, or 09/363-7000. Fax 09/363-7010. www.skycitygrand.co.nz. 316 units. NZ$370 (US$259) luxury suite; NZ$510 (US$357) executive suite; NZ$3,600 (US$2,518) grand suite. Long-stay, off-peak, and special deals available. AE, DC, MC, V. Valet parking NZ$25 (US$18). **Amenities:** 2 restaurants (DINE by Peter Gordon [fusion cuisine] and The Terrace Bar & Restaurant); 2 bars; heated indoor lap pool; gym; East West Day Spa, specializing in Eastern-style holistic treatments; Jacuzzi; sauna; concierge; tour bookings; business center; secretarial services; 24-hr. room service; massage; babysitting; laundry service; same-day dry cleaning; nonsmoking rooms; currency exchange; on-call doctor/dentist; access for travelers w/disabilities. *In room:* A/C, TV, dataport, minibar, fridge, coffeemaker, hair dryer, iron, safe.

Devonport

ACCOMMODATIONS ■
Esplanade Hotel **7**
Peace & Plenty Inn **9**
Villa Cambria **1**

DINING ◆
Cod Piece **6**
Da Ciccio **5**
Monsoon **5**

ATTRACTIONS ●
Devonport Museum & Gardens **2**
Holy Trinity Anglican Church **10**
Mount Victoria Cemetery **4**
North Head Maritime Park **11**
Royal New Zealand Navy Museum **3**
Windsor Reserve **8**

Ferry
Mountain

MODERATE

Braemar on Parliament Street 🥝🥝, 7 Parliament St. (© **0800/155-4363** in NZ, or 09/377-5463; fax 09/377-3056; www.AucklandBedandBreakfast.com), is a new B&B just a short walk from High Street. The three-story Edwardian gentleman's town house, built in 1903, has four rooms—some en suite, some private bathroom—priced from NZ$180 to NZ$325 (US$126–US$227). You'll be hard-pressed to find any other quality B&B this handy to downtown activities, restaurants, and transport systems. The **President Plaza Hotel Auckland** 🥝, 1 Hobson St. (© **0800/773-743** in NZ, or 09/356-1000; www.presidentplaza.co.nz), in the heart of the city overlooking Viaduct Harbour, is also a great value, with rooms from NZ$149 to NZ$320 (US$104–US$224).

Duxton Hotel 🥝🥝🥝   There is something intangibly serene about the Duxton. Maybe it's the leafy, tree-lined street it sits in, or the green park it overlooks. Either way, it's quieter and more intimate than some of the bigger hotels. Treat yourself to a special deluxe spa package that includes breakfast and a king-size Jacuzzi with shutters opening onto the main room. Apartments with full laundry facilities and kitchens are also a big plus. Just 6 years old, this little oasis of calm demands your attention.

100 Greys Ave. © **0800/655-555** in NZ, or 09/375-1800. Fax 09/375-1801. www.duxton.com. 154 units. NZ$197 (US$138) deluxe; NZ$225 (US$157) deluxe spa; NZ$253 (US$177) 1-bedroom suite; NZ$281 (US$197) 1-bedroom apartment; NZ$450 (US$315) 2-bedroom apartment. Long-stay, off-peak, and special deals available. AE, DC, MC, V. Valet parking NZ$15 (US$11) per day. **Amenities:** Restaurant (The Grill [contemporary New Zealand]); bar; outdoor heated pool; guest access to small gym across road; Jacuzzi; concierge; tour bookings; car rentals; business center; 24-hr. room service; massage; babysitting; laundry service; same-day dry cleaning; nonsmoking rooms; currency exchange; on-call doctor/dentist; airport transport; access for travelers w/disabilities. *In room:* A/C, TV, dataport, kitchenette, minibar, fridge, coffeemaker, hair dryer, iron.

The Sebel Suites 🥝🥝   If you're a fan of all things nautical, you'll feel right at home at the ever-popular Sebel Suites, where big views take in the comings and goings of the Viaduct Basin. Right in the middle of the action, with classy restaurants and bars galore right on the doorstep, this all-suite accommodations was built for the America's Cup. Suites are fresh and crisp, and all marina suites have a separate living room and balconies looking over the water. If you like being within easy reach of a good time, The Sebel is for you—and given its prime location, you'll find the rates extremely reasonable.

85–89 Customs St. W. © **0800/937-373** in NZ, or 09/978-4000. Fax 09/978-4099. www.mirvachotels.com.au. 132 units. From NZ$337 (US$236) city studio suite; NZ$394 (US$276) 1-bedroom city suite; NZ$506 (US$354) 1-bedroom marina suite; NZ$562 (US$393) 1-bedroom deluxe or executive marina suite. Special deals available. AE, DC, MC, V. Valet parking NZ$25 (US$18). **Amenities:** Heated pool and gym across the road (NZ$8/US$5.60) for guest use; concierge; tour bookings; 24-hr. room service; laundry service; dry cleaning; nonsmoking rooms; on-call doctor/dentist. *In room:* A/C, TV, dataport, fully equipped kitchen, minibar, fridge, coffeemaker, hair dryer, iron, safe-deposit boxes.

INEXPENSIVE

Auckland Central Backpackers, 229 Queen St. (© **09/358-4877**; fax 09/358-4872; www.acb.co.nz), is just steps off the waterfront and close to the Britomart Transport Exchange. Dorm beds go for around NZ$25 (US$18).

Auckland City YHA 🥝   Formerly a budget hotel, this seven-story building is well suited to backpacker accommodations. Rooms are simple but of good size. Everything is clean and tidy, and if you're not sold on its excellent location close to Karangahape Road, you'll be won over by the excellent sun decks, TV lounge, kitchen/dining room, and smart little bistro cafe overlooking the city. It has lockers, bike storage, a book exchange, and a travel center. There are more twin share and double rooms here than at Auckland International (see below).

City Rd. and Liverpool St. © **0800/278-299** in NZ, or 09/309-2802. Fax 09/373-5083. www.yha.co.nz. 160 beds (none with bathroom). From NZ$22 (US$15) dorm bed per person; NZ$64 (US$45) twin/double. NZ$3 (US$2.10) extra per person per night for non–YHA members. AE, MC, V. **Amenities:** Cafe; tour bookings; car rentals; coin-op laundry; nonsmoking rooms; on-call doctor/dentist. *In room:* No phone.

Auckland International Hostel-YHA ☆☆   This hostel opened in mid-1999 in a large converted office block, so everything is clean, modern, and comfortable. It's one of the best hostels in the country, with over 50,000 guests a year. Security is tight. It's just a 5-minute walk to central city. This is the flagship YHA hostel; its sister establishment, Auckland City YHA (see above), is only 100m (328 ft.) away. This facility has a communal lounge, a smokers' room, bike and luggage storage, and large new kitchens.

1–35 Turner St. (P.O. Box 68-149). © **0800/278-299** in NZ, or 09/302-8200. Fax 09/302-8205. www.yha.co.nz. 170 beds. From NZ$24 (US$17) 4-share dorm; NZ$90 (US$63) en-suite twin/double. NZ$3 (US$2.10) extra per person per night for non–YHA members. AE, MC, V. Limited off-street parking NZ$5 (US$3.50); reservation required. **Amenities:** Tour bookings; car rentals; laundry; nonsmoking rooms. *In room:* No phone.

IN PONSONBY
VERY EXPENSIVE
Mollies ☆☆☆   This grand old 1870s home has been extensively renovated and expanded to provide 12 stylish suites and apartments. If you take the upstairs level, you'll have a balcony; downstairs rooms open onto the garden. Nothing has been spared to create upmarket interiors filled with antiques and smart furniture. The location is handy to Ponsonby Road restaurants, bars, and boutique shopping. Mollies combines the comforts of home with the privacy of apartment living. A member of Small Luxury Hotels of the World, it has accumulated plenty of international accolades.

6 Tweed St. © **09/376-3489.** Fax 09/378-6592. www.mollies.co.nz. 12 suites. NZ$411–NZ$512 (US$287–US$358) driver/nanny room; NZ$546 (US$382) junior suite; NZ$889 (US$622) villa suite; NZ$1,114 (US$779) premier villa suite. Off-season rates and weekend deals available. Rates include breakfast, predinner drinks, canapés, and limousine inner city transfers. AE, DC, MC, V. Free off-street parking. **Amenities:** Bar; nearby fitness center; downstairs recreation area; tour bookings; car rentals. *In room:* A/C in apts, TV, dataport, fully equipped kitchens, hair dryer, iron.

MODERATE
The Great Ponsonby Bed & Breakfast ☆☆   This immaculately restored villa will delight you, as will hosts Sally James and Gerard Hill. It's quiet, yet within walking distance of the best of Ponsonby, and the comfortable rooms reflect a colorful Pacific mood. Three suites have both bathtubs and showers. The lovely Dunedin Room has its own deck, while the upstairs Penthouse has a sitting room and balcony. Don't overlook the Palm Garden studios if you want extra space and privacy; some of these come with kitchenette, minibar, and VCR. There's a sunlit lounge bulging with books and magazines, verandas to unwind on, and breakfasts to linger over.

30 Ponsonby Terrace. © **0800/766-792** in NZ, or 09/376-5989. Fax 09/376-5527. www.greatpons.co.nz. 11 units. NZ$180–NZ$360 (US$126–US$252). Rates include breakfast. AE, MC, V. Free off-street parking. **Amenities:** Use of bikes; tour bookings; car rentals; laundry service. *In room:* TV, dataport, coffeemaker, hair dryer, iron.

INEXPENSIVE
The Brown Kiwi Travellers Hostel ☆   This 100-year-old house is on a quiet street just a block from the main Ponsonby action. The best deals here are the two rooms in the lovely little garden house, a purpose-built corrugated-iron dwelling tucked among

> ## *Moments* One Tree Hill
>
> A stroll in **Cornwall Park** in Epsom is a must. You'll find fields with grazing sheep, charming walks, and One Tree Hill, where early European settlers planted a sacred totara tree to honor the birth of a child. Stop first at the **Cornwall Park Visitor Centre** (⟨© 09/630-8485; www.cornwallpark.co.nz) for maps and information on self-guided walks.

banana palms and ponds. It serves as a double or triple facility and is less sardinelike than the in-house rooms. Overall, this place offers a good atmosphere and a terrific garden courtyard in which to while away summer days and nights.

7 Prosford St. ⓒ/fax 09/378-0191. www.brownkiwi.co.nz. 32 beds (none with bathroom). NZ$22–NZ$24 (US$15–US$17) dorm per person; NZ$54–NZ$66 (US$38–US$46) twin/double. MC, V. **Amenities:** Bar; tour bookings; car rentals; coin-op laundry; nonsmoking rooms. *In room:* Hair dryer, iron, safe.

IN MOUNT EDEN/EPSOM
VERY EXPENSIVE
Florence Court ⓐⓐⓐ *(Finds)*   It's not often you can stay in a New Zealand Historic Places Category 1 property, and the 1,115-sq.-m (12,000-sq.-ft.) Florence Court exceeds all others. This first-class example of fine Edwardian architecture offers superlative accommodations amid the opulence of Louis XV antiques. Quite apart from savoring the plush comforts of huge rooms, you'll spend hours exploring this vast mansion set on .8 hectares (2 acres) of beautiful gardens. Film stars, heads of state, and prime ministers have all sampled the tranquillity.

6 Omana Ave., Epsom. ⓒ 09/623-9333. Fax 09/623-9330. www.florencecourt.co.nz. 4 units, 1 cottage. NZ$1,068 (US$747) suite or cottage. Long-stay rates and special deals negotiable. Rates include breakfast, airport transfers, and predinner cocktails. MC, V. Free valet parking. **Amenities:** 5-course dinner prepared by chef, by prior arrangement; nearby golf course; tennis court; access to nearby health club; bike rentals; billiard room; concierge; tour bookings; car rentals; secretarial services; limited room service; massage; babysitting; laundry service; same-day dry cleaning; nonsmoking rooms; on-call doctor/dentist. *In room:* TV, coffeemaker, hair dryer, iron, safe.

INEXPENSIVE
Bavaria Bed & Breakfast Hotel ⓐ *(Value)*   It says FREE STATE OF BAVARIA on the gate and, as you can imagine, Rudi and Ulricke Stephan get a lot of German guests. But it's a cosmopolitan establishment in a quiet, leafy neighborhood, equally enjoyed by large numbers of Americans and Canadians. The three upstairs rooms are the sunniest, and all have doors leading out onto the balcony. All units have en-suite bathrooms. The big old villa is close to Mount Eden village, where there are several restaurants and cafes, and you can catch buses on nearby Dominion Road heading into the city, which is 10 minutes away.

83 Valley Rd., Mount Eden. ⓒ 09/638-9641. Fax 09/638-9665. www.bavariabandbhotel.com. 11 units. NZ$139–NZ$145 (US$97–US$101). Off-season and long-stay rates available. Rates include breakfast. MC, V. Free off-street parking. **Amenities:** Tour bookings; car rentals; nonsmoking rooms; on-call doctor/dentist. *In room:* Dataport, hair dryer and iron upon request.

IN PARNELL/NEWMARKET
To get to Parnell if you don't have a car, take The Link bus from Queen Street, which travels down Customs Street and along Beach Road to Parnell Rise. Sadly, most of the best B&Bs in this area have closed or are not what they used to be. If you want a

middle-of-the-road hotel in a pleasant setting, try **Kingsgate Hotel Parnell,** 92–102 Gladstone Rd. (© **0800/782-5489** in NZ, or 09/377-3619). It's just across the road from a quiet park with 5,000 rosebushes and has 117 rooms priced from NZ$120 to NZ$160 (US$84–US$112).

IN REMUERA
EXPENSIVE

Aachen House *ﾑﾑﾑ* If you're looking to sloth it out in total elegance, surrounded by stunning antiques and top service, Joan McKirdy's Edwardian villa is for you. Suites are furnished with the busy executive in mind, with two direct-dial phones, a fax hookup, and a classic writing desk, plus a modern en-suite bathroom and big super-king-size beds. The Victoria, with its own lounge and balcony, is particularly enticing. The house is 4km (2½ miles) from downtown; bus service is a block away. I don't like to use the word "perfect" too much, but this little boutique hotel fits the description.

39 Market Rd., Remuera. © **0800/222-436** in NZ, or 09/520-2329. Fax 09/524-2898. www.aachenhouse.co.nz. 9 units. NZ$300–NZ$700 (US$210–US$490). Rates include predinner drinks, breakfast. Long-stay, off-peak, and special deals available. AE, DC, MC, V. Free off-street parking. Children under 16 not accepted. **Amenities:** Teahouse in garden; nearby golf course; tour bookings; car rentals; courtesy car; secretarial services; laundry service; same-day dry cleaning; nonsmoking rooms; on-call doctor/dentist. *In room:* TV, dataport, coffeemaker available, hair dryer, iron available, safe.

Cotter House *ﾑﾑﾑ* *Finds* Gloria Poupard-Walbridge has taken this exquisite 1847 British Regency–style mansion and turned it into a stunning B&B operation. You'll gasp at the splendor when you walk through the door. Cotter House is a heritage building overflowing with antiques, fine international art, dramatic window treatments, and luxurious marble bathrooms—a lavish haven for the discerning traveler. The two-room suite is my pick, but you can take the whole house if you like, or have exclusive use of the 1892 ballroom for formal gatherings, cocktail parties, or weddings. And Gloria's cooking will knock your socks off. Her fabulous French breakfasts are the *pièce de résistance.*

4 St. Vincent Ave., Remuera. © **09/529-5156.** Fax 09/529-5186. www.cotterhouse.com. 4 units. NZ$650 (US$455) 2-bedroom Bronze suite; NZ$500 (US$350) Blue Provencal; NZ$450 (US$315) Oriental; NZ$500 (US$350) Burgundy suite; NZ$2,278 (US$1,593) entire property per day. Extra person NZ$98 (US$69). Long-stay and special packages available. Rates include 4-course breakfast and airport transfers. Dinner on request. AE, DC, MC, V. Free off-street valet parking. Children under 11 not accepted. **Amenities:** House bar; heated outdoor pool; nearby golf course; exercise pavilion; courtesy car; business services; massage; babysitting; laundry facilities; dry cleaning; nonsmoking rooms; on-call dentist/doctor. *In room:* TV/DVD, dataport, shared minibar and coffeemaker, hair dryer, iron, safe.

MODERATE

The Devereux Boutique Hotel *ﾑ* Antigua, Cairo, Provence, Tuscany, the Pacific—they're all at The Devereux, where creative hands have created a global atmosphere in an 1890s villa. Rooms are a colorful parade of nations, some fiery and

---

Finds **Scented Heaven**

You don't have to be a rose lover to appreciate the intoxicating perfumes that rise from Parnell's beautiful rose gardens at **Dove-Myer Robinson Park.** The 5,000 rose bushes in formal beds make the park the perfect picnic spot. And look out for the gorgeous and historic little **St. Stephen's Chapel,** one of the city's first churches. Access to both is off Gladstone Road and Judges Bay Road.

Moments **Sunset Views**

Take a picnic basket and go up the easy 10-minute bush walk to the top of Mount Hobson in Remuera. Watch the sun go down over wonderful 360-degree views of the harbor and city. Access to Mount Hobson Reserve is signposted on Remuera Road, just before you reach the village.

---

vibrant, others restful and serene. Go around the world without worrying about jet lag; just lie back and enjoy. The three suites have both spa bathrooms and showers. The Devereux is similar in size to Aachen House but feels more contemporary and much less formal.

267 Remuera Rd., Remuera. © 09/524-5044. Fax 09/524-5080. www.devereux.co.nz. 10 units. NZ$186–NZ$285 (US$130–US$199). Rates include breakfast and airport transfers. Long-stay, off-peak, and special deals available. AE, DC, MC, V. Free off-street parking. **Amenities:** Nearby golf course and tennis courts; bike rentals; tour bookings; car rentals; secretarial services; massage; babysitting; laundry service; same-day dry cleaning; on-call doctor/dentist. *In room:* TV, dataport, minibar, coffeemaker upon request, hair dryer, iron and safe upon request.

IN DEVONPORT/BIRKENHEAD
EXPENSIVE

Stafford Villa ✶✶✶ *Finds*   Guests lavish praise upon the Stafford Villa's upmarket B&B experience. Once home to a missionary family, the old two-story home, set in a quaint and tranquil Victorian suburb, was transformed by the industrious Mark and Chris Windram. Chris spent many years marketing small luxury hotels and resorts around the world, so she has a pretty keen idea of what makes a good holiday experience. The two rooms are lush and indulgent—"just a little over the top," says Chris, who believes guests like something different. You can breakfast in the conservatory, take a 5-minute walk to the ferry, and be in downtown Auckland just 10 minutes later.

2 Awanui St., Birkenhead Point. © 09/418-3022. Fax 09/419-8197. www.staffordvilla.co.nz. 2 units. NZ$365–NZ$395 (US$255–US$276). Rates include full breakfast and airport transfers. Long-stay, special deals, and weekend packages available. AE, DC, MC, V. Free off-street parking. **Amenities:** Nearby golf course; car rentals; massage; babysitting; laundry service; same-day dry cleaning; nonsmoking rooms. *In room:* TV/VCR, dataport, coffeemaker, hair dryer.

MODERATE

Devonport has numerous excellent B&Bs in this price range. As well as those below, and if you like to be in the center of the village, you can unwind at the newly renovated **Esplanade Hotel** ✶✶, 1 Victoria Rd. (© **09/445-1291;** fax 09/445-1999; www.esplanadehotel.co.nz), which has 15 character-filled rooms with en-suite bathrooms, plus a suite and a two-bedroom penthouse apartment. Rates range from NZ$275 to NZ$725 (US$193–US$508).

Peace & Plenty Inn ✶✶✶ *Moments*   If you're a romantic, you will love this gorgeous old home, which Judy Machin has transformed into the ultimate sumptuous, floral-themed haven. Every room has an en suite—two with bath and shower, the rest shower only. One has a fridge. The downstairs Albert is the smallest unit but has the best bathroom; the Windsor is the biggest. Three upstairs rooms are sunny, with views and balconies. The whole place oozes character and ambience. If you love the subtropical garden, don't miss the garden suite.

6 Flagstaff Terrace, Devonport. © **09/445-2925**, Fax 09/445-2901, www.peaceandplenty.co.nz. 7 units. NZ$230–NZ$295 (US$161–US$206). Long-stay and off-peak rates available. Rates include breakfast. MC, V. **Amenities:** Nearby golf course and tennis courts; tour bookings; car rentals; massage; babysitting; laundry service; same-day dry cleaning; nonsmoking rooms; on-call doctor/dentist; ferry transport. *In room:* TV, dataport, coffeemaker, hair dryer, iron.

Villa Cambria *Finds*   Clive and Kate Sinclair have marvelous senses of humor—you'll love the warmth of their household. The Sinclairs have lived in Asia, and the house is filled with beautiful collectibles from their travels. An Oriental calm emanates from every room. The Raffles in particular is a serene blue-and-white enclave; the black-and-white Al Cuds and the Loft, both outside the main house, are yummy, too, and offer a little more privacy.

71 Vauxhall Rd., Devonport. © **09/445-7899**. Fax 09/446-0508. www.villacambria.co.nz. 5 units. NZ$180–NZ$250 (US$126–US$175). Rates include breakfast and airport and ferry transfers. Long-stay and off-season deals available. AE, MC, V. Free off-street parking. Children under 12 not accepted. **Amenities:** Nearby golf course; tour bookings; car rentals; nonsmoking rooms. *In room:* TV and fridge in garden loft, coffeemaker, hair dryer, iron.

IN THE WESTERN SUBURBS

Wine lovers might like to consider the luxuries of **Vineyard Cottages** , 1011 Old North Rd. (© **0800/846-800** in NZ, or 09/411-8248; www.vineyard-cottages.co.nz). The exclusive cottages (around NZ$250/US$175) sit amid Matua Valley Wines vineyards in the heart of the Waimauku wine-growing region, just 30 minutes from central Auckland.

Beach lovers should consider **Bethells Beach Cottages,** 267 Bethells Rd. (© **09/810-9581;** www.bethellsbeach.com). They have two sunny holiday cottages set in lush, private gardens—the ultimate Kiwi getaway—for around NZ$250 to NZ$350 (US$175–US$245). If you favor a bush environment, opt for **Rangiwai Lodge** , 29 Rangiwai Rd., Titirangi (© **09/817-8990;** www.accommodation-nz.com), just a 4-minute walk from Titirangi Village. It has a heated indoor pool, and all rooms have a private deck and en-suite bathroom. Rates are from NZ$300 to NZ$350 (US$210–US$245).

IN CLEVEDON/EASTERN SUBURBS

The all-new **Point View Lodge** , 316 Point View Dr., Howick (© **09/537-5678;** www.pointview.co.nz), has three beautiful rooms that go for around NZ$350 to NZ$450 (US$245–US$315). **Birchwood Settlers Cottage** , RD3, Clevedon (© **09/292-8729;** birchwood@xtra.co.nz), is about 30 minutes south of Auckland on a large farm. The cottage, nestled in orchards, costs around NZ$250 (US$175).

NEAR THE AIRPORT

If you have an early-morning flight or you're checking into Auckland at night and want a quick bed, give one of the following a call. **Jet Inn Hotel** , 63 Westney Rd., Mangere (© **0800/538-466** in NZ, or 09/275-4100; www.jetinn.co.nz), gets many recommendations; rooms cost NZ$120 to NZ$245 (US$84–US$171). **Kiwi International Airport Hotel** , 150 McKenzie Rd., Mangere (© **0800/801-919** in NZ, or 09/256-0046; www.kiwihotel.co.nz), is a modern complex with 49 rooms; prices start around NZ$100 (US$70). It has a 24-hour courtesy coach to the airport (an 8-min. ride), plus a restaurant and cocktail bar. **Centra Auckland Airport,** Kirkbridge and Ascot roads, Airport Oaks (© **0800/080-236** in NZ, or 09/275-1059; www.southpacific.ICHotelsgroup.com), has 242 rooms for NZ$145 to NZ$201 (US$101–US$141).

4 Where to Dine

You get no points for finding a brilliant restaurant in Auckland; there are too many of them for that to be considered a feat. The predominant cuisines are ethnic and Pacific Rim, the latter being that variable trend of combining the freshest, high-quality ingredients with whatever cultural element (theoretically Pacific-based) grabs the chef's fancy. As you can imagine, the interpretations are endless.

Although there are restaurants scattered all over the city, you'll find they rub shoulders with each other in the Viaduct Basin area and along Ponsonby and Parnell roads—still the trendiest areas and favorites with big spenders. There is also a good haul along the downtown waterfront, at Mission Bay, and in Devonport and Takapuna on the North Shore. You can take your pick from innumerable Italian/Mediterranean-style eateries with starched white tablecloths and timber floors, and fashionable California/New York–style brasseries and elegant bistros.

If you've singled out a popular favorite, it's a good idea to make reservations, especially on weekends, but in many cases you can simply stroll and choose. Tipping is perfectly in order but is not a custom anywhere in New Zealand.

A word on wine: New Zealand restaurants are generally classified as licensed (to sell beer, wine, and spirits) or BYO (bring your own). Some stipulate wine only or are unlicensed.

IN INNER CITY

EXPENSIVE

Among the top dining choices in the inner city, don't pass up the traditional Japanese experience of **Katsura** ★★★, in the Carlton Hotel (✆ **09/366-5628**), where you can expect to part with large numbers of dollars for mouthwatering morsels in an elegant, authentic atmosphere. **White** ★★★, in the Hilton (✆ **09/978-2000**), is a superb dining experience for all the senses—predictably, the decor is all white. **Otto's** ★★★, in the Ascott Metropolis (✆ **09/300-9595**), offers fine dining with superb service and food that is almost impossible to fault.

Harbourside ★★, first floor, Ferry Building, Quay Street (✆ **09/307/0556**), is a chic place with great views and seriously good seafood. Two others not to be missed are **The Grove** ★★, St. Patrick's Square, 55 Albert St. (✆ **09/368-4129**), a new, groovy favorite with terrific food; and **O'Connell Street Bistro** ★★★, O'Connell and Shortland streets (✆ **09/377-1884**), a tiny but perfect 28-seat restaurant that's big on international style and flavors—definitely a place for special moments. **Soul** ★★, Hobson and Customs Street West (✆ **09/356-7249**), is now an institution in a prime Viaduct Basin location with fabulous people-watching potential. Top chefs, an open-air style,

---

Finds **Quick & Easy**

For fresh takeaway salads, seek out **Salad Works,** 30 Chancery St. (✆ **09/368-7101**), where you can mix and match assorted green leaves with vegetables, fish, meat, and the dressing of your choice. There are ready-made choices if your imagination fails you. **Suju,** 37 Chancery St. (✆ **09/309-3006**), is a terrific little soup-and–fresh juice bar. Nearby, the London chain **Wagamama,** Level 2, Metropolis Building, 1 Courthouse Lane (✆ **09/359-9266**), is a snazzy noodle bar offering fresh and tasty Japanese food served on long communal tables.

TELEPHONE TIPS

To call New Zealand from another country: *Dial the international access code (U.S. or Canada **011**, U.K. **00**, Australia **0011**), followed by the country code **64**, followed by the area code (known as **STD**, or subscriber toll dialing), dropping the zero, then the six- or seven-digit local number.*

To make a direct international call from New Zealand: *Dial **00**, followed by the country code (U.S. or Canada **1**, U.K. **44**, Australia **61**, Ireland **353**), then the area code, and the local number.*

To call within New Zealand: *Dial the STD (including the 0), followed by the local number. If you're calling within a city, dial only the local number.*

Directory assistance within New Zealand: *Dial **010**.*

International operator: *Dial **0170**.*

For further information, see Fast Facts in Chapter 2.

METRIC CONVERSIONS

TEMPERATURE

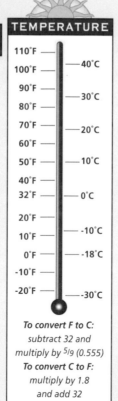

110°F
100°F — 40°C
90°F
80°F — 30°C
70°F — 20°C
60°F
50°F — 10°C
40°F
32°F — 0°C
20°F
10°F — -10°C
0°F — -18°C
-10°F
-20°F — -30°C

To convert F to C:
subtract 32 and
multiply by 5/9 (0.555)
To convert C to F:
multiply by 1.8
and add 32
32°F = 0°C

LIQUID VOLUME

To convert	multiply by
U.S. gallons to liters	3.79
Liters to U.S. gallons	0.26
U.S. gallons to imperial gallons	0.83
Imperial gallons to U.S. gallons	1.20
Imperial gallons to liters	4.55
Liters to imperial gallons	0.22

1 liter = 0.26 U.S. gallon
1 U.S. gallon = 3.8 liters

DISTANCE

To convert	multiply by
inches to centimeters	2.54
centimeters to inches	0.39
feet to meters	0.30
meters to feet	3.28
yards to meters	0.91
meters to yards	1.09
miles to kilometers	1.61
kilometers to miles	0.62

1 ft = 0.30 m   1 mile = 1.6 km
1 m = 3.3 ft   1km = 0.62 mile

WEIGHT

To convert	multiply by
Ounces to grams	28.35
Grams to ounces	0.035
Pounds to kilograms	0.45
Kilograms to pounds	2.20

1 ounce = 28 grams
1 pound = 0.4555 kilogram
1 gram = 0.04 ounce
1 kilogram = 2.2 pounds

ISBN 0-471-74700-9
52199
9 780471 747000

My, what an inefficient
way to fish.

Ring toss, good. Horseshoes, bad.

Faster! Faster! Faster!

We take care of the fiddly bits, from
providing over 43,000 customer reviews
of hotels, to helping you find our best
fares, to giving you 24/7 customer service.
So you can focus on the only thing
that matters. Goofing off.

travelocity®
You'll never roam alone.™

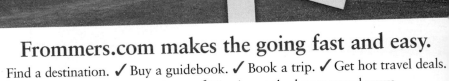

Do the Hokey Pokey

A blend of vanilla ice cream with pieces of toffee, Hokey Pokey ice cream is unique to New Zealand and was first manufactured by the Meadowgold Ice Cream Company of Papatoetoe, Auckland, in the 1940s.

and the best New Zealand fish anywhere make it a winner with international travelers and the business crowd. For something entirely different, head for **Wildfire,** Shed 22, Princes Wharf, Quay Street (© **09/353-7595;** www.wildfirerestaurant.co.nz), to sample Brazilian churrasco barbecue cuisine—lots of meat and a wild South American dance atmosphere as the night wears on.

DINE INTERNATIONAL FUSION   Founder of London's legendary Sugar Club restaurant, top New Zealand chef Peter Gordon is in charge of the menu at this brand-new upmarket eatery. Floating circles of dimmed light, artwork, and an inventive menu make it worth seeking out. Kick off with Japanese-inspired starters or pan-fried scallops, leaving space for crab-crusted hapuka, roast duck breast, or prime beef filet. They have a great New Zealand wine list.

In the SKYCITY Grand Hotel, 90 Federal St. © **09/363-7030.** Reservations required. Main courses NZ$28–NZ$36 (US$20–US$25). AE, DC, MC, V. Daily 6pm–late.

Euro PACIFIC RIM/BISTRO   This place started with a hiss and a roar during the America's Cup challenge and, unlike many, has maintained consistently high standards of food and delivery. It's a favorite with all ages, including lunching businessmen, the who's who, and visitors keen to sample one of the city's best bistros. The day I enjoyed a fine chicken salad here, the sun was beaming down, the staff was friendly, and all seemed well with the world.

Shed 22, Princes Wharf. © **09/309-9866.** Reservations recommended. Main courses NZ$25–NZ$35 (US$18–US$25). AE, DC, MC, V. Daily 11am–late.

The French Café CONTEMPORARY EUROPEAN   I've never heard a bad word about this perpetual award winner. Come here if you savor sensational, finely crafted dishes that you will remember forever. From the foie gras to the roast duckling, you'll be sighing with pleasure. Better yet, you don't have to take out a bank loan to dine in this sophisticated little gem, which sits proudly in one of the seedier parts of town.

210 Symonds St. © **09/302-2770.** Reservations required. Main courses NZ$25–NZ$35 (US$18–US$25). AE, D, MC, V. Mon–Sat 6:30pm–late.

Prime MODERN NEW ZEALAND   It's easy to see why Prime is so popular with the business-lunch crowd. Salmon filet on polenta rösti and the signature rabbit, served by one of the best and friendliest staffs in the city, make it a must-visit. The restaurant has great views toward the Hilton hotel. The nearby espresso bar pours 700 cups a day—grab good coffee here, because it's hard to find in Auckland.

PriceWaterhouseCoopers Tower, 188 Quay St. © **09/357-0188.** Reservations recommended. Main courses NZ$16–NZ$26 (US$11–US$18). AE, D, MC, V. Daily 7am–7pm.

MODERATE

Mexican Café MEXICAN   Now an institution, this restaurant has served reliable, reasonably priced meals in a lively, colorful atmosphere for more than 2 decades. The

A Cheap Feed at the Food Halls

If you're after a dollar-stretching fill up, the city has plenty of food courts, where even NZ$5 to NZ$15 (US$3.50–US$11) will satisfy the hunger pangs. One of the most popular is in **Downtown Shopping Centre,** QEII Square on Quay Street. It's open Monday through Thursday from 7am to 6pm, Friday from 7am to 8pm, and Saturday and Sunday from 7am to 4pm. There is an international food boulevard at **SKYCITY Metro,** 291–297 Queen St., open daily from 9am until late. **Food Alley,** Albert Street, across from the Stamford Plaza hotel, is another good one, with nine different ethnic cuisines represented; it's open daily from 10am to 10pm and is licensed to serve alcohol.

At the **Atrium Food Gallery,** Atrium Shopping Centre, between Victoria and Wellesley streets, you'll find everything from McDonald's to pasta, kabobs, Chinese, sushi, and a bakery. It's open Monday through Thursday from 7am to 6pm, Friday from 7am to 9pm, Saturday from 7am to 6pm, and Sunday from 7:30am to 6pm. **Victoria Park Market,** 210 Victoria St. W., has an international food court that's open from 9am to 6pm daily, as well as several licensed cafes and a McDonald's. The major suburban shopping malls also have reasonably priced food courts offering a variety of food-stuffs. **Ponsonby International Foodcourt,** Ponsonby Road and Pollen Street, gets high marks for its selection and indoor-outdoor dining areas above Ponsonby Snooker. It's open daily 10am until 10pm.

menu is huge, the servings generous, and the enchiladas divine. For the best fun, go on a Tuesday, Wednesday, or Thursday night when the cafe schedules live Latin music. And don't overlook the rare tequila supply.

Upstairs, 67 Victoria St. W. ℭ **09/373-2311.** Reservations recommended. Main courses NZ$15–NZ$25 (US$11–US$18). MC, V. Daily noon–late.

IN PONSONBY/HERNE BAY
EXPENSIVE

Also try the upmarket Italian cafe **Prego** *ÆÆ*, 226 Ponsonby Rd. (ℭ **09/376-3095**).

Chandelier *ÆÆÆ* ITALIAN-INSPIRED   If you're the type who believes eating out should be a complete celebration, something a little indulgent, then head for Chandelier, an over-the-top glamour restaurant and lounge bar. It's right next door to SPQR and draws an equally avant-garde crowd. The Italian-inspired interior and food are consistently good—spoil yourself!

152 Ponsonby Rd. ℭ **09/360-9315.** Reservations recommended. Main courses NZ$25–NZ$35 (US$18–US$25). AE, DC, MC, V. Daily 5pm–late.

SPQR Café & Bar *ÆÆ* INTERNATIONAL   If you want to see trendy Ponsonby at its strutting best and most colorfully diverse, come to SPQR. The menu is just a few strides above average, but it's the atmosphere and the people-watching that make it such a winner. In what was once a tire-retread shop, now stylishly spartan with stainless steel and concrete, the film and media crowd, the gay community, and your average run-of-the-mill Joe Bloggs all lean about looking supercool and hungry. SPQR serves up tasty morsels such as paper-thin Roman pizza with unusual toppings until well after midnight. (See "The Club & Bar Scene" under "Auckland After Dark," later in this chapter.)

150 Ponsonby Rd. ℂ 09/360-1710. Main courses NZ$25–NZ$35 (US$18–US$25). AE, DC, MC, V. Mon–Fri noon–2am; Sat–Sun 10am–2am.

Vinnies Restaurant ★★★ *Moments* MODERN FRENCH/EUROPEAN   Vinnies invariably appears on any top-five list of Auckland restaurants. Its wall full of awards draws attention to the chefs' superior level of culinary artistry and innovation. It's acknowledged as the place to go to if you aspire to (or claim) sophisticated urban tastes. The interior is romantic, the service tops. Owner Prue Barton also has a dedicated wine program in operation with two sommeliers. Hire out the private dining room if you feel like spoiling yourselves.

166 Jervois Rd., Herne Bay. ℂ 09/376-5597. Reservations recommended. Main courses NZ$29–NZ$36 (US$20–US$25). AE, DC, MC, V. Mon–Sat 6:30pm–late.

MODERATE

Bella ★★ ITALIAN BISTRO   Come here for a late-afternoon drink in the sun and stay for tasty, reasonably priced Italian-style fare. The pasta and breads are handmade on the spot.

165 Ponsonby Rd. ℂ 09/360-2656. Main courses NZ$23–NZ$28 (US$16–US$19). AE, DC, MC, V. Daily noon–late.

Benediction ★★ *Finds* CAFE   Trendy but largely undiscovered by the wider population, Benediction is in a stylish adaptation of the old Symonds Street stables and is popular for breakfast and lunch. The counter food is especially good, and there's a slight down-home feel about the place that makes you want to linger. It's very hip with 20- and 30-something locals, especially those from the record and media industry.

30 St. Benedict St., Newton. ℂ 09/309-5001. Main courses NZ$15–NZ$25 (US$11–US$18). AE, MC, V. Daily 7am–5pm.

Charlie White's ★★ CONTEMPORARY NEW ZEALAND   If you're a meat eater or a follower of the South Beach Diet, you'll love this place. From big steaks to organic calves' liver, you'll be in your element. Service can be slow, but the helpings are more than generous.

Angelsea St. and Ponsonby Rd. ℂ 09/360-5153. Main courses NZ$25–NZ$28 (US$18–US$19). AE, DC, MC, V. Daily 7am–late.

Dizengoff ★★ CAFE   When Dizengoff opened several years ago, everyone wanted to be here—or, more precisely, to be seen here. The place is invariably filled with stylish types who like to pick delicately at their healthy bagels and sip strange health drinks without mussing up their lip gloss. All that aside, the food is just as tasty as it

---

Finds **The Healthy Stuff**

The organic lifestyle is catching on fast. The upmarket **Total Wellbeing,** 145 Ponsonby Rd. (ℂ 09/378-2020), provides organic groceries and takeaway food items. **Musical Knives,** 272 Ponsonby Rd. (ℂ 09/376-7354), is Auckland's best vegetarian restaurant. The menu also features organic wines. **The Organic Kitchen,** 266 Ponsonby Rd. (ℂ 09/378-0201), is a cafe that will tempt you back to good health.

Moments **Dining with a Difference**

If you're looking for something different, then **Finale,** 350 Karangahape Rd. (*©* **09/377-4830;** www.350finale.co.nz), is for you. Help yourself to a delicious buffet and sit back for outrageous cabaret entertainment provided by the glamorous drag queen extravaganza.

---

is healthy, and if you can squeeze into this swirling den of style, you'll certainly relish the big brunchy-style breakfasts.

256 Ponsonby Rd. *©* **09/360-0108.** Main courses NZ$16–NZ$25 (US$11–US$18). AE, DC, MC, V. Daily 7am–5pm.

Villa d'Vine *✸✸* FRENCH/ITALIAN COUNTRY   This casual but classy little restaurant focuses on authentic flavors and ambience. Styled after the rustic eating houses of Provence and Tuscany, it employs French-trained chefs who specialize in traditional rotisserie meats, fresh pasta, and lots of fresh herbs. Affordably priced classics in a warm, inviting interior make this a great place to relax with a glass of good wine.

204 Jervois Rd., Herne Bay. *©* **09/376-2001.** Main courses NZ$22–NZ$28 (US$15–US$19). AE, MC, V. Tues–Sat 5pm–late.

INEXPENSIVE

Atomic Café *✸✸* *Kids* CAFE   Everyone seems to love Atomic, especially on weekends. The food is good and the atmosphere terrific. The brick-lined interior snakes out back to a little enclosed courtyard—a lovely place for brunch, and the kids can get loose in the sandpit. There's a blackboard menu with hints of Asia in miso soups and soba noodles, supplementing the offerings of bagels, pancakes, and other breakfast fillers. There's nothing "designery" about Atomic; it's slightly frayed at the edges, in fact, but it has genuine warmth that is very appealing.

121 Ponsonby Rd. *©* **09/376-4954.** NZ$15–NZ$25 (US$11–US$18). No credit cards. Mon–Fri 6am–6pm; Sat–Sun 8am–5pm.

IN MOUNT EDEN/EPSOM

Try **One Tree Grill** *✸✸*, 9 Pah Rd., Greenwoods Corner, Epsom (*©* **09/625-6407**), a smart little restaurant with a cute-as-a-button bar upstairs. It's hugely popular with locals. **GPK,** 234 Dominion Rd., Mount Eden (*©* **09/623-1300**), serves great pizzas and has a good bar atmosphere. Another highly recommended option is **Bowmans** *✸✸*, 597 Mount Eden Rd., Mount Eden (*©* **09/638-9676**), which puts many inner city establishments to shame with its top service and consistently good food. **Molten** *✸✸✸*, 42 Mount Eden Rd., Mount Eden (*©* **09/638-7236**) is another suburban gem producing great meals bound to impress.

Circus, Circus *✸✸* *Finds* CAFE   This little gem is filled with circus memorabilia and show posters, along with food and staff that make it worth visiting. The front section is a bit of a tight fit, but you can always spill out onto the pavement or find a shady spot in the rear courtyard. Select from a big blackboard menu that includes terrific eggs Benedict with salmon, lots of other brunch favorites, excellent-value panini, waffles, pan-fried kidneys, and delectable counter cakes. Circus is a popular village haunt where you'll get a feel for the eclectic Mount Eden community.

447 Mount Eden Rd., Mount Eden Village. *©* **09/623-3833.** NZ$15–NZ$25 (US$11–US$18). AE, DC, MC, V. Daily 7am–4:30pm.

IN PARNELL/MISSION BAY/NEWMARKET

EXPENSIVE

In contrast to Ponsonby's artsiness, Parnell attracts a trendy corporate crowd—the work-hard, play-hard crew. The result is icons such as **Veranda Bar & Grill** 𝒢𝒢, or VBG, 279 Parnell Rd. (☎ **09/309-6289**), where expensive Pacific Rim cuisine and a party atmosphere reign supreme. For the finest dining in town, head for **Antoines** 𝒢𝒢𝒢, 333 Parnell Rd. (☎ **09/379-8756**), which attracts a well-heeled clientele with rich French cuisine and impeccable service; or **The George** 𝒢𝒢𝒢, 144 Parnell Rd. (☎ **09/358-2600**), which turns out impeccable meals in the company of an extensive wine list. All of the above can be pricey, so go with a fat wallet.

Cibo 𝒢𝒢 MODERN NEW ZEALAND   Almost 17 years old, Cibo has proven that a restaurant with all the right ingredients will endure. Elegant, favored by the business crowd, and popular for special occasions, it serves up the likes of duck leg confit with buttered beans, and honey-glazed lamb shank, with an assurance that guarantees return visits. You might need a map or a friendly local to point you in the direction, but it's worth the hunt.

Axis Building, 91 St. Georges Bay Rd., Parnell. ☎ 03/303-9660. Reservations recommended. Main courses NZ$25–NZ$30 (US$18–US$21). AE, MC, V. Mon–Fri noon–late.

Hammerheads Restaurant & Bar 𝒢𝒢 *Kids* SEAFOOD   Just when you thought you were sick of fish, you can trust Hammerheads to serve up completely new flavor surprises. In its 16 years in the Navy League buildings next to Kelly Tarlton's Underwater World, Hammerheads has gathered numerous awards. Dishes such as grilled snapper with potato gnocchi, artichoke hearts, fennel, and citrus sauce; and tempura-battered terakihi with crispy fried potato, fresh lime, and wasabi mayonnaise are part of the reason. Almost anything that swims in the sea is likely to appear on the menu here, presented with an immense amount of style. A kids' menu is available, and the big sail-covered balcony is a great place to watch waterfront action.

19 Tamaki Dr., Okahu Bay. ☎ 09/521-4400. Reservations required for dinner. Main courses NZ$26–NZ$36 (US$18–US$25). AE, DC, MC, V. Daily 11:30am–late.

Mikano 𝒢𝒢 INTERNATIONAL   Mikano is all about fabulous architecture, vibrant color, sensational sea views, good jazz, fine wine, and innovative food. It has won numerous awards for its eclectic, often themed menu—from the temporary Italian menu, grilled quail with grapes and verjuice, and roasted veal with porcini mushrooms and braised radicchio. The wine list is vast, and the sofas in the bar are just the place to sample it.

1 Solent St., Mechanics Bay (off Tamaki Dr.). ☎ 09/309-9514. Reservations recommended. Main courses NZ$25–NZ$36 (US$18–US$25). AE, DC, MC, V. Mon–Fri 11:30am–late; Sat 5:30pm–late; Sun 9:30am–late.

MODERATE

You'll find the best coffee in Parnell at **Dunk** 𝒢𝒢, 297 Parnell Rd. (☎ **09/377-2414**), next door to the post office. It also does a great-value breakfast.

In Newmarket, the **Turkish Café Bar, Grill & Pizza** 𝒢, 76–82 Broadway (☎ **09/520-2794**), has tasty Turkish and Middle Eastern dishes, plus Italian wood-fired pizzas served up in a contemporary interior, *plus* belly dancers on Wednesday, Friday, and Saturday nights. If you love Japanese food, opt for **Rikka** 𝒢, 73 Davis Crescent, Newmarket (☎ **09/522-5277**).

Tips Parnell Parking

For a "secret" spot—go down Parnell Road, and at the sea end of the village, turn right into Garfield Road. Immediately to your right, on the corner, is a small parking area that allows 120 minutes of free parking.

Iguacu Restaurant & Bar ⚘ PACIFIC RIM   Iguacu deserves full marks for its fabulous interior. Giant silver-framed mirrors lend a grandiose air to an environment made light and airy by a glazed ceiling; earthy colors and big windows to the street keep you in touch with reality. Food here is generally very good. It's a favorite spot for the lunching business crowd. See also "The Club & Bar Scene" under "Auckland After Dark," later in this chapter.

269 Parnell Rd. ℂ 09/358-4804. Reservations recommended. Main courses NZ$25–NZ$36 (US$18–US$25). AE, DC, MC, V. Mon–Fri 11am–late; Sat–Sun 10am–late.

Portofino ⚘⚘ *Finds* NORTHERN ITALIAN   When you're exhausted and just want to eat quickly and well, Portofino will oblige with delicious pastas, pizzas, and chicken and veal dishes. It's small, dark, cozy, and terribly popular, so get in early if you want a guaranteed spot. Watch the chefs cooking, enjoy the friendly staff, and leave without spending a fortune. Portofino has several other city locations—the best is on Viaduct Basin—but the Parnell eatery still scores more for atmosphere.

156 Parnell Rd. ℂ 09/373-3740. Main courses NZ$20–NZ$25 (US$14–US$18). AE, MC, V. Daily 11am–late.

IN REMUERA

New on the scene in Remuera is **The Maple Room** ⚘⚘⚘, 93–95 Upland Rd., Benson Road Village, Remuera (ℂ **09/522-1672**), which is scoring big points for its tapas-style dishes and main courses like duck risotto and mint-and-chile lamb rump. It's open Monday through Friday from 11:30am until late, weekends from 9am to 3pm. **Jada,** 305 Remuera Rd. (ℂ **09/522-2130**), is a popular little Italian-style option in the main Remuera village. **Sierra Café** ⚘⚘, Clonbern and Remuera roads (ℂ **09/523-1527**), is definitely the best cafe in the area, with amazingly good counter food. Pick up freshly baked pies, quiches, frittatas, and extravagant cakes for an over-the-top picnic. Tucked behind the Remuera shops, the **Thai Village** ⚘⚘, 415 Remuera Rd. (ℂ **09/523-3005**), has a nice ambience and can always be trusted to deliver an excellent dining experience. **Café Jazz** ⚘, 563 Remuera Rd., Upland Village (ℂ **09/524-0356**), is another nice, moderately priced spot for lunch or a light evening meal. It offers standard New Zealand cafe fare, such as sandwiches, salads, and pizza.

IN DEVONPORT/BIRKENHEAD

Another Devonport standout is **Monsoon** ⚘⚘, 71 Victoria Rd. (ℂ **09/445-4263**), a snappy little Thai/Malaysian place. Because it's so popular, either go early or reserve. The catchily named **Cod Piece** ⚘⚘, 26 Victoria Rd. (ℂ **09/446-0877**), serves up good old fish and chips and burgers. Birkenhead Point has a surprising array of eating choices. **Hayashi** ⚘⚘⚘, 261 Hinemoa St., Birkenhead (ℂ **09/418-3011**), is a standout Japanese restaurant that successfully mixes the traditional with contemporary flair. **Mezze,** 98 Hinemoa St., Birkenhead (ℂ **09/480-1598**), is a great little tapas bar and brasserie.

Da Ciccio ★★ *Finds* ITALIAN/PIZZERIA   Da Ciccio is an intimate little spot run by Italians, a place where the divine smell of garlic permeates every nook and cranny, a place where you can be sure of a good meal and a good time. Staff members here were as friendly as any I encountered anywhere in Auckland. The menu focuses on pizzas and traditional pasta dishes such as penne *arrabbiata* and ever-delicious spaghetti marinara, overflowing with tomato, tuna, shrimp, anchovies, and mussels. It's BYO, so take your own wine; it also has a good takeaway menu.

99 Victoria Rd. ☎ **09/445-8133**. Reservations required. Main courses NZ$20–NZ$26 (US$14–US$18); pizzas around NZ$20 (US$14). AE, DC, MC, V. Mon–Fri 6pm–late; Sat–Sun noon–late.

5 Exploring Auckland

If you're short on time, the best thing to do is leap aboard the **Explorer Bus** ★★★ (see "Getting Around," earlier in this chapter) and see as much as you can.

THE TOP FOUR ATTRACTIONS

Auckland Museum ★★★ *Kids*   Auckland's imposing museum building stands in the Auckland Domain on the rim of an ancient volcano surrounded by parks and gardens. It has the largest collection of Maori and Polynesian artifacts in the world, and for this reason alone is worth a visit.

Major refurbishment of the museum is complete, and the extensive **Maori Treasures Gallery** is a must-see. Key attractions in this area are the impressive 25m (82-ft.) war canoe chiseled from one enormous totara trunk and covered with intricate carvings. That same artistry is reflected in the 26m (85-ft.) meetinghouse, with its carved and painted walls and rafters. Also on display are magnificent greenstone weapons, tools, and feather cloaks. Three times a day—at 11am, noon, and 1:30pm—concerts by the Manaia Maori Performance Group bring the culture to life.

Pacific Pathways is a moody area housing a world-renowned collection of Pacific artifacts; *New Zealand at War: Scars on the Heart* tells an emotional story of New Zealand in conflict, from the Land Wars of the 1840s to its present-day peacekeeping operations. The first-floor **Natural History Galleries** showcase everything from dinosaur skeletons to live seaside rock pools. It's a fascinating area well supported by the superb **Discovery Centre.** My favorite gallery is the thought-provoking **Wild Child,** which focuses on the experiences that shaped a colonial childhood.

This first-rate museum experience gives a marvelous introduction to New Zealand history and culture. To get the most from it, allow 2 to 3 hours minimum. An on-site cafe is open during museum hours.

Auckland Domain. ☎ **09/309-0443**, or 09/306-7067 for recorded Infoline. www.aucklandmuseum.com. Admission to permanent collection by donation (NZ$5/US$3.50 suggested); charges for special exhibitions may apply. Maori cultural performance NZ$15 (US$11) adults; NZ$11 (US$7.90) seniors, students, and YHA card holders; NZ$7.50 (US$5.20) children. Daily 10am–5pm. Closed Dec 25 and Apr 25 (ANZAC morning). Wheelchair access throughout. Explorer Bus every 30 min.; Link bus from and to downtown every 10 min.

Sky Tower ★★★ *Kids*   In the first 18 months after it opened in August 1997, Sky Tower drew over a million visitors, making it New Zealand's most popular paid attraction. At 328m (1,076 ft.), it is the tallest building in the Southern Hemisphere, affording unforgettable views over the sprawling mass of Auckland. It has three observation decks, including an outdoor area, a glass lift and glass floor panels, multilingual

---

Fun Fact **Afraid of Heights?**

Sky Tower has been designed to provide a high level of performance in the event of earthquakes, severe winds, storms, or fire. It is built to withstand winds gusting to 200kmph (124 mph); it has protected fire refuges; and analysis shows it would stay standing in an earthquake of 8.0 magnitude on the Richter scale occurring within 20km (12 miles) of the tower. So put aside your fears (if I can, anyone can), and have a breathtaking experience.

---

audio guides, and a revolving restaurant. Access to the observation decks is on three glass-fronted elevators, which can whiz up the building in a speedy 40 seconds.

The Lower Observation level is accessible by stairs and has a coffee shop. The Main Observation level features the latest technology, with live weather feeds and touch computer screens giving geographical information. The Outdoor Observation area holds high-powered binoculars and is open to the elements. The Sky Deck is the highest public viewing area, with 360-degree views through seamless glass.

SKYCITY, Victoria and Federal sts. ⓒ 0800/759-2489 in NZ, or 09/363-6000. Fax 09/363-6010. www.skycity auckland.co.nz. Admission to observation decks NZ$18 (US$13) adults, NZ$8 (US$5.60) children 5–14, NZ$44 (US$31) families. Admission to Sky Deck NZ$3 (US$2.10) extra. To ensure entry, make a reservation. AE, DC, MC, V. Daily 8:30am–late. Underground parking for small fee.

Kelly Tarlton's Antarctic Encounter & Underwater World *Kids*   In your wildest dreams, you might have imagined a live underground penguin colony; at Kelly Tarlton's **Penguin Encounter,** it's an amazing reality. For full insight into this unique self-sustaining population of king and gentoo penguins, make sure you pick up the free brochure, which details the establishment of a full simulated Antarctic environment, complete with saltwater pools, in the heart of subtropical Auckland. You'll be able to board heated, soundproof Snow Cats and enter the frozen landscape.

Just as awe-inspiring is **Underwater World,** the dream and final project of the late Kelly Tarlton, a famous New Zealand diver. At Underworld World, visitors travel on a moving walkway through an acrylic tunnel under the ocean. Surrounded by giant stingrays, eels, sharks, and over 1,500 fish, you're treated to a diver's view without having to wear the wet suit. A new exhibit, **Stingray Bay,** shows off the remarkable creatures at close quarters. This area also includes the adjacent NIWA Interactive Room for kids, a refreshment kiosk, and large educational touch screens. This is a special attraction for all ages; allow 45 minutes to 2 hours.

23 Tamaki Dr., Orakei. ⓒ 0800/805-050 in NZ, or 09/528-0603. Fax 09/528-5175. www.kellytarltons.co.nz. Admission NZ$28 (US$19) adults, NZ$22 (US$15) students over 15 with ID, NZ$12 (US$8.40) children 5–14, free for children under 5. Special rates for families and seniors available. AE, DC, MC, V. Nov–Feb daily 9am–8pm; March–Oct daily 9am–6pm. Wheelchair access provided. Take Mission Bay city bus, Explorer Bus, or Fullers Harbour Explorer. Free Kelly Tarlton's shuttle calls at several inner city hotels four times daily 9:30am–5:30pm. Free parking.

Auckland Art Gallery   Recognized as the leading New Zealand art gallery, Auckland Art Gallery holds more than 10,000 New Zealand and European works. The Main Gallery emphasizes historical collections; guided tours begin at 2pm daily. The New Gallery, opened across the street in 1995, houses a magnificent contemporary collection of new ideas, new works, and new artists. This is where you'll find the McCahon Room, which displays works by the late Colin McCahon, New Zealand's most respected modernist artist. The gallery has an ongoing program of family days, tours, lectures, and holiday programs.

Main Gallery: Wellesley and Kitchener sts. ℂ **09/307-7700,** or 09/309-0831 for recorded information. Fax 09/302-1096. www.aucklandartgallery.govt.nz. Free admission; fees for some touring shows. New Gallery: Wellesley and Lorne sts. ℂ **09/307-4540.** Free admission to downstairs galleries; NZ$7–NZ$10 (US$4.90–US$7) for temporary and touring exhibitions. Both galleries: Daily 10am–5pm. Closed Good Friday and Dec 25.

THE VIADUCT BASIN

For the first time in the 152-year history of the America's Cup, a village was created to support syndicates, corporations, super-yachts, and the public together in one venue. This is Auckland's Viaduct Basin, a glistening creation that includes new apartment blocks, hotels, restaurants, cafes, bars, shops, markets, and every facility an earnest yachtie could ever want.

Between October 1999 and March 2000, and again from October 2002 to March 2003, the village was the place to soak up the excitement of the America's Cup challenge. Millions of visitors crammed in over the two periods, along with more than 2,000 competitors and team personnel, plus 200 international media representatives during each challenge.

In addition to the America's Cup action, the village played host to up to 80 **super-yachts** on each occasion, the largest gatherings in the Southern Hemisphere, turning Auckland into a Pacific Monte Carlo. Superyachts are luxury motor and sailing vessels in excess of 30m (98 ft.) long, ranging in value from NZ$4 million to over NZ$40 million (US$2.8 million–US$28 million). Viaduct Harbour can accommodate 88 superyachts of up to 50m (164 ft.).

Visitors can experience grand-prix sailing on an authentic America's Cup yacht, *NZL 40,* built for the 1995 San Diego Challenge. You can be as involved as you want in the crewing action; it's suitable for all ages and levels of ability. For information on the daily sailings from Viaduct Harbour, call **SailNZ** (ℂ **0800/724-569** in NZ, or 09/359-5987; www.sailnz.co.nz). The price per person is NZ$125 (US$87) for 2 hours of sailing, NZ$195 (US$136) for a 3-hour match race.

The Viaduct Basin development has changed the face of Auckland forever, providing a fistful of fabulous restaurants, clubs, and bars that have endured—despite the fact that Team New Zealand relinquished the America's Cup in the 2002–03 challenge. It is a marvelous place to explore, and given that some of Auckland's best eateries are here, you'd be silly to miss it.

Viaduct Harbour has also been a stopover point in the epic Volvo Ocean Race (formerly the Whitbread Round-the-World Race).

Moments Sky Jump

When we talk about special moments, this may not be what you had in mind, but one thing's for sure: You won't forget this experience in a hurry. **Sky Jump** is one of New Zealand's wackiest adrenaline rushes—perhaps the ultimate! For details on this 192m (630-ft.) controlled free-fall from the Southern Hemisphere's tallest tower, call ℂ **0800/759-586** in NZ, or 09/368-1835, or check www.skyjump. co.nz. It costs NZ$195 (US$136) and operates daily from 10am to 6pm, weather permitting (closed Jan 1 and Dec 25).

Value **Auckland Super Pass**

Get four of Auckland's leading attractions for one unbelievable price—a discount of over 25%. **Sky Tower, Kelly Tarlton's, Fullers Auckland,** and **Rainbow's End** have combined for this great offer, which can be used over a 2-week period and includes a pass to revisit whichever attraction you liked the best. Purchase the pass from any one of the included attractions or from the Auckland Visitor Information Centre. It costs around NZ$69 (US$48) for adults and NZ$39 (US$27) for children.

WALKING OVER WATER

Bring on the nerves of steel for one of Auckland's newest attractions—**Harbour Bridge Experience** (℃ 09/361-2000; www.ajhackett.com). Based on a concept similar to the successful Sydney activity, walkers are guided underneath and over the top of Auckland Harbour Bridge. The 1½-hour adventure begins with a full briefing by a professional guide at the base complex. Guests are then fitted with overgarments, radio headsets, and safety harnesses. It's achievable for people of almost all ages and all fitness levels, but you must be over 7 and preferably not have a fear of heights. The walk costs NZ$65 (US$46) for adults and children. Discounts for seniors are available. A bungy/bridge climb combo is NZ$140 (US$98), NZ$200 (US$140) families; see "Outdoor Activities & Spectator Sports," later in this chapter. You can take a bus or a short walk from city hotels; pickup service is available on request. There's limited parking at the site.

OTHER MUSEUMS, MONKEYS & MORE

Museum of Transport Technology and Social History *(Kids)*   This is the largest museum of transport and technology in the country, covering 16 hectares (40 acres) in Western Springs, 4.8km (3 miles) from the city center. You'll find trams, trains, steam engines, aircraft, and more. The museum houses major collections of road transport, historical buildings, and medical and dental equipment displays. You can take a tram ride (every 20 min.) from the Great North Road entrance past the zoo to the **Sir Keith Park Memorial** (there's a small charge). Displays here include interesting military exhibits, rail memorabilia, and one of the most impressive collections of historical aircraft in Australasia, including the only Solent Mark IV flying boat in the world. There are some great hands-on exhibits to keep you amused. Allow 2 hours.

805 Great North Rd., Western Springs. ℃ 09/846-0199. Fax 09/846-4242. www.motat.org.nz. Admission NZ$18 (US$13) adults, NZ$12 (US$8.40) children 5–16 and seniors, NZ$28 (US$19) families. Daily 10am–5pm. Closed Dec 25. Explorer Bus.

New Zealand National Maritime Museum   The National Maritime Museum is perfectly placed—right in the heart of the America's Cup action. Inside are intricate working displays and fascinating exhibitions documenting 1,000 years of New Zealand maritime history. Watch traditional craftsmen restoring historical vessels, wood turning, and working on sails. Of course there's an exhibit on America's Cup history. Plus, you get the chance to hit the high seas yourself: The historic scow *Ted Ashby* gives 45- to 60-minute rides Tuesday, Thursday, Saturday, and Sunday at noon and 2pm. It's definitely the cheapest cruise you'll find. The 14 galleries and interactive displays in this acclaimed museum will keep you busy for at least 2 hours.

Hobson Wharf, Viaduct Basin. ℂ 0800/725-897 in NZ, or 09/373-0800. Fax 09/377-6000. www.nzmaritime.org. Admission NZ$12 (US$8.40) adults, NZ$6 (US$4.20) children, free for children under 5, NZ$28 (US$19) families. Museum Combo (museum entry plus Ted Ashy harbor cruise) NZ$19 (US$13) adults, NZ$12 (US$8.40) children, NZ$48 (US$34) families. AE, DC, MC, V. Summer daily 9am–6pm; winter daily 9am–5pm. Closed Dec 25.

Auckland Zoo

Within 5 minutes of city high-rises, you can watch and hear Suma-tran tigers snarl, lions roar, and monkeys chatter. Over 1,000 birds and animals from every continent make their home in this outstanding parkland, recognized as one of Australasia's leading zoos. It is home to New Zealand's largest collection of native and exotic species. You can meet kiwi, tuatara, and other locals at the Daily Native Fauna Encounter. Or you can visit the beach and see shore birds and little blue penguins. You can also watch sea lions through a spectacular underwater viewing window. At the McDonald's South American Rainforest, troops of spider monkeys, bonnet macaques, squirrel monkeys, and siamangs swing from branch to branch. Check out Pridelands for giraffes, zebras, lions, and rhinos. And visit the zoo's two most famous residents, Kashin and Burma, in their state-of-the-art elephant house. Ask about the special Backstage Pass (bookings required), or treat the kids to a Safari Night sleepover and barbecue.

Motions Rd., Western Springs. ℂ 09/360-3800, or 09/360-3819 for recorded information. Fax 09/368-3818. www. aucklandzoo.co.nz. Admission NZ$16 (US$11) adults, NZ$12 (US$8.40) students and seniors, NZ$8 (US$5.60) children 4–15. Family passes available. AE, DC, V. Daily 9:30am–5:30pm (last admission 4:15pm). Closed Dec 25. Explorer Bus or Pt. Chevalier 045, which departs from Downtown Centre, Inner City. Wheelchairs available. Free parking.

Butterfly Creek

Just minutes from Auckland International Airport and built over a large wetland, Butterfly Creek shows off more than 800 free-flying tropical butter-flies. The big butterfly house is a delight. Complete with waterfalls, ponds, lush foliage, turtles, fish and exotic birds, it allows you to get up close to stunningly color-ful butterflies. If you're lucky, you'll see the world's largest moth, which has a wingspan of up to 280 millimeters (11 in.).

Tom Pearce Dr. ℂ 09/275-8880. Fax 09/275-1110. www.butterflycreek.co.nz. Butterfly House NZ$11 (US$7.70) adults, NZ$6 (US$4.20) children 3–15, NZ$25–NZ$40 (US$18–US$28) families; Red Admiral Express NZ$3 (US$2.10) per person; Buttermilk Farm NZ$5 (US$3.50) adults, NZ$4 (US$2.80) children. Daily 9am–5pm; Papillon Bar & Café 7:30am–late.

Snowplanet

If you want to polish up your ski or snowboard skills before heading south, take a trip over the Harbour Bridge and let loose in one of the largest indoor snow resorts in the world and the first snowdrome in Australasia. You can guarantee snow here 365 days of the year, and young and old can have a ball. It features three lifts, a terrain park, and a separate learners' area.

91 Small Rd., Silverdale. ℂ 09/427-0044. www.snowplanet.co.nz. Admission for 1 hr. NZ$24 (US$17) adults, NZ$19 (US$13) children under 13; day pass NZ$59 (US$41) adults, NZ$49 (US$34) children; rental NZ$14 (US$9.80) adults, NZ$9 (US$6.30) children. Daily 9am–midnight.

BeesOnline Honey Centre

It would be silly to call this a honey of an excursion, but I'm going to anyway. You'll love this beautifully designed attraction, which reveals the inner workings of a beehive. Set in picturesque countryside beside two small lakes, the modern, ecofriendly center showcases production, honey tastings, and bee-related products and gifts. After a visit, you can dine at the award-winning cafe.

791 St. Hwy. 16, RD3, Waimauku, Auckland. ℂ 09/411-7953. Fax 09/411-5216. www.beesonline.co.nz. Free admis-sion. Mon–Fri 9am–4pm; Sat–Sun 9am–5pm.

Tips **The Gallery Guide**

The bimonthly booklet, *The Auckland Gallery Guide,* which includes information about leading galleries and their exhibitions. is available free from information centers and art galleries. Its user-friendly maps are a great help. For galleries and exhibitions, call ℭ **09/378-4070** or fax 09/378-4063.

HISTORIC HOUSES

Alberton   This is perhaps the finest of all Auckland's historic homes that are open to the public. The once-simple farmhouse, built in 1863, grew into the fairy-tale mansion that stands today. Owned by the New Zealand Historic Places Trust, it provides an intimate glimpse into Victorian life.

100 Mount Albert Rd., Mount Albert. ℭ **09/846-7367.** Fax 09/846-1919. www.historic.org.nz. Admission NZ$7.50 (US$5.20) adults, NZ$3.50 (US$2.40) unaccompanied children, free for accompanied children and members of overseas heritage organizations. NZ$15 (US$11) for 3 Auckland Historic Places Trust Properties, including Ewelme and Highwic (see below). Wed–Sun 10:30am–noon and 1–4:30pm. Closed Good Friday and Dec 25.

Ewelme Cottage   This house was built for the Rev. Vicesimus Lush from 1863 to 1864 and named for Ewelme Village in England. The roomy kauri cottage is authentically preserved, right down to its 19th-century wallpaper. It contains an important collection of more than 800 books.

14 Ayr St., Parnell. ℭ/fax **09/379-0202.** www.historic.org.nz. Admission NZ$7.50 (US$5.20) adults, free for accompanied children. Fri–Sun 10:30am–noon and 1–4:30pm. Closed Good Friday and Dec 25. Explorer Bus to Parnell Village.

Highwic   Highwic is one of New Zealand's finest Gothic Revival houses. Built in 1862, it gained additions modeled from an American pattern book in 1873. Its distinctive architecture and gardens offer insight into the lives of the wealthy Victorian family who retained possession of it until 1978.

40 Gillies Ave., Epsom. ℭ **09/524-5729.** Fax 09/524-5575. www.historic.org.nz. Admission NZ$7.50 (US$5.20) adults, free for accompanied children. Wed–Sun 10:30am–noon and 1–4:30pm. Closed Good Friday and Dec 25.

ESPECIALLY FOR KIDS

Most of Auckland's major attractions—Kelly Tarlton's, the Discovery Centre at Auckland Museum, the Auckland Zoo, Sky Tower, and the Museum of Transport Technology and Social History (all described above)—will give the kids hours of fun. **Artstation,** 1 Ponsonby Rd., Newton (ℭ **09/376-3221;** www.aucklandcity.govt.nz/artstation), is a community arts center and gallery offering classes for all ages.

Rainbow's End Theme Park ℛℛℛ *Kids* *Value*   This is New Zealand's premier adventure playground, with 9 hectares (22 acres) devoted to crazy rides and attractions for children. For those under 10, there's a Dream Castle with its own miniature roller coaster, carousel, and Ferris wheel. Older kids will scream their lungs out on New Zealand's only double-loop roller coaster, and there's more fun to be had on the log flume, on the pirate ship, in the Enchanted Forest, and in an abandoned mine. Add bumper boats, cars, and virtual theater, and the whole family will be glad you came.

Great South and Wiri Station roads, Manukau City. ℭ **0800/438-672** in NZ, or 09/262-2030. Fax 09/262-1958. www.rainbowsend.co.nz. All-day Super Pass (includes unlimited rides) from around NZ$39 (US$27) adults, NZ$29

(US$20) children 4–13, free for children under 4. Mini Pass (includes any 3 rides) around NZ$25 (US$18) per person, NZ$8 (US$5.60) for any additional rides. Family passes available. At, DC, MC, V. Feb–Dec daily 10am–5pm; Jan daily 10am–10pm. Closed Dec 25. Free parking. Take the Manukau motorway exit 15 min. south of Auckland and drive 400m (1,312 ft.) to the end of the Rainbow.

Fun Factory &&& *Kids*   If you feel like a 25-minute drive out of the city, head across the Harbour Bridge to Silverdale, where you'll find this great spot for kids up to the age of 12. It provides a big range of holiday programs and daily activities. Adults can either stay with the kids or leave them supervised and go for a wander on a nearby beach. Parties are a specialty.

5 Agency Lane, Silverdale. © 09/427-8390. Fax 09/427-8390. funfactory@xtra.co.nz. Admission weekdays NZ$4.50 (US$3.15) 12–23 months, NZ$6 (US$4.20) 2–12 years; weekends and holidays NZ$7 (US$4.90) for children of all ages; adults with children under 12 months free. Drop & Shop (in which parents can drop off kids while they go shopping) NZ$10 (US$7) 1 hr., NZ$15 (US$11) 2 hr., NZ$20 (US$14) 3 hr.

PARKS & GARDENS

The Auckland area has 22 regional parks, covering 37,038 hectares (91,484 acres) and more than 500km (310 miles) of walking tracks. The **Auckland Domain** &&&, the city's oldest park, is an imposing crown of green just minutes from the city center. Within it, the **Wintergarden,** the steamy **Tropical House,** and **Fernz Fernery** are botanical showcases for indigenous and exotic plant specimens. Admission is free; the Wintergarden is open daily from 10am to 4pm. There are also extensive formal gardens, sweeping lawns, statuary, duck ponds, sports grounds, and dozens of picnic spots. Summer Sundays bring free jazz and rock concerts in the band rotunda, chamber music in the Wintergarden, and megaconcerts on the sports fields. Call © **09/ 379-2020** or fax 09/571-3757 for details. There are several well-signposted entrances to the Auckland Domain. Two of the busiest are on Stanley Street and Parnell Road. There are also entrances on Grafton Road and Park Road.

   Cornwall Park && is a true urban oasis; with **One Tree Hill Domain,** it forms the largest park in Auckland. The two parks fan out from the hill and are grazed by sheep and cattle. Stone walls, beautiful avenues of oak trees, and dozens of pretty walkways

---

Tips Photo Ops

Of course you can't beat the 360-degree view from **Sky Tower** (p. 125), and once you've seen that, all others seem to pale by comparison—with the exception perhaps of shots taken on your **Auckland Bridge Climb.** An old favorite is **One Tree Hill,** accessible through the very pretty **Cornwall Park.** The obelisk is visible from everywhere in the city. Like Mount Eden, it was once a Maori *pa* (fort) dating from the 14th century. The one tree that dominated its profile was, sadly, damaged by a Maori activist in 1996. It has been replaced by a grove of small trees that have yet to reach a significant height. **Mount Eden** is an extinct volcano and Auckland's highest natural point. It boasts terrific views of the city, the harbor, and Hauraki Gulf. **North Head Maritime Park** in Devonport offers a different perspective—looking back at the city from North Shore. You'll get great photos of the cityscape from here.

Moments **Day Spa Delights**

Day spas are sprouting all over Auckland. The most luxurious is **Spa de Servilles** ✾✾✾, Level 1, Shed 20, Princes Wharf (© **09/309-9086**; www.servilles. co.nz), which will lull you into luxury and sloth at the touch of a finger. It's the nearest you'll get (in New Zealand) to sophisticated European spas. Half- and full-day treatments range from NZ$260 to NZ$895 (US$182–US$626). And boys—don't forget, you can enjoy these indulgences, too! Also worth checking out is **Spa at the Hyatt** ✾✾✾, Hyatt Regency hotel (© **09/355-1234**), a stunning new facility that has six exquisite treatment rooms, a 25m (82-ft.) lap pool, saunas, Jacuzzi, steam room, juice bar, and fully equipped gym. Also new is **East West Day Spa** ✾✾✾, SKYCITY Grand Hotel, 123 Albert St. (© **09/303-4777**; www.east spa.com), which focuses on Eastern-style holistic skincare, massage, and beauty treatments. **Bliss** ✾✾, Crown Plaza Hotel, 128 Albert St. (© **09/368-4698**; www. blissreflexology.com), offers traditional Chinese reflexology in a stylish, relaxing inner city haven.

wind their way through this haven. Access is off Manukau Road at Royal Oak and Greenland West and Campbell roads. **Cornwall Park Visitor Centre** (© **09/630-8485;** www.cornwallpark.co.nz) has information on walks in the park.

The **Parnell Rose Garden** and **Dove-Myer Robinson Park** (named after a popular former city mayor) are off Gladstone and Judges Bay roads in Parnell. One of the city's first churches, little St. Stephen's Chapel, is also here.

The **Auckland Botanic Gardens** ✾, 102 Hill Rd., Manuwera (© **09/267-1457;** www.aucklandbotanicgardens.co.nz), cover 64 hectares (158 acres). It's home to the famous **Ellerslie Flower Show** (see "Special Events," earlier in this chapter), and more than 10,000 plants flourish here. The gardens are open daily from 7am to 8pm in summer and 7am to 6pm in winter; the visitor center is open Monday through Friday from 8am to 4pm, Saturday and Sunday from 10am to 4pm; the cafe is open daily from 8:30am to 4:30pm. Guides for organized groups are available Monday through Friday. Call © **09/266-3698,** e-mail botanicgardens@arc.govt.nz, or ask at the visitor center. To get here from the city, travel south and take the Manuwera motorway exit, turn left onto Hill Road, and drive to the entrance.

Also worth a look are **Eden Gardens,** 24 Omana Ave., Mount Eden (© **09/638-8395;** www.edengarden.co.nz). They're open daily 9am to 4:30pm; the on-site cafe is open from 10am to 4pm. Admission is NZ$5 (US$3.50) adults, NZ$3.50 (US$2.40) seniors, free for children. Once a quarry, it is now a showplace for an amazing collection of rhododendron, vireya, hibiscus, bromeliads, palms, and many other subtropical species.

WINE OUT WEST

Greater Auckland is home to more than 80 vineyards. Henderson Valley is the country's oldest grape-growing area, dating to the arrival of Croatian and other Northern Hemisphere immigrants in the early 1900s. Today, the western suburbs and areas north to Kumeu are a major grape-growing region. Cabernet sauvignon is the most commonly planted grape; merlot and pinot noir are also important. Chardonnay and sauvignon blanc are the main white varieties. Most West Auckland wineries also draw fruit from other regions, mostly Gisborne, Marlborough, and Hawkes Bay. The Henderson and Kumeu areas are the most accessible for a day's outing. They're about 30 minutes from central city. Waiheke Island is about 30 to 40 minutes away by ferry; it's by far the prettiest region and worth the time.

You'll find a good cluster of wineries along Lincoln Road and Henderson Valley Road, and nestled in the surrounding hills. The small townships of Kumeu, Huapai, and Waimauku also have a good selection. For information on wine tours, see "Organized Tours & Cruises," below. For further details on the area, pick up the free brochure *Winemakers of West Auckland* from the visitor center. Following are the notables.

Babich Wines ☘, 10 Babich Rd., Henderson (© **09/833-7859**; www.babich wines.co.nz), is only 20 minutes from central city and is open for tastings Monday through Friday from 9am to 5pm, Saturday from 9am to 6pm, and Sunday from 11am to 5pm. One of the most picturesque wineries, it has a pleasant picnic area near its shop. It often has vintages going back to 1990.

Soljans Estate ☘, 366 St. Hwy. 16, Kumeu (© **09/412-5858**; www.soljans.co.nz), produces internationally competitive wines. It has cellar sales and tastings and a cafe and winery complex; daily winery tours (11:30am–2:30pm) followed by a tasting cost around NZ$12 (US$8.40) per person. The winery is open daily 9am to 5:30pm; the cafe, Monday through Friday 10am to 4pm, weekends 9am to 4pm.

Nobilo Vintners, 45 Station Rd., Huapai (© **09/412-6666**; www.nobilo.co.nz), is the country's fourth-largest winemaker. Tours cost around NZ$10 (US$7) per person and begin at set times Saturday through Monday. The winery is open Monday through Friday from 9am to 5pm, weekends from 10am to 5pm.

Matua Valley Wines ☘, Waikoukou Road, Waimauku (© **09/411-8301**; www. matua.co.nz), produced the first New Zealand sauvignon blanc over 25 years ago. The winery is open Monday through Saturday, 10am to 5pm, and Sunday from 11am to 4:30pm. The Hunting Lodge, an excellent fine-dining restaurant on-site, is run separately. There is also a lovely picnic area.

For information on Waiheke Island wineries, see "A Side Trip to Waiheke Island," later in this chapter.

If you're short on time, call at **NZ Winemakers Centre** ☘☘☘, Shop 7, National Bank Centre, Victoria and Elliot streets (© **09/379-5858**; www.nzwinemakerscentre. co.nz), where you'll find an extensive range of varietals from most New Zealand regions. It offers tax-free wine sales, wine tastings, worldwide home delivery, and wine-tour information. It's open daily 9:30am to 7:30pm (closed Good Friday, Easter, and Dec 25).

DOING DEVONPORT

TAKING THE FERRY   Catching the **Fullers Ferry** ☘☘☘ to Devonport is one of the nicest day's outings you can have in Auckland. Make your way to the Ferry Building on Quay Street (© **09/367-9111**) and take to the water. You'll get great views of the city, Viaduct Basin, and the America's Cup Village as you head out aboard the catamaran *Kea*. The ferry operates daily every half-hour from 7:15am to 8pm and every hour from 8pm to 11pm. The round-trip fare is around NZ$9 (US$6.30) adults, NZ$5 (US$3.50) children. If you're planning to base yourself in Devonport, buy a 10-trip or weekly ferry pass.

DEVONPORT VILLAGE ATTRACTIONS   The village of Devonport is all about atmosphere, charm, historic buildings, the arts, and cafes. It has a summer holiday feel, even in the middle of winter, and especially on weekends. Stop at the **Devonport Visitor Information Centre,** 3 Victoria Rd. (© **09/486-8670;** www.tourismnorth shore.org.nz), where you can find out about things to see and do. It's open Monday through Friday from 8am to 5pm, weekends and public holidays from 8:30am to 5pm.

The two historic backbones of the village are Victoria and Church streets, now the main business area. Many of the buildings here date to the first European settlement; a brochure for *The Old Devonport Walk* gives you all the details as you wander.

There are three excellent white-sand beaches in close range—**Devonport,** a good swimming spot with a playground; **Cheltenham,** a safe tidal beach; and **Narrow Neck Beach,** with safe swimming and a playground. **Mount Victoria** sits near the business center and allows great harbor views, and **North Head** was a significant defense spot for both Maori and the Europeans. The volcanic hill was further developed during World War II, and it's honeycombed with underground tunnels, chambers, and gun emplacements. **Devonport Explorer Tours** (© **09/357-6366;** www.devonporttours. co.nz) can take you here on a 1-hour minibus tour for around NZ$30 (US$21) per adult (including ferry ride); booking ahead is essential. Alternatively, you can get an all-day pass for around NZ$25 (US$18) that allows you to leave the bus at any point and pick it up again on the next tour.

At the colorful **Art by the Sea** ☝, King Edward Parade and Church Street (© **09/ 445-6665**), you'll find top-quality work by New Zealand artists. It's right next door to cafes and across the road from the sea; hours are Sunday through Friday from 10am to 5pm, Saturday from 10am to 5:30pm. **Peter Raos Glass Gallery** ☝☝☝, Shop 5, 2 Queens Parade (© **09/445-4278;** www.raos.co.nz), is also worth checking out for handmade art glass by a local resident.

The **Devonport Village Market,** Devonport Community House, 32 Clarence St. (© **09/445-3068**), takes place on the second Sunday of every month from 10am to 3pm. It features entertainment, 70 crafts and food booths, and more.

Two museums to visit are the **Devonport Museum,** 31A Vauxhall Rd. (© **09/445-2661**), open Saturday and Sunday from 2 to 4pm; and the **Navy Museum,** Spring Street (© **09/445-5186**), open daily from 10am to 4:30pm. If you decide to stay for dinner, there are numerous restaurants and cafes (see "Where to Dine," earlier in this chapter). For something completely different, check out **Devonport Chocolates** ☝☝, 17 Wynyard St., Devonport (© **09/445-6001;** www.devonportchocolates.co.nz), where you can see chocolate being made. The shop is open Monday through Thursday 9:30am to 5:30pm, Friday 9am to 5pm, and weekends 10am to 4pm.

ORGANIZED TOURS & CRUISES

You can book several half- and full-day tours of the city and its environs at the visitor center. The half-day tours cover sightseeing highlights, while all-day tours usually include something of the east or west suburbs, the zoo, and the vineyards.

Mike's Garden Tours (© **09/846-5350;** fax 09/846-5315; www.mikesgardentours. co.nz) are the only ones that combine sightseeing with private garden visits. There are several options, ranging in price from NZ$90 to NZ$100 (US$63–US$70) for adults.

New Zealand Tourism Award winner **Auckland Adventures** ☝ (© **09/379-4545;** www.aucklandadventures.com) gets high praise for its specialty packages, which include nature tours, beach/bush walks, mountain biking, Maori culture, group abseiling, and camp and winery tours Prices range from NZ$95 to NZ$130 (US$66–US$91).

Tamaki Hikoi ☆☆ (© 0800/282-5526 in NZ; www.aucklandnz.com), is a 4-hour Maori walking tour through Auckland. A guide from the Ngati Whatua tribe retells legends, beginning at the dormant volcano of Mount Eden. After a picnic lunch, you continue past local landmarks, finishing at the downtown waterfront. The tours costs around NZ$90 (US$63) for adults, NZ$60 (US$42) for children 5 to 14. It's an easy to moderate walk, mainly on road surfaces. Wear sensible walking shoes.

Bush & Beach ☆ (© 0800/423-224 in NZ, or 09/837-4130; www.bushand beach.co.nz) will take you out to the wild west coast to experience the elemental side of Auckland. Half- or full-day tours can include a gannet colony, winery visits, and virgin rainforest. They cost NZ$95 to NZ$130 (US$66–US$91) per person.

A good-value experience is **Geo Tours** ☆ (© 09/525-3991; www.volcanoshop. com). Geologist Murray Baker will give you the lowdown on everything volcanic, including visits to craters, cones, lava flows, and ash layers. Prices for Auckland or regional volcanic tours start at NZ$95 (US$66) for a half-day and NZ$150 (US$105) for the full-day option.

For a range of tours with a Maori flavor, contact **Potiki Adventures** (© 0800/692-3836 in NZ; www.potikiadventures.com). From a Northland marae stay to gathering shellfish and learning about flax weaving and Maori plant medicine, the company can organize personalized itineraries or take you on a full-day tour (around NZ$135/US$94 per person).

One of the best wine tours is with **Auckland Wine Tasting Tours** ☆ (© 09/630-1540; www.winetrailtours.co.nz). It specializes in taking small groups to leading growers. Half- and full-day tours cost NZ$95 to NZ$195 (US$66–US$136) per person. The full-day Matakana tour (around NZ$160/US$112 per person) introduces you to the wines of one of the loveliest rural areas near the city. **Auckland Fine Wine Tours** ☆☆ (©/fax 09/849-4519; www.insidertouring.co.nz) has a great choice of half-day food and wine tours for NZ$120 to NZ$150 (US$84–US$105) and full-day tours from NZ$130 to NZ$240 (US$91–US$168). The Great Auckland Food Tour is especially good. It introduces you to cheese making, ice cream, a busy fish market, delis, a chocolate boutique, a distillery, and a winery. The price (around NZ$200/US$140 per person) includes a cafe lunch.

On The Road Tours (© 09/630-7692; www.ontheroad.co.nz) operates a good range of city tours. Prices for half-day tours start at around NZ$50 (US$35) per person. If you're a keen beer drinker, you might like to try **Lionzone,** the Lion beer experience, 380 Khyber Pass Rd., Newmarket (© 09/358-8366; www.lionzone.co.nz). Lion Brewery is the home of New Zealand's biggest beer brand, and Steinlager is its flagship international beer. Tours begin daily at 9:30am, 12:15pm, and 3pm.

If you feel like striking out on your own, join **Kawau Kat Cruises,** Pier 3, Quay Street, downtown (© 0800/888-006 in NZ), which will deliver you to Rangitoto Island. The schedule gives you plenty of time to climb the 700-year-old dormant volcano. Walk through basalt lava, the world's largest pohutukawa forest, and lava tunnels (take a torch) in the company of native birds. Trips leave Pier 3 daily at 9:40am, 10:30am, 11:40am, 1:40pm, and 3pm. The last return is at 5pm. The price is around NZ$20 (US$14) for adults, NZ$12 (US$8.40) for children.

ON THE WATER

With 96 boat charter companies, Auckland won't deprive you of an opportunity to get out on the waves. **Fullers Auckland,** Ferry Building, Quay Street (© **09/367-9111;** www.fullers.co.nz), is one company that makes it easy. One of its best-value deals if you're on a tight itinerary is the **Harbour Cruise,** a 1½-hour sightseeing excursion that shows off Viaduct Harbour, Devonport Naval Base, and the Harbour Bridge, with coffee and commentary. Fares are NZ$30 (US$21) for adults, NZ$15 (US$11) for children. The cruise includes a return ticket to Devonport so passengers can visit the seaside village at their leisure, or on any scheduled Fullers sailing. Tours depart from Pier 3, Quay Street, at 10:30am and 1:30pm. Fullers also has a Volcanic Explorer option that visits Rangitoto Island (around NZ$55/US$38 per adult, NZ$25/US$18 per child) and several Waiheke Island Explorer options, including a Waiheke Wine Tour for around NZ$68 (US$48) per person.

After winning the America's Cup twice, New Zealand is big on yachting. **The Pride of Auckland,** at the National Maritime Museum, Quay Street (© **09/373-4557;** www.prideofauckland.com), offers five daily events, including a 2½-hour dinner cruise for around NZ$95 (US$66); the price includes admission to the National Maritime Museum. The Maritime Museum's own cruises on heritage vessels are a little cheaper, but the luncheon cruise has a boxed lunch as opposed to a sit-down meal; it's also shorter and on an entirely different type of vessel. All are excellent experiences.

If you want tall ship sailing, the *Soren Larsen* (© **0800/767-365** in NZ, or 09/411-8755; www.sorenlarsen.co.nz), star of *The Onedin Line,* is your vessel. You can book day sails, coffee cruises, or holiday voyages, which include a 5-night sailing cruise between Auckland and the Bay of Islands. Auckland day trips start at around NZ$98 (US$69) per person, longer voyages at NZ$1,280 (US$895).

Sail New Zealand (© **0800/724-569** in NZ, or 09/359-5987; www.sailnz.co.nz), offers a variety of tours in both Auckland and the Bay of Islands. *NZL 40, NZL41,* and *Lion New Zealand* are all available for sailing or match-race tours (see "The Viaduct Basin," earlier in this chapter).

6 Outdoor Activities & Spectator Sports

OUTDOOR PURSUITS

AIR BUNGY   The **Sky Screamer,** Albert and Victoria streets, just down from Sky Tower (© **09/377-1328**), will send you skyward with a maximum adrenaline rush at 200kmph (124 mph). Prices start at NZ$35 (US$25) per person. Open 11am to late.

BUNGY JUMPING   **A.J. Hackett Bungy Auckland,** Westhaven Reserve (bottom of Curran St.), Herne Bay (© **0800/462-8649** in NZ, or 09/361-2000; www.aj hackett.com), is the world's first harbor bridge bungy. For around NZ$90 (US$63), you leap out over Waitemata Harbour. Or double up and include the Harbour Bridge Experience for about NZ$140 (US$98).

CANYONING   **Canyonz,** 240 Penrose Rd., Mount Wellington, Auckland (© **0800/ 422-696** in NZ, or 09/815-9464; www.canyonz.co.nz), offers a range of energetic adventures on Auckland's west coast and in the Coromandel Peninsula (see chapter 6). Costs range from NZ$165 (US$115) for the Blue Canyon adventure to NZ$225 (US$157) per person for a Coromandel excursion to Sleeping God Canyon, where you can slither down a 300m (984-ft.) waterfall.

CLIMBING The **Birkenhead Indoor Climbing Wall,** Mahara Avenue, Birkenhead ((C) **09/418-4109;** www.indoorrockclimbing.co.nz), is open daily from 10am to 10pm.

FOUR-WHEEL-DRIVE BIKING If "real" adventure in the country is your thing, call **4 Track Adventures,** Restall Road, Woodhill Forest ((C) **0800/487-225** in NZ, or 09/420-8104; www.4trackadventures.co.nz). Its quad bikes are easy to ride, and you don't need previous experience. Expect to pay around NZ$125 (US$87) per person for a 1-hour safari. Van pickup from central hotels and backpackers is available for NZ$30 (US$21).

GOLF You'll find more than 40 golf courses in the Auckland region. For details, call the **Auckland Visitor Golf Association** ((C)/fax **09/522-0491**), Monday through Thursday between 9am and 5pm, and ask for the course nearest you and current greens fees. Or start at the top at **Gulf Harbour Golf Course & Country Club** ((C) **09/424-0971;** www.gulf-harbour.co.nz), a world-class 18-hole course where you pay around NZ$120 (US$84) for 18 holes, including cart hire.

HORSEBACK RIDING The Auckland region is home to about 20 riding operations. The visitor center can give you advice about the outfitter nearest you. One of the closest to the inner city is **Valley View Riding** ((C) **09/837-0525**), in Henderson.

KAYAKING Ian Ferguson, MBE (Member of the British Empire—awarded for outstanding contributions, in this case to sport) is one of New Zealand's top athletes; he has competed in five Olympic games, won four gold medals and one silver, and in 1996 was named New Zealand Olympian of the century. He is also the man behind **Fergs Kayaks** ☆☆ (see more on Fergs Kayaks in chapter 11). Located at **Ian Ferguson Marine Sports Centre,** 12 Tamaki Dr., Okahu Bay ((C) **0800/333-999** in NZ, or 09/529-2230; www.fergskayaks.co.nz), it offers several kayaking options; the most fun, perhaps, is the Rangitoto Night Trip, which involves a 75-minute paddle out to the island and a 45-minute walk to the top of Rangitoto for a spectacular night view of Auckland. The trip leaves at 6pm, returns by 11pm, and costs around NZ$75 to NZ$80 (US$52–US$56) per person.

MOUNTAIN BIKING Downhill mountain biking—my kind of stuff—is what you get with **Auckland Adventures** ((C) **09/379-4545;** www.aucklandadventures. co.nz). Its 9-hour excursion takes in the best of West Auckland and costs about NZ$100 per person; biking time varies from 1 to 3 hours, depending on your level of fitness. **Adventure Cycles**, 36 Customs St. E. ((C) **09/309-5566;** www.adventure-auckland.co.nz), organizes self-guided cycle tours for NZ$15 (US$11) per half-day and NZ$90 (US$63) per week. It's open daily 7am to 7pm.

SAILING You'll find numerous brochures about sailing charters at the visitor center, and the staff there can help you decide. See also "Organized Tours & Cruises," above. If you'd like to learn the basics, contact **Penny Whiting Sailing School** ☆☆ ((C) **09/376-1322;** fax 09/376-4595; www.pennywhiting.com).

SCUBA DIVING **Divercity Charters,** 128 Wairau Rd., Glenfield ((C) **09/444-7698,** or boat phone 025/519-651), can take you to seven top dive sites near Auckland, including marine reserves. Call for current charter rates.

SKY DIVING You'll forget all the other views once you get airborne with Auckland's only 7-day parachute center, **Skydive Auckland,** Mercer Skydiving Centre

(© **0800/865-867** in NZ, or 09/373-5778; www.skydiveauckland.com). It offers free pickup service.

SURFING   New Zealand Surf Tours (© **09/832-9622**; www.newzealandsurftours. com) offers 1-day surf tours (NZ$99/US$69), 1- and 2-day surf schools (NZ$120–NZ$189/US$84–US$132) and a 5-day surf tour (NZ$699/US$489) in the Auckland and Northland regions.

SWIMMING   Accessible from Tamaki Drive (where there's frequent bus service from Britomart), the beaches at Judges Bay, Okahu Bay, Mission Bay, Kohimarama, and St. Heliers Bay are popular inner-harbor swimming spots. If you want pool swimming, the visitor center has an excellent brochure that details 10 major complexes.

WALKING   An easy, enjoyable walk is along the promenade of **Tamaki Drive** 𝒜𝒜, which takes you from the inner city around to the pleasant seaside suburbs of Mission Bay and Kohimarama. **One Tree Hill, Cornwall Park,** and **Mount Eden** all offer a bit of physical exertion. If you really want to explore, contact **Waitakere Wilderness Walks** (©/fax **09/838-9007**; www.wildwalk.co.nz). It offers 1- and 2-day walks and photographic excursions in the unspoiled west coast. An excellent self-guided trek is the **Coast to Coast Walk** 𝒜𝒜𝒜, a 4- to 6-hour walk through the inner city and suburbs. A comprehensive map available from the visitor center shows the 16km (10-mile) route.

SPECTATOR SPORTS

For information on current events, contact the **Auckland Visitor Information Centre** (© **09/979-2333;** fax 09/979-2334; reservations@aucklandnz.com), or check out the events listings at www.eventsauckland.com.

HORSE RACING   The **Auckland Cup** (© **09/524-4069;** fax 09/524-8680) takes place on New Year's Day at Ellerslie Race Course. It's the biggest day in New Zealand thoroughbred racing, with over 30,000 on course.

Alexandra Park Raceway, Greenland West Road, Epsom (© **09/630-5660;** www. alexpark.co.nz), mounts the **Lion Red Auckland Trotting Cup Carnival,** an extravaganza that includes the NZ$100,000 (US$70,000) Great Northern Derby for 3-year-olds and the NZ$250,000 (US$175,000) Lion Red Trotting Cup. Regular **Night Trotting** meetings are on Friday and Saturday nights.

For more information on horse racing, call the **Recorded Racing Information Service** (© **09/520-7507**).

MARATHON   The **Round the Bays Run** (© **09/525-2166**) is held around Tamaki Drive each March.

RUGBY   Check with the visitor center for current schedules of **All Blacks** and fiercely fought provincial rugby games nationwide. The rugby season runs from April to September. For rugby and league match information, contact **New Zealand Rugby Football Union** (© **04/499-4995**) or **New Zealand Rugby Football League Inc.** (© **09/524-4013**).

TENNIS   The **ASB Bank Classic,** in January, attracts women tennis players from around the world; the **Heineken Open,** the men's event, generally follows the women's event, also in January. Call © **09/373-3623** or fax 09/373-3625 for details.

7 Shopping

Most shops are open Monday through Friday from 9am to 5:30pm, with many staying open late on Thursday and Friday. Saturday hours are normally 10am to 4pm, although some shops stay open all day. Many are also open on Sunday. Several free shopping guides are available at the visitor center.

Tip: If you have the store mail your purchases back home, you won't have to pay the 12.5% GST—and you won't have to lug them all around the country. Alternately, **Pak Mail,** 466 Lake Rd., Takapuna (© **0800/725-6245** in NZ, or 09/486-1475; www.pakmail.co.nz), will pick up your purchases and insure, pack, and freight them home for you. Even extra luggage can be shipped; no size limits apply.

DUTY-FREE DELIGHTS DFS Galleria Customhouse, Customs and Albert streets (© **0800/388-937** in NZ, or 09/308-0700), is New Zealand's most luxurious duty- and tax-free department store. It offers complimentary shuttle service, free delivery of purchases to the airport, and currency exchange. It's open daily from 10am to 10pm. For a list of all New Zealand duty-free stores, pick up the free *Duty Free & GST Free Shopping Guide* at the airport or visitor center. If you shop at an off-airport duty-free store, be sure you have your airline ticket with you.

INNER CITY

Shoppers seeking the latest in cutting-edge fashion and design can pick up the pocket-size **Auckland Fashion Guide** from the Visitor Information Centre and then head for the **High Street–Vulcan Lane–O'Connell Street areas** *ϭϭϭ* (www.hotcity.co.nz). This is the place to go for leading New Zealand fashion houses, accessories, art, coffee, and interesting food. It's where you'll find international fashion hotshots **Karen Walker, Zambesi,** and **World.** Also here are excellent bookstores such as **Unity** (© **09/307-0731**) and **Touchwood** (© **09/379-2733**). The lovely and innovative **Pauanesia** *ϭϭ*, 35 High St. (© **09/366-7282**), sells the very best in contemporary New Zealand and Pacific homeware. **The Vault,** 13 High St. (© **09/377-7665**), is the perfect place for reasonably priced New Zealand and international design items—everything from jewelry to stationery to small gifts. The new **Chancery shopping area** (© **09/368-1863**) is also here. It's packed with international brand stores and exclusive fashion names. If

---

Tips **Antiques Hunting**

The most popular concentrations of antiques stores are around the Epsom area and in Parnell, Remuera, Ponsonby, and the inner city. **Lord Ponsonby Antiques,** 86 Ponsonby Rd. (© 09/376-6463), is as good a place as any to start. Also in Ponsonby is **Piper Antiques,** 159 Ponsonby Rd. (© 09/376-9000).

In Parnell, look for **John Stevens Antiques,** 377 Parnell Rd. (© 09/377-4500); in Epsom, you'll find **Auckland Antique Shop,** 465 Manukau Rd. (© 09/630-4048), and **Country Antiques,** 489 Manukau Rd. (© 09/630-5252). In Remuera, look for **Antiquities,** 89 Great South Rd. (© 09/520-0353), **Barry Thomas Antiques,** 93 Great South Rd. (© 09/520-4090), **Abbey Antiques,** 87 Great South Rd. (© 09/520-2045), and several others on the same stretch of Great South Road.

Finds **Great Tastes**

To satisfy your gourmet tastes or pick out tasty morsels for a picnic, head for **Kapiti Shop**, 136–142 Fanshawe St. (© **09/377-2473**; www.kapiticheeses.co.nz), which has a huge selection of premium New Zealand cheeses—and make sure you try Kapiti's ice cream. It's divine! **Zarbo**, 24 Morrow St., Newmarket (© **09/ 520-2721**; www.zarbo.co.nz), carries an excellent range of delicious items. **Pandoro**, 427 Parnell Rd., Parnell (© **09/358-1962**), and 290 Dominion Rd., Mount Eden (© **09/631-7416**), is an authentic Italian bakery offering organic, non–genetically modified, and additive-free products. **Vinotica**, 47–49 The Strand, Parnell (© **09/358-3339**; www.vinotica.co.nz), stocks a selection of the finest fresh produce, cheeses, meats, deli items, and baked goods. And enjoy the sights and sounds of an authentic working fish market at **Auckland Fish Market**, Sanfords, Jellicoe Street, near Viaduct Harbour (© **09/379-1490**; www.aucklandfish market.co.nz). It has a daily early-morning auction and a seafood school.

you're a *Lord of the Rings* fan, check out the big range of movie collectibles and jewelry at **DMC**, 61 High St. (© **09/303-4757**; www.lotrshop.co.nz).

All manner of stores line **Queen Street** from top to bottom, but don't overlook the little side streets running off it; here you'll often find excellent specialty shops, such as **Compendium**, 5 Lorne St. (© **09/300-3212**), which has an impressive collection of quality New Zealand craft work. It schedules regular exhibitions of glass, jewelry, pottery, wood, sculpture, clothes, and furniture. **Fingers** ★★, 2 Kitchener St. (© **09/ 373-3974**), is Auckland's most established New Zealand jewelry collective. If you want to take home a special swimsuit, head for **Blue Dude**, 6 Durham St. E. (© **09/ 309-5017**; www.swimwear.co.nz), where you'll find a full range for the entire family. If you're into hiking and camping, don't go past **Specialty Maps**, 46 Albert St. (© **09/307-2217**). It carries a large range of maps, compasses, guidebooks, and travel accessories of all kinds. **Kura Gallery**, 188 Quay St. (© **09/302-1151**; www.kura gallery.co.nz), has a great range of original New Zealand art and crafts.

For good clusters of specialty stores, also check out **Queen's Arcade**, Queen and Customs streets (© **09/358-1777**), where you'll find two levels of excellent shops. **Downtown Shopping Centre**, near the waterfront, is another mall of upmarket shops and boutiques; check out **All at Sea**, on the ground floor (© **09/300-5079**; www.marinetheme.co.nz), which has nautical gifts and handcrafted sailing ships.

PONSONBY/HERNE BAY/K'ROAD

Although better known for its wealth of eateries, Ponsonby also has some terrific specialty design stores and boutiques, with an emphasis on housewares, fashion, and furniture. Karangahape Road is worth browsing for its diversity and cultural mix. Check out www.ponsonbyroad.co.nz for details.

PARNELL/NEWMARKET

Shopping Parnell is a special experience, albeit an expensive one, with everything from Timberland to Cartier. You'll find all sorts of exclusive gifts in a rabbit's warren of little historic buildings, restored to picturesque splendor, that stretch along a mile of Parnell Road. Be sure to investigate **Höglund Art Glass**, 285 Parnell Rd. (© **09/300-6238**;

The Markets

Everyone makes a big deal about **Victoria Park Market,** 210 Victoria St. W. (✆ **09/309-6911;** www.victoria-park-market.co.nz), but I find it a tedious shuffle between jaded retail outlets. It's different, I'll grant it that, but different doesn't necessarily mean better. More than 100 outlets purvey everything from the ridiculous to the bizarre. There are some interesting things, but you have to look carefully; a lot of it is junk. It's open daily 9am to 6pm.

For an excellent Pacific experience, definitely visit the **Otara Market** *かかか*, Newbury Street, Otara (✆ **09/274-0830**), held Saturday from 6am to noon. It's the largest Polynesian market in the world, with larger-than-life personalities, exotic foods and smells, wonderful tapa cloth, flax mats and baskets, and bone carvings. **Mangere Town Centre Market** (✆ **09/275-7078**), on Saturday from 6am to 2pm, offers a free multicultural show between 10am and noon. It's behind the Farmers Trading Co. building, with entrances off Mascot and Orly avenues.

K'Rd. Market, K'Road, Motorway Overbridge (✆ **09/377-5086**), runs Saturday from 10am to 4pm and features crafts and clothes. The **K'Rd. Trash & Treasures Collectibles Market** (✆ **021/644-604**) is in the K'Rd. Car Park Sunday from 6 to 11am.

Avondale Market, Avondale Racecourse, Ash Street, Avondale (✆ **09/818-4931**), on Sunday from 6am to noon, has a strong Polynesian and Asian influence. It features a mass of fruit, vegetables, new and used clothes, and bric-a-brac. The **Aotea Square Markets,** The Edge, Queen Street (✆ **09/309-2677**), take place Friday and Saturday from 10am to 6pm; they feature New Zealand fashion labels, retro gear, foods, fabric, jewelry, and furniture.

www.hoglund.co.nz), a beautiful store with original work by leading glassblowers Ola and Marie Höglund. Click on to www.parnell.net.nz for more information about this area.

Passion for Paper *かか*, 217 Parnell Rd. (✆ **09/379-7579**), is one of my favorites. It has divine papery goods imported from Italy. **Woolly for You,** 237 Parnell Rd. (✆ **09/377-5437**), carries a variety of knitwear in wool, mohair, and angora as well as sheep products. **Elephant House,** 237 Parnell Rd. (✆ **09/309-8740**), has a large range of New Zealand–made goods, with over 300 artisans represented.

Many think New Zealand chocolate rivals Swiss chocolate in quality. For a sample, seek out **Chocolate Boutique Café,** 323 Parnell Rd. (✆ **09/377-8550;** www.chocolate boutique.co.nz). There's even chocolate (hot and iced) to drink, and something for the diabetic, too.

Newmarket is a favorite fashion district for locals, especially on Saturday. This is also where you'll find **Two Double Seven Shopping Centre,** 277 Broadway, a five-story, block-long building oozing with retail opportunity. Broadway (the main street) has great shoe shops with many international labels represented. Check www.new market.net.nz for more information.

> **Moments   South Seas Souvenirs**
>
> To get a feel for Auckland's Polynesian nature, visit the Tongan women who sell tapa cloth on Saturday mornings outside the Tongan Church on Richmond Road, between Chamberlain and Dickens streets. You'll get superb bark cloth at good prices.

8 Auckland After Dark

Auckland has something for everyone—the adventurous, the sophisticated, the young, and the young at heart. From 24-hour casinos and live theater to cinema, clubs, pubs, bars, and dance spots, you can party all the way to breakfast time.

For information about current cultural and entertainment events in the city, contact **Ticketek**, Aotea Centre (© 09/307-5000; www.ticketek.co.nz), which provides easy credit card booking with next-day courier delivery. It also makes bookings around the country—a good way to save time and avoid disappointment. The free newspaper *Tourist Times* also lists current happenings.

THE PERFORMING ARTS

The Edge, 50 Mayoral Dr. (© 09/309-2677; www.the-edge.co.nz), is the cultural core of Auckland. Located in the central area bordered by Mayoral Drive and Albert, Wellesley, and Queen streets, it includes the modern Aotea Centre, the impressive Auckland Town Hall, and the Civic Theatre, which has undergone a NZ$40-million (US$28-million) refurbishment. The **Aotea Centre** (© 09/307-5060), opened in 1990 by Dame Kiri Te Kanawa, features theater, ballet, dance, opera, major stage productions, art exhibitions, and lots of local drama. The **Auckland Town Hall** is the city's best-known building. It reopened in 1997 following a NZ$32.8-million (US$23-million) restoration. The Great Hall seats over 1,600 and is modeled after the Gewandhaus Concert Hall in Leipzig, Germany, which was bombed during World War II. It is regarded as one of the finest acoustically tuned concert halls in the world, and schedules regular performances by the Auckland Philharmonia and the New Zealand Symphony Orchestra. For listings of events at The Edge, call © 09/307-5060 or go to www.akcity.govt.nz.

The **SKYCITY Theatre** is the newest addition to the city's performance venues. The 700-seat theater features state-of-the-art technology and major local and international performers in dance, theater, rock, pop, jazz, and cabaret. For details on events, call © 0800/759-2489 or visit www.skycity.co.nz.

The **Maidment Theatre** at Auckland University (© 09/308-2383) is well known for New Zealand drama and theater sports; the **Bruce Mason Centre,** in Takapuna (© 0800/005-959 in NZ, or 09/488-2940), offers a little of everything.

THE LIVE MUSIC SCENE

Pick up the free *Auckland What's On* guide from the visitor center for the latest on the music scene. You'll find jazz and rhythm-and-blues gigs at places such as **London Bar,** Wellesley and Queen streets (© 09/373-3864); **Deschlers,** High Street (© 09/379-958), which is popular with the 20- to 30-something after-work crowd; and **Gables Tavern,** Jervois Road and Kelmarna Avenue, Herne Bay (© 09/376-4994). The **Alto Casino & Bar** at Skycity (© 09/363-6368) also has live jazz performances.

The **Devonport Folk Music Club** meets in the Bunker, Mount Victoria, Devonport (© **09/445-2227**), Monday evenings at 8pm; new faces are welcome.

For rock, blues, and jazz, head for **Java Jive,** 308 Ponsonby Rd. (© **09/376-5870**); **Temple Bar,** 486 Queen St. (© **09/377-4866**), which has open mic and jam nights, solo acts, and bands; and **Devonport Bar & Brasserie,** 5 Victoria Rd., Devonport (© **09/445-3142**).

If Irish music is your thing, you'll find it at **Danny Doolan's,** Viaduct Basin (© **09/ 358-2554**), where there's live entertainment on Thursday, Friday, and Saturday nights; **The Dogs Bollix,** Karangahape and Newton roads (© **09/376-4600**), which schedules piano nights and jam sessions; and **The Bog,** 196 Parnell Rd., Parnell (© **09/377-1510**).

The **Mexican Café,** 67 Victoria St. W. (© **09/373-2311**), has live Latin music every Wednesday and Thursday.

THE CLUB & BAR SCENE

No matter how many nightspots I list here, I'll always overlook somebody's favorite. If you want a night with the work-hard, play-hard business crowd, head for Parnell; older, richer, devil-may-care types flock to Viaduct Harbour and its many nighttime haunts. The younger, funky, black-clothed set hangs out in High Street/Vulcan Lane in the inner city; most of the all-night clubs, drag queens, and gay bars are along Karangahape Road; and Ponsonby is a favored upmarket place for drinks, dinner, and a general wind-up before hitting the club scene.

INNER CITY   If you want to check out the yachting scene, head for **The Loaded Hog,** Viaduct Harbour, Hobson and Quay streets (© **09/366-6491**), where the pace is fairly frisky after a day on the water. **Spy Bar,** 204 Quay St., Viaduct Harbour (© **09/377-7811**), is Auckland's top after-hours bar for a sophisticated older crowd. Brand new on the scene is (the very chic) **Chic,** 201 Quay St., Viaduct Harbour (© **09/377-5360**), where exotic fabrics, lavish "beds," and plush pillows set the mood for a seductive night out with the glam crowd. **Plum,** Viaduct Harbour (© **09/357-0980**), has fabulous cocktails, a friendly staff, and great retro music.

Minus 5, Princes Wharf (© **09/377-9865**), is the "coolest" experience in town. Everything from the walls to the glasses is made of ice, and the temperature is a constant –5°F (–21°C), so make the essential booking and don your warmest coat. **Crow Bar,** 26 Wyndham St. (© **09/366-0398**), is a classy little "rich" joint that's trendy in the wee small hours. **Honey,** 5 O'Connell St. (© **09/369-5639**), is a sophisticated spot offering over 30 varieties of champagne and New Zealand's very own vodka label, 42-Below—the cocktails are winners. **Galatos,** 17 Galatos St. (© **09/303-1928**), is a plush bar that veers towards the alternative international gig scene with live funk, soul, hip-hop, and jazz.

Coco Club, Fort Lane, City (© **09/309-3848**), an upmarket alley bar for sophisticates, offers vintage champagne by the glass; and **Match Lounge Bar,** Hopetoun and Pitt streets, City (© **09/379-0110**), is a slick little joint designed to accommodate an intimate crowd with plenty of quieter spots for conversations. Don your glad rags for this one and arrive late if you want to appear cool. **Khuja Lounge,** 536 Queen St. (© **09/377-3711**), is a Latino/hip-hop/funk DJ scene popular with the 20s and 30s crowd; and **Fu,** 166 Queen St., downstairs (© **09/309-3079**), is the dark, gritty home to purists of hip-hop, drum and bass, and breaks.

KARANGAHAPE ROAD/PONSONBY Suede, 213 Symonds St. (© 09/366-3906), previously the corner bar Tonic, is a favorite with a mixed crowd of locals; **Club 4:20,** 373 Karangahape Rd. (no phone), is the place to find out all about New Zealand's growing hip-hop scene.

SPQR, 150 Ponsonby Rd. (© 09/360-1710), is the staple of Ponsonby Road. It has a great bar scene late Friday and Saturday nights; you'll see all sorts, both gay and straight, indulging in cocktails with fanciful names such as Horny Monkey and the Slapper. **Chandelier,** 152 Ponsonby Rd. (© 09/360-9315), is just the place for a quiet drink in an opulent environment. **Lime,** 167 Ponsonby Rd. (© 09/360-7167), is the smallest bar of all, and everyone, just everyone, is determined to be first or second here—after that, there's always a queue to get in.

Sponge, 198 Ponsonby Rd. (© 09/360-0098), attracts a younger dance crowd; **Orchid,** 152b Ponsonby Rd. (© 09/378-8186), beautifully appointed in 1970s Asian style, serves the best cocktails; and **Whiskey,** 210 Ponsonby Rd. (© 09/361-2666), is the best late-night scene on Friday and Saturday. The very popular **Malt,** 442 Richmond Rd., Grey Lynn (© 09/360-9537), has the feel of a local corner pub with a bit more warmth and style.

PARNELL/NEWMARKET **Iguacu,** 269 Parnell Rd., Parnell (© 09/358-4804), has established a reputation for hedonism. A business crowd tends to let loose here on Friday and Saturday nights, and it's pretty much a case of anything goes—certainly lively, and certainly a pickup joint of the first degree. **The George,** 144 Parnell Rd. (© 09/358-2600), draws the fashionable Parnell set on Friday and Saturday nights. A younger hip crowd looking for good house music favors **Denim,** 207 Parnell Rd.,

Placing Your Bets: A Night at the Casino

Auckland's **SKYCITY Casinos,** Victoria and Federal streets (© 0800/759-2489 in NZ, or 09/363-6000; www.skycity.co.nz), receive over 12,000 visitors per day! The **SKYCITY Casino** is the largest in New Zealand. This vast expanse of 88 gaming tables (blackjack, roulette, craps, Caribbean stud poker, baccarat, tai sai, pai gow, and money wheel), an 80-seat keno lounge, and more than 1,200 slot machines is not the most stimulating of environments—unless you're keen to try your luck. Everyone is earnest and intent, as well they might be, given the amount of money changing hands. Still, it's worth a look, if nothing else. The upmarket **Alto Casino & Bar** *, on the third level, is much more stylish and intimate. It has live music and a strict dress code (jackets for men; jeans, shorts, active sportswear, and sports shoes not permitted). It opens at 4pm and continues through the night. The **SKYCITY Members Club** is a more exclusive, invitation-only gaming room.

You may not be interested in gambling, but I think a visit to SKYCITY is essential at some point in your visit to Auckland. The casinos are not the only aspect of this multifaceted complex. It holds several excellent restaurants, the Sky Tower, the SKYCITY Theatre complex, and one of the best contemporary New Zealand art collections in the country. The casinos are open 24 hours a day, every day.

Parnell (© 09/337-0227). The Paddington, 117 St. Georges Bay Rd., Parnell (© 09/309-3586), might seem cast adrift in industrial land between Parnell and the city, but it's a big hit with the advertising crowd and designers after work. Don't be put off by the big-screen televisions; it gets more glamorous later in the evening. In Newmarket, there's the slightly unruly, "boys' night out" atmosphere of The Penny Black (© 09/529-0050), Khyber Pass and Broadway.

THE GAY SCENE

It's hard to keep up with Auckland's ever-changing gay scene—especially when you're not gay. But I have it on good authority that Urge, 490 Karangahape Rd. (© 09/307-2155), is a good bar for the "more masculine" crowd. Just be sure to wear leather! Staircase Nightclub & Bar, 334 Karangahape Rd. (© 09/374-4278), is a gay-friendly scene, as is Kamo, 382 Karangahape Rd. (© 09/377-2313). The suggestively named Flesh Nightclub & Lounge Bar, 15–17 O'Connell St., City (© 09/336-1616), is popular; Lateshift, 25 Dundonald St. (© 09/373-2657), the men's safe-sex cruise club, is going strong.

9 A Side Trip to Waiheke Island ★★★

This divine little paradise is just 35 minutes from downtown Auckland by ferry; of its permanent population of about 8,000, nearly 1,000 commute to the city each day to work. In summer, the island's population swells to over 30,000 as visitors come to languish in the enchanting mix of white-sand beaches, lush native bush, green farmland, top wineries and vineyards, and swish little cafes and restaurants. I strongly recommend that you stay at least 1 or 2 nights.

ESSENTIALS

GETTING THERE   By Ferry   Fullers Ferries (© 09/367-9111; www.fullers.co.nz) offers regular service (20 sailings daily) from downtown Auckland to Waiheke Island. Ferries depart from Pier 2, Quay Street, in central city. Most sailings are met by buses, shuttles, and taxis at Matiatia, near the main township of Oneroa. The Fullers trip takes 35 minutes and costs around NZ$26 (US$18) round-trip for adults, NZ$13 (US$9.10) for children.

The Subritzky (© 09/534-5663; www.subritzky.co.nz) passenger and vehicular ferry leaves from Half Moon Bay, Pakuranga, and arrives at the Kennedy Point Wharf farther east across the Surfdale Causeway. Ferries run every hour daily between 6am and 6pm. The fare is around NZ$120 (US$84) round-trip for a car and driver. Passengers without cars pay about NZ$27 (US$19) adults, NZ$15 (US$11) children. Reservations are essential.

Pine Harbour Ferry, Jack Lachlan Drive, Pine Harbour, Auckland (© 09/536-4725; www.pineharbour.co.nz), operates regular service to Waiheke between 8:30am and 5:40pm, with extended hours between December 27 and January 31. The round-trip fare is around NZ$20 (US$14) adults, NZ$10 (US$7) children. It's a shorter, cheaper ferry trip, but you have to drive farther on the Auckland side if you're staying in the city.

By Tour   Fullers Waiheke Island Explorer Tour ★★ (© 09/367-9111) gives you the option of being met on the island by a bus and taken on one of four tours, which last from 1½ hours to all day. It's an excellent option if you're short on time. This option departs daily at 10am and costs around NZ$48 (US$34) for adults, NZ$24 (US$17) for children 5 to 15 years old.

ORIENTATION The island is approximately 19km (12 miles) long and has 90km (56 miles) of coastline, 40km (25 miles) of which is white-sand beaches. **Oneroa,** the largest shopping village on Waiheke, is a 15- to 20-minute uphill walk from Matiatia Wharf, where the passenger ferries dock. It's a 10-minute drive from the Kennedy Point Wharf, where the vehicular ferry docks. This western end of the island has the most settlement around **Sandy** and **Enclosure bays** and **Palm Beach. Ostend** and **Surfdale** also have shops and cafes. The best supermarket is at Surfdale.

GETTING AROUND **By Car** If you don't want to take a car to the island, pick up a rental when you arrive. **Waiheke Rental Cars** ✦, Matiatia Wharf (© **09/372-8635;** www.waihekerentalcars.co.nz), has good hourly rates and offers pickup and key drop-off service. **Waiheke Auto Rentals,** Matiatia Wharf (© **09/372-8998;** www.waihekerentals.co.nz), is another option. Four-wheel-drive vehicles, scooters, motorbikes, and mountain bikes are also available. For bicycle rental, contact **Bike Hire Waiheke Island** (© **09/372-7937;** www.4waiheke.co.nz/bikehire.htm), open daily from 8:30am. Rates begin at NZ$30 (US$21) per day.

By Bus **Waiheke Bus Company** (© **09/372-8823;** fax 09/372-9207) serves most bays and beaches at the west end of the island. Pick up a schedule from bus drivers or at the visitor center. Inquire about the **All-Day Bus Pass,** which costs around NZ$14 (US$9.80) per adult, NZ$8 (US$5.60) per child, and NZ$30 (US$21) per family.

By Motorcycle For a unique perspective on the island, go pillion with **Waiheke Harley-Tours** (© **09/372-9012**). Steve Marshall will give you a memorable tour of all the best spots.

VISITOR INFORMATION The **Waiheke Island Visitor Information Centre,** Artworks, 2 Korora Rd., Oneroa (© **09/372-9999;** fax 09/372-9919; www.4waiheke.co.nz), is open daily from 9am to 5pm in summer, 9am to 4pm in winter. Its staff has extensive knowledge of available accommodations on the island and rents over 100 local properties. There is also an information kiosk at Matiatia Wharf. Book accommodations months ahead for the hugely popular **Easter Jazz Festival** (www.waihekejazz.co.nz), because Aucklanders flock to the island for the event. The **Waiheke Island Wine Festival** (© **09/372-7676;** www.waihekewinefestival.co.nz), in February, is a great chance to taste the island's terrific, award-winning wines. Tickets go on sale in October.

For more information on Waiheke Island, check out www.waihekenz.com, www.4waiheke.co.nz, and www.gotowaiheke.co.nz.

Tips **Booking Ahead**

Make life easy for yourself and contact **Waiheke Island Booking Centre,** Shop 2, 116 Oceanview Rd., Waiheke (© **09/372-3377;** www.waihekebooking.co.nz). It can take care of accommodations, tours, rental cars, and activities. If you want to find your own rental home, try **Waiheke Unlimited,** Box 403, Surfdale (© **09/372-7776;** www.waihekeunlimited.co.nz), which books more than 200 rental properties.

EXPLORING THE ISLAND

In Oneroa, visit the upgraded **Artworks Community Arts Centre,** Kororoa Road (© **09/372-6900**), where you'll find a wide range of works from the many resident artists and craftspeople on the island. It's open daily from 10am to 4pm. Nearby is the fascinating **Whittakers Musical Museum** ✸✸ (© **09/372-5573;** www.musical-museum.org), where Lloyd and Joan Whittaker will hold you spellbound with their live performances (about NZ$12/US$8.40) on a range of antique musical instruments, including organs, concertinas, pianolas, and mouth organs.

The **Waiheke Island Historic Village & Museum,** 165 Onetangi Rd. (© **09/372-2970** or 09/372-5168), is overlooked by a fortified Maori settlement site first inhabited 700 years ago. There are old cottages with collections of furniture, books, documents, and photographs. It's open Monday, Wednesday, and weekends year-round, and daily during school holidays and in summer, from noon to 4pm. Catch the Onetangi Bus no. 1 to get there.

Be up early to experience a bit of local culture at the **Ostend Market** ✸, Ostend Hall, corner of Ostend Road and Belgium Street. A parade of local pottery, island-made goods, fruits and vegetables, herbal remedies, massage, plants, herbs, and more, it's held every Saturday from 8am to 1pm. On Sunday between 10am and 2pm, visit the **Oneroa Market,** Artworks Courtyard, Ocean View Road, where you'll find musicians, performers, crafts, and food.

Another "must" activity is a drive to the glorious **Onetangi Bay** ✸✸✸—in my mind, one of the best beaches in New Zealand. Here you can swim and surf in crystal-clear water with views as far as the eye can see. If you want to feel the true spirit of freedom, take it all off at the western end of **Palm Beach,** a small bay used for nude swimming.

If you'd like a peek into a fabulous private garden, check out Lance and Kay Peterson's **Te Whau Garden** (© **09/372-6748;** lance.kay@circlepacific.co.nz), which features a stunning combination of art and native bush. Even better is **Connells Bay Waiheke Sculpture Park** ✸✸✸, Cowes Bay Road (© **09/372-8957;** www.connells-bay.co.nz), where you'll find a superb display of work by top New Zealand sculptors set into the magnificent landscape. There are also around 100 artists living on the island, many with open studios; grab the *Waiheke Island Art Map* from the visitor center and take your pick.

A good way to see the mysterious east end of the island is to join the **Rural Mail Run** (about NZ$20/US$14 per person). It leaves at 8:30am Monday through Friday; for details and bookings, call © **09/372-9166.** Another excellent way to get a feel for Waiheke is to go with **Ananda Tours** ✸✸ (© **09/372-7530** or 021/471-355; www.ananda.co.nz). It offers art studio, wine, and walking tours with knowledgeable guides; prices begin at NZ$65 (US$46) per person. Speaking of walking, pick up the excellent *Waiheke Walkways* ✸✸ brochure from the visitor center. It outlines and maps out nine wonderful island walks, which have been upgraded.

Another fabulous way to see the island is to **Drive The Loop** ✸✸✸, a 1-day self-drive tour that starts and finishes at Waiheke Auto Rentals on Matiatia Wharf (see "Getting Around," above). The company provides the rental vehicle and loop tour package, which includes maps with all the most interesting people and places highlighted. It takes 4 to 8 hours (65km/40 miles), depending on how often you stop, and costs NZ$100 to NZ$150 (US$70–US$105), depending on the vehicle category. For information, call © **09/372-8998,** or fax 09/372-9822.

VISITING VINEYARDS

To the surprise of many, more than 40 vineyards operate on Waiheke Island, where the Mediterranean-style climate is perfect for growing grapes (and olives). Some of the country's best red wines come from the island. Before you start exploring, pick up the free *Waiheke Winegrowers' Map* from the visitor center, or check out the Waiheke Winegrowers' Association website, www.waihekewine.co.nz. Plan your visits around eating time, because several growers have excellent restaurants.

The leader among the Waiheke vineyards is undoubtedly **Stonyridge** ✺✺✺, 80 Onetangi Rd. (✆ **09/372-8822;** www.stonyridge.co.nz). In 1987, Stonyridge produced the first Larose vintage, which was immediately judged one of the world's top red wines by the London World Guide to Cabernet. It has the dreamiest vineyard, with an incredibly picturesque view from its restaurant, which is one of the nicest places on the island to dine (lunch only; see "Where to Dine," below). Winery tours begin at 11:30am on Saturday and Sunday; admission is about NZ$12 (US$8.40) for adults, free for children.

Mudbrick Vineyard & Restaurant ✺✺✺, 126 Church Bay Rd., Oneroa (✆ **09/ 372-9050;** www.mudbrick.co.nz), is another magical setting for a meal. **Gold Water Estate,** 18 Causeway Rd., Putiki Bay (✆ **09/372-7493;** www.goldwaterwine.com), is a small premium winegrower producing top cabernet/merlots—although it's seldom open. It offers tasting sessions and tours by arrangement. **Peninsula Estate,** 52A Korora Rd., Oneroa (✆ **09/372-7866;** fax 09/372-7840), is open for tasting and sales from 1 to 4pm daily in summer. It's acclaimed for its cabernet/merlot.

Kennedy Point Vineyard ✺, 44 Donald Bruce Rd., Kennedy Point (✆ **09/372-5600;** www.kennedypointvineyard.com), has a winery and tasting room in a beautiful setting. **Te Whau Vineyard** ✺✺✺, 218 Te Whau Dr. (✆ **09/372-7191;** www. tewhau.com), has a smart little cafe that serves lunch. Tours are NZ$10 (US$7) per person. With more than 500 cellared wines, Te Whau houses the most diverse collection of New Zealand wine in the world. **Passage Rock Wines** ✺✺✺, 438 Orapiu Rd. (✆ **09/372-7257;** www.passagerockwines.co.nz), is in a tranquil bay. Its award-winning wines have grabbed international attention—as have its wood-fired pizzas.

If you want to take a wine tour, contact **Jaguar Wine Tours** (✆ **09/372-7312; www.waihekejaguartours.co.nz**). Fullers also offers vineyard tours; see "Getting There: By Tour," above, for more information.

WHERE TO STAY

The island has plenty of good backpacker and hostel options, priced from NZ$20 to NZ$60 (US$14–US$42) per person per night; contact the information center (✆ **09/372-9999**) for details.

Finds **The Good Oil**

Waiheke is fast becoming known for its premium extra-virgin olive oils. Around 20,000 trees grow on the island; harvest season is April through May or June. There is no better place to start sampling than **Rangihoua Estate** ✺✺✺, 1 Gordons Rd. (✆ **09/372-6214;** www.rangihoua.co.nz). The Frantoio Room is open Monday through Saturday during January and February; otherwise tours and tasting are held every Saturday from 11am until 4pm, or by appointment.

You'll find plenty to be pleased about at **The Estate Church Bay** ☆☆, 56 Church Bay Rd. (© **09/372-2637;** www.theestatechurchbay.com). Four beautiful rooms overlook vineyards and country views. **Matiatia Olive Estate** ☆☆, 10 Alan Murray Lane, Matiatia Harbour (© **09/372-4272;** www.matiatiaoliveestate.co.nz), near the passenger ferry, has four lovely rooms.

The Boatshed ☆☆☆   There's a real feel of New Zealand about this gorgeous spot above the beach, overlooking little Oneroa. To call it "relaxed luxury" is a little undefined, but I think you'll love the clean-cut elegance of the marine-themed suites. The Boatshed offers terrific sea views from private balconies and every comfort, right down to heated bathroom floors. For something special, go for the three-story Lighthouse suite, which has a private top-floor lounge and a first-floor bedroom with commanding views and a balcony. Ground-floor rooms are more spacious. You may never want to leave.

Tawa and Huia sts. © 09/372-3242. Fax 09/372-3262. www.boatshed.co.nz. 5 suites. NZ$500–NZ$800 (US$350–US$560). Rates include breakfast and airport and ferry transfers. Off-season rates available. AE, DC, MC, V. Free off-street parking. Children under 12 not accepted. **Amenities:** All-day dining; bar; nearby golf course; outdoor Jacuzzi; watersports equipment and bike rentals on request; tour bookings; car rentals; massage; laundry service; dry cleaning; nonsmoking rooms. *In room:* TV/VCR, dataport, minibar, fridge, coffeemaker, hair dryer, iron, safe.

Giverny Inn ☆☆   Gabrielle Young and Bruce McLelland have fashioned lovely accommodations on a bush-clad hill with 180-degree sea views. The upstairs, in-house suite is all about romance; in the lush garden, you'll find a one-bedroom restored cottage and a two-bedroom cottage with two bathrooms. Each cottage has a kitchenette. Giverny Inn is peaceful, plush, and not to be missed.

44 Queens Dr. © 09/372-2200. Fax 09/372-2204. www.giverny.co.nz. 3 units. NZ$405–NZ$495 (US$283–US$346). MC, V. Rates include breakfast. **Amenities:** Jacuzzi; car rentals; tour bookings; massage; laundry service. *In room:* TV, minibar, coffeemaker, hair dryer.

Te Whau Lodge ☆☆☆ *Value*   Gene O'Neill and Liz Eglinton have an unbeatable combination: a brand-new lodge; awesome views; dynamite culinary skills; and relaxed, friendly personalities. Built to blend with the landscape, the lodge utilizes timber finishes and that intrinsic New Zealand building material, corrugated iron. Every spacious room has its own theme, its own bathroom, and its own fabulous balcony. Gene and Liz will take care of all your activity bookings. and just when you think it can't get any better, Gene will present you with one of his delectable four-course dinners.

36 Vintage Lane, Te Whau Point, Waiheke. © 09/372-2288. Fax 09/372-2218. www.tewhaulodge.co.nz. 4 units. NZ$410 (US$287). Rates include breakfast, predinner drinks and canapés, and airport and ferry transfers. Sat dinner B&B with predinner drinks and canapés NZ$610 (US$427). Dinner Sun–Fri NZ$50–NZ$100 (US$35–US$70). AE, DC, MC, V. Free off-street parking. Children under 12 not accepted. **Amenities:** Bar; nearby golf course; outdoor Jacuzzi; watersports equipment rental; bike rentals; tour bookings; car rentals; 24-hr. room service; massage; laundry service; nonsmoking rooms. *In room:* TV/VCR on request, dataport, coffeemaker, hair dryer, iron.

WHERE TO DINE

One of the best Waiheke restaurants is **Te Whau Vineyard Café** ☆☆☆, 218 Te Whau Dr. (© **09/372-7191**). *Wine Spectator* rated it one of the top New Zealand restaurants for wine lovers, and it has an amazing collection of over 500 New Zealand wines. It offers lunch Wednesday through Monday from 11am to 5pm, dinner Friday and Saturday from 6:30 to 11pm.

At **Mudbrick Vineyard & Restaurant** 🏵🏵, Church Bay Road, Oneroa (℃ **09/ 372-9050**), diners gaze out over rolling farmland to the waters of Hauraki Gulf while enjoying French rural cuisine; main courses are priced from NZ$26 to NZ$36 (US$18–US$25). **Stonyridge Café & Vineyard** 🏵🏵, 80 Onetangi Rd. (℃ **09/372- 8822**), serves excellent Pacific Rim cuisine in a glorious romantic setting. It serves lunch only, daily in summer and on Saturday and Sunday in winter. Main courses cost around NZ$26 to NZ$30 (US$18–US$21); reservations are required.

In Oneroa village, you'll find residents amassed at **Salvage,** Ocean View Road (℃ **09/372-2273**), for coffee, snacks, lunch, and dinner. The food is reasonable, but I think you'll be far more impressed by my favorite—**Nourish Café** 🏵🏵🏵 , 3 Belgium St., Ostend (℃ **09/372-3557**). It has a fresh seasonal menu with main courses around NZ$25 (US$18), as well as a great range of cakes and baked goods. It's open daily from 8am, with late nights on Thursday, Friday, and Saturday. The expert hosts at **Ajadz Indian Cuisine** 🏵🏵, Artworks, Oneroa (℃ **09/372-2588**), offer authentic tandoori and curry dishes from northern and southern India. It's open Tuesday through Sunday for lunch and dinner. **Vino Vino** 🏵🏵, behind Green Hills Wines & Spirits, Oneroa (℃ **09/372-9888**), is another local favorite for its big Mediterranean platters and full a la carte dining on a huge deck with stunning views. **Spice,** 153 Ocean View Rd. (℃ **09/372-7659**), is a great place for coffee and picnic supplies.

10 A Side Trip to Great Barrier Island

Imagine pristine white-sand beaches empty of people; imagine lush mountains and a vast network of walking tracks. Add rare birds and plant life, a permanent population of less than 1,000, and a seductive, laid-back lifestyle, and you have New Zealand's fourth-largest landmass, Great Barrier Island. The Department of Conservation administers over 70% of the island, and locals like to say that there are more conservationists per square inch than anywhere else in New Zealand.

This seductive paradise is *the* place if you're looking for a unique New Zealand experience. It's New Zealand as it used to be—all 285 sq. km (111 sq. miles) of it. It's isolated, yet it's only a 35-minute plane ride from our biggest city. It's a place the locals call "the Barrier" and I call "heaven." Get yourself there and you'll remember it forever.

ESSENTIALS
GETTING THERE   By Plane   Great Barrier Airlines (℃ **0800/900-600** in NZ, or 9/275-9120; www.greatbarrierairlines.co.nz), runs daily flights to the island from Auckland International Airport and North Shore Aerodrome. **Mountain Air Great Barrier Xpress,** Domestic Terminal, Auckland International Airport (℃ **0800/222- 123** in NZ, or 09/256-7025; www.mountainair.co.nz), also has daily flights to the island. Most flights land at Claris airfield in the center of the island; some land at Okiwi airfield, 8km (5 miles) from Port Fitzroy. The 35-minute trip costs around NZ$150 (US$105) round-trip.

By Ferry   Ferries land at Tryphena, at the southern end of the island. **Subritzky SeaLink,** 45 Jellicoe St., Auckland Viaduct (℃ **0800/732-546** in NZ, or 09/300-5900; www.subritzky.co.nz), runs 4½- to 5-hour trips to the island daily in summer and 4 days a week in winter (timetables vary). The *Eco Islander* has two theaters with plasma screens showing movies and documentaries, a cafe, and a reading room on board. The long trip can be grueling when the sea is rough. Round-trip fares are around NZ$91 (US$64) adults, NZ$76 (US$53) seniors and students, NZ$61 (US$43) children, NZ$311 (US$218) for a car. I think it's far better to pay a little more for the short flight. And don't worry about taking a car—it's easy to pick up a cheap rental at the Claris airfield. **Fullers Ferry** (© **09/367-9111;** www.fullers.co.nz), is a much faster (2½-hour) trip, but its timetable service operates only in high season (roughly, Dec–Jan).

ORIENTATION

Great Barrier Island is approximately 15km (9⅓ miles) wide and 30km (19 miles) long, with Mount Hobson (621m/2,037 ft.) rising in the center. The island landscape is rugged, and much of it is inaccessible by road. The west coast is characterized by steep, forested ranges that run down to the sea; the east coast offers sweeping, white-sand beaches and rolling hills. The main areas of settlement are **Port Fitzroy** in the north; **Claris, Whangaparapara,** and **Okupu** in the center, and **Tryphena** in the south. Good roads connect them all. Claris and Tryphena are the main villages, though neither is much more than a few shops, cafes, a pub, and a post office. Port Fitzroy boasts one store, a dive station, and a boat club. There are no banks on the island. Be prepared to pay more for basic supplies than you would on the mainland.

GETTING AROUND

By Car   Reasonably priced rental options include **GBI Rent A Car & Adventure Rentals,** Mulberry Grove, Tryphena, and Claris airfield (© **09/429-0062;** gbi. rentacar@xtra.co.nz), which has a wide range of vehicles and offers free delivery to Claris airfield and Tryphena Wharf. Prices start at around NZ$60 (US$42) per day. **Aotea Car Rentals** (© **09/429-0055;** www.aoteatransport.co.nz), offers a similar service and prices from around NZ$90 (US$63) per day.

By Bus and Shuttle   There is no scheduled public transport on the island, but regular bus services meet boats and planes. **Great Barrier Buses** (© **09/429-0474**) has daily service to walking tracks, beaches, and Port Fitzroy. A 1-day pass costs around NZ$45 (US$32). **Aotea Transport** (© **09/429-0055**) runs a "People and Post" bus from Tryphena to Port Fitzroy daily between November and February.

By Bike   Rental mountain bikes are available from **GBI Rent A Car & Adventure Rentals** (© **09/429-0062;** gbi.rentacar@xtra.co.nz) for around NZ$40 to NZ$50 (US$28–US$35) per day. **Paradise Cycles,** Tryphena (© **09/429-0474**), has multi-day special deals.

VISITOR INFORMATION

The **Great Barrier Island Visitor Information Centre,** Hector Sanderson Road, Claris (© **09/429-0033;** fax 09/429-0660; www.greatbarrier.co.nz), is open from 9am until 4pm daily. The staff has extensive knowledge of the island and offers a pre-booking service for holidays on the island. In January, the **Port Fitzroy Mussel Fest** (© **09/429-0072**) provides stalls, entertainment, and as many succulent mussels as you think you can eat. The annual **Santa Parade,** in December at the Claris Sports Club, has a legendary reputation for fun.

EXPLORING THE ISLAND

Great Barrier has a rich history. Maori have inhabited the island for over 1,000 years, and Europeans created a thriving timber industry, milling the huge stands of native kauri trees for the shipbuilding industry. The island was a whaling station until the 1960s, and the relics of old stamping batteries attest to a rich gold- and silver-mining history. The remains of the **Oreville Stamping Battery** are beside the road on the way to Whangaparapara. Also in this area you'll find the very popular **Kaitoke Hot Springs Track,** which leads to natural hot springs in a creek. Use the toilet by the roadside—it's the last one you'll see for a while. The springs are 45 minutes in. Don't forget insect repellent.

Farther north, at Port Fitzroy, you must visit Tony Bouzaid's **Glenfern Sanctuary** ♦♦♦, Glenfern Road (© 09/429-0091; www.fitzroyhouse.co.nz). Take his guided walk and be witness to one of the most wonderful native wildlife sanctuaries anywhere. Over 8,000 trees have been planted as part of an ongoing reforestation project, and timber boardwalks make the walk easy. Tony also offers multiday tramp-sail packages that might include a visit to the otherwise inaccessible Sven Stellin of **Barrier Gold,** a backyard enterprise making a range of kanuka oil products on the shore of Wairahi Bay.

Even farther north, you'll find the **S.S. _Wairarapa_ Walkway** at the very beautiful (and deserted) **Whangapoua Beach.** The steamer _Wairarapa_ wrecked on cliffs near Miners Head on October 29, 1894, with the loss of around 130 lives. A little gravesite at the northern end of the beach serves as a reminder of one of New Zealand's worst shipping disasters.

A range of tracks crisscross **Mount Hobson,** a focal point for keen trampers. There are stunning views from the top on a clear day, and the summit is the main nesting ground for the rare black petrel. It's at least a 2-hour round-trip walk. A signposted side track will take you to **Kaiaraara Kauri Dam,** one of the tallest kauri dams, built over 70 years ago to transport logs out of the forests. If you feel like a steep climb, you'll find the remains of two more dams farther upstream.

In Okupu is a delightful surprise: **Young's Museum** ♦♦, 212 Blind Bay Rd. (© **09/429-0388**). Christine Young, spurred on by the memory of her father, has put together the cutest little museum you'll find anywhere. It's a real Kiwi experience, with Christine showing you through her father's astounding collection of old photographs that depict early life on the island. Phone ahead for an appointment.

A good number of **artists and sculptors** live on the island; the visitor center can furnish a brochure detailing their whereabouts.

If the great outdoors is more your style, call Richard Lintott of **Foromor Fishing Charters** ♦♦♦, 149 Sandhills Rd., Medlands Beach (© **09/429-0033**; www.great barrier.co.nz). You can try your hand at saltwater fly fishing or get him to take you out to the impressive **gannet colonies** on the west coast of the island. **Aotea Kayak Adventures,** Mulberry Grove, Tryphena (© **09/429-0664**; aoteakayak@hotmail. com), offers night kayak trips, sunset paddles, and harbor kayak cruises. Prices range from NZ$35 to NZ$65 (US$25–US$46).

WHERE TO STAY

If you plan on traveling to Great Barrier Island during the summer months, book your accommodations well in advance. In Port Fitzroy, **Fitzroy House** ♦, Glenfern Road (© **09/429-0091**; www.fitzroyhouse.co.nz), has a three-bedroom, self-contained cottage; rates start at NZ$140 (US$98). On a hill above Okupu Beach, you'll find a real gem in self-contained **Bay Lodge Cottage** ♦♦, P.O. Box 28, Claris (© **09/429-0916**; www.lodgings.co.nz/baylodge.html), for NZ$195 (US$137). Owners Neil and

Carole Wright will ply you with chilled wine, freshly baked bread, fruit, and flowers. The cottage is just up the hill from John Mellars' boutique vineyard.

At the top end of the market, you won't regret a hilltop stay at **Earthsong Lodge** ✮✮✮, 38 Medland Rd., Tryphena (© **09/429-0030;** www.earthsong.co.nz), where Trevor and Carole Rendle cook amazing meals as part of the NZ$896 (US$627) room rate. At **Mount Saint Paul Lodge** ✮✮, 29 Kaitoke Lane, Claris (© **09/429-0861;** www.mountstpaullodge.co.nz), you'll enjoy big, luxurious rooms for NZ$750 (US$525).

If you like the idea of leaping from a king-size bed onto the beach, settle yourself into Richard and Sandy Lintott's modern beachfront home, **Foromor Lodge** ✮✮✮, 149 Sandhills Rd., Medlands Beach (© **09/429-0335;** fax 09/429-0395; www.great barrier.co.nz). Nodding off to sleep to the rhythm of the waves is a special kind of luxury. A cottage that sleeps four costs NZ$175 (US$122), and rooms in the lodge are NZ$230 (US$161).

If you're after an especially romantic setting, stay at **Oasis** ✮✮✮, 50 Medland Rd., Tryphena (© **09/429-0021;** fax 09/429-0034; www.barrieroasislodge.net), which is just that—a private retreat enclosed in lush garden foliage, right beside Michael and Penny Gardiner's tiny vineyard. The home is filled with fascinating collectibles, and you'll swoon over the Gardiners' cooking. Rates are NZ$300 (US$210) and include breakfast.

WHERE TO DINE

Don't get too excited about dining possibilities on the island—they're few and far between, and relatively expensive compared to the city. **Claris Texas Café** ✮✮✮, Claris (© **09/429-0811**), is one of the best choices. It serves hearty breakfast fare, tasty lunches, and good coffee daily. You can eat out in the courtyard overlooking fields and idly wonder what might have become of the rest of the world. **Oasis, Earthsong Lodge,** and **Mount Saint Paul Lodge** (see "Where to Stay," above), are all open to casual diners. Bookings are essential at all three. The menu at Oasis is international; Earthsong specializes in French and nouveau cuisine; and Mount Saint Paul's specialty is provincial French and Italian cuisine.

Things are more modest at **Tipi and Bobs Waterfront Restaurant** in Tryphena. You can expect good-value meals, especially if you like fresh fish and chips. **Currach Irish Pub,** Pa Beach, Tryphena (© **09/429-0211**), offers excellent seafood.

11 Out from Auckland

For information about Northland and the Coromandel Peninsula, see chapter 6.

EN ROUTE TO NORTHLAND: THE HIBISCUS COAST

Located 48km (30 miles) north of Auckland, the Hibiscus Coast comprises the communities of Silverdale, Whangaparoa, Orewa, Waiwera, and Puhoi. The area is a 45-minute drive from Auckland, and InterCity coaches offer service that makes a day's outing a reasonable option.

The **Hibiscus Coast Information Centre,** 214A Hibiscus Coast Hwy. (next to KFC), Orewa (© **09/426-0076;** hbcvic@rodney.govt.nz), is open Monday through Friday from 10am to 5pm, Saturday and Sunday from 10am to 4pm.

On the drive north, stop at **Waiwera Thermal Resort** ✮✮, State Highway 1 (© **0800/924-937** in NZ, or 09/427-8800; www.waiwera.co.nz), open Sunday through Thursday from 9am to 10pm, Friday and Saturday from 9am to 10:30pm. Nineteen indoor and outdoor pools are kept at 82°F to 113°F (28°C–45°C); there are both private and communal pools. The cost is around NZ$22 (US$15) for adults, NZ$12 (US$8.40) for children 5 to 14, NZ$5 (US$3.50) for kids under 5, and NZ$55 (US$38) for families.

EN ROUTE TO THE COROMANDEL PENINSULA: THE PACIFIC COAST HIGHWAY

The Pacific Coast Highway is not exactly a highway, certainly not in the American sense of the word. Rather, it is a combination of roads that make up one of the best scenic routes in the country, following the coastline from Auckland all the way to Hawkes Bay. Along the way, it delivers you to Coromandel Peninsula via the very pretty **Seabird Coast** *.

It's worth stopping here for two things: **Kaiaua Fisheries Licensed Seafood Restaurant & Takeaways** (© 09/232-2776), open daily from 9am to 9pm, serves some of the best fish and chips in the country. And once you've filled your empty stomach, check out the **Miranda Shorebird Centre** *, East Coast Road (©/fax 09/232-2781; www. miranda-shorebird.org.nz), where you'll find information about the millions of migratory birds that swing by here on their way north. The 8,500 hectares (20,995 acres) of tidal flats are a big attraction for wading birds and bird-watchers alike.

You can also relax in one of the largest hot mineral pools in the Southern Hemisphere or unwind in a private Jacuzzi at **Miranda Hot Springs Thermal Pools** (© 07/867-3055). It's open Monday through Thursday from 8am to 9pm, Friday and Saturday from 8am to 10:30pm.

Northland & Coromandel

Northland—*Te Tai Tokerau*, or "Birthplace of a Nation"—is one of nature's best playgrounds, but surprisingly visitors often overlook it. The Bay of Islands is what most people know of Northland. This is home to the fabulous Waitangi National Reserve, where the Treaty of Waitangi was signed between Maori and European settlers in 1840; this is also where visitors are best catered to in Northland. Beyond that, the region offers an idyllic summer lifestyle that seems to last year-round.

Northland's peninsular shape offers two contrasting coastlines: white scenic beaches that curve around sheltered coves and harbors to the east, and long stretches of wild, dune-backed beaches and kauri forests pounded by the Tasman Sea to the west.

Northland is made up of six distinct areas: Warkworth and the Kowhai Coast just north of Auckland; Whangarei and the east coast; the Bay of Islands; the Far North; Hokianga; and the Kauri Coast. The population is sparse—in the Far

North area alone, there are 7,252 sq. km (2,800 sq. miles) of farmland and forest occupied by just 53,000 people. Only three towns—Kaitaia, Kaikohe, and Kerikeri—have more than 4,000 residents. Clearly, you'll have large patches all to yourself, so start exploring.

Coromandel, like Northland, has long been a haven for New Zealand holidaymakers. It's closer to Auckland than most of Northland, but it has less to offer in terms of accommodations and organized tourism. Certainly the scenery is just as dramatic, and you'll get that same surfeit of remote beaches and laid-back lifestyle. Leaving Auckland and following the Pacific Coast Highway will take you into Coromandel's quaint, sometimes tatty seaside townships, around endless beaches and bays, and over rugged hill country into the heart of an area made famous by logging, gold mining, gum digging, alternative lifestyles, and artists. There's a raw quality to the Coromandel Peninsula that even the fledgling tourist industry hasn't yet tamed.

1 Bay of Islands & the Far North ★★★

Bay of Islands: 233km (144 miles) N of Auckland; Cape Reinga: 440km (273 miles) N of Auckland

The essential personal items for this area are swimsuit, sunglasses, and suntan lotion—perhaps a fishing rod or a wet suit if you're so inclined. With endless beaches, over 144 islands, and warm, clear blue waters to play in, you'll need little else. Recreation is king up here. There's great fishing, excellent diving, and a climate with average winter temperatures ranging from 45°F to 61°F (7°C–16°C) and summer days of 57°F to 77°F (14°C–25°C).

The Bay of Islands features three little townships: **Paihia/Waitangi, Russell,** and **Kerikeri.** In the Far North, the hot spots are **Doubtless Bay; Kaitaia,** the largest town; and up that last thin finger of land to **Cape Reinga,** believed to be the departing point for the spirits of the Maori dead.

> **(Tips Don't Miss the Best!**
>
> Don't be like the majority of visitors, who go only as far as the Bay of Islands. Some of the best beaches, natural landscapes, and tranquil retreats lie much farther north. It makes sense to travel up an extra day or two, rather than staying in the Bay of Islands and, at best, taking a long 12-hour bus trip to Cape Reinga and back. Go the extra mile: You won't regret it.

ESSENTIALS

GETTING THERE & GETTING AROUND   By Plane   There are three Northland airports: Whangarei, Kerikeri, and Kaitaia. **Air New Zealand Link** (✆ 0800/737-000 in NZ, or 09/357-3000) has daily service from Auckland to Kerikeri, with a shuttle bus to Paihia, and daily service from Auckland to Kaitaia. Charter flights are available with **Salt Air Bay of Islands** (✆ 09/402-8338; www.saltair.co.nz); **Mountain Air** (✆ 09/256-7025; www.mountainair.co.nz); or **Skylink Air Charter** (✆ 09/422-7018; www.skylink.co.nz).

By Coach (Bus)   Both **InterCity** (✆ 09/913-6100; www.intercitycoach.co.nz) and **Northliner Express** (✆ 09/307-5873; www.northliner.co.nz) have daily service between Auckland and Paihia, Kerikeri, and Kaitaia. Both offer discounts to VIP backpackers and seniors. **Kiwi Experience** (✆ 09/366-9830; www.kiwiexperience.com) offers well-priced 1-, 2-, and 3-day tours to the Bay of Islands and Cape Reinga. There's no local bus service in the Bay of Islands, Doubtless Bay, or Kaitaia.

By Car   If you plan to spend a few days in this area, pick up the free *Twin Coast Discovery Highway* map from any visitor center. It's an easy drive however you do it, with beautiful coastal views and rolling farmland all the way. Rather than going straight to the Bay of Islands (about a 3-hr. drive), you might want to explore the Warkworth and Whangarei areas, which are described later in this chapter in "Whangarei & Beyond." The drive from Auckland direct to Kaitaia via the east coast takes about 4 to 5 hours. Northland's west coast is also worth a visit if you have the time. The best plan is to go up the east side and drive back to Auckland via the west coast.

If you arrive via plane or bus, rental cars are available through **Budget,** in the Paihia Holiday Shoppe, corner of Selwyn and Williams roads, in the ASB Bank Building, Paihia (✆ 09/402-8568; www.budget.co.nz).

By Ferry   If you stay in Russell but want to eat in Paihia, you'll need to take the passenger ferry that connects the two. It's the only inexpensive means of getting from one shore to another, and it runs hourly beginning at 7am and ending at 7:30pm. In summer, crossings are extended to 10:30pm. Fares are around NZ$5 (US$3.50) each way for adults, NZ$2.50 (US$1.75) for children 5 to 15. If you miss the last boat, you can take the slightly more expensive water taxi. *Note:* The ferry from Paihia carries pedestrians only. If you're driving to Russell, take the car ferry at Opua. No reservations are needed; the ferry shuttles back and forth every 10 minutes, daily from 7am to 10pm, and costs around NZ$10 (US$7) one-way for a car and driver and NZ$1 (US70¢) per extra passenger. Campervans cost around NZ$15 (US$11) and motorcycles NZ$4 (US$2.80) one-way.

By Water Taxi   The **Island Water Taxi** (book at the visitor center) offers 24-hour service; fares depend on the time of day and the number of passengers.

Northland

Cape Reinga
North Cape
Te Paki

Northland
Auckland
NORTH ISLAND
SOUTH ISLAND
Wellington
Christchurch
Dunedin

Pukenui
Karikari Peninsula
Matai Bay
Tokerau Beach
Doubtless Bay
Taipa
Taupo Bay
Stephenson Island
Awanui
Mangonui
Tauranga Bay
Cavalli Islands
Kaitaia
Cable Bay
Coopers Beach
Whangaroa
Ahipara
Kaeo

PACIFIC OCEAN

Broadwood
Waipapa
Kerikeri
Bay of Islands
Cape Brett
Waitangi
Mitimiti
Rawene
Ohaeawai
Haruru Falls
Russell
Paihia
Opononi
Taheke
Kaikohe
Oakura Bay
Hokianga Harbour
Omapere
Waimamaku
WAIPOURA KAURI FOREST
Tawai
Whananaki
TROUNSON KAURI PARK
Hikurangi
Matapouri
Aranga
Parakao
Kamo
Tutukaka
Kaihu
Avoca
Whangarei
Maungatapere
Mauou
Poor Knights Islands
Mamaranui
Baylys Beach
Dargaville
Onerahi
One Tree Point
Marsden Point
McLeod Bay
Ruakaka
Glinks Gully
Waipu
Hen & Chicken Islands

Tasman Sea

Paparoa
Maungaturoto
Ruawai
Matakoha
Kaiwaka
Rototuna
Tinopai
Wellsford
Pakiri
Kaipara Lighthouse
Pouto
Hateo North
Tapora
Tauhes
Leigh
Kaipara Harbour
Mangakura
Warkworth
South Head
Martins Bay
Orewa
Kaukapakapa
Silverdale
Whangaparoa
Helensville
Takapuni
Waitakere
Henderson
Auckland

0   30 mi
0   30 km
N

By Tour   Several companies in Auckland offer 1-, 2-, and 3-day tours to the Bay of Islands and beyond. For good value and personal service, contact **Great Sights** (© **0800/744-487** in NZ; www.greatsights.co.nz). **Northliner Express** (© **09/307-5873;** www.northliner.co.nz) also has a range of packages and good-value **backpacker passes.** Tours to Cape Reinga operate from Bay of Islands, Doubtless Bay, and Kaitaia (see "To Cape Reinga," below).

ORIENTATION   **Paihia** and **Waitangi** basically form one settlement, which is the hub of the region's commercial and visitor action. All tours and cruises for the Bay of Islands start here. It's a short (1.6km/1-mile) walk to Waitangi, where the historic Treaty House is located. The main street is Marsden Road, which runs along the waterfront. Williams Road is a one-way street perpendicular to the coast; many of the shops are here.

Russell is a tiny community across the water. The Strand runs along the waterfront. Most of the charter boats in the area are anchored here; access is by ferry.

Kerikeri is a 20-minute drive north from Paihia. Once you turn off State Highway 10 onto Kerikeri Road, you'll find most of the main attractions and eateries.

In **Doubtless Bay,** the little fishing village of **Mangonui** (82km/51 miles from Paihia) is the core settlement. **Coopers Beach, Cable Bay, Taipa,** and **Tokerau Beach** are all within a few minutes of Mangonui. From Cable Bay, the coast swings in a huge arc of fabulous remote beaches all the way up to **Karikari Peninsula.**

Kaitaia is the major town of the Far North, 116km (72 miles) south of Cape Reinga. To the southwest lies the small town of **Ahipara** at the base of **Ninety Mile Beach,** which runs all the way up to the Cape.

VISITOR INFORMATION   You'll find the **Bay of Islands i-Site Visitor Centre,** The Wharf, Marsden Road, Paihia (© **0800/363-463** in NZ, or 09/402-7345; fax 09/402-7314; www.fndc.govt.nz). Hours are 8am to 5pm in winter, 8am to 8pm in summer. Get your Kerikeri information here, too. Online, go to www.northlandnz.com, www.twincoast.co.nz, www.russell.gen.nz, www.paihia.co.nz, or www.kerikeri.co.nz.

The **Far North i-Site Visitor Centre** is at Jaycee Park, South Road, Kaitaia (© **09/408-0879;** fax 09/408-2546; www.fndc.govt.nz). It's open daily from 8:30am to 5pm, closed only December 25. For information on Ahipara, Ninety Mile Beach, and Far North activities, see www.ahipara.co.nz or www.topofnz.co.nz.

SPECIAL EVENTS   **Waitangi Day** on February 6 is a national holiday and cultural day and Paihia is the focus events. In late January the **Bay of Islands Sailing Week Regatta** is staged. The **Russell Spring Festival** is held in early September; and the **Bay of Islands Jazz and Blues Festival** (© **09/402-7345**) runs day and night from early to mid-August at various venues around Paihia and Russell.

EXPLORING THE TOWNS
IN PAIHIA/WAITANGI
Waitangi Treaty Grounds ✸✸✸   Even if you're not interested in history, I guarantee you'll love it here. This 506-hectare (1,250-acre) reserve has had a massive facelift, and quite apart from its historical importance, there are fabulous boardwalks through beautiful parklike grounds and mangrove swamps. It's somewhere you can comfortably spend 2 hours.

It was on the grounds of the small Georgian house that the Confederation of Chiefs signed the first treaty with the British government. The treaty granted to the Maori the rights of British subjects in exchange for recognition of British sovereignty. (See appendix A for more information.) The home of James Busby from 1832 to 1880, the broad lawn was the scene of colorful meetings between Maori and Pakeha during the treaty negotiations on February 6, 1840. Inside, you'll see a facsimile of the treaty written in Maori, an exhibition of James Busby's family mementos, and rooms with period furnishings.

The reserve is also home to one of the most magnificent *Whare Runanga* (meeting-houses) in the country, complete with an inspiring sound-and-light show. The house contains elaborately carved panels from all the Maori tribes in New Zealand. Just below the sweeping lawn, on Hobson's Beach, is an impressive 35m-long (115-ft.) Maori *waka* (war canoe) made for the treaty centennial celebrations from three giant kauri trees.

If your visit coincides with the February 6 celebration of **Waitangi Day,** you'll find the center of activity is the Waitangi National Trust Estate. There's lots of Maori song and dance, plus Pakeha officials in abundance, dressed to the nines in uniforms of then and now. Reserve way ahead, as it's a huge family day with crowds of vacationing Kiwis in attendance.

Waitangi Treaty Grounds, Waitangi. (C) **09/402-7437.** Fax 09/402-8303. www.waitangi.net.nz. Admission NZ$10 (US$7) adults, free for children 14 and under. Waitangi Garden tours plus admission NZ$20 (US$14). Apr–Sept daily 9am–5pm; Oct–Mar daily 9am–6pm. Closed Dec 25.

Culture North 𝕽𝕽   Located in the Waitangi Estate grounds, this addition to the cultural program has been a finalist in the New Zealand Tourism Awards. It tells the 1,000-year story of the Maori people from the discovery of New Zealand through to the present day. Combining drama with a stunning light and dance show, it's sure to please. It's a 2-hour program, and they provide hotel pickup service. They also provide guided tours of the treaty grounds, a marae visit, and other Maori cultural experiences.

Waitangi, RD2, Okaihau. (C)/fax **09/402-5990** or 09/401-9301. www.culturenorth.co.nz. Admission NZ$45 (US$32) adults, NZ$23 (US$16) children 3–15. Tour of treaty grounds NZ$20 (US$14) per person. Mon, Wed–Thurs, and Sat 7:30–9:30pm.

IN RUSSELL

Russell is a veritable minefield of historic sites. This is where the great Maori chief Hone Heke burned everything except the mission property, and chopped down the flagstaff (four times) in defiance of British rule.

Tips Heritage Journeys

For a truly unique cultural experience, you can now join two separate Maori tour groups in a traditional *waka* (canoe). **Taiamai Tours** ((C) **027/290-7047** in NZ, or 09/405-9990 evenings; www.taiamaitours.co.nz) invites you to paddle a canoe alongside members of the Ngapuhi tribe. It's the more traditional of the two experiences and includes traditional prayers, speechmaking, a visit to a sacred island, and a stopover at a mussel bed. It departs from Horotutu Beach at Paihia at 10am, 1pm, and 3pm (weather permitting) and costs from NZ$50 (US$35) adults, NZ$25 (US$18) children. **Te Waka Tours** ((C) **09/402-7017;** nicktipene@hotmail.com) takes you to Russell and back in an outrigger canoe. Hear stories, sing songs, and enjoy the scenery on a 2½-hour trip that costs from NZ$65 (US$46).

If you plan to wander the historic sites, first visit the **Russell Museum** *ℰ*, 2 York St. (℃/fax **09/403-7701;** rslmuseum@xtra.co.nz), open daily from 10am to 4pm (or 5pm in summer). Admission is around NZ$5 (US$3.50) for adults and NZ$1 (US70¢) for children. You can learn all about Maori-European contact and pick up heritage brochures pointing out other sites in the village. Behind the museum, check out the **Bay of Islands Maritime Park Headquarters and Visitors Centre,** The Strand (℃ **09/403-7685;** fax 09/403-7649). Its free 15-minute audiovisual *The Land is Enduring* gives an overview of Maori-European history in the area. It's open from 8:30am to 4:30pm (or 5pm in summer).

Farther down The Strand, you'll find **Pompallier** *ℰℰ* (℃ **09/403-9015;** www.historic.org.nz). Built in 1841, this is New Zealand's oldest surviving Roman Catholic building. It housed a printing press used from 1842 to 1849 to print religious documents in the Maori language. Today, along with the press, there's a working tannery and bookbindery. Tours are given at 10:15am, 11:15am, 1:15pm, and 3:15pm. Admission is NZ$5 (US$3.50) for adults and free for children.

For a look at the oldest wooden church in New Zealand, go to **Christ Church,** Church Street and Robertson Road. You can't miss the dear little building surrounded by colorful flowering hibiscus bushes. It's open from 9am to 5pm.

IN KERIKERI

The pretty town of Kerikeri has the most to offer in the Bay of Islands in the way of land-based attractions. Visiting the **Kerikeri Basin** *ℰℰℰ* is essential if you want to continue the historic theme. It's home to New Zealand's oldest stone building, the **1835 Stone Store.** Next door you'll see **Kemp House,** the first mission house and the oldest wooden house in the country. **Northern Steamship Company** (℃ **0800/944-785** in NZ, or ℃/fax 09/407-9229; www.steamship.co.nz) offers 1-hour cruises of Kerikeri Inlet aboard SS *Eliza Hobson,* departing from The Stone Store between 11am and 2pm in summer (reduced sailings in winter). The cost is NZ$25 (US$18) for adults, NZ$10 (US$7) for children, and NZ$65 (US$46) for a family.

Above the Basin is the well-preserved **Kororipo *Pa*,** a fort occupied by the fearsome chief Hongi Hika; across the river from the *pa* site is **Rewa Village** *ℰℰ* (℃ **09/407-6454**), a full-scale reconstruction of a *kainga* (fortified pre-European Maori fishing village). It's open daily; admission is NZ$5 (US$3.50) for adults and NZ$1 (US70¢) for children.

Garden enthusiasts should also enjoy **Wharepuke Subtropical Garden,** 190 Kerikeri Rd., Stone Store Hill (℃ **09/407-8933;** fax 09/407-8975; www.sub-tropicals.co.nz),which is a growing "art gallery" of subtropical plants. It's open daily 7:30am to 6pm. A self-guided tour costs NZ$5 (US$3.50) and tours (maximum six people) are NZ$20 (US$14) per person by appointment. **The Parrot Place** *ℰℰ*, 1 Mission Rd., Kerikeri (℃ **09/407-5146**), will delight with its collection of multicolored parrots from Asia, Australia, Africa, New Guinea, South America, and the Solomon Islands. Admission is around NZ$5 (US$3.50) adults and NZ$2.50 (US$1.75) for school-age children.

Kerikeri is also home to a thriving arts community. Pick up the free brochure *The Kerikeri Art & Craft Trail ℰℰℰ*, which details 17 excellent outlets within a few kilometers of Kerikeri. **Keriblue Ceramics** *ℰℰ*, 560 Kerikeri Rd. (℃ **09/407-4634;** fax 09/407-5588; www.keriblue.co.nz), is especially fine. It's open 9:30am to 5pm daily. Directly opposite is the **Kauri Workshop** (℃ **09/407-9196;** kauriw@xtra.co.nz), where you can watch Brian Cliffin making swamp kauri bowls.

You haven't lived until you've savored the unspeakably indulgent pleasures of **Makana Confections** 𝔊𝔊𝔊 (© **09/407-6800;** www.makana.co.nz), right beside the Kauri Workshop. The hand-dipped chocolates are indescribable—try them yourself at the tasting bar and watch the whole process through glass windows; it's open daily 9am to 5:30pm. Then sample the 100% homemade and natural taste sensations produced by **Bay of Islands Ice Cream Company** 𝔊𝔊, 84 Kerikeri Rd. (© **09/407-8136;** fax 09/407-8109).

To sample Northland wines, head for **Cottle Hill Winery,** Cottle Hill Drive (© **09/407-5203;** www.cottlehill.co.nz), open daily 10am to 5pm with tastings for NZ$5 (US$3.50); **Marsden Estate Winery,** Wiroa Road, Kerikeri (© **09/407-9398;** www.marsenestate.co.nz), open daily 10am to 5pm September through June, and 10am to 4pm Tuesday to Sunday July and August; or **Bishops Wood Estate,** 1329 St. Hwy. 10 (© **09/407-9628;** bishopswood@value.net.nz), open daily 10am until late.

For fine New Zealand–made skincare products, free of all synthetic preservatives or synthetic parabens, check out the highly successful **Living Nature** 𝔊𝔊𝔊, State Highway 10 (© **0508/548-464** in NZ, or 09/407-7895; www.livingnature.com).

IN THE FAR NORTH

The **Wagener-Subritzky Homestead,** Houhora Heads Road, RD4, Kaitaia (© **09/409-8850;** wagenerpark@xtra.co.nz), was the area's first, built in 1860, and its original inhabitants owned or leased almost all the land between Awanui and Cape Reinga—about 12,600 hectares (31,122 acres). Admission is NZ$15 (US$11) for adults and NZ$7.50 (US$5.25) for children, and it is open on request every day except Christmas Day and Good Friday. It's a 40km (25-mile) drive north of Kaitaia, signposted off the Main Road to Cape Reinga. The scenery is stunning, and there's also a cafe, a souvenir shop, dinghies for hire, bullock rides, fabulous beach swimming, a backpackers lodge, and a campground.

The other must-see is the **Ancient Kauri Kingdom** 𝔊𝔊, State Highway 1, Awanui (©/fax **09/406-7172;** www.ancientkauri.co.nz), 7km (4⅓ miles) north of Kaitaia. You can view massive 30,000- to 50,000 year-old kauri logs that have been hauled from the Northland swamps, then see the fine furniture and crafts that are made from them. It's open daily, and admission is free. You can also see the remnants of ancient buried kauri forests, over 42,000 years old, at **Gumdiggers Park,** Heath Road, Waiharara (© **09/406-7166;** www.gumdiggerspark.co.nz). It's 25km (16 miles) north of Kaitaia and is open daily. It will also give you an insight into the tough lives of the early gum-digging pioneers.

In the Taipa area, **Matthews Vintage Collection,** State Highway 10, 5km (3 miles) north of Taipa (© **09/406-0203;** winm-lynk@xtra.co.nz), has an extensive array of restored vintage cars, tractors, and farm and domestic equipment; **Butler Point Whaling Museum,** Butler Point, Hihi Road, Mangonui (© **09/406-0006;** www.butlerpoint.co.nz), features Capt. William Butler's residence (1847) and whaling memorabilia; and **Laurel's Soaps & Gifts,** Waterfront Road, Mangonui (© **09/406-0939;** laurels@xtra.co.nz), is home to New Zealand's largest producer of 100% natural handcrafted soaps and skincare products.

ORGANIZED TOURS & CRUISES

There's no need to prebook before arriving in town, as there are plenty of operators; by shopping around, you'll get better deals. The only exception is between December 23 and January 15. If you're planning to visit then, you'll need to reserve ahead.

Family-owned **Kings,** Maritime Building, Waterfront, Paihia (© **0800/222-979** in NZ, or 09/402-8288; www.kings-tours.co.nz), has a wide selection of tours. The most popular is the **Bay in a Day Tour** 🐬🐬, which includes swimming with dolphins, a trip to the Hole in the Rock (a large natural rock formation that rises up from the ocean with a hole in it, forming a tunnel that boats can pass through), and boom netting off the back of the boat. It costs about NZ$95 (US$67), runs from 9:30am to 4pm, and includes an island stopover for lunch (bring your own).

Fullers Bay of Islands, Maritime Building, Waterfront, Paihia (© **0800/653-339** in NZ, or 09/402-7421; www.fullers-bay-of-islands.co.nz), also has several tours; for a full day, its best is the **Supercruise,** which combines the Cream Trip and the Hole in the Rock cruise. This costs from NZ$95 (US$67) for adults and NZ$48 (US$34) for children.

TO CAPE REINGA

You'll be hard-pressed to find more dazzling seascapes than those on your way to **Cape Reinga** 🐬🐬🐬. The cape is situated at the top of Aupouri Peninsula, which features famous **Ninety Mile Beach** and three magnificent harbors: **Parengarenga,** with silica sand so white you need dark glasses; **Houhora;** and **Pukenui.** The **Cape Reinga Lighthouse** stands above the battling currents of the Tasman Sea and the Pacific Ocean coming together.

Private cars are not allowed on Ninety Mile Beach, which can be hazardous because of tidal sweeps, quicksand, run-off channels, sand holes, and plankton build-up. Leave the driving to the experts: Take one of the numerous coach tours to the cape, and you'll be able to make the return trip down the hard-packed sands, stopping first at the mountainous **Te Paki sand dunes** 🐬🐬🐬 and **quicksand stream.**

Note: The round-trip from the Bay of Islands to Cape Reinga by private car takes about 7 hours—and that's not allowing for decent stops en route. A day tour from

---

Moments **Swimming with Dolphins**

Dolphin lovers, rejoice. There are plenty of these gorgeous creatures in the waters of Bay of Islands. The common dolphins often pass through, and there's a resident population of bottle-nosed dolphins. Four operators are licensed to swim with dolphins: **Kings** (© **09/402-8288**), which charges around NZ$95 (US$67) for adults and NZ$50 (US$35) for children; **Fullers Dolphin Adventures** (© **09/402-7421**), with rates of NZ$99 (US$69) for adults and NZ$50 (US$35) for children; **Dolphin Discoveries** (© **09/402-8234**; www.dolphinz.co.nz), charging NZ$99 (US$69) for adults and NZ$59 (US$41) for children; and **Carino Yacht Charters** (© **09/402-8040**; info@sailingdolphins.co.nz), with rates of around NZ$80 (US$56) per adult and NZ$40 (US$28) per child for a full day's sail, snorkeling, beach games, and dolphin swimming. The Kings trip is the longest (6½ hours) and is the only combo trip that includes boom netting, the Hole in the Rock, and dolphin swimming. It should be noted that swimming with dolphins has its critics and supporters. You may want to visit the Whale and Dolphins Conservation Society's website at www.wdcs.org. For more information about responsible travel in general, check out these websites: Tread Lightly (www.treadlightly.org) and the International Ecotourism Society (www.ecotourism.org).

Kaitaia is a more reasonable alternative. I'd strongly advise you to spend an extra night and stay at Doubtless Bay or Kaitaia so you can do the area justice without feeling rushed.

FROM PAIHIA   You can take a full-day Cape Reinga tour with **Kings** (© 09/402-8288) for around NZ$95 (US$67) per adult and NZ$48 (US$34) per child. **Fullers Northland** (© 09/402-7421)—the more family oriented of the two—also has a full-day tour taking in slightly different things along the way; it costs about NZ$115 (US$81) with lunch, NZ$99 (US$69) without lunch. **Awesome Adventures,** Maritime Building, Paihia (© 09/402-6985; www.awesomenz.com), is less formal, attracts a younger crowd, and stops at a fish-and-chip shop to eat. It costs NZ$95 (US$67) for a full day and is less likely to have children on board. See "Organized Tours & Cruises," above, for more information.

FROM KAITAIA   Go with a full-day excursion from **Sand Safaris Cape Reinga Tours,** 221 Commerce St., Kaitaia (© 0800/869-090 in NZ, or 09/408-1778; www.sandsafaris.co.nz), or **Harrisons Cape Runner Tours,** 123 North Rd., Kaitaia (© 0800/227-373 in NZ, or 09/408-1033; www.ahipara.co.nz/caperunner). The cost is around NZ$55 (US$39) for adults and NZ$35 (US$25) for children.

FROM MANGONUI (DOUBTLESS BAY)   You can do a day tour with **Paradise Connexion** (© 09/406-0460).

OUTDOOR PURSUITS

BEACHES   The farther north you go, the better and more deserted the beaches get. Those on **Karikari Peninsula** 🜲🜲🜲 have always been my favorites, but good swimming beaches dominate the whole northeast coast, from Auckland up.

FAST BOATING   **Excitor,** Maritime Building, Paihia (© 09/402-7020; www.excitor.co.nz), can take you out to the Hole in the Rock in *Excitor* for around NZ$68 (US$48) for adults, NZ$34 (US$24) for children 14 and under. Also charging similar rates is **Kings'** *Mack Attack* (© 09/402-8180).

FISHING   Light-line fishing is affordable; the visitor center in Paihia can furnish you with a list of fishing charters. Most supply rods and bait and run 3- to 5-hour trips. Snapper fishing is especially popular; it ranges from NZ$50 to NZ$120 (US$35–US$84) for a 4-hour boat trip.

GOLF   You can arrange to play at the beautiful 18-hole waterfront **Waitangi Golf Club** (©/fax 09/402-7713; www.waitangigolf.co.nz). Greens fees are around NZ$40 (US$28) per person. Club, shoe, and cart hire available.

KAYAKING   **Coastal Kayakers,** Paihia (© 09/402-8105; www.coastalkayakers.co.nz), can take you to explore waterfalls, mangrove swamps, and a deserted island. No experience is necessary. A 4-hour trip costs NZ$50 (US$35); a full-day trip is NZ$70 (US$49). Farther north in the Tauranga Bay area, **Northland Sea Kayaking,** Tauranga Bay Road, Northland (© 09/405-0381; northlandseakayaking@xtra.co.nz), is more of a wilderness experience, with accommodations provided on private beaches. Full and half-day tours range from NZ$60 to NZ$80 (US$42–US$56).

MOUNTAIN BIKING   You can rent bikes for around NZ$10 (US$7) per hour or from NZ$25 (US$18) per day from **Bay Beach Hire,** Marsden Road, Paihia (© 09/402-7905). It also rents catamarans, kayaks, dinghies, motors, windsurfers, and rowboats.

> ### Tips Sailing Away
>
> You won't find any shortage of charter yachts and yacht tours. The Kiwi Expe-
> rience (backpacker) crowd tends to favor **"She's a Lady" Island Sailing Adven-
> tures** (© 0800/724-584 in NZ, or 09/402-8119; www.bay-of-islands.com), which
> include knee boarding, fishing, and two island stops in the NZ$85-to-NZ$90
> (US$60–US$63) full-day outing; or **Straycat Sailing** (© 09/402-6130), which offers
> catamaran outings from 10am to 4pm for NZ$75 per adult and NZ$45 (US$32)
> per child (includes lunch). For the best value, consider **Gungha's Super Cruise**
> (© 0800/478-900 in NZ, or 09/407-7930; www.bayofislandssailing.co.nz), which
> has both the 14m (46-ft.) *Gungha* and a 20m (64-ft.) maxi yacht, *Gungha II*. It
> gets lots of repeat business for the full-day sailings, which include a scenic tour
> of the Bay of Islands with at least one island stopover and a yummy lunch for
> around NZ$75 (US$53) per adult. It has departures from Kerikeri, Paihia, and
> Russell. For a 3-day sailing adventure, join the friendly crew of **Ecocruz,** P.O. Box
> 91, Paihia (© 0800/432-6278 in NZ, or 025/592-153; www.ecocruz.co.nz), for
> around NZ$495 to NZ$575 (US$347–US$403). For a tall-ship adventure, step back
> in time with a voyage on the *R. Tucker Thompson,* Opua Wharf, Opua (© 0800/
> 882-537 in NZ, or 09/402-8430; www.tucker.co.nz). It sails from October to the
> end of April and costs NZ$110 (US$77) for adults and NZ$55 (US$39) for chil-
> dren. If you want to try New Zealand's fastest commercial sailing catamaran,
> contact the company called **Sail on the Edge,** Paihia (© 0800/724-569 in NZ, or
> 09/402-7900; www.sailnz.co.nz). Its 7m-long (72-ft.), 12m-wide (40-ft.) vessel is
> capable of speeds in excess of 30 knots. A day's outing costs around NZ$140
> (US$98) for adults, NZ$90 (US$63) for children.

PARASAILING   For a bird's-eye view of the islands, soar with **Flying Kiwi Parasail**
(© 09/402-6078 or 021/359-691; www.parasail-nz.co.nz) for NZ$70 to NZ$85
(US$49–US$60).

SCUBA DIVING   Several operators visit the Greenpeace *Rainbow Warrior* wreck.
Reliable companies include **Dive North** (© 09/402-7079; www.divenorth.co.nz),
Paihia Dive Hire (© 09/402-7551; www.divenz.com), and **Octopus Divers** (© 09/
407-4900; octopus@xtra.co.nz). It's an hour's boat ride to the Cavalli Islands, where
you'll find the wreck in 25m (82 ft.) of water off Matauri Bay. Prices start around
NZ$200 (US$140) for a wreck trip.

SKYDIVING   Bay of Islands SkyDive Centre (© 0800/427-593 in NZ, or 09/
402-6744 or 021/756-758; www.skydive4fun.com) can ease you out of an aircraft and
into the skies for NZ$200 (US$140), and you won't soon forget the sensation of floating over those stunning islands.

WALKING   Around the Bay of Islands, you can't go past the boardwalks and walkways in the **Waitangi National Trust Estate** . The visitor center in Paihia can
furnish details of all the trails, as well as the very good booklet *Walking in the Bay of
Islands Maritime and Historic Park* (NZ$3/US$2.10). The **Park Visitor Centre** in
Russell, P.O. Box 134 (© 09/403-7685; fax 09/403-7649), or the **Ranger Station** in
Kerikeri (© 09/407-8474) can help with trail maps and details. There are also some
beautiful campsites, some on uninhabited islands in the bay, with nominal per-night

fees. You must reserve with the park rangers in Russell. Try the **Kerikeri River Walk**—it's an easy 1-hour hike to **Rainbow Falls.**

WHERE TO STAY

Remember one important fact if you want to stay in the Bay of Islands: From December to January, the population swells from a mere 2,000 to over 30,000. Reserve well in advance.

Paihia has the biggest concentration of motels and hotels, while Russell and Kerikeri offer more bed-and-breakfast options. Paihia is definitely the most convenient place to stay if you intend to take lots of tours and participate in organized activities. It also has the better food outlets, and you won't have to worry about missing the last ferry to Russell. Russell is the place to be if you want a quiet spot—for most of the time, there are far fewer people here, but I wouldn't go so far as to say that it's less touristy. Rates below include 12.5% GST and free parking.

Backpacker Paradise

Backpackers will think they've arrived in paradise: Paihia is the best-serviced backpacker town in the country. There are around 10 top-quality backpacker lodges, most of them cheek-by-jowl on Kings Road. **Pipi Patch Lodge**, 18 Kings Rd., Paihia (℃ **0800/005-127** in NZ, or 09/402-7111), attracts a lot of the Kiwi Experience buses. It's just 50m (164 ft.) from the beach and has a pool set in a sunny courtyard; every room has its own bathroom. **Lodge Eleven Backpackers-YHA** 𝒜, MacMurray and Kings roads, Paihia (℃/fax **09/402-7487**; www.yha.co.nz), is highly rated; every room has its own shower and toilet. Located 100m (328 ft.) from the beach, the place is immaculate and has personalized service.

Peppertree Lodge 𝒜𝒜, 15 Kings Rd., Paihia (℃ **09/402-6122**; www.peppertree.co.nz), was built for backpacker comfort and is seen by many as the best of the best. **The Pickled Parrot Backpackers Lodge,** Grey's Lane (℃ **0508/727-768** in NZ, or 09/402-6222; www.pickledparrot.co.nz), is the smallest backpacker lodge and offers free breakfast. **Captain Bob's Backpackers,** 44 Davis Crescent (℃/fax **09/402-8668**; Tommys@xtra.co.nz), has awesome ocean views from a quiet elevated location. **The Mousetrap Backpackers,** 11 Kings Rd. (℃ **09/402-8182**; www.mousetrap.co.nz), is another small one (25 people only) in a big old house with sunny balconies.

Centabay Lodge, 27 Selwyn Rd. (℃ **09/402-7466**; www.centabay.co.nz), is the closest to the bus stop, wharf, shops, and beach, and has a range of accommodations, good communal facilities, and a friendly atmosphere. Last but not least is the **Saltwater Lodge** 𝒜𝒜, 14 Kings Rd. (℃ **0800/002-266** in NZ, or 09/402-7075; www.saltwaterlodge.co.nz), which has top facilities and private bathrooms in every unit. New on the scene is the well-endowed **Bay Adventurer Apartments & Backpacker Resort,** 28 Kings Rd. (℃ **0800/112-127** in NZ, or 09/402-5162; www.bayadventurer.co.nz); its swimming pool and Jacuzzi are big draws.

If you want information about Department of Conservation campsites in Northland, contact **Department of Conservation Visitor Centre,** 92 Otaika Rd., Whangarei (© 09/430-2007).

IN PAIHIA/OPUA

In addition to the options listed below, you might try the reasonably priced **Paihia Pacific Resort Hotel** ℛ, 27 Kings Rd. (© **0800/744-442** in NZ, or 09/402-8221; www.paihiapacific.co.nz)—it's 35 units (NZ$150–NZ$190/US$105–US$133) are away from the main hotel stretch, surrounded by palm trees and lush gardens.

Bay of Islands Lodge ℛℛℛ *(Finds)*   Just 2 years old, this sophisticated custom-built gem is tucked into a bush-clad hillside with just native birds for company. Simply put, it's divine. From the French oak floors and the large, stylish living rooms to the big bedrooms with decks and state-of-the-art fittings, you'll want for nothing. It's beautifully done and fabulous value.

St. Hwy. 11, Paihia Rd., Opua. ©/fax **09/402-6075.** www.bayofislandslodge.co.nz. 4 units. NZ$450–NZ$580 (US$315–US$406). Rates include breakfast and open bar. Dinner NZ$95 (US$67) per person, by arrangement. Off-peak rates. AE, MC, V. Well signposted on Paihia Rd., just after Opua Hill, before you enter the township. 5 min. by car from Paihia. **Amenities:** Heated outdoor pool; nearby golf course and tennis courts; tour bookings; car rentals; courtesy transport to Paihia; free laundry service; nonsmoking rooms; on-call doctor/dentist; airport transfers; access for travelers w/disabilities w/elevator. *In room:* TV/VCR, dataport, hair dryer, safe.

Cliff Edge by the Sea ℛℛℛ   If views are important to you, they don't come better than this and yes, it is definitely on the cliff edge. It has a more family-home atmosphere than Bay of Islands Lodge and is a member of Select Hotels. Hosts Peter and Glennis Meier go out of their way to ensure privacy and the best of comforts. Peter is also a superb chef. The Waitangi room has a big corner Jacuzzi and four-poster bed; the Kowahi is cool; Okiato has the best view; and in Waikare, you can wake to the sunrise.

3 Richardson Rd. W., Opua. ©/fax **09/402-6074.** www.cliffedge.co.nz. 4 units. NZ$380–NZ$480 (US$266–US$336). Rates include breakfast and open bar. Dinner NZ$95 (US$67) per person by arrangement. AE, MC, V. Off-peak rates. Located 5 min. by car from Paihia. As you rise over Opua Hill, S11 forks. Right is the Russell car ferry at Opua; left takes you to Paihia. Go straight ahead to English Bay, wind downhill and Richardson Rd. W. is the 3rd on the right. **Amenities:** Nearby golf course; cliff-edge Jacuzzi; sauna; tour bookings; car rentals; courtesy transport to Paihia; massage; free laundry service; nonsmoking rooms; on-call doctor/dentist; airport transfers. *In room:* TV/VCR, dataport, hair dryer, safe.

Copthorne Hotel & Resort ℛ *(Value)*   This is a standard hotel in a unique and stunning location, right beside Waitangi National Trust, the sea, and a wealth of walking opportunities. Factor in quietness and one of the best outdoor swimming pool complexes in the country and you'll understand why this one's easy to recommend. Eighty-five percent of the recently refurbished (2005) rooms are king/splits with either sea views (premium) or garden views (standard). The one-level Hibiscus wing overlooks the pool and in the Seaspray wing every room has a deck or balcony. Don't be put off by tour groups; there's room for everyone.

Tau Henare Dr., Paihia. © **0800/808-228** in NZ, or 09/402-7411. Fax 09/402-8200. www.copthornebayofislands. co.nz. 145 units. NZ$146–NZ$200 (US$102–US$140). Long-stay and off-peak rates. B&B deals on special packages. AE, DC, MC, V. Located around the bay from Paihia township—5 min. by car; 25-min. walk. **Amenities:** Restaurant; bar; outdoor solar-heated pool; nearby golf course; outdoor all-weather tennis courts; Jacuzzi; bike rentals; tour bookings; car rentals; courtesy transport to Paihia every hour; secretarial services; 24-hr. room service; massage; babysitting; coin-operated washers/dryers; laundry service; same-day dry cleaning; nonsmoking rooms; foreign-currency exchange; on-call doctor/dentist; airport transfers; limited access for travelers w/disabilities. *In room:* TV, dataport, minibar, fridge, coffeemaker, hair dryer, iron, safe.

Sanctuary Palms ★★★ *Value*   Three gorgeous, modern, self-contained apartments, each with their own character, sit high over Paihia township (which is a 5-minute walk away) offering style, luxury, and privacy. The ground-floor room, Moulin Rouge, has a stunning bathroom and, like all the apartments here, truly feels like your home away from home. This is an ideal place for families, two couples traveling together, or the perfect romantic getaway. The upstairs Pasifika has a bigger lounge and balcony with a bush outlook; and the cool Waterfall room opens onto the garden waterfall.

31 Bayview Rd., Paihia. © **09/402-5428.** Fax 09/402-5427. www.sanctuarypalms.com. 3 units. NZ$350–NZ$450 (US$245–US$315). MC, V. Rates include a welcome food basket. Special packages available. **Amenities:** Nearby golf course; tour bookings; car rentals; massage; full laundry in each apt; nonsmoking rooms; on-call doctor/dentist; airport transfers. *In room:* TV/VCR, dataport, full kitchens, fridge, coffeemaker, hair dryer, iron.

IN RUSSELL

A lot of the lodgings on this side of the water are high-priced for what you get, so shop around. Personally I think you get value for money in the Paihia-Opua area. For a budget-conscious stay, head for the **Top 10 Holiday Park,** Longbeach Road, Russell (© **09/403-7826;** fax 09/403-7221; russelltop10@xtra.co.nz). **Kimberley Lodge,** 2 Pitt St. (© **09/403-7090;** www.lodges.co.nz), is a beautiful home right in the middle of the village, but its rates—NZ$692 to NZ$804 (US$484–US$563), dinner around NZ$100 (US$70) per person—are on the steep side. More modestly priced are the **Te Maiki Villas** ★, Flagstaff Road (© **0800/156-777** in NZ, or 09/403-7046; www.temaikivillas.co.nz). Its nine smart three-bedroom villas have spectacular views and go from around NZ$175 to NZ$325 (US$123–US$228).

You might also enjoy the bright, refurbished, and unique **Triton Suites,** 7 Wellington St., Russell (© **09/403-8067;** www.tritonsuites.co.nz), which are close to town and have big Jacuzzis. **Aomotu Lodge,** 6 Ashby St., Russell (© **09/403-7693;** www.aomotulodge.com), has four beautifully appointed suites with spacious en suites in a character-filled home for around NZ$350 (US$245).

Eagles Nest ★★★ *Finds*   It's hard to find the words to adequately describe this sublime retreat. Daniel and Sandie Biskind found the perfect place for their world-class sanctuary and spared no expense in creating something you'll remember forever. Sacred Space is the main house, which contains three luxury suites—the living room converts to an in-house theater at the flick of a switch. Across the gorgeous pool is the two-story honeymoon love nest known as First Light Temple, and on a far hill, The Cottage offers a more low-key version of this sumptuous style. The core philosophy at Eagles Nest is: relax, regenerate, rejuvenate. It's an experience you'll relish and want to relive, over and over again.

60 Tapeka Rd., Russell. © **09/403-8333.** Fax 09/403-8880. www.eaglesnest.co.nz. 11 rooms in 4 self-contained units. NZ$2,025–NZ$3,938 (US$1,418–US$2,757). Rates include breakfast and airport transfers; dinner at extra charge. Long-stay, off-peak, and special deals available. AE, DC, MC, V. Drive up and over Flagstaff Hill in Russell township; Tapeka Rd. is the 2nd left after the brow of the hill. **Amenities:** Exclusive dining room (spa cuisine) w/10,000-bottle wine cellar; heated outdoor pool; helicopter access to Kauri Cliffs luxury golf club; Jacuzzi; sauna; gym equipment in each villa; free bikes; concierge; tour bookings; car rentals; secretarial services; massage; babysitting; laundry service; dry cleaning; nonsmoking rooms; on-call doctor/dentist; airport transfers; access for travelers w/disabilities. *In room:* A/C in 1 villa, TV/VCR, fax, dataport, kitchen, minibar, fridge, coffeemaker, hair dryer, iron, safe.

Orongo Bay Homestead ★   This is a simple, tranquil haven in what was New Zealand's first American Consulate in the 1860s. It's a charming old home set amid acres of big trees and organically certified gardens. The Consul's Room is the best in the house, with wonderful garden views, but my favorite is the Retreat, which is built out over a stream, with doors opening onto a balcony where you can sit and watch the ducks in complete silence. If you want even more privacy, go for the two Barn Rooms that sit across the stream in a lovely meadow. Delicious dinners are derived from the garden's organic produce; in summer, these are enjoyed on the veranda.

Aucks Rd., RD1, Russell. (C) **0800/242-627** in NZ, or 09/403-7527. Fax 09/403-7675. www.thehomestead.co.nz. 4 units. NZ$650 (US$455). Rates include breakfast; 4-course organic dinner by arrangement. Long-stay, off-peak rates, and special deals available. AE, DC, MC, V. **Amenities:** Bar; nearby golf course; sauna; tour bookings; massage; laundry service; nonsmoking rooms; on-call doctor/dentist; airport transfers; access for travelers w/disabilities. *In room:* Dataport, fridge in 2 units, coffeemaker, hair dryer, iron.

IN KERIKERI

Kerikeri YHA Hostel, 144 Kerikeri Rd. ((C) **09/407-9391;** www.yha.co.nz), has twin, dorm, and family rooms from NZ$20 to NZ$24 (US$14–US$17) per person, plus tent sites. New on the B&B scene is the very pleasing **Pukanui Bed & Breakfast** 𝔊, 322 Kerikeri Rd., Kerikeri ((C) **09/407-7003;** www.pukanui.co.nz), which has three rooms with en-suite bathrooms in a contemporary home surrounded by a mandarin orchard and subtropical gardens. Guest rooms (NZ$130–NZ$175/US$91–US$123) overlook a swimming pool and are just a 10-minute walk to town.

Kauri Cliffs 𝔊𝔊𝔊 *(Moments)*   Set on 2,630 hectares (6,500 acres) of rolling coastal farmland, Kauri Cliffs golf club and lodge offers world-class facilities with an unforgettable view—not to mention the par-72 David Harman–designed golf course that sweeps along the cliff tops (voted 49th best in the world by *Golf* magazine). If you want premium pampering in a breathtaking setting, this is the place—luxury and comfort are a given, and every whim can be catered to. Rooms are spacious, bathrooms luxurious, and style greets you at every turn. It's much bigger and more extensively appointed than Eagle's Nest in Russell, but it has that same distinctive mark of quality that discerning international travelers expect. A new world-class health spa will be completed in 2006—just another reason to linger in "paradise."

Matauri Bay, 25 min. northeast of Kerikeri. (C) **09/405-1900.** Fax 09/405-1901. www.kauricliffs.com. 22 units. NZ$1,125–NZ$2,200 (US$788–US$1,540) suites; NZ$5,175–NZ$6,187 (US$3,623–US$4,330) cottage. Rates include predinner drinks, hors d'oeuvres, a la carte dinner, full breakfast, use of all facilities except golf, and airport transfers. Off-season rates and special deals available. AE, DC, MC, V. Located 20 min. from Kerikeri Airport; detailed driving instructions provided on request. **Amenities:** Restaurant (gents require jacket); several bars; outdoor heated pool; world-class golf course on property; 2 tennis courts; large gym; 2 outdoor Jacuzzis; mountain bikes; concierge; car rentals; business services; salon; massage; babysitting; laundry service; same-day dry cleaning; nonsmoking rooms; on-call doctor/dentist. *In room:* TV/DVD, dataport, kitchenette, minibar, fridge, coffeemaker, hair dryer, iron, safe.

The Summer House 𝔊𝔊   If you're garden lovers, you'll be right at home here among citrus orchards and subtropical gardens. Hosts Christine and Rod Brown are passionate about plants and their peaceful retreat will seduce you into a long stay. The two upstairs bedrooms both have showers and views over the pond. But my preference is for the self-contained, downstairs semidetached suite, which has a Pacific theme and a much bigger bathroom.

424 Kerikeri Rd. (C) **09/407-4294.** Fax 09/407-4297. www.thesummerhouse.co.nz. 3 units. NZ$175–NZ$275 (US$123–US$193). Rates include breakfast. Long-stay and off-season rates available. MC, V. No children under 12. **Amenities:** Tour bookings; car rentals; courtesy car; laundry service; same-day dry cleaning; nonsmoking rooms; on-call doctor/dentist. *In room:* Kitchenette in self-contained suite, minibar, coffeemaker, hair dryer, iron.

IN THE FAR NORTH

For a special treat, take yourself to the Karikari Peninsula, where you'll find some of the best beaches in New Zealand. You'll also find the superlative **Carrington** 𝔊𝔊𝔊,

Maitai Bay Road, Karikari Peninsula (℃ **09/408-7222;** www.carrington.co.nz), set amidst 3,000 hectares (7,410 acres) of rolling coastal land. It offers 10 spacious, modern suites that open onto wide verandas with beach views. Separate villas provide three-bedroom comforts with golf-course views. A resort par excellence, it's well worth going the extra mile. In Doubtless Bay, one of the best spots is **Beach Lodge** 𝍢, 121 St. Hwy. 10, Coopers Beach (℃/fax **09/406-0068;** www.beachlodge.co.nz). Its five delightful, two-bedroom, self-contained units are just a few paces from the white-sand beach; rates are NZ$385 to NZ$500 (US$270–US$350). The very pleasing **Taipa Bay Beach Resort** 𝍢𝍢, 22 Taipa Point Rd. (℃ **09/406-0656;** www.taipabay.co.nz), is 7km (4⅓ miles) north of Mangonui village. Their 32 suites and apartments allow you to enjoy sand and surf at your doorstep for around NZ$215–NZ$335 (US$151–US$235).

In Kaitaia are several motel options. You'll get a basic but comfortable sleep at **Sierra Court Motor Lodge,** 65 North Rd. (℃ **0800/666-022** in NZ, or 09/408-1461; fax 09/408-1436), for around NZ$95 to NZ$115 (US$67–US$81). It has a sheltered swimming pool, private Jacuzzi, game room, and play area. Further north at Houhora Heads, you'll find great waterfront camping at **Wagener Holiday Park & Backpacker Cabins** (℃ **09/409-8564;** www.northlandholiday.co.nz). Nonpowered sites cost around NZ$15 (US$11) per adult; powered sites are about NZ$30 (US$21) per night. Backpacker beds range from NZ$20 to NZ$25 (US$12–US$18) per person. At Ninety Mile Beach, try **Siesta Guest Lodge** 𝍢, 38 Tasman Heights, Ahipara (℃ **09/409-2011;** www.ahipara.co.nz/siesta), where you'll find four rooms from NZ$150 to NZ$275 (US$105–US$193). Farther south, near Dargaville and Waipoua Forest, check out **Waipoua Lodge** 𝍢𝍢𝍢, State Highway 12, Katui, Northland (℃ **09/439-0422;** www.waipoualodge.co.nz). This very welcome upmarket addition to Northland's west coast is a must. It features four stylish apartments set in gardens separate from the 120-year-old main villa and dining room.

WHERE TO DINE

The biggest and best concentration of restaurants and cafes is in Paihia, but there are some close rivals in nearby Kerikeri. As always in the provinces, service tends to wax and wane. **Caffe Over The Bay,** first floor, The Mall, Marsden Road, Paihia (℃ **09/402-6066**), still enjoys one of the best eatery locations in town but the food and service are not what they used to be. If you're only after coffee and a snack, I'd suggest you're better off in **Blue Marlin Café,** Marsden Road at street level below (no telephone), where they do an excellent range of burgers and light meals. **Café Jerusalem** 𝍢𝍢, 24 Kings Rd., Paihia (℃ **09/402-5001**), is very popular for its delicious Middle Eastern fare and good coffee. It's open 11am to 11pm daily. **Beach House Café** 𝍢, 16 Kings Rd. (℃ **09/402-7479**), gets the local vote for terrific gourmet burgers; and **The Sugar Boat Restaurant** 𝍢𝍢, Waitangi Bridge, Paihia (℃ **09/402-7018**), offers excellent meals in a unique ship setting.

IN PAIHIA

Bistro 40 𝍢 NEW ZEALAND CUISINE   Situated on Paihia's waterfront underneath Only Seafood, this sister establishment focuses on matching fine New Zealand flavors with top New Zealand wine brands. It's consistently recognized as one of the best in Paihia and while there's a strong seafood emphasis, they also offer steaks and venison. Save room for the tiramisu!

40 Marsden Rd., Paihia. © 09/402-7444. Reservations recommended. Main courses around NZ$30 (US$21). AE, DC, MC, V. Daily 6pm–late. Closed Dec 25.

Only Seafood 🍴🍴 SEAFOOD   The name says it all—seafood takes center stage here in a smart, white-walled, timber-floored interior. Start with delicious sushi and raw fish salads, then tuck into mains like a salmon filet filled with oysters, oven baked and served with sauce Provençale, or marinated, chargrilled, and served with teriyaki sauce. If you're a seafood lover, you'll be in seventh heaven.

40 Marsden Rd. (upstairs), Paihia. © 09/402-6066. Main courses NZ$25–NZ$28 (US$18–US$20). AE, DC, MC, V. Daily 5pm–late.

Waikokopu Café 🍴🍴 *(finds)* CAFE/LIGHT MEALS   Waikokopu wins with its dreamy lakeside, bush-enclosed location and its well-priced light meals. The menu changes regularly, but generally features delicious seafood like seared scallops with lightly curried banana served on jasmine rice oozing with peanut sauce. If your wallet is feeling thin, pig out on the pancake pileup—a stack of wild-berry pancakes topped with Greek yogurt, drizzled with honey, or served with bacon, banana, and maple syrup. Vegetarians and children are attended to, and you can't beat sipping a good espresso while sitting out on the timber deck overlooking the water.

Treaty Grounds, Waitangi. © 09/402-6275. Reservations required for dinner in summer. Main courses NZ$20–NZ$25 (US$14–US$18). MC, V. Daily 9am–5pm.

IN RUSSELL

The Gables, The Strand (© **09/403-7618**), has previously won widespread praise, but it seems to have lost its gloss and is overpriced compared to some of the competition. **The Duke of Marlborough,** The Strand (© **09/403-7829**), gets good comments for sound pub-style food but variable service, and **Gannets** 🍴, on York Street (© **09/403-7990**), scores the most points for tasty, good-value meals in a simple interior. The broadbill fish steaks are excellent. **York Street Café,** opposite the museum (© **09/403-7360**), has great coffee and a wonderful seafood chowder and you can sit inside, or in the outdoor courtyard. **Omata Estate** 🍴🍴, Aucks Road, Russell (© **09/ 403-8007**), is part of a luxury lodge and winery on the water's edge, nearer the Opua Ferry Landing than Russell itself, but it gets good reviews for its 6-course degustation menu and dishes like confit of salmon and scallops with lime risotto. Make sure you make a reservation. **Kamakura** 🍴🍴🍴, on The Strand (© **09/403-7771**), is my pick for the best on this side of the water. It's a sophisticated upmarket restaurant where "Pacific Rim cuisine meets Mediterranean with a touch of Japanese." You'll get the finest local produce and seafood, including fresh New Zealand crayfish blended into first-class meals with a high level of creativity. It's open daily, 11am until late.

IN KERIKERI

I had one of my nicest meals in the whole country at **Kina Kitchen** 🍴🍴, Cobblestone Mall, Kerikeri Road (© **09/407-7669**). Some locals seemed surprised by that—they'd warned me that service isn't always up to scratch. However, that applies to most places in New Zealand's provincial centers, and sometimes you just have to look past it, focusing instead on the quality of the food. A couple of others worthy of mention are **Fishbone** 🍴, 88 Kerikeri Rd. (© **09/407-6065**), a very popular local cafe for light lunches (Mon–Sat 8:30am–4pm, Sun 9am–2pm); and **Marsden Estate Winery** 🍴🍴, Wiroa Road, Kerikeri (© **09/407-9398**), which serves fabulous antipasto platters with estate-grown wine on a grape-covered courtyard overlooking lakes and vineyards. If you're looking for the best picnic food in town, don't drive past **Kerikeri Bakehouse Café** , Kerikeri Road (✆ **09/407-7266**), open daily from 7am to 5pm, supplying the most astounding range of edibles you'll find for hundreds of miles!

Pure Tastes 𝒜𝒜𝒜 ASIAN/INTERNATIONAL   Whatever else you do, don't miss this culinary gem, tucked away down a side street. Chef Paul Jobin and his team have combined cooking school/cafe/restaurant in a winning format. The menu has a seafood emphasis with strong Asian overtones—Penang fish curry, Asian wok toss, and Thai crispy beef are cases in point. It's bright and delicious and the homemade ice creams are real winners.

Fairway Dr., Kerikeri. ✆ 09/407-6510. Main courses NZ$16–NZ$27 (US$11–US$19). MC, V.

Rocket Café 𝒜 CAFE/LIGHT MEALS   This little gem is worth a stop on your way into Kerikeri. The food and coffee here are great. You'll get bulging calzones, freshly baked pies and quiches, and the best muffins for miles around. It's a pretty setting, with big windows looking out to kiwifruit vines, bougainvillea, and orange trees. There's even a playground for children, should they become irksome at the dinner table.

Kerikeri Rd., just off St. Hwy. 10. ✆ 09/407-3100. Lunch main courses NZ$15–NZ$22 (US$11–US$15). DC, MC, V. Daily 8:30am–5pm.

2 Whangarei & Beyond ⭑⭑

169km (105 miles) NE of Auckland; 62km (38 miles) S of Paihia; 58km (36 miles) E of Dargaville

On my last visit to Whangarei (pop. 46,000), the place seemed dreary and dull—but not any longer. Like so many provincial New Zealand towns, it's got its act together and the development of the Town Basin has given it a fresh sparkle. With international yachts moored quayside and a sprouting of cafes, galleries, and gift stores, it's a pleasant place to wander.

If you're a keen scuba diver, you'll certainly want to base yourself here—nearby **Tutukaka** and the **Poor Knights Islands** are the supreme diving spots. They're part of a fascinating marine reserve and one of the world's top dive locations. Big-game fishing is the other star attraction, and if you consider shark cage diving an attraction, well, that's here, too.

Approximately 1 hour south of Whangarei and 1 hour north of Auckland is the village of **Warkworth,** at the heart of the Kowhai Coast. It gives access to the very pretty **Sandspit/Matakana area,** where you can catch a ferry to Kawau Island or visit a range of excellent swimming beaches. It's not exactly off the beaten track, but Sandspit offers some fine accommodations and the chance to mellow out away from fellow tourists. In recent years, the area has become increasingly popular and you'll now find a number of enjoyable low-key attractions here.

ESSENTIALS

GETTING THERE & GETTING AROUND   By Plane Whangarei is a 40-minute flight from Auckland with **Air New Zealand Link** (✆ **0800/737-000** in NZ), which provides service several times a day. **Great Barrier Airlines** (✆ **0800/ 900-600**) flies to Whangarei from Auckland on Friday and Sunday. The **Airport Shuttle** (✆ **09/437-0666**) offers passenger service to Whangarei.

By Coach (Bus)   Both **InterCity** ((C) 09/913-6100) and Northliner Express ((C) 09/307-5873) pass through Warkworth and Whangarei several times a day.

By Car   Warkworth is about 1 hour north of Auckland; Whangarei is 2 hours away. The highway between Auckland and Whangarei has a high incidence of accidents, so drive carefully. If you need a rental car, the major companies have offices at the airport.

VISITOR INFORMATION   The **Whangarei Information & Travel i-Site,** 92 Otaika Rd., Whangarei ((C) **09/438-1079;** fax 09/438-2943; www.whangareinz.org.nz), is open daily from 8:30am to 5:30pm in summer and Monday through Friday from 8:30am to 5pm, weekends from 9:30am to 4:30pm in winter. For more information, check out www.whangarei.co.nz.

The **Warkworth i-Site Centre,** 1 Baxter St., Warkworth ((C) **09/425-9081;** fax 09/425-7584; www.warkworth-information.co.nz), is open daily from 9am to 5:15pm year-round (closed Dec 25).

EXPLORING THE TOWNS
IN WHANGAREI

I'd begin with a browse around the **Town Basin** ✿✿✿. This is where you'll find, among other things, the world's largest sundial and **Clapham's Clocks, The National Clock Museum** ((C) 09/438-3993; www.claphamsclocks.co.nz), a rather zany collection of timepieces, clocks, and music boxes; an in-house Austrian clockmaker; and a gift store. It's open daily 9am to 5pm (closed Dec 25) and costs NZ$8 (US$5.60) for adults, NZ$6 (US$4.20) for seniors and students, NZ$4 (US$2.80) for children, and NZ$16 (US$11) family.

Whangarei Museum ✿, including the Kiwi House, Heritage Park, and Clarke Homestead, is on State Highway 14 (the road to Dargaville), 3 minutes from downtown ((C) **09/438-9630;** www.whangareimuseum.co.nz). It's open daily from 10am to 4pm and costs NZ$8 (US$5.60) for all attractions. The **Native Bird Recovery Centre** (beside the museum) ((C) **09/438-1457**), is open Monday through Friday, 10am to 4pm.

The **Whangarei Art Museum,** Cafler Park Rose Gardens, Water Street ((C) **09/430-7240**), features local and national exhibitions and is open daily 9am to 5pm. If you've ever wondered how paper is made, check out **The Paper Mill** ✿, 300 Otaiki Rd. ((C) **09/438-2652;** www.thepapermill.co.nz), which offers 40-minute papermaking tours (9:30am–2:30pm). The mill is open Monday through Friday, 10am to 3pm.

Gardeners meanwhile, will get a special joy out of **The Quarry Gardens** ✿✿, Russell Road ((C) **09/437-7210;** www.whangareiquarrygardens.org.nz),which have changed an old quarry site into a lush subtropical display with numerous tracks linking to the Coronation Scenic Reserve.

For one of the most unexpected attractions in New Zealand, head for **Zion Wildlife Gardens** ✿✿✿ , Gray Road, Kamo ((C) **09/435-0110;** www.zionwildlifegardens.co.nz), where you'll find rare white tigers, white lions, and other magnificent endangered big cats. Guided tours operate daily at 9:30am, 11am, 2pm, and 3:30pm and take about 1½ hours. The cost is NZ$60 (US$42) per adult and NZ$30 (US$21) children. Touching the animals is not permitted on these tours, but if you're brave and rich, pay NZ$250 (US$175) per person (by appointment) and Craig, The Lion Man, will take you to meet his favorite cats, allowing you to pat one of the animals. Minimum age is 16 years.

Into the Deep Blue Sea

Why stay on land when there's so much to see underwater? I've never fan-cied myself in a wet suit, but I can see the advantages if you plan to explore the magnificent marine environment off the Tutukaka Coast and the Poor Knights Islands (1 hr. offshore by boat). **Tutukaka,** 30 minutes from Whangarei, is the gateway to the **Poor Knights Island Marine Reserve** , where crystal-clear waters near the edge of the continental shelf are bathed in subtropical currents. Sheer cliff faces, sea caves, tunnels, and archways are teeming with a range of sealift, including subtropical fish not usually found in New Zealand waters.

The reserve was rated as one of the top 10 diving spots in the world by Jacques Yves Cousteau and is strictly controlled by the Department of Con-servation with regard to fishing zones and restricted areas; make sure you go fishing or diving with a licensed operator. The main operator is **Dive! Tutukaka,** The Poor Knights Dive Centre, Marina Road, Tutukaka, Whangarei (© **0800/288-882** in NZ, or 09/434-3867; www.diving.co.nz), which offers a full range of snorkeling and diving options. Its staff members know all the best places—there are over 100 to choose from. Some of the team are also award-winning underwater photographers, so if that's what gets your heart ticking, you're in the right place. They have the largest dedicated dive char-ter fleet in New Zealand, accompanied by fully qualified dive guides and dive masters. They also offer a Twin Wrecks dive adventure on the scuttled ex-naval ships, *Tui* and *Waikato,* which were prepared for adventure diving before being sunk to diver-friendly depths.

Private tours with the tiger cubs cost NZ$200 (US$140) adults and NZ$50 (US$35) children ages 2 to 12 years.

Get a glimpse of local life at the **Whangarei Growers' Market** , held every Saturday morning in the Whangarei Forum North Carpark (off Rust Ave.), from 6am until 10:30am.

IN WARKWORTH

You'll find a nice little cluster of activities in the Sandspit and Matakana areas just a few minutes out of Warkworth. There are several crafts outlets, among them **Morris & James Country Pottery & Café** , 48 Tongue Farm Rd., Matakana (© **09/ 422-7116;** www.morrisandjames.co.nz), makers of quality terra-cotta and glazed pots, tiles, platters, and decorative ceramics; it's open daily with free guided pottery tours Monday through Friday at 11:30am.

Don't miss **Zealandia Sculpture Garden** , 138 Mahurangi West Rd., Wark-worth (© **09/422-0099**). Created by leading New Zealand sculptor, Terry Stringer, it features a sculpture park surrounded by farmland. It's open "seven hours, seven days, for seven months" (mid-October to Easter), with guided tours at 11am and 2pm.

No trip to this area is complete without a cruise or ferry ride from Sandspit Wharf to **Kawau Island** . Sir George Grey, an early governor of New Zealand, built the

Mansion House 150 years ago. It's now restored and open for visits, and on the grounds you'll find the descendants of his "Australian imports": wallabies, kookaburras, and rosellas. **Kawau Kat Cruises** (✆ **0800/888-006** in NZ, or 09/425-8006; www.kawaukat.co.nz) offers a fun outing on the **Royal Mail Run** 🎯🎯, which leaves the wharf each day at 10:30am and visits all the bays and Mansion House. It costs around NZ$50 (US$35) for adults, NZ$20 (US$14) for children, and NZ$100 (US$70) for a family. If you'd like to stay on Kawau Island, David and Helen Jeffery of **Kawau Island Experience** , North Cove, Kawau Island (✆ **09/422-8831;** www.sailingholiday.co.nz), offer both two rooms (NZ$150/US$105) and half-day, full-day, overnight, or extended cruises on their yacht, priced from NZ$400 (US$280).

The other major attraction is **Goat Island Marine Reserve,** 4km (2½ miles) northeast of Leigh and about 40 minutes from Warkworth. It was established in 1975 as New Zealand's first marine reserve and is a mecca for divers. If you'd like to explore the marine life here, the **Glass Bottom Boat** at Leigh (✆ **09/422-6334;** www.glass bottomboat.co.nz), offers a 45-minute trip on *Aquador,* or an excellent, 30-minute "round the islands" trip.

WHERE TO STAY
IN WHANGAREI

Whangarei has a good selection of motels; you can find out about them at the visitor center. Backpackers will find top-line comforts at **Bunkdown Lodge,** 23 Otaika Rd., Whangarei (✆ **09/438-8886;** www.bunkdownlodge.co.nz), from NZ$20 (US$14) per person. Jan Malcolm provides a lovely en-suite room with its own lounge (NZ$165–NZ$190/US$116–US$133) at **Sail Inn,** 148 Beach Rd., Onerahi, Whangarei (✆ **09/ 436-2356;** sailinn@xtra.co.nz). It has great views, your own Jacuzzi, and is just 5km (3 miles) from town. At Jackson's Bay, 15 minutes from Whangarei, you'll find a stylish hideaway that sleeps eight at **Jackson Bay Retreat** (✆ **021/158-3154;** www.jacksons bayretreat.co.nz). This three-level, four-bedroom home sits in native bush, is fully self-contained and has its own beach at the end of a bush track. Rates run from around NZ$250 to NZ$450 (US$175–US$315).

Mulryan's   Val and Kevin Ryan have poured so many loving hours into the restoration of their two-story 1896 villa that you wonder how they have the energy left to be such great hosts. This is a terrific rural experience with fruit from the orchard, honey from the hives, and herbs from the garden. Two upstairs rooms have balconies overlooking the garden. Both rooms are attic style, one with en suite and one with a private bathroom—the latter bathroom is the largest. A great stopover if you're heading north.

Crane Rd., Whangarei (well signposted just off St. Hwy. 1) ✆ 09/435-0945. Fax 09/435-5146. www.mulryans.co.nz. 2 units. NZ$225–NZ$245 (US$158–US$172). Rates include breakfast. No children under 12. AE, DC, MC, V. **Amenities:** Outdoor pool; nearby golf course; grass tennis court; Jacuzzi; nonsmoking rooms. *In room:* Fridge, coffeemaker, hair dryer, shared iron.

IN WARKWORTH

Tera del Mar, 140 Rodney Rd., Leigh, Warkworth (✆ **09/422-6090;** www.teradel mar.co.nz), is about 25km (16 miles) from Warworth but well worth the drive through pretty countryside. It offers five lovely, big bedrooms and four bathrooms. **Takatu Lodge & Vineyard** , 518 Whitmore Rd., Matakana (✆ **09/423-0299;** www. takatulodge.co.nz), is a stunning new, contemporary property set amid a working vineyard.

The Saltings Estate & Vintner's Haven This double-barreled delight is truly enchanting. Terry and Maureen Baines have three gorgeous en-suite rooms in their own home, and just a stroll away is a separate self-contained guesthouse that can accommodate seven adults. The added bonus is that it overlooks the small vineyard and winery. Allow for the fact that you may never want to leave and stay at least 2 nights! It's idyllic.

1210 Sandspit Rd., Warkworth ✆ **09/425-9670.** Fax 09/425-9674. www.saltings.co.nz. 6 units. NZ$225–NZ$255 (US$158–US$179) Saltings standard rooms; NZ$255–NZ$295 (US$179–US$207) Saltings deluxe suite; NZ$200–NZ$240 (US$140–US$168) Vintner's standard room; NZ$295–NZ$495 (US$207–US$347) Vintner's 1- or 2-bedroom apt. Rates include full breakfast at Saltings. Breakfast provisions for Vintner's rooms NZ$40 (US$27) per couple. Long-stay and off-peak rates available. Minimum 2-night stay. No children under 12. Saltings closed Dec 21–Jan 2. MC, V. **Amenities:** Laundry facilities for Vintner's guests; nonsmoking rooms. *In room:* Dataport, kitchen and kitchenette in Vintner's Haven, coffeemaker, hair dryer.

WHERE TO DINE

Numerous new cafes and restaurants have sprung up in Whangarei, and you'll get a good overview by picking up the free brochure *Eating Out in Whangarei.* Making an impression is award-winning **A'Deco** ★★★, 70 Kamo Rd., Whangarei (✆ **09/459-4957**), which is highly praised for its modern, fine dining in an elegant Art Deco residence. It's open Tuesday through Saturday for dinner and Wednesday through Friday for lunch. Award-winning **Tonic** ★★, 239 Kamo Rd. (✆ **09/437-5558**), is less formal and offers modern French-style cuisine in a cozy 30-seat restaurant; it's open daily from 6pm. Both charge city prices—in the realm of NZ$25 to NZ$30 (US$18–US$21) for main courses. **Killer Prawn** ★, 26–28 Bank St. (✆ **09/430-3333**), remains one of Whangarei's most popular dining establishments with its ultimate seafood, big steaks, chicken, and sizzling lamb dishes. Personally I find it a little lacking in charm, without the class of Tonic and A'Deco but perfectly fine for a reasonable meal. It's open Monday through Saturday from 11am and Sunday from 5pm. Three cafes are worth noting: **Fresh** ★★★, 12 James St. (✆ **09/438-2921**), which has an excellent all-day menu and is open Monday through Friday 8am to 5pm, and Saturday 8am to 2pm; **Bob** ★★, 29 Bank St (✆ **09/438 0881**), which serves good coffee and deli food; and **Caffeine Espresso** ★★, 4 Water St. (✆ **09/438-6925**), which has a lively, older, funkier atmosphere and is open Monday through Friday 7am to 3pm and weekends 7am to 2pm.

In Warkworth, stop by the visitor center for the good brochure listing restaurants as well as attractions and accommodations. About 10 minutes out of town is one of the best spots, **Heron's Flight Vineyard & Café** ★★, 49 Sharp's Rd., Matakana (✆ **09/422-7915;** www.heronsflight.co.nz), where you'll find fine wines, good coffee, and food; you can stroll among grapes, figs, roses, and olives. It's open daily from 10am to 6pm for delicious light lunches. Main courses cost from NZ$15 (US$11), and its romantic vineyard environment makes it a winner. **Mariposa Palm Café** ★★, 253 Point Wells Rd., Matakana (✆ **09/422-7597**), is another delightful cafe destination, this one set amid a subtropical garden and nursery. It's open daily 9am to 4pm. **The Pizza Construction** ★, Snells Beach (✆ **09/425-5555**), just 5 minutes from Sandspit, is a big hit with locals for its extensive menu that goes way beyond great pizzas.

EN ROUTE BACK TO AUCKLAND, VIA THE WEST COAST

If you came up to the Far North from Auckland on Highway 1, you may want to return on a longer, less direct route that takes in the **Waipoua Kauri Forest** ★★★

and the **Trounson Kauri Park.** If you do this, be sure to also enjoy the scenic beauty of **Hokianga Harbour.**

The kauri is the giant of the New Zealand native forest, and at Waipoua the largest trees are over 1,000 years old. Look for **Tane Mahuta (God of the Forest)** , the largest known kauri in New Zealand, and **Te Matua Ngahere (Father of the Forest),** by volume the second-biggest known tree in the country. These and other special trees are signposted on the tourist drive through the forest. You'll find the **Kauri Coast i–Site Information Centre** at 65 Normanby St., Dargaville (© **09/439-8360;** www.kauricoast.co.nz).

The **Kauri Museum,** Church Road, Matakohe (© **09/431-7417;** www.kaurimuseum.com), is south of Dargaville and worth visiting. It's open daily 8:30am to 5:30pm from November to April and 9am to 5pm in winter. Admission is NZ$12 (US$8.40) adults, NZ$3 (US$2.10) children. In this area, consider staying at Guy and Linda Bucchi's very charming **Petite Provence** , 703c Tinopai Rd., Matakohe (© **09/431-7552;** www.petiteprovence.co.nz), where the three lovely rooms cost NZ$130 (US$91) each.

3 The Coromandel Peninsula ★★

119km (74 miles) E of Auckland

At the height of the gold rush in the late 1800s, the towns of the Coromandel Peninsula were heavily populated and thriving. Thames, now seen as the gateway to the peninsula, had a population of nearly 20,000 and between 80 to 90 pubs. Today, there are around 7,000 permanent residents and just four pubs, and it's still the biggest town on the peninsula. There's a sense of that more colorful history all along the west coast, but as in Northland, most of the action is on the picturesque east coast.

This scenic finger of land, reaching into the sea between Auckland and the Bay of Plenty, is famous for its jagged western coastline and its balmy eastern beach recesses that provide endless opportunity for swimming, diving, boating, fishing, and general lazing about. Thousands of New Zealanders have been doing just that for decades. Big, bush-covered ranges divide the two coasts and offer the ultimate challenge for fit trampers, and there are quaint attractions scattered throughout.

You can comfortably reach the base of the Coromandel Peninsula from Auckland in just 1½ hours, and from Rotorua in 2¾ hours. While it's feasible to do most of the peninsula in a day trip, try to spend a couple of extra days in the area and explore more of what it has to offer.

ESSENTIALS

GETTING THERE & GETTING AROUND   By Plane   Air Coromandel/ Great Barrier Airlines (© **0800/900-600** in NZ, or 09/275-9120; www.gbair.co.nz) runs daily services and scheduled scenic flights between Whitianga and Auckland, Great Barrier Island, the Bay of Islands, Waiheke Island, Rotorua, and Tauranga.

By Ferry   Kawau Kat (© **0800/888-006** in NZ, or 09/425-8006; www.kawaukat.co.nz) operates between Auckland and Coromandel town. The trip takes 2 hours and costs around NZ$75 (US$53) one-way for adults and NZ$45 (US$32) children.

By Coach (Bus)   InterCity (© **09/913-6100**) runs regular services between Auckland, Whitianga, and Coromandel. The **Coromandel Busplan Pass** allows travel from Auckland to Thames, the loop through Coromandel and Whitianga and back to Thames, and either on to Rotorua or back to Auckland for around NZ$100 (US$70).

By Car   If you're coming from Auckland: Drive south on State Highway 1 for about 50km (31 miles), then turn east on State Highway 2. About 34km (21 miles) later, you'll pick up State Highway 25 to Thames. If you want to head straight to the east coast beaches of Whitianga, Tairua, and Pauanui: Take the direct route, signposted EASTERN BEACHES, turning right at Kopu (St. Hwy. 26) away from Thames. Approximately 1km (½ mile) from this point, turn left onto State Highway 25a, which is the direct route. If you follow the Pacific Coast Highway through Thames and Coromandel town: Turn left at Kopu and follow the PCH "Hook" signs. This is a terrific trip, but if your destination is the east coast beaches, it will add at least 1 to 1½ hours to your journey. If you're traveling up the west side of the peninsula, through Whitianga to Pauanui, pass through Tairua township and continue south until you reach the service station on the left. This is where you turn off to Pauanui (there's a small sign) and travel north again.

The road from Colville village, north of Coromandel town, to the top of the peninsula is unpaved all the way and takes around 1½ hours. It's a stunning trip, but not recommended for the fainthearted. It is dirt only, very steep, narrow, and often a one-way lane with no room for passing—plus steep drops to the ocean. If you want to explore this area, I strongly advise you to join **Coromandel Discovery Tours,** 316 Tiki Rd., Coromandel (✆ **07/866-8175;** www.coromandeldiscoverytours.co.nz).

By Taxi   Contact **Mercury Bay Taxi,** in Whitianga, at ✆ **07/866-5643.**

VISITOR INFORMATION   The **Thames i–Site Visitor Centre,** 206 Pollen St., Thames (✆ **07/868-7284;** fax 07/868-7584; www.thames-info.co.nz), is open Monday through Friday from 8:30am to 5pm, Saturday, Sunday and public holidays 9am to 4pm. The **Coromandel i–Site Visitor Centre,** 355 Kapanga Rd., Coromandel (✆ **07/866-8598;** fax 07/866-8527; www.coromandeltown.co.nz), is open in summer, daily from 9am to 5pm; and in winter, Monday through Saturday from 9am to 5pm, Sunday 10am to 2pm. The **Whitianga i–Site Visitor Centre,** 66 Albert St., Whitianga (✆ **07/866-5555;** fax 07/866-2205; www.whitianga.co.nz), is open Monday through Friday

---

Tips   **A Word on Driving**

Remember that getting to places on the peninsula often takes longer than you think. Many of the roads are narrow and winding and, off State Highway 25, generally unsealed (unpaved). Thames to Coromandel village takes almost 2 hours driving through numerous little coastal settlements. There are pretty beaches aplenty to stop at along the way, BUT **DRIVE CAREFULLY!** North of Coromandel township, the roads become significantly worse. Rental-car companies previously forbade vehicles from traveling here, but if you stick to the Pacific Coast Highway path (St. Hwy. 25), you're generally okay. The route from Coromandel to Whitianga takes about 1 hour by State Highway 25 (recommended for rentals), and a similar length of time on the "infamous" 309 route, which has 24km (15 miles) of unsealed road and is narrow and winding. It may be scenic with some interesting stops along the way, but State Highway 25 is far less harrowing.

from 9am to 5pm, Saturday and Sunday from 9am to 1pm. Pick up the free 72-page *Coromandel Visitor's Guide* at any one of the above locations.

The Thames office of the **Department of Conservation** is on Kauaeranga Valley Road (© 07/867-9080).

Coromandel Peninsula is well served with websites. You can find information on the region at any of the following: www.thecoromandel.com, www.mercurybay.co.nz, www.webtrails.co.nz, www.thepeninsula.co.nz, www.whitianga.co.nz, www.pacificcoast. co.nz, and www.waihi.org.nz.

SPECIAL EVENTS For details of the colorful 2-week annual **Pohutukawa Festival,** held every November to celebrate the red-flowering native pohutukawa trees that line the coast, call © 07/876-9832, fax 07/867-9398, or check www.pohutukawafest. com. In early February, Coromandel town celebrates with the **Coromandel Flavours Festival.** Contact the visitor center for details.

EXPLORING THE PENINSULA

Personally, I prefer Northland, but Coromandel has an intangible, rustic quality that makes it rather alluring. Certainly, from a purely physical point of view, there's nothing quite like the sight of New Zealand's famous pohutukawa in full scarlet bloom (in Dec and Jan), against black rock and white beach, for mile after endless mile.

There are good walks around Paeroa (near the Karangahake Gorge), Waihi, Whangamata, Tairua, Whitianga, Colville, Coromandel, and Thames. Information on the **Coromandel Forest Park** is available at the Department of Conservation office in Thames (see "Visitor Information," above). There's also a DOC office in Coromandel township at the i-Site Visitor Centre.

In Thames, you'll find historic mining areas well signposted. For gold-mining tours in the Thames area, try **Goldmine Experience,** Main Road, State Highway 25, Thames (©/fax **07/868-8514;** www.goldmine-experience.co.nz), which offers a guided tour through an operational, 19th-century Stamper Battery and into one of the richest goldmines of the time. They're open daily from 10am to 4pm in summer.

From 1885 over 30 schools of mining provided practical training for gold miners; the largest of those, the **Thames School of Mines Museum** 𝒦𝒦, Brown and Cochrane streets (© **07/868-6227**), is open daily from 11am to 4pm in summer (reduced winter hours). In complete contrast, you can escape into the Tropics at the **Butterfly and Orchid Garden,** Victoria Street, Thames (© **07/868-8080;** www.butterfly.co.nz). They're 3km (1¾ miles) north of the town and are open daily 10am to 4pm. Or maybe you'd enjoy a tour of **The Thames Natural Soap Company** 𝒦𝒦, at Pollen and Grey streets, Thames (© **0800/326-777;** www.naturalsoap.co.nz). Tours run Monday through Friday at 11am, 1pm, and 3pm; the cost is NZ$10 (US$7) for adults, NZ$7 (US$4.90) for children 5 to 13. Allow an hour and you'll get a soap gift. They also have a great shop for gifts to take home.

If you feel like a wander, pick up the *Historic Grahamstown* brochure and check out the town's past. Add in a visit to **Thames Historical Museum,** corner of Pollen and Cochrane streets, Grahamstown, Thames (© **07/868-8509**), which is open daily, 1 to 4pm. Admission is NZ$4 (US$2.80) adults and NZ$2 (US$1.40) for children. Youngsters might also enjoy **Thames Small Gauge Railway,** Brown Street (© **07/868-9707**), which costs NZ$1 (US70¢) per ride and runs most Sundays from 11am to 3pm.

As you head north, just beyond Tapu, turn east off State Highway 25 and go 6.5km (4 miles) to the spectacular **Rapaura Watergardens** 𝒦𝒦, 586 Tapu-Coroglen Rd.,

---

Finds Waterfall Walk

The **Waiau Falls** are 11km (7 miles) east of Coromandel. A 5-minute walk from the 309 Road ends at the foot of the falls. The **309 Kauris,** 1km (½ mile) farther east, are the finest, easily accessible stand of kauri trees on the peninsula. It's a delightful 10-minute bush walk to see them.

Tapu, Thames Coast (©/fax **07/868-4821;** www.rapaurawatergardens.co.nz). Numerous paths meander through the 26 hectares (64 acres) of gardens and 14 water-lily ponds, which are open daily from 9am to 5pm. Admission is around NZ$12 (US$8.40) for adults and NZ$5 (US$3.50) for children. About 2.5km (1½ miles) past Rapaura Gardens, stop at Tapu and ask directions to one of nature's oddities, the **"square kauri,"** a 2,500-year-old kauri whose trunk is a perfect square. **Te Mata Beach** *☞*, also at Tapu, is a good hunting ground for specimens of carnelian-agate gemstones.

In Coromandel is the **Driving Creek Railway and Pottery** *☞☞*, 410 Driving Creek Rd. (© **07/866-8703;** www.drivingcreekrailway.co.nz). Barry Brickell, an accomplished potter, owns the country's only narrow-gauge mountain railway, which passes through replanted native forest. There are usually at least two departures daily costing from NZ$17 to NZ$20 (US$12–US$14) for adults and around NZ$35 (US$25) per family. The station is 2.5km (1½ miles) from Coromandel town, and the 1-hour trip covers 3km (2 miles) of track.

Pick up the *Coromandel Craft Trail* brochure, which details over 30 of the peninsula's craftspeople, or visit **Weta Design** *☞☞*, 46 Kapanga Rd., Coromandel Town (© **07/866-8823;** www.wetadesign.co.nz), which shows work by New Zealand's top artists and craftspeople. It's open 9:30am to 6pm in summer and from 10am to 5pm in winter. **Waitati Gardens** *☞*, 485 Buffalo Rd., Coromandel Town (© **07/866-8659;** waitatigardens@xtra.co.nz), are a pleasant horticultural diversion (admission is NZ$5/US$3.50); and make sure you visit the weird and whimsical at **Waiau Waterworks** *☞☞☞*, 309 Road, Coromandel (© **07/866-7191;** www.waiauwaterworks.co.nz). This haven of strange, water-based sculptures and gadgets is a great place for kids—as long as they're well supervised. It's open daily from 9am to 5pm in summer; admission is around NZ$10 (US$7) for adults and NZ$5 (US$3.50) for children ages 5 to 15.

On the east coast, Whitianga has the excellent **Mercury Bay Historical Museum,** opposite the wharf (© **07/866-0730**), featuring exhibits dating from 800 to 950 A.D. For something entirely different, visit **Mill Creek Lavender** *☞☞*, 445 Mill Creek Rd. (© **07/866-0088;** www.millcreeklavender.co.nz), a sweet-smelling haven open to visitors from 10:30am to 5pm weekends, between October and Easter, or by appointment. At **Bay Carving** *☞☞*, The Esplanade, Whitianga (© **07/866-4021;** bay carving@xtra.co.nz),you can carve your own bone souvenir in 2 to 3 hours. They're open from 9am daily and carving costs from NZ$40 (US$28) per person, per piece, depending on the design chosen.

A fun activity is taking the **Whitianga Water Transport** (© **07/866-5925**) passenger ferry to the Ferry Landing. It operates daily from 7:30am to 10:30pm (extended hours from Christmas Day to the end of Jan). Once at the Ferry Landing, you can link up with **Hot Water Beach ConXtions** (© **07/866-2478**) and go to Hahei, Hot

Water Beach, Cathedral Cove, and other area attractions. The bus costs around NZ$25 (US$18) per person for the day's outing.

At **Hot Water Beach** 𝄞𝄞𝄞 , inquire about the time of the next low tide—thermal water heats parts of this beach for 2 hours on either side of low tide. That's when you can dig a hole in the sand, settle in, and soak in the hot saltwater that comes up from underground springs.

ORGANIZED TOURS

The best tour companies are located at Pauanui but their tours cover the whole peninsula. **Johansen & Wincorp Adventures** 𝄞𝄞, Pauanui Beach (☎/fax **07/864-8731;** www.coromandel.co.nz) offers a wide range of hikes, nature treks, and guided and personalized tours. Their Twilight Glow Worm Experience is a lot of fun and all tours include some history of the region, as well as information on Maori medicines and foods of the forest. Tours range in price, but are around NZ$80 (US$56) per person. **Aotearoa Lodge & Tours,** 70 Racecourse Rd., Whitianga (☎ **07/866-2807;** www. tournz.co.nz), specializes in multiday tours of Coromandel Peninsula, Rotorua, and East Cape, departing Auckland daily. Its 3-day "A Touch of Coromandel" tour is about NZ$800 (US$560) per person.

Kiwi Dundee Adventures 𝄞𝄞𝄞 , Bond and Harbourview Road, Whangamata (☎/fax **07/865-8809;** www.kiwidundee.co.nz), is the brainchild of passionate outdoors enthusiast Doug Johansen and his partner, Jan Poole. Doug is one of New Zealand's foremost nature guides, and he and Jan offer a range of full-day tours. Day tours are priced from NZ$190 (US$133) per person, including lunch. They also have several upmarket 3-day tours running between Auckland, Coromandel, and Rotorua, offering top-level accommodations for two to six people. These are priced on application and according to the accommodation used.

Take to the water in the **Glass Bottom Boat** 𝄞𝄞 (☎ **07/867-1962;** www.glass bottomboatwhitianga.co.nz), to see a little of the area's amazing marine life; or join **Ocean Wave Tours** 𝄞𝄞 (☎ **0800/806-060** in NZ; www.oceanwave.co.nz) to explore sea caves and islands for about 2 hours, for around NZ$50 (US$35) per adult and NZ$40 (US$28) children.

OUTDOOR PURSUITS

BEACHES   Whangamata is a top surfing and swimming beach. **Cooks Beach** has safe swimming and lovely picnic areas, while **Buffalo Beach** is good for swimming and shellfish collecting—both are in the Mercury Bay area.

FISHING   There are numerous boat charter operations based in Whitianga, Whangamata, and Waihi, and the visitor centers have masses of brochures. Tairua Beach offers excellent surf-casting. Coromandel's northern islands provide excellent snapper fishing. For an organized fishing experience, try **Coromandel Charters** (☎ **07/866-7167;** www.corocharters.co.nz), who offer half- and full-day excursions.

GOLF   The **Mercury Bay Golf & Country Club,** Golf Road, Whitianga (☎ **07/ 866-5479**), is an 18-hole course; greens fees are about NZ$20 to NZ$30 (US$14–US$21) **Matarangi 18-Hole Golf Links & Resort** (☎ **07/866-5394;** www. matarangi.co.nz) is one of New Zealand's top 10 courses; and **Coromandel Golf Club,** Hauraki Road, Coromandel (☎ **07/866-8539**), is a scenic 9-hole course; fees are NZ$20 (US$14) for nonmembers. **Thames Golf Club** (☎ **07/868-9062**) is a par-70, 18-hole course; greens fees are around NZ$25 (US$18) per person.

Finds **Cathedral Cove**

This gorgeous sheltered cove is part of the Hahei Marine Reserve and famous for its large sea cave. The beach and cave are accessible by walkway from Hahei.

HORSE TREKKING   Riders with a sense of adventure might like to try the guided horse treks into the rugged Coromandel Ranges offered by **Rangihau Ranch,** Rangihau Road, Coroglen (© **07/866-3875;** Rangihau@xtra.co.nz). They're halfway between Whitianga and Tairua. Or experience an outback sheep station with **Twin Oaks Riding Ranch,** State Highway 25, Kuaotunu Road, Whitianga (© **07/866-5388;** www.twinoaksridingranch.co.nz), which charges around NZ$30 (US$21) for a 2-hour trek.

KAYAKING   **Cathedral Cove Sea Kayaking** ✸✸✸ (© 07/866-3877; www.seakayaktours.co.nz) operates from Hahei and offers daily tours from October to May. It's a fabulous way to see beaches, islands, caves, and coves—no experience is necessary. Try the fascinating 3½-hour Volcanic Coast tour, which costs about NZ$70 (US$49).

MOUNTAIN BIKING   **Mercury Mountain Biking,** 8 Kudu Dr., Whitianga (© **07/866-4993** or 025/922-9743), has exclusive access to two tracks for tours. They also hire bikes. North of Coromandel, you'll find a testing track between Stony Bay and Fletcher Bay, which takes about 2 hours each way. There are also good tracks in the Carter Holt Harvey (CHH) forests south of Tairua and at Whangamata. To get into these areas, you need to register at the CHH office, just north of Whangamata (© **07/865-8473**), or at one of the visitor centers in the area.

SCUBA DIVING   The waters around Whitianga are ideal for diving. **Cathedral Cove Dive,** Hahei Beach Road, Hahei (© **09/866-3955;** www.hahei.co.nz), has dive trips for certified divers, plus PADI dive courses for all levels, in the marine reserve or in the waters beyond. Snorkeling trips in divine locations are offered as well.

WINDSURFING   **Seafari Windsurfing,** 18A Centennial Dr., Whitianga (© **07/866-0677**), offers windsurfing hire (from NZ$25/US$18) and tuition from NZ$40 (US$28), wetsuit included. You can also hire kayaks from NZ$10 (US$7).

WHERE TO STAY

North Islanders flock to Coromandel Peninsula during December and January, when you'll need to book well ahead. In the off season, you'll get motel beds at laughably good rates. Lodgings on the east coast are generally nicer than those on the Thames side.

Van and caravan sites in **Conservation Lands** are available on a first-come, first-served basis; camping fees are from NZ$5 (US$3.50) per adult and NZ$2 (US$1.40) per school-age child. For details, contact the **Department of Conservation,** P.O. Box 78, Thames (© **07/868-6381;** or the **Kauaeranga Visitor Centre** (© **07/867-9080;** www.doc.govt.nz).

The rates given below include the 12.5% GST.

IN OR NEAR THAMES

Tuscany on Thames ✸✸, Jellicoe Street, Thames (© **07/868-5099;** www.tuscanyonthames.co.nz), is a smart, new motel complex with a swimming pool and 14 units with lovely bathrooms with double Jacuzzis. **Thames Gateway Backpackers** ✸, 209 Mackay St., Thames (© **07/868-6339**), is a small, comfortable stay ("just like home")

right beside the Thames Information Centre and the InterCity bus stop. They'll set
you up in dorm beds or double/twins and give you free bikes to get around town.

Coastal Motor Lodge 🦜🦜   Tararu is a great place for migratory seabirds and brilliant sunsets, and a chalet at Coastal Motor Lodge is just the place to enjoy them. The
spacious A-frame chalets sleep two and have cute kitchens and balconies. Everything
is spotless, and the two units for travelers with disabilities are especially big. The front
unit near the road is particularly cozy, with bathtub, shower, and queen-size and single beds. The complex is set in parklike grounds just across the road from the water
(not a swimming beach, unfortunately).

608 Tararu Rd. (Coromandel Coast Rd.), Thames. ✆ **07/868-6843.** Fax 07/868-6520. www.stayatcoastal.co.nz. 15 units.
NZ$120–NZ$190 (US$84–US$133). Long-stay and off-peak rates available. AE, DC, MC, V. Located 1.5km (1 mile) north
of Thames. **Amenities:** Nearby golf course; Jacuzzi; massage; babysitting; laundry service and coin-op laundry; nonsmoking rooms. *In room:* TV, dataport, kitchenette, fridge, coffeemaker, hair dryer, iron.

IN OR NEAR COROMANDEL

Anchor Lodge 🦜🦜, 448 Wharf Rd., Coromandel Town (✆ **07/866-7992;** www.
anchorlodgecoromandel.co.nz), is a very nice 14-unit motel complex in a native bush
setting 400m (1,312 ft.) from the town center.

Driving Creek Villas 🦜🦜 *Finds*   Two boutique villas are located in a private bush
setting and fitted out with all the modern goodies. Each villa has two bedrooms, one
bathroom, a big lounge, and a private garden. Listen to native birds singing outside
your window, as you unwind in these cute self-contained havens.

21a Colville Rd., Coromandel Town. ✆ **07/866-7755.** Fax 07/866-7753. www.drivingcreekvillas.com. NZ$245
(US$172). Extra person NZ$25 (US$18). Breakfast available on request. Long-stay and off-peak rates available. MC, V.
Amenities: Nearby golf course and tennis courts; free bikes; car rentals; massage; laundry service; airport transfers. *In
room:* A/C, TV/DVD/CD, full kitchen, coffeemaker, hair dryer, iron.

Flax Bach 🦜   If a delightful 1960s Kiwi holiday cottage set in a small citrus orchard
sounds tempting, head for this two-bedroom hideaway (sleeps five) just across the
road from a safe swimming beach, backed by Department of Conservation native forest and right next door to the coastal walkway.

Long Bay Rd., Coromandel Town. ✆ **09/419-5005** or 021/855-645. www.flaxbach.co.nz. NZ$100 (US$70) for 4 people, NZ$25 (US$18) extra person. Minimum 1-week stay during Christmas period and 2-night minimum stay rest of
year. No credit cards. **Amenities:** Linen and cleaning service on request; kitchen; fridge; TV; books and games; ham-
mock; barbecue; nonsmoking rooms.

IN OR NEAR WHITIANGA

The small, friendly **Cat's Pyjamas Backpackers' Lodge,** 4 Monk St., Whitianga
(✆/fax **07/866-4663;** www.cats-pyjamas.co.nz), is in the center of town; beds start at
NZ$18 to NZ$20 (US$13–US$14) per person. **The Waterfront Motel** 🦜🦜, 2 Buffalo Beach Rd., Whitianga (✆ **07/866-4498;** www.waterfrontmotel.co.nz), is one of
the newer motel complexes across the road from the beach, and it has good facilities
and rooms from NZ$130 to NZ$300 (US$91–US$210). If you want a self-contained
hideaway for around NZ$120 (US$84) with breakfast by a tranquil river 10 minutes
from Whitianga, go for **Riverside Retreat,** 309 Road, RD1 (✆ **06/377-3035;** www.
riverside.co.nz).

Mercury Bay Beachfront Resort 🦜🦜   Friendly hosts Kate and Paul Dimock have
a terrific establishment here. In a matter of seconds, you can walk from your comfortable room to the sparkling sands of Buffalo Beach. Upstairs units have balconies;

downstairs, a private patio opens onto the garden and beach. All rooms are cool, clean, and comfortable.

111–113 Buffalo Beach Rd., Whitianga. © 07/866-5637. Fax 07/866-4524. www.beachfrontresort.co.nz. 8 units. NZ$165–NZ$265 (US$112–US$186) standard; NZ$225–NZ$295 (US$158–US$207) luxury unit. Extra person NZ$20 (US$14). Long-stay and off-peak rates available. AE, DC, MC, V. **Amenities:** Nearby golf course; Jacuzzi; free watersports equipment, bikes, fishing rods, and golf clubs; babysitting; coin-op laundry; nonsmoking rooms. *In room:* TV, dataport, kitchen, fridge, coffeemaker, hair dryer, iron.

Villa Toscana ★★★ *(Moments* Giorgio and Margherita Allemano have replicated a Tuscan villa high on a hill overlooking native bush and the ocean, where they take great pleasure in welcoming guests from all over the world. Their fully self-contained, two-bedroom guest suite has its own entrance, deck, garden, barbecue, and outdoor Jacuzzi. You'll find no fault with the spacious, airy bedrooms. The decor is simple—lots of traditional Italian tiles and marble—plus a large bathroom with Italian fixtures, a granite kitchen and a wide lounge for relaxing at the end of a busy touring day. Giorgio is happy to show you his underground wine cellar and, as a marine biologist and keen fisherman, he has plenty to talk about. Don't miss the genuine Italian gourmet dinners. It's not cheap but it's a fully Italian experience that you'll remember long after leaving.

Ohuka Park, Whitianga. © 07/866-2293. Fax 07/866-2269. www.villatoscana.co.nz. 1 2-bedroom suite. NZ$720 (US$504) 1–2 people; NZ$840 (US$588) 3 people; NZ$960 (US$672) 4 people. Rates include breakfast and Whitianga Airport transfers. Off-season rates available. MC, V. Located 4km (2½ miles) north of Whitianga. **Amenities:** Dinners on request; nearby golf course; 2 nearby outdoor tennis courts; 11m (35-ft.) Bertram game fishing launch for hire at NZ$900 (US$630) per day; kayaks; free mountain bikes; massage; babysitting; laundry service; nonsmoking rooms; private helipad; on-call doctor/dentist. *In room:* TV/DVD, dataport, kitchen, fridge, coffeemaker, hair dryer, iron, washing machine.

IN PAUANUI/TAIRUA

Colleith Lodge ★★, P.O. Box 25, Tairua (© 07/864-7970; www.colleithlodge.co.nz), has three very nice, modern B&B rooms with en-suite bathrooms overlooking a lap pool; and **Harbourview Bed & Breakfast** ★★, 179 Main Rd., Tairua (© 07/864-7040; www.harbourviewlodge.co.nz), also has three en-suite rooms and a swimming pool. Both make an ideal base for exploring the peninsula.

Puka Park Resort ★★★ There's been a major upgrade at this idyllic hideaway and if you're a discerning traveler who expects nothing but the best, you'll love being spoiled—it's the premier upmarket accommodation on the peninsula. Built 18 years ago, this series of exquisite "treehouses" climbs uphill, away from the main lodge, and is completely enclosed by native bush. But you won't have to walk or carry a thing; service is tops here and every scrap of luggage is attended to by the smiling (and incredibly fit) staff. Standard chalets contain a shower-only bathroom; superiors are larger with both tub and shower. Executive chalets have separate lounge/dining areas, while the luxurious Royal Puka Suite is a free-standing two-story, three-bedroom chalet with everything you're ever likely to need on an indulgent holiday.

Mount Ave., Pauanui Beach. © 07/864-8088. Fax 07/864-8112. www.pukapark.co.nz. 48 units. From NZ$302–NZ$428 (US$211–US$300) standard treehut; NZ$371–NZ$473 (US$$260–US$331) superior bush; NZ$473–NZ$574 (US$331–US$402) executive; NZ$1,373–NZ$1,474 (US$961–US$1,032) Royal Puka Suite. NZ$51 (US$36) each extra person. Rates include breakfast on special deals only. Winter rates available. AE, DC, MC, V. Drive into Pauanui with the Waterways Development on your left, go through the roundabout and onto a second roundabout where Puka Park Resort is signposted. Make a hard right onto Pauanui Beach Rd.; turn right at the second street onto Mount Ave. and follow this as far as you can. Turn left and go uphill to the resort. **Amenities:** Restaurant; bar; heated outdoor pool; nearby 10-hole golf course; tennis court; gymnasium; day spa beauty treatments; outdoor Jacuzzi; sauna; rental watersport equipment; free bikes; concierge; tour bookings; business center; car rentals; massage; babysitting; laundry service; 3-day dry-cleaning service; nonsmoking rooms; foreign-currency exchange; on-call doctor/dentist. *In room:* TV, dataport, minibar, fridge, coffeemaker, hair dryer, iron, safe.

IN WHANGAMATA

Brenton Lodge   This lodge's super location overlooks the whole of Whangamata town and beaches. You get the best of John and Rosa Ashton's lovely gardens surrounding the delicious bedrooms with crisp cotton sheets, bathrobes, beach towels, and fresh flowers. Lavender Cottage is the farthest from the main house and has the best view; Rose Cottage is all fresh and white with sloping ceilings; and the Garden Room above the main house is a blue-and-white haven overlooking the pool. To top it all off, a gourmet breakfast is served in your room or alfresco on your private balcony.

2 Brenton Place, Whangamata. ©/fax **07/865-8400**. www.brentonlodge.co.nz. 3 cottages. NZ$325 (US$228). Extra person NZ$100 (US$70). Rates include breakfast. AE, MC, V. **Amenities:** Outdoor pool; nearby golf course; Jacuzzi; laundry service; nonsmoking rooms; on-call doctor/dentist. *In room:* Kitchenette, coffeemaker, hair dryer, iron.

WHERE TO DINE
IN THAMES

Sealey Café, 109 Sealey St. (© **07/868-8641**), in an old villa, offers light lunches and coffee. It's the best of a limited choice; it's open daily from 11am until late, and live jazz is featured on Sunday afternoons. **Sola Café,** 720B Pollen St. (© **07/868-8781**), is probably your best good-coffee choice. They have a small vegetarian menu and are open daily 9am to 4pm and for dinner on Friday nights. Or try **The Billy Goat Café,** 444 Pollen St. (© **07/868-7384**), which serves good coffee and fresh counter food from 7:30am to 4pm Monday through Friday.

IN COROMANDEL

Driving Creek Café, 180 Driving Creek Rd. (© **07/866-7066**), just north of town in an old villa, serves delicious meals using local and organic produce. It's open Wednesday through Sunday, from 9:30am to 4pm and is THE place to get a feel for local culture—it's a laid-back venue set in the bush, with a piano planted in its center. The **Success Café,** 104 Kapanga Rd. (© **07/866-7100**), is a nice place for a light lunch or a quiet evening meal. It serves local seafood in a relaxed environment; open daily in summer from 9am to 6pm, with reduced hours in winter. **Umu,** 22 Wharf Rd. (© **07/866-8618**), features local seafood, New Zealand lamb and beef, plus vegetarian dishes and great coffee. All food is available as takeaway meals and they're open daily from noon for lunch and dinner.

Peppertree Restaurant & Bar, 31 Kapanga Rd. (© **07/866-8211**), is probably the best eatery in town, and its dinners present seafood, sushi, mussel fritters, local beef, and fresh vegetables in interesting combinations. It's open daily from 10:30am until late in summer, 11am to 9pm in winter. If you'd like a snack of fresh daily smoked fish, mussels, scallops, salmon, or roe, then head for **The Coromandel Smoking Company,** 7 Tiki Rd. (© **07/866-8793**). It's open daily from 8am until 6pm.

IN WHITIANGA

One of my favorite Whitianga spots is **Café Nina,** 20 Victoria St. (© **07/866-5440**), open daily in summer from 8am to 10:30pm and winter from 9am to 5:30pm. You'll get the best coffee and counter food in town at this 100-year-old miner's cottage tucked away in a small back street. It's hugely popular and always has a mixed, slightly alternative crowd.

The Fireplace ★★, 9 The Esplanade (✆ **07/866-4828**), is a great waterfront spot with a courtyard, great seafood, wood-fired pizzas, and good service. They're open daily from 11am to late; be sure to make a reservation. **The Eggsentric Café** ★★, 1047 Purangi Rd., Flaxmill Bay (✆ **07/866-0307**), is near Cooks Beach and just a ferry ride from Whitianga itself. It has a great atmosphere and a chef who does inspiring and delicious things with fresh seafood. They're open Tuesday through Friday 10:30am till late, and weekends 9am until late. **Salt Bar and Café,** 1 Blacksmith Lane, Whitianga (✆ **07/866-5818**), is reasonably new; if you're in for a good time over gourmet meals with a strong Thai flavor this is your spot. It's open daily from 11am until late.

IN PAUANUI/TAIRUA

The one thing lacking in Pauanui is good eateries. You can go upmarket and have no regrets at **Puka Park Resort** ★★★ (p. 183), or you can take the passenger ferry (NZ$5/US$3.50, every hour until 1am in summer) across to Tairua and dine at **Manaia** ★★, 228 Main Rd., Tairua (✆ **07/864-9050**); or at **The Old Mill** ★★, 1 The Esplanade, Tairua (✆ **07/864-7884**), which is the more formal of the two.

IN WHANGAMATA

Café Rossini, 646 Port Rd. (✆ **07/865-6117**), is an unpretentious daytime cafe open 9am–4pm daily. It also opens for dinner Friday and Sunday (6pm–late) from mid-November to April.

EN ROUTE TO TAURANGA

Katikati, known locally as "The Mural Town," is south of Waihi on State Highway 2. In 1996, a festival was held to celebrate the painting of its 20th outdoor mural since 1991 and to reinforce its image as the mural town of New Zealand. For information on the town and surrounding Bay of Plenty area, call into the **Mural Town Visitor Centre,** 34 Main Rd., Katikati (✆ **07/549-1658;** katikatiinfo@wbopdc.govt.nz).

EN ROUTE TO HAMILTON

From Waihi, take State Highway 2 through the Karangahake Gorge and at Paeroa, turn onto State Highway 26. Follow this 76km (47 miles) to Hamilton.

7

Waikato & Bay of Plenty

Forty percent of New Zealand's total population—that's nearly 1.5 million people—lives within a 242km (150-mile) radius of the Waikato district. First settled by the Maori, who recognized its agricultural potential and appreciated its temperate climate, the Waikato is rich in natural resources and is a leading food producer. Its biggest natural asset is the Waikato River, the longest river in New Zealand.

The seaside townships of Tauranga, Te Puke, the mural town of Katikati, and Mount Maunganui, one of the country's most popular beach resorts, are the main components of the Bay of Plenty. Forget woolly sheep, and start thinking fuzzy kiwifruit because that's what this area is famous for—1,677,279,378 kiwifruit were exported from Tauranga in 1998. The area grows 80% of the country's NZ$700-million (US$490-million) export kiwifruit crop. It's also a place of mellow summers; great surf and beaches; big game fishing; long, lazy holidays; and the biggest retired population in the country. It literally is a bay of plenty.

1 Hamilton & the Waikato ✦

127km (79 miles) S of Auckland; 107km (66 miles) NE of Rotorua; 107km (66 miles) E of Tauranga

Unfortunately for Hamilton, its proximity to Auckland (just a 1-hr. drive) means it's often overlooked as a sightseeing destination. Many travelers pass through the city heading south, usually to the famed Waitomo Caves in south Waikato or to Rotorua and Taupo.

If you want to linger awhile, though, you'll discover the hot springs and horse-racing world of Matamata township; the rich Maori culture of Ngaruawahia and more hot springs at Waingaro; the surf and beaches of Raglan; and the antiques and Kentucky-like thoroughbred world of Cambridge.

Hamilton—the country's largest inland city (pop. 106,000)—is a commercial and industrial center. There's something bland about the place despite its pretty face, but there's always a hint of change in the air.

ESSENTIALS

GETTING THERE & GETTING AROUND **By Plane** **Air New Zealand National & Link** (© 0800/767-767 in NZ) plus **Origin Pacific** (© 0800/302-302 in NZ) provide daily service to Hamilton Airport (www.hamiltonairport.co.nz). **Freedom Air International** (© 0800/600-500 in NZ; www.freedomair.com) also operates flights to Australia. The airport is about 15 minutes south of the city. A shuttle service is provided by **Roadcat Transport** (© 07/823-2559) or **Airport Shuttle** (© 07/843-7778).

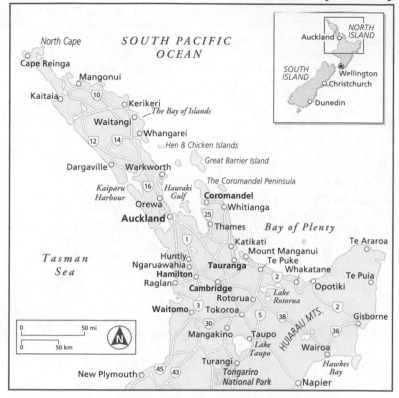

By Coach (Bus)   Both **InterCity (© 09/913-6100)** and **Newmans (© 09/913-6200)** link Hamilton to other major centers.

By Train   The **Tranz Scenic** Overlander route passes through Hamilton on the route between Auckland and Wellington. Call **© 0800/802-802** for timetables and reservations.

By Car   Hamilton is on State Highway 1 (St. Hwy. 1), so you'll pass through it heading north or south. It's usually slightly over an hour's drive from Auckland, but the stretch of road between the two cities is notorious for bad accidents that result in fatalities. *Note:* Please take particular notice of all yellow-line road markings, which designate no-passing sections of a highway. It's 1 to 1½ hours to Rotorua, Tauranga, or Taupo.

For rental cars call **Waikato Car Rentals,** Brooklyn Road, Hamilton (**© 0800/154-444** in NZ, or 07/855-0094; www.waikatocarrentals.co.nz).

By Taxi   **Hamilton Taxi Society (© 0800/477-477** or 07/847-7477; www.hamilton taxis.co.nz) operates a 24-hour service.

ORIENTATION   Both State Highway 1 and the Waikato River run through the heart of Hamilton. Victoria Street is the main street, and the main shopping area fills a compact area around it. The central area is easily negotiated on foot or by car.

VISITOR INFORMATION   The **Hamilton Visitor Information Centre** (© 07/
839-3580; www.waikatonz.com) is in the new Transport Centre on the corner of
Anglesea and Bryce streets. It's open Monday through Friday from 8:30am to 5pm,
Saturday 9am to 4pm, Sunday and public holidays from 10am to 4pm; closed December 25. The **i-Site Waitomo Information Centre,** 21 Waitomo Caves Rd., Waitomo
(© **07/878-7640;** fax 07/878-6184; www.waitomoinfo.co.nz), is open 8am to 8pm
in summer, 8am to 5pm in winter. **Cambridge Information Centre,** corner of Queen
and Victoria streets, Cambridge (© **07/823-3456;** fax 07/823-3457; www.
cambridge.net.nz), is open Monday through Friday from 9am to 5:30pm and weekends 10am to 4pm in summer; and in winter, Monday through Friday from 9am until
5:30pm, weekends 10am to 4pm. **Information Raglan** is at 4 Wallis St., Raglan (© 07/
825-0556; fax 07/825-0557; www.raglan.org.nz), and is open Monday through Friday from 10am to 5pm, and Saturday, Sunday, and holidays from 9am to 4pm.

SPECIAL EVENTS   The **Hamilton Gardens Summer Festival** (© 07/856-3200)
is held in mid-February each year. **Balloons Over Waikato** (© 07/839-3580) is a
spectacular event featuring over 30 hot-air balloons in mid-April. The **NZ National
Agricultural Fieldays** (© **07/843-4499;** www.fieldays.co.nz) is a huge event staged
at Mystery Creek in mid-June. It attracts nearly 150,000 national and international
visitors. For further information on Waikato events, contact **Events Hamilton** (© 07/
838-6679; www.hamilton.events.co.nz).

EXPLORING THE AREA

To learn about activities in the smaller rural towns of Morrinsville, Matamata, Ngaruawahia, Te Aroha, and Te Awamutu, pick up brochures from the Hamilton visitor
center.

IN HAMILTON

Riverboat fans will get great pleasure from the **MV *Waipa Delta*** ✦ (© **0800/472-
335** or 07/854-7813; fax 07/854-9419; www.waipadelta.co.nz). Modeled on paddle
steamers of the last century, this floating restaurant/cruise vessel has a range of tours:
a luncheon cruise from 12:30 to 2pm˙ (NZ$40/US$28); a scenic afternoon tea cruise
from 3 to 4pm (NZ$20/US$14); and a moonlight dinner cruise with live entertainment (NZ$55/US$39). Children ages 5 to 14 are half price, and family passes are
available.

   Hamilton Gardens ✦✦, Cobham Drive (© **07/856-3200;** www.hamiltongardens.
co.nz), is the region's most popular visitor destination. It consists of 58 hectares (143
acres) of specialty gardens along the banks of the Waikato River. You don't have to be
a gardener to appreciate the serenity of the Japanese Garden or the beauty of the herb
garden. The Gardens Terrace restaurant and the Gardens Café are both open daily
from 10am to 5pm in summer and until 4pm in winter. **Hamilton Lake** and its 56-
hectare (138-acre) reserve is also a pleasant place for a quiet wander. It's just outside
the central business district.

   The **Waikato Museum of Art & History** ✦✦✦, Victoria and Grantham streets, Private Bag (© **07/838-6606;** www.waikatomuseum.org.nz), and **Exscite** ✦✦✦ (© 07/
838-6553; fax 07/838-6571) are especially good value for children. The museum has a
fine display of Maori art and carving from the area's Tainui people. Exscite is a madhouse
of colorful fun designed as a learning environment for children. Museum admission is
by donation; Exscite costs around NZ$6 (US$4.20) for adults, NZ$5 (US$3.50) for

---

Kids The Sweet Stuff

At **Chocolate Expo,** Donovans Chocolates, 137 Maui St., Hamilton (© 07/847-5771; www.donovanschocolates.co.nz), you can buy from the factory store or linger in the cafe. On the other side of town, **Candyland,** 75 Henry Rd., Taupiri (© **07/824-6818;** www.candyland.co.nz), is New Zealand's largest candy shop. Visit the Candy Museum, watch chocolates being made, or create your own lollipop at the candy-making show. The show costs NZ$8 (US$5.60) for adults and NZ$5 (US$3.50) for children under 12. Candy demonstrations are at 10:30am and 1pm on weekends and holidays.

---

children, and NZ$20 (US$14) per family. Both are open daily from 10am to 4:30pm (closed Dec 25).

Hamilton Zoo and the **FreeFlight Sanctuary** ☀, Brymer Road (© **07/838-6720;** www.hamiltonzoo.co.nz), is a 21-hectare (52-acre) retreat for birds and animals; it's 5 minutes off State Highway 1, west of Hamilton. It's open daily from 9am to 5pm. They also have late night openings (until 8pm) on Wednesdays and Saturdays in January and on Saturdays in February. And if you're at this end of town, you might consider going a bit farther to **Waingaro Hot Springs** ☀ (©/fax **07/825-4761;** waingaro. hot.springs@clear.net.nz); it's 23km (14 miles) west of Ngaruawahia (about 30 min. from Hamilton). Big waterslides, thermal mineral pools, bumper boats, and barbecues make this a terrific family outing. It's open daily from 9am to 10pm.

When it turns dark, you might like to try your luck in Hamilton's new casino complex, **Skycity Riverside Hamilton,** 346 Victoria St. (© **07/834-4900;** www.sky riverside.co.nz), which has 20 gaming tables, 300 gaming machines, plus bar and restaurant facilities. It's open daily 9am to 3am.

IN CAMBRIDGE

This pretty oak-filled town of 11,000 is the bright star of the Australasian bloodstock industry—sort of a miniature Kentucky, if you like. Its old homes and rolling green fields make it a delightful spot for a day visit from Hamilton, or a stopover on your journey south. In the last 2 years, it has become more lively and it deserves at least a 1-night stopover.

The **Cambridge Thoroughbred Lodge,** on State Highway 1, 6km (3¾ miles) south of Cambridge (© **07/827-8118;** www.cambridgethoroughbredlodge.co.nz), is home to the **NZ Horse Magic Show.** The 1-hour shows are given Tuesday through Sunday at 10:30am; bookings are essential. The cost of NZ$12 (US$8.40) for adults, NZ$5 (US$3.50) for children ages 3 to 14, and NZ$25 (US$18) per family includes a tour and horse ride. In addition, casual tours are given from 10am to 3pm daily and cost NZ$5 (US$3.50) for adults and NZ$3 (US$2.10) for children. If you fancy **"A Night at the Trots,"** head to the **Cambridge Raceway,** Taylor Street, Cambridge (© **07/827-5506;** www.cambridgeraceway.co.nz), for the thrill and excitement of live harness and greyhound racing.

The **Cambridge Country Store** ☀☀, 92 Victoria St. (© **07/827-8715;** www. cambridgecountrystore.co.nz), is a wonderful place to loosen your purse strings. You'll find a wide range of top New Zealand arts and crafts in this old converted church. It's open daily from 8:30am to 5pm. **All Saints Café** (© **07/827-7100**), upstairs, is the perfect place to contemplate your purchases. It's open Monday through Saturday 8:30am to 4:30pm and 9am to 4:30pm on Sunday.

The town is also a treasure trove of antiques. Antiques fairs are in September and April and the Cambridge Information Centre has a good brochure that lists the best antique dealers in Hamilton and Cambridge. If you're in the mood for a stroll, pick up the *Heritage Trail* brochure, which details heritage sites in town.

Nearby **Lake Karapiro**—8km (5 miles) from town—is also a pleasant outing for boating, sailing, water-skiing, swimming, and rowing. If you're lucky, you might even spy one of New Zealand's Olympic rowing champions in training. Cambridge is home to the gold medal-winning Evers-Swindell twins, Georgina and Caroline.

IN WAITOMO: EXPERIENCING THE CAVES

The busy little pocket of tourist activity that is Waitomo is the exception in the otherwise quiet, cow-filled south Waikato pasture. The tiny village owes its existence to the remarkable limestone caves 70 km (43 miles) south of Hamilton.

You can get to the area via the **Waitomo Shuttle Bus** (© **0800/808-279** in NZ, or 07/873-8279), which connects to InterCity and Newmans coach services and Tranz Scenic trains in nearby Otorohanga. They also connect with Freedom Air at Hamilton Airport. **Waitomo Wanderer Scenic Shuttle** (© **0508/926-337** in NZ, or 07/873-6108; www.waitomotours.co.nz) offers daily service between the caves and Rotorua. Kiwi Experience and Magic Travellers also run to the area. If you're driving from the north, take State Highway 1 south to State Highway 3, just south of Otorohanga, and turn west at the signpost for Waitomo Caves.

The **Museum of Caves & i-Site Visitor Centre,** 21 Waitomo Caves Rd., Waitomo (© **07/878-7640;** www.waitomo-museum.co.nz), is open daily from 8am to 8pm in summer, from 8am to 5:30pm in winter. Admission to the museum itself is NZ$5 (US$3.50) for adults and free for children.

The caves *are* what make Waitomo a visitor destination, and the best among them are the **Waitomo Glowworm Caves** ✸✸✸ , Waitomo Caves Road (© **07/878-8227;** www.waitomocaves.co.nz). The caves' most impressive feature is **"The Cathedral"** ✸✸✸ , which rises 14m (46 ft.) and is an acoustically perfect auditorium that has been the site of performances by the Vienna Boys' Choir and Dame Kiri Te Kanawa. Your tour takes you through 250m (820 ft.) of stunning underground scenery, culminating in the glowworm caves. A cafe and shop complex are also on site.

If you have time, include **Aranui Cave** ✸✸—15 minutes down the road—which doesn't have glowworms, but does have the most spectacular natural formations; you're allowed to take photographs here. Tickets for both are sold at the Waitomo Glowworm Cave ticket office.

Tours in the Glowworm Cave include a magical boat ride through the **Glowworm Grotto.** These leave daily every half-hour from 9am to 5pm, and hourly in the Aranui Cave from 10am to 3pm. A two-cave combination ticket costs about NZ$48 (US$34) per adult and NZ$23 (US$16) per child; a one-cave ticket costs NZ$30 (US$21) at Waitomo Caves and NZ$28 (US$20) at Aranui Cave, and children pay half price. The best time to visit the Glowworm Grotto is mid- to late afternoon, when the crowds are smaller. If the weather is cool, bring a sweater because it's even cooler underground.

After being closed to the public for 15 years, **Ruakuri** reopened in June 2005. Laced with myth and legend, Ruakuri ("den of dogs") was first discovered by Maori almost 500 years ago. It takes its name from the pack of wild dogs that lived in the cave entrance.

Underworld Adventures

The Legendary Black Water Rafting Company 𝕬𝕬𝕬 (② **0800/228-464** in NZ, or 07/878-6219; www.blackwaterrafting.co.nz) started the whole cave rafting business 17 years ago. The highlight of its trips is a 1.5m (5-ft.) jump off an underground waterfall. Black Labyrinth is the gentler of the options. The 3-hour excursion includes cave tubing—you float through the caves on a rubber tube. It costs NZ$85 (US$60) per person; you must be over 12 and 40 kilograms (88 lb.). Black Abyss is for those over 16 and is a much more energetic 5-hour affair that includes abseiling and rock climbing; the cost is NZ$160 (US$112) per person. This company also has a fabulous little cafe and a free Jacuzzi for cavers.

   Waitomo Adventures Ltd. (② **0800/924-866** in NZ, or 07/878-7788; www.waitomo.co.nz) has four rather endearingly named adventures: Tumu Tumu Toobing, which involves lots of swimming and floating over 4 hours (around NZ$95/US$67); Haggas Honking Holes, which is the most action-packed with three abseils in waterfalls, rock climbing, and groveling—you need to be very fit, agile, and brave for this one (NZ$165/US$116); Lost World, which has a huge 100m (328-ft.) abseil into the Lost World (about NZ$225/US$158); and Lost World All Day Epic, which adds lots more wet stuff (about NZ$355/US$249).

   While a number of companies will take you underground, only one delivers a genuine caving experience with a qualified instructor: **Absolute Adventure** (② **0800/787-323** in NZ; www.absoluteadventure.co.nz). It's by far the most physically demanding of Waitomo's activities and includes abseiling, traversing high ledges, bridging, rock climbing, squeezing and crawling through narrow passages, and climbing waterfalls. A 2-hour trip costs NZ$120 (US$84) and the 4-hour trip costs NZ$165 (US$116).

Tours of the cave now depart from the **Ruakuri Information Centre,** at the Legendary Black Water Rafting Co, 585 Waitomo Caves Rd. (② **0800/222-323;** www.ruakuri.co.nz), daily (except Dec 25) at 9am, 11am, 1pm, and 3pm. Admission costs NZ$45 (US$32) adults, NZ$15 (US$11) children ages 5 to 14.

   If you'd rather stay above ground, why not tackle the new **Dundle Hill Walk** (② **0800/924-866** in NZ, or 07/878-7788; fax 07/878-6266; www.waitomowalk.com). During this 2-day, clearly marked, self-guided walk through native bush, forestry, and farmland, you'll walk about 12km (7.4 miles) a day and stay at Dundle Hill hut. It requires moderate fitness and costs NZ$50 (US$35) adults, NZ$20 (US$14) children.

WHERE TO STAY
IN HAMILTON

If you want rural charm 20 minutes from Hamilton, ring Peter and Daphne Searle at **Uliveto Country Stay & Olive Grove** 𝕬, 164 Finlayson Rd., Ngahinapouri, Hamilton (② **07/825-2116;** www.uliveto.co.nz), which has two lovely rooms. Near the airport, **Hamilton Airport Motor Inn** 𝕬𝕬, Airport Road (② **0800/106-679** in NZ, or 07/843-8412; www.airportinn.co.nz), has rooms from NZ$95 to NZ$145 (US$67–US$102). Backpackers can try **YHA Hamilton,** 1190 Victoria St. (② **0800/278-299** in NZ, or 07/838-0009; www.yha.co.nz), where dorms are NZ$20 to NZ$24 (US$14–US$17) per person.

   All rates include 12.5% GST and free parking.

Novotel Tainui ★★ *Value*   This is still one of my favorite hotels—there's just something open and welcoming about the place, and for the price, you get great amenities. New in 1999, its large rooms have contemporary decor and overlook either the city or the river. All have desks and nice bathrooms; there are two slightly larger standard rooms on each floor. If you want reliable service and immaculate rooms, Novotel offers great value—and all rooms were given a complete soft-furnishings refurbishment in 2005.

7 Alma St., Hamilton. © 0800/450-050 in NZ, or 07/838-1366. Fax 07/838-1367. www.accorhotels.co.nz. 177 units. NZ$170–NZ$350 (US$119–US$245). Rates include airport transfers. Long-stay and special deals available. AE, DC, MC, V. Valet parking NZ$10 (US$7). **Amenities:** Restaurant; bar; nearby golf course; small gym; indoor Jacuzzi; sauna; children's programs; concierge; tour bookings; car rentals; secretarial services; salon; 24-hr. room service; massage; babysitting; laundry service; same-day dry cleaning; nonsmoking rooms; on-call doctor/dentist. *In room:* A/C, TV w/pay movies, fax in executive suites, dataport, minibar, fridge, coffeemaker, hair dryer, iron, safe.

Rydges Le Grand Hotel ★★   Rooms of an extraordinary size are the lasting memory of Le Grand, which opened as a boutique hotel in 1994. The style feels like that of a small European hotel, with high ceilings, tiled balconies, and huge potted palms. It's much more traditional than the Novotel down the road (see above). This is one of the nicer Hamilton places, and it's right in the heart of shopping and restaurant zones.

Victoria and Collingwood sts., Hamilton. © 07/839-1994. Fax 07/839-7994. www.rydges.com. 38 units. NZ$149–NZ$250 (US$104–US$175) standard; NZ$250–NZ$450 (US$175–US$315) deluxe; NZ$350–NZ$450 (US$245–US$315) executive and honeymoon suites. Long-stay and weekend rates available. AE, MC, V. **Amenities:** Restaurant; bar; concierge; tour bookings; car rentals; business center; secretarial services; 24-hr. room service; massage; babysitting; laundry service; same-day dry cleaning; on-call doctor/dentist. *In room:* A/C, TV, dataport, minibar, fridge, coffeemaker, hair dryer, iron.

IN CAMBRIDGE

Park House, 70 Queen St., Cambridge (© 07/827-6368; www.parkhouse.co.nz), has three B&B rooms in a smart Georgian home, ranging from NZ$130 to NZ$160 (US$91–US$112). Bill and Pat Hargreaves will make sure you are well looked after.

Huntington Stables Retreat ★★★ *Finds*   This luxury retreat in the middle of lush Waikato farmland is a real find. They've done everything right, and their two stable suites skimp on nothing. One has a king-size bed, the other a super-king-size/twin setup; all smartly furnished rooms are generous in size, plus there's a beautiful pool, Jacuzzi, and sauna right outside the back door. The luxurious bathrooms feature shower and bath, and Egyptian cotton towels; and French doors open out from your private lounge to a deck overlooking farmland. From the wine cellar to the well-stocked pantry and fridge, you'll be exceedingly well looked after with every comfort at your fingertips. I was reluctant to leave.

106 Maungakawa Rd., RD4, Cambridge, 2351. © 07/823-4120. Fax 07/823-4126. www.huntington.co.nz. 2 units. From NZ$390–NZ$450 (US$273–US$315). Rates include breakfast provisions and airport transfers. Long-stay and weekend packages available. AE, DC, MC, V. No children under 12. **Amenities:** Outdoor pool; nearby golf course; Jacuzzi; sauna; massage; laundry service; nonsmoking rooms; on-call doctor/dentist. *In room:* TV/VCR, dataport, kitchen, fridge, coffeemaker, hair dryer, iron.

The Mews ★★ *Value*   Every comfort has been accounted for in this smart motel complex. All units have fabulous double Jacuzzis—after a day on the road, I can think of nothing better than filling it with bubbles and soaking. Don't drive past this picturesque stone-and-shingle complex—it's even better on the inside.

20 Hamilton Rd., Cambridge. © 07/827-7166. Fax 07/827-7163. www.cambridgemews.co.nz. 12 units. NZ$140 (US$98) studio; NZ$145 (US$102) 1-bedroom unit; NZ$200 (US$140) 2-bedroom apt. Extra person NZ$20 (US$14).

Rates include airport transfers. Long-stay, off-peak, and special deals available. AE, DC, MC, V. **Amenities:** Nearby golf course; tour bookings; car rentals; laundry service; same-day dry cleaning; nonsmoking rooms; on-call doctor/dentist. *In room:* TV, dataport, kitchen, fridge, coffeemaker, hair dryer, iron.

Thornton House 🍁🍁   Christine Manson and David Cowley have opened the doors of their gorgeous 1902 villa, providing two rooms that are bound to please. The Blue Room is smaller, cozy, and moody with a shower-only en suite. The bigger Garden Room has a tub, an extra single bed, and a door to the veranda. Both are beautifully decorated with stereos and CD selections. The town center is just a 5-minute walk away, but because this is so much a family home, you may just want to stay indoors.

2 Thornton St., Cambridge 📞 07/827-7567. Fax 07/827-7568. www.thorntonhouse.co.nz. 2 units. From NZ$195–NZ$230 (US$137–US$161). Rates include breakfast. Long-stay rates available. AE, DC, MC, V. **Amenities:** Nearby golf course and tennis courts; tour bookings; car rentals; massage; laundry service; same-day dry cleaning; nonsmoking rooms; on-call doctor/dentist; airport transfers. *In room:* TV, dataport, coffeemaker, hair dryer.

IN WAITOMO

Given the nature of this place, I'm surprised no one has thought to build an underground hotel. Perhaps it would be better than some of the aboveground choices: The pickings are slim here. Caving backpackers should look in the direction of the new and sparkling **Kiwi Paka YHA** 🍁🍁🍁, Hotel Road, Waitomo (📞 07/878-3395; www.kiwipaka-yha.co.nz), which opened in 2002, providing excellent chalets. Dorm rooms are from NZ$25 (US$18) per person and NZ$60 (US$42) double; chalets with private bathrooms are NZ$75 to NZ$120 (US$53–US$84). They're only a 2-minute walk from the caves and have state-of-the-art facilities as well as a great little cafe. Another option is **Juno Hall Backpackers and Waitomo Horse Trekking** 🍁🍁, Main Road, Waitomo (📞/fax 07/878-7649). Its new farmhouse-style hostel has dorm rooms around NZ$20 (US$14), doubles around NZ$50 (US$35), and triple and family rooms from NZ$65 to NZ$85 (US$46–US$60). A nice B&B in Waitomo, **Abseil Breakfast Inn,** Waitomo Caves Village (📞 07/878-7815; www.abseilinn.co.nz), has four rooms from NZ$120 to NZ$150 (US$84–US$105).

   Kamahi Cottage, 229 Barber Rd., RD5, Otorohanga (📞/fax 07/873-0849; www.kamahi.co.nz), is 30 minutes from Waitomo Caves and is the nicest B&B in the area. They have a charming self-contained, one-bedroom cottage for NZ$225 (US$158). As an alternative, you can try the **Waitomo Caves Hotel,** Lemon Point Road, Waitomo (📞 07/878-8204; www.waitomocaveshotel.co.nz), but I consider it highly overrated. It's a shame that this fabulous old building with its rich history and terrific location has been allowed to fall into such a state. At best, the hotel provides a tidy level of budget-quality accommodations. At worst, it is desperately in need of a major revamp. Rooms run from NZ$130 (US$91).

WHERE TO DINE
IN HAMILTON

The visitor center has a helpful free *Dine Out* guide. You'll find the bulk of the best restaurants, cafes, bars, and nightspots in a tight cluster in and around the south end of Victoria Street.

   The favorite trendy restaurant (at press time) is **Domaine** 🍁🍁🍁, 575 Victoria St. (📞 07/839-2100), which attracts a mixed business crowd during the day and has just enough flair to keep you coming back. **Hydro Majestic** 🍁🍁🍁, 33 Jellicoe Dr., Hamilton East (📞 07/859-0020), is favored for its funky kitsch atmosphere and great food.

Cullen's, Marketplace, Hood Street, Hamilton (© 07/838-3618), is also very popular, though I found it less stylish than the two above.

Tables On The River ✱, 12 Alma St. (© 07/839-6555), which overlooks the river, still gets top marks from many, but I think there's a better over-the-river setting at the Novotel's **Caffe Alma** (see "Where to Stay," above). Also popular is **The Balcony Restaurant and Bar,** next door to Tables (© 07/838-3133), and yes, it also has river-view dining. For the best breakfasts and lunches, go to **Scott Epicurean Café** ✱✱✱, 181 Victoria St. (© 07/839-6680); it's open daily.

Another good choice is **Escaba** ✱, 237 Victoria St. (© 07/834-3131), which, despite its stark interior, has friendly staff and well-priced food. Just down the road, **Metropolis Caffé** ✱, 211 Victoria St. (© 07/834-2081), has excellent coffee, vegetarian meals, and a slightly crazy interior popular with a crowd in their 20s and 30s. Next door is **Iguana** (© 07/834-2280), which deserves a mention for its sushi, gourmet pizzas, comfy booths, and fast-paced night scene. **Barzurks,** on Victoria Street, opposite Rydges Le Grand Hotel, is sought out for its superb pizzas and laid-back atmosphere. **Museum Café** ✱✱, 1 Grantham St. (© 07/839-7209), offers dinner Tuesday through Saturday and over-the-river cafe service throughout the day.

IN CAMBRIDGE

At last! The Cambridge dining scene has something to skite about. **Onyx** ✱✱✱, 70 Alpha St., Cambridge (© 07/827-7740), should be your first port of call. Here you'll find fabulous wood-fired pizzas, great salads, and tasty seafood platters. **Instone Café** ✱✱, 85 Victoria St., Cambridge (© 07/827-8590), is open for great coffee and snacks daily 7am to 7pm; and **Essenza** ✱✱, State Highway 1, on the way to Hamilton (© 07/823-1515), is an unexpectedly good coffee emporium cast amid the fields. Another rural option is the hidden gem called **The Boatshed Café** ✱✱, RD2, Amber Lane, Cambridge (© 07/827-8286), which overlooks Lake Karapiro and also runs a rental kayak operation that takes you through a canyon sparkling with glowworms.

IN WAITOMO

About the best you'll find in these parts is Blackwater Rafting's **Long Black Café** ✱, Main Road (© 07/878-7361), where the counter food includes good vegetarian fare, and a working espresso machine is a good sign. They have all-day breakfasts and excellent coffee. Alternatively, try **Morepork Pizzeria & Café** ✱, at Kiwi Paka YHA, School Road, Waitomo (© 07/878-3395); it's open daily for breakfast, lunch, and dinner.

2 Tauranga & Bay of Plenty ✱✱✱

208km (129 miles) SE of Auckland; 86km (53 miles) NW of Rotorua

Tauranga is no longer the sleepy place of my childhood holidays. Somewhere along the way, it has transformed itself into a sort of miniature version of Australia's Gold Coast. Today, it is New Zealand's second-fastest-growing area after Queenstown. It has a population of about 100,000 and boasts 2,400 hours of sunshine per year. Tauranga and its nearby beachfront neighbor, Mount Maunganui, are confident, thriving urban centers, and no matter what time of year you visit, you'll be spoiled with choices for anything related to outdoor beach-driven activity.

ESSENTIALS

GETTING THERE **By Plane** Air New Zealand National & Link (© 0800/ 767-767 in NZ), as well as **Origin Pacific** (© 0800/302-302), operate daily flights from Tauranga and Whakatane to Auckland, Wellington, and Christchurch.

By Coach (Bus) InterCity (© 09/913-6100) and **Newmans** (© 09/913-6200) both operate daily services between Tauranga and Auckland, Napier, Rotorua, Taupo, Thames, and Wellington. The **Magic Travellers** (© 09/358-5600) buses also stop in Tauranga en route to Rotorua.

By Car Drive south from Auckland on State Highway 1, then go east on State Highway 2. From the Coromandel Peninsula, take Highway 25 or 26 to Waihi and pick up Highway 2. The trip takes around 3 hours. If you're coming from Hamilton, the trip takes 1½ hours, and from Rotorua, around 1 hour.

ORIENTATION Once you get used to the frequent roundabouts, you'll find this an easy city to navigate. **Edgewater** is the beautifully paved product of multimillion-dollar inner city redevelopment. It's one of the prettiest downtown areas in the country. **Cameron Road** is the main arterial route. The toll bridge offers a short cut to **Mount Maunganui,** where you'll find that Project Phoenix has converted the downtown shopping area into a palm-filled promenade that's hard to beat. **Ocean Beach** features great stretches of sand and a growing number of high-rise apartments and holiday homes. More than 60km (37 miles) of continuous white-sand beach runs from Mount Maunganui to Whakatane.

GETTING AROUND Some distance out from Tauranga, expect to share the road with a scary number of huge trucks, all bound for the port. The traffic flow is fast and often congested. Public transport is limited within Tauranga itself. Walk if you can.

VISITOR INFORMATION The **Tauranga i–Site Visitor Centre,** Civic Centre, 95 Willow St., Tauranga (© **07/578-8103;** fax 07/578-7020; www.tauranga.govt.nz), is open daily, 8:30am to 5:30pm. Pick up a free copy of the excellent *Bay of Plenty Visitor Guide.* The **Mount Maunganui i–SiteVisitor Centre** is on Salisbury Avenue (© **07/575-5099;** fax 07/578-7020; trgvin@tauranga.govt.nz). The **Katikati Information Centre** is at 36 Main Rd. (© **07/549-1658;** fax 07/549-1798; katikatiinfo@ wbopdc.govt.nz). For more information on the area, check out www.bayof plentynz.com, www.cityoftauranga.co.nz, and www.tauranga.co.nz.

SPECIAL EVENTS Tauranga and Mount Maunganui offer a profusion of summer events that cover everything from ironman competitions and yachting regattas to beauty pageants and jazz festivals. Pick up the free Oceanfest guide to summer events at the visitor center, call © **07/577-7209,** or visit www.tauranga.govt.nz/events for more information.

EXPLORING THE AREA
IN & NEAR TAURANGA

Sun, sea, and surf rule here. But before you take to the water, take a look at **Kiwi360** (© **07/573-6340;** www.kiwi360.com), on the main Rotorua/Tauranga highway 5km (3 miles) south of Te Puke. It's definitely different, and if you want insight into this multi-million-dollar industry, this is the place—and it's great for kids, too. There are daily tours through orchards and theme parks, a kiwifruit souvenir shop, and a restaurant.

The mural town of **Katikati** is worth a brief stopover. Ask at the visitor center for the location of some of the town's many professionally painted street murals. And take a dip in the thermal **Sapphire Springs,** Hot Springs Road (✆ **07/549-0768;** sapphire.springs@xtra.co.nz), set in 31 hectares (78 acres) of native bush.

In Tauranga, the **Elms Mission House,** Mission and Chapel streets (✆ **07/577-9772;** www.theelms.org.nz), is one of the finest examples of colonial architecture of its time (1847). The house is open Wednesday, Saturday, Sunday, and public holidays from 2 to 4pm and costs NZ$5 (US$3.50) for adults, NZ50¢ (US35¢) for children. If you're interested in more of the town's history, pick up the excellent brochure *Historic Tauranga* from the information center.

Garden enthusiasts can pick up the *Garden Trail* brochure at the visitor center. If you don't want to do the whole tour, at least visit the **Cascades Fountain Garden** ✿✿, 170 Plummers Point Rd., Tauranga (✆/fax **07/548-0554;** www.cascade.orcon.net.nz). Open daily from 10am to 10pm, the gardens are filled with unique water features with night lighting. Admission costs less than NZ$10 (US$7). **McLaren Falls Park** ✿✿, McLaren Falls Road, Tauranga (✆ **07/577-7000**), is another lovely stop. It consists of 170 hectares (420 acres) of lakeland park set amid pastoral farming and horticulture, containing one of the best botanical tree collections in the North Island. If you have a license, you can fish for trout, or simply enjoy the arboretum and numerous walking tracks.

If wine is your passion, go to **Mills Reef Winery & Restaurant,** Moffat Road, Bethlehem, Tauranga (✆ **0800/645-577** in NZ, or 07/576-8800; www.millsreef. co.nz); and while you're in the area, call in to **Prenzel of Tauranga,** 171 Moffat Rd. (✆ **07/579-2668;** www.prenzel.com), who are the distillers of delicious liqueurs, schnapps, flavored olive oils, and cooking products. They're open daily and offer free shop tastings.

Just south of Tauranga, three more stops are creating a buzz. **Te Puke Vintage Auto Barn** ✿✿, Te Puke–Rotorua Highway (✆ **07/573-6547;** www.vintagecars.nzhere. com), offers the chance to view over 100 vintage and classic vehicles, daily from 9am to 5pm. **Mossop's Honey Shoppe** ✿, State Highway 29 (✆ **07/543-0971;** www. mossopshoney.co.nz), has an interesting live bee display and a myriad of honey-based products and gifts. At the **Comvita Visitor Centre** ✿✿, Wison Road South, Paengaroa (✆ **0800/493-782** in NZ; www.comvita.com), 9km (5½ miles) south of Te Puke, you'll find a multi-award-winning heart of natural health and bee products, with over 100 honeys to sample.

The most spectacular of Tauranga's attractions is nearby **White Island** ✿✿✿ , New Zealand's only active marine volcano. Among the operators offering aerial excursions are **Vulcan Helicopters** (✆ **0800/804-354** in NZ, or 07/308-4188; www.vulcanheli.co.nz) and **East Bay Flight Centre** (✆ **07/308-8446;** fax 07/308-8042). Both operate out of Whakatane. **White Island Tours,** 15 Strand St. E., Whakatane (✆ **0800/733-529** in NZ, or 07/308-9588; www.whiteisland.co.nz), will put you on a luxury launch and give you a 6-hour guided tour with lunch and safety gear included. Don't despair if you don't make it to White Island from here, as there are several Rotorua operators, which also offer great flights.

IN MOUNT MAUNGANUI

The town is named after the small mountain, but it is now often referred to by its Maori name, **Mauao.** The biggest attraction here has always been **Ocean Beach** ✿✿✿ , famed for its surf and great swimming. **The Mount** 🟊🟊 itself has a network of lovely walkways. The full 3.5km (2.2-mile) walk around the Mount takes about an hour. You can also climb to the top of its 252m (827 ft.), which takes about 2 hours. Pick up the free *Walker's Guide to Mauao* from the visitor center.

At the base of the Mount, on Adams Avenue, the **Mount Maunganui Hot Salt Water Pools** 🟊🟊🟊, Adams Ave. (© **07/575-0868;** h2omanagement@xtra.co.nz), is a modern complex where you can soak away all your aches and pains in water warmed to 102°F (39°C); the active and children's pools are 90°F (32°C). Private pools and massage services are available. Hours are Monday through Saturday from 6am to 10pm and Sunday from 8am to 10pm. Admission is around NZ$5 (US$3.50) for adults and NZ$3 (US$2.10) for children. Massage costs NZ$55 (US$39) for 1 hour.

OUTDOOR PURSUITS

DOLPHIN SWIMMING   Several companies offer the opportunity to get in the water with the common dolphins that live in the bay. Try **Butler's Swim With Dolphins,** Pier J, Tauranga Marina, Keith Alan Drive, or Salisbury Wharf, Mount Maunganui (© **0508/288-537** in NZ, or 07/578-3197; www.swimwithdolphins.co.nz). Expeditions depart Tauranga daily at 8:45am and the Mount at 9:15am for a full-day outing. For information on the ethics of swimming with dolphins, see the section on ecotourism in chapter 2.

FISHING   Blue Ocean Charters, Coronation Pier, Tauranga (© **07/578-9685;** www.blueoceancharters.co.nz), offers half- and full-day reef fishing, day and overnight hapuka fishing, and ecotrips to Mayor Island.

FOUR-WHEEL-DRIVE ADVENTURES   Longridge Fun Park (© **0800/867-386** in NZ, or 07/533-1515; www.longridgepark.co.nz) is at Paengaroa on State Highway 33, a half-hour south of Tauranga. Open from 9am, they have self-drive 4WD cars costing around NZ$70 (US$49) for adults and NZ$30 (US$21) for children for 3km (2 miles) of fun.

JET-BOATING   There are reliable thrills to be had with **Longridge Jet** (© **0800/867-386** in NZ, or 07/533-1515; www.longridgepark.co.nz).

SEA KAYAKING   Oceanix Sea Kayaking Expeditionz, Mount Maunganui (© **07/572-2226;** www.oceanix.co.nz), specializes in sea kayaking and snowboarding tours from around NZ$95 (US$67).

SKYDIVING   Tauranga Tandem Skydiving at Tauranga Airport (© **07/576-7990;** freefall@xtra.co.nz), is your best bet. A basic jump will cost around NZ$200 (US$140).

SURFING   Hibiscus Surf School, Mount Maunganui (© **07/575-3792**), offers exclusive personal tuition with surf instructor Rebecca Taylor, who will quickly bring you up to speed on local surf and ocean conditions. Prices range from NZ$80 (US$56) for 2 hours to NZ$230 (US$161) for 6 hours.

WHITE-WATER RAFTING   There's no shortage of rafting operators. **Wet 'n' Wild Rafting** 🟊, 2 White St., Rotorua (© **0800/462-7238** in NZ; www.wetnwildrafting. co.nz), operates on five rivers in this region, offering a wide range of adventures depending on your level of experience. You can add more fun by combining rafting with jet-boating, a helicopter ride, and mountain biking.

WHERE TO STAY

Every summer, more than 60,000 New Zealanders make their annual holiday pilgrimage to Tauranga and Mount Maunganui. If you plan to come here between December and February, book well in advance. All rates below include 12.5% GST and free parking.

IN & NEAR TAURANGA

You'll find most motels on Waihi Road and 15th Avenue. The **Tauranga YHA** is at 171 Elizabeth St. (© **0800/278-299** in NZ, or 07/578-5064; www.yha.co.nz). The new and classy **Hotel on Devonport** ✦✦✦ , 72 Devonport Rd., Tauranga (© **07/ 578-2668;** www.hotelondevonport.net.nz), is a boutique establishment right in the center of the city. Rooms are big and modern.

Ridge Country Retreat ✦✦✦ Finds   This gorgeous small boutique lodge and spa provides just about anything you could wish for in a smart, contemporary environment on 14 hectares (35 acres) of sloping hills and native bush just out of the city. It has fabulous facilities, including a whole range of beauty therapies and massages, and rooms are big and sumptuous. Bathrooms are also large and very well appointed. It's all about understated luxury and a chance to recharge, revitalize, and replenish, say Joanne O'Keeffe and Penny Oxnam. Newer and more stylish than Cassimir, this is a choice you won't regret.

300 Rocky Cutting Rd., Welcome Bay, Tauranga. © **07/542-1301.** Fax 07/542-2116. www.rcr.co.nz. 11 units. NZ$890–NZ$980 (US$623–US$686). AE, MC, V. Rates include full breakfast, predinner drinks, and 5-course dinner. Off-season rates available. No children under 12. **Amenities:** Heated outdoor lap pool; nearby golf course; tour bookings; car rentals; some business services; massage; laundry service; same-day dry cleaning; nonsmoking rooms. *In room:* A/C, TV/VCR, fax, dataport, minibar, fridge, coffeemaker, hair dryer, iron, safe.

IN MOUNT MAUNGANUI

Pacific Coast Backpackers, 432 Maunganui Rd. (© **0800/666-622** in NZ, or 07/574-9601; www.pacificcoastlodge.co.nz), is just a few hundred meters from the beach and downtown. Dorm beds start at NZ$20 (US$14). **Baywatch Motor Inn,** 349A Maunganui Rd. (© **0800/229-928** in NZ, or 07/574-7744; www.baywatch motorinn.co.nz), provides excellent rooms, all with Jacuzzis.

Puerta del Sol Golfing Retreat ✦✦✦ Finds   If you weren't planning on visiting Mount Maunganui, change your mind and head for Puerta del Sol, a luxurious slice of Mexico right in the middle of New Zealand. It's upmarket, personalized, private—in short, one of the best B&Bs in the country. Look out from the yucca-surrounded swimming pool to the Mount Maunganui Golf Course, a championship course just a few steps away. All suites feature Mexican ranch decor, balconies, king-size beds, and robes and other extras.

214 Ocean Beach Rd., Mount Maunganui. © **07/575-8665.** Fax 07/575-8695. www.puertadelsol.co.nz. 3 units. From NZ$350–NZ$450 (US$245–US$315). Rates include continental breakfast and airport transfers; dinner by arrangement. Long-stay and off-peak rates available. AE, MC, V. No children under 12. Closed in July. **Amenities:** Outdoor pool; 18-hole international golf course on rear boundary; nearby tennis courts; Jacuzzi; bike rentals; massage; laundry service; next-day dry cleaning; nonsmoking rooms. *In room:* TV, dataport, minibar, fridge, coffeemaker, hair dryer, iron.

WHERE TO DINE
IN TAURANGA

The dining scene in this area has taken off, and you'll probably miss restaurants and cafes every time you blink. There's a cluster of very good ones on the Strand, in the

Wharf Street area, and on Devonport Road between Spring and Elizabeth streets. Pick up the free *Dine Out* guide from the visitor center.

Shiraz Café ❀, 12 Wharf St. (© **07/577-0059**), is tops for coffee and good Mediterranean and Middle Eastern food. There's a great courtyard out back, or you can people-watch at pavement tables. Try **Spinnakers Restaurant & Bar,** Tauranga Bridge Marina (© **07/574-4147**), on the water's edge, for fabulous seafood and a wide range of breakfast, lunch, and dinner offerings; or **Bravo** ❀❀, Red Square, Tauranga (© **07/578-4700**), a consistent award winner serving up delicious meals, gourmet pizzas, and good coffee. It's open daily from 9am until late.

Tucked away in the Old Yacht Club Building, at the south end of The Strand, **Harbourside Brasserie & Bar** ❀❀❀ (© **07/571-0520**) is eternally popular. It's open daily from 10:30am until late; there's a strong seafood slant to its excellent menu and the views are unmatched. For something a bit different, head for **Kestrels @ The Landing** ❀❀❀, The Strand, water's edge (© **07/928-1123**), where you can dine onboard the historic vessel *Kestrel* (or on the landing). It's open daily until late. Amphora **Café & Bar** ❀❀, 43 The Strand (© **07/578-1616**), is a stylish place for coffee overlooking the waterfront. **Collar & Thai** ❀❀, Goddards Centre, 21 Devonport Rd. (© **07/577-6655**), is a popular local haunt serving the best Thai curries. It's open for lunch Tuesday to Friday from 11:30am, and for dinner, Monday through Sunday, from 5:30pm until late.

A little out of the center of town, you won't be disappointed by **Somerset Cottage** ❀❀❀, 30 Bethlehem Rd. (© **07/576-6889**). A more expensive option, yes, but it's the winner of numerous awards and just the place for a special occasion. It's open for lunch Wednesday through Friday, and for dinner Tuesday through Sunday.

IN MOUNT MAUNGANUI

The favorite here is **Thai-phoon Restaurant** ❀❀, 14a Pacific Ave. (© **07/572-3545**). **Astrolabe Café & Bar** ❀❀, 82 Maunganui Rd. (© **07/574-8155**), is big on space and style (Spanish). **Zambezi Bar & Café,** 108 Maunganui Rd. (© **07/575-4202**), does a good job catering to vegetarians, with superb platters and fresh salads, plus monthly live shows. The cafe gets a younger crowd. If you're in the mood for good coffee and snacks, try **Ajo's Café,** 520 Mount Maunganui Rd. (© **07/575-5667**), or **Back Porch** ❀, Central Parade (© **07/575-3337**).

EN ROUTE TO ROTORUA

As you head south to Rotorua on State Highway 2, you'll pass through **Te Puke,** the "Kiwifruit Capital of the World." Here's where you'll find **Kiwi360** (see "Exploring the Area," above). The road is good for the hour-long journey, but it gets crowded with lots of heavy logging trucks headed for the port in Tauranga; *drive with care.*

8

Rotorua, Taupo & Tongariro National Park

Rotorua sits on the edge of one of the most awesome and concentrated volcanic areas in the world. In every direction is tangible evidence of a riotous geological past extending back millions of years. The Te Arawa people settled the area in the mid–14th century, and their descendants began tourism in the area in the 19th century, guiding visitors to the famous Pink and White terraces. The 1886 eruption of Mount Tarawera destroyed the terraces, but the legendary Maori hospitality lives on. Coupled with enough daredevil activities to rival Queenstown's reputation as New Zealand's adventure capital, the famous welcome continues to draw international visitors at a rate of 1.5 million a year.

Volcanic activity was also responsible for the formation of Lake Taupo. In A.D. 186, an enormous eruption—estimated to have been 100 times greater than that of Mount St. Helens in 1980—tore a savage hole 32km (20 miles) wide, 40km (25 miles) across, and 183m (600 ft.) deep. Today, we're thankful for that. Where would New Zealand holidaymakers be without the cool blue waters that provide ideal conditions for fishing, water-skiing, and boating?

South of Taupo lies Tongariro National Park, home to three volcanoes. Tongariro was New Zealand's first national park (the world's second after Yellowstone), and today it is a winter playground for skiers and a perfect place for summer tramping. Unfortunately, Mount Ruapehu's eruptions create havoc from time to time—the last 8 years ago, when its eruptions ruined any possibility of a successful ski season and many businesses suffered.

1 Rotorua ★★★

221km (137 miles) SE of Auckland; 86km (53 miles) S of Tauranga

You'll smell Rotorua long before you see it. The sulfuric aroma in the air is an unmistakable prelude to geothermal things to come. This natural wonderland and the 11 major lakes in the area are the draw for visitors. In fact, *Travel & Leisure* readers voted Rotorua 10th in the 1996 poll of the Top 10 Cities in the World.

Rotorua has long had a reputation for being too touristy, but the recent NZ$35-million (US$25-million) revamp of the city inspired heaps of new adventures and attractions, giving Rotorua added energy and enthusiasm. And if you're interested in Maori culture, this is the most accessible place to find it. A third of the population of 70,000 is Maori; that's the highest percentage of any city in the country.

ESSENTIALS
GETTING THERE By Plane Air New Zealand National and Link (© 0800/767-767 in NZ) provides daily service to all other major centers. **Super Shuttle**

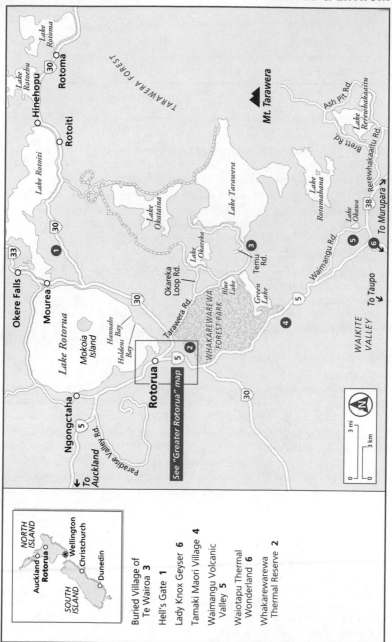

NORTH ISLAND

Auckland
Rotorua

Wellington
Christchurch

SOUTH ISLAND

Dunedin

Buried Village of
Te Wairoa **3**

Hell's Gate **1**

Lady Knox Geyser **6**

Tamaki Maori Village **4**

Waimangu Volcanic
Valley **5**

Waiotapu Thermal
Wonderland **6**

Whakarewarewa
Thermal Reserve **2**

Tips **Sore Feet?**

A sheltered seat and a free, hot, thermal footbath are right outside the main entrance to the visitor center and Bus Stop. Go ahead and take your shoes off and soak your weary feet for a few minutes.

(© 07/349-3444) provides daily transfers to and from the airport, 15 minutes out of town, for around NZ$15 (US$11).

By Coach (Bus)   InterCity, Newmans, Magic Travellers, and Kiwi Experience all provide service to Rotorua. Contact **The Bus Stop,** 67 Fenton St. (© 07/348-179; fax 07/348-6044), for coach and ferry bookings throughout New Zealand.

By Car   Centrally located Rotorua is only a 1-hour drive from the cities of Taupo, Hamilton, and Tauranga; a 3-hour drive from Auckland; and a 5-hour drive from Wellington. Roads in the area are excellent, but Rotorua is in the heart of the forestry industry, which means a heavy volume of large, fast-traveling logging trucks. Take care at all times.

ORIENTATION   Rotorua sits in the curve of Lake Rotorua's southwestern shore, spreading inland in a neat pattern. **Fenton Street** is the main drag and the main area for souvenir shops. It runs from the lake for 3.4km (2 miles) south to **Whakarewarewa Village** (just call it "Whaka," as the locals do), the area's most accessible thermal reserve. The center of town is not large. **Tutanekai Street** is the main shopping street; **City Focus,** under the sail-like structure, is in the middle of it all.

Note: Don't wander in Kuirau Park after dark. Make sure to remove all valuables from cars, and lock those cars, too.

GETTING AROUND   City and suburban buses run approximately every hour on weekdays, less frequently on weekends. You'll find taxis at the visitor center and on Fenton Street, or you can call © 07/348-5079. If you need a car, call **The Rental Car Centre,** 14 Ti St. (© 07/349-3993; rotorua@therentalcarcentre.co.nz).

VISITOR INFORMATION   Rotorua i-Site Visitor Centre & Travel Office, 1167 Fenton St. (© 0800/768-678 in NZ, or 07/348-5179; fax 07/348-6044; www. rotoruanz.com), is open daily from 8am to 6pm in summer, 8am to 5:30pm in winter. It provides travel and sightseeing reservations, currency exchange, luggage storage, a cafe and restaurant, an excellent souvenir shop, and showers and toilets. The visitor center's guide booklets are an excellent value.

Travel information is also available at **AA Travel Centre,** 1121 Eruera St. (© 07/ 348-3069; fax 07/346-2034). The **Map & Track Shop,** 1225 Fenton St. (©/fax 07/ 349-1845), open daily from 9am to 6pm, offers a mind-boggling array of maps, plus hut passes, hunting permits, and fishing licenses. The **Redwoods Visitor Centre, Whakarewarewa Forest,** Long Mile Road, Rotorua (© 06/346-2082; fax 07/347-3372; www.redwoods.co.nz), provides information on the extensive walking tracks in Whakarewarewa Forest and Redwood Grove. It's open daily 8:30am to 6pm in summer; 8:30am to 5pm winter and 10am to 4pm weekends, year-round. For more information on the area, check www.rotorua.co.nz and www.rdc.govt.nz.

Pick up a free copy of *Thermal Air,* an excellent little publication listing activities, attractions, eateries, and events. The local newspaper, the *Daily Post,* also has event listings.

FAST FACTS   The **post office,** Hinemoa Street (© **07/347-7851**), is open Monday through Friday from 7:30am to 5pm, Saturday 8am to 4pm, and Sunday 10am to 3pm. **Thomas Cook,** Fenton and Hinemoa streets (© **07/348-0640**), is open Monday through Friday from 9am to 5pm, Saturday 9:30am to 12:30pm. For Internet access, try **The Cyber World,** 1174 Haupapa St. (© **07/348-0088**), or **Cybershed,** 1176 Pukuatua St. (© **07/349-4965**). **Nomads Cyber Café,** 1195 Fenton St., near the visitor center (© **07/348-3288**), also offers breakfast, lunch, and snacks.

SPECIAL EVENTS   The route of the **Rotorua Marathon** (©/fax **07/348-8448**) goes around Lake Rotorua. This very serious competition takes place in late April or early May. In early November, more than NZ$25,000 (US$17,500) in prizes is up for grabs in the **International Trout Fishing Tournament** (© **07/332-3617**). In late January, **Opera in the Pa** (© **07/348-9047**) presents New Zealand's best young Maori, European, and Polynesian opera voices in the sacred grounds of the Rotowhio Marae at the New Zealand Maori Arts & Crafts Institute.

EXPLORING ROTORUA

Although the major thermal areas and Maori culture remain very popular, **Mount Tarawera** ✸✸✸ now plays a big part in Rotorua tourism. It has a strong mystical history for the Maori, and I keep hearing rave reports about four-wheel-drive and fly-over crater tours. If your time is short, the four must-see/must-do attractions are the **Buried Village; Rotorua Museum;** either of the geothermal reserves, **Waiotapu** or **Waimangu;** and a scenic flight over **Mount Tarawera.** This is easy to manage in 2 days. Visit the museum first or last for a comprehensive overview of Mount Tarawera's role. And pick up the *Passport to Rotorua's Finest Attractions* brochure from the visitor center—it details the bus service that frequents 18 leading attractions.

THE MAJOR SIGHTS & ATTRACTIONS
In the City Area
Rotorua Museum of Art & History ✸✸✸   Set in the world-famous Bath House, the Rotorua Museum has a new lease on life. After an injection of millions on refurbishment and a fabulous state-of-the-art cinema experience, plus the restoration of the Blue Baths, it's well worth a visit, especially if you want insight into the Mount Tarawera eruption of 1886. The restored section of the Great South Seas Spa is equally fascinating. People came from all over the world to visit the spa and were encouraged to take "electric baths," a rather bizarre practice that saw electric currents fed into the bathwater. There is also an excellent exhibition of the treasures *(taonga)* of the Arawa people.

Government Gardens, Rotorua. © **07/349-4350.** Fax 07/349-2819. www.rotoruamuseum.co.nz. Admission (includes Blue Baths) NZ$12 (US$8.40) adults, NZ$6 (US$4.20) children. Summer daily 9am–8pm; winter daily 9am–5pm. Tours at 9:30am, 11am, 2pm, and 4pm. Closed Dec 25.

Polynesian Spa ✸✸✸ *(Moments)*   Don't leave town without indulging in this divinely soothing experience. The jewel in this watery crown is the **Lake Spa** complex, with

---

Fun Fact Sacred Lake

Of the 11 major lakes in the area, most are ideal for swimming and watersports—except Lake Rotokakahi, the Green Lake. This lake is sacred *(tapu)* to the Maori and, therefore, off limits for swimming, boating, and fishing.

Tips **Saving on the Sights**

A number of offers represent significant savings on the leading attractions. Check at the visitor center or its website (www.rotoruanz.com) for the latest **Rotorua Hot Deals.** New packages and deals are added regularly throughout the year; they typically include Tamaki Tours, Polynesian Spa, Agrodome, Skyline Skyrides, and many other star attractions.

four Japanese Rotem Buro pools at different temperatures, set among rocks and waterfalls beside the lake. Add to that the **Lake Spa Retreat,** where you can lie back and have delicious things done to your body in the name of stress release and relaxation. (Try the mud-and-ginger body wrap, and you'll be happier than a pig in mud.) This is the upmarket area of the complex: You get extra service, a private bar, a lounge, and meals, and it's well worth the cost. The **Family Spa** is another top addition. It has a warm freshwater pool with toddlers' pool and mini-waterslide; adults can enjoy two adjacent hot mineral pools while they supervise the brood. The complex has 28 bathing pools in total, including 17 private pools.

Adults have the use of a large hot mineral pool plus the three adjacent Priest Spa acidic pools, famous for their curative effects on ailments such as arthritis and rheumatism. The water in these pools comes from acidic springs, and the temperature varies from 102°F to 108°F (39°C–42°C). The water in all other pools is quite different. It's soft alkaline water, which flows from a boiling spring 100m (328 ft.) from the complex and is cooled by the addition of the town's water. The Polynesian Spa is incredibly popular, so you'll seldom be alone unless you opt for a private pool or Luxury Spa experience.

Government Gardens, lakefront end of Hinemoa St. ✆ **0508/765-977** in NZ, or 07/348-1328. Fax 07/348-9486. www.polynesianspa.co.nz. Admission adults-only pool and Priest Spa NZ$15 (US$11); Lake Spa NZ$30 (US$21) adults; NZ$13 (US$9.10) children; private pools NZ$12 (US$8.40) adults, NZ$4 (US$2.80) children, NZ$28 (US$19) families; massage NZ$70 (US$49) for 30 min., NZ$140 (US$98) for 1 hr.; lockers NZ$2 (US$1.40); swimsuit or towel rental NZ$4 (US$2.80) with NZ$5 (US$3.50) deposit. AE, MC, V. Daily 6:30am–11pm.

Te Puia ★★★ Te Puia encompasses the Geothermal Valley, the Maori Cultural Experience, and the New Zealand Maori Arts & Crafts Institute. The highlight of the thermal reserve is definitely the effusive **Pohutu Geyser.** It usually erupts 10 to 25 times a day to a height of 16 to 20m (53–66 ft.). This steamy little valley is also known for its mud pools, which average 194°F to 203°F (90°C–95°C). The 1½-hour guided tour is a good option, allowing you a chance to learn about the culture and the thermal activity. It includes a look through a replica of a Maori village and the New Zealand Maori Arts & Crafts Institute, established in 1963 to foster traditional Maori carving and weaving skills. You'll see carvers and weavers at work and ride the Waka Express train into new geothermal areas. If this is your first experience with Maori culture, I'd spend about 2 to 3 hours here and see one of the live performances as well—either the midday concert or the evening Mia Ora performance, which includes a full *hangi* (earth oven) meal.

Hemo Rd., Rotorua. ✆ **0800/837-842** in NZ, or 07/348-9047. Fax 07/348-9045. www.tepuia.com. Tour with Maori guide and midday concert from NZ$22 (US$15) adults, NZ$11 (US$7.70) children 5–15; Mia Ora—Essence of Maori performance from NZ$75 (US$52) adults, NZ$40 (US$28) children; combo package (general admission, cultural show, and dinner) from NZ$88 (US$62) adults, NZ$46 (US$32) children 5–15. AE, MC, V. Summer daily 8am–6pm; winter daily 8am–5pm. Guided tours hourly 9am–5pm.

Greater Rotorua

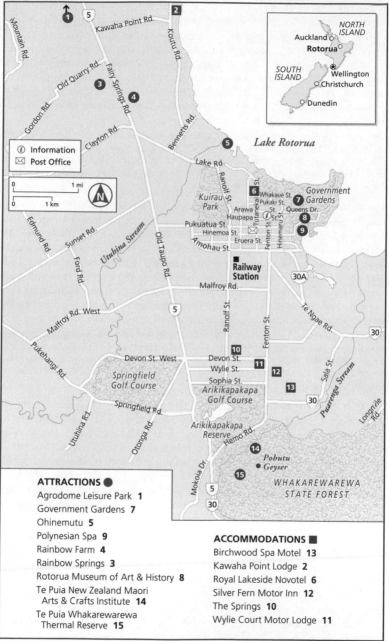

NORTH ISLAND
Auckland
Rotorua
SOUTH ISLAND
Wellington
Christchurch
Dunedin

Mountain Rd.
Kawaha Point Rd.
Koutu Rd.
Gordon Rd.
Old Quarry Rd.
Fairy Springs Rd.
Clayton Rd.
Bennetts Rd.
Lake Rotorua
Lake Rd.

ⓘ Information
✉ Post Office

0   1 mi
0   1 km
N

Edmund Rd.
Sunset Rd.
Utuhina Stream
Ford Rd.
Old Taupo Rd.
Malfroy Rd. West
Pukehangi Rd.
Malfroy Rd.
5

Ranolf St.
Kuirau Park
Whakaue St.
Pukaki St.
Government Gardens
Queens Dr.
Arawa St.
Haupapa St.
Tutanekai St.
Fenton St.
Hinemaru St.
Pukuatua St.
Hinemoa St.
Eruera St.
Amohau St.

Railway Station
Malfroy Rd.
30A
Te Ngae Rd.
30

Fenton St.
Ranolf St.
Devon St. West
Devon St.
Wylie St.
Sophia St.
Springfield Golf Course
Springfield Rd.
Arikikapakapa Golf Course
Sala St.
Puarenga Stream
Longmire Rd.
30

Uluhina Rd.
Otonga Rd.
Arikikapakapa Reserve
Hemo Rd.
Mokoia Dr.
5
30
Pohutu Geyser
WHAKAREWAREWA STATE FOREST

ATTRACTIONS ●
Agrodome Leisure Park **1**
Government Gardens **7**
Ohinemutu **5**
Polynesian Spa **9**
Rainbow Farm **4**
Rainbow Springs **3**
Rotorua Museum of Art & History **8**
Te Puia New Zealand Maori Arts & Crafts Institute **14**
Te Puia Whakarewarewa Thermal Reserve **15**

ACCOMMODATIONS ■
Birchwood Spa Motel **13**
Kawaha Point Lodge **2**
Royal Lakeside Novotel **6**
Silver Fern Motor Inn **12**
The Springs **10**
Wylie Court Motor Lodge **11**

In Nearby Ngongotaha

Skyline Skyrides ★★ *Kids*   Skyline Skyrides is far and away the number-one visitor attraction in Rotorua, and for the panoramic views from Mount Ngongotaha alone, the ride up is definitely worth it. Entertain the kids with crazy ways to descend—the regular scenic luge, an advanced luge track, an adventure flying fox, the sidewinder, or the chairlift. A new attraction is the Sky Swing, which hoists three passengers to over 36m (120 ft.) before swinging them out over Mount Ngongotaha at speeds up to 140kmph (87 mph). A restaurant and food court are up here if you feel peckish.

Fairy Springs Rd., Rotorua. ⓒ 07/347-0027. Fax 07/348-2163. www.skylineskyrides.co.nz. Gondola from NZ$20 (US$14) adults, NZ$9 (US$6.30) children 5–14; luge ride NZ$7.50 (US$5.25); gondola and 5 luge rides NZ$37 (US$26) adults, NZ$27 (US$19) children; gondola family pass NZ$48 (US$34). Gondola and 6-luge-ride family pass from NZ$70 (US$49). Gondola and lunch NZ$43 (US$30) adults. Daily 9am–late. Nighttime luge Thurs–Sat. In the suburb of Ngongotaha 4.6km (3 miles) north of town on St. Hwy. 5.

Agrodome ★★ *Kids*   Not everyone wants to come face to face with 19 different sheep breeds in one place at one time, but if you do, this is your chance. You can also see a shearing display and a working sheepdog demonstration, tour the 160-hectare (395-acre) farm on horseback, or find yourself something satisfyingly woolly in the souvenir shop. There's a range of adventure activities here, too—helicopters, jet-boating, bungy jumping (see "Outdoor Pursuits," below, for details)—plus a chocolate factory, a pearl farm, a restaurant, and a woolen mill. You pay individually for these. All in all, it's a great one-stop show that should keep the kids happy. And don't forget to ask about the wide range of adventure packages, which provide multiple activities at a reduced rate.

Western Rd., Ngongotaha. ⓒ **0800/339-400** in NZ, or 07/357-1050. Fax 07/357-5307. www.agrodome.co.nz. Admission to Agrodome Show from NZ$20 (US$14) adults, NZ$10 (US$7) children, NZ$55 (US$38) families. Agrodome Farm Tour from NZ$25 (US$18) adults, NZ$12 (US$8.40) children 5–15, NZ$60 (US$42) families; Agrodome Show and Farm Tour combo from NZ$40 (US$28) adults, NZ$20 (US$14) children, NZ$80 (US$56) families. AE, MC, V. Daily 8:30am–5pm. Shows daily 9:30am, 11am, and 2:30pm.

Paradise Valley Springs ★ *Kids*   From sheep to trout in a few easy minutes, and an unexpected bonus: lions! This very pretty place has delightful bush walks through a wildlife sanctuary, trout-filled streams, and a wetlands area. There is also an underwater viewing cave and a spawning stream where you can hand-feed the trout. When there are suitably sized lion cubs in-house, you might be able to pet them—something the kids will love.

473 Paradise Valley Rd., Ngongotaha. ⓒ **07/348-9667**. Fax 07/349-3359. www.paradisev.co.nz. Admission NZ$22 (US$15) adults, NZ$12 (US$8.40) children 5–15. AE, MC, V. Daily 8am–dark (last ticket sales 5pm). Lion feeding daily 2:30pm.

Rainbow Springs Nature Park & Kiwi Encounter ★★ *Kids*   As at Paradise Valley Springs (above), you'll find water teeming with trout. But instead of lions, you'll get kiwi and tuatara, and the farm show here is definitely a hands-on experience: You can try hand milking a cow, riding a bull, churning butter, or cuddling a piglet. The 50-minute show includes a shearing demonstration. Both the springs and the farm across the road have shops filled to brimming with sheepskin products and souvenirs. Kiwi Encounter is unique in that it presents "conservation in action"—the raising of kiwi chicks from eggs for release into the wild. The excellent tour will give you a terrific insight into these rare birds and how they are being saved from extinction.

Fairy Springs Rd., Ngongotaha. ⓒ **0800/724-626** in NZ, or 07/350-0440. Fax 07/350-0441. www.rainbowsprings. co.nz and www.kiwiencounter.co.nz. Admission around NZ$25 (US$18) adults, NZ$15 (US$11) children 5–15; Kiwi Encounter tour around NZ$27 (US$19) adults, NZ$17 (US$12) children; combo NZ$45 (US$32) adults, NZ$25 (US$18) children. AE, MC, V. Daily 8am–5pm. Shows daily 10:30am, 11:45am, 1pm, 2:30pm, and 4pm. Guided springs tours 11:45am and 1pm.

Just Outside Rotorua

Buried Village of Te Wairoa 🖝🖝   The Buried Village has undergone a big revamp, along with the establishment of a museum and upgrading of the picturesque waterfall walk. The museum displays many of the objects unearthed after the Mount Tarawera eruption buried the small village of Te Wairoa in 1886. A meandering pathway set among trees and meadows by the Te Wairoa Stream connects the Buried Village's excavated dwellings. You'll see remains of a flour mill, Maori *whare*, stores, the Rotomahana Hotel, and more. Thirty-minute guided tours (included in the admission price) begin at various times. Allow 1 to 2 hours for your visit. To book a comprehensive morning or afternoon tour from Rotorua city, phone ℂ **07/362-8287.**

If you feel like eating, I recommend bypassing the cafe here and heading just down the road to the Landing Café (p. 217).

Tarawera Rd., RD5, Rotorua. ℂ/fax **07/362-8287.** www.buriedvillage.co.nz. Admission from NZ$22 (US$15) adults, NZ$6 (US$4.20) children 6–15, NZ$45 (US$32) families. AE, MC, V. Summer daily 9am–5:30pm; winter daily 9am–4:30pm. Closed Dec 25. 15 min. from the city on a scenic drive past the Blue and Green lakes.

MAORI CULTURAL EXPERIENCES

It's easy to be completely confused by the number of Maori cultural experiences available in Rotorua. Basically, they all offer a hangi (earth-oven feast) and a song-and-dance performance. The hangi is the traditional Maori method of cooking. A large pit is filled with a wood fire topped by stones; when the stones are heated through, baskets of food are placed on top and covered with damp cloths. Earth is then shoveled over to create a natural oven. After about 3 hours, dinner is unveiled, with intermingling flavors of various foods lightly touched by wood smoke.

The best concert and hangi is at **Tamaki Maori Village** (see below). The **World of Maori,** Rotoiti Tours (ℂ **0800/476-864** in NZ, or 07/348-8969; www.worldofmaori. co.nz), operates from the Rakeiao Marae, home of the Ngati Rongomai tribe on the shores of Lake Rotoiti. The good, authentic experience includes Maori performance and hangi, and the cost of around NZ$80 (US$56) adults, NZ$40 (US$28) children 6 to 13 includes the 20-minute drive to the marae.

All of the major hotels have nightly hangi and concerts. Of these, the **Royal Lakeside Novotel** 🖝🖝, Tutanekai Street (ℂ **0508/446-244** or 07/346-3888; www.novotel. co.nz), is definitely the best. It's a little more expensive than some others, but the show presents a good balance between old and new. The steamed hangi (not as strong as the earth-cooked version) is beautifully presented and has lots of extras. While you eat, a contemporary Maori guitarist performs and traces the history of Maori in tourism. Although you don't get the feel of a marae here, a strong and consistently good performance group sings in several languages. It costs around NZ$75 (US$52) per person and runs from 6:30 to 9pm.

A visit to **Whakarewarewa Thermal Village** 🖝🖝🖝, Tyron Street, Rotorua (ℂ **07/ 349-3463;** www.whakarewarewa.com), will give you insight into the workings of a modern, real-life Maori village set among geothermal activity. It's open daily from 8:30am to 5pm, with guided tours between 9am and 4pm and cultural performances at 11:15am and 2pm daily. You can also experience ancient Maori customs and traditions, learn Maori rituals and beliefs, and view sacred freshwater springs at **Mitai Village,** 196 Fairy Springs Rd., Rotorua (ℂ **07/343-9132;** www.mitai.co.nz). It's open daily with a concert and hangi performance from 6:30pm to 9:45pm.

Tips **A Free Experience**

Don't overlook the fact that you can make your own way to **Ohinemutu Maori Village,** on Rotorua's lakefront. Follow the lake road around past the Royal Lakeside Novotel, and just by the first little group of shops, turn into Houkotuku Street. Turn right into Ariariterangi Street and drive to the historic Tamatekapua meetinghouse, cemetery, and church. Always ask permission before entering. You'll see tons of natural thermal activity in the area, much of it steaming up in people's gardens.

Another lovely way to immerse yourself in Maori legend is by taking a trip to **Mokoia Island** (see "Get Out on the Water," below). Or call on Sonny Corbett of **Sonny's World Maori Stories & Legends Tours** *☆☆*, 23b King St., Rotorua (© **07/ 349-0290;** www.sonnysworld.co.nz), to immerse you in things Maori. His tours to a marae will teach you all about Maori protocols in these sacred places. Half-day tours (8:30am–12:30pm) are NZ$70 (US$49) per person; full-day tours are NZ$140 (US$98) per person. Private full-day tours cost NZ$600 (US$420) per couple.

And if you'd like to experience paddling a traditional-style Maori canoe *(waka),* join **Mana Adventures,** Rotorua lakefront (© **07/346-8595;** www.manaadventures. co.nz), which will take you out in an 11m (36-ft.), 16-person *waka tangata* (people's canoe).

Tamaki Maori Village & Realm of Tane *☆☆☆*   This family company has taken top honors in the New Zealand Tourism Awards. The re-created, presettlement Maori village, 15 minutes from the city, presents tribal life as it used to be. Carving, weaving, *moko* (tattooing), singing, dancing, chanting, and cooking are all part of the living-village experience. At night, you can enjoy one of the best Maori performances and genuine hangi meals in Rotorua. The Realm of Tane, in Rotorua itself, is a blend of guided tour, character theater, and storytelling on a series of indoor sets. The 1-hour show (at noon, 1:30, 3, and 4:30pm), tells the story of Maori migration to New Zealand. It is an ideal scene setter or follow-up to the village experience.

1220 Hinemaru St., Rotorua. © **07/346-2823.** Fax 07/347-2913. www.maoriculture.co.nz. Hangi and concert NZ$90–NZ$93 (US$63–US$65) adults, NZ$55–NZ$58 (US$38–US$41) children 5–15; Realm of Tane NZ$30–NZ$33 (US$21–US$23) adults, NZ$15–NZ$18 (US$11–US$13) children. Prices include evening pickup from city accommodations. Combo deals and family passes available. AE, DC, MC, V. Summer shows 6–9pm and 8–11pm; winter shows 5:30–8pm and 7:30–10pm. Closed Dec 25. The village is on St. Hwy. 5, 20 min. north of Taupo.

ORGANIZED TOURS

You'll find heaps of brochures for half- and full-day tours at the visitor center. Most of the tours take in the main geothermal attractions and are similarly priced.

One of the best tours is **Destination Tarawera** *☆☆☆*, which begins with a pickup from your lodging by **Mt. Tarawera New Zealand Ltd.** (© **07/349-3714;** www.mt-tarawera.co.nz). You'll either be driven or helicoptered up Mount Tarawera via Kaingaroa Forest and take a guided walk through and around the craters. If you choose the helicopter option, you'll be whisked off the mountaintop to fly over nine craters and follow the 15km (9½-mile) path of the 1886 eruption to Waimangu Volcanic Valley. You return to Rotorua via the volcanic crater lakes. It's about 4 amazing hours altogether, and costs around NZ$415 (US$290) per person for the helicopter option and NZ$125 (US$87) adults for a 4WD.

You have new walking-tour options. **Nature Connection** (© 07/347-1705; www.natureconnection.co.nz) offers a morning walk at Waimangu Volcanic Valley and an afternoon walk in Whirinaki Forest ✿✿✿, which is a terrific combination by anyone's standards. **Walking Legends** (© 07/345-7363; www.walkinglegends.com) operates fully guided 4-day treks from Rotorua, in the Lake Waikaremoana Track ✿✿✿ in Te Urewera National Park, 150km (93 miles) southeast of Rotorua. It has its own launch to transport passengers and luggage to and from the start and finish of the track. You'll get into real outback country with this one.

For tours that explore Maori culture and history, call **Rotoiti Tours** or **Sonny's World Maori Stories & Legends Tours** (see "Maori Cultural Experiences," above).

OUTDOOR PURSUITS

Rotorua is teeming with fast-paced opportunity, and everything is within easy reach. Ten minutes in one direction and you get jet-boating, zorbing (see below), luging, bungy jumping, four-wheel-drive safaris, off-roading, and horseback riding; just 20 minutes from Rotorua on the Tauranga Highway, you can raft the highest Grade V waterfall in the Southern Hemisphere, leap in a jet boat, or go mountain biking, walking, or off-roading.

BUNGY JUMPING At **Rotorua Bungy & Swoop,** Agrodome (© 07/357-4747; www.rotoruabungy.co.nz), you can leap from a 43m (141-ft.) tower for around NZ$90 (US$63). And just when you thought things couldn't get any more insane, they go and invent New Zealand's first **Swoop.** For just NZ$45 (US$32) per person, you can be strapped into a hang-gliding harness with two others and lifted 40m (131 ft.) in the air. Pull the ripcord and experience the feeling of flying at 130kmph (81 mph) with a G-force factor of 3.

CLIMBING **The Wall,** 1140 Hinemoa St. (© 07/350-1400), offers indoor and outdoor climbing adventures; it's open daily from 10am until late. The cost starts at about NZ$25 (US$18) for adults.

Tips Get Out on the Water

Mokoia Island Tours, the Lakefront (© 0800/862-784 in NZ, or 07/348-6634; www.mokoia-island.com), incorporates the *Lakeland Queen* paddle boat, Skatcat, and Mokoia Island Guided Tours. The Skatcat provides a fast lake-cruising option in a catamaran with daily half-hour (NZ$30/US$21 adults, NZ$15/US$11 children) and 1-hour cruises (NZ$55/US$38 adults, NZ$25/US$18 children) departing the Rotorua lakefront. The 1-hour tours go around Mokoia Island; the 1½-hour trip (NZ$70/US$49 adults, NZ$35/US$25 children) offers guided walks on the island. All tours depart from the Rotorua lakefront.

The *Lakeland Queen* carries 140 passengers and offers breakfast, lunch, or dinner cruises. Breakfast cruises (about NZ$50/US$35 for adults, NZ$30/US$21 for children) depart at 7 and 8am; the luncheon buffet cruise (NZ$50/US$35 for adults, NZ$30/US$21 for children) departs at 12:30pm and returns at 1:30pm. The evening lake cruise and dinner, from 4:45pm to 8:30pm, includes a four-course menu and costs around NZ$85 (US$60) for adults, NZ$50 (US$35) for children. The evening cruise, island culture experience, and four-course dinner returns around 9:30pm and costs NZ$145 (US$101) for adults and NZ$85 (US$60) for children.

Bubble, Bubble, Toil & Trouble: The Geothermal Attractions

When you enter this region, you quickly realize there's something hard at work under your feet. Steam rises out of gutters and along roadsides, and you can never be entirely sure where the next hiss and roar will come from. Volcanic and geothermal activity has always played a major role in the landscape here, so be sure to experience it yourself. The visitor center has information on shuttle services to the main geothermal areas. These usually cost NZ$20 to NZ$40 (US$14–US$28); in some cases, prices include admission to the chosen area.

Twenty minutes south of Rotorua, you'll find **Waimangu Volcanic Valley** ☆☆ (☏ 07/366-6137; www.waimangu.com). Created on June 10, 1886, by Mount Tarawera's impressive blowout, Waimangu is the only hydrothermal system in the world wholly formed in historic times as a result of a volcanic eruption. Today, you can walk through the valley and look at the many features, the best 75% of which fall during the first 45 minutes of the 1½-hour walk. These include **Frying Pan Lake,** the world's largest hot-water spring, and the impossibly turquoise **Inferno Crater** ☆☆—a mysterious lake where the level rises and falls on a regular 38-day cycle. The valley is open daily from 8:30am to 5pm. The walk costs from NZ$30 (US$21) for adults and NZ$10 (US$7) for children ages 6 to 16. If you do the walk and boat cruise, a total of 3 hours, the cost is around NZ$55 to NZ$60 (US$38–US$42) for adults and NZ$15 (US$11) children. For the boat ride alone you pay from NZ$35 (US$25) adults and NZ$10 (US$7) children.

Personally, I'd do just the first 45 minutes of the above walk, skip the boat cruise altogether, and head 10 minutes farther south to **Waiotapu Thermal Wonderland** ☆☆☆ (☏ 07/366-6333; www.geyserland.co.nz).Waiotapu is a much more intensive and colorful geothermal exhibition. It's open daily from 8:30am to 5pm, and you'll want to allow 1 to 1½ hours. You can go it alone or with a guided tour, and once again, the bulk of the best attractions are within the shorter (30- to 40-min.) walk. The best features here are the reliable **Lady Knox Geyser,** which performs around 10:15am daily; the spectacular **Champagne Pool** ☆☆; New Zealand's largest bubbling **mud pool;** and the vivid green **Devil's Bath**—the greener the water, the higher the

FISHING   Within minutes of the city, you can be in the thick of some of the best wild trout fishing in the country. Lakes Tarawera, Okataina, and Rotoiti offer the best chance of catching a trophy fish. They're open for fishing from October to the end of June and hold both wild and stocked trout. The greatest trout population per acre is in Lake Rotorua, where wild fighting rainbow trout average 2 to 4 pounds and brown trout 5 to 7 pounds. Make sure you get your Rotorua fishing license before you start.

Bryan Colman Trout Fishing ☆☆, 32 Kiwi St., Rotorua (☏ 07/348-7766; www. TroutFishingRotorua.com), is a top guide—the longest-serving in Rotorua—who offers light tackle trolling and fly- and spin fishing for rainbow trout for NZ$95 (US$66) per hour.

arsenic content. Admission is around NZ$23 (US$16) for adults, NZ$8 (US$5.60) for children 5 to 15, and NZ$55 (US$38) per family.

Forty-five minutes south of Rotorua, you'll find the **Hidden Valley Orakei Koraka Geyserland Resort** &&& (© **07/378-3131**; www.orakeikorako.co.nz), a pocket wonderland of geysers, hot springs, boiling mud, and the majestic Aladdin's Cave on the shores of Lake Ohakuri. This little valley of incredible beauty is preserved by its isolation and inaccessibility—it can only be reached by boat (no extra charge). Boats don't run on a timetable; you can cross at any time. You might want to save this for the journey south—Taupo is just 25 minutes away. Allow at least an hour for a good look around. As in any geothermal area, stay on the formed pathways to avoid danger. The resort is open daily from 8am to 4:30pm. Admission is around NZ$23 (US$16) for adults, NZ$8 (US$5.60) for children under 16, and NZ$54 (US$38) per family. To get there, turn off on State Highway 5, just after Golden Springs at Mihi Bridge.

Hell's Gate & Wai Ora Spa &&& (© **07/345-3151**; www.hellsgate.co.nz) is 15km (9⅓ miles) northeast of Rotorua on State Highway 30 to Whakatane. This Maori-owned reserve is steeped in culture, and its 8 hectares (20 acres) of thermal activity are different every day—and magnificent in the rain. Reputedly the fiercest of the thermal valleys, it features hot-water lakes, sulfur formations, Rotorua's only mud volcano, and the largest boiling whirlpool in New Zealand. It also offers a range of spa experiences, including massage and mud baths. Don't forget to ask about cheaper combo packages. It's open from 9am to 8:30pm daily (closed Dec 25). Admission is NZ$25 (US$18) for adults, NZ$10 (US$7) for children under 16, NZ$60 (US$42) per family. For the Hell's Gate Mud Bath & Spa, you pay NZ$70 (US$49) adults, NZ$30 (US$21) children, NZ$160 (US$112) family.

If you want to get a glimpse of geothermal action in the city free of charge, head for **Kuirau Park,** off Pukuatua and Ranolf streets. This is the site of the huge spontaneous eruption in 2000, and you can still see the dead trees and white ash in the cordoned-off area. There are steaming vents everywhere, and it is vital that you stay on formed pathways. Stay out of the park at night.

FLIGHTSEEING   **Volcanic Air Safaris,** Memorial Drive (© **0800/800-848** in NZ, or 07/348-9984; www.volcanicair.co.nz), has a range of helicopter and floatplane tours, from an 8-minute, NZ$60 (US$42) floatplane or helicopter spin over the city to 3-hour volcanic tours all the way out to **White Island** && in the Bay of Plenty (NZ$665/US$465 per person by helicopter, NZ$395/US$276 by floatplane). Its most popular offering is the helicopter/floatplane trip to **Mount Tarawera** &&, including a landing and tour of Orakei Korako; it costs NZ$320 (US$224).

FOUR-WHEEL-DRIVE ADVENTURES   Test your nerve at **Off Road NZ** &&, 193 Amoore Rd. (© **07/332-5748**; www.offroadnz.co.nz), 20 minutes north of the city off State Highway 5. The four-wheel-drive bush safari departs daily, every hour from 9am to 5pm, and costs around NZ$80 (US$56) per person. You'll find yourself in tunnels, waterfalls, mud, and more mud. Otherwise, try out the 12-lap sprint car racetrack built to test the best at NZ$30 (US$21) per driver.

GOLF   The Arikikapakapa course at the **Rotorua Golf Club,** 399 Fenton St. (© 07/348-4051; www.rotoruagolfclub.co.nz), is a gently undulating, all-weather course with an international reputation. Greens fees are about NZ$60 (US$42), and club hire is NZ$25 (US$18). A new attraction is the 21-bay driving range, **Government Gardens Golf,** Government Gardens (© 07/348-9126; www.governmentgardensgolf.co.nz). It's open daily from 7am to 9pm and costs NZ$18 to NZ$20 (US$13–US$14) for 18 holes. And there's ideal family fun at **Short Golf,** 146 Sala St. (© 07/348-3531; www.action-nz.co.nz), with a 9-hole course that everyone can enjoy.

HORSEBACK RIDING   **The Farmhouse,** Sunnex Road, Rotorua (© 07/332-3771; farmhouse@xtra.co.nz), is the largest horse-trekking facility in New Zealand, with over 100 horses for all ages and abilities. It's a working farm and homestay as well, and all gear is provided.

JET-BOATING   You can spin out on the **Agrojet** at Agrodome (© 07/357-2929; agrojet@xtra.co.nz) for NZ$40 (US$28) per adult, NZ$30 (US$21) per child. Or leap aboard **Longridge Jet,** which is based much farther out, south of Te Puke on State Highway 3 (© 0800/867-386 in NZ, or 07/533-1515; www.funpark.co.nz). A ride costs around NZ$75 (US$52) for adults, NZ$45 (US$32) for children.

KAYAKING   Take it easy on Rotorua's lovely lakes with **Adventure Kayaking** (© 07/348-9451; www.adventurekayaking.co.nz). Half-day paddles with a thermal pool swim cost from NZ$80 (US$56); full-day tours are NZ$110 (US$77); and individual kayak hire goes for around NZ$45 (US$32) per seat per day.

LUGING   See the "Exploring Rotorua" section, earlier in this chapter, for information about the endlessly popular **Skyline Skyrides luge** 🌟🌟 (© 07/347-0027; fax 07/348-2163).

MOUNTAIN BIKING   Go it alone on rented bikes from **Bike Rotorua** (© 07/346-1717), and head for the trails at Redwoods Forest, Whakarewarewa. You'll pay NZ$35 (US$25) for a half-day, NZ$50 (US$35) for a full day. Or team up with the crew at **Planet Bike** (© 07/348-9971; www.planetbike.co.nz), which caters to all levels. Prices start at NZ$30 (US$21) per person for 2 hours. Half-day tours and full-day adventure combos are available. For an extra thrill, go downhill from the Skyline Gondola with **Edzown** (© 07/346-1717). A day pass gives you unlimited access to the gondola, bike trails, chairlift, and luge rides. The shop is open Friday through Sunday from 9am.

SKYDIVING   Leap out over Rotorua at around 2,850m (9,348 ft.) with **NZOne–The Ultimate Jump** (© 07/345-7520; www.nzone.biz). Be prepared to drop around NZ$275 (US$192).

WALKING   Apart from numerous strolls around the various lakes, the **Whakarewarewa Forest** 🌟🌟🌟 has six well-marked walking tracks for all ages and levels of fitness. You can spend half an hour or a whole day making your way through the forest. The beautiful **Redwood Memorial Grove Track** 🌟🌟🌟 is the most popular. It meanders through giant 60m (197-ft.) California coastal redwoods and takes 30 minutes from the forest visitor center on Long Mile Road. Also popular is the **Motutara Walkway** 🌟🌟, which wanders around the lakefront to Sulphur Bay. The 1½-hour walk passes through unusual "moonscape" outcrops of sulfur along the way.

Whirinaki Rainforest Guided Walks ☞☞☞, Whirinaki Forest (℗ **0800/869-255** in NZ, or 07/377-2363; www.rainforest-treks.co.nz), offers 1- to 3-day fully catered treks led by professional Maori guides, starting at Rotorua or Taupo. You'll pay NZ$155 (US$108) for a 1-day ecocultural walk; NZ$285 (US$199) per person for a 1-day privately guided walk; or NZ$745 (US$521) for the 3-day Rainforest Trek. For a full inventory of walks in the area, call at the **Map & Track Shop,** 1225 Fenton St. (℗/fax **07/349-1845**). Its multiday walks operate only from October through April. One-day walks are available all year.

WHITE-WATER RAFTING   If you want world-rated championship rafting guides, head for **Kaituna Cascades Raft & Kayak Expeditions,** Trout Pool Road, Okere Falls, Rotorua (℗ **0800/524-8862** in NZ, or 07/345-4199; www.kaitunacascades.co.nz). It'll give you the best time you've ever had, including a 7m (23-ft.) drop over the Southern Hemisphere's highest commercially rafted waterfall. The company operates on the Kaituna, Rangitaiki, and Wairoa rivers. Prices range from NZ$68 to NZ$95 (US$48–US$66), depending on the river. **River Rats** (℗ **0800/333-900** in NZ, or 07/345-6543; www.riverrats.co.nz) is another excellent company. It operates on the above rivers, plus the Tongariro.

ZORBING   Where else can you find yourself inside a giant plastic bubble, with the option of being wet or dry as you roll 250m (820 ft.) down a steep, slippery slope? It's like nothing you've ever done before. A wet or dry ride costs NZ$45 (US$32). Children can try the mini-zorb on flat terrain for around NZ$12 (US$8.40). The zorb is at Agrodome, Western Road, Ngongotaha (℗ **07/357-5100;** www.zorb.com).

WHERE TO STAY

There are at least 14,000 visitor beds in Rotorua, so you shouldn't have any trouble finding one to suit you. The major hotels have recently finished significant renovations, and Fenton Street is a veritable motel mile. Many motels in Rotorua provide private heated Jacuzzis in each unit. Be warned, though: These are not all thermal pools. New motel complexes are not allowed to draw off the city's geothermal reserves, so check first if you want a thermal pool. If you're interested in a personalized hospitality experience, pick up the *Rotorua Farm and Homestay* brochure at the visitor center.

Rates below include 12.5% GST and parking.

VERY EXPENSIVE

Opened in 2004, **Peppers on the Point** ☞☞, 214 Kawaha Point Rd., Rotorua (℗ **07/348-4868;** www.peppers.co.nz), is a grand 1930s home that has been remodeled into a stylish seven-suite lodge with fabulous lake views. Large rooms with stylish bathrooms go for around NZ$600 to NZ$700 (US$420–US$490), which includes dinner and breakfast. And look out for another new beauty, **Lodge @ 199** ☞☞, 199 Spencer Rd. (℗ **07/362-8122;** www.199.co.nz), due to open on the shores of Lake Tarawera in late 2005. This special four-suite haven will appeal to romantics with its silk-draped ceilings and over-the-water suite. Nestled on the water's edge, it will provide beautiful accommodations, dinner, and breakfast for NZ$600 to NZ$800 (US$420–US$560).

Kawaha Point Lodge ☞☞ *finds*   Hosts Tony and Margaret Seavill have converted their lakeside home into a top-notch small lodge that focuses on the personal touch, and 8 years on, word of their fabulous rooms and superb service has spread. Five rooms are in the main building, and three others are attached with separate access. All have high-end furnishings and roomy en-suite bathrooms, feather duvets and pillows, and extras such as robes, complimentary port, and homemade biscuits.

171 Kawaha Point Rd., Rotorua. © 07/346-3602. Fax 07/346-3671. www.kawahalodge.co.nz. 8 units. NZ$726–NZ$946 (US$508–US$662). Rates include breakfast, dinner, and airport transfers. Long-stay and off-peak rates available. AE, DC, MC, V. Take St. Hwy. 5 from central city; after 5 min., turn right to Kawaha Point Rd. just before Skyline Skyrides. Turn left at the shops, then take first right. **Amenities:** 4-course dinner prepared by chef; bar; outdoor pool; 3 nearby golf courses; sauna; tour bookings; massage; babysitting; laundry service; same-day dry cleaning; nonsmoking rooms; on-call doctor/dentist. *In room:* A/C, TV on request, dataport, minibar, fridge, coffeemaker, hair dryer, iron.

Okareka Lake House ★★★ *(Finds)*   Splendor to take your breath away with top service as a keystone—what more could you want? This brand-new lakeside property 15 minutes outside Rotorua has to be one of the top lodges in New Zealand. Small, secluded, and sumptuous, it has a homey ambience that will seduce you the minute you walk in. It's more intimate than many of the bigger lodges in the same price bracket. All double rooms are spacious, with modern en-suite bathrooms. The master bedroom suite has its own lounge, office, and private Jacuzzi.

Lake Okareka. © 07/349-8123. www.okareka.co.nz. 5 units. NZ$2,000 (US$1,398). Rates include breakfast, predinner drinks, and dinner. AE, DC, MC, V. 15 min. from Rotorua Airport. **Amenities:** Bar and large wine cellar; nearby golf and tennis courts; 2 Jacuzzis (1 w/main suite); tour bookings; car rentals; business facilities; library and entertainment theater; massage; same-day dry cleaning; nonsmoking rooms; on-call doctor/dentist. *In room:* AC, TV/DVD/VCR/CD, dataport, minibar, fridge, coffeemaker, hair dryer, iron.

Treetops Lodge & Estate ★★★   The sublime Treetops Lodge is unique among New Zealand's first-rate lodges, and one of the best, in my view. It's perfect for nature lovers and those who appreciate the finer things in life. Set on 1,000 hectares (2,470 acres) of wilderness game reserve, which includes an 800-year-old forest, and surrounded by 24,300 hectares (60,000 acres) of Department of Conservation land, Treetops opened in January 2000 half an hour outside Rotorua. It is a true sanctuary that specializes in big-game hunting and peaceful retreat. It's all about world-class luxury. Once nestled into your big, stylish suite, savoring the valley or lake vistas, you'll think you're in paradise. Every suite is appointed with top-quality furnishings in the best of taste. Rooms and huge bathrooms are exquisite in every detail. Guests in lodge suites have exclusive use of a kitchen; villas have kitchenettes.

351 Kearoa Rd., RD1, Horohoro. © 07/333-2066. Fax 07/333-2065. www.treetops.co.nz. 12 units. NZ$1,834 (US$1,283) lodge suite; NZ$2,171 (US$1,518) villa. Extra person NZ$450 (US$315). Children under 12 NZ$338 (US$236). Rates include breakfast, predinner cocktails, dinner, selected lodge activities, and airport transfers. Long-stay rates and special deals available. AE, DC, MC, V. 30 min. from central city. **Amenities:** Bar; nearby golf course and pool; watersports equipment rentals; bike rentals; 100km of walking and jogging tracks; unguided trout fishing in private lake; game room; concierge; tour bookings; car rentals; business services; 24-hr. room service; massage; babysitting; same-day dry cleaning; nonsmoking rooms; on-call doctor/dentist. *In room:* TV/DVD/VCR, dataport, minibar, fridge, coffeemaker, hair dryer, iron, safe.

EXPENSIVE

Duxton Hotel Rotorua ★★ *(Value)*   If you favor the peace and quiet of an out-of-town lakeside location, then the relatively small Duxton is for you. A recent multimillion-dollar refurbishment elevated the property to a very high standard. Rooms look out to lake and garden views. Some have Jacuzzis with shutters that fold open to the bedroom, and all are roomy and stylishly furnished. Just 15 minutes out of town, the Duxton is also a destination in its own right and incredibly good value for money.

366 St. Hwy. 33, Okawa Bay, Rotorua. © 0800/655-55 in NZ, or 07/362-4599. Fax 07/362-4594. www.duxton.com. 44 units. NZ$320 (US$224) garden room; NZ$343 (US$240) lakeview room; NZ$365 (US$255) lakeview suite. Long-stay and off-peak rates available. Rates include airport transfers and transport to nearby thermal springs. AE, DC, MC, V. **Amenities:** Restaurant; bar; outdoor heated pool; tennis court; boat jetty; pontoon boat for trips to private hot pools; business

center; concierge; tour bookings; car rentals; room service; free guest laundry; same day dry cleaning; nonsmoking rooms; helipad; on-call doctor/dentist; currency exchange. *In room:* TV, dataport, minibar, fridge, coffeemaker, hair dryer, iron.

Royal Lakeside Novotel ★★

This is definitely one of the better Rotorua hotels, and the closest to central city and the main restaurant beat. Opened in 1996, it was extensively refurbished in 2005 and now has a classic, international style that's very easy on the eye. It's a multicultural hotel (with part-Thai ownership) that boasts a quiet atmosphere and a cosmopolitan staff with ready smiles. You'll be spoiled by the terrific amenities. The lakeview superior rooms are the most popular, but parkside units are generally quieter. The eight king suites have spa bathrooms, and two executive suites are split-level, with mezzanine bedrooms. The Royal Suite is simply spectacular—and yes, members of the Thai royal family use it. The Atlas Brasserie puts on fabulous buffet dinners.

Lake end of Tutanekai St., Rotorua. ℂ **0800/776-677** in NZ, or 07/346-3888. Fax 07/347-1888. www.accorhotels. com. 199 units. NZ$163–NZ$326 (US$114–US$228) superior; NZ$416 (US$291) junior suite; NZ$563 (US$394) king or executive suite; NZ$3,938 (US$2,757) Royal Suite. Long-stay, off-peak, and special deals available. AE, DC, MC, V. **Amenities:** 2 restaurants; bar w/live jazz Fri night; heated indoor pool; nearby golf course; small gym; spa; 4 private geothermal whirlpools; sauna; concierge; tour bookings; car rentals; business center; secretarial services; 24-hr. room service; massage; babysitting; laundry service; same-day dry cleaning; nonsmoking rooms; on-call doctor/dentist. *In room:* A/C, TV w/pay movies, dataport, minibar, fridge, coffeemaker, hair dryer, iron.

MODERATE

For a range of very smart lodgings, check out **Jack & Di's Lakeview Accommodation** ★★, 5 Arnold St., Rotorua (ℂ **0800/522-526** in NZ, or 07/357-4294; www. jackanddis.co.nz). The five options include a charming waterfront cottage, a city penthouse apartment, a friendly lodge, and a lakefront resort. Prices range from around NZ$150 to NZ$400 (US$105–US$280).

Birchwood Spa Motel ★

Everything in the good-size studios and apartments here is pristine and sparkling clean. Three upstairs units have double Jacuzzis in the bathrooms, and most others have self-filled Jacuzzis in cute private patios. Bathrooms are a bit small. The complex is just 2 minutes from Whakarewarewa Thermal Reserve, the Rotorua Golf Club, and the Redwood Forest. It's 2km (1¼ miles) from central city, a 25-minute walk. Birchwood provides a comfortable stay with very helpful hosts.

6 Sala St. and Trigg Ave., Whakarewarewa, Rotorua. ℂ **0800/881-800** in NZ, or 07/347-1800. Fax 07/347-1900. www. birchwoodspamotel.co.nz. 17 units. NZ$95–NZ$120 (US$66–US$84) studio; NZ$115–NZ$135 (US$80) 1-bedroom; NZ$155–NZ$180 (US$108–US$126) 2-bedroom. Extra person NZ$15 (US$11). Rates include airport transfers. Long-stay and off-peak rates available. AE, DC, MC, V. Take Fenton St. toward Taupo and turn left at roundabout; the motel is a few doors down. **Amenities:** Nearby golf course; private Jacuzzi in 10 units; tour bookings; car rentals; limited room service from nearby hotel; nearby massage; babysitting; laundry service; coin-op laundry; same-day dry cleaning; nonsmoking rooms; on-call doctor/dentist. *In room:* TV, dataport, kitchenette, fridge, coffeemaker, hair dryer, iron.

The Springs ★★

Guests have a choice of four sumptuous rooms with king-size beds, fine linens, walk-in wardrobes, lovely en-suite bathrooms, and doors to a private terrace. The lavish Paradise Spring room has just been refurbished in wheat and black silk and looks stunning. Murray and Colleen Ward treat you well, and the tall hedges give this central residential property a sense of privacy.

16 Devon St., Rotorua. ℂ **07/348-9922.** Fax 07/348-9964. www.thesprings.co.nz. 4 units. NZ$325 (US$227). Rate includes breakfast. DC, MC, V. Closed July–Aug. Children under 14 not accepted. **Amenities:** Nearby golf course; tour bookings; same-day dry cleaning; nonsmoking rooms. *In room:* TV, dataport, coffeemaker, hair dryer, iron.

Wylie Court Motor Lodge ★ *Kids*

Rooms at the 18-year-old Wylie Court are nothing flashy, but after a good revamp, they're comfortable and offer definite benefits for families. For a start, every unit has its own thermally heated outdoor Jacuzzi, and the whole place is set amid beautiful gardens with two playgrounds. Accommodations come in a number of different configurations; most are split-level with mezzanine beds. Each executive suite can sleep up to eight and contains two bedrooms, two bathrooms, a full kitchen, and a bigger Jacuzzi. This place has much more of a family atmosphere than Silver Fern, down the road, which tends to have more honeymooners and business guests.

345 Fenton St., Rotorua. ℂ 0800/100-879 in NZ, or 07/347-7879. Fax 07/346-1494. www.wyliecourt.co.nz. 36 units. NZ$140 (US$98) studio and cedar block; NZ$165 (US$115) executive. Extra person NZ$20 (US$14). Children under 10 NZ$10 (US$7). Rates include airport and bus transfers. Long-stay, off-peak, and special deals available. AE, DC, MC, V. **Amenities:** Restaurant (dinner only); bar; heated outdoor pool; nearby golf course; 2 playgrounds; car rentals; babysitting; laundry service; coin-op laundry; same-day dry cleaning; nonsmoking rooms; on-call doctor/dentist; access for travelers w/disabilities. *In room:* TV, dataport, kitchenette, fridge, coffeemaker, hair dryer, iron.

INEXPENSIVE

Hot Rock Backpackers 🐦🐦 *Value*   If you want a fun, central location with great facilities, you couldn't do better than this backpackers, which has been a finalist in the New Zealand Tourism Awards. Some rooms are tidier than others, but overall the place has a good atmosphere. The 10 motel-like double rooms with their own kitchen facilities are an excellent value. Most rooms have balconies and bathrooms. Two indoor thermal pools are emptied and cleaned each day.

1286 Arawa St., Rotorua. ℂ 0800/223-363 in NZ, or 07/348-8636. Fax 07/348-8616. www.acb.co.nz/hotrock. 33 units, 140 beds. NZ$22 (US$15) dorm bed without linens; NZ$25 (US$18) per person shared room with bedding and en-suite bathroom; NZ$65 (US$46) per person twin/double with en-suite bathroom. Singles available on request. Long-stay rates available. MC, V. **Amenities:** Popular Lava Bar; heated outdoor pool and 2 indoor mineral pools; nearby gym; tour bookings; car rentals; coin-op laundry; nonsmoking rooms.

Kiwi Paka YHA 🐦🐦 *Value*   Kiwi Paka is a bit farther out of town than the inner city backpacker establishments, but its guests enjoy a far bigger range of award-winning budget accommodations, better social facilities and amenities, and a quieter residential area. Everyone congregates in the cafe or the Kiwi Tasting Bar. The communal kitchen, dining room, and lounge were renovated in late 1999; added amenities such as the large thermal pool and the courtesy coach confirm this as a top-quality budget stay.

60 Tarewa Rd., Rotorua. ℂ 07/347-0931. Fax 07/346-3167. www.kiwipaka-yha.co.nz. 250 beds. Shared facilities: NZ$20 (US$14) per person bunk room; NZ$23 (US$16) per person twin/double; NZ$27 (US$19) per person single. En-suite chalets: NZ$60 (US$42) twin/double; NZ$75 (US$52) triple; NZ$100 (US$70) quad. Linen charge NZ$2 (US$1.40). Rates include airport and bus transfers. MC, V. Children under 12 not accepted. **Amenities:** Café Brasserie (lunch and dinner); bar; heated lit outdoor pool; game room; tour bookings; car rentals; coin-op laundry; nonsmoking rooms; on-call doctor/dentist.

WHERE TO DINE

Not so long ago, finding even a decent cup of coffee here was a struggle. These days, it's different. There's a growing cafe scene, much of it concentrated at the lake end of Tutanekai Street, known as "The Streat." Rotorua also has around 50 restaurants—everything from Turkish to Korean, Indonesian to Italian. For a family dining experience with great views, feast 600m (1,968 ft.) up at **Aorangi Peak Restaurant,** Mountain Road, Ngongotaha (ℂ **07/347-0046**). It pays to reserve a table. **Capers Epicurean,** 1181 Eruera St. (ℂ **07/348-8818**), is a terrific place for picnic goodies, delicious lunches, and coffee. It's open Tuesday through Saturday from 7:30am until late. And don't forget to try the traditional **Maori hangi** while you're in Rotorua (see "Maori Cultural Experiences" under "Exploring Rotorua," earlier in this chapter). Pick up the free dining guide and "The Streat" cafe brochure at the visitor center.

EXPENSIVE

Atlas Brasserie Restaurant ⭐⭐ *(Value)* INTERNATIONAL/THAI Dining at the Atlas is like eating in a giant conservatory with strong Asian overtones. It's colorful, light, airy, and always busy. The resident Thai chef lends the cuisine a strong Thai emphasis. Spicy seafood with green vegetables and fresh basil served on rice noodles isn't a bad way to start. Manuka smoked lamb rump served on kumara (sweet potato) mash, with mint *jus* and herb Yorkshire pudding, is just as likely to appeal. Look out for the great-value seafood buffets (around NZ$45–NZ$50/US$32–US$35) on Friday and Saturday nights, and the Thai buffet on Thursday night.

In the Royal Lakeside Novotel, Lake end of Tutanekai St. ✆ 07/346-3888. Reservations recommended. Main courses NZ$24–NZ$32 (US$17–US$22). AE, DC, MC, V. Daily 6am–10:30pm.

Bistro 1284 ⭐⭐⭐ *(Finds)* NEW ZEALAND/INTERNATIONAL My lasting memory of Bistro 1284 is of the incredibly friendly and personal service, and the good reports keep coming back. Add the fact that the food was divine and the atmosphere simply stylish, and you have a winning recipe. It's definitely the most "citified" of Rotorua's restaurants, and with menu items such as grilled scallops with ginger cream sauce and salmon caviar, you can be sure your taste buds will be tickled.

1284 Eruera St. ✆ 07/346-1284. Reservations required. Main courses NZ$24–NZ$32 (US$17–US$22). AE, DC, MC, V. Tues–Sat 6pm–late.

MODERATE

Landing Café ⭐⭐ *(Finds)* NEW ZEALAND This is a delightful stopover if you're anywhere out in the Blue and Green lakes or the Buried Village area. It's about 30 minutes from the city along a scenic road, and the food is more than worth the drive. I rate the mussel chowder very highly, and venison medallions with mustard mash have a band of fans. Desserts are the perfect way to end a meal in front of a roaring fire. This is also a top lunch spot where you can look out over the jewel-like waters of Lake Tarawera. You can also take a scenic cruise on Lake Tarawera from here.

Tarawera Rd. ✆ 07/362-8502. Reservations required for dinner. Main courses NZ$21–NZ$30 (US$15–US$21). DC, MC, V. Daily 9am–late.

Lime Caffeteria ⭐⭐⭐ CAFE/LIGHT MEALS This is my favorite Rotorua haunt. It's light, bright, and as fresh as a squeezed lime. The food is divine. You haven't lived until you've sampled the amazing blueberry and custard brioche! But there's more to Lime than small, tasty snacks and good coffee. It also turns out a delectable range of lunch options, like duck and shiitake wonton soup with bok choy and star anise; and blue brie, fig, and pine nut filo parcels with green-grape salad. Don't forget to buy a few picnic treats to munch while you're out walking.

1096 Whakaue St. ✆ 07/350-2033. Main courses NZ$15–NZ$25 (US$11–US$18). MC, V. Daily 8am–4:30pm.

Relish ⭐⭐ CAFE/PIZZERIA Drop in for coffee or a light lunch, linger over one of the delicious pizzas turned out on the wood-fired oven, or choose from the a la carte menu. You'll be glad you indulged. Chicken teriyaki pizza gets my vote, but you might prefer an evening meal of Middle Eastern spiced duck breast. It's a casual dining environment, ideal after a busy day of sightseeing.

1149 Tutanekai St. ✆ 07/343-9195. Reservations required for dinner. Main courses NZ$20–NZ$30 (US$14–US$21). MC, V. Daily 8am–late.

INEXPENSIVE

Fat Dog Café 🏵🏵 *Value* CAFE/LIGHT MEALS   This place is tops for atmosphere, a fact that people of all ages seem to have discovered. You'll find them here draped over old chairs and sofas—everyone from a whole herd of mountain bikers to someone who could be your granny. Food is not only cheap, it's also incredibly tasty and, dare I say it, healthy! There's a fabulous selection of counter food and a simple blackboard menu that lists the old adolescent favorites such as nachos and pies. Vegetable bakes, lasagnas, bagels, and salads can all be followed by something sweet and delicious, washed down with the best espresso in Rotorua. A funky little dive that's all color and charming chaos.

1161 Arawa St. ℂ 07/347-7586. Main courses NZ$12–NZ$25 (US$8.40–US$18). AE, DC, MC, V. Daily 8am–late.

River Monster Japanese Restaurant 🏵🏵 *Value* JAPANESE   Casual sushi bars are the best invention in the world, and this one continues an increasingly popular tradition of healthy, tasty, and budget-priced food. You can eat in or take away any of the specialized rice dishes. Sushi, sashimi, noodles, tempura, and teriyaki dishes are all represented. Make sure you indulge in dessert—a choice of green tea, pumpkin, or black sesame handmade ice cream, or all three.

1139 Tutanekai St. ℂ 07/346-0792. Main courses NZ$12–NZ$25 (US$8.40–US$18). AE, DC, MC, V. Tues–Sun 10am–late.

SHOPPING

Pick up the excellent *Rotorua Arts Trail* brochure from the visitor center. It gives names and contact details of many of the city's best artists, jewelers, and craftspeople.

The best places to shop for Maori arts and crafts are **Tamaki Maori Village,** State Highway 5 (ℂ 07/346-2823), which has one of the best displays of indigenous work in the country; **Te Puia's New Zealand Maori Arts & Crafts Institute,** at Whakarewarewa Thermal Reserve (ℂ 07/348-9047), where you'll find superb carvings; and **The Best of Maori Tourism,** Haupapa Street (ℂ 07/347-4226), which has contemporary and traditional crafts and especially good weaving and carved gourds.

A stunning new Maori-owned gallery, **Te Raukura** 🏵🏵🏵, Tutanekai and Haupapa streets (ℂ 07/921-0070), is well worth a stop if you're looking for something classy and indigenous to take home.

Simply New Zealand, Tourism Rotorua Centre, 1161 Fenton St. (ℂ 07/348-8273; www.simplynewzealand.com), has an excellent range of New Zealand–made merino wool knitwear, delightful toiletries, and a host of souvenirs. **Rainbow Springs** and **Agrodome** (see "The Major Sights & Attractions," earlier in this chapter) have good shops for wool products. At the **Jade Factory,** 1288 Fenton St. (ℂ 07/349-3968; www.jadefactory.com), you can watch the creative process of carving jade as it happens. For contemporary New Zealand art, visit **Madhouse Store & Gallery,** 1093 Tutanekai St., across from the Royal Lakeside Novotel (ℂ 07/347-6066; www.madhousedesign.co.nz).

ROTORUA AFTER DARK

Rest assured, there is more to Rotorua's nightlife than Maori hangi and concert performances. For a start, pick up a free copy of *Thermal Air,* which will point you in the direction of some of the best places to go.

There's an Irish pub in every town, and in Rotorua that's **O'Malley's Irish Bar,** 1287 Eruera St. (ℂ 07/347-6410), which schedules live music most Friday and Saturday nights. **Clarke's Lakeview Bar** 🏵, in the Royal Lakeside Novotel, Tutanekai Street, is a good place to meet for drinks. You'll find locals mixing with hotel guests, and Friday nights bring live music and happy-hour prices. Another good hotel nightspot is **The Mezz Bar** ✿, in Rydges on Fenton Street.

Backpackers will invariably have a good night at Hot Rock Backpackers' **Lava Bar,** 1286 Arawa St. **The Pig & Whistle City Bar,** 1182 Tutanekai St. (✆ **07/347-3025**), has a boutique brewery and hearty pub-style meals, with live music on Friday and Saturday. **Fuze City Bar** ✿✿, Lake End, Tutanekai Street (✆ **07/349-6306**), is open from 3pm until late Tuesday through Saturday and offers a smart environment for evening drinks, tapas, and gourmet pizza.

EN ROUTE TO TAUPO

It's a short drive to Taupo, just 84km (52 miles) over excellent roads. Throughout this area, watch out for logging trucks. If you haven't already done so, this could be a good time to call at one of the three main geothermal reserves, especially the **Hidden Valley Orakei Korako Geyserland Resort,** which is closer to Taupo than to Rotorua (see "Exploring Rotorua," earlier in this chapter). Eight kilometers (5 miles) before you reach Taupo, look for the steamy **Wairakei Geothermal Power Station,** which harnesses all that underground energy to furnish electric power.

2 Taupo ✿

287km (178 miles) SE of Auckland; 84km (52 miles) S of Rotorua; 155km (96 miles) NW of Napier

I've always found Taupo somewhat disappointing, but many New Zealanders practically worship this little lakeside town. Certainly, from a visitor's point of view, it makes a perfect central base from which to take in the area attractions, and the local council invested NZ$1 million in 2002 to redevelop central areas of the town, so it's looking quite spruce. It's within half a day's drive of the Hawkes Bay wine region, the mountains and ski fields of Tongariro National Park, the thermal wonderland of Rotorua, the white-sand surf beaches of Bay of Plenty, and the glowworms of Waitomo.

Taupo itself also has its merits—the vast sparkling waters of Lake Taupo are perfect for boating, water-skiing, and fishing; there are thermal pools, plenty of accommodations, some good, fast-paced outdoor activities, and a small permanent population of 22,000, which more than doubles in summer. There are also a number of new attractions and accommodations that make it a worthy stop.

ESSENTIALS

GETTING THERE & GETTING AROUND   By Plane   Air New Zealand Link (✆ **0800/737-000**) flies to Taupo from Auckland and Wellington five times a day, with connections to other destinations. In winter, **Mountain Air** (✆ **0800/922-812;** www.mountainair.co.nz) has daily flights between Auckland and the Chateau and Turangi Airports. For a taxi or airport shuttle, call ✆ **07/378-5100.**

By Coach (Bus)   InterCity and **Newmans** buses arrive and depart from the Taupo Travel Centre on Gasgoine Street (✆ **07/378-9032**). **Magic Travellers** and **Kiwi Experience** also serve Taupo. **Guthreys Express** (✆ **0800/759-999** in NZ, or 07/376-0027) has daily services from Taupo to Auckland, Rotorua, and National Park village, which is in Tongariro National Park. **The Connection Bus** (✆ **07/378-9955;** www.paradise tours.co.nz), runs between the Rotorua and Taupo visitor centers around three times a day for the ridiculously low fare of about NZ$17 to NZ$22 (US$12–US$15) one-way. There is no local bus service.

By Taxi   For service in and around Taupo, call **Taupo Taxis** (✆ **07/378-5100**).

By Car   State highways 1 and 5 pass through Taupo. All roads in the area are excellent, but drive with care in winter (when they're icy) and when there's a heavy flow of logging trucks. The drive to Rotorua is 45 minutes; to Waitomo or Napier, 1½ hours; to Hamilton or Tauranga, 2 hours; and to Palmerston North, 3 hours.

By Bicycle   To rent a bike, contact **Cycle World,** 30 Spa Rd. (℃ **07/378-6117**), or **Rent-A-Bike Taupo,** 106–108 Rifle Range Rd. (℃ **07/378-7947**). Taupo is particularly geared for cyclists, with dedicated lanes, shared paths, and numerous recreational off-road rides.

ORIENTATION   Taupo spreads along the northeastern tip of the lake, where the Waikato River, New Zealand's longest, flows out of Lake Taupo's Tapuaeharuru Bay. The main road is **Tongariro Street.** Perpendicular to that are **Heu Heu** and **Horomatangi streets,** two of several that form the main shopping area. Tongariro Street runs into **Lake Terrace,** the continuation of State Highway 1 that runs around the lake and takes you to most of the motels. The settlements of **Acacia Bay** and **Jerusalem Bay** are just across on the western shore of the lake.

VISITOR INFORMATION   The **Taupo i-Site Visitor Centre** (℃ **07/376-0027;** www.laketauponz.com) is easy to find—it's on Tongariro Street, the main road through Taupo. It has a wide selection of brochures and can arrange fishing guides and licenses, tours, and activities. It also sells stamps, phone cards, and souvenirs. Hours are 8:30am to 5pm daily.

FAST FACTS   The **post office** is at the corner of Ruapehu and Horomatangi streets; it's open Monday through Friday from 8:30am to 5pm. Internet access is available at **Internet Outpost,** 11 Tuwharetoa St. (℃ **07/376-9920**). It's open 9am to 11pm daily.

SPECIAL EVENTS   The last Saturday in November is the **Lake Taupo Cycle Challenge** (℃ **07/378-1546;** www.cyclechallenge.org.nz). In October, more than 3,000 cyclists gather for the **Powerade Day-Night Thriller** (℃ **07/378-0455;** www.event promotions.co.nz), the largest mountain-bike event of its kind in the world. The annual **Lake Taupo International Fishing Tournament** (℃ **07/377-3026;** www.troutfishing tournament.org.nz) is in April; the annual **Levene Half Marathon** (℃ **07/378-1546;** www.taupohalfmarathon.org.nz) takes place in August.

EXPLORING TAUPO

Most of Taupo's interesting attractions are just north of the town in a cluster around the Wairakei Tourist Park. The visitor center has a good brochure on this area. At the top of the hill as you leave town heading north, turn right onto Huka Falls Road and stop first at the **Huka Falls Lookout** ✹✹✹ . The falls themselves aren't huge, but they are impressive for the speed at which the blue-green water of the Waikato River moves over the 24m (79-ft.) drop. You can walk alongside the gorge on a path and across the rushing water on a footbridge, which provides a safe but thrilling way to enjoy the falls. You can also walk to the falls from Taupo (see "Outdoor Pursuits," below).

After you visit the other attractions in this area, divert down Aratiatia Road on your way back into town to see the **Aratiatia Rapids.** The gates of the dam above the rapids open every day at 10am, noon, 2pm, and 4pm from October to March. In less than 10 minutes, the dry riverbed goes from an empty basin of boulders to a raging river. After about half an hour, the gates close, the released water flows downstream, and the dry bed reappears. It's fascinating to watch. The best view is about 5 minutes' walk downstream, but you can also observe from the lookout.

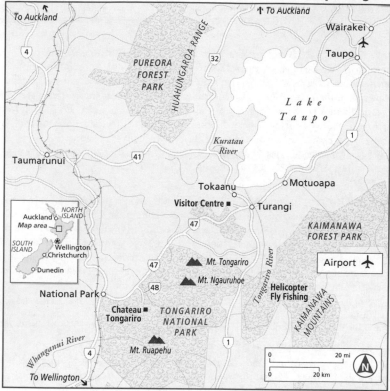

Lake Taupo Region

The **Lake Taupo Museum and Art Gallery,** Story Place (☎ **07/378-4167;** www.taupo museum.co.nz), is open daily from 10:30am to 4:30pm. It holds several art galleries, displays of Maori art and culture, and a wide selection of exhibits related to fishing, the timber industry, geology, and the lake. Admission is around NZ$4 (US$2.80) for adults.

Honey Hive 𝓚 (Kids)   After your stop at the Huka Falls Lookout, get back on the Huka Falls Road Tourist Loop and continue to the Honey Hive. Dare I say it? The place is buzzing with activity, and you don't need to be a bee enthusiast to appreciate the astounding array of bee-related products inside. You'll see an excellent range of gifts, from cosmetics and fruit wines to chocolate bees and woolly bees. Suffice it to say that this makes a pleasant change from sheep. Also on site is the Bees Knees Café, but don't go getting too excited about that—it definitely needs a revamp.

Huka Falls Loop Rd. ☎ **07/374-8553.** www.honeyhivetaupo.com. Free admission. Daily 9am–5pm.

Volcanic Activity Centre 𝓚𝓚𝓚 (Value)   The Taupo volcanic region is one of the world's largest, spanning 282km (175 miles), and this is the best place in the country to get an understanding of what's bubbling underfoot. Along with 3-D maps of the area, there are touch-screen computers, a working model of a geyser, a tornado machine, an earthquake simulator, interactive volcanoes, and fabulous short films on all aspects of volcanic and geothermal activity. Allow at least an hour for a worthwhile visit.

Huka Falls Rd. © **07/374-8375.** Fax 07/374-8370. www.volcanoes.co.nz. Admission NZ$8 (US$5.60) adults, NZ$4 (US$2.80) children, NZ$20 (US$14) family pass. Mon–Fri 9am–5pm; Sat–Sun 10am–4pm. Closed Good Friday, Dec 25, and till noon Apr 25.

Prawn Farm *(Kids)*   This is the place to see Malaysian river prawns happily getting fat in Wairakei's geothermally heated prawn farm. Interesting 30-minute tours operate hourly between 11am and 4pm. You can feed the prawns by hand, then end your visit at the Prawn Works Bar 'n' Grill, where you can eat the ones that grew the fattest. It's a lovely setting overlooking the Waikato River. You can also jet-boat from here (see "Outdoor Pursuits," below). The restaurant has a special kids' menu and play areas; for an extra charge, you can play Killer Prawn Golf after eating.

Huka Falls Rd. © **0800/697-7296** in NZ, or 07/374-8474. Fax 07/374-8063. www.prawnfarm.co.nz. Admission around NZ$10 (US$7) adults, NZ$4 (US$2.80) children, NZ$20 (US$14) per family. Daily 9:30am–5pm; evening dining Dec 26 to mid-Feb. Closed Dec 25.

Wairakei Natural Thermal Valley   This attraction is worth visiting if you enjoy geysers, mud pools, and other strange geothermal phenomena. Call first at the Wairakei Geothermal Visitor Centre for guided steam-field and historical tours that will give you insight into geothermal power generation. And check out **Wairakei Terraces**, next to Wairakei Steamfield (© **07/378-0913;** www.wairakeiterraces.co.nz), where, in a mysterious steamy setting, you'll learn about Maori legends and history. The establishment also offers an evening concert, hangi, and a Maori village tour.

Just off St. Hwy. 1. © **07/374-8004.** Fax 07/374-8656. Geothermal tours NZ$18 (US$13) adults, NZ$9 (US$6.30) children; the Terraces NZ$18 (US$13) adults, NZ$9 (US$6.30) children, NZ$50 (US$35) family. Maori cultural experience NZ$75 (US$52) adults, NZ$38 (US$26) children. Daily 9am–5pm. Closed Jan 1, Good Friday, and Dec 25–26.

SOAKING IN TAUPO HOT SPRINGS

Set in the unique natural Onekeneke Thermal Valley, **Taupo Hot Springs Spa**, behind the De Brett Thermal Resort and the Outrigger Terraces Resort, State Highway 5 (the Napier-Taupo Hwy.), Taupo (© **07/377-6502;** www.taupohotsprings.com), has been a favorite bathing spot for over 100 years. The water here is said to be the ultimate in providing therapeutic relief for muscular, bone, and skin ailments. Pools are filtered, drained, and cleaned every night. The pool complex is not as big, as modern, or as attractive as Rotorua's Polynesian Spa (p. 203), but it's definitely cheaper and feels just as good, and there is no sulphur in the water here. Facilities include 12 private pools, a children's pool, two Jacuzzis, a hydroslide, a volleyball court, *pétanque*, and a barbecue area. Admission to the public pools costs around NZ$12 (US$8.40) for adults, NZ$5 (US$3.50) for children; NZ$5 (US$3.50) giant dragon slide; barbecue hire NZ$10 (US$7). Private pools cost NZ$12 (US$8.40) for adults, and spa treatments range from NZ$20 to NZ$150 (US$14–US$105). The complex is open daily from 7:30am to

---

Finds **Hot Dip**

If you're walking the very pleasant Huka Falls Track, test out the hot stream that runs into the Waikato River at the Spa Park end of the track—but as in all geothermal pools, *don't* put your head under! Just after the start of the track, you'll cross a bridge over the stream. Access to the pool is below that. It's popular with Magic Traveller and Kiwi Experience types, so don't expect to always be alone.

> **Kids Just for Kids**
>
> **Lilliput Farm,** 136 Link Rd. (© 07/378-2114), is a 4-hectare (10-acre) treat for kids who like animals. They can hand-feed 20 different species and enjoy pony and donkey rides. The farm is open Monday to Friday 10am to 2pm, weekends 10am to 4pm. Admission is NZ$7 (US$4.90) adults, NZ$5 (US$3.50) children, NZ$20 (US$14) families. The **Creative Café,** 13 Marama Arcade, Taupo (© 07/ 377-0261; www.thecreativecafe.co.nz), lets kids paint their own ceramics while mum and dad enjoy coffee. It's open Wednesday through Monday.

9:30pm. As part of a 5-year expansion plan, the day spa will expand in 2006, and plans are afoot for the addition of several more private pools.

If you don't have time for a soak in Taupo, you can stop at the **Tokaanu Thermal Pools,** at the south end of Lake Taupo (see "En Route to Tongariro National Park," later in this chapter).

CRUISING THE LAKE

Taupo is New Zealand's biggest lake, with four options for heading out on the water: the replica steamboat *Ernest Kemp,* the motor launch *Cruise Cat,* the old yacht *Barbary,* and the steam launch *Alice.* The first three follow a similar path and pass the **Maori rock carvings** ★★, which are accessible only by boat. **Ernest Kemp Scenic Tours** (© 07/378-3444; ernikemp@reap.org.nz) operates 2-hour cruises daily for around NZ$30 (US$21) per adult, NZ$15 (US$11) per child. It is essential to book through the visitor center or the Taupo Boat Harbour office. The **Cruise Cat Experience** (© 07/378-0623; www.chrisjolly.co.nz) covers a longer distance than the *Ernest Kemp* in a shorter time. The tour operates daily from 11:30am to 1pm and costs around NZ$40 (US$28) for adults, NZ$20 (US$14) for school-age children. The *Barbary* **Carvings Cruise** (© 07/378-3444) departs at 10am, 2pm, and 5pm and costs around NZ$35 (US$25) for adults, NZ$12 (US$8.40) for children. The **Steam Launch** *Alice* (© 07/378-3444) offers a 1-hour cruise from Pier 41, Taupo Boat Harbour, on Saturday and most Sundays at 11am, 12:30pm, and 2pm. It costs NZ$15 (US$11) adults, NZ$6 (US$4.20) children, free for children under 5.

ORGANIZED TOURS

The fun way to start your visit to Taupo is by leaping aboard the double-decker bus for the **Discover Taupo Town Tour** (© 07/377-0774; www.taupotours.com). The 1951 vintage bus will take you on a 20-minute spin around town (in summer only) for around NZ$8 (US$5.60) for adults, NZ$4 (US$2.80) for children 2 to 15, NZ$20 (US$14) families. Tours depart every 2 hours between 10am and 4pm.

Paradise Tours (© 07/378-9955; www.paradisetours.co.nz) has a range of half-day excursions to local attractions (from around NZ$44/US$31 per adult), plus full-day tours to Rotorua, Napier, and Waitomo. **Haka Trails** ★★ (© 07/377-6016; www.hakatrails.co.nz), offers a range of Maori excursions and experiences. For a unique evening, try the Marae Sleepover, which begins in the late afternoon. You'll sleep in the *whare tipuna* (ancestral house), visit thermal pools, and eat dinner and breakfast for NZ$250 (US$175) per person. Another Maori-run operation is **Mist Maiden Tours** (© 07/376-5436), which offers half- and full-day tours in and around

Taupo, ranging in price from NZ$180 to NZ$250 (US$126–US$175). The 7-hour day tours include a visit to a local marae.

OUTDOOR PURSUITS

BIKING Bike tours and rentals can be arranged through **Rapid Sensations,** Wairakei Tourist Park (② **0800/353-435** in NZ, or 07/378-7902; www.rapids.co.nz). Its tours go to the Craters of the Moon thermal area, a 2½-hour ride that costs around NZ$75 (US$52) per person. Rentals are about NZ$50 (US$35) for a half-day. In Taupo, you can also rent bikes from **Cycle World,** 30 Spa Rd. (② **07/378-6117**). For more information, including tours, suppliers, and recommended cycle tracks, pick up the excellent brochure *Cycling Around Lake Taupo.*

BUNGY JUMPING You don't even have to jump to be impressed by the scenery that surrounds the 47m (154-ft.) bungy platform cantilevered out over the Waikato River. Call **Taupo Bungy,** 202 Spa Rd. (② **0800/888-408** in NZ, or 07/377-1135; www.taupobungy.co.nz). You'll pay around NZ$100 (US$70) for the experience. The company offers free pick-up from accommodations for jumpers. The bungy operates 9am until 7pm in summer (closed Dec 25).

CLIMBING Try something a bit different at **Rock 'n' Ropes,** State Highway 5, Wairakei, Taupo (② **0800/244-508** in NZ, or 07/374-8111; www.rocknropes.co.nz). If you've ever dreamed of being part of a circus act, this is your chance to polish up on rope walking, trapezing, rock climbing, and assorted other airborne fun. Courtesy transport to the site is available. A giant swing costs NZ$15 (US$11); the Adrenalin Combo is NZ$40 (US$28). It's open 10am until 5pm.

FISHING More than 100 years have passed since the first trout fry were released into the Lake Taupo region. Today, their plump descendants are one of the main draws. It's the best of New Zealand's best trout fishing. You'll need a special Taupo-issued fishing license, which can be good for a day to a full season. Remember that the minimum legal size is 45 centimeters (18 in.) and the daily limit is three. The visitor center can give you a list of the dozens of fishing guides in the area. Two we recommend are **Chris Jolly Outdoors** (② **07/378-0623;** www.chrisjolly.co.nz), which is great for large groups; and professional guide **Grant Bayley** (② **07/377-6105;** www.fishhunttaupo.com), who offers both tuition for beginners and local knowledge for experts.

FLIGHTSEEING Scenic rides in **Taupo's Floatplane** (② **07/378-7500;** www.tauposfloatplane.co.nz) leave from the lakefront near Taupo Boat Harbour; they range from a 10-minute flight to a 2-hour White Island excursion for around NZ$350 (US$245). Ask about the 10-minute backpacker special for four people, at around NZ$65 (US$46) per person. **Mountain Air** ✲✲✲ (② **0800/922-812** in NZ, or 07/892-2812; www.mountainair.co.nz) offers breathtaking flights over the Volcanic Plateau.

⌒Tips Fun Savings

If you plan on making the rounds of adventure activities, check out the savings package deals represent. The visitor center will point you in the direction of seasonal savings; for year-round package deals, contact **MaxBuzz** (www.maxbuzz.co.nz), which offers combos for Taupo Tandem Skydiving, Taupo Bungy, Huka Jet, and Holy Cow.

FOUR-BY-FOUR BIKING   Quad bikes are all the rage, and **Taupo Quad Adventures,** 24km (15 miles) north of Taupo on State Highway 1 (© **07/377-6404;** www. 4x4quads.com), offers rides through native bush, farms, and forest trails for NZ$70 to NZ$95 (US$49–US$66) per bike for a 1-hour ride. It also offers longer trips.

GOLF   **Wairakei International Golf Course** ★★★ , State Highway 1 (© **07/374-8152;** www.wairakeigolfcourse.co.nz), is rated among the top 20 golf courses in the world outside the United States. Book well ahead; greens fees are around NZ$80 (US$56) for affiliated and NZ$150 (US$105) for nonaffiliated members. The **Taupo Golf Club,** 32 Centennial Dr. (© **07/378-6933;** www.taupogolf.co.nz), is one of only two New Zealand clubs to have two 18-hole courses. You have the choice of the Centennial Championship Course or the Tauraha Course. Greens fees are around NZ$35 (US$25) for affiliated and NZ$50 (US$35) for nonaffiliated members.

HORSE TREKKING   **Taupo Horse Treks,** Karapiti Road, Wairakei Tourist Park (© **07/378-0356;** www.taupohorsetreks.co.nz), offers 1- to 2-hour treks through pine forests and thermal areas. One-hour tours cost around NZ$35 (US$25) per horse, NZ$60 (US$42) per horse for 2 hours.

JET-BOATING   Two operators work two completely different areas of the Waikato River. **Huka Jet** ★★★ , Wairakei Tourist Park (© **0800/485-2538** in NZ, or 07/374-8572; www.hukajet.com), specializes in impressive 360-degree spins and close-ups of Huka Falls. It charges around NZ$80 (US$56) for adults, NZ$50 (US$35) for children for a 30-minute adventure. **Rapids Jet,** Rapids Road, Aratiatia (© **0800/727-437** in NZ, or 07/378-5828; www.rapidsjet.com), runs farther upstream in the fast waters of the Aratiatia Rapids; prices are NZ$75 (US$52) per adult, NZ$40 (US$28) per child.

KAYAKING   Paddle over the turquoise-blue waters of the Waikato River with **Canoe & Kayak** (© **0800/529-256** in NZ; www.canoeandkayak.co.nz). A guided trip includes a soak in hot springs. For lake kayaking, call **Kayaking Kiwi** (© **0800/529-255** in NZ, or 07/378-7902; www.kayakingkiwi.com); it offers rock drawing and volcanic kayaking trips priced from NZ$85 (US$59).

SWIMMING   The completely revamped and extended **AC Baths,** Avenue and Spa roads (© **07/376-0350;** www.taupovenues.co.nz), opened in 2003. New indoor and outdoor pools, nine private pools, 2 hydro-slides, a Jacuzzi, a sauna, and a cafe make it well worth a visit in summer, when Taupo gets fiercely hot.

WALKING   The visitor center's excellent *Taupo Walkways* brochure outlines the area's 10 most popular tracks. They range from 15 minutes to 1½ hours in length. One option is the 3km (2-mile) walk from Spa Park, in Taupo, along the riverbank to Huka Falls (2 hr. round-trip). You can carry on to Aratiatia Rapids, which takes another 2 hours.

WHITE-WATER RAFTING   The guides with **Kiwi River Safaris** (© **0800/723-8577** in NZ, or 07/377-6597; www.krs.co.nz) know their stuff. They've had a minimum of 5 years' full-time experience and are qualified swift-water rescue technicians, with first aid and CPR certification updated annually. Options include daily Grade III-IV trips on Rangitaiki River and float trips on the Waikato River. The Grade IV-V trips on Wairoa River are for serious thrill seekers and happen only 26 days a year, when the hydro waters are released. Prices start at around NZ$95 (US$66) per person. **Rapid Sensations Adventures** (© **0800/353-435;** www.rapids.co.nz) offers a range of rafting adventures on the Tongariro, Mohaka, and Motu rivers. Prices start at NZ$55 (US$38).

Moments **Lakeside Hole-in-One** ☆☆

If it feels like your lucky day, or perhaps you've given up on Lotto, try Taupo's crazy **"Great Lake Hole in One" Challenge** (© 07/378-8117). It's addictive, it's fun, and, to my mind, it's impossible. The truth is, it's not. Apparently, more than 200 people have managed to make it, winning fabulous prizes, including trips to Europe, bungy jumps, and dinners. The object is to stand on the shoreline and whack a golf ball 115m (378 ft.) over the water in the hope that it will fall directly into the tiny hole in the middle of a floating pontoon. Balls cost NZ$1 (US70¢) each, NZ$15 (US$11) for 18, and NZ$20 (US$14) for 25. A red hole-in-one wins a trip for two to Europe; an ace in one of the 12-inch-wide blue-and-white holes will earn you local lodgings, attractions, products, adventure packages, or dinners. And can you believe it? There's about one winner per week! You can take a shot daily from 9am to 5pm, depending on weather conditions.

WHERE TO STAY

The Point Villas ☆☆☆ , Whakamoenga Point, Taupo (© **07/825-4756;** www.the pointvillas.com), offers some stunning modern accommodations top-quality rooms and gorgeous bathrooms in a divine bush setting overlooking Lake Taupo.

If you'd like to rent a home for your stay, contact **Westerman Property Solutions** (© **07/378-6163;** www.holidayhometaupo.co.nz), which has a selection of more than 100 two- to five-bedroom homes ranging from NZ$100 to NZ$400 (US$70–US$280) per night.

All rates below include 12.5% GST and parking.

VERY EXPENSIVE

Huka Lodge ☆☆☆   When an upmarket lodge has been around as long and won as many awards as Huka, you might be inclined to approach it with reverence and trepidation. That would be a mistake. They're all human here, and the key to enjoying Huka is to cast aside preconceptions and simply wallow. It's hard to find fault with the setting, the facilities, or the rooms. I've heard some negatives about stuffy service, and even experienced it myself on one occasion, but things seem to have loosened up a bit. Guest rooms want for nothing, and the public spaces, especially the wine cellar and the Trophy Room, are divine. Once all alone in this price bracket in New Zealand, Huka faces increasing competition from new players in the field and can't afford to be complacent, regardless of awards. However, it still has a certain something that none of the others has yet acquired.

Huka Falls Rd., Taupo. © **07/378-5791.** Fax 07/378-0427. www.hukalodge.co.nz. 20 units, 1 cottage. NZ$2,464–NZ$4,500 (US$1,723–US$3,147) double or double suite; NZ$7,976–NZ$11,081 (US$5,578–US$7,749) cottage. NZ$450 (US$315) per person Christmas Day/New Year's Eve surcharge. Minimum 3-night stay Dec 22–Jan 5. Rates include breakfast, cocktails, 5-course dinner, airport transfers, and use of lodge facilities. Off-peak rates available. AE, DC, MC, V. From St. Hwy. 1, turn onto Huka Falls Rd. and follow signs; lodge is 300m (984 ft.) upstream from Huka Falls. **Amenities:** Bar and wine cellar with biggest private collection in New Zealand (more than 30,000 bottles); heated pool; nearby golf course; all-weather tennis court; 2 Jacuzzis; use of bikes; concierge; tour bookings; car rentals; secretarial services; limited room service; massage; babysitting; laundry service; overnight dry cleaning; nonsmoking rooms; currency exchange; on-call doctor/dentist; airport transfers; access for visitors w/disabilities. *In room:* A/C, dataport, minibar, fridge, coffeemaker, hair dryer, iron, safe.

Lake Taupo Lodge ☆☆   This is a big lakeside home offering everything from Frank Lloyd Wright–inspired architecture and parklike gardens to attentive service by the owners, Gary and Shirley Akers. The 20-year-old lodge is a member of Small Luxury Hotels of the World, and Andrew Harper is one of many to have lavished praise upon it. That said, the interior is beginning to look slightly dated and in need of a freshening. The lake suite has the best lake views and the biggest bathroom; four of the rooms have Jacuzzis.

41 Mapara Rd., Acacia Bay, Taupo. (C) 07/378-7386. Fax 07/377-3226. www.laketaupolodge.co.nz. 7 units. NZ$1,294–NZ$1,338 (US$905–US$936) deluxe; NZ$1,564–NZ$1,676 (US$1,094–US$1,172) executive. Rates include breakfast, 4-course dinner, and airport transfers. Long-stay, off-peak, and B&B rates available. 5 min. north of Taupo in Acacia Bay. Children under 12 not accepted. **Amenities:** Bar; nearby golf course; outdoor lit tennis court; billiard room; bike rentals; car rentals; massage; laundry service; same-day dry cleaning; nonsmoking rooms. *In room:* TV/VCR, dataport, minibar, coffeemaker, hair dryer.

MODERATE

There are over 70 motels in Taupo alone, but they fill up fast on weekends and during summer holidays, so book ahead. In addition to the listings below, **Wairakei Resort** 𝒢𝒢, State Highway 1, Wairakei (𝒞 **0800/737-678** in NZ, or 07/374-8021; www.wairakei.co.nz), is a good base; it's just 7km (4⅓ miles) out of town and in the heart of most of the attractions. Its 187 rooms go for NZ$150 to NZ$350 (US$105–US$245). **Quest Resort** 𝒢𝒢, 9 Tui St., Taupo (𝒞 **0800/350-005** in NZ, or 07/378-7487; www.questtaupo.co.nz), has excellent modern, two- and three-bedroom villas and great amenities, including a heated pool and hot plunge pool. Special deals can be accessed through the website.

Baycrest Lodge 𝒢𝒢   Built in 1997, Baycrest is one of Taupo's best motels. It's a first-class establishment just minutes from the town center. Upstairs units all have spacious bathrooms with Jacuzzis, plus balconies overlooking the lake; downstairs units have their own individual courtyard, each with a private thermal tub. All rooms have European fittings and lovely furnishings. The new 2- to 3-bedroom apartment is great value for families or friends traveling together. It has two large bathrooms. Everything was refurbished in 2004.

79 Mere Rd., Taupo. (C) **0800/229-273** in NZ, or 07/378-3838. Fax 07/378-4007. www.baycrest.co.nz. 16 units. NZ$175 (US$122) studio; NZ$210 (US$149) 2-bedroom executive; NZ$300 (US$210) 2-bedroom apartment; NZ$400 (US$280) 3-bedroom apartment. Long-stay and off-peak rates available. AE, DC, MC, V. **Amenities:** Bar; heated outdoor pool; in-ground hot thermal tubs in ground-floor patios; several nearby golf courses and golf practice net; tour bookings; car rentals; secretarial services; limited room service; babysitting; laundry service; coin-op laundry; same-day dry cleaning; nonsmoking rooms; on-call doctor/dentist. *In room:* TV, dataport, kitchenette, fridge, coffeemaker, hair dryer, iron.

Outrigger Terraces Resort 𝒢𝒢 𝒱𝒶𝓁𝓊𝑒   This landmark hotel has had a massive dose of modernity to convert it into a very pleasant stay just above Taupo Hot Springs Spa—to which guests have discounted access. Rooms in the small 1889 colonial building are not vast, but they're comfortable and convenient. The two suites are bigger and certainly the best value; each has a TV/DVD. By 2006, the hotel is slated to gain 60 one-, two-, and three-bedroom apartment suites, along with new amenities like a heated lap pool. The air-conditioned suites will have full kitchens.

(Finds Local Treasure

For lovely forest walks and mountain-bike tracks, head for **Craters of the Moon Park,** on Poihipi Road. Head north from Taupo, cross the bridge, and at the top of the long hill turn onto the road to Kinloch (Poihipi Rd.). The park is about 5km (3 miles) farther on. Make sure you lock your car in this area.

80–100 Napier-Taupo Hwy. ℂ 0800/555-075 in NZ, or 07/378-7080. Fax 07/378-4174. www.outrigger.com. 80 units. NZ$185 (US$129) thermalview room; NZ$195 (US$136) lakeview room; NZ$265 (US$185) suite. Enquire for new apt prices. Long-stay, off-peak, and special rates available. Drive south from Taupo township, go around the lake, and turn left onto the Napier-Taupo Hwy. The complex is about 1km (⅔ mile) up on the left. **Amenities:** 2 restaurants; 2 bars; heated indoor lap pool; several nearby golf courses; all-weather outdoor tennis court; gymnasium; Jacuzzi; sauna; bike rentals; tour bookings; car rentals; courtesy transport to town and golf courses; business services; 24-hr. room service; massage; babysitting; coin-operated laundry; laundry service; same-day dry cleaning; nonsmoking rooms; currency exchange; on-call doctor/dentist; airport transfers; access for travelers w/disabilities. *In room:* Dataport, minibar, fridge, coffeemaker, hair dryer, iron.

INEXPENSIVE

Pukeko Cottage ⚘, 15a Charles Crescent, Rainbow Point, Taupo (ℂ 06/879-9472; www.pukekocottage.co.nz), is a little self-contained gem a short walk from the lake just south of town. It has two bedrooms and goes for around NZ$150 (US$105) per night, NZ$10 to NZ$15 (US$7–US$11) for additional guests. For something more modest, go for backpacker accommodations at the **Rainbow Lodge,** 99 Titiraupenga St. (ℂ 07/378-5754; www.rainbowlodge.co.nz), where beds go for NZ$22 to NZ$60 (US$15–US$42). The **Taupo Top 10 Holiday Park,** 28 Centennial Dr. (ℂ 07/378-6860; www.taupo top10.co.nz), is an award-winning park with a wide range of cheap accommodations.

WHERE TO DINE

I'm told there are around 60 restaurants in Taupo, and I'd like to know where they're all hiding. Although there's no shortage of places to eat, "shining stars of cuisine" are a bit thin on the ground. As is the case anywhere in New Zealand, restaurants and cafes keep reinventing themselves and changing their names, styles, and menus. A delicious lunch or summer evening meal at **Prawn Farm** ⚘⚘ (p. 222), Huka Falls Road (ℂ 07/374-8474), is worth your attention. It's the world's only geothermally heated prawn farm, and the prawn platter need not make you feel guilty. **Pimentos,** 17 Tamamutu St. (ℂ 07/377-4549), is another good choice for tasty dinners. It has an eclectic menu—from sautéed prawns to sweet-chile-and-mint-glazed lamb shanks—generally well presented. It's open Wednesday through Monday.

The popular **Soleil** ⚘⚘, 43 Ruapehu St. (ℂ 07/376-5759), serves global cuisine with an Asian focus at dinner Tuesday through Sunday. **Huka Vineyard Restaurant** ⚘⚘, Wishart Estate Vineyard, 58 Huka Falls Rd. (ℂ 07/378-5426), is open for lunch daily (from 10am). It's in a 100-year-old barn and specializes in wine and food matches.

Pick up freshly baked picnic goodies at **Deli Twenty-One** ⚘⚘, 34 Horomatangi St. (ℂ 07/378-8772). Phone ahead and specify your preferences, and the staff will put it all together for you. Or you can swing by, grab a table, and enjoy good coffee and a snack. Open daily from 8am to 5pm. And don't miss **Flax** ⚘⚘, 5 Horomatangi St. (ℂ 07/377-8052), a great little cafe with local color.

The Brantry Restaurant ⚘⚘ CONTEMPORARY NEW ZEALAND If you managed to find Zest (below), The Brantry is just a few doors away. Tucked into a two-story 1950s house, it gets rave reviews from the locals for its moody interior and good food. It's one of the pricier options in town, but dishes like stuffed lamb rump will leave you pleased to have made the effort.

45 Rifle Range Rd. (ℂ 07/378-0484. Reservations recommended. Main courses NZ$25–NZ$30 (US$18–US$21). AE, MC, V. Tues–Sat 6pm–late.

Replete Café ⚘ DELI/CAFE Trying to get lunch at Replete is like queuing for tickets to a sold-out show; everyone wants a piece of the action. The service can be flustered, but the food does tend to be good—great salads and pies. Replete appears to be Taupo's favorite daytime haunt for all ages, especially 30- to 40-something business types.

45 Heu Heu St. (€) 07/377-3011. Lunch main courses NZ$10–NZ$20 (US$7–US$14). AE, DC, MC, V. Daily 8:30am–5pm.

Zest *☆☆* CAFE   Wedged between a fruit shop and a suburban butchery, this little gem is well worth hunting out. Make sure you find it. It's immensely popular with in-the-know locals—especially the ladies—who appear to delight in its reliable coffee and tasty soups and salads. There is always a freshly baked array of sweet temptations to end with.

65 Rifle Range Rd. (€) 07/378-5397. Main courses NZ$8–NZ$15 (US$5.60–US$11). AE, MC, V. Mon–Fri 9am–4pm; Sat–Sun 9am–2pm.

TAUPO AFTER DARK

The core of Taupo's nightlife is geared toward backpackers. If you want to make a quiet start to the evening, head for **19th Hole,** at Wairakei International Golf Course, State Highway 1 ((€) 07/374-8152), where you can enjoy a drink and chat. **Holy Cow,** upstairs at Tongariro and Tuwharetoa streets ((€) 07/378-0040), is definitely the happening place for the young crowd. Anything goes, especially dancing on the tables. The **Gravity Bar,** Tongariro Street ((€) 07/377-4469), is another lively spot. If you feel like a good beer followed by a quieter dining experience, head for **Plateau** *☆☆*, 64 Tuwharetoa St. ((€) 07/377-2425), which celebrates Kiwi music and a range of Montieths' craft beers. For a touch of the Irish, head to **Finn MacCuhal's Irish Pub,** Tongariro and Tuwharetoa streets ((€) 07/378-6165), where you can enjoy a Guinness and rowdy music.

EN ROUTE TO TONGARIRO NATIONAL PARK

The 94km (58-mile) drive from Taupo to Tongariro National Park is an easy one along the eastern shore of Lake Taupo. At the southern end of the lake, stop at **Turangi** if trout fishing is your passion. The **Tongariro River** is one of the best-known trout-fishing sites in the world (see chapter 3). If you have time, also detour to **Tokaanu Thermal Pools.** Even if you don't swim, there's a nice nature walk. Or call in at the **National Trout Centre** *☆☆*, south of Turangi ((€) 07/386-9243; www.doc.govt.nz), which features interactive displays and an award-winning underwater viewing chamber that allows you to observe trout in their natural habitat.

State Highway 47 cuts off from State Highway 1 to lead you through plateau tussock land to State Highway 48 and the entrance to park headquarters. It's clearly signposted. As you leave Lake Taupo behind, you enter a world dominated by the grand volcanic landscape.

3 Tongariro National Park *☆☆*

99km (61 miles) SW of Taupo; 141km (87 miles) NE of Wanganui

Tongariro National Park is New Zealand's oldest national park and, as of 1990, a World Heritage Area in recognition of its outstanding natural and cultural features. It is a place of extremes and surprises that will make you ponder your own diminutive reality.

The park can be explored from one of two main areas—**National Park** and **Whakapapa villages** on the western side of the mountains, or **Turoa Ski Resort** and **Ohakune township** to the south.

The core of the park consists of the sacred peaks Tongariro, Ngauruhoe, and Ruapehu, which were presented to the people of New Zealand in 1887 by Te Heuheu Tukino IV, Paramount Chief of the Tuwharetoa tribe. At 2,797m (9,174 ft.), **Mount Ruapehu** is the highest mountain on the North Island and is the principal skiing spot in the region. Its **Crater Lake,** filled with acidic tepid water, has a bottom layer of 6m (20 ft.) of sulfur mud, which acts as a barrier between the water and the molten rock below. In June 1996, this active volcano erupted, surprising scientists monitoring its activity. A few days earlier, they had downgraded its danger rating after 8 months of relative inactivity following the spectacular eruptions of September and October 1995. Before that, Ruapehu had been quiet for 8 years. Up-to-date information on Ruapehu is at www.geo.mtu.edu/volcanoes/new.zealand/ruapehu.

Mount Ngauruhoe rises 2,290m (7,513 ft.), smolders constantly, and from time to time (the last in 1975) sends showers of ash and lava from its crater.

Mount Tongariro is the lowest and northernmost of the three, measuring 1,968m (6,455 ft.). It is also the focus of Maori legends. The peaks are at the end of a volcanic chain that extends all the way to the islands of Tonga, 1,610km (1,000 miles) away. Their origin is fairly recent in geological terms, dating back only about 2 million years.

The weather in Tongariro National Park is always changeable and can be savage regardless of the season. Trampers and skiers should always seek the latest track and weather details before venturing into the park.

ESSENTIALS

GETTING THERE & GETTING AROUND   By Plane   Mountain Air Xpress (✆ **0800/922-812** in NZ; www.mountainair.co.nz) has daily service linking Auckland with Mount Ruapehu. It also has a range of ski-flight packages.

By Train   The **TranzRail** (✆ **0800/802-802**) *Overlander* trains stop at National Park and Ohakune.

By Coach (Bus)   InterCity (✆ **07/378-9032**) provides service to the national park. **Whakapapa Express** (✆ **0800/828-763** in NZ, or 07/377-0435) offers daily ski and mountain transport between Taupo, Ohakune, and Whakapapa. **Ruapehu Ski Shuttle** (✆ **0800/331-995** in NZ, or 09/379-8886; fax 09/379-8151) serves National Park village, Whakapapa, and Ohakune from Auckland Sunday through Wednesday and on Friday.

By Car   Highway 1 runs along the eastern side of the park; Highway 4 goes through National Park Village on the western side; Highways 47 and 48 bring travelers from the south shore of Lake Taupo into the heart of the park; and Highway 49 turns off State Highway 1 at Waiouru at the south end of the park and travels to Ohakune. Mount Ruapehu is a 4-hour drive from either Auckland or Wellington.

VISITOR INFORMATION   The **Whakapapa Visitor Centre** is in the village of Whakapapa at the end of State Highway 48 (✆ **07/892-3729;** fax 07/892-3814; whakapapavc@doc.govt.nz). It's open daily from 6pm in summer, 8am to 5pm in winter (closed Dec 25). It provides current volcanic, weather, and track information, as well as hut and camping passes, maps and brochures, hunting permits, and other items. The center has exhibits on the natural and human history of the park along with two excellent audiovisual displays, *The Sacred Gift of Tongariro* and *The Ring of Fire.* Information about the Whakapapa Ski Field, 7km (4⅓ miles) above the village, is also available.

The **Ruapehu Visitor Centre,** 54 Clyde St., Ohakune (✆ **0800/782-7348** in NZ, or 06/385-8427; fax 06/385-8527; www.destinationruapehu.com), is open weekdays from 9am to 5pm, weekends from 9am to 3:30pm. For information online, go to www.mtruapehu.com. You can reach the Ohakune **Department of Conservation** office at ✆ **06/385-0010.** The **Turangi i-Site Visitor Centre,** Ngawaka Place, Turangi

(© **0800/288-726** in NZ, or 07/386-8999; fax 07/386 0074; www.laketauponz.com), is another useful stop. It's open daily from 8:30am to 5pm. For information on National Park Village, go to www.nationalpark.co.nz.

Make sure you pick up the free brochure *Tongariro Action—Do It,* available at any visitor center.

The **telephone area code (STD)** for the west side of the national park is **07;** for Ohakune, it is **06.**

EXPLORING THE PARK
ON THE SLOPES
Skiing is *the* activity in season (June–Oct), when the weather and Mount Ruapehu permit. The 1996 eruption closed the two main fields—Whakapapa and Turoa—for 2 years, and a mild winter in 1999 didn't improve things, but the situation appears to have recovered. Combined, these two fields offer over 700 hectares (1,730 acres) of patrolled, skiable terrain (and almost the same amount off-trail), with facilities and geographical variety to satisfy any skier. Whakapapa and Turoa will always be the names of the two ski areas, but since 2001, they've been united under one brand, Mount Ruapehu—New Zealand's largest ski area. You can get seamless lift passes to ski on either field; the company operates bus service between the two.

The **Whakapapa Ski Area** (© **07/892-3738;** www.mtruapehu.com), above the Grand Chateau, is heavily populated compared to South Island fields, which is its biggest disadvantage. There's something for everyone in terms of skiing, but be careful that you don't sail over bluffs. A lot of skiers stay in the club huts on the field. Whakapapa's sister resort is Copper Mountain, in Colorado, with which it shares some reciprocal privileges. Contact the ski area for details. Ski lifts operate daily from 8:30am to 3:45pm and cost NZ$75 (US$52) for adults, NZ$45 (US$32) for youth; for the lower mountain (beginners' area), they cost NZ$60 (US$42) adults, NZ$35 (US$25) for children. Packages including lift passes, rental, and lessons cost around NZ$80 (US$56) for adults, NZ$55 (US$38) for children.

The Whakapapa summer operation (Dec–Apr, 9am–4pm daily) includes guided Crater Lake walks (NZ$75/US$52 adults, NZ$50/US$35 children); and scenic chairlift rides (NZ$20/US$14 adults, NZ$10/US$7 children).

Whakapapa Shuttle (© **07/892-3716**) offers the best transport to the mountain, which costs NZ$15 (US$11) round-trip from National Park Village.

Many prefer **Turoa Ski Resort** (© **06/385-8456;** www.mtruapehu.com), above Ohakune, because it draws fewer people. It boasts the longest vertical drop of any ski area in Australasia, plus an abundance of gullies for snowboarders. There are also accommodations and restaurants in Ohakune. Ski lifts operate daily from 9am to 3:45pm and cost the same as at Whakapapa (above). Turoa is open only in winter (late June to early Nov). **Snow Express** (© **06/385-9280**) offers the best transport, which departs from Ohakune's Junction Ski Shop every half-hour and costs NZ$15 (US$11) round-trip.

Skiers and snowboarders can find more information on these ski fields and others in chapter 3. For the latest snow conditions and ski information, call **Snowphone** (© **0900/99-444** in Turoa, or 0900/99-333 in Whakapapa).

ON THE TRACKS: A TRAMPER'S PARADISE
Walking in Tongariro National Park is spectacular, to say the least, and there are plenty of possible routes. Pick up the Department of Conservation's brochure *Whakapapa Walks* for an introduction to some of the best. **Taranaki Falls** ✿ is a 2-hour, 6km

(3.75-mile) circular track that starts above Whakapapa Village and takes in both native bush and stark tussock vegetation. Taranaki Falls plunges 20m (66 ft.) over the edge of a large lava flow, which erupted from Ruapehu 15,000 years ago. **Silica Rapids Walk** is a 2- to 3-hour loop track that also starts above Whakapapa Village. It takes you through a beech forest, past streams and the rapids, and through subalpine plants and swamp as it returns to Bruce Road, 2km (1.3 miles) above the starting point.

The best walk of all is also the toughest—the famous **Tongariro Crossing** &&&. Regarded as New Zealand's greatest 1-day walk, it takes you between Tongariro and Ngauruhoe, over the most stunning volcanic landscapes in the country. It involves an 800m (2,625-ft.) altitude gain and a couple of very sharp but short stretches. People of all fitness levels can generally cope, but many underestimate the climate at altitude. Forget the fact that it is summer and take plenty of warm clothing, as conditions change fast and furiously. It is important to organize transport at both ends of the walk. Contact the **Tongariro Track Transport** (© 07/892-2870) or **Howard's Lodge Transport,** Carroll Street, National Park Village (© **07/892-2827;** www.howardslodge.co.nz). For more details on the Tongariro Crossing, refer to the "Tramping" section in chapter 3.

ON YOUR BIKE

An essential information source for mountain bikers in this area is the pocket-size publication *Volcanic Plateau Mountain Bike Rides,* written and published by Kennett Brothers in association with the Department of Conservation and printed on waterproof paper. It details a host of rides in the area, including the highly regarded 42nd Traverse. The booklet costs around NZ$10 (US$7) and is for sale at visitor centers and bike stores in the area.

The **42nd Traverse** &&& is one of the most popular bike rides on the North Island. It covers old logging tracks through remote native bush and has an overall descent of 570m (1,870 ft.) through spectacular scenery. Depending on your enthusiasm for the task, it takes anywhere from 3 to 7 hours to complete. You'll need to organize transport to and from your vehicle; **Howard's Lodge,** Carroll Street, National Park Village (©/fax **07/892-2827;** www.howardslodge.co.nz), or **Ski Haus,** Carroll Street, National Park Village (© **07/892-2854;** www.skihaus.co.nz), can arrange that for you. Howard's Lodge also offers guided rides.

WHERE TO STAY

Ohakune and National Park villages offer a good range of winter accommodations, but Whakapapa Village has fewer choices. You'll need to book well ahead to beat New Zealand skiers to the best beds. In summer, the area is popular with trampers and mountain bikers, and because some accommodations close after the ski season, it's still wise to reserve ahead. Rates given below include 12.5% GST.

IN OHAKUNE

This is where you'll find the greatest variety of accommodations, and it's only about an hour to Whakapapa, making it a good base. **Powderhorn Chateau** &&, bottom of Mountain Road (© **06/385-8888;** www.powderhorn.co.nz), is a member of Unique Hotels & Lodges and is the closest accommodations to the mountain on the Turoa side. It's definitely the best the town has to offer. It was built in 1995 and has 32 well-appointed rooms with private bathrooms for around NZ$160 to NZ$210 (US$112–US$149). Luxury apartments that sleep six go for NZ$700 (US$490) per night, with significantly lower off-peak rates. **Ossie's Ski Apartments & Chalets,** 59 Tainui St. (© **06/385-8088;** www.ossies-ohakune.co.nz), offers 13 two-story chalets with lovely Scandinavian-style timber interiors. Prices start around NZ$120 (US$84), good value for the money. In winter, you'll find smart lodgings at **Beechers Lodge Motel,** Turoa Alpine Village (☎ **06/385-8771;** beechers@actrix.gen.nz). Eight rooms have en suites and sleep two to five people each. Facilities include a restaurant, bar, spa, and sauna; rates range from NZ$100 to NZ$160 (US$70–US$112).

IN NATIONAL PARK VILLAGE

Centrally located just west of Whakapapa Ski Area, National Park Village has a nice selection of good-value, low-cost accommodations. It's also the only place that offers a view of all three mountains. **Howard's Lodge** ✿✿, Carroll Street (☎/fax **07/ 892-2827;** www.howardslodge.co.nz), is a friendly spot with backpacker dorm beds and simple twins, doubles, and quads with shared facilities, plus deluxe rooms with en-suites. Dorm beds are NZ$20 to NZ$24 (US$14–US$17) per person; standard rooms are NZ$60 to NZ$85 (US$42–US$60); deluxe rooms are NZ$80 to NZ$150 (US$56–US$105). **Ski Haus** ✿, Carroll Street (☎ **07/892-2854;** www.skihaus. co.nz), is big on atmosphere and offers a choice of bunks or private double rooms, all with bathrooms nearby. Dorm beds are NZ$20 to NZ$25 (US$14–US$18), doubles NZ$75 (US$52). **National Park Backpackers & Climbing Wall** ✿✿, Finlay Street (☎/fax **07/892-2870;** www.npbp.co.nz), is a new complex that's drawing a big crowd to its indoor climbing wall. Dorm beds are NZ$18 to NZ$20 (US$13–US$14); doubles with en-suites start at around NZ$50 (US$35).

IN WHAKAPAPA VILLAGE

This small alpine village has limited accommodations unless you take a Whakapapa On-Snow package deal and stay in one of the on-field ski clubs (see the "Skiing & Snowboarding" section in chapter 3). **Whakapapa Holiday Park** (☎ **07/892-3897;** whakapapaholpark@xtra.co.nz) has heated cabins, a self-contained lodge that sleeps 32, caravan and tent sites, and a fully stocked store. Prices start around NZ$44 (US$31) for cabins, NZ$65 (US$46) for the lodge, and NZ$12 (US$8.40) per person for caravan and tent sites. **Skotel Alpine Resort,** Whakapapa Village (☎ **0800/ 756-835** in NZ, or 07/892-3719; www.skotel.co.nz), has everything from backpacker rooms to smart deluxe units and self-contained chalets. There's a restaurant, a good sauna and Jacuzzis, and a fun-filled bar during ski season. Superior rooms and chalets are around NZ$160 (US$112); rates are higher in ski season.

The **Grand Chateau** ✿✿, Whakapapa Village (☎ **0800/242-832** in NZ, or 07/892-3809; www.chateau.co.nz), is the grande dame of the area. Built in 1929, the glorious old building has a New Zealand Historic Places Trust category I classification. Most guest rooms have been refurbished recently, and a big extension of 40 new rooms is now on stream. This is where you'll find the nicest rooms. The junior suites are especially good value; if you feel like splashing out, go for the gorgeous, big Te Heu Heu suite (NZ$750/US$525) and enjoy your own fireplace, Jacuzzi, and telescope. You pay top dollar—NZ$180 to NZ$450 (US$126–US$315)—in winter and get a much better rate in summer. If you're traveling as a family, a better value is the Chateau's **Fergussons Villas** ✿, behind the Grand Chateau (☎ **0800/733-944**). The nine self-contained villas are bright, cozy, and a great place for long stays. Rates are around NZ$185 to NZ$240 (US$129–US$168). Villa guests enjoy access to the Grand Chateau's facilities, including a heated indoor pool, sauna, gym, bars, and restaurant.

WHERE TO DINE
IN OHAKUNE

Ohakune has the best range of eateries, but be aware that some of them close in summer. **Powderkeg Restaurant and Bar** 👫👫, at Powderhorn Chateau (© **06/385-8888**), is a good winter bet for hearty meals and heaps of partying. It offers brasserie-style food. A more subdued, semi–fine dining atmosphere characterizes Powderhorn's other year-round restaurant, **The Matterhorn.** There's always good food at **The Fat Pigeon Cafe** 👫👫, bottom of Mountain Road (© **06/385-9423**), where you can relax in a charming garden setting. **The Mountain Rocks Café & Bar,** Clyde and Goldfinch streets (© **06/385-8295**), is the newest eatery where you can enjoy everything from big breakfasts to hearty dinners. It has a nice courtyard for outdoor summer dining.

IN NATIONAL PARK VILLAGE

The dining scene is finally improving here, although it is still rather limited, and open hours are unpredictable at best. **Ski Haus Restaurant & Bar,** Carroll Street (© **07/892-2854**), is open year-round for breakfast and dinner, serving filling fare such as steaks, chicken dishes, and a few vegetarian offerings. **Eivins Off Piste Café Bar,** State Highway 4, National Park (© **07/892-2844**), is now in a new building, and the breakfasts, lunches, and dinners are guaranteed to fill a gap—if the place is open! **Basekamp Gourmet Burger Bar,** Carroll Street (© **07/892-2872**), is good for pizzas and chunky burgers—try the venison and lamb burgers. The newest eatery, **Station Café,** National Park Railway Station, Station Road (© **07/892-2881**), is proving popular, but it, too, is often closed during the day.

IN WHAKAPAPA VILLAGE

Your best meals here will be at the **Ruapehu Restaurant** 👫👫 (© **07/892-3809**) at the Grand Chateau (see "Where to Stay," above). The Chateau's **Pihanga Cafe** is open from 11:30am until late, and although it's long overdue for a decor revamp, the reasonably priced meals (all under NZ$20/US$14) will fend off hunger pangs. That's the best I can say about it. Across the road, **Fergussons Café** has counter food, light meals, and good coffee daily from 8:30am to 5pm, but it won't be winning prizes anytime soon, either. **Skotel** (© **07/892-3719;** see "Where to Stay," above) has a restaurant open to casual diners for breakfast and dinner. Once again, food is of the no-fuss, filling variety, but you'll find a great party atmosphere here in winter.

EN ROUTE TO GISBORNE

There are two ways of getting to Gisborne from Rotorua. You can either drive along the Bay of Plenty route past Whakatane to Opotiki, and then cut through the Waioweka Gorge (St. Hwy. 2), or you can allow much more time and follow the East Cape Road (St. Hwy. 35), which takes in stunning scenery on the easternmost point of New Zealand.

The Cape drive will take 6 to 7 hours. This is probably the least-visited part of the country. Take great care on this road; there is often wandering stock, and locals don't always obey the road rules. For information on the East Cape Road and its attractions, see chapter 9.

The short route from Opotiki to Gisborne on State Highway 2 will take just 3 hours, but much of it is steep and winding through the Waioweka Gorge. It's faster, but it's boring compared to the East Cape Road.

EN ROUTE TO HAWKES BAY

Head back to Taupo, where you'll turn onto the Napier-Taupo Highway, State Highway 5. The journey follows excellent roads and takes around 1½ hours.

9

Gisborne & Hawkes Bay

Gisborne and the East Cape epitomize all that's special about New Zealand— stunning unspoiled scenery, rich culture and history, white-sand beaches, fabulous wines, and friendly, hospitable people. Gisborne, the most isolated city in the country, lies just south of the sparsely populated East Cape in Poverty Bay and is separated by mountain ranges from both Bay of Plenty and Hawkes Bay.

Nearby Mount Hikurangi, the tallest nonvolcanic mountain on the North Island at 1,839m (6,032 ft.), is the first point on mainland New Zealand the sun touches each day, and Gisborne the first city in the world to see the light.

It is the place where both Maori and European voyagers first set foot on land.

The *waka* (canoe) *Horouta* brought the first Maori settlers of the Great Migration from Hawaiiki over 1,000 years ago, and Captain James Cook stepped ashore at Kaiti Beach in Gisborne in 1769.

The Hawkes Bay region, 215km (133 miles) to the southwest, shares many of the same alluring natural features and has more than 30% of the country's finest vineyards. The adjacent cities of Napier and Hastings and the smaller community of Havelock North curve along the coast.

Both Gisborne and Hawkes Bay are blessed with mild climates, long hours of sunshine, and fertile soil—the perfect combination for horticulture. The landscape is a patchwork of orchards, market gardens, pasture, and vineyards.

1 Gisborne & the East Cape ✸✸

293km (182 miles) NE of Rotorua; 298km (185 miles) SE of Tauranga; 504km (312 miles) SE of Auckland

Gisborne (pop. 31,000) had its big moment when it welcomed in the first light of the new century. There were hopes that the NZ$9.5-million revamp of the city would signal a bright, rich future for the area, but I think things have pretty much reverted to the same old quiet, provincial atmosphere that always prevailed. Mind you, the beautification was much needed, and it's good to see the place looking tidier and slightly more alive.

However, the small-town atmosphere is part of Gisborne's charm, and we shouldn't overlook the fact that it is a prosperous river port city and commercial center. It moves at a relaxed pace (and some days that's an understatement) and enjoys 2,200 hours of sunshine annually with summer temperatures consistently above 77°F (25°C), often rising above 95°F (35°C).

Apart from being the country's second-largest grape-growing district and the self-appointed Chardonnay Capital, this area is also the last genuine bastion of bicultural society largely unaffected by tourism. That bicultural heritage is evident everywhere, in the use of the Maori language in everyday life and in the fact that 45% of the population is Maori—the highest proportion of people of Maori descent anywhere in New Zealand.

If you'd like to experience an isolated part of the country that is more like New Zealand "used to be," then come to Gisborne and the East Cape.

ESSENTIALS

GETTING THERE & GETTING AROUND   **By Plane   Air New Zealand Link**
(✆ **06/867-1608**) operates daily flights from major New Zealand cities. Don't be
shocked by the fact that aircraft share the runway with a railway line. Planes give way
to the freight trains, and there are no problems. For airport transport, call **Link Shuttles** (✆ **06/867-4765**).

By Coach (Bus)   InterCity (✆ **06/868-6196**) offers daily bus service to Gisborne
from Auckland, Wellington, and Rotorua. **Coachrite** (✆ **06/868-9969**) travels to
Hastings Monday through Friday. City buses operate Monday through Friday only,
but Gisborne is better explored by car or taxi.

By Shuttle   Shuttle buses provide transportation around East Cape between Opotiki
and Gisborne. They leave daily from the visitor centers in both towns, which can provide information on schedules and fares.

By Taxi   Call the **Gisborne Taxi Society** (✆ **06/867-2222**).

By Car   No matter which route you take to Gisborne—via East Cape, via Waioweka
Gorge, or via Napier—you're in for a long and winding drive. By far the most interesting way, via East Cape, is also by far the longest. To make the most of the rich culture and stunning scenery in this area, you really need to stop overnight halfway (at
Hicks Bay perhaps). Otherwise, be prepared to be on the road for 8 to 10 hours once
you leave Opotiki.

ORIENTATION   Gisborne is on the northern shore of Poverty Bay, where the
Waimata and Taruheru come together to form the Turanganui River, the country's
shortest river at just 1,200m (3,936 ft.). The city center is compact. **Gladstone Road**
is the main thoroughfare. **Centennial Marine Drive** runs from the bustling port area
around the bay to the mouth of the Waipaoa River. Most of the best restaurants are
around the port area at the north end of Gladstone Road.

   Opotiki lies at the eastern end of Bay of Plenty. It is the gateway to the **East Cape
Road,** which is the final leg of the Pacific Coast Highway (St. Hwy. 35).

   Wairoa, 99km (61 miles) south of Gisborne at the mouth of the Wairoa River, is
the gateway to the wilderness areas of Urewera National Park and Lake Waikaremoana. The 3-day tramp around the lake is one of the Department of Conservation's
Great Walks of New Zealand (see chapter 3).

VISITOR INFORMATION   The **Gisborne i-Site Visitor Centre,** 209 Grey St.,
across from Pizza Hut (✆ **06/868-6139;** fax 06/868-6138; www.gisbornenz.com), is
open daily from 8:30am to 5:30pm in summer, 8:30am to 5pm in winter (closed Dec
25). You can also find information on the area at www.destinationgisborne.co.nz and
www.pacificcoast.co.nz.

   The **Wairoa i-Site Visitor Centre** is at the corner of State Highway 2 and Queen
Street, Wairoa (✆ **06/838-7440;** fax 06/838-3821; www.wairoanz.com). It is open
8:30am to 5pm weekdays, 10am to 4pm weekends. The **Opotiki i-Site Visitor Centre** is at the corner of Elliot and St. John streets, Opotiki (✆/fax **07/315-8484;** info
centre@odc.govt.nz).

FAST FACTS   The **post office** is at 74 Grey St., Gisborne. It's open Monday
through Friday from 9am to 5pm. For **Internet access,** inquire at the visitor center
(see above).

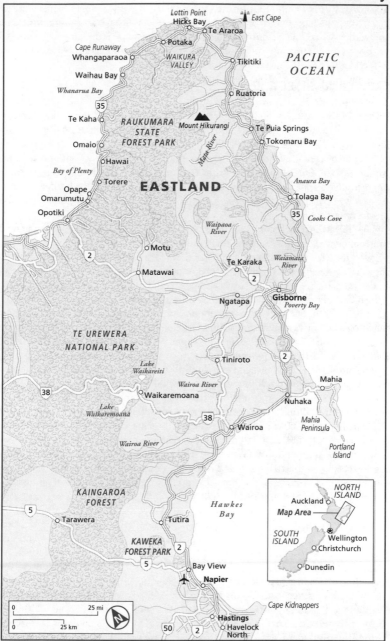

Lottin Point
Hicks Bay
East Cape
Te Araroa
Cape Runaway
Potaka
Whangaparaoa
WAIKURA VALLEY
PACIFIC OCEAN
Waihau Bay
Tikitiki
Whanarua Bay
Ruatoria
35
Te Kaha
RAUKUMARA STATE FOREST PARK
Mount Hikurangi
Te Puia Springs
Omaio
Tokomaru Bay
Hawai
Bay of Plenty
Torere
EASTLAND
Anaura Bay
Opape
Omarumutu
Tolaga Bay
Opotiki
35
Cooks Cove
Waipaoa River
Motu
2
Te Karaka
Waiamata River
Matawai
2
Gisborne
Ngatapa
Poverty Bay
TE UREWERA NATIONAL PARK
2
Lake Waikareiti
Tiniroto
38
Waikaremoana
Wairoa River
Mahia
Lake Waikaremoana
Nuhaka
38
Mahia Peninsula
Wairoa
Wairoa River
Portland Island
KAINGAROA FOREST
Hawkes Bay
NORTH ISLAND
Auckland
Map Area
5
Tarawera
Tutira
SOUTH ISLAND
Wellington
KAWEKA FOREST PARK
2
Christchurch
5
Bay View
Napier
Dunedin
0   25 mi
0   25 km
Cape Kidnappers
Hastings
Havelock North
50   2

SPECIAL EVENTS   The **Gisborne Opera Festival,** every 3 years (the next one will be in 2006), includes a week of opera and arts together with Maori culture, wine trails, and garden visits. The **Gisborne Wine & Food Festival** ⊛ is on Labour Weekend in October. For information, call ⓒ **0800/447-667** in New Zealand. For details on all Eastland area events, contact the visitor center.

EXPLORING GISBORNE

To get a panoramic view of Poverty Bay, the city, and the harbor and rivers, head for **Kaiti Hill Lookout.** It's signposted at the northern end of Gladstone Bridge, and you can drive all the way to the brick semicircular lookout point. A statue of Captain Cook looks out to Young Nick's Head, at the opposite end of the bay. At the foot of Kaiti Hill is one of New Zealand's largest carved Maori meetinghouses, **Te Poho-o-Rawiri Marae** ⊛⊛ (ⓒ **06/868-5364**). Visits can be arranged by appointment, providing an opportunity to see a living gallery of Maori art in the exceptionally detailed *tukutuku* (woven wall panels) and *kowhaiwhai* (painted scroll ornamentation) patterns painted on the rafters.

The **Tairawhiti Museum** ⊛⊛, 18–22 Stout St. (ⓒ **06/867-3832**; www.tairawhiti museum.org.nz), is one of the best small provincial museums in the country. It has displays on the Maori and European history of the area as well as geological and natural history, decorative arts, and maritime history. Admission is free. It's open Monday through Friday from 10am to 4pm, and Saturday, Sunday, and public holidays from 1:30 to 4pm (closed Good Friday and Dec 25). The **East Coast Museum of Technology,** Main Road, Makaraka (ⓒ **06/868-8254**; www.ecmot.8m.com), is 6km (4 miles) from the city. Its huge collection of vintage farm machinery, fire engines, and general equipment from a bygone era is open daily from 9:30am to 4:30pm. Admission is around NZ$3 (US$2.10) for adults, NZ$1 (US70¢) for children.

The internationally renowned **Eastwoodhill Arboretum** ⊛⊛⊛, 2392 Wharekopae Rd., Ngatapa (ⓒ **06/863-9003**; www.eastwoodhill.org.nz), lies 35km (22 miles) and 20 minutes west of Gisborne. It is an extraordinary testament to one man's passion for trees. This magnificent 70-hectare (173-acre) woodland park was the life's work of William Douglas Cook, who began planting the bare site in 1910. Today, it holds more than 3,500 species of 750 tree genera, making it the largest arboretum in New Zealand. The arboretum is a haven for scientists, photographers, and garden enthusiasts alike. Allow at least 1½ hours and plan to have a picnic under the maples. It's open year-round daily from 9am to 5pm (closed Good Friday and Dec 25); admission is around NZ$8 (US$5.60) for adults.

For a tour of other attractions in the Ngatapa Valley area, contact **Trev's Tours,** 200 Campbell Rd., Ngatapa (ⓒ **06/863-9815**; trevstours@xtra.co.nz). He charges around NZ$100 (US$70) per person for a 6-hour tour of the valley highlights—and don't forget to ask about his other interesting options, including food and wine tours.

Hackfalls Arboretum, Tiniroto Road, 1 hour from Gisborne (ⓒ **06/863-7091**; hackfalls@xtra.co.nz), has one of the biggest collections of maples and oaks in New Zealand. It's open daily; admission is NZ$5 (US$3.50) per person. **Bermuda Palms Plantation,** 11 Murphy Rd., Wainui Beach, 15 minutes from Gisborne (ⓒ **06/867-7095**; rjbodle@xtra.co.nz), is open to visitors for NZ$5 (US$3.50) per person. **Gisborne Botanical Gardens,** Aberdeen Road, are a pleasant distraction on the banks of the Taurheru River in the heart of town. Admission is free. Pick up the *Gardens to Visit* brochure from the visitor center if you're interested in even more greenery.

A DROP OF WINE

Gisborne is New Zealand's second-largest producer of chardonnay grapes (after Marlborough), growing over a third of the national crop. The area also produces significant quantities of award-winning Riesling and a wide range of other varieties. Pick up the *Wine Trail Guide* at the visitor center, fix yourself a picnic, and head out to explore. *Note:* Not all wineries are open to the public all the time, so it pays to phone ahead for hours. As well as those below, check out **Waiohika Estate,** 75 Waimata Valley Rd. (© **06/867-4670**), for wine tastings and garden visits; **Amor-Bendall,** 145 Wairere Rd., Wainui Beach (© **021/859-435**), for chardonnay and pinot gris; and **TW Chardonnay** 😊😊, Back Ormond Road (© **021/864-818;** call for an appointment) for very good vineyard tours and tastings.

   Taste Tairawhiti 😊😊, Gisborne Wine Company (© **06/863-1285;** www.gisborne winecompany.co.nz), arranges winery tours. The 3- to 4-hour tour takes visitors to eight wineries and vineyards and costs NZ$60 (US$42) per person. A picnic hamper is available for NZ$10 (US$7) per person. The price includes wine tasting and a cheese platter at The Works (see below). **House of Wine** 😊😊, Brunton Road, Gisborne (© **06/863-2794**), presents the area's artisan winemakers and wine tastings (NZ$5/US$3.50 per person). It's open Monday through Saturday from 10am to 5pm. If you'd like to learn the secrets of cider making, visit **The Cidery,** 91 Customhouse St., Gisborne (© **06/868-8300**), home to New Zealand's leading cider producer, Bulmer Harvest. It's open weekdays 9am to 5pm, weekends 10am until 3pm.

The Milton Vineyard 😊😊   Milton Vineyard was established in 1984 as New Zealand's first commercial, fully certified organic winery. It's known for its Riesling, chenin blanc, and late-harvest dessert wines. It's set in a superb garden with a picnic area.

119 Papatu Rd., Manutuke. © **06/862-8680.** Fax 06/862-8869. milton@bpc.co.nz. Summer daily 10am–5pm, or by appointment year-round.

Montana Wines 😊😊   Established in 1934, this is New Zealand's leading winemaker and wine exporter. The company has wineries in Auckland, Marlborough, Hawkes Bay, and Gisborne. The Gisborne winery produces the Ormond Estate, Patutahi Estate, Saints, and Montana labels—some of the country's best chardonnay. And check out the newest addition, **The Lindauer Cellars,** Solander Street (© **06/868-2757;** gisborne cellardoor@montanawines.co.nz), which is open daily December through February, and Tuesday through Saturday from March to November.

Lytton Rd., Gisborne. © **06/867-9819.** Fax 06/867-9819. Daily 9am–5pm.

The Works & Longbush Wines 😊😊   The Thorpe family has worked its vineyards for more than 35 years and now produces three ranges of Gisborne-made wines under the Woodlands, Longbush, and Nick's Head labels. It focuses on chardonnay and merlot. You can taste the production at The Works, a restaurant and wine bar.

The Works, Esplanade, Inner Harbour, Gisborne. © **06/863-1285.** Daily 10am–6pm.

A SPOT OF CULTURE

Rotorua may have the most accessible concentration of Maori culture in the country, but Eastland is one of the few places in New Zealand where strong cultural and tribal affiliations are still evident in day-to-day activities. The Maori language is part of everyday life here.

   The area is home to more than 100 working marae (village commons), which still form a focal point for most Maori communities. They are used regularly for meetings, celebrations, funerals, and family and tribal functions. Many can be viewed by arrangement, but there are two important rules to remember: You must not take photographs inside marae anywhere in New Zealand, and you must not smoke or take food inside. In many, you will also have to remove your shoes.

The remnants of ancient *pa* sites (Maori fortresses) abound throughout the region. Among the most notable are the one at Ngatapa and another in the hills to the north of Waikohu. The district also has a large number of *kohanga reo* (early-childhood education centers) and *kura kaupapa* (primary schools) where only Maori is spoken. Most other schools in the region have bilingual units.

You can see Maori culture at work and play in the many small communities around the East Cape Road.

EXPLORING THE EAST CAPE ✸✸✸

State Highway 35 between Opotiki and Gisborne is a memorable 334km (207-mile) journey. The road is etched into the coastline, rewarding the traveler with an ever-changing vista of the South Pacific. In summer, scarlet pohutukawa trees border the bright blue bays, and all along the way you'll see deserted white-sand beaches that afford innumerable opportunities for walking and fishing.

Make sure you get a copy of **Jason's Pacific Coast Highway Touring Guide** (www.jasons.com), free from visitor centers throughout the North Island. As well as providing a detailed, very readable map, it illustrates highlights along the way.

The route is also a genuine cultural experience. Many of the larger bays are centers of Maori settlements, usually surrounding their home marae. At **Te Kaha,** the Tukaki meetinghouse in the marae has an elaborately carved lintel, which you can view by asking permission. **Whangaparaoa** is where the great migration canoe *Tainui* landed, and Potaka is the northern boundary of the Ngati Porou tribe. Hicks Bay, not quite midway, has marvelous views and the **Tuwhakairiora meetinghouse** ✸✸, one of the finest examples of carving on the cape. The carving was carried out in 1872 and is dedicated to local members of Ngati Porou who died in overseas wars. Turn left at the general store to reach the meetinghouse.

Not far from Hicks Bay, the road descends to sea level and follows a narrow bay to **Te Araroa.** Here you'll find the country's oldest (600 years) and largest pohutukawa tree and a wealth of Maori history. A 20-minute side trip from here will bring you to the picture-book vista of the historic **East Cape Lighthouse** ✸✸. The track to the 1906 lighthouse must be covered on foot; it leads up 700 steps.

⌒Moments Sunrise at Mount Hikurangi

At 1,839m (6,032 ft.), Mount Hikurangi is the first point on mainland New Zealand to see the sunrise each day. At the summit are nine carved sculptures. A walking track to the top crosses private property, but because it is sacred to the Maori, you must gain permission from **Te Runanga o Ngati Porou,** who have offices in Ruatoria (© **06/864-9004** or 06/867-9960). An excellent alpine hut on the higher reaches allows early-morning climbs to see the sunrise. Hut fees are around NZ$5 (US$3.50) per person; bookings are essential. Four-wheel-drive tours are also available.

The next settlement is Tikitiki, where the historic **St. Mary's Church** stands like a sentinel above the road. Built as a memorial to Ngati Porou soldiers who died in World War I, it is one of New Zealand's most ornate Maori churches.

Next stop, just a short diversion off the main road, is **Ruatoria,** the center of Ngati Porou. Although scattered around the country, they compose New Zealand's second-largest Maori tribe. For more information on the local Ngati Porou tribe, check out the website www.ngatiporou.iwi.nz. It lists a network of indigenous tour operators on the east coast, from Gisborne north to Potaka, who are committed to providing authentic, culturally appropriate experiences.

There are four marae at **Tokomaru Bay** ☆☆, plus a glorious sweep of beach and a selection of interesting old unused buildings. (Take care when swimming in the ocean here.)

The road then leads to **Tolaga Bay** ☆, which has one of the longest free-standing jetties in New Zealand, plus, rather unexpectedly, the **Tolaga Bay Cashmere Company** ☆☆, 31 Solander St. (© **06/862-6746;** www.cashmere.co.nz), which produces fine merino, cashmere, and silk knitwear. The company's high-fashion garments are renowned throughout Australasia. This shop, which specializes in wholesale prices and seconds, is open in summer Monday through Saturday from 9am to 4pm, Sunday 10am to 2pm. It is closed on winter weekends. Tolaga Bay is 54km (33 miles) north of Gisborne.

The **Ernest Reeve Walkway** ☆, at the northern end of Tolaga Bay, leads to a lookout on the cliffs, overlooking the bay. The stunning views are worth capturing on film. Allow an hour for the return walk.

To get the best from the East Cape region, consider a guided tour tailored to your interests. **Rose's Tiki Tours** ☆ (©/fax **06/867-1687;** t.rose@actrix.co.nz), specializes in tours of Eastland. For something different, try **Whalerider Tours** ☆☆ (© **06/ 868-6139;** fax 06/868-6138; www.gisbornenz.com) with Hone Taumaunu, cultural consultant for the highly successful New Zealand movie *Whalerider.* He will take you on a tour of the Whangara settlement and into the house where much of the movie was filmed. The 3-hour tour departs from Whangara (directions from visitor center) and costs around NZ$50 to NZ$60 (US$35–US$42) per person.

OUTDOOR PURSUITS

BEACHES   Gisborne has three major swimming beaches, **Midway, Waikanae,** and **Wainui.** Lifeguards patrol all three in season. **Kaiaua Beach,** 60km (37 miles) north of Gisborne and 6km (3¾ miles) off State Highway 35, is good for fishing, swimming, and picnics. **Anaura Bay,** 77km (48 miles) north of Gisborne and 6km (3¾ miles) off State Highway 35, was Captain Cook's second landing spot in New Zealand. It has a beautiful beach of unspoiled golden sand, offering safe swimming and good fishing. A 3.5km (2-mile) bush walk gives wonderful scenic views; allow 2½ hours. You can make marae visits here; there is a motor camp as well.

FISHING   In this area, you can do anything from freshwater fly-fishing for brown trout to game fishing for marlin in the Pacific. For the independent angler, the Pacific Coast Highway is the ultimate route for surf-casting, game fishing, and diving. Local knowledge is plentiful, and visitors can take a shortcut to success by contacting local fishing clubs or taking advantage of guides and charter services. Saltwater fishing does not require a license. For wilderness brown and rainbow trout fishing, call **Safari Adventures,** Taumata Road, Rere, Gisborne (© **06/867-0872;** www.nzsafari.co.nz), which also offers accommodations and saltwater game fishing.

The Motu, Waioweka, Hangaroa, and Ruakituri rivers offer some of the finest freshwater fishing. Licenses are required for all freshwater fisheries. Call **Fish & Game New Zealand's Trout Line** (© 0800/876-885 in NZ). For the **Gisborne Fishery Office,** call © 06/868-7160, or check out www.fish.govt.nz.

GOLF   Poverty Bay Golf Club, Awapuni and Lytton roads, Gisborne (© 06/867-4402; povertybaygc@paradise.net.nz), is one of the top 10 18-hole courses in the country. Fees range from NZ$15 to NZ$25 (US$11–US$18).

HORSE TREKKING   One of the best horse-trekking operations around is **Waimoana Horse Treks,** Lysnar Street, Wainui Beach (©/fax 06/868-8218; waimoana@ihug.co.nz). Just 5km (3 miles) north of Gisborne, the treks take you over beaches and through native bush and farmland. One- and 2-hour rides run daily between 10am and 2pm.

HUNTING   New Zealand Safari Adventures, Tangihau Station, Rere (© 06/867-0872; www.nzsafari.co.nz), is an outdoor playground 30 minutes from the city where you can hunt trophy red deer, elk, mountain goat, or Hokonui ram with experienced guides.

SNORKELING WITH SHARKS   Get face to face with mako sharks—from the safety of a cage, of course. **Surfit Shark Cage Experience** ✿✿✿, 48 Awapuni Rd., Gisborne (© 06/867-2970; www.surfit.co.nz or www.sharks.co.nz), will take you out into reef waters teeming with the marine predators from November to April. The 5-hour experience costs around NZ$250 (US$175), which seems like a lot of money to terrify yourself—but think of the stories you can tell afterward.

SURFING   The popular surf beaches are **Makorori Point** ✿✿, **Pouawa, Sponge Bay,** and **Kaiaua. Midway Beach** has the famous Gisborne pipe, known for its deep barrel rides, and **Waikanae** and **Wainui beaches** are also good for surfing and bodyboarding. **Kaiti Beach,** around the Gisborne Port and harbor area, offers excellent sailboarding and yachting. The visitor center staff will point you in the direction of numerous other surf breaks. For surf lessons and board hire, call **Gisborne Surf School** (© 06/868-3484; www.gisbornesurfschool.co.nz). Prices for board hire start at NZ$25 (US$18) for a half-day, NZ$40 (US$28) for a full day. Lessons start at NZ$45 (US$32) per person for 2 hours.

SWIMMING   Gisborne Olympic Pool Complex, Centennial Marine Drive (© 06/867-6220; fax 06/867-4953), is open daily from 6am to 8pm. It has indoor and outdoor pools, a dive pool, a spa and therapy pool, a 98m (321-ft.) hydroslide, and a toddlers' pool.

WALKING   Good walking abounds in this area. For an easy amble, pick up the free brochure *Gisborne, An Historic Walk,* which leads around the inner city on a 1- to 3-hour wander. *Walks of the Eastland Region* (available at the visitor center), is a more comprehensive appraisal of excellent walks in the whole region. **Waikoko Country Walks,** 457 Pehiri Rd., Gisborne (© 06/863-7069; fax 06/863-7006), will take you on a 2-day walk across farmland to Eastwood Hill Arboretum, with a return on a different country route. This costs around NZ$300 to NZ$350 (US$210–US$245) per person and includes meals and accommodations. Superserious trampers who want to investigate the wilderness areas of the remote **Te Urewera National Park** should contact the Department of Conservation, Aniwaniwa Visitor Centre, Private Bag, Wairoa (© 06/837-3803). Apart from the famous multiday Lake Waikaremoana Great Walk, there are at least 15 short and day walks in this area.

WHERE TO STAY

In addition to the listings below, you may want to check out the bright and colorful **Gisborne YHA Hostel,** 32 Harris St. (📞 **06/867-3269;** yha.gis@clear.net.nz), which is close to town and offers dorm beds for around NZ$20 to NZ$25 (US$14–US$18).

All rates here and below include 12.5% GST and parking.

Cedar House 🎯🎯 *Value*   You'll be glad you discovered this two-story Edwardian gem when you set foot in the enormous, well-appointed guest rooms with either en-suite or private bathroom facilities. Built in 1909 for a prominent local family, the house has undergone extensive renovation, and Derek and Carole Green love to share the stunning result. New Zealand native timbers are polished afresh, and there's a big upstairs guest lounge with a TV/VCR, and two verandas where you can while away the hours. After you've explored the town, which is just a short walk away, you can sink back into quality bed linens or soak in a big bathtub—you have to do something to earn that big breakfast!

4 Clifford St., Gisborne. 📞 **06/868-1902.** Fax 06/867-1932. www.cedarhouse.co.nz. 4 units. From NZ$210 (US$149). Long-stay rates and special deals available. Rates include breakfast. Dinner on request from NZ$65 (US$46) per person. AE, MC, V. **Amenities:** Nearby golf course; tour bookings; laundry service; nonsmoking rooms. *In room:* Dataport, minibar, coffeemaker, hair dryer.

One Orange 🎯🎯   The quirkily named One Orange is a complete contrast to Cedar House (above): It's a contemporary designer pad near the beach. Owners Robbie Greenslade and Michael Parkin (he's an architect) have created a gem where you'll be able to wallow in modern comforts. The self-contained studio apartment has a sunny deck with rural and beach views and all the privacy you might want. The queen-size bed comes with the best linen finishes, and big towels are on hand if you decide to visit the beach across the road. Robbie is one of only two women in the country registered with the New Zealand Professional Fishing Guides Association. She's also a great cook; wine-matched dinners are a specialty. An additional king-size room with en suite can be booked in conjunction with the apartment.

98 Wairere Rd., Wainui Beach. 📞 **06/868-8062.** Fax 06/863-1263. www.oneorange.co.nz. 1 apt (additional room by arrangement). From NZ$200 (US$140). Rates include breakfast provisions. Minimum 2-night stay. MC, V. **Amenities:** Tour bookings; car rentals; laundry service; nonsmoking rooms. *In room:* TV, dataport, kitchen, minibar, fridge, coffeemaker, hair dryer, iron.

Opou—A Country House 🎯🎯🎯 *Moments*   This unexpected treasure—a historic 120-year-old mansion set in 12 hectares (30 acres) of gardens and filled with European and Asian antiques—will have you sighing with pleasure within the first 5 minutes. Hosts Robin Bickford and Manav Garewal spent 27 years in the diplomatic service before turning their talents to fine cuisine and welcoming guests. The large rooms all open onto big verandas. Two rooms have en suites, two have adjacent private bathrooms; all are beautifully finished.

95 Whakato Rd., Manutuke, Gisborne. 📞 **06/862-8732.** Fax 06/862-8042. www.opoucountryhouse.co.nz. 4 units. NZ$675 (US$472). Dinner by arrangement. AE, MC, V. Off-peak rates available. Near the small village of Manutuke, 10km (6¼ miles) from Gisborne. **Amenities:** Outdoor pool; several nearby golf courses; bike rentals; tour bookings; car rentals; courtesy airport transfers; babysitting; laundry service; dry cleaning; nonsmoking rooms; on-call doctor/dentist. *In room:* TV, dataport, hair dryer.

Portside Hotel 🎯🎯 *Value*   Opened in December 2004, the Portside brings a new level of smart and much-needed apartment-style accommodations to Gisborne. Studio rooms are a little on the small side, but if you opt for the one-bedroom suite, you'll be more than happy. They have bigger kitchens, laundry facilities, and a big corner bath and shower. Two-bedroom suites sleep four, and connecting rooms mean flexibility. Prices are unbelievably good.

2 Reads Quay, Gisborne. ℂ 06/869-1000. Fax 06/869-1020. www.portsidegisborne.co.nz. 62 units. NZ$125–NZ$135 (US$87–US$94) studio; NZ$145–NZ$155 (US$101–US$108) 1-bedroom suite; NZ$230–NZ$250 (US$161–US$175) 2-bedroom suite. AE, DC, MC, V. Long-stay rates and special B&B packages available. **Amenities:** Outdoor lit pool; nearby golf course; small gym; car rentals; laundry service; same-day dry cleaning; nonsmoking rooms; on-call doctor/dentist; airport transfers; access for travelers w/disabilities. *In room:* A/C, TV/DVD, dataport, kitchen or kitchenette, minibar, fridge, coffeemaker, hair dryer, iron.

WHERE TO DINE

In the postmillennium vacuum, Gisborne eateries seem to have declined rather than improved. Service is often near appalling, the meals disappointing. All that saves some places is their location. But don't despair—there are one or two gems. In addition to those below, try your luck at the **Poverty Bay Club,** Childers Road and Customhouse Quay (ℂ **06/868-9179**), open Tuesday through Saturday from noon until late. Main courses here are about NZ$30 (US$21)—big-city prices that lack a little big-city quality. **Café Villaggio** ⚜, 57 Balance St. (ℂ **06/868-1611**), tucked into an Art Deco house in a suburban shopping center, has especially good pizzas. It's open Tuesday through Saturday from 9:30am until late, Sunday 9:30am to 3pm.

Bookshop Café ⚜⚜⚜ CAFE   This is my new Gisborne favorite. The place's own billing says it all—serious food and serious coffee. Located above Muirs Bookshop, with plenty of good books and magazines to browse, you'll find fabulous counter food, a delightful little balcony overlooking the main street, and the best coffee in Gisborne. It's the perfect place for coffee or a light lunch.

62 Gladstone Rd. ℂ 06/869-0653. Main courses NZ$10–NZ$15 (US$7–US$11). AE, MC, V. Mon–Fri 8:30am–4pm; Sat–Sun 9:30am–3pm.

Ruba ⚜⚜ CAFE   In the grand old Union Steamship Company building, this hidden-away treat is worth seeking out. It serves terrific breakfasts, excellent coffee, and a lunch menu that's more creative than that at some of the town's bigger eateries. Take rum-and-lime-marinated chicken on a flour tortilla, for instance, or prawn and mussel chowder. A long pine table covered in magazines sets the casual mood. You won't regret a visit.

14 Childers Rd. ℂ 06/868-6516. Main courses NZ$12–NZ$18 (US$8.40–US$13). AE, MC, V. Mon–Sat 7am–4pm; Sun 9am–3pm.

Verve Café ⚜ CAFE/INTERNATIONAL   Not only is this one of those refreshingly scruffy local haunts that abounds in personality, but it's also a two-time winner of the Regional Best Café award. It comes minus pretensions, and you'll find an incredibly mixed crowd enjoying the excellent coffee and simple food. It's especially popular with backpackers and surfers, but all ages congregate here. The menu includes everything from antipasto platters and nachos to pastas, curries, salads, and preparations of fish, lamb, beef, and chicken. This is Gisborne at its laid-back best. You won't leave hungry, and you will have tasted the local culture.

121 Gladstone Rd., Gisborne. ℂ 06/868-9095. Reservations recommended for dinner. Main courses NZ$12–NZ$26 (US$8.40–US$18). AE, MC, V. Mon–Sat 8:30am–10pm; Sun 8:30am–3pm.

The Wharf Café, Bar & Restaurant ⚜ *Overrated* PACIFIC RIM   The location is unbeatable, but sadly, neither the food nor the service was equal to it on the night of my visit. One can only hope the duty chef was simply having a bad day and that things will have improved by the time this is in print. The menu reads well—seared scallops, roasted pork loin, snapper filet with Gruyère potatoes—but the place begs for an overhaul of staff and delivery.

60 The Esplanade, Shed No. 1, The Wharf, Gisborne. © **06/868-4876.** Reservations recommended. Main courses NZ$28–NZ$35 (US$19–US$25). AE, DC, MC, V. Daily 9am–late. Closed Dec 25–26.

EN ROUTE TO NAPIER

The 216km (134-mile) drive along State Highway 2 from Gisborne to Napier passes through a wealth of picturesque natural scenery: rugged high-country sheep stations, lush native bush, Lake Tutira, and a breathtaking view of Poverty Bay from the top of the Wharerata Hills, 37km (23 miles) outside the city. Between Poverty and Hawkes bays, **Morere Hot Springs Scenic Reserve** ⚲ (© **06/837-8856;** morere.hot.springs@xtra. co.nz) is signposted on the highway. It makes a nice stop-off point for a bush walk (there are six tracks, which take from 10 min.–2½ hr. round-trip), a picnic, or a soak in the pools (both thermal and cold). Admission to the public pools is around NZ$5 (US$3.50) for adults, NZ$3 (US$2.10) for children; private pools cost around NZ$3 (US$2.10) extra. They're open daily from 10am to 7pm.

2 Hawkes Bay ⚲⚲⚲

216km (134 miles) SW of Gisborne; 423km (262 miles) SE of Auckland; 228km (141 miles) SE of Rotorua

Napier is bursting at the seams with pride, and so it should be: It is the prettiest little city in New Zealand. It boasts an unbeatable combination of fabulous climate, elegant Art Deco architecture, as much award-winning wine as anyone could want, plus sea, surf, and pretty vineyards—and, combined with Hastings and Havelock North, the best selection of unique boutique accommodations in the country.

It hasn't always been this good. In 1931, a massive earthquake demolished the whole of Napier and nearby Hastings, killing hundreds of people. But like the phoenix, Napier rose again, this time on new ground lifted out of the harbor by the force of the earthquake. Rebuilt during the Depression, the town opted for the Art Deco and Spanish mission architecture so popular at the time. As a result, Napier (pop. 54,298) easily claims one of the world's largest collections of buildings in these styles.

Hastings (pop. 67,428) is something of a nonentity by comparison. It does have some fine Spanish mission architecture, plus Te Mata Peak, with the best views in the district, and it's closest to the famous gannet colonies. It also has excellent wineries and some great accommodations.

Havelock North (pop. 8,507) is a genteel community surrounded by wineries, farms, and fruit orchards. It boasts some of the best-regarded private schools and some of the oldest commercial wine cellars in the country.

ESSENTIALS

GETTING THERE & GETTING AROUND   By Plane   Air New Zealand (© **06/ 833-5400**) provides daily service between Napier/Hastings and Auckland, Wellington, and Christchurch, with connections to other key centers. **Origin Pacific Airways** (© **0800/302-302** in NZ; www.originpacific.co.nz), also offers scheduled flights to Napier. The airport is a 5-minute drive from Napier City and a 20-minute drive from Hastings. Shuttle service (© **06/879-9766**) into Napier costs about NZ$15 (US$11).

By Coach (Bus)   InterCity (© 09/913-6100) and **Newmans** (© 09/913-6200) provide daily bus service between Napier/Hastings and Auckland, Gisborne, Rotorua, Taupo, Tauranga, and Wellington. **Magic Travellers** (© 09/358-5600) and **Kiwi Experience** (© 09/366-9830) both include Napier/Hastings on their routes. Monday through Friday, **Coachrite Connections** (© 06/868-9969) operates regular bus service between Hawkes Bay towns.

By Car   An extensive highway system links the region to key North Island cities: Wellington on State Highway 2; Rotorua/Taupo on State Highway 5; Gisborne on State Highway 2; and Auckland via Taupo on State Highway 1 and State Highway 5. The drive from Auckland is 5 hours; from Wellington, 4 hours; from Rotorua, 2½ hours; from Gisborne, 2 hours; and from Taupo, 1½ hours. Three excellent, free touring guides cover this area: Pacific Coast Highway (www.pacificcoast.co.nz), Thermal Explorer Highway, and the Classic New Zealand Wine Trail. Pick up copies at your nearest visitor center.

By Taxi   A **Napier Taxis** (© 06/835-7777) stand is at Clive Square.

ORIENTATION   The pride of Napier is **Marine Parade,** a beautiful stretch of waterfront lined with stately Norfolk pines. **Kennedy Road,** the main thoroughfare, diagonally bisects the town. The fishing wharf suburb of **Ahuriri,** around **Bluff Hill,** is home to nice shops and restaurants. The best beach is **Westshore Beach** in Westshore Domain, part of the new-land legacy of the 1931 disaster.

Hastings lies 20 minutes south of Napier, and Havelock North is 5 minutes southeast of Hastings.

VISITOR INFORMATION   The **Napier i-Site Visitor Centre,** 100 Marine Parade, Napier (© 06/834-1911; fax 06/835-7219; www.hawkesbaynz.com), is open Monday through Friday from 8:30am to 5pm, and Saturday, Sunday, and holidays from 9am to 5pm (closed Dec 25). It has extended hours from December 26 to March 31.

The **Hastings i-Site Visitor Centre,** Russell Street North, Hastings (© 06/873-5526; fax 06/873-5529; www.hastings.co.nz), is open Monday through Friday from 8:30am to 5pm, Saturday from 9am to 4pm, and Sunday from 9am to 3pm, with extended summer hours (closed Dec 25).

For a calendar of events in the area, check www.hawkesbaynz.com. For accommodations listings, check www.napieraccommodation.com.

FAST FACTS   The chief **post office** is on Dickens Street, Napier (© 06/835-3725). For Internet access, try **Cybershed,** 177 Hastings St., Napier (© 06/834-3055), or **Cybers Internet Café,** 98 Dickens St., Napier (© 06/835-0125), open 8:30am to midnight. **The Chemist Shop Napier,** 32 Munroe St. (© 06/834-0884), is open daily 8am to 9pm.

SPECIAL EVENTS   The **Harvest Hawkes Bay Wine and Food Festival** 🎯🎯🎯 (© 06/834-1911; www.harvesthawkesbay.co.nz), during the first week of February, provides an opportunity to sample a wealth of food and wine in one location. The **Brebner Print Art Deco Weekend** 🎯🎯🎯 draws up to 18,000 people for wining, dining, dancing, jazz, vintage cars, and special walks and tours. Most participants dress in 1920s and 1930s fashions. It's on the third weekend in February. For details, contact the **Art Deco Trust** in Napier (© 06/835-0022; www.artdeconapier.com).

EXPLORING HAWKES BAY

Napier is the focus of most of Hawkes Bay's paid attractions, but you'll find the bulk of the wineries in the Hastings/Havelock North area. *Tip:* Check out the Napier on

Parade pass, which includes reduced admission and a return free visit to one of the attractions along Marine Parade. It costs NZ$34 (US$24) for adults, NZ$19 (US$13) children, and NZ$99 (US$69) for a family, and includes Marineland, the National Aquarium, Par 2 Golf, and Ocean Spa Napier. In the summer, ask about the Mega-pass at the visitor center.

IN NAPIER

THREE MARINE ATTRACTIONS The **National Aquarium of New Zealand** ✸✸✸ , Marine Parade (© **06/834-1404;** www.nationalaquarium.co.nz), opened in March 2002. This NZ$8.3-million (US$5.8-million) project replaced the old Aquarium on Marine Parade, south of Marineland, and built on it to include a huge ocean tank with an acrylic tunnel, plus new themed exhibits. Napier opened the first public aquarium in New Zealand in 1956, and it now holds the most comprehensive collection. Response to the attraction exceeded all expectations, and its themed sleepovers for children and the interactive displays are a big hit. It's as close to the ocean as you can get without getting your feet wet.

The aquarium's magnificent architecture imitates the form of a stingray. Exhibits include tuatara, kiwi, piranha, crocodile, and every sea creature you could imagine. Kids have lots of hands-on activities, and feeding times (the reef tank at 10am, the ocean tank at 2pm) are always exciting. Allow 1 to 2 hours for a good visit. Admission costs NZ$25 (US$18) for adults, NZ$15 (US$11) for seniors, NZ$12 (US$8.40) for children under 14, and NZ$45 (US$32) per family. Diving in the oceanarium costs NZ$50 (US$35), plus NZ$5 (US$3.50) for the tank and NZ$25 (US$18) for hire dive gear. The Behind the Scenes Tour runs twice daily and costs NZ$25 (US$18) for adults, NZ$12 (US$8.40) for children, including admission. The aquarium is open daily 9am until 7pm in summer and until 5pm in winter.

Just down the road is the ever-popular **Marineland of New Zealand** ✸✸ , Marine Parade (© **06/834-4027;** www.marineland.co.nz), where two female common dolphins are the star performers. You get free admission if you bring fish for the dolphins; otherwise, it's NZ$11 (US$7.70) for adults, NZ$5.50 (US$3.85) for children. You can also swim with the dolphins. This is a rich, worthwhile experience, but be aware that the dolphins' mood will determine whether you'll be able to touch them. There are five swimming sessions per day (limited to two people at a time). Marineland also has performing seals, sea lions, a penguin recovery workshop, and several species of marine birds. Ask about the Touch and Feed Dolphins Tour (NZ$16/US$11 adults, NZ$8.50/US$5.90 children), the Penguin Recovery Workshop (NZ$16/US$11), Swim with Dolphins (NZ$55/US$38), Marine Animal Encounter (NZ$16/US$11 adults, NZ$8.50/US$5.90 children), and Photos with Penguins (NZ$8/US$5.60 each). The center is open daily from 10am to 4:30pm (closed Dec 25). The ticket price includes admission to Lilliput Model Railway, a miniature railway attraction inside the Marineland buildings.

The Seahorse Farm ✸✸ , Main Road, Awatoto, Napier (© **06/834-0998;** www.theseahorsefarm.co.nz), offers commercial seahorse farm tours and insight into over 75,000 of the mysterious little sea creatures for around NZ$10 (US$7) for adults, NZ$5 (US$3.50) for children, and NZ$25 (US$18) per family. Tours are at 10am, 1pm, and 3pm.

THE MUSEUMS Chief among museum attractions is **Hawkes Bay Museum** ✸✸ , 65 Marine Parade (© **06/835-7781;** www.hawkesbaymuseum.co.nz). Check out the splendid semipermanent, award-winning exhibition *Nga Tukemata—The Awakening,*

Finds   **Classy Crafts**

Statements Gallery ☆☆☆ , Tennyson and Hastings streets, Napier (© **06/834-1331;** www.statementsgallery.co.nz), is one of my favorite places for finding that extra-special piece of colorful New Zealand art glass, beautiful hand-crafted New Zealand jewelry, and ceramics you'll want to take home. It also stocks paintings, prints, and sculptures.

which presents the art of local Ngati Kahungunu people. A dinosaur exhibit features fossil discoveries from northern Hawkes Bay, and an audiovisual presentation tells the story of the 1931 earthquake. Admission is around NZ$8 (US$5.60); hours are daily from 9am to 6pm October through May, daily from 10am to 5pm June to September.

For something a bit different, look into the **Juke Box Museum,** 158 Main Hwy., Clive (© **06/870-0775;** fax 06/870-0713). It's open daily from 9:30am to 5pm; adults pay NZ$5 (US$3.50) admission. The nearby **British Car Museum,** 63 East Rd., Te Awanga (© **06/875-0561** or 025/231-3916), parades more than 90 cars. It's open Saturday and Sunday from 10am to 4pm and by appointment. Admission is NZ$5 (US$3.50) for adults, NZ$2 (US$1.40) for children.

Not quite a museum, but almost, is **Trainworld,** 88 Dickens St., Napier (© **06/835-8045**). Up to 37 miniature trains operate on 800m (2,625 ft.) of track in one of the world's largest 00-gauge model railways. It's open daily from 10am to 5pm; admission is around NZ$8 (US$5.60) for adults, NZ$5 (US$3.50) for children, and NZ$18 (US$13) per family.

FUR, FRUIT, FEATHERS & WOOL   For everything you ever wanted to know about the opossum but were afraid to ask, head for **Opossum World,** 157 Marine Parade (© **06/835-7697;** www.opossumworld.co.nz). See how the opossum trapper lives, look through a working boutique tannery, and buy furry crafts and souvenirs. They may be cute, but the animals are an ecological nightmare—over 70 million of them in the wild eat 21,000 tons of foliage each night. The museum is open daily from 9am to 5pm.

Twenty-four kilometers (15 miles) south of Napier, visit **Pernel FruitWorld,** 1412 Pakowhai Rd., Hastings (© **06/878-3383;** www.pernel.nzliving.co.nz). You've tried wine tasting; now try fruit tasting in the fruit bowl of New Zealand. Pernel grows over 85 different varieties of pip and stone fruits. Leap aboard its unique apple wagon for a tour of the 32-hectare (79-acre) working orchard and fruit pack house. Visit during September or October, and you'll find the place a picturesque show of blossoms. On site are a shop, cafe, and museum. It's open daily from 9am to 4pm. Hourly tours cost around NZ$10 (US$7) for adults, NZ$5 (US$3.50) for children, and NZ$25 (US$18) per family. Or feast on freshly picked field strawberries and ice cream at **The Strawberry Patch,** Havelock Road, Havelock North (© **06/877-1350**). It's open daily from mid-October to mid-March, Monday through Saturday from 8:30am until 6pm, Sunday 9am to 5:30pm.

For an insight into the workings of an ostrich farm, take a guided tour of **Kalimna Ostrich Park,** 126 Poraiti Rd., Napier (© **06/844-9242**). You can take a farm tour and buy eggs, feathers, and carved eggs. Admission is around NZ$10 (US$7) for adults, NZ$5 (US$3.50) for children, and NZ$25 (US$18) per family.

(Fun Fact** Not Just Hamburgers**

What do you get when you mix a passion for burgers and a commitment to historic preservation with the Art Deco capital of the world? McDeco McDonald's, situated in fine Deco style on Gloucester Street, Taradale, Napier (© **06/844-2992**).

And if you still haven't learned all there is to know about sheep, visit **Classic Sheepskins,** 22 Thames St., off Pandora Road (© **06/835-9662;** www.classicsheepskins.co.nz). It offers free 25-minute tours through its tannery, daily at 11am and 2pm. The shop sells sheepskin products at factory prices and offers worldwide mailing service. The shop is open Monday through Friday from 7:30am to 5pm, Saturday and Sunday from 9am to 4pm.

AN ART DECO AMBLE   The city of Napier is virtually a museum of Art Deco and Spanish mission architecture, built from 1931 to 1933, after the earthquake. Over 70 years later, the buildings are remarkably unchanged. A map outlining a 1½- to 2-hour self-guided walk through the downtown area and another showing a more extensive scenic drive are available for about NZ$5 (US$3.50) each at the visitor center and at the **Art Deco Shop** 🌟🌟, 163 Tennyson St. (© **0508/278-332** in NZ, or 06/835-0022; www.artdeconapier.com). Open daily from 9am to 5pm (closed Dec 25), it stocks a wide range of brochures and terrific Art Deco gifts.

Guided walking tours 🌟🌟 run all year. Bookings are not necessary; just go to the Art Deco Shop and inquire about the next tour. The 1-hour **Morning Walk** leaves from the visitor center at 10am daily (except Dec 25). It includes an Art Deco booklet and ends at the Art Deco Shop, where you can watch a video. This walk is NZ$10 (US$7) for adults, free for children. The **Afternoon Walk** begins at the Art Deco Shop at 2pm, daily from October through June and on Wednesday, Saturday, and Sunday from July to September. The 2-hour program includes an introductory slide presentation, an Art Deco booklet, and a 1½-hour walk. The cost is NZ$15 (US$11) for adults. A 1-hour vintage car tour of Art Deco landmarks in a 1934 Buick costs NZ$99 (US$69), maximum three people.

IN HASTINGS

The **Hawkes Bay Exhibition Centre,** 201 Eastbourne St. E. (©/fax **06/876-2077;** hbec@inhb.co.nz), is the region's major venue for touring exhibits of paintings, sculpture, crafts, and historical material. It has a cafe and a shop specializing in local crafts. The center is open Monday through Friday from 10am to 4:30pm; Saturday, Sunday, and holidays from 11am to 4pm (closed Dec 25).

Driving to the top of **Te Mata Peak** 🌟🌟🌟, about 11km (7 miles) from Hastings, is a must-do activity. Take Havelock Road to Te Mata Peak, then to Simla Avenue to Te Mata Peak Road, and ascend the 393m (1,289-ft.) peak. On a clear day, the grand limestone ridge between beach and city offers panoramic views across the Ruahine, Kaweka, and Maungaharuru ranges, with the volcano Ruapehu visible in the distance. There are also walking tracks in the forest as you ascend.

GANNET GAZING   Australian gannets have been nesting at **Cape Kidnappers** 🌟🌟🌟 since the 1870s, with numbers steadily increasing to around 6,500 pairs. This makes it the largest and most accessible mainland gannet colony in the world. The sanctuary affords stunning views and is open to the public from October to April. The best time to

A Taste of the Wineries

This region is home to New Zealand's oldest winemaking establishments, and with over 40 wineries to choose from, you're bound to find a glass of something pleasing. Hawkes Bay's conditions are ideal for late-maturing varieties such as cabernet sauvignon and Riesling. Chardonnay, sauvignon blanc, and sweet dessert wines from this area are also prized. Most wineries are open daily, with free tours, tastings, and sales. At least 10 also feature restaurants. Make sure you pick up the free Hawkes Bay Winery Guide and map from the visitor center. New vineyards and wineries are opening all the time.

Craggy Range Winery ☆☆☆, 253 Waimarama Rd., Havelock North (© 06/873-7126; www.craggyrange.com) opened in 2003. It's the brainchild of Americans Terry and Mary Peabody and is already producing excellent chardonnay, sauvignon blanc, and merlot. **Te Mata Estate,** 349 Te Mata Rd., Havelock North (© 06/877-4399; www.temata.co.nz), has been erected in stages since 1870. It's been voted New Zealand's top winery. **Trinity Hill** ☆, 2396 Hwy. 50, Hastings (© 06/879-7778; www.trinityhill.com), is a modern winery with picnic hamper–style food available during the summer. It has a bent toward chardonnay and bordeaux-style reds. **Te Awa Farm Winery** ☆☆☆, 2375 Hwy. 50, Hastings (© 06/879-7602; www.teawafarm.co.nz), produces bordeaux-style reds and top label chardonnay and has one of the best winery restaurants, serving great lunches daily.

Vidal Estate, 913 St. Aubyn St. E., Hastings (© 06/876-8105; www.vidal.co.nz), was founded in 1905 and produces many prize-winning wines. Its popular restaurant is open for lunch and dinner daily. **Alpha Domus** ☆☆, 1829 Maraekakaho Rd., Hastings (© 06/879-6752; www.alphadomus.co.nz), is a tiny boutique operation that makes outstanding bordeaux-style reds. **Clearview Estate** ☆☆, 194 Clifton Rd., Te Awanga, RD2, Hastings (© 06/875-0150; www.clearviewestate.co.nz), has a very pretty lunch restaurant. Its blissful seaside location among grapevines and olive and avocado trees makes it a winner. **Brookfields Vineyards & Restaurant,** Brookfields Road, Meeanee, Taradale, Napier (© 06/834-4615; www.brookfieldsvineyards.co.nz), is another popular restaurant and vineyard setting closer to town. Brookfields' wines are fruit driven and age well.

Mission Estate Winery, 198 Church Rd., Taradale, Napier (© 06/845-9350; www.missionestate.co.nz), was founded by the Catholic Society of Mary in 1851. You can dine in the historic seminary building Monday through Saturday nights. **Church Road Winery** ☆, 150 Church Rd., Taradale, Napier

view the birds is from early November to late February. If you want to go it alone, drive 21km (13 miles) south to Clifton Domain; then it's a 2-hour walk along 8km (5 miles) of sandy beach. *Note:* The walk *must* be done at low tide because the high tide rides all the way up to the base of steep cliffs. Be sure to check with the Napier or Hastings visitor centers or with the **Department of Conservation,** Napier (© 06/834-3111), about tide times.

(© **06/844-2053**; www.churchroad.co.nz), is another of the older wineries. Established in the late 1890s, it contains the first wine museum in New Zealand. It also stages summer concerts; a restaurant serves daily lunches. **Sacred Hill Winery** ✿✿, 1033 Dartmoor Rd., Puketapu, Napier (© **06/844-0138**; www.sacredhill.com), occupies a divine hilltop setting and serves outdoor summer lunches on weekends from November to Easter.

A TOTAL WINE & FOOD DESTINATION   If you have a weakness for fine food and fine wines, then you must visit **Sileni Estates Winery & Epicurean Centre** ✿✿✿, Maraekakaho Road, Hastings (© **06/879-8768**; www.sileni.co.nz). You'll find a divine little gourmet-food store, a fabulous restaurant, the wine cellar, a culinary school, and more, all in a striking piece of architecture set among vineyards. The center is open daily from 10am to 5pm. The restaurant opens for lunch at 11am daily in summer.

WINE TOURS   One of the most down-to-earth and personalized tours is with **Grant Petherick Exclusive Wine Tours** ✿✿✿ , 805 Fitzroy Ave., Hastings (©/fax **06/876-7467**; www.flyfishingwinetours.co.nz). He takes two to six people at a time, and everyone raves about him. Tours for two people cost NZ$360 (US$252) for a half-day, NZ$630 (US$441) for a full day.

Grape Escape (© **0800/100-489** in NZ; www.grapeescapenz.co.nz) puts you in the capable and experienced hands of Greg Beachen. His half-day tour (1–5pm) takes in four to five wineries and costs around NZ$45 (US$32). The full-day gourmet tour includes local food producers, markets, and a picnic platter, and costs NZ$115 (US$80) per person.

If you feel like exercising, call **On Yer Bike Winery Tours** ✿✿✿ , 129 Rosser Rd., Hastings (© **06/879-8735**; www.onyerbikehb.co.nz). Its flat-terrain tours are suitable for anyone and cycle past olive groves, orchards, ostrich farms, and horse studs (in addition to six wineries), giving you a back-road view of this charming region. You have a choice of rickshaws, tandem cycles, or mountain bikes; the tour team will collect any wine you purchase along the way. Tours range from NZ$50 to NZ$85 (US$35–US$59) per person, and you should allow up to 5 hours. If you don't have time for a winery tour, head downtown to **Swig,** 19 Carlyle St., Napier (© **06/835-7999**; shop@swig.co.nz), where you'll find a palatable range of the region's finest wines in one easily accessible destination. The prices are excellent. Swig is open Monday through Saturday from 10:30am to 7:30pm.

There are two main organized tours, which basically differ in the form of transport. **Gannet Safaris Overland** (© **0800/427-232** in NZ, or 06/875-0888; www.gannetsafaris.com) offers half-day tours in an air-conditioned coach from September to April; no walking is required. The 3½-hour trip departs daily at 9:30am and 1:30pm and costs about NZ$60 (US$42) for adults, NZ$35 (US$25) for children. **Gannet Beach Adventures** (© **0800/426-638** in NZ, or 06/875-0898; www.gannets.com) transports you by tractor and trailer for around NZ$30 (US$21) per adult, NZ$20

Tips **Kidnappers Escape**

Stop by the visitor center to pick up the excellent free brochure and map *Kidnappers Escape* 𝒦𝒦𝒦, which details all artists, craftspeople, accommodations, and tours in this especially picturesque area. The trail starts at Clive, which is a 5-minute drive from Napier, Hastings, or Havelock North, and covers the 12km (7½-mile) coastal stretch out to Clifton. A great day out. For more information, check www.kidnappersescape.com.

(US$14) per child. It includes 20 to 30 minutes of walking and lasts 4 hours. Tours operate from October through early May.

IN HAVELOCK NORTH

At **Arataki Honeyland,** 66 Arataki Rd. (© **0800/272-825** in NZ, or 06/877-7300; www.aratakihoneyhb.co.nz), you can see into the world of the honeybee through glass walls. It's one of the largest beekeeping enterprises in the country. Visitors can take a tour of the honey factory (daily at 1:30pm), taste the honey, and browse in the gift shop. It's open Monday through Saturday from 8:30am to 5pm, Sunday and public holidays 9am to 4pm, and costs NZ$10 (US$7) per person; call ahead to arrange a tour.

OUTDOOR PURSUITS

BALLOONING   Waft skyward from Hastings with **Early Morning Balloons** (©/fax **06/879-4229;** www.early-am-balloons.co.nz). Flight time is around 1 hour, but allow 4 hours total. The cost of about NZ$275 (US$192) per person includes breakfast.

CANOEING   Sail 'n Surf, Pandora Road and Humber Street, Ahuriri, Napier (©/fax **06/835-0684**), rents canoes and windsurfers for use in a safe tidal waterway. A single canoe costs about NZ$20 (US$14) for 1 hour.

FISHING   Grant Petherick Fly Fishing, 805 Fitzroy Ave., Hastings (©/fax **06/876-7467;** www.flyfishingwinetours.co.nz), caters to anglers of all abilities and offers full- and half-day trips for nymph and dry fly-fishing. Saltwater fishermen should contact **Out of the Blue Boat Charters** (© **06/875-0188;** outofthebluecharters@clear.net.nz), which charges around NZ$500 (US$350) for a full day's fishing.

GOLF   A new highlight is **Cape Kidnappers Golf Course** 𝒦𝒦𝒦 , 448 Clifton Rd., Te Awanga (© **06/875-1900;** www.capekidnappers.com), recently judged one of the best new courses in the world by *Travel & Leisure Golf Magazine.* The **Napier Golf Club,** Waiohiki, State Highway 50, Taradale, Napier (© **06/844-7913**), is an excellent 18-hole course just minutes from the city. Greens fees are around NZ$35 (US$25) for affiliated members, NZ$55 (US$38) for nonaffiliated players.

HORSE TREKKING   Coastal Horse Treks (© **06/836-7626;** nicola.smale@ xtra.co.nz) offers farm and beach treks for around NZ$30 (US$21) per person per hour for all levels of ability.

JET-BOATING   Travel down Hawkes Bay's Ngaruroro River with **Riverside Jet** (© **06/874-3841;** www.riversidejet.co.nz). The price for 30 minutes is around NZ$50 (US$35) for adults, NZ$40 (US$28) for children.

WHITE-WATER RAFTING **Riverland Outback Adventures,** RD2, Napier ((📞 06/834-9756; riverlnds@xtra.co.nz), has Grade I and II scenic fun runs on the upper reaches of the Mohaka River right through to Grade IV and V white-water action. Participants must be at least 13 years old.

WHERE TO STAY

Stylish accommodations abound in Hawkes Bay, as a stop at the visitor center will quickly confirm. The endless choices include dozens of gorgeous little self-contained cottages, many of them in association with vineyards. Rates listed below include 12.5% GST and parking.

IN NAPIER

Summer visitors may well fancy camping in this balmy climate. If that's the case, head straight for **Kennedy Park Top 10 Park** 🏕, Storkey Street, off Kennedy Road (📞 **0800/457-275** in NZ, or 06/843-9126; www.kennedypark.co.nz), which has a grand history

---

Kids **Especially for Kids**

Treat yourself to a moment's rest by letting the kids loose at **Splash Planet** 🏕🏕, Grove Road, Hastings (📞 06/876-9856; www.splashplanet.co.nz). The park has everything from go-carts, bumper boats, a pirate ship, and a train to castles, a continuous river-raft ride, an activity pool, a safe toddlers' pool, miniature golf, and more. It's open daily October to April from 10am to 6pm (closed May–Sept). Admission is around NZ$25 (US$18) for adults, NZ$20 (US$14) for children under 16, NZ$90 (US$63) per family.

In Napier, you'll find lots of fun at **Onekawa Aquatic Centre,** Maadi Road, Onekawa (📞 06/834-4150; www.onekawaaquatic.co.nz). As well as swimming, you can play volleyball, miniature golf, touch rugby, and basketball. It's open daily from 6am to 9pm. For more watery fun, visit **Ocean Spa Napier** 🏕🏕🏕, 42 Marine Parade, Napier (📞 06/835-8553; napier@h2o management.co.nz), which features toddler pools, lap pools, sauna and massage facilities, beauty therapy, and a cafe. It's open Monday through Saturday from 6am to 10pm, Sunday 8am to 10pm. Admission fees start at NZ$6 (US$4.20) for adults, NZ$4 (US$2.80) for children, NZ$16 (US$11) for families. Private spas cost NZ$8 (US$5.60) for adults, NZ$6 (US$4.20) for children.

Another great place to burn off energy is **Kiwi Adventure Company** 🏕🏕🏕, 58 West Quay, Ahuriri, Napier (📞 06/834-3500; www.kiwi-adventure.co.nz). It has climbing walls for beginners to experts and also offers kayak lessons and rentals, plus custom-made adventure trips. It's open Tuesday through Friday from 3 to 9pm, Saturday and Sunday 10am to 6pm. Indoor rock climbing costs NZ$15 (US$11) for 12 and over, and NZ$12 (US$8.40) for children under 12. Kayaking costs NZ$145 (US$101). **Jungle Junction,** Bridge and Waghorne streets, Ahuriri, Napier (📞 06/833-7077), is an indoor adventureland for children up to the age of 10. It's open Tuesday through Sunday from 9:30am until 5:30pm. Admission is NZ$7 (US$4.90) for children 3 to 10, NZ$5 (US$3.50) for children under 3, free for adults.

of treating generations of New Zealanders to a fabulous stay. Set on 2.8 hectares (7 acres) with a pool and a playground, it's a great place for kids. Prices range from NZ$85 to NZ$135 (US$59–US$94). Backpackers will find good digs at **Napier YHA,** 277 Marine Parade (© **06/835-7039;** www.yha.co.nz), just across the road from major attractions and close to town. Beds range from NZ$21 to NZ$56 (US$15–US$39).

If you want to be immersed in fine New Zealand art, head for Napier's loveliest inner city spot, **The ApARTment** ☆☆☆ , Emerson Street (© **025/450-314** in NZ, or 06/834-1943; www.artapartment.co.nz). A stylish three-bedroom apartment in a restored central city historic building costs NZ$450 (US$315) for the master suite and NZ$75 (US$52) for each extra room. The new **Te Pania Hotel** ☆☆, 45 Marine Parade, Napier (© **06/833-7733;** www.scenic-circle.co.nz), is also worth checking out. Its 107 bright, airy rooms are a much more modern experience than The County Hotel (below). Rates range from NZ$220 to NZ$500 (US$154–US$350).

Cobden Villa ☆☆ *Finds*   Americans Amy and Cornel Walewski fell in love with Napier and its Art Deco heart, bought an 1870 villa, and completely restored it in Art Deco style. The gorgeous guest rooms reek of a bygone era. The biggest, Chiparus, has a big bathroom and a luxurious Jacuzzi. All open onto porches. If you're a fan of this period, don't miss it—Cornel's 1938 Buick is a bonus.

11 Cobden Rd., Napier. © 06/835-9065. Fax 06/833-6979. www.cobdenvilla.com. 3 units. NZ$395–NZ$495 (US$276–US$346). Long-stay rates available. MC, V. From the north end of Marine Parade, turn left into Coote Rd., then right into Thomson Rd. Follow up the hill and turn left into Cobden Rd. **Amenities:** Nearby golf course and tennis courts; massage; laundry service; same-day dry cleaning; nonsmoking rooms; airport transfers; access for travelers w/disabilities. *In room:* A/C, hair dryer, iron.

The County Hotel ☆☆ *Value*   This is a very English-style boutique hotel in a faithfully restored Edwardian building right in the heart of Napier. It underwent a major refurbishment in 2002, when ownership changed, and everything seems much improved. The hotel gained six new rooms, two of which can become two-bedroom suites. The bar and restaurants were made over and extended, and the library grew by more than 1,000 books. Service is attentive, and the rooms are good-size and more than comfortable. It's a terrific central location, with restaurants and many attractions within walking distance.

12 Browning St., Napier. © 0800/843-468 in NZ, or 06/835-7800. Fax 06/835-7794. www.countyhotel.co.nz. 18 units. NZ$250–NZ$320 (US$175–US$224) Queen or Spa room; from NZ$500 (US$350) suite. Rates include airport transfers. Long-stay and off-peak rates available. AE, DC, MC, V. **Amenities:** Restaurant; bar; nearby spa and sauna; bike rentals; tour bookings; car rentals; secretarial services; 24-hr. room service; babysitting; laundry service; dry cleaning; nonsmoking rooms; on-call doctor/dentist. *In room:* A/C, TV, fax, dataport, minibar, fridge, coffeemaker, hair dryer, iron.

Deco City Motor Lodge ☆ *Value*   As far as motels go, this is one of the best. You'll find spacious rooms, all with big Jacuzzis; the two-bedroom units have two TVs and two telephones each. Some rooms are air-conditioned. Built in Art Deco style, the complex is designed to pamper business and leisure travelers alike. You won't be disappointed.

308 Kennedy Rd., Onekawa, Napier. © 0800/536-6339 in NZ, or 06/843-4342. Fax 06/843-7565. www.decocity.co.nz. 31 units. NZ$115 (US$80) studio; NZ$125 (US$87) 1-bedroom; NZ$145 (US$101) 2-bedroom; NZ$160 (US$112) 3-bedroom house. Extra person NZ$15 (US$11). Long-stay and off-peak rates available. AE, DC, MC, V. **Amenities:** Outdoor pool; nearby golf course; children's playground; tour bookings; car rentals; secretarial services; babysitting; laundry service; coin-op laundry; same-day dry cleaning; nonsmoking rooms; on-call doctor/dentist. *In room:* TV, dataport, kitchen, minibar, fridge, coffeemaker, hair dryer, iron.

The Master's Lodge ⭐⭐⭐ *Finds* Once owned by tobacco baron Gerhard Husheer (the master), the gracious home has been restored to its original splendor and is now under the ownership of Larry and Joan Blume. The two large suites have million-dollar views over the city and bay, and their elegant appointments are faultless. One has a private bathroom, the other an unbelievably stylish en suite with an elevated tub. Vibrant color prevails throughout, and you'll feel very much at home.

10 Elizabeth Rd., Bluff Hill, Napier. ℂ 06/834-1946. Fax 06/834-1947. www.masterslodge.co.nz. 2 units. NZ$980 (US$685) includes breakfast; NZ$1,320 (US$923) includes breakfast, predinner drinks, hors d'oeuvres, 4-course dinner, use of all facilities, and access to Ocean Swimming complex. Special deals available. AE, MC, V. Children under 12 not accepted. **Amenities:** Bar; access to nearby pool and spa; nearby golf course and tennis courts; watersports equipment; bike rentals; concierge; car rentals; massage; laundry service, same-day dry cleaning; nonsmoking rooms; on-call doctor/dentist. *In room:* Dataport, hair dryer, iron, safe.

IN HASTINGS

For a gorgeous cottage stay, you'll be hard-pressed to beat the style and comfort of **Millar Road** ⭐⭐⭐, 83 Millar Rd., Hastings (ℂ 06/875-1977; www.millarroad. co.nz), where two cottages overlook a pool and vineyards. Each cottage sleeps four; they cost NZ$500 (US$350) per cottage, or NZ$950 (US$664) for both. There is a 2-night minimum stay. If summer camping is your thing, head for **Hastings Top 10 Holiday Park,** 610 Windsor Ave., Hastings (ℂ 06/878-6692; www.hastingsholiday park.co.nz). It is right beside the swimming complex Splash Palace, making it an ideal spot for children.

Hawthorne Country House ⭐⭐ Hawthorne Country House is a lovely Edwardian home, filled with spectacular Art Nouveau stained glass and set among 100-year-old trees. Each spacious guest room has its own en-suite bathroom and individual color scheme; all open directly onto a veranda leading to the garden. The two front rooms are my favorites. Their polished wooden floors resonate with history, and the pure cotton linens, feather duvets, bathrobes, and complimentary port or sherry add to the indulgence. The guest lounge comes complete with fresh cookies, fruit, tea- and coffeemaking facilities, a TV/VCR, and delicious sofas in front of a roaring fire.

420 St. Hwy. 2, Hastings. ℂ/fax 06/878-0035. www.hawthorne.co.nz. 5 units. NZ$235–NZ$270 (US$164–US$189). Rates include breakfast. Long-stay and off-peak rates available. MC, V. **Amenities:** Nearby golf course; tour bookings; laundry room; nonsmoking rooms; on-call doctor/dentist; access for travelers w/disabilities. *In room:* Fridge, coffeemaker, hair dryer, iron, no phone.

IN HAVELOCK NORTH

This is where you'll find the biggest concentration of fabulous cottage, B&B, and new apartment accommodations. **Black Barn Vineyards** ⭐⭐⭐, Black Barn Road (ℂ 06/ 877-7985; www.blackbarn.com) offers the best among them. They include **Summerlee** (from NZ$1,000/US$700 per night for three couples), **The Beach House** (from NZ$600/US$420 for three bedrooms), **Rush Cottage** (from NZ$290/US$203 per night), and **The Black Barn** (NZ$490/US$343 per night, sleeps four). All are seriously classy. **Brompton Apartments** ⭐⭐⭐, 39 Havelock Rd. (ℂ 06/877-0117; www.brompton.co.nz), are ideally situated right in the heart of the village. They're spacious, tasteful, and modern, with big bathrooms and private courtyards. One apartment has three bedrooms. The property has a heated outdoor pool and tennis courts. Rates range from NZ$140 to NZ$230 (US$98–US$161); a cooked breakfast costs NZ$15 (US$11).

The Woolshed Apartments $\mathcal{R}\mathcal{R}$, 106 Te Mata Rd. (© **06/877-0031;** www.woolshed apartments.co.nz), lie within a 5-minute walk of the village. Prices for the 17 fully equipped two-bedroom, serviced apartments start at NZ$185 (US$129), plus NZ$20 (US$14) for each extra adult and NZ$10 (US$7) for each extra child. For a quiet country escape, head to **Cape South Cottages** $\mathcal{R}\mathcal{R}$, 55 Waipuka Rd. (© **06/874-7736;** www. capesouthcottages.co.nz), where you'll find a cute-as-a-button two-bedroom cottage with a stylish interior. It costs NZ$280 (US$196) for two, NZ$50 (US$35) for each additional person. Guests have the use of the family's heated outdoor swimming pool.

Mangapapa Lodge $\mathcal{R}\mathcal{R}\mathcal{R}$ Falling into bed in any one of the Mangapapa suites is a must-repeat performance. This member of the Small Luxury Hotels of the World group is set among acres of orchards, and there is nothing stuffy about this luxurious retreat. In the main house, the Marcon is a wonderful room with a huge bathroom; of the cottage suites, I took a particular fancy to the Oxford. Every room has fresh flowers, fruit baskets, and the like. You'll rest easy here.

466 Napier Rd., Havelock North. © **06/878-3234.** Fax 06/878-1214. www.mangapapa.co.nz. 12 units. NZ$1,052 (US$736) dinner and B&B lodge room; NZ$690 (US$483) B&B lodge room; NZ$1,614 (US$1,129) dinner and B&B executive suite; NZ$1,252 (US$876) B&B executive suite. Rates include airport and town transfers. Off-peak rates available. AE, DC, MC, V. **Amenities:** 2 dining rooms; bar; heated outdoor pool; nearby golf course; lit grass tennis court; huge indoor Jacuzzi; sauna; use of bikes; tour bookings; car rentals; secretarial services; limited room service; babysitting; same-day dry cleaning; nonsmoking rooms; on-call doctor/dentist. *In room:* A/C, TV/VCR, dataport, minibar, fridge, coffeemaker, hair dryer, iron, safe.

WHERE TO DINE

Including the wineries (see "A Taste of the Wineries," p. 250), Hawkes Bay has a number of good restaurants and cafes. Wineries are, in the main, concentrated around the Hastings/Havelock North area, while most good restaurants and cafes are in Napier. Of the wineries, **Sileni Estate** and **Vidal Estate** both have excellent restaurants, and Craggy Range Winery's **Terroir** (see below) is not to be missed.

IN NAPIER

In addition to the establishments below, you'll eat well at **Provodore** $\mathcal{R}\mathcal{R}$, 60 West Quay, Ahuriri (© **06/834-0189**), which offers modern New Zealand cuisine with Asian and Mediterranean influences. It's open for lunch and dinner Tuesday through Friday. In the same area, **East Pier** $\mathcal{R}\mathcal{R}$, Hardinge Road, Ahuriri (© **06/834-0035**), right on the beach, serves lunch and dinner daily. It's relaxed and focuses on modern New Zealand cuisine. Another good bet is **Exchange** $\mathcal{R}\mathcal{R}$, Te Pania Hotel, Marine Parade, Napier (© **06/833-7733**), which is open daily from 6pm. For an Art Deco experience, try **Chambers** $\mathcal{R}\mathcal{R}$, at The County Hotel, 12 Browning St., Napier (© **06/ 835-7800**), which is always consistent, open from noon until late. For excellent meals at reasonable prices, try **Soak** $\mathcal{R}\mathcal{R}$, at Ocean Spa Napier, Marine Parade (© **06/835-7888**), which is open daily from 9am to 9pm. It's a super place to enjoy a long, lazy brunch from the casual cafe style menu. If seafood is your preference, try **The Mussel Boys** $\mathcal{R}$, 39 Marine Parade, Napier (© **06/835-2183**). It takes a lot to beat a plate full of New Zealand green-lipped mussels and chunks of freshly baked bread. The restaurant is open daily from late morning until late.

Ujazi $\mathcal{R}\mathcal{R}\mathcal{R}$ CAFE   Almost everyone loves Ujazi—there's just something warm and inviting about the place. It's all about shabby chic, great food, and excellent value for the money. It's considered *the* place for a hearty brunch, and with tables spilling out

Moments Foodie Heaven

A wealth of local gourmet-food producers have joined forces to create the **Hawkes Bay Wine Country Food Trail** ⭐⭐⭐. Pick up the free map at the visitor center and make your way to some of the tastiest spots in these parts. The choices are endless—handmade chocolates, breads, olives, wine, ice cream, honey, and more. All this culminates in the **HB Food Group Farmers' Market** ⭐⭐⭐, held at the Hawkes Bay Showgrounds, Kenilworth Road, Hastings (☎ **06/877-1001;** www. savourhawkesbay.co.nz), every Sunday from 8:30am to 12:30pm, and at Lower Emerson Street, Napier, every Wednesday from 3:30 to 7pm October to March.

Take home some heaven in a jar in the form of exquisite, traditional preserves from **The Squirrel's Pantry** ⭐⭐⭐, 162 Te Mata Mangateretere Rd., Hastings (☎ **06/877-4457**), in a delightful orchard setting. It's open Tuesday through Saturday from 9am to 5:30pm December through February, 9am to 5pm March through November. I can never resist the divine fruits marinated in rum, whiskey, and other spirits.

---

onto the pavement, it's a great people-watching spot. The menu includes soups, pastas, salads, focaccia melts, and a tasty range for vegetarians.

28 Tennyson St. ☎ **06/835-1490**. Lunch main courses NZ$12–NZ$26 (US$8.40–US$18). MC, V. Daily 8am–5pm (varies seasonally).

IN HASTINGS

Your best bets in this area are the winery restaurants (see "A Taste of the Wineries," p. 250). **Sileni Estates Restaurant** ⭐⭐⭐, 2016 Maraekakaho Rd. (☎ **06/879-8768**), is a shining star among them. And don't forget to explore the Epicurean Centre and Wine Discovery Centre while you're there. You'll find gourmet pizzas, bar snacks, and a diverse crowd at **The Corn Exchange,** Stortford Lodge, 118 Maraekakaho Rd. (☎ **06/870 8333**). It has a good bar feel and a local wine list; it's open daily from 10:30am until late. **Madelaine's,** Heretaunga Street (☎ **06/878-6745**), makes good coffee and lunch food—it's part of the gift shop of the same name. **Clifton Bay Café & Bar** ⭐⭐, Clifton Road, Hastings (☎ **06/875-0096**), is out of town on the way to Cape Kidnappers, but it's worth the trip. It serves terrific breakfast and lunch daily in summer from 10am to 4pm.

IN HAVELOCK NORTH

Options are limited here, but locals swear by the good-value food and lively atmosphere at the **Rose and Shamrock Village Inn,** Napier Road and Porter Drive (☎ **06/877-2999**), styled after an authentic Irish bar. The nearby **Olive Tree Café,** 7 Joll Rd. (☎ **06/877-0222**), is a simple spot that serves excellent light lunches and delicious counter food. And **Diva Bar & Bistro,** Village Court, Napier Road (☎ **06/877-5149**), is a pleasant cafe bar for a light evening meal.

To savor that real New Zealand tradition—fish and chips—head for **Dunk's Fish & Chip Shop,** 16 Joll St. (☎ **06/877-5108**). It's the best around. For picnic fare, ring **Cuccini Café Deli,** 9 Middle Rd. (☎ **06/877-8392**). For one of the best vineyard meals, head to **Black Barn Bistro** ⭐⭐⭐, Black Barn Road (☎ **06/877-7985**), a stylish bistro set among vines. There's no better place to admire the scenery and sample the fruits of the land.

Terroir ✸✸✸ FRENCH COUNTRY   Big open fireplaces, soaring ceilings, and culinary drama underpin a French-style rustic menu that will have your mouth watering in minutes. Rated one of the top 13 winery restaurants in the world in 2004 by *UK Wine Spectator,* it's guaranteed to impress. You can watch your chickens on the open-fire rotisserie, swoon over wood-fired fish, or savor traditional coq au vin, spit-roasted lamb, and classic duck dishes. It's a big culinary adventure, and the high point of Hawkes Bay dining.

Craggy Range Winery, 253 Waimarama Rd. ☎ 06/873-0143. Main courses NZ$25–NZ$35 (US$18–US$25). AE, DC, MC, V. Daily from noon; express dining 3–6pm; dinner 6pm–late.

NAPIER AFTER DARK

Night owls looking for a bit of action will do well to head for **Shed 2,** West Quay, Ahuriri (☎ **06/835-2202**), which has lots of loud music, a big-screen TV, and good food at good prices. It's popular with a young crowd. Next door, there's a more sedate atmosphere in **Caution** ✸✸, West Quay, Ahuriri (☎ **06/835-0028**), a lounge bar serving great cocktails and vintage Hawkes Bay wines. **O'Flaherty's Irish Pub,** Hastings Street, has regular live Irish music and is big on atmosphere; right next door you'll find **The Big Chill Nightclub** and **Shooters 2 Bar** (☎ **06/878-5290**), where wild times can be had by one and all. More Irish fun is at **Rosie O'Grady's Irish Bar,** Hastings Street, Napier (☎ **06/835-8689**). **Churchill's Champagne & Snug Bar,** in The County Hotel, 12 Browning St., Napier (☎ **06/835-7800**), is a small corner bar with over 100 wines and champagnes to choose from.

EN ROUTE TO NEW PLYMOUTH

Contrary to expectations you might have of simply driving east to west from Napier to New Plymouth, by far the quickest way is to drive *south* from Napier. Pass through Waipukurau and Dannevirke, on State Highway 2 connecting with State Highway 3 at Woodville and traveling on to Palmerston North. Continue on State Highway 3 to Wanganui, and then up to New Plymouth. This 412km (255-mile) trip should take about 5 hours without stops. The roads are excellent, and you'll be driving through prime farmland for most of the journey.

10

Taranaki & Wanganui

Situated between Auckland and Wellington, Taranaki is the westernmost province of the North Island. Its major city is New Plymouth, a busy port on the coast of the Tasman Sea. Taranaki is a leading dairy-farming region, an energy center with major reserves of natural gas and oil, and home to Mount Egmont, now known as Mount Taranaki. The region is also famous for its lush gardens and beautiful parks.

Southeast of Taranaki is Wanganui, one of the major towns of the area now known as the River Region, which includes the provinces of Manawatu, Horowhenua, Tararua, Whanganui, and Rangitikei. Until recently, Wanganui did not play a significant part in overseas visitors' itineraries, but its leading light—the broody Whanganui River, the longest navigable river in New Zealand—is worth exploring. A number of good outdoor activities center on the river, and the town will give you an idea of the workings of small-town New Zealand.

1 New Plymouth: Gateway to Egmont National Park

412km (255 miles) W of Napier; 164km (102 miles) NW of Wanganui; 369km (229 miles) SW of Auckland

You get the feeling that being left out on the western tip of the North Island has had benefits for New Plymouth. As if to compensate, the residents have provided themselves with excellent cultural amenities, stunning gardens, and fabulous nature walks.

Then there are the cows, the milk, the cheese, the world's biggest dairy factory at nearby Hawera, and some of the prettiest rolling green pasture you'll see anywhere in the country. Above all, literally, is Mount Taranaki, the Fuji-like jewel in the Egmont National Park crown, which attracts hundreds of trampers, mountaineers, rock climbers, and casual walkers. Be prepared to be surprised by this buzzy little city of 66,000 people.

ESSENTIALS
GETTING THERE & GETTING AROUND **By Plane** **Air New Zealand Link** and **Origin Pacific** provide daily flights from Auckland, Wellington, and Wanganui, with connecting service to other cities. Call © 06/755-2250 for flight information. The New Plymouth Airport is approximately 8km (5 miles) from the city, a 10- to 15-minute drive. **Withers Coachlines** (© 06/751-1777) provides shuttle service to and from the airport.

By Coach (Bus) **InterCity** (© 06/759-9039) and **Newmans** (© 06/759-6080) provide daily coach service. **New Plymouth City Services** (© 06/758-2799) operates local city buses.

By Shuttle **Cruise NZ Tours,** 8 Baring Terrace (© 06/758-3222; www.kirkstall.co.nz), departs New Plymouth daily at 7:30am for the North Egmont Visitor Centre at Egmont National Park, returning to the city at 4:30pm. Reservations are essential; the trip costs around NZ$40 (US$28) round-trip.

By Car   New Plymouth is reached on State Highway 3 from Wanganui via Stratford and from the north via Waitara; or on State Highway 45, the coastal highway, via Opunake.

By Taxi   Call **New Plymouth Taxis** (℗ **06/757-3000**) or **Energy City Cabs** (℗ **06/757-5580**).

ORIENTATION   Devon Street East and **Devon Street West** are the main thoroughfares. Running parallel and to the north are the one-way streets **Powderham** and **Courtenay,** and to the west, **Vivian** and **Leach streets.** The main road into the city from the south is **Eliot Street.** Once you've memorized the one-way pattern, it's very easy to find your way around. The small towns of Stratford and Hawera lie to the south of New Plymouth.

VISITOR INFORMATION   The **New Plymouth Visitor Centre,** Puke Ariki, 65 St. Aubyn St. (℗ **06/759-6060;** fax 06/759-6073; www.newplymouthnz.com), is open Monday through Friday from 9am to 6pm (Wed until 9pm), and Saturday, Sunday, and public holidays from 9am to 5pm (closed Dec 25). You can also find information on the area at www.taranaki.com.

   Information South Taranaki, 55 High St., Hawera (℗ **06/278-8599;** fax 06/278-6599; www.stdc.co.nz), is open year-round Monday through Friday from 8:30am to 5:30pm, with additional hours November through February; and Saturday and Sunday from 10am to 3pm (closed Dec 25).

SPECIAL EVENTS   During October's **Taranaki Rhododendron Festival,** more than 100 private and public gardens open their gates. The **TSB Bank Festival of Lights** ✿✿ (℗ **06/759-6060**) takes place in Pukekura Park, nightly from late December through early February, weather permitting. Call the visitor center for details of other events, or check the events calendar on the website.

EXPLORING THE TOWNS
IN NEW PLYMOUTH

For thought-provoking contemporary art, head for **Govett-Brewster Art Gallery** ✿✿✿ , Queen Street (℗ **06/758-5149;** www.govettbrewster.org.nz). Major works by world-renowned New Plymouth–born kinetic artist Len Lye, who spent most of his life in New York, are here, accompanied by an ongoing program of changing exhibitions. The gallery is open daily from 10:30am to 5pm. Entry is by donation.

   The Taranaki Museum underwent massive renovations during 2001–02 and reopened in 2003 as **Puke Ariki** ✿✿✿ , 1 Ariki St. (℗ **06/758-4544;** www.pukeariki.com). The impressive two-wing complex rises up in the heart of the city, a groundbreaking knowledge center that houses the full public library, the museum, and the visitor information center—which flow into one another. An air bridge connects the two wings. The museum showcases a major repository of Taranaki history, including many Maori treasures associated with the Taranaki tribes. "Treasures" is the name that encompasses all gallery spaces, each one focusing on different components of the Taranaki experience. Make sure you check out **Taranaki Stories,** which details the region's tumultuous Maori land wars through to pioneer history and current Taranaki residents. The complex has two cafes (see "Where To Dine," below) and a large grass park. The museum is open Monday through Friday from 9am to 6pm, and Saturday, Sunday, and holidays from 9am to 5pm. Admission is free.

   The **TSB Bank Bowls New Zealand Museum,** Dean Park, Brooklands Road (℗ **06/758-0284;** bowlsnzmuseum@xtra.co.nz), has the well-deserved distinction of being the

only lawn-bowling museum in the world—over 8,000 entries on lawn bowling's history. The museum is open by appointment only; call first.

Three beautifully restored historic buildings you can visit are **Richmond Cottage,** Ariki Street; **Te Henui Vicarage,** 290 Courtenay St.; and **The Gables Colonial Hospital,** Brooklands Park Drive. The visitor center can supply details on their hours.

If you'd like to know more about the region's energy reserves, visit the **Maui Production Station Display Centre,** Tai Road, Oaonui, South Taranaki, on the west side of the mountain on State Highway 45 (© **06/757-7171;** www.stos.co.nz). It's New Zealand's largest gas processing plant and offers a host of information and interactive displays. The center is open daily, and admission is free. The **Methanex New Zealand Motunui Plant,** Main Highway, Motunui (© **06/754-9700**), is the world's first synthetic fuel plant. Its information center has models and a video display and is open daily 8am to 8pm.

Outdoorsy types might like to cruise the **Sugar Loaf Islands Marine Park,** off the coast of New Plymouth. **Chaddy's Charters** (© **06/758-9133;** fax 06/759-9095) will accommodate you on an English lifeboat. The 1-hour cruise takes you to the cluster of small islands, which are home to an astoundingly rich plant, bird, and wildlife population. The trip costs around NZ$30 (US$21) for adults, NZ$15 (US$11) for children.

And if you want to explore a quaint slice of rural life, pick up a map from the visitor center and drive around the little knob of coast, formally State Highway 45, otherwise known as **Surf Highway.** As well as the premier surf spots, you'll find many small towns, access to Egmont National Park walking tracks, and more. The area has suddenly taken off, and a number of excellent new attractions have sprung up. You'll find superb New Zealand–made jewelry at **Ringcraft Moana,** 109 Surrey Hill Rd., Oakura (© **06/752-7772;** www.nzpearl.co.nz), open Monday through Friday 9am to 4pm. **Emacadamia,** The Nutcracker Suite, 219 Surrey Hill Rd., Oakura (© **06/752-7793;** www.emacadamia.co.nz), is a macadamia-nut orchard offering factory tours and a delicious range of macadamia goodies. It's open Sunday from 1:30 to 4:30pm. **The Egmont Soap Factory,** 33 Tasman St., Opunake (© **06/761-8707**), produces environmentally friendly products, including vegetable oil and natural herbal soaps. There are also a good number of potteries around the coast. You'll find them all detailed on the Surf Highway 45 map available from the information center.

IN HAWERA

In Hawera, a 50-minute drive south of New Plymouth, you'll find what is widely acclaimed as the best private museum in New Zealand. The **Tawhiti Museum** ✦✦✦ , 401 Ohangai Rd. (©/fax **06/278-6837;** www.tawhitimuseum.co.nz), is the brainchild of Nigel and Teresa Ogle. It uses life-size exhibits and scale models—all made by Nigel—to capture the history of South Taranaki. The Tawhiti Bush Railway operates, weather permitting, on the first Sunday of each month. The museum, once a cheese factory, is open December 26 through January daily from 10am to 4pm; February through May Friday through Monday from 10am to 4pm; and June through August Sunday only. Admission is NZ$8 (US$5.60) for adults, NZ$2 (US$1.40) for children 5 to 15, and free for children under 5. The railway costs NZ$3 (US$2.10) for adults, NZ$1 (US70¢) children.

And while we're talking about offbeat provincial attractions, don't overlook **Dairyland Café Display Centre** ✦✦, on the corner of State Highway 3 and Whareroa Road, 2km (1¼ miles) south of Hawera (© **06/278-4537;** www.fonterra.com). This is the largest, most efficient dairy-manufacturing site in the world. You can enjoy a simulated milk-tanker ride and view excellent audiovisual displays on the New Zealand dairy industry. There are also state-of-the-art farm tours (by arrangement), and you can take tea and dairy delicacies in Taranaki's only revolving cafe. The center is open daily from 9am to 5pm. Admission to the display area costs NZ$3 (US$2.10) adults, NZ$2 (US$1.40) children and seniors, NZ$8 (US$5.60) families.

If you're an Elvis fan, make an appointment to check out the **Elvis Presley Memorial Room,** 51 Argyle St., Hawera (© **06/278-7624**), and view the collection of records and souvenirs.

VISITING GARDENS GALORE

The *Taranaki Visitor's Guide,* available free from any of the region's visitor centers, lists 25 public and private gardens that are open to the public. That's just the beginning. **Pukekura Park & Brooklands** ☆☆☆ , accessible from Fillis Street, Brooklands Road, or Victoria Road, is a double hit of exquisite parkland that includes walkways, the Brooklands Zoo (open daily 9am–5pm), playgrounds, a beautiful fernery (open daily 8am–4pm), lakes, fountains, waterfalls, and specialist gardens. It's a free must-visit spot in any season. Between Christmas and February, try to visit the park at night to see the stunning **TSB Bank Festival of Lights** ☆☆.

The **Pukeiti Rhododendron Trust** ☆☆, 2290 Carrington Rd., RD4, New Plymouth (© **06/752-4141;** www.pukeiti.org.nz), has a world-class collection of rhododendron, azalea, and viraya set in centuries-old rainforest. It's a 30-minute drive from New Plymouth on Carrington Road and is open daily from 9am to 5pm September through March (closed Dec 25); and daily from 10am to 3pm April through August. There are a cafe, shop, and display center. Admission is NZ$10 (US$7) adults, NZ$9 (US$6.30) seniors, free for children under 16.

Two more must-see gardens offer free admission. **Tupare,** 487 Mangorei Rd., New Plymouth (© **06/765-7127**), is open daily from 9am to 5pm. **Hollard Gardens,** Upper Manaia Road, Kaponga, South Taranaki (© **06/765-7127**), is open daily from 9am to 5pm. Kaponga, a small rural village, is approximately 1 hour from New Plymouth. From New Plymouth, head south on State Highway 3 to Stratford and take the right-hand turn toward Dawson Falls. Take a left just past the village of Mahoe to get to Kaponga. The main season is September through March.

EXPLORING EGMONT NATIONAL PARK

The 33,534-hectare (82,829-acre) area surrounding Mount Taranaki/Mount Egmont was established as Egmont National Park in 1900. Centered on the volcanic cone of Mount Taranaki, with more than 140km (87 miles) of walks and tracks, the area is made up of subalpine forest, volcanic landforms, mountain streams and waterfalls, rainforest, and alpine herb fields. There are panoramic views of Taranaki province from the summit of the mountain, which is just 30km (19 miles) from New Plymouth.

The North Egmont entrance to the park is a 25-minute drive from New Plymouth; for shuttle transport, see "Essentials," above. The **North Egmont Visitor Centre,** Egmont Road, Egmont Village (© **06/756-0990**), displays geologic and botanic exhibits related to the park. It's open daily in summer from 8am to 4:30pm, and late March to late September Wednesday through Sunday from 9am to 4pm. *Note:* Mountain weather can be harsh and changeable; care is needed above the tree line at all times. Always check conditions with the Department of Conservation, Stratford (© **06/765-5144**), before a climb or hike.

> ### (Finds) Dawson Falls
>
> Dawson Falls, off Manaia Road, Kaponga, is well worth a visit. The 17m (54-ft.) falls are just 20 minutes from the parking lot, along a safe and attractive path in the bush. The **Dawson Falls Visitor Centre** (© 025/430-248) has a public exhibit with information on the history of the mountain and its flora and fauna. The visitor center is open in summer (mid-Nov to early Feb) daily from 8:30am to 4:30pm; winter, Wednesday through Sunday from 8:30am to 4:30pm. You'll also find a lodge, a waterfall lookout, many walking trails, and picnic areas. The falls are a 1-hour drive from New Plymouth. Head south on State Highway 3 to Stratford and take the signposted right-hand turn to the falls.
>
> If you want to stay on Mount Taranaki, **Dawson Falls Mountain Lodge,** Upper Manaia Road, Egmont National Park (©/fax **06/765-5457**; www.dawson-falls.co.nz), 45 minutes south of New Plymouth and 20 minutes west of Stratford, has 11 Swiss chalet–style rooms, a sauna and a plunge pool, a restaurant, and a very appealing honeymoon room.

Major attractions in the park include walking tracks, rock-climbing areas, delightful picnic spots, and waterfalls. The **Maunganui Ski Fields** (© **06/756-5493**) are on the Stratford side of the park in the area known as East Egmont. Follow the signs off Pembroke Road in Stratford. The ski area has T-bar and rope tows, a canteen, ski patrol, and instructors. For conditions, call **Snowphone** (© **06/767-7669**) or **Metphone** (© **0900/999-06; NZ99¢/US70¢** per minute).

MacAlpine Guides (© **0800/866-484** in NZ, or 027/441-7042, or 06/751-3542 after hours; www.macalpineguides.com) can provide advice on rock climbing, mountaineering, summit climbs, tramping, rafting, abseiling, bridge swinging, and kayaking.

OUTDOOR PURSUITS

BIKING   Cycletours Taranaki (© **06/756-7727**; fax 06/756-7716; tours@cycletaranaki.co.nz) will tailor a tour of the region's quiet back roads to suit all ages and levels of fitness. **Joe's Cycles** (© **06/754-7065**) rents mountain bikes and tandem cycles for NZ$15 to NZ$20 (US$11–US$14) for 2 hours.

DAM DROPPING   Kaitiaki Tours (© **0800/336-376** in NZ, or 021/461-110; www.damdrop.com) offers a range of adrenaline-pumping activities based around the Waingongoro River. They include fast-paced water sledging and tipping yourself over a dam on something inflatable. Three-hour excursions start at NZ$85 (US$59) adults, NZ$60 (US$42) children.

FISHING   Ultimate Fishing Adventures (© **027/224-9992** or 06/759-2345) will take you game fishing, fresh- or saltwater fly-fishing, bottom fishing, or sea fishing. In summer it also has evening fishing packages.

GOLF   Taranaki is home to 20 courses, including the **New Plymouth Golf Club Ngamotu Links,** Devon Road, Bell Block (© **06/755-1349**). The 18-hole, par-72 championship course is on magnificent parklike grounds and has a bar, pro shop, and restaurant. Greens fees are NZ$30 (US$21) for affiliated and NZ$40 (US$28) for nonaffiliated players.

KAYAKING **Taranaki Outdoor Adventures** (🕾 **0800/200-6254** in NZ; www. adventurelodgetaranaki.co.nz) is expert in sea, surf, and river kayaking. Throw in a bit of bridge-swinging, rock climbing, and abseiling, and you have the ideal one-stop shop.

SURFING **Surf School Taranaki** (🕾 **06/752-8283** or 027/450-8283; surf@black diamondsafaris.co.nz) offers 2-hour surfing sessions for beginners through advanced surfers who are at least 6 years old. The price is NZ$50 (US$35) per person with a minimum group size of three.

SWIMMING The **New Plymouth Aquatic Centre,** Kawaroa Park (🕾 **06/759-6060**), is open Monday through Friday from 6am to 8:30pm, weekends and public holidays from 8:30am to 7pm (closed Dec 25). It offers a range of heated indoor and outdoor pools, hydroslides, and a steam room. **Taranaki Mineral Pools,** 8 Bonithon Ave., New Plymouth (🕾 **06/759-1666**), were established in 1914 and now provide a host of modern massage and beauty treatments to follow a hot soak in one of the private or group pools. They are open in summer Monday 9am to 8pm; Tuesday 9am to 5pm; Wednesday through Friday 9am to 9pm; Saturday noon to 9pm; and Sunday 2pm to 8pm. Private pools cost NZ$25 (US$18) per couple.

WALKING A wide range of walks, from easy to energetic, crisscross the New Plymouth area. The visitor center produces a series of super little foldout pamphlets and maps that highlight the best walks.

WHERE TO STAY

A lot of pleasant things have happened to the Taranaki accommodations scene in the last 2 years, chief among them the addition of the smart offerings described below. **Mataro Lodge** ✦✦✦ , 676 Mataro Rd., Urenui (🕾 **06/752-3926;** www.mataro.co.nz), is a modern country retreat with three beautiful rooms 20 minutes north of New Plymouth. Prices start at NZ$400 (US$280). **Taranaki Country Lodge** ✦, 169 Hursthouse Rd., New Plymouth (🕾 **0800/395-863** in NZ, or 06/755-0274; www.taranakicountry lodge.co.nz), has two suites set amid rolling Taranaki farmland; you'll pay at least NZ$250 (US$175).

All rates here and below include the 12.5% GST and parking.

Airlie House ✦✦ (Value) This beautifully restored 110-year-old villa is tucked under big trees in the inner city, just a few minutes' walk from town and the popular mineral pools. The lovely downstairs Drawing Room is a big, sunny haven with a super-king-size bed, a window seat, and shower-only en suite. For the money, though, you can't beat the modern one-bedroom apartment upstairs, which has its own kitchen. There's a second downstairs suite with a private bathroom, and two upstairs rooms for use by one three-person party.

161 Powderham St., New Plymouth. 🕾 **06/757-8866.** www.airliehouse.co.nz. 3 units, 1 apt. NZ$135–NZ$150 (US$94–US$105). Rollaway NZ$35 (US$25). Rates include breakfast. Long-stay rates negotiable. AE, MC, V. **Amenities:** Nearby golf course and tennis courts; babysitting; laundry service; same-day dry cleaning; nonsmoking rooms; on-call doctor/dentist. *In room:* TV, dataport, coffeemaker, hair dryer.

Nice Hotel & Bistro ✦✦✦ New Plymouth's only small luxury hotel offers stylish rooms with individual charm. You'll find feather duvets, contemporary artwork, and generous bathrooms with double Jacuzzis or massage showers. The hotel is right in the heart of the city and it has its own popular restaurant downstairs. The suite is divine and has its own private lounge, fireplace, and grand piano. It's a cut above the usual hotel room.

71 Brougham St., New Plymouth. (✆ 06/758-6423. Fax 06/758-6433. www.nicehotel.co.nz. 8 units. NZ$225 (US$157) room; NZ$300 (US$210) suite. Rates include airport transfers. Long-stay rates and special deals available. AE, DC, MC, V. Head onto Leach St. and turn right onto Brougham. Children under 12 not accepted. **Amenities:** Restaurant and private dining rooms; bar; several nearby golf courses; gym across the street; use of bikes; tour bookings; courtesy car; secretarial services; massage; laundry service; same-day dry cleaning; nonsmoking rooms; on-call doctor/dentist. *In room:* TV, dataport, minibar, fridge, coffeemaker, hair dryer, iron.

The Waterfront Hotel 🐓🐓 *Value*   Location, location, location—this place has it, right beside the new museum and bustling inner city developments overlooking the ocean. Just 3 years old, The Waterfront has smart, uncluttered rooms (some connecting). Oceanview units are the most sought after. I fell in love with the three big, one-bedroom apartments, which have roomy bathrooms, Jacuzzis, leather furniture, modern kitchens, and laundry facilities—and yes, they overlook the ocean. Units on the top two floors of the three-story building have air-conditioning. Crisp design and unbeatable value make the hotel popular with corporate and international travelers.

1 Egmont St., New Plymouth. (✆ 0508/843-928 in NZ, or 06/769-5301. Fax 06/769-5302. www.waterfront.co.nz. 42 units. NZ$135–NZ$400 (US$94–US$280). MC, V. Breakfast, long-stay, and off-peak rates available. **Amenities:** Restaurant (Salt); bar; nearby golf courses and tennis courts; free membership to town gymnasiums; tour bookings; car rentals; business and secretarial services; 24-hr. room service; massage; babysitting; laundry service; same-day dry cleaning; nonsmoking rooms; currency exchange; on-call doctor/dentist; airport transfers; access for travelers w/disabilities. *In room:* TV/DVD, dataport, minibar, fridge, coffeemaker, hair dryer, iron.

WHERE TO DINE

Prepare to be surprised by the standard of cuisine in this little provincial outback. For a town of its size, it has an unbelievable number of very good eateries. The Plymouth Hotel's **Orangery Restaurant** 🐓🐓 (✆ 06/758-0589) offers fine a la carte dining every night from 6pm. **Andre L'Escargot Restaurant & Bar** 🐓🐓🐓, 37–43 Brougham St. (✆ 06/758-4812), is an elegant New Plymouth institution; it's still good dining, but it's now facing competition from a few other top choices. It's open Monday through Saturday from 11am until late.

   Nice Hotel & Bistro 🐓🐓 (✆ 06/758-6423) also gets lots of votes (see "Where to Stay," above). I found **Metropol Café Restaurant & Bar** 🐓🐓, King and Egmont streets (✆ 06/758-9788), to be very good for quick lunches and light evening meals. It's open daily from 10am until late. **Café Arborio** 🐓🐓🐓, in Puke Ariki (✆ 06/758-4544), is an Italian cafe by day and licensed restaurant by night. It gets my vote as the best in town. It's on the first floor on the North Wing of the new museum and library complex and is one of the "in" spots. It's open 9am to late, and the food is divine. In the South Wing you'll find a great spot for coffee at **Daily News Café** (✆ 06/758-4544), an espresso bar with a great stack of newspapers and magazines to read.

   Another top-quality new addition is **Pankawalla** 🐓🐓🐓, 85 Devon St. W. (✆ 06/758-4444), a classy Indian restaurant that you wouldn't normally expect to find in the provinces. It's open daily from 6pm.

   For the best coffee, head straight for **Mookai** 🐓🐓, 67 Devon St. W. (✆ 06/759-2099), open daily early to late; and **Chaos** 🐓🐓, Brougham Street (✆ 06/759-8080), which combines deli, cafe, and bakery.

   MacFarlanes Caffe, 1 Kelly St., Inglewood (✆ 06/756-6665), 20 minutes southeast of New Plymouth, is popular for brunch. It has excellent coffee and a nighttime atmosphere that is about as raging as it gets in Taranaki. It's open Sunday through Thursday from 9am to 5pm, Friday and Saturday from 9am to late.

EN ROUTE TO WANGANUI

The 2½-hour drive from New Plymouth to Wanganui goes through some of the best dairy farmland in New Zealand. Regardless of the time of year, the rolling landscape is generally green and lush. You'll pass through the rural towns of Inglewood, Stratford, Hawera, and Waverley before reaching Wanganui.

2 Wanganui (★

164km (102 miles) SE of New Plymouth; 141km (87 miles) SW of Tongariro National Park; 193km (120 miles) N of Wellington; 252km (156 miles) SW of Napier

There's tourism potential in Wanganui, and the town has finally become aware of it. In the past few years it has transformed itself from a rather grubby little river town to something much prettier. Now that the inner city has a smart face, attention is turning to the long-awaited beautification of the town's major beach suburb, Castlecliff.

The single-biggest draw in the area is the history-rich **Whanganui River.** This moody snake of a river is the second longest in the North Island and the longest navigable waterway in the country. It flows 290km (180 miles) from the upper reaches of Tongariro National Park to the Tasman Sea, where, at its mouth, you find **Wanganui township.** The river has always had a special place in Maori history. A long history of discontent between Maori and Pakeha over its use and ownership hopefully was settled with the mid-1999 Waitangi Tribunal decision to hand the river back to the Maori people.

The Whanganui River flows through **Whanganui National Park,** most of which is accessible only by boat or on foot. The population of the greater Whanganui District is 45,000, and the area is blessed with 2,084 hours of sunshine annually.

ESSENTIALS

GETTING THERE & GETTING AROUND   By Plane   Wanganui Airport, 10 minutes outside the town center, is served daily by **Air New Zealand** (© 0800/737-000 in NZ; www.airnz.co.nz).

By Coach (Bus)   InterCity (© 09/913-6100) and **Newmans** (© 09/913-6200) provide service between Wanganui and Auckland, New Plymouth, National Park Village (in Tongariro National Park), and Wellington. **White Star Passenger Services,** 161 Ingestre St. (© 06/347-6677), operates local town buses.

By Car   Wanganui is on state highways 3 and 4. It is 2½ hours from New Plymouth or Wellington, 3 hours from Taupo, and 4 hours from Rotorua.

By Taxi   Call **Wanganui Taxis** (© 06/343-5555).

VISITOR INFORMATION   The **i-Site Wanganui Visitor Centre,** 101 Guyton St., Wanganui (© 0800/926-426 in NZ, or 06/349-0508; fax 06/349-0509; www.wanganui nz.com), is open in summer Monday through Friday from 8:30am to 6pm, Saturday and Sunday from 9am to 3pm; and in winter Monday through Friday from 8:30am to 5pm, Saturday and Sunday from 10am to 3pm.

SPECIAL EVENTS   Garden lovers may like to visit during the biennial **Wanganui Blooming Artz Festival** (© 06/348-7840). The next festival is in October 2007. The biennial **Wanganui Arts Festival** (© 06/348-7840), in March (next in 2006), is a

---

Tips **Heart of Glass**

Chronicle Glass Studio & Tours, 2 Rutland St., Wanganui (© 06/347-1921), is a collective of three local glass blowers, Katie Brown, Lyndsay Patterson, and Karen Ellet. Watch them in action and browse in the contemporary mezzanine gallery, which features a wide range of collectible glass art produced by Wanganui glass artists. The studio is open Monday through Friday 9am to 5pm, weekends 10am to 4:30pm.

12-day feast of performing arts. The October **Jazz Boat Festival** (© 06/343-7742) attracts international performers to events that include riverboat cruises.

WHAT TO SEE & DO
THE MAIN ATTRACTIONS

The **Sarjeant Gallery** 🌟🌟🌟 , Queen's Park, Wanganui (© 06/349-0506), is one of the finest provincial galleries in the country. It boasts a large contemporary photographic collection and stunning architecture. Admission is free. The gallery is open Monday through Sunday from 10:30am to 4:30pm, holidays from 1 to 4:30pm.

Nearby you'll find the **Whanganui Regional Museum** 🌟🌟, Watt Street, Wanganui (© 06/345-7443; www.wanganui-museum.org.nz), which is renowned as New Zealand's finest provincial museum. It has rare collections of Maori canoes, artifacts, and moa bones. It's open daily 10am to 4:30pm. Admission is NZ$2 (US$1.40) for adults, NZ60¢ (US40¢) for children under 15, NZ$5 (US$3.50) for families.

Ohorere Gardens, 1778 Papaiti Rd., Wanganui (©/fax 06/342-5848), is a private garden on the banks of the Whanganui River, 4km (2½ miles) from the city center. You'll see camellias, rhododendrons, more than 100 varieties of old roses, and ponds. It's open September through April on Wednesday and Sunday from 10am to 4pm. The entry fee of NZ$5 (US$3.50) includes tea and coffee.

If you feel up to climbing hundreds of steps, cross the river to **Durie Hill Elevator and Tower.** Located opposite the Wanganui City Bridge at the bottom of Victoria Avenue, it begins with a pedestrian tunnel that takes you to the historic elevator, which in turn rises 66m (216 ft.) through the hill to the summit. You can then take the 191 narrow spiraling steps up the Memorial Tower for unparalleled views. Check with the visitor center for hours. For a lovely, quiet wander close to town, it takes a lot to beat **Virginia Lake** 🌟🌟, on Great North Road on St. John's Hill. The lake is bordered by pleasant bush walks, hundreds of ducks waiting to be fed, a free-flying bird aviary that you can walk through, and a coin-operated fountain that shows off with brilliant colored displays at night.

If you are interested in the arts, you'll be pleased to hear that some of New Zealand's top artists live in the area. Pick up the *Arts & Cultural Trail, Arts Guide,* and *Whanganui Artists Open Studios* brochures from the information center. They cover a wealth of painters, printmakers, sculptors, jewelers, potters, and glass artists.

A SCENIC DRIVE TO PIPIRIKI

River Road, the only road that leads into Whanganui National Park from Wanganui, is narrow and winding but very scenic. Staying on River Road for approximately 1½ hours will lead you to the tiny settlement of Pipiriki, 79km (49 miles) upstream from

Wanganui. Many marae lie along the river, and you'll pass the historic Maori mission of Jerusalem, once home to the famous New Zealand poet James K. Baxter.

EXPLORING WHANGANUI RIVER & WHANGANUI NATIONAL PARK

The Whanganui River has its origins high on Mount Tongariro. There the river is a mere alpine stream, but it gathers water from Mount Ngauruhoe and Mount Ruapehu as it descends through the Central Volcanic Plateau, toward Taumarunui, Wanganui, and finally the Tasman Sea.

There are 239 listed rapids along the Whanganui, but it is a Grade II river and therefore popular with canoeists of all levels. Many begin their river adventures at the Taumaranui end, making their way south to Wanganui. This trip can take 5 to 6 days, and the Department of Conservation maintains huts along the way for overnight stays.

In 1987, the huge, largely inaccessible, and remote bush areas surrounding the middle reaches of the Whanganui River were designated a national park, becoming the second-largest tract of native bush on the North Island. Several of the original routes for the early Maori and European inhabitants have been cleared, providing some of the most isolated wilderness tramping in New Zealand—the 3-day **Maungaparua** and **Matemateonga tracks** (see "On Foot," below) are accessible only by canoe or jet boat.

One of the most popular spots in the park is the **Bridge to Nowhere,** which was built in 1917 deep in the bush across the Mangaparua Gorge to give access to the last pioneering settlement of the New Zealand government. The isolated settlement failed in 1942, but the bridge remains. You'll need to travel upstream (see "By Jet Boat," below) and then walk 40 minutes, along some steep sections and narrow tracks, to reach the bridge.

If you'd like to spend the day picnicking, head to **Hipango Park Reserve,** 26km (16 miles) upriver from Wanganui. The 2-acre native bush reserve with recently upgraded barbecue pits and toilets is a popular destination for boat tours (see "By Riverboat," below). For details of **Journeys on the Whanganui,** a collection of river packages, visit www.whanganuiriver.co.nz.

There are a number of exciting ways to experience the Whanganui River and Whanganui National Park. Here are a few examples:

BY AERIAL CABLEWAY The **Flying Fox** ⑂⑂, Wanganui (©/fax **06/342-8160;** www.theflyingfox.co.nz), is a unique river experience. A little patch of civilization in the middle of nowhere is accessible by an aerial cableway, or "flying fox." Once you've negotiated this awesome swing across the river, you can enjoy charming cottage accommodations or bush campsites (see "Where to Stay," below). The Flying Fox is in the national park, 45 minutes from Wanganui. To reach it, take a jet-boat tour or drive up River Road and cross the river on the aerial cableway. Several tours stop here (see "By Bus," below).

Tips **A Traditional Marae Visit**

If you would like to meet local Maori at the **Koriniti Marae,** Whanganui River Road, Wanganui (© **06/342-8198;** fax 06/348-0398; www.koriniti.com), call first to make sure you do not interrupt private events like *tangi* (funerals). Visitors are welcome to take photographs at the marae and to look through the Whare Toanga (museum). There is no charge, but a *koha* (donation) is welcome.

BY BUS   If a 14-seat air-conditioned bus is your style, you can join the popular **Whanganui National Park Rural Mail Tour** ☆☆. Call **Take It Easy Tours** (✆ 06/ 344-7465; fax 06/344-7462). The tour runs from 7:30am to 2:30pm and covers 190km (118 miles), delivering mail to remote farms, schools, and marae. You can stay overnight at the Flying Fox or at Jerusalem Backpackers, where the Catholic nuns put you up for the night. The day trip costs around NZ$35 (US$25).

BY CANOE   If you want to find out about the historic Maori myths and legends of the river, go with Niko Tangaroa of **WakaTours** ☆☆, 17a Balance St., Raetihi (✆/fax 06/385-4811; www.wakatours.co.nz). His 3-day guided canoe tour takes you to historic sites with overnight stays at riverside marae. It's a rare experience that costs NZ$560 (US$392) for adults, NZ$460 (US$322) for students 12 to 17 years old, including all meals. A minimum of four people is required per tour, and 4- to 5-day packages are available. Another option is **Wades Landing Outdoors,** RD2, Owhango (✆/fax 07/895-5995), which charges NZ$95 (US$66) and up per person for a 1-day excursion. Note that Wades Landing is in Taumaranui, where many canoeists launch for a trip on the river.

BY JET BOAT   **Bridge to Nowhere Jet Boat Tours,** Pipiriki, RD6, Wanganui (✆ 0800/480-308 in NZ, or 025/480-308; fax 06/348-7133; www.bridgetonowhere tours.co.nz), operates in the most beautiful part of the river. Its most popular 4-hour tour to the Bridge to Nowhere costs around NZ$90 (US$63) and is suitable for all ages. The jet boat/canoe option allows you to enjoy a leisurely paddle downstream for NZ$80 to NZ$135 (US$56–US$94) per person. **Pipiriki Jet Boat Tours,** 2513 RD6, Pipiriki (✆ 0800/862-743 in NZ; or 06/385-3246; www.pipirikitours.co.nz), also runs Bridge to Nowhere jet-boat rides for NZ$90 (US$63) per person. Its 45-minute ride through deep, moss-covered ravines to the home of the endangered native blue duck costs NZ$40 (US$28) per person.

BY RIVERBOAT   The Waimarie Paddle Steamer was built in 1890, sank in 1952, and was salvaged in 1993. Since then, it has been painstakingly rebuilt at the **Whanganui Riverboat Centre & Museum,** 1A Taupo Quay (✆/fax 06/347-1863; www.wanganui. org.nz/riverboats). Daily cruises travel 13km (8 miles) up the Whanganui River to Upokongaro, then return to the city. The center is open Monday through Friday from 9am to 4pm, Saturday and Sunday 10am to 4pm. The cost is NZ$30 (US$21) for adults, NZ$12 (US$8.40) for children 5 to 15, NZ$75 (US$52) per family.

ON FOOT   Contact the **Department of Conservation,** Whanganui Area Office, 74 Ingestre St., Wanganui (✆ 06/345-2402; www.doc.govt.nz), for information on a range of walks. In brief, the **Skyline Walk** requires 6 to 8 hours and affords views of Mount Ruapehu and Mount Taranaki. The **Matemateaonga Track** takes 3 to 4 days; the 3-day **Mangapurua Valley Walk** includes the famous **Bridge to Nowhere. Whanganui River Jet,** Wades Landing Outdoors, RD2, Owhango (✆/fax 07/895-5995 or 025/797-238), offers a complete charter service for trampers wanting to use either of these tracks. It will drop you off and pick you up at prearranged times on the riverbanks. Cost is around NZ$125 (US$87) per person.

OUTDOOR PURSUITS

BEACHES   **Castlecliff Beach,** 9km (5½ miles) from the city center, is a typical West Coast beach with black-iron sand and lots of driftwood. It's good for swimming and surfing. Wild **South Beach,** obviously to the south of the city, is great for long beach-combing walks, while **Mowhanau** is a pretty swimming beach surrounded by *papa* cliffs (a cross between a mudstone and sandstone formation, which is soft and slippery). It has a playground and good picnicking areas. Head north on the highway to New Plymouth and turn left onto Rapanui Road; continue another 9km (5½ miles).

BIKING   City Cycle Tours (© **06/343-7130**) offers cycle packages that include bikes and helmets.

FLIGHTSEEING   Get yourself into the bright-yellow **Wanganui Aero Work Tiger Moth** (© **06/345-3994**) for a 20-minute flight over the city, river, and Tasman Sea.

GOLF   The **Wanganui Golf Club,** Belmont Links, Clarkson Avenue, Wanganui (© **06/344-4481**), is an 18-hole championship course.

MOUNTAIN BIKING   Lismore Forest, just minutes from central Wanganui, has some of the best mountain-bike tracks in the region. You can rent bikes from **Wanganui Pro-Cycle Centre,** 199 Victoria Ave., Wanganui (© **06/345-3715;** fax 06/345-3331). Rentals are around NZ$45 (US$32) per day.

WHERE TO STAY

Accommodations are not Wanganui's strong point. There are no major hotels, probably no more than 30 motel complexes, around 30 homestays or farmstays, nothing truly upmarket, and fewer than half a dozen backpacker establishments.

If remote is what you're after, try **The Flying Fox** ⚔, P.O. Box 333, Wanganui (©/fax **06/342-8160;** www.theflyingfox.co.nz), where two cottages go for NZ$110 to around NZ$120 (US$77–US$84), and one gypsy cart is NZ$70 (US$49). Everything sits under old walnut trees, and hosts Annette and John make natural beers and organic meals. *Remember:* You'll have to cross the river on a flying fox (see "By Aerial Cableway" under "Exploring Whanganui River & Whanganui National Park," above), and it's 45 minutes upriver from Wanganui.

Even more remote, for those who truly do want to get away from it all, is **Bridge to Nowhere Lodge,** Ramanui Landing, Whanganui River (© **0800/480-308** in NZ; fax 06/348-7122; www.bridgetonoweretours.co.nz), where Joe and Mandy offer rooms, breakfast, and dinner for NZ$250 (US$175), or self-catering for NZ$70 to NZ$90 (US$49–US$63).

Arles Bed & Breakfast, 50 Riverbank Rd., RD3, Wanganui (©/fax **06/343-6557;** www.arles.co.nz), has four units in the house (two with shared bathroom) and one self-contained two-bedroom flat for NZ$120 to NZ$140 (US$84–US$98).

All rates listed include the 12.5% GST and parking.

Arlesford House ⚔⚔⚔ (Finds)   Just 8km (5 miles) north of Wanganui, this stunning country homestead is famed for its royal visitors. Built in 1934 almost entirely of native timbers and set in a beautiful garden, it exudes warmth and character. Upstairs rooms are huge, especially the Regency, which has a gorgeous bathroom sunroom that overlooks the garden. The Victoria also has a generous en-suite bathroom; two other big rooms have good-size private bathrooms. The cottage has a kitchen. Try to stay more than 1 night, because once you get here, I guarantee you won't want to leave.

202 St. Hwy. 3, RD4, Wanganui. © **06/347-7751.** Fax 06/347-7561. www.arlesfordhouse.co.nz. 4 units in house; 3 units in cottage. NZ$197–NZ$220 (US$138–US$154). Rates include breakfast. Long-stay, off-peak, and weekend packages available. MC, V. **Amenities:** Outdoor pool; nearby golf course; tennis court; laundry service; nonsmoking rooms; access for travelers w/disabilities in cottage. *In room:* TV, dataport, coffeemaker, hair dryer, iron.

Rutland Arms Inn ⚔   This is one of the better hotel-style lodgings in Wanganui. All rooms are large and well appointed, with feather duvets and cotton sheets; four

units have Jacuzzis. The Taylor Suite is my favorite—very big and very sunny. The original 1800s building was completely renovated in 1996. The Rutland has an English-style bar on the ground floor, along with a restaurant and the Courtyard Café.

48–52 Ridgway St., Wanganui. © 0800/788-5263 in NZ, or 06/347-7677. Fax 06/347-7345. www.rutland-arms. co.nz. 8 units. NZ$115–NZ$180 (US$80–US$126). Rates include breakfast. Long-stay and off-peak rates available. AE, DC, MC, V. **Amenities:** Restaurant; bar; nearby gym; limited room service; babysitting; laundry service; same-day dry cleaning; nonsmoking rooms; on-call doctor/dentist. *In room:* TV, fax, dataport, minibar, fridge, coffeemaker, hair dryer, iron.

Siena Motor Lodge This 1997 complex is definitely worth your attention. It's right on the main street, just down from the shopping center and near a number of eateries. All rooms have premium-quality beds and CD players. My pick for value and comfort is room no. 9, a corner studio with its own Jacuzzi and private courtyard.

335 Victoria Ave., Wanganui. © 0800/888-802 in NZ, or 06/345-9009. Fax 06/345-9935. www.siena.co.nz. 10 units. NZ$125–NZ$145 (US$87–US$101). AE, DC, MC, V. **Amenities:** Nearby golf course; nearby tennis courts; self-service laundry; same-day dry cleaning; nonsmoking rooms; access for travelers w/disabilities. *In room:* A/C, TV, DVD, dataport, kitchen, minibar, fridge, coffeemaker, hair dryer, iron.

Tamara Backpackers Lodge Rory Smith believes in keeping things clean and comfortable and providing a good kitchen and a friendly atmosphere. The house, once a maternity hospital and then a private hotel, overlooks the river and is an easy walk to town. The fabulous rear garden has hammocks under giant palm trees. No dorms have more than four beds.

24 Somme Parade, Wanganui. © 06/347-6300. Fax 06/345-8488. www.tamaralodge.com. 40 beds. NZ$20 (US$14) dorm bed; NZ$34–NZ$44 (US$24–US$31) single; NZ$44–NZ$54 (US$31–US$38) double. Rates include airport transfers. MC, V. **Amenities:** Nearby golf course; use of bikes; game room; tour bookings; car rentals; coin-op laundry; nonsmoking rooms; TV lounge. *In room:* No phone.

WHERE TO DINE

Indigo , Majestic Square (© **06/348-7459**), is the new cafe and bar that everyone is talking about—and with good reason. It brings a little of the city to the Wanganui dining scene, and that can't be a bad thing. Indigo has a great setting in the heart of town and very nice outdoor areas. It's open from 8am until 5pm Sunday through Tuesday and until late Wednesday through Friday.

Big Orange/Ceramic Wine Bar , 51 Victoria St. (© **06/348-4449**), operates as a cafe by day and a restaurant and bar by night. The lunch menu includes some excellent light meals, but the service is notoriously slow.

Redeye Café , 96 Guyton St. (© **06/345-5646**), has plenty of character, although it doesn't seem to appeal to a lot of the older locals, who classify it as noisy with bad service. It's certainly a student haunt that plays no-compromise music, but I wouldn't bypass it. It's open Monday through Friday from 8am until late, Saturday from 9:30am until late. **Jolt Coffee** , 19 Victoria Ave. (© **06/345-8840**), has good coffee and a bit more style. It's open Monday through Friday 7:30am to 5:30pm, Sunday 1 to 5pm (closed Sat).

More popular with the over-35s is **Legends,** 25 Somme Parade (© **06/345-7575**), overlooking the river. Although the meals are tasty and the surroundings pleasant, I prefer the grittiness of Redeye. It's open Monday through Friday 10:30am until late, weekends from 10am. **Vega** , Taupo Quay and Victoria Avenue (© **06/345-1082**), is a popular fine-dining restaurant that many consider the best in town. **Stellar,** 2 Victoria St. (© **06/345-7278**), offers good-value, tasty meals, especially pizzas and desserts, daily from 5pm until late.

EN ROUTE TO WELLINGTON

You can get to Wellington in two ways—on State Highway 1 down the coast via Levin, Waikanae, and Paraparaumu (the better road), or via Palmerston North, the Wairarapa, through Masterton, Carterton, Greytown, and Featherston. Both trips take about 2½ hours, but the Wairarapa journey begs for a few stop-offs that may well eat up some of your time. If you go this way, I strongly suggest you spend a night in the area (see "Where to Stay" in the "A Side Trip to Wairarapa" section in chapter 11). The **i-Site Palmerston North Visitor Centre,** 52 The Square, Palmerston North (© **06/350-1922;** fax 06/350-1929; www.manawatunz.co.nz), can help with accommodations and local highlights.

If you travel down the coast road, be sure to drop by the **Southward Car Museum** ᖵᖵ, near Paraparaumu, 45 minutes north of Wellington (© **04/297-1221;** www.southward.org.nz). Even if you're not auto-inclined, I think you'll find it interesting. The museum is open daily from 9am to 4:30pm. A little farther south on the Kapiti Coast, it's worth making even a brief stop at the Lindale Centre, where you'll find the fabulous **Kapiti Cheese Company** ᖵᖵᖵ (© **04/298-1352**), along with a range of New Zealand crafts stores. **The Kapiti Coast Visitor Information Centre,** Centennial Park, State Highway 1, Otaki (© **06/364-7620;** www.kapiti coast.govt.nz), can provide accommodations and adventure details for this increasingly popular holiday area. It's open Monday through Friday 8:30am to 5pm, weekends 9am to 4pm.

11

Wellington

Wellington is, without doubt, my favorite New Zealand city. I've always seen it geographically as a miniature Hong Kong—there's a beautiful curved harbor surrounded by hillsides dotted with houses and elegant high-rises clustered into a central fist. There is an immediacy and a vibrancy here that you don't get in other New Zealand cities.

Once seen as a stuffy, bureaucrat-filled political capital, Wellington has reinvented itself to become New Zealand's entertainment and cultural capital and the fastest-growing weekend destination in the country.

With the opening of the long-awaited Te Papa, the national museum of New Zealand, the waterfront is alive again. The Courtenay Place neighborhood has one of the best bar, cafe, and restaurant scenes in the country, and some say there are enough restaurants per capita to rival New York City.

Galleries, theaters, and shops abound, and the beauty of Wellington is that so much is within walking distance. It's a compact place with a pronounced cosmopolitan elegance, and an exciting corporate component adds to the rich urban atmosphere: Morning, noon, and night, "the suits," as they are affectionately called here, crowd the streets.

The British originally called the harbor Port Nicholson, and it wasn't until after the 1839 visit of the Duke of Wellington that the city was renamed in his honor. The seat of government was moved here from Auckland in 1865.

Today's Wellington is diverse and sophisticated. The fact that it can be extremely cold and windy here in winter is understandable if you consider the fact that there's little between the capital and Antarctica to stop the gales. And the fact that so much of this city—filled with many glass-fronted high-rises—sits on a major fault line seems to be of such little concern to its inhabitants that I almost feel picky raising the issue. Speaking of raising, it's interesting to note that a large portion of Wellington's waterfront playground is on reclaimed land (just like Hong Kong)—much of it forced up by a giant 1855 earthquake and finished off by clever acts of reclamation.

1 Orientation

ARRIVING

BY PLANE   **Wellington International Airport** is 8km (5 miles) southeast of the city. The quickest route passes through Mount Victoria via a two-lane tunnel. A more circuitous, but more scenic, route travels via Oriental Parade. The trip usually takes 15 to 20 minutes, although it can exceed 30 minutes at peak traffic times.

Wellington Airport operates both international and domestic business from the same building. It is served by the following international airlines: **Air New Zealand** (© 0800/737-000 in NZ, or 04/388-9737), **British Airways** (© 09/966-977),

Lufthansa (ℭ 0800/945-220 in NZ), Qantas Airways (ℭ 0800/808-767), Singapore Airlines (ℭ 04/499-0271), and Polynesian Airlines (ℭ 0800/800-993).

Leading domestic airlines that fly into Wellington are Air New Zealand (ℭ 0800/737-000 in NZ), Air New Zealand Link (ℭ 04/388-0695), and Soundsair Ltd. (ℭ 0800/505-505). For arrival and departure information, call ℭ 04/388-9900.

The Wellington Airport Visitor Information Centre (ℭ 04/385-5123; fax 04/385-5137; www.wellington-airport.co.nz) is on level one of the main terminal building. Staff members can assist with booking accommodations, TranzRail, Interislander ferries, and long-distance coaches. It's open daily from 7am to 8pm.

The terminal has three restaurants: Red Rocks, for pizza and pasta; The Bays, for bakery, grill, and ice-cream items; and Cooked Strait, for wine and tapas or full meals. There are also car-rental desks, duty-free stores, gift shops, a Travelex Foreign Exchange service open during all international flight times, and ATMs. Coin-operated lockers can be found on the ground floor.

Super Shuttle (ℭ 04/387-8787) operates between the airport, the city, and the railway station Monday through Friday. It costs around NZ$15 (US$11) per person. Several shuttle operators provide door-to-door service at higher fares.

The express bus Stagecoach Flyer, Ridewell Service Centre (ℭ 0800/801-7000 in NZ, or 04/801-7000; www.stagecoach.co.nz), goes right into central city and then on to Waterloo Interchange in Lower Hutt. It operates every 30 minutes, 365 days a year from 5:30am to 8:20pm and an All Day Star Pass costs NZ$9 (US$6.30) per person. Single-ride tickets are also available. The trip from the airport to central-city stops takes about 45 minutes.

A taxi between the city center and the airport costs NZ$20 to NZ$35 (US$14–US$25), depending on the destination. The fare to Lower Hutt is approximately NZ$50 to NZ$60 (US$35–US$42). Taxi stands are directly outside the main terminal. If you have any problems with your taxi driver, call Wellington Airport Operation (ℭ 04/385-5124).

BY TRAIN & COACH (BUS)   Most long-distance trains depart from the Wellington Railway Station, on Waterloo Quay. For long-distance rail information, call ℭ 0800/802-802 in New Zealand, or 04/498-3413. Most major hostels and hotels are within a short taxi ride of the station.

For coach information, call InterCity (ℭ 09/913-6100) or Newmans (ℭ 09/913-6200). Both of these coach lines operate out of the railway station. Kiwi Experience (ℭ 09/366-1665) and the Magic Travellers Network (ℭ 09/358-5600) also stop in Wellington.

BY CAR   Wellington is reached via highways 1 and 2. It's 195km (121 miles) from Wanganui (approximately 2 hr.); 460km (285 miles) from Rotorua (approximately 4–5 hr.); and 655km (406 miles) from Auckland (approximately 7–8 hr.). The motorway terminates right in the city.

BY FERRY   For information on the Interislander Wellington-Picton ferry, call ℭ 0800/802-802 or check www.interislander.co.nz. Be aware that there are two ferry operators working between Wellington and Picton. The three conventional Interislander ferries operate all year. Strait Shipping Ltd., Waterloo Quay (ℭ 0800/844-844 in NZ; www.bluebridge.co.nz), operates Bluebridge Cook Strait Ferry traveling to Picton daily at 3am and 1pm, and Picton to Wellington daily at 8am and 7pm. There are no 3am or 8am sailings on Mondays, and it costs NZ$120 (US$84) for cars,

Wellington

NORTH ISLAND

Auckland

SOUTH ISLAND

Wellington

Christchurch

Dunedin

(i) Information

✉ Post Office

‖‖‖ Pedestrian Mall

Central Terrace

Fairlie

Devon

Kelburn Parade

Glasgow

St. John

Waiteata

McKenzie

The Terrace

Palmer

Inverlochy

Vivian

Buller

MacDonald

Motorway Tunnel

Percival

Arlington

Torrens

Webb

Tonks

Abel Smith

Claytons

Walter

Victoria

Willis

O'Reilly

Allenby

Church

Boulcott

Dixon

Cuba St

Hopper

Arthur

Kelvin

Wigan

Bute

Ghuznee

Cuba Mall

Manners Mall

Wellington Information Centre

Martin Sq.

Buckle

Frankville

Haining

Frederick

Marion

Leeds

Egmont

Furness

Taranaki

Inglewood

Manners

Opera House Lane

(i)

Town Hall

Civic Square

Harris

Tasman

Jessie

Mount Cook Terminal

Sussex

Francis

Ebor

Tory

Jacobs

Holland

BASIN RESERVE

Barker

Fifeshire

Vivian

College

Lorne

Tennyson

Alpha

Courtenay Place

Allen

Wakefield

Cable

Barnett

Nelson

Cambridge Terrace

Kent Terrace

Blair

Chaffers

Lloyd

Moir

Armour

Tutchen

Prine

Moncrieff

Brougham

Edge Hill

Levy

Lipman

Marjoribanks St.

Fallowfield

Caroline

Roxburgh

Hood

Oriental

Overseas Terminal

Porritt Av.

Queen

Elizabeth

Batham

Austin

Herd

Parade

0   0.2 mi

0   0.2 km

N

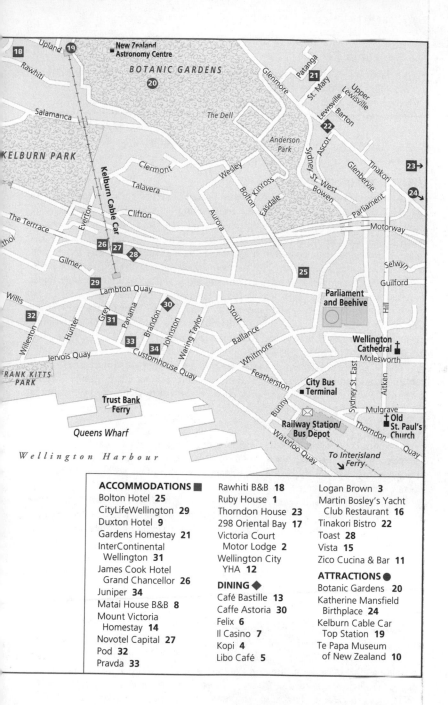

ACCOMMODATIONS ■
Bolton Hotel **25**
CityLifeWellington **29**
Duxton Hotel **9**
Gardens Homestay **21**
InterContinental
  Wellington **31**
James Cook Hotel
  Grand Chancellor **26**
Juniper **34**
Matai House B&B **8**
Mount Victoria
  Homestay **14**
Novotel Capital **27**
Pod **32**
Pravda **33**

Rawhiti B&B **18**
Ruby House **1**
Thorndon House **23**
298 Oriental Bay **17**
Victoria Court
  Motor Lodge **2**
Wellington City
  YHA **12**

DINING ◆
Café Bastille **13**
Caffe Astoria **30**
Felix **6**
Il Casino **7**
Kopi **4**
Libo Café **5**

Logan Brown **3**
Martin Bosley's Yacht
  Club Restaurant **16**
Tinakori Bistro **22**
Toast **28**
Vista **15**
Zico Cucina & Bar **11**

ATTRACTIONS ●
Botanic Gardens **20**
Katherine Mansfield
  Birthplace **24**
Kelburn Cable Car
  Top Station **19**
Te Papa Museum
  of New Zealand **10**

> ### *Tips* Public Relief
>
> Free public toilets are at 69 sites throughout the city. Staffed facilities are at the ANZ Building (at the corner of Lambton Quay and Featherston St.). You'll also find restrooms at all major attractions and several department stores.

NZ$45 (US$32) for adults, and NZ$25 (US$18) for children one-way. Their trip is cheapest but it takes 3 hours 20 minutes.

VISITOR INFORMATION

The **Wellington i–Site Visitor Information Centre,** 101 Wakefield St., Civic Square (© 04/802-4860; fax 04/802-4863; www.wellingtonnz.com), is open Monday through Friday from 8:30am to 5:30pm (Tues till 5pm) and Saturday and Sunday from 9:30am to 4:30pm. It provides details of regional attractions and has the best range of free guides in the country. It also has a range of tiny pocket-size leaflets and cards on everything from transport systems to shopping, art, fashion, and free walking tours. Staff members can book accommodations and attractions; arrange transport; and sell stamps and phone cards. It also has an e-mail center and cafe.

For information on Lower and Upper Hutt areas, contact **Hutt City i-Site Visitor Centre,** 25 Laings Rd., Lower Hutt (© 04/560-4715; fax 04/939-4716; www.hutt city.info) or **Upper Hutt Visitor Information Centre,** 6 Main St., Upper Hutt (© 04/527-2141; fax 04/527-9818; www.upperhuttcity.com).

The free weekly publications *Capital Times* and *City Voice* are available at the visitor center and leading hotels and cafes. Both have details on local happenings. If you're a keen follower of the performing arts, check at the visitor center for availability of discounted day-of-performance tickets.

SPECIAL EVENTS

Wellington is home to the country's biggest cultural event, the biennial **New Zealand International Arts Festival** ✸✸✸ (© 04/473-0149; www.nzfestival.telecom.co.nz). It features international works and the best of New Zealand talent in everything from opera to jazz, dance to comedy.

A major spin-off from the festival is the growth of the **Wellington Fringe Festival** ✸✸ (© 04/495-8015; www.fringe.org.nz), which is a completely separate event run at the same time. It's now an annual event celebrating offbeat productions and innovative art forms.

Summer City Festival (© 04/801-3500; www.feelinggreat.co.nz), staged during January and February each year, launches Wellington's events calendar with more than 70 free activities such as the Teddy Bears' Picnic, the Rock Barge Concert on Oriental Parade, a Pacific Islands Festival, and Summer Shakespeare in the Botanic Gardens Dell.

Wellington Race Cup Meeting offers more than NZ$1 million (US$700,000) in stakes during 3 days of racing, and is an integral part of New Zealand's Summer Racing Carnival. The meeting attracts the best horses and jockeys around. The first 2 days of racing are held during Wellington's Anniversary Weekend (late Jan), and the Cup race itself is held the following Saturday. In between are street parades, golf tournaments, and other events. For more information, contact the Wellington Racing Club (© 04/801-4000; www.trentham.co.nz).

Montana World of Wearable Art ✸✸✸ (✆ 03/548-9299; www.worldof wearableart.com) is a theatrical costume spectacle not to be missed, now staged annually at the Events Centre Wellington in mid-September and early October. This 2-hour visual extravaganza attracts international entrants and sell-out audiences of over 22,000—not bad considering it started in Nelson in 1987 in a leaky tent with just 200 people watching.

Montana Wellington International Jazz Festival (www.jazzfestival.co.nz) features a superb roster of national and international jazz musicians performing modern jazz through the classics (mid- to late October at various city locations).

Martinborough Country Fair ✸✸ (✆ 06/306-9043) is a popular gathering of crafts artisans from around the country. Held the first Saturday in February and the first Saturday in March, it attracts about 30,000 visitors. Martinborough is about an hour's drive northeast of Wellington.

Golden Shears (✆ 06/378-7373; www.goldenshears.co.nz) is a 3-day international shearing contest that includes wool handling and sheep and goat shearing. It's held in late February or early March in Masterton, 103km (64 miles) northeast of Wellington.

In November, catch a special 50-minute festival train from Wellington to the **Toast Martinborough Wine, Food & Music Festival** ✸✸✸ (✆ 06/306-9183; www.toast martinborough.co.nz). Shuttles run a continuous circuit within a 10km (6-mile) area of Martinborough's town square to Martinborough vineyards, where tastings take place with the winemaker.

CITY LAYOUT

The main focal point of **inner city** is the harbor. The new Te Papa national museum fronts this water, as does the Queen's Wharf dining and shopping complex. Unlike the rest of the city, the CBD (Central Business District) is generally flat and easily negotiable. The best **shopping** is along Lambton Quay and Willis Street; Manners Street and Cuba Mall also have plenty of stores. They are less upmarket, but Cuba Mall especially is one of the hippest areas, known for its edgy boutiques and design stores. The inner area of Lambton Quay, Willis Street, and The Terrace is home to many of the nation's **corporate headquarters** and thus is second home to "the suits." Several leading hotels and apartment complexes are also in this area, so if you base yourself here, you won't need a car to see most of the major attractions and shops—but you will need earplugs for a truly sound sleep.

The heaviest concentration of **bars** and **eateries** is between Courtenay Place and Wakefield Street and the lanes running between them, especially Blair and Allen streets. Most of the inner city is safe, but I wouldn't go lurking around Cuba Mall after closing time, especially the top end, which has always been seen as the heart of the seedier side of the sex industry. Manners Mall is no more appealing late at night. Courtenay Place on Thursday, Friday, and Saturday nights is the center of nightlife, but there are often numerous people about who have consumed more than their fair share of alcohol and who may not be entirely open to reason. Generally, though, personal safety rules are the same as in any other international city—use common sense and don't wander about dark places alone in the middle of the night. Many central city areas are now under security camera surveillance.

THE NEIGHBORHOODS IN BRIEF

Thorndon This neighborhood sits right on the fault line, but that hasn't detracted from real-estate values here. It's seen as one of the premier suburbs because of its beautiful historic buildings, its views, and its proximity to the inner city. There are some excellent bed-and-breakfasts within walking distance of Parliament Buildings, the city, the Botanic Gardens, and Tinakori Village, a fashionable little spot for shopping and eating. The area's only downsides are the noise from the motorway, the heavy traffic on Tinakori Road, and the lack of both off- and on-street parking.

Mount Victoria This is where I would live if I thought I could afford anything bigger than a letterbox. It's very close to the Courtenay Place end of town, everything is within walking distance, and it's filled with gorgeous (slightly less perfect) wooden houses. It's also quieter. Parking is generally earmarked for residents only during business hours, but you'll be fine after 6pm.

Kelburn Kelburn is easily accessed via the cable car from Lambton Quay, which runs up to the Botanic Gardens and Victoria University. Homes in this area are sought after for their especially good harbor and city views.

Oriental Bay This part of town offers prime real estate just 800m (about half a mile) around the water's edge from the inner city and Mount Victoria. Again, it's a great place to stay, with several hotels and private high-rise apartments stretched out along Oriental Parade, which is a favorite playground for in-line skaters, walkers, and runners. There are hints of San Francisco here, I'm told, plus a few excellent cafes and restaurants and beautiful city and harbor views.

Evans Bay This area is far less inspiring. It's farther out, around the point, and its prime attraction is its proximity to the airport.

Lower Hutt A city within a city— Lower Hutt is the ninth largest in New Zealand. It's across the harbor from Wellington proper and accessed via a short motorway drive, usually about 15 minutes in good traffic. This is where you'll find the fabulous Dowse Art Museum, but I have to scratch my head to think of other reasons why you would stay here instead of inner city.

2 Getting Around

Wellington is blessed with an excellent public transport system, and you can easily see the best attractions without a car.

BY BUS   Call **Ridewell** (© **04/801-7000**) for information on all urban services. Buses operate daily 7am to 11pm on most routes and the visitor center can give you a comprehensive city map that shows major bus routes and timetables. Timetables are also available from newsstands. The main city bus terminal, **Lambton Interchange,** is adjacent to the main railway station on the corner of Bunny and Featherston streets. The easiest places to catch buses in central city are Lambton Quay, Willis Street, Dixon Street, Cuba Mall, Courtenay Place, and the railway station.

The NZ$5 (US$3.50) **Daytripper Pass** gives you unlimited travel on the City Circular Bus and Stagecoach Wellington routes 1 to 49. With this pass, you can also take two children under 16 after 9am on weekdays and all day on weekends. The **Star Pass** is NZ$9 (US$6.30) and gives one person a day's unlimited travel on all Stagecoach Wellington, City Circular, and Cityline Hutt Valley bus services. Both passes can be purchased from your bus driver. The NZ$15 (US$11) **Capital Explorer Pass** gives you a full day of unlimited travel after 9am on a wide range of train and bus services in and around Wellington, Hutt Valley, and the Kapiti Coast.

The **City Circular** is a terrific bright-yellow bus taking in the 10 top spots of the city every 10 minutes. One circuit costs NZ$3 (US$2.10) for adults. The route includes stops at Parliament, Lambton Quay, Kirkcaldies Department Store, the cable car, Queen's Wharf, Te Papa, the Civic Centre, Courtenay Place, and several other shopping areas. It operates Monday through Saturday from 6am to 11pm and Sunday and holidays from 8am to 10:30pm. You can also use the Stagecoach Star Pass, Daytripper Pass, or group passes; tickets can be purchased from the driver.

Newlands Coach Service operates bus routes 50 to 59 from central Wellington to the northern suburbs. Purchase tickets from the driver; these buses arrive on Featherston Street and leave from Lambton Exchange.

BY TAXI   There are taxi stands in front of the railway station; in the Lambton Quay shopping area between Grey and Hunter streets; on Bond Street just off Willis Street; on Dixon Street between Cuba and Victoria streets; and on Cambridge Terrace near Courtenay Place. For service, call **Black & Gold Taxis** (© **04/388-8888**) or **Wellington Combined Taxis** (© **04/384-4444;** www.taxis.co.nz). You'll pay a NZ$1 (US70¢) surcharge if you phone for a taxi.

BY TRAIN   **Tranz Metro** operates daily electric train service from Wellington to its outer suburbs. Trains arrive at the railway station on Bunny Street; everything is an easy walk or bus ride from there. You can save money with the purchase of a **Family Pass** (NZ$15/US$11), which gives unlimited travel for a day. Call © **04/801-7000** or check www.tranzmetro.co.nz for timetable information.

BY CAR   If you can avoid using a car in downtown Wellington, do so; you'll save yourself a lot of hassles. Traffic congestion is significant during the week and parking can be a problem. If you do drive, there are 10 major parking buildings in central city. All are well signposted and are open 24 hours. Rates range from NZ$2 to NZ$10 (US$1.40–US$7) per hour. There are also pay-and-display parking areas, where a machine dispenses a ticket to be displayed in your car window. On Saturday and Sunday, parking is free in all metered pay-and-display areas and in council parking buildings, but the time limits still apply. If you exceed them, you can expect a fine. Parking in resident parking zones is also a costly business if you get caught. Ask at the Visitor Information Centre about NZ$4 (US$2.80) per day parking vouchers.

Also be aware that, from 2005 to 2007, Wellington's new NZ$40-million inner city bypass will be taking shape. The project may cause a few traffic delays initially—in the Ghuznee Street and Terrace Tunnel areas—but most major construction should be completed by the end of 2006. Alternative road routes within the city will be well marked.

BY CABLE CAR   The cable car takes you from Lambton Quay straight up to the Botanic Gardens, with a Victoria University stop on the way. It runs daily every 10 minutes from 7am to 10pm Monday through Friday, 8:30am to 10pm Saturday, 9am to 10pm Sunday and public holidays. A round-trip ticket costs NZ$3.60 (US$2.50) for adults, NZ$2 (US$1.40) for children 5 to 15. Family and senior discounts are available. For information, call © **04/472-2199.**

BY FERRY   The **Dominion Post Ferry** runs daily between Queen's Wharf, Somes Island, Eastbourne, and Days Bay Wharf. The trip to Days Bay takes 30 minutes one-way, and Eastbourne Village is a good 10- to 15-minute trip from Days Bay. The one-way fare costs around NZ$8 (US$5.60) for adults and NZ$4 (US$2.80) for children; a family return pass is NZ$40 (US$28). Call ℂ **04/494-3339** or 04/499-1282 or check www.eastbywest.co.nz for timetable information.

FAST FACTS: Wellington

American Express The foreign exchange bureau is in the Cable Car complex, 280–292 Lambton Quay (ℂ **04/473-7766;** fax 04/473-7765). It's open Monday through Friday from 8:30am to 5pm.

Area Code Wellington's telephone area code (STD) is **04.**

Babysitters Most hotels and B&Bs can arrange babysitters, or you can call Wellington Nanny Connections at ℂ **04/384-1135.**

Dentist For 24-hour service, phone ℂ **04/801-5551.**

Doctor For emergency doctor referrals, call ℂ **04/472-2999.**

Embassies & Consulates The **U.S. Embassy** is at 29 Fitzherbert Terrace, Thorndon (ℂ **04/462-6000);** the **Canadian High Commission** is at 61 Molesworth St. (ℂ **04/473-9577);** and the **British High Commission** is at 44 Hill St. (ℂ **04/924-2888).**

Emergencies Dial ℂ **111** to call the police, report a fire, or request an ambulance.

Hospitals Wellington Hospital is on Riddiford Street, Newtown (ℂ **04/385-5999).**

Internet Access The **Email Shop,** 175 Cuba St. (ℂ **04/384-1534),** has a full range of Internet and computer services; it's open daily from 9am to 10pm. It also has outlets at the **Wellington i–Site Visitor Information Centre** (see "Visitor Information," above). For other options, try **Cybernomad,** 43 Courtenay Place (ℂ **04/801-5964),** which offers high-speed Internet service, or **Cyber Spot Internet,** 180 Lambton Quay (ℂ **04/473-0098).**

Newspapers Wellington's morning newspaper, the *Dominion,* and evening paper, the *Evening Post,* are both published Monday through Saturday. On Sundays, get the best paper in the country, the *Sunday Star Times.* Overseas newspapers are sometimes available at newsstands and in the reading room of the National Library, Molesworth Street (ℂ **04/474-3000).**

Pharmacies There are late-night pharmacies at 17 Adelaide Rd., Wellington (ℂ **04/384-4944),** and 729 High St., Lower Hutt (ℂ **04/567-5345).**

Police See "Emergencies," above.

Post Office The main post office is at 7 Waterloo Quay (ℂ **04/496-4065).** Collect poste restante mail at NZ Post, 43 Manners St. (ℂ **04/473-5922).** New Zealand Post shops are open Monday through Friday from 9am to 5pm.

---

3 Where to Stay

If you've been here before, don't be tricked into thinking Wellington has a bunch of new hotels. There are one or two new ones, but in fact several existing properties have just changed ownership and names. And remember that everything in Wellington is geared for the corporate market. Hotel and motel rates are significantly higher Monday through Thursday, but you can pick up exceptionally good deals on the weekends, especially during the off season. There has been a big increase in inner city apartment developments, and some exceptional values rise right off the heart of Lambton Quay and The Terrace, placing you perfectly in the heart of everything. Although there is a wide range of home-stay options, there are not as many upmarket B&Bs in the suburbs as there are in, say, Christchurch or Auckland.

One new hotel is **Novotel Capital** &&, 133–137 The Terrace (© **0800/444-422** in NZ, or 04/918-1900; www.novotel.co.nz), where rooms range from NZ$158 to NZ$338 (US$111–US$237). It's very much a corporate hotel, but its five stylish suites offer great value.

All rates include 12.5% GST and free off-street parking unless otherwise stated.

IN INNER CITY
VERY EXPENSIVE
InterContinental Wellington &&&   Seen as Wellington's most luxurious hotel, this is the sort of place where you could rub shoulders with the rich and famous—or at least the cosmopolitan and corporate. Now 15 years old, it underwent a big makeover in 2001. It's right in the heart of the CBD, and if you give in to indulgence, you'll love the top service and classy environment. The higher the price, the better it gets—and there's no doubt in my mind that the top-floor Club rooms are pampering at its best. These have divine bathrooms with huge Jacuzzis and lots of other perks, including access to the Club Lounge. Ten accessible units are available for travelers with disabilities.

Grey and Featherston sts., Wellington. © **0800/442-215** in NZ, or 04/472-2722. Fax 04/472-4724. www.intercontinental.cm/wellington. 231 units. NZ$435 (US$305) deluxe queen/twin; NZ$525 (US$368) club king/twin; NZ$750 (US$525) executive suite; NZ$2,300 (US$1,610) presidential suite. Extra person NZ$25 (US$18). Children under 16 stay free in parent's room. Long-stay, off-peak rates, and special deals available. AE, DC, MC, V. Valet parking NZ$15 (US$11) Mon–Fri, NZ$10 (US$7) Sat–Sun. **Amenities:** 2 restaurants (Chameleon Restaurant [award-winning international] and Arizona Bar & Grill [Tex-Mex]); 2 bars; fabulous high-rise heated indoor pool; well-equipped gym; Jacuzzi; sauna; day spa and beauty treatments; concierge; tour desk; car rentals; courtesy car; business center; secretarial services; adjacent salon; 24-hr. room service; massage; babysitting; laundry service; same-day dry cleaning; nonsmoking rooms; club-level rooms; on-call doctor/dentist. *In room:* A/C, TV, dataport, minibar, fridge, coffeemaker, hair dryer, iron, safe.

EXPENSIVE
CityLife Wellington: A Heritage Hotel && ⟨Value⟩   You won't find a better apartment, at a better price, in a better location. Smack in the middle of Wellington's Golden Mile, CityLife rises seven levels above Lambton Quay, and it's no surprise to learn that rooms are often booked several weeks ahead. Take one of the executive suites as your modern home away from home. They're large, tastefully appointed, and fully self-contained with laundry facilities; three have big balconies. Opened in 1995 in a refitted commercial building and given a soft revamp in 2004, CityLife is an unbeatable value.

300 Lambton Quay, Wellington. © **0800/368-888** in NZ, or 04/922-2800. Fax 04/922-2803. www.citylifewellington.co.nz. 70 units. NZ$355 (US$249) studio; NZ$437 (US$306) 1-bedroom suite; NZ$496 (US$347) 2-bedroom suite; NZ$567 (US$397) 2-bedroom director's suite; NZ$650 (US$455) 3-bedroom ambassador's suite. NZ$35 (US$25) for extra rollaway beds. Long-stay rates and special deals available. AE, DC, MC, V. Limited off-street parking. In 2006, CityLife will be closed Feb 3–6, Apr 6–9, Oct 27–31, and Nov 1–9. The car entrance is at 14 Gilmer Terrace, off

Boulcott St.; go past the Plimmer Hotel and to the end of Gilmer Terrace. **Amenities:** Breakfast cafe; small gym; car rentals; business center; babysitting; laundry service; same-day dry cleaning; nonsmoking rooms. *In room:* TV/VCR, dataport, kitchen, minibar, fridge, coffeemaker, hair dryer, iron, washer/dryer.

Duxton Hotel ★★★   So you want style, luxury, service, award-winning cuisine, and a great location all wrapped up in one? The Duxton delivers. Ideally across the street from Te Papa and the Michael Fowler Centre, and close to Courtenay Place, it offers nine levels of top comfort and attracts everyone from leisure and corporate travelers to international dignitaries. Built in 1987, all of the generously proportioned rooms have harbor or city views; deluxe units have marble bathrooms with separate tub and shower. The club-level suites go up another notch in comfort and are well worth the extra price—especially if you get a weekend deal. Breakfast is also included in the tariff of club-level rooms. Fourteen accessible units are available for travelers with disabilities. It wouldn't hurt to pack earplugs just in case harbor activity disturbs you, but all rooms are double-glazed. Half of the hotel underwent a major refurbishment in late 2005 to early 2006.

170 Wakefield St., Wellington. © **0800/475-292** in NZ, or 04/473-3900. Fax 04/473-3929. www.duxton.com. 192 units. NZ$320 (US$224) deluxe; NZ$445 (US$312) Club; NZ$557 (US$390) Club suite; NZ$1,238 (US$867) Presidential suite. Extra person NZ$28 (US$20). Long-stay rates available. AE, DC, MC, V. Valet parking NZ$15 (US$11) per day. **Amenities:** Restaurant; bar; well-equipped gym; concierge; tour desk; car rentals; business center; 24-hr. room service; massage; babysitting; same-day dry cleaning; laundry service; nonsmoking rooms; club-level rooms; on-call doctor/dentist. *In room:* A/C, TV w/pay movies, dataport, minibar, fridge, coffeemaker, hair dryer, iron.

MODERATE

Bolton Hotel ★★★ *Finds*   Brand new in 2005, this multistory, apartment-style hotel has an elegance and style that exceeds some of its bigger capital city cousins. Owners have paid meticulous attention to guest preferences and rooms abound with luscious textural fabrics and unexpected extra touches—a comprehensive minibar, for instance, that includes an umbrella and disposable raincoat, the importance of which can't be overestimated in Wellington. It's colorful, crisp, modern, and close to the heart of the city. What more could you want?

Corner of Bolton and Mowbray sts., Wellington. © **0800/996-622** in NZ, or 04/472-9966. Fax 04/472-9955. www.boltonhotel.co.nz. 142 units. NZ$185–NZ$200 (US$130–US$140) studio; NZ$245–NZ$260 (US$172–US$182) 1-bedroom suite; NZ$300 (US$210) 2-bedroom suite. Long-stay, off-peak, and special deals available. AE, DC, MC, V. Valet parking NZ$12 (US$8.40) per day. **Amenities:** Restaurant (Mediterranean/NZ); tiny lobby cafe (Brioche); heated indoor lap pool; excellent gym; Jacuzzi; sauna; concierge; car rentals; babysitting; laundry service; same-day dry cleaning; nonsmoking rooms; on-call doctor/dentist; access for travelers w/disabilities. *In room:* A/C, TV, dataport, kitchen in all but 24 units, minibar, fridge, coffeemaker, laundry facilities in suites, hair dryer, iron.

James Cook Hotel Grand Chancellor ★★ *Value*   This 34-year-old hotel has earned its reputation for great rates in a prime location with friendly staff. A big makeover in 2004 saw the lobby revitalized and the addition of new Club Rooms on

---

Tips **All Girls**

If you want to stay in an all-girls environment, check out the **Mermaid Guesthouse for Women**, 1 Epuni St., Aro Valley, Wellington (©/fax **04/384-4511**; www.mermaid.co.nz). Rates in the restyled Victorian villa are from NZ$75 to NZ$145 (US$53–US$102). They also have a 1-bedroom apartment, **Qbissima**, at 51–75 Webb St., minutes from the city center, from NZ$110 to NZ$155 (US$77–US$109).

Level 26, providing complimentary breakfast and extra amenities in the Club Lounge. For the little extra you pay, these 17 slick Club Rooms are the pick of the bunch. Another two floors will be refurbished in 2006. With its bustling city outlook, direct access to shopping on Lambton Quay, and commerce on The Terrace, this hotel is the perfect base for business or pleasure—and don't forget to ask about the cheaper weekend rates.

147 The Terrace, Wellington. (C) **0800/699-500** in NZ, or 04/499-9500. Fax 04/499-9800. www.grandhotels international.com. 260 units. From NZ$185–NZ$450 (US$130–US$315). Long-stay, off-peak, and special deals available. AE, DC, MC, V. Valet parking NZ$10 (US$7) per day. **Amenities:** 2 restaurants; 2 bars; gym; day spa and beauty treatments; concierge; tour desk; car rentals; business center; mobile hairdresser; 24-hr. room service; massage; babysitting; same-day dry cleaning; nonsmoking rooms; on-call doctor/dentist. *In room:* A/C, TV, dataport, minibar, fridge, coffeemaker, hair dryer, iron.

Victoria Court Motor Lodge ℛℛ *Finds*   Stay in this smart new complex and you can forget all about driving your car. It's just a hop, skip, and jump from central shopping and restaurants. What's more, the 25 units have much to offer in terms of value and comfort. The two-bedroom units especially are a gift for families or two couples traveling together, and when you see the smart kitchens, you might even feel inclined to cook.

201 Victoria St., Wellington. (C) **04/472-4297.** Fax 04/385-7949. www.victoriacourt.co.nz. 25 units. NZ$145–NZ$210 (US$102–US$147). Extra persons NZ$15 (US$11). MC, V. Long-stay, off-peak, and weekend rates available. Free off-street parking. Victoria St. is one-way heading west, so make sure you enter it off Ghuznee St., not Vivian St. **Amenities:** Babysitting; laundry service; coin-op laundry; same-day dry cleaning; nonsmoking rooms. *In room:* TV, dataport, kitchenette or full kitchen, fridge, coffeemaker, hair dryer, iron.

INEXPENSIVE

Wellington City YHA ℛℛ   This is without doubt the best backpacker establishment in Wellington. It hums with activity as guests of all ages settle into crisp, colorful rooms—private or bunk style—and the international staff seems to know everything there is to know about the city. Location is a prime attraction, and rooms are well situated for sunshine and harbor views. A complete refurbishment was carried out in 2001, doubling the size of the establishment. Internet and postal services are available, and a group lounge acts as a great social spot. There is a well-equipped kitchen, plenty of quiet intimate spaces, and a supermarket just across the road. All transport and other YHA bookings can be made on the premises.

Cambridge Terrace and Wakefield St., Wellington. (C) **04/801-7280.** Fax 04/801-7278. www.yha.co.nz. 320 beds. NZ$24–NZ$26 (US$17–US$18) quad share en suite; NZ$21–NZ$23 (US$15–US$16) 6-share, with or without en suite; NZ$84–NZ$90 (US$59–US$63) double with en suite, NZ$64–NZ$68 (US$45–US$48) double with shared bathrooms. Nonmembers pay additional NZ$3 (US$2.10) per person per night. Off-peak rates available. MC, V. Car-park building nearby. **Amenities:** Game room; tour bookings; car rentals; coin-op laundry; nonsmoking rooms; communal kitchens; dining rooms; Internet room. *In room:* Hair dryer and iron available upon request.

IN THORNDON/KELBURN

Gardens Homestay ℛℛ   Neil Harrop and Sally Guinness like to say that guests are simply friends they haven't met yet. As the inventor of New Zealand's Fly By Wire ride, Neil has an extensive knowledge of tourism, which he delights in sharing with those lucky enough to score a bed in this grand 1892 Victorian home filled with antiques. The large two-bedroom, upstairs suite (one smallish bathroom) is ideal for two couples or family members traveling together. It's quiet and private, and has lovely views over one of Wellington's premier residential areas.

11 St. Mary St., Thorndon, Wellington. ℂ **04/499-1212.** Fax 04/499-8383. www.gardenshomestay.co.nz. 2-bedroom suite. NZ$256–NZ$395 (US$179–US$277). Off-peak rates available. Rates include breakfast. MC, V. Closed July–Aug. **Amenities:** Heated outdoor pool; free bikes; babysitting; free laundry; same-day dry cleaning; nonsmoking rooms. *In room:* Dataport, hair dryer, iron.

Rawhiti Boutique Bed and Breakfast ★★ *Finds*

Stand in Annabel Leask's "secret garden" tucked away behind her gorgeous two-story Victorian, hillside home high above the city and you get a real feel for just how picturesque this city can be. Inside, you'll find two lovely downstairs rooms bathed in sunlight and open to memorable views. The gold room is the larger one, with a bigger bathroom, but the blue king/twin room is equally charming. Annabel has strong interests in all the arts, speaks French, and has lived internationally. Her home is close to the university and just a few steps from the Wellington Cable Car.

40 Rawhiti Terrace, Kelburn, Wellington. ℂ **04/934-4859.** Fax 04/973-4859. www.rawhiti.co.nz. 2 units. NZ$200–NZ$264 (US$140–US$185). Rates include breakfast. Long-stay and off-peak rates available. MC, V. From The Terrace, turn onto Salamanca Rd., which veers left into Kelburn Parade. Go past the university, turn right up the hill at the roundabout and first right into Rawhiti Terrace. **Amenities:** Nearby golf club and tennis courts; tour bookings; car rentals; laundry service; same-day dry cleaning; nonsmoking rooms; on-call doctor/dentist. *In room:* TV, dataport, fridge in 1 room, coffeemaker, hair dryer, iron.

Ruby House ★★ *Value*

Elizabeth Barbalich is a natural hostess—lively, charming, and always smiling. The three-level guesthouse she has created below her grand family home is bound to please. Imagine French-country style meeting Kiwi ingenuity and you'll get the picture. There's one guest room on each level, so privacy is a given. The top room has a deck but a smaller bathroom. The lower room—the Luciano—is my favorite, with its own patio and claw-foot tub. Two units have VCRs. The shared kitchen, dining area, and living room exude freshness. It's just 1 minute from the Botanic Gardens and cable car.

14b Kelburn Parade, Kelburn, Wellington. ℂ **04/934-7930.** Fax 04/934-7935. www.rubyhouse.co.nz. 3 units. NZ$185–NZ$250 (US$130–US$175). Minimum 2-night stay. Rates include breakfast. Rates for entire house negotiable; long-stay and off-peak rates available. AE, DC, MC, V. Free off-street parking. From The Terrace, turn onto Salamanca Rd., which veers left to Kelburn Parade. The house is down a narrow driveway set among the university buildings. **Amenities:** Nearby tennis courts and gym; massage; babysitting; laundry service; same-day dry cleaning; nonsmoking rooms. *In room:* TV, dataport, hair dryer, iron.

Thorndon House ★

Warmth and welcome are aplenty in this grand old wooden house where Markus and Gabi Landvogt delight in offering personalized guest attention. Nothing seems to be too much trouble. Lotta is the biggest of the two upstairs bedrooms and outside, the very cute back garden cottage is a little honey with a bit more privacy. You're a little farther away from Tinakori Road's traffic noise here, and I can't believe you won't sleep soundly.

17 Park St., Thorndon, Wellington. ℂ **04/499-0503.** Fax 04/499-0504. www.thorndonhouse.co.nz. 2 rooms, 1 cottage. NZ$150–NZ$190 (US$105–US$133) room; NZ$220 (US$154) cottage. Long-stay and off-peak rates available. MC, V. Rates include breakfast. **Amenities:** Tour bookings; car rentals; babysitting; laundry service; same-day dry cleaning; nonsmoking rooms. *In room:* TV, dataport, coffeemaker, hair dryer.

IN MOUNT VICTORIA/ORIENTAL PARADE

If you like books, you'll be happy at **Booklovers Bed and Breakfast** ★, 123 Pirie St., Mount Victoria (ℂ **04/384-2714;** www.booklovers.co.nz), where Jane Tolerton offers three large rooms in her Victorian home for about NZ$160 to NZ$175 (US$112–US$123). It's just a short walk from Courtenay Place.

Mount Victoria Homestay ☆ The visitors' book at Bill and Coral Aitchison's inner city home is filled with glowing reports on their hospitality and generosity—"hosts from Heaven," they're called. Their 1920s Edwardian villa was completely restored in 2002 and everything—from the Wedgwood and Spode dinnerware to hearty breakfasts to the tranquil garden courtyard where guests enjoy evening drinks—illustrates Coral's attention to detail. Two upstairs guest rooms are quiet and private yet just a few minutes' walk from some of the capital's best restaurants and nightlife.

11 Lipman St., Mount Victoria, Wellington. © 04/802-4886. Fax 04/802-4877. www.mountvictoria.co.nz. 2 units. NZ$220 (US$154). Rates include breakfast. MC, V. **Amenities:** Courtesy airport transport by arrangement; babysitting; laundry service; same-day dry cleaning; nonsmoking rooms; on-call doctor/dentist. *In room:* TV, dataport, minibar, fridge, coffeemaker, hair dryer, iron.

298 Oriental Bay ☆☆☆ *Finds* Take one Parisian-style town house built in 1928 in one of Wellington's most gorgeous bays; install stunning antiques, lavish chandeliers, and charming hostess, Susan Bilbie; and you have a top bed-and-breakfast stay. There are two sumptuous rooms, both with lovely marble en-suite bathrooms. I fell in love with the divine Summer House, situated up behind the main house with its own brick courtyard, and I expect you will too. It's perfectly placed among restaurants, just 3 minutes from the city and 10 minutes from the airport, and where else could you get private lessons from New Zealand's 1998 billiard champion, or tinkle on a baby grand piano? This is unequivocally Wellington's best B&B experience.

298 Oriental Parade, Oriental Bay. ©/fax 04/384-4990 or 021/113-5960. www.298.co.nz. 2 units. NZ$500 (US$350). Rate includes breakfast and predinner drinks. AE, MC, V. **Amenities:** Nearby pool; nearby golf course; gym equipment; laundry service; same-day dry cleaning; billiard table and billiard lessons by arrangement; nonsmoking rooms. *In room:* TV, dataport, minibar, fridge, coffeemaker, hair dryer.

NEAR THE AIRPORT

Brentwood Hotel ☆ The 37-year-old Brentwood has been given a thorough makeover in recent years and it looks a whole lot more inviting. The downstairs poolside superior rooms get my vote for better space, corner Jacuzzis, and overall comfort—there's only four of them, so be in early. The hotel is a popular conference venue and often hosts tour buses and sports teams, who usually stay upstairs. Keep an eye out for the new studio apartments and suites coming on stream after 2006. Overall, a modest property but perfectly adequate if you want is a bed before an early departure.

16 Kemp St., Kilbirnie, Wellington. © 0508/273-689 in NZ, or 04/920-0400. Fax 04/920-0401. www.brentwoodhotel.co.nz. 119 units. NZ$126–NZ$160 (US$88–US$112). Rates include airport transfers. Long-stay, off-peak, and weekend rates available. AE, DC, MC, V. 5 min. from airport by car. **Amenities:** Restaurant; bar; outdoor lit pool; nearby golf course; access to nearby gym; car rentals; business center; 24-hr. room service; massage; babysitting; laundry service; coin-op laundry; same-day dry cleaning; nonsmoking rooms; free airport transport. *In room:* TV, dataport, minibar, fridge, coffeemaker, hair dryer, iron.

Home Stay at Evans Bay ☆☆ *Finds* Multilingual Leisha Schuitema has traveled extensively, adores meeting people, and "doesn't feel alive" until she has dipped her hands into her cooking bowls. She'll spoil you with edible delicacies and a warm welcome beyond compare. Two upstairs rooms are sunny and bright. One has its own en-suite bathroom (shower only), the other a private bathroom with tub and shower. You'll feel very much at ease in this modern home filled with Leisha's own paintings and collections of china. It's just 10 minutes at most from the airport and enjoys beautiful harbor views.

4/378 Evans Bay Parade, Evans Bay, Wellington. ℂ **04/386-1504.** Fax 04/386-1503. www.homestayevansbay.co.nz. 2 units. NZ$200–NZ$250 (US$140–US$175). Rates include breakfast; dinner by arrangement. Long-stay and off-peak rates available. AE, MC, V. **Amenities:** Nearby pool, golf course, and tennis courts; tour bookings; car rentals; laundry service; same-day dry cleaning; nonsmoking rooms; on-call doctor/dentist; airport transport. *In room:* TV, dataport, coffeemaker, hair dryer.

Matai House B&B 👉👉 *(Finds)*   Walk through the front door here and you can almost see your next plane taxiing down the airport runway across the harbor. Guest rooms are in the private, lower area of a charming, two-story home. Two gorgeous suites with an adjoining lounge and harborview balconies feature heavenly king-size beds with down comforters and elegant en-suite bathrooms. With a separate guest entrance, this is an ideal spot for a family or two couples traveling together.

41 Matai Rd., Haitaitai, Wellington. ℂ **04/934-6985.** Fax 04/934-6987. www.mataihouse.co.nz. 2 units. NZ$200–NZ$250 (US$140–US$175). MC, V. Rates include breakfast and airport transfers. No children under 12. **Amenities:** Nearby golf course; tour bookings; car rentals; laundry service; same-day dry cleaning; nonsmoking rooms. *In room:* TV, dataport, fridge, coffeemaker, hair dryer, iron.

4 Where to Dine

Wellington used to have the best concentration of restaurants and cafes of any city in New Zealand, but Auckland has edged it out. However, it's still crammed with a variety that reflects its cosmopolitan population. Everything is within walking distance and priced for all budgets. The visitor center's *Wine & Food Guide* gives an excellent introduction to many of the leading lights. Ethnic restaurants—Turkish, Greek, Indian, Thai, Mongolian, Japanese, Malaysian, Chinese, Korean, and more—abound and are found in the biggest concentration around Cuba Street and Courtenay Place. Cuba Street is also the hippest place to eat on a budget and there are a number of vegetarian eateries in this area. There has been a big explosion of Indian restaurants and Malaysian *roti* eateries, and if you've tried these delicious pancakes with their rich curries, you'll know how addictive they can be.

And don't forget the suburbs: Thorndon, Mount Victoria, Oriental Parade, and Eastbourne, just for starters, have little pockets of culinary magic. At least one new restaurant or cafe opens every week.

Situated strategically between the ever-expanding wine-growing regions of Marlborough and Wairarapa, Wellington couldn't be better placed to introduce you to the sublime delights of New Zealand's finest wines. It's wall-to-wall food and wine out here—go for it!

IN INNER CITY

In addition to those reviewed below, **Boulcott Street Bistro** 👉👉, 99 Boulcott St. (ℂ **04/499-4199**), is regarded as one of the city's finest upmarket restaurants. They don't take reservations so it's first in, first served. For something more casual, try the ground floor of **Bouquet Garni,** 100 Willis St. (ℂ **04/499-1095**), which is also an enduring favorite. Upstairs is more expensive and more formal.

EXPENSIVE

Citron 👉👉👉 CONTEMPORARY EUROPEAN   Intimate, tiny, and luxurious are words that spring to mind when you think of chef Rex Morgan's culinary haven. Booked out weeks in advance, it takes you on a taste extravaganza with a fixed-price menu or the pricier nine-course degustation menu with little refreshers tucked between courses. Visitors might like to try New Zealand venison on a Brussels sprout

> ## *Tips* Quick Caffeine Fixes
>
> Apart from the other cafes reviewed in this section, you'll find excellent coffee and good atmosphere at **One Red Dog**, 9–11 Blair St. (© 04/384-9777); **Masi,** 49 Willis St. (© 04/473-3550); **Midnight Espresso** , 178 Cuba St. (© 04/384-7014); **Caffe L'Affare** , 27 College St. (© 04/385-9748); **Emporio,** 28 Grey St. (© 04/470-0122); **Expressaholic,** 128–130 Courtenay Place (© 04/384-7790); **Toast** , 120 The Terrace (© 04/499-1656); **Starbucks** (© 04/472-4861), now firmly ensconced in several city locations, including the Old Bank Arcade & Chambers, on Lambton Quay (© 04/922-0624), and also on The Terrace and on Willis Street. And for constant reliability, you can't go past **Arabica** (© 04/473-7697), opposite the InterContinental hotel on Grey Street.

purée with Maori potato ravioli and honeyed *horopito* (fern shoots). Whatever you settle on, you'll leave satisfied and impressed.

270 Willis St. © **04/801-6263.** Reservations essential. Fixed menu from NZ$60 (US$42); degustation menu from NZ$95 (US$67). AE, DC, MC, V. Dinner Tues–Sat from 6pm.

Il Casino NORTHERN ITALIAN From the intimate luxury of the Moet Room and Piano Bar to the divine garden room and casual pizzeria, Il Casino presents the very best of Venetian cuisine. You'll be spoiled by the attentive European service that has cemented the restaurant's reputation over the past 25 years. Try *Filetto di Bue Alla Pescatora*—prime beef filet medallions sautéed in clarified butter and garnished with poached prawn tails with cherry-and-orange glaze. You'll come away wishing you lived in Italy.

108–112 Tory St. © **04/385-7496.** Reservations recommended. Main courses NZ$25–NZ$35 (US$18–US$25); NZ$35 (US$25) 3-course pretheater menu. AE, DC, MC, V. Mon–Fri noon–2pm; Mon–Sat 6pm–late.

Logan Brown INTERNATIONAL Ask about Wellington's best restaurant, and the name Logan Brown will be mentioned consistently. It's all leather-upholstered booths, white-clothed tables, Corinthian pillars, and chandeliers big enough to swing on in what was once a banking chamber. The food is billed as "honest and simple." The wine list is lengthy with an uneven balance between French (they win) and New Zealand offerings. Funnily enough, you'll find this culinary star cast adrift in the city's red-light area—not that that should affect your decision to try the epicurean offerings of the most splendid restaurant interior in town. Service is impeccable, but it can be stuffy.

Tip: If you want to sample Logan Brown without emptying your wallet, go for the pretheater set menu: three light courses for NZ$35 (US$25) daily from 6 to 7:30pm. Also offered is a three-course Bankers Lunch Menu for the same price.

Cuba and Vivian sts. © **04/801-5114.** Reservations recommended. Main courses NZ$35 (US$25). AE, DC, M, V. Mon–Fri for lunch from noon; daily from 5:30pm.

MODERATE

If you enjoy Indian food, **Great India Restaurant** , 141 Manners St. (© 04/384-5755), comes highly recommended; it's open midday to 2pm for lunch Monday through Friday, and 5pm until late daily. Reservations are advised. For tangy Asian-style flavors, head for **Zing,** corner of Wakefield and Blair streets (© 04/385-0111). Their Lazy Brunch is a favorite on weekends from 10:30am and they're also open for lunch and dinners daily.

Finds **Deli Fixings**

Whether you want to stock up on picnic food or just sit and enjoy coffee with a fine range of edibles, don't miss these inner city delis and bakeries. **Dixon Street Gourmet Deli,** 45 Dixon St. (© **04/384-2436**), has a glowing reputation as long as my arm; and **Smith the Grocer,** in the Old Bank Arcade, Lambton Quay (© **04/473-8591**), is tucked in between leading fashion stores. Both have a wide range of specialty items to take home, plus delicious ready-to-eat treats for the moment. **Bordeaux Bakery,** 220 Thorndon Quay (© **04/499-8334**), and **Le Moulin,** 248 Willis St. (© **04/382-8118**), are two superlative French bakeries; and for Italian-style breads, try **Pandoro,** 2 Allen St. (© **04/385-4478**). **Real Earth Organic Café,** 96 Victoria St. (© **04/470-7752**), has an unrivalled organic menu for both vegetarians and nonvegetarians.

Caffe Astoria *★* MODERN CAFE/LIGHT MEALS   This upmarket cafe has a prime setting in the center of Lambton Quay's little green space, and it's well patronized by businesspeople and earnest-looking Wellingtonians with a slightly professorial look about them. It's a great place to unwind with a bottle of wine, a good coffee, or a delicious snack. Its big interior is always full and buzzing, and it's a popular brunch spot on weekends. There's something quintessentially Wellington about it that shouldn't be missed.

159 Lambton Quay. © **04/473-8500.** Main courses NZ$15–NZ$25 (US$11–US$18). MC, V. Mon–Thurs 7am–7:15pm; Fri 7am–8:15pm; Sat–Sun 9am–4pm.

Chow *★★* SOUTHEAST ASIAN   The fact that Chow now has two inner city locations is an indication of its popularity. It's gone for a casual yet modern, stylish interior and its extensive range of noodles, grills, steamed dishes, and salads combined with wine, sake, cocktails or teas, have made it a winner with busy professionals. Servings are small so order two or three menu choices. It's the sort of place you keep going back to because you know you'll always leave happy.

45 Tory St. and 11 Woodward St. © **04/382-8585** or **04/473-4474.** Main courses NZ$19–NZ$25 (US$13–US$18). AE, MC, V. Daily noon–midnight.

Felix *★★* *Value* DELI/CAFE   A favorite with both suits and the artsy crowd, the lively Felix consistently offers a wide range of lip-smacking deli delights. The all-day breakfast menu offers a number of choices that extend as far out as udon noodles in spicy lemon-grass broth with fresh fish, mussels, and clam meat . . . or was that the lunch menu? It's a slick little operation, with fast service despite the queues waiting for seats. If you have a sweet tooth, consider the jaffa (orange-chocolate) tart with a star anise marmalade and crème fraîche—one of the many indulgences I enjoyed as I watched the Wellington world whirl past the full-glass frontage.

Wakefield and Cuba sts. (opposite Town Hall). © **04/499-5528.** Main courses NZ$15–NZ$26 (US$10–US$18). DC, MC, V. Mon–Fri 7:30am–late; Sat–Sun 8:30am–late.

Hummingbird *★* PACIFIC RIM   With a superbly broody, moody interior—all chocolate brown, dark timber, and leather—Hummingbird has always been a big favorite for lunches, and the chef presents a wide range of appetizer-size dishes in the belief that we should all eat like hummingbirds—savoring small amounts regularly. It's loud and relaxed when full and a good choice for a quick snack before going on to the movies or the theater. For the real fun stuff, come at night for a lively bar scene. There's also a popular late supper every night until 3am and live music on Sundays.

22 Courtenay Place. ℂ **04/801-6336.** Reservations recommended. Main courses NZ$15–NZ$30 (US$10–US$21). AE, DC, MC, V. Mon–Fri 11am–late; Sat–Sun 10am–late.

Juniper ⁂ MODERN PACIFIC RIM   As the name suggests, there's a big gin list at this stylish and moody spot decorated with brown suede, dark wooden tables, and flickering candles. Tiger prawns served with coconut, rock melon, and lime-chile dressing, or lamb's fry with cabernet jus are just two of the tempters that make it popular with inner city corporates.

Johnston St., CBD. ℂ **04/499-3668.** Reservations recommended. Main courses NZ$21–NZ$25 (US$14–US$18). AE, DC, MC, V. Daily 10am–late.

Kopi ⁂ *Value* MALAYSIAN   Kopi almost has more awards than main courses, and if you love Asian food, you can't do better than the delicate flavors of its roti and curries. Try *pulut udang*—parcels of sticky rice filled with spiced shrimps and wrapped in roti. It's a narrow little restaurant (with both upstairs and downstairs seating) and you'll be close to other diners, but that somehow adds to the warmth of the place. I found the service friendly and efficient, and the food just as delicious as its mammoth reputation has always claimed it to be.

103 Willis St. ℂ **04/499-5570.** Reservations required. Main courses NZ$20–NZ$25 (US$14–US$18). AE, DC, MC, V. Daily 10am–late.

Lido Café ⁂ *Value* CAFE   No matter what time of day you come here, you'll find a decent smattering of people to make things interesting. Lido has always been popular for its tasty meals, and its location opposite the City Council makes it a popular lunch spot with the working crowd. This is a laid-back place, far from formal, and you can sit inside or out—see and be seen. The interior is looking a little tatty, but the place is still tickling my taste buds with a menu that scans the continents.

Wakefield and Victoria sts. ℂ **04/499-6666.** Main courses NZ$15–NZ$26 (US$10–US$18). AE, DC, MC, V. Mon–Fri 7:30am–late; Sat–Sun 9am–late.

Pod ⁂ INTERNATIONAL   This large, contemporary, fully glazed space with high ceilings—open to full view from the street—can seem a little vast and unwelcoming at first glance. But it's carved out a good name with the business crowd. And after you try its tasty dishes like braised lamb shanks, seared Cervena (venison), and fresh pan-fried fish at sensible prices, it's easy to see why.

Corner of Victoria and Willeston sts. ℂ **04/939-7073.** Main courses NZ$16–NZ$20 (US$11–US$14). AE, DC, MC, V. Mon 9am–4pm; Tues 9am–late; Wed–Fri 7:30am–late; Sat 10am–late.

Pravda ⁑ CONTEMPORARY EUROPEAN   The name, the pictures of Lenin, the sparkling chandeliers, the dark-wood paneling, and long, dining hall style all suggest something Russian, but the big brasserie menu takes a broader leap. Expect quality midprice dishes like seared salmon or grouper with fennel and potato purée. It's sophisticated and doubles as a terrific cafe.

107 Customhouse Quay. ℂ **04/801-8858.** Main courses around NZ$24 (US$17). AE, MC, V. Mon–Fri 7:30am–late; Sat 9am–3pm.

Zico Cucina & Bar ⁂ *Finds* ITALIAN CAFE   Franco Zanotto left his role as executive chef at the famous Il Casino restaurant to start up this divine little cafe, and for that we can all be truly thankful. He's created just the right mix of relaxed informality,

---

> **⌒Tips Food Courts**
>
> Wellington has good food courts. The best is **Gourmet Lane,** in the BNZ Centre,
> 1 Willis St. This place is a dream for dollar-wise travelers, as even NZ$8 (US$6)
> will fill the gaps. The choices include Chinese, burgers, gourmet pies, barbecue,
> and more. It's open Monday through Thursday from 8am to 5pm, Friday from
> 8am to 8pm, and Saturday from 10am to 3pm. Another popular choice is the
> **Reading Food Court** at Reading Cinema, Courtenay Place Central (℃ **04/801-
> 4601**). The **Wellington Market,** at Cable and Taranaki streets (℃ **04/801-8991**),
> has 14 ethnic food shops providing cheap eats. It's open Friday through Sunday
> from 10am to 5:30pm.

---

great-tasting food, and fun service. It's a family affair—his wife and sons also attend
to your culinary needs—and the menu is so vast I had forgotten the first offerings
before I read through to the last. Pizzas, seafood and veal dishes, and numerous pastas all deserve sampling.

8 Courtenay Place. ℃ **04/802-5585.** Reservations required. Main courses NZ$18–NZ$28 (US$12–US$20). AE, DC,
MC, V. Mon–Fri 10:30am–late; Sat–Sun 5:30pm–late. Closed Dec 25–26 and Jan 1–3.

INEXPENSIVE

New Dynasty 𝕽𝕽, 25 Tory St. (℃ **04/384-3288**), is a great place for traditional Chinese *yum cha* lunch—fat little dumplings and the like. The **Krazy Lounge** 𝕽𝕽, 132
Cuba St. (℃ **04/801-6652**), is a slightly bohemian favorite with all ages, known for
its simple but substantial fare. **The Green Parrot,** Taranaki and Wakefield streets
(℃ **04/384-6080**), is a backpacker regular that's been serving up big, old-fashioned
meals for the past 29 years. On Courtenay Place are numerous **kabob houses** that stay
open late. Well-priced Italian food is found at **Nicolini's,** 26 Courtenay Place (℃ **04/
802-4442**). **One Red Dog,** 9–11 Blair St. (℃ **04/384-9777**), has cheap wood-fired
pizzas and good service.

IN THORNDON/KELBURN

For a laid-back spot to put a smile on your face, head for **Backbencher Pub & Café,**
34 Molesworth St. (opposite Parliament; ℃ **04/472-3065**), where you'll find a great
pub atmosphere that lightheartedly mocks the local parliamentarians. It's best
summed up as cheap and cheerful. In Kelburn, seek out the pocket-size delights of
Kelburn Café, 87–89 Upland Rd., Kelburn (℃ **04/475-8381**), which is open daily
9am to 5pm, serving great coffee and fabulous cakes.

Francois 𝕽𝕽𝕽 FRENCH COUNTRY   Francois came on the scene about 5 years
ago and it has never looked back. It's tucked into an elegant colonial cottage near the
Beehive, where the French owner and his French chef turn out signature dishes like
duck confit, snails, pickled ox tongue, and Provençal-style seafood casseroles. The
interior is smart and simple. Recommendations come thick and fast for this place, so
even if you're not staying in the area, give it a try.

10a Murphy St., Thorndon. ℃ **04/499-5252.** Reservations required. Main courses NZ$25–NZ$35 (US$17–US$24).
AE, DC, MC, V. Tues–Fri noon–2pm; Mon–Sat from 6pm.

Maria Pia's 𝕽𝕽𝕽 ITALIAN COUNTRY   Just around the corner from Francois,
this gorgeous little family-owned and -operated trattoria was another instant success

from the minute it opened its doors. Also sited in an old building, it has a warm, low-key interior that doesn't distract you in any way from the divine fresh pasta that is made, by hand, by Italian-born Maria every day.

55–57 Mulgrave St., Thorndon. © **04/499-5590.** Reservations required. Main courses NZ$22–NZ$32 (US$15–US$22). AE, MC, V. Tues–Fri 11:30am–2:30pm; Tues–Sat 5:30–11:30pm.

Tinakori Bistro ⟡⟡ MODERN NEW ZEALAND   This cute restaurant, right in the heart of Tinakori Village, is a delightful place for an evening meal. You probably won't have a wild time here—the mood is generally pretty restrained—but the food is very good. Chargrilled Cervena with aubergine parmigiana, risotto cake and port sauce, or roasted herb-infused lamb loin are typical offerings.

328 Tinakori Rd. © **04/499-0567.** Reservations recommended. Main courses NZ$24–NZ$30 (US$17–US$21). AE, DC, MC, V. Mon–Fri noon–2pm; daily 6–10:30pm.

IN MOUNT VICTORIA/ORIENTAL PARADE

Another good choice in this neighborhood is **Vista,** 106 Oriental Parade (© **04/385-7724**). It's open daily for breakfast, lunch, and dinner. **The White House Restaurant,** 232 Oriental Parade (upstairs; © **04/385-8555**), is a top-priced option you'll hear recommended time and again. It draws the corporates and the romancers and serves fine New Zealand food with great sea views. And for one of the few decent Greek restaurants, go to **Theo's Greek Taverna,** 13 Pirie St., Mount Victoria (© **04/801-8806**), a new shining star and open Tuesday through Sunday for dinner. It's been judged New Zealand's Best Greek Restaurant for 2 years running. Try to go Thursday, Friday, or Saturday nights for the music and party atmosphere.

Café Bastille   FRENCH PROVINCIAL   Judged Wellington Restaurant of the Year in 2005, business is brisk here and you'll definitely need to book ahead if you want to savor old favorites like French onion soup, coq au vin, and Provencal fish soup. You might also consider the rabbit kidneys, chicken livers, and pigs' ears. With its sunny yellow interior, timber floors, French posters, and mirrors, it feels like a friendly neighborhood cafe.

16 Majoribanks St., Mount Victoria. © **04/382-9559.** Reservations essential. Main courses NZ$22–NZ$28 (US$15–US$20). AE, DC, MC, V. Daily 5:30pm–late.

Martin Bosley's Yacht Club Restaurant   MODERN NEW ZEALAND   Previously reserved as the exclusive dining domain of members of the Royal Port Nicholson Yacht Club, this bright and classy spot has opened its doors to the wider public—and for that we can be truly thankful. You'll get some of the best dishes in Wellington here—luscious seafoods served in myriad ways from an all-round creative menu. Try the smoked eel mousse or the oyster broth. Service is pleasant and confident and the waterside location is almost unbeatable.

Royal Port Nicholson Yacht Club, 103 Oriental Parade, Oriental Bay. © **04/385-6963.** Reservations recommended. Main courses NZ$30–NZ$35 (US$21–US$24). AE, DC, MC, V. Mon–Fri noon–3pm; Thurs–Fri 6pm–late.

NEAR THE AIRPORT

To call this area a culinary backwater is an understatement, but there are modest coffee and light snack offerings at **Café'n'ate Greta Point,** 307 Evans Bay Parade (© **04/386-3884**), which is open daily.

5 Exploring Wellington

The city's major attraction is Te Papa, the new national museum of New Zealand. It opened in 1998 and since then it has received well over 7 million visitors—30% from overseas. As New Zealand's largest cultural investment and Wellington's most exciting attraction, Te Papa is playing a major role in increasing visitor numbers to the capital city.

In 2000, the city also opened a state-of-the-art 40,000-seat stadium, which hosts top international performing artists and sporting action. Another new attraction is the Karori Sanctuary. Locally referred to as the city's best-kept secret, these 252 hectares (623 acres) of regenerating forest are just minutes from the city center. Visitors can walk in the bush surrounded by wildlife and birdcalls.

THE TOP ATTRACTIONS

Museum of New Zealand—Te Papa Tongarewa ★★★ (Kids)   One of the largest national museums in the world, Te Papa is redefining the word *museum*. Built at a cost of NZ$317 million (US$222 million), it is believed to be 5 years ahead of anything of its kind in the world, combining interactive technology with stunning world-class displays that tell the story of New Zealand—its history, art, and natural environment. Advanced motion simulators take visitors back in time to the explosive formation of New Zealand and the prehistoric landscape, and in the present you can try virtual-reality bungy jumping, shear a sheep, or ride on the back of a whale.

Te Papa is also a partnership between Pakeha (the majority culture of European descent) and Maori culture. It includes a range of magnificent exhibitions featuring **Manu Whenua** ★★, some of the country's most significant Maori treasures, as well as **Te Marae** ★★, a unique 21st-century carved meetinghouse. Visitors can share in formal Maori welcomes and *iwi* (tribal) ceremonies, see how the Maori navigated the Pacific, and learn the stories behind the carvings and the Treaty of Waitangi.

The second level contains **Mountains to Sea,** which puts the spotlight on the natural world. From minuscule insects to the gigantic skeleton of a 21m (69-ft.) pygmy blue whale, it presents both the familiar and the bizarre of New Zealand's natural inhabitants. **Mana Pasifika** explores how Pacific Island cultures have influenced and affected New Zealand. **On the Sheep's Back** examines the place of those friendly, woolly creatures in the lives of New Zealanders, often in a surprising and witty manner. **Passports** ★★ explores the migrant story of New Zealand in a fantastic exhibition and audiovisual presentation that is one of the highlights of the museum.

Spread over five levels, the museum includes much more and warrants at least half a day's exploration. It's playful, imaginative, bold, and more than impressive. It is an essential destination if you're keen to learn more about New Zealand. Few people leave unmoved. It's stunningly high-tech and loads of fun. On top of that, the architecture isn't bad, either.

Special guided tours must be prebooked. The 60-minute **Introducing Te Papa Tour** runs at 10:15am and on the hour to 3pm through summer (Nov 1–March 31), and twice daily at 10:15am and 2pm in winter. It costs NZ$10 (US$7) for adults and NZ$5 (US$3.50) for children. Request foreign-language guides at the time of booking. A self-guided tour booklet is available at the information desk for NZ$2 (US$1.40), an excellent investment.

Te Papa has two eateries: Te Papa Café serving excellent New Zealand cuisine; and Espresso Bar for coffee and snacks. It also has a superb gift shop, **Te Papa Store,** featuring original crafts and top Maori designs.

Cable St., on the Waterfront, Wellington. ℂ **04/381-7000**. Fax 04/381-7070. www.tepapa.govt.nz. Free admission; fees for some activities, guided tours, and short-term exhibitions. Interactive displays NZ$2–NZ$8 (US$1.40–US$5.60); children's rides NZ$8–NZ$10 (US$5.60–US$7). Daily 10am–6pm (Thurs till 9pm). Parking NZ$4 (US$2.80) per hour.

Wellington Cable Car ✸✸ *(Moments)*

This splendid little 4½-minute trip takes you to some of the best views you'll see anywhere. Pray for fine weather, as Wellington city and the harbor look spectacular from up here on a cloudless day. It's also the best way to access the Wellington Botanic Garden (see below); and there is a fine little Cable Car Museum (ℂ **04/475-3578;** www.cablecarmuseum.co.nz) at the top, detailing the 100-year history of the service. The museum has free admission and is open weekdays from 9:30am to 5pm and weekends and holidays from 10am to 4:30pm.

Cable Car Lane, 280 Lambton Quay (next to McDonald's) and Upland Rd., Kelburn, Wellington. ℂ **04/472-2199**. www.wellingtonnz.com/cablecar. Round-trip fare NZ$3.60 (US$2.50) adults, NZ$2 (US$1.40) children, NZ$10 (US$7) per family. Mon–Fri 7am–10pm; Sat 8:30am–10pm; Sun and holidays 9am–10pm. Car runs every 10 min., from the top and bottom at the same time.

Wellington Botanic Garden ✸✸

The Botanic Garden brochure and map available at the Wellington visitor center or Treehouse Visitor Centre within the gardens will help you make the most of your time in this leafy enclave. Established in 1868, the gardens have been managed by the Wellington City Council since 1891. They cover 25 hectares (62 acres), presenting a mix of protected native forest, conifer varieties, and plant collections with seasonal floral displays. The Lady Norwood Rose Garden is a colorful spectacle from November to May, with blooms flourishing in 106 formal beds. The Begonia House and Garden Café shows off tropical and temperate plants, including orchids and the main lily pond, and the Bolton Street Memorial Park includes the historic cemetery. The chapel is open daily from 10am to 4pm.

The **Carter Observatory** (ℂ **04/472-8167;** www.carterobservatory.org) is another key attraction within the gardens. This is your chance to see the wonders of the Southern Hemisphere's night sky. From November through April, it's open Sunday through Tuesday from 10am to 5pm, Wednesday through Saturday from 10am until late; from May through October, Sunday through Thursday 11am to 4pm, Friday through Saturday 11am until late.

Access to the gardens is from the Cable Car or Centennial entrance off Tinakori Rd., Thorndon, Wellington. ℂ **04/ 499-1400** for Treehouse Visitor Centre. www.wbg.co.nz. Free admission. Daily sunrise–sunset. No. 12 Karori Bus from Lambton Quay stops outside Founders entrance on Glenmore Rd. Parking available along Glenmore Rd. and in the public lot adjacent to the Lady Norwood Rose Garden.

Katherine Mansfield Birthplace ✸ *(Finds)*

Anyone of a literary bent will get a great deal of pleasure from a visit to Katherine Mansfield's restored birthplace. New Zealand's most distinguished author and a short-story writer of world renown, Mansfield was born into the Beauchamp family in 1888. She left Wellington at age 19 for Europe, where she kept company with the likes of Virginia Woolf, T. S. Eliot, and D. H. Lawrence. The Beauchamp house has been meticulously restored. If you're familiar with Mansfield's stories, you'll get a sense of what inspired them as you walk about the family home.

25 Tinakori Rd., Thorndon, Wellington. ℂ/fax **04/473-7268**. www.katherinemansfield.com. Admission NZ$6 (US$4.20) adults, NZ$4 (US$2.80) seniors and students, NZ$2 (US$1.40) children. Victorian teas by arrangement. Tues–Sun 9am–4pm. Closed Mon, Dec 25, and Good Friday. No. 14 Wilton Bus stops at nearby Park St.

Wellington Zoo ★★ (Kids) Wellington Zoo is renowned for its work with endangered species, such as the Sumatran tiger, chimpanzee, white-cheeked gibbon, and Malayan sun bear. It's also the only place in the capital to see the famous brown kiwi (the Kiwi House is open daily 10am–4pm) and the tuatara. The newest exhibit is the Tropical River Trail, which highlights a rainforest habitat, birdlife, and several species of primates. In February and March, look out for **Wild Summer Nights** ★★, when you can spend an evening at the zoo with a picnic (food outlets are available on the grounds) and listen to jazz or blues among the animals. Another new interactive feature is the **Close Encounters** ★★★, which offers the chance to hand feed a red panda (age requirement of over 6 years), a giraffe (over 7), the big cats (over 12), or to spend a full day with a zookeeper tending the animals (over 18).

200 Daniell St., Newtown, Wellington. ℂ 04/381-6755. Fax 04/389-4577. www.wellingtonzoo.com. Admission NZ$10 (US$7) adults, NZ$5 (US$3.50) children 3–16, NZ$30 (US$21) family; NZ$60–NZ$400 (US$42–US$280) for Close Encounters, bookings required. Daily 9:30am–5pm. Closed Dec 25. No. 10 or 23 bus to Newton Park from the railway station.

The Parliament Buildings ★★ New Zealand's Parliament Buildings are on Molesworth Street in the city center and include the distinctive beehive-shaped building that is the administrative headquarters. They reopened to the public in 1995 after undergoing a NZ$165-million refurbishment. You can visit Parliament daily free of charge. The 1-hour tours include the Edwardian neoclassical **Parliament House,** the Victorian-Gothic **Parliamentary Library,** and, if the group is not too large, the 1970s-style **Beehive.** If you want to see and hear history in the making, call first to check when the House is sitting. The Debating Chamber makes for fascinating spectator sport.

The refurbished buildings also present outstanding examples of New Zealand art. The most impressive of all is the spectacular work by Malcolm Harrison, which occupies the three-story height of the new Galleria. The Maori Affairs Select Committee Room, at the front of Parliament House, is another interesting feature, worth visiting for the remarkable carvings and weavings specially commissioned for it.

Across the road, the **Old Government Building** is also worth a look. It's the second-largest wooden building in the world and now houses the University Law Faculty. And since you're in the vicinity, you could also check out the **National Library of New Zealand,** 70 Molesworth St. (ℂ 04/474-3000; www.natlib.govt.nz). The ground-floor National Library Gallery showcases the art and history collections of the Alexander Turnbull Library and is open Monday through Friday from 9am to 5pm, Saturday from 9am to 4:30pm, and Sunday from 1 to 4:30pm. The **Alexander Turnbull Library,** in the same building, is the research wing of the National Library, specializing in New Zealand and the Pacific. Books, serials, recordings, manuscripts, and archives are on the first floor and newspapers on the lower ground floor. On the second floor, visitors can peruse files of photographs. Drawings, paintings, and maps are available for research by appointment.

Parliament Buildings, Molesworth St., Wellington. ℂ 04/471-9503. www.ps.parliament.govt.nz. Free admission. Tours given hourly Mon–Fri 10am–4pm; Sat 10am–3pm; Sun noon 3pm. Closed Dec 25, Dec 26, Good Friday, New Year's Day, Jan 2, and Waitangi Day (Feb 6). City Circular Bus stops at gates of Parliament.

MORE ATTRACTIONS

City Gallery Wellington ★★★ City Gallery has a reputation for challenging viewers with the best of contemporary visual art—everything from painting, sculpture, film, and video to industrial and graphic design and architecture. It's not everyone's

> ## (Tips Wellington for Free
>
> • **Take in the Scenery from Mount Victoria:** Take a leisurely drive to the top and enjoy the spectacular views in all directions, or allow an hour or so to walk up the well-marked tracks, enjoy the sights, and return down a different route.
> • **Savor Botanic Beauty:** Enjoy the lush greenbelt in the heart of the city. Check out the Carter Observatory and the sculptures in the gardens.
> • **Explore Te Papa:** Don't overlook the possibility that one visit to the stunning Te Papa National Museum of New Zealand simply may not be enough!
> • **Tour the Beehive:** Hope that a Parliamentary session coincides with your visit and stay and listen to the debates. Enjoy the artwork, too.
> • **Wander Along Oriental Parade:** Amble along the waterfront, enjoying the architecture, the cafes, the views, and the buzz of activity as Wellingtonians race past on in-line skates and bikes.
> • **Get Wet in the Bucket Fountain:** A popular city landmark since 1969 when it was unveiled as the centerpiece of the new Cuba Mall, the fountain surprises, soaks, and delights adults, children, and dogs alike.

cup of tea, but if you want to find out what's happening in the New Zealand world of contemporary art, it's one of the best places to start. The gallery has a fully licensed cafe, bar, and restaurant.

Civic Sq., 101 Wakefield St., Wellington. ℂ **04/801-3952.** Fax 04/801-3950. www.city-gallery.org.nz. Admission by donation; some international exhibitions may carry an entry charge. Daily 10am–5pm. Free exhibition tours every Sat–Sun at 2pm. Closed Dec 25.

The Dowse 🀫🀫🀫   If you found City Gallery a bit too intellectual (some people do), it will be well worth your while taking a trip out to the Dowse Art Museum, which has the best collection of New Zealand crafts art in the country. A varied and changing exhibition program features contemporary ceramics, jewelry, glass, textiles, wood, sculpture, and photography, most of it exceedingly pleasing to the eye.

45 Laings Rd., Lower Hutt. ℂ **04/570-6500.** Fax 04/569-5877. www.dowse.org.nz. Free admission; fees for some special exhibitions. Mon–Fri 10am–4pm; Sat–Sun and holidays 11am–5pm. Closed Dec 25. Situated 20km (12 miles) from Wellington city. Take the train to Waterloo Station and walk down Knights Rd. to the museum, or catch the Eastbourne/Big Red bus, which departs hourly from Courtenay Place to Queensgate.

Karori Wildlife Sanctuary 🀫🀫   Opened to the public at the beginning of 2001, this 252-hectare (623-acre) reservoir catchment is now a safe haven for native birds. Only minutes from the central city, it is now home to rare native wildlife such as kiwi, saddlebacks, and tuatara, which were reintroduced after all pests and predators had been removed from the valley. Enjoy a 1½-hour guided bush walk and learn about the history of the area as well as plans for the continuing development of this unique inner city greenbelt.

31 Waiapu Rd., Karori, Wellington. ℂ **04/920-9200.** Fax 04/920-9000. www.sanctuary.org.nz. Admission NZ$8 (US$5.60) adults, NZ$4 (US$2.80) children, NZ$20 (US$14) family. Guides and nocturnal tours at extra cost. Dec–Mar daily 10am–5pm; Apr–Nov Mon–Fri 10am–4pm, weekend and public holidays 10am–5pm. Closed Dec 25. Access is

Kids Especially for Kids

If you're ready to let the kids loose, head for **Capital E,** Civic Square, Victoria Street (© **04/913-3720**; www.capitale.org.nz), open daily from 10am to 5pm. This wonderful place combines a varied program of exhibitions, events, and theater especially designed for families. It's all about fun, entertainment, and education. Call for current programs and admission prices.

Lollipop's Playland & Café, Level 1, Wellington Trade Centre, Victoria and Ghuznee streets (© **04/384-4466**; www.lollipops.co.nz), is another inner city fantasyland that has been created to entertain children up to age 12. It has a merry-go-round, a model racetrack, indoor basketball, a bowling alley, dress-up clothes, climbing frames, and facilities for drawing and collage-making. Best of all is a maze of tubular staircases and slides that ends in a sea of over 11,000 plastic balls. Children need to be supervised, or you can hire a "playcarer" to make sure the kids are safe while you enjoy a break in the cafe. Admission is NZ$9 (US$6.30) for ages 4 to 11; NZ$6 (US$4.20) for ages 12 months to 23 months. They're open Monday through Friday 9:30am to 5:30pm and weekends 9:30am to 6pm.

Story Place, at Te Papa, Cable Street (© **04/381-7000**; www.tepapa.govt. nz), is a magical world of dress-ups, storytelling, songs, and art activities for children 5 years and under. There are daily 45-minute sessions from 10:15am to 4:30pm and admission is NZ$2 (US$1.40). Tickets can be purchased at Te Papa's Information Desk on Level 2 of the museum.

Older kids will get a buzz out of **Wet & Wild,** Frank Kitts Park, The Waterfront (© **04/235-9796**), where they can let loose on in-line skates, in paddleboats, or on water bikes. It's open daily December through February, weather permitting.

from Waiapu Rd. (turn left when emerging from the Karori side of the Karori Tunnel). Take Bus no. 12, 17, 18, 21, 22, or 23. Travel past the entrance to Waiapu Rd. Disembark at the first stop after Karori Tunnel. The Sanctuary is an easy 5-min. walk at the end of Waiapu Rd.

Museum of Wellington City & Sea   There's been a NZ$12.5-million (US$8.75-million) refurbishment at this newest of Wellington's museums, housed in a historic icon, the 1892 Bond Store. The history of the area is presented in six galleries with audiovisual displays, cinema screens, and traditional exhibitions of memorabilia and photographs. Make sure you see **Wahine Gallery,** which is a memorial to the 1968 marine tragedy in Cook Strait; and **A Millennium Ago,** where Maori legends are combined with special effects. If you want an intense glimpse into Wellington's past, this is the place to get it.

The Bond Store, Queens Wharf, Wellington. © **04/472-8904.** Fax 04/496-1949. www.museumofwellington.co.nz. Admission NZ$2 (US$1.40) per person. Tours every Sat at 11am. Daily 10am–5pm. Closed Dec 25. The City Circular bus stops here.

Pataka   This modern gallery, 15 minutes north of the city, in Porirua, celebrates the cultural diversity of the region. It showcases the very best of Maori, Pacific Island, and New Zealand art, all of which gives you excellent insights into the region's heritage. If you're interested, there's also a chance to buy a piece of New Zealand art from their very good sales gallery.

Corner Norrie and Parumoana sts., Porirua City. (C) **04/237-1511.** Fax 04/237-4527. www.pataka.org.nz. Admission free. Mon–Sat 10am–4:30pm; Sun 11am–4:30pm. Take the motorway heading north and exit at Porirua. Free parking.

ORGANIZED TOURS & CRUISES

If your time is limited, you'll get a comprehensive view of Wellington by booking with **Hammond's Wellington Sightseeing Tours** ⚶⚶ ((C) **04/472-0869;** www.wellington sightseeingtours.com). Their Wellington City Sights Tour covers the financial and commercial area, Parliament buildings, and Botanic Gardens; they go up to Mount Victoria lookout and then around the coastal bays, returning to the city via View Road. It costs NZ$45 (US$32) for adults and NZ$23 (US$16) for children. The Palliser Bay Seal Colony & Lord of the Rings Tour visits numerous filming sites such as Hobbiton Woods, Rivendell, and the Great River Anduin, and takes in terrific Wairarapa scenery. It costs NZ$160 (US$112) for adults and NZ$80 (US$56) for children. A light lunch is included. Wally and his son Lance run the operation, giving it a personalized flavor with good commentary. Their 2½-hour tours depart daily at 10am and 2pm.

Flat Earth ⚶⚶⚶ ((C) **0800/775-805** in NZ, or 04/977-5805; www.flatearth.co.nz) has a range of excellent specialty tours, including three Lord of the Rings options priced from NZ$275 (US$193) per person; Maori Treasures tours priced from NZ$220 (US$154) per person for a half-day; and excellent Capital Arts Tours that immerse you in the city's art and architecture for NZ$325 (US$228) for four people for half a day.

Zest Food Tours ⚶⚶⚶ ((C) **04/801-9198;** www.zestfoodtours.co.nz) is another excellent new business. Its Walking Gourmet (daily 9:30am–1pm) costs NZ$195 (US$137) per person and introduces you to the capital's lively food scene. Taste Wellington (daily 9:30am–3pm) costs NZ$500 (US$350) per person and includes coffee roasting, top specialty food stores, a wine-matched lunch at an award-winning restaurant, and a visit to the home of a local food writer. Tours can be tailored to specific interests.

Wellington Explorer Tour ((C) **0800/287-287** in NZ, or 04/478-8315; www.new lands.co.nz), run by Newlands Coach Service, offers a wider range of themed city tours: the Historic Capital, the Government Capital, and the Green, Cultural, Mythological, or Wild Capital. It has an excellent record of visitor satisfaction; guides are friendly and informative. **Day Trippa Tours** ((C) **04/970-0056;** www.daytrippa.co.nz) has daily tours departing Wellington at 10am for Nga Manu Nature Reserve and the Lindale Centre. As well as viewing native birds and reptiles, you get the chance to go shopping. The tours return at 4pm and cost NZ$99 (US$69) per person.

Seal Coast Safari ⚶⚶ ((C) **0800/732-527** in NZ, or 04/929-7839; www.sealcoast. com) offers a completely different outing that departs daily from the visitor center at 10:30am and 1pm. For NZ$69 (US$48) for adults, children half price, you'll spend 2¾ hours taking the coastal road to the seals at Red Rocks. **Walk Wellington** ⚶ ((C) **04/ 384-9590;** walkwellington@xtra.co.nz), on the other hand, gives you a fabulous introduction to the city. The Essential Wellington tour is NZ$20 (US$14) per person and departs from the Visitor Centre. Call (C) **04/802-4860** for bookings and departure times. If you feel like an airborne thrill, buzz through the city skies in a bright-red helicopter with **HeliPro** ⚶⚶, Shed 1, Queens Wharf ((C) **04/472-1550;**

www.helipro.co.nz). You can do the City Panorama for around NZ$75 (US$53) or the South Coaster spin for around NZ$135 (US$95) per person.

ON THE WATER

For a launch trip, contact **Shed 5** (© **04/499-9069;** www.shed5.co.nz), about cruising options priced NZ$45 to NZ$75 (US$32–US$53) per person; or Paul Gubb of **Sweet Georgia Cruising** (© **025/452-641**), which offers luxury charters with a gourmet galley and wine cellar.

Another option is a Somes Island excursion with the **Dominion Post Ferry** (see "Getting Around," earlier in this chapter). Simply take the ferry and stop off on the island, picking up a return ferry a few hours later. The island recently reopened to the public after 100 years of restricted access. In recent times, it has served as a quarantine station and before that as a prisoner-of-war camp. It has been replanted and developed as a wildlife refuge and has walking tracks and great views.

6 Outdoor Pursuits

ADVENTURE AVIATION   Experience the exhilaration of open-cockpit flying in a classic 1942 Tiger Moth biplane over the Kapiti Coast. Fly up to 1,050m (3,500 ft.), where you'll loop the loop and do barrel rolls and stall turns. Pay around NZ$150 (US$105) for 20 minutes of hair-raising aerobatics, or NZ$110 (US$77) for a more sedate coastal scenic flight. Contact **Kapiti Aero Club** (© **04/902-6536;** bj007@ paradise.net.nz).

CLIMBING   **Fergs Kayaks,** Queens Wharf (© **0800/333-999** in NZ, or 04/499-8898; www.fergskayaks.co.nz), has the largest indoor climbing wall in the country. Entry is from NZ$12 (US$8.40) for adults, NZ$8 (US$5.60) for children. It's open daily from 9am to 8pm, later in summer. Farther afield, **Top Adventures,** The Energy Centre, 453 Hutt Rd., Lower Hutt (© **04/589-9181;** www.topadventures.co.nz), is a great base for all sorts of energetic activity. Its climbing facility is great for beginners and experts. For casual visits, adults pay NZ$14 (US$9.80) and children up to 14 pay NZ$10 (US$7).

GOLF   There are a number of courses within 25 minutes of Wellington city. **Paraparaumu Beach Golf Club,** 376 Kapiti Rd., Paraparaumu Beach (© **04/298-4561**), is an 18-hole, par-71 course rated one of the top 50 courses in the world by *Golf Digest.* Greens fees are NZ$85 (US$60), club rental is NZ$35 (US$25), and carts are NZ$30 (US$21). Reserve well in advance. **Hutt Golf Club,** Military Road, Lower Hutt (© **04/567-4722**), is an 18-hole, par-70 course where you'll pay NZ$45 (US$32) for a round. Clubs are NZ$30 (US$21), a trundler or pull cart is NZ$10 (US$7), and a cart costs NZ$35 (US$25). **Karori Golf Club,** South Makara Road, Wellington (© **04/476-7337**), is an 18-hole, par-70 course; a round costs around NZ$30 (US$21) during the week and NZ$40 (US$28) on weekends. Clubs, including a trundler, are about NZ$25 (US$18).

IN-LINE SKATING   This is a great way to explore Oriental Parade. Skates can be hired from **Fergs Kayaks,** Queens Wharf (© **04/499-8898;** www.fergskayaks.co.nz), for NZ$12 (US$8.40) per hour. Daily rates available.

KAYAKING   **Fergs Kayaks,** Queens Wharf (© **04/499-8898;** www.fergskayaks. co.nz), is owned by New Zealand's legendary canoeist and Olympic gold medallist Ian Ferguson. You can either do the self-paddle thing for NZ$12 (US$8.40) per person per hour, or join a guided group. Try the night harbor tour, around NZ$50 (US$35) per person for 2½ hours of paddling, with soup and snacks at the end. **Tamarillo Sea-Kayaking,** Kapiti (© **025/244-1616;** fax 04/239-9789), offers a more remote, nature-based sea-kayak experience around Kapiti Island, one of New Zealand's most famous conservation reserves. Instruction is given to those with no previous experience. The all-day adventure includes a chartered launch trip to and from the island and costs around NZ$150 (US$105). Birders will love this one.

MOUNTAIN BIKING   This is one group that truly celebrates Wellington's hilly terrain. You have the choice of everything from a leisurely ride around the bays to a spine-chilling route that includes a vertical cliff face. For bike rentals, call **Pins Cycles,** Willis and Boulcott streets (© **04/472-4591**), or **Penny Farthing Cycles,** 89 Courtenay Place (© **04/385-2279**). **Marty Taylor** (© **025/498-560**), will set you up and take you to the best places, as will **Mud Cycles** (© **04/476-4961;** www.mud cycles.co.nz), which is next to Wellington's Mountain Bike Park in Karori. **Mountains To Sea Bike Adventures** (© **04/383-8130;** www.mikesbikes.co.nz) has tours for small groups of all fitness levels from wobbly beginners to thrill seekers.

SCUBA DIVING   Explore Wellington's unique underwater coastline with **Dive Spot,** 9 Marina View, Mana (© **04/233-8238;** www.divespot.co.nz), which offers training, rentals, and dive trips.

SWIMMING   The **Wellington Regional Aquatic Centre,** 62 Kilbirnie Crescent, Kilbirnie (© **04/387-8029**), has four heated pools: a lap pool, a learners' pool, and adjoining junior and toddler pools with an access ramp for people in wheelchairs. There are also diving facilities, Jacuzzis, saunas, a sun deck, a cafe, and a YMCA fitness center. The **Freyberg Pool,** 139 Oriental Parade (© **04/384-3107**), is an easy walk from most inner city accommodations.

TENNIS   The **Wellington Renouf Tennis Centre,** 20 Brooklyn Rd., Central Park (© **04/384-6294;** fitz@ihug.co.nz), has 14 outdoor courts and four indoor courts. It's open Monday through Friday from 6am to 11pm, Saturday and Sunday from 8am to 11pm. A cafe and bar are on the premises.

WALKING   There are endless walking opportunities in Wellington. The most obvious that spring to mind are a quiet amble through the **Botanic Gardens** or around **Oriental Parade,** or a more taxing climb up any one of the many **Mount Victoria** tracks. The visitor center has a wide range of excellent Heritage Trail brochures, which give you the chance to learn and discover as you go. They also have a terrific range of more than ten Explore Wellington brochures, which detail various themed walks in different areas of the city. Included is the popular Five Lunchtime Walks, all of 40 or 50 minutes duration within the central city area.

7 Shopping

Wellington is such a compact city that it's easy for visitors to find their way around and to wander at ease. You can pick up the free *Wellington Shopping Guide* and *The Fashion Map* at the visitor center. From the department and designer stores of Lambton Quay (nicknamed the Golden Mile) up Willis Street to the funkier side of town on Cuba Street, you'll find markets, alternative boutiques, secondhand stores, and great cafes. It's all easy and shopper-friendly. Store hours are usually Monday through Friday from 9am to 5:30pm, Saturday from 9am to 4:30pm, and Sunday from 10am to 2pm.

Tips Shopping for Souvenirs

The always-popular **Simply New Zealand,** 13 Grey St. (© **04/472-6817**), has a huge range of gifts, jewelry, and crafts as well as wool knitwear, Maori carvings, and America's Cup souvenirs. **Te Papa Store** ***, Te Papa, Cable Street (© **04/381-7000;** mail@tepapa.govt.nz), has one of the best selections of New Zealand arts, crafts, and souvenirs in the city. Everything is top quality and attractively laid out, and you don't pay local tax (GST) if you're mailing gifts overseas. **Art Works,** 117 Customhouse Quay (© **04/473-8581;** artworksnz@xtra.co.nz), is another great source of high-quality New Zealand arts and crafts. New on the scene and making an impression in two locations is **Ora** **, 58 Guthrie St., Lower Hutt (© **04/939-9630)** and 23 Allen St., City (© **04/384-4157;** www.ora.co.nz), open daily 9am to 4pm. Both galleries feature a comprehensive selection of top quality handmade New Zealand artworks in glass, fiber, ceramics, native timbers, and mixed media.

Other worthy places to browse top-notch arts, crafts, and jewelry are **Tamarillo,** 102–108 Wakefield St., opposite the visitor center (© **04/473-6095); Avid,** 48 Victoria St. (© **04/472-7703); Kura,** 19 Allen St. (© **04/802-4934;** www.kuragallery.co.nz); and **Vessel,** 87 Victoria St. (© **04/499-2321**). And for all things woolly, drive around the bays to **Sheepskin Warehouse,** Evans Bay Parade, Greta Point (© **04/386-3376;** fax 04/386-3379). New Zealand has the best technology in the world for sheepskin products, and if you doubt that, come here. An overseas shipping service is available and GST is deductible.

The best place to start is **Lambton Quay,** which has three linked arcades, and **Capital on Quay,** at 250 Lambton Quay (© **04/473-8868**). There are boutiques, a heap of shoe stores, music shops, and excellent bookstores. It's also where you'll find Wellington's most famous department store, **Kirkcaldie & Stains** (© **04/472-5899**), offering traditional service and quality merchandise since 1863. **Jumpers,** Harbour City Centre, Lambton Quay (© **04/499-9915**), has Wellington's largest range of New Zealand knitwear.

Look out for the NZ$20-million (US$14-million) redevelopment of the historic Bank of New Zealand building on Lambton Quay. It's now the **Old Bank Arcade & Chambers,** a stunning retail arcade after the style of Sydney's Queen Victoria Arcade. It has attracted interest from top national and international retail stores and includes cafes, restaurants, and designer clothing stores. **Vibrant Hand-knits,** Lee Andersen's Designer Gallery, Old Bank Arcade (© **04/472-8720**), has a unique collection of New Zealand-designed and -produced knitwear.

As you move onto **Willis Street,** you'll find more fashion, books, and music aplenty. Turn down **Manners Street** and make your way into the weird and wonderful **Cuba Street** area, which gets more interesting the higher up the mall you go. Look out for **Hemporium,** 151 Cuba St. (© **04/385-2907**), which sells everything made of hemp, including clothing. **Iko-Iko,** 144A Cuba St. (© **04/385-0977**), has kooky gifts for the people who think they have everything—an inflatable armchair, for

Tips **The Markets**

James Smith Market, Second Floor, 55 Cuba St., at Manners Street (© **04/ 801-8812**), features 25 shops open daily. You'll see African wares, New Zealand souvenirs, new and used clothing, crafts, palmistry and tattoos, tarot readings, a House of Magic, shoes, gifts, and plenty more. The **Wellington Market,** Taranaki and Wakefield streets (© **04/801-8991**), features everything old and new and resembles more the old-style marketplace, with collectibles, clothing, furniture, souvenirs, and a food court with lots of ethnic stalls. It's open Friday through Sunday and all public holidays from 10am to 5:30pm. And if you want fresh produce, head to the **Moore Wilson Fresh Food Market,** at Moore Wilson's on Lorne Street (© **04/384-9906**), where you'll find a wealth of organics, fish, flowers, breads, and other edibles. **Jackson Street Market,** corner of Jackson and Elizabeth streets, Petone (© **04/939-2811**) features fine goods and gourmet products and is held Sunday mornings from 9am to 1pm.

instance. If you want your future predicted, your sexual preferences catered to, your body pierced or tattooed, or simply a cup of damn good coffee, you're in the right area.

Another good specialty-store area is the **Tinakori Road Village.** Much more upmarket than Cuba Street, it's not overly big, just a few smart little gift stores, galleries, and the like. My favorite is **Millwood Gallery,** 291b Tinakori Rd., Thorndon (© **04/473-5178**), an art-and-book boutique filled to the gills with divine papery offerings. It specializes in original works of art based on Wellington and has a range of cards and gift wraps. Another goody here is **The Lily House,** 320 Tinakori Rd., Thorndon (© **04/499-3399**). It has fabulous displays of colorful New Zealand–made ceramics and all sorts of household and garden accessories.

8 Wellington After Dark

This is one city where you won't run out of things to do after dark. Start by checking the current issues of *Capital Times* and *What's On,* both free and available at visitor centers and many cafes.

THE PERFORMING ARTS

Wellington is home to the largest performing-arts festival in the country (see "Special Events," earlier in this chapter); it is also home to the National Orchestra and Opera, the Royal New Zealand Ballet, and four thriving professional theater companies. In addition, you'll find the National Dance and Drama Centre, the New Zealand School of Dance, and the New Zealand Drama School, all based in the capital.

A rejuvenated **Westpac St. James Theatre,** 77–83 Courtenay Place (© **04/802-4060;** www.stjames.co.nz), opened its doors in 1998 after a NZ$21-million (US$15-million) refurbishment project, and this fine Edwardian venue now combines a preserved heritage theater with state-of-the-art technology. Apart from staging top-quality musical shows, it is also the new and permanent home of the Royal New Zealand Ballet Company.

The city has a healthy professional theater scene. The **Downstage Theatre,** in Hannah Playhouse, Courtenay Place, corner of Cambridge Terrace (© **04/801-6946;**

www.downstage.co.nz), presents first-rate theater in an exciting, award-winning structure. Downstage's year-round season presents its own productions and the best touring shows, including classics, contemporary drama, comedy, and dance, with an emphasis on quality New Zealand works. Tickets are around NZ$35 (US$25) for most shows.

Circa Theatre, 1 Taranaki St. (© **04/801-7992;** www.circa.co.nz), sits grandly beside Te Papa. It produces quality and generally innovative productions. You can enjoy a preshow meal at its licensed cafe.

Bats Theatre, 1 Kent Terrace (© **04/802-4175;** www.bats.co.nz), is seen as the country's top developmental theater, presenting new and experimental plays and dance at great prices.

Embassy Theatre, 10 Kent Terrace (© **04/384-7657;** www.deluxe.co.nz), was refurbished for the world premiere of *The Lord of the Rings: The Return of the King*. The combination of sumptuous 1920s decor with a giant screen and state-of-the-art digital sound, not to mention its cafe and bar, makes it well worth a visit.

THE CLUB & BAR SCENE

It's simple: When it gets dark, the party starts, and again, the compact nature of the city is a blessing for those looking for a good time. There are late-night bars and dance venues aplenty, and if you want to bypass the quiet start and head straight for the action, then **Courtenay Place** it is. I have to say, though, that the large number of drunken youths in this area on Thursday, Friday, and Saturday nights is almost enough to put me off—almost. The reality is that there are enough bars in this part of town for all ages to find a comfortable niche, and anyone over 25 who has outgrown the vomiting-in-the-street trick need only look around for a place that suits his or her mood. Be warned though—the Wellington bar scene is ever-changing and venues listed here may have changed names and owners by the time you arrive.

The "in" places for the older crowd (that's 30 plus) are always changing, but you'll be safe if you start with **The Monkey Bar,** 25 Taranaki St. (© **04/802-5090**), which is a sleek lounge bar with a great cocktail list and live music Wednesday through Friday. It's actually under the also-trendy **Zibibbo,** 25–29 Taranaki St. (© **04/385-6550**), which inhabits the old central police building. You can get great Spanish-Italian food here along with sophisticated nightlife. **The Establishment,** 14–16 Courtenay Place (© **04/382-8654**), is pitched to the younger 20s to 30s crowd. It has an intimate lounge and bar upstairs, but downstairs it's all about dancing. Down the street is the very cool, and very sexy **Go Go,** upstairs at 26C Courtenay Place (© **04/384-4709**), also favored for its younger dance music scene.

Tips **A Night at the Movies**

All Wellington cinemas offer discounted tickets for daytime and Tuesday-night screenings. Students and seniors also get a discount. Look in the newspapers for schedules. Try the **Embassy Theatre,** 10 Kent Terrace (© **04/384-7657**), with a giant screen and a new sound system; **Hoyts Cinemas,** which has two multi-screen complexes in Manners Mall and Manners Street; or **Rialto Cinemas,** Cable Street and Jervois Quay (© **04/385-1864**), a three-theater complex. **Penthouse Cinema & Café,** 205 Ohiro Rd., Brooklyn (© **04/384-3157**), is the city's only suburban theater and draws a loyal local crowd.

Tips Beer Literacy

If you're a beer lover, Wellington will please you to no end. I'd start with **Tasting Room,** 2 Courtenay Place (© **04/384-1159**), which is New Zealand's tenth Monteith's Craft Beer Bar. They know all about creative beer and food matching. **Bodega,** 101 Ghuznee St. (© **04/384-8212**), is Wellington's original ale house serving the city's only hand-drawn ales. It has 17 different tap beers and a massive selection of imports. **Shed 22 Brewing Co.,** corner of Taranaki and Cable streets (© **04/381-2282**), has great harbor views and you can sit back and see why these beers are international award winners. **The Courtenay Arms,** 26–32 Allen St. (© **04/385-6908**), is a real English ale house with premium imported British ales on tap.

One of the coolest new places to be seen at is the very posh **Arbitrageur** ✵✵✵, 125 Featherston St. (© **04/499-5530**), where you'll find sophisticated club style, over 60 of the best wines, and an interior that will win over any wine purist's heart. It's open Monday through Thursday from 11:30am to 9pm and Friday 11:30am until 10pm.

Mini Bar, 24 Courtenay Place (© **04/801-5015**), is a good, stylishly retro place to meet before heading off elsewhere. **Motel** ✵✵✵, Forrester's Lane (© **04/382-8585**), has also gone the retro way, creating an exotic mood that includes sculptures and oriental lamps. It's very suave and runs adjacent to the ever-popular Chow restaurant.

Molly Malones, Taranaki Street and Courtenay Place (© **04/384-2896**), is the biggest and busiest Irish bar in town, with live music every weekend. Also in this area is the hugely popular **Coyote,** 63 Courtenay Place (© **04/385-6665**), which attracts a mixed and generally rowdy crowd.

At the other end of town, **Shed 5,** Queens Wharf (© **04/499-9069**), is the Friday-night meeting spot for the business crowd; and **Diva,** 37 Dixon St. (© **04/385-2987**), is favored by those looking for a quiet start to the evening. There are also interesting bar and dance choices in the Cuba and Willis streets area, which tend to be a bit less concerned with fashion and making an appearance.

THE GAY SCENE

The visitor center has folders full of information related to the gay scene, including gay-friendly accommodations and nightspots other than those listed here. **Pound Club,** Level 1, Oaks Complex, Dixon Street (© **04/384-6024**), is a popular meeting place with lounge bar, night club, and regular shows. **Sanctuary,** Courtenay Place (© **04/384-1565**), is a men's cruise club open Tuesday through Sunday from 8pm. Gay women looking for a place to meet others should head for **Girlszone,** held in the Pound Club every Tuesday night. There's a gay sauna at **Checkmate,** 20 Garrett St. (© **04/385-6556**), and another at **Wakefield Health Club,** 15 Tory St. (© **04/385-4400**). If you want to find out more about the gay scene, call the **Gay Switchboard** (© **04/473-7878**). The line is open nightly from 7:30 to 10pm for information and support. **Gay Line Wellington** (www.gayline.gen.nz) is also a useful first stop. **Lesbian Line** (© **04/499-5567**) operates Tuesday, Thursday, and Saturday, 7:30pm to 10pm, offering information on accommodations, sporting events, and counseling services.

9 A Side Trip to Wairarapa ★★★

Don't be fooled by the quiet rural exterior and quaint, sleepy villages; there's a lot happening in the Wairarapa. This is the place of wine, warmth, and more wine. And we're not talking hobby vineyards—Wairarapa is home to some of the world's finest boutique vineyards, and built around that draw card is the biggest array of boutique accommodations you'll find anywhere in New Zealand.

Just over an hour's drive from Wellington across the winding Rimutaka Hills (take care driving in winter), you'll find a spread of productive farmland hemmed in by the rugged Tararua Ranges to the west and the dramatic Pacific Ocean to the east.

Twenty years ago, Wellingtonians scarcely gave Wairarapa a second look; now it's one of their hottest weekend getaway spots. Most of the activity is centered on **Martinborough,** and here's where you'll find the biggest changes. Hong Kong businessman Mike Laven bought the old **Martinborough Hotel** (p. 311) and turned it on its head. It's now one of the premier accommodations in the area. Not content to rest on his laurels, our Mr. Laven simply picked up the old Station Hotel in **Masterton,** a little farther north, moved it to Martinborough, and turned it into a restored office, retail, and wine complex.

It's entrepreneurial action and foresight such as these that have seen Martinborough and its southern neighbors, **Featherston** and **Greytown,** really take off. Wharekauhau Country Estate at Palliser Bay is a stunning addition to the Small Luxury Hotels of the World group, and there are new shops, cafes, and lodgings opening all the time. The **Toast Martinborough Wine, Food & Music Festival** attracts over 9,000 fans every year, the Martinborough Craft Fair is an annual favorite, and there are numerous outdoor activities to keep you amused if you ever run out of wine to taste.

ESSENTIALS

GETTING THERE   From central Wellington, take the northern motorway, driving around the harbor toward Lower Hutt, and follow the signs to Wairarapa. Once on this route, you head over the Rimutaka Hills and arrive in Featherston, the southernmost village in Wairarapa, around 1½ hours later.

If you're entering the area from the north, it takes 3 hours from Napier and 1 hour from Palmerston North to reach Masterton. Flying to Martinborough from Wellington by helicopter takes just 15 minutes.

VISITOR INFORMATION   In Masterton, the **Masterton Visitor Centre,** 316 Queen St. (© **06/370-0909;** fax 06/378-8451; www.wairarapanz.com), is open daily and should be your first stop. If you're not intending to drive the extra 30 minutes north from Featherston/Martinborough, check out the office at 18 Kitchener St., Martinborough (© **06/306-9043;** martinborough@wairarapanz.com).

EXPLORING THE AREA

About 27km (17 miles) north of Masterton on State Highway 2, **Pukaha Mount Bruce National Wildlife Centre** ★★ (©/fax **06/375-8004;** www.mtbruce.doc.govt. nz) is New Zealand's main center for the captive breeding of endangered species. Wheelchair-accessible walkways wind through rainforest and aviaries where threatened birds such as the kiwi and stitchbird are making a comeback. Make your first stop the excellent audiovisual display, which will help you understand what the center is all about, and then pick up the free walkway guide. Admission is NZ$8 (US$5.60) for adults and free for children. Guided walks are NZ$15 (US$11) per

---

Tips **A Word on ATMs**

There are no automatic teller machines in Martinborough, so come with enough cash to last your stay.

---

person, or NZ$45 (US$32) for a family. It's open daily from 9am to 4:30pm; the eels are fed at 1:30pm and the kaka (native parrots) at 3pm.

The artistically minded might like to investigate **Aratoi-Wairarapa Museum of Art & History,** Bruce and Dixon streets, Masterton (© 06/370-0001; www.aratoi. co.nz), which is open daily from 10am to 4:30pm, showcasing local talent.

Fifteen minutes from Martinborough, you'll find **Kahutara Canoes** (© 06/308-8453; www.wairarapa.co.nz/kahutara), where John and Karen McCosh offer a variety of trips on the scenic Ruamahanga River. Canoes range from large Canadian craft down to one- and two-person kayaks. Trips last from 1 to 5 hours and cost from NZ$40 (US$28) adults and NZ$15 (US$11) children for a half-day excursion. John is likely to introduce you to his **Taxidermy Gallery,** a log cabin containing a veritable zoo of animals that no longer need feeding—everything from lions and tigers to alligators, deer, turtles, and birds.

Heading south toward Cape Palliser, look out for **Putangirua Pinnacles** ☆☆☆ , a world-class example of badlands erosion. The pinnacles were formed in the past 120,000 years by heavy rain eroding an ancient gravel deposit, and it's worth the 30-minute walk off the road to see these spectacular formations. Quite eerie, and great photographic material. Farther around the coast, you'll find the cute fishing village of **Ngawi** and the country's largest breeding area for **New Zealand fur seals.**

The **Hau Nui Wind Farm,** New Zealand's first commercial wind farm, is 21km (13 miles) southeast of Martinborough on White Rock Road. Seven huge turbines are spaced along a 540m (1,771-ft.) ridge and make a dramatic silhouette against the skyline. The site itself is not open to the public, but you can check out a viewing area with information about the project.

Patuna Chasm Walkway (© 06/306-9966; www.patunafarm.co.nz), 17km (11 miles) from Martinborough, is the region's best natural attraction. A 4-hour tramp through farm and bush takes you to a fascinating limestone gorge filled with fossils, ferns, stalactites, waterfalls, and eels. Your guide will show you the best swimming spots, so bring your swimsuit, sturdy shoes, and spare clothes. The walk is open October through April and costs around NZ$30 (US$21) for adults, NZ$20 (US$14) for children. Bookings are essential. You'll find an adventure ropes course and horse trekking at the same base.

More adventures can be found with **McLeod Quad Adventures,** Hautotara, Martinborough (© 0800/494-335 or 06/306-8846; www.mcleodsadventures.co.nz), which offers quad-bike journeys across farmland and through rivers and bush. A 2½-hour trip costs around NZ$120 (US$84) one person per bike; NZ$30 (US$21) per pillion passenger. Reservations are essential.

If walking is your thing, consider the 3-day **Tora Coastal Walk** (© 06/307-8115 or 06/307-8862; www.toracoastalwalk.co.nz), which takes you through native bush and river valleys, staying at a different hill-country farm each night. It costs around NZ$160 (US$112), which includes accommodations and luggage cartage. It's open from October 1 through April 30 and bookings are essential.

There are also numerous fine **gardens** in the Wairarapa. The visitor center's *Wairarapa Escape Planner* lists great gardens along with other attractions of the region. The *Garden Trails* brochure lists 10 South Wairarapa gardens.

The Wairarapa is also a major orchard area. If you feel like fresh fruit while you're in Greytown, go to **Murphys Orchard,** 67 Reading St. (© **06/304-9551**), which produces nectarines, apricots, peaches, and 14 plum varieties in January and February; **Palmers Berryfruit Gardens,** Main Road North (© **06/304-9125**), which grows almost every berry fruit you can name; and **Pinehaven Orchards,** Udy Street (© **06/304-9699**), home to the now-famous Gala apple variety, developed in the 1940s.

THE WINERIES

The high sunshine hours and low autumn rainfall of the Martinborough region have been major factors in the international success of the small boutique wineries in this area. It is distinguished from other New Zealand wine areas by the high proportion of red-wine grape plantings and by its reputation for quality pinot noir. Most wineries are open for tastings while stocks permit, and some are open year-round. There are over 25 vineyards in the Martinborough area alone, and large tracts of grapes have also been planted at Gladstone and Masterton. The best time to visit is from late October to early March, when new wine stocks have been released. To find out more about winemaking in this region, go to www.nzwine.com. Conducted group tours to area wineries can be made only by prior arrangement. Contact the Martinborough visitor center (© **06/306-9043**), which can also supply the free brochure *Martinborough & Wairarapa Wine Trails.*

When it comes to selecting the best of the bunch, it's pretty subjective, but local opinion consistently swings in the direction of **Dry River Wines,** Puruatanga Road, Martinborough (© **06/306-9388;** fax 06/306-9275), a small low-tech winery specializing in the Alsace varietals pinot gris, Gewürztraminer, and Riesling as well as chardonnay, pinot noir, and sauvignon blanc. The majority of its wines are sold by mail order within a few weeks of release, so it's unlikely you'll find the place open.

Ata Rangi Vineyard, Puruatanga Road, Martinborough (© **06/306-9750;** www. atarangi.co.nz), makers of an internationally acclaimed pinot noir, has been operating for almost 22 years. It has an excellent tasting room for sampling the flagship pinot noir along with celebre, chardonnay, and a summer rosé.

Palliser Estate Wines, Kitchener Street, Martinborough (© **06/306-6019;** www.palliser.co.nz), is a leading force in this area. It produces award-winning pinot noir, chardonnay, sauvignon blanc, and Riesling. Wines are produced under the Palliser Estate and Pencarrow labels. Palliser is open daily for cellar sales.

Martinborough Vineyard, Princess Street, Martinborough (© **06/306-9955;** www.martinborough-vineyard.co.nz), was one of the original four vineyards in the area. It's open daily from 11am to 5pm for tasting and is dedicated to producing pinot noir, chardonnay, Riesling, sauvignon blanc, and pinot gris. Its star is the award-winning pinot noir.

Te Kairanga, Martins Road, Martinborough (© **06/306-9122;** www.tkwine.co. nz), open daily from 10am to 5pm, is one of the most popular vineyards. It produces a wide range, including pinot noir, chardonnay, cabernet sauvignon, and sauvignon blanc.

Others worth visiting are the very pretty **Gladstone Vineyard,** Gladstone Road, RD2, Carterton (© **06/379-8563;** www.gladstone.co.nz), which has weekend lunches between November and March; **Margrain Vineyard,** Ponatahi Road, Martinborough

Quirky Shopping

The **Paua Shell Factory Shop,** 54 Kent St., Carterton (✆ **06/379-6777;** www.pauashell.co.nz), is an attraction in its own right. It gets over 50,000 visitors a year and has a huge range of jewelry and souvenirs at factory prices. It's open daily and there are factory tours and video presentations to enjoy. **Martinborough Cheese Shop,** 8 Kitchener St., Martinborough (✆ **06/306-8383),** features specialty cheeses and local delicacies, including wines and olive oils, and is open daily from 10am to 5pm. **Saratoga Dairy Goats,** Caveland Road, Gladstone, Masterton (✆ **06/372-7074;** www.saratoga.co.nz), produces handcrafted goat cheeses, while **Kingsmeade Cheese,** Olivers Road, Masterton (✆ **06/377-5252;** www.kingsmeadecheese.co.nz), is the medal-winning maker of sheeps' milk cheese. **Olivo Olive Grove,** Hinakura Road, Martinborough (✆ **06/306-9074),** has award-winning extra virgin and infused olive oils, with tastings and sales most weekends.

(✆ **06/306-9292;** www.margrainvineyard.co.nz), with a rather divine villa accommodations; and **Walnut Ridge Vineyard,** 159 Regent St., Martinborough (✆/fax **06/306-9323;** www.walnutridge.co.nz).

Martinborough Wine Centre, in Martinborough Village (✆ **06/306-9040;** www.martinboroughwinecentre.co.nz), represents 30 of the region's 40 vineyards. If you're short on time, or visiting out of the main wine season, this is the perfect place to get a comprehensive overview. Tastings cost NZ$10 to NZ$12 (US$7–US$8.40) per person. A delightful cafe/delicatessen and retail store are on-site. Every Sunday from 10am to 2pm, the center stages the **Martinborough Country Market**—the perfect place for wines, breads, organic produce, fish, local cheeses, preserves, and much more. If you're interested in wine tours of this region, contact **Five Star Tours,** Wellington (✆ **04/479-1356;** fax 04/479-6403), who offer a day tour (including lunch), for around NZ$150 (US$105) per person. A half-day tour is NZ$95 (US$67).

MUSEUM MANIA

Nowhere have I come upon so many museums, covering such a wide variety of themes. Here are a few for you to investigate. The **Fell Locomotive Museum,** Fitzherbert Street, Featherston (✆ **06/308-9779;** fell.loco.museum@xtra.co.nz), houses the only remaining Fell engine in the world. It's open daily 10am to 4pm. Admission is NZ$4 (US$2.80) adults, NZ$2 (US$1.40) children, NZ$10 (US$7) family. Next door is the **Heritage Complex** (✆ **06/308-9458),** which displays early settler memorabilia and the Japanese POW camp history. It's open daily 10am to 4pm; entry is by donation.

Ken Burgiss's **Memorabilia Museum,** 5 Woodward St., Featherston (✆ **06/308-9352),** features cameras, toys, moneyboxes, bottles, and more. **Mainly Military Museum,** at the corner of Daniell and Revans streets, Featherston (✆ **06/308-6336;** ivank@xtra.co.nz), has a display of wartime memorabilia. It's open Saturday and Sunday from 10:30am to 3pm and by appointment.

Cobblestones Museum, 169 Main St., Greytown (✆ **06/304-9687),** has historic displays and a blacksmith's shop. It's open daily from 9am to 4:30pm. Admission is around NZ$5 (US$3.50) for adults, NZ$3 (US$2.10) for children. **Martinborough**

Colonial Museum, The Square, Martinborough (© **06/306-9736**), is open Saturday and Sunday from 2 to 4pm. Admission is by donation.

Mount Bruce Pioneer Museum, 18km (11 miles) north of Masterton on State Highway 2 (© **06/372-5859;** h.christensen@xtra.co.nz), is Wairarapa's largest working museum with over 3,000 items on display. It's open daily from 9am to 5pm; admission is NZ$5 (US$3.50) for adults. The **Pointon Collection of Cars & Costume,** No. 2 McKinstry Rd., Te Ore Ore, Masterton (© **06/378-6710;** www. pointoncollection.co.nz), has displays of vintage and veteran cars, tools, and vintage costumes. It's open daily from 10am to 4pm.

WHERE TO STAY

You'll be spoiled for choice here. This region is one of the best in the country when it comes to terrific accommodations. There are over 100 self-contained cottages alone, most of them cute as buttons. There are endless numbers of homestays and several top-quality upmarket options as well. The visitor center has two excellent booklets, *A Taste of Greytown* and *Martinborough Accommodation.*

As well as the very expensive listing below, you'll find superb lodgings at **Longwood** 👌👌, Longwood Road, Featherston (© **06/308-8289;** www.longwood.co.nz). Longwood is a rare experience in what is reputably New Zealand's largest private home, set in parklike gardens. The huge en-suite bedrooms and three divine cottages within the grounds are a must-visit. Lodge rooms are around NZ$900 (US$630), which includes dinner, bed, and breakfast; cottages are from NZ$150 (US$105) bed-and-breakfast plus NZ$50 (US$35) each extra person.

The 12.5% GST is included in the rates below.

VERY EXPENSIVE

Wharekauhau Country Estate 👌👌👌   Set amid 2,000 hectares (5,000 acres) of a working sheep station, this little piece of paradise sits in splendid isolation overlooking the rugged seas of Palliser Bay. It's highly rated by Andrew Harper (www.andrew harpertravel.com), among others, and you'll be paying top dollar for the sublime comforts of a cottage suite with all the best trimmings—big four-poster beds, dressing room, luxurious bathrooms with great views, and private verandas. It's a member of Small Luxury Hotels of the World and has won several New Zealand Tourism Awards. This is warmth, elegance, and style at its best. You'll be pleased you went the distance.

Western Lake Rd., Palliser Bay, RD3, Featherston. © **06/307-7581.** Fax 06/307-7799. www.wharekauhau.co.nz. 18 units. From NZ$1,879–NZ$1,946 (US$1,315–US$1,362) cottage suites; from NZ$4,612 (US$3,228) 2-bedroom Chateau Wellington, from NZ$6,497 (US$4,548) 3 bedrooms; from NZ$1,772 (US$1,240) Wharepapa 3-bedroom cottage. Cottage suite rates include breakfast, predinner drinks and canapés, 4-course gourmet dinner. Off-peak rates and special deals available. AE, DC, MC, V. Closed mid-July for 3 weeks. **Amenities:** Bar; heated indoor pool; all-weather tennis court; gym; outdoor Jacuzzi; free bikes; concierge; tour bookings; car rentals; massage; babysitting; laundry service; nonsmoking rooms; foreign-currency exchange; access for travelers w/disabilities. *In room:* TV on request, dataport, minibar, fridge, coffeemaker, hair dryer, iron.

MODERATE TO INEXPENSIVE

In Greytown, you'll find good rooms at **Kuratawhiti Bed & Breakfast,** 40 Kuratawhiti St. (© **06/304-9942;** www.kuratawhiti.co.nz). Also in Greytown, you'll find four delightful rooms at **Westwood** 👌👌, 82 West St. (© **06/304-8510;** www. westwood.greytown.co.nz), priced from NZ$195 to NZ$$250 (US$137–US$175). But the star in Greytown is without a doubt **The White Swan** 👌👌👌 , Main Street (© **06/304-8894;** www.thewhiteswan.co.nz), which has eight stunning rooms that you won't want to leave. Rates range from an unbelievably reasonable NZ$130 to NZ$260 (US$91–US$182).

Literally dozens of superb self-contained cottages are listed at the visitor center.

Peppers Martinborough Hotel *&&* This old beauty has been given a new life and a brush of contemporary interior design. It's a favorite weekend spot with Wellingtonians and a fine place to base yourself for vineyard exploration. Each of the large guest rooms has a different decor. There are nine units in the main hotel building and seven luscious new rooms in the garden courtyard; all have excellent bathrooms and king-size beds. The upstairs units in the main hotel open onto the balcony and have outdoor seating; the Riddiford and the Weld rooms are especially charming. The courtyard rooms are bigger and more modern; of these, my favorites are the Barton and Sheko.

The Square, Martinborough. © **06/306-9350.** Fax 06/306-9345. www.peppers.co.nz. 16 units. NZ$285 (US$203). Off-peak rates and special wine-escape packages available. Rates include breakfast. AE, DC, MC, V. **Amenities:** Restaurant; 2 bars; nearby golf course and tennis courts; tour bookings; car rentals; babysitting; dry cleaning; nonsmoking rooms; access for travelers w/disabilities. *In room:* A/C in some rooms, TV, dataport, minibar, fridge, coffeemaker, hair dryer, iron.

WHERE TO DINE

The Slow Food Café & Restaurant *&&*, 290 High St., Masterton (© **06/377-5100**), is a welcome addition to the sleepy culinary scene of Masterton. It has great wood-fired pizzas and tasty dishes cooked according to slow food principles. It's open daily from 9am till late. **Café Cecille** *&&*, Queen Elizabeth Park, Masterton (© **06/370-1166**), has a great reputation for its good service and lamb and beef dishes. Set in the middle of a leafy park, it's open Monday through Friday, 10am until late, and weekends 9am until late.

Main Street Deli Café *&&*, 88 Main St., Greytown (© **06/304-9022**), is open daily for all meals and continues to attract a team of happy regulars. Across the road you'll find a fabulous array of baked goods and good coffee at **The French Baker** *&&*, 81 Main St., Greytown (© **06/304-9569**); and Salute, 83 Main St., Greytown (© **06/304-9825**), serves up consistently good Mediterranean-style food. It's open Tuesday through Sunday from noon. Another local favorite is **Lilac Dining Room,** White Swan Country Hotel, Main Street, Greytown (© **06/304-8894**), which is open for breakfast, lunch, and dinner.

Just out of Featherston village, **The Tin Hut** *&&*, State Highway 2, Tauherenikau (© **06/308-9697**), gets rave reviews from the locals for its excellent pub-style fare in a revamped interior.

The Village Café, The Wine Centre, Kitchener Street, Martinborough (© **06/306-8814**), serves up tasty food and some of the region's best wine and cheeses. Don't overlook the divine meals at **The Bistrot** *&&&*, Martinborough Hotel (© **06/306-9350**). You'll also want to consider the new **French Bistro** *&&*, 3 Kitchener St., Martinborough (© **06/306-8863**), which is a small, charming spot with a menu that changes daily. **Est** *&&&*, Memorial Square, Martinborough (© **06/306-9665**), is another culinary gem that shouldn't be missed. It has an innovative menu and a great wine list; it's open Wednesday through Sunday, 11am until late.

12

Marlborough & Nelson

So, here you are on the South Island—the Mainland—home to 900,000 people. (Over 2,700,000 live on the North Island and two-thirds of them north of Taupo, so there will be days when you think you have the huge and spectacular South Island all to yourself.) There's less traffic here, but you'll be traveling greater distances between major towns, and when you arrive at a few places, you may well think you have stepped back in time.

The stunning southern landscape—big, majestic, unforgiving—is dominated by the central spine of the Southern Alps, and anyone who lives here has enormous respect for its grandeur. You'll soon see why.

If you cross over from Wellington on the Cook Strait ferry, your introduction to the south will be at Picton, which sits at the head of the beautiful Marlborough Sounds. Nearby is Blenheim, at the heart of Marlborough's famous winemaking province. To the west lies Nelson, the sunniest place in New Zealand and home to more vineyards, fine beaches, and the most accessible concentration of top artists and craftspeople in the country.

The greater Nelson province is geographically made up of five distinct areas, each with its own character: Nelson-Richmond, the urban heart; Motueka, the horticultural heartland; Abel Tasman National Park, a paradise of bush-wrapped beaches and crystal-clear waters; Golden Bay, heaven cast between two great national parks; and St. Arnaud–Murchison, an alpine-lakes area in the heart of Nelson Lakes National Park.

1 Picton & Blenheim ★★

Picton: 146km (91 miles) E of Nelson; Blenheim: 117km (73 miles) SE of Nelson

Picton and Blenheim are the two main towns of Marlborough province, an area best known as New Zealand's largest and most spectacular wine region. Both townships are quiet and easygoing. Blenheim, the larger of the two, has a population of 25,000. Picton, a quaint waterfront village at the head of Queen Charlotte Sound, has a population of just 3,600, and its main claim to fame is that it's the arrival point for ferries from Wellington. Unfortunately, many travelers think that's the end of its attributes, when in fact it is also the stepping-off point for the unspoiled tranquil charms of the Marlborough Sounds. With over 1,500km (930 miles) of shoreline, the sounds—Queen Charlotte, Kenepuru, and Pelorus—are ideal for sailing, kayaking, fishing, and bush walking. You'd be silly to miss them.

ESSENTIALS

GETTING THERE & GETTING AROUND   By Plane   Air service to Picton from Wellington is provided by **Soundsair** (✆ **0800/505-005** in NZ; www.soundsair.com). **Air New Zealand Link** (✆ **0800/737-000**) flies into nearby Blenheim. The Picton Airport (also known as Koromiko Airport) is approximately a 10-minute drive from Picton's town center. The Blenheim Airport is 10km (6 miles) from the town center. **Marlborough Shuttle Services** (© **03/572-9910**) provides airport and ferry transfers in Picton and Blenheim.

By Train   The TranzCoastal provides daily rail service between Picton and Christchurch. The trip takes about 5½ hours. Contact **Tranz Scenic** (© **0800/872-467** in NZ; www.tranzscenic.co.nz) for more information.

By Coach (Bus)   Coach service into both Picton and Blenheim is provided by **Inter-City** (© **09/913-6100**). The trip from Christchurch takes 5 hours; from Nelson, 2 hours. Picton, and Kaikoura farther south, are both included in the routes of **Magic Travellers** (© **09/358-5600**) and **Kiwi Experience** (© **09/366-9830**).

By Car   Most rental-car companies request that you turn in one car in Wellington (on the North Island) and pick up a new one in Picton. However, you can take cars and campers on the ferry should the need arise. If you're driving from Nelson, the trip takes about 2 hours; from Christchurch, 4 to 5 hours.

By Ferry   For timetables and information on the **Interislander,** call © **0800/802-802.** For information on **Strait Shipping** ferries, call © **0800/844-844.** See also "Arriving" under "Orientation" in chapter 11.

By Water Taxi   Picton doesn't have a local bus system, but water taxis from the **Cougar Line** (© **0800/504-090** in NZ, or 03/573-7925; www.cougarlinecruises. co.nz) provide regular service throughout Queen Charlotte Sound. **Endeavour Express** (© **03/573-5456;** www.boatrides.co.nz) also has regular service; or call **West Bay Water Transport** (© **03/573-5597;** www.westbay.co.nz) each way.

By Taxi   **Blenheim Taxis** (© **0800/802-225** or 03/578-0225) serves Blenheim, Picton, and the Sounds. It has cars, 10-seater vans, and a wheelchair hoist available.

ORIENTATION   It's difficult to get lost in Picton. The town faces Queen Charlotte Sound and the small shopping area is centered on High Street. London Quay runs along the foreshore, with the ferry terminal at one end and the town wharf at the other.

Blenheim is not quite so straightforward, despite its small size. Its layout has always puzzled me and no matter how many times I visit, I always go around in circles. Be sure to pick up a map at the visitor center!

VISITOR INFORMATION   The **Picton i-Site Visitor Centre,** The Foreshore, Picton (© **03/520-3113;** fax 03/573-5021; www.destinationmarlborough.com), is in the same building as the **Department of Conservation** (the latter only in the building Oct–Apr), and is open daily 8:30am to 6pm in summer, 8:30am to 5pm in winter. The Blenheim office is at The Railway Station, Sinclair Street, State Highway 1, Blenheim (© **03/577-8080;** fax 03/577-8079). It's open December to March from 8:30am to 6pm, and weekends from 9am to 5pm; March to November, it's open weekdays from 8:30am to 5pm, and weekends from 9am to 4pm.

Other useful websites: www.marlborough.co.nz, www.picton.co.nz, www. marlborough4fun.co.nz (for events listings), and www.marlboroughweb.com.

EXPLORING BLENHEIM & PICTON
WET ADVENTURES: GETTING OUT ON THE WATER
It's not a question of *whether* you'll go out on the water in Marlborough Sounds, but rather *which* vessel you'll be on. The ferries from Wellington provide a good introductory view as they make their way toward Picton, but for a closer look you'll need to

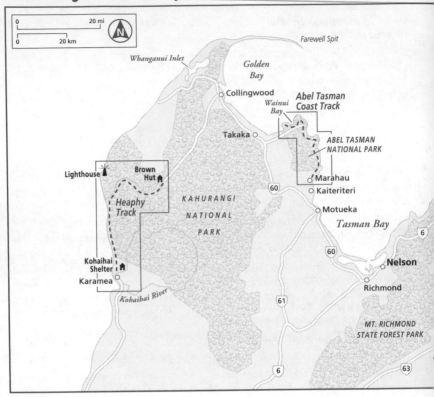

go out on a smaller, more specialized boat. The **Cougar Line,** The Waterfront, Picton (© **0800/504-090** in NZ, or 03/573-7925; www.cougarlinecruises.co.nz), has a range of cruise options in Queen Charlotte Sound. If your time is limited, take the short cruise, which departs from Picton at 10am and returns at 1:30pm. Also offered are a twilight cruise during peak season and a popular cruise-and-walk option to suit all levels of fitness. All day tours cost NZ$58 (US$41) per person.

Another option is the 4-hour **Queen Charlotte Sound Mail Run Cruise** operated by **Beachcomber Cruises,** London Quay, Picton (© **03/573-6175;** www.beach combercruises.co.nz). Or try the **Pelorus Mail Run** (© **03/574-1088;** www.mail-boat.co.nz), which departs Tuesday, Thursday, and Friday from Havelock at 9:30am and costs around NZ$95 (US$67) for adults, free for children. Tea and coffee is supplied, but bring your lunch. A courtesy coach is available to and from Picton.

Sea kayaking is one of the best ways to get intimate and up close to the Sounds. I had my first-ever kayaking experience here and now I'm hooked. Two recommended outfitters to go with are **Sea Kayaking Adventure Tours,** Anakiwa Road, RD1, Picton (© **0800/262-5492** in NZ, or 03/574-2765; www.nzseakayaking.com), which has day trips from NZ$85 (US$60); and **Marlborough Sounds Adventure Company** ✶✶✶ , London Quay, Picton (© **0800/283-283** in NZ, or 03/573-6078; www.marlboroughsounds.co.nz). The latter company is the larger of the two and has more

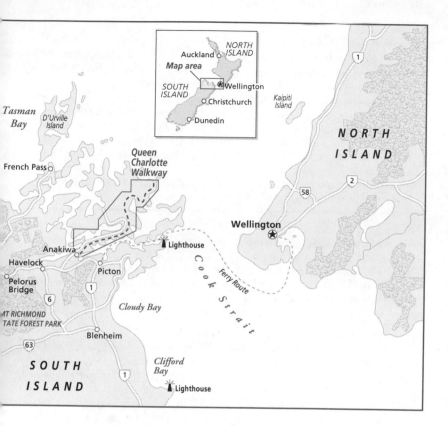

In the inset map:

SOUTH ISLAND

NORTH ISLAND

Auckland

Map area

Wellington

Kaipiti Island

Christchurch

Dunedin

Main map labels:

Tasman Bay

D'Urville Island

French Pass

Queen Charlotte Walkway

NORTH ISLAND

Anakiwa

Havelock

Pelorus Bridge

Picton

Lighthouse

Wellington

Cook Strait

Ferry Route

6

1

Cloudy Bay

MT RICHMOND TATE FOREST PARK

58

2

1

63

Blenheim

SOUTH ISLAND

Clifford Bay

Lighthouse

boats, more extensive trips, and the most central Picton base. Its most popular trip is the 1-day excursion for around NZ$95 (US$67) per person.

For those who like sailing, **Compass Charters,** 20 Beach Rd., Waikawa Marina, Picton (© **0800/101-332** in NZ, or 03/573-8332; www.compass-charters.co.nz), is the South Island's largest charter company. They have budget to luxury-yacht and launch cruises—skippered or self-drive—priced according to the vessel and duration. Renwick-based **Affinity Cruises** (© **0800/862-334** in NZ, or 03/572-7223; www. affinitycruises.co.nz) offers excellent 2-, 5-, or 7-day cruises with private cabins.

If you're a food, wine, and water lover, opt for the **Marlborough Travel Greenshell Mussel Cruise** ✿✿✿ (© **0800/990-800** in NZ, or 03/577-9997; www.marlborough travel.co.nz). This terrific half-day outing takes you into the stunning Sounds environment, visiting a Greenshell' mussel farm, where you'll be treated to a feast of yummy, freshly steamed mussels with a complimentary glass of Marlborough Sauvignon Blanc. The tour operates November through March, departing Havelock and Picton at 1:30pm daily and from Portage Resort Hotel at 3pm daily. It costs NZ$95 (US$67) from Portage and Havelock and NZ$125 (US$88) from Picton, and is worth every cent.

Although passengers on any of these vessels may see dolphins, **Dolphin Watch Ecotours,** Picton Foreshore (© **0800/9453-5433** in NZ, or 03/573-8040; www.

Kids Especially for Kids

There's a real treat in store for young and old alike at the new **Seahorse World Aquarium** ✵✵✵, Picton Foreshore (☎ 0800/800-081 in NZ, or 03/573-6030; www.seahorseworld.co.nz). Watch tiny, mysterious seahorses court and dance, see thousands of babies at various stages of growth, and find out about the mysteries of the male pregnancy. On top of that, there's a 6m (20-ft.) preserved giant squid—only one of two examples in the Southern Hemisphere. Kids can also get up close and personal with crayfish, sharks, stingrays, and the multitudes of fishes that thrive in New Zealand waters. Fish are fed at 11am and 2pm and there are free guided tours (excluding entry fee) at 10am, noon, 1pm, and 3pm. Check out the fossil displays and ask about the new ecotours to the natural paradise of Blumine Island in Marlborough Sounds.

naturetours.co.nz), makes these lovely creatures the focus of its naturalist tours. A 4-hour guided ecotour costs from NZ$75 (US$53), NZ$45 (US$32) for children. They also have an excellent a bird-watcher's tour for a similar price.

If you have fishing on your mind, call up Havelock-based **Chris Hobbs Snapper Fishing Charters** (☎ 03/574-2911; www.tsuribaka-fishing.co.nz/chrishobbs) and ask for details about his 5- and 10-hour charters.

THE QUEEN CHARLOTTE WALKWAY ✵✵✵

If you're like me and love walking but hate carrying things, the Queen Charlotte Walkway is just for you. It's a 1- to 4-day experience with amazing views and not a pack in sight. That's because kind people in boats do all the pack lifting and transferring of your goodies for you. Even better, you don't have to stay in cramped huts or tents, as there are smart lodgings along the way. There's lots more information about this walk in the "Tramping" section in chapter 3, but briefly, the 71km (44-mile) walking track passes through lush coastal forest, around coves and inlets, and along skyline ridges with breathtaking views of Queen Charlotte and Kenepuru sounds. If you've got time, try the excellent kayak/walk combos offered by **Wilderness Guides,** 3 Auckland St., Picton (☎ 0800/266-266 in NZ, or 03/520-3095; www.wilderness guidesnz.com). You can also tackle the track on mountain bikes. **Cycle Adventure Tours Downunder,** 1 Auckland St., Picton (☎ 03/573-8565; www.cyclenz.com) has 1-day bike rentals from NZ$45 (US$32) and 1- to 3-day guided tours from around NZ$160 (US$112).

WINE, WINE & MORE WINE

It doesn't matter what time of year you visit Marlborough, because the weather is invariably balmy (with a few frosty winter mornings), and there's always wine to drink if all else fails. If you stand on any high point, you'll see grapevines spread across the rolling landscape in all directions as far as the eye can see. In just over 25 years, Marlborough has established itself as one of the world's premier wine-producing regions. There are around 60 wineries in the area; many have restaurants, most have tastings, and some have galleries or crafts shops. Pick up the free *Marlborough Winemakers* map from the visitor center before setting off, or check out www.winemarlborough.net.nz. Following are a few wineries of note.

Sleeping among the Grapes

There are a growing number of vineyard accommodations for visitors to choose from. **Le Grys Homestay & Premium Wines** 𝕮𝕮, Le Grys Vineyard, Conders Bend Road, Renwick (© **03/572-9490**; www.legrys.co.nz), offers a divine mud-block cottage for around NZ$250 (US$175), plus NZ$45 (US$32) each extra person, and a room in the main house for NZ$140 (US$98). **Isabel Lodge,** 72 Hawkesbury Rd., Renwick (© **03/572-8300**; www.isabel estate.com), has three rooms for NZ$95 (US$67). Another option is **Straw Lodge** 𝕮𝕮𝕮, 17 Fareham Lane, Blenheim (© **03/572-9767**; www.trailsof marlborough.co.nz), where two lovely private vineyard suites have their own courtyard and facilities. Rooms are from NZ$195 to NZ$245 (US$137–US$172). **Vintners Retreat** 𝕮𝕮, 55 Rapaura Rd., Blenheim (© **03/572-7420**; www.vintnersretreat.co.nz) has 14 stylish two- and three-bedroom, self-contained villas nestled among the vines ranging in price from NZ$295 (US$207). At **St. Leonards Vineyard Cottages** 𝕮, 18 St. Leonards Rd., Blenheim (© **03/577-8328**; www.stleonards.co.nz), choose from four delightful, self-contained cottages for NZ$90 to NZ$270 (US$63–US$189).

More than 27 years ago, **Montana Brancott Winery,** State Highway 1, Main Road South, Riverlands (© **03/578-2099**; www.montanawines.co.nz), planted the first vines in the region, and today it's New Zealand's largest winery. Tours leave Monday through Saturday from 10am to 3pm. The wine shop and the huge (and sometimes noisy) Montana Brancott Restaurant are open daily from 9am to 5pm.

Those with an eye for good wines will be familiar with **Cloudy Bay** 𝕮𝕮𝕮, Jacksons Road, Blenheim (© **03/520-9140**; www.cloudybay.co.nz). Its name is well known internationally, and 75% of its acclaimed sauvignon blanc is exported. It also produces chardonnay, cabernet merlot, and a sparkling wine, Pelorus. It's open for tasting and sales daily from 10am to 4:30pm (closed Dec 25 and Good Friday).

Allan Scott Wines & Estates 𝕮𝕮, Jacksons Road, Blenheim (© **03/572-9054**; www.allanscott.com), is just across the road and has a good vineyard restaurant called Twelve Trees. The winery produces chardonnay, sauvignon, and Riesling. The cellar is open for tasting daily from 9am to 5pm; the restaurant opens daily for lunch at noon.

Hunter's Wines, Rapaura Road, Blenheim (© **03/572-8489**; www.hunters.co.nz), is home to Jane Hunter, acclaimed as one of the five best women winemakers in the world. The winery is hugely popular with tour groups. The dated restaurant is open daily from noon until late; the wine shop, Monday through Saturday from 9:30am to 4:30pm and Sunday from 11am to 3:30pm.

Grove Mill 𝕮𝕮𝕮, Waihopai Valley Road, Renwick (© **03/572-8200**; www.grovemill.co.nz), is well worth a visit, especially if you're also an art lover. In addition to producing medal-winning chardonnay, Riesling, and cabernet sauvignon, its gallery features exhibitions of nationally recognized New Zealand artists. It's open daily from 11am to 5pm.

Highfield Estate 𝕮𝕮, Brookby Road, Blenheim (© **03/572-9244**; www.highfield.co.nz), which produces classic varietal wines, has wine tastings, cellar door sales, and a restaurant with stunning views. It's open daily from 10:30am to 5pm.

Wairau River Wines ✸✸✸, corner of Rapaura Road and State Highway 6, Blenheim (✆ **03/572-9800**; www.wairauriverwines.com) has one of the best winery restaurants in the Marlborough region—a reliable brasserie with an innovative blackboard menu at reasonable prices. It's housed in an charming mud-brick building, has cellar-door sales, and is open daily 10am to 5pm.

Cellier Le Brun ✸✸, Terrace Road, Renwick (✆ **03/572-8859**; www.lebrun.co.nz), has a delightful cafe. French winemaker Daniel Le Brun established the vineyard in 1980, and with 12 generations of champagne making behind him, he's truly established in his new venture.

Gillan Estate Wines, Rapaura Road, Blenheim (✆ 03/572-**9979),** combines award-winning architecture with excellent wine and food, while **Lawson's Dry Hills Winery,** Alabama Road, Blenheim (✆ **03/578-7674**; www.lawsonsdryhills.co.nz), also has a very good reputation for its wines and fine dining.

Johanneshof Cellars, State Highway 1, Koromiko (✆ **03/573-7035**; Johanneshof.Cellars@xtra.co.nz), has spectacular underground wine cellars blasted into the hillside. **Huia,** Boyces Road, Blenheim (✆ **03/572-8326**; www.huia.net.nz), is an up-and-coming winery open for tastings daily from 10am to 4:30pm. **Herzog's Winery & Restaurant** ✸✸✸, 81 Jeffries Rd., Blenheim (✆ **03/572-8770**; www.herzog.co.nz), has burst onto the scene with a now-famous luxury gourmet restaurant (see "Where To Dine," below).

WINERY TOURS Vine To Wine, Blenheim (✆ **03/578-8459**; sheenagrey@xtra.co.nz), offers 4- and 8-hour winery tours with wine expert Sheena Grey. She will take you on an in-depth tour around Marlborough vineyards, introducing you to growers and winemakers. Professionally tutored wine tastings are also available at several wine cellar doors. Tours are priced from NZ$260 (US$182) for one person and NZ$80 (US$56) for each additional person. The **Sounds Connection** ✸✸✸, 10 London Quay, Picton (✆ **0800/742-866** in NZ, or 03/573-8843; www.sounds connection.co.nz), has half- and full-day tours from NZ$55 (US$39). Its groups are smaller than some larger companies, and you can choose the vineyards. If you want some exercise while you see the wineries, call **Wine Tours By Bike** ✸✸✸, 106 Jeffries Rd., Blenheim (✆ **03/572-9951**; www.winetoursbybike.co.nz), which will take you on an exploration of its favorite cycling roads, scenic spots, vineyards, wineries, arts, crafts, and olive or fruit farms. Stop at a vineyard for lunch (extra cost) and soak up the quiet calm of this divine area. The tour is NZ$60 (US$42) per person, plus NZ$120 (US$84) per day or NZ$25 (US$18) per hour for a guide.

WHERE TO STAY

Book early if you want to stay in Picton, which is a busy place during the summer months. Blenheim has a larger range of accommodations, including many delightful self-contained cottages and vineyard stays (see "Sleeping Among the Grapes," above).

IN PICTON & THE SOUNDS

In addition to Picton township, there are quite a few lodgings just waiting for you in the Marlborough Sounds. Prime among them is the very stylish **Bay of Many Coves Resort** ✸✸✸, Queen Charlotte Sound (✆ **0800/579-9771** in NZ, or 03/579-9771; www.bayofmanycovesresort.co.nz), which has one-, two-, and three-bedroom self-contained apartments priced from NZ$300 to NZ$700 (US$210–US$490). It also has an excellent restaurant open to casual diners. **Lochmara Lodge** ✸, Lochmara Bay, Queen Charlotte Sound (✆/fax **03/573-4554**; www.lochmaralodge.co.nz), is a lovely

(Finds) Taste Sensations

Marlborough is home to around 120 olive groves and a number of commercial presses. At the first New Zealand Extra Virgin Olive Oils Awards in 2002, Marlborough growers won more than 30% of all awards. A number of growers welcome visitors and you can get a list of their names from the visitor center, or contact the Marlborough branch of **Olives New Zealand** (www.olives nz.org.nz). Olive oils are among the treats at **Prenzel Distilling Company,** Sheffield Street, Riverlands Estate (off St. Hwy. 1) ((C) **0800/272-639** in NZ, or 03/ 578-2800; www.prenzel.com). They also produce a delicious range of liquors, schnapps, and gin.

And to satisfy your sweet tooth, you can now visit Northland's **Makana Confections** ⟨⟨⟨⟨⟨, premier chocolate makers, which has set up a not-to-be-missed shop on the corner of Rapaura and O'Dywer roads, Blenheim ((C) **03/570-5370;** www.makana.co.nz).

---

spot with 11 rooms at NZ$70 to NZ$90 (US$49–US$63). The **Lazy Fish Guest House,** Queen Charlotte Sound ((C)/fax **03/579-9049;** www.lazyfish.co.nz), is also pleasant, in a restored colonial homestead just 8m (26 ft.) from the sea. Accommodations extend from private rooms in the homestead to secluded cabins in the bush. Rooms here are priced from NZ$395 (US$277).

The Gables, 20 Waikawa Rd. ((C) **03/573-6772;** www.thegables.co.nz), which has three bedrooms (NZ$110–NZ$135/US$77–US$95) plus two cottage suites (NZ$135–NZ$150/US$95–US$105), is a good, entertaining B&B stay. For great value backpacker accommodations, **The Villa Backpacker's Lodge,** 34 Auckland St., Picton ((C) **03/573-6598;** www.thevilla.co.nz) is hard to beat.

Jasmine Court Travellers' Inn ⟨⟨⟨   David and Joan Lennox run the best motel in Picton, and you won't find much to complain about in their immaculate complex. From the Villeroy & Bosch china to CD players with classical music, quality is at the forefront. Every room features local original art and bathrooms with top-quality fittings—one even has a 14-jet shower! The Lennoxes will store your luggage and car if you're walking the tracks; there's also a small day room to relax in if you need a spot after checking out.

78 Wellington St., Picton. (C) **0800/421-999** in NZ, or 03/573-7110. Fax 03/573-7211. www.jasminecourt.co.nz. 14 units. NZ$125–NZ$185 (US$88–US$130). Long-stay and off-peak rates available. AE, DC, MC, V. No children under 12. **Amenities:** Nearby golf course; tour bookings; car rentals; small business center; secretarial services; laundry service; same-day dry cleaning; nonsmoking rooms. *In room:* TV/VCR, CD player, dataport, kitchen, fridge, coffeemaker, hair dryer, iron.

The Portage Resort Hotel ⟨⟨⟨ (Finds)   The Portage has been providing hospitality for more than 100 years, but in its latest guise, and thanks to a 5-year revamp that began in 2001, there's much to be recommended here. For a start, the Kenepuru Sounds setting is breathtaking. The rest of the world may as well not exist. All rooms—from backpacker style through to deluxe suites—look out over the water. They're simple rooms and the bathrooms maybe a little small in some cases, but this is offset by splendid public areas and a location to die for, just 10 minutes from Picton by water taxi.

Kenepuru Sound, Marlborough. © 0800/762-442 in NZ, or 03/573-4309. Fax 03/573-4362. www.portage.co.nz. 35 units. From NZ$170–NZ$295 (US$119–US$207). NZ$35 (US$25) children 5–12 years; NZ$50 (US$35) each additional person over 12 years. Off-peak rates available. AE, DC, MC, V. **Amenities:** 2 restaurants (Te Weka [contemporary NZ]; Snapper Café [light meals]); 2 bars; outdoor pool; nearby 9-hole golf course via water taxi; Jacuzzi; watersports equipment rentals; bike rentals; children's program; courtesy transfer to and from Torea Bay for water taxi; babysitting; laundry service; nonsmoking rooms; on-call doctor/dentist. *In room:* Dataport, kitchenette, minibar on request, fridge, coffeemaker, hair dryer, iron.

Sennen House ☆☆ One of Picton's grand old colonial homes, Sennen House— built in 1886—today provides five terrific self-contained suites, each with its own private entrance. They're all large and well appointed, with generous bathrooms and living areas. The Banks suite has its own balcony, and the Cooks has its own fireplace. Set in big gardens with a native bush backdrop, it's quiet and peaceful, yet only a short drive to the township and ferries.

9 Oxford St., Picton. © 03/573-5216. www.sennenhouse.co.nz. 5 units. From NZ$295–NZ$695. (US$210–US$499) Long-stay and off-peak rates available. Rates include predinner drinks and breakfast. AE, MC, V. **Amenities:** Nearby golf course; laundry service; same-day dry cleaning; courtesy car; nonsmoking rooms. *In room:* TV, dataport, kitchenette, fridge, coffeemaker, hair dryer.

The Yacht Club Hotel ☆ *Value* This is the place to watch. Now halfway through a major revamp, this 35-year-old property has some beautiful, brand-new, self-contained apartments that are hard to beat for value. More are coming on stream in the next 2 years. Rooms in the existing hotel are also being upgraded, so until the mission is complete, there's a mixed bag there. Go for roomy executive rooms with their quirky circular king-size beds and bigger bathrooms. Best of all, the hotel's right in the heart of Picton.

25 Waikawa Rd., Picton. © 0800/991-188 in NZ, or 03/573-7002. Fax 03/573-7727. www.theyachtclub.co.nz. 35 hotel units, 6 apts. NZ$155 (US$109) business; NZ$175 (US$123) deluxe; NZ$195 (US$137) executive; from NZ$300 (US$210) apartments. Long-stay, off-peak, and special deals. AE, DC, MC, V. **Amenities:** 2 restaurants (The Chart Room and The Boatshed Bar & Café); outdoor heated pool; golf course nearby; all-weather outdoor tennis court, spa, sauna, and gymnasium by 2007; tour desk; car rentals; massage; babysitting; coin-operated laundry; free ferry pickup. *In room:* TV, dataport, kitchens in apts, minibar, fridge, coffeemaker, hair dryer, iron.

IN BLENHEIM

If you're looking for a place with individuality and style, try **Hotel d'Urville** ☆☆, 52 Queen St., Blenheim (© **03/577-9945;** www.durville.com), which has 10 lovely themed rooms priced from NZ$373 (US$261). **Old St. Mary's Convent** ☆☆, Rapaura Road, Blenheim (© **03/570-5700;** www.convent.co.nz), is a unique stay in a restored 100-year-old convent. Its four rooms are vast and cost between NZ$300 and NZ$500 (US$210–US$350). The honeymoon suite is gorgeous, and there's even a small church on the property. **Uno Piu** ☆, 75 Murphys Rd., Blenheim (© **03/578-2235;** www.unopiu.co.nz) offers lovely bed-and-breakfast homestead accommodations plus a delightful, self-catering, two-bedroom mud-block cottage set in its own garden. You can also wallow in the home swimming pool.

WHERE TO DINE

As well as the cafes and restaurants reviewed below, don't forget about all the winery restaurants. You'll find them listed on the free winery map from the visitor center.

IN PICTON

Picton eateries come and go, but one enduring favorite is **Le Café,** London Quay, Picton (© **03/573-5588**)—casual, friendly, reliable, and open daily. If you'd like a special dining experience, get a water taxi and head for Portage Resort's **Te Weka Restaurant** ✿✿✿ (© **03/573-4309**), which serves divine New Zealand food—salmon, mussels, tuna, lamb, venison—and wine in a gorgeous bush-clad setting adjacent to their funky Retro Lounge Bar.

The Chart Room Restaurant ✿✿✿ CONTEMPORARY NEW ZEALAND Some locals will tell you this place is overpriced, but I suggest you ignore them. This is a welcome little slice of city in a small seaside town. Nautically themed, it edges out all others in town in terms of decor and presentation, and taste sensations like chargrilled eye filet of beef with potato and olive-oil tart, broad beans, and merlot jus are well worth the higher dollars you pay. Once you've immersed your taste buds in the subtle flavors they present, you WILL be back for more.

The Yacht Club Hotel, 25 Waikawa Rd., Picton. © 03/573-7002. Main courses NZ$25–NZ$32 (US$18–US$22). AE, DC, MC, V. Summer daily noon–late; winter daily 6–9pm.

Expresso House ✿✿ CAFE/PACIFIC RIM This is Picton's smartest little cafe. With its polished timber floors and austere white interior, you could be forgiven for thinking you've ended up in the city. An outdoor courtyard for summer dining brings it all back to earth, though, and you'll find an all-day menu with treats such as lemon and salmon fettuccine or chicken on rye with lemon-caper sauce and a delicious range of flavored breads. Nighttime specials include rare baked filet of beef with wasabi cream and filet of salmon with lime glaze.

58 Auckland St., Picton. © 03/573-7112. Main courses NZ$18–NZ$26 (US$13–US$18). MC, V. Summer daily 11am–late; winter Thurs–Tues 11am–8pm.

IN HAVELOCK

New to the Havelock scene is the delightful **Slip Inn Café Restaurant & Wine Bar** ✿✿, Havelock Marina, Havelock (© **03/574-2345**), which is open daily from 7am until late. It offers unimpeded views over the marina and Pelorus Sound, as well as great value with seafood dishes and pizza priced around NZ$17 (US$12).

The Mussel Boys ✿ SEAFOOD The giant mussel shells on the restaurant roof are a dead giveaway—this is the place for the freshest, tastiest mussels you'll find anywhere. They're grown locally and treated with the utmost culinary care. Fresh steamers are served whole in their shell in special pots; fresh flats are grilled on the half shell and topped with something tasty; and the mussel raft is a long, soft roll filled with cornmeal-coated pan-fried mussels on salad with a chile mayonnaise. Mmmmm. Need I say more?

73 Main Rd., Havelock. © 03/574-2824. Reservations required for dinner. Main courses NZ$15–NZ$25 (US$11–US$18). MC, V. Summer daily 11am–9:30pm; winter Sun–Thurs noon–7pm, Fri–Sat open late. At Havelock, St. Hwy. 6, 40 min. from Picton.

IN BLENHEIM

Herzog ✿✿✿, Herzog Winery, 81 Jeffries Rd., RD3, Blenheim (© **03/572-8770**), surpasses all others in the Marlborough region. It's fine dining at its best. In addition to a general menu, it offers a five-course gourmet menu from around NZ$150 (US$105) per person. It's open mid-October through May for dinner Tuesday through Sunday. **Hotel d'Urville Restaurant & Bar** ✿✿, 52 Queen St. (© **03/577-9945**), established itself early as a place for top, innovative cuisine and after a couple of jaded years, seems to have made a glorious comeback. It offers an impressive local wine list (more than 60 selections) and an award-winning menu. Open daily for dinner, 6:30pm to 10pm; bookings are essential.

For coffee to jump start your day, try **CPR Express,** 1c Main St., Blenheim (© **03/ 579-5040**), where they roast their own beans. Also check out **Figaro's,** 8 Scott St., Blenheim (© **03/577-7277**), to find more excellent coffee along with great snacks, salads, and a menu that changes daily. It's open Monday to Friday, 7:30am to 3:30pm, Saturday 9am to 1pm.

HEADING SOUTH: EN ROUTE TO CHRISTCHURCH

If you're going south, the drive to Christchurch is approximately 4 hours. This is a perfect opportunity to stop off in Kaikoura or the wine-growing area of Waipara in North Canterbury. If you plan to do either, allow a whole day for the trip. For details on Kaikoura and its famous whale-watching excursions, see "Side Trips from Christchurch" in chapter 13.

HEADING NORTH: EN ROUTE TO NELSON

The **Queen Charlotte Drive** offers wonderful views of the Marlborough Sounds, but it's a narrow, winding road that needs to be driven with great care. It's a drive worth doing, with several good lookout stops along the way. The road meets up with State Highway 6 at the little village of Havelock; you then continue east to Nelson. The whole trip should take about 2 hours.

2 Nelson, Richmond & Motueka ★★★

144km (89 miles) W of Picton; 226km (140 miles) NE of Westport; 424km (263 miles) N of Christchurch

Nelson is the sunniest playground in New Zealand. Its 2,500 hours of annual sunshine, tranquil waters, gold-sand beaches, vineyards, and craft activities make it one of the most popular destinations in the country. And the good thing is, this applies to winter as well. While the rest of the country is lashed with foul winter chills, Nelson sits in a sheltered haven, blissfully unaware of everyone else's discomfort.

Perhaps this accounts for why the area is one of the last bastions of alternative lifestylers, especially in the Takaka–Golden Bay area. Immigrating Europeans and Americans have sought it out, too, so you'll find plenty of mixed accents among the locals.

The combined population of Nelson City and nearby Richmond is about 51,000. An hour's drive east is the small town of Motueka, population 12,000, and between the two is an area rich in tourist pickings. This is where you'll find most of the 300 full-time artists and craftspeople. It's thick with orchards, vineyards, galleries, quaint shops, and cafes, and a visit here should not be rushed. It's a laid-back province that quickly convinces you that laid-back is best.

ESSENTIALS

GETTING THERE   By Plane   Nelson City Airport is the fourth-busiest airport in New Zealand, with regular direct flights to and from Auckland, Wellington, Christchurch, and major provincial centers. It's serviced by **Air New Zealand Link** (© **0800/767-767;** www.airnz.co.nz) and **Origin Pacific Airways** (© **0800/302-302;** www.originpacific.co.nz). **Super Shuttle** (© **03/547-5782**) operates regularly between the airport and the city center for around NZ$15 (US$11) one-way.

By Coach (Bus)   InterCity, 27 Bridge St., Nelson (© **03/548-1538;** www.intercity coach.co.nz), connects Nelson to Christchurch via Kaikoura/Marlborough or the Lewis Pass. Both **Kiwi Experience** (© **09/366-9830**) and the **Magic Travellers Network** (© **09/358-5600**) include Nelson on their schedules. There are several local bus

Central Nelson

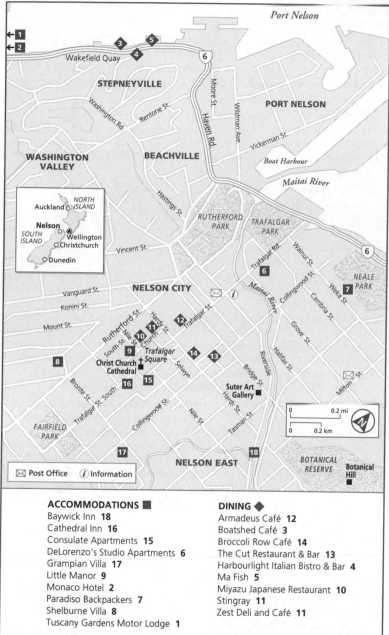

Port Nelson

STEPNEYVILLE

Wakefield Quay

PORT NELSON

Boat Harbour

Maitai River

WASHINGTON VALLEY

BEACHVILLE

NORTH ISLAND
Auckland
Nelson
SOUTH ISLAND
Wellington
Christchurch
Dunedin

RUTHERFORD PARK

TRAFALGAR PARK

NEALE PARK

NELSON CITY

Trafalgar Square

Christ Church Cathedral

Suter Art Gallery

FAIRFIELD PARK

NELSON EAST

BOTANICAL RESERVE
Botanical Hill

0   0.2 mi
0   0.2 km

☒ Post Office   ⓘ Information

ACCOMMODATIONS ■
Baywick Inn **18**
Cathedral Inn **16**
Consulate Apartments **15**
DeLorenzo's Studio Apartments **6**
Grampian Villa **17**
Little Manor **9**
Monaco Hotel **2**
Paradiso Backpackers **7**
Shelburne Villa **8**
Tuscany Gardens Motor Lodge **1**

DINING ◆
Armadeus Café **12**
Boatshed Café **3**
Broccoli Row Café **14**
The Cut Restaurant & Bar **13**
Harbourlight Italian Bistro & Bar **4**
Ma Fish **5**
Miyazu Japanese Restaurant **10**
Stingray **11**
Zest Deli and Café **11**

companies that link all towns within the region. Details are available from the visitor center.

By Car   The scenic drive from Picton to Nelson, via Queen Charlotte Sound (narrow and winding) or State Highway 6 (more direct), takes approximately 2 hours without stops. (The scenic route takes about a half-hour longer than the State Highway.) If you're coming from the West Coast, the drive from Westport takes approximately 3½ hours; from Christchurch via Lewis Pass, about 5 hours, or via Kaikoura-Blenheim, 6 hours.

By Taxi   Taxis pick up passengers outside the Majestic Theatre on Trafalgar Street and on Bridge Street opposite the Suburban Bus Company. For pickup, call **Nelson City Taxis** (© 03/548-8225), **Sun City Taxis** (© 03/548-2666), or **Motueka Taxis** (© 03/528-7900).

ORIENTATION   Two landmarks will keep you oriented in Nelson: Trafalgar Street (the main street) and Church Hill, owned by Christ Church Cathedral and surrounded by lush lawns. The steps leading up to the church are a local gathering point. If there is any trouble at all to be had in Nelson, you'll usually find it in this area after dark.

Most shops, cafes, and restaurants are at Trafalgar and Halifax streets, although you'll find a few eateries around the bay on the waterfront. The waterfront road leads to Richmond township, which is 14km (8½ miles) and approximately a 10-minute drive away.

Past Richmond, you turn right over the railway bridge and take the Coastal Highway (St. Hwy. 60) to Motueka township, a 1-hour drive. Motueka itself is a straightforward little town built around the main highway at the mouth of the Motueka River. On the way to Motueka, stop off at the delightful little village of Mapua—it's just five minutes off the main highway. The wharf area particularly is home to a number of excellent cafes, galleries, and attractions.

VISITOR INFORMATION   The **Nelson i-Site Visitor Centre,** at 77 Trafalgar St. (© 03/548-2304; fax 03/546-7393; www.nelsonnz.com), is open Monday through Friday from 8:30am to 5pm, and 9am to 4pm on weekends and public holidays. It now occupies a stylish new complex that incorporates a large gift store and a display center. Make sure you watch the fabulous video of the region's attractions. Major bus lines also arrive and depart from here. The **Department of Conservation** counter at the visitor center is staffed only from October to Easter. The **Motueka i-Site Visitor Centre** is on Wallace Street, Motueka (© 03/528-6543; fax 03/528-6563; www. abeltasmangreenrush.co.nz).

FAST FACTS   The post office is at the corner of Halifax and Trafalgar streets, diagonally opposite the visitor center. There is handy Internet access at the visitor center, or at **Internet Outpost,** 35 Bridge St. (© 03/539-1150), and **Boots-Off Travellers Centre,** 53 Bridge St. (© 03/546-8789).

SPECIAL EVENTS   Sadly, the **Montana World of Wearable Art Awards** (www. worldofwearableart.com) are no longer held in Nelson; they've transferred to Wellington in the interests of coping with larger audiences. (See "Special Events" in chapter 11). The **Nelson Jazz Festival** runs from late December to early January. The **Sealord Summer Festival** runs from December through February. Late January's **Taste Nelson Wine & Food Festival** is one of the biggest in the country. For details on all these events, contact the visitor center.

Going Green: The Gardens

Nelson's balmy climate is perfect for gardening, and you'll find many superb private gardens open to the public during spring and summer. Pick up the free brochure and map *Gardens of the Nelson Region* at the visitor center. It describes 25 gardens in the region and lists all major events associated with gardening in the area.

EXPLORING THE AREA

The Summertime Bus is an excellent way to see Nelson's best attractions. Tickets and bus stops are available from the Visitor Information Centre, or from the bus driver: NZ$5 (US$3.50) for a circuit, NZ$10 (US$7) for an all-day pass, and NZ$20 (US$14) family day pass. The bus leaves from the Visitor Information Centre on the hour from 10am to 4pm. It operates weekends only from November 6 until December 5; then every day (except Dec 25) from December 11 until February 6; and then weekends only until March 27.

NELSON'S TOP MUSEUMS & HISTORIC BUILDINGS

Nelson Provincial Museum, Trafalgar and Hardy streets (✆ 03/547-9740; www. museumnp.org.nz), is relocating from its previous site at Stoke and is expected to reopen at the Trafalgar Street site in central Nelson in late 2006. There is also a name change in the wind as this book goes to press, so ask at the visitor center for new details and new admission prices. The museum houses one of the largest historic photographic collections in the country, along with an important Maori artifact collection and a comprehensive reference library on local history. It's open daily from 9am to 5pm; the Research Facility is open Monday through Friday from 12:30 to 4:30pm.

In Stoke, a suburb of Nelson, you'll find the **Broadgreen Historic House,** 276 Nayland St., Stoke (✆ 03/547-0403; fax 03/547-0409), a restored two story cob house built in the mid-1850s. This New Zealand Tourism Award winner has 11 rooms furnished to faithfully represent a family home of the period. It's open daily from 10:30am to 4:30pm; call for winter hours. Admission is around NZ$5 (US$3.50) for adults and NZ$1 (US70¢) for children.

In central Nelson, it's worth visiting the **South Street Historic Precinct.** Just off Nile Street West behind the Rutherford Hotel, this cute little street captures the feel of a past era. Sixteen working-class cottages built between 1863 and 1867 remain intact and are still inhabited. Nearby, on top of Church Hill, is **Nelson Cathedral,** 367 Trafalgar St. (✆ 03/548-1008; nelson.cathedral@clear.net.nz). It's open daily free of charge to visitors, in summer from 8am to 6pm and in winter from 8am to 5pm. Built of local Takaka marble, the cathedral is known for its striking stained glass, carved features, and unique free-standing organ. Car and fashion buffs—jointly or separately—will enjoy the **World of Wearable Art & Collectible Car Complex,** 95 Quarantine Rd., Nelson (✆ 03/547-4573; fax 03/547-0856; www.wowcars.co.nz), which presents not only collectible cars, but a stunning museum collection of past entries and winners of the internationally renowned World of Wearable Arts Awards. It's open daily from 10am to 6pm in summer and from 10am to 5pm in winter. Admission is NZ$15 (US$11) for adults, NZ$12 (US$8.40) for seniors, and NZ$7 (US$4.90) for children. They also offer family concessions and there's a shop and gallery on-site.

> (*Tips* **Liquid Sunshine**
>
> Nelson olive oils are rapidly gaining recognition nationally and internationally, as some of the best you'll taste anywhere. If you're a fan of dipping, drizzling, and pouring, give in to temptation and visit some of the following. *Note:* It pays to call first to make sure they're open for direct sales. **Moutere Grove,** 979 Central Rd., Upper Moutere (© 03/543-2232; www.mouteregrove.co.nz), has a free tour and organic olive oil tastings by appointment only. **Hau Plains Olive Oil,** 543 High St., Motueka (© 03/528-6391; www.hauplains.co.nz), is open most days for sales and tastings. Others to look out for are: **Frog's End Estate,** Westdale Road, Richmond (© 03/544-0570; frogsend@netaccess.co.nz); **Tasman Bay Olives,** Horton Road, Tasman (© 03/540-2084; www.olivesnewzealand. com); and **Mount Heslington Olives,** 89 Mount Heslington Rd., Brightwater (© 03/542-3727; mt-heslington@clear.net.nz).

Across town, the **Founder's Historic Park,** 87 Atawhai Dr. (© **03/548-2649;** www.founderspark.co.nz), is a replica of a historic village containing many of the old buildings and artifacts of Nelson. Special attractions include Dr. Bush's Windmill, the Port Nelson Exhibition, vintage and horse-drawn vehicles, fire engines, and a working train. It's open daily from 10am to 4:30pm (closed Good Friday and Dec 25); admission is NZ$5 (US$3.50) for adults, NZ$2 (US$1.40) for children, and NZ$13 (US$9.10) per family.

Last, but definitely not least, is **The Suter Te Aratoi o Whakatu** ✹✹✹ , 208 Bridge St. (© **03/548-4699;** www.thesuter.org.nz), the region's public art museum. Collections include works by 19th-century New Zealand artists with strong Nelson ties, such as John Gully, Lindauer, and Van der Velden. There's an excellent crafts shop and a bush-clad cafe overlooking Queens Gardens. It's open daily from 10:30am to 4:30pm and admission is NZ$3 (US$2.10) adults, NZ$1 (US70¢) for students and NZ50¢ (US30¢) for children. *Please note:* The Suter is planning to close at the end of February 2006 until October 2007 for major refurbishment.

THE MOUTERE HILLS WINERIES

Most of Nelson's 18 or so wineries are scattered along the rolling Moutere Hills and the alluvial Waimea Plains. The wines—Riesling, chardonnay, sauvignon blanc, Gewürztraminer, cabernet franc, merlot, cabernet sauvignon, and pinot noir—have intense fruit flavors, good acidic balance, and weight. A number of wineries have tasting rooms and restaurants. For more details on Nelson wineries, tap into the **Nelson Winemakers Association** website at www.nelsonwines.co.nz.

The visitor center has a leaflet and a very clear map pinpointing the best of the area's wineries, or you can take a wine tour with **JJ's Quality Tours** ✹✹, 10 Musgrave Crescent, Tahunanui (© **0800/568-568** in NZ, or ©/fax 03/545-1855; www.jjs.co.nz). It costs from NZ$50 (US$30) for a half-day tour. **Bay Tours,** 48 Brougham St., Nelson (© **0800/229-868** in NZ, or 03/545-7114; fax 03/545-7119; www.Bay ToursNelson.co.nz), also offer an excellent range of gourmet wine tours. If you're short on time, hot-foot it straight to the **Regional Wine Centre** ✹✹, 67 Aranui Rd., Mapua (© **03/540-2526;** fax 03/540-2561; Flavour@NelsonConnect.co.nz), which features a showing of the region's best wines, olive oils, beers, and gourmet foods. It includes a wine and taste center, a cafe, and a restaurant.

Moments **To Market, To Market**

You'll gain a terrific insight into local activities if you go to the **Nelson Market** ☆☆☆, in Montgomery Square (ⓒ **03/546-6454**). It's held every Saturday from 8am to 1pm and offers fine crafts, fresh food and produce, and a whole heap of the unexpected. **Monty's Sunday Market** is held every Sunday from 8:30am to 1pm in the same place and features more bric-a-brac, clothing, and oddments.

One of the best-known producers is **Neudorf Vineyards** ☆☆☆, Neudorf Road, Upper Moutere (ⓒ **03/543-2643;** www.neudorf.co.nz). Set in a picturesque vineyard, the winery offers prearranged tastings of its prize-winning chardonnay, Riesling, pinot noir, and sauvignon blanc. It's open Monday through Saturday from 10:30am to 5pm, September through May; and noon until 4pm from June through August.

Siefried Estate Vineyard and Restaurant, Main Road, Appleby, Richmond (ⓒ **03/544-1555;** www.seifreid.co.nz), has a large restaurant and tasting room, open daily from 10am to 5pm. A winery tour and tasting is around NZ$10 (US$7) per person, by appointment, Monday through Saturday. Dinner is available in the restaurant Friday and Saturday evenings from 6pm.

Denton Winery, Awa Awa Road, Upper Moutere (ⓒ/fax **03/540-3555**), is another popular choice for a personalized tasting and restaurant experience; it's open from Labour Day weekend to Easter, daily from 11am to 5pm.

Moutere Hills Vineyard ☆☆, Eggers Road, Upper Moutere (ⓒ/fax **03/543-2288;** www.mouterehills.co.nz), serves beautifully presented light meals in its converted wool-shed winery, along with Riesling, sauvignon blanc, and chardonnay. It's open from October 24 to Easter, daily from 11am to 6pm.

Waimea Estates, 22 Appleby Hwy. (ⓒ **03/544-6385;** www.waimeaestates.co.nz), produce all the main wine types, and their cafe and cellar door are open daily all year from 10am to 5pm.

SHOPPING FOR ARTS & CRAFTS

The essence of Nelson province is found in its abundance of top-quality arts and crafts—by far the best concentration anywhere in New Zealand. There are over 300 practicing artists and 40 galleries and studios. Start by purchasing a copy of *Nelson Regional Guide Book: Art In Its Own Place* (NZ$20/US$14), available at the Nelson visitor center, which also distributes the free *Tourist Guide to Nelson Potters, Nelson Inner City Shopping Guide,* and *Nelson City Art Trail.* If you're driving to Motueka, pick up the free brochure *Nelson's Coastal Way—Mapua & Coastal Villages,* which highlights top craftspeople, vineyards, and cafes. And check out www.nelsonarts.org.nz.

South Street Gallery, 10 Nile St. (ⓒ/fax **03/548-8117;** www.nelsonpottery.co.nz), is well stocked with work by 25 top potters; it's open Monday through Friday from 9am to 5pm and weekends 10am until 4pm. **Jens Hansen Gold & Silversmith** ☆☆☆, 320 Trafalgar Sq. (ⓒ **03/548-0640;** www.jenshansen.com), is a name associated with fine-quality New Zealand–made gold and silver jewelry—*and* the handmade rings and jewelry used in the trilogy *Lord of the Rings.* It's open Monday through Saturday 9am until 5pm in summer and 9am until 5pm weekdays in winter. **Dean Hawkins Jeweller** ☆☆, 240 Trafalgar St. (ⓒ **03/548-0387;** dhjeweller@xtra.co.nz), is another

---

Finds Cool Crafts

One of the loveliest little galleries around is **The Coolstore Gallery** ☆☆☆, 7 Aranui Rd., Mapua (© **03/540-3778**; www.coolstoregallery.co.nz), located in a converted apple coolstore on Mapua Wharf. It displays a wide range of contemporary art and crafts from the region's best artisans. It's open daily from 10am until 5pm. Just down the road, you'll find it hard to suppress a smile at **Laughing Fish Studio,** 24 Aranui Rd., Mapua (© **03/540-3940;** www.laughing fishstudio.co.nz), where large ladies cavort across everything from plates to wall works. And hat lovers will rejoice at **Serious Straw** ☆☆, 144 Aranui Rd., Mapua (© **03/540-3262;** www.hats.co.nz), which makes and imports a gorgeous range of fashionable and funky straw hats. If you can't make it to Mapua, they have a stall at Nelson's Saturday and Sunday markets.

---

worth checking out; and **Red** ☆☆, 1 Bridge St. (© **03/548-2170;** red gallery@clear.net.nz), is a terrific place for contemporary fine art, jewelry, and New Zealand crafts. **Flame Daisy,** 324 Trafalgar Sq. (© **03/548-4475**), is a new glass art gallery, with a wide variety of items at cheaper prices than the gorgeous Höglund Glass range (see below). If you're looking for something a bit different, **Refinery,** 3 Halifax St., Nelson (© **03/548-1778**), is likely to deliver. It stocks work from artists dedicated to recycling—everything from old cutlery and metal to timber, rubber, and tiles. It's open Monday through Saturday from 10am until 4pm.

Farther afield, **Craft Habitat** is a consortium of crafts shops on the corner of Champion and Salisbury roads in Richmond (© **03/544-1488;** email address **Paul.laird@xtra.co.nz**). Potter **Steve Fullmer** ☆☆☆, Baldwin Road, Tasman (© **03/ 526-6765;** fullmer.gallery@xtra.co.nz), is one of the country's best. His gallery is open daily 10am until 5pm in summer and Wednesday through Sunday in winter. **Royce McGlashen Pottery** ☆☆☆, 128 Ellis St., Brightwater (© **03/542-3585;** pottery@ ts.co.nz), is another high point. When it comes to color, some of the nicest pottery around is produced by **Katie Gold** ☆☆☆, Main Road, Upper Moutere (© **03/543-2544;** katie_gold@paradise.net.nz).

If you like beautiful glass pieces, don't miss **Höglund Art Glass International Glass Centre** ☆☆☆, Landsdowne Road, Richmond (© **03/544-6500;** www.nelson. hoglund.co.nz). Ola and Marie Höglund worked at Orrefors and Kosta Boda before emigrating from their native Sweden, and their skills have translated into stunning, colorful handblown glassware. You can watch the action in the studio daily from 9am to 5pm (closed Dec 25 and Good Friday). There's also a cafe and they have a second gallery in Nelson's Rutherford Hotel on Trafalgar Square. They also have tours (NZ$15/US$11 adults) that enlighten you to the history of glass and its processes. And don't worry about having to cart your favorite piece home—they offer an international shipping service.

ESPECIALLY FOR KIDS

Give the kids their own time out at **Nelson Fun Park** (© **03/548-6267**), adjacent to Tahunanui Beach, just a 5-minute drive from central city. They can unwind on the hydroslide, play miniature golf, or have fun on bumper boats. **Natureland Zoological Park** (© **03/548-6166;** www.naturelandzoo.co.nz) is also at Tahunanui Beach, open daily from 9am to 4pm. It gives children a chance to get up close to wallabies,

> **Tips Six Times the Fun**
>
> If you want to try a bit of everything and save money at the same time, check out combo deals with the Nelson Visitor Centre. If you invest in several activities, you'll pay far less, which is a big consideration when you're traveling with a family.

meerkats, otters, monkeys, and exotic birds and costs from NZ$5 (US$3.50) for adults and NZ$2 (US$1.40) for children.

Chipmunks Adventure Playground, 311 Hardy St. (© **03/548-7055;** www.chipmunks.co.nz), is ideal for younger children (up to 11 years). It has an adventure playground, birthday party packages, and an under-3 play area. Admission is around NZ$6 (US$4.20) per day; it's open daily from 9:30am to 6pm.

Touch the Sea Aquarium ☆☆☆, 8 Aranui Rd., Mapua (©/fax **03/540-3557;** seatouch@xtra.co.nz), is a charming little aquarium on Mapua Wharf. Kids get to put their hands in special tanks to discover the mysteries of sea urchins, starfish, and various shells and fish. It's worth the admission of around NZ$6.50 (US$4.55) for adults, NZ$4 (US$2.80) for children, and NZ$16 (US$11) per family. There's also a playroom and an excellent gift store.

OUTDOOR PURSUITS

For a complete overview of outdoor activities in the region, it's best to start at one of the visitor centers, which have a wide range of brochures. There are three national parks within easy driving distance; that alone raises dozens of outdoor possibilities.

BEACHES Nelson has dozens of fabulous beaches. Close to the city, the best bet is **Tahuna Beach,** which offers excellent swimming. Farther afield, just past Motueka, you'll find the hugely popular **Kaiteriteri Beach** ☆☆☆, a favorite with Cantabrians,

CAVING Lovers of dark underground spaces will enjoy exploring **Ngarua Caves,** Takaka Hill, Motueka (© **03/528-8093;** mte@xtra.co.nz). These marble caves feature the skeletal remains of New Zealand's extinct flightless bird, the moa, and a 45-minute guided tour is offered on the hour from 10am to 4pm. Entry is NZ$13 (US$9.10) for adults and NZ$4 (US$2.80) for children. There are more caves at Takaka (see "Exploring Golden Bay" in the "Abel Tasman National Park & Golden Bay" section, later in this chapter).

FISHING Bait up those hooks and get out there! The fish are awaiting in lakes, rivers, streams, and the ocean. There's good on-shore fishing at Connolly's Quay on Rocks Road, the western end of Tahuna Beach, Boulder Bay, and Cable Bay. When it comes to stalking trout, call John Brunwin of **Fly Fishing New Zealand,** 97 Murphy St., Nelson (© **03/548-9145;** www.flyfishnewzealand.com). His prices start at NZ$500 (US$350) per day for one to two people.

FLIGHTSEEING When you get up in the air over this stunning province, you'll truly understand why so many people love it. **Abel Tasman Air,** Motueka Airfield, Motueka (© **0800/304-560** in NZ, or 03/528-8290; www.abeltasmanair.co.nz), offer a range of scenic flight packages. One of the nicest is Fly & Dine, which delivers you some of the region's special spots. Helicopter fans should buzz into the skies with **Nelson Helicopters,** Tangmere Place, Nelson Airport (© **0800/450-350** in NZ, or 03/547-1177; www.nelsonhelicopters.co.nz). Try their Three National Parks 1-hour scenic tour; or visit *Lord of the Rings* filming sites.

FOUR-WHEEL-DRIVE ADVENTURES   Just 10 minutes from central Nelson, you can don your helmet, get on a 4×4 motorbike, and go for it over your choice of testing tracks. **Happy Valley Adventures** &&, 194 Cable Bay Rd., Nelson (© **0800/ 157-300** in NZ, or 03/545-0304; www.happyvalleyadventures.co.nz), is the place to call. Prices range from NZ$75 to NZ$130 (US$53–US$93) per rider (extra for pillion passengers). Or you can fly on a hire wire for over 3km (1¾ miles)—assuming you've nothing better to do—for NZ$85 (US$60) adults, NZ$55 (US$39) children.

GOLF   **Nelson Golf Club,** Bolt Road, Tahunanui, Nelson (© **03/548-5028;** fax 03/548-5028), is an 18-hole course open daily. Greens fees are NZ$28 (US$20) for affiliated members and NZ$38 (US$27) for nonaffiliated members. **Greenacres Golf Club,** Best Island, Richmond (© **03/544-6441;** fax 03/544-8420), also has 18 holes and is open daily; nonaffiliated members pay NZ$30 (US$21). **Motueka Golf Club,** Harbour Road, Motueka (©/fax **03/528-8998**), charges NZ$25 (US$18) for nonaffiliated members for 18 holes. **Motueka Golf Range,** Chamberlain Street, Motueka (© **03/526-7774;** www.motuekagolfrange.co.nz), is open from 10am until 8pm and costs around NZ$8 (US$5.60) for a bucket of balls.

HORSE TREKKING   **Stonehurst Farm Horse Treks,** Stonehurst Farm, Clover Road, Richmond (© **0800/487-357** in NZ, or 03/542-4121; www.stonehurstfarm. co.nz), gives visitors the chance to enjoy the freedom of 400 hectares (988 acres) of wide-open spaces on a sixth-generation-owned farm. The 1- to 4-hour treks explore varied scenery (hill country, river areas, plains, and farmland), and cost from NZ$35 to NZ$90 (US$25–US$63).

KAYAKING   If you don't have time to kayak in the unforgettable Abel Tasman, at least take to the waters near Nelson with **Cable Bay Kayaks,** Cable Bay Road, Nelson (© **0508/222-532** in NZ, or 03/545-0332; nick.cablebaykayaks@clear.net.nz). They specialize in half- and 1-day tours that take in bird colonies, caves, and coves from around NZ$50 to NZ$95 (US$35–US$67) per person.

MOUNTAIN BIKING   **Natural High,** 52 Rutherford St., Nelson (© **0800/444- 144** in NZ, or 03/546-6936; www.cyclenewzealand.com), offers guided bike excursions, from a 2-hour tour of the city sights and waterfront to multiday South Island tours and off-road adventures. **Eazibike,** 17 Rochfort Dr., Richmond (© **0800/200- 282** in NZ, or 027/420-0845; eazibike@clear.net.nz), has bikes from NZ$20 (US$14) and tours on quiet country roads visiting potteries and wineries. **Mapua Adventures,** Mapua Wharf, Mapua (© **03/540-3833;** www.mapuaadventures.co.nz), makes it easy for you to explore this gorgeous area by bike. Rentals start at around NZ$10 (US$7).

PARAGLIDING   **Adventure Paragliding,** 80 Quebec Rd., Nelson (© **0800/111- 611** in NZ, or 03/546-6863; www.skyout.co.nz), charges around NZ$150 (US$105) for a tandem flight.

ROCK CLIMBING   **Vertical Limits Climbing & Adventure Centre,** 34 Vanguard St. (© **0508/837-842** in NZ, or 03/545-7511; www.verticallimits.co.nz), is the largest indoor climbing center in New Zealand. It offers indoor rock climbing, abseiling, and guided climbing and caving adventures with qualified instructors. A shot at the climbing walls costs around NZ$18 (US$13) for adults, NZ$15 (US$11) for students, and NZ$12 (US$8.40) for children under 10. It's open Monday through Friday from 10am to 9pm and weekends from 10am to 6pm.

A Walk to Remember

A walk along Boulder Bank—the thin strip of land that reaches out from Nelson into the sea—is an unusual and exhilarating experience. Take water, sun protection, and a windbreaker for this 2½-hour, 8km (5-mile) walk, which begins and ends at Boulder Bank Drive.

SKYDIVING   Skydive Abel Tasman, 16 College St., Motueka Airport (© **0800/ 422-899** in NZ, or 03/528-4091; www.skydive.co.nz), has free-fall tandem skydives with instructors from NZ$260 (US$182).

SURFING & WINDSURFING   The best surfing is at **Snappers Point,** north of Boulder Bank Drive. The eastern end of **Tahuna Beach** and **Atawhai,** north off State Highway 6, are popular areas for windsurfing at high tide.

WALKING   Just about anywhere in Nelson is suited to walking. From a leisurely stroll to full multiday treks, you'll be in your element. For information on multiday walks, see "Tramping" in chapter 3. Also check out the "Abel Tasman National Park & Golden Bay" section, later in this chapter.

For a charming city walk, find the Maitai River off Nile Street and follow the signposted walkway to the locals' favorite swimming spot—Girlie's Hole. Another good 45-minute walk traces Nelson's old water system up through the native bush to old dams built in the 1870s. Go to Brook Motor Camp; there's a parking area by the dam, and the trail leads on from here. Within 5 minutes, you'll be in native bush and a quiet valley. There are steps and handrails on the trail.

If you'd like to walk with the birds, go along Motueka Sandspit and enjoy the views across Tasman Bay to D'Urville Island and Nelson City. This is an internationally important seabird habitat and is home to many varieties that come here to breed. (Please keep dogs away from the southern end of the spit.) It's part of the Motueka Walkway, which is detailed in a brochure available at the visitor center. Access the walkway from the end of Staples Street.

WHITE-WATER ADVENTURES   Ultimate Descents New Zealand, Motueka (© **0800/748-377** in NZ, or 03/523-9899; www.rivers.co.nz), seems to have every possible white-water activity covered. It offers a wide range of outings by kayak, raft, river bug, or sled (which involves going through white water lying face-down on the sled), from Grade II to the savage Grade V on rivers throughout the greater Nelson province. Half-day to multiday rafting and kayaking trips for all ages cost from NZ$105 to around NZ$1,000 (US$74–US$700).

WHERE TO STAY

Nelson isn't short of beds, but if you're visiting over the December-to-January period, you'll be competing with thousands of New Zealanders who descend upon the area. Book early! There is a wide range of accommodations—including lots of smart B&Bs and excellent backpacker offerings—and with one or two exceptions, most are incredibly well priced. The rates given below include 12.5% GST and free parking.

IN NELSON

At **Te Puna Wai Lodge** ☞☞, 24 Richardson St., Nelson (© **03/548-7621;** www. tepunawai.co.nz), every comfort is attended to in two rooms and an apartment for around NZ$200 to NZ$300 (US$140–US$210). A very good motel is the 27-unit **DeLorenzo's Studio Apartments** ☆☆, 51 Trafalgar St. (© **03/548-9774**; www.delorenzos.co.nz), where accommodations go for around NZ$175 to NZ$195 (US$123–US$137).

Expensive

Consulate Apartments ☆☆☆   Elegant, sophisticated, and understated, these three large, serviced apartments make the most of what was once the base for an Italian consul. Each apartment has modern facilities of the highest quality—one even has a piano for your use. Two have two bedrooms and the other has one, and they're just a 2-minute walk from the main street.

353 Trafalgar Sq. © **03/545-8200**. Fax 03/548-4156. www.consulateapartments.co.nz. 3 units. From NZ$400–NZ$800 (US$280–US$560). Minimum 2-night stay. Rates include breakfast provisions. AE, DC, MC, V. Beside the Cathedral. **Amenities:** Nearby golf course; tour bookings; car rentals; massage and beauty treatments; laundry facilities; laundry service; same-day dry cleaning; nonsmoking rooms; airport transfers. *In room:* A/C, TV/VCR/DVD/CD, fax, dataport, kitchen, fridge, coffeemaker, hair dryer, iron.

Moderate

Baywick Inn ☆☆ *Value*   Canadian Janet Southwick and her New Zealand husband, Tim Bayley, are back after spending 20 years in Canada, and they're doing a fabulous job of hosting guests at a terrific price. Janet had her own restaurant in Toronto, so expect great food. Upstairs rooms in their 115-year-old home have plenty of space and character; the Parkdale has a huge step-down bathroom complete with claw-foot tub and shower, plus its own sunroom. And if you're suffering from pet deprivation, the resident wire-haired fox terrier is a sucker for attention. All this just 5 minutes' walk from town.

51 Dommet St., Nelson. © **03/545-6514**. Fax 03/545-6517. www.baywicks.com. 3 units. NZ$140–NZ$175 (US$98–US$123). Long-stay and off-peak rates available. Rates include breakfast. Dinner by arrangement. MC, V. No children under 12. *In room:* TV, coffeemaker on request, hair dryer, iron, no phone.

Cathedral Inn ☆☆ *Value*   The well-appointed rooms all have en-suite bathrooms, though some are on the small side with shower only; if you want a tub, request the Queen room. The old-style furnishings match the vintage of the 1870s house. There is a central upstairs guest snug with fridge, microwave, and ironing facilities, and a huge dining/sitting room downstairs. You'll get plenty of privacy and comfort here.

369 Trafalgar St. S., Nelson. © **0800/883-377** in NZ, or 03/548-7369. Fax 03/548-0369. www.cathedralinn.co.nz. 7 units. NZ$210–NZ$290 (US$147–US$203). Rates include breakfast. Long-stay and off-peak rates available. AE, MC, V. No children under 12. **Amenities:** Jacuzzi; bike rentals; laundry service; same-day dry cleaning; nonsmoking rooms; airport transfers. *In room:* TV, dataport, coffeemaker, hair dryer.

Value Backpacker Beds

Nelson is blessed with quality accommodations at affordable prices—there are at least 10 backpacker establishments in the town. In addition to Paradiso (see below), you'll find good value at **Nelson City YHA**, 59 Rutherford St. (© **03/545-9988**; www.yha.co.nz); and **The Green Monkey**, 129 Milton St. (© **03/545-7421**; www.thegreenmonkey.co.nz). **Club Nelson**, 18 Mount St. (© **03/548-3466**; www.nelsonbackpackers.co.nz), is in a sunny, quiet street and a swimming pool is among its excellent facilities.

Grampian Villa ★★★ *finds*   John and Jo Fitzwater take to the role of hosts like ducks to water and their two-storied historic Victorian villa reflects the passion they have for the tourism industry. All four rooms are large, with excellent bathrooms and balconies, or veranda access. The upstairs Observatory room has the biggest bathroom, but my personal favorite is the luscious burgundy-and-gold downstairs Mr. Gibbs room. By 2006 they will offer four lower-priced rooms in a separate house across the street.

209 Collingwood St. © **03/545-8209.** Fax 03/548-7888. www.grampianvilla.co.nz. 4 units. NZ$250–NZ$350 (US$175–US$245). Rates include breakfast. MC, V. Long-stay rates available. No children under 12. **Amenities:** Bike rentals; massage; laundry service; same-day dry cleaning; nonsmoking rooms; on-call doctor/dentist; access for travelers w/disabilities. *In room:* TV, dataport, minibar, fridge, coffeemaker, hair dryer, iron.

The Little Manor ★★ *Moments*   This magical place offers storybook charm. The cottage is right in the heart of Nelson's historic South Street area, yet it presents all the modern amenities you could hope for. Angela Higgins leaves you entirely to yourself in the self-contained, 4.5m-wide (15-ft.) confines of this little "doll's house," but not before you have experienced her terrific hospitality. Don't be deceived by its small frontage: Apart from its downstairs bathroom, laundry, minute kitchen, living/dining room, and front office, there are two upstairs bedrooms, a huge deck, and a cozy landing for reading. And if you miss out on this, ask about Angela's Little Retreat—a contemporary apartment with just as much appeal.

12 Nile St., Nelson. © **03/545-1411** or 021/247-1891. Fax 03/545-1417. the.little.manor@xtra.co.nz. 2 units. Cottage NZ$240 (US$340), extra person NZ$45 (US$32); apt NZ$195–NZ$250 (US$137–US$175). Rates include breakfast basket delivered to your door. Long-stay and off-peak rates available. AE, DC, MC, V. **Amenities:** Nearby golf course; car rentals; nearby health center and massage; babysitting; laundry service; same-day dry cleaning; nonsmoking rooms; on-call doctor/dentist. *In room:* A/C in apartment, TV/DVD, dataport, kitchen, fridge, coffeemaker, hair dryer, iron.

Monaco Hotel ★★ *Value*   If you're a fan of English heritage–style architecture, you'll love this new spot on water's edge. Exposed rustic beams, thick walls, and brick interior finishes give the impression of a little English country pub, yet rooms (of varying sizes and styles) have modern amenities. Pay a little extra for a luxury room complete with big Jacuzzi, or enjoy a value-priced two-bedroom villa set apart from the main hotel building in an English garden filled with climbing roses.

6 Point Rd., Nelson. © **03/547-8233.** Fax 03/547-8244. www.monacoresort.co.nz. 36 units. NZ$195 (US$137) deluxe hotel; NZ$250 (US$175) luxury hotel; NZ$281–NZ$310 (US$197–US$217) villas. Long-stay, off-peak, and special deals available. AE, DC, MC, V. **Amenities:** Restaurant; bar; nearby golf course; concierge; tour bookings; car rentals; massage; laundry service; same-day dry cleaning; nonsmoking rooms; on-call doctor/dentist; access for travelers w/disabilities. *In room:* TV/DVD, dataport, kitchens in villas, minibar, fridge, coffeemaker, hair dryer, iron.

Shelbourne Villa ★★★   Wayne and Val Ballantyne have converted their two-storied 1929 villa into a pleasurable oasis offering four lovely room choices. I'd opt for The Loft if you like a modern look, plenty of space, and balcony views. Like the Master Suite, it has its own fireplace and king-size bed. The downstairs Garden Suite is also very appealing and has a separate living room and kitchenette. Wherever you end up sleeping, you won't be disappointed.

21 Shelbourne St. © **03/545-9059.** Fax 03/546-7248. www.shelbournevilla.co.nz. From NZ$200–NZ$300 (US$140–US$210). Rates include breakfast. MC, V. **Amenities:** Nearby golf course; tour bookings' car rentals; laundry service; nonsmoking rooms. *In room:* A/C, TV/DVD In lounge, dataport, kitchenette in Garden Suite, fridge, coffeemaker, hair dryer, iron.

Inexpensive

Paradiso Backpackers ❀❀ *Finds*   You can expect a crowd at Paradiso—it's definitely the most popular Nelson backpacker stay. One look at its fabulous pool, its conservatory kitchen/dining room, and its quirky lounge set up in an old bus, and you realize why. Bedrooms might be pretty standard and boring, but they're comfortable, and with all the other luxuries on hand, who cares?

42 Weka St., Nelson. ℭ **0800/269-667** in NZ, or 03/545-7128. Fax 03/546-7533. www.backpackernelson.co.nz. 95 beds (shared bathrooms), 9 units with en-suite bathrooms. NZ$89–NZ$119 (US$62–US$83). Long-stay and off-peak rates available. AE, MC, V. **Amenities:** Outdoor heated pool; Jacuzzi; sauna; car rentals; laundry service; nonsmoking rooms. *In room:* No phone.

IN TAHUNANUI-RICHMOND

Tahuna Beach Holiday Park, 70 Beach Rd., Tahunanui, Nelson (ℭ **0800/500-501** in NZ, or 03/548-5159; www.tahunabeachholidaypark.co.nz), is the largest motor camp in New Zealand, accommodating several thousand travelers a night during the summer months. It has motel units, tourist and standard cabins, and tent sites—not to mention a fabulous atmosphere. A good motel in this area is **Tuscany Gardens Motor Lodge** ❀❀, 80 Tahunanui Dr., Tahunanui (ℭ **0800/887-226** in NZ, or 03/548-5522; www.tuscanygardens.co.nz).

IN MOTUEKA/MAPUA

Motueka township itself doesn't contain an abundance of nice accommodations, but outlying areas have rich pickings for those wanting a peaceful country stay. **Bronte Lodge** ❀❀, Bronte Road East, near Mapua (ℭ **03/540-2422;** www.BronteLodge.co.nz), is one such place, with two luxury suites and two villas ranging from NZ$440 to NZ$540 (US$308–US$378). **Mahana Escape** ❀❀, 750 Old Coach Rd., Mahana (ℭ **03/540-3090;** www.mahanaescape.co.nz), is a colorful B&B with four rooms from around NZ$175–NZ$320 (US$123–US$224); and **Kimeret Place** ❀❀, Bronte Road East, Mapua (ℭ **03/540-2727;** www.kimeretplace.co.nz), has two B&B rooms and two apartments that are bound to please.

Very Expensive

Motueka River Lodge ❀❀❀   Now 16 years old, this custom-built lodge set in the forested countryside has developed a patina of understated exclusivity. It's the perfect spot for keen fishermen, as it overlooks Motueka River, famous for its wild brown trout. Or if you just want to languish in high comfort with none of the stuffiness of some upmarket stays, you can easily do so here. All guest rooms are beautifully appointed with superb bathrooms. The deluxe rooms are my favorites, although the stable room with its separate lounge is a close second.

Hwy. 61, Ngatimoti, Motueka. ℭ **03/526-8668.** Fax 03/526-8669. www.motuekalodge.co.nz. 5 units. NZ$1,350 (US$945) suite; NZ$1,687 (US$1,181) deluxe suite. Extra person NZ$150 (US$105). Rates include breakfast, predinner cocktails, 5-course dinner, and airport transfers. 2-night minimum. MC, V. The lodge is 50 min. by car from Nelson. No children under 12. **Amenities:** Bar; all-weather tennis court; Jacuzzi; tour bookings; massage; laundry service; nonsmoking rooms; airport transfers. *In room:* Hair dryer, iron, no phone.

Paratiho Farms ❀❀❀ *Moments*   I was speechless the first time I rounded a grassy hillock and saw Paratiho. This magnificent property, set on an 800-hectare (1,976-acre) working farm, was opened in 2000 by an American couple, Robert and Sally Hunt. Highly rated by *Condé Nast Traveler,* this member of the Small Luxury Hotels of the World group is perhaps the most luxurious, the most personalized, and the most unique of any in New Zealand. It certainly has one of the highest tariffs, but the six huge suites (in three cottages, separate from the main lodge) are filled with every conceivable thing you could need. If you want the ultimate private indulgence, opt for the gorgeous three-bedroom Farm Cottage.

545 Waiwhero Rd., RD2, Upper Moutere, Nelson. © 03/528-2100. Fax 03/528-2101. www.paratiho.co.nz. 6 units. NZ$2,250 (US$1,575) suite; NZ$300 (US$210) per person per night for Farm Cottage, minimum 2 persons per night. Rate for entire property available. Rate includes all meals, beverages, wine, unlimited use of on-site recreational facilities, and airport transfers. AE, DC, MC, V. The lodge is a 15-min. drive inland from Motueka or 45-min. drive from Nelson Airport. No children under 12. **Amenities:** Meals prepared by top chef; bar; heated outdoor pool; golf putting green; all-weather tennis court; well-equipped gym w/sonarium (a cross between a sauna and steam room); spa; tour bookings; car rentals; laundry service; same-day dry cleaning; nonsmoking rooms; on-call doctor/dentist. *In room:* A/C, TV, dataport, minibar, fridge, coffeemaker, hair dryer, iron, safe.

Expensive

Wairepo House *ᏏᏏᏏ*   In a fourth-generation apple and pear orchard, this big colonial homestead oozes romance. With nearly a hectare (over 2 acres) of woodland gardens (including a giant chess set), this peaceful, rural oasis begs a lingering stay. Richard and Joyanne Easton will make sure it's everything you hoped for. The big two-bedroom Peony Suite on the top floor is the most spacious and has a double Jacuzzi, lounge, kitchen, and balcony. Others open onto the pool and garden.

22 Weka Rd., Mariri, Tasman. © 03/526-6865. Fax 03/526-6101. www.wairepohouse.co.nz. 5 units. NZ$350–NZ$595 (US$245–US$417). NZ$55 (US$39) per person per night for extra adults. Rates include breakfast, canapés, and predinner drinks. MC, V. **Amenities:** Outdoor heated pool; grass tennis court; *petanque;* garden chess; tour bookings; guided orchard tours; car rentals; laundry service; nonsmoking rooms. *In room:* TV/CD, dataport, kitchenette in Peony Suite, minibar, coffeemaker, hair dryer, iron.

Moderate

Aporo Pondsiders *ᏏᏏᏏ (Finds*   Mike and Marian Day have come up with a gem of an idea—three supercute, self-contained cottages overhanging an ornamental pond in a peaceful rural environment. You'd be silly to miss them! Staggered for privacy, they have king-size beds and modern furnishings with a small kitchen, living room, and balcony overlooking the water. Pick up the binoculars and watch herons and shags, row in the dinghy, or walk in the woods.

Permin Rd., Tasman. © 03/526-6858. Fax 03/526-6258. www.aporo.co.nz. 3 units. NZ$250 (US$202) 1-bedroom cottage; NZ$400 2-bedroom cottage. Rates include breakfast hamper. MC, V. 30 min. from Nelson and 10 min. from Motueka. **Amenities:** Laundry facilities; nonsmoking rooms. *In room:* TV/CD, dataport, kitchen, coffeemaker, hair dryer, iron.

Inexpensive

Bakers Lodge *ᏏᏏ*, 4 Poole St., Motueka (© **0800/800-102** in NZ, or 03/528-0102; www.bakerslodge.co.nz), has 74 beds over 16 rooms priced from NZ$20–NZ$22 (US$14–US$15) for dorms and NZ$60–NZ$96 (US$42–US$67) for double and en-suite rooms.

WHERE TO DINE

Nelson is the seafood capital of New Zealand, so it isn't unreasonable to expect top seafood in the area's restaurants. Combine that with a wealth of horticultural produce, world-renowned wines, and a casual atmosphere, and the stage is set for some memorable dining. There's been a rush of new cafes—not all worth visiting—and you won't be short of an opportunity to dine well.

IN NELSON

For the best coffee in Nelson, go straight to **Morrison Street Café** *ᏏᏏ*, 244 Hardy St., Nelson (© **03/548-8110**). It's open Monday through Friday from 7:30am until

Finds Mouthwatering Morsels

If you're a chocolate-lover, you will never forgive yourself if you don't hunt down **Rosy Glow** ✿✿✿, 20 Harley St., Nelson (© **03/548-3383**). It's tucked into a little side street behind the police station. You won't miss it—it's painted a bright baby pink. Once inside, you can indulge in a huge range of exquisite, very rich, dark-chocolate treasures. See if you can hold out till the 9am opening time.

For the best and biggest range of ice cream in town, head for **Penguino Gelato Café** ✿✿✿, 85 Montgomery Sq., Nelson (© **03/545-6450**), where you'll find 18 flavors made from traditional Italian recipes. Try the gelato, sorbet, sundaes, bambinos for children, and big four-flavor cone for the ambitious. They're open daily in summer.

4pm; from 8:30am until 3pm on Saturday; and from 9am until 3pm on Sunday. **Armadeus Café** ✿, 284 Trafalgar St. (© **03/545-7191**), is the place to go if you have a sweet tooth. The Austrian owner is a dab hand with delicious, and probably very fattening pastries and chocolate goodies. There's a full dinner menu with an Austrian bent as well. They're open daily from 8:30am. **Lambretta's Café Bar** ✿, 204 Hardy St. (© **03/545-8555**), remains popular for light meals and a good time. It's invariably packed with people enjoying pastas, pizzas, and seafood dishes from 8:30am until late daily.

You can't help but meet locals at **The Oyster Bar** ✿✿✿, 115 Hardy St., Nelson (© **03/545-8955**), where you can down oyster shooters in vodka, a range of saucy cocktails, and fresh sushi and oysters. It's tiny and open Tuesday through Saturday from 5pm until late. There's more excellent Japanese cuisine at **Miyazu Japanese Restaurant** ✿✿✿, Rutherford Hotel, Nelson (© **03/548-2299**), where you can watch slick Japanese chefs preparing your meal in front of you. They're open Monday through Saturday from 6pm. **Harbourlight Italian Bistro & Bar** ✿✿✿, 341 Wakefield Quay, Nelson (© **03/546-6685**), is in the historic Harbourlight Store building with breathtaking views of the Nelson waterfront. It has an Italian-style menu that relies on fresh and organic local produce and is now one of the best restaurants in town.

Boatshed Café ✿✿ SEAFOOD   The over-the-water setting of this busy Nelson landmark is a terrific feature, and while it continues to deliver good seafood meals in a memorable location, the service and staff's attitudes fluctuate a little more than is desirable. You can hand pick your own wriggly crabs or lobster and have them delivered to the pot for the chef's attention, or select from a large seafood menu.

350 Wakefield Quay, Nelson. © **03/546-9783**. Reservations required for dinner. Main courses NZ$28–NZ$32 (US$20–US$22). AE, DC, MC, V. Daily 9am–late.

Broccoli Row Café ✿✿ *Value* VEGETARIAN/SEAFOOD   Whenever I'm in Nelson, I head straight to Broccoli Row for reliably good food with flair. It's a little winner with a warm, intimate interior and a delightful courtyard. If you're a vegetarian, you'll think you've landed in heaven. The soups are always tasty, and there's a range of counter food for lunch, along with a regularly changing blackboard menu.

5 Buxton Sq., Nelson. © **03/548-9621**. Reservations recommended for dinner. Main courses NZ$18–NZ$25 (US$13–US$18). AE, DC, MC, V. Mon–Sat 9:30am–9:30pm. Closed June, Dec 25, and Jan 1.

Tips **Raise Your Glass**

With a strong hop-growing history, it's not surprising that Nelson delivers on the beer front. Two to visit are **Founders Organic Brewery** ✻✻✻, Founders Historic Park, 87 Atawhai Dr., Nelson (📞 **03/548-4638**; www.biobrew.co.nz), the country's first certified organic brewery complete with a cafe that serves great lunches; and **Mac's Brewery** ✻✻✻, 660 Main Rd., Stoke (📞 **03/547-0526**; www.macs.co.nz), where they make a range of premium, award-winning beers and offer brewery tours at 11am and 2pm daily for NZ$10 (US$7). They're open 10am until 5pm.

The Cut Restaurant & Bar ✻✻✻ MODERN NEW ZEALAND   The Cut, along with Harbourlight and Appleman's in Richmond, is the most favored eatery in the area. Set in an early-1900s house, it's taken a simple, stylish approach to fine dining—all polished wood and white tablecloths and for 3 years running has won Nelson's best restaurant award. The rib-eye steak gets rave reviews, and the spiced lamb is worth a mention. There are Mediterranean overtones to the menu, which features lots of game in winter. Also try the fish dishes and the divine desserts.

94 Collingwood St., Nelson. 📞 **03/548-9874.** Reservations required. Main courses NZ$26–NZ$32 (US$18–US$22). AE, DC, MC, V. Daily 6pm–late; Tues–Sat 6pm–late in winter.

Harry's Bar ✻✻ PACIFIC/ASIAN   Locals seem very happy with Harry's and that's usually a good sign. Sited in old legal chambers, it has a reputation for serving consistently excellent meals with an emphasis on Asian flavors. The modern interior, built around glass and lighting effects, can distract you from the sometimes patchy service. It's lively, especially in the early evening when locals gather for predinner drinks.

306 Hardy St., Nelson. 📞 **03/539-0905.** Reservations recommended. Main courses NZ$22–NZ$30 (US$15–US$21). AE, MC, V. Summer Thurs–Tues 11am–late; winter Tues–Sat 6pm–late.

Ma Fish ✻ SEAFOOD   Upstairs at the Nelson Yacht Club, this is an excellent family-friendly restaurant that, understandably, makes a big deal over the local fish catch. Watch ships and boats while you tuck into fish "a thousand ways."

322 Wakefield Quay, Nelson. 📞 **03/539-1307.** Main courses NZ$20–NZ$30 (US$14–US$21). AE, DC, MC, V. Mon–Fri 4pm–late; Sat–Sun noon–late.

Stingray ✻✻✻ CAFE   It's a smart operator who can successfully combine fabulous organic and healthy vegetarian fare with a diverse menu that includes steaks, Thai marinated chicken, and pizza in one of the hippest meeting places in town. Come here for amazing smoothies, fresh juices, organic salads, coffee, or champagne and tapas at the start of an evening out.

8 Church St., Nelson. 📞 **03/545-8957.** Main courses NZ$15–NZ$25 (US$11–US$18). AE, MC, V. Daily 8am–late.

Zest Deli & Café ✻✻✻ CAFE/DELI   You won't know where to start when you walk through the doors of this "giant food basket." It's one of the best little finds in Nelson, tucked between Hardy Street and Selwyn Place, just across the street from the equally delicious Stingray. This place—with fresh food (especially the pies and pastries) and coffee, plus a wide range of gourmet gift products—is worth looking for.

5 Church St., Nelson. 📞 **03/546-7064.** Daily 7:30am–10pm. NZ$10–NZ$20 (US$7–US$14). MC, V.

IN RICHMOND

One of the popular casual favorites in the area is **The Honest Lawyer Country Pub** ★, 1 Point Rd., Monaco, Nelson (© **03/547-8850**), which is not actually in the country at all, but near Nelson Airport. It's a replica of a classic English pub, offering breakfast, lunch, and dinner daily from 7am till late. **Appleman's Restaurant** ★★★, 294 Queen St., Richmond (© **03/544-0601**), is the one consistently recommended by locals. Innovative preparations of lamb, beef, venison, and seafood set it apart from most other menus and hoist it into the top three of the greater Nelson region. It's open daily from 6pm.

IN MOTUEKA/MAPUA

The Smokehouse ★★, Shed 3, Mapua Wharf, Mapua (© **03/540-2280**), hangs out over the turquoise depths of Mapua Estuary, and the menu is completely dominated by fish dishes, many of them using the smoked product prepared on the premises. It's well signposted from the main highway and well worth the sidetrack. It's open daily from 9am to 9pm. Another good bet here is **Flax Restaurant & Bar** ★★★, Shed 1, Mapua Wharf (© **03/540-2028**), which is open daily for lunch and dinner, from 10:30am. **The Naked Bun Patisserie** ★★, 66–68 Aranui Rd., Mapua (© **03/540-3656**), is a European-style patisserie, where you'll get not only divine sweet things, but also organic breads and very tasty savory snacks. It's open daily from 6am to 5pm and has indoor and outdoor dining. There are also dining opportunities at some of the local wineries (see "The Moutere Hills Wineries," earlier in this chapter). It has a fabulous location overhanging the estuary, terrific service, and divine food. In Motueka, **Blast Espresso** ★★, 145 High St. (© **03/528-0087**), is a reliable bet for good coffee and, if you need it, gluten-free food.

3 Abel Tasman National Park & Golden Bay ★★★

Marahau, the southern gateway to the park: 67km (42 miles) NW of Nelson; Takaka, the gateway to Golden Bay: 109km (68 miles) NW of Nelson

Abel Tasman is New Zealand's smallest national park. It protects 23,000 hectares (56,810 acres) of easily accessible coastline, offering unbeatable gold-sand beaches and forested headlands. Marahau and Totaranui are the main gateways to the park, a 1½- and 2½-hour drive, respectively, from Nelson.

Farther north, Golden Bay sits peacefully beyond the twists and turns of Takaka Hill, opening out in a spread of forested parks and golden beaches. The scenery is breathtaking, and the area draws many visitors keen to hike the Abel Tasman's Coastal Track and Kahurangi's Heaphy Track. Today, it is a fertile mix of dairy farming and artsy alternative lifestyles—a reflection of the number of people who've reached this corner of the world and found they didn't want to leave.

ESSENTIALS

GETTING THERE & GETTING AROUND   By Plane   Vincent Aviation Ltd. (© **0800/846-236** in NZ) has scheduled flights between Wellington and Takaka, plus Heaphy Track and Abel Tasman National Park connections. Several other small operators, including **Abel Tasman Air** (© **0800/304-560** in NZ; www.abeltasmanair.co. nz), also service this area.

By Coach (Bus)   Abel Tasman Coachlines, 27 Bridge St., Nelson (© **03/548-0285;** www.abeltasmantravel.co.nz), operates regular service from Nelson to Kaiteriteri, Marahau, Totaranui, and Abel Tasman National Park, daily year-round. It also

---

> ⌒Tips   **A Scenic Alternative**
>
> Take a fast spin on **Exhilarator** 𝒦𝒦𝒦 , Wakefield Quay, Nelson (© **03/548-8066;**
> www.exhilarator.co.nz), which departs Nelson daily at 9:30am, noon, and 4pm.
> A 2-hour round-trip to Abel Tasman National Park is around NZ$60 (US$42).

---

provides connecting service to Kahurangi National Park and the north entrance to the Heaphy Track. **KBus,** P.O. Box 1079, Blenheim (© **0800/881-188** in NZ, or 03/ 578-4075; www.kbus.co.nz), has scheduled service between Picton, Blenheim, Motueka, Nelson, Abel Tasman, Golden Bay, and Heaphy Track, plus service between Collingwood and Takaka.

By Shuttle   Trek Express (© **0800/128-735** in NZ, or 03/540-2042; www.trek express.co.nz) operates a four-wheel-drive shuttle to Kahurangi Park and all other major hikes in the area.

By Car   The trip from Nelson to Takaka via State Highway 60 takes about 2 hours and includes a long, steep, winding section crossing Takaka Hill. To reach Marahau, turn right at the bottom of Takaka Hill, just past Motueka, and drive through Kaiteri- teri. The trip takes about 1½ hours.

VISITOR INFORMATION   The **Department of Conservation,** King Edward Street, Motueka (© **03/528-9117**), provides information on the national parks and huts available on the tracks. The **Golden Bay i-Site Visitor Centre,** Willow Street, Takaka (© **03/525-9136;** www.nelsonnz.com), is open from 9am to 5pm daily in summer and 9am until 4pm in winter. The **Farewell Spit Visitor Centre & Café,** RD1, Collingwood, Golden Bay (© **03/524-8454;** fax 03/524-8259), is open daily most of the year and has informative displays on the upper reaches of Golden Bay. Further information on Golden Bay can be found at www.goldenbay.net.nz.

EXPLORING ABEL TASMAN NATIONAL PARK 𝒦𝒦𝒦

Abel Tasman is the jewel among popular national parks. It's a sea kayaker's paradise, and it's great for swimming and fishing. The **Abel Tasman Coastal Track** (see chap- ter 3 for details on this track) is one of the Department of Conservation's eight iden- tified Great Walks and the only coast track of its kind in the country. It can be done in 3 to 5 days, or combined with water taxis or sea kayaks for added interest.

Sea kayaking is probably the best way to see the area, and **Abel Tasman Kayaks** 𝒦𝒦𝒦 , Marahau Beach, RD2, Motueka (© **0800/732-529** in NZ, or 03/ 527-8022; www.abeltasmankayaks.co.nz), pioneered the activity in this region. It has a large base with secure car parking and hot showers. A range of trips is available year- round. The most popular is the 1-day guided Beaches and Islands excursion for NZ$99 (US$69). It also has a 3-day fully catered Enchanted Coast tour for NZ$595 (US$417) and a 2-day kayaking-and-walking tour starts at NZ$240. Prices include pickup and transport from Motueka. Return transport to Nelson costs NZ$14 (US$9.80). **Ocean River Sea Kayaking** 𝒦𝒦𝒦 , Marahau Beach Road, RD2, Motueka (© **0800/732-529** in NZ, or 03/527-8022; www.seakayaking.co.nz), specializes in independent freedom rentals from NZ$69 (US$48) per person per day. They'll give you all the instruction you need and you can unwind at the end in the company's hot tub!

> **⌐Tips Time Factor**
>
> Don't forget, if you're being picked up from Nelson for any of these park excursions, you'll have to allow 1½ hours each way on a bus. You'll leave Nelson at 7:15am, 8:30am, or 3:40pm, returning 1:55, 5:15, 6, or 7:15pm. There's only one bus in winter (from the end of Apr to Oct), leaving Nelson at 8:30am, returning at 6pm.

Abel Tasman Wilson's Experiences ✸✸✸, 265 High St., Motueka (© **0800/223-582** in NZ, or 03/528-2027; www.abeltasman.co.nz), operates buses, launches, and beachfront lodges. It's an award-winning family-owned business run by the Wilson family, who pioneered tourism in the park in 1977. They arrange 1- to 5-day guided walks and sea-kayaking trips that include stays at their Torrent Bay Lodge and Homestead Lodge at Awaroa Bay. All trips can be arranged as walking only, or walking/sea kayaking combinations, and skilled guides and chefs provide quality experiences and meals. During high season, a 1-day guided sea kayaking trip costs from NZ$96 (US$67); a 2-day walk or sea kayak trip is NZ$682 (US$407) for adults and NZ$472 (US$330) for children; the 3-day guided option is NZ$998 (US$699) for adults, NZ$798 (US$559) for children 8 to 14; the 5-day walk costs NZ$1,470 (US$1,029) for adults and NZ$1,029 (US$720) for children. Rates are lower from mid-April to mid-October. Scenic cruises are also offered on the company's **Vigour Taxi Service** and **Vista Cruises.** Prices for these start around NZ$50 (US$35) for adults.

Abel Tasman Aqua Taxi ✸✸✸, Marahau, RD2, Motueka (© **0800/278-282** in NZ, or 03/527-8083; www.aquataxis.co.nz), has a 3-hour cruise that visits points of interest along the park beaches and the fur-seal colony on Tonga Island. The price ranges from around NZ$50 to NZ$75 (US$35–US$53). If you're short on time, do the cruise if nothing else, or you'll miss seeing this spectacular unspoiled coast.

For a terrific guided walk, look no further than **Kahurangi Guided Walks** ✸✸, Dodson Road, Takaka, Golden Bay (© **03/525-7177**; www.kahurangiwalks.co.nz). They offer 1-, 3-, or 5-day walking trips in the Abel Tasman and Kahurangi National Parks. There are excellent half-day trips for those on a tight schedule, starting from around NZ$30 to NZ$40 (US$21–US$28) per person. **Bush and Beyond Guided Walks** ✸✸, 35 School Rd., Motueka (© **03/528-9054;** www.naturetreks.co.nz), have day and multiday walks priced from NZ$120 (US$84).

WHERE TO STAY
Kaiteriteri Beach has a wealth of accommodations, but you'll have to book months in advance. At Marahau Beach, backpackers and campers should check out **The Barn,** Harvey Road, Marahau (© **03/527-8043;** fax 03/527-8440), the closest lodgings to the park, with a shared dorm, double/twin rooms, and motor-home or tent sites from NZ$20 to NZ$60 (US$14–US$42). **Marahau Beach Camp,** Franklin Street, Marahau (©/fax **03/527-8176;** www.abeltasmanmarahaucamp.co.nz), also has backpacker and camping facilities. More upmarket are the eight rooms at **Abel Tasman Ocean View Chalets** ✸, Beach Road, Marahau, RD2, Motueka (© **03/527-8232;** www.accommodationabeltasman.co.nz), with rates of NZ$138–NZ$205 (US$97–US$144) for four people in their 1- and 2-bedroom chalets.

My pick for this area is **Awaroa Lodge** ✸✸✸, Abel Tasman National Park (© **03/528-8758;** www.awaroalodge.co.nz), which has 26 modern rooms from around

NZ$300–NZ$400 (US$210–US$280). It's tucked into the northern end of the park, is a feature destination of the Abel Tasman Coastal Track, and has its own restaurant. There is no road access. You reach the lodge via foot, kayak, water taxi, helicopter or small, fixed-wing aircraft. **Abel Tasman Marahau Lodge** ★★, Marahau Beach, RD2, Motueka (✆ **03/527-8250;** www.abeltasmanmarahaulodge.co.nz), has 12 smart studio units with en-suite bathrooms for NZ$160 to NZ$250 (US$112–US$175). It's not the Hilton, but you do get great service, a magical setting, and incredible silence.

EXPLORING GOLDEN BAY ★★★

The main town near Golden Bay is Takaka, which has an astoundingly small population of 1,100. Another 28km (17 miles) north is Collingwood, which is even smaller. While in Takaka, you can peek in at the **Golden Bay Museum & Gallery,** Commercial Street (✆/fax **03/525-9990**), open Monday through Saturday from 10am to 4pm. There are also several working artists in the area, and the free brochure *Arts of Golden Bay,* available from the visitor center (✆ **03/525-9136**), details the locations and visiting hours of 11 of the best.

Golden Bay is rich in natural attractions, and one of the best known is **Te Waikoropupu Springs** ★★, called Pupu Springs by the locals. Here you'll find rushing water claimed to be the clearest freshwater in the world. It's signposted just north of Takaka township.

Cave formations are also common; one of the most famous, **Harwood's Hole,** plummets an awesome 183m (600 ft.) straight down. The visitor center can supply you with details. There are three other cave systems worth investigating. **Ngarua Caves,** 20km (12 miles) from Motueka on Takaka Hill (✆ **03/528-8093**), are easily negotiated and feature stalactites aplenty and the skeletal remains of the extinct moa. Guided tours are given on the hour between 10am and 4pm from mid-September to June 7. Admission costs around NZ$13 (US$9.10). **Te Anaroa & Rebecca Caves,** Rockville, Golden Bay (✆ **03/525-6044**), have easy access and the best glowworms. They're very beautiful, but some of the rooflines are low and narrow, which may put you off if you're claustrophobic. Admission is around NZ$15 (US$11) for adults and NZ$6 (US$4.20) for children; call for tour times. **Rawhiti Caves,** also in Golden Bay (✆ **03/525-7177**), cost around NZ$15 (US$11) for adults and NZ$7 (US$4.90) for children. It takes a 40-minute bush walk to reach the caves, where you're greeted with a huge entrance and a steep descent. You need to be agile for this outing, and it's not recommended for children under 5.

Local rock climbers know all about the many attributes of **Payne's Ford Scenic Reserve,** near Takaka. The limestone bluffs they favor dominate the area; a track through the reserve follows an old tramway line. You'll find excellent swimming holes in the nearby Takaka River.

All along the road from Takaka to Collingwood, you'll see signs pointing to the coast. Each beach is different, but much of the bay is shallow; swimming at high tide involves a lot less walking. Tata Beach is deeper.

Another 26km (16 miles) north of Collingwood is the base of **Farewell Spit,** a unique sand spit 35km (22 miles) long and 800m (about half a mile) wide. All along its length are sand dunes as high as seven- to eight-story buildings. The birdlife here is amazing, as it is a migratory stopover for several species. The **Farewell Spit Nature Tour** (✆ **03/524-8188;** www.farewell-spit.co.nz) departs from the Collingwood Post Office building; times vary with the tidal conditions. It's a 6½-hour trip that costs NZ$80 (US$59) adults, NZ$50 (US$35) children under 15 years. A full meal is included and you get a comprehensive commentary by a local driver.

Farewell Spit Eco Tours *⋆⋆*, Tasman Street, Collingwood ((*C* **0800/808-257** in NZ, or 03/524-8257; www.farewellspit.com), has a range of superb tours to Farewell Spit. Most popular is the Lighthouse trip, a 5½-hour trip that costs around NZ$70 (US$49) for adults and NZ$45 (US$66) for children ages 5 to 15. There are also special bird-watching trips by arrangement that range from NZ$70 to NZ$95 (US$49–US$67) for adults. Bring binoculars and a camera.

Another great Golden Bay outing is the **Scenic Mail Run** *⋆⋆* ((*C* **03/524-8188**; fax 03/524-8091), which leaves from the Collingwood Post Office at 10:30am Monday through Friday. The 5½-hour trip costs around NZ$60–NZ$75 (US$42–US$53) and includes lunch.

For information on the **Heaphy Track** and **Kahurangi National Park,** see "Tramping" in chapter 3.

WHERE TO STAY

Sans Souci Inn *⋆*, 11 Richmond Rd., Pohara Beach ((*C*/fax **03/525-8663;** www.sanssouciinn.co.nz), is an ideal beach stay near Takaka if you're into simplicity and style. The seven-unit grass-roofed inn, run by a young Swiss couple, is a divine hideaway with a Japanese feel. Mediterranean floor tiles, low futon-style beds, and scented Lawson cypress ceilings give it a unique character. Doubles are NZ$90 (US$63) and a restaurant is on-site.

Farther north, **Collingwood Homestead** *⋆⋆*, Elizabeth Street, Collingwood ((*C* **03/524-8079**; www.collingwoodhomestead.co.nz), is one of the best home stays in the region. It's hard to find fault with the personalized hospitality and four large bedrooms with brand-new modern bathrooms. Rates are NZ$265 (US$186), which includes a wonderful breakfast.

WHERE TO DINE

It's easy to recommend the **Wholemeal Café** *⋆⋆*, 60 Commercial St., Takaka ((*C* **03/525-9426**). It has the best food in the area, and you can't help feeling it's horrendously healthy as well as delicious. It's also a great place to pick up picnic fare. The cafe is open in summer daily from 7:30am to 9:30pm, and, after Easter, Sunday through Tuesday from 8:30am to 5pm, Thursday through Saturday from 8:30am until late.

Near Collingwood, **Paddlecrab Kitchen,** Farewell Spit, Puponga ((*C* **03/524-8708**), will surprise you with the standard of its food. It may be well out on a geographical limb, but combine its incredible location with inventive cuisine, courteous service, and good-value dining and you'll find it was worth the extra miles. It's open daily from October through April from 8am until 10pm, and from 10am until 4pm from August through September. It's closed for June and July. At Pohara, enjoy a wide choice of seafood and gourmet pizzas at **Penguin Café & Bar,** 818 Abel Tasman Dr., Pohara ((*C* **03/525-6126**). It's open daily in summer from 9am.

13

Christchurch & Canterbury

Christchurch may have a reputation for being the most English and the most conservative of New Zealand's major cities, but it's far from quiet and subdued—and let's not get carried away with hype: It's not *that* English. A river, a few parks, and old buildings do not, England make. That said, it's a picturesque city that's worth more than a cursory glance.

Christchurch's modern airport provides the gateway to the South Island, affectionately known as "The Mainland" by those who live here. It is the third-largest city in New Zealand—a prosperous place that is home to 337,000 people who enjoy the lowest annual rainfall of any of the four major cities, the greatest temperature extremes, and 2,120 hours of sunshine annually.

With one-eighth of its area devoted to public parks, reserves, and recreation grounds, and with the 186-hectare (459-acre) Hagley Park smack in its center, you shouldn't be surprised to find Christchurch tagged New Zealand's Garden City. This verdant core, along with the Avon River, a spread of Victorian architecture, and the avenues and squares, are almost entirely responsible for the reputation of "Englishness." Plus, with over 50 adventure products to offer, the city is a mecca for anyone who likes a racy edge to his or her holiday. Whether you choose leisurely days discovering the city's cultural foundation or adrenaline-pumping outdoor activities, you'll find that conservative old Christchurch can dish up a few surprises.

The province of Canterbury, stretching from the Southern Alps to the Pacific Ocean, has legendary physical attractions, from ski fields and fishing rivers to the Port Hills tramping tracks and east coast beaches. Day-trip options from Christchurch include Kaikoura, Akaroa, Hanmer, Arthur's Pass, and Methven—each presenting its own version of provincial hospitality, rural escapism, and heart-stopping outdoor adventure.

1 Orientation

ARRIVING

BY PLANE Christchurch has frequent air service from all major centers via Air New Zealand and Air New Zealand Link as well as Air Nelson and Origin Pacific (see "Getting Around" in chapter 2). **Christchurch International Airport** is 10km (6 miles) from Cathedral Square and it receives direct flights from several countries. The new international terminal features everything travelers will need, including boutique shopping and a **Visitor Information Centre** (© 03/353-7783; www.christchurch-airport.co.nz). The **Visitor Information Centre** in the domestic terminal (© 03/353-7774) will book accommodations and transportation at no charge. Also here are car-rental firms, a bank, a florist, a bookstore, a confectionery store, a hair salon, Internet kiosks, a restaurant, a souvenir shop, and a duty-free store. For further international airport details, check www.christchurch-airport.co.nz.

Christchurch

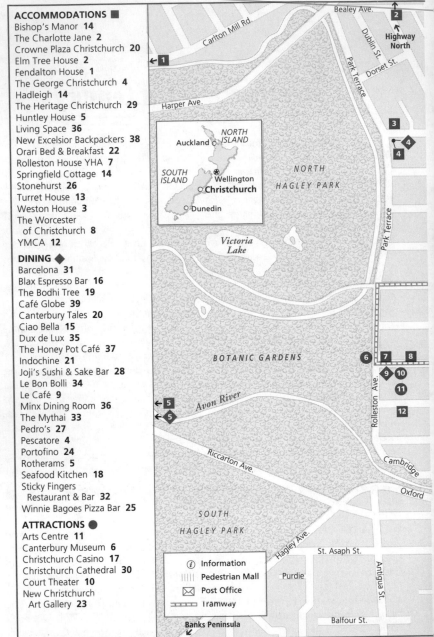

ACCOMMODATIONS ■
Bishop's Manor **14**
The Charlotte Jane **2**
Crowne Plaza Christchurch **20**
Elm Tree House **2**
Fendalton House **1**
The George Christchurch **4**
Hadleigh **14**
The Heritage Christchurch **29**
Huntley House **5**
Living Space **36**
New Excelsior Backpackers **38**
Orari Bed & Breakfast **22**
Rolleston House YHA **7**
Springfield Cottage **14**
Stonehurst **26**
Turret House **13**
Weston House **3**
The Worcester
 of Christchurch **8**
YMCA **12**

DINING ◆
Barcelona **31**
Blax Espresso Bar **16**
The Bodhi Tree **19**
Café Globe **39**
Canterbury Tales **20**
Ciao Bella **15**
Dux de Lux **35**
The Honey Pot Café **37**
Indochine **21**
Joji's Sushi & Sake Bar **28**
Le Bon Bolli **34**
Le Café **9**
Minx Dining Room **36**
The Mythai **33**
Pedro's **27**
Pescatore **4**
Portofino **24**
Rotherams **5**
Seafood Kitchen **18**
Sticky Fingers
 Restaurant & Bar **32**
Winnie Bagoes Pizza Bar **25**

ATTRACTIONS ●
Arts Centre **11**
Canterbury Museum **6**
Christchurch Casino **17**
Christchurch Cathedral **30**
Court Theater **10**
New Christchurch
 Art Gallery **23**

Bealey Ave.

Carlton Mill Rd.

Highway
North

Dublin St.

Dorset St.

Park Terrace

Harper Ave.

NORTH
ISLAND
Auckland

SOUTH
ISLAND
Wellington
Christchurch
Dunedin

NORTH
HAGLEY PARK

Park Terrace

Victoria
Lake

BOTANIC GARDENS

Rolleston Ave.

Avon River

Riccarton Ave.

Cambridge

Oxford

SOUTH
HAGLEY PARK

Hagley Ave.

St. Asaph St.

Purdie

Antigua St.

ⓘ Information
||||| Pedestrian Mall
✉ Post Office
▭▭▭▭ Tramway

Banks Peninsula

Balfour St.

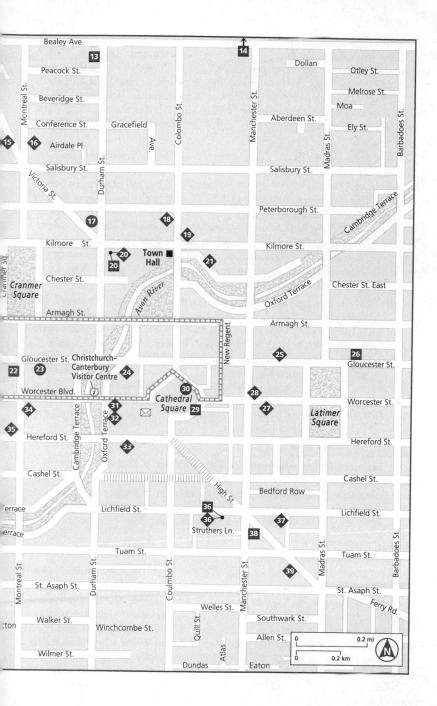

Several shuttle companies operate between the airport and central city. **Super Shuttle** (© **03/365-5655**) runs daily 24 hours and charges around NZ$18 to NZ$20 (US$13–US$14). The **City Flyer Bus** (© **03/366-8855**) departs from the airport and from Worcester Street, near the Square, opposite Regent Theatre and calls at the Bus Exchange before returning to the airport. It leaves on the half-hour Monday through Friday, on the hour Saturday and Sunday. For a 20-minute taxi ride, call **First Direct** (© **03/377-5555**). The fare to central city should be NZ$22 to NZ$30 (US$15–US$21).

BY TRAIN & COACH (BUS)   Train service to and from Christchurch has been greatly reduced as railway companies rationalize their operations. The TranzAlpine (Greymouth), and the *Coastal Pacific* (Picton) are the only two still running. For information, call **Tranz Scenic** at © **0800/843-596.** The **Christchurch Railway Station** is on Clarence Street, in Addington. Regular shuttles run from the station to the city.

InterCity (© **0800/468-372** or 03/379-9020) covers most of the South Island, offering service between Christchurch, Dunedin, Fox and Franz Josef Glaciers, Greymouth and the West Coast, Wanaka, Queenstown and Mount Cook, Invercargill, Timaru, Picton, and Kaikoura. If you prefer something cheaper, go with **Kiwi Experience** (© **03/377-9810**).

BY CAR   If you're coming from the north, you'll drive in on State Highway 1 (St. Hwy. 1) and enter the city through the northwest suburbs of Papanui and Merivale. It's 4 to 5 hours from Picton and 2½ hours from Kaikoura. From Dunedin, via Timaru and Ashburton, you'll also be on State Highway 1. It takes 5 hours from Dunedin, 2 from Timaru. From the southwest, via Lake Tekapo and Geraldine, travel on Highway 79 to Highway 77 and then Highway 73; this takes you to Mount Hutt and over the Rakaia River. If you're coming from the West Coast, you'll go over Arthur's Pass and enter Christchurch at Upper Riccarton. This trip takes 4 hours. Christchurch is 366km (227 miles) north of Dunedin, 350km (217 miles) south of Picton, and 254km (157 miles) southeast of Greymouth.

VISITOR INFORMATION
The **Christchurch & Canterbury i-Site Visitor Centre** is in the Old Chief Post Office Building, Cathedral Square West (© **03/379-9629;** fax 03/377-2424; www. christchurchnz.net). It's open Monday through Friday from 8:30am to 5pm; Saturday, Sunday, and holidays from 8:30am to 4pm (longer hours in summer). Useful websites are www.bethere.org.nz or www.whatsonchristchurch.co.nz.

SPECIAL EVENTS
Christchurch is the festival capital of New Zealand—no matter when you visit, it's bound to coincide with a festival of some sort. The **World Buskers Festival** ❊❊❊ (© **03/377-2365**), from mid- to late January, is the largest street performance festival in the Southern Hemisphere. You'll be treated to jazz and comedy shows, as well as acts of juggling, contortionism, and more. In February, the city bursts into bloom with the **Garden City Flowers & Romance** (© **03/365-5403**). The annual **Wine and Food Festival** ❊❊ (© **03/358-1648**) also takes place in February. The **Christchurch Arts Festival** ❊❊❊ (© **03/365-2223**) is staged every 2 years in July and showcases international talent. The next one will be held in 2007. **Showtime Canterbury** ❊❊, featuring the **Canterbury A & P Show** (© **03/941-6840**), is an absolute tradition in this part of the world. Staged the second week of November, it features thoroughbred and standardbred racing.

CITY LAYOUT

Cathedral Square (also known as the Square) is the center point, around which the main roads are laid out in a grid system, surrounded by four main avenues—Bealey, Moorehouse, Deans, and Fitzgerald. The winding Avon River meanders 24km (15 miles) from the west of Christchurch, through the city and out to sea. The Port Hills, south of the city, are an ever-present landmark from which you can always get your bearings. Colombo Street is the main street running north-south to the Port Hills.

THE NEIGHBORHOODS IN BRIEF

Fendalton This is the heart of Christchurch conservatism and money—the southern equivalent of Auckland's Remuera. You'll find wonderful old homes and beautiful tree-lined streets, but its retail center is small, unimaginative, and easily bypassed altogether in favor of Merivale shopping. There are few accommodations in this area.

Merivale Those among the moneyed set who consider themselves a little more contemporary throng to Merivale to shop and dine. Located between Papanui and inner city, it is an attractive suburb, close to the heart of things, and it offers a good number of B&Bs along with "Motel Mile," which stretches south along Papanui Road from Merivale Mall to Bealey Avenue. Always safe, in all senses of the word, it is a pleasant place to be, and you can walk here from the heart of the city in about 30 minutes.

St. Albans This older suburb lies adjacent to Merivale to the east—some would call it the poor man's Merivale, but now that most of the old villas have been significantly renovated, real-estate prices are a little out of the "poor" league. There is no real retail heart here and just a few lodgings—predominantly at the Bealey Avenue end of the suburb, where there is another good selection of motels.

Inner City I recommend finding accommodations in inner city, which generally consists of the area within the four main avenues: Deans, Bealey, Moorehouse, and Fitzgerald. Most of the major hotels are close to Cathedral Square (known as the Square) and the shopping on Colombo Street, City Mall (the pedestrian-only zone of Cashel St.), and Manchester and High streets. The main restaurant/bar zone is situated on Oxford Terrace, which borders the Avon River and connects with the lower end of City Mall. Hagley Park is a short walk.

Hagley Park/Botanic Gardens Theoretically still inner city, this compact area just west of the central business district is easily defined by its proximity to Hagley Park and the Botanic Gardens. It is generally the area west of Montreal Street, along Park Avenue, and through to Deans Avenue on the west side of the park. You'll find excellent accommodations and some of the major attractions, such as the Canterbury Museum, the Arts Centre, and the new Art Gallery. It's a 5- to 10-minute walk along Worcester Boulevard (serviced by the tram) to the Square and the visitor center.

Riccarton/Ilam Riccarton is on the western side of Hagley Park, and apart from its huge shopping mall, a proliferation of cheap Asian restaurants, and a Sunday market, it has little for me to recommend. The area between Riccarton and Fendalton is known as Ilam, and this is where you'll find Canterbury University tucked into a beautiful leafy enclave.

Sumner Once a holiday spot for Christchurch residents, Sumner has long since become a suburb of the city itself. It's a delightful place about 15 to 30 minutes from the city. The neighborhood is characterized by steep hillsides dotted with prime real estate with stunning views of the city and coast, as well as by quaint holiday homes that still sit near the beach. It's easily accessed by bus, has a cute village feel, and offers a thriving social life with at least 20 cafes and restaurants. In summer, the young surfing crowd gathers on the Esplanade, and there's generally volleyball and beach fun aplenty.

Lyttelton This is a quaint port village over the Port Hills from Christchurch, a 20- to 30-minute drive away. You'll either love it or hate it; Lyttelton seldom gets reactions in between. Quaint, to some, turns out to be ugly and gray to others. It has few lodgings and is considerably less convenient for Christchurch sightseeing. However, a visit here makes for a nice drive. Head out to Sumner and go up over the Port Hills and down into Lyttelton. You can then return to the central city via the tunnel. (Of course, you can use the tunnel both ways for a quicker trip.)

2 Getting Around

BY PUBLIC BUS All local buses operate out of the **Bus Exchange,** Colombo and Lichfield streets (© **03/366-8855;** www.metroinfo.org.nz). North-south buses are based on Colombo Street; east-west buses are based within the building. **Red Bus Limited** (© **0800/733-287** in NZ, or 03/379-4260; www.redbus.co.nz), operates the majority of these urban bus services, with others provided by **Leopard Coachlines (Urban Cat)** (© **03/73-8100**). The **Bus Info Centre** is on the second level of the building for details on the complete service. Zoned fares range from NZ$2 to NZ$6 (US$1.40–US$4.20). For information and details on all-day passes, contact **Bus Info** (© **03/366-8855;** www.metroinfo.org.nz).

Check out the advantages of a **Red Bus Explore Christchurch Day Pass.** Its network of routes enables you to explore Christchurch for NZ$7 (US$4.90) per person or NZ$15 (US$11) per family. Purchase it from your bus driver or Metro Info in the Bus Exchange, which is open daily 7:30am to 5:30pm. If you're planning an evening out, consider the **Midnight Express Service** 𝒜𝒜, which leaves on four major suburban routes on the hour between midnight and 4am. Just look out for the distinctive purple buses, or call Bus Info for route details. It will save you the hassle of finding car parks and it costs just NZ$5 (US$3.50).

Tips A Note on Safety

Like any large city, Christchurch has its criminal element, but if you use common sense, there's no reason why you should see any evidence of it. It's generally considered not a good idea to wander about in Cathedral Square alone after midnight, and most inner city streets east of Manchester Street need a little more caution. It also pays to give Latimer Square a wide berth if you're alone after dark. The inner city, especially around City Mall and Oxford Terrace, is generally safe, as there are always plenty of people about at all hours and security cameras now operate in some areas.

> **_Tips_ An Easy Introduction**
>
> If you're in town for a few days and want to get a feel for the inner city, head for the Square and look for the red-and-black **Personal Guiding Service** kiosk. Trained guides—they're in red and black too—offer daily 2-hour walking tours at 10am and 1pm from October through April, and at 1pm from May through September. Tours also depart 15 minutes earlier from outside the nearby Visitor Centre. For more information, call ✆ **03/379-9629.**

A suburban bus system, **The Orbiter,** allows you to travel around the outskirts without having to go into central city. The bright-green buses run every 15 minutes during the day and every half-hour in evenings and on weekends. They cost NZ$2 (US$1.40). The **Metro Star,** is an extension of that cross-suburban service, linking all the major suburban shopping malls. Its orange buses runs every 15 minutes Monday through Friday and every 30 minutes on evenings and weekends. It uses a long-term electronic card system, which is prepaid and can be used on all other buses. Cash is accepted, but it's more expensive and you only get one free transfer, as opposed to unlimited transfers with Metrocards.

The upstairs information center at the Bus Exchange has take-away timetables and all the information you'll need.

BY SHUTTLE   The free central-city electric shuttle is bright yellow; its pickup points are designated by bright-yellow street towers. The shuttle travels between the Casino, Town Hall, Victoria Square, Cathedral Square, City Mall, South City, Smiths City, and Hoyts 8 on Moorehouse Avenue at 10-minute intervals during the day, 15-minute intervals at night. The service does not operate on Christmas Day, Boxing Day, New Year's Day, or Good Friday.

BY PRIVATE BUS   The **City Circuit Bus** (✆ **03/332 6012** or 021/217 3975; fax 03/332-6598) offers transportation to the area's most popular attractions: The **Plains Circuit** goes to Willowbank Kiwi House, the Antarctic Centre, Air Force World, Orana Park, Riccarton Mall, and Mona Vale Gardens, while the **Port Circuit** goes to Ferrymead Historic Park, the Gondola, Lyttelton Port, Sumner Beach, and Gethsemane Gardens. Both start at the visitor center in the Square. The cost is NZ$22 (US$15) for one circuit or around NZ$35 (US$25) for both.

BY TRAMWAY   Christchurch's short but pleasant tramway (✆ **03/366-7830;** www.tram.co.nz) runs from Cathedral Square down Worcester Boulevard, crossing the Avon River to the Arts Centre. From here, it turns right to Rolleston Avenue and travels on to Armagh and New Regent streets and back to the Square. It operates from 9am to 9pm in summer and until 6pm in winter; one circuit takes 25 minutes and there are 11 stops along the route. Tickets are available on board at NZ$13 (US$9.10) for adults (children under 16 ride for free) and you can hop on and off the tram as often as you like for 2 days.

BY TAXI   There are taxi stands scattered around the inner city and at all transport terminals. **First Direct** (✆ **03/377-5555**) has a reputation for being the best priced. For taxis that can accommodate wheelchairs, call ✆ **03/379-9788.**

BY CAR   If you want to see only the main central-city sights, you probably won't need a car; you can make the most of free shuttles and cheap tour buses for those farther-afield destinations. And don't forget the Midnight Express bus (see above) if you're staying late in the city. If you do have a car, driving in Christchurch is straightforward. Most on-street parking is metered or has time limits. It's a good idea to make use of the centrally located municipal parking buildings, most of which offer your first hour's parking free. They are well signposted on Kilmore Street over the Crowne Plaza Hotel; in Cashel Street near the Grand Chancellor Hotel; on Lichfield Street near the Durham Street intersection; on Oxford Terrace near the Main Library; on Manchester Street near the intersection with Armagh Street; and under the new Art Gallery on Gloucester Street. You'll find free car parking in Hagley Park during the day—entrance is at the end of Armagh Street.

BY BICYCLE   Christchurch is a biker's heaven—it's flat (except for the Port Hills), and motorists are used to a high volume of bicycle traffic. There are cycle lanes set aside in many areas, especially in the northwest suburbs, where there's quite a bit of university bike traffic. For information on rentals, see "Outdoor Pursuits," later in this chapter.

ON FOOT   Most of the main central-city attractions are well placed for easy walking—especially in the Arts Centre/Botanic Gardens area. Shopping areas are fairly far-flung, but you can make use of the free electric shuttle or the very reasonably priced tram to take the load off your feet every so often.

FAST FACTS: Christchurch

American Express The office at 773 Colombo St. (© **0800/263-936** in NZ) accepts mail for cardholders, issues and changes traveler's checks, and replaces lost and stolen traveler's checks and American Express cards.

Area Code The telephone area code (STD) is **03.**

Babysitters **Tuam Street Early Learning Centre,** 161 Tuam St. (© **03/365-6364**), open Monday through Friday from 8am to 5:30pm, can be contacted for babysitting services. Many hotels can also furnish evening babysitters.

Currency Exchange The **ANZ Bank Bureau de Change,** at Hereford and Colombo streets, in Cathedral Square (© **03/371-4714**), is open Monday through Friday from 8:30am to 4:30pm.

Disabled Services Contact **Disability Information Service,** 314 Worcester St. (© **03/366-6189**; fax 03/379-5939; dis@disinfo.co.nz), open Monday through Friday from 9am to 4:30pm.

Doctors For referrals, emergencies, or medical care, contact **After Hours Surgery,** Colombo Street and Bealey Avenue (© **03/365-7777**).

Emergencies Dial © **111** to call the police, report a fire, or request an ambulance.

Hospitals **Christchurch Hospital,** Oxford Terrace and Riccarton Avenue (© **03/364-0640**), has an Accident and Emergency Department.

Internet Access Try **Vadal.Net,** 57–59 Cathedral Square (© **03/377-2381**).

Pharmacies Go to **Urgent Pharmacy,** 931 Colombo St. (© **03/366-4439**).

Post Office The main post office is at 140 Hereford St. and is open Monday through Friday from 9am to 5pm. For all post offices, call © **0800/501-501.**

3 Where to Stay

I recommend staying in the inner city or near Hagley Park, within the four major avenues (see "City Layout," above), so you're within walking distance of the main attractions. The stretch of Papanui Road from Bealey Avenue to the suburb of Merivale is known as "Motel Mile" and also provides a good range of easily accessible accommodations.

The latest smart addition to the Canterbury accommodations scene is Christchurch's first genuinely luxurious, privately owned lodge, which opened in late 2003. **Otahuna Lodge** ⭐⭐⭐, RD2, Rhodes Road, Tai Tapu, Christchurch (© **03/329-6333;** www.otahuna.co.nz), is located just 20 minutes outside Christchurch in one of the region's grandest old homes. The 10 units are gigantic and introduce a new level of style to the Christchurch accommodations market. It is, in a word, fabulous. Lodge rooms cost NZ$900 (US$630); suites range from NZ$1,350 to NZ$2,025 (US$945–US$1,418), and each extra person costs NZ$282 (US$197).

The peak season is December through February, when you should book well ahead. All rates quoted include the 12.5% GST and free off-street parking unless otherwise stated.

IN INNER CITY
EXPENSIVE
Crowne Plaza Christchurch ⭐⭐⭐   The Crowne Plaza is still seen by many as Christchurch's number-one luxury hotel. It's hard to miss its architectural dominance of Victoria Square, and what really sells the place is its central-city location and its unquestionably high level of service. All rooms were recently refurbished with elegant contemporary furniture; many units have excellent city views. The Club rooms occupy the two top floors and have extra touches and access to Club Lounge with free breakfast and cocktails. It's worth paying the extra to get the space and bigger bathrooms they offer. Although not quite as refined as The George (see below) in my view, it's still a good choice.

Kilmore and Durham sts., Christchurch. © **0800/110-888** in NZ, or 03/365-7799. Fax 03/365-0082. www.crowne plaza.co.nz. 298 units. NZ$383 (US$268) standard; NZ$450 (US$315) Club Room; inquire for rates in Governor's Suite and Presidential Suite. Long-stay and special deals available. AE, DC, MC, V. **Amenities:** 3 restaurants; 3 bars; nearby golf course; gym; free bikes; concierge; tour desk; car rentals; comprehensive business center; 24-hr. room service; massage; babysitting; laundry service; same-day dry cleaning; nonsmoking rooms; on-call doctor/dentist. *In room:* A/C, TV w/pay movies, dataport, minibar, fridge, coffeemaker, hair dryer, iron.

MODERATE
The Heritage Christchurch ⭐⭐   At The Heritage, you have the choice of charm and character from the colonial past in the Old Government Building, or contemporary indulgence in the large rooms of the adjacent Heritage Tower. Both buildings were part of a NZ$16-million (US$11-million) conversion undertaken in 1997. In the tower, I especially like the split-level one-bedroom suites, which have a separate lounge, walk-in wardrobe, air-conditioning, and mezzanine bedroom. The sought-after heritage suites in the OGB also feature mezzanine bedrooms, along with open dining areas, kitchens, and laundry facilities, making them ideal for long stays. The marvelous location puts you close to everything, but I like the Crowne Plaza rooms better.

28 Cathedral Sq., Christchurch. © **0800/936-936** in NZ, or 03/377-9722. Fax 03/377-9881. www.heritagehotels. co.nz. 134 units in Heritage Tower; 40 units in Old Government Building (OGB). Heritage Tower: NZ$280 (US$196) deluxe tower; NZ$350 (US$245) executive; NZ$390 (US$273) penthouse studio; NZ$505 (US$354) penthouse suite.

OGB: NZ$365 (US$256) 1-bedroom suite; NZ$475 (US$333) 2-bedroom suite; NZ$790 (US$553) 3-bedroom suite. Long-stay and special deals available. AE, DC, MC, V. Valet parking NZ$15 (US$11). **Amenities:** Restaurant; bar; heated indoor lap pool; nearby golf course; well-equipped gym; day spa and salon; Jacuzzi; sauna; concierge; tour desk; car rentals; business center; 24-hr. room service; massage; babysitting; laundry service; same-day dry cleaning; nonsmoking rooms; on-call doctor/dentist. *In room:* TV w/pay movies, dataport, minibar, fridge, coffeemaker, hair dryer, iron.

Riverview Lodge ✹✹ 🄥alue   This lovely Edwardian home in a quiet residential area, just a 15-minute walk from the Square, features spacious rooms with private balconies overlooking a leafy garden and the Avon River. The gorgeous new Churchill suites are in a separate home two doors away. They're even more charming—and great value for all the space you get. And don't forget to ask about their two cute restored cottages.

361 Cambridge Terrace, Christchurch. ©/fax **03/365-2860.** www.riverview.net.nz and www.moacottages.co.nz. 4 units in lodge (2 Churchill suites); 2 cottages. NZ$170–NZ$240 (US$119–US$168). Long-stay and off-peak rates available. Rates include breakfast. MC, V. Limited off-street parking. Find the intersection of Bealey and Fitzgerald aves.; Riverview is just a block away. Don't try following Cambridge Terrace—it's long, sometimes one-way, and sometimes disappears altogether. **Amenities:** Free kayaks, bikes, and golf clubs; laundry service; same-day dry cleaning; nonsmoking rooms. *In room:* TV, hair dryer, iron, no phone.

INEXPENSIVE

Living Space ✹ 🄥alue   A funky cross between a hotel and an independent apartment block, Living Space is ideal for families, or couples traveling together. It offers basic studios, roomier apartments from one to four bedrooms, and secure access via swipe cards. You'll be right in the heart of the city, a step away from the Bus Exchange, in one of the brightest, most colorful stays in town. There are communal kitchens, theaters, a library, dining rooms, laundries, and masses of art on the walls.

96 Lichfield St. © **0508/454-846** in NZ, or 03/964-5212. Fax 03/964-5245. www.livingspace.net. 110 units. From NZ$85–NZ$95 (US$60–US$67) studio; NZ$140 (US$98) 1- and 2-bedroom apts; NZ$180 (US$126) 3-bedroom apt;

Inner City Backpackers

New and improved backpacker stays have sprouted in the inner city region. The best is the well-awarded **Stonehurst** ✹✹✹, 241 Gloucester St. (© **0508-786-633** in NZ, or 03/379-4620; www.stonehurst.com), which has a wide range of accommodations from dorms to tourist motels and flats. **New Excelsior Backpackers** ✹✹, Manchester and High streets (© **0800/666-237** in NZ, or 03/366-7570; www.newexcelsior.co.nz), is in one of the city's old hotels, smack in the middle of town. Most dorms have four or six beds; the majority of rooms have sinks. The fabulous rooftop deck is the jewel in the crown. **Star Times Backpackers** ✹, 56 Cathedral Square (© **0800/982-225** in NZ, or 03/982-2225; www.startimes.co.nz), is right in the Square and always busy; and **Christchurch City Central YHA**, 273 Manchester St. (© **0800/278-299** in NZ, or 03/379-9535; www.yha.co.nz), has 166 beds in dorm and double arrangements. **Rolleston House YHA**, 5 Worcester Blvd. (© **03/366-6564**; www.yha.co.nz), is much smaller than its sister operation, but is better located in the cultural precinct and close to many major attractions. **Base Backpackers** ✹✹, 56 Cathedral Square (© **0800/227-369** in NZ, or 03/982-2225; www.basebackpackers.com), is perfectly located in Cathedral Square and has a popular bar and theme nights.

NZ$220 (US$154) 4-bedroom apt. Long-stay rates available. AF, MC, V. **Amenities.** Several nearby restaurants; car rentals; 24 hr. computer suite; games lounge w/pool table; 2 DVD movie theaters; coin-operated laundries; library; full commercial kitchens on every floor; swipe-card security; on-call doctor/dentist. *In room:* TV, kitchenette, fridge.

NEAR HAGLEY PARK
EXPENSIVE

The George Christchurch ★★★ (*Value*)   The George is a member of the Small Luxury Hotels of the World group, and its attention to detail is hard to fault. Sleek, cool, and modern, it typifies the new breed of boutique hotels that focus energy on individual guest needs. The George has also annexed an old adjacent homestead, which is now The Residence; it has two luxury suites and one studio apartment, plus a formal dining room, lounge, and kitchen for those booking the whole property. I can think of no better place in town to indulge yourself—you get everything you pay for. It's quieter and more elegant than the Crowne Plaza.

50 Park Terrace, Christchurch. ✆ **0800/100-220** in NZ, or 03/379-4560. Fax 03/366-6747. www.thegeorge.com. 57 units in hotel; 3 units in The Residence. NZ$399 (US$280) standard; NZ$445 (US$312) executive; NZ$821 (US$575) suite. Residence rooms can be booked individually, or the entire property can be booked for exclusive use. Long-stay rates and special deals available. AE, DC, MC, V. **Amenities:** 2 restaurants; bar; nearby 9-hole golf course; floodlit AstroTurf tennis court; access to off-site gym w/Jacuzzis and sauna; free bikes; concierge; tour desk; car rentals; secretarial services; 24-hr. room service; massage; babysitting; free laundry service; same-day dry cleaning; nonsmoking rooms; concierge-level rooms; on-call doctor/dentist. *In room:* A/C, TV w/pay movies, fax, dataport, minibar, fridge, coffeemaker, hair dryer, iron, safe.

The Weston House ★★   Few have been disappointed with the architectural splendor of this Georgian-style home, a Category 1 Historic Places Trust building. Ideally located just across from Hagley Park, it offers two large rooms in what were once the servants' quarters—one upstairs, one down. Guests are spoiled with extras such as heated bathroom floors, a private sitting area upstairs, and a walk-in wardrobe downstairs. The house is divine, no question, although I think bedrooms at The Worcester, a few blocks away, have more style.

62 Park Terrace, Christchurch. ✆ **03/366-0234.** Fax 03/366-5254. www.westonhouse.co.nz. 2 units. NZ$360–NZ$390 (US$252–US$273). Rates include airport transfers. Long-stay rates and special deals available. AE, DC, MC, V. No children under 12. **Amenities:** Nearby golf course and tennis courts; tour bookings; car rentals; courtesy car; laundry service; same-day dry cleaning; nonsmoking rooms; on-call doctor/dentist. *In room:* TV, dataport, minibar, fridge, coffeemaker, hair dryer, iron.

The Worcester of Christchurch ★★★ (*Value*)   This superb B&B is the only one in Christchurch with its own gallery. Host Maree Ritchie has been an art dealer for the past 22 years, and the home she shares with her husband, Tony Taylor, is filled with paintings, sculpture, and antiques. Rooms are well appointed with fine furnishings, fresh flowers, and chocolates. The Worcester suite overlooks Worcester Boulevard and has its own dressing room, while the Godley suite has its own lounge. This gem of a Victorian house is directly across from the Arts Centre; you couldn't wish for a better location. The three nearby self-contained West Fitzroy apartments, a couple of blocks away, are swish, contemporary, and closer to inner city. They can be taken singly, or together to provide extra bedrooms.

15 Worcester Blvd., Christchurch. ✆ **0800/365-015** in NZ, or 03/365-0936. Fax 03/364-6299. www.worcester.co.nz or www.westfitzroy.co.nz. 2 units in house; 3 apts at West Fitzroy. NZ$380–NZ$395 (US$266–US$277) suite; NZ$215–NZ$350 (US$151–US$245) each apt. Rates include airport transfers and breakfast and predinner drinks in house. Long-stay rates available in apts. AE, DC, MC, V. No children under 12 in house. **Amenities:** Nearby golf course and tennis courts; on-site gym at apt; laundry service; same-day dry cleaning; nonsmoking rooms. *In room:* TV, dataport, kitchens in apts, fridge, coffeemaker, hair dryer, iron.

MODERATE

Orari Bed & Breakfast 🏃🏃 (value)   Sited directly across Montreal Street from the new Christchurch Art Gallery and right in the heart of the cultural precinct, Orari gets top marks for perfect positioning. And you'll be hard-pressed to find a better value-for-money stay in this area. It's a fabulous big old house, built in 1893, and its splendid timbers have been beautifully restored. Rooms are clean-cut and smart, spacious and comfortable. All but two have en suites (the other two have private bathrooms). Big, stylish living rooms and a yummy breakfast add to its charms.

Gloucester and Montreal sts. ℂ 03/365-6569. Fax 03/365-2525. www.orari.net.nz. 10 units. NZ$160–NZ$198 (US$112–US$139). Off-peak rates available. Rates include breakfast. AE, DC, MC, V. Closed June–July. **Amenities:** Nearby golf course and tennis courts; nonsmoking rooms. *In room:* Coffeemaker, hair dryer.

INEXPENSIVE

YMCA 🏃🏃 (value)   Three words spring instantly to mind—value, location, and liveliness. There's a constant flow of traffic of all ages here, and the modern six-story building is perfectly situated just across from the Arts Centre and Botanic Gardens. The apartments have kitchenettes, while the deluxe units have bathrooms and TVs. Each person in a 5-, 6-, or 10-bunk room gets a locker with a key. Overall, this is probably the most upmarket of Christchurch's hostels.

12 Hereford St., Christchurch. ℂ 0508/962-224 in NZ, or 03/365-1586. Fax 03/365-1386. www.ymcachch.org.nz. 42 dorm beds, 34 units with shared bathrooms; 25 units with private bathrooms. From NZ$22 (US$15) dorm bed; NZ$65 (US$46) standard room; NZ$95 (US$67) deluxe room; NZ$115–NZ$145 (US$81–US$102) 1-bedroom apt; NZ$150 (US$105) 2-bedroom apt. Long-stay rates available. AE, DC, MC, V. **Amenities:** Cafe and dining room; nearby golf course and tennis courts; full-scale gym; discount on fitness classes and climbing wall; sauna; children's programs during school holidays; massage; babysitting; laundry service and coin-op laundry; same-day dry cleaning; nonsmoking rooms. *In room:* Dataport in deluxe rooms, kitchen in 2 apts, fridge in deluxe and apts, hair dryer in deluxe rooms, no phone.

IN FENDALTON/MERIVALE/ST. ALBANS

EXPENSIVE

Motels abound in this area and most offer good deals. There's also good bed-and-breakfast rooms at **Fendalton House** 🏃, 50 Clifford Ave., Fendalton (ℂ **0800/374-298** in NZ, or 03/355-4298; www.fendaltonhouse.co.nz), priced NZ$200 to NZ$220 (US$140–US$154).

The Charlotte Jane 🏃🏃🏃   At this smart boutique hotel, no stone is unturned when it comes to comfort. This stunning old mansion—formerly a Victorian school for young ladies—has been converted into a haven of luxury, and if you like big rooms, you'll be in your element here. Bathrooms are equally huge, some with monster Jacuzzis. All units have bidets, antiques, and luscious bedding. The house next door—now Henderson House—has been added to provide a restaurant and extra accommodations. It's just a 5-minute walk to Merivale and approximately 15 minutes to the city.

110 Papanui Rd., Christchurch. ℂ 03/355-1028. Fax 03/355-8882. www.charlotte-jane.co.nz. 10 units in The Charlotte Jane; 2 units in adjacent Henderson House. NZ$395 (US$277) luxury; NZ$500 (US$350) superluxury and honeymoon suites. Off-peak rates available. Rates include gourmet breakfast. AE, DC, MC, V. No children under 15. **Amenities:** Restaurant; bar; nearby golf course; concierge; tour bookings; car rentals; laundry service; same-day dry cleaning; nonsmoking rooms; on-call doctor/dentist. *In room:* TV/VCR, dataport, coffeemaker, hair dryer, iron.

MODERATE

Bishop's Manor 🏃🏃🏃   Every suite here is huge and there's both a bath and a shower in each of them. On top of that, you have the graciousness of a fine old home, the beauty of extravagant draperies, and the peace of a quiet suburban street. The West

(Moments) Historic Retreat

You'll have to be in quick if you want to stay in the divine little gem that is **Jack's Cottage** 🌸🌸🌸, Tauton Gardens, Governor's Bay Road, Governor's Bay (📞 **03/329-9746**; fax 03/329-9546; www.tauntongardens.co.nz). Located in the middle of Barry and Lyn Sligh's beautiful, 2-acre woodland garden, this little 1860s cottage has been fully restored into the quaintest sleep you'll find anywhere. It has its own kitchen and a beautiful bathroom and you can roam the gardens at will. It's about a 25-minute drive over the Port Hills from Christchurch and about a 15-minute drive around the bays from Lyttelton. It costs NZ$250 to NZ$300 (US$175–US$210), which includes breakfast supplies and laundry service.

---

suite is by far the largest (it has two bedrooms, a dressing room, and a sheltered balcony), but I like the rich colors of the South suite and the classic golds and creams of the East suite. All suites are upstairs and there's a big living room as well.

14 Bishop St., St. Albans. 📞 **03/379-7990**. Fax 03/379-7991. www.bishopsmanor.co.nz. 4 units. NZ$280–NZ$370 (US$196–US$259). Long-stay and off-peak rates available. Rates include breakfast. Dinner by arrangement. AE, DC, MC, V. **Amenities:** Nearby golf course and tennis courts; tour bookings; car rentals; massage; babysitting; laundry service; same-day dry cleaning; nonsmoking rooms; on-call doctor/dentist. *In room:* TV, dataport, fridge, coffeemaker, hair dryer, iron.

Elm Tree House 🌸🌸   Built in 1920, this lovely two-storied home is just a few steps from Merivale Mall and numerous cafes and restaurants. Rooms are big—all with en suites, one with bathtub—and the original wood paneling throughout gives it a warm, intimate old-world feeling. The Honeymoon and Franz Josef suites are the sunniest and nicest (upstairs), but I can't imagine anyone complaining about any of the accommodations here. Unlike The Charlotte Jane (see above), this is an owner-hosted operation.

236 Papanui Rd., Merivale. 📞 **03/355-9731**. Fax 03/355-9753. www.elmtreehouse.co.nz. 6 units. NZ$235–NZ$325 (US$165–US$228). Long-stay and off-peak rates available. Rates include breakfast and predinner drinks. AE, MC, V. Children under 12 allowed by arrangement only. **Amenities:** Nearby golf courses and tennis courts; nearby gym; tour bookings; car rentals; laundry service; same-day dry cleaning; nonsmoking rooms. *In room:* TV, dataport, coffeemaker, hair dryer, iron.

Hadleigh 🌸🌸   Located on a quiet, residential street, this gorgeous two-storied home exudes charm. The gold Goddard Room is the biggest, but it only has a queen-size bed. I prefer the sunny Cartwright Room, which has a much bigger bathroom, a bath, and a king-size bed. I think it's the pick of the bunch. Two other more modest suites both have two bedrooms and a shared bathroom each. I think Elm Tree bedrooms are the best value for your money, but Hadleigh has lovelier living rooms and shared spaces.

6 Eversleigh St., St. Albans. 📞/fax **03/355-7174**. www.hadleigh.co.nz. 4 units. NZ$295–NZ$360 (US$207–US$252). AE, MC, V. Rates include predinner drinks, canapés, and breakfast. **Amenities:** Nearby golf course; billiard room; tour bookings; car rentals; courtesy car to city and trains; babysitting; laundry service; same-day dry cleaning; nonsmoking rooms; on-call doctor/dentist; access for travelers w/disabilities. *In room:* TV, kitchen in apt, coffeemaker, hair dryer.

Springfield Cottage 🌸🌸🌸 (Moments)   My own home is only a few blocks from this darling cottage, but I want to shift here immediately. Built in the 1870s and renovated with a modern kitchen, it's a romantic stopover that I'm sure you'll love. It has a big back garden, a barbecue for your use, and two lovely little sitting rooms. If you're the independent type, it will suit you perfectly.

137 Springfield Rd., St. Albans. ℭ 03/377-3168. www.springfieldcottage.co.nz. Self-contained cottage for two. NZ$170–NZ$300 (US$119–US$210). B&B rate NZ$30 (US$21) extra. Minimum 2-night stay. Long-stay and off-peak rates available. MC, V. No children. **Amenities:** Tour bookings; car rentals; laundry facilities; nearby dry-cleaning service; nonsmoking rooms; on-call doctor/dentist. *In room:* TV/DVD/CD, dataport, kitchen, fridge, coffeemaker, hair dryer, iron.

INEXPENSIVE

Turret House   If you're looking for big bedrooms at a reasonable rate, Turret House delivers them. Pam and Michael Hamilton's grand old inner city home has en-suite rooms done out with traditional furnishings. It's hardly a 10-minute walk into town and there's a big breakfast to set you up for the day.

435 Durham St. N. ℭ **0800/488-773** in NZ, or 03/365-3900. Fax 03/365-5601. www.turrethouse.co.nz. 8 units. NZ$95–NZ$150 (US$67–US$105). Rates include breakfast. MC, V. **Amenities:** Nearby golf course; tour bookings; rental cars; bike rentals; laundry service; same-day dry cleaning; nonsmoking rooms. *In room:* TV, coffeemaker, hair dryer.

IN SUMNER

There are two delightful beach stays here, both located in self-contained apartments, situated close to the Metro bus route and 15 minutes from town. **Sumner Apartments** ꞏꞏ, The Esplanade, Sumner (ℭ **03/354-4483;** www.sumnerapartments. co.nz), has one-, two-, or three-bedroom apartments just across the road from Sumner's white-sand beach. **Grey Sands of Sumner** ꞏꞏ (ℭ **03/326-4275;** www.elements ofsumner.co.nz), has a two-bedroom apartment with laundry facilities and two secure carparks; it's also a stone's throw from the beach.

Moments **Rural Retreats**

Imagine waking up in the morning to total silence, snow-capped mountain peaks, and an endless spread of perfect rolling green. This is what you get when you stay at **Terrace Downs High Country Resort** ꞏꞏꞏ, Coleridge Road, Rakaia Gorge, Canterbury (ℭ **0800/465-373** in NZ, or 03/318-6943; fax 03/318-6942; www.terracedowns.co.nz), which is located 45 minutes northwest of Christchurch. Complete with one of New Zealand's top 18-hole golf courses, it provides accommodations in stylish villas and chalets, beautifully crafted from local stone and timber. It's close to Mount Hutt ski fields and some of the best fishing around. Tariffs start around NZ$250 (US$175) for a studio and run to around NZ$650 (US$455) for a modern four-bedroom home. I found the terrace villas just perfect.

For something more modest and closer to Christchurch, visit Merrilies Rebbeck, who will welcome you at **Ballymoney Farmstay** ꞏꞏ, Wardstay Road, RD, Christchurch (ℭ **03/329-6706;** fax 03/329-6709; www.ballymoney.co.nz), located in the very pretty Tai Tapu area, just 15 minutes from central Christchurch. She has two guest suites (NZ$180/US$126, breakfast included), a gorgeous garden, and a small farm filled with an amazing array of special animals. For the whole package that includes a farm tour, you'll pay NZ$270 (US$189). Look out for the stunning white peacock.

NEAR THE AIRPORT

If you've just landed in Christchurch and urgently need sleep, try **Copthorne Hotel Commodore** ☆☆, 449 Memorial Ave. (© **0508/266-663** in NZ, or 03/358-8129; www.commodore.net.nz), which has 135 rooms from NZ$202 (US$141) for a premium room to NZ$250 (US$175) for very good business rooms.

Huntley House ☆☆☆ *(finds)*   I walked into Huntley House and never wanted to leave. It deserves every superlative you can think of, with "opulent" and "elegant" on top of the list. A grand old home combined with modern new apartments built in the same period style, it hides down a long, leafy drive just 7 minutes in either direction from the city and the airport. I fell in love with the plushness of the five homestead rooms, but the modern one-bedroom suites and two-bedroom apartments overlooking the pool are equally enticing. Opened in December 2004, this is now one of Christchurch's top stays.

67 Yaldhurst Rd., Upper Riccarton. © **03/348-8435.** Fax 03/341-6833. www.huntleyhouse.co.nz. 17 units. NZ$669 (US$468) Garden Room; NZ$781 (US$547) Garden Suite and Homestead Room; NZ$1,119 (US$783) 2-bedroom Garden Suite; NZ$669 (US$468) the Cabin. NZ$55 (US$39) each extra person. Rates include breakfast, airport transfers, and evening cocktails. Off-peak rates and special packages available. AE, DC, MC, V. **Amenities:** Restaurant; bar; outdoor heated pool; nearby golf courses and tennis courts; library; pool and snooker room; tour bookings; car rentals; massage; babysitting; laundry in 2 apts; laundry service; same-day dry cleaning; nonsmoking rooms; on-call doctor/dentist; airport transfers; access for travelers w/disabilities. *In room:* TV, dataport, kitchen in 8 new rooms, minibar, fridge, coffeemaker, hair dryer, iron, safe.

Outrigger at Clearwater Resort ☆☆☆ *(Value)*   Much nicer than other airport-hotel options, Clearwater has the advantage of a rural situation, not to mention its 18-hole international golfing resort facilities—and all for a very pleasing price. Set amid 186 hectares (465 acres) of greenery, golf courses, and trout-filled lakes, it's a short drive to the airport and rooms are modern, chic, individual, and beautifully cantilevered out over the water. The hotel rooms and suites are great value, and the larger terrace apartments (eight only) are perfect for long stays, friends, or families. It opened in 2003 and construction on future facilities—including a swimming pool and health spa—is still underway.

Clearwater Ave., Harewood, Christchurch. © **0800/555-075** in NZ, or **03/360-1000.** Fax 03/360-1001. www. outrigger.com. 97 units. NZ$245 (US$172) lakeside room; NZ$313 (US$219) lakeview suite; NZ$380 (US$266) lakefront and quay suite; NZ$549 (US$384) lakeside villa; NZ$633 (US$443) apt and terrace villa. Rates include airport transfers. Long-stay, off-peak, and special rates available. AE, DC, MC, V. **Amenities:** Restaurant (The Lakes); bar and wine cellar; 18-hole championship golf course, home of the Clearwater Classic Australasian PGA tournament; 2 outdoor lit tennis courts; gym and spa by 2007; on-site freshwater fishing guide and lessons; bike rentals; concierge; tour bookings; car rentals; courtesy car; 24-hr. room service; massage; babysitting; laundry facilities in suites and apts; same-day dry cleaning; nonsmoking rooms; on-call doctor/dentist. *In room:* A/C, TV/VCR/DVD, dataport, minibar, fridge, coffeemaker, hair dryer, iron.

4 Where to Dine

You can make a pig of yourself in a region renowned for its lamb, seafood, produce, and world-class wines. Christchurch has the highest ratio of eateries per capita of any New Zealand city—though it's not the only city to claim that. You'll get a bunch of options in one spot at Oxford Terrace, known to locals as "The Strip." Lunchtime is the most crowded; after 11pm, it transforms itself into more of a nightclub scene. The best restaurants though, tend to be tucked away in more low-key places.

See the map on p. 344 to locate some of the establishments mentioned below.

IN INNER CITY
EXPENSIVE

Canterbury Tales ☆☆☆ MODERN NEW ZEALAND   Canterbury Tales presents you with edible works of art that taste just as good as they look. This is a forever-award-winning establishment where you can feel completely at ease with the friendly service. It's not big on atmosphere and the regularly changing menu is far from cheap, but you'll be offered the best of everything. The place is dangerously close to taking "the modern minimalist plate" to ridiculous lengths, but what you do get exhibits a skillful blend of flavors. Free-range organic chicken with rocket and bacon risotto, poached fava beans, port jus, and rocket pistou is just one sampling.

Crowne Plaza Christchurch, Kilmore and Durham sts. ☎ 03/365-7799. Reservations required. Main courses NZ$27–NZ$48 (US$19–US$34). AE, DC, MC, V. Summer Tues–Sat 6pm–late; winter Thurs–Sat 6pm–late.

Indochine ☆☆ (Moments) ASIAN/NEW ZEALAND   Tucked into a dark avenue that runs between Colombo and Manchester streets, Indochine is a sophisticated little spot that blends Asian culinary influences with the best of New Zealand produce and a rich, slightly bordello-like interior. The mezzanine dining area is the perfect spot to linger over delicious dim sum and everything from squid to roast pork belly. It won't be everyone's cup of tea, but if you're an adventurous diner and you like good service, it's the place for you. It's a favorite with the arts crowd and doubles as a classy cocktail bar.

209 Cambridge Terrace. ☎ 03/365-7372. Reservations recommended. Main courses NZ$22–NZ$30 (US$15–US$21). AE, MC, V. Daily from 5pm.

Minx Dining Room ☆☆☆ (Finds) MODERN NEW ZEALAND   Be prepared for a few surprises at this racy new joint themed around the Hillman Minx car. It's part of a whole new retail and restaurant complex, and popularity coupled with an open kitchen makes it noisier than some may like. But it's a stylish playground for the city's aspiring socialites. The daily changing menu is invariably good and features the likes of roast quail, squid-ink risotto with scallops, and assorted fish dishes.

96 Lichfield St. ☎ 03/374-9944. Reservations required. Main courses NZ$25–NZ$32 (US$18–US$22). AE, DC, MC, V. Daily 10am–late.

Pedro's ☆☆ SPANISH   For nearly 26 years, Pedro Carazo has been bringing the best of Basque to Christchurch. Market-fresh seafood forms the core of the menu,

---

(Finds) Currying Favor

Indian restaurants have popped up all over Christchurch like pappadoms in hot oil. The **Raj Mahal** ☆☆☆, at Manchester and Worcester streets (☎ 03/366-0521), is considered best of the bunch. A few of the best of the rest are **India Cottage** ☆, 71 Kilmore St. (☎ 03/377-5337); **Little India Bistro & Tandoor** ☆☆, Gloucester and New Regent streets (☎ 03/377-7997); **Tulsi** ☆, Gloucester and Manchester streets (☎ 03/377-8999); **Tandoori Palace** ☆☆, 475 Papanui Rd., Merivale (☎ 03/352-9520); and **Two Fat Indians** ☆, 112 Manchester St. (☎ 03/371-7273). And a new, very decorative suburban treat is **Mantra** ☆☆☆, 72–74 North Avon Rd., Richmond Village (☎ 03/389-9997), which is my favorite. Go the short distance out of the city center to find it. It's open daily for lunch from 11:30am and from 5pm for evening dining.

> **Finds   Classy Cafe**
>
> If you've stepped out on the trendy retail strip of Victoria Street, make sure you take a side step near the clock tower and veer over to **Blax Espresso Bar** ★★★, corner of Montreal and Victoria streets (℃ **03/366-8982**). It's all white and bright, and you need to be in early to snare one of their delectable pain au chocolat, or their fought-over caisseponch. Blax is open 7:30am to 4pm Monday through Saturday.

with *lots* of garlic. Regulars keep coming back to enjoy the noisy, relaxed atmosphere and the always charming Pedro, who likes to mingle with his guests. Food is divine, from the paella to the *gambas al ajillo* (garlic prawns). And it's all served up on the traditional Spanish crockery that Pedro buys on his regular trips home.

143 Worcester St. ℃ 03/379-7668. Reservations recommended. Main courses NZ$25–NZ$32 (US$18–US$22). AE, MC, V. Tues–Sat 6–11pm.

The Seafood Kitchen ★★ NEW ZEALAND SEAFOOD   Anyone who enjoys a good seafood meal will love this place. The menu is defined by the fish the chef chooses fresh from the markets each morning, so you can't always be assured of returning for your favorites, but every day is a taste discovery. A low-key decor, friendly staff, and good service all enhance fabulous meals. You won't be disappointed.

Corner of Colombo and Peterborough sts. ℃ 03/365-6543. Reservations required. Main courses NZ$25–NZ$38 (US$18–US$27). AE, DC, MC, V. Tues–Sat 6pm–late.

MODERATE

Barcelona ★★ INTERNATIONAL   Timber floors and questionable acoustics make this popular place noisier than it ought to be. That said, it's the best of the restaurants along The Strip—and you can always dine outside. The menu presents an eclectic selection that roams across Asia, Europe, and the Pacific in its inspiration, dishing up everything from a delicious field mushroom risotto to pan-fried groper with kumara and capers.

Corner of Oxford Terrace and Worcester St. ℃ 03/366-2100. Reservations recommended. Main courses NZ$22–NZ$30 (US$15–US$21). AE, DC, MC, V. Daily 11am–late.

Bodhi Tree ★★★ *Value* BURMESE   You'll have to beat back the crowds to get into what is claimed to be New Zealand's only Burmese restaurant. It's a place of humble decor, small taste plates, and sensational flavors that you'll remember for hours after. Make sure you try the pickled tea salad and the sautéed squid with chile and basil. You can keep ordering as many little dishes as you like until you're full.

808 Colombo St. ℃ 03/377-6808. Reservations essential. Main courses NZ$15–NZ$20 (US$11–US$14). AE, DC, MC, V. Tues–Sun from 6pm.

Ciao Bella ★★ MODERN NEW ZEALAND   If you're after award-winning lamb and beef, try this small, classy restaurant. It hit the scene as a brilliant little architectural gem several years ago and it has sustained a reputation for good food and long lunches. It's a favorite with architects and radio staff who inhabit the area.

131 Victoria St. ℃ 03/371-7288. Reservations recommended. Main courses NZ$25–NZ$32 (US$18–US$22). AE, DC, MC, V. Tues–Thurs 11:30am–late; Fri–Sat 10am–late; Sun 10am–4pm.

The Mythai 🍴🍴🍴 *Value* THAI   A Friday night at The Mythai should be on every-one's itinerary, but make sure you reserve since I'm not the only one who feels this way. East meets west here, with a Kiwi proprietor and two Bangkok chefs producing authentic Thai food. The atmosphere is always lively, and group dinners can some-times get boisterous. If you order *Gaeng Keow Wan Gai*, chicken with sweet green curry and coconut cream, you won't regret it. Everything is available for takeout.

84 Hereford St. ⓒ **03/365-1295**. Fax 03/365-1285. Reservations required for dinner Fri–Sat. Main courses NZ$16–NZ$28 (US$11–US$20). AE, DC, MC, V. Mon–Fri 11am–late; Sat 5pm–late.

Portofino 🍴🍴🍴 ITALIAN   I personally celebrated when Auckland's Portofino made an appearance in Christchurch. The chain has a long history of polished restau-rant service and excellent, well-priced fare. In Christchurch, it has established a sexy little restaurant—all mood and mirrors—with a bountiful wine display, cute Italian waiters, and all the edible favorites from calzone and linguini through scampi, veal, scallops, prawns, and pastas.

182 Oxford Terrace. ⓒ **03/377-2454**. Reservations recommended for dinner. Main courses NZ$20–NZ$32 (US$14–US$22). AE, DC, MC, V. Mon–Fri 11:30am–late; Sat–Sun 4:30pm–late.

Sticky Fingers Restaurant & Bar 🍴 MODERN NEW ZEALAND   Big umbrel-las mark the entrance to this popular spot, and you'll find all types enjoying the try-hard interior. If you can, grab one of the comfortable booths. The menu includes salads, steak, lamb, fish, pasta, and pizza in generous servings. It's a popular haunt for lunching businessmen and after-work drinkers. Service can be patchy, but Sticky Fin-gers isn't alone in that, I'm sorry to say.

Clarendon Towers, Oxford Terrace. ⓒ **03/366-6451**. Fax 03/366-6452. Reservations recommended for dinner. Main courses NZ$24–NZ$28 (US$17–US$20). AE, DC, MC, V. Daily 8am–very late.

Winnie Bagoes Pizza Bar 🍴🍴🍴 PIZZA   Winnie Bagoes gourmet pizzas are among the most scrumptious in town, and the lively atmosphere encourages you to stay and eat in. The Florentine pizza, for one example, presents apricot chicken, cashew nuts, and cream cheese. There's also a range of pastas, calzones, and salads, and if you've got a sweet tooth, a dessert pizza. Unbeatable for atmosphere and consistency.

194 Gloucester St. ⓒ **03/366-6315**. Reservations recommended Fri–Sun. Main courses NZ$12–NZ$26 (US$8.40–US$18). AE, DC, MC, V. Mon–Fri 10am–late; weekends from 6pm.

Tips Espresso Hits

Gasping for a good coffee? Then head for **Hummingbird**, 165 Victoria St. (ⓒ **03/ 379-0826**), where a whole team of regulars can attest to consistently good brews. The **Daily Grind Express** is another good choice with several city loca-tions—at 168 Armagh St. (ⓒ **03/377-4959**), and under the Clarendon Building, Oxford Terrace and Worcester Street (ⓒ **03/377-8836**), for a start. Both serve great counter food and fresh juices. **C1 Espresso** 🍴🍴, 150 High St. (ⓒ **03/366-7170**), is more funky and rough around the edges, but it has the best coffee. **Vic's Café & Bake** 🍴🍴, 132 Victoria St. (ⓒ **03/366-2054**), combines good coffee with an award-winning array of freshly baked European breads.

Moments **Meals on Wheels**

For Christchurch's most moving dining experience, leap aboard the **Tramway Restaurant,** in Cathedral Square near the Police Kiosk (© **03/366-7511** for reservations). It operates from 7:30 to 11pm and does about five circuits of the tramway during your meal. Main courses are priced from around NZ$30 (US$21) and meal packages start at NZ$54 (US$38) per person for a three-course meal. There are better dining experiences, but this one has novelty value.

INEXPENSIVE

Café Globe ☆☆ *Value* CAFE If you want to throw yourself into the center of student and arty life, this is the place. Situated in the older, funkier part of town near Christchurch Polytechnic's Schools of Jazz and Fashion and tucked between quaint secondhand stores and designer boutiques, the Globe is always busy. The interior is low-key, and the portions generous. Sought out for its coffee, it also does a hearty breakfast. It has the best vegan muffins in town and a good range of vegetarian food that includes salads, pastas, panini, and more. Licensed for wine drinkers, it's a great place for people-watching and a favored hangout for many artists.

171 High St. © **03/366-4704.** Main courses NZ$10–NZ$22 (US$7–US$15). AE, DC, MC, V. Mon–Fri 7am–4pm; Sat–Sun 8:30am–4pm; Fri from 6pm.

The Honey Pot Café ☆ CAFE If you're in the mood for a big, wholesome breakfast, stop by The Honey Pot. It has a warm, casual atmosphere, and if you can get through its "Full Breakky" of two eggs with house sausages, grilled tomatoes, bacon, fried mushrooms, onions, hash browns, and an espresso, you're doing better than me. The lunch and dinner menus offer pizzas, gourmet sandwiches, and desserts. It's not salubrious, but if you're on a budget it can fill the gaps.

114 Lichfield St. © **03/366-5853.** Breakfast main courses NZ$10–N7$20 (US$7 US$14). MC, V. Mon–Fri 7am–late; Sat–Sun 8am late.

NEAR HAGLEY PARK
EXPENSIVE

Le Bon Bolli ☆☆ FRENCH Award-winning chef Phillip Kraal has brought the ambience of the Left Bank to Christchurch. Le Bon Bolli has won numerous awards and it's right in the heart of Worcester Boulevard activity. You get the choice of casual brasserie downstairs, or formal French (at considerably higher prices) upstairs. The brasserie is one of the best places in town for delicious salads—smoked chicken with lettuce, French beans, hard-boiled eggs, new peas, and melon in creamy herb mayonnaise is a case in point. Upstairs, you might try the baked rump of spring lamb rolled in fresh herbs and garlic with red-wine-braised leeks served on a vegetable rosti and sautéed lamb's brains.

Montreal St. and Worcester Blvd. © **03/374-9444.** Fax 03/374-9442. Reservations required upstairs. Main courses NZ$16–NZ$26 (US$11–US$18) brasserie; from NZ$60 (US$42) for 3-course dinner upstairs. AE, DC, MC, V. Brasserie daily 10am–11pm; upstairs restaurant noon–2pm and 6:30pm–late.

Pescatore ☆☆☆ PACIFIC RIM Pescatore has an established reputation for innovative cuisine. It even boasts a mention in the *New York Times*. The food is undoubtedly delicious, but at the risk of seeming picky, I think the place is getting a little carried away with its minute portions—given the prices, one does like to go home feeling as if a full meal has been eaten. The menu offers Canterbury lamb, Akaroa salmon, Golden Bay crab and scallops, and the famously decadent Fang au Chocolate. Pescatore is a pricey option, but it's popular with local foodies. The decor is understated and unassuming and the service very attentive.

The George Hotel, Park Terrace. © 03/371-0257. Reservations required. Main courses NZ$32–NZ$79 (US$22–US$55); degustation menu from NZ$85 (US$39), with suggested wines NZ$150 (US$105). AE, DC, MC, V. Tues–Sat 6–10pm.

Rotherams 🏵🏵🏵 *Moments* INTERNATIONAL   This is a tucked-away culinary jewel in the midst of Riccarton retail heartland. It's most definitely worth searching out and savoring. You'll get some of the best meals in the most romantic ambience of almost any restaurant in the city. Personally, I like it best of the top-rated restaurants. Service is attentive, presentation first class, flavors divine, and the wine list impressive. If you have something special to celebrate (and who needs a reason?), let Swiss owner/ chef Martin Weiss spoil you to bits.

42 Rotherma St., Riccarton. © 03/341-5142. Reservations required. Main courses NZ$25–NZ$40 (US$18–US$28). AE, DC, MC, V. Mon–Sat from 6pm.

INEXPENSIVE

Dux de Lux 🏵 VEGETARIAN/SEAFOOD   If you're young and looking for a good time, head for the Dux, especially Thursday, Friday, and Saturday nights when it features live bands; there's live jazz on Tuesdays. The Dux is an avid supporter of the New Zealand music scene and hosts the best talent in town, from loud guitar rock to smooth drum-and-bass grooves. It batch-brews its own beers and has won best lager at the Australian International Beer Awards. When it comes to food, it features satisfying meals at a decent price. Vegan and most cultural dietary requests can be accommodated. Now 26 years old, the Dux has a superb laid-back weekend atmosphere, as people crowd into the courtyard and watch the activity of the nearby market stalls.

The Arts Centre, Montreal and Hereford sts. © 03/366-6919. Main courses NZ$20–NZ$26 (US$14–US$18). AE, DC, MC, V. Daily 11:30am–11pm.

Le Café 🏵🏵 *Kids* CAFE   This is a popular spot for coffee after a show at Court Theatre, and the outside dining under the trees is always a big hit. A great place for people-watching, but things get pretty hectic at times, so expect to wait. The menu includes light meals—nachos, focaccia, pizza, burgers, Caesar salad. Le Café's bakery is another choice farther into the Arts Centre. Everything is made fresh daily—Italian ciabatta, German-style sourdough and rye, and traditional Kiwi meat pies—and makes good picnic fare if you're heading for the gardens.

The Arts Centre, Worcester Blvd. © 03/366-7722. Reservations accepted for breakfast only. Main courses NZ$15–NZ$22 (US$11–US$15). AE, DC, MC, V. Sun–Thurs 7am–midnight; Fri–Sat 24 hr.

Finds **Vegetarian Hits**

Head down Colombo Street to find **The Lotus Heart,** 595 Colombo St. (© 03/ 379-0324), for plenty of vegan and gluten-free options. Just a few doors away is **Aiki Japanese Organic Kitchen** 🏵, 599 Colombo St. (© 03/366-1178), which combines 99% health with inventive Asian favorites. **Mainstreet Café,** Colombo and Salisbury streets (© 03/365-0421), has a long history of tantalizing taste buds with well-priced meals to suit any taste.

> **Tips Gourmet Takeaway**
>
> For the best gourmet takeout meals in Christchurch, go to **Traiteur of Merivale,** at the corner of Papanui and Aikmans roads (℃ **03/355-7750**). It has a weekly changing menu with several starters, mains, and desserts, plus pasta and salad options, all well priced.

IN FENDALTON/MERIVALE

In heartland Merivale (just behind the mall on Aikmans Road), you'll find a fistful of swanky eateries rubbing shoulders in a sunny, shared courtyard filled with grassy patches, potted trees, and grape vines. It becomes quite a party on a warm summer's day.

Aikmans Café Bar ☆☆ INTERNATIONAL   The pioneer of good dining in Merivale, Aikmans, now under new ownership, continues to deliver good food and a great summer atmosphere. The interior—warm, mellow, and intimate—makes a smart statement in one of Christchurch's smartest neighborhoods. It's recently been extended to include a vine-enclosed courtyard, which is a terrific spot on a sunny day. The menu—which offers all-day breakfasts, lunches, and dinner—ranges from waffles to pastas and pizzas, plus creative mains such as ostrich salad, escalopes of pork flamed in Frangelico, and charred lamb tenderloin with honey-roasted kumara.

154 Aikmans Rd., Merivale. ℃ **03/355-2271.** Reservations recommended. Main courses NZ$18–NZ$30 (US$13–US$21). AE, DC, MC, V. Daily 8:30am–late.

Brigittes Espresso Bar ☆ *Kids* CAFE   Half the population of Merivale seems to enjoy weekend brunch at Brigittes, so make sure you book ahead. The homey interior looks out onto the street and opens up to a sheltered courtyard. You'll find all the usual breakfast options, including eggs Benedict and eggs Florentine, plus lunch and dinner choices such as honey-glazed chicken on salad greens served with lime-ginger soy dressing.

Aikmans Rd. and Papanui Rd., Merivale. ℃ **03/355-6150.** Reservations recommended. Main courses NZ$16–NZ$26 (US$11–US$18). AE, DC, MC, V. Mon 8:30am–6pm; Tues–Sat 8:30am–10pm; Sun 10am–4pm; public holidays from 10am.

JDV ☆☆☆ MODERN NEW ZEALAND   This is where fashionable black garb and gold jewelry are ranked as highly as the coconut-and-ginger duck curry with sticky rice cake, steamed bok choy, lychees, and charred lime. Movers and shakers (along with the rich and slothful), gather here to pay homage to the chefs' penchant for unexpected flavor mixes and reliably delicious meals. Start and/or end the night in the upstairs martini bar.

The Mall, Aikmans Rd., Merivale. ℃ **03/964-3860.** Reservations recommended. Main courses NZ$25–NZ$35 (US$18–US$25). AE, DC, MC, V. Daily 11:30am–late.

Tutto Benne ☆☆ *Value* ITALIAN   Felice and Paulette Mannucci have run a succession of excellent eateries in Christchurch for nearly 3 decades. This latest effort is a little gem. At this pizzeria meets small neighborhood restaurant, the full menu gallops across 15 pizza types, pastas, risottos, and traditional delicacies like veal saltimbocca with prosciutto, sage, and marsala. And we should never forget the Italian cassatta!

192 Papanui Rd., Merivale. ℃ **03/355-4744.** Reservations recommended. Main courses NZ$20–NZ$30 (US$14–US$21). AE, DC, MC, V. Daily 5pm–late.

IN SUMNER

A trip to Sumner wouldn't be complete without a visit to **Coffee Culture Ltd.** ☆☆, 28 Mariner St. (© **03/326-5900**). There's also a branch at 160 Cashel Mall, Christchurch (© **03/377-8825**), plus four suburban cafes in Cashmere, Durham Street, Riccarton, and Shirley. Desserts and coffee are their specialty. **The Cornershop Bistro** ☆☆, 32 Nayland St. (© **03/326-6720**), is an excellent neighborhood restaurant that's casual and competent, presenting everything from racks of lamb to fresh groper filets.

Café Rock ☆☆ *Kids* CAFE If you're going to the beach to eat, it makes sense to sit where you can see it. With sidewalk seating and the sand just across the street, the Rock has a relaxed, casual atmosphere. The value-for-money food includes wholesome breakfasts—frittata with smoked salmon, capers, and spring onions is a tasty sample—and lunch options of curries, pastas, salads, ciabatta, and soups. Dinner brings forth dishes such as grilled oven beef with oven-dried tomato, pistachio, basil, and feta butter on potato rosti with roast-garlic confit and beef jus. You'll find everyone from surfies and singles to trendies and families unwinding here. Service can be patchy but it's worth enduring.

22A Esplanade, Sumner. © 03/326-5358. Reservations recommended. Main courses NZ$18–NZ$25 (US$13–US$18). MC, V. Daily from 8:30am for coffee, 9:30am–11pm for meals.

Ruptured Duck Pizzeria & Bar ☆ *(Value)* *Kids* PIZZA It's worth a trip to Sumner just to savor Ruptured Duck's vegetarian calzone, which bulges with artichoke hearts, pesto, garlic, eggplant, onions, mushrooms, tomato, broccoli, sun-dried tomatoes, and an aioli topping. The smoked chicken and brie pizza with a thick apricot or cranberry base, topped with roasted bell peppers and chicken, is always a favorite. The laid-back interior has two balconies and a buzzy atmosphere.

4 Wakefield St., Sumner. © 03/326-5488. Main courses NZ$18–NZ$28 (US$13–US$20). MC, V. Daily noon–10pm; bar from 7pm.

OTHER PALATABLE CONSIDERATIONS

Caffe Roma ☆, 176 Oxford Terrace (© **03/379-3879**), is popular for breakfast and lunch. **The Metro** ☆, Kilmore and Manchester streets, opposite the Town Hall (© **03/374-4242**), is great for after-show coffee. **Gannets** ☆☆, 818 Colombo St. (© **03/379-2387**), is popular for seafood, and at Victoria Street and Bealey Avenue, you'll find the classy little wine bar **Saggio di Vino** ☆☆☆ (© **03/379-4006**).

Sala Sala ☆☆☆, 184 Oxford Terrace (© **03/379-6975**), is one of the best Japanese restaurants in town. **Retour** ☆☆☆, Cambridge Terrace (© **03/365-2888**), is a

---

Finds **Berry, Berry Nice**

You get two chances to pick fresh berries and then sit down in smart little on-farm cafes for a meal, or coffee and berry-based treats. Take a drive through the pretty lanes of the Halswell area and find **Otahuna Berries Raspberry Café** ☆☆☆, Rhodes Road, Tai Tapu (© **03/329-6687**). It's about a 20-minute drive out of town. Head out towards Tai Tapu on the main highway to Akaroa and you'll see it signposted down Rhodes Road on your left. Pig out on *the* most divine cakes when you get there. **Berryfields' Sweethearts Restaurant** ☆☆, 161 Gardiners Rd., Harewood (© **03/359-5630**), is in the opposite direction, near the airport. It's more of a restaurant experience and attracts a more mature crowd.

delicious dining experience in a unique band rotunda setting; and for good-value meals in a contemporary setting, go to **Oasis** 𝒢𝒢, at the corner of Madras and Chester Street East (☏ **03/363-2800**).

5 Exploring Christchurch

Christchurch prides itself almost equally on its arts, sports, history, and gardens. There are a number of theaters and art galleries, along with several excellent museums, parks, and gardens to explore. Attractions and events are listed in the daily newspaper, *The Press,* and in the monthly *Tourist Times,* available free at the visitor center.

See the map on p. 344 to locate some of the attractions listed below.

THE TOP ATTRACTIONS

The hub of the city center and an excellent starting point is **Cathedral Square.** There are several restaurants, hotels, duty-free shops, and attractions within an easy stroll. It's also where you'll find the **Wizard of Christchurch,** who performs daily at 1pm in summer and when the weather cooperates in winter. The Wizard stands above the crowd on a ladder, ranting and raving about all things from bureaucracy, love, and religion to Americans and politicians. He's an essential Christchurch personality—quirky, smart, and not to be trifled with intellectually. Be sure you know what you're talking about if you pick an argument. You'll also find **Chalice** 𝒢𝒢 here. It's a massive new sculpture created by internationally renowned, Christchurch-based sculptor Neil Dawson.

Canterbury Museum 𝒢𝒢𝒢 *(Kids)*   Perfectly placed on the edge of the Botanic Gardens within a stone's throw of the Arts Centre, the Canterbury Museum is a must. Check out the excellent Antarctic display, a must-see before going out to the International Antarctic Centre. Also look for the superb Natural History Discovery Centre, where you can happily pull open drawers and inspect the contents of jars and cases. The quaint Victorian Canterbury street is interesting, and there's an excellent Maori section. The museum is about to begin major extensions and redevelopment, with completion expected in 2007–2008, but this should not interfere with an interesting visit. Allow 2 hours.

Rolleston Ave. ☏ **03/366-5000.** Fax 03/366-5622. www.canterburymuseum.com. Free admission; Discovery Centre NZ$2 (US$1.40); fees for special exhibits. Oct–Mar daily 9am–5:30pm; Apr–Sept daily 9am–5pm. Free guided tours Tues–Thurs 3:30–4:30pm. Closed Dec 25.

Arts Centre 𝒢𝒢 *(Kids)*   You can't go to Christchurch and not visit the Arts Centre. Originally home to Canterbury University College from 1873 to 1975, it begs leisurely exploration. Quite apart from the lovely Gothic architecture, it presents a rabbits' warren of over 40 retail outlets selling New Zealand–made arts and crafts and heaps of things to interest kids, including great food stalls. You'll find some pretty bizarre goods, but overall the standard is high. There are excellent buys in leather, wool, wood, and crafts.

Court Theatre is housed in the original Engineering Building and Hydraulics Lab, the **Academy Cinema** is in the old Boys' High Gym, and the **Southern Ballet** now occupies the Electrical Engineering Lab and the Mechanical Engineering Lab. There are several good eating spots (Dux de Lux and Le Café are described on p. 362; the Boulevard Cafe, E-Caf Internet Café, and Annie's Wine Bar & Restaurant are also popular). Buskers and performers add color to the weekend market, and you can take a NZ$8 (US$5.60) tour daily or by appointment (☏ **03/363-2836**).

Bounded by Worcester Blvd., Rolleston Ave., Hereford St., and Montreal St. ℂ 03/363-2836. www.artscentre.org.nz. Free admission. Most crafts and retail outlets daily 10am–4pm; market and food fair Sat–Sun 10am–4pm; restaurant and cafe hours vary.

Christchurch Art Gallery Te Puna o Waiwhetu ✸✸✸

I love the flashiness of this new and sparkling architectural icon that has rapidly established itself as the place to go since its 2003 opening. Curving glass facades and spectacular outdoor sculpture aside, it has one of the largest permanent collections in New Zealand, and with eight new gallery spaces, there's plenty of space for both contemporary and historic displays. The collection of over 5,500 paintings, sculptures, prints, drawings, and crafts emphasizes work from the Canterbury region, but there are regular touring international and national shows as well.

And don't overlook the new book and gift shop. It has some terrific New Zealand–made goods—as does the in-house craft gallery, **Form.** A sculpture garden and cafe/restaurant complete the picture, making this a must-visit attraction. Next door is the **Centre of Contemporary Art** (ℂ **03/366-7261**), which is also worth a visit for its exhibitions of New Zealand contemporary art.

Worcester Blvd. and Montreal St. ℂ **03/941-7300.** Fax 03/941-7301. www.christchurchartgallery.org.nz. Free admission; fees for special exhibits. Daily 10am–5pm (Wed till 9pm). Closed Dec 25. Free guided tours daily at 11am and 2pm, and Wed at 6:30pm and 7:30pm. Cafe Mon–Fri 9:30am–late; Sat 8am–late; Sun 8am–5:30pm. Underground parking, entrance off Gloucester St.

Botanic Gardens ✸✸✸ (Kids)

The turquoise-and-yellow Peacock Fountain just inside the main gate on Rolleston Avenue is a handy marker that can't be missed. This is the best point of entry to the lush 23 hectares (57 acres) of deservedly world-renowned gardens. Even if you've never considered yourself the slightest bit green-thumbed, there's something magical about this place. Sweeping lawns, fragrant rose gardens, and some of the oldest exotic trees in New Zealand provide spectacular displays year-round. The Avon River and its huge duck population add interest. The kids can run loose, feed the ducks, and frolic in the playground. Don't miss the lush tropical greenhouse, or the heavenly scented rose gardens adjacent to it. I also love the little alpine garden area and the two ponds that border the rhododendron and azalea gardens.

Rolleston Ave. ℂ **03/372-2840.** www.ccc.govt.nz/parks. Free admission. Free guided tours on foot depart at 9am on first Tues of every month from Botanic Gardens Information Centre, adjacent to the restaurant. A tour vehicle operates daily 10am–4pm and costs around NZ$10 (US$7); join it at the restaurant near the info center or by the Peacock Fountain on the half-hour. Grounds daily 7am to 1 hr. before sunset; conservatories daily 10:15am–4pm; information center Sept–Apr daily 10:15am–4pm, May–Aug daily 11am–3pm. The no. 17 bus and the tram provide convenient access to the Rolleston Ave. entrance.

International Antarctic Centre ✸✸✸ (Kids)

If you've always wanted to romp with penguins, stroke a leopard seal, climb aboard a snowmobile, explore a snow cave, and feel the icy wind chills of Antarctica, this is probably as close as you'll ever get. The penguins may be man-made and the leopard seals stuffed, but everything about this attraction is of superb value. It takes more of a geographic/natural history approach than the Canterbury Museum's Antarctic exhibition, and if you see both, you'll have a healthy appreciation for life on the ice. Considered one of New Zealand's leading attractions, it gives you a feel for modern Antarctic life through sophisticated sound-and-light shows, a spine-tingling audiovisual presentation, and interactive exhibits. The center is suitable for visits of 30 minutes or half a day, but spending 1 to 2 hours is ideal. Two wheelchairs are available for use by the public.

The newest attraction here is the **Antarctic Hagglund Ride** ★★★ , the only one of its type in the world. Its 45-minute tour gives you a unique insight into the planning of Antarctic journeys. It's well worth the extra money and a big hit with kids.

Orchard Rd., adjacent to the Christchurch International Airport. (✆ **0508/736-4846** in NZ, or 03/353-7798. Fax 03/353-7799. www.iceberg.co.nz. Admission NZ$25 (US$18) adults, NZ$15 (US$11) children 5–15, NZ$65 (US$46) per family; group rates available. Antarctic Combo (admission plus Hagglund ride): NZ$35 (US$25) adults, NZ$15–NZ$25 (US$11–US$18) children 15 and under, NZ$99 (US$69) family. Snowphones available in 6 languages for NZ$8 (US$5.60). AE, DC, MC, V. Oct–Mar daily 9am–8pm; Apr–Sept daily 9am–5:30pm. The center is a 15-min. drive from central city and an 8-min. walk from the Christchurch Airport Terminal. The city/airport bus runs to the center every half-hour; the complimentary Super Shuttle runs from the airport to the center. Free parking.

Christchurch Cathedral ★   If you want a bird's-eye view over the square and inner city, climb the 133 steps in the 120-foot Christchurch Anglican Cathedral tower. You won't be alone—well over 300,000 visitors per year wend their way into the cathedral, making it one of the South Island's most visited attractions. Construction was begun in 1864, just 14 years after the first settlers arrived, and was completed in 1904. Today, it's New Zealand's most famous Gothic Revival church and Christchurch's most important landmark. The cathedral is open for prayer during the weekdays; Holy Communion is celebrated daily.

Cathedral Sq. (✆ **03/366-0046.** www.christchurchcathedral.co.nz. Free admission to cathedral; tower NZ$4 (US$2.80) adults, NZ$1.50 (US$1.05) children, NZ$8 (US$5.60) per family. NZ$2.50 (US$1.75) fee to use your camera in the cathedral. NZ$4 (US$2.80) for guided tour. Summer Mon–Sat 8:30am–7pm, Sun 7:30am–7:30pm; winter daily 8:30am–5pm. Guided tours 11am–2pm. Cathedral choir sings a half-hour choral evensong Tues–Wed 5:15pm, Fri 4:30pm, Sun 10am; young choristers sing service Fri 4:30pm (except during school holidays). Most buses pass through the square.

Southern Encounter Aquarium & Kiwi House ★ *Kids*   Visit this attraction if you won't get a chance to swim with dolphins or whale-watch in Kaikoura. It's all here on film in a fascinating 25-minute sequence that takes in the mysteries of underwater Fiordland and New Zealand birdlife as well. You can get your hands wet in the touch tank, see fly-tying demonstrations in the fishing lodge, and gaze upon the engineering marvel that holds 92 tons of seawater behind four glass panels, each weighing 750 kilograms (1,658 lb.) and leaning out at a 45-degree angle. A diver gets in with giant eels at feeding time (11am, but subject to change); marine species are fed at 3pm. Well-situated near the visitor center, it makes a good diversion; however, if you're short on time, opt for the International Antarctic Centre or Orana Park instead.

Cathedral Sq. (✆ **03/359-7109.** Fax 03/359-4330. www.southernencounter.co.nz. Admission NZ$12 (US$8.40) adults, NZ$5 (US$3.50) children, NZ$29 (US$20) per family, free for kids 3 and under. Group discounts available. MC, V. Daily 9am–4:30pm. Feeding times: trout and salmon 1pm, marine fish 3pm, special feeds 11am. Kiwi on display 10am–4:45pm. Closed Dec 25. Enter through Christchurch Visitor Centre or T&Ski Shop.

ADDITIONAL ATTRACTIONS

Animal lovers who are short on time may have to choose between Orana Park and Willowbank Wildlife Reserve. Both are closer to the airport than to central city, so either could make a good last-minute stop. Personally I'm a big-cat fan, so I'd opt for Orana, where things African are to the fore. But if you want a guaranteed sighting of a kiwi before you leave New Zealand, go to Willowbank.

Orana Park ★★★ *Kids*   There's something quite magical about getting up close and personal with Harold the Rothschild giraffe and his four lanky pen mates. You can feed them and fondle their ears and they won't mind a bit, but don't try that with the park's lions, tigers, and cheetahs. Set in 80 attractively laid-out hectares (198 acres), the park is New Zealand's largest wildlife reserve. You'll see few fences and cages here—the emphasis is on a natural environment, which seems to agree with the cheetahs, the only successfully breeding ones in Australasia (10 or so new cubs in the past 12 years). At 3:55pm daily, you can see them make a dash for their raw-meat supper, which is attached to a fast-moving lure. The main lion feeding time is 2:30pm daily. This is the only place in Christchurch to see a tuatara, and there's a nocturnal kiwi house as well, but the one at Willowbank is bigger and better. If you're in a hurry, take the park's 40-minute free shuttle circuit.

743 McLeans Island Rd. (℃) 03/359-7109. Fax 03/359-4330. www.oranawildlifepark.co.nz. Admission NZ$16 (US$11) adults, NZ$6 (US$4.20) children 5–14, NZ$38 (US$27) per family. Group rates available. MC, V. Daily 10am–5pm. Closed Dec 25. The park is a 25-min. drive from central city and is well signposted from the airport. Free parking.

Willowbank Wildlife Reserve   Willowbank is billed as New Zealand's premier wildlife park, showcasing one of the most complete selections of native and non-indigenous wildlife in their natural environments. It has the country's largest collection of kiwis, and you won't find any glass between you and the feathers. It takes a few minutes for your eyes to adjust to the dimly lit nocturnal house, but if you're patient and quiet, you will see a kiwi. This is guaranteed if you take a guided tour at 11:30am or 2:30pm. Night tours of the New Zealand Kiwi Experience are at 7:30, 8:30, and 9:30pm. A new feature is the Ko Tane Cultural Performance at 5:30 and 6:30pm.

60 Hussey Rd. (℃) 03/359-6226. Fax 03/359-6212. www.willowbank.co.nz. Admission NZ$20 (US$14) adults, NZ$10 (US$7) children. Ko Tane from NZ$16 (US$11) adult, NZ$12 (US$8.40) children. Group discounts available. AE, DC, MC, V. Daily 10am–10pm. Take Harewood Rd. and turn right to Gardiners Rd.; turn right again to Hussey Rd. It's a 15-min. drive from the city. The Best Attractions bus also calls here.

Science Alive   This is a thinking person's outing, and it may be the quietest your children ever get on your entire holiday. Adults seem to have as much fun as the kids as they come to grips with tsunami makers, tightropes, and a host of interactive exhibits. Stop by the excellent gift shop and eat your fill afterward at Galileo's Cafe, or take in a movie on one of the eight screens across the foyer.

392 Moorehouse Ave. (℃) 03/365-5199. Fax 03/365-5189. www.sciencealive.co.nz. Admission NZ$10 (US$7) adults, NZ$7 (US$4.90) children 2–5, NZ$7 (US$4.90) student, NZ$25 (US$18) for 4 people. Group discounts available. Mon–Fri 1–9pm; Sat–Sun and public holidays 10am–9pm. Located within the Hoyts 8 complex. The free, yellow electric shuttle stops here every 10 min. Free parking at rear of complex.

Crossing the Harbor

Take the stunning scenic drive over the Port Hills to Lyttelton and once you've explored the little village, leap aboard the **Diamond Harbour Ferry** (℃ **03/366-8855**), located on Lyttelton Wharf. For the small sum of NZ$8 (US$5.60) for adults and NZ$4 (US$2.80) for children, you can travel across to the other side of the harbor and back. It's a walk uphill once you get there, but you can catch your breath over coffee, or a cool beer at historic **Godley House** (℃ **03/329-4880; www.godleyhouse.co.nz**). A ferry run can also drop you off at **Quail Island** for the day. This former quarantine station and leper colony was also used by Scott and Shackleton as home base for their Antarctic expeditions. It abounds with interesting walks and historic points of interest. Get dropped off by **Black Cat Cruises**, B Jetty, Port of Lyttelton (℃ **0800/436-574**; www.blackcat.co.nz).

Double Deal

Get two rides for the price of one with the **Double Deal** offered by **Christchurch Gondola** (© **03/384-0700**) and **Christchurch Wildlife Cruises** (© **03/328-9078**). Pay just NZ$54 (US$38) for adults and NZ$19 (US$13) for children ages 4 to 14.

Air Force Museum   If you've got a hankering to indulge your passion for flight, this past winner of Best New Zealand Attraction is your place. Two hours will give you a good overview of flight simulators, the history hall, the restoration hangar, and displays of planes—everything from Spitfires and Skyhawks to Tiger Moths.

45 Harvard Ave., Wigram. © **03/343-9532**. Fax 03/343-9533. www.airforcemuseum.co.nz. Admission NZ$15 (US$11) adults, NZ$9 (US$6.30) seniors, NZ$5 (US$3.50) children, NZ$28 (US$20) family. AE, MC, V. Daily 10am–5pm. Closed Dec 25. Take the City Circuit Bus or bus no. 5, 51, 81, or 82 from central city. Located at Wigram Air Base, a 15-min. drive from the center, via Riccarton Rd. or Blenheim Rd., both of which merge into Main South Rd.

Ferrymead Heritage Park   The 8.2-hectare (20-acre) historic park offers a look at life in early colonial Christchurch, with buildings, streets, fashions, and other paraphernalia of a bygone era. There's a schoolhouse, jail, operating bakery, and cooperage and livery stable, along with a 1.5km (1-mile) trolley link between the two main areas of the park. This could be a stopover to or from the Mount Cavendish Gondola, which is also accessed off Bridle Path Road.

Ferrymead Park Dr., Ferrymead. © **03/384-1970**. Fax 03/384-1725. www.ferrymead.org.nz. Admission NZ$10 (US$7) adults, NZ$5 (US$3.50) children 5–15, NZ$25 (US$18) per family. Tram runs Sat–Sun for small fee. Daily 10am–4:30pm. Closed Dec 25. Take Ferry Rd. east and take the first right after Heathcote Bridge, or take the no. 35 bus.

Christchurch Gondola   The Christchurch Gondola may not have quite the same breathtaking impact as the Queenstown equivalent, but for unparalleled views westward over the city and the Canterbury Plains to the Southern Alps, and for the full sweep of Pegasus Bay and the Pacific Ocean all the way up to the Kaikoura Ranges, you can't beat it. Perched on the crater rim of an extinct volcano, 445m (1,460 ft.) above sea level, the Gondola complex features the Time Tunnel Heritage Show, with a Canterbury video presentation and a walkthrough exhibition.

If you want to take the Freedom Walk in the Port Hills, pay for the gondola ride up and then walk down any of the numerous hill tracks to Sumner Beach (allow 2 hr.), from which you can catch a bus back to the city, or to Lyttelton, also about 2 hours. Wear sturdy walking shoes—the tracks are steep and can be slippery. The **Mountain Bike Adventure Co.** (© **0800/424-534;** www.cyclehire-tours.co.nz) is another option for your descent. Reservations are essential and can be made at the visitor center (© **03/379-9629**).

10 Bridle Path Rd. © **03/384-0700**. Fax 03/384-0703. www.gondola.co.nz. Admission NZ$18 (US$13) adults, NZ$8 (US$5.60) children 5–15. Discounts for families, seniors, and students. Oct–Apr daily 10am–midnight; winter noon–10pm. The lower terminal is 15 min. from the city center. Take Ferry Rd. and head east; take the first right over the Heathcote Bridge. Or take the Best Attractions bus, which calls here, or the no. 28 Lyttelton bus. Free parking.

PARKS & GARDENS

Christchurch isn't called the Garden City for nothing, and taking pride of place among them all are the **Botanic Gardens**, described under "The Top Attractions," above.

Mona Vale, 63 Fendalton Rd. (© **03/348-9660** or 03/348-7011; fax 03/348-7011), has 5.5 hectares (14 acres) of rolling lawns, rose gardens, fountains, and a grand turn-of-the-20th-century homestead, all open to the public free of charge. The homestead restaurant serves lunch from noon to 2pm, morning and afternoon teas from 10am to 3:30pm. Reservations are essential. Guided garden tours are held daily from November through March.

The **Avon River** runs along the border of Mona Vale, and a punting excursion will give you a peek into some of the beautiful private gardens on the river. The punts operate October through April, daily from 9am to 4:30pm, or on request. The cost is around NZ$25 (US$18) for 20 minutes, NZ$30 (US$21) for 30 minutes.

The 2½-hour **Garden Drive,** described in **Christchurch Scenic Drive Guide** brochure at the visitor center, includes both the Botanic Gardens and Mona Vale. Although much of the tour highlights architecture rather than actual gardens, it will give you a good look around the northwest suburbs, where there are many exquisite private home gardens.

Two other self-guided drives in the same brochure cover the **Port Hills Drive** 𝒜𝒜𝒜 and the **Avon River Drive,** which are not exactly garden tours, but will give you an excellent overview of the city and its natural landscape. The Port Hills Drive is especially worth doing for its spectacular views from Alps to ocean.

During the 4-day **Cathedral Garden Festival,** many of Christchurch's private gardeners throw open their gates. It's held annually in late November. Ask at the visitor center for more information.

If you take the spectacular drive up Dyer's Pass Road and over the Port Hills to Governor's Bay, you'll find a cluster of private gardens open to the public (ask at the visitor center for details). Barry Sligh at **Taunton Gardens** 𝒜𝒜 (© 03/329-9746) is an enthusiastic plant breeder whose stunning 2 hectares (5 acres) of woodland gardens are open Tuesday through Sunday from September to April for NZ$10 (US$7). Just down the road is one of the most famous structured gardens in New Zealand: **Ohinetahi** 𝒜𝒜𝒜 (© 03/329-9852), owned by architect Sir Miles Warren and open by appointment for NZ$20 to NZ$25 (US$14–US$18).

THE WINERIES

There are now over 40 wineries in the Canterbury region, making this the fourth-largest winemaking area in the country. The combination of long hours of sunshine; stony, free-draining soils; low rainfall; extended autumns; and cool winters produces grapes with complex and developed flavors. The region is well suited to the production of red wines such as cabernet, merlot, and pinot noir. The main growing areas are Waipara, Christchurch, and Banks Peninsula.

For details on February's **Christchurch Food & Wine Festival,** call © 03/371-1761, and for March's **Waipara Wine & Food Festival,** call © 0800-166-071.

The visitor center's brochure on the *Waipara Valley Wineries Wine Trail* has a map showing the main wineries. The *Christchurch & Canterbury Gourmet Guide* (NZ$5/US$3.50) also has a concise list of the major wineries.

Finds **Well Oiled**

If you're in the Waipara Valley, make sure you visit **Athena Olive Groves** 𝒜𝒜𝒜, 164 MacKenzies Rd., Waipara (© 03/314-6774; www.athenaolives.co.nz), and try their fabulous range of extra virgin and flavored olive oils, plus their pickled olives. Open daily from 10am until 5pm.

Wine Tours

Canterbury Vin de Pays Tours (© 03/357-8262; www.vindepays.co.nz) has a range of options from NZ$85 to NZ$115 (US$60–US$81). Its tours visit Waipara (5 hr.) and Akaroa wineries (6 hr.), all of which offer tastings and many of which have restaurants. The day trip to Akaroa also includes a visit to a cheese factory and lunch at a quality restaurant. **Adventure Canterbury** (© 0800/847-455 in NZ; www.adventurecanterbury.com), also offers a half-day tour of the Waipara winery region.

Colmonell Wine Trail ☆☆ (© 03/314-6805 or 025/227-6120) has a wagon trail ride through Waipara wineries for around NZ$30 (US$21); reservations are required. Just leap into one of the six covered wagons, and you'll be taken at a leisurely pace to seven local wineries. The wagons leave from the Waipara Hotel Carpark in Waipara Village at 11:30am. It's an excellent value and lots of fun. If you need transport from Christchurch to Waipara, take the **Hanmer Connection** (© 0800/377-378) shuttle for about NZ$20 (US$14) one-way. It leaves from the Christchurch visitor center, with hotel pickups by arrangement.

Canterbury House Vineyards ☆   You can't miss these huge stone buildings just before the Waipara River Bridge. Americans Michael and Nancy Reid vacationed in New Zealand some years ago and fell in love with the country. Their first vines were planted in 1994, and pinot noir is their flagship. The Reids plan to add a barrel hall, function facilities, and larger restaurant enclosing a cloistered courtyard. Expect lots of tour groups.

St. Hwy. 1, Waipara. © 03/314-6900. Fax 03/314-6905. www.canterburyhouse.com. Daily 10am–5pm for tastings, NZ$5 (US$3.50) per person. AE, DC, MC, V. Dinner Fri–Sat.

Daniel Schuster Wines ☆☆☆   A few kilometers north of Waipara Valley in the Omihi area, this picturesque vineyard is well worth a visit, if only to meet with international wine consultant and owner, Danny Schuster. You can visit the tasting room and peruse wine for sale, or take a more comprehensive cellar tour and enjoy barrel tastings with the winemaker by prior arrangement. The vineyard produces pinot noir, chardonnay, and Riesling.

192 Reeces Rd., Omihi, North Canterbury. © 03/314-5901. Fax 03/314-5902. www.danielschusterwines.com. MC, V. Wines cost NZ$19–NZ$60 (US$13–US$42) per bottle. Daily 10am–5pm.

Morworth Estate ☆☆   This is a new state-of-the-art winery with a contemporary restaurant complex. Established in 1993, the vineyard has quickly established a reputation for the production of excellent sauvignon blanc, pinot noir, chardonnay, rosé, Gewürztraminer, pinot gris, and Riesling varieties.

Block Rd., RD6, Christchurch. © 03/349-5014. Fax 03/349-5017. www.morworth.com. Tastings NZ$5 (US$3.50) per person. Restaurant Wed–Sun 10am–4pm; dinner by prior arrangement.

Pegasus Bay Winery & Restaurant ☆☆   This small vineyard and winery are run by the Donaldson family, who have been seriously involved with wine for over 30 years. A new 100-seat restaurant serves top-quality cuisine. Specialties include sauvignon/semillon, chardonnay, merlot cabernet, pinot noir, and Riesling.

Stockgrove Rd., Amberley. © **03/314-6869.** Fax 03/314-6861. www.pegasusbay.com. Tastings NZ$5 (US$3.50) per person. AE, DC, MC, V. Winery daily 10:30am–5pm; restaurant daily noon–4pm. Closed Dec 25–26 and Jan 1. Located 5km (3 miles) north of Amberley.

Rossendale Wines   Located in the charming Tai Tapu Valley area, at Halswell, on the perimeter of Christchurch, Rossendale has a established tradition of good wine and good food. Wines available here including Riesling, Gewürztraminer, sauvignon blanc, merlot, and pinot noir.

168 Old Tai Tapu Rd., Halswell. © **03/322-9684.** Fax 03/322-9273. www.rossendale.co.nz. Daily 10am–late.

Trents Estate Vineyard & Restaurant   This charming setting is built around a 125-year-old historic chicory kiln, which has been cleverly converted into a rustic restaurant. It is surrounded by pinot noir, chardonnay, and Riesling grapes.

Trents Rd., Templeton. © **03/349-6940.** Fax 03/349-6940. www.trentsvineyard.co.nz. Thurs–Sun 11am–4pm; Fri–Sat 11am–late.

Waipara Springs Winery & Restaurant   This is one of the oldest vineyards in the Waipara region. It produces premium-quality sauvignon blanc, Riesling, chardonnay, cabernet sauvignon, and pinot noir grapes from its own 20 hectares (49 acres). It has accumulated numerous medals overseas and in New Zealand, including a Gold Medal for its 1996 cabernet sauvignon, a Silver Medal for the 1997 sauvignon blanc, and a Gold for its 1997 Riesling.

St. Hwy. 1, Waipara. ©/fax **03/314-6777.** www.waiparasprings.co.nz. Daily 11am–5pm for tastings and sales. Closed Dec 24–25.

ORGANIZED TOURS

For a good overview of Akaroa and Banks Peninsula, call up **Canterbury Trails** (© **03/337-1185;** www.canterburytrails.co.nz), which offers comprehensive day tours to the area that include a nature harbor cruise or an opportunity to swim with dolphins. If mountain scenery is more your thing, take the trip to Arthurs Pass National Park, which can also include a ride on the TranzAlpine train (one-way). Prices begin around NZ$260 (US$182).

One Night Outdoors   (© **03/942-2230;** www.onenightoutdoors.com) is a 2-day guided wilderness walk, complete with a night out under the stars—and you'll be amazed at how many stars are visible in the southern skies! It's a perfect trip if you're short on time, or if you want an introduction to walking in New Zealand's mountain wilderness. The informed guides will teach you how to ensure safety. Prices start at NZ$260 (US$182) per person.

In the food and drink line, **Taste Canterbury**   (© **03/326-6753;** www.good things.co.nz) offers a terrific set of personalized gourmet food and wine tours of the

---

Moments **Maori Magic**

Tucked away in suburban Christchurch sits the largest urban marae and carved ancestral house (Aoraki) in New Zealand. **Nga Hau E Whau National Marae** , 250 Pages Rd., Linwood (© **03/388-7685;** www.nationalmarae.co.nz), offers a number of daytime and evening cultural experiences and you'll be impressed by the bounty of fine Maori carving on site. This is the best place in the South Island to enjoy an authentic, traditional hangi, and cultural experience.

An Unforgettable Train Trip

The **TranzAlpine** 𝄞𝄞𝄞 is rated as one of the five most spectacular train journeys in the world, and you can't fail to be impressed by the scenery as you make your way from Christchurch in the east to Greymouth in the west. The train travels over the Canterbury Plains; through the heart of the Southern Alps; and through tunnels, beech forests, and massive river gorges to the West Coast. It's a must-do for anyone visiting the South Island.

The return-day excursion costs around NZ$117 (US$82) to Arthur's Pass and NZ$162 (US$113) to Greymouth, with cheaper rates for children. If you take the Arthur's Pass option, you'll have 5 hours there before the train returns, but there are many excellent bush walks in the area and a couple of nice cafes (see "Side Trips from Christchurch," later in this chapter).

If you go to Greymouth, you'll have only 1 hour in the township before the train returns to Christchurch—not a lot of time to do much more than wander about. Check out the "Greymouth & Lake Brunner" section in chapter 14 for possible activities.

The train leaves from Christchurch's main railway station at 1 Clarence St., Addington. For reservations and further information, contact **Tranz Scenic** (© **0800/872-467** in NZ; www.tranzscenic.co.nz). Food is available on the buffet car, or you can bring your own picnic. The train makes six stops during the journey.

greater Canterbury region. Mavis Airey is a knowledgeable guide and food writer and her half-day tours costs NZ$100 (US$70) per person (or NZ$170/US$119 per person for a full day). You'll get a lovely overview of rural Canterbury on the Akaroa and Ellesmere tours. I strongly recommend them.

Canterbury Brewery Tour, 36 St. Asaph St., Christchurch (© **03/371-3290;** www.canterburybrewery.co.nz), has a 1½-hour tour through the museum and working brewery, followed by beer tasting. It runs Monday through Friday at 10am and 12:30pm, plus Saturday at 1pm and costs NZ$12 (US$8.40) for adults, NZ$6 (US$4.20) for children, and NZ$25 (US$18) per family. Bookings are essential.

After all that, you can go on an invigorating 3-hour jaunt in the Port Hills (NZ$40/US$29) with **Ian McLeod's Walkaway Tours** (© **03/942-6072;** www.walkaway.co.nz). He offers several scenic and ecotours, plus a very good full-day **Gallivanting City Shopping Tour** 𝄞𝄞𝄞 that can include designer clothing, jewelry, antiques, art galleries, antiquarian books, interior decor, or a mix of them all. It costs NZ$180 (US$126) per person, including lunch, wine, and coffee, and it's a great introduction to the city.

And for something entirely different again, allow a full day for the **TranzAlpine & High Country Explorer** 𝄞𝄞𝄞 (© **0800/863-975;** www.high-country.co.nz). You'll never forget this standout adventure, which sees you speeding up the Waimakariri River in a 400hp Chevy-powered Hamilton jet and delivered to the doors of a four-wheel-drive vehicle. You'll then be taken 20km (12 miles) through spectacular, otherwise inaccessible high country to Flock Hill Resort, where you can indulge in the classic Kiwi smorgasbord lunch. You are then taken up to Arthur's Pass village for the 2-hour journey back to Christchurch on board the TranzAlpine (see "An Unforgettable Train Trip," below). This superb tour is a great value at around NZ$300 (US$210). It departs from Christchurch at 9am and returns at 7pm. Take a sweater or jacket at any time of year and don't forget your camera. There's dynamite scenery along the way!

Canterbury Leisure Tours (© 0800/484-485 in NZ, or 03/384-0999; www.leisure tours.co.nz) has a comprehensive selection of half- and full-day tours that cover everything from whale-watching in Kaikoura (see "Side Trips from Christchurch," later in this chapter) to wine trails, sheep-farm tours, horse trekking, Mount Cook, Hanmer Springs (see "Side Trips from Christchurch," later in this chapter), and more.

And if you *still* haven't gotten *Lord of the Rings* out of your system—and believe me, plenty haven't—you're a sure thing for **Hassle-Free Tours'** adventures. Call © 0800/427-753 in NZ or 03/354-6050, or visit the website at www.hasslefree.co.nz to find out about their 4WD excursions that deposit you in the thick of Edora, the capital city of the Rohan people of the film trilogy. The cost is around NZ$200 (US$140).

6 Outdoor Pursuits

BEACHES   Christchurch has three main beaches—Sumner, Taylor's Mistake, and New Brighton. Originally a quiet holiday suburb, **Sumner** is now favored by city dwellers on weekends. Its attractive beach is a magnet for swimmers, surfers, and volleyball players. There are plenty of good cafes, restaurants, and bars (see "Where to Dine," earlier in this chapter). Lots of families, lots of young people.

Taylor's Mistake is a surfie hangout (see "Surfing," below) with some quaint old holiday homes tucked into the cliffs. There's a good walk around the cliff tops from Taylor's Mistake to Boulder Bay. (Directions are on a big board to the right of the parking area behind the surf club.) The beach is over the hill from Sumner and is best accessed by car. Once past Scarborough Hill, there's no place else to go but down to Taylor's Mistake.

There has been a rush of redevelopment at **New Brighton.** It's a good place to take the kids for fishing, safe swimming, and surfing. All in all, a better beach experience awaits at Sumner.

BIKING   Christchurch has a reputation as a cyclist's paradise because of its overall flat terrain. Bike lanes are marked off in several parts of the city, and parking lots provide bike racks. For rentals, contact **City Cycle Hire** (© 0800/343-848 in NZ, or 03/339-4020; www.cyclehire-tours.co.nz), which will deliver bikes to your accommodations. Road bikes cost NZ$20 (US$14) per half-day; mountain bikes are NZ$45 (US$32) per full day.

BOATING   **Punting** is a fun activity, especially since someone else is doing all the work. You'll spot the young men in straw hats pushing their way up the Avon River at the junction of Oxford Terrace and Worcester Boulevard. You can reserve a ride at the visitor center and pay around NZ$12 (US$8.40) per person for a 20-minute round-trip to the Town Hall, NZ$18 (US$13) for a 30-minute round-trip to the Retour Restaurant. You can also get tickets from the landing stage at Worcester bridge. Punts depart daily 9am to dusk. Punting is also available at Mona Vale Gardens (see "Parks & Gardens," earlier in this chapter).

If canoeing is your thing, rent one from **Antigua Boatsheds,** 2 Cambridge Terrace (© 03/366-5885; www.boatsheds.co.nz), for NZ$8 to NZ$15 (US$5.60–US$11) per hour. It opens at 9am; the last boats go out at 5pm.

CLIMBING Get the inside scoop at **Bivouac Outdoor** 𝘙𝘙𝘙 , 76 City Mall, near the Bridge of Remembrance (© **03/366-3197;** www.bivouac.co.nz), where you can also buy *Port Hills Climbing* (NZ$25/US$18). In summary: **Castle Rock** and **The Tors** are good for all levels; **Rapaki** is good for beginner to intermediate climbers; and **Lyttelton Rock** is for the more adventurous. **Castle Hill** in Arthur's Pass has hundreds of climbs for mixed levels and is excellent for bouldering. Or head to the **YMCA Indoor Rock Climbing Wall,** 12 Hereford St. (© **03/366-0689;** www.ymcachch. org.nz), which is open daily from 8am to 10pm and costs NZ$8 (US$5.60) for adults, NZ$5 (US$3.50) for children; it's an extra NZ$5 (US$3.50) for harness hire and NZ$5 (US$3.50) for shoe hire.

DOLPHIN-WATCHING **Christchurch Wildlife Cruises,** 17 Norwich Quay, Lyttelton (© **0800/436-574** in NZ, or 03/328-9078; www.blackcat.co.nz), has an afternoon dolphin-watching cruise, departing daily at 1:30pm all year. It costs NZ$49 (US$34) for adults and NZ$20 (US$14) for children. They also operate dolphin-watching cruises in Akaroa (see "Side Trips to Christchurch," later in this chapter). You'll find free parking near the wharf, or you can catch the no. 28 bus from the city to Lyttelton. A free shuttle also connects with each cruise.

FISHING The South Island has some of the last examples of true wilderness fishing in an unspoiled environment. The visitor center has a multitude of brochures. For a personalized ecotourism experience, contact Guy Heard of **Game Heard** (© **03/351-5664**), or **Complete Angler,** Barbadoes and Cashel streets (© **03/366-9885;** www.completeangler.co.nz), for guided trout and salmon trips and everything you ever needed to know about fishing.

GOLF The Canterbury region boasts over 40 courses. **Russley Golf Club,** 428 Memorial Ave., near the airport (© **03/358-4748**), has reasonably flat, well-bunkered greens and is one of the premier courses in New Zealand. It is open by arrangement. Greens fees are around NZ$60 (US$42). **Harewood Twin Courses,** 371 McLeans Island Rd. (© **03/359-8843;** www.harewoodgolf.co.nz), is the largest golf club in the South Island, with two 18-hole courses. **Christchurch Golf Club** (sometimes referred to as Shirley), 45 Horseshoe Lake Rd. (© **03/385-2738**), has well-groomed, primarily flat fairways. It's open most days; greens fees are NZ$90 (US$63). **Clearwater Resort,** Johns Road (© **03/360-1003;** www.clearwaternz.com), is a par-72 course and casual players will pay NZ$125 (US$88) for a round of golf. The **Terrace Downs Country Resort and Golf Club** (© **0800/465-373** in NZ, or 03/318-6943; www. terracedowns.co.nz) has opened in Rakaia, a 50-minute drive from Christchurch, at the base of the Mount Hutt ski field and on the banks of the Rakaia Gorge. The par-72 course has 70 bunkers, eight lakes, rolling fairways, and spectacular views; and nonaffiliated fees of around NZ$110 (US$77).

HORSE TREKKING For a delightful forest and beach ride, contact **Parkgrove Stables** (© **03/385-2508;** www.adventurecanterbury.com). It caters to both beginners and experienced riders. A 1-hour farm and forest trek is around NZ$40 (US$28). Or head over the hills to Charteris Bay and join a farm and bush trek with **Orton Bradley Horse Treks** 𝘙𝘙, Orton Bradley Park (© **03/329-4900;** www.obhorsetreks.co.nz). They're 30 minutes from the city and you'll see terrific harbor views along the way.

HOT-AIR BALLOONING There is no other place in the world where it's possible to fly from the center of a city, in view of the ocean, toward snow-capped mountains.

Up, Up and Away (© 03/381-4600; www.ballooning.co.nz) charges NZ$220 (US$154) for adults and NZ$180 (US$126) for children for a special first-light experience. Free transport is provided from city locations.

ICE-SKATING   Alpine Ice Sports Centre, 495 Brougham St., Opawa (© 03/366-9183), is open daily; admission is NZ$12 (US$8.40) for all ages and NZ$35 (US$25) for a family pass, which includes skate rental. Spectators are free.

JET-BOATING   Several operators offer exhilarating spins up the Waimakariri River. The longest established is **Waimak Alpine Jet** (© 0800/263-626 in NZ, or 03/318-4881; www.waimakalpinejet.co.nz). It's a little farther out of town than **Jet Thrills** (© 0800/847-455; www.adventurecanterbury.com), a 15-minute drive away, but both give you something to squeal about. Prices start around NZ$70 to NZ$99 (US$49–US$69) per person.

KAYAKING   To have a go at white-water kayaking, call **Bivouac Outdoor** (© 03/366-3197). If sea kayaking is your preference, call **Top Sport Kayaking,** 1091 Ferry Rd. (© 03/384-0405; www.topsport.co.nz). Beginners will go to the smooth waters of the Estuary or the Heathcote River. Both white-water and sea-kayaking lessons are available.

MOUNTAIN BIKING   The Port Hills are a favorite place for mountain biking. The **Mountain Bike Adventure Co.** (© 0800/424-534) makes it possible to take the Christchurch Gondola to the top and then bike down one of the hill tracks or the road. The cost is around NZ$50 (US$35). The gondola operates daily from 10am to midnight October through April, noon to 10pm in winter. Mountain-biking reservations can be made at the visitor center.

PARAGLIDING   Nimbus Paragliding (© 0800/111-611 in NZ, or 03/389-1999; www.nimbusparagliding.co.nz) was the early pioneer of Canterbury paragliding and has pilots who will assist you in leaping off one of three superb Port Hills sites. Four to 10 minutes of flying will cost NZ$140 (US$98) tandem. A paragliding school with 1- to 11-day courses is also available. Seriously addicted paragliders could consider **Nimbus Paragliding Adventure Tours,** which provides all flying equipment, campervans, and a New Zealand–wide itinerary covering the best flying sites (see chapter 3).

SKYDIVING   If you feel ready for that ultimate adrenaline rush, ring **Skydivingnz.com** (© 03/343-5542; www.skydivingnz.com). You'll be attached to its highly experienced tandem instructor. Free-fall skydiving over Hagley Park costs NZ$245 (US$172) from 9,000 feet. Courtesy transport is provided to the Wigram Control Tower in Hornby.

SURFING   Sumner Beach is an ideal spot for novices. Brighton Beach has hard-breaking waves and is suitable for intermediate and advanced surfers. Taylor's Mistake is a good dumper with powerful waves. The **Eastcoast Boardriding Co.,** 1091 Ferry Rd. (© 03/384-3788; www.eastcoast.co.nz), on the foreshore behind the gas station just before the Ferrymead Bridge on the way to Sumner and Taylor's Mistake, rents boards from around NZ$30 (US$21) for 2 hours, NZ$60 to NZ$70 US$62–US$49) for a day. They're open daily from 9am to 6pm.

SWIMMING   Get your head wet at **QEII Park,** Travis Road, on the way to New Brighton (© 03/383-4313; www.ccc.govt.nz). There are four heated indoor pools, including a crazy hydroslide made up of 220m (722 ft.) of twisting tubes. Right in town is the new **Centennial Leisure Centre,** Armagh Street (© 03/941-6853), which has a gym, lap pool, leisure pools, spas, and saunas.

WALKING The visitor center has several brochures detailing city walks. One of the best is *Christchurch City Centre Walks* ⭐, which gives three easy 45-minute options that take in city landmarks. *River Walks of Christchurch* ⭐⭐ details 13 walks for all ages.

Taking to the Slopes

There are excellent ski fields within 2 hours of Christchurch. Closest among them are the five main fields of the Arthur's Pass area—Porter Heights, Mount Cheeseman, Broken River, Craigieburn Valley, and Temple Basin—all 1 to 1½ hours from the city. **Porter Heights** (℃ 03/318-4002; www.porterheights.co.nz) is the closest commercial field. It has the longest downhill drop in New Zealand, and although the facilities are pretty basic, it has a variety of terrain and stunning views. It's good for all skill levels. **Mount Cheeseman** (℃ 03/379-5315; www.mtcheeseman.com) is a club field and the second closest to Christchurch. It's good for all skiers and snowboarders, but it's not as big as the others. **Broken River** (℃ 03/318-7270; ski@brokenriver.co.nz) is another club field and a bit more rugged; it has rope tows only. **Craigieburn Valley** (℃ 03/365-2514; www.craigieburn.co.nz) is a club field 1¼ hours away, perfect for intermediate and advanced skiers. **Temple Basin** (℃ 03/377-7788; www.temple basin.co.nz), a club field beyond Arthur's Pass, has the most reliable snow in Canterbury facing the sun. It's a steep and enclosed field, and skiers say that if you can ski at Temple Basin, you can ski anywhere in the world. It's a snowboarder's paradise, too.

North Canterbury also has **Mount Lyford** (℃ 03/315-6178; www.mt lyford.co.nz), a privately owned commercial field 1 hour from Kaikoura and 1½ to 2 hours north of Christchurch; and **Mount Olympus** (℃ 03/329-1727; www.activenz.co.nz/mt-olympus), a club field in the back of the Craigieburn range, set in a wide south-facing basin, that offers a variety of runs on uncrowded slopes.

Farther afield is **Mount Hutt Ski Area,** Main Road, Methven (℃ 03/302-8811; www.nzski.com); it's right in the heart of the Southern Alps and is recognized internationally as having the longest number of skiable days in Australasia. It's located 90 minutes south of Christchurch by car. Although it's the most developed commercial field in Canterbury, it's very popular because it's well serviced by T-bars and chairlifts, and good shuttles are available. It's quite crowded here, and it isn't every skier's favorite. It doesn't have the same good fall line as Porter Heights, but it does have much better après-ski and on-field facilities. *Note:* It's important to read all signs here. If they say CLOSED, they mean it—it can get dangerous here because the weather closes in very quickly. It's a long haul up the mountain, and chains are necessary for a good part of the season. For a snow report, call ℃ 0900/99-SNO.

Note: Addicted skiers tell me you should never go anywhere in the Porter Heights range or Mount Hutt when Canterbury's infamous nor'west wind blows; apparently it's often raining in the mountains then and you'll be plagued by horrendous winds.

The more energetic will find the 4-day, 35km (22-mile) **Banks Peninsula Track** 🐾🐾🐾 worthwhile (see "Akaroa" under "Side Trips from Christchurch," later in this chapter); there's also the 3-day, 43km (27-mile) **Kaikoura Coast Track** 🐾🐾. **Arthur's Pass National Park,** 150km (93 miles) west of Christchurch, is another tramper's heaven (see "Side Trips from Christchurch," below). The new 3-day guided **Christchurch to Akaroa Walk** might also appeal. Call **Tuatara Tours** (© 0800/377-378 in NZ, or 03/962-3280; www.tuataratours.co.nz) for details. It costs around NZ$990 (US$693) per person, which includes accommodations. Or call **New Zealand Hiking Safaris** (© 0800/697-232 in NZ; www.hikingnewzealand.com), who have a range of superb multiday treks. It's based in Lyttelton but offers treks all over New Zealand.

WHITE-WATER RAFTING **Rangitata Rafts** (© 0800/251-251 in NZ, or 03/696-3735; www.rafts.co.nz) will take pleasure in introducing you to the Rangitata River's Grade V rapids. You'll start the adventure with a relaxed lunch rather than hard work. That comes later as you go through safety briefs, practical training, and a natural progression to the intense Grade IV and V section. End with hot showers and a barbecue. All this will cost around NZ$158 (US$111). The day trip includes transport from Christchurch. If you drive yourself there it costs NZ$148 (US$104) per person.

WINDSURFING One of the best windsurfing spots is the estuary near the turnoff to Heathcote Valley on Ferry Road. **Eastcoast Boardriding Co.** 🐾, 1091 Ferry Rd. (© 03/384-3788; www.eastcoast.co.nz), on the foreshore behind the gas station just before the Ferrymead Bridge, can set you up. All its instructors are Level II or higher, and among them is four-time New Zealand windsurfing champion Hamish Bayly. The cafe on the premises is a great meeting place for surfies and the like.

7 Shopping

THE MALLS

The city has a number of suburban malls. **Westfield Riccarton** 🐾🐾 (© 03/348-4119) has more than 100 shops; the bus stops right outside the door. **Northlands Mall,** in Papanui (© 03/352-6535), has 67 stores. **The Palms,** in Shirley (© 03/385-3067), has more than 85 stores, a big entertainment complex, and good bus services. The recently revamped, upmarket **Merivale Mall** 🐾🐾 (© 03/355-9692) is smaller, but features a more expensive range of designer stores and boutiques. All malls are open daily.

THE MARKETS

The **Arts Centre,** on Worcester Boulevard (© 03/366-0989; p. 365), offers a good range of everything from quirky to quality, especially during the open market weekends when the courtyard swells with purveyors of all things.

Tips **Made in New Zealand**

Head for **Untouched World,** 155 Roydvale Ave. (© 03/357-9399; www.untouched world.com), where you'll find a stunning range of top-quality, New Zealand–made wool garments in a delightful setting with a top-end restaurant and native garden. Phone for courtesy transport. **Wild South Adventure Clothing,** 685 Colombo St. (© 03/379-7330), also sells excellent garments in natural fibers.

> **Finds** **Retail on High**
>
> Some of my favorite stores are in High Street, and chief among them is the girly paradise **Cosi Fan Tutte** ᏪᏪᏪ, 167 High St. (ⓒ **03/365-0001**), which stocks everything a seriously feminine woman could ever want. A few doors along, **One Big Sugar Bowl** ᏪᏪ (ⓒ **03/377-3600**) will also appeal to all your senses with lovely costume jewelry, underwear, and accessories. **Decodence**, 151 High St. (ⓒ **03/982-8332**), is a good place for Art Deco finds; and **inform** ᏪᏪᏪ, 158 High St. (ⓒ **03/366-3893**) is where you'll find more beautiful contemporary jewelry by Koji Miyazaki (owner of Form in the Christchurch Art Gallery) and other reputable New Zealand jewelers.

Riccarton Rotary Market ᏪᏪ (ⓒ **03/339-0011**), which you'll find Sundays from 8am at Riccarton Racecourse, on Racecourse Road, Upper Riccarton, is supposedly New Zealand's biggest outdoor market and attracts over 300 vendors. Arrive early to get the best bargains. The goods are predominantly secondhand, but there are some good buys in sheepskin products and crafts. You'll need to sift through everything as there's a lot of junk.

CITY SHOPPING SPOTS

Back in the city, **New Regent Street** ᏪᏪ is an architectural highlight on the central-city tram route. It features a mix of boutiques, restaurants, and cafes and is generally very lively. If you're walking, it runs between Gloucester and Armagh streets.

For antiques and interesting secondhand stores, walk the length of **High Street** between Litchfield and Tuam streets. You'll find more stores scattered along **Manchester Street,** predominantly between Cambridge Terrace and Cashel Street. **W. Holliday & Sons** ᏪᏪᏪ, 20 Papanui Rd., St. Albans (ⓒ **03/355-4117**), is a fifth-generation enterprise with the best imported antiques. **Wayne Wright Antiques** ᏪᏪ, 88 Victoria St. (ⓒ **03/366-1116**), is a close second. For classical and decorative antiques from Europe, visit **Morrison & West Antiques** ᏪᏪ, The Old Council Chambers, 1 Sumner Rd., Lyttelton (ⓒ **03/328-8380**).

Victoria Street, north of the Crowne Plaza through to Bealey Avenue, is now home to a lovely range of boutique gift, fashion, design, furniture, and interior decor stores, with plenty of cafes and restaurants along its length for a much-needed shopper's rest.

Top-quality New Zealand arts, crafts, and jewelry can be found at **Form Gallery** ᏪᏪᏪ, in the new Christchurch Art Gallery (ⓒ **03/377-1211;** www.form.co.nz). If you don't find what you want, **Cave Rock Gallery** ᏪᏪ, on the Hereford Street side of the Arts Centre (ⓒ **03/365-1634**), will almost certainly fill some gaps.

There is a **Regency Duty-Free Shop** at 736 Colombo St. (ⓒ **03/379-1923**). And it's in this area and into the Square that you'll find a wide range of gift stores selling souvenirs and clothing.

J. Ballantyne & Co., at City Mall and Colombo Street (ⓒ **03/379-7400**), is still seen as *the* department store in Christchurch. It has been operating with distinctive style for over 100 years and its newly opened Contemporary Lounge is a must visit for top international clothing and accessories brands that can't be found elsewhere in the South Island.

City Mall (at the end near the Bridge of Remembrance) has a cluster of designer fashion shops—especially **Flame** and **ZFA,** along with **Plume** ᏪᏪ (ⓒ **03/355-1112**), which stocks the four top New Zealand designers—Karen Walker, Nom*d, World, and Zambesi. Fashion lovers should also cruise High Street, where individual designer boutiques are in the biggest concentrations.

For excellent New Zealand–made contemporary gifts, go to **The Vault** ✿✿✿ (© **03/379-5399**), which is also in this area, or **Wild Places** (© **03/365-2533**).

Map World ✿✿✿ , 173 Gloucester St. (© **03/374-5399;** www.mapworld.co.nz), is New Zealand's most comprehensive specialty map shop, stocked to the brim with guidebooks and topographic maps.

Delectable New Zealand foodstuffs ideal as picnic fare or take-home gifts can be found at **Good Things** ✿✿, 163 High St. (© **03/366-3894;** www.goodthings.co.nz). It stocks over 50 cheeses cut fresh from the block and specializes in New Zealand wines and local products. Also worth checking out for top food lines is **Kapiti Cheeses Christchurch,** 12–18 Moorhouse Ave. (© **03/377-7077;** www.kapiticheeses.co.nz), which has a wide range of gift hampers, wine, and cheese.

8 Christchurch After Dark

Christchurch has a variety of nightlife, but lacks the range and color of Wellington and Auckland. Find out about weekend happenings by reading the "Entertainment" section of Friday's *Press,* or consult the "What's On" section of the *Tourist Times.* For information on the music scene, contact the **Christchurch Civic Music Council** (© **03/366-3310;** cmc@netaccess.co.nz).

THE PERFORMING ARTS

The city has a regular program of concerts, plays, musicals, and dance performances held at the **Town Hall,** on Kilmore Street (© **03/377-8899**), and the **Theatre Royal,** 145 Gloucester St. (© **03/366-6326**).

The **Court Theatre,** in the Arts Centre, Worcester Boulevard (© **0800/333-100** in NZ, or 03/963-0870; www.courttheatre.co.nz), is the home of the best professional theater company in New Zealand. Shows range from Shakespeare to contemporary American and British theater to the best New Zealand plays. Tickets for most shows are around NZ$30 (US$21).

The **WestpacTrust Entertainment Centre** (© **03/377-8899**) is another venue. The center covers a large area, and the two main entrances are on Jack Hinton Drive, which runs off Lincoln Road, and Wrights Road, which runs off Blenheim Road.

THE CLUB & BAR SCENE

The most visible evidence of Christchurch nightlife is to be found along Oxford Terrace, or **"The Strip,"** as it's known locally. This is the hub of the lively cafe and bar scene. Come 11pm, the mood changes as the place is infiltrated by the 18-to-30 age group and the music is pumped up accordingly. If you're single, under 40, hungry for the inebriated attentions of the opposite sex, and ready for just about anything, you'll have a great time here; if you're none of the above, you'll probably get the urge to move on around midnight. In this area, **Azure** (© 03/365-6088), **Coyote** (© 03/366-6055), **All-Bar-One** (© 03/377-9898), and **Viaduct** (© 03/377-9968) have popular dance floors, which get so packed you can barely move. Next door to Viaduct is its partner, **Di Lusso** (© 03/377-9968), which presents a stylish little lounge bar that mixes good music and cocktails—chiefly for the 30s crowd. The **Tap Room** (© 03/365-0547) is probably the nicest of this cluster of bars and attracts a wider age group.

Rootes Bar, under Minx Dining Room, 96 Lichfield St. (© 03/374-9944), is the latest stylish spot for everyone from gorgeous girls on the make to businessmen on the prowl and the happy cocktail set. Just down the road you'll find **Eye Spy**, 56 Lichfield St. (© 03/379-6634), a place of lush cocktails and funky house music. **Triptych**, corner of Armagh and Colombo streets (© 03/365-3735), is a classy, inner city lounge bar where you can lean back in leather sofas in front of the fire. **Ciao Bella's Premium Bar**, 131 Victoria St. (© 03/371-7288), is packed tight with media and architectural types on a Friday night; and **Indochine**, 209 Cambridge Terrace (© 03/365-7372), is the sophisticated hangout of choice for the arts crowd. **Bar D'O,** 817 Colombo St. (© 03/365-2393), is an intimate, late-night hangout; and **Mansion,** upstairs, 76 Lichfield St. (© 03/366-0939), is popular with a younger crowd and is the final stop for many in the early hours of Sunday morning.

If sports bars are more your style, you won't find one bigger than **Holy Grail,** 98 Worcester Blvd. (© 03/365-9816), which has huge screens and a 24-hour license. **Legends,** 46 Bedford Row (© 03/366-5596), is another in this vein; and **The Loaded Hog,** Manchester and Cashel streets (© 03/366-6674), is a popular starting point for the 20- to 30-something crowd.

The **Southern Blues Bar,** 198 Madras St. (© 03/365-1654), opens nightly from 7:30pm until very late and attracts an audience ages 25 to 75. There's live music every night, ranging from jazz to Latin and rock. Another good jazz bar is **Sammy's Jazz Review** ☆☆☆, 14 Bedford Row (© 03/377-8618). **Foam** ☆☆, 30 Bedford Row (© 03/365-2926), has a lovely mix of intimate and wide-open spaces, plus very good jazz nights. In Merivale, **Zanzibar** ☆☆, Merivale Mall, Aikmans Road (© 03/355-5577), hums on a Thursday and Friday night and is a well-established "meat market." Adjacent **JDV,** Aikmans Road (© 03/964-3860), has a gorgeous little martini bar that rocks until late, especially on Thursday nights.

The **Dux de Lux,** in the Arts Centre (© 03/366-6919; p. 362), is the place to be if you're into loud local bands and a pretty full-on bar environment. It's a favorite for 20- and 30-year-olds, who spill out into the paved courtyard area. Great boutique brews, too.

Hedging Your Bets

The **Christchurch Casino,** Victoria Street, across from the Crowne Plaza (© **0800/227-466** in NZ, or 03/365-9999; www.christchurchcasino.co.nz), opened in 1994 and was New Zealand's first. In 11 years, it's had well over 5 million visitors (60% local). It's probably the only boutique casino in Australasia that features a more classical European style, setting it apart from its Auckland equivalent's money-churner atmosphere. You'll find over 350 gaming machines as well as blackjack, baccarat, Caribbean stud poker, American roulette, keno, and Tai Sai. Café Caesars is open for light meals; there are several bars; and the Grand Café is worth a visit in itself for its excellent food. You must be at least 20 to enter; dress codes are strict—no jeans or denim of any kind, and no thongs, T-shirts, or active sportswear. Free shuttles operate to and from local hotels and motels. Open 24 hours a day, 7 days a week.

Tips   The Gay Scene

Christchurch is a very "polite" city, and its gay scene is less overt than in the bigger cities. Here's what I've unearthed: **Chameleon Bar,** corner of Tuam and Colombo streets (© **03/365-5648**), is open Thursday and Friday 7pm to late, Saturday 8pm until late and Sunday 3pm until late. **Cruz,** upstairs, Ministry Nightclub complex, 90 Lichfield St. (© **03/379-2910**), is Christchurch's only gay bar nightclub and is open Tuesday through Sunday 7pm until late. **Menfriends,** upstairs, 83 Lichfield St. (© **03/377-1701**), is a sauna and cruise club; **The Box,** upstairs, 146a Lichfield St. (© **03/377-4748**), is a gay video and cruise lounge; and **Divas Boutique,** 146a Lichfield St. (© **03/379-3446**), is a social lounge where cross-dressers and transvestites can meet, Tuesday through Saturday, noon until 9pm. They have regular cross-dressing parties every Saturday night. For more information, check www.gaynz.com.

MOVIES

Currently, the biggest multiplex is **Hoyts 8,** 392 Moorehouse Ave. (© **03/366-6367**). The **Regent on Worcester,** 94 Worcester St. (© **03/377-8095**), is a fine, centrally placed four-cinema complex right beside the Square. And the **Academy** ★★ (© **03/366-0167**) and the **Cloisters** (© **03/366-0167**), located in the heart of the Arts Centre, show national and international art-house films. An eight-theater complex opened at **The Palms** in Shirley in late 2003 and another at **Westfield Riccarton** (see "Shopping," above).

9 Side Trips from Christchurch

AKAROA ★★★

There's a rather off-putting, winding hill road between Christchurch and Akaroa—but the scenery is wonderful and you shouldn't let a few steep twists and turns deter you from visiting this little French-inspired whimsy on the shores of Akaroa Harbour.

From the time you reach the breathtaking setting of the **Hilltop Café & Bar** (© **03/325-1005**), a country pub worth a visit, overlooking Akaroa and the harbor, you'll be seduced by this dramatic volcanic landscape. Jean Langlois, an early French explorer, took word of it back to France, and in 1840, two ships and a handful of settlers arrived to colonize the site. They were too late—the British had beaten them to it when they signed the Treaty of Waitangi the year before. The French abandoned their plan, but the settlers stayed on, casting about names such as Le Bons Bay, Duvauchelle, and French Farm. Today, you'll still find "rues" here, not streets.

In recent years, the community of about 800 residents has pulled up its promotional socks, and you'll find a growing number of excellent lodgings, restaurants, and shops. The Maori word *akaroa* means "long harbor," and that's exactly what dominates the village and its activities.

ESSENTIALS

GETTING THERE   From Christchurch, follow State Highway 75 to Akaroa, passing through Halswell Village and Little River, up over the hills and down around Akaroa Harbour. Two shuttle companies operate regularly from Christchurch. **French**

Connection (© **0800/800-575** in NZ, or 03/366-4556; www.akaroafrenchconnection. co.nz), has daily departures from Christchurch Visitor Centre and a complimentary pick-up service from inner city accommodations. The **Akaroa Shuttle** (© **0800/ 500-929;** www.akaroashuttle.co.nz), charges around NZ$20 (US$14) per person round-trip for the direct shuttle service. Both make the 1-hour trip daily; reservations are essential.

VISITOR INFORMATION The **Akaroa Information Centre** is in the old post office building, 80 Rue Lavaud (©/fax **03/304-8600;** www.akaroa.com).

EXPLORING THE TOWN & HARBOR

A small **museum,** made up of four historic buildings on Rue Lavaud (© **03/304- 1013;** akmus@xtra.co.nz), has lively displays and good Maori collections. It's open daily from 10:30am to 4:30pm. The **Langlois-Eteveneaux Cottage** was partly pre-fabricated in France around 1846 and is probably the oldest in Canterbury. The **Old French Cemetery** was the first consecrated burial ground in Canterbury and is just off Rue Pompallier. The old **lighthouse,** which was in service from 1880 to 1980, is also interesting.

If you're artistically inclined, pick up the brochure for the self-guided **Artisan's Trail of Banks Peninsula** 🎎, which leads to the homes and studios of 11 local artists and craftspeople. You'll need at least a day, as many of them are scattered farther afield in the surrounding bays.

One thing every visitor should do is experience the harbor firsthand. **Pohatu Sea Kayaking** (© **03/304-8552;** www.pohatu.co.nz), offers guided kayak tours in the Flea Bay Marine Reserve and you should see lots of penguins. **Dolphin Experience Akaroa,** 61 Beach Rd. (© **0508/365-744** in NZ, or 03/304-7726; www.dolphin sakaroa.co.nz), gives you the chance to spend time in the water with the Hector's dolphins. From November through April, their dolphin trips depart daily at 6am, 9am, noon, and 3pm. From May through October, tours run at 9am and noon only.

Akaroa Harbour Cruises 🎎🎎 *The Cat* takes 90 people and offers great views throughout the 2-hour scenic cruise, which visits a salmon farm, a *paua* pearl farm, and bird-life sites. You have to be quite unlucky on this trip *not* to see the charming Hector's dolphins. The company's 3-hour dolphin-swimming trip gives you a chance to have a close encounter. See the section on ecotourism in chapter 2 for more information on swimming with dolphins.

Main Wharf. © 0800/436-574 in NZ, or 03/304-7641. Fax 03/304-7643. www.canterburycat.co.nz. Scenic nature cruise NZ$49 (US$34) adults, NZ$20 (US$14) children. YHA discounts available. May–Sept daily 1:30pm; rest of year daily 11am and 1:30pm. Dolphin swimming NZ$95–NZ$105 (US$67–US$74) adults, NZ$75–NZ$85 (US$53–US$60) children. May–Sept daily noon; rest of year 6, 8:30, 11:30am, and 1:30pm. Parking at base of wharf and along the waterfront.

Finds **Pit Stop**

If you feel like a break before crossing the hill, stop at the **Little River Gallery** 🎎🎎, Main Road, Little River (© **03/325-1944;** www.littlerivergallery.com), where you'll find a wide range of New Zealand–made arts and crafts. And right beside the gallery is the excellent **Little River Store & Café.** Both are open daily—the gallery from 9:30am to 5:30pm, the store from 7:30am to 7:30pm, and the cafe from 9am to 6pm.

> ### *Finds* The Big Cheese
>
> As you drop down from the hills into Barrys Bay on your drive to Akaroa, keep
> an eye out on the left for **Barry's Bay Cheese** ⟨⟨⟨ (© **03/304-5809;** fax 03/304-
> 5814), makers of mouthwatering traditional cheeses—everything from award-
> winning cheddars to Maasdam, gouda, edam, and havarti, to name just a few.
> During the cheese-making season (usually Oct–Apr), you can watch cheese-
> making activities every second day, through the viewing gallery window.
> There's a shop and I advise you to stock up! They're open daily.

WALKING THE WALK

Consider this: 35km (22 miles) of unspoiled coastal farmland scenery; undisturbed
colonies of fur seals, penguins, and dolphins; sheltered turquoise bays; the rustic comforts of trampers' huts; and enough moderate exertion to keep you honest. This is
what you get with the **Banks Peninsula Track** ⟨⟨⟨ (© **03/304-7612;** www.banks
track.co.nz). The track twice climbs to 600m (1,968 ft.) and features rugged, exposed
headlands, so a reasonable level of fitness is required. The season runs from October
1 to April 30. The cost is around NZ$200 (US$140), which includes transport from
Akaroa to the first hut, 4 nights' accommodations, track registration, and landowners'
fees. The 2-day tramp is recommended only for those with a high level of fitness and
costs around NZ$125 (US$88) per person.

The **Southern Bays Track** (©/fax **03/329-0007**) offers three unguided and guided
options over the southern coastlines, cliffs, valleys, bush, and peaks of Banks Peninsula, descending into the Little River village via the Okuti Valley. For those who like
challenge without the hassle, the guided walk, with packs carried by someone else, has
got to be a dream option. The season runs from mid-October to the end of May. Call
for prices.

WHERE TO STAY

In addition to those listed below, I recommend the following options. **Kahikatea
Country Retreat** ⟨⟨⟨ , Wainui Valley Road (© **03/304-7400;** fax 03/304-7430;
www.kahikatea.com), has a romantic cottage in a prime rural position overlooking
Akaroa Harbour. It's about 22km (14 miles) from Akaroa itself. **Chez la Mer Backpackers,** 50 Rue Lavaud (©/fax **03/304-7024;** www.chezlamer.co.nz), has shared
bunkrooms for NZ$22 (US$15) per person, and twins/doubles for NZ$53 to NZ$64
(US$37–US$45). Set in a historic building, it has a picturesque charm and an ideal
main-street location.

Rates given include 12.5% GST.

Maison de la Mer ⟨⟨⟨ *(Moments)*   Bruce and Carol Hyland's last B&B in Devonport was my favorite in all of New Zealand. Their new Akaroa venture has all that
same romance, class, and hospitality transferred south. For privacy, opt for The
Boathouse, a self-contained apartment set apart from the main house that has its own
kitchen. Two luscious rooms in the main house have wide sea views. The Fleur de Lys
has a private sunroom.

1 Rue Benoit, Akaroa. © **03/304-8907.** Fax 03/304-8917. www.maisondelamer.co.nz. 3 units. NZ$295 (US$207).
Rates include breakfast. AE, MC, V. Closed July–Aug. No children under 12. **Amenities:** Nonsmoking rooms. *In room:*
TV/DVD, dataport, kitchen in The Boathouse, minibar, fridge, coffeemaker, hair dryer, iron.

Mill Cottage 🏵🏵🏵 *(Finds)* I cannot imagine anyone *not* falling in love with the exquisite historic Mill Cottage, a restored gem, decorated in William Morris style and surrounded by a garden full of trees and roses. It has a queen and two single bedrooms, a kitchen, and living room. Host Louisa and Cliff also offer a suite in the main house, comprising a queen bedroom, sitting room, and two single beds in a second bedroom.

81 Rue Grehan, Akaroa. ℂ **03/304-8007.** www.akaroa.gen.nz. 2 units. NZ$275–NZ$350 (US$193–US$245). Long-stay and off-peak rates available. Rates include breakfast. AE, DC, MC, V. **Amenities:** Tour bookings; massage; babysitting; nonsmoking rooms; on-call doctor/dentist. *In room:* TV in main house, dataport, kitchen in cottage, fridge, coffeemaker, hair dryer, iron.

Wilderness House 🏵🏵 *(Value)* This big two-storied home, set in a large garden, is just a short stroll from the heart of the village. It oozes old-world charm and, of the four rooms, I like the elegant botanically themed Nalder Room the best. Mind you, the claw-foot tub was a draw card in the Walker Room and the private balcony and French Provincial style of the Shepherd Room were just as appealing. You even get to wander in a tiny private vineyard as part of the deal.

42 Rue Grehan, Akaroa. ℂ **03/304-7517.** Fax 03/304-7518. www.wildernesshouse.co.nz. 4 units. NZ$240 (US$168). Long-stay and off-peak rates available. Rates include breakfast. MC, V. No children under 12. **Amenities:** Laundry service; dry cleaning; nonsmoking rooms. *In room:* Fridge, coffeemaker, hair dryer, iron.

WHERE TO DINE

For excellent picnic fare, head to **Akaroa Bakery,** 51 Beach Rd. (ℂ **03/304-7663**), open daily from 7:30am to 4pm. It has specialty breads, sandwiches, pies, and cakes baked fresh each day.

Bully Hayes Bar & Café 🏵 MODERN NEW ZEALAND Locals will tell you that the food here is "up and down," and that's certainly been my experience. The presentation is smart and maximizes the superb waterfront location, and there's something to be said for sipping a glass of Canterbury wine out on the terrace. One of the most popular menu items is minted lamb tossed with fresh vegetables served on kumara (sweet potato) mash. Overall, it could be better, but I still come here for the setting.

57 Beach Rd. ℂ **03/304-7533.** Reservations recommended. Main courses NZ$20–NZ$30 (US$14–US$21). AE, DC, MC, V. Mon–Fri 10am–late; Sat–Sun 8:30am–late.

Moments **On the Run**

One adventure that shouldn't be missed is the **Eastern Bays Scenic Mail Run** 🏵🏵🏵 (ℂ **03/304-7873,** or call the visitor center). Join mailman Gerry Trott and his wife, Anita, who make this 120km (74-mile), 4-hour journey around some pretty hair-raising Banks Peninsula roads every day. They deliver mail, papers, and freight to the isolated farms and communities of the peninsula, and they'll take up to eight passengers along for the ride. They'll even stop to let you take photos—and believe me, you'll want to. And have you ever heard of a mailman who stops to offer a picnic of tea and scones at a picturesque beach along the way? The Mail Run departs from the visitor center Monday through Saturday at 9am. It costs around NZ$38 (US$27); reservations the day before travel are essential.

Finds A Beach Diversion

On the way to or from Akaroa on State Highway 75, take a detour to **Lake Ellesmere**. It measures 287 sq. km (111 sq. miles), but it's only 2m (6½ ft.) deep at its deepest point and is home to thousands of Australian black swans and other birds. And for a dramatic seascape, don't go past **Birdlings Flat** 禽禽, in the same area. The seas are very dangerous on this stone-covered beach, so don't attempt swimming under any conditions. It's signposted off the main highway about 30 to 40 minutes from Christchurch.

C'est La Vie Bistro/Café 禽禽禽 FRENCH You'll pay city prices here, but what other Akaroa restaurant can claim a well-deserved review in the *New York Times*? The menu generally includes seafood specialties and treats such as quail wrapped in speck and sauce burgundy. The duck à l'orange is legendary. The 12-year-old bistro has an intimate interior with space for 24 in two seatings.

33 Rue Lavaud. ☎/fax **03/304-7314.** Reservations recommended. Main courses NZ$28–NZ$35 (US$20–US$25). MC, V. Daily 6pm–late. Closed July–Sept.

ARTHUR'S PASS 禽禽
Arthur's Pass, named after Arthur Dudley Dobson, who discovered it in 1865, connects Canterbury and Westland. Nestled in the Southern Alps on State Highway 73, the pass has become a destination in its own right, and Arthur's Pass village (pop. minuscule) has a growing range of modest accommodations. The area has several ski fields (see "Taking to the Slopes," earlier in this chapter) and many short walks; Arthur's Pass National Park is a favorite with trampers. If you like a dramatic landscape and weather conditions to match, this is the place for you.

ESSENTIALS
GETTING THERE   From Christchurch, take State Highway 73 to Arthur's Pass National Park. The alpine village of Arthur's Pass is 2 hours from Christchurch and your halfway mark to the West Coast. You can also go by train on the TranzAlpine (see "An Unforgettable Train Trip" on p. 373) or by bus with **Coast to Coast** (☎ **0800/ 800-847;** www.coast2coast.co.nz). Another option is a 1-day tour from Christchurch with **Travel Pioneer** (☎ **0800/808-070**) or **Peninsula & Alpine Tours** (☎ **03/384-3576;** fax 03/384-3971). The only daily afternoon service is provided by **Alpine Coaches** (☎ **0800/274-888**).

VISITOR INFORMATION   The **Arthur's Pass Visitor Centre,** State Highway (73 Main Road), P.O. Box 8, Arthur's Pass (☎ **03/318-9211;** fax 03/318-9210), is a good place to start. The weather in this area can be extremely changeable, and the center staff will be able to advise you on all safety issues related to walking tracks. Open daily, except December 25.

WALKING ON THE WILD SIDE
Snow, avalanches, and over 4,000 millimeters (160 in.) of rain a year have their impact on the walking tracks here. Despite these changing conditions, the area has numerous 2- to 3-day tramps and many shorter walks that bring you up close to thundering waterfalls, wild rivers, dripping beech forests, and a wealth of birdlife.

A lot of them are also tough going and require a degree of skill in personal navigation using maps and compasses. Make sure you're tackling something within the range of your ability, and no matter what the weather is like when you set off, *always* bring plenty of warm clothing. Pick up the Department of Conservation's two brochures, *Walks in Arthur's Pass National Park* and *Arthur's Pass Village Historic Walk*, at the visitor center.

Two short walks worth doing are **Devil's Punchbowl Waterfall** 𝒻 and **Bridal Veil.** Each takes 1 to 1½ hours. The **historic village walk** 𝒻 is a pretty 1½-hour wander that can be accomplished easily if you've stopped off at Arthur's Pass on the return TranzAlpine journey.

WHERE TO STAY

For the modest sum of NZ$110 to NZ$120 (US$77–US$84), you can take a bed at **Arthur's Pass Chalet Restaurant & Accommodation,** Main Road (© **03/318-9236;** www.arthurspass.co.nz). Its 11 units are right in the heart of the little township.

Grasmere Lodge 𝒻𝒻𝒻 *(Moments)*   This is the New Zealand equivalent of an English country-house hotel where an intimate number of guests receive the very best personal service. It's also a member of the Small Luxury Hotels of the World group, and hosts Oliver Newbegin and his wife, Vicki Harraway, are experts in unobtrusive pampering. Six rooms in the original lodge and six suites in the grand new homestead spare nothing in comfort. All of the spacious units have robes, slippers, underfloor heating, sheepskin foot rugs, sherry, tea and coffee, cookies, and electric blankets. Bathrooms are fabulous on all counts.

St. Hwy. 73, Cass. © 03/318-8407. Fax 03/318-8263. www.grasmere.co.nz. 12 units. NZ$1,400 (US$980) lakeview rooms; NZ$1,710 (US$1,197) mountainview rooms; NZ$2,025 (US$1,418) chalet and cottage suites. NZ$1,800 (US$1,260) Mountain Chalet & River View Cottage (2 couples or more sharing); NZ$197 (US$138) per person surcharge Dec 25. Rates include breakfast, predinner canapés, 5-course dinner, and transfer from TranzAlpine stop at Mount White Bridge. AE, DC, MC, V. Located 120km (74 miles) from both Greymouth and Christchurch. Inquire in advance about acceptance of children under 12. **Amenities:** Restaurant; bar; heated outdoor pool; tennis court; limited fitness equipment; free bikes and canoes; concierge; tour bookings; secretarial services; massage, laundry service; nonsmoking rooms. *In room:* Dataport, coffeemaker, hair dryer, iron.

Wilderness Lodge   Nature lovers will want to stay at this wonderful high-country lodge, where hosts Gerry McSweeney, ecologist/conservationist extraordinaire, and his wife, Anne Saunders, have developed a very special experience. Although it's not nearly as luxurious as Grasmere, the lodge offers superior outdoor activities and informed, guided nature tours. All rooms overlook the Waimakariri valley and mountain peaks and there are four new alpine lodges for a bit of extra pampering. I recommend a 2-night minimum stay to fully enjoy the property.

St. Hwy. 73, Arthur's Pass. © 03/318-9246. Fax 03/318-9245. www.wildernesslodge.co.nz. 24 units (all with private bathroom). From NZ$660 (US$462) mountain lodge rooms; from NZ$980 (US$686) alpine lodges. Surcharge for Dec 25 and 31 and Jan 1. Off-peak rates available. Rates include breakfast, dinner, use of lodge facilities, and guided nature and farm activities. AE, DC, MC, V. **Amenities:** Restaurant; bar; lounge; 24-hr. room service; massage; laundry service; nonsmoking rooms; access for travelers w/disabilities. *In room:* Dataport, fridge, coffeemaker, hair dryer, iron.

KAIKOURA

The seaside settlement of Kaikoura is located halfway between Christchurch and Picton on the rugged east coast. Waves lap at its toes and huge mountains stretch away from its shoulders. It's a stunning combination that never fails to impress and these days the population of approximately 3,200 never misses a beat in capitalizing on natural attributes.

Hot & Steamy

Hanmer Springs Thermal Pools & Spa, 1 Jacks Pass Rd. (✆ **0800/442-663** in NZ, or 03/315-7511; www.hanmersprings.co.nz), have attracted visitors for over 100 years. The complex boasts nine open-air thermal pools, three sulfur pools, sauna and steam rooms with plunge pool, four private thermal suites, a 25m (16-ft.) heated freshwater pool, a family activity pool with two waterslides, a gym, and therapeutic massage facilities. The water in the pools is maintained at a temperature between 89.6°F and 104°F (32°C–40°C). The Garden House Café overlooks the whole complex. The pools are open daily from 10am to 9pm. Adults pay NZ$10 (US$7) admission or NZ$12 (US$8.40) for a day pass; children pay NZ$5 (US$3.50). Now attracting over 500,000 visitors a year, the springs are planning a NZ$1-million (US$700,000) development to expand current facilities. This will include a new day-spa facility and picnic areas.

Hanmer Springs is 1½ hours northeast of Christchurch. It's a picturesque drive, but be careful in winter, when icy conditions can make the roads dangerous. Take Highway 1 out of Christchurch and go 45 minutes to the left-hand Hanmer turnoff just over the Waipara River Bridge. It's well signposted the rest of the way. If you don't have a car, call the **Hanmer Connection** (✆ **0800/377-378** in NZ, or 03/962-3280; www.hanmerconnection.co.nz), which operates daily between Christchurch and Hanmer. Bookings are essential. It costs NZ$25 (US$18) one-way, NZ$45 (US$32) round-trip.

The **Hanmer Springs i-Site Visitor Centre,** Amuri Avenue (✆ **03/315-7128;** fax 03/315-7658; www.hurunui.com), is open daily from 10am to 5pm.

If you'd like to stay overnight in Hanmer Springs, try the **Cheltenham House** 👬, 13 Cheltenham St. (✆ **03/315-7545;** www.cheltenham.co.nz). Len and Maree Earl have 34 years' worth of local knowledge and an elegant 1930s home with six sunny, spacious bedrooms; central heating and electric blankets will insulate you against those icy, 14°F (–10°C) winter mornings. The house is set in large gardens, a 2-minute stroll to the Hamner Springs

Chief among them is the marine bounty—several breeds of whales, dolphins, seals, and thousands of sea birds. Once a sleepy hollow that virtually closed down in the winter, Kaikoura is now a thriving little town that is especially energetic and interesting during the tourist season.

ESSENTIALS

GETTING THERE   Traveling on State Highway 1, Kaikoura is an easy 2½-hour drive from Christchurch—unless you use this opportunity to stop over in the Waipara wine region, in which case you should allow a whole day. It is approximately 2 hours south of Blenheim. You can also go by train and the **TranzCoastal** (✆ **0800/872-467** in NZ; www.tranzscenic.co.nz) is certainly a lovely trip. As a return day trip from Christchurch, it costs NZ$76 (US$53) for adults and NZ$48 (US$34) for children. That gives you around 5½ hours to explore Kaikoura or go whale-watching. It departs

Thermal Pools and Spa. This is great style at an unbelievably good price—NZ$170 to NZ$210 (US$119–US$147) a night. Another good B&B option is **Albergo Hanmer** 🌟🌟🌟, 88 Rippingale Rd., Hanmer (© **0800/342-313** in NZ, or 03/315-7428; www.albergohanmer.com), which has four spacious rooms ranging in price from NZ$175 to NZ$240 (US$123–US$168) for an en-suite room; NZ$220 to NZ$290 (US$154–US$203) for the cottage; and NZ$380 to NZ$560 (US$266–US$392) for the new, stylish, three-bedroom alpine villa. The new **Heritage Hanmer Springs** 🌟, 1 Conical Hill Rd. (© **0800/368-888** in NZ, or 03/315-7021; www.heritagehotels.co.nz), is another excellent choice, with 65 stylish rooms from NZ$208 (US$146).

For a host of excellent, fast-paced activities all centered in one place, contact **Thrillseekers Canyon** 🌟🌟🌟, 839 Main Rd., Hanmer Springs (© **03/315-7046;** www.thrillseekerscanyon.co.nz), which is open daily 9am to 5:30pm offering everything from bungy jumping and jet-boating to river rafting and assorted combos. Walkers *must* investigate **Hanmer Forest** 🌟🌟🌟, which provides a web of pretty walkways through stunning collections of exotic trees. There's an excellent forest brochure at the visitor center that outlines the best woodland, forest, and alpine walks. Make sure you take your camera!

There is now a host of excellent eateries in Hanmer. **The Old Post Office Restaurant** 🌟🌟 (© **03/315-7461**) is probably the best restaurant in Hanmer, and by all accounts it could give plenty of city establishments a run for their money. Main courses run NZ$28 (US$20). It's open Tuesday through Saturday from 6pm until late; reservations are essential. Another must is **Malabar** 🌟🌟🌟, Alpine Pacific Centre, 5 Conical Hill Rd. (© **03/315-7745**), which has a delicious Asian-Indian menu; and for the best coffee, go straight to **Powerhouse Café** 🌟🌟🌟, Jack's Pass Road (© **03/315-5252**), or **Springs Deli Café** 🌟🌟🌟, 47 Amuri Ave. (© **03/315-7430**). The latter has a fabulous range of takeout picnic food.

Christchurch at 7:30am and returns at 7pm. One-way fares are also available. **Hanmer Connection** (© **0800/377-378;** www.hanmerconnection.co.nz) provides a shuttle service to Kaikoura via Hanmer Springs on Tuesday, Thursday, and Saturday; and **InterCity** (© **09/913-6100**) and **Newmans** (© **09/913-6200**) both pass through the township.

VISITOR INFORMATION   The **Kaikoura i-Site Visitor Centre,** is located at the south end of the town's main carpark, Westend (© **03/319-5641;** www.kaikoura.co.nz or www.naturallykaikoura.co.nz). It has comprehensive displays of all the town's attractions and can organize transport.

SPECIAL EVENTS   Do your utmost to be in Kaikoura for the first week of October, when the town hosts **Seafest** 🌟🌟🌟 in Takahanga Domain (© **0800/473-2337;** www.seafest.co.nz), a crazy and delicious celebration of the ocean and its extravaganza of tastes.

WALKING THE WALK

The **Kaikoura Coast Track** 🐾🐾🐾 , Medina, 1250 Conway Flat Rd., Cheviot (© **03/ 319-2715;** www.kaikouratrack.co.nz), begins almost an hour south of Kaikoura and takes you across an historic sheep station, up into tussock land, down into bush valleys, and along a beach beneath cliffs embedded with 8,000-year-old tree stumps and fossils. It's 3 days in country otherwise inaccessible to you and for NZ$135 (US$95) per person, it's money very well spent. You sleep in farm cottages along the way and home-cooked meals can be provided.

Kaikoura Wilderness Walk 🐾🐾🐾 (© **0800/945-337** in NZ, or 03/319-6966; www.kaikourawilderness.co.nz), is a comfortable 2-day hiking experience over 17km (11 miles) in the Puhi Peaks Nature Reserve, a remote area that is home to rare wildlife. You'll overnight at Shearwater Lodge, which was built in 2004 in a precipitous location that has to be seen to be believed. The 2- to 3-day guided walk, all meals, and accommodations cost NZ$695 (US$487) per person. Only available from October through April, this is a more mountainous, wilderness experience than the more farm-based Kaikoura Track. Both are well worth doing.

WHERE TO STAY

Nikau Lodge 🐾🐾, corner of State Highway 1 and Deal Street, Kaikoura (© **03/319- 6971;** www.nikaulodge.com), has six B&B rooms (five with en-suites, one with a private bathroom), plus a two-bedroom cottage, with prices ranging from NZ$125 to NZ$225 (US$88–US$158).

All rates quoted below include the 12.5% GST and free off-street parking unless otherwise stated.

Hapuku Lodge 🐾🐾🐾 *(Value)*   You won't believe your eyes when you see the level of style and quality you get here for the oh-so-reasonable price. It is, without doubt, one of the smartest small contemporary lodges in the country and you'll love the deep, restful silence of nights spent in this out-of-town location. Handcrafted furniture; big, well-designed bathrooms; and generous beds all add up to a fantastic stay. If you want extra space and privacy, opt for the apartment above the olive mill. And in 2006, six new, stand-alone treehouses should be added.

Hapuku Rd., just off St. Hwy. 1, Kaikoura. © **0800/521-568** in NZ, or 03/319-6559. Fax 03/319-6557. www.hapuku lodge.com. 7 units. From NZ$320–NZ$390 (US$224–US$273). NZ$50 (US$35) each extra person. Long-stay, off-peak, and special rates available. Rates include breakfast. AE, DC, MC, V. Located 12km (7½ miles) north of Kaikoura township. **Amenities:** Restaurant/cafe; bar; free bikes; tour bookings; courtesy transport; business services; laundry service; nonsmoking rooms; on-call doctor/dentist; airport transfers to Kaikoura; access for travelers w/disabilities. *In room:* TV/DVD/CD, dataport, fridge, coffeemaker, hair dryer, iron.

Finds Wine on High

Make sure you don't drive past **Kaikoura Winery,** 140 St. Hwy. 1 (© **03/319- 7966;** www.kaikourawines.co.nz), perched high above the ocean on limestone cliffs, to the south of the town. It's worth a stop for some of the most scenic wine tasting you'll ever experience. The ocean views are wonderful and they have a very impressive underground cellar. You're welcome to have a picnic there and they have gourmet food available. It's open daily from 10am until 5:30pm and tours are held on the hour.

Marine Experiences in Kaikoura

Whales and other marine mammals are the primary draw of Kaikoura, but be aware that you'll be fighting for a place with hundreds of others *and* that it's all weather dependent. **Whale Watch Kaikoura** ✿✿✿ (✆ **0800/655-121** in NZ, or 03/319-6767; www.whalewatch.co.nz) gives you a close encounter with the giant sperm whale. Book well ahead for this awesome adventure. It offers four 2½-hour tours daily on two types of vessels. The fare is around NZ$125 (US$88) for adults, NZ$60 (US$42) for children (not suitable for kids under 3). You may also spot dolphins, fur seals, and seabirds. If you're prone to seasickness, make sure you take the appropriate medication because even the sight and smell of others being sick around you is enough to upset the sternest gut. This is a slick, well-managed operation and the films and videos first-rate, but I found there was something slightly manic about it all and you spend most of the trip waiting to see a whale's tail from about 30m away.

Wings Over Whales (✆ **0800/226-629** in NZ, or 03/319-6580; www.whales.co.nz) offers an airborne perspective to whale-watching via a 30-minute flight that costs from NZ$135 (US$95) per person. If you're short on time, this is probably the best alternative.

Encounter Kaikoura ✿✿ (✆ **0800/733-365** in NZ, or 03/319-6777; www.encounterkaikoura.co.nz) has tours for watching and/or swimming with Dusky dolphins, the most playful and acrobatic of all the dolphins. The cost is NZ$115 (US$81) for adults, NZ$105 (US$74) for children under 15. Reserve well in advance. I'd also recommend their **Albatross Encounter** ✿✿✿, which gets you up close and personal with the area's astounding seabird population. Make sure you take your camera for this one. It costs around NZ$60 (US$42) for adults and NZ$30 (US$21) for children. **Dive Kaikoura** (✆ **0800/728-223** in NZ, or 03/319-6622; www.scubadive.co.nz) is a fun activity that operates several times a day and can be enjoyed by the whole family. The Seal Swim is NZ$70 (US$49) for adults, NZ$50 (US$35) for children; diving costs NZ$100 (US$70) for adults. Reservations are recommended. **Seal Swim Kaikoura** (✆ **0800/732-579** in NZ, or 03/319-6182; www.sealswimkaikoura.co.nz), operates October through May and has seal swims priced from NZ$50 to NZ$70 (US$35–US$49).

Sea Kayak Kaikoura ✿✿✿ (✆ **0800/452-456** in NZ; www.seakayakkaikoura.co.nz), operates from September 15 to May 10, and provides one of the loveliest ways of getting a feel for the richness of Kaikoura's marine environment. You'll have fur seals diving around your kayak and seabirds diving down from above. This is definitely what I'd be doing if I only had a day in Kaikoura. They offer half-day trips for NZ$65 (US$46) for adults and NZ$50 (US$35) for children.

Kincaid Lodge ★★   Located 6km (3¾ miles) north of Kaikoura, this old farm homestead, built in 1903, now has a new life. Helen Costley is an enthusiastic young hostess and her rooms are spacious with nice bathrooms. The whole property is set in a peaceful garden well back from the main highway, with farm animals peering over the fence. It's definitely overpriced compared to the much more stylish Hapuku Lodge up the road, but it's a lovely stay nonetheless.

611 Main North Rd., Kaikoura. (℃ **03/319-6851**. Fax 03/319-6801. www.kincaidlodge.co.nz. 4 units. NZ$495–NZ$557 (US$347–US$390). Long-stay rates available. Rates include breakfast. AE, MC, V. No children under 12. **Amenities:** Tennis court; free bikes; babysitting; laundry service; nonsmoking rooms. *In room:* Fridge, coffeemaker, hair dryer, iron.

WHERE TO DINE

New cafes and restaurants are popping up in Kaikoura like mushrooms on a damp day. For the size of the place, there's more than enough to choose from. **Hapuku Café** ★★★ , State Highway 1, 12km (7½ miles) north of Kaikoura (℃ **03/319-6558**), is more than worth the short trip out of town. It serves delicious lunches—everything from venison medallions on rosti to salmon filo with spinach salad—which can be enjoyed on the grape-enclosed patio, or in the rustic, timbered cafe interior. **Hislops Café** ★★ , 33 Beach Rd., Kaikoura (℃ **03/319-6971**), is another excellent cafe, albeit a less architecturally handsome one. It has an organic focus and the food is always great. **Finz of South Bay** ★★ , South Bay Parade (℃ **03/319-6688**), is still seen by locals as the best formal restaurant and although the sea views are great, the decor here always gives me a stomachache. That said, their seafood dishes are excellent. **Encounter Kaikoura** ★★★ , West End (℃ **03/319-6777**), is my preferred hit for a delicious lunch, or coffee and a snack. They have an excellent menu, fabulous counter food, and a busy, modern environment that teems with people of all nationalities.

EN ROUTE TO THE WEST COAST & THE GLACIERS

From Christchurch, take State Highway 73 through the magnificent landscape of Arthur's Pass National Park. In 2 hours, you'll get to the village of Arthur's Pass, your halfway point to the West Coast. You'll then pass over the new Otira Viaduct, which takes care of the worst and most dangerous part of the journey. Continue to proceed with caution, though, especially when it's snowing. From Otira, it's another 1 to 1½ hours to Greymouth on the West Coast. If you're traveling straight down to Franz Josef and Fox glaciers, follow State Highway 6 all the way. You can expect the drive to the glaciers to take another 3 to 5 hours, depending on how often you stop.

Moments   **A Cultural Exchange**

Maurice and Heather Manawatu of **Maori Tours Kaikoura** ★★★ ((℃ **0800/866-267** in NZ, or 03/319-5567; www.maoritours.co.nz), will send you away with some of your loveliest New Zealand memories. They'll take you on a journey through Kaikoura's rich Maori history to ancient Maori sites, and you'll explore a beautiful stand of native bush, learning about the traditional uses of plants by Maori. Wear sensible walking shoes and take along a sense of humor and a willingness to participate. The 3- to 4-hour tour costs NZ$85 (US$60) for adults and NZ$45 (US$32) for children.

14

West Coast & the Glaciers

This is a unique part of New Zealand, where people approach life with a laid-back attitude and a strong sense of community. It's a place of majestic landscapes, rich history, and colorful characters, and you'll be hard-pressed to find anything slick or superficial here.

Greenstone was the first treasure of these wild and beautiful shores. It's still the best place in the country to purchase contemporary jade carvings. Gold and timber have also shaped the course of coast history, and both continue to figure prominently in what you'll experience here.

More than anything, though, the dramatic landscape draws visitors. Almost 80% of the West Coast land area is protected under the Department of Conservation, and five of the country's 13 national parks are wholly or partially in the region. The rainforests of the West Coast are among the most diverse in New Zealand, and few places in the temperate world contain such a variety of vegetation. Naturally, these forests are well sustained by the West Coast's notoriously high rainfall, so bring a raincoat, lots of insect repellent, and a sense of humor—you'll need all three!

From its subtropical north to its rainforested south, the West Coast is diverse and always interesting. Where else in the world could you find an icy glacier just a few kilometers from a sandy beach?

1 Westport ✦ & Karamea ✦✦✦

Westport: 101km (63 miles) N of Greymouth; 226km (140 miles) SW of Nelson

The drive to **Westport** (pop. 6,000) is better than actually arriving here. This funny little township is slightly shabby and smells of coal. I think calling it the "Adventure Capital of the West Coast" is stretching it a bit, but the area's mild climate and coastal to subtropical mountain scenery do provide an ideal setting for outdoor activities such as white-water rafting, jet-boating, horse trekking, caving, and rock climbing. For the not-so-adventurous, there's excellent sea and river fishing, gold panning, and a variety of scenic and historic walks.

Traveling 1½ hours north to **Karamea** is worth the time and effort. This little corner of paradise is snuggled into the warm northwest part of the South Island and is, in fact, much farther north than Wellington. It is the terminal point of the Heritage Highway, the gateway to the Kahurangi National Park—the beginning of a natural heaven.

ESSENTIALS

GETTING THERE & GETTING AROUND   **By Plane**   **Air New Zealand Link** (© 0800/737-000) flies daily to Westport from Wellington.

By Coach (Bus)   Westport is serviced daily by **InterCity** (© 09/913-6100). Both **Magic Travellers** (© 09/358-5600) and **Kiwi Experience** (© 09/366-9830) also include Westport on their schedules.

To get from Westport to Karamea, go with either **Cunningham's Coaches** (© 03/789-7177), which charges NZ$15 (US$11) per person one-way, NZ$8 (US$5.60) for bikes; or **Karamea Express** (© 03/782-6757), which charges around NZ$18 (US$13). Both make the trip Monday through Friday and connect with other bus services to Nelson, Greymouth, Hokitika, and Christchurch. **Drive Me Wild Hikers' Transport** (© 0800/945-369 in NZ, or 03/546-8876; www.drivemewild.co.nz), offers transport on both sides of Heaphy Track. From Karamea, they travel to Nelson via Westport and Motueka on the day you finish walking.

By Car   Westport can be reached on Highway 6 from Greymouth in the south in about 2 hours, or from Nelson via the Buller Gorge in approximately 3½ hours. All roads are good, but look out for single-lane bridges and those that share the bridge with trains—a unique West Coast feature.

Karamea is just 100km (62 miles) north of Westport, but you should allow 1½ to 2 hours for the trip, as at least 26km (16 miles) of it is steep and winding. It's a beautiful drive over the Karamea Bluff, descending into bush landscape and then along the coast. And look out for truck drivers who dominate the road!

VISITOR INFORMATION   The **Westport i-Site Information Centre,** 1 Brougham St. (© **03/789-6658;** fax 03/789-6668; www.westport.org.nz), opposite the post office, is open in summer daily from 9am to 7pm, and in winter Monday through Friday from 9am to 4pm.

The **Karamea Information & Resource Centre,** RD6, Karamea (© **03/782-6652;** fax 03/782-6654; www.karameainfo.co.nz), is opposite the Karamea Store in the tiny village of **Market Cross.** From November to April, it's open daily from 9am to 5pm; May to October, Monday through Friday from 9am to 5pm, Saturday 9am to 1pm. There is also a post office here along with a garage, crafts outlet, and cafe. Just beyond Market Cross are the Karamea Tavern, the police station, motels, and The Last Resort (p. 398). Everything is within walking distance, but the entrance to the Heaphy Track and Kahurangi National Park is another 15km (9⅓ miles) farther on at the end of State Highway 67.

EXPLORING WESTPORT

Coal Town Museum, Queen Street South (©/fax **03/789-8204**), gives you the chance to walk through a true-to-life coal mine, complete with sound effects from the deep bowels of the earth. Even if you're not lured here by these promises, you'll find an interesting repository of historical artifacts. Check out the new displays of maritime and pioneering history. In summer, the museum is open daily from 9am to 4:30pm (closed Dec 25), with extended hours over the Christmas and New Year period; Admission is around NZ$8 to NZ$10 (US$5.60–US$7) for adults, NZ$3 to NZ$4 (US$2.10–US$2.80) for children.

If you want an insight into the rugged history of the Westport area, try the local guides at **Outwest Tours** (© **0800/688-937;** www.outwest.co.nz), who will take you on personalized tours of old coal mining and off-the-beaten-track areas, like **Stockton Mine** ✸✸, New Zealand's largest coal mine, 750m (2,500 ft.) above sea level on the Stockton Plateau. You'll travel in 4×4 Unimog vehicles, traversing rivers and generally taking on everything in your path. It won't always be smooth, but it will be exciting.

OUTDOOR PURSUITS

ABSEILING & ADVENTURE CAVING   **Norwest Adventures Ltd.** ✸✸, Main Road, Charleston (© **0800/011-6686** in NZ, or 03/789-6686; www.caverafting.com),

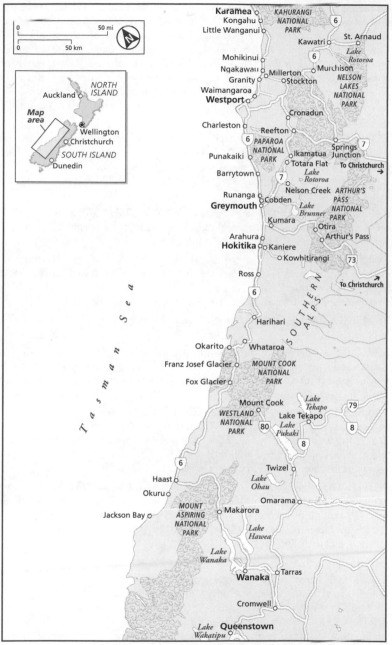

can introduce you to the mystery and intrigue of the underworld. The Adventure Caving trip costs NZ$280 (US$196) and requires high levels of fitness for people ages 16 and over—don't try it if you get claustrophobic or are afraid of heights. The Metro Cave tour is a delightful 2- to 3-hour walk through rainforest to see spectacular cave formations and glowworms (NZ$75/US$53). The Underworld Rafting experience involves making your way by raft along underground stream passages and out into the Nile River rapids. Some consider it a tamer adventure than that offered by Wild West Adventure in Greymouth (p. 402). It's a 4- to 5-hour trip that costs around NZ$150 (US$105) per person.

ECORAFTING   Half- and multiday white-water rafting expeditions are available with **Eco-Rafting Adventures NZ** *&&*, 108 Mawhera Quay, Greymouth (© **0508/ 669-675**; www.ecorafting.co.nz). A half-day rafting trip costs around NZ$100 (US$70) per person, a full day about NZ$150 (US$105). Multiday trips begin at about NZ$250 (US$175) per day.

KAYAKING   **Ultimate Descents,** Buller Gorge (© **0800/748-377**; www.rivers.co.nz), offers three types of kayaks for all skill levels on Grade 2 to 3 rivers. You must be 13 years and over to participate in the 4½-hour trips.

SWING BRIDGE   If you haven't found enough ways to test your nerves already, enlist in a walk across New Zealand's longest swing bridge. **Buller Gorge Swingbridge & Adventure Park** *&*, State Highway 6, Buller Gorge (© **03/523-9809**; www.bullergorge.co.nz), offers a heart-pumping distraction 1 hour from Westport.

SURFING   Chief among the best beaches is **Tauranga Bay,** 15 minutes south of Westport.

SWIMMING   There are just two words to sum up swimming on any of the West Coast beaches—*extreme care!* Undertows are common and an ever-present hazard on beaches exposed to the westerly swell. Always seek local advice about safe areas. If you're uncertain, *never* get wet!

WALKING   **Tauranga Bay** *&&&* is a popular place to explore beaches, coastline, and seal colonies. There is a good-quality short track through the area, specially designed to accommodate wheelchairs. The seal-colony walk is 20 minutes round-trip, and the Cape Foulwind Walkway *&&&* is 1½ hours. The Department of Conservation's brochure with maps of both walks is available at the visitor center.

WHITE-WATER RAFTING   Call **Buller Adventure Tours** *&&*, in Buller Gorge (© **0800/697-286** in NZ, or 03/789-7286; www.adventuretours.co.nz), which also offers jet-boating and horse-trekking tours. Ecorafting starts at around NZ$100 (US$70), white-water rafting at around NZ$110 (US$77), horse treks at NZ$70 (US$49), and jet-boating at NZ$75 (US$53).

WHERE TO STAY

If you're looking for classy, upmarket accommodations in Westport, stop now—you won't find any. You will, however, find one or two smart, moderately priced options that are bound to bring a satisfied smile to your face. Campers can head for **Westport Holiday Park,** 31–37 Domett St., Westport (© **03/789-7043**; www.westportholidaypark. co.nz), which has chalets, tent and caravan sites, and bunk rooms in a native bush setting. **The Happy Wanderer,** 56 Russell St., Westport (© **03/789-8627**; www.westportyha backpackers.co.nz), is a small YHA-affiliated hostel with a separate bed-and-breakfast lodge, with dorms for NZ$20 (US$14) and double/twin units for NZ$45 (US$32). **Archer House** ☆☆, 75 Queen St., Westport (© **03/789-8778;** www.archerhouse.co.nz), has three large bedrooms (two with en-suite bathrooms), in a beautifully restored character home. They're probably the best B&B rooms in town and they cost NZ$150 (US$105).

All rates quoted below include the 12.5% GST and free off-street parking unless otherwise noted.

Chelsea Gateway Motor Lodge ☆☆ *Value*   This property is definitely the best Westport has to offer. Rooms range from studios to one-, two-, and three-bedroom units. The three-bedroom unit is a fabulous apartment-style dwelling with two king bedrooms and a bathroom upstairs, and a second bathroom and a twin room downstairs. Six units have big Jacuzzis. All rooms are smoke-free.

330 Palmerston St., Westport. © **0800/660-033** in NZ, or 03/789-6835. Fax 03/789-6379. www.nzmotels.co.nz. 20 units. NZ$110–NZ$190 (US$77–US$133). Rates include transfers. Long-stay rates available. AE, DC, MC, V. **Amenities:** Nearby golf course; children's playground; coin-op laundry; same-day dry cleaning; nonsmoking rooms. *In room:* TV, dataport, kitchenette, fridge, coffeemaker, hair dryer, iron.

River View Lodge ☆   Riverview's hillside garden is a big hit with everyone who visits. Good-size rooms are simply decorated and have stunning views of the river. Tea and coffee, sweets, and homemade cookies are placed in rooms daily. Each unit has both a shower and a tub. And for those who like to sit and contemplate life, there are timber decks with a panoramic outlook.

St. Hwy. 6, Lower Buller Gorge Rd., Westport. © **0800/184-656** in NZ, or 03/789-6037. Fax 03/789-6037. www.rural lodge.co.nz. 4 units. NZ$190–NZ$250 (US$133–US$175). Long-stay and off-peak rates available. Rates include breakfast. MC, V. Closed June. Take St. Hwy. 6 and go 7km (4⅓ miles) in the direction of Reefton. Just a 10-min. drive from Westport. No children under 12. **Amenities:** Nearby golf course; tennis court; laundry service; nonsmoking rooms. *In room:* TV, dataport, coffeemaker, hair dryer.

WHERE TO DINE
The notion of culinary excellence and innovation has yet to hit Westport and if it's your first West Coast destination, it will give you the chance to get used to the West Coast dining style, which, at best, can be described as laid-back. **Bailies,** 187 Palmerston St. (© **03/789-7289**), has the largest family menu in town for light meals and good takeaway pizzas; **Serengeti Restaurant,** Westport Motor Hotel, 207 Palmerston St. (© **03/789-7889**), is open daily for a la carte meals and Sunday smorgasbords. A new player on the scene since my last visit is **Currtino's Yellow House Café** ☆, 243 Palmerston St. (© **03/789-8765**), and it's as close as I get to putting the flicker of a star on anything in town. It's open Monday through Friday from 8am until late, and weekends from 9am until late, delivering the nicest meals—spice-rubbed pork served with apple chutney indicates they're at least trying.

Bay House Café & Restaurant ☆☆ *Finds* INTERNATIONAL   This is definitely the little dining gem of the West Coast. Situated about 15 minutes southwest of Westport at Tauranga Bay, it has a dramatic location overlooking the beach and food that more than measures up. Try the seafood salad, featuring smoked salmon, king prawns, and sautéed calamari in a citrus dressing. Steamed Thai mussels, open steak sandwiches, pastas, and chicken satay are other menu offerings. Eat your fill, then walk around to view the seal colony.

Tauranga Bay, Westport. ©/fax **03/789-7133.** Reservations required. Main courses NZ$22–NZ$27 (US$15–US$19); NZ$45–NZ$55 (US$32–US$39) 3-course dinner menu. AE, MC, V. Daily 10am–late. Closed May–Sept.

Tips **Filling Up**

Before you leave Westport, heading to either Nelson or Greymouth, fill your car with petrol. There are no more petrol stations until you hit Murchison, or 87km (54 miles) south near Greymouth.

EXPLORING KARAMEA ✸✸✸

Caught between the wild Tasman Sea on one side and the bush-clad mountains of Kahurangi National Park on the other, Karamea (pop. 650) is a thin slither of subtropical paradise. As the gateway to the Kahurangi, it offers a host of natural attractions, and it is to Karamea that Heaphy Track walkers go at the end of their 4- to 6-day tramp. Much of the coastline is wild and rugged, with rocky points and narrow beaches backed by steep cliffs. Nikau palms, rainforest, and dairy-farm pastures all flourish in the warm temperatures, and the limestone landscape contains many spectacular caves.

Tops on your list should be a visit to **Oparara Arch** ✸✸✸, the biggest limestone arch of its type in the Southern Hemisphere. The drive to the arch takes approximately 1 hour through rainforest. If you're short on time, go straight to **Oparara Basin Guided Tours & Helicopter Charter Karamea** (© 03/782-6111; www.adventures nz.co.nz). It has the best range of excursions, including spectacular helicopter views over a fascinating landscape. The **Guided Honeycomb Hill Caves Tour,** Karamea Information Centre, Market Cross (© 03/782-6652; www.karameainfo.co.nz), takes you into to the restricted **Honeycomb Cave area** ✸✸✸, which was discovered in 1980. Now managed by the Department of Conservation, it's in pristine condition, complete with moa bones. Most people are completely blown away by the experience. The full 4-hour **Honeycomb Tour** includes equipment, transport, guide, and lunch and costs around NZ$85 (US$60) for adults and NZ$55 (US$39) for children under 12. *Please note:* These caves are protected and access is by guided tour only. The full **Oparara Basin Tour** takes 8 hours and includes canoeing down the Oparara River, exploring the rainforest, and visiting the Oparara and Honeycomb caves. You'll need warm clothing and a good degree of fitness. **The Last Resort,** 71 Waverley St., Karamea (© 03/782-6617), can organize white-water heli-rafting trips, scenic helicopter flights, and canoeing trips. The Karamea River is one of the few Grade 5 rivers in New Zealand. They also hire mountain bikes for about NZ$30 (US$21) per day.

OUTDOOR PURSUITS

CANOEING   Hire a canoe from **The Last Resort** (© 03/782-6617; www.last resort.co.nz) or **Karamea Motors** (© 03/782-6757). You can also hire canoes on an hourly basis from around NZ$15 to NZ$20 (US$11–US$14) per hour. Paddle in the safe estuaries, but be aware of tidal changes and keep away from river mouths.

FISHING   There are over 322km (200 miles) of accessible heli-fishing on several backcountry rivers. **The Last Resort** (see "Canoeing," above) can organize heli-fishing trips and guides. The 40km (25 miles) of coastline is suitable for surf casting, and the Karamea River is a trout fisherman's heaven. Trout licenses can be obtained from the **Karamea Hardware Store,** State Highway 67, Market Cross, on a daily, weekly, or annual basis.

The whitebait season is from September 1 to November 14. Whitebait are the young of three main species of migrating fish. They're considered a delicacy and found predominantly on the West Coast. There are special rules and regulations for white-baiters, so make sure you get a copy of them from the Department of Conservation or the Karamea Information & Resource Centre.

MOUNTAIN BIKING   Mountain biking is prohibited in Kahurangi National Park, but if you'd like to ride in other areas, **The Last Resort** and **Karamea Motors** (see "Canoeing," above) have bikes for rent.

WALKING   There are two major hikes in this area—the famous **Heaphy Track** ✺✺✺, which is suitable for trampers of all ages, and the **Wangapeka Track,** which is better suited to the well-equipped tramper. Both tracks take about 4 days and both require hut ticket passes available from the Karamea Information & Resource Centre. Parts of the Wangapeka Track have been washed out by flooding, so always check first with the information center to make sure it is open. For more information on both tracks, see "Tramping" in chapter 3.

There are also many excellent short walks. For the **Nikau Loop Walk,** drive to the Kohaihai River mouth at the start of the Heaphy Track. The walk is suitable for all ages and takes 40 minutes. **Heaphy Hut Walk** ✺✺✺ gives you a 5-hour taste (round-trip) of the Heaphy Track. Guided walk companies operating in this area include **Kahurangi Guided Walks,** Dodson Road, Takaka, Golden Bay (✆ **03/526-7177;** www.heaphey-track.co.nz), and **Bush and Beyond Guided Treks,** 35 School Rd., Motueka (✆ **03/528-9054;** www.naturetreks.co.nz). See chapters 3 and 12 for further information.

WHERE TO STAY

Bridge Farm Motels (✆ **0800/527-263** in NZ, or 03/782-6955; fax 03/782-6745; www.karameamotels.co.nz), just over the Old Karamea Bridge, 500m (1,640 ft.) from the township, is new, pink, and ideal for families or travelers aiming to spend a few days in the area. Studio and one- and two-bedroom units are NZ$95 to NZ$140 (US$67–US$98).

The Last Resort ✺✺ (Finds)   This fabulous grass-roofed complex may well surprise you. First opened as budget accommodations in 1991, they now offer another tier of comfort in en-suite units and three cottages. The latter are the biggest, with full cooking facilities and two bedrooms each. There is also a good restaurant and bar, following the same Mediterranean style and incorporating huge native timber beams from the forest floor.

71 Waverly St., P.O. Box 31, Karamea. ✆ **0800/505-042** in NZ, or 03/782-6617. Fax 03/782-6820. www.lastresort.co.nz. 30 units. NZ$70 (US$49) backpacker or lodge room with shared bathroom; NZ$80 (US$56) lodge room with en-suite bathroom; NZ$100 (US$70) studio with en-suite bathroom; NZ$140 (US$98) cottage with accessible facilities for travelers with disabilities. Long-stay and off-peak rates available. AE, DC, MC, V. 800m (2,624 ft.) from local shops, 5km (3 miles) from beach. Bus service pickup from door. No children under 12. **Amenities:** Restaurant; cafe; 2 bars; nearby golf course; Jacuzzi; miniature golf; watersport rentals; bike rentals; car rentals; massage; laundry service; nonsmoking rooms. *In room:* TV, kitchens in cottages, hair dryer, iron, no phone in some units.

EN ROUTE TO GREYMOUTH: PUNAKAIKI

The drive between Westport and Greymouth is simply stunning, with some of the best coastal views in the country. There are many walkways leading to a variety of natural attractions. Chief among them is the world-famous **Punakaiki Pancake Rocks and Blowholes** ✺✺✺, the main feature of the 10-minute **Dolomite Walk** in the heart of the **Paparoa National Park.** These strange pancakelike limestone formations were pushed up from the ocean floor by seismic action 30 million years ago. For the best show, try to visit the rocks at high tide with a westerly swell running; water comes surging into the deep caverns below and can spout up to 9m (30 ft.) in the air. The rocks are 45km (28 miles) north of Greymouth on the coast section of State Highway 6. If you're on an InterCity coach, the bus will stop here to enable you to do the 20-minute round-trip walk. The track is wide, well maintained, and easily negotiable.

Across the road from the track entrance, you'll find a busy gathering of little cafes and crafts stores, along with the **Punakaiki-Paparoa National Park Visitor Centre,** P.O. Box 1, Punakaiki (© **03/731-1895;** fax 03/731-1896; www.punakaiki.co.nz). The **Department of Conservation** (© **03/731-1895;** punakaikivc@doc.govt.nz) is in the same building; it is open daily 9am to 5pm year-round. **Punakaiki Crafts** ✿✿ (©/fax **03/731-1813;** www.punakaikicrafts.co.nz) is a cooperative with the best, most innovative arts and crafts on the coast. It's open daily from 8:30am to 6pm. There's an excellent espresso outlet here, too.

There are plenty of other excellent short walks in the area. Both the **Truman Track** ✿✿ and the **Punakaiki Cavern** are under 1 hour and suitable for the entire family. The Truman includes a stroll through coastal forest to a beach with caves and a waterfall. The visitor center has a leaflet detailing all walks in the area.

Punakaiki Horse Treks (© **03/731-1839;** www.pancake-rocks.co.nz) offers a variety of activities exploring the rich park environment, including nature tours of the magnificent Punakaiki Valley in an eight-wheeled amphibious vehicle, and horse treks through bush and beach environments. The latter start at NZ$95 (US$67) per person for a 2½-hour ride. They're open for business from the third week of October through the first week of May.

Punakaiki Canoes, State Highway 6, Punakaiki (© **03/731-1870;** info@river kayaking.co.nz), will take you upstream on the Pororari River, through a stunning gorge cut from limestone cliffs. It's suitable for all ages and experience levels and costs around NZ$40 (US$28) per person for 2 hours and around NZ$50 to NZ$60 (US$35–US$42) for a full day. Guided trips start at about NZ$75 (US$53).

WHERE TO STAY

Many travelers now stop over in Punakaiki on the trip from Nelson to the West Coast. It's an excellent place for a rest before heading south to the glaciers.

Punakaiki Rocks Hotel & Villas ✿✿, State Highway 6, Punakaiki (© **0800/ 786-2524** in NZ, or 03/731-1163; www.punakaiki-resort.co.nz), opened in 2001 with bright new rooms right on the beach from around NZ$150 (US$105). It's the closest to the Pancake Rocks and includes a restaurant overlooking the beach. **Paparoa Park Motel,** State Highway 6, Punakaiki (© **0800/727-276** or 03/731-1883; www. paparoa.co.nz), is just a short distance south of the Pancake Rocks over the Punakaiki River. It has tidy native-timber studios and family units.

The Rocks Homestay ✿✿, 33 Hartmount Place (© **0800/272-164** in NZ, or 03/731-1141; www.therockshomestay.com), is 3km (2 miles) north of Punakaiki; their three rooms cost NZ$130 to NZ$170 (US$91–US$119). They also manage a modern, self-contained house that sleeps four for NZ$160 to NZ$200 (US$112–US$140) and another that sleeps seven for NZ$220 to NZ$400 (US$154–US$280).

Farther south, 29km (18 miles) from Punakaiki and 15km (9⅓ miles) north of Greymouth, **Breakers Seaside Bed & Breakfast,** 9 Mile Creek, State Highway 6

(© **03/762-7743;** www.breakers.co.nz), has four en-suite rooms for around NZ$150 to NZ$250 (US$105–US$175). Ask for the Breakwater Room for fabulous views.

2 Greymouth & Lake Brunner

101km (63 miles) SW of Westport; 45km (28 miles) N of Hokitika; 290km (180 miles) SW of Nelson

I've always felt Greymouth was rather well named. Personally, it's never been a town to inspire a long stopover, despite the fact that it is centrally placed and has the best access to Nelson and Christchurch.

It is, however, part of a rich history. The Grey River was the landing place for Maori canoes on the hunt for greenstone, or *pounamu*—the jade that was Westland's most prized possession. Even today, the Grey River gap has great significance in Maori myth, and greenstone is just as prized as ever. The discovery of gold in the 1860s also left its mark on the area.

With a population of 11,000, Greymouth is kept busy with coal and timber exports. It is the largest town and the commercial heart of the West Coast, and most goods and services are available here—although some of them could do with a bit of a crank-up. If you're trying to decide whether to stay in Greymouth or travel another 45km (28 miles) to Hokitika, keep in mind that Greymouth has better food outlets, while Hokitika has a greater range of attractions and tourist shopping. The best accommodations in the central West Coast area lie between the two (see "Where to Stay," under "Hokitika: Greenstone, Glowworms & Gold," later in this chapter).

ESSENTIALS

GETTING THERE & GETTING AROUND   By Plane   Daily flights between Christchurch and Hokitika are operated by **Air New Zealand Link** (© **0800/737-000** in NZ). A shuttle service carries visitors the extra 30 minutes by road to Greymouth.

By Train   The **Tranz Scenic** TranzAlpine route (© **0800/843-596** in NZ) runs daily between Christchurch and the Greymouth railway station on Mackay Street and will stop in Moana (at Lake Brunner) on request. This is New Zealand's best rail experience (see chapter 13 for more details).

By Coach (Bus)   InterCity (© **09/913-6100**) buses reach Greymouth from Queenstown, Fox Glacier, Franz Josef, Nelson, and Westport. Both **Kiwi Experience** (© **09/ 366-9830**) and **Magic Travellers** (© **09/358-5600**) include Greymouth on their routes. A daily shuttle bus stops at Lake Brunner en route to Christchurch.

By Car   Greymouth is reached via Highway 6 from both the north and the south. Highway 7 brings travelers from the east coast via Lewis Pass, and Highway 73 takes you through Arthur's Pass National Park on the road from Christchurch. The trip from Nelson takes approximately 4 to 5 hours; from Christchurch, 4 hours.

VISITOR INFORMATION   The **Greymouth i-Site Visitors Centre,** in the Regent Theatre Building, at Herbert and Mackay streets (© **0800/473-966** in NZ, or 03/768-5101; fax 03/768-0317; www.greydistrict.co.nz), is open in summer Monday through Friday from 8:30am to 7pm, Saturday 9am to 6pm, Sunday and public holidays 10am to 5pm (closed Dec 25). It has reduced hours in winter, closing at 5:30pm Monday through Friday. It also functions as the Department of Conservation agency for the region.

EXPLORING GREYMOUTH

If you're a history buff, you'll find that **Shantytown** ★★ (© 0800/742-689 in NZ, or 03/762-6634; www.shantytown.co.nz) has been rather well done. Situated amid native bush, the replica West Coast gold-mining town includes over 30 buildings. A steam train operates on a 20-minute bush track, and a stagecoach will rattle you over an old bush road. You can also pan for gold and visit an operating sawmill. It's open daily from 8:30am to 5pm. Admission is around NZ$15 (US$11) for adults, NZ$10 (US$7) for children 5 to 13, with family concessions. To get here, drive 8km (5 miles) south of Greymouth to Paroa, make a left, and go another 3km (2 miles) inland. *Note:* At press time, a NZ$12-million (US$8.4-million) redevelopment plan had just been announced for Shantytown. On completion in around 3 years, this will include introductory experiences, a new theater, and a national train-restoration center.

For a summary of the region's artistic talents, head for **Left Bank Art Gallery** ★, 1 Tainui St. (© 03/768-0038; www.leftbankart.co.nz), daily from 10am to 5pm. It has changing exhibitions (NZ$2/US$1.40 admission), an excellent shop featuring the work of 70 West Coast artists, and the New Zealand Pounamu Jade Collection. It's closed Sunday and Monday in winter.

If you prefer something a little more intoxicating, go to **Monteith's Brewing Company** ★★, Turumaha and Herbert streets (© 03/768-4149; www.monteiths.co.nz), to book the NZ$10 (US$7) brewery tour and tasting. Tours are given Monday through Friday at 10am, 11:30am, and 2pm, and on weekends at 11:30am and 2pm.

OUTDOOR PURSUITS

CAVE RAFTING   **Wild West Adventure Company** (© 0800/147-483 in NZ, or 03/768-6649; www.nzholidayheaven.com), has a 5-hour Dragon's Cave Rafting Trip for around NZ$125 (US$88), taking you deep into a subterranean wonderland of lakes, glowworms, and waterfalls. If you include an abseiling option, it costs around NZ$200 (US$140).

GOLF   **Greymouth Golf Club,** Golf Links Road, Kaiata (© 03/768-5332), is 3km (1¾ miles) from town, has 18 holes, and welcomes visitors. Green fees are from NZ$15 (US$11).

MOUNTAIN BIKING   For the best information on mountain bike trails and rentals contact Tony Coll at **Colls Sportsworld,** 53 Mackay St. (© 0800/282-344 in NZ, or 03/768-4060).

Finds   **A Blackball Experience**

Go off the beaten path and discover the quaint historic village of Blackball, 28km (17 miles) northeast of Greymouth in the Grey Valley. Started as a base for transient gold seekers in 1864, it's a lingering testimony to the way life used to be on the coast. Visit the "famous" **Formerly the Blackball Hilton,** 26 Hart St. (© 03/732-4705; www.blackballhilton.co.nz), an original West Coast pub, for a beer, a casual meal, or a low-key overnight stay; and stop off at the award-winning **Blackball Salami Company,** Hilton Street (© 03/732-4111), which makes sausages and salami—low-fat venison and beef versions are a specialty.

OFF ROAD ADVENTURES Five kilometers (3 miles) north of Greymouth, you can tackle **On Yer Bike** (© **0800/669-372** in NZ, or 03/762-7438; www.onyerbike. co.nz) on either a four-wheeled bike or the amphibious eight-wheeled Argo. A 1-hour Explorer bike ride costs around NZ$70 (US$49). One hour on a go-cart will set you back around NZ$90 (US$63).

SURFING The main breaks are on **Cobden** and **Blaketown** beaches, both sign-posted about 5 minutes north of central Greymouth, and farther north at **9-mile Beach.**

WALKING The **Point Elizabeth Walkway** 🏃🏃 starts at Rapahoe and follows the coast south around the headland to the Cobden Beach road end. The track takes under 2 hours one-way. If the tide is low, return along the beach. Go in early evening to enjoy one of Greymouth's fabulous sunsets.

Wild West Adventure (see "Cave Rafting," above) has details on 83 walks within **Te Ara Pounamu** 🏃🏃🏃, the Greenstone Pathway—a spectacular 720km (446-mile) route that has been followed for hundreds of years by Maori traders. Walks range from 30-minute wanders to multiday options; some are guided. **Walks & Drives** (© **03/768-4090**) has a wide range of guided walks from a few hours to several days anywhere on the West Coast or the greater South Island.

WHITE-WATER RAFTING **Wild West Adventure Company** (© **0800/147-483** in NZ, or 03/768-6649; www.nzholidayheaven.com) has a wide range of rafting packages that can include trail rides, helicopters, walking, or drinking champagne in natural hot pools surrounded by rainforest. There are three popular Hot Rock options. The 5-hour guided walk, raft, and hot pools trip costs around NZ$200 to NZ$$250 (US$140–US$175). If you include a helicopter ride, the price rises to around NZ$400 to NZ$450 (US$280–US$315).

ORGANIZED TOURS

Kea West Coast Tours, 152 Golf Links Rd. (© **0800/532-868** in NZ, or 03/768-9292; www.keatours.co.nz), has a number of tours to the glaciers, Punakaiki, Shanty-town, and Blackball. These range in price from around NZ$55 (US$39) per person to NZ$190 (US$133) per person for the Twin Glaciers and Lake Matheson Tour.

Off Beat Tours (© **0800/270-960** in NZ, or 03/732-3749; www.offbeattours.co.nz) goes all the way south to the glaciers and all the way north to Karamea and the spectacular Oparara Limestone Arches. Prices range from NZ$75 (US$53) for a half-day tour to around NZ$200 (US$140) for the full-day glacier trip.

For one of the best-value scenic flights, seek out **Air West Coast** 🏃🏃🏃 at Greymouth Airport (© **03/738-0524;** www.airwestcoast.co.nz). The four-seater Cessna 172 takes you all the way down to Milford Sound. It's a full figure-eight trip that also covers the glaciers, Mount Cook, valleys, rivers, forests, and lakes. The 3½-hour flight costs around NZ$685 (US$480) per person for two. Keep in mind that you'll pay close to that for some of the scenic flights out of Queenstown that are shorter and cover far less territory. A shorter flight to Mount Cook and the glaciers will cost NZ$315 (US$221) per person, minimum two people.

WHERE TO STAY

Greymouth Seaside Top 10 Holiday Park, 2 Chesterfield St. (© **0800/867-104** in NZ, or 03/768-6618; www.top10greymouth.co.nz), has tent and caravan sites, cabins, motel units, and a backpacker bunkhouse. Backpackers have some fun choices in

---

⟨ *Tips* **Shopping for Greenstone**

You can hold out and peruse a far wider range of greenstone options in Hokitika, or you can accept local word that **Jade Boulder Gallery,** 1 Guinness St., Greymouth (✆ **0800/523-326** in NZ, or 03/768-0700; www.jadeboulder.com), is the best source of quality jade carving on the West Coast. Owner Ian Boustridge's work is in collections all around the world. He carves the bigger pieces on display at the gallery. You'll also see other souvenir items such as wooden bowls, hand-knit sweaters, and furniture. Light meals are available at the Jade Boulder Café. If you're looking for top-quality New Zealand jade, I'd recommend you start here. The gallery is open daily from 8:30am to 9pm in summer and 8:30am to 5pm in winter.

---

the fish-themed **Neptunes,** 43 Gresson St. (✆ **0800/003-768** in NZ, or 03/768-4425), which has a free Jacuzzi; the animal-themed **Noahs Ark Backpackers,** 16 Chapel St. (✆ **0800/662-472** in NZ, or 03/768-4868; www.noahsarkbackpackers.co.nz); and **Global Village Backpackers,** 42–54 Cowper St. (✆ **03/768-7272;** globalvillage@minidata.co.nz), which has a charming riverside setting and has been completely refurbished with new beds throughout.

All rates given here include the 12.5% GST and free off-street parking.

At Your Leisure 🌟🌟   Norm and Carmel Kelly's peaceful hillside home has one of the best views in Greymouth and their two upstairs guest rooms are well sited for the stunning sunsets. The blue Tasman room has the biggest bathroom with bath and shower; and the Kowhai is a bit smaller and cozier. Breakfast is served overlooking the fern-clad garden with the windows thrown wide open.

10 Tindale Rd., Greymouth. ✆ **03/768-5496.** Fax 03/768-5497. www.atyourleisure.co.nz. 2 units. NZ$150 (US$105) Kowhai; NZ$180 (US$126) Tasman. Rates include breakfast. Long-stay and off-peak rates available. MC, V. **Amenities:** Nearby golf course; tour bookings; car rentals; courtesy transport to town; babysitting; laundry service; same-day dry cleaning; nonsmoking rooms; on-call doctor/dentist; train and airport transfers. *In room:* TV, coffeemaker, hair dryer.

Kingsgate Hotel 🌟🌟 *(Value*   This is my choice for the best lodging in Greymouth. It offers smart, spacious guest rooms with everything you'll need on-site. The six-floor hotel tower contains 42 premium rooms that were refurbished in 2004. Seven family suites are available as well. The property is within walking distance of restaurants and attractions; it has a better in-house restaurant than Hotel Ashley. Many tour groups and business travelers frequent the place.

32 Mawhera Quay, P.O. Box 337, Greymouth. ✆ **0800/805-085** in NZ, or 03/768-5085. Fax 03/768-5844. www.kingsgate hotels.co.nz. 102 units. From NZ$105 (US$74) standard and premium rooms; from NZ$135 (US$95) family suite; from NZ$165 (US$116) suites. Off-peak and long-stay rates available. AE, DC, MC, V. **Amenities:** Restaurant; bar; gym; concierge; tour desk; secretarial services; 24-hr. room service; babysitting; laundry service; coin-op laundry; same-day dry cleaning; nonsmoking rooms; on-call doctor/dentist. *In room:* TV, dataport, minibar, fridge, coffeemaker, hair dryer, iron.

Rosewood Bed & Breakfast 🌟   This restored 1920s home is minutes of the town center. Four big bedrooms have en suites, and the fifth has a private bathroom. The Mona room upstairs is the nicest and has the best bathroom, although the front room downstairs is very pleasant, with a window seat looking out into the garden.

20 High St., Greymouth. ✆ **0800/185-748** in NZ, or 03/768-4674. Fax 03/768-4694. www.rosewoodnz.co.nz. 5 units. NZ$150–NZ$200 (US$105–US$140). Off-peak rates available. Rates include breakfast. MC, V. **Amenities:** Courtesy car; laundry service; nonsmoking rooms. *In room:* TV, dataport, coffeemaker and fridge available, hair dryer, iron.

WHERE TO DINE

Apart from the eateries reviewed below, the restaurants at Quality Kings Hotel and Hotel Ashley also serve good meals. Both veer toward the more formal—or as formal as things get on the West Coast. For good coffee, Internet, and adventure atmosphere, try **dp.one Café,** 108 Mawhera Quay (© **03/768-4005**). **Café 124 on Mackay,** 124 Mackay St., Greymouth © **03/768-7503**), has reasonable all-day food, but the service is patchy at best. **Trawlers Seafood Restaurant,** 14–16 Tarapuhi St., Greymouth (© **03/768-9254**), has the smartest restaurant interior and good meals, but the service if often hopeless. I'll say it again: Don't expect dining miracles on the West Coast.

Bonzai Pizzeria & Café PIZZERIA/LIGHT MEALS   Try the Pescara pizza, smothered in mussels, shrimps, squid, fresh fish, lemon, and Parmesan. You can get coffee and counter food all day, and in the evenings the laid-back atmosphere includes light meals such as seafood chowder, steaks, nachos, pasta, and fish.

31 Mackay St., Greymouth. © **03/768-4170**. Pizzas and light meals NZ$12–NZ$25 (US$8.40–US$18). AE, DC, MC, V. Mon–Sat 7am–late; Sun 3pm–late.

Jones's Café ☆☆ CAFE/LIGHT MEALS   Locals will tell you this little cafe offers the best food, the best service, and the best atmosphere. The interior is unremarkable, but the coffee is the most consistent in town.

37 Tainui St., Greymouth. © **03/768-6468**. Main courses NZ$16–NZ$26 (US$11–US$18). No credit cards. Daily 11am–9pm.

The Smelting House Café ☆☆ *Value* CAFE/LIGHT MEALS   I appreciate the laid-back atmosphere of this cafe, situated in the old bank building. It's gained a solid reputation for good coffee and tasty snacks. There's a range of pasta dishes, soups, and salads for lunch or a light early-evening meal, plus delicious cakes. Appetizing, affordable, and always filled with travelers, cyclists, and families.

102 Mackay St., Greymouth. © **03/768-0012**. Main courses NZ$10–NZ$25 (US$7–US$18). No credit cards. Daily 8am–5pm.

A SIDE TRIP TO LAKE BRUNNER ☆☆

Lake Brunner and the little township of Moana, situated on its northern shore, lie 30 minutes east of Greymouth. It's a peaceful, scenic diversion serviced by both the TranzAlpine train and a daily shuttle bus—and, I regret to say, great clouds of greedy sand flies that you'll spend your hours swatting away. Access by road is via Arthurs Pass or Lewis Pass, which makes it a good stopover point if you're heading north or south.

The lake and surrounding rivers have some of the best trout fishing in the South Island. The prime time for fishing is between October and April. The Greymouth i-Site Visitor Centre has a big list of guides and will point you in the right direction for the best spots. Just make sure you get a license first.

If you find the tranquil nature of this location appealing and you decide to stay over, you'll find a motel complex, a motor camp, and the old **Moana Hotel,** Ahau Street, Moana (© **03/738-0388;** www.moanahotelmotel.co.nz), which offers inexpensive motel/hotel rooms and cabins. If you prefer a more upmarket option, stay at **Lake Brunner Lodge** ☆☆, Mitchells, RD1, Kumara, Westland (©/fax **03/738-0163;** www.lakebrunner.com), on the unpopulated side of the lake. It has 11 rooms and has recently been upgraded. The tariff ranges from NZ$620 to NZ$765 (US$434–US$536).

Dining out is a little more limited. Your best option is **Stationhouse Café,** Koe Street, Moana (© **03/738-0158**), where pastas, steaks, and roast lamb range from NZ$16 to NZ$30 (US$11–US$21). It's a pretty setting overlooking tiny Moana Railway Station and the lake, but a trifle overpriced and you have to take the service as you find it. It's open daily from 10:30am until late.

EN ROUTE TO HOKITIKA

This 45km (28-mile), 30-minute drive south follows the coastline closely along mostly flat farmland. Nothing too inspiring, but there are hints of the Southern Alps that await when you turn away from the Tasman Sea farther south. About 32km (20 miles) from Greymouth, you'll cross the **Arahura River,** where Maori found huge supplies of greenstone.

3 Hokitika: Greenstone, Glowworms & Gold

45km (28 miles) S of Greymouth; 147km (91 miles) N of Franz Josef Glacier

As you drive into the quiet, rather forlorn-looking township of Hokitika, you'll find it hard to believe that it was once a boisterous, rowdy "Goldfields Capital," where more than 35,000 miners and prospectors patronized more than 102 hotels and kept the dance halls roaring. As many as 80 boats would be docked at the wharves, many of them waiting to transport gold out of the area.

Sadly for Hokitika, the gold supply was finite; when the rush died, so did the wild, carefree days. The economy took a downward turn, and the livelihood of most of today's 4,000 residents is based on farming, forestry, and tourism. But the town is renowned for the Wildfoods Festival, held each March, and it is *the* place to buy crafts on the West Coast. During the summer months, it's probably the cheeriest and busiest of the West Coast towns. It has 1,850 sunshine hours annually and 2,783 millimeters (111 in.) of rainfall—keep your wet-weather gear handy if you're staying for any length of time.

ESSENTIALS

GETTING THERE   By Plane   There is air service via **Air New Zealand Link** (© **0800/737-000** in NZ) between Hokitika and Christchurch.

By Train   Access to the nearest rail service is in Greymouth (see "Greymouth & Lake Brunner," earlier in this chapter).

By Coach (Bus)   InterCity (© **09/913-6100**) has daily departures from Hokitika to Nelson, Westport, Greymouth, and Fox Glacier. Both **Magic Travellers** (© **09/ 358-5600**) and **Kiwi Experience** (© **09/366-9830**) pass through Hokitika on their way from Greymouth to the glaciers.

By Car   Hokitika is reached from the north and south via Highway 6.

VISITOR INFORMATION   The **Westland Visitor Information Centre** is in the Carnegie Building, Tancred and Hamilton streets, Hokitika (© **03/755-6166;** fax 03/ 755-5011; www.westlanddc.govt.nz). It's open December through April, daily from 8:30am to 6pm; May through November, Monday through Friday from 8:30am to 5pm and Saturday and Sunday from 10am to 4pm. Twenty-five minutes south of Hokitika, the **Ross Goldfields Visitor Information & Heritage Centre,** 4 Aylmer St., Ross (© **03/755-4077;** www.ross.org.nz), is open daily from 9am to 5pm in summer and 9am to 3:30pm in winter. Try your hand at gold panning for NZ$6.50 (US$4.55).

Moments Wildfoods Festival

If you're in the area around the second Saturday in March, stop in Hokitika for the **Hokitika Wildfoods Festival** ✹✹✹ (© **0800/494-539** in NZ, or 03/755-8321; www.wildfoods.co.nz). On the easy side of things, you'll be able to sample wild pig, venison, wild herbs, honey, and fish from local waters; the much braver visitor might like to try possum pâté, wild goat, wriggling grubs, and the unmentionable parts of a variety of animals. The general motto here is close your eyes, swallow, and ask questions later! Admission is around NZ$22 (US$15) for adults, NZ$5.50 (US$3.85) for children, and ticket numbers are limited to 19,000 each year.

Note: If you're traveling farther south, Hokitika is the last stop for banks, ATMs, pharmacies, and major supermarkets until you reach Wanaka, 450km (279 miles) away.

EXPLORING HOKITIKA

To gain insight into the history of this little town, pick up the *Hokitika Heritage Walk* brochure at the visitor center or the West Coast Historical Museum.

The **West Coast Historical Museum,** Tancred and Hamilton streets (© **03/755-6898;** hokimuseum@xtra.co.nz), features reconstructions and artifacts of the 19th-century "Alluvial placer" gold-mining era on the West Coast. Wood and slab dwellings display household furnishings. A typical bar, horse-drawn vehicles, mining tools, and pictorial records of the harbor's maritime history are among the wealth of items you'll see. Gold panning is an all-weather attraction in the miner's hut. The museum is open daily from 9:30am to 5pm. Admission is NZ$5 (US$3.50) for adults, NZ$1 (US70¢) for children.

If you're traveling with kids, **Jacquie Grant's Eco World & National Kiwi Centre** ✹✹, 64 Tancred St. (© **03/755-5251;** kiwi.house@xtra.co.nz), is worth a visit. The stars here are the 63 rather repulsive, but nonetheless fascinating, giant eels. The eldest is over 80 years old, and some weigh up to 25 kilograms (55 lb). Try to visit during their feeding (ring ahead for times), and try a spot of hand feeding. It also features Australasia's largest tropical aquarium, with an indoor lake, giant trout, birds, and reptiles. It is open daily, from 9am to 5pm. Admission is NZ$13 (US$9.10) for adults, NZ$7 (US$4.90) for children, and NZ$33 (US$23) per family. It incorporates the **National Kiwi Centre,** which has live kiwi displays.

Take to the water on a Scenic Waterways **Paddle Boat Cruise** ✹, Main Road South (© **03/755-7239** or 03/756-8002; www.paddleboatcruises.com). A dreamy tour down tranquil Mahinapua Creek is just the thing to do on a leisurely afternoon (2pm daily). Keep a look out for the beautiful white herons that may be in residence. The 1½-hour cruises cost around NZ$25 (US$18) for adults and NZ$12 (US$8.40) for children. Make reservations in advance at the visitor center.

Staying afloat, call up **Due West Canoe Safaris** ✹✹ (© **0800/383-9378** in NZ, or 03/755-6717; www.duewest.co.nz) for a fabulous paddle on Lake Mahinapua, or take a river trip and feel the thrill of riding rapids.

EXPLORING LAKE KANIERE SCENIC RESERVE ✹✹✹

This beautiful nature reserve, centered on one of the South Island's largest lakes, is just 18km (11 miles) from Hokitika. If you don't have time to stay and explore, there's a lovely 58km (36-mile) circular scenic drive past the lake and back through Kakatahi Valley farmlands.

Lingering, however, will be rewarded by vistas of the lake ringed by unspoiled forests with a backdrop of distant mountains. You'll find an information kiosk and toilets at the landing, where the road first comes to the water's edge. There are picnic tables, fireplaces, and toilets at Sunny Bight. This is also the starting point for two walks: the **Kahikatea Forest Walk** *, a 10-minute stroll through the forest; and the **Lake Kaniere Walkway** **, a 3½-hour trek that features beaches, rainforest, and birdlife. Pick up advance information on the walks at the visitor center in Hokitika.

SHOPPING

In peak season, shopping takes on the nature and dimensions of a sport in Hokitika, as the human contents of buses spill out into the vicinity of Tancred Street. All of the following stores are open daily.

The Gold Room   You'll see it here in every form—from raw nuggets and flakes to top-quality crafted jewelry. If you want a unique piece with a bit of character, you could well find it here. 37 Tancred St. ℂ/fax **03/755-8362.**

Hokitika Craft Gallery   Nineteen of the West Coast's top artisans have brought their work together under one roof. Look out for contemporary works in fiber, wood, pottery, jade, leather, wool, glass, and bone. My pick is the furniture by top craftsman Marc Zuckerman. 25 Tancred St. ℂ **03/755-8802.** Fax 03/755-8803.

Hokitika Glass Studio   Excuse me if I don't rave about glass penguins (plenty do; they're the most popular item), but if you can see past them, there are some stunning glass works here. Bowls, platters, and gorgeous perfume bottles are my picks. 28 Tancred St. ℂ **03/755-7775.**

House of Wood   This little shop has the best range of handcrafted wooden items. Browse the creative boxes, lovely bowls, and wooden toys. You can also watch wood-turners at work in the studio. 29 Tancred St. ℂ/fax **03/755-6061.**

Jade Factory   The studio generally has up to seven carvers at work. A big selection of excellent-quality jewelry is for sale. 41 Weld St. ℂ **03/755-8007.** Fax 03/755-7804.

The Sheep Station   Look out for the monster sheep and you're there! Aside from some pretty wacky novelty items, you'll find an excellent selection of merino wool and possum fur knitwear and rugs here. 20 Sewell St. ℂ **03/756-8090.**

Moments Bright Lights: Spotting Glowworms for Free

When people talk about the bright lights of Hokitika, they don't mean a dazzling display of neon and inner city activity. It's much more likely that they're referring to the largest outdoor gathering of glowworms in New Zealand. Head north, to the edge of the town, and there, right on the edge of the main road (St. Hwy. 6), is a charming, easily accessed dell that shines bright every evening. The glowworms thrive in the moist atmosphere of the wooded banks. Make sure it's properly dark before you visit, speak quietly, and don't turn on torches (flashlights), or these shy critters will vanish. It's free, quite magical, and well worth the effort of groping your way through darkness.

Westland Greenstone Ltd. This is a good place to see greenstone and *paua* jewelry being made. The showroom has a wide range of the finished products at factory prices. 34 Tancred St., between Weld and Hamilton sts. Ⓒ/fax **03/755-8713.**

William Steyn Stone Painter I have a compulsion to buy every one of this man's exquisitely painted beach stones. Steyn came to Hokitika from South Africa and, inspired by the rock paintings of the ancient San people of the Kalahari Desert, he has combined his graphic artist talents with local materials to produce unique New Zealand gifts. 41 Weld St. Ⓒ **03/755-5362.**

WHERE TO STAY

Two of the best spots on the whole of the West Coast are just out of the main township (see reviews of Villa Polenza Boutique Lodge and Rimu Lodge, below). Campers will find a good deal at the **Hokitika Holiday Park,** 242 Stafford St. (Ⓒ **0800/ 465-436** in NZ, or 03/755-8172; www.hokitika.com/holidaypark). It has tent and caravan sites, cabins, and flats. **Mountain Jade Backpackers,** 41 Weld St., Hokitika (Ⓒ **0800/838-301** in NZ, or 03/755-8007; fax 03/755-7804), has roomy dorms with beds costing from NZ$50 to NZ$80 (US$35–US$56).

EXPENSIVE

Villa Polenza Boutique Lodge ✸✸✸ *(Finds* These are without question the best accommodations on the entire West Coast. Fourth-generation West Coaster Russell Diedrichs and his creative wife, Trina, have built an Italian-style villa atop a raw hillside overlooking Hokitika, and inside have created a stylish contemporary oasis. Extras such as down duvets, robes, and liqueurs and chocolates all add to the serious pampering. The bright-blue Azzurra Suite is something special, featuring an unforgettable bathroom complete with large tub, separate shower, bidet, toilet, and dressing room. And for a bathing experience with a difference, there are two gas-heated pools set side by side in the bushy privacy of the hillside, overlooking the vast seascape.

143 Brickfield Rd., RD2, Hokitika. Ⓒ **0800/241-801** in NZ, or 03/755-7801. Fax 03/755-7901. www.villapolenza.co.nz. 3 units. NZ$400–NZ$550 (US$280–US$385). Extra person NZ$100 (US$70). Off-peak rates available. Rates include breakfast and airport, train, and bus transfers; dinner by arrangement. MC, V. Travel north from Hokitika town center, turn onto Hampden St. (which becomes Hau Hau Rd.), and turn left onto Brickfield Rd. It's a 5-min. drive from the center. No children under 12. **Amenities:** Nearby golf course; 2 heated private outdoor baths; laundry service; nonsmoking rooms. *In room:* Hair dryer, iron, no phone.

MODERATE

Rimu Lodge ✸✸✸ *(Value* Peter and Helen Walls have built a real gem on the top of a spur, overlooking bush-clad slopes and the Hokitika River. You'll be hard-pressed to find a more serene and tranquil setting, or better views. Four big suites (two up, two down) will bring an instant smile to your face. They're modern, spacious, and gorgeous. The two upstairs rooms have bigger bathrooms.

33 Seddons Terrace Rd., Hokitika. Ⓒ **03/755-5277.** Fax 03/755-5237. www.rimulodge.co.nz. 4 units. NZ$225–NZ$275 (US$158–US$193). AE, MC, V. Off-peak rates available. Rates include breakfast, canapés, and predinner drinks. Drive south over the Hokitika River Bridge and turn left into Arthurstown Rd. Travel 4km (2½ miles) to a T-junction and turn right. Drive past Rimu Hotel on the right, go uphill, and Seddons Terrace Rd. is the second on your left. No children under 12. **Amenities:** Nearby golf course; tour bookings; car rentals; courtesy transport to Hokitika; massage; laundry service; dry cleaning; nonsmoking rooms; on-call doctor/dentist; access for travelers w/disabilities. *In room:* Fridge, coffeemaker, hair dryer.

Teichelmann's Bed & Breakfast ✸✸ *(Value* Brian Ward and Barbara Flanagan transformed this iconic Hokitika B&B, making it lighter, brighter, and lovelier. The upstairs Wilson room—creamy and luscious—is my favorite. The sun pours in, and the room has a king-size and larger-than-normal single beds plus a private bathroom. Four other in-house rooms have en suites. If you're lucky, you might be able to nab the cute garden suite with its big Jacuzzi. Overall a terrific stay for the price.

20 Hamilton St., Hokitika. (℗ **0800/743-742** in NZ, or 03/755-8232. Fax 03/755-8239. www.teichelmanns.co.nz. 6 units. From NZ$175–NZ$195 (US$123–US$137). Off-peak rates available. Rates include breakfast. MC, V. Directly opposite the visitor center. No children under 12. **Amenities:** Nearby golf course; tour bookings; car rentals; limited laundry service; nonsmoking rooms; on-call doctor/dentist; train and airport transfers; access for travelers w/disabilities. *In room:* Coffeemaker, hair dryer.

WHERE TO DINE

The once popular **Trappers Restaurant,** 131–137 Revell St. (℗ **03/755-6859**), is open limited hours and does not always impress locals with its quality or service. It specializes in wild food and game in rustic atmosphere.

Sister Browne's Cafe ✶✶, 23 Weld St. (℗ **03/755-8581**), serves light lunches, including vegetarian, vegan, and gluten-free fare, and possibly the best coffee in Hokitika. **Tasman View Restaurant,** in the Southland Hotel, 111 Revell St. (℗ **03/755-8344**), is popular for its Friday-night smorgasbord and balcony dining; and **Stations Restaurant** ✶✶, corner of Cement and Blue Spur roads (℗ **03/755-5499**), is an encouraging new addition just a short drive out in the country.

Café de Paris ✶✶, 19 Tancred St. (℗ **03/755-8933**), provides what may be the best meals in town. The French owner has always swung his menu in favor of things European and when service is not patchy, you'll dine well.

EN ROUTE TO FRANZ JOSEF & FOX GLACIERS

Note: There are no banks or ATMs in either glacier village, so remember to get money before going south—you won't be able to do so again until you get to Wanaka, some 450km (279 miles) away. Credit cards are accepted in most places, though. If you're driving nonstop to Wanaka, allow 6 to 7 hours. The drive to Franz Josef from Hokitika takes about 2 hours.

If you're in the **Whataroa** area (35km/22 miles north of Franz Josef) during the November-to-February nesting season of the white heron *(kotuku),* book one of the **White Heron Sanctuary Tours** ✶✶✶ (℗ **0800/523-456** in NZ, or 03/753-4120; www.whiteherontours.co.nz). Entry to the country's only white-heron nesting colony is by permit and starts with a 20-minute jet-boat ride. You then walk through native rainforest accompanied by a guide. The excursion costs around NZ$100 (US$70) for adults, NZ$50 (US$35) for children.

A little farther west, **Okarito Lagoon,** 10km (6 miles) off State Highway 6, is a beautiful spot where **Okarito Nature Tours** ✶✶ (℗ **03/753-4014;** www.okarito.co.nz) can introduce you to the wonders of New Zealand's largest unmodified wetland. Its guided kayak tours are priced from NZ$75 (US$53) per person. Kayak rental is about NZ$40 (US$38) per person for 2 hours, NZ$60 (US$42) per person for a full day.

4 Franz Josef & Fox Glaciers ✶✶✶

Franz Josef: 188km (117 miles) S of Greymouth; 24km (15 miles) N of Fox Glacier

It seems improbable that you could find a glacier on a South Pacific island and ice in a temperate rainforest, but that's New Zealand for you—full of surprises. Nowhere else in the world outside arctic regions will you find glaciers just 305m (1,000 ft.) above sea level and just 12km (7½ miles) from the sea.

The two glaciers are just a small part of the 115,000-hectare (284,050-acre) **Westland National Park,** an impressive area of high mountains, glacial lakes, and rushing rivers. The park is popular for tramping, mountain climbing, fishing, canoeing, hunting, and horse trekking. In 1990, the combined Mount Cook/Westland National Parks, Fiordland National Park, Mount Aspiring National Park, and all the significant adjacent natural areas were incorporated into a single vast **Southwest New Zealand World Heritage Area (Te Wahipounamu),** which contains about 10% of New Zealand's total land area, or 2.6 million hectares (6.4 million acres). The World Heritage Highway traverses the northern third of this region and is largely confined to the West Coast side of the Main Divide.

So what are the differences between Franz Josef and Fox glaciers and their townships? Fox Glacier is longer and has better helicopter and walking options; Franz Josef village has a better visitor center and is busier overall, with superior food and lodging options. Just a short distance apart, the drive should nonetheless be undertaken with care.

ESSENTIALS
GETTING THERE   By Coach (Bus)   InterCity (© 09/913-6100) provides regular transport to the glaciers from north and south. Both **Magic Travellers** (© 09/358-5600) and **Kiwi Experience** (© 09/366-9830) include the glaciers on their itineraries as well.

By Car   The World Heritage Highway (St. Hwy. 6) follows the coast from Whataroa to Franz Josef Glacier to Fox Glacier to Haast and over the Haast Pass. The Department of Conservation's *World Heritage Highway Guide* suggests places to stop along the way. Roads in this area should always be treated with respect, especially in wet or icy conditions.

GETTING AROUND   I'd be surprised if you can't walk the full length of either village in just 10 minutes. Bike rentals are available in both, and you can travel between the two via InterCity coach.

VISITOR INFORMATION   The **Westland National Park Visitor Centre,** State Highway 6, P.O. Box 14 (© 03/752-0796; www.doc.govt.nz), is in the center of its village, as is its counterpart, the **Fox Glacier Visitor Centre,** Westland National Park, State Highway 6, P.O. Box 99 (© 03/751-0807; www.glaciercountry.co.nz). Their displays, literature, and activities are essential to a full appreciation of the area and they're open 8:30am until 6pm in summer and 8:30am until 4:45pm in winter, with a 1-hour closure at noon.

EXPLORING THE GLACIERS
Ask at the two visitor centers about the schedule for nature lectures, slide presentations, and guided walks—and see the excellent *Flowing West* movie at the **Alpine Adventure Centre,** Main Street, Franz Josef (© 03/752-0793), or at **Fox Heli Services,** Alpine Guides Building, Fox Glacier (© 03/751-0866).

The visitor centers administer the alpine and tramping huts available for overnight hikers, and keep track of trampers and climbers as well—it is essential to check conditions and register your intentions before setting out. The centers' displays give a complete rundown on the formation of glaciers, the movement of ice, the mountains, the history of the region, and more.

Your sightseeing at the glaciers can be as costly or as inexpensive as your budget dictates. There are several options that can put a rather unfriendly hole in your budget, but these are among the most spectacular travel experiences in the world and are therefore worth every cent. If you'd rather, there are plenty of self-guided walks in the area, many of which give good views of the glaciers.

The silence of any fine morning in glacier country is ruptured by the frenetic buzz of **helicopters.** It's one of the best ways to see and appreciate the natural splendor of this area. Equally amazing are the **guided glacier walk** and the **heli-hike,** which combines both.

The choice of what to do may not turn out to be as agonizing as you think—the weather could very easily decide for you. To say that the weather here is unpredictable is an understatement, and even when it appears fine and sunny on the ground, conditions up on the glacier may preclude a helicopter landing. If your time is short, take the first flight available lest you miss out.

Several operators offer glacier hikes. **The Helicopter Line** ★★★ (✆ **0800/807-767** in NZ, 03/752-0767 in Franz Josef, or 03/751-0767 in Fox Glacier; www.helicopter.co.nz) is the biggest heli-tourism operator in New Zealand. Its most popular trip is the 30-minute twin glacier option with snow landing for around NZ$250 (US$175). **Glacier & Southern Lakes Helicopters** (✆ **0800/800-732** in NZ, 03/752-0755 in Franz Josef, or 03/751-0803 in Fox Glacier; www.heli-flights.co.nz), has a 30-minute twin glacier trip with an 8- to 10-minute névé landing from NZ$230 (US$161). **Fox and Franz Josef Heliservices** (✆ **0800/800-793** in NZ, 03/751-0866 in Fox Glacier, or 03/752-0793 in Franz Josef; www.scenic-flights.co.nz) also offers a comprehensive range of flights, with a 30-minute flight going for around NZ$230 (US$161).

Another option that everyone raves about is the **heli-hike** ★★★, which you can do with either the Helicopter Line (see above for contact information) or **Alpine Guides Fox Glacier** ★★★ (✆ **0800/111-600** in NZ, or 03/751-0825; www.foxguides.co.nz). For around NZ$265 (US$186), Alpine Guides flies you to a high glacier level to spend 3½ hours exploring spectacular ice formations. The helicopter then returns to pick you up. It's suitable for all fitness levels, but does require some agility.

Guided glacier walks are yet another possibility. Alpine Guides (see above) has both half- and full-day options on Fox Glacier. An expert guide will lead the way, chipping steps in the ice for you; you'll go up into the icefall, walk among the crevasses, and listen to the deep-throated grumble of the moving glacier. Hobnailed boots, waterproof parkas, heavy socks, and a walking stick are provided. The cost of the 3- to 4-hour trip is around NZ$65 (US$46) for adults; a full-day option is NZ$95 (US$67).

In Franz Josef, **Franz Josef Glacier Guides** (✆ **0800/484-377** in NZ, or 03/752-0763; www.franzjosefglacier.com) offers half-day hikes from NZ$90 (US$63); a full-day glacier adventure for NZ$150 (US$105); glacier valley ecotours for NZ$50 (US$35) for adults, NZ$25 (US$18) for children; and heli-hike options for NZ$240 to NZ$400 (US$168–US$280). It also has a slower, more informative half-day walk for the less agile.

Last but not least, **Mount Cook Ski Planes** ★★ (✆ **0800/368-000** in NZ, 03/752-0714 on the West Coast, or 03/430-8034 at Mount Cook; www.mtcookskiplanes.com), offers a fabulous-value specialist experience. This is New Zealand's only fixed-wing glacier landing and when you land up on the snow, and the engines are switched off, you're in total silence. This makes for a very different experience compared to a helicopter glacier landing. The twin glacier excursion takes 50 minutes and costs from NZ$270 (US$189) for adults. The 60-minute Glacier Magic trip costs from NZ$335 (US$235).

BEYOND THE GLACIERS: WHAT TO SEE & DO

Skydive NZ ★★★ (© **0800/751-0080** in NZ, or 03/751-0080; www.skydivingnz. co.nz) takes you up around the side of Mount Cook and over some of the most awesome scenery in the country. Then lucky you gets to jump 2,700m (8,856 ft.) for around NZ$275 (US$193).

Ferg's Kayaks, 20 Cron St., Franz Josef (© **0800/423-262** in NZ, or 03/752-0230; www.glacierkayaks.com), has a 3-hour guided kayak tour on the mirrorlike Lake Mapourika for around NZ$70 (US$49). They also offer scooter hire, which is a fun way to get around the village.

Dave Hetherington, at **Alpine Trophies** (© **03/751-0856**) or **Alpine Adventure Centre** (© **03/752-0793;** fax 03/752-0764), is the man to introduce you to a spot of guided hunting or fishing.

The West Coast's wet weather is great news for rafters; if you want to see how brave you really are, join **Rivers Wild** ★★, Franz Josef (© **0800/469-453** in NZ, or 021/748-371; www.riverswild.co.nz), for an unforgettable day on otherwise inaccessible Grade 4 and 5 rivers. You'll get there by helicopter, departing Franz at 7:30am. There's also have a range of multiday hike and raft options.

Walkers and trampers should stop by either visitor center to collect Department of Conservation material on the numerous tracks in the area. The **Copland Track** ★★ is a popular overnight round-trip that gives you a glimpse of Westland's spectacular scenery, with the natural hot pools at Welcome Flat an added attraction. Rainfall in the area is high, so come well equipped and always sign in (and out) before undertaking any hike.

Another walk takes you to a **seal colony at Gillespies Beach** ★★★, a 21km (13-mile) drive from Fox village. Take Cook Flat Road–Lake Matheson Road from the village and follow the signs to the beach. The last 11km (7 miles) of the road is unpaved. Allow 3 hours round-trip.

If all this exercise seems positively tedious, why not take a quiet after-dark amble to Fox's mini **glowworm dell?** Wait until it's very dark, and keep quiet. There is a short track just off the main road opposite the BP gas station. There is a small charge for adults, but children enter free.

WHERE TO STAY

During peak season, accommodations are woefully short in these parts. You'll be competing for rooms with lots of tour groups. On top of that, some hotels are overpriced for what they offer. My best advice is to book well ahead or travel outside the summer months; otherwise, you may find yourself staying as far away from the glaciers as Greymouth. You can experience the glaciers without staying overnight in Fox or Franz Josef townships, but the advantage of sleeping here is being close enough to jump on flights when there's a break in the weather.

IN FRANZ JOSEF

The **Franz Josef Top 10 Holiday Park,** Main Road (© **0800/467-897** in NZ, or 03/752-0735; www.mountainview.co.nz), has tent and powered sites, cabins, a lodge,

Moments **Lake Matheson & Lake Mapourika**

Lake Matheson, 5km (3 miles) from Fox Glacier township, shows up on all the postcards, but what the pretty pictures don't show is the wonderful **Lake Matheson Walk** 🌟🌟, an easy track around the lake that takes about 1½ hours. You'll enjoy great views of Mount Cook (on the right) and Mount Tasman (to the left), and if you go to the lake before dusk, you can watch the mountains turn pink in the sunset—along with plenty of other sightseers doing exactly the same thing. When the lake and air are still, you'll be able to get one of those famous photographs of the mountains perfectly reflected in the water. **Café Lake Matheson** is at the parking area where the walk starts; it's open daily from 7am to 5pm.

Lake Mapourika, 9km (5½ miles) north of Franz Josef, is the largest lake in Westland National Park and deserves attention for its arresting reflections and setting. You can swim and fish, or opt for a peaceful kayak trip (see **Ferg's Kayaks** under "Beyond the Glaciers: What to See & Do," above).

tourist cabins, and flats. **Rainforest Retreat & Backpackers,** Cron Street, Franz Josef (© 0800/873-346 in NZ, or 03/752-0220; www.rainforestretreat.co.nz), is nestled in native rainforest and provides some lovely, reasonably priced options for travelers on a budget. Another smart new option for a few more dollars is **Glenfern Villas** 🌟🌟, State Highway 6, Franz Josef (© 0800/453-633 in NZ, or 03/752-0054; www.glenfern. co.nz), where you'll find very comfortable 1- and 2-bedroom villas with fully equipped kitchens. Plus, they're just a short walk to village shops and cafes.

The rates provided here include 12.5% GST and free off-street parking.

Punga Grove Motor Lodge 🌟🌟 *Value*   This gorgeous spot surrounded by huge tree ferns and rainforest is my pick for the best value in the area. The seven rainforest studios built in 2003 are the best of all. They have big Jacuzzis, leather furnishings, and look directly into the forest. Among the original choices, the two-bedroom suite is especially appealing, with a big kitchen. Four other units have two levels with rooms looking directly into the treetops. They're shady, inviting, and well situated for long stays. The complex is in a quiet location, 150m (492 ft.) from shops and restaurants.

Cron St., Franz Josef. © 0800/437-269 in NZ, or 03/752-001. Fax 03/752-0002. www.pungagrove.co.nz. 20 units. From NZ$170–NZ$$180 (US$119–US$126) queen studio; NZ$185–NZ$205 (US$130–US$144) 1-bedroom suite; NZ$220–NZ$240 (US$154–US$168) 2-bedroom suite; NZ$235–NZ$260 (US$165–US$182) rainforest studio. Long-stay, off-peak, and family rates available. AE, DC, MC, V. Turn off St. Hwy. 6 to Cowan St., then left to Cron St. Children under 12 in family units only. **Amenities:** Tour bookings; coin-op laundry; nonsmoking rooms; access for travelers w/disabilities. *In room:* TV, dataport, kitchenette, fridge, coffeemaker, hair dryer, iron.

Westwood Lodge 🌟🌟   If you're after tranquillity, Westwood is for you. Just out of town, the timbered interiors create a pleasant country-style decor and all suites have en-suite bathrooms. A new luxury suite features a Jacuzzi and double sinks. Main lodge spaces have big fireplaces and mountain views and will put you in a sociable mood.

St. Hwy. 6, Franz Josef. © 03/752-0112. Fax 03/752-0111. www.westwood-lodge.co.nz. 9 units. NZ$495–NZ$595 (US$347–US$417) dinner, bed, and breakfast; NZ$395–NZ$495 (US$277–US$347) bed-and-breakfast. Dinner by arrangement NZ$45 (US$32) per person. AE, DC, MC, V. 2km (1¼ miles) north of the village. No children under 12. **Amenities:** Bar; billiards room; tour bookings; courtesy car; massage; laundry service; nonsmoking rooms. *In room:* TV, dataport, fridge, coffeemaker, hair dryer, iron.

IN FOX GLACIER

Glacier Country Hotel ✦, State Highway 6, P.O. Box 32, Fox Glacier (© **0800/ 696-963** in NZ, or 03/751-0847; www.scenic-circle.co.nz.), is the baby of the Scenic Circle Hotels group. You can expect modest accommodations at affordable prices, often well below the rack rates. Built in the late 1960s, it's right in the heart of the village and is older and smaller than the Franz Josef Glacier Hotels (owned by the same company). You'll find new motel rooms at **The Westhaven** ✦✦, Fox Glacier (© **0800/369-452** in NZ, or 03/751-0084; www.thewesthaven.co.nz), right in the heart of the action.

Te Weheka Inn ✦✦   These central accommodations opened in two stages in 2001 and 2002 and provides one of the nicer stays in Fox Glacier. Rooms are spacious with king-size or twin beds and they have balcony views toward the village. Bathrooms are also a decent size and have a bathtub as well as a shower. There's an upstairs guest lounge and library where you can relax and a sunny dining room for breakfast. By 2006, expect a Jacuzzi, a sauna, and a gymnasium on stream.

St. Hwy. 6, Fox Glacier. © **0800/313-414** in NZ, or 03/751-0730. Fax 03/751-0731. www.teweheka.co.nz. 21 units. NZ$310–NZ$345 (US$217–US$242). Extra adult NZ$70 (US$49). Long-stay and off-peak rates available. Rates include breakfast. AE, MC, V. **Amenities:** Restaurant (summer only); gym; Jacuzzi; sauna; free bikes; tour bookings; coin-operated laundry; nonsmoking rooms; access for travelers w/disabilities. *In room:* TV, dataport, fridge, coffeemaker, hair dryer, iron.

WHERE TO DINE
IN FRANZ JOSEF

If you've decided to do your own cooking, head for **Fern Grove Food Centre,** Main Road (© **03/752-0177**), open from 7:45am until late, especially for fresh bread and Mrs. Mac's famous meat pies. The **Blue Ice Café** ✦✦, Main Road (© **03/752-0707**), serves pizza, is fully licensed, and gets raves for the best cafe atmosphere in glacier country. **Beeches Café & Bar** ✦✦, Main Road (© **03/752-0721**), is a more expensive option with reasonably good food and all-day service.

The **Alice May** ✦, Main Road (© **03/752-0740**), has cheap family dining with lots of steaks and the best chips in town, in quantities to satisfy the biggest appetite. **The Landing** ✦✦, Main Road (© **03/752-0229**), is a popular sports bar serving pizza, snacks and platters. It's nothing fancy, but service is good (mostly) and it's a good value-for-money option; it's open daily 10am till late in summer and 4 to 10pm in winter.

Finds Flights of Fancy

If you have an eye for top-quality craftsmanship, you'll enjoy the displays at **Flights of Fancy** ✦✦✦, Main Road, Franz Josef (© **03/752-0242;** fax 03/752-0232). It's where you'll find a stylish collection of some of the best New Zealand arts and crafts—definitely the finest store of its sort in this part of the West Coast. It's open 8am to 9pm in summer (closed Dec 25), 9am to 5:30pm in winter.

Finds Back to Nature

Nature-lovers will get a real thrill out of spending a few nights at **Wilderness Lodge Lake Moeraki,** 30km (19 miles) north of Haast (© **03/750-0881;** www. wildernesslodge.co.nz), which has forged a solid international reputation in ecotourism. Rates range from NZ$500 to NZ$700 (US$350–US$490) and include accommodations, breakfast, dinner, use of lodge facilities, and daily guided nature trips. There are numerous outdoor activities available, from kayaking, walking, and fishing to seal- and bird-watching.

IN FOX GLACIER

The **Fox Glacier General Store** 𝕗𝕗, Main Road (© **03/751-0829**), sells everything from foodstuffs and hot meat pies to camping supplies, hardware, and boots. It's open daily from 8am till late. **Alpine Guides Hobnail Café** 𝕗, Main Road (© **03/751-0005**), right next to the Alpine Guides booking office, has a constant traffic of eager adventurers. It's open for breakfast, lunch, and all-day snacks, and the simple timber-tabled interior is always bustling and sunny.

Café Neve 𝕗𝕗, Main Road (© **03/751-0110**), has a terrific range of pizzas along with delicious counter food and dinner dishes such as venison _osso buco_ served on a kumara (sweet potato) mash with steamed vegetables. Another possibility is the traditional West Coast whitebait omelet with fresh herbs. It's open from 9am till late and is definitely one of the nicest options. **Café Lake Matheson** 𝕗, Lake Matheson Road (© **03/751-0878**), has a fabulous aspect beside the lake, a nice "woody" interior and great-value light meals.

Cook Saddle Café and Saloon, Main Road (© **03/751-0700**), is a Tex-Mex favorite with backpackers. It has good ambience in true eclectic West Coast style—a trophy head here, an animal skin there. Venison burgers, Boss Hogg ribs, and Texas T-bone all speak of a slightly displaced sense of geography, but if a full stomach and a good night are your intention, then you've come to the right place. **The Plateau Café & Bar,** corner of Sullivan Street and State Highway 6 (© **03/751-0058**), is a nice spot in the Glowworm Forest Building, open for lunch and dinner daily with homemade baking all day.

EN ROUTE TO HAAST

Just 1 hour south of Fox Glacier (62km/38 miles) is **The Salmon Farm Café** 𝕗𝕗, State Highway 6, South Westland (© **03/751-0837**). The menu is predictably "fishy," with both fresh and smoked salmon dishes in abundance. It's open daily from 7am to 7pm, with shorter winter hours.

Farther south, the magnificent vistas from the **Knight's Point View Point** are worth a stop to take in sandy coves, bush-clad hillsides, rocky headlands, and ocean views.

Haast itself is 121km (75 miles) south of Fox Glacier. The **South Westland World Heritage Visitor Centre** is at the junction of State Highway 6 and Jackson Bay Road (© **03/750-0809;** fax 03/750-0832; haastvc@doc.govt.nz). The center has excellent exhibits on coastal highlights. It's open daily from 8:30am; mid-April to early November, it closes at 4:30pm; early November to December 25 and February 7 to mid-April, it closes at 6pm; and December 26 to February 6, it closes at 7pm.

EN ROUTE TO WANAKA

The highway between Haast and Wanaka is magnificent, moss-covered, and often misty. It follows the course of the Haast River for much of the way. High peaks rise up on either side of the road. The route took 40 years to build and is 563m (1,847 ft.) above sea level. The Department of Conservation has created many walks along the way. Traveling nonstop, the trip to Wanaka should take 2 to 3 hours. Be prepared to make camera stops along the way of stunning waterfalls and river views.

EN ROUTE TO QUEENSTOWN

Highway 6 is good traveling all the way to Wanaka. From there, the trip to Queenstown will take around 1½ hours. You drive around the edge of Lake Dunstan, which was formed behind the Clyde Dam. Bypassing Cromwell township, you then travel through the stone fruit orchards of the Cromwell area. After passing through the Kawarau River Gorge, you come into Gibbston Valley and on into Queenstown.

If you're a competent driver, you could also go to Queenstown via the Crown Range. It's unsuitable for caravans and can be slippery and icy in winter, but the views from the top are stunning and it's 30 minutes shorter than State Highway 6.

15

Queenstown & Environs

The southwestern section of the South Island holds some of New Zealand's greatest natural beauty. At its heart, the Fiordland National Park is but a small portion of Te Wahipounamu, the South West New Zealand World Heritage Area—2.6 million hectares (6.4 million acres) that make up about 10% of New Zealand's total landmass.

The area gives a whole new meaning to the word "wilderness," and you don't have to be a pack-carrying tramper to appreciate its grandeur. From mountain peaks, lakes, and rivers to native bush, waterfalls, rural towns, and more organized tours and adventures than anywhere else in New Zealand, you'll find plenty to satisfy your recreational appetite.

Before you hit Queenstown farther south, you'll come to Wanaka, a lakeside settlement that serves as the gateway to the Mount Aspiring National Park and World Heritage Area. It's a pretty town that quickly seduces you into a state of total relaxation. Mount Cook, which the Maori named *Aoraki* ("the cloud piercer"), is the highest point in New Zealand. It lies close to the West Coast, but the only road access is from the south, turning off State Highway 8, approximately 2 hours north of Wanaka.

Queenstown is undeniably the hub of it all. Spreading out from the foot of the Remarkables on the northeastern shore of Lake Wakatipu, it's an international resort, and ever since gold was discovered in the region in the 1860s, the town has been on a winning streak.

Just over the hill as the crow flies, Te Anau is the hub for exploring Fiordland National Park. Situated on the tranquil shores of Lake Te Anau, this little township is renowned as a walking capital. It is the stepping-off point for several world-famous tracks—the Milford, Routeburn, Hollyford, Greenstone, Kepler, and Dusky. It is also the departure point for explorations of Milford Sound, once astutely described by Rudyard Kipling as the eighth wonder of the world.

1 Wanaka: Gateway to Mount Aspiring National Park ★ ★

145km (90 miles) S of Haast; 117km (73 miles) N of Queenstown

Either you warm to Wanaka or you don't. It's often seen as a very quiet, less self-important version of Queenstown, or to put it another way, as Queenstown was 20 years ago. Often overlooked by visitors on the move between the West Coast and Queenstown, Wanaka is the perfect place to spend a couple of days recharging. There has been a huge amount of growth in the town in the last 5 years, with much-needed new accommodations, restaurants, shops, and tourism operators opening for business.

And one last key thing to remember about Wanaka, which is often overlooked in favor of Queenstown in relation to Milford Sound: If you plan to fly to Milford, keep in mind that if you fly from Wanaka instead of Queenstown, you will get a longer flight over a different route—one that takes in great swaths of the Mount Aspiring National Park, not seen on the Queenstown flights.

ESSENTIALS

GETTING THERE By Plane Air New Zealand (© **0800/737-000** in NZ; www.airnewzealand.co.nz), provides a daily service from Christchurch. **Aspiring Air** (© **0800/100-943** in NZ, or 03/443-7943; www.nz-flights.com) has three flights a day from Queenstown.

By Coach (Bus) InterCity (© **09/913-6100**) provides coach service linking Wanaka to the West Coast, Christchurch, Dunedin, Mount Cook, Queenstown, Te Anau, and Milford Sound. **Kiwi Experience** (© **09/366-9830**) and **Magic Travellers** (© **09/358-5600**) both include Wanaka on their routes. **Wanaka Connexions** (© **03/443-9122;** www.wanakaconnexions.co.nz) runs between Wanaka and Queenstown several times a day, and also has a daily service to Invercargill, Dunedin, and Christchurch.

By Car Wanaka is reached via the Haast Pass from the West Coast. It's a 4-hour drive from the glaciers. Highway 6 connects it to Cromwell and Queenstown, 1½ hours to the south. Highway 89, the Cardrona Road over the Crown Range, is a more direct and impressive route that takes around 1 hour (if you stop to admire the views). Once narrow, winding, and treacherous, it's now fully paved and is, in fact, the highest tar-sealed road in Australasia. Wanaka is a 5-hour drive from Christchurch and 3½ hours from both Dunedin and Te Anau.

VISITOR INFORMATION The **Lake Wanaka i-Site Visitor Centre,** 100 Ardmore Rd., is in the log cabin on the lakefront (© **03/443-1233;** fax 03/443-1290; www.lakewanaka.co.nz). It's open daily May to mid-September from 9am to 5pm, late September through April from 8:30am to 6:30pm (closed Dec 25). The **Department of Conservation,** Ardmore Street and Ballantyne Road (© **03/443-7660;** fax 03/443-8777; www.doc.govt.nz), provides information on Mount Aspiring National Park and all DOC tracks in the area. The DOC is open November through April daily from 8am to 4:45pm, and in winter Monday through Friday from 8am to 4:45pm, Saturday and Sunday from 9:30am to 3:45pm.

FAST FACTS The fastest and cheapest Internet access is offered by **Bits & Bytes,** corner of Helwick and Brownston streets (© **03/443-7078**). For medical matters, go to **Wanaka Medical Centre,** 21 Russell St. (© **03/443-7811**). The **Post Office** is on Ardmore Street, as you drive into Wanaka.

SPECIAL EVENTS Wanaka Rodeo (© **03/443-7736**) is held in early January. **Rippon Rock Festival** (© **03/443-1833**) is a biennial open-air music festival in a vineyard in early February. **Silverstone Race To The Sky** (**www.racetothesky.com**) draws international motorsport junkies to an annual Easter hill climb. April's **Warbirds Over Wanaka International Air Show** (© **03/356-0297;** www.nzfpm.co.nz) combines classic vintage and veteran aircraft, machinery, fire engines, and tractors with dynamic Air Force displays and aerobatic teams in the natural amphitheater of the Upper Clutha Basin. It's held every second Easter in even-numbered years. In autumn, celebrate the **Festival of Colour** (www.festivalofcolour.co.nz), 5 days of intense arts, dance, theater, and music. The next festival will be held in April 2007. There are also numerous ski festivals during winter; the visitor center has details.

EXPLORING WANAKA

There's fun to be had at **Stuart Landsborough's Puzzling World** 𝕽𝕽, on State High-way 89, 2km (1¼ miles) from Wanaka (© **03/443-7489;** www.puzzlingworld.co.nz). Since 1973, Stuart Landsborough (also known as Professor Puzzle) has drawn thou-sands of visitors to the confusing passageways of his elaborate Great Maze. The crazy Tilted House and Leaning Clock Tower will further test your perceptions. Admission is NZ$10 (US$7) for adults and NZ$7 (US$4.90) for children, and it's open daily from 8:30am to 5:30pm. Allow 1 to 2 hours for your visit.

The **New Zealand Fighter Pilots' Museum** 𝕽𝕽𝕽 , Skyshow Centre, Wanaka Air-port, 10km (6 miles) southwest of Wanaka (© **03/443-7010;** www.nzfpm.co.nz), is home to the largest collection of flyable World War II fighter planes in the Southern Hemisphere. You can investigate the airplanes, interactive displays, film footage, and scale model aircraft. The Skyshow Centre is also home to a collection of alpine fighter aircraft, Biplane Adventures, Tandem Skydive, Wanaka Helicopters, Aspiring Air, and the Flight Deck Café. Admission is NZ$8 (US$5.60) for adults, NZ$4 (US$2.80) for children, and NZ$20 (US$14) per family. It's open daily from 9am to 4pm (till 6pm Dec 27–Jan 27).

Take a break at **Wanaka Beerworks** 𝕽𝕽, State Highway 6 (© **0800/273-9754** in NZ, or 03/443-1865; www.wanakabeerworks.co.nz), which is wedged between the two museums. This little boutique brewery with a cozy bar and tasting room is open from 9am until 5pm daily (tours and tastings 2pm daily).

Rippon Vineyard 𝕽𝕽𝕽 , Mount Aspiring Road (© **03/443-8084;** www.rippon. co.nz), is run by Rolfe and Lois Mills, pioneer grape-growers in Central Otago, and their vineyard location overlooking Lake Wanaka is simply stunning. It's open for tast-ings (NZ$5/US$3.50) and sales December through April, daily from 11:30am to 5pm; and July through November, daily from 1:30 to 4:30pm.

ORGANIZED TOURS

For rugged outdoor fun, **Criffel Peak Safaris** 𝕽𝕽𝕽 (© **0800/102-122** in NZ, or 03/443-1711; www.criffelpeaksafaris.com) offers tours on four-wheel all-terrain quad bikes priced from around NZ$125 (US$88) for a 2-hour tour. You must be at least 16 and have a car driver's license. **Wanaka Sightseeing** (© **03/443-1855;** www. wanakasightseeing.co.nz; www.lordoftheringstours.co.nz), offers wine, walking, and lifestyle tours, plus a *Lord of the Rings* tour for NZ$280 to NZ$290 (US$196–US$203) per person. Camera buffs will enjoy an outing with photographer and nat-uralist, Gilber van Reenen of **Clean Green Photo Nature Tours,** Ballantyne Road,

---

Moments The Big Screen

Get real local flavor at **Cinema Paradiso** 𝕽𝕽𝕽 , 1 Ardmore St. (© **03/443-1505;** www.paradiso.net.nz), Wanaka's only movie theater. It's quite possibly the wackiest place you'll ever experience. Seats take the form of old sofas and cush-ions in the aisles, and a Morris Minor car has been installed for a drive-in feel. You'll get a personalized, off-the-wall introduction from the owner, and there's a 30-minute intermission for quick cafe meals—and yes, they will hold the movie until you're finished eating. Showtimes are at 6 and 8:30pm daily; admis-sion is NZ$12 (US$8.40) for adults, NZ$8 (US$5.60) for children.

Wanaka (© 03/443-7951; www.cleangreen.co nz), who will tailor a photographic expedition to suit your interests. You'll pay from NZ$70 (US$49) per person.

OUTDOOR PURSUITS

CANYONING   Contact **Deep Canyon Experience** (© 03/443-7922; www.deep canyon.co.nz), pioneers of the sport in New Zealand. You'll get a tobogganing, abseiling, and swimming adventure guaranteed to thrill. The 7½-hour adventure costs around NZ$195 (US$137), which includes lunch. They operate November through April and offer a range of day trips from NZ$195 to NZ$660 (US$137–US$462) per person.

CLIMBING   There's a lot of excellent, stable climbing in the area. **Wanaka Rock Climbing & Abseil Adventures,** 7 Apollo Place St. (© 03/443-6411; www.wanaka rock.co.nz), can introduce you to all the best places. You'll pay from NZ$99 (US$69) for a range of options.

ECORAFTING   This is an easy adventure for less active people. It's all about learning as you paddle, and guides will enlighten you about flora and fauna along the way. From September to April, **Pioneer Rafting** 𝕽𝕽 (© 03/443-1246; ecoraft@xtra.co.nz) conducts half- and full-day excursions down the Upper Clutha. This is not whitewater rafting, and the trip is suitable for anyone from ages 8 to 80. A half-day trip costs NZ$115 (US$81) for adults and NZ$75 (US$53) for children.

FISHING   Opportunities abound in the Wanaka area, with plenty of guides operating on the rivers and lakes. **Lakeland Adventures** (© 03/443-7495; www.lakeland adventures.co.nz) charges from around NZ$250 (US$175) for guided trout fishing for three people. **Southern Lakes Fishing Safaris** (©/fax 03/443-9121; www.southern lakesfishing.co.nz) specializes in fly-fishing for all levels of experience and charges from NZ$580 (US$406) for a full day for one to two people.

FLYING   **Aspiring Air** (© 0800/100-943 in NZ, or 03/443-7943; www.nz-flights. com) has a variety of scenic flights in the Mount Aspiring area from NZ$140 (US$98) per person. Their Milford Sound flight with included boat cruise costs around NZ$365 (US$256) for adults and NZ$225 (US$158) for children. **Aspiring Helicopters** (© 03/443-4000; www.alpineheli.co.nz), can give you a 20-minute scenic flight over Wanaka for around NZ$150 (US$105) per person, or why not treat yourself to their alpine picnic flight—a 2-hour adventure with gourmet treats for NZ$270 (US$189) per person.

GOLF   **Wanaka Golf Club,** Ballantyne Road, Wanaka (© 03/443-7888; www. wanakagolf.co.nz), is a challenging 18-hole course with astounding views. There is a well-stocked pro shop and it costs NZ$50 (US$35) for 18 holes, or NZ$30 (US$21) for 9 holes.

HORSE TREKKING   By far the best outfitter is **Backcountry Saddle Expeditions** 𝕽𝕽, 25km (16 miles) south of Wanaka on State Highway 89 (© 03/443-8151; www.ridenz.com), which has 2-hour treks for around NZ$65 (US$46). A full-day trek costs NZ$180 (US$126) per person. Transport is available from Wanaka at a cost of NZ$5 (US$3.50) per person.

JET-BOATING   The best jet-boating is with **Wilkin River Jets** 𝕽𝕽𝕽, State Highway 6, Makarora (©/fax 03/443-8351; www.wilkinriverjets.co.nz), which is between Fox Glacier and Wanaka. Locals say it's better than the much-lauded Dart River experience at Glenorchy, near Queenstown. Priced around NZ$75 (US$53), it's also cheaper and offers a mix of thrill riding and the softer approach, so you get a good feel for this remote region. They also offer combos that include a helicopter flight, bush walk, and river jet from NZ$280 (US$196) per person. **Clutha River Jet,** Lakeland Adventures, 100 Ardmore St., Wanaka (© 03/443-7495; www.lakelandadventures.co.nz), is conveniently placed on the lakefront and will spin you across the lake to enter the mighty Clutha River. It's a fast-paced, 6-minute adventure.

KAYAKING **Alpine Kayak Guides,** 11 Mount Iron Dr. (© 03/443-9023; www.alpinekayaks.co.nz), has half- and full-day trips on three rivers, ranging in difficulty from beginner to experienced. Trips last 8 hours and run daily from October to April. Costs start at NZ$95 (US$67) and include equipment, lessons, and lunch. You can rent kayaks for a lake paddle from **Lakeland Adventures** (© 03/443-7495), for NZ$20 to NZ$40 (US$14–US$28) per hour.

MOUNTAIN BIKING The Department of Conservation's leaflet on bike trails in the Wanaka area is available from its office at Ardmore Street and Ballantyne Road (© 03/443-7660). Mountain bikes can be rented from **Racer's Edge/Mountain Bikes Unlimited,** 99 Ardmore St. (© 03/443-7882; www.racersedge.co.nz), for NZ$45 (US$32) per day. **Alpine & Heli Mountain Biking** (© 03/443-8943; www.mountainbiking.co.nz) conducts guided half- or full-day, overnight, and heli-biking trips from November through April. The half-day trips cost around NZ$150 (US$105) and are designed for the not-so-fit biker who likes the idea of a 90% down-hill ride. Good bikes are also available from **Lakeland Adventures,** next door to the information center (© 03/443-7495), for NZ$10 (US$7) per hour, and there are excellent biking tracks around the lake.

SKIING **Cardrona Ski Field** is 40 minutes from Wanaka on State Highway 89. The more challenging **Treble Cone Ski Field** is also 40 minutes away. In addition, you'll find cross-country skiing and heli-skiing in the Harris Mountains. And for Nordic skiing, head to the **Waiorau Nordic Field,** in the Cardrona Valley. For further information on all ski fields in this area, see chapter 3.

WALKING Walking opportunities in Mount Aspiring National Park vary from easy strolls through lowland forest to tramps on mountain tracks that may take several days. Brochures and information can be obtained from the Department of Conservation office. **Edgewater Adventures,** 59A Brownston St. (© 03/443-8422; www.adventure.net.nz), has a wide range of guided half- and multiday treks priced from NZ$100 (US$70) per person. At **Diamond Lake,** 20 minutes from town, you'll find the Diamond Lake and Rocky Mountain Track, which takes 1½ hours from the car park to the summit. For a more remote walk, call **Siberia Experience** ⊛⊛⊛ (© 0800/345-666 in NZ, or 03/443-8666; www.siberiaexperience.co.nz), offering a combo of scenic flight, jet boat, and a 3-hour walk in remote beech forests for NZ$235 (US$165) for adults and NZ$190 (US$133) for children. Their guided experiences are unique and some of the best in the region. Just make sure you take plenty of insect repellent to keep the notoriously greedy sand flies at bay! Fit, adventurous travelers might like to be tested by a remote wilderness experience with **Wild Walks** ⊛⊛, 10a Tenby St., Wanaka (© 03/443-4476; www.wildwalks.co.nz). Their specialist mountain guides take just five people maximum into remote backcountry locations. Overnight trips range in price from NZ$600 to NZ$1,400 (US$420–US$980).

But if all you really want is a light amble, follow my footsteps around the lovely, tree-covered tracks of the lake. Start at the information center and simply follow your nose. Even if you don't exert yourself, it will leave your conscience clear for dinner.

WHERE TO STAY

If you're looking for accommodations with style and character, you'll definitely find them in the Wanaka area. There has been a lot of development in the township itself, especially around the lake edge and quality lodges and bed-and-breakfasts are increasing in numbers. You won't be short of a good stop here but you will need to book well ahead if you're planning to stay between November and March. Wanaka is a favorite playground for New Zealanders.

All rates quoted include the 12.5% GST and free off-street parking unless otherwise noted.

VERY EXPENSIVE

Whare Kea Lodge ★★★ *Finds*   Tucked away from the public eye, Whare Kea offers style and luxury at its most sublime. Walk through the door and you'll be overwhelmed by one of the most remarkable residential views in the country. This monster of a house has huge bedrooms with verandas, deep bathtubs, dual-sided showers, and top-quality furnishings. A classy hideaway for those who want to indulge.

Mount Aspiring Rd., P.O. Box 115, Wanaka. ✆ **03/443-1400**. Fax 03/443-9200. www.wharekealodge.com. 6 units. NZ$1,000 (US$700) deluxe; NZ$1,400 (US$980) master suite. Long-stay and off-peak rates available. Rates include breakfast, dinner, and use of all facilities. AE, DC, MC, V. Follow signs on Mount Aspiring Rd., 5 min. west of Wanaka township. No children under 14. **Amenities:** Bar; Jacuzzi; game room; organized summer and winter activities w/professional guides; secretarial services; massage; laundry service; nonsmoking rooms; helipad. *In room:* TV, dataport, minibar, fridge, coffeemaker, hair dryer, iron.

EXPENSIVE

Wanaka Stonehouse ★★, 21 Sargood Dr., Wanaka (✆ **03/443-1933;** www.wanaka stonehouse.co.nz), now under new ownership, is a quietly residential B&B that has gone upmarket with an extensive revamp of facilities. The four en-suite rooms are light and airy with an alpine feel; a bigger ground-floor suite is ideal for families. There's a Jacuzzi and sauna to help you unwind at the end of the day. Prices range from NZ$345 to NZ$395 (US$242–US$277).

Lakeside Apartments ★★ *Value*   There's no question in my mind that the opening of these centrally located lakeside apartments has introduced a new level of classy, value-for-money accommodations to Wanaka. All apartments have three bedrooms, but you can take one or two bedrooms if you prefer a cheaper option and still get two big bathrooms, a fabulous modern kitchen, and tons of space. Well appointed, right beside some of the town's best eateries, and just a stroll to the water, they're hard to beat. The penthouses are vast and have gigantic lakeview terraces on the top level.

9 Lakeside Rd., Wanaka. ✆ **0800/002211** in NZ, or 03/443-0188. Fax 03/443-0189. www.lakesidewanaka.co.nz. 63 units. NZ$395–NZ$595 (US$277–US$417) superior; NZ$445–NZ$645 (US$312–US$452) deluxe; NZ$495–NZ$695 (US$347–US$487) premier; NZ$695–NZ$895 (US$487–US$627) penthouse. Long-stay, off-peak, and special deals available. AE, DC, MC, V. **Amenities:** Heated outdoor pool; nearby golf course; 2 Jacuzzis; tour bookings; bike rentals; car rentals; business center; secretarial services; laundry in each apt; nonsmoking rooms. *In room:* TV/DVD/CD, dataport, kitchen, fridge, coffeemaker, hair dryer, iron.

Minaret Lodge ★★★ *Finds*   Open since 2002, this smart B&B option is full of surprises (and that includes a *Lord of the Rings* room), and exceeds all expectations. The dining and living room facilities are contained within a stylishly renovated home in a peaceful residential neighborhood, and three purpose-built chalets are set in a .8-hectare (2-acre) garden with an attractive spa and sauna complex a short stroll across the lawn. Once you're inside the chalets, you'll relax instantly. Beds are big and bathrooms are well appointed. If you want more space, take the suite chalet, which includes a tastefully finished lounge and en suite with both bathtub and shower. There is perhaps a greater sense of privacy here than at other similarly priced B&B options in Wanaka.

34 Eely Point Rd., Wanaka. © **03/443-1856.** Fax 03/443-1856. www.minaretlodge.co.nz. 5 units. NZ$350–NZ$500 (US$245–US$350). MC, V. Rates include predinner drinks and full gourmet breakfast. Off-peak rates available. No children under 12. **Amenities:** Tennis court; Jacuzzi; sauna; bike rentals; car rentals; courtesy car by arrangement; some business services; laundry service; same-day dry cleaning; nonsmoking rooms. *In room:* A/C, TV/DVD/CD, fax, dataport, fridge, coffeemaker, hair dryer, iron, safe.

River Run *Value* When you see the facilities at River Run, you'll know you've got one of the best lodge deals in the country. John Pawson and Meg Taylor have built with imagination and flair: Everything smacks of originality and every room is arranged with comfort in mind, with generous beds, fine linens, and superb marble bathrooms. John and Meg are outdoor types who love mountaineering and climbing, and John also tends their 170-hectare (420-acre) mixed farm that borders the Clutha River. River Run is a heavily hosted experience and Meg is a superb chef.

Halliday Rd., RD2, Wanaka. © **03/443-9049.** Fax 03/443-8454. www.riverrun.co.nz. 5 units. NZ$320–NZ$460 (US$224–US$322). Exclusive use of lodge NZ$1,800 (US$1,260) per night, minimum 5 nights. Dinner NZ$80 (US$56) per person. Winter packages available during ski season. AE, DC, MC, V. 6-min. drive east of central Wanaka. Turn off St. Hwy. 6 to Halliday Rd.; continue to stone gates and drive through to River Run. No children under 12. **Amenities:** Bar; outdoor Jacuzzi; free bikes; tour bookings; massage; laundry service; nonsmoking rooms. *In room:* TV/VCR, dataport, hair dryer.

MODERATE

Edgewater Resort *Value* Situated right on the shores of Lake Wanaka, Edgewater is a favorite with New Zealanders who like resort-style accommodations. There's a welcoming atmosphere here that is hard to beat and style tends toward that of a high-country fishing lodge. All units, which have been extensively upgraded recently, offer balconies or terraces. In short, it's a friendly, comfortable 18-year-old development that has aged well and oozes Kiwi atmosphere. If you like space, go for the great-value one-bedroom suites, which have bigger bathrooms with double baths.

Sargood Dr., P.O. Box 61, Wanaka. © **0800/108-311** in NZ, or 03/443-8311. Fax 03/443-8323. www.edgewater.co.nz. 104 units. NZ$220 (US$154) hotel room; NZ$325 (US$228) 1-bedroom suite; NZ$495 (US$347) 2-bedroom apt. Package deals available. AE, DC, MC, V. A 20-min. stroll to town center. **Amenities:** Sargoods Restaurant; bar; 9-hole putting green; 2 all-weather tennis courts; Jacuzzi; sauna; playground; concierge; room service; massage; babysitting; laundry facilities in suites; laundry service; Wanaka Airport transfers on request; nonsmoking rooms. *In room:* TV, dataport, minibar on request, fridge, coffeemaker, hair dryer, iron.

Mountain Range *Finds* If you want breathtaking views of three mountain ranges, peace and quiet, and luxurious rooms with beautiful bathrooms, Mountain Range delivers. Stuart Pinfold and Melanie Laaper are terrific young hosts—they've been recommended by many—and their rooms are delicious. They're different than River Run, but there's that same sense of understated luxury and comfort that makes them one of my favorite Wanaka spots. Ask for the McKerrow room if you want a giant bathtub, or the loft room for coziness and great views.

Heritage Park, Cardrona Valley Rd., Wanaka. © **03/443-7400.** Fax 03/443-7450. www.mountainrange.co.nz. 7 units. NZ$265–NZ$290 (US$186–US$203). Long-stay, off-peak, and special deals available. Rates include breakfast. MC, V.

Just off Cardona Valley Rd., 2km (1¼ miles) outside Wanaka. No children under 12. **Amenities:** Nearby golf course; courtesy transport to Wanaka; secretarial services; laundry service; nonsmoking rooms; on-call doctor/dentist. *In room:* Dataport, hair dryer.

Oakridge Pool & Spa Resort ☆☆ (Value)

New owners have taken this establishment and shaken it by the scruff of the neck, turning it into a much more upmarket stay. Extensive new developments include stylish, modern apartments; a new lodge building with a popular restaurant and a fabulous pool complex; and a day spa that will set you drooling. All up, it's a great value location and the one-bedroom apartments (some up, some down) are the best.

Corner of Cardona Valley Rd. and Studholme Rd. (℃) **0800/869-262** in NZ, or 03/443-7707. Fax 03/443-7750. www. oakridge.co.nz. 77 units. From NZ$140–NZ$180 (US$98–US$126) resort room; NZ$200 (US$140) studio; NZ$240 (US$168) 1-bedroom apt; NZ$320 (US$224) 2-bedroom apt; NZ$25 (US$18) each extra person. Long-stay rates and special packages available. AE, DC, MC, V. **Amenities:** Restaurant (The Hub [contemporary New Zealand]); bar; 2 outdoor heated pools; nearby golf course; day spa beauty treatments; 7 Jacuzzis; sauna; children's activity program; tour bookings; car rentals; courtesy transport to Wanaka; limited room service; massage; babysitting; laundry facilities in apts; laundry service; dry cleaning; nonsmoking rooms; on-call doctor/dentist; airport transfers; access for travelers w/disabilities. *In room:* TV/DVD, dataport, kitchen or kitchenette, fridge, coffeemaker, hair dryer, iron.

Te Wanaka Lodge ☆☆

Passionate Australian skiers Graeme and Andy Oxley took over Te Wanaka in 2000. Their lodge and cottage have terrific living rooms with a family feel, and the dining-room table is just about big enough to ski down. Every unit is well designed, with balconies, queen-size or twin beds, and showers (some with TVs as well). Although the bathrooms are a bit small, it's not a big deal when there are other comforts to enjoy.

23 Brownston St., Wanaka. (℃) **0800/926-252** in NZ, or 03/443-9224. Fax 03/443-9246. www.tewanaka.co.nz. 13 units, 1 cottage. From NZ$180–NZ$190 (US$126–US$133) lodge; NZ$195–NZ$205 (US$137–US$144) cottage. Rates include breakfast and transfers to bus. Long-stay and off-peak rates available. AE, MC, V. No children under 12. **Amenities:** Bar; nearby golf course; outdoor Jacuzzi; bike rentals; limited business facilities; massage; laundry service; nonsmoking rooms. *In room:* TV in some rooms, dataport, fridge in cottage, hair dryer.

Wanaka Springs ☆☆

Another lovely addition in 2000 and a NZ Tourism Award finalist, Wanaka Springs is the purpose-built lodge of Murray and Lyn Finn. Rooms here envelope you in warmth and rich color, and garden views (with decks) add a restful quality. Bathrooms are big and modern, and the main living spaces are lovely. At the end of a hard day, there's nothing better than relaxing in their eight-seater Jacuzzi in the garden.

21 Warren St. (℃) **03/443-8421.** Fax 03/443-8429. www.wanakasprings.com. 8 units. NZ$295–NZ$330 (US$207–US$231). Rates include breakfast. Long-stay rates negotiable. MC, V. 3 min. from town. **Amenities:** Nearby golf course; nearby gym; Jacuzzi; tour bookings; laundry service; nonsmoking rooms. *In room:* Dataport, coffeemaker, hair dryer.

INEXPENSIVE

The Purple Cow Backpackers, 94 Brownston St., P.O. Box 367, Wanaka ((℃) **0800/ 772-277** in NZ, or 03/443-1880; www.purplecow.co.nz), is frequented by budget-minded travelers from throughout the world. It's just a step or two from town and has dorm beds from NZ$22 (US$15) per person and doubles for NZ$64 (US$45).

WHERE TO DINE

There are plenty of places to eat in Wanaka. **Sargoods Restaurant** ☆☆, Edgewater Resort ((℃) **03/443-8311**), serves remarkably good international cuisine from an a la carte menu with main courses priced from around NZ$25 to NZ$32 (US$18–US$22). **The Hub** ☆☆, Oakridge Spa Resort ((℃) **03/443-7707**), is another with a lovely environment and an excellent, more-European-styled menu. It's more casual than Sargoods. **Bombay Palace** 🐧🐧, upstairs, Pembroke Mall (✆ **03/443-6086**), has the best Indian food and curries in town. The **Doughbin Bakery,** on the lakefront (✆ **03/443-7290**), is the best place to stock up on picnic fare, and **Tuatara Pizza Co.,** 72 Ardmore St. (✆ **03/443-8186**), is definitely *it* for pizzas. If you want to unwind before dinner, go to the bar above Relishes, **Apartment One** 🐧🐧, 99 Ardmore St. (✆ **03/443-4911**), accessed behind the building. It has great cocktails that you can enjoy on a big balcony.

Ambrosia Restaurant 🐧🐧🐧 INTERNATIONAL/PACIFIC RIM

A new team has taken over the town's leading culinary light, high on a hill overlooking town. Once you've tried the prosciutto-wrapped chicken breast, beef filet, or pan-seared salmon—with tasters and sorbets between courses—you'll appreciate why this is one of the best and most charmingly intimate eateries in Wanaka.

76 Golf Course Rd. ✆ 03/443-1255. Reservations required. Main courses NZ$26–NZ$32 (US$18–US$22). AE, DC, MC, V. Dec–Mar Fri–Sun noon–2pm; year-round Tues–Sun from 6pm.

Café Fe 🐧🐧 CAFE/NEW ZEALAND

Set on the edge of a new housing area just out of town, this lovely, semirural spot has adopted simple, barnlike architecture. As the sun beams in throughout the day, you can enjoy delicious breakfasts, light lunches, or just excellent coffee and perhaps a coconut and macadamia muffin. Anyone who's anyone is seen here sooner or later.

Corner of Orchard Rd. and Cardrona Rd. ✆ 03/443-4683. Reservations advised for lunch. Main courses NZ$15–NZ$22 (US$11–US$15). AE, DC, MC, V. Daily 7:30am–5pm.

Café Gusto 🐧🐧 MODERN NEW ZEALAND

Right next to Lakeside Apartments under the very popular Missy's Kitchen, Gusto draws you in with bright yellow furniture on a sunny patio overlooking the lake. The most "city" in style of the Wanaka eateries, it has delicious lunch and casual evening dining selections: aubergine and Parmesan risotto, Moroccan spiced lamb backstraps on couscous, venison burgers, and Greek lamb salad, to name a few. Colorful, bright, and popular with locals and visitors alike, it's a great place to start.

1 Lakeside Dr. ✆ 03/443-6639. Main courses NZ$18–NZ$26 (US$13–US$18). AE, MC, V. Daily 8am–late.

Kai Whakapai Café & Bar 🐧🐧 *Value* NEW ZEALAND/CAFE

The most visible and definitely the most popular of Wanaka's casual cafes, this one is oozing with smiles and good food at sensible prices. Quite apart from the divine pizzas, croissants, and fresh pastas, much of it with a vegetarian slant, this place is expert at promoting the pleasures of pie eating. You can pig out on chocolate, quince, coconut, boysenberry, apple, or banana cream pie.

Lakefront, Wanaka. ✆ 03/443-7795. Main courses NZ$15–NZ$30 (US$11–US$21). AE, DC, MC, V. Daily 7am–late.

Missy's Kitchen 🐧🐧🐧 PACIFIC RIM

Always broad in its focus, Pacific Rim cuisine comes peppered with a few international touches at this extremely popular Wanaka restaurant. Palm-sugared quail, for instance, is not exactly of Pacific origin, but you won't be complaining when you sink your teeth into it. Casual by day and moody by night, with a menu that combines a wealth of interesting flavors and a big wine list, Missy's is sure to endure. It has the best wine list in Wanaka and probably the most professional service.

Level 1, 80 Ardmore St. ✆ 03/443-5099. Reservations recommended. Main courses NZ$23–NZ$32 (US$18–US$22). AE, MC, V. Daily 6pm–late (Sat–Sun from 10am).

Relishes Café 🐟🐟 INTERNATIONAL   Relishes has been a top spot for years and I've had some of my nicest fish meals here. If you need proof of popularity, people are turned away in droves for lack of space. It's a simple, country-style interior, nothing flashy, but the baked blue cod served with hazelnut and lemon butter left a memorable impression. Roasted duck breast with mushroom ragout and wilted spinach sounded just as appetizing.

1/99 Ardmore St., Wanaka. 📞 **03/443-9018.** Reservations recommended. Main courses NZ$22–NZ$30 (US$15–US$21). AE, MC, V. Daily 6pm–late.

Te Tawara o Wanaka 🐟🐟 MODERN NEW ZEALAND   Take the successful barnlike formula of sister property Café Fe and replicate it in a stylish, evening restaurant, and you have a winner. The focus is on local produce and dishes like roast belly pork with caramelized winter pears, or chargrilled venison with white polenta and mustard-seed glaze will have you begging for more. Service is professional and attentive and the ambience pleasing.

Corner of Orchard Rd. and Cardona Rd. 📞 **03/443-4411.** Reservations recommended. Main courses NZ$25–NZ$32 (US$18–US$22). AE, DC, MC, V. Tues–Sat 5pm–late.

White House Bar & Café 🐟🐟 MEDITERRANEAN/MIDDLE EASTERN   Peter Scott is a man of forthright ideas, and his restaurant philosophy is built on "underwaiting"—no fuss, no flap. He's seriously into understatement, which doesn't always go down well with the locals, but you'll be hard-pressed to find fault with the food. Beetroot, chargrilled vegetables, and polenta salad enjoyed in a charming Greek villa–style environment is not a bad way to kill time. Middle Eastern spiced chicken, calamari, and mussels are all here to be enjoyed, inside or outside. For a civilized, low-key restaurant with a big fireplace and no pretensions, you shouldn't miss the White House.

33 Dunmore St., Wanaka. 📞 **03/443-9595.** Reservations recommended. Main courses NZ$18–NZ$28 (US$13–US$20). MC, V. Daily 11am–11pm.

EN ROUTE TO MOUNT COOK

If you plan to drive to Mount Cook from Wanaka, expect to get there in 2½ hours on excellent roads. Rejoin State Highway 6 and travel south to Highway 6A, which links you to State Highway 8. From Queenstown, the trip to Mount Cook takes about 4 hours.

2 Mount Cook ⭐

263km (163 miles) NE of Queenstown; 331km (205 miles) SW of Christchurch

Mount Cook Village is known throughout the world for its alpine beauty and remoteness. It sits within the 70,000 hectares (173,000 acres) of **Mount Cook National Park,** some 753m (2,470 ft.) above sea level and surrounded by 140 peaks over 2,100m (6,888 ft.) high, 22 of which are over 3,000m (9,840 ft.). Most famous of all is **Aoraki–Mount Cook,** which rises 3,695m (12,120 ft.) into the sky. *Aoraki* means "cloud piercer" in Maori. A third of the park is permanent snow and ice, and the **Tasman Glacier,** at 29km (18 miles) long and 3km (2 miles) wide, is the longest known glacier outside arctic regions. More difficult to get onto than Fox or Franz Josef glaciers, it's still accessible for exhilarating downhill skiing.

    In recent years, Mount Cook Village has suffered a reputation for being rather shabby and expensive, but major developments from 2001 have brought forth big improvements.

Tips Be Prepared

If you're driving up to Mount Cook Village during winter, make sure you have antifreeze fluid in your car radiator.

ESSENTIALS

GETTING THERE   Air New Zealand Link (© 0800/737-000 in NZ) has regular flights to Mount Cook from Christchurch, Queenstown, and Te Anau. There is a daily **InterCity** (© 03/379-9020) link between Mount Cook and Christchurch, Queenstown, and Timaru. **The Cook Connection,** Twizel (© 0800/266-526 in NZ; www.cookconnect.co.nz), offers daily trips from Lake Tekapo and Twizel to Mount Cook from October through May between 8am and 8pm. By car, Mount Cook is reached via State Highway 80 and great care should be taken on all roads in the area during autumn and winter when surfaces become icy and slippery. Twizel is 45 minutes from Mount Cook World Heritage Park and is the base for a number of tourism businesses operating in the Mount Cook area.

ORIENTATION   A T-intersection at the end of the highway marks the entrance to Mount Cook Village. Turn left and you'll pass Glencoe Lodge, a modern motor hotel, the youth hostel, Alpine Guides Mountain Shop, and finally the Aoraki–Mount Cook National Park Visitor Centre. Turn right at the intersection and you'll pass Mount Cook Chalets before reaching the peak-roofed, internationally famous Hermitage Hotel, which now includes a modest grocery store and post office.

VISITOR INFORMATION   The **Aoraki–Mount Cook Visitor Centre,** Bowen Drive, P.O. Box 5, Mount Cook Village (© 03/435-1186; fax 03/435-1080; www.doc.govt.nz), is open daily from 8:30am to 6pm in summer and 8:30am to 5pm in winter (closed Dec 25). Department of Conservation officers can give you the latest information on weather, track, and road conditions. Trampers and mountaineers must check in and sign the intentions register before entering the park. Officers can also fill you in on high-altitude huts, hut passes, picnic grounds, and recommended walks in the area.

The **Lake Pukaki Visitor Centre,** State Highway 8, Pukaki (© 03/435-3280; fax 03/435-3283; www.mtcook.org.nz), is another good resource. **Alpine Guides,** Main Road, Mount Cook (© 03/435-1834; fax 03/435-1898; www.alpineguides.co.nz or www.heliskiing.co.nz), can also provide a wealth of information on alpine activities, schedules, and fees. For information on Mount Cook ski areas, connect to **www.nzski.com**.

EXPLORING THE AREA

Clearly, the mountains are the main attraction here. The Mount Cook area is also the access point for the beautiful **Tasman Glacier.** If you missed the scenic glacier flights at Fox and Franz Josef, you'll have another chance here. Go with award-winning **Air Safaris** ✸✸ (© 0800/806-880 in NZ, or 03/680-6880; www.airsafaris.co.nz). Its 50-minute Grand Traverse leaves from Lake Tekapo and flies over the McKenzie Basin and lakes, around Mount Cook, over 12 major glaciers, across the Main Divide to the Westland World Heritage National Parks, to the West Coast Glaciers, and back to Lake Tekapo. This stunning flight costs from NZ$250 (US$175) for adults and NZ$170 (US$119) for children. **Mount Cook Ski Planes,** Mount Cook Airport

(℗ **0800/800-702** in NZ, or 03/430-8034; www.mtcookskiplanes.com), is the only company licensed to land scenic flights on Tasman Glacier and in Mount Cook National Park. Their stunning fixed-wing flights cost from NZ$210 to NZ$410 (US$147–US$287).

The Helicopter Line (℗ **0800/650-651** in NZ, or 03/435-1801; www.helicopter. co.nz) has several tours, such as the Alpine Explorer, a 30-minute flight which covers Mount Cook, the Main Divide, and Tasman Glacier, plus a snow landing, for around NZ$280 (US$196) per person. All helicopter operations in the Mount Cook area are based at Glentanner Helicopter Base, 15 minutes from Mount Cook Village. All fixed-wing craft operate from Mount Cook Airport.

Skiers will head for the Tasman Glacier during the June-to-October season, but know in advance that skiing here is neither cheap nor for novices. Skiing on the glaciers involves two runs of about 11km (7 miles) each, with ski planes returning you to the top after the first run and flying you out at the end of the day. The glacier is perfect for intermediate-grade skiers; it's a long distance, but not steep. The full-day excursion costs from NZ$650 (US$455) and can be booked through **Alpine Guides** (℗ **03/435-1834;** www.alpineguides.co.nz), which also rents ski and climbing equipment and can organize guides to take you **mountain climbing** as well.

If you prefer something a little less expensive, park conservation offices can furnish a map of easy walks, which take anywhere from half an hour to half a day—you'll be able to commune with Mother Nature to your heart's content.

Discovery Tours, 10 Jollie Rd., Twizel (℗ **0800/213-868** in NZ, or 03/425-0114; www.discoverytours.co.nz), has several guided activities including walks, 4WD excursions, mountain biking, fishing, heli-biking, farm visits, and a *Lord of the Rings* tour, starting from NZ$30 (US$21) per person. **Glacier Explorers** 𝔯𝔯𝔯 , Mount Cook Village (℗ **03/435-1077;** www.glacierexplorers.com), can take you on an unbelievable 3-hour boat ride on Tasman Glacier Lake for NZ$105 (US$74) for adults and NZ$50 (US$35) for children. These tours only operate from October through May (providing the lake is not frozen), and they include a 15-minute drive followed by a 30-minute walk to the lake.

WHERE TO STAY & DINE

Almost all of the accommodations in Mount Cook Village are owned by the same company, so you'll have minimal bargaining power, but call before you arrive as there are daily specials available, especially at the **Hermitage Hotel, Glencoe Motels and Chalets,** Terrace Road (℗ **0800/686-800** in NZ, or 03/435-1809; www.mountcook.com). This old faithful fell from grace for a few years, but after a NZ$15-million (US$11-million) refurbishment, begun in 2001, it is a much better bet than it used to be. Sixty new rooms were added along with a complete overhaul of all public spaces. Since then, all motels and chalets have also been completely renovated. It has rates of NZ$550 to NZ$710 (US$385–US$497) including buffet dinner and breakfast, and NZ$800 to NZ$880 (US$560–US$616) in the Aoraki Wing, including four-course dinner and breakfast; but don't forget those specials. The on-site **Panorama Restaurant** has lost its stuffy edge and now offers nice, comfortable dining.

Glencoe Lodge (℗ **03/435-1809;** fax 03/435-1879), has 57 rooms from NZ$410 (US$287), including breakfast. Motel studios run NZ$225 to NZ$280 (US$158–US$196) and chalets NZ$220 to NZ$240 (US$154–US$168), including breakfast. Glencoe is home to **Chamois Bar & Lounge,** which has great pub food and is favored by the locals for its lively atmosphere.

The **Mount Cook YHA Hostel,** Bowen Drive and Kitchener Avenue (© **0800/ 278-299** in NZ, or 03/435-1820; www.yha.co.nz), has 70 beds in 17 rooms, including six twins and two doubles. The cost is NZ$25 (US$18) per dorm bed, NZ$64 (US$45) for a twin or a double. It has the best shop in the village, plus a sauna, video library, TV lounge, luggage lockers, and a ski drying room. Bookings are essential from November to April.

Camping and **caravanning** are permitted in Mount Cook National Park at designated sites; water and toilets are available. If you use these facilities, remember that fires are prohibited within park boundaries. Check with the park visitor center for locations and conditions. Hikers and mountaineers have the use of 12 huts in the park, which have bunks and emergency radios. Only the Mueller Hut is within easy reach of the casual tramper. The others are at high altitudes and you need to be an experienced, expert climber to reach them. Fees for overnight use of the huts is about NZ$20 (US$14) per person, and arrangements must be made at the National Park Visitor Centre.

Rather than staying in Mount Cook Village itself, you might prefer to spend the night in one of the surrounding towns: Twizel, Fairlie, Tekapo, Omarama, and Kurow are all within a 2-hour drive and have motels, B&Bs, and home stays aplenty.

EN ROUTE TO QUEENSTOWN

State Highway 6 is good traveling all the way from Wanaka to Queenstown; the trip takes around 1½ hours. You'll drive around the edge of Lake Dunstan, which was formed behind the Clyde Dam. Bypassing Cromwell township, you then travel through the stone fruit orchards of the Cromwell area. As an introduction to the rapidly expanding wine industry in this area, stop at **The Big Picture** ✰✰✰ , State Highway 6, Cromwell (© **03/445-4052;** www.wineadventure.co.nz). It has an excellent interactive wine film and tasting auditorium, a good cafe and restaurant, and a tasty selection of goodies from the area's wineries and boutique culinary producers. It's past the Cromwell turnoff on the left and open daily from 9am until 8pm. After passing through the Kawarau River Gorge, you come into Gibbston Valley and on into Queenstown.

You could also go to Queenstown via the Crown Range. You'll be rewarded by spectacular views and a slightly shorter travel time than on the State Highway 6 route.

3 Queenstown ✰✰✰

404km (250 miles) SW of Franz Josef; 263km (163 miles) SW of Mount Cook; 117km (73 miles) S of Wanaka; 172km (107 miles) NE of Te Anau

Queenstown has over 1 million visitors a year, and you don't have to be a genius to figure out why. We've all heard the endless hype about it being the adventure capital of the world, and there are certainly enough crazy activities here to challenge the strongest, but Queenstown offers much more. Don't be put off by comments that it's touristy, un-Kiwi, crowded, and overrated. Sure, the streets are dominated by booking offices, but Queenstown has excellent shopping, restaurants, cafes, and clubs as well. And in many adrenalin-seeking ways, it encapsulates much of what New Zealand is about.

Famed for its international winter ski profile, Queenstown is also a brilliant spring, summer, and fall destination. This is when you get the best of its scenic beauty, easy walks, and endless opportunities to relax. Thrill seeking may be touted as the major attraction, but you can just as easily go fishing, golfing, gold panning, wine tasting, or boating. One thing is certain: You won't run out of things to do.

Central Queenstown

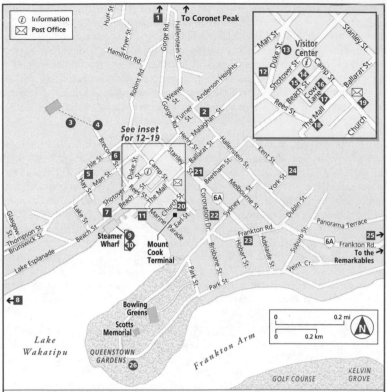

To Coronet Peak

(i) Information
☒ Post Office

Huff St.
Fryer St.
Hamilton Rd.
Gorge Rd.
Hallenstein St.
Robins Rd.
Weaver St.
Anderson Heights
Turner St.
Malaghan St.
Henry St.
Gorge Rd.
Brecon St.
Isle St.
Man St.
Hay St.
Lake St.
Shotover St.
Beach St.
Duke St.
Rees St.
Camp St.
Stanley
The Mall
Ballarat St.
Marine Parade
Church St.
Earl St.
Coronation Dr.
Beetham St.
Melbourne St.
Sydney St.
Hobart St.
Adelaide St.
Brisbane St.
Park St.
Kent St.
York St.
Dublin St.
Suburb St.
Veint. Cr.
Panorama Terrace
Frankton Rd.
To the Remarkables
6A
See inset for 12–19

Glasgow St.
Thompson St.
Brunswick St.
Lake Esplanade
Beach St.

Steamer Wharf
Mount Cook Terminal
Bowling Greens
Scotts Memorial

Lake Wakatipu

QUEENSTOWN GARDENS

Frankton Arm

GOLF COURSE
KELVIN GROVE

0   0.2 mi
0   0.2 km
N

Visitor Center
Man St.
Duke St.
Shotover St.
Beach St.
Rees St.
Cow Lane
The Mall
Camp St.
Stanley St.
Ballarat St.
Church

ACCOMMODATIONS ■
Aurum Hotel & Suites **21**
Balmoral House **24**
Brown's Boutique Hotel **5**
The Dairy **6**
Eichardt's Private Hotel **11**
Garden Court Suites & Apartments **23**
The Heritage **8**
Matakauri Lodge **8**
Millbrook Resort **1**
Mountvista Boutique Hotel **22**
Parkroyal Queenstown **7**
The Point **25**
Punatapu **8**
Queenstown House **2**
Queenstown YHA **8**
Shotover Lodge **1**
Sofitel Queenstown **12**
The Spire **20**
White Shadows Country Inn **1**

DINING ◆
Boardwalk Seafood Restaurant & Bar **10**
The Bunker **16**
Fishbone Bar & Grill **14**
Fraser's Bar & Grill **10**
Joe's Garage **19**
Old Man Rock **17**
Solera Vino **15**
Tatler **18**
Wai Waterfront Restaurant **10**

ATTRACTIONS ●
Department of Conservation Office **13**
Kiwi & Birdlife Park **4**
Queenstown Gardens **26**
Skyline Gondola **3**
Steamer Wharf/ TSS *Earnslaw* **9**

NORTH ISLAND
Auckland
SOUTH ISLAND
Wellington
Christchurch
Queenstown
Dunedin

It seems as though the whole world suddenly wants to live in Queenstown, and the town has experienced a phenomenal growth in development in the last 2 years. The inner commercial area has several new retail, office, and restaurant complexes, with more under construction and residential expansion is also in a boom phase. A whole new town is currently being considered for development near the airport at Frankton and if that goes ahead, it will provide many more retail, social, economic, and residential possibilities. New hotels and apartment complexes are also currently under construction and by mid-2006, several of these should be open for business.

ESSENTIALS

GETTING THERE & GETTING AROUND   By Plane   Queenstown is well serviced by **Air New Zealand National** and **Air New Zealand Link** (© 0800/ 737-000 in NZ) from such cities as Christchurch, Auckland, Wellington, and Rotorua. Air New Zealand also has a weekly flight from Sydney year-round and a weekly flight from Brisbane during ski season. The Air New Zealand Travel Centre is at 41 Shotover St., Queenstown (© 03/441-1900). **Qantas** (© 0800/808-767 in NZ) also has a weekly flight direct from Sydney and Brisbane in winter and **Origin Pacific** (© 0800/302-302 in NZ), flies in under a Qantas codeshare partnership.

Super Shuttle (© 03/442-3639; www.supershuttle.co.nz) will drop you off downtown for around NZ$15 (US$11) per person; the **Airport Bus** (© 03/442-6647) goes between the airport and major accommodations (every half-hour), for around NZ$5 (US$3.50). A **taxi** (© 03/442-7788) to the town center costs about NZ$20 (US$14).

By Coach (Bus)   InterCity (© 03/442-2800) runs between Queenstown and Christchurch, Dunedin, Fox Glacier, Franz Josef, Invercargill, Milford Sound, Mount Cook, Te Anau, and Wanaka. The InterCity depot is at the visitor center, Camp and Shotover streets (© 03/442-2800). **Kiwi Experience** (© 09/366-9830), **Magic Travellers** (© 09/358-5600), and **Backpackers Express** (© 03/442-9939) all service Queenstown as well.

The **Shopper Bus** (© 03/441-4471) provides transportation in and around town, to major accommodations, and to the airport from 6:45am to 11:15pm. Most one-way trips are about NZ$2.50 to NZ$5 (US$1.75–US$3.50). It departs from Camp Street 15 minutes after the hour and from the airport on the half-hour, from 7:30am to 7:30pm.

By Car   Allow a full day (6 hr.) from Christchurch, 3½ hours from Dunedin, 5½ hours from Franz Josef, 2½ hours from Te Anau, 5 hours from Milford Sound, and 2½ hours from Invercargill. All roads leading into town are excellent. All major rental-car companies have offices in Queenstown.

By Taxi   Call **Queenstown Taxis** (© 03/442-7788) or **Alpine Taxis** (© 03/442-6666). Fares from the town center to most accommodations are between NZ$5 (US$3.50) and NZ$15 (US$11).

ORIENTATION   Queenstown is a compact town, with most shops, restaurants, and amenities within easy walking distance. There is no public bus system, but the Shopper Bus (see above) provides excellent all-day service. The central shopping area is bordered by Marine Parade on the lakefront, Camp Street to the north of that, and Shotover Street, which runs into Lake Esplanade. Focus on Beach Street, Rees Street, and The Mall for shopping.

The historic village of Arrowtown is 20km (12 miles) to the northeast. A calm counterbalance to the frenetic pace of Queenstown, Arrowtown is one of New Zealand's last little frontier towns. Glenorchy, now billed as the "Gateway to Paradise," is a 40-minute drive around the west arm of Lake Wakatipu.

VISITOR INFORMATION   The **Queenstown i-SiteVisitor Centre,** Clocktower Centre, Shotover and Camp streets (℡ **0800/668-888** in NZ, or 03/442-4100; fax 03/442-8907; www.queenstown-vacation.com), is open daily from 7am to 7pm in summer and from 7am to 6pm from Easter to the end of October. It sells stamps; sends faxes and e-mail; exchanges currency; and makes reservations for accommodations, transport, and activities. The **Real Journeys Visitor Centre** is on the Steamer Wharf, Beach Street, Queenstown (℡ **0800/656-503** in NZ, or 03/442-7500; fax 03/442-7504; www.realjourneys.co.nz). **New Zealand Reservations** (℡ **0800/804-111** in NZ, or 03/355-9902; www.newzealandreservations.co.nz) can assist with accommodations, sightseeing, and activity bookings. The **Department of Conservation Information Centre,** 37 Shotover St. (℡ **03/442-7933**), is the place to go for information on walking trails and national parks.

While at the visitor center, pick up a copy of the *Queenstown Today & Tonight* brochure. For a critical lowdown on what to do, get *Itag* and the *Backpackers' Guide to Queenstown.* Also look for the two free tourist papers, *The Mountain Scene* and *Qt Visitor Information.*

Get an online introduction to the area at www.newzealand-vacation.com, www.queenstownnz.co.nz, www.queenstownadventure.com, www.queenstownvisitorguide.com, and www.arrowtown.com.

SPECIAL EVENTS   The visitor center can provide details on a vigorous program of special events held in the area throughout the year. Here's a small sampling of what you can expect.

In January, riders from all over the South Island participate in the famous **Glenorchy Races,** which include bareback riding and attract thousands of spectators. The **Queenstown Jazz Festival** (℡ **03/442-9516;** www.queenstownjazz.co.nz), presents 10 days of top jazz. The **Arrowtown Autumn Festival** (℡ **03/442-1570**) runs the week after Easter. Now in its 20th year, it features market days and street entertainment celebrating the gold-mining era. The **Queenstown Winter Festival** (℡ **0800/337-8482;** www.winterfestival.co.nz) is the perfect excuse for 9 days of unadulterated madness and mayhem in July. It features a big opening ceremony and Mardi Gras, ski events, and street entertainment, and just about anything goes. The **Spring Carnival** (℡ **03/442-4615;** www.nzski.com), held in mid-September at the Remarkables Ski Resort, presents a feast of snow-related sports and social activities.

FAST FACTS: Queenstown

American Express   The office is at 59 Beach St. (℡ **03/442-7730**).

Area Code   The telephone area code (STD) for Queenstown is **03**.

Currency Exchange   Try **Thomas Cook,** 34 Camp St. (℡ **03/442-6403**), or **BNZ Bureau de Change,** 11–13 Rees St. (℡ **03/442-5810**).

Dentists   For 24-hour service, call ℡ **03/442-7274,** 03/442-8580, or 03/442-2711.

Doctors The **Queenstown Medical Centre** is on Isle Street (© **03/441-0500**).

Emergencies For police, fire, or ambulance services, dial © **111**.

Internet Access **Internet Outpost,** open from 8:30am to 11:30pm, charges NZ$6 (US$4.20) per hour. **Budget Communications,** above McDonalds in O'Connell's Mall (© **03/441-1562**), is open daily from 9am until 11pm and charges from NZ$3 (US$2.10) per hour.

Pharmacy **Bradley's Pharmacy,** 19 Rees St. (© **03/442-8338**), is open from 8am to 10pm. After hours, call © **03/442-9140**.

Post Office The post office is on Camp Street (© **03/442-7670**). It's open Monday through Friday from 8:30am to 8pm, Saturday from 9am to 8pm, and Sunday 10am to 6pm.

EXPLORING THE AREA
IN QUEENSTOWN

There is no better place to appraise Queenstown than from the **Skyline Gondola** 🌟🌟🌟 (© **03/441-0101;** www.skyline.co.nz), which takes you up to **Bob's Peak.** The view is breathtaking. You can stay for lunch or dinner at the buffet restaurant or cafe (see "Where to Dine," later in this chapter). The gondola operates from 9am until the restaurant closes around midnight, with a round-trip fare of NZ$19 (US$13) for adults, NZ$9 (US$6.30) for children. The complex includes shops and an 800m (2,624-ft.) luge.

The 30-minute thrills-and-spills film *Kiwi Magic,* Embassy Cinemas, The Mall (© **03/442-7862;** www.kiwimagic.co.nz), tempts you with fast-paced action and costs NZ$10 (US$7) for adults and NZ$5 (US$3.50) for children. Ring the theater for daily screening times.

The **Kiwi & Birdlife Park** 🌟, Brecon Street (© **03/442-8059;** www.kiwibird.co.nz), is in tranquil 3.2-hectare (8-acre) surroundings near the base of the gondola. Allow 30 to 40 minutes to see the birdlife and reptiles close at hand. Along with three daily conservation shows (11am, 1pm, and 3pm), they have several rare birds that can't be seen anywhere else. A recent addition is the early Maori hunting village, and you can attend a night show followed by dinner in the restaurant and a Maori performance. Admission is NZ$23 (US$16) for adults, NZ$10 (US$7) for children 5 to 15; the night show and dinner with performance costs NZ$88 (US$62) for adults and NZ$40 (US$28) for children.

If wildlife is your passion, take the 20-minute drive out to Kelvin Heights to **Deer Park Heights** 🌟🌟 (© **03/442-2005;** www.thedeerpark.co.nz). Pay just NZ$20 (US$14) per car at the toll gate and then drive 5km (3 miles) through herds of red deer, wapiti, fallow deer, and the goatlike Himalayan thar that roam in large enclosures on 800 hectares (1,977 acres). It's a working farm, and you'll see animals at all stages of development. There are also tame animals that enjoy being fed by hand. All this plus spectacular views from 550m (1,804 ft.) above Queenstown, an old Korean film set, several filming locations for *Lord of the Rings,* and bountiful picnic spots. The scenic tours are from around NZ$50 (US$35) per person, and a jet boat and 3-hour scenic tour combo (departing Queenstown at 10am and 2pm daily) is NZ$140 (US$98) for adults and NZ$75 (US$53) for children.

Goldfields Mining Centre ⊛, in Kawarau Gorge (℗ **03/445-1038**; www.goldfields mining.co.nz), is open daily from 9am to 5pm. The goldfields of this region were among the richest in the world in the early 19th century, and Goldfields is the official gold-mining demonstration site. It's a 40-minute drive through the Kawarau Gorge on the way to Cromwell, so if you're on your way to Wanaka or Dunedin, stop in. You have to walk over a narrow but stable bridge that crosses high above the river; and if you've got a fear of heights like me, you might shake in your boots a bit. But if I can do it, so can you. It costs around NZ$15 (US$11) for adults and NZ$8 (US$5.60) for children. Jet-boating from here costs NZ$75 (US$53) for adults, NZ$45 (US$32) for children.

If you have an interest in the arts, take the self-drive **Wakatipu Arts Trail** ⊛⊛, which takes you through the pretty back roads between Queenstown and Arrowtown, visiting eight well-known artists and craftspeople. Pick up the brochure from the visitor center and allow at least a morning to appreciate fine watercolors, oils, wood art, and jewelry.

Kids Especially for Kids

Queenstown doesn't overflow with children's activities. Many of the adventures have minimum age requirements, but one that doesn't is **Family Adventures** ⊛⊛⊛ (℗ **03/442-8836**), which encourages families to take part in its scenic four-wheel-drive excursion into Skipper's Canyon to watch the famous Pipeline bungy, Flying Fox, and jet boat in action, before embarking on a 1½-hour gentle rafting tour down the safest section of the Shotover River. The cost is from NZ$150 (US$105) for adults and NZ$110 (US$77) for children, who must be over 3 years old.

Caddyshack City ⊛⊛, 25 Brecon St. (℗ **03/442-6642**), is an indoor miniature-golf experience that makes for lots of laughs. Open daily from 10am to 8pm, it costs around NZ$20 (US$14) for adults, NZ$12 (US$8.40) for children 5 to 14, and NZ$50 (US$35) per family. Kids under 5 cannot play, but pushchairs are provided.

Off-Road Adventures Kids Quads, 61a Shotover St. (℗ **03/442-7858**), has a supervised kids' four-wheeler circuit and training is given. A 50cc Suzuki costs NZ$2 (US$1.40) per minute for up to 30 minutes.

Go Vertical Bungy ⊛⊛, Brecon Street (℗ **0800/124-224** in NZ; www.go vertical.co.nz), is below the gondola, offering children's harnessed trampoline activities. For more sedate fun, head for **Destination Art,** 31 Ramshaw Lane, Arrowtown (℗ **03/442-1772**; www.destinationart.co.nz), where daily children's classes in a full range of arts and crafts are held from 10am until noon and cost NZ$40 (US$28).

Kiwi & Birdlife Park ⊛ (see above) gives kids a good introduction to conservation and New Zealand birdlife. The **Skyline Luge** ⊛⊛⊛ (see "Outdoor Pursuits," later in this chapter) is great fun for all ages, as is Real Journey's **Walter Peak Farm Excursion** (see "Lake Cruises" below), which includes a steamship cruise and a farmyard tour where children can help feed the animals.

IN NEARBY ARROWTOWN

For an enjoyable outing and a less hectic pace, drive out to the once-thriving gold-mining town of Arrowtown. It sprang up on the banks of the Arrow River when gold was discovered here in 1862. Many of the quaint original buildings remain, along with stunning avenues of trees planted in 1867. In autumn, the whole town glows with colorful foliage. To get a better understanding of the town's history, go to the **Lake District Museum** ⚘, 49 Buckingham St. (© **03/442-1824;** www.museumqueenstown.com). Admission is NZ$6 (US$4.20) for adults, NZ$1 (US70¢) for children; it's open daily from 8:30am to 5pm.

Although there is no longer a Chinese community in Arrowtown, you can take a stroll in the restored **Chinese Camp,** on Bush Creek at the northern end of town. The camp was once occupied by the Chinese gold-mining community in the late 19th century. Look out for **Ah Lum's General Store** and the tiny dwellings tucked under rocky outcrops.

Other places to explore include the **Royal Oak Hotel,** 47 Buckingham St. (© **03/442-1700**), one of the oldest licensed hotels in Central Otago, where you can still enjoy a drink and a hearty round of pub food; the **Old Gaol,** on Cardigan Street; and **St. John's Presbyterian Church,** which dates back to 1873, at Durham and Berkshire streets. Overall, Arrowtown in very pretty but in peak tourist season it's about as "touristy" as touristy gets. It's much better in autumn when the crowds have dissipated and the leaves are falling.

ORGANIZED TOURS

Start with the sedate **Queenstown-Arrowtown Double Decker Bus Tour** ⚘⚘ (© **03/441-4421;** fax 03/441-4021), which gives a bird's-eye view of the Wakatipu Basin without leaving the ground. It includes a 1-hour stop in Arrowtown; you can also leave the bus there in the morning and go back to Queenstown on the afternoon return trip. It costs NZ$38 (US$27) for adults and NZ$17 (US$12) for children and departs daily from the top of Camp Street at 10am and 2pm, returning at 1pm and 5pm.

For information on **Wine Trail** tours, see "The Wineries," below.

Trilogy Trail (© **0800/676-264** in NZ, or 03/442-2207; www.trilogytrail.com) is operated by people who were involved in the making of the *Lord of the Rings* trilogy, and they'll give you an insight into Middle Earth, visiting filming locations by air or road. Tours run from 2½ to 5 hours. A 4WD tour costs NZ$125 (US$88) for adults, NZ$63 (US$44) for children; a flying/landing tour runs from NZ$315 to NZ$665 (US$221–US$466) for adults.

Of the operators taking four-wheel-drive tours into Skippers Canyon, **Skippers Canyon Heritage Tours** ⚘⚘⚘ (© **0800/271-617** in NZ, or 03/442-5949; www.queenstown-heritage.co.nz), run by Bill Forsyth, is one of the best. Bill is the fourth generation of a family who were among the first Skippers settlers, and both his grandparents and his great-grandparents are buried in the historic Skippers Cemetery. The half-day tour is limited to four to six people and culminates in a delicious picnic on the edge of the cliff overlooking the A. J. Hackett bungy jump. The cost is NZ$115 (US$81) per person.

Nomad Safaris ⚘⚘⚘ (© **0800/688-222** in NZ, or 03/442-6699; www.nomadsafaris.co.nz), has exclusive rights to guide in the old mining towns of Macetown and Seffersstown, taking you through spectacular Otago scenery along the way. They also offer two 4WD "Safari of the Rings" tours, visiting *Lord of the Rings* filming locations.

Of their 20 drivers, eight have been extras in the film trilogy and all have an in depth knowledge of Tolkien's work that is bound to satisfy the most dedicated fans. They are the only company offering dedicated *Lord of the Rings* tours, and their experience is by far the best. For the most landscape diversity, take the Wakatipu Basin tour; for the most film locations and more remote scenery, take the Glenorchy tour. Both are 4 hours long and cost NZ$130 (US$91) for adults, NZ$65 (US$46) for children.

Goldseeker Tours ★★, Queenstown (✆ **03/441-2460;** www.queenstown-gold seekers.co.nz), will splash you through 20 river crossings in the remote areas of Arrow Gorge in your pursuit of gold and a good time. The half-day tour costs around NZ$95 (US$67) for adults and NZ$60 (US$42) for children 17 and under.

Photo Safaris Queenstown ★★, Queenstown Centre for Creative Photography (✆ **03/409-0272**), will take you on an unforgettable 7-hour 4WD photographic trip, teaching you all the tricks for getting the best out of your camera. This costs NZ$270 (US$189) per person. They also have a range of photographic workshops priced from NZ$370 (US$259) per person.

If you want to tour in style, contact **Limousine Line** (✆ **03/442-2040;** www. limousineline.co.nz). Its knowledgeable drivers give clients a unique, personal experience based on their interests and time constraints.

LAKE CRUISES

If you need a moment of serenity, get aboard the 1912 vintage steamship **TSS Earnslaw** and cruise across Lake Wakatipu in style. Affectionately known as the "Lady of the Lake," it departs on 1½-hour cruises to Walter Peak up to six times a day, year-round (with a reduced winter schedule). Cost is NZ$38 (US$27) for adults and NZ$15 (US$11) for children. Passengers with more time can disembark at Walter Peak on the 3½-hour farm excursion, which includes a country-style morning or afternoon tea (NZ$58/US$41 adults, NZ$15/US$11 children). Alternatively, from October to mid-April, you can take a 40-minute horse trek across the foothills, enjoy a delicious Walter Peak barbecue, or splurge on the evening dining excursion, which features a three-course carvery buffet and a shortened farmyard tour. Contact **Real Journeys,** Steamer Wharf (✆ **0800/656-503** in NZ, or 03/442-4846; www.realjourneys.co.nz).

For a highly personalized lake cruise, call **Yvalda Boat Cruises** ★★★ (✆ **027/ 434-5555** in NZ; www.cruising.net.nz). The MV *Yvalda* is a classic ketch-rigged motor launch built in Scotland in 1936 and used by Sir Winston Churchill during World War II for meetings with his generals. Today the vessel provides daytime and overnight cruises for up to six people. The ketch is a real gem and the whole experience is a tranquil, friendly getaway from Queenstown's adventure madness. Two-hour daytime cruises depart daily from the jetty just beyond The Bathhouse Restaurant on the lakefront at 10am and 1:30pm and cost from NZ$75 (US$53) per adult. Overnight cruises (price on application) depart at 5pm and return at 9am.

THE WINERIES

There's new gold in this picturesque valley—liquid gold, in the form of prize-winning wine! Central Otago's rugged hillsides are clad in lush vineyards that produce some of the country's most distinctive wines. Pinot noir, chardonnay, sauvignon blanc, pinot gris, and Riesling varieties are well suited to the hot summer days and cool nights. Since 1990, Central Otago pinot noir has topped its class five times in national wine competitions. Pick up the free brochure *The Central Otago Wine Trail,* which maps out the major wineries. The three best are close to Queenstown—Gibbston Valley Wines,

Peregrine, and Chard Farm. Rippon Vineyard is in Wanaka; Felton Road, Mt. Difficulty, and Olssen's are at Bannockburn, near Cromwell; and Springvale Estate, William Hill, Briar Vale Estate, and Black Ridge are in the Clyde/Alexandra area.

New vineyards are coming on stream all the time as the region's 686 hectares (1,694 acres)—and expanding—mature and many are developing new winery and restaurant complexes. There are now over 71 vineyards in the region. The Queenstown and Wanaka Visitor Centres can provide a comprehensive map and brochure of the Central Otago wine industry to make your self-drive exploration more satisfying and straightforward. For more information check www.otagowine.com.

Amisfield Winery 🌾🌾   Ten minutes from Queenstown is this small producer of pinot noir, aromatic whites, and methode traditionelle wines. They have an underground barrel hall, a cellar-door facility, and a small bistro near picturesque Lake Hayes.

10 Lake Hayes Rd., Queenstown. ℂ 03/442-0556. www.amisfield.co.nz. Daily 10am–6pm.

Chard Farm Vineyard 🌾🌾   This is one of the most spectacularly situated vineyards in the country. Straddling a narrow ledge between rugged mountains and the Kawarau River Gorge, it's reached via a narrow, unpaved road 100m (328 ft.) above the river. Available wines include chardonnay, pinot noir, Riesling, sauvignon blanc, pinot gris, and Gewürztraminer.

St. Hwy. 6, just past the Kawarau bungy bridge (20 min. from Queenstown). ℂ 03/442-1006. www.chardfarm.co.nz. Daily 10am–5pm (weekends from 11am). Wine NZ$15–NZ$70 (US$11–US$49) per bottle.

GVW Winery 🌾🌾🌾   A stop for lunch here is a must. It's the most visited winery in Australasia, with not only great food but also a divine setting. As pioneers of winemaking in Central Otago, Gibbston has set high standards. Many of its wines are stored in the climatically controlled wine cave, which was blasted out of a rocky outcrop behind the restaurant. The pinot noir has twice topped its class in national competitions, and the chardonnay, sauvignon blanc, and Riesling have won over 40 medals. Connoisseurs will enjoy the tour through the caves and the tasting of four wines. There is also a large gift store and delicatessen on-site and next door, Gibbston Valley Cheesery makes and sells top quality regional cheeses.

St. Hwy. 6, 25 min. from Queenstown. ℂ 03/442-6910. Fax 03/442-6909. www.gvwines.com. Daily 10am–5pm. Wine NZ$19–NZ$60 (US$13–US$42) per bottle. Cave tour NZ$11 (US$7.70).

Mt. Difficulty Wines 🌾🌾   You won't regret a trip into the Bannockburn area and this is where you'll find Mt. Difficulty Wines producing excellent pinot noir, Riesling, chardonnay, sauvignon blanc, pinot gris, and merlot. They also have a very pleasant cafe open for lunch at noon.

Felton Rd., Bannockburn. ℂ 03/445-3445. Fax 03/445-3446. www.mtdifficulty.co.nz. Summer daily 10:30am–5pm; winter daily until 4:30pm. Wine NZ$22–NZ$75 (US$15–US$53) per bottle.

Peregrine 🌾🌾   Named after the falcon now found only in the Central Otago region, Peregrine is a relatively new player on the scene. Success has come early, though, and its 1998 sauvignon blanc won New Zealand, Australian, and United Kingdom trophies. The opening of its new architecturally designed restaurant complex, with a distinctive curved wing-shaped roof, has cemented it as one of the classiest wineries to visit. They produce good pinot noir, pinot gris, Riesling, sauvignon blanc, chardonnay, and rosé.

Tips **The Wine Tours**

The best of the bunch is still **Queenstown Wine Trail** ✹✹✹ (🕾 **0800/827-8464** in NZ, or 03/442-3799; www.queenstownwinetrail.com). Its 4½-hour tour has the most informed commentary and includes Gibbston Valley Wines (with lunch at the restaurant), Chard Farm Vineyard, Wentworth Estate, and the Taramea Winemakers Centre. The cost is NZ$89 (US$62) and it operates all year. Their Summer Sampler tour runs October through March and costs NZ$110 (US$77). If you can't get into this one, try **Appellation Central Wine Tours** ✹✹✹ (🕾 **03/442-0246**; www.appelationcentral.co.nz)—the only tour company that will take you to the rapidly expanding Bannockburn and Cromwell vineyard regions, where many of the best new vineyards are. It has two daily options, one including lunch in the historic town of Clyde. Prices range from NZ$135 to NZ$175 (US$95–US$123) per person.

St. Hwy. 6, 5 min. past Gibbston Valley Wines. 🕾 **03/442-4000.** www.peregrinewines.co.nz. Daily 10am–5pm. Wine NZ$19–NZ$55 (US$13–US$39) per bottle.

SIDE TRIPS TO MILFORD SOUND ✹✹✹

If you don't have time to make the long drive to Milford Sound (see "Milford Sound," later in this chapter), there are numerous operators offering trips from Queenstown. Flying is money well invested, as the long 1-day coach trips can be exhausting and you'll spend most of your time on a bus. If you are planning to drive yourself, I definitely recommend spending a night at Te Anau before undertaking the journey to Milford Sound. That way, your Milford trip can be taken at a leisurely pace, and you can stop along the way to enjoy the scenery.

For fixed-wing scenic flights from Queenstown to Milford, go with **Queenstown Air** (🕾 **03/442-2244;** www.queenstownair.co.nz), which offers a variety of flight and cruise combos from around NZ$300 (US$210); or **Air Wakatipu** (🕾 **03/442-3148;** www.flying.co.nz), with Milford options priced from around NZ$240 (US$168).

If flying and driving are not options, don't despair. **Great Sights Queenstown** (🕾 **03/442-9445;** www.greatsights.co.nz) and **Real Journeys** (🕾 **0800/656-503;** www.realjourneys.co.nz) both offer coach trips from Queenstown. Allow at least 12 hours for a trip of this nature, of which approximately 10 hours will be spent on the bus. A better option is to coach in and fly out, which saves time and lets you see the landscape from two different perspectives, but if the weather closes in—and it often does—you'll end up coaching both ways.

Real Journeys also offers a range of flight and scenic-cruise options priced from NZ$345 to NZ$375 (US$242–US$263). Their Coach and Nature Cruise (Oct–Apr) from Queenstown is NZ$200 (US$140) for adults, NZ$100 (US$70) for children. It cruises on the new boat *Milford Mariner,* with an on-board nature guide. A coach/nature cruise/fly package (Oct–Apr) from Queenstown is NZ$499 (US$349) for adults, NZ$295 (US$207) for children. A coach/scenic cruise/fly package (all year) from Queenstown costs NZ$494 (US$346) for adults, NZ$292 (US$204) for children. You can book all Real Journey excursions at its visitor center at Steamer Wharf (🕾 **03/442-7500;** fax 03/442-7504). It has excellent coaches, comfortable cruising vessels, informed drivers, and interpretation in four languages other than English.

OUTDOOR PURSUITS
IN QUEENSTOWN

There's no doubt Queenstown has more crazy, boundary-testing activities per square mile than anywhere else in New Zealand.

BIKING **Queenstown Bike Hire,** 23 Beach St. (© 03/442-6039), rents road and mountain bikes, tandems, and scooters; ask for a map that details the popular rides around town. **Outside Sports and Dr. Bike,** top of The Mall (© 03/442-8883), rents road and mountain bikes. It also supplies mountain-bike trail maps. Rentals range from NZ$40 to NZ$80 (US$28–US$56) per day. Serious mountain bikers should consider the guided tours provided by **Gravity Action** (© 03/441-1021; www.gravityaction. com), and **Vertigo Mountain Bikes** (© 03/442-8378; www.heli-adventures.co.nz).

BUNGY JUMPING There are four bungy-jumping sites in Queenstown. So what's the difference between them all? **A. J. Hackett Bungy** ☆☆☆ (© 0800/286-495 in NZ, or 03/442-7122; www.ajhackett.com) now operates them all.

Kawarau Suspension Bridge, at 43m (141 ft.) high, was the world's first commercial bungy operation, and since it was the "original," it seems to hold a special place in jumpers' hearts. It's great for water touches in the Kawarau River and is 23km (14 miles) from Queenstown. The full package, including jump, T-shirt, video, photos, and transport, costs NZ$140 (US$98). Allow 1 to 3 hours. At the top of Bob's Peak, **The Ledge** is 47m (154 ft.). This is what you might call an urban bungy experience that has two angles—the Wild Side and the Mild Side. You can also jump at night. Pay NZ$140 (US$98) for the jump, a T-shirt, and the gondola ride; allow 1 hour. The **Ledge Sky Swing** also operates here and costs NZ$110 (US$77). The **Nevis Highwire Bungy** ☆☆☆ is Hackett's newest venture. At 134m (440 ft.) over the Kawarau River, it takes over from the Pipeline as the tallest bungy site in New Zealand. The full pack here costs NZ$220 (US$154); it's NZ$199 (US$139) for a jump and transport only. **The Pipeline** is set 102m (335 ft.) above the Shotover River in Skippers Canyon, so it, too, has that wonderful Skippers Canyon Road access. The pipeline was originally used to carry water across the canyon to sluice the terraces for gold. It was restored in 1993 and today incorporates a walkway and bungy platform. The basic drive/jump option costs NZ$160 (US$112). **The Thrillogy** is a three-jump combo for NZ$299 (US$209).

CANYONING **12 Mile Delta Canyoning** (© 03/441-4468; www.xiimile.co.nz) does half-day trips for NZ$140 to NZ$225 (US$98–US$158). Allow 3 hours, 1½ of them wet. It also offers a heli-canyon combo.

⎛Moments Up, Up & Away

For an unforgettable adventure, call up experienced Queenstown helicopter pilot Louisa "Choppy" Patterson at **Over the Top** ☆☆☆ (© 0800/123-359 in NZ, or 03/442-2233; www.flynz.co.nz). Something of a legend in these parts, Choppy knows all the magic picnic spots thousands of feet up in the mountains. She can land you there, leave you with a champagne lunch in total solitude, and return later to drop you back into civilization. This truly memorable excursion will cost NZ$340 (US$238) per person. Don't miss this unique chance for adventure!

FISHING   The visitor center can advise you on several recognized trout-fishing operators with prices ranging from NZ$85 (US$60) per hour to NZ$500 (US$350) for a full day. **Queenstown Fishing Guides & Charters** (© 03/442-5363; www.wakatipu.co.nz), offers lake trolling, fly-fishing, and lure fishing. Or try **Over The Top Fly Fishing** (© 0800/123-359 in NZ, or 03/442-2233; www.flynz.co.nz), for a truly out-of-the-way guided heli-fly-fishing experience.

FLY BY WIRE   This odd new adventure fires you away from the earth at speeds up to 170kmph (105 mph). **Fly by Wire** ☆ (© 03/409-0030; www.flybywire.co.nz) charges NZ$160 (US$112) for 5 minutes of excitement while strapped into a rocket, which is attached to a strong wire. Minimum age is 15. Watch the video at Network Car Rentals, on Shotover Street, to see what you're getting yourself into.

GOLF   The ultimate in Queenstown golf is **Millbrook Resort** ☆☆☆, Arrowtown (© 0800/800-604 in NZ, or 03/441-7010; www.millbrook.co.nz), where you'll pay around NZ$125 (US$88) for the par-72, Bob Charles–designed course. Carts, equipment, instruction, and a free shuttle from Queenstown are available. The 18-hole **Queenstown Golf Club** ☆☆☆, Kelvin Heights (© 03/442-9169), is a full-service course with NZ$55 (US$39) green fees and NZ$45 (US$32) for club rental.

HORSE TREKKING   There are a number of horse-trekking operators who charge from NZ$50 to NZ$100 (US$35–US$70). **Moonlight Stables** ☆☆☆ (© 03/442-1229; www.moonlightcountry.com) is on the 324-hectare (800-acre) Doonholme Farm, 15 minutes from Queenstown. Well-mannered horses and experienced guides offer full- or half-day treks through spectacular landscapes and deer farms for NZ$75 (US$53) adults and NZ$45 (US$32) children. **Shotover Stables** (© 03/442-9708), is just 6 minutes out of town at Arthur's Point.

HOT-AIR BALLOONING   **Sunrise Balloons** ☆☆☆ (© 0800/468-247 in NZ, or 03/442-0781; www.ballooningnz.com) will give you a memorable experience floating silently over the Wakatipu Basin at dawn. The price—NZ$295 (US$207) for adults, NZ$195 (US$137) for children under 12—includes a champagne breakfast after landing.

JET-BOATING   **Shotover Jet** ☆☆☆ (© 0800/746-868 in NZ, or 03/442-8570; www.shotoverjet.com) is perhaps the best-known operator and the biggest adrenaline rush. You'll pay from NZ$95 (US$67) for adults and NZ$55 (US$39) for kids to blast through narrow rocky canyons in as little as 10 centimeters (4 in.) of water for 30 minutes. **Kawarau Jet** (© 0800/529-272 in NZ, or 03/442-6142; www.kjet.co.nz) departs from the main town pier and skates across Lake Wakatipu to the Kawarau and Shotover rivers. The 45- to 60-minute trip costs NZ$85 (US$60) for adults, NZ$45 (US$32) for children (see "Money-Saving Combos," below, for other options).

LUGE   The **Skyline Luge** ☆☆☆ (© 03/441-0101; www.skyline.co.nz) is 800m (2,624 ft.) of downhill fun for NZ$7 (US$4.90) per ride per person. Various packages on offer include several rides and gondola transport. It operates from 9am to dusk; tickets are available from the Skyline Gondola terminals.

PARAPENTING/HANG GLIDING/PARAGLIDING   **Queenstown Paragliding School** (© 0800/727-245 in NZ; www.extremeair.co.nz) will give you a day's course in the basics for NZ$195 (US$137). There are approximately 15 **tandem parapente** operators, most working above the gondola on Bob's Peak; prices are around NZ$170 to NZ$200 (US$119–US$140) for an introductory tandem flight.

RIVER BOARDING/RIVER SURFING If you thought surfing was restricted to the ocean, forget it. Now you can cling to a specially designed boogie board, don a helmet, and go for it down churning river rapids. **Serious Fun River Surfing** (© 0800/737-468 in NZ, or 03/442-5262; www.riversurfing.co.nz) goes down a 7km (4-mile) stretch of the Kawarau River for NZ$140 (US$98). You'll progress from flat water to Grade IV rapids with instruction as you go along. No experience is necessary, but confidence in the water is. Trips are conducted from October to May. **Mad Dog River Boarding** (© 0508/623-364 in NZ, or 03/441-1386; www.riverboarding. co.nz) charges NZ$140 (US$98) to go through the Roaring Meg section of the Kawarau River, which includes Grades II and III rapids.

ROCK CLIMBING **The Rung Way** (© 03/441-0074; www.rungway.co.nz) has a carefully constructed Via Ferrata system of rungs, ladders, and wire ropes in high rocky places that will test the best of you. It's a fully guided experience at three different levels of ability, priced from NZ$149 (US$104) for 3 to 5 hours.

SKIING From late June to September, the international ski crowd flocks to Queenstown to enjoy the accessible slopes of **Coronet Peak;** the least-crowded slopes of the **Remarkables;** the best family fields at **Cardrona;** and the most challenging slopes at **Treble Cone.** For the ultimate rush, try a day of heli-skiing or heli-boarding with **Harris Mountain Heliski** (© 03/442-6722; www.heliski.co.nz), **HeliGuides** (© 03/442-7733; www.flynz.co.nz), or **Glacier Southern Lakes Heliski** (© 03/442-3016; www.heli-flights.co.nz). For more information on skiing and snowboarding in the area, see chapter 3.

SKYDIVING For NZ$245 to NZ$395 (US$172–US$277), **NZONE** (© 03/442-5867; www.nzone.biz) will fly you over awesome scenery and then drop you out to fall at speeds of up to 200kmph (124 mph).

WALKING Three well-known multiday walks start in the Queenstown vicinity. See "Tramping" in chapter 3 for information on the **Routeburn,** the **Greenstone Valley,** and the **Grand Traverse Tracks.** Each starts near the little township of Glenorchy, at the far end of Lake Wakatipu, 47km (29 miles) from Queenstown. It's also possible to sample these great walks by going in several hours and back out again on the same day. Alternatively, you can do the **Routeburn Encounter Guided Day Walk** ✸✸✸ (© 0800/768-832 in NZ, or 03/442-8200; www.routeburn.co.nz) from November to April, with transport from Queenstown provided. The track rises 230m (754 ft.) over 6.5km (4 miles) and is suitable for reasonably active people. Take warm and waterproof clothing and good boots.

The **Department of Conservation Information Centre,** 37 Shotover St. (© 03/442-7935), open daily from 8am to 8pm, can furnish details on short walks around Queenstown as well as those farther afield. There are at least 10 walks of 1 to 8 hours in and around town. There are also several excellent walks around **Lake Wakatipu,** including the pleasant and easy **Bobs Cove Track and Nature Trail** ✸✸, which starts 14km (9 miles) from Queenstown on the road to Glenorchy.

Experienced naturalist Richard Bryant of **Guided Walks of New Zealand** ✸✸✸ (© 0800/455-712 in NZ, or 03/442-7126; www.nzwalks.com) specializes in treks with nature interpretation. He offers half- and full-day options with a maximum of seven people, costing from around NZ$100 to NZ$350 (US$70–US$245).

There are also pleasant walks and trails in and around **Arrowtown.** Pick up the Department of Conservation brochure, which details all these walks, their conditions,

> **Tips Money-Saving Combos**
>
> If you want to try a variety of activities, look into money-saving combos. Most booking agents around Queenstown can fill you in on all the details and several adventure operators have their own money-saving combinations. **Info & Track,** 37 Shotover St. (📞 **03/442-9708;** www.infotrack.co.nz), can tell you about packages such as the **Shotover High Five** 🐦🐦, which combines the Shotover Jet with a helicopter ride to Skyline for luge rides, the *Kiwi Magic* movie, and a gondola ride down. This 3½-hour "softer" option costs NZ$195 (US$137) for adults. The **Awesome Foursome** 🐦🐦🐦 is a popular full-day option that combines the Nevis Highwire Bungy with the Shotover Jet, a spectacular helicopter ride, and a Shotover raft trip. Designed for the adrenaline junkie, it costs NZ$475 (US$333). The **Shotover Trio** combines the Shotover Jet with a helicopter ride and rafting for NZ$279 (US$195). **Queenstown Combos** (📞 **0800/ 423-836** in NZ, or 03/442-7318; www.combos.co.nz) has about 14 different packages and can make reservations for you. Prices start at around NZ$175 (US$123). **Action Combos** (📞 **0800/723-8464** in NZ, or 03/442-9792; www.rafting. co.nz) offers a range of rafting-based combos that include bungy, helicopter rides, and jet-boats.

and fitness requirements. For weather forecast information, call **MetPhone** (📞 **0900/ 99-903;** www.metservice.co.nz).

WHITE-WATER RAFTING The Shotover and Kawarau rivers are top spots for white-water rafting. The Kawarau trips are generally better for those who are rafting for the first time. The Shotover trips are much more challenging and are usually accompanied by safety kayaks. **Challenge Rafting** 🐦🐦 (📞 **0800/423-836** in NZ; www.raft.co.nz) charges around NZ$150 (US$105) for its Shotover raft trip and around NZ$140 (US$98) for the Kawarau trip. Allow 4 to 5 hours at Grades III to V rapids. **Queenstown Rafting** (📞 **0800/723-846** in NZ; www.rafting.co.nz) operates similar trips priced from NZ$139 (US$97). **Extreme Green Rafting** 🐦🐦🐦 (📞 **03/ 442-8517;** www.nzraft.com) is a smaller operator with more competitive prices. It also has an Upper Shotover Scenic option, which includes a flight or drive to the top of the river. This full-day outing is a passive rather than high-adrenaline activity, suitable for all ages and levels of fitness.

IN NEARBY GLENORCHY

Glenorchy is a tiny village surrounded by rugged high country, mountains, glacier-fed lakes, and ancient beech forests—*Lord of the Rings* country, in fact. Much of the filming was done in this remote area. It's also the latest hot spot in southern tourism. Just 40 minutes away, it's now a base for several tour operators, all of which offer transport from Queenstown.

FUNYAKING Sitting in an inflatable Canadian-style canoe and floating downstream at 8kmph (5 mph), enjoying the scenery, is my idea of a sensible adventure. With **Funyaks** 🐦🐦🐦 (📞 **03/442-9992;** www.dartriver.co.nz), you'll jet-boat up the Dart River for 75 minutes (or you can go by 4WD vehicle, if you prefer), then canoe back down to Glenorchy in stable inflatable canoes. No need for daredevil confidence—it's a family trip guaranteed to please everyone. The price is from NZ$255 to NZ$275 (US$179–US$193) and includes transfers, guides, and lunch.

HORSE TREKKING   The **Dart Stables** ✶✶ (© **0800/474-3464** in NZ, or 03/442-5688; www.dartstables.com) has exclusive riding territory in the high country of the 200-hectare (494-acre) Wyuna Station and sole rights to trek through Department of Conservation areas. Treks are available for all abilities and range from 2 hours to overnight excursions, priced from NZ$105 (US$75) per person (NZ$125/US$89 per person with transport from Queenstown).

JET-BOATING   **Dart River Safaris** ✶✶✶ (© **0800/327-8538** in NZ, or 03/442-9992; www.dartriver.co.nz) provides one of the best jet-boating experiences in New Zealand. The Safari combines jet-boating with walks in ancients forests and visits to *Lord of the Rings* sites at Paradise. It departs Glenorchy at 9am and 1pm. Allow 6 hours in total and expect to pay NZ$179 to NZ$199 (US$125–US$139).

WALKING   Glenorchy is the departure point for the **Routeburn,** the **Greenstone and Caples,** and the **Rees and Dart** tracks, all of which are internationally renowned. Get information at the **Department of Conservation,** Glenorchy Visitor Centre, Glenorchy (© **03/442-9937;** www.glenorchyinfocentre.co.nz). See also "Tramping" in chapter 3.

SHOPPING

Queenstown has an excellent range of New Zealand–made goods, from sheepskin products, leather, and outdoor wear to fine crafts, pure wool hand-knits, and jewelry. Most shops are open daily to 10pm, and many offer overseas packaging and postal services. Pick up the free *Queenstown Dining & Shopping Guide* at the visitor center.

Several new upmarket shopping complexes have opened since 2003, and in late 2005, 15 stylish stores opened on the ground floor of the new Sofitel Hotel.

Moments Body Business

When the stress of being a tourist gets the better of you, turn your attention to one of Queenstown's new pampering services. Among them all, **Body Sanctum** ✶✶✶ , 12 Man St. (© **03/442-8006;** www.bodysanctum.co.nz), comes most highly recommended. Men and women alike can feel the benefits of aromatherapy, sports massage, shiatsu, reflexology, and a wide variety of beauty therapy services. You can also unwind at the **Millbrook Resort Day Spa** ✶✶✶ , Malaghan Road (© **03/441-7000;** fax 03/441-7007); it's the biggest and classiest and offers a full range of wet and dry massage therapies, a hair salon, facials, beauty treatments, manicures, and pedicures—all set within the restful acres of Millbrook. **Aspects Beauty & Health Day Spa,** 53 Shotover St. (© **03/442-7389;** www.aspectsofbeauty.co.nz), can rejuvenate the weariest traveler with a wide range of massage therapies, body wraps, Jacuzzis, and manicures. **Hush Spa** ✶✶ , Level 2, The Junction, corner of Gorge and Robins Road (© **03/409-0901;** www.hushspa.co.nz), will soothe you with exotic body therapies, massage rituals, and facial treatments; and **The Art of Rest,** First Floor, 10 Athol St. (© **03/442-4336**), will bring you back to life (post–jet lag) with flotation-enhanced massage. If you're not sure what that is, trust me, it's worth finding out.

The **O'Connells Shopping Centre,** Camp and Beach streets (℗ **03/442-7760**), has 25 stores offering everything from food and fashion to knitwear, jewelry, and contemporary art. If you missed **Canterbury New Zealand** (℗ **03/442-4020**) in other major centers, you'll find it here.

Gallery Oceanic ☆☆☆, 43b Beach St. (℗ **03/442-6076;** www.oceanicgallery. co.nz), has the most impressive selection of arts and crafts by New Zealand artisans, followed closely by the **Bonz Gallery,** upstairs in **Bonz New Zealand** ☆☆, 8–10 The Mall (℗ **03/442-5398**), a top outlet for original designs in 100% merino wool handknit sweaters and jackets. **Goldfields Jade and Opal,** top of The Mall (℗ **03/442-9356**), and **The Opal Centre,** Beach and Rees streets (℗ **03/442-8239**), have the finest collections of investment opal jewelry.

For one of the biggest selections of sheepskins, woolen jerseys, leisurewear, jewelry, wooden carvings, confectionery, and local honeys and jams, go to **DF Souvenirs,** 32 The Mall (℗ **03/442-5275**). Another good source of all of the above is **The Mountaineer Shop,** Beach and Rees streets (℗ **03/442-7460**). *Lord of the Rings* fans will find endless amusement at **All Things Lord of the Rings,** 19 Shotover St. (℗ **0800/688-222** in NZ; www.lordoftheringsnz.com), which has Middle Earth memorabilia coming out its ears. And if you have a sweet tooth, don't miss **The British Lolly Shop,** Church Lane (℗ **03/441-2274;** www.thebritishlollyshop.com), which seems an awfully long way from home to me, but some among you may be glad of that. You'll find another very cute little gift store at **Vesta** ☆☆☆, Williams Cottage, Marine Parade (℗ **03/442-5687;** www.vestadesign.co.nz), which is hardly bigger than a doll's house, yet manages to present some excellent New Zealand art, design work, and a tiny cafe.

Untouched World ☆☆☆, The Mall (℗ **03/442-4992;** www.untouchedworld.com), is a fabulous source of exclusive men's and women's apparel—especially merino mink garments that combine 100% New Zealand merino wool with possum fur for pure luxury.

WHERE TO STAY

There are now around 19,000 visitor beds in this small town, ranging from backpackers to new apartments, international-class hotels, and luxury lodges. It pays to book well in advance. Should you arrive without reservations, head for the **Queenstown Travel & Visitor Centre,** in the Clocktower Centre, Shotover and Camp streets (℗ **03/442-4100;** fax 03/442-8907), and ask for assistance. The rates below include 12.5% GST and free off-street parking unless otherwise noted.

IN QUEENSTOWN
Very Expensive
Eichardt's Private Hotel ☆☆☆ *Finds*   Voted the Best Small Hotel in the World by Andrew Harper (www.andrewharpertravel.com) in 2003, Eichardt's takes on the best of any luxury accommodations in New Zealand and comes up trumps. It's one of my favorite places in New Zealand. It's small, but in this case, size doesn't count. It is first class in every respect. The luxurious rooms have great views and big skylit bathrooms with lavish bathtubs, showers, and heated floors. You'll get all the modern conveniences in an exquisite interior that draws on the original building's history. Service is detailed, interior design mouthwatering, and its central location a bonus. It deserves the many accolades pouring in from all corners of the world.

Marine Parade, Queenstown. © 03/441-0450. Fax 03/441-0440. www.eichardts.co.nz. 5 units. From NZ$1,595 (US$1,139) lakeview suite; NZ$1,375 (US$963) mountainview suite. NZ$250 (US$175) each extra person; NZ$200 (US$140) per person Christmas/New Year supplement. Long-stay rates available. Rates include breakfast and airport transfers. AE, DC, MC, V. **Amenities:** Restaurant; bar; nearby golf course; concierge; massage; babysitting; laundry service; same-day dry cleaning; nonsmoking rooms; on-call doctor/dentist. *In room:* A/C, TV/DVD/stereo, dataport, kitchenette, minibar, fridge, coffeemaker, hair dryer, iron, safe.

Sofitel Queenstown ✪✪✪   This is New Zealand's first Sofitel hotel—and with bigger rooms, wired concierge, and espresso machines in every room, it's setting a new standard for service. Rooms are classic yet sensual, bathrooms are orchid-filled and complete with LCD screens over the bath. It's right in the center of town surrounded by new shops and restaurants. A sophisticated stay for the discerning traveler.

8 Duke St., Queenstown. © 0800/444-422 in NZ, or 03/450-0045. Fax 03/450-0046. www.sofitel.com. 82 units. From NZ$610 (US$427) deluxe; NZ$698 (US$489) executive suite; NZ$2,025 (US$1,418) penthouse; NZ$90 (US$63) surcharge on lakeview rooms. Long-stay, off-peak, and special packages available. AE, DC, MC. V. Valet parking NZ$15 (US$11) day. **Amenities:** 3 restaurants (Italian, Pacific Rim, and European); 3 bars; nearby golf course and tennis courts; gym; day spa and beauty treatments; Jacuzzi in penthouse suites; bike rentals; ski drying and storing area; concierge; tour bookings; car rentals; business center; shopping arcade w/15 stores; salon; 24-hr. room service; massage; babysitting; guest laundry and laundry service; same-day dry cleaning; nonsmoking rooms; executive-level rooms; butler service; foreign-currency exchange; on-call doctor/dentist; airport transfers; access for travelers w/disabilities. *In room:* A/C, TV/DVD/CD, dataport, kitchen in penthouses, minibar, fridge, espresso machine, hair dryer, iron, safe.

The Spire ✪✪✪ *Value*   Small, sensual, and classy, this new boutique hotel blends contemporary design with modern technology and upmarket comfort. All of the rooms are gorgeous, with hints of Japanese Zen simplicity. Bathrooms are big and well-designed and all beds offer king-size comfort. It's slightly bigger than Eichardt's, more contemporary, and at half their prices, a very good deal. Spoil yourself.

3–5 Church Lane. © 03/441-0004. Fax 03/441-0003. www.thespirehotels.com. 10 units. NZ$995 (US$697). Rates include breakfast and airport transfers. AE, DC, MC, V. **Amenities:** Restaurant (Tues–Sat dining from 6pm); bar; nearby golf course and tennis courts; concierge; tour bookings; car rentals; secretarial services; room service; massage; babysitting; same-day dry cleaning; nonsmoking rooms; foreign currency exchange; on-call doctor/dentist; airport transfers; access for travelers w/disabilities. *In room:* A/C, TV/DVD/CD, dataport, minibar, fridge, coffeemaker, hair dryer, iron, safe.

Expensive

The Dairy Private Luxury Hotel ✪✪   Once a 1920s general store, The Dairy has grown beyond a simple B&B and, under new ownership, it has undergone a very pleasing transformation and significant upgrade. Bedrooms are beautifully decorated and there are excellent social spaces, including a roaring fire and reading room. Best, your hostess Elspeth will spoil you with delicious afternoon tea scones. Always a well-loved spot just a stroll from town, it now sets a new benchmark for similarly priced options like Browns and Mountvista.

10 Isle St., Queenstown. © 03/442-5164. Fax 03/442-5166. www.thedairy.co.nz. 13 units. NZ$355–NZ$390 (US$249–US$273) deluxe; NZ$385–NZ$420 (US$270–US$294) premium. Long-stay and off-peak rates available. Rates include breakfast. AE, MC, V. Limited off-street parking. It's a 150m (492-ft.) uphill walk from town center. **Amenities:** Bar; Jacuzzi; free bikes; car rentals; massage; laundry service; same-day dry cleaning; nonsmoking rooms; access for travelers w/disabilities. *In room:* TV, coffeemaker, hair dryer, iron.

Mountvista Boutique Hotel   This small hotel comes highly rated by *Condé Nast Traveler.* Just steps away from Queenstown Gardens, it has the quiet intimacy that discerning travelers have come to expect. Spacious en-suite rooms are on three levels; 12 of them have big double baths, and 8 have balconies. All have big beds, comfortable chairs, and lots of room to lounge about in. If you like a smaller, more intimate hotel stay, this is perfect. Host Murray Inwood will go out of his way to indulge you and tempt you with evening canapés and local wines each evening before sending you out to try the local restaurant scene.

4 Sydney St., Queenstown. © **03/442-8832.** Fax 03/442-4233. www.mountvista.com. 14 units. From NZ$330 (US$231) deluxe; NZ$395 (US$277) suites. Long-stay and off-peak rates available. Rates include predinner drinks and breakfast. AE, DC, MC, V. No children under 12. **Amenities:** Nearby golf course; sauna; car rentals; some business services; massage; laundry service; same-day dry cleaning; nonsmoking rooms. *In room:* A/C, TV/VCR, dataport, mini-bar, fridge, coffeemaker, hair dryer, iron, safe.

Queenstown House   Owner Louise Kiely has remodeled this unique accommodations into something between a small boutique hotel and a B&B. The property has eight delightful rooms in the main house (refurbished in 2005) and seven new villa suites in an adjacent building. Each has its own special charm—I especially love the Hunting Room—but for best views, go for the Baron Room. Apartment suites in the new block are much bigger and have their own decks, large sitting rooms and a modern kitchen. Louise has personality-plus and encourages guests to meet for predinner drinks in the cozy living room. A delicious breakfast is served in the dining room overlooking the lake and township—which, it should be noted, is only a short walk downhill.

69 Hallenstein St., Queenstown. © **03/442-9043.** Fax 03/442-8755. www.queenstownhouse.co.nz. 15 units. NZ$250–NZ$295 (US$175–US$207) in main house; NZ$395–NZ$695 (US$277–US$487) villas; NZ$795 (US$557) 2-bedroom villa. Rates include breakfast and predinner drinks. AE, DC, MC, V. Some off-street parking available. **Amenities:** Nearby golf course; babysitting; self-serve laundry; same-day dry cleaning; nonsmoking rooms. *In room:* TV, dataport in villa suites, hair dryer.

MODERATE
Aurum Hotel & Suites   Bright, new, contemporary—with big living areas, good-size bathrooms, and lovely kitchens—the apartments here are more intimate than those at The Point (and smaller); and they have proximity to town on their side. Great value, great views. The Aurum shares reception and gym facilities with its sister property, the adjacent A-Line Hotel, which also has good value, but older rooms.

27 Stanley St., Queenstown. © **0800/696-963** in NZ, or 03/442-4718. Fax 03/442-4715. www.scenic-circle.co.nz. 84 units. From NZ$292 (US$204) superior room; NZ$360 (US$252) 1-bedroom suite; NZ$556 (US$390) 2-bedroom suite; NZ$225–NZ$292 (US$158–US$204) A-Line Hotel room. Long-stay and off-peak rates negotiable. AE, DC, MC, V. It's a 5-min. downhill walk to town; Shopper Bus stops nearby. **Amenities:** Restaurant; bar; nearby golf course; fitness center; Jacuzzi; sauna; courtesy shuttle to town; room service; massage; babysitting; laundry facilities; laundry service; same-day dry cleaning. *In room:* TV, dataport, kitchen, minibar, fridge, coffeemaker, hair dryer, iron, safe.

Balmoral House   Les and Cis Walker love hosting. Their modern hillside home with antique furnishings has four excellent rooms. The upstairs honeymoon suite has a double Jacuzzi with a view, but I liked the size and intimacy of the green room with its king-size and single bed, plus seating to enjoy the stunning views. There's a big self-contained two-bedroom suite downstairs with two bathrooms, ideal for families or two couples.

24 York St. © **03/442-7209.** Fax 03/442-6499. www.zqnbalmoral.co.nz. 4 units. NZ$250 (US$175) queen; NZ$295 (US$207) king; NZ$325 (US$228) honeymoon suite; NZ$50 (US$35) each extra person. Off-peak rates available. AE, DC, MC, V. From Frankton Rd. turn right into Dublin St. and drive up to the giveway sign. Balmoral is directly across the street. **Amenities:** Nearby golf course; free bikes; tour bookings; car rentals; babysitting; laundry service; same-day dry cleaning; nonsmoking rooms; on-call doctor/dentist. *In room:* TV, DVD, and kitchen in downstairs suite, fridge, coffeemaker, hair dryer, iron.

Brown's Boutique Hotel *finds*   You'll be right at home at Brown's if you want a good-value stay with character and knowledgeable local hosts. Nigel Brown (a former NZ ski champion) and his wife, Bridget, know Queenstown inside out and their host, Alex, has his own fan club. The hillside, Tuscan-style property with great views offers spacious rooms with big bathrooms and luxurious beds. Size-wise, it's on a par with The Dairy and Mountvista, and while it's a little more modest than both, it's no less inviting.

26 Isle St., Queenstown. ℭ **03/441-2050.** Fax 03/441-2060. www.brownshotel.co.nz. 10 units. NZ$260–NZ$280 (US$182–US$196). Long-stay and off-peak rates available. Rates include breakfast. AE, DC, MC, V. 3-min. walk to town. **Amenities:** Nearby golf course; tour bookings; car rentals; laundry service; dry cleaning; nonsmoking rooms; on-call doctor/dentist. *In room:* TV, dataport, minibar, fridge, coffeemaker, hair dryer, iron.

Garden Court Suites & Apartments 🗛🗛 *Value*   Once an average motel, Garden Court has taken itself into a new league with the addition of fabulous contemporary apartments at a reasonable price. On top of that, the existing studios have also been revamped. They slope down, away from the road, so there's no traffic noise; among these, the two-bedroom apartments are the best value, with a cozy living area, kitchen, and bathroom downstairs and two bedrooms and a second toilet upstairs. If you want style and comfort, you won't find much to complain about in the new apartment block. Its bathrooms are simply great—well lit, spacious, and with combination tub/showers. Fourteen new one-bedroom apartments overlook the lake and are the quietest.

41 Frankton Rd., Queenstown. ℭ **0800/427-336** in NZ, or 03/442-9713. Fax 03/442-6468. www.gardencourt.co.nz. 54 units. NZ$168 (US$118) studio suite; NZ$220 (US$154) 1-bedroom apt; NZ$233 (US$163) 2-bedroom family; NZ$308 (US$216) 2-bedroom luxury apt. Extra person NZ$35 (US$25). Long-stay and off-peak rates available. AE, DC, MC, V. 400m (1,312 ft.) from town center, opposite Millennium Hotel; on Shopper Bus route. **Amenities:** Breakfast restaurant; bar; nearby golf course; Jacuzzi; tour desk; secretarial services; coin-op laundry; same-day dry cleaning; nonsmoking rooms. *In room:* TV/VCR, dataport, kitchen, fridge, coffeemaker, hair dryer, iron.

The Heritage 🗛🗛🗛   This is a big hotel with an intimate boutique feel. Just 10 years old, it's idyllically set in an alpine forest and offers traditional hotel-style rooms as well as apartment-style suites with kitchen and laundry facilities. Accommodations are in three wings, but the walkways between them and the main lodge are not covered—umbrellas are provided. Take a one-bedroom lakeside suite and savor the 2m-wide (7-ft.) Hollywood king-size bed, marble bathroom, and entertainment system. The staff is incredibly friendly, the property is quiet, and you'll quickly get that home-away-from-home feel. Twenty stylish new villas came on stream in 2003, and these will be popular with families and long-stayers.

91 Fernhill Rd., Queenstown. ℭ **0800/368-888** in NZ, or 03/442-4988. Fax 03/442-4989. www.heritagehotels.co.nz. 177 units. NZ$218 (US$153) deluxe; NZ$265 (US$186) studio suite; NZ$405 (US$284) 2-bedroom suite; NZ$628 (US$440) villas. NZ$52–NZ$80 (US$36–US$56) surcharge on lakeview rooms. Rates include airport transfers. Long-stay and off-peak rates and special deals available. AE, DC, MC, V. Drive through town and go up the hill at the Fernhill roundabout. It's a 15-min. walk to town. **Amenities:** Restaurant; bar; indoor/outdoor heated pool; small exercise room; spa; Jacuzzi; sauna; concierge; car rentals; courtesy shuttle to town; 24-hr. room service; massage; babysitting; coin-op laundry; same-day dry cleaning/laundry service; nonsmoking rooms; on-call doctor/dentist. *In room:* TV, VCR in suites, dataport, kitchenette in suites, minibar, fridge, coffeemaker, hair dryer, iron, safe.

The Point 🗛🗛 *Value*   Don't freak out when you get to the top of the driveway: It may be a steep descent to the apartments staggered down the hillside overlooking the lake, but it's well worth it. These units have some of the best views of any lodging in Queenstown. On top of that, you get new, fully furnished luxury and space at a ridiculously reasonable price. The five studios are especially good value, but if you want the ultimate, request apartment no. 2, which is the size of a small house with three bedrooms, two bathrooms, gas fire, and Jacuzzi. Rooms here are much bigger than most other apartments listed above, making them ideal for families or couples traveling together.

239 Frankton Rd., Queenstown. ℂ 0800/222-239 in NZ, or 03/441-1899. Fax 03/441-1898. www.thepointqueenstown. co.nz. 25 units. NZ$125 (US$88) studio; NZ$200 (US$140) 1-bedroom apt; NZ$250 (US$175) 2-bedroom apt, 4 people; NZ$400 (US$280) 3-bedroom apt, 6 people; NZ$500 (US$350) 4-bedroom apt, 8 people. Extra person NZ$45 (US$32). Long-stay and off-season rates available. AE, DC, MC, V. 1.5km (1 mile) from center of town; served by Shopper Bus. **Amenities:** Nearby golf course; tennis court; small exercise room; tour bookings; car rentals; massage; babysitting; self-serve laundry; same-day dry cleaning; nonsmoking rooms. *In room:* TV/DVD/CD, dataport, kitchen, minibar, fridge, coffeemaker, hair dryer, iron.

INEXPENSIVE

Creeksyde Camper Van Park, 54 Robins Rd. (ℂ 03/442-9447; www.camp.co.nz), is definitely the Mercedes of campgrounds, situated in what was once a nursery—so there are trees and plants aplenty, plus room for 50 campervans, all with power outlets and water and waste hookups. There are also completely self-contained units and budget lodge rooms, all within a 5-minute walk of town. The charge is from NZ$27 (US$19) for tent and van sites, NZ$46 to NZ$52 (US$32–US$36) for lodge rooms, NZ$62 (US$43) for deluxe cabins, and NZ$90 to NZ$120 (US$63–US$84) for motel rooms. New holiday units are from NZ$132 (US$92).

Pinewood Lodge 🎭🎭 *Value*   Rob and Roz Greig have created one of the best budget options on the South Island. The series of little houses dots a tree-covered hillside, and brand-new complexes, housing a dorm area, kitchens, and lounges, rival many pricier operations. There's a real family feel about this place, the perfect choice if you want quality budget digs and a sociable atmosphere.

48 Hamilton Rd., Queenstown. ℂ 0800/746-3966 in NZ, or 03/442-8273. Fax 03/442-9470. www.pinewood.co.nz. 26 units. From NZ$24 (US$17) dorm bed; NZ$50–NZ$70 (US$35–US$49) double/twin; from NZ$100 (US$70) family unit. Extra person NZ$15 (US$11). AE, DC, MC, V. An easy 5-min. walk to town center, close to the Kiwi & Birdlife Park. **Amenities:** Jacuzzi; bike rentals; game room; tour desk; car rentals; courtesy shuttle to town; laundry service; coin-op laundry; nonsmoking rooms; access for travelers w/disabilities. *In room:* TV in some units, no phone.

YHA Queenstown Lakefront 🎭   This friendly, always-busy hostel recently underwent a big upgrade that smartened up the whole place. The result makes for a comfortable, economic stay just across the road from Lake Wakatipu, a pretty 15-minute walk into town. There are family rooms as well as the usual dorm and double/twin configurations; a small on-site shop sells the essentials.

88–90 Lake Esplanade, Queenstown. ℂ 0800/278-299 in NZ, or 03/442-8413. Fax 03/442-6561. www.yha.co.nz. 147 beds. NZ$25–NZ$35 (US$18–US$26) dorm; NZ$50–NZ$70 (US$35–US$49) double. MC, V. **Amenities:** Tour bookings; coin-op laundry; nonsmoking rooms. *In room:* No phone.

JUST OUT OF TOWN
Very Expensive
Matakauri Lodge 🎭🎭🎭   Matakauri Lodge opened on New Year's Eve 1999, and has rapidly established a reputation as one of the most romantic of New Zealand's exclusive lodges. Built from Queenstown schist with cedar walls and beech floors, it exudes a natural, informal style that quickly lulls you into a state of inert bliss. Views from the duplex chalets will take your breath away, and there is no better place to savor them than in the huge double Jacuzzi that takes pride of place in each of the 15-sq.-m (161-sq.-ft.) bathrooms. A polished and exceedingly friendly staff attends to every comfort. When you lie back in your mezzanine bedroom overhanging Lake Wakatipu each night, you'll be thankful you made this choice.

Closeburn, Glenorchy Rd., Queenstown. ℂ 03/441-1008. Fax 03/441-2180. www.matakauri.co.nz. 7 units. NZ$1,320–NZ$1,700 (US$924–US$1,190). Off-peak rates available. Rates include breakfast, predinner drinks, 3-course dinner, use of all facilities, and airport transfers. AE, DC, MC, V. Just over 5km (3 miles), a 7-min. drive, out of

Queenstown on the road to Glenorchy. **Amenities:** Bar; golf driving net; small exercise room; Jacuzzi; sauna; tour bookings; car rentals; massage; babysitting; laundry service; same-day dry cleaning; nonsmoking rooms. *In room:* A/C, TV/VCR, dataport, minibar, fridge, coffeemaker, hair dryer, iron.

Punatapu ✸✸✸   This exclusive retreat is all about pampering and pleasure. Set in a pristine alpine landscape in a secluded cove above Lake Wakatipu, it's the sort of place sought out by the rich and famous for privacy, security, and personalized, highly creative comfort. Now 10 years old, Punatapu quickly established itself as a leader in the luxury stakes. Rooms are lavishly decorated and spacious with all the comforts you'd expect for the price—and all have recently been refurbished. The Barn Studio is my pick for something special. Overall it has a more sumptuous decor and a few more facilities than nearby Matakauri, including the chance to meet a leading New Zealand artist-in-residence in the summer. There is also a new cooking school, a home theater, and a gymnasium under construction. The in-house chef showcases many distinctly New Zealand products in the sumptuous meals. If you'd like a divine coastal setting, ask about Punatapu's newly refurbished house at Karitane, near Dunedin.

Glenorchy Rd., P.O. Box 1252, Queenstown. ✆ **03/442-6624.** Fax 03/442-6229. www.punatapu.com. 4 units. NZ$2,000 (US$1,400). Rates include breakfast, predinner drinks and canapés, dinner, and airport transfers. Rates for B&B only or exclusive use on request. Long-stay rates available. AE, DC, MC, V. Closed June. 12km (7 miles) from Queenstown on the Glenorchy Rd. No children under 12. **Amenities:** Bar; small heated outdoor pool; nearby golf course; fully equipped gym; Jacuzzi; sauna in Punatapu suite nearby bike rentals; tour desk; car rentals; massage; laundry service; same-day dry cleaning; nonsmoking rooms; resident doctor. *In room:* Mobile A/C units on demand, TV/VCR, fax, dataport, fridge, coffeemaker, hair dryer, iron, safe.

NEAR ARROWTOWN
Very Expensive
Millbrook Resort ✸✸✸ *Value*   Many locals will tell you Millbrook is overrated, but personally I can't fault the quantity and quality of facilities here. It has luxury accommodations and international-caliber golf at unbeatable rates, plus the best giant bathtubs in the country. Opened in 1992, this award-winning resort is a destination in itself. The pricier cottages and villas are ideal for families or friends traveling together, while the generously sized village inn rooms offer the best value. Every comfort is attended to with 2m-wide (7-ft.) beds, fireplaces, and walk-in wardrobes. All this overlooks one of the best championship golf courses in the country. There are good walks between restaurants, spa facilities, and your room.

Malaghans Rd., Arrowtown, Private Bag, Queenstown. ✆ **0800/800-604** in NZ, or 03/441-7000. www.millbrook.co.nz. 170 units. NZ$390 (US$273) village inn; NZ$440 (US$308) villa suite; NZ$600 (US$420) hotel villa; NZ$600–NZ$900 (US$420–US$630) cottages; NZ$900–NZ$1,600 (US$630–US$1,120) Fairway Homes. Rates include breakfast. Special deals available. AE, DC, MC, V. 20 min. from Queenstown and 3 min. from Arrowtown. **Amenities:** 3 restaurants; bar; heated indoor pool; 18-hole golf course designed by Bob Charles, pro shop, driving and putting greens; 3 tennis courts (1 all-weather, 2 grass); extensive gym; day spa; 2 Jacuzzis and 1 Japanese hot pool; saunas; bike rentals; children's holiday programs; concierge; tour desk; car rentals; courtesy shuttle to Queenstown; limited room service; massage; babysitting; laundry service; same-day dry cleaning; nonsmoking rooms; on-call doctor/dentist. *In room:* TV/VCR, dataport, kitchen in some units, minibar, fridge, coffeemaker, hair dryer, iron.

Expensive
Shotover Lodge ✸✸ *Value*   Steve and Jeanette Brough are friendly, experienced hosts who delight in sharing their new, purpose-built spot in an unbeatable location overlooking the Shotover River. They've kept it small—just three en-suite rooms—to make sure their guests get the best of their undivided attention. Once you've sampled Jeanette's outstanding gourmet breakfast and predinner canapés, you won't want to budge. She sets a very high standard for other hosted accommodations to match.

Rooms are big, relaxed, and airy with commanding mountain and river views, and all three (two in the barn) are detached from the main house for added privacy. All in all, it's rather like staying with your best friends in their big country house.

61 Atley Rd., Arthurs Point, Queenstown. © **03/441-8037.** Fax 03/441-8058. www.shotoverlodge.com. 3 units. NZ$478 (US$333). Off-peak rates available. Rates include predinner drinks, hors d'oeuvres, and breakfast. MC, V. From Queenstown, take the road to Arrowtown/Coronet Peak, go down over the Shotover River Bridge. Atley Rd. is 500m (1,640 ft.) farther on, on the right. Follow the signs to the lodge. A 5-min. drive from town. **Amenities:** House bar; nearby golf course; spa; cliff-top Jacuzzi; tour bookings; car rentals; massage; babysitting; dry cleaning; nonsmoking rooms. *In room:* TV, dataport, minibar, fridge, coffeemaker, hair dryer, iron.

White Shadows Country Inn 🌟🌟🌟 *(Moments* Set on 4 hectares (10 acres) of terraced gardens, lawns, and ponds, this romantic hideaway opened in 1999. Since then, hosts William Bailey and Michael Harris have impressed hundreds of international guests. Two guest suites are in a separate, secluded stone cottage with its own private courtyard. Rooms are plush and en-suite bathrooms have glass roofs. Wood beams, stone fireplaces, fine linens, and gourmet breakfasts are just a few of the reasons you should stay here.

58 Hunter Rd., RD1, Queenstown. © **03/442-0871.** Fax 03/442-0872. www.whiteshadows.co.nz. 2 units. NZ$695 (US$487). Rates include breakfast. AE, MC, V. Closed mid-Apr to mid-Oct each year. No children under 15. **Amenities:** Several nearby golf courses; outdoor Jacuzzi; free bikes; tour bookings; laundry service; dry cleaning; nonsmoking rooms; airport transfers. *In room:* TV/DVD, minibar, fridge, coffeemaker, hair dryer, iron, safe.

Moderate

There are charming rooms at **Arrowtown Old Nick Bed and Breakfast** 🌟🌟, 70 Buckingham St., Arrowtown (© **0800/653-642** in NZ, or 03/442-0066; www.old nick.co.nz). The tariff ranges from NZ$120 to NZ$175 (US$84–US$123), including breakfast, for two rooms in the main house that share a bathroom, and a further three rooms with en-suites in The Stables.

Arrowtown Lodge 🌟🌟 *(Finds* This architecturally designed gem consists of four semidetached cottages that replicate something of Arrowtown's gold-rush heritage. Built of mud bricks, but providing modern conveniences, the cottages offer privacy and a definite ambience that captures something of the spirit of the area. All have underfloor heating and patios. You'll get charm and 21st-century comfort here at an unbelievably reasonable rate.

7 Anglesea St., Arrowtown. © **0800/258-802** in NZ, or 03/442-1101. Fax 03/442-1108. www.arrowtownlodge.co.nz. 4 units. NZ$160–NZ$200 (US$112–US$140). MC, V. Rates include breakfast. Long-stay and off-peak rates available. Coming into Arrowtown off Malaghan Rd., turn left to Berkshire Rd. Anglesea St. is the 3rd street on the right. 20-min. drive to Queenstown and a 2-min. walk to Arrowtown center. **Amenities:** Public pool next door; nearby golf course (at Millbrook); free bikes; courtesy transport to airport and Queenstown; laundry service; nonsmoking rooms. *In room:* Dataport, coffeemaker, hair dryer.

The Old Ferry Hotel Guesthouse 🌟 If you like a sense of history, the Ferry Hotel building (ca. 1872) is the place for you. It has been lovingly restored and now oozes history in its comprehensive displays of photographs and memorabilia. Rooms all have individual charms, but take the en-suite unit if you want a bit more space. It has a fireplace and access to the vine-draped front veranda. The living room and farmhouse kitchen are delightful social spots, and the quaint rural environment is about as peaceful as you could ever imagine.

Spence Rd., RD1, Queenstown. © **0800/111-804** in NZ, or 03/442-2194. Fax 03/442-2190. www.ferry.co.nz. 2 units. NZ$215–NZ$265 (US$151–US$186). MC, V. Whole house rates on request. Rates include breakfast and airport and Queenstown transfers. Long-stay and off-peak rates available. Take St. Hwy. 6 from Queenstown for 11km (7 miles) and just over the Shotover River Bridge, turn left to Lower Shotover Rd., then immediately left again to Spence Rd. It's 10 min. from both Arrowtown and Queenstown. **Amenities:** Nearby golf course; tour bookings; car rentals; limited business facilities; laundry service; massage; babysitting; nonsmoking rooms. *In room:* Hair dryer, iron, no phone.

IN NEARBY GLENORCHY

There's a bit of everything in Glenorchy, from cheap backpackers to a very upmarket lodge. **Glenorchy Hotel** (✆ 03/442-9902; fax 03/442-9912; www.glenorchynz.com) is a classic Kiwi country-style hotel with nine rooms and backpacker accommodations for 18; **Glenorchy Holiday Park & Backpackers** (✆ 03/442-7171; glenpark@ queenstown.co.nz) has all the usual campground facilities, plus lodge rooms and cabins. Located between the Greenstone and Routeburn tracks, gorgeous little **Kinloch Lodge** ✸✸ (✆ 03/442-4900; www.kinlochlodge.co.nz) offers bunks and private rooms with shared facilities in a setting you'll always remember. Drive 45 minutes north of Queenstown and then take a 3-minute boat ride across the lake to the low-cost comforts of this outback gem.

Very Expensive

Blanket Bay ✸✸✸   This is luxury at its most sublime, and so it should be for one of the highest rates in the country. Opened in December 1999, this Small Luxury Hotels of the World member is set on sprawling grounds on the bush-clad fringes of Lake Wakatipu. At the heart of the lodge is a 9m-high (30-ft.) great room with a massive log fireplace and antique wooden floors. No expense has been spared in the construction of the spacious guest rooms. All beds are king-size, and all bathrooms have double sinks and separate showers and tubs. High-fidelity sound systems and private balconies are in every room. Designed as an exclusive haven, Blanket Bay promises a lot—and delivers.

Blanket Bay, Glenorchy. ✆ **03/442-9442.** Fax 03/442-9441. www.blanketbay.com. 13 units. NZ$1,451 (US$1,016) lodge room; NZ$2,239 (US$1,567) lodge suite; NZ$2,239 (US$1,567) chalet suite; NZ$2,690 (US$1,883) stateroom. Extra person NZ$343 (US$240). Rates include breakfast, predinner cocktails, dinner, and carte blanche use of sports equipment and facilities. AE, DC, MC, V. Closed for 3 weeks in June. Near Glenorchy, a 45-min. drive from Queenstown. Water and helipad access and limousine transport can be booked. No children under 13. **Amenities:** 2 dining rooms; 2 bars; heated outdoor pool; nearby golf course; well-equipped gym; Jacuzzi; 2 steam rooms; free watersports equipment; free bikes; game room w/complimentary bar; concierge; tour desk; car rentals; business center; massage; laundry service; dry cleaning; nonsmoking rooms. *In room:* A/C, TV/VCR/DVD, dataport, minibar, fridge, coffeemaker, hair dryer, iron, safe.

WHERE TO DINE

Queenstown is filled with an ever-changing array of good cafes and restaurants. Locals think **Habebes** (✆ 03/442-9861), in Wakatipu Arcade off Rees Street, serves the best salads in town. Its Lebanese and vegetarian offerings seem eternally popular. **Winnies** ✸, 7 The Mall (✆ 03/442-8635), is cheered for its gourmet pizzas and rustic interior. The **Skyline Gondola Restaurant** (✆ 03/441-0101) is as much an experience as a meal. Enjoy lavish lunch and evening buffets accompanied by spectacular views. A buffet dinner including gondola ride is around NZ$65 (US$46) and lunch is around NZ$50 (US$35).

IN QUEENSTOWN

Expensive

Boardwalk Seafood Restaurant & Bar ✸✸✸ SEAFOOD   Everything here is as consistent as always. After 11 years in operation, it's established itself as a leading light, especially for its innovative and impeccable presentation of seafood, steak, and lamb. Try barbecued kingfish, lightly peppered and served with grilled vegetables and

---

Finds **Winning Wines**

Gantley's Restaurant, 172 Arthur's Point Rd., Arthur's Point (*©* **03/442-8999**), has an extensive wine list with over 250 selections, showcasing some of the most outstanding wines produced in New Zealand. One of only four New Zealand restaurants to win an Award of Excellence from *Wine Spectator* magazine for "having one of the most outstanding restaurant wine lists in the world," Gantley's is also the only New Zealand restaurant to have received the award five times. Main courses range from NZ$30 to NZ$40 (US$21–US$28), and they're open daily from 6:30pm; they offer courtesy transport from Queenstown.

---

smoked tomato dressing, or baked salmon steak marinated in lime, lemon grass, and ginger, served on steamed baby greens with roasted cashews. Despite the competition from new fine-dining players, award-winning Boardwalk is always mentioned in top recommendations.

Steamer Wharf, Beach St. *©* **03/442-5630.** Reservations required. Main courses NZ$29–NZ$34 (US$20–US$24). AE, DC, MC, V. Daily 6pm–late.

Eichardt's House Bar *✿✿✿ Finds* CONTEMPORARY NEW ZEALAND   For a sublime lunch experience (or just coffee and cake), treat yourself to the oh-so-classy environs of Eichardt's House Bar, in the private hotel building on the ground floor. Just five tables add to the air of exclusivity, so be in quick. New Zealand crab and scallop cake, wild pork pies, Moroccan chicken, and delicious vegetarian dishes have all featured on this top menu. Small but big on atmosphere, it's a must. It's also a great cocktail spot at night, before or after dinner.

Ground Floor, Eichardt's Private Hotel, Marine Parade. *©* **03/442-0450.** Reservations recommended. Main courses NZ$24–NZ$30 (US$17–US$21). AE, DC, MC, V. Daily 11am–11pm; lunch only noon–2pm.

Solera Vino *✿✿✿* NEW ZEALAND/MEDITERRANEAN   My most recent meal here was simply outstanding. Tucked into the little window seat of the tiny restaurant, with a romantic fire roaring and reflections flickering across white plaster walls, the mood was set for roast duck breast with six spices and thyme honey, or rack of lamb roasted with thyme, cumin, and olive crust and served with zucchini and aubergine gateau.

25 Beach St. *©* **03/442-6082.** Reservations required. Main courses NZ$28–NZ$38 (US$20–US$27). AE, MC, V. Daily 6pm–late.

Tatler *✿✿* ASIAN/PACIFIC   This is one of the justifiably favored restaurants in Queenstown. The dark-timbered interior sets up an instant atmosphere and meals (tops in presentation) are consistently well flavored and tasty. Whether it's chile lemon chicken stir-fry with Asian noodles, roast Mediterranean vegetables, seafood chowder, or chicken coconut curry on basmati rice, Tatler is what I call a sure thing. I go there every time I'm in Queenstown.

5 The Mall. *©* **03/442-8372.** Reservations recommended for dinner. Main courses NZ$22–NZ$30 (US$15–US$21). AE, MC, V. Daily 10am–late.

Wai Waterfront Restaurant *✿✿✿* MODERN NEW ZEALAND   Taking over the old location of Lagos on Steamer Wharf, Wai (Maori for "water") was a winner from the beginning. Its heavy focus on fresh seafood and oysters is well complemented by the water lapping directly outside its doors, and summer outdoor tables give it a festive feel. If you like fresh oysters, you'll be in seventh heaven (when they're in season, that is), and you should try them with lime sorbet and vodka, or baked in an herb Parmesan crust. Beyond that, venison, beef, lamb, duck, and ostrich also feature on an exciting menu.

Steamer Wharf, Beach St. © 03/442-5969. Reservations required, especially for a waterfront table. Main courses NZ$29–NZ$40 (US$20–US$28). AE, DC, MC, V. Daily 11am–late.

Moderate

Fishbone Bar & Grill ✸✸ SEAFOOD   If I could have a restaurant in my backyard, it would be this one. It's wacky and colorful, the decorative fish-filled interior is a joy, and the seafood meals rate among the best I've had. South Island salmon smoked over Canadian sycamore wood chips and served with aioli was mouthwatering; the blue cod dishes are reliably good; and for a well-priced fill-up, you can't pass up a Fishbone burger bulging with fish filet. Service is filled with humor and desserts are to die for—complete with a chocolate fish.

7 Beach St. © 03/442-6768. Main courses NZ$20–NZ$32 (US$14–US$22). AE, DC, MC, V. Daily 5:30pm–late.

Old Man Rock ✸ *Value* MODERN NEW ZEALAND   If you want fast, casual, and tasty, this cafe/bar will deliver. Staff members have an extra dose of personality, and the interior features lots of timber, stone walls, and a fireplace and sofas. The menu darts across pastas, delicious pizzas, salads, and beer-battered fish. It has a big following of 20- and 30-somethings and connects with Chico's nightclub upstairs.

The Mall. © 03/442-8968. Main courses NZ$14–NZ$25 (US$9.80–US$18). AE, MC, V. Daily 9am–2am.

Inexpensive

Joe's Garage ✸✸✸ *Finds* CAFE   Although trendily hard to find, you *must* seek out Joe's because in my mind, it is the best coffee provider in QT. It's a case of American roadie-style cafe meeting Queenstown hip—and strangely, it works. It's little more than a garage, virtually unadorned but for the buzzy atmosphere and chatty locals. Sit up at the counter while you wait for a strong espresso, bacon and bun, panini, or burger. This is my favored Queenstown cafe; I just can't keep away from it.

(*Moments* Treasure Hunt

Every city has them—those luscious little culinary secrets that locals like to keep for themselves. I won't win friends in Queenstown for this, but I'm going to tell you about **The Bunker** ✸✸✸, Cow Lane (© 03/441-8030). And don't think that just because I've given you the address, you're going to be able to find it easily. It hides behind a very unassuming door and just assumes that people who are hungry and passionate enough, will find it. And once you do unearth it, you won't regret the hunt. It's a tiny restaurant with a huge reputation for classy haute cuisine, an intimate atmosphere, and an impressive collection of single malt whiskeys. Venison, lamb, scampi, quail, and duck all take their place on an innovative menu that will most definitely make a hole in your wallet. It's open from 5pm until 5am, by which time you'll probably be bankrupt but hugely satisfied.

Camp St., beside the post office (the little brown building with a flag over the door). © 03/442-5282. Most menu items under NZ$18 (US$13). AE, MC, V. Daily 7am–5pm.

Vesta ✿✿✿ *(Finds* CAFE   For a truly unique coffee experience mixed with history, contemporary design, and quirky retail opportunity, head for Vesta. This tiny espresso bar (with snacks and light meals) is tucked into the back of Queenstown's oldest house (1864) and modern art and design appear against a backdrop of the original, peeling 1800s floral wallpapers. Don't miss it and be prepared to loosen your wallet on goodies to take home.

Williams Cottage, Marine Parade, Queenstown. © 03/442-5687. Menu items NZ$5–NZ$20 (US$3.50–US$14). AE, MC, V. Daily 9am–5pm.

IN NEARBY ARROWTOWN

Café Mondo ✿✿ CAFE   Easy to miss, this little gem is tucked down the bottom of an arcade, where it fronts on to a sunny courtyard. Inside, the interior is unassuming, the food superb. Favored for its big breakfasts, it also presents delicious treats like corn-and-feta fritters, salmon rosti, Asian beef salad, and chicken stacks for lunch, or relaxed evening meals.

Ballarat Arcade, Arrowtown. © 03/442-0227. Reservations recommended for dinner. Main courses NZ$14–NZ$29 (US$9.80–US$20). AE, MC, V. Daily 8am–late.

Pesto ✿✿ *(Value* ITALIAN/PIZZA   Baby sister to Saffron, Pesto offers a classy, copper-clad casual setting in which to bite into some of the most succulent pizzas in this part of the world. Pasta with anchovies, tomato, Italian sausage, spinach, and lemon chile oil will also tempt. All ages gather in the sunny courtyard and the super-cool interior.

18 Buckingham St. © 03/442-0131. Reservations recommended. Pastas NZ$15–NZ$18 (US$11–US$13); pizzas NZ$15–NZ$28 (US$11–US$20). AE, DC, MC, V. Daily 5pm–late.

Postmaster's House ✿✿✿ CONTEMPORARY NEW ZEALAND/EUROPEAN   This is another feather in Arrowtown's rather surprising culinary cap. Who would have expected this tiny village to dish up another top eatery after Saffron? Come here to enjoy a restored historic building, an elegant interior, and delicious meals that might include leg of venison with red-onion goat-cheese tart with black-truffle jus, or bouillabasse and foie gras. Sink back in your leather chair with a glass of the region's best wine and resign yourself to indulgence.

Buckingham St., Arrowtown. © 03/442-0991. Reservations essential. Main courses NZ$28–NZ$36 (US$20–US$25). AE, DC, MC, V. Daily 6pm–late.

Saffron 🦆🦆🦆 *Finds* MODERN NEW ZEALAND When you're named in *Condé Nast Traveler's* list of the 100 Best Tables in the World (2001), you've got a lot to live up to, but Saffron seems to be managing the stress rather well. It's currently considered one of the most serious fine-food places in the region. Book ahead, because people are coming from miles around to enjoy Bollinger by the fireside before meals such as Thai duck and lemon-grass curry with two rices.

18 Buckingham St. ② 03/442-0131. Reservations required. Main courses NZ$29–NZ$40 (US$20–US$28). AE, DC, MC, V. Daily 11am–late.

IN NEARBY GLENORCHY

Glenorchy is a bit lean on dining options, but you won't starve. **Glenorchy Hotel** (② 03/442-9902) has a terrace cafe and restaurant with a la carte, stone grill, and bistro dining; and **Glenorchy Café** (② 03/442-9958) can fill the gaps with snacks and light meals in a casual atmosphere. **Kinloch Lodge** 🦆🦆 (② 03/442-4900) has the best menu, with the likes of Thai rare beef salad, mushroom and Parmesan risotto, or a large platter of local cheeses, meats, and breads.

QUEENSTOWN AFTER DARK

Midwinter in Queenstown is a night owl's paradise. There's plenty happening all year, of course, but once the town fills up with international visitors, anything can, and often does, happen.

Queenstown now has two casinos. **SKYCITY Queenstown Casino,** 16–24 Beach St. (② 03/441-0400; www.skyalpine.co.nz), has over 70 gaming machines and the usual table games such as roulette, blackjack, and baccarat. Also here are Wild Thyme Bar & Restaurant and live entertainment on Friday and Saturday nights. It's open daily from noon to 4am. **Wharf Casino,** Steamer Wharf (② 03/441-1495; www. wharf-casino.co.nz), is a boutique operation with much the same on offer in the way of games. It's open daily from 11am to 3am. In both cases, you must be over 20 and smartly dressed to enter.

Those with wild times on their mind head for **Chico's Restaurant & Bar** 🦆🦆, on The Mall (② 03/442-8439). It has great food, live entertainment, and dancing from 10:30pm until late. **The Edge Niteclub** 🦆, Camp and Man streets (② 03/442-4144); **The World,** Shotover Street (② 03/4426757); and **Triple M,** Shotover Street (② 03/442-7853), are all part of the recognized backpacker scene. **Shooters Bar,** 10 Brecon St. (② 03/442-4144), is dominated by pool tables and a football crowd. **The Dux de Lux,** 14 Church St. (② 03/442-9688), draws big crowds with its specialty beers and great atmosphere.

Most people 35-plus tend to hang out at **Fraser's Bar & Grill** 🦆🦆🦆, in the Steamer Wharf Complex (② 03/442-5111), where there's occasional live music. Also in this area, you can freeze your tail off in the name of a good time at **Minus 5,** Steamer Wharf (② 03/442-6050), in the company of hand-sculpted ice and vodka cocktails. If you like things a little hotter, try **The Boiler Room,** Steamer Wharf (② 03/441-8066), which entices with "an element of corruption."

Those of you who like a sense of discovery in your nightlife may want to hunt for "the B bars"—a cluster of nightspots started up by Queenstown entrepreneur Al Spary. **The Bunker** 🦆🦆🦆, Cow Lane (② 03/441-8030), is favored by a 20s-to-40s crowd and plays on no advertising, no signs, and the fact that it's hard to find. Equally obscure is **Bardeaux** 🦆🦆, Eureka Arcade, off The Mall (② 03/442-8284), a sophisticated late-night wine and cocktail bar. **Barup,** next to Bardeaux (② 03/442-7707), is an exclusive Swiss chalet–type of wine and cocktail bar; ask around among the locals and you might get shown the way.

It's all class and cocktails at **Eichardt's House Bar** ✿✿✿, Marine Parade (© 03/ 441-0442), which is one of most people's favorites; and by the time this book hits the shelves, the Sofitel's Champagne Lounge will likely be another trendy hangout for the moneyed crowd.

EN ROUTE TO TE ANAU

Te Anau is a 172km (107-mile) drive from Queenstown on excellent roads. Follow State Highway 6 to Kingston at the south end of Lake Wakatipu, where you'll have the option of taking a ride on the historic *Kingston Flyer* (© 03/248-8848; www. kingstonflyer.co.nz), a pre-1930s passenger train pulled by steam engines. The train departs at 10:15am and 3:45pm daily from October 1 to April 30. The round-trip takes 1½ hours and costs around NZ$35 (US$25) return for adults, NZ$15 (US$11) for children. The train is owned and operated (on track set in 1878) by TranzRail.

Continue on State Highway 6 through the tiny township of **Athol** and then turn west onto State Highway 94 over the summit of **Gorge Hill,** along the **Mararoa River,** and through sheep and cattle country to **Te Anau,** nestled beside the largest lake on the South Island.

4 Te Anau ✿✿

172km (107 miles) SW of Queenstown; 116km (72 miles) S of Milford Sound; 157km (97 miles) NW of Invercargill

Te Anau is the hub of Fiordland National Park, a magnificent 1.2-million-hectare (3-million-acre) World Heritage Site filled with scenic wonders, serenity, mystery, and some of the best walking tracks in the world. The little resort township is built around the foreshore of Lake Te Anau, the largest of the South Island lakes. It has a permanent population of about 3,000, which swells to over 10,000 in summer. If you're coming to explore Fiordland's waterfalls, virgin forests, mountains, rivers, and lonely fiords, this is the place to base yourself.

Lake Te Anau is a wonder in itself. Its eastern shoreline, where the township is located, is virtually treeless, with about 76 centimeters (30 in.) of annual rainfall, while its western banks are covered in dense forest nurtured by more than 254 centimeters (100 in.) of rain each year. What attracts visitors to New Zealand's second-largest lake are the opportunity for watersports and the proximity to Milford Sound, 116km (72 miles) away. The sound, which is actually a fiord, reaches 23km (14 miles) in from the Tasman Sea, flanked by sheer granite peaks and traced by playful waterfalls. Its waters and surrounding land have been kept in as nearly a primeval state as humans could possibly manage without leaving it totally untouched. In fine weather or pouring rain, Milford Sound exudes a powerful sense of nature's pristine harmony and beauty.

Milford Sound may be the most famous and accessible of the fiords, but Doubtful Sound is the deepest and, according to some, the most beautiful. Even farther south, Dusky Sound may well qualify as the most remote and mysterious of the famous trio.

ESSENTIALS

GETTING THERE   By Plane   Air services to Te Anau and Fiordland are provided by **Air Fiordland Ltd.** (© 03/249-7505; fax 03/249-7080). Charter flights are also available.

By Coach (Bus) Daily coach service runs between Te Anau and Christchurch, Dunedin, and Invercargill via **InterCity** (© **03/379-9020**). Daily service also runs to Te Anau and Milford Sound from Queenstown. And numerous shuttle bus companies make daily trips, too. Information is available at the visitor centers in Queenstown, Invercargill, and Te Anau.

By Car From Queenstown, take State Highway 6, then State Highway 94 (see "En Route to Te Anau," above, for details).

ORIENTATION Te Anau's main street is State Highway 94, called Milford Road within the township, with the post office, restaurants, grocery stores, and most shops. The majority of hotels and motels are on Lakefront Drive, which stretches attractively around the lake. The township is tiny and very easy to negotiate on foot or by car.

VISITOR INFORMATION The **Fiordland i-Site Visitor Centre,** Lakefront Drive, P.O. Box 1, Te Anau (© **03/249-8900;** fax 03/249-7022; fiordland-isite@real journeys.co.nz), sits at the lake end of Milford Road. It shares the same office as **Real Journeys** (© **0800/656-501** in NZ, or 03/249-7416; www.realjourneys.co.nz). Hours are daily from 8:30am to 5:30pm. The **Fiordland National Park Visitor Centre,** Lakefront Drive, P.O. Box 29, Te Anau (© **03/249-7924;** fax 03/249-7613; www.doc.govt.nz), is a must for anyone contemplating doing either short walks around Te Anau or the well-known multiday tramps—Hollyford, Routeburn, Milford, Kepler, and Caples. It's open daily from 8:30am to 8pm in January, from 8:30am to 4:30pm April 24 through October 24, and from 8:30am to 6pm the rest of the year. For more information, go to www.fiordland.org.nz.

SPECIAL EVENTS The **Fiordland Summer Festival Weekend** (© **03/249-7959**), held in January, includes a celebrity debate, rodeo, garden tours, harness racing, arts and crafts, food stalls, and street entertainment. The **Kepler Challenge** and the **Luxmoore Grunt** (© **03/249-9596;** www.keplerchallenge.co.nz), are tough international ultra-marathon races held in December each year.

EXPLORING TE ANAU & THE SOUNDS

Milford and Doubtful sounds are the primary draws of this area, and in Te Anau you'll discover a number of options for exploring one or both. You can drive, fly, or take a coach to Milford Sound from Te Anau (see "Milford Sound" later in this chapter), and you can fly over or take a scenic cruise through Doubtful Sound.

You'll quickly discover that people in Te Anau are reluctant to recommend one sound or one excursion above another, so explore the choices carefully. Consider your available time and the amount of money you want to spend. My advice would be to drive to Milford and, if you can, overnight on one of the boats; then, if you're still keen to see Doubtful and Dusky sounds, take the 40-minute flight. Not only does this take

---

Natural Mystery

For an excellent cinematic introduction to the greater Fiordland region—much which, you will never lay eyes on otherwise—make sure you see *Ata Whenua-Shadowland,* a stunning and unforgettable cinematic journey. Call **Fiordland Cinema,** The Lane, Te Anau (© **03/249-8812;** www.fiordlandcinema.co.nz), for session times.

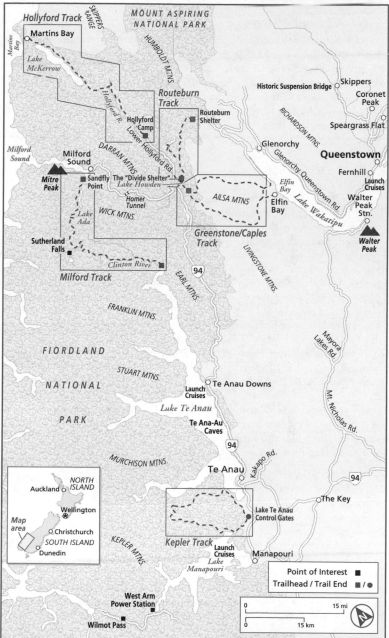

Te Anau & Fiordland

Hollyford Track

Martins Bay

Martins Bay

Lake McKerrow

SKIPPERS RANGE

MOUNT ASPIRING NATIONAL PARK

HUMBOLDT MTNS.

Hollyford R.

Hollyford Camp

Lower Hollyford Rd.

Routeburn Track

Routeburn Shelter

Historic Suspension Bridge

Skippers

Coronet Peak

RICHARDSON MTNS.

Speargrass Flat

Glenorchy

Queenstown

DARRAN MTNS.

Milford Sound

Milford Sound

Sandfly Point

The "Divide Shelter"

Lake Howden

Homer Tunnel

AILSA MTNS.

Glenorchy Queenstown Rd.

Elfin Bay

Elfin Bay

Fernhill

Walter Peak Stn.

Launch Cruises

Mitre Peak

WICK MTNS.

Lake Ada

Lake Wakatipu

Walter Peak

Sutherland Falls

Clinton River

Milford Track

EARL MTNS.

94

Greenstone/Caples Track

LIVINGSTONE MTNS.

FRANKLIN MTNS.

FIORDLAND

NATIONAL

PARK

STUART MTNS.

MURCHISON MTNS.

Launch Cruises

Te Anau Downs

Lake Te Anau

Te Ana-Au Caves

94

Te Anau

Katapo Rd.

MAYORA Lakes Rd.

Mt. Nicholas Rd.

94

The Key

KEPLER MTNS.

Kepler Track

Lake Te Anau Control Gates

Launch Cruises

Lake Manapouri

Manapouri

NORTH ISLAND

Auckland

Wellington

Map area

Christchurch

SOUTH ISLAND

Dunedin

Point of Interest ■

Trailhead / Trail End ■ / ●

West Arm Power Station

Wilmot Pass

0   15 mi

0   15 km

N

Tips **A Sound Difference**

Real Journey's Doubtful Sound cruise has English-only commentary and no food other than picnic lunches available. It's a longer cruise than the Milford Sound option and much more remote. You'll see far fewer people at Doubtful—and given that there are around 100 buses a day going into Milford, that says a lot. Milford Sound is more dramatic and awe-inspiring, but Doubtful is a lot more untouched and remote. You're also far more likely to see wildlife at Doubtful—not that the dolphins are on the payroll!

---

just a fraction of the cruise time, but you also get a thrilling perspective of otherwise inaccessible areas.

Air Fiordland, Town Centre, Te Anau (© **0800/107-505** in NZ, or 03/249-7505; www.airfiordland.com), has several Milford Sound flight packages, some combining cruise options, plus an excellent 40-minute flight over Doubtful Sound.

Southern Lakes Helicopters, Lakefront Drive (© **03/249-7167;** www.southern lakeshelicopters.co.nz), has a 50-minute flight over Doubtful Sound that passes soaring peaks and waterfalls. The highlight is the flight into Campbell's Kingdom, which is accessible only by helicopter. Prices for all their flights are on application. **Fiordland Helicopters,** Te Anau Airport (© **03/249-7575;** www.fiordlandhelicopters.co.nz), offers trips that range from 15 minutes to 1½ hours. It's a little cheaper than Southern Lakes, but it's based farther out of town and runs only one helicopter.

If a full-day bus tour (from Te Anau) is more your style, join the "Discover Milford Sound" tour run by **Great Sights** (© **0800/744-487** in NZ; www.greatsights.co.nz). It runs daily, departing 10:15am from Te Anau Travel Centre and returns at 5:15pm. It costs around NZ$120 (US$84) for adults and NZ$60 (US$42) for children. You can include lunch for an extra NZ$25 to NZ$30 (US$18–US$21) per person. Another good option is the popular **Milford Sound Barbecue Bus** ✿✿ (© **0800/421-045;** www.milford.net.nz), which departs from either Queenstown or Te Anau. It's a smaller group tour and includes a classic barbecue lunch in spectacular Hollyford Valley rather than on the cruise boats.

DOUBTFUL SOUND ✿✿✿

Doubtful Sound makes an idyllic day excursion from Lake Manapouri. At 21m (69 ft.), it's the deepest of the fiords. Filled with ancient rainforest, cascading waterfalls, towering peaks, and abundant wildlife, it's an unforgettable experience. An air of complete silence, broken only by birdcall, adds to the mystery.

Doubtful Sound is 10 times bigger than Milford, and although it can't boast Mitre Peak, its still waters mirror 1,200m (3,936-ft.) **Commander Peak.** Another difference between the two sounds is that you always know Milford is close to civilization because of the buzz of aircraft going to and from the airstrip and the multitude of buses that make their way there on a daily basis. Doubtful is much more remote.

There's no way to get to Doubtful Sound on your own. Real Journeys (see "Visitor Information," above) transports visitors from Manapouri, then takes a launch trip to the West Arm, followed by a 20km (12-mile) coach trip to Deep Cove in Doubtful Sound. The coach takes you up and over Wilmot Pass, 662m (2,171 ft.) above sea level, stopping on the way to visit **Manapouri Power Station,** where you spiral 225 eerie meters (750 ft.) downward to view the seven immense underground turbines. A second launch then takes you out into the sound, and if you're lucky, you'll spot the resident pod of 60 or more dolphins, fur seals, and rare crested penguins. You'll get close enough to waterfalls to feel the spray, and you'll be able to savor total silence when the captain shuts off the engine.

Real Journey's Doubtful Sound day excursions will introduce you to their brand new catamaran, which came on stream in November 2005, replacing the *Commander Peak*. It carries 150 passengers over two decks and departs daily from Manapouri with connecting coaches from Queenstown or Te Anau. Visitors can self-drive from Queenstown in 2½ hours and from Te Anau in 40 minutes. Reservations are essential. From Manapouri, the Wilderness trip costs NZ$215 (US$151) for adults, NZ$45 (US$32) for children. From Te Anau, add about NZ$20 (US$14), and another NZ$22 (US$15) for a preordered picnic lunch. From October to May, Real Journey's offers overnight cruises on the *Fiordland Navigator*. It offers a range of accommodations for up to 70 passengers, from en-suite cabins to quad-share bunks. From Manapouri, adults pay NZ$475 (US$333) for a twin share and NZ$315 (US$221) for a bunk; children pay NZ$238 (US$167) for a cabin.

THE MILFORD TRACK & OTHER WALKS

Most dedicated trampers consider the famous **Milford Track** ❀❀❀ the finest anywhere in the world. Four days are required to walk the 54km (33 miles) from Glad Jetty at Lake Te Anau's northern end to Sandfly Point on the western bank of Milford Sound. Other popular walks in this area are the **Hollyford Valley,** the **Routeburn,** and the **Kepler.** For more information, see "Tramping" in chapter 3.

OTHER OUTDOOR PURSUITS

FISHING   Fiordland offers unsurpassed opportunities for wilderness trophy trout fishing. The best fishing is in the Eglinton Valley. Ian Murray of **Fish 'n' Trips** (📞 **03/ 249-7656;** fax 03/249-7663) clearly has a sense of humor. If you want a guided wilderness fishing experience, call him. **Fiordland Guides** ❀❀, 472 Te Anau-Milford Hwy. (📞 **03/249-7832;** www.fiordlandlodge.co.nz), can take you on a terrific fishing trip for NZ$350 (US$245) for a half-day, NZ$600 (US$420) for a full day, or NZ$100 (US$70) per hour.

Moments All A-Glow ❀❀

The **Te Anau Glowworm Caves** excursion on Lake Te Anau is operated by **Real Journeys,** Lakefront Drive, Te Anau (📞 **0800/656-501** in NZ, or 03/249-7416; www.realjourneys.co.nz). This adventure runs year-round and includes an underground boat ride into the glowworm grotto. The geologically young caves (only about 15,000 years old) have 200m (656 ft.) of passages, which are still being formed by water cascading down the cave tiers at a rate of 55,000 gallons per minute. On the second level of the waterbed, you'll see the glowworm grotto. If you want to enjoy the 16km (10-mile) lake cruise to the caves, take the daylight option (NZ$49/US$34 adults, NZ$15/US$11 children). The evening options run from October to April. A major revamp of the caves' underground walkway system is planned, with completion due in 2006. The caves will remain open during the building program.

HORSERIDING Pay NZ$70 (US$49) for a horse trek through beautiful landscapes with **High Ride Adventures,** 865 Wilderness Rd. (© **03/249-8591;** www. highride.co.nz). They pick up tours at 9:30am and 2pm, and in summer at 6pm.

KAYAKING Fiordland Wilderness Experiences, 66 Quintin Dr. (© **03/249-7700;** www.fiordlandseakayak.co.nz), offers guided sea-kayaking options ranging in length from 1 to 6 days. It goes to Milford, Dusky, and Doubtful Sounds and Lake Manapouri. See the section on "Milford Sound," below, for further kayaking options.

WHERE TO STAY

Reserve well ahead for visits between Christmas and February. Once the peak season is over, you can expect to get some incredibly good deals. There are numerous motel complexes along the waterfront; and travelers interested in a B&B stay should consider the old-world charms of **Te Anau Lodge** ☆, 52 Howden St., Te Anau (© **03/249-7477;** www.teanaulodge.com). Originally a convent, this grand old building has been relocated to a new garden and restored to offer seven rooms with en-suite bathrooms. Backpackers are well served in Te Anau and one of the nicest is **Te Anau Backpackers Lodge,** 48 Lakefront Dr. (© **0800/200-074** in NZ, or 03/249-7713; www. teanaubackpackers.co.nz), where dorm beds are from NZ$25 (US$18) and doubles cost NZ$60 to NZ$75 (US$42–US$53).

VERY EXPENSIVE

Fiordland Lodge ☆☆☆ _Value_ Ron and Robynne Peacock are responsible for this gem of a rural lodge that sits on a tussock-covered ridge overlooking Lake Te Anau. Think stylish tree house and you won't be far wrong. Wood is the focus and I'll be amazed if you don't come away impressed. I especially love the creative way they use logs to support the bathroom basins. Take one of the smart lodge rooms for in-house comforts, or opt for the privacy and romance of one of the two quaintest little log cabins. Either way, this will be one of your most impressive New Zealand stays.

472 Te Anau-Milford Hwy. © 03/249-7832. Fax 03/249-7449. www.fiordlandlodge.co.nz. 12 units. NZ$760–NZ$820 (US$532–US$574) lodge rooms; NZ$980–NZ$1,040 (US$686–US$728) executive suite; NZ$360–NZ$420 (US$252–US$294) log cabins, sleep 4. Off-peak and exclusive packages available. In-house lodge room rates include dinner, bed, and breakfast; cabin rates, breakfast only. AE, DC, MC, V. 5km from Te Anau. Turn right into no. 472. When road forks into 3, take the center driveway and follow to top. **Amenities:** Restaurant; bar; nearby golf course; courtesy transport to Te Anau; resident fishing and nature guide; massage; laundry service; nonsmoking rooms; access for travelers w/disabilities. _In room:_ TV/VCR, dataport, fridge, hair dryer.

MODERATE

The Cat's Whiskers Bed & Breakfast ☆☆ Quiet rooms open onto a sunny garden courtyard at the rear of Lindsay and Anne Marie Bernstone's contemporary lakeside home. Just across the street from the Fiordland National Park Visitor Centre and a 10-minute walk from the center of town, it has location and quiet on its side. All rooms are comfortable and colorful, with en-suite bathrooms. The family room downstairs is spacious, but doesn't see as much sun as the upstairs units—the king-size-bed room overlooks the lake and park, while others have their own balconies. There is separate outdoor access for guests, which adds to the privacy you can enjoy here.

2 Lakefront Dr., Te Anau. ©/fax 03/249-8112. www.catswhiskers.co.nz. 4 units. NZ$155–NZ$170 (US$109–US$119); NZ$30 (US$21) each extra person. Rates include breakfast. Winter rates negotiable. MC, V. **Amenities:** Nearby golf course; laundry facilities; nonsmoking rooms. _In room:_ TV, fridge, coffeemaker, hair dryer, no phone.

Te Anau Hotel & Villas ☆☆ If you prefer privacy away from the tour groups and tramping groups who frequent this hotel, spend the extra money and go for one of the deluxe villa suites set in rose gardens around the pool. You can also get interconnecting rooms for families or couples traveling together. The hotel is dated in parts, but let's not forget it was originally built in 1965 and refurbishment is ongoing. Overall, it offers an acceptable level of comfort and service.

64 Lakefront Dr., Te Anau. (🅒 0800/223-687 in NZ, or 03/249-9700. Fax 03/249-7947. www.teanauhotel.co.nz. 112 units. NZ$265–NZ$450 (US$186–US$315). Long-stay and winter rates available. AE, DC, MC, V. **Amenities:** Restaurant; bar; heated outdoor pool; nearby golf course; Jacuzzi; sauna; tour desk; car rentals; courtesy car; business services; limited room service; massage; babysitting; laundry; nonsmoking rooms; foreign-currency exchange; on-call doctor/dentist; access for travelers w/disabilities. *In room:* TV, dataport, kitchen in villa suites; minibar, fridge, coffeemaker, hair dryer, iron.

WHERE TO DINE

The dining scene is slowly improving, but there's still room for innovation and snappier service. Just remember that if you come here out of the main tourist season, several eateries close for the winter months. Apart from the listings below, the **Mackinnon Room,** at Te Anau Hotel (see "Where to Stay," above), is a reliable restaurant with an extensive menu. For something more low-key, try **Pop-In Cafe,** 92 Lakefront Dr. (🅒 03/249-7807), where light meals take the form of meat pies, sandwiches, salads, and fries. It's a good place to stock up on picnic food; it also has Internet access. It's open daily from 7am. **Ming Garden Chinese Restaurant,** Loop Road (🅒 03/249-7770), is the best of the Asian restaurants, and **La Toscana Pizzeria** 🅐🅐, Uptown (🅒 03/249-7756), is one of the town's better culinary bets. It's open from 5:30pm. For good coffee, head for **Naturally Fiordland** 🅐🅐, 62 Town Centre (🅒 03/249-7111). They also have fabulous smoothies, squeezed juices, soups, and teas; they're open from 9am to late.

Bailiez Restaurant, Café & Bar 🅐 (Value) INTERNATIONAL/MEXICAN

Bailiez draws a mixed crowd, from singles to families. Stone fireplaces and comfy sofas add a loungelike character to the restaurant. The Mexican section of the menu is popular. Fish, game, and light snacks also feature on an all-day menu, along with traditional treats such as cranberry venison. It's nothing fancy, but it serves up a hearty meal.

Luxmore Resort Hotel, Milford Rd. (🅒 03/249-7526. Main courses NZ$22–NZ$28 (US$15–US$20). AE, DC, MC, V. Daily 9am–late.

Recliff Café 🅐🅐 NEW ZEALAND/INTERNATIONAL

Step into a cute old cottage refitted with a contemporary bar and moody little dining rooms. The menu here is fresh and inviting, incorporating all food types in a healthy, modern way. You'll find it frequented by backpackers and older folks alike, who come to enjoy a lively atmosphere that includes guitar music. Offerings range from Fiordland venison to orange roughy grilled with a chile-and-coriander-herb crust and served with a fresh Greek salad and tzatziki. Vegetarians and vegans are well taken care of.

12 Mokonui St. (🅒 03/249-7431. Main courses NZ$22–NZ$30 (US$15–US$21). MC, V. Summer daily 4pm–1am; call for winter hours.

Sandfly Café 🅐🅐 CAFE

You know you're in the deep south when a cafe decorates its computers with possum fur! Quirky, charming, and friendly, this is my favorite Te Anau cafe. People of all ages and walks of life congregate here on stools and sofas, for the excellent coffee, tasty salads, soups, and hot paninis.

9 The Lane, Te Anau. (🅒 03/249-9529. Main courses NZ$15–NZ$25 (US$11–US$18). MC, V. Daily 8am–6pm.

EN ROUTE TO DUNEDIN

If you've already visited Milford Sound and are planning to travel to Dunedin from Te Anau, the drive will take about 4½ hours over good roads. Take State Highway 94 across Gorge Hill into Lumsden, across the Waimea Plains to the milling center of Gore, through farmlands to Clinton, and across rolling downs to Balclutha. From there, take State Highway 1 north along the coast past Milton and Lookout Point, where you'll get your first look at Dunedin. Along the way, you might stop at **Wapiti Handcrafts Ltd.,** on Mossburn's main street; it makes and sells deerskin fashions.

5 Milford Sound ★★★

119km (74 miles) NE of Te Anau; 286km (177 miles) NW of Queenstown

No matter when you visit or what the weather is like, your memories of Milford Sound are bound to be special. Its 14 nautical miles leading to the Tasman Sea are lined with mountain peaks that rise sharply out of the water to heights of 1,800m (5,904 ft.). Forsters fur seals laze on rocky shelves, and dolphins play in water that reaches depths of 600m (1,968 ft.). The sound's entrance is so hidden when viewed from the sea that Captain Cook sailed right by without noticing it when he charted the waters some 200 years ago.

It rains a lot in Milford Sound, and that's an understatement. And while I'm on negatives, it can't be stressed enough that weather in this area is extremely changeable, even in summer, so come prepared. As many have found, reading about the cold and rain in midsummer is one thing, experiencing it quite another. Over 927 centimeters (365 in.) fall annually, so be prepared to get wet. The sound is a mystical, moody place when it rains. You may not glimpse the mountaintops or Mitre Peak through the mist, but you'll see hundreds of waterfalls cascading down spectacular cliff faces. In dry conditions, there are only three or four permanent waterfalls in the sound.

In summer, coaches pour in at a rate of 100 per day for the launch cruises—that's up to 5,000 people joining you for a look at this special place. If you're prepared to overlook this rather cramped state of affairs, you'll be rewarded with grand, unforgettable landscapes.

THE MILFORD ROAD

The road to Milford Sound is world-famous. Although it can be completed in 2 hours, allow at least 3 so you can stop to look at the many natural attractions along the way. Highway 94 from Te Anau leads north along the lake, with islands and wooded distant shores on your left. The drive is often a slow one, especially in wet conditions, as you make your way through steep gorges and between walls of solid rock and moss-covered inclines. I would discourage anyone from taking a motorhome on this road as it is narrow, steep, and winding with a lot of bus traffic—and if that doesn't put you off, the dark, narrow tunnel will. The road is usually very busy in summer and there can be

Tips **Warning**

During the winter months, take the NO STOPPING—AVALANCHE ZONE signs along the Milford Road very seriously. No matter how much you want to stop and take a photograph, don't—it could cost you your life.

delays, especially at Homer Tunnel. *Remember:* There are no fuel stops between Te Anau and Milford, so make sure your tank is full. This is NOT a road you want to be "marooned" on—in any season. During the winter months, all drivers on Milford Road are required by law to carry chains for their vehicles. Road conditions can be checked on www.milfordroad.co.nz, or by calling © **0900/33-222** in NZ (calls cost NZ$1/US70¢ per minute).

Be sure to stop for pictures at the **Mirror Lakes.** The road winds down the **Eglinton** and **Hollyford valleys,** through the astoundingly narrow and steep **Homer Tunnel,** and down into the majestic **Cleddau Valley,** to Milford Sound. Before you go, stop by the **Fiordland National Park Visitor Centre,** Lakefront Drive, Te Anau (© **03/249-7921;** fax 03/249-7613; www.doc.govt.nz), for information on Fiordland National Park. Ask specifically for the pamphlet *The Road To Milford* (about NZ$3/US$2.10), which describes each mile of the journey. It's not a bad idea to go armed with sand-fly repellent, too.

Homer Tunnel, about 101km (63 miles) into the journey, is a major engineering marvel: a 1.2km (¾-mile) passageway first proposed in 1889, begun in 1935, and finally opened in 1940. It wasn't until 1954 before a connecting road was completed and the first private automobile drove through. There's no lighting in the tunnel and it's very narrow. Drive with extreme care!

About 6km (3¾ miles) past the tunnel, stop and walk to **The Chasm.** The pleasant 15-minute round-trip goes through mossy undergrowth and beech forest to see a rather wonderful feat of natural erosion on the **Cleddau River.**

EXPLORING THE SOUND

To be fully appreciated, Milford Sound must be seen from the deck of one of the cruise vessels. **Real Journeys,** Lakefront Drive, Te Anau (© **0800/656-502** in NZ, or 03/249-7416; www.realjourneys.co.nz), operates a bewildering array of cruises—both daytime and overnight options. Prices differ depending on whether you join the activity in Queenstown, in Te Anau, or at Milford Sound, and whether you have coach, car, fixed-wing, or helicopter connections. A popular day option is the **Coach and Nature (or Scenic) Cruise,** which departs Queenstown at 6:45am and returns at 8:30pm; the cost is NZ$195 (US$137) scenic cruise or NZ$200 (US$140) nature cruise for adults, NZ$98 (US$67) scenic cruise or NZ$100 (US$70) nature cruise for children. If you go coach both ways, don't expect to be back in Queenstown until around 8pm, but also be aware that flights in and out of Milford are completely weather dependent and you may have to bus it if your flight is canceled. The Coach and Nature Cruise only operates October through April and if you choose to fly one-way you will pay close to twice the above prices.

You can overnight on Milford Sound in Real Journey's *Milford Mariner,* which features 30 en-suite cabins and includes kayaking and trips in tender vessels, a three-course buffet, and breakfast; rates are NZ$390 (US$273) for adults, NZ$195 (US$137) for children. The *Milford Wanderer* sleeps 61 in quad-share bunk-style compartments; NZ$264 (US$184) quad-share for adults, NZ$132 (US$92) quad-share for children. The MV *Friendship* sleeps 12 in backpacker-style accommodations; prices are NZ$264 (US$185) for adults, NZ$132 (US$92) for children, from October through April.

Milford Sound Red Boat Cruises (© **0800/264-536** in NZ, or 03/441-1137; www.redboats.co.nz) has been a tradition here since 1957. It has four boats operating day cruises only. The cost of NZ$49 to NZ$65 (US$34–US$46) for adults and

> **Tips Avoiding the Crowds**
>
> If possible, avoid going into Milford Sound at the peak tourist times of 12:30 to 1:30pm. Cruise sailings during the lunch period are the prime tour-bus time, and you will face long queues and higher prices.

NZ$12 (US$8.40) for children gets you a cruise lasting 1 hour and 45 minutes. Pre-ordered picnic lunch options are available and Great Sights coaches from Queenstown and Te Anau connect with all cruises.

Both of the above cruise companies will take you to **Milford Deep Underwater Observatory** *ℛℛ* (℃ 03/249-9442; www.milforddeep.co.nz), where you'll descend over 10m (33 ft.) beneath the fiord surface to observe the vibrant underwater community. It costs NZ$28 (US$20) extra above your cruise price, or if you go on the Milford Deep Shuttle, it costs NZ$49 (US$34) per adult and children under 15 are free.

Walking is another marvelous activity in this area if you have the time. The Fiordland National Park Visitor Centre in Te Anau (see "Te Anau," earlier in this chapter) will furnish you with details on guided outings that climb into the peaks, meander along the shore, or take you close to waterfalls. One to consider is the much-praised **Trips 'n' Tramps** (℃ 03/249-7081; www.milfordtourswalks.co.nz), which has a 1-day walk on the Milford Track as part of a small group of 12 for around NZ$140 (US$98) per person.

Kayaking may be the most popular activity here after the cruises. Your best bet is **Rosco's Milford Sound Sea Kayaks,** State Highway 94, Deepwater Basin, Milford Sound (℃ **0800/476-726** in NZ; www.kayakmilford.co.nz). These easygoing excursions offer an extraordinary way to experience the sound. You don't have to be super-fit or have previous kayaking experience. Most popular is the Sunriser Wildlife 'n' Waterfall trip, which departs at 7:30am and returns by 1:30pm. This costs around NZ$110 (US$77). There is also a package for Milford Track walkers who can begin their trip by yacht, sailing across Lake Te Anau to start the Milford Track. They end their 4-day wilderness adventure with a relaxed ecopaddle from Sandfly Point back to Milford Sound. This costs around NZ$150 (US$105).

WHERE TO STAY

The historic Mitre Peak Lodge provides accommodations only to members of guided Milford Track parties. The hotel dates from 1891, when Elizabeth Sutherland (wife of the sound's first settler) established a 12-room boardinghouse to accommodate seamen who called into the sound.

Milford Sound Lodge   You'll need to enjoy communing with nature to savor a stay here. It's the only land-based accommodations in Milford Sound and is basic, no frills, and generally filled with young backpackers, but the complex is set in splendid surroundings and has been refurbished recently. Most of the simple rooms have four beds and little else. There's a lounge, cooking and laundry facilities, and a restaurant that provides counter meals.

St. Hwy. 94 (Private Bag, Te Anau), Milford Sound. ℃ **03/249-8071.** Fax 03/249-8075. www.milfordlodge.com. 24 units (with shared bathrooms). NZ$22–NZ$25 (US$15–US$18) dorm bed; NZ$63 (US$44) double. MC, V. **Amenities:** Pizzeria and coffee lounge; tour bookings; courtesy shuttle for Milford Track independent walkers to meet boat and coach services; laundry room.

16

Dunedin, Southland & Stewart Island

Dunedin, the "capital" of Otago province; Southland; Invercargill; and Stewart Island have generally been lumped together as the south of the south; if visitors tend to overlook any part of the country, it would be this one. This is unfortunate because the area offers some of the most diverse and fascinating flora and fauna; some of the quaintest, "real New Zealand" townships; and probably one of the least harried travel experiences of all.

Southland extends as far northwest as Lake Manapouri and as far east as Balclutha. It is the country's coolest and rainiest region, yet the even spread of its rainfall is the very foundation of its economy—the production of grass and grass seed, which in turn supports large numbers of sheep and dairy farms. Southland also has the longest daylight hours in New Zealand, and the Percy Burn Viaduct (near Tuatapere) is believed to be the largest wooden rail viaduct remaining in the world.

The area's coastline saw early settlement by Maori sealers and whalers. Today, the region's fishing industry is a major force—its contributions include those succulent Bluff oysters and crayfish (rock lobsters) you've devoured in your New Zealand travels.

Invercargill is a convenient central base for exploring the region. It lies an easy 2-hour drive from Fiordland and 2½ hours from Dunedin, via Highway 1. It is the central focus of Southland—the only place in New Zealand where Scottish heritage has left a distinctive accent among the people, which you'll notice in the way many people roll the letter *r*. It is a place of incredible friendliness and hospitality, and the only spot in the world where people can see living tuatara, the only lizard left from the dinosaur age.

Stewart Island, the third-largest island of New Zealand, is an area of raucous birdcall, lush native vegetation, and unchanged Kiwi habits—which goes for both the human and the ornithological species.

1 Dunedin ★★

283km (175 miles) S of Queenstown; 366km (227 miles) S of Christchurch; 220km (136 miles) N of Invercargill

Dunedin is a southern gem—sometimes gray, bleak, and freezing in winter, but a gem nevertheless. It has dramatic scenery and some of the finest historic buildings in the country, and the immediacy of its funky university life lends an alternative air to what is inherently a strongly Scottish Presbyterian base.

With a population of about 120,000, Dunedin is New Zealand's fourth-largest city and the second largest in the South Island. The city itself is vital, and you'll quickly notice that the streets are filled with young people. It's the main business center for

Dunedin

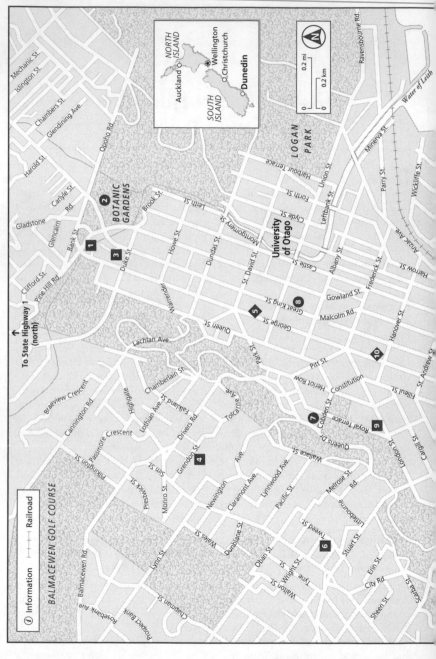

Otago Harbour

BELLEKNOWES GOLF COURSE

The Octagon

The Oval

← To Airport/State Highway 1 (south)

Otago province, and nearby Otago Peninsula is home to several internationally recognized reserves, where some of the world's rarest wildlife can be viewed year-round in their natural habitats.

The splendor of many of its grand city buildings reflects Dunedin's economic and cultural preeminence in Victorian New Zealand, and today it has a justly deserved reputation as one of the best-preserved Victorian and Edwardian cities in the Southern Hemisphere. The original 344 Scottish settlers, who arrived in the area in March 1848, would be proud if they could witness the outcome of their early endeavors.

Things can be, and often are, a little different down here. Where else could you find a kilt shop in New Zealand, plus a thriving population of alternative musicians and artists, a castle, New Zealand's only whiskey distillery, a haggis maker, a colony of albatross, some of the best student pubs in the country, and a chocolate factory? It's a slightly disconcerting mix that will charm the socks off you.

ESSENTIALS

GETTING THERE   By Plane   Freedom Air International (© **0800/600-505** in NZ; www.freedomair.com), has daily flights between Dunedin and Sydney and Brisbane. **Air New Zealand,** at the corner of The Octagon and Princes Street (© **0800/ 737-000** in NZ, or 03/479-6594; www.airnz.co.nz), provides service between Dunedin and Auckland, Wellington, and Rotorua in the North Island, and Christchurch and Invercargill in the South Island. **Origin Pacific** (© **0800/302-302** in NZ, or 03/547-2020; www.originpacific.co.nz) has daily flights to Christchurch. **Stewart Island Flights** (© **03/218-9129;** www.stewartislandflights.com) has flights to and from Stewart Island on Monday, Wednesday, Friday, and Sunday.

The Dunedin airport is inconveniently placed 40 minutes out of the city, and taxis charge approximately NZ$45 to NZ$60 (US$32–US$42) for the trip into town. You'd be well advised to take one of the shuttles that run to the city at regular intervals. The **Dunedin Taxis Airport Shuttle** (© **0800/505-010** or 03/477-7777) charges NZ$15 to NZ$20 (US$11–US$14) to most parts of central city. **City Taxis** (© **03/ 477-1771**) also offers a similarly priced service from the airport.

By Coach (Bus)   InterCity (© **09/913-6100**) provides coach service between Dunedin and Christchurch, Invercargill, Picton, Queenstown, Te Anau, and Timaru. The bus terminal is at 205 St. Andrew St. (© **03/477-8860**). **Bottom Bus,** The Octagon, Dunedin (© **0800/304-333** in NZ, or 03/434-7370; www.bottombus.co.nz), has a full southern circuit, which includes a Milford Sound Cruise for NZ$375 (US$263). It offers discounts to travelers with YHA, VIP, and BBH backpacker cards.

By Car   Dunedin can be reached via state highways 1 and 87. It is 366km (227 miles) and approximately 5 hours' drive south of Christchurch; 220km (136 miles) and approximately 3 to 4 hours northeast of Invercargill; and 3 hours from Queenstown inland through Central Otago. The Southern Scenic Route from Invercargill is another alternative. It passes through the forested coastal Catlins area and is well worth the slight diversion from State Highway 1.

ORIENTATION   All good cities have a heart, and Dunedin is no exception. Rather than a square, though, it has a tree-lined octagon, which acts as a central meeting place. This is where you'll find the visitor center, bus terminals, the main art gallery, and a host of cafes and bars. It boasts a statue of Scotland's beloved poet, Robert Burns (whose nephew was Dunedin's first pastor), grassy areas under trees, and a giant chessboard. The Octagon divides the city's main street into George Street to the north and

Princes Street to the south. A popular shopping area is to be found in the George Street section (see "Shopping," later in this section). The city center is at the head of Otago Harbour, and is encircled by a 200-hectare (500-acre) strip of land, the Green Belt.

GETTING AROUND   By Bus   Most city buses (© 03/477-2224) leave from the vicinity of The Octagon. Four different companies provide service for the same prices, but all use different numbering systems and do different city runs. Your best bet is to get bus timetables from the visitor center on The Octagon. There is frequent service during the week, but it's a little spotty on weekends. The fares are by zone and range from NZ$1.10 to NZ$3.50 (US80¢–US$2.45) per section.

By Taxi   Taxi stands can be found at The Octagon, at all terminals, and near the Chief Post Office. Or call **Dunedin Taxis** (© 03/477-7777) or **City Taxis** (© 03/477-1771).

By Car   Once you familiarize yourself with the one-way systems and the interrupted street pattern around The Octagon, Dunedin is easy to negotiate. Most central streets have metered parking, and there's a municipal parking building near City Hall and a car park in the Meridian Shopping Centre.

VISITOR INFORMATION   The **Dunedin i-Site Visitor Centre,** 48 The Octagon (© **03/474-3300;** fax 03/474-3311; www.cityofdunedin.com or www.dunedinnz.com), is set in the magnificently restored Municipal Chambers. It's open Monday through Friday from 8:30am to 5pm, and Saturday, Sunday, and holidays from 9am to 5:30pm. In summer, the office remains open until 6pm. You can also contact **Tourism Dunedin,** 193 Princes St. (© **03/471-8042;** fax 03/471-8021; www.dunedinnz.com).

SPECIAL EVENTS   Dunedin has an all-year program of festivals and events. To find out about them, check at the visitor center.

The **Dunedin Festival Fortnight** in February and March presents themed weekends, exhibitions, outdoor concerts, family activities, and sporting and cultural events. At the same time is the **id Dunedin Fashion Show** (www.id-dunedinfashion.com), where the city's many designers showcase their work on the Dunedin Railway Platform in front of international media. In early March, you can taste the best of the region at **Taste Otago,** when restaurants, food producers, winemakers, and breweries set up in Woodlaugh Gardens for a weekend of indulgence. To see the city at its most Scottish, time your visit to coincide with **Scottish Week,** in mid-March, when there are daily concerts, Highland and Scottish dancing, pipe bands, and more than likely a spot of haggis making.

In May, the **Regent Theatre 24-hour Book Sale** ✪ offers up over 300,000 volumes in the country's largest sale of secondhand books. It all started as a way to raise funds for the theater's restoration, and it's become a successful, established event filled with fun, live entertainment, and great bargains. In the third week of October, **Dunedin Rhododendron Festival** celebrates the exotic beauty of Dunedin's most famous flower. A happy combination of soil and climate makes the city one of the finest rhododendron-growing areas in the world. More information about Rhododendron Week and its private garden tours is available by calling © **03/467-7241** or going to www.cityofdunedin.com.

Fun Fact **Scottish Roots**

Dunedin is the ancient Gaelic name of Edinburgh in Scotland, and Otago University, the oldest in New Zealand, was modeled after Glasgow University.

FAST FACTS: Dunedin

Area Code The telephone area code (STD) for Dunedin is **03**.

Automobile Association The **AA** is at 450 Moray Place (© **03/477-5945**, or 025/386-122 after hours; fax 03/477-9760), and is open Monday through Friday from 8:30am to 5pm. For breakdowns, phone © **0800/500-222**.

Dentists Raymond J. George, Level 7, at The Octagon and George Street (© **03/477-7993**), provides 24-hour service.

Doctors Go to the **Travellers Medical & Vaccination Centre,** 169 Eglinton Rd., Mornington (© **03/453-6121**).

Emergencies For police, fire, or ambulance service, dial © **111**.

Internet Access **Arc Internet Café,** 135 High St. (© **03/474-1135**), is open from 10am until late.

Pharmacies **The Pharmacy,** 1 block from The Octagon at 267 George St. (© **03/477-9953**), is Dunedin's only 7-day pharmacy.

Post Office The Chief Post Office is at 343 Princes St. (© **03/477-3517**); there's another at 233 Moray Place (© **03/474-0932**).

Restrooms There are good public restrooms on Municipal Lane on the Upper Octagon, between the visitor center and the public library. Open Monday through Saturday from 8:30am to 8:30pm and Sunday from 9am to 5pm.

EXPLORING DUNEDIN

Swing by the visitor center to watch the half-hour video *Dunedin Discovered,* which will give you an overview of the region. Also pick up a sightseeing map and look for the *Walk the City* brochure (NZ$3/US$2.10). There are terrific scenic drives around the city and on the peninsula, and the visitor center has plenty of maps and brochures to show you where to go and what to look out for along the way. One of your first stops should also be the Otago Museum (see below). Its new gallery, "Southern Land, Southern People," will bring more meaning to your visit.

TAKING IN THE VIEWS

There are three good lookout points from which to view the city and its environs: **Mount Cargill Lookout,** 8km (5 miles) from the city center (turn left at the end of George St., then left on Pine Hill Rd. to its end, and then right onto Cowan Rd., which climbs to the summit); **Centennial Lookout,** or Signal Hill (turn onto Signal Hill Rd. from Opoho Rd., then drive 3km [1¾ miles] to the end of Signal Hill Rd.); and **Bracken's Lookout** (at the top of the Botanic Gardens), which was named after poet Thomas Bracken, who wrote the words to New Zealand's national anthem.

MUSEUMS, GALLERIES & HISTORIC HOMES

Otago Museum 𝕶𝕶𝕶 *Kids*   Established in 1868, this is New Zealand's fourth-largest museum with over 1.7 million items; most people are surprised by the depth of its large ethnographic, natural-history, and decorative-arts collections. It also has the best Pacific and Southern Maori collections in the country.

The museum has undergone an NZ$18-million (US$13-million) upgrade and increased its size by 70%. Along with a new and improved foyer, cafe, and shop, you'll find a new special-exhibitions gallery, a stylish atrium, a new 6-minute introductory video (the best way to begin your visit), and a stunning gallery called **"Southern Land, Southern People"** 🐸🐸, which tells the human and natural-history story of the southern region. Allow an hour for this new section and to get the best from it take a guided tour, which can be prebooked.

Visitors can meet the extinct giant moa in a gallery that includes the museum's world-class collection of complete moa skeletons and one of the few complete moa eggs in the world; and fans of old-style museums should not miss the new **Animal Attic** 🐸, which replicates the Victorian timbered gallery of the museum as it was in 1868. It's my favorite museum space—unforgettable for its visual impact and zany collections of stuffed animals (which kids will love), birds, and New Zealand spiders. And don't overlook the fun factor of **Discovery World,** one of those terrific places for children where you end up playing yourself. Allow 2 hours for a good look around.

419 Great King St., P.O. Box 6202, Dunedin. ⓒ **03/474-7474.** Fax 03/477-5993. www.otagomuseum.govt.nz and www.discoveryworld.co.nz. Free admission to museum; admission to Discovery World NZ$8 (US$5.60) adults, NZ$4 (US$2.80) children, NZ$15 (US$11) per family. Southern Land Tour NZ$10 (US$7) per person. Mon–Fri 10am–5pm; Sat–Sun noon–5pm. Closed Good Friday and Dec 25.

Otago Settlers Museum 🐸🐸 This is Otago's museum of social history, tracing the stories of those who have made the region home—from the original Maori inhabitants to the sturdy Scottish pioneers, the rough-and-ready gold miners to the business entrepreneurs who followed them. Exhibitions are comprehensive, presenting even the most detailed engineering and scientific facts in a readily accessible manner. There are also exhibits on the Kai Tahu Maori communities of Otago; an ever-popular transport collection (engine buffs will be in heaven); and a Penny Farthing cycle you can actually ride. A new gallery features the 19th-century settlers' shipboard experience, which includes a mock-up of the steerage of a sailing ship. Allow an hour for a quick overview.

31 Queens Gardens, Dunedin. ⓒ **03/477-5052.** Fax 03/474-2727. www.otago.settlers.museum.co.nz. Admission NZ$6 (US$4.20) adults, NZ$4 (US$2.80) seniors and students, free for children. No charge for exhibitions. Mon–Sun 10am–5pm. Research department Mon–Fri 10am–1pm; NZ$12 (US$8.40) entry fee. Museum closed Good Friday and Dec 25.

Dunedin Public Art Gallery 🐸🐸 When the Dunedin Public Art Gallery opened in 1996, art lovers throughout the country celebrated. The new space is one of the best in New Zealand, and has received acclaim for both its architecture and its collection— one of the best in Australasia. There are significant holdings of European art, Japanese prints, and French Impressionist works, along with a comprehensive collection of contemporary and early New Zealand art. The shop stocks a good range of art-related products.

30 The Octagon, Dunedin. ⓒ **03/474-3240.** Fax 03/474-3250. www.dunedin.art.museum. Free admission; charges for special exhibitions. Daily 10am–5pm. Closed Good Friday and Dec 25. Special tours available by arrangement.

Olveston 🐸🐸🐸 *Finds* Olveston is one of New Zealand's best-known stately homes and if, like me, you have a passion for grand old homes, it should definitely be on your agenda. Designed by London architect Sir Ernest George, the 35-room, Jacobean-style mansion was built between 1904 and 1906 by the much-traveled and very prosperous Theomin family. It sits on an acre of tree-sheltered grounds, and since it was bequeathed to Dunedin in 1966, it has been carefully maintained in virtually its original state. David Theomin had a passion for Eastern decorative arts, and he filled his home with bronze, cloisonné, ivory, ceramics, jade, and over 250 paintings. On top of its unique interior finery, the house itself is a work of art and pays homage to the

Kids Chocolate Heaven

Chocolate lovers and fans of *Charlie & the Chocolate Factory*, rejoice! The famous **Cadbury World** ✦✦, 280 Cumberland St. (© **03/467-7967;** www.cadbury world.co.nz), is open. This unique, interactive chocolate-themed center offers daily guided tours of New Zealand's most famous—and favorite—chocolate factory every half-hour from 9am until 3:15pm. Immerse yourself in the process and sample treats along the way. A full tour takes about 75 minutes, but be aware that many of the most interesting processes are "secret" and you don't get to see them. I found that a little disappointing. It costs NZ$15 (US$11) for adults, NZ$8 (US$5.60) for children ages 5 to 15, and NZ$38 (US$27) for a family. A retail outlet here also offers special "tour only" prices.

skills of 19th-century craftsmen. Those with reservations are given preference; house viewing is by 1-hour guided tour only. Reservations are required for the 2-hour painting tours.

42 Royal Terrace, Dunedin. © 03/477-3320. Fax 03/479-2094. www.olveston.co.nz. Admission NZ$15 (US$11) adults, NZ$4 (US$2.80) children. Guided tours given daily at 9:30 and 10:45am, noon, 1:30, 2:45, and 4pm.

OTHER HIGHLIGHTS

Forgive me for not walking up **Baldwin Street,** which, according to the *Guinness Book of World Records,* is the world's steepest street. I couldn't face the 270 steps that take you to the top, or the footpath and its impossible gradient. Just minutes from the city center, this little street tricks you with a gentle beginning. It then rears dramatically skyward to come to a dead end on the hillside. If you're hale and hearty and have something to prove, this could be a good test, and I believe the views from the top are worth it. And if you want a certificate to prove to your friends back home that you had what it takes, then stop by the **World's Steepest Street Tourist Shop,** 282 North Rd. (© **03/473-0923**). To get to Baldwin Street, take the Normandy bus to North Road; Baldwin is the 10th street on the right past the Botanic Gardens. And remember, if you drive to the top, there's only a very tight turnaround space and only one way out—down the way you came!

Dunedin's **Railway Station** warrants more than a cursory glance. This marvelous old Flemish Renaissance–style structure was designed by George A. Troup and built between 1904 and 1906. Troup won the Institution of British Architects Award for his efforts and was later knighted. Built of Kokonga basalt with Oamaru limestone facings, the station's most prominent feature is its large square clock tower. Equally impressive are the Aberdeen granite pillars supporting arches of the colonnade across the front, the red Marseilles tiles on the roof, and the colorful mosaic floor (more than 725,000 Royal Doulton porcelain squares) in the massive foyer depicting a "puffing billy" engine. Look for the replica of Dunedin's coat of arms and the stained-glass windows above the balcony.

PARKS & GARDENS

The 28-hectare (69-acre) **Dunedin Botanic Gardens** (© **03/477-4000;** botanic@ cityofdunedin.com) were the first to be established in New Zealand, in 1869. At the northern end of George Street, they feature the world-renowned Rhododendron Dell.

Nestled into native bush with magnolia, cherry, and maples, the Dell features over 3,000 rhododendron plants and has spectacular masses of blooms from October to December. You can also see the comprehensive native-plant collection, an Edwardian conservatory garden, rock gardens, and rose gardens. The gardens are open daily from dawn to dusk, free of charge. A kiosk restaurant offers light snacks and morning and afternoon teas; a shop and information center are also on the grounds. All three are open daily from 10am to 4pm.

For information on Dunedin's famous October **Rhododendron Festival,** go to www.cityofdunedin.com.

EXPLORING OTAGO PENINSULA

Otago Peninsula is simply spectacular, especially on a clear day. It has some of the finest views of the southern coastline and is one of New Zealand's most renowned ecotourism areas, with several excellent wildlife centers. You can book tours of the peninsula through the visitor center, or pick up the free *Visitors' Guide to the Otago Peninsula,* which features a comprehensive map of attractions, arts and crafts, accommodations, and restaurants. The 33km (20-mile) peninsula curves around one side of Otago Harbour. It's an easy road, although some portions are unpaved, and it takes you past quaint coastal boatsheds and quiet settlements. The listings below cover Otago's highlights.

Royal Albatross Centre ✸✸✸   It seems a cruel irony that a magnificent bird such as the royal albatross, which can stay in the air for weeks on end, should make such an ungainly landing when it finally decides to come down to earth. But we can be thankful that it has chosen to do so at Taiaroa Head, the only mainland colony of albatross in the world. One-hour tours will show you the birds only; 90-minute tours add the tunnel complex of the old Fort Taiaroa and the last working example of an Armstrong Disappearing Gun. The best times to visit are January and February, when the chicks are hatching; in late afternoon, you'll see courtship displays. After 6:30pm, the sea breezes come up, and juveniles come in from the sea. It's important to remember, though, that this is wildlife and there are no guarantees. Sometimes you can see birds as close as 3.6m (12 ft.) away, sometimes much farther. But with binoculars and a telephoto camera lens, you're bound to get good results. During the mating season, the main observatory is closed, and viewing is from an alternative spot a little farther away. It's a 2-minute walk up a path to the observatory; mobile carts are available for visitors with disabilities. A souvenir shop, cafeteria, and wildlife displays are on the grounds.

Moments **Brew Stop**

Tours of **Speight's Brewery Heritage Centre** ✸✸✸, 200 Rattray St., Dunedin (✆ **03/477-7697;** www.speights.co.nz), cost NZ$18 (US$13) for adults, NZ$15 (US$11) for students, and NZ$5 (US$3.50) children ages 5 to 15. For that you'll spend about 1½ hours looking at the brewing processes of this "Pride of the South," with tastings and a sample of the product at the end. Speight's has been favoring us with its fine ales since 1876, and the tour gives a good overview of the industry. Make sure you see the stunning Otago video presentation at the end—it made my little Kiwi heart burst with pride. Tours are limited to 25 people and run daily at 10am, 11:45am, and 2pm, with an extra 7pm tour Monday through Thursday.

Moments **Close Encounters**

If you're traveling with kids—or even if you're not—don't miss the **New Zealand Marine Studies Centre & Westpac Aquarium** ✿✿✿, Portobello, Otago Peninsular (🕿 **03/479-5826**; www.marine.ac.nz). I can't keep my hands out of things, so I delighted in being able to delve into marine tanks—although it goes without saying that you should first see who's living in there. After all, there's no point in losing a finger to a lobster. You can help feed the sea critters every Wednesday and Saturday from 2pm to 3pm; or take one of the daily guided tours at 10:30am. The center is open daily from noon to 4:30pm. If you're heading out to the view the albatrosses, it's on your way.

Taiaroa Head. 🕿 **03/478-0499.** Fax 03/478-0575. www.albatross.org.nz. Free admission to Albatross Centre. Daily 1-hr. Albatross Tour: NZ$28 (US$20) adults, NZ$14 (US$9.80) children; Daily 90-minute Taiaroa Tour, including Armstrong Disappearing Gun: NZ$33 (US$23) adults, NZ$16 (US$11) children; Fort Taiaroa Tour: NZ$12 (US$8.40) adults, NZ$6 (US$4.20) children; Albatross Insight NZ$8 (US$5.60) adults, NZ$4 (US$2.80) children. Center open daily 9am–7pm. Closed Dec 25. Tour reservations required; call visitor center on The Octagon or the Albatross Centre directly.

Penguin Place ✿✿✿   When you consider that every yellow-eyed penguin has 200 feathers per square inch, you realize there's likely to be a whole lot of preening going on in the heart of this excellent conservation project. The 1½-hour tour begins with an informative talk and slide presentation; you're then driven 5 minutes across farmland to an extensive network of tunnels and hides that took 8 years to build. Here you'll be able to watch the world's rarest penguins at close quarters without disturbing them. Fifteen years ago, there were eight breeding pairs; today, there are over 35 pairs in the colony, which represents 20% of New Zealand's mainland yellow-eyed population. You'll need sensible walking shoes, as there's at least 500m (1,640 ft.) of walking involved, much of it uphill and steep. But you'll be rewarded with fabulous coastal views, colonies of fur seals, possibly Hooker sea lions if you're lucky, and incredible, swirling tangles of sea kelp—all fantastic photographic opportunities.

Pakihau Rd. 🕿 **03/478-0286.** Fax 03/478-0257. www.penguin-place.co.nz. Admission from NZ$33 (US$23) adults, NZ$12 (US$8.40) children. MC, V. Tours given Nov to mid-Mar 10:15am–7:45pm; reservations required. Tours depart from the McGrouther Farm on Harrington Point Rd. It is well signposted and just 5 min. before the Royal Albatross Centre.

Larnach Castle ✿✿   Larnach Castle may be small by European standards, but it's clear William Larnach had more than a simple bungalow in mind when he set about constructing this marvelous edifice in 1871. No doubt keen to impress his French heiress wife, he hired 200 workmen for 3 years just to build the shell; a host of European master craftsmen took another 12 years to complete the interior. The carved foyer ceiling alone took three craftsmen 6½ years to finish. The Georgian hanging staircase is the only one in the Southern Hemisphere, and it sits comfortably with the best of everything that Larnach incorporated.

   Larnach came to New Zealand from Australia in the late 1860s to set up the first Bank of Otago. He later became a Member of Parliament, but with three marriages behind him and a family history dotted with scandal and misfortune, he committed suicide in the Parliament Buildings in Wellington. (His first two wives both died at the age of 38, and his third dealt him a fatal emotional blow by dallying with the son from his first marriage.) After his death, the crown used the castle as a mental hospital. For the past 34 years, it has been the home of Margaret Barker and her family, who have committed themselves to its restoration. Pick up the self-guiding pamphlet at the reception area and wander as you wish. If you'd like to stay in the castle lodge or stables, see "Where to Stay," later in this chapter.

Highcliff Rd. (© **03/476-1616.** Fax 03/476-1574. www.larnachcastle.co.nz. Admission to castle and grounds N7$18 (US$13) adults, NZ$8 (US$5.60) children; grounds only NZ$10 (US$7) adults, NZ$3 (US$2.10) children. Daily 9am–5pm. Closed Dec 25. Take Portobello Rd. 3km (2 miles) north of Glenfalloch Woodland Garden and follow the signs inland.

Glenfalloch Woodland Garden ★   On the shores of Otago Harbour, 9km (5½ miles) from Dunedin, Glenfalloch (Gaelic for "Hidden Valley") makes a perfect stop-off point for tea or coffee during your peninsular excursion. It's peaceful in this historic 30-hectare (74-acre) garden, and you'll find superb displays of rhododendrons and azaleas. Full lunches are available in the licensed cafe.

430 Portobello Rd. (© **03/476-1006.** Fax 03/476-1137. www.glenfalloch.co.nz. Donations appreciated. Daily dawn–dusk; cafe daily from 11:30am–4pm. Restaurant closed May–Sept. Tours Mon–Fri by arrangement, NZ$6.50 (US$4.55).

ORGANIZED TOURS

Dunedin is blessed with a number of excellent tour operators who provide enjoyable sightseeing the easy way. You'll find a profusion of pamphlets at the visitor center on The Octagon. During summer months, it pays to reserve early.

Many of the operators are geared toward peninsula exploration. For around NZ$60 (US$42), **Wild South** ★ (© 03/474-3300; www.wilddunedin.co.nz) will guide you to the Yellow-eyed Penguin Reserve. You'll also observe several species of wading birds in their natural habitat, fur seals, sometimes Hooker sea lions, albatross, and various seabirds. The 6-hour trip requires a reasonable degree of fitness, warm clothing, and good footwear, as you'll be walking 2 hours out of the 6 and there are steep inclines.

Take the hedonistic approach to touring with **Luxury Chauffeurs** (© 03/477-3144; fax 03/477-3145; www.luxurychauffeurs.co.nz). It has a 4-hour **Dunedin Scenic Tour** for around NZ$110 (US$77) per person, which focuses on historic buildings; and a very good 8-hour **Eco Tour,** which includes the Royal Albatross Centre, Larnach Castle, and other peninsular highlights for around NZ$200 (US$140) per person.

Outdoor types will find pleasure in the sea-kayak, rafting, walking, and mountain bike tours offered by **Wild Earth Adventures** ★★★ (© 03/473-6535; www.wild earth.co.nz). Its **Ocean Discovery Kayak Tour** takes you along wild beaches and soaring sea cliffs to the albatross colony and offers amazing photographic opportunities. It

---

Moments **Hair-Raising Fun**

If you think ghosts don't exist, think again. Andrew Smith's **Hair Raiser Ghost Walk** ★★ (© 03/477-2258; hairraisertours@xtra.co.nz) might convince you otherwise. Get behind the city's beautiful architecture and discover the truth behind many famous ghost sightings, the wandering habits of the supernatural, and The Octagon fires. Based on fact, not fiction, it's not for the faint-hearted and there's no guarantee of a good night's sleep afterwards. No garlic or crucifixes allowed. Tours leave from outside the visitor center Wednesday and Friday at 6pm and cost NZ$20 (US$14) per person. No credit cards.

(*Finds*) **A Passion for Fashion**

The best way to get a feel for Dunedin's thriving fashion industry is to join Jeannie Hayden on her inner city tour, **Passion for Fashion** ✿✿✿ (© 03/478-0614; www.walkthetalk.co.nz). She'll take you to design studios, fashion workrooms, jewelry studios, avant-garde fashion stores, and some of the city's best retailers. The morning fashion tour (9:30am–2pm) includes coffee and lunch and costs NZ$120 (US$84) per person; the afternoon jewelry tour (3–6pm) includes coffee and early-evening drinks and costs NZ$75 (US$53) per person. I could have done it all over a second time.

---

costs NZ$99 (US$69) per person. For something special, try the 3-hour **Botanical Gardens Native NZ Plant Tour,** which runs morning and afternoon and costs NZ$75 (US$53) per person. If you're of an energetic bent and feel like challenging yourself with Dunedin's hills, their 4-hour **Mountain Bike Tour** will sort you out for a mere NZ$99 (US$69) per person.

Country Tours (© 03/467-5041; fax 03/467-5071) brings you back to solidly grounded land experiences. Louise Foord, an expert at what lies beyond the main roads—gardens, history, architecture, wildlife—will tailor a tour to your personal requirements.

Also popular is **Elm Wildlife Tours** ✿✿✿ (© 0800/356-563 in NZ, or 03/454-4121; www.elmwildlifetours.co.nz); twice voted New Zealand's best wildlife tour, it gives you a sound insight into the habits of various penguin species, fur seals, and sea lions. Viewing hides give you a close encounter and options range from NZ$69 to NZ$105 (US$48–US$74).

COACH (BUS) TOURS

Citibus Newton Tours, Princes Street and Transport Place (© 03/477-5577; www.transportplace.co.nz), conducts excellent tours of varying duration, all with guides providing valuable insight into the area's highlights, along with the occasional anecdote to liven things up. All tours may be booked directly with Citibus Newton or at the visitor center. Pickups from your lodging can be arranged. The **Essential Dunedin** ✿✿ tour departs five times per day from the visitor center. The fare for this double-decker bus ride is NZ$18 (US$13) per adult, NZ$9 (US$6.30) per child under 15. The **Wildlife Tour** runs from Dunedin to Taiaroa Head and back (NZ$65–NZ$80/US$46–US$56 for adults, NZ$33–NZ$$40/US$23–US$28 for children) and allows you to get on and off the bus at any of the key points. Itinerary options include the albatross colony, penguin colony, and Larnach Castle. There are up to six runs a day from October to March and two during winter months. And if you want a special glimpse into heartland New Zealand that even many New Zealanders haven't seen, book **Track and Trail** ✿✿✿, which combines a 4-hour coach tour between Queenstown and Pukerangi, traveling through remote landscapes, with an unforgettable 2-hour trip on the Taieri Gorge Train (See "A Train Trip to Taieri Gorge," below). The journey costs NZ$115 (US$81) for adults, NZ$58 (US$41) for children.

CRUISING THE PENINSULA

A number of cruise options can show you the wildlife delights of Otago Peninsula. The visitor center has a comprehensive selection of brochures and a helpful staff to help you sort out your priorities.

Locals are quick to tell you about the fantastic value offered through the family-owned and -operated **Monarch Wildlife Cruises** ★★★, Wharf and Fryatt streets (© **0800/666-272** in NZ, or 03/477-4276; www.wildlife.co.nz) Established in 1983 by owners with degrees in biology and a wealth of experience on research vessels, Monarch won the New Zealand Tourism Awards Natural Heritage category in 1994 and the Ecotourism category in 1997. The crew are experienced Department of Conservation officers or have degrees in zoology, so there's not much you won't be able to find out about albatross, New Zealand fur seals, yellow-eyed penguins, and other species you're likely to pass. If you're short on time, opt for the 1-hour albatross cruise from Wellers Rock, which costs NZ$32 (US$22) for adults, NZ$12 (US$8.40) for children. (Remember that Wellers Rock is a 45-min. drive from central city.) Monarch also has full harbor cruises from Dunedin lasting just over 5 hours. Dress warmly and take your camera; if you're unsure about which option to take, note that the most popular is the cruise-and-bus trip that includes a guided tour of Penguin Place—it gives you a taste of everything. They run half-day tours from NZ$75 to NZ$110 (US$53–US$77) and full-day options from NZ$170 to NZ$200 (US$119–US$140).

OUTDOOR PURSUITS

BEACHES   New Zealanders don't often utter the two words "Dunedin" and "beaches" in the same breath, but the truth is, there are at least eight or nine magnificent, unspoiled, white-sand beaches within an easy drive of Dunedin. You may not always want to swim in the coolish waters, but from a scenic point of view, they're worth a visit. **St. Kilda** and **St. Clair** are probably the best known, made famous by a dedicated band of wet-suited surfies. A short drive north to the Port Chalmers area reveals **Long Beach, Aromoana,** and **Purakanui,** and on Otago Peninsula, **Pilot's Beach** (near the Albatross Centre), **Victory Beach, Sandfly Bay,** and **Seal Point** are all generally deserted and beautiful. Closer to town you have **Tunnel Beach,** which is accessed through private property and a tunnel. Ask the staff at the visitor center for driving instructions. You'll find great walks on **Brighton Beach,** a 20-minute drive south of Dunedin.

BIKING   Dunedin may be hilly, but there are great cycling opportunities, especially out on the peninsula. Rent a bike from **Browns,** Lower Stuart Street (© **03/477-7259**).

If you're more into fat tires, the visitor center's excellent brochure *Mountain Bike Rides in Dunedin* outlines all the best tracks, including the very popular **Central Otago Rail Trail** ★★★ (© **03/474-6909**; www.centralotagorailtrail.co.nz), a 5- to 6-day excursion that takes you into Middlemarch and Central Otago. It's an unforgettable trip through stunning scenery and dinky small towns.

FISHING   Nearby Port Chalmers is known for its stellar salmon and trout fishing from October to April. If you want to try your hand at shark fishing, deep-sea fishing, saltwater, or light-tackle sportfishing, call **Otago Harbour Salmon Fishing Charters,** 7 Henderson St., Mornington, Dunedin (© **03/453-6614**), or inquire at the Dunedin visitor center for other options. Ted Bensemann of **Wannabe Fishin'** (© **03/489-0088;** www.wbfishing.com), knows all the best local spots for trout fishing and hunting.

GOLF   The **Otago Golf Club Balmacewen Course** (© **03/467-2099;** www.otago golfclub.co.nz) has been operating since 1896. It's an 18-hole championship course with a fully stocked pro shop. Affiliated members pay around NZ$55 (US$39), non-affiliated pay NZ$75 (US$53). **St. Clair Golf Club** (© **03/487-7076;** www.stclair golf.co.nz) is also popular; greens fees are NZ$25 (US$18) affiliated and NZ$35

(US$25) nonaffiliated. **Tahuna Park Golf Driving Range,** Victoria Road, St. Kilda (© **03/455-0445;** www.0900golfer.co.nz), is open from 9am until dark, with clubs for hire. A bucket of balls costs around NZ$10 (US$7).

HORSE TREKKING   Bums 'n' Saddles Horse Treks (© **03/488-0097**) will put the wind in your hair as you ride along white-sand beaches. The treks are suitable for all abilities and cost around NZ$35 to NZ$40 (US$25–US$28) for 2 hours.

SEA KAYAKING   Otago Harbour is the perfect playground for sea kayakers. You can explore the spectacular sea cliffs teeming with wildlife, or turn your hand to a surf landing on an isolated beach. Contact **Wild Earth Adventures** (see above in "Organized Tours"), for the best outings.

SURFING   Head for **St. Clair** and **St. Kilda** beaches on the Esplanade. This is the center of Dunedin's surfie activity.

A Train Trip to Taieri Gorge

The **Taieri Gorge Railway** ✸✸✸ (© **03/477-4449;** www.taieri.co.nz) is more than a small jaunt on a train—it is an award-winning journey through history and spectacular scenery that is otherwise inaccessible to the public. No matter what time of the year, you'll be impressed with both the scenic beauty and the sheer engineering feat of the railway's construction. The 75km (47 miles) of rail, including 12 tunnels, and the magnificent Wingatui Viaduct took 42 years to build, beginning in 1879. Make sure you get *Your Guide to the Taieri Gorge* when you board the train, so you can follow your progress through to the tiny township of Middlemarch, the final stopping point—a funny little backwater of a place where bachelors need hard-to-find wives. Once here, you can get off and, if you're not interested in finding the bachelors, you can link up to a coach to Queenstown; mountain bike, walk, or horseback ride—which will take you several days; or stay on the train for the return trip.

From October 1 through April, the Dunedin-Middlemarch return train runs Friday and Sunday morning. It leaves Dunedin Railway Station at 9:30am, has a 45-minute stop at Middlemarch, and returns to Dunedin at 3:25pm. It costs NZ$71 to NZ$75 (US$50–US$53) round-trip for adults. Students get a 20% discount; one child per adult rides free, with each extra child paying around NZ$20 (US$14). The shorter 4-hour trip to Pukerangi (19km/12 miles short of Middlemarch) runs daily at 2:30pm, returning 6:30pm, and costs NZ$63 to NZ$67 (US$44–US$47). Both trips include at least two photo stops, excellent ongoing commentary, and a buffet car for snacks and drinks. An adults-only car and a wheelchair-accessible carriage (book in advance) are available. For a coastal train experience, leap aboard the **Seasider,** which departs on selected Wednesdays and Saturdays in the summer season. I haven't tried this one yet, but I'm assured that the wild coastline on the trip north to Palmerston, makes it more than worthwhile. You can make it a return trip, or link with a gold mine tour. It costs NZ$53 to NZ$57 (US$37–US$40).

Moments **Salt, Sea & Surf**

St. Clair Hot Salt Water Pool, at St. Clair Beach, is a 25m (82-ft.) outdoor pool right beside the ocean and, if your bones are aching from too much walking, a soak in the therapeutic waters will do you a world of good. The pool's sea-watwer is heated to a pleasing 82°F (28°C) and you can hear waves crashing on the nearby shore. It's open from late October through March from 6am until 7pm. Admission is around NZ$5 (US$3.50). Ask about their pool parties, which include fun activities, games, and a barbecue.

SWIMMING   If the ocean seems too daunting, head for **Moana Pool,** Littlebourne Road and Stuart Street (© **03/474-3400** for pool information, 03/477-7792 for waterslides, or 03/471-9782 for Flippers Early Childhood Centre). There's been a NZ$10.8-million (US$7.6-million) revamp here, with a new leisure pool and lap and diving pool now open. The waterslides are fully enclosed tubes; you can opt for a slow or fast descent. Other watery options include scuba instruction, aqua-fitness classes, underwater hockey, and water polo. Or laze around in the cafe while the kids run wild in the play area. Flippers Early Childhood Centre is for children under 5. It's open daily to give parents time off. And if all that activity proves to be too much for you, call **Moana Pool Physiotherapy** (© **03/477-2881**) to have body stresses eliminated.

WHERE TO STAY

Dunedin provides the usual range of lodgings, from backpacker hostels to motels to fine hotels. But what I love most about the area is its very fine choice of heritage homestays and B&Bs, many of which are in exquisite Victorian-style buildings. At certain times of the year, midrange options are heavily booked because of university activities, so make your reservations early. Rates given below include the 12.5% GST and free off-street parking.

IN TOWN
Expensive

Fletcher Lodge 🌀🌀🌀   This house is a stunning example of Dunedin's unique architecture. Built by one of New Zealand's leading industrialists in 1924, it features impressive detailing such as the Wedgwood ceiling and frieze in the music room and stained-glass inserts in almost every window. Keith and Ewa Rozecki-Pollard carried out major refurbishments in 2003, adding two new suites to an already glowing fold. All guest rooms contain desks and sofas, plus luxurious touches such as underfloor heating in the tiled bathrooms and sumptuous bedding that begs you to sleep in. Fletcher Lodge welcomes a wide range of overseas visitors, ambassadors, diplomats, and businesspeople. Definitely a place for the discerning traveler.

276 High St., Dunedin. © **0800/843-563** in NZ, or 03/477-5552. Fax 03/474-5551. www.fletcherlodge.co.nz. 6 units. NZ$225 (US$158) standard; NZ$350 (US$245) premium; NZ$450–NZ$550 (US$315–US$385) deluxe. Long-stay rates available. Rates include breakfast. AE, DC, MC, V. **Amenities:** Nearby golf courses; Jacuzzi; tour bookings; massage; laundry service; same-day dry cleaning; nonsmoking rooms. *In room:* TV, dataport in deluxe rooms only, coffeemaker, hair dryer, iron.

One Royal Terrace 🌀🌀 *Moments*   From the huge crystal chandelier in the entry hall and hanging staircase to the velvet-finished windows, this big, two-storied Victorian beauty combines old-world charm with modern comforts. It's more ornate than the other old homes listed below and if you're not happy here I'll eat my Victorian hat. Ian and Glenda Begg are passionate rally car drivers and you'll love the lavish touches they've added to their three big rooms. The Gold Room is especially romantic.

1 Royal Terrace. © 03/479-0772. Fax 03/479-0775. www.oneroyalterrace.co.nz. 3 units. NZ$300–NZ$495 (US$210–US$347). Long-stay and off-peak rates available. Rates include breakfast. MC, V. **Amenities:** Nearby golf courses and pools; tour bookings; nonsmoking rooms. *In room:* TV/CD, dataport, coffeemaker, hair dryer.

Moderate

If you're looking for a smart motel close to town, you'll be hard-pressed to find anything better than the new **Motel on York** 𝒜𝒜, 47 York Place (© **0800/006-666** in NZ, or 03/477-6120; www.motelonyork.co.nz), which is just two streets off The Octagon. Its 23 units offer all the comforts of a good little boutique hotel.

Elgin House 𝒜𝒜   Roger and Carolyn Rennie live in the converted attic of their impressive three-storied home, leaving the three luxurious bedroom spaces on the ground floor to you. The Inglenook is the biggest, with a fireplace and a romantic window seat overlooking a cottage garden. The Garden Room and the Oriel share a private bathroom and are let together to a single party. Drawing, dining room, and kitchen are all on the center floor and it's here you can unwind with the Rennies and a bottle of local wine after a big day of sightseeing.

31 Elgin Rd., Mornington, Dunedin. © **0800/272-940** in NZ, or 03/453-0004. www.elginhouse.co.nz. 3 units. NZ$250–NZ$295 (US$175–US$207). Rates include breakfast. MC, V. Children under 12 by arrangement. **Amenities:** Nearby golf course; home theater; same-day dry cleaning; nonsmoking rooms; airport transfers by arrangement. *In room:* TV, dataport, coffeemaker, hair dryer, iron.

Hyland House Dunedin 𝒜   Take three 1911 historic terrace houses and totally restore them, adding all the modern conveniences, and you get this unique cluster of accommodations. Broken down in to 10 private, self-contained guest rooms, it offers space and comfort for a reasonable price. Nine of the suites include bathtubs and all have their own entrance and views over Woodhaugh Valley and Dunedin Botanic Gardens. There's a shopping center nearby and you're within walking distance of the city.

1003–1011 George St. North. © 03/473-1122. Fax 03/473-6066. www.hylandhouse.co.nz. 10 units. From NZ$125–NZ$170 (US$88–US$119) queen suite; NZ$195–NZ$240 (US$137–US$168) queen/twin suite. Long-stay and off-peak rates available. AE, DC, MC, V. **Amenities:** Nearby golf course; tour bookings; laundry service; same-day dry cleaning; nonsmoking rooms; access for travelers w/disabilities. *In room:* TV, dataport, kitchenette, fridge, coffeemaker, hair dryer, iron.

Mahara Bed & Breakfast 𝒜𝒜𝒜 *(Finds)*   I like to pretend I'm a princess when I stay in Mahara's vast Annie Lees suite—it's just a character weakness I have. That aside, Mahara is definitely for you if you love character homes, quiet leafy suburbs, and a warm welcome. You can't help but be impressed by the magnificent timber and stained-glass features of this 1901 Queen Anne Revival Edwardian mansion. The Leebank Room is more intimate and sexy, with luscious burgundy taffeta drapes and fur-covered lamps. Both have en-suite bathrooms and everything has recently been refurbished to the highest standard.

2 Fifield St., Dunedin. © 03/467-5811. Fax 03/467-5587. www.mahara.co.nz. 2 units. NZ$195–NZ$350 (US$137–US$245). Rates include breakfast. Long-stay and off-peak rates available. AE, DC, MC, V. Free street parking. **Amenities:** Nearby golf course; babysitting; laundry service; same-day dry cleaning; nonsmoking rooms. *In room:* TV, dataport, hair dryer, iron.

Peacocks ★★ *Value*   It's a tough life when you have to saunter from one gorgeous Victorian mansion to the next, but someone has to do it! And when you end up in a place like Peacocks, you realize how charmed life can be. The five lovely rooms here are hard to choose between. All have en suites and lovely antique beds. It's just a short walk downhill to town, but that means a steep uphill climb home.

304 York Place. © **0800/327-333** in NZ, or 03/474-1300. Fax 03/473-1160. www.stationmasters.co.nz. 5 units. From NZ$250–NZ$350 (US$175–US$245). Long-stay and off-peak rates available. Rates include breakfast. MC, V. **Amenities:** Nearby golf course; tour bookings on request; laundry and laundry service; same-day dry cleaning; nonsmoking rooms; on-call doctor/dentist. *In room:* TV, fridge, coffeemaker, hair dryer, iron.

Scenic Circle Dunedin City Hotel ★★ *Value*   The City Hotel is small, modern, and close to town—just 1 block off The Octagon and near plenty of shops and eateries. You can opt for city or harbor views and rooms are spacious and fresh, with good bathrooms. I spent 3 days here and could have happily stayed longer because of its all-round convenience and compact little gym that I always had to myself. For more space, pay a little extra for the superior room.

Corner of Princes and Dowling sts. © **0800/696-963** in NZ, or 03/470-1470. Fax 03/470-1477. www.scenic-circle.co.nz. 110 units. NZ$200 (US$140) standard; NZ$220 (US$154) superior. Weekend rates available. AE, DC, MC, V. Valet parking. **Amenities:** Restaurant; bar; nearby golf course; gym; concierge; tour bookings; car rentals; room service; guest laundries and laundry service; same-day dry cleaning; nonsmoking rooms; access for travelers w/disabilities. *In room:* TV, dataport, minibar, fridge, coffeemaker, hair dryer, iron.

The Stationmaster's Cottage ★ *Finds*   If you like your own space and privacy, you'll love this little cottage. It's a cozy, self-contained getaway that hides behind a fringe of vines and flowers next door to Peacocks. There are two double bedrooms and one twin, each simply decorated and sharing the large, family bathroom. A quaint kitchen and small living room complete the picture. Beware: once settled in, you may need to be levered out with a shoe horn!

300 York Place. © **0800/327-333** in NZ, or 03/474-5994. Fax 03/473-1160. www.stationmasters.co.nz. Self-contained 3-bedroom cottage. From NZ$250 (US$175); NZ$35 (US$25) each extra person. Long-stay and off-peak rates available. Breakfast food supplied. MC, V. **Amenities:** Tour bookings; car rentals; laundry facilities; dishwasher; nonsmoking rooms; access for travelers w/disabilities. *In room:* TV/DVD, kitchen, fridge, coffeemaker, hair dryer, iron.

Inexpensive

You'll find reasonably priced B&B digs at **Deacons Court,** 342 High St., Dunedin (© **0800/268-252** in NZ, or 03/477-9053; www.deaconscourt.co.nz). They have rooms with en-suite or private bathroom facilities in a large, Victorian home from NZ$100 to NZ$140 (US$70–US$98). Closer to town, you'll find a similar stay at **Tower House,** 9 City Rd. (© **03/477-5678;** www.thetowerhouse.co.nz), where the tariff is also from NZ$100 to NZ$140 (US$70–US$98).

Manor House Backpackers ★★   Manor House is one of the most popular backpackers in Dunedin. There's nothing "packed-in" about the place, as beds are spread throughout two divine old houses situated next door to each other. Each house has a shared lounge, bathroom, and kitchen areas, and they're set in nice gardens. Clean and tidy seems to be the order of the day. It's especially popular with Germans, Brits, and Israelis.

28 Manor Place, Dunedin. © **0800/477-0484** in NZ, or 03/477-0484. Fax 03/479-2009. www.manorhousebackpackers.co.nz. 55 beds (with shared bathrooms). NZ$22 (US$15) per person dorm bed; from NZ$55 (US$39) twin/double. Long-stay and special deals available. MC, V. Limited off-street parking. **Amenities:** Free bikes; game room; tour bookings; car rentals; coin-op laundry; nonsmoking rooms; access for travelers w/disabilities. *In room:* No phone.

ON OTAGO PENINSULA

There are certainly enough things to see on the peninsula to justify an overnight stay. At **Nisbet Cottage** 🌺🌺, 6A Elliffe Place, Shiel Hill, Dunedin (© **03/454-5169;** www.natureguidesotagoe.co.nz), hosts and nature guides Ralf and Hildegard can advise you on the area's natural history and unique birdlife. They specialize in nature-based accommodations packages, in which you tie up 2 or more nights' stay with guided wildlife tours of Dunedin, Otago Peninsular, and the Catlins. There are three lovely guest rooms with en-suite bathrooms and stunning views over Dunedin Harbor. Two- or 3-night tour packages range from NZ$1,050 to NZ$1,770 (US$735–US$1,239) and include breakfast, tour, and picnic lunch.

Larnach Lodge 🌺🌺 Larnach Castle (see "Exploring Otago Peninsula," earlier in this chapter) provides an imposing backdrop to the lodge's 12 spacious, themed rooms, which all have magnificent views. (There are no lodgings in the castle itself.) The Gold Rush Room features a king-size bed made from an old cart found on the castle grounds, complete with four huge wheels and the driver's seat and brakes attached to the end. There's a hint of the Wild West about it that doesn't quite fit the elegance of the rest of the lodge and castle. That aside, beds are divinely comfortable and bathrooms are generous. If you want to enjoy dinner in the castle's formal dining room, book by 5pm. Overall, an excellent place to base yourself for peninsula exploration, but a bit far out if you want town action.

Larnach Castle, 145 Camp Rd., Otago Peninsula © **03/476-1616.** Fax 03/476-1574. www.larnachcastle.co.nz. 12 units. NZ$210–NZ$240 (US$147–US$239) standard; NZ$250–NZ$270 (US$175–US$189) premium. Also 6 units (with shared bathrooms) in stables from NZ$100 (US$70). Rates include breakfast. MC, V. **Amenities:** Dining room; pre-booked babysitting; coin-op laundry; nonsmoking rooms; access for travelers w/disabilities. *In room:* TV, fridge, coffeemaker, hair dryer, no phone.

WHERE TO DINE

As a university town, Dunedin is home to many establishments that cater to students. Restaurants are therefore less stratified than in other New Zealand cities, and you'll find everyone—students, businesspeople, families, elderly couples—dining happily together in most places. There are plenty of budget options and quirkily named cafes and bars.

For a firsthand taste of university social life, head for **The Governor's Café,** 438 George St. (© **03/477-6871**), open daily from 8am to midnight. For good coffee, go to **ReFuel Bar,** 640 Cumberland St. (© **03/479-3875**), which is next to the dental school, also in the thick of university life. It's open during university semesters, Monday through Friday 11am until late and Saturday 7pm to late. **Plato** 🌺🌺, 2 Birch St., Inner Harbour Warehouse Area (© **03/477-4235**), is a good restaurant choice for service and great original tastes. Take a cab, as it's easy to get lost in the wharf area.

EXPENSIVE

Bell Pepper Blues 🌺🌺🌺 MODERN NEW ZEALAND Chef/owner Michael Coughlin is one of New Zealand's best-known prize-winning chefs. With his wife, Marianne, he has established an unpretentious restaurant with a focus on fine food—meals you remember long afterwards for their flavor and stylish presentation. It's an intimate, heavily booked spot, so reserve ahead for such culinary pleasures as smoked duck terrine, or chocolate tart with a compote of nectarines, raspberry coulis, and vanilla cream. Widely regarded as one of Dunedin's best dining experiences, it also offers a delicious light lunch menu in the adjacent Chile Club, which doubles as restaurant bar at night.

474 Princes St ℂ 03/474-0973. Reservations required. Main courses NZ$25–NZ$35 (US$18–US$25). AE, DC, MC, V. Wed–Fri noon–2pm; Mon–Sat 6:30pm–late.

High Tide ⭑⭑ *Finds* SEAFOOD   If you find High Tide at all, you should be congratulated, as it's on the waterfront amid a rabbit's warren of dark wharf streets. But it's definitely worth the hunt—or more sensibly, the cab ride—as it serves up fantastic seafood dishes and a host of other creative menu offerings. This could be your one chance to try roast New Zealand mutton bird with kumara (sweet potato) crisps, fresh watercress salad, and green-peppercorn vinaigrette. The low-key interior gives way to big harbor views on light summer nights, the service is friendly and attentive, the wine list is more than adequate, and desserts are a perfect indulgent ending to a memorable dining experience.

29 Kitchener St. ℂ 03/477-9784. Reservations recommended. Main courses NZ$25–NZ$32 (US$18–US$22). AE, MC, V. Tues–Sun from 6pm. Turn left off the road that takes you to the albatross colony, just along from Watercooled Sports.

Table Se7en ⭑⭑ INTERNATIONAL   There's a slither of big-city style in this upstairs eatery that looks over the main shopping street. You can relax at the bar before tucking into artistically presented treats like herb-crusted filet of pork with fragrant kumara, caramelized apples, sautéed spinach, and almond flakes. If that doesn't tempt you, try beef steak with a touch of chimichurri, or harissa-crusted, herb-smoked venison. It's not only their name they've gotten clever with—the menu is just as cool.

Level 1, corner of Hanover and George sts. ℂ 03/477-6877. Reservations recommended. Main courses NZ$25–NZ$32 (US$18–US$22). AE, MC, V. Mon–Sat noon–3pm; dinner from 6pm.

MODERATE

Bean Scene ⭑⭑ CAFE/MODERN NEW ZEALAND   You'll have to beat back the crowds of locals who favor this smart little cafe, but once in, you won't regret the wrestle for a table. Lunch or early-evening meals here are fresh and tasty. My favorite was a very, very delicious (and filling) porcini, wild mushroom, and red-wine risotto drizzled with truffle oil—I ate it for 3 days running. You'll find gluten-free, dairy-free, and vegetarian options here, as well as plenty to satiate meat lovers.

16 The Octagon. ℂ 03/471-7372. Reservations for evening dining. Main courses NZ$18–NZ$30 (US$13–US$21). AE, MC, V. Mon–Fri 7:45am–late; Sat 9am–late.

Mazagram Espresso Bar ⭑⭑ *Finds* ESPRESSO BAR   One of my favorite Dunedin haunts, this places is a must-visit treat if you're a coffee connoisseur. You'll find yourself crammed into a tiny roastery with just four little marble tables (there are more tables outside). Mazagram supplies most of Dunedin's leading cafes. It does a mean brew and can also tempt you with a sweet to accompany your coffee.

Upper Moray Place. ℂ 03/477-9959. Cakes NZ$6—NZ$10 (US$4.20–US$7). No credit cards. Mon–Fri 8am–6pm; Sat 10am–2pm.

Nova ⭑⭑ ITALIAN/ASIAN   No visit to Dunedin is complete without a visit to trendy Nova. Step down off The Octagon into this smart, city-style cafe oozing ambience, and you'll find everything from delicious breakfast classics such as bagels and panettone to an easy mix of Italian and Asian dinner dishes. Seafood gumbo is a favorite—thick, spicy soup of seafood, bacon, and sausage served with toasted rye—or select from wok-fried vegetables, risotto of the day, steamed mussels, and lasagna, among others. Everyone comes to Nova, especially tourists and locals of an artistic bent, stepping in from the adjacent Public Art Gallery.

Dunedin Public Art Gallery, 29 The Octagon. © **03/479-0808.** Reservations recommended. Main courses NZ$18–NZ$28 (US$13–US$20). AE, DC, MC, V. Mon–Fri 7am–11pm; Sat 9am–midnight; Sun 9am–11pm.

Strictly Coffee ✿✿✿ CAFE   I almost got a chill up my spine when I discovered this cute, hidden-away place down a back alley. It's just my sort of place—slightly disheveled in a shabby-chic kind of way, unpretentious, friendly, and known to anyone who's anyone. On top of that, you get excellent coffee—fresh from their own roastery that you can huddle beside if you feel so inclined—sweet, savory treats and good magazines. They've also wised up to the fact that opening early saves caffeine-deprived lives!

23 Bath St. © **03/479-0017.** Cafe food NZ$5–NZ$12 (US$3.50–US$8.40). AE, MC, V. Mon–Fri 8am–5pm.

INEXPENSIVE
Jizo Café/Bar ✿✿ JAPANESE   I love to sit in this plain little restaurant and watch the chefs flinging my sushi together with an aplomb that leaves me breathless and hungry. This is the best place to sample cheap, authentic Japanese food in a casual environment. Service is snappy and the staff speaks both Japanese and English. It has a full sushi menu, udon, katsus, and seafood, vegetarian, and meat dishes, not to mention an impressive range of Japanese beers and sake. All this *and* jazz music. It could only happen in Dunedin.

56 Princes St. © **03/479-2692.** Main courses NZ$10–NZ$20 (US$7–US$14). AE, DC, MC, V. Mon–Sat 11am–9pm (Fri till 10pm).

SHOPPING
Dunedin offers excellent shopping, with most stores open Monday through Thursday from 9am to 5:30pm, Friday from 9am to 9pm, and Saturday and Sunday from 10am to 1pm (some later).

A good place to park your car and start browsing is the new **Meridian Shopping Centre,** George Street (© **03/477-1129**), which has over 40 specialty stores and an international food court. For a Kiwi memento to take home, check out **The New Zealand Shop** (© **03/477-3379**), in the Civic Centre, next door to the visitor center on The Octagon. It's open Monday to Thursday 9am to 5.30pm, Friday 9am to 6pm, Saturday 9:30am to 4:30pm, and Sunday 10am to 4pm—and will even open just for you if you call ahead. It'll pack and post your order overseas, too.

If you want something with a "bonny wee Scottish" flavor, head for **The Scottish Shop,** 187 George St. (© **0800/864-686;** scottish.shop@xtra.co.nz). It has a wide

---

⸨Finds⸩ Gourmet Gifts

Everyday Gourmet Ltd. ✿✿, 446 George St., Dunedin (© **03/477-2045**), provides instant gourmet satisfaction and the chance to find the perfect, unusual gifts for friends and family back home. Quite apart from the delicious counter food and light meals on offer, there are shelves bulging with products from near and far. I've decided it's easier to give into temptation than to resist. You'll find New Zealand–made items that will surprise and delight: the country's best olive oils, sauces, honey, preserves, chocolates, and cheeses, all presented in attractive gift packs. While you try to decide what to buy, enjoy the terrific coffee. It's open Monday through Friday from 9am to 6pm, Saturday from 10am to 3pm.

---

range of tartan and heraldic goods, right down to tartan ties. **Helean Kiltmakers,** 8 Hocken St., Kenmure (© **03/453-0233**), continues the theme with made-to-measure kilts.

Hides, 185 George St. (© **03/477-8927**), has top-quality Dunedin-made sheepskin and leather jackets, while **Glen's Leather & Accessories,** 192 Castle St. (© **03/477-3655**), offers good-value lambskin and leather products. **Kathmandu Ltd.,** 144 Great King St. (© **03/474-5178**), will see you right for all your outdoor gear.

For top-quality, one-of-a-kind New Zealand designer jewelry, you can't do better than **Fluxus Contemporary Jewellery,** 99 Stuart St. (© **03/477-9631**). This cooperatively run gallery exhibits the works of leading New Zealand jewelers such as Kobi Bosshard, Georg Beer, and Lyn Kelly. Exquisitely detailed pieces beg to be purchased!

The award-winning **University Book Shop,** 378 Great King St. (© **03/477-6976;** www.unibooks.co.nz), offers just about anything you're likely to want to read. It's just across the road from the Otago Museum and open Monday through Friday from 8:30am to 5:30pm, Saturday from 9:30am to 1:30pm.

Meanwhile, I challenge any woman to resist the swirls of lace, lush fabrics, contemporary jewelry, and assorted temptations found in my favorite store, **Domus Elegans** ✸✸✸, 385 Moray Place (© **03/474-0385**), a truly romantic gift and antique collectibles store that I'd like to have much closer to my home.

Milford Galleries, 18 Dowling St. (© **03/477-7727**), is the best dealer showing contemporary New Zealand art.

International doll artistry is best displayed at **Jan McLean Originals,** 494 George St. (© **03/479-2909;** www.janmcleandolls.com). Jan designs and sculpts limited-edition porcelain dolls and has a large selection of limited-edition collectible teddy bears. Open Monday through Saturday from 10am to 2pm.

DUNEDIN AFTER DARK

Dunedin's nightlife ranges from its legendary university swill holes where drunken, animal-like behavior is de rigeur to smart, upmarket wine bars and, now, to a boutique casino. There are also two good theaters, a multiscreen movie theater, and several cafes that double as live-music venues.

THE PERFORMING ARTS   The **Fortune Theatre,** Stuart Street and Upper Moray Place (© **03/477-8323;** www.fortunetheatre.co.nz), plays a major part in the cultural life of Dunedin with a wide range of performances, from Shakespeare to contemporary New Zealand works. The theater is in a historic late-1800s building. Its season runs from February to December. Tickets cost around NZ$30 to NZ$32 (US$21–US$22) for adults and NZ$15 to NZ$20 (US$11–US$14) for students.

The **Regent Theatre,** on the Lower Octagon (© **03/477-8597;** fax 03/477-4726), hosts a range of national and international performances. Check the local paper for the current schedule of concerts. Also look out for the Dunedin Sinfonia concert series brochure at the visitor center. Ticket prices vary.

THE BAR, CAFE & PUB SCENE   We can thank the student population for much of the color in Dunedin's after-dark scene. Their favorite hangouts include the legendary **Gardens Tavern** (affectionately known as "The Gardies"), 697 Castle St., Dunedin North (© **03/477-6593**)—chance it if you dare! **ReFuel Bar,** 21 Frederick St. (© **03/477-2575**) has The Lounge and Fusion Bars, which provide a changing array of nightly entertainment.

> ⌒*Moments* **Back Alley Pleasures**
>
> Hunt for the *piece de resistance* of Dunedin bars, the very suave, very hard to find gem, **Pequeno** ⋆⋆⋆, Lower Ground Floor (they really mean "underground"), Savoy Building, 50 Princes St. (⌀ **03/477-7830**). Alternatively, if you can find a friendly local to direct you, you can access it from a steep, dark alley off Upper Moray Place. I was taken here by Andrew of Hair Raiser Ghost Walk, so it stands to reason he would pick the darkest, seediest entry. Once inside though, it is a salubrious and classy little den—all fur, leather, and artistic Dunedin types out for a good time. Definitely a place for grown-ups, and they have a terrific wine and cocktails list.

The **Royal Albert Mine Host Bar,** 387 George St. (⌀ **03/477-2952**), is a slight improvement for those in an older age group. The **Lone Star Café & Bar,** 417 Princes St. (⌀ **03/474-1955**); **Bennu Café & Bar,** 12 Moray Place (⌀ **03/474-5055**); and the **Ra Bar,** 21 The Octagon (⌀ **03/477-6080**), are currently deemed to be the happening spots for good food and a lively bar atmosphere for anyone over 25.

Bacchus Winebar, upstairs at 12 The Octagon (⌀ **03/474-0824**), is a nice enough place overlooking The Octagon. It never really takes off in terms of a wild night out—it's more of a sedate place to savor good company and good wine in a smoke-free environment.

For a funky Dunedin night out, you can't beat the **Arc Café Bar,** 135 High St. (⌀ **03/474-1135**). You'll find a wide cross section of society here, all blending amiably and listening to live music.

MOVIES   There are six big screens at the **Hoyts 6 Cinema,** 33 The Octagon (⌀ **03/477-7019**). It has a licensed cafe and bar and plenty of parking at the rear. There is also a new **Rialto 3** theater complex on Upper Moray Place. The **Metro Cinema,** Moray Place, shows artsy movies.

EN ROUTE TO INVERCARGILL

You could drive from Dunedin to Invercargill in roughly 2½ to 3 hours via State Highway 1, passing through the small Southland townships of Balclutha, Gore, and Edendale. This pleasant drive will take you past farmland and mile after mile of grazing sheep.

But now that I've personally experienced the **Southern Scenic Route** ⋆⋆⋆ via the **Catlins** ⋆⋆⋆ for the first time, I urge you to consider taking an extra day to explore this rich, unspoiled coastline. I spent a leisurely 7 hours getting from Dunedin to Invercargill, taking as many side routes as I could, and I never regretted a second of it. The region contains the most significant area of native forest on the east coast of New Zealand, and walking tracks will take you through tall podocarps such as rimu and totara.

Keep in mind, though, that rain falls in this area 214 days a year, so chances are you're going to get wet. However, a lot of the rainfalls occur overnight and won't disrupt your sightseeing. Be sure to pick up the visitor center's brochure on the Southern Scenic Route (St. Hwy. 92), so you can make informed decisions about the stops you make. It is also important to note that many of the roads are unpaved, and if you're unfamiliar with this sort of driving, knock 20kmph (12 mph) off your speed, concentrate, keep in the road grooves, and don't overreact if you skid.

Leaving Dunedin, your first diversion should be to the wildlife-rich area of **Nugget Point** ℱ, signposted just south of Balclutha. Gloriously undisturbed coastline awaits, and from here all the way to Waikawa, you'll find a rich vein of scenic opportunity. Chief among them will be **Purakaunui Falls,** accessed by a 20-minute round-trip walk through beech and podocarp forest; **Cathedral Caves** ℱ, an 80-minute round-trip walk along the beach at low tide only; and the spectacular curve of **Tautuku Bay,** 2km (1¼ miles) south of Papatowai. If you see nothing else, the hilltop view of this bay alone makes the trip worthwhile.

Farther south, you'll find one of the world's finest fossil forests, which can be viewed at low tide at **Curio Bay.** This sea-washed rock terrace dates back 160 million years and is the original floor of a Jurassic subtropical forest of kauri trees, conifers, and other trees growing at a time when grasses had not evolved. At low tide, you can easily make out the stumps and fallen logs that were petrified after being buried in volcanic ash, then raised when the sea level changed.

Another worthwhile stop is **Slope Point.** As the name suggests, the strong winds here are responsible for the rather strange, bent-over form of the trees. Wear warm clothing, as the winds lash in off Foveaux Strait. This is the southernmost point of the South Island, and if you're here on a fine day, you'll be pleased with the views.

The Southern Scenic Route continues on to Te Anau—a total trip of 440km (273 miles) from Dunedin. The Catlins side of the journey is by far the most interesting leg, and it's easy to see why this area is one of the new frontiers of New Zealand tourism. There's a range of moderately priced motels, B&Bs, and backpacker accommodations along the way if you decide to stop over. There are brochures for many of these at the Owaka Information Centre. For more information on the route, call ℂ **0800/723-642** (in New Zealand) or 03/214-9733, or go to www.southland.org.nz.

2 Invercargill ✸

190km (118 miles) S of Queenstown; 217km (135 miles) SW of Dunedin

Asked to name six great things about Invercargill, most people hesitate and scratch their heads. The 53,000 residents of this southernmost city would be justifiably indignant. They'll quickly tell you that people from Invercargill are among the friendliest in the country, that the city has the best seafood, and that it makes a perfect base for exploring some of the country's finest scenery in Fiordland, the Catlins, and Stewart Island. Nor should we overlook the fact that Southland is the capital of country music in New Zealand.

Originally settled by Scottish immigrants, the city's prosperity has been founded on the lush grasslands of Southland, and today several million sheep and cattle graze the flat pastures that surround it. Invercargill is the province's major service center, with more than 1,000 motel and hotel beds.

This once swampy bogland first attracted Europeans keen to establish a flax-milling industry. It was surveyed in 1856 by New Zealand's first surveyor general, J. Thomson, who wisely mapped out the main streets (named after Scottish rivers) 40m (131 ft.) in width, still giving the city its distinctive spacious character. Southlanders continue to be seen as a hardy, practical, gregarious lot, and they'll make sure your stay here is a memorable one.

ESSENTIALS

GETTING THERE & GETTING AROUND   By Plane   Air New Zealand (© 0800/737-000 in NZ) has service between Invercargill and Auckland and Wellington on the North Island, and Christchurch and Dunedin on the South Island. **Stewart Island Flights** (© 03/218-9129; www.stewartislandflights.com) has daily scheduled flights to Stewart Island. The airport is 2.5km (1½ miles) from the city center. **Spitfire Shuttles** (© 03/214-1851) provides transport to and from the city. Invercargill Airport was due to be lengthened in 2005, enabling direct flights from Australia. For more information, go to www.airport.southlandnz.com.

By Coach (Bus)   InterCity (© 03/214-0598) has coach service between Invercargill and Christchurch, Dunedin, Queenstown, Te Anau, and Timaru. The bus depot is also on Leven Street. Look out for **The Freebie,** a free local shuttle service connecting inner city businesses. It runs Monday through Friday, every 15 minutes between 9:30am and 5:45pm. For information on connecting bus routes, call © **03/ 218-7108.**

By Car   Invercargill can be reached on Highway 6 from Queenstown or Highway 1 from Dunedin. See the information on the Southern Scenic Route under "En Route to Invercargill," above. The **Automobile Association** office is 47–51 Gala St. (© **03/ 218-9033**).

By Taxi   Call **Blue Star Taxis Ingill Ltd.,** Tay and Jed streets (© **03/218-6079**), or **Taxi Co.,** 200 Clyde St. (© **03/214-4478**).

ORIENTATION   Invercargill's streets are laid out in grid patterns. The main thoroughfares are Tay Street (an extension of St. Hwy. 1) and Dee Street (an extension of St. Hwy. 6). Many of the principal shops and office buildings are found at their intersection. Queens Park is an 81-hectare (200-acre) green oasis in the center of town.

VISITOR INFORMATION   The **Invercargill i-Site Visitor Centre,** in the Southland Museum and Art Gallery, Victoria Avenue (© 03/214-6243; fax 03/218-4415; www.visit.southlandnz.com), is open Monday through Friday from 9am to 5pm, Saturday and Sunday from 10am to 5pm (closed Dec 25). The **Department of Conservation,** State Insurance Building, 7th Floor, Don Street (© 03/214-4589; fax 03/ 214-4486), is open Monday through Friday from 8am to 5pm. For more information, contact **Venture Southland** (© 03/211-1429; fax 03/211-1401; www.venturesouthland. co.nz). Its website also provides information on Stewart Island. For more information on this area check www.visitinvercargillnz.com.

FAST FACTS   The **Central Post Office** is at 1 Don St. **Southland Hospital,** Kew Road (© **03/218-1949**), has 24-hour emergency care. You can get prescriptions filled at **UFS Dispensary,** 76 Tay St. (© **03/218-9393**), or, for after-hours service, 90 Kelvin St. (© **03/218-4893**). For Internet access, try **Comzone.net,** 45 Dee St. (© **03/214-0007**), where they charge around NZ$4 (US$2.80) per hour.

EXPLORING THE AREA
MUSEUMS, GALLERIES & ARCHITECTURE

It's hard to miss the big white pyramid of the renovated **Southland Museum and Art Gallery** ☆☆ (© 03/218-9753; www.southlandmuseum.com), on Gala Street near the main entrance to Queens Park. A wide range of exhibits brings the region to life. The biggest attraction of all, the **Tuatarium** ☆☆☆, should not be missed. Here you'll

Southland

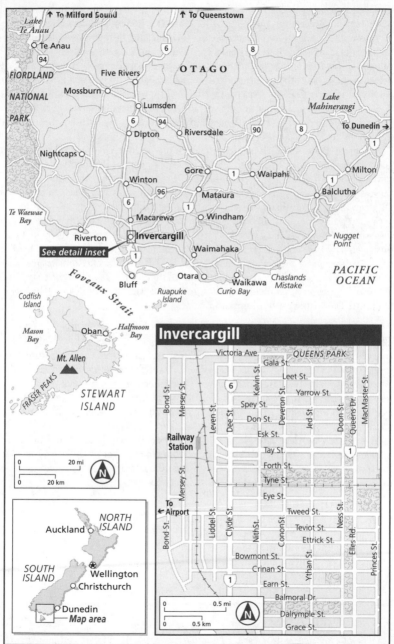

To Milford Sound
To Queenstown

Lake Te Anau

Te Anau

94

FIORDLAND

6

8

OTAGO

Five Rivers

Mossburn

NATIONAL

Lumsden

PARK

6   94

Dipton   Riversdale

90

8

Lake Mahinerangi

To Dunedin →

1

Nightcaps

Gore   1   Waipahi

Milton

1

Winton

96

Mataura

Balclutha

6

1

Te Waewae Bay

Macarewa   Windham

Riverton   Invercargill

See detail inset

Nugget Point

1

Waimahaka

PACIFIC OCEAN

Bluff   Otara   Waikawa   Chaslands Mistake

Ruapuke Island   Curio Bay

Foveaux Strait

Codfish Island

Mason Bay

Oban   Halfmoon Bay

Mt. Allen

FRASER PEAKS

STEWART ISLAND

0   20 mi
0   20 km

N

NORTH ISLAND

Auckland

SOUTH ISLAND

Wellington

Christchurch

Dunedin

Map area

Invercargill

Victoria Ave.   QUEENS PARK

Gala St.

Leet St.

6

Kelvin St.

Yarrow St.

MacMaster St.

Bond St.

Mersey St.

Leven St.

Dee St.

Spey St.

Deveron St.

Jed St.

Doon St.

Queens Dr.

Don St.

Esk St.

1

Railway Station

Tay St.

Forth St.

Tyne St.

Eye St.

Tweed St.

To Airport

Bond St.

Mersey St.

Liddel St.

Clyde St.

Nith St.

Conon St.

Teviot St.

Ettrick St.

Ness St.

Elles Rd.

Princes St.

Bowmont St.

Ythan St.

Crinan St.

1

Earn St.

Balmoral Dr.

Dalrymple St.

Grace St.

0   0.5 mi
0   0.5 km

N

find the fascinating tuatara—strange prickly reptiles that are descendants of the dinosaurs and now exceptionally rare. The museum breeding program is the only one in the world. As tuatara are nocturnal, they may be hard to spot during the day. The highlight is Henry, now over 100 years old, who, along with the successfully breeding Albert and his concubines, Mildred and Lucy, may show his face. Another excellent museum attraction is the comprehensive audiovisual program on New Zealand's **Sub-Antarctic Islands** 🐧🐧, an area of international importance because they have some of the world's last remaining areas of vegetation unmodified by humans. The museum is open Monday through Friday from 9am to 5pm; Saturday, Sunday, and holidays from 10am to 5pm. Admission is free.

Anderson Park Art Gallery, 91 McIvor Rd., Invercargill (© **03/215-7432**) is housed in a fine Georgian-style residence set on 24 hectares (59 acres) of landscaped gardens. You'll find this architectural delight 7km (4⅓ miles) north of the city, just a short drive east along McIvor Road, which runs off North Road. It's open daily from 10:30am to 5pm. Admission is free, except during exhibitions.

Speaking of things old, *Invercargill Heritage Trail* is an excellent brochure produced by the New Zealand Historic Places Trust and available at the visitor center. It highlights 19 of the city's finest architectural specimens, including St. Mary's Basilica, on Tyne Street, and the town's famous 43m (139-ft.) red-brick Romanesque water tower. There is a similar brochure for nearby Bluff; and the *Invercargill City Spirit Walk* brochure details a 1-hour walk through the inner city, following history in sculptures, landmarks, and information panels.

PARKS & GARDENS

The main entrance to **Queens Park** is near Southland Museum and Art Gallery. This cool green 81-hectare (200-acre) oasis is a perfect place to wander and it features some beautiful trees. You'll find formal rose gardens, a rhododendron walk, an iris garden, a Japanese garden, a wildlife sanctuary, a walk-through bird aviary, duck ponds, a winter garden, tennis courts, and an 18-hole golf course. The aviary has a good parrot collection and is best visited in early morning or late afternoon, when the birds are most active.

Maple Glen Gardens and Nursery, in nearby rural Wyndham (© **03/206-4983;** www.mapleglen.co.nz), is a remarkable private garden and exotic bird haven that every gardener should see. It's open Sunday through Friday from 2 to 4pm and Saturday from 9am to 5pm. A guided walk costs NZ$5 (US$3.50) per person.

A SIDE TRIP TO BLUFF

If time permits, take a drive to Bluff to find **Tiwai Smelter Tours,** NZ Aluminium Smelters Ltd., Private Bag, Invercargill (© **03/218-5494;** www.comalco.com). This free tour is much more interesting than you might think and is available weekdays at 10am, with only three tours per week. Bookings are essential; there are special clothing requirements for safety reasons. Children under 12 will not be admitted. **Bluff's**

⌕Tips Picnic Time

Look out for the visitor center's handy green brochure that outlines *Invercargill's Picnic Areas.* It describes 16 ideal picnic spots and where to find them.

Finds **Hidden Gems**

If you're looking for an interesting country drive out of Invercargill, go to **Cosy Nook** 🐸🐸, a delightful fishing settlement on one of the wildest coastlines in the world. Near Riverton, it's well signposted from State Highway 99. You'll find cute old fishing boats and cottages and some creative signage. **Riverton Rocks Beach** is also a treat, with gorgeous little green pebbles all over the place. It's about a 45-minute drive from Invercargill. Just over the hill to the southwest, you'll find **Colac Bay**—one big horseshoe swoop of surfing heaven, with a cluster of little cottages on the foreshore.

Maritime Museum, Foreshore Road (© **03/212-7534;** bluffmuseum@netscape.net.nz), is open daily and presents good coverage of Southland's maritime history. Bluff is 27km (17 miles) south of Invercargill. In Invercargill, get on Dee Street, which becomes State Highway 1; the drive will take about 30 minutes. The **Paua Shell House** 🐸🐸, 258 Marine Parade (no phone), is open 9am until 5pm daily and is a testament to one couple's passion for this iconic New Zealand shell. I guarantee you'll never ever see anything else like it!

ORGANIZED TOURS

If you haven't already explored the Catlins area (see "En Route to Invercargill," earlier in this chapter), join **Lynette Jack Scenic Sights** (©/fax **03/215-7741** or 025/338-370). Lynette has tours from 2 hours to a full day that explore not only the Catlins, but also Bluff, Riverton, and Western Southland. To sightsee in total comfort, contact **Ambassador Limousines** (© **03/217-4504** or 025/339-889). Personalized tours of Southland for up to 12 people can also be arranged with **Athol Bennie** (© **03/235-2827;** fax 03/235-2826). Both **Southeast Air** (© **03/214-5522;** fax 03/214-5520) and **Southern Wings Air Charter** (© **03/218-6171;** www.southernwings.co.nz) offer chartered scenic flights around Southland.

OUTDOOR PURSUITS

BEACHES   Oreti Beach, 9.5km (6 miles) west of Invercargill, out past the airport, is safe for swimming. This broad expanse of sand stretches from Omaui at the southern end right around to Riverton. There are surf patrols in attendance during summer.

BIKING   Single and tandem bikes can be hired from **Wensley's Cycles,** Tay and Ninth streets (© **03/218-6206;** fax 03/218-6368).

FISHING   There are numerous fishing opportunities in Southland, many within 30 minutes of Invercargill. The famous **Mataura River** offers some of the best trout fishing in the world. The season in most areas opens October 1 and goes to April 30. There are exceptions, so check the regulation guide available at the visitor center. The team at **Outdoor World,** Tay Street (© **03/214-2052**), can advise you on the best spots and the best tackle. **Len Prentice** (©/fax **03/216-4447**) is a well-respected guide for dry fly and upstream nymph fishing to sighted rainbows and browns, and **Alan Wilson** (©/fax **03/217-3687;** dryfly@southnet.co.nz) can help with wilderness and heli-fishing.

WALKING   There are numerous fine walks within an hour's drive of Invercargill. You can read about them in the Department of Conservation's excellent brochure *Day*

Walks from Invercargill, available at the visitor center. **Sandy Point Domain,** 7km (4¼ miles) west of the city, has attractive walking tracks through totara forest and sand dunes. The **Foveaux Walkway** in Bluff is a 2-hour walk around Bluff's rugged coastline. The track begins at Ocean Beach Road and ends at Stirling Point, or vice versa. The 30-minute **Glory Track** starts at Stirling Point and finishes at Gunpit Road. A little farther afield, the **Tuatapere Humpridge Track** 🌟🌟, 31 Orawia Rd., Tuatapere (✆ **0800/486-774** in NZ, or 03/226-6739; www.humpridgetrack.co.nz), is fast gaining a reputation as an excellent 3-day walk for those of moderate to high fitness levels. Tuatapere is 86km (53 miles) from Invercargill and 100km (62 miles) from Te Anau on the Southern Scenic Route.

WINDSURFING The best area for windsurfing is at **Awarua Bay.** Gear rental is available at **Anderson Wind and Surfing,** 204 Spey St. (✆ **03/214-4283**).

WHERE TO STAY

Most of the 1,000 or so beds available in Invercargill are in the budget and moderately priced range, with little to offer in the bed-and-breakfast or expensive bracket. One thing the area can boast, though, is its wide range of home- and farmstay options scattered throughout the surrounding farmland. Pick up the visitor center's brochure detailing 15 of these home- and farmstays. The rates given below include the 12.5% GST and free off-street parking.

MODERATE

Ascot Park Hotel 🌟🌟 This is deemed Invercargill's top spot, and although it's a bit too far out of town (4km/2½ miles) to be convenient, it does have silence on its side—unlike the Kelvin Hotel (see below). All rooms were refurbished in 2000. The four deluxe units are a good pick if you like heaps of space. The suites are perfect for two couples or a family. The motel units come complete with kitchens. The hotel is favored by sports teams, tour groups, and independent travelers.

Tay St. and Racecourse Rd., Invercargill. ✆ **0800/272-687** in NZ, or 03/217-6195. Fax 03/217-7002. www.mainstay.co.nz or www.ilt.co.nz. 96 units. From NZ$165 (US$116) standard; NZ$175 (US$123) superior; NZ$180 (US$126) deluxe; NZ$320 (US$224) suite; from NZ$100 (US$70) motel units. Extra person NZ$20 (US$14). AE, DC, MC, V. **Amenities:** Restaurant; 2 bars; heated indoor pool; nearby golf course; small exercise room; Jacuzzi; sauna; children's play area; courtesy car; secretarial services; limited room service; massage; babysitting; laundry service; same-day dry cleaning; nonsmoking rooms; airport transfers. *In room:* A/C, TV, dataport, minibar, fridge, coffeemaker, hair dryer, iron.

Balmoral Lodge Motel 🌟🌟 *Value* This is one of the best motel complexes I've stayed in—and definitely the best value for the money. Built 22 years ago, it has been maintained in tip-top condition and the latest upgrades were completed in 2002. Room nos. 12 through 28 are particularly smart. Most are spacious mezzanine units with lounges; all are centrally heated. Grab the honeymoon suite if you can and indulge yourself in its four-poster bed and big Jacuzzi. Twelve new units opened in 2005.

265 Tay St., Invercargill. ✆ **0800/225-667** in NZ, or 03/219-9050. Fax 03/217-5755. www.ilt.co.nz. 38 units. From NZ$105 (US$74) studio; NZ$110 (US$77) 1-bedroom unit; NZ$125 (US$88) 2-bedroom unit or suite. Extra person NZ$20 (US$14). Off-peak and long-stay rates available. AE, DC, MC, V. All InterCity buses stop outside. A 15-min. walk from town. **Amenities:** Laundry service and coin-op laundry; same-day dry cleaning. *In room:* TV, dataport, kitchen, fridge, coffeemaker, hair dryer, iron.

Kelvin Hotel 🌟 This hotel was completely refurbished in 2001, taking it into the well-priced midrange bracket. It's pretty much a standard facility, but rooms are all fresh and light. Bathrooms are small but smart, all with combination tub/showers (and Jacuzzis in sixth-floor rooms). Room no. 601 is the corner honeymoon suite, with great views over the city. Molly O'Grady's in-house restaurant has an Irish theme and is very popular with locals. This is a hard-to-beat central-city location, right in the middle of the main shopping streets, but unfortunately is also prone to a lot of noise, especially on weekends.

Kelvin and Esk sts., Invercargill. © 0800/802-829 in NZ, or 03/218-2829. Fax 03/218-2827. www.ilt.co.nz or www.mainstay.co.nz. 60 units. From NZ$135 (US$95) deluxe; NZ$190 (US$133) suite. Extra person NZ$20 (US$14). Packages and long-stay rates negotiable. AE, DC, MC, V. **Amenities:** Restaurant; 2 bars (Irish, casino); nearby golf course; nearby gym; room service; laundry service; same-day dry cleaning. *In room:* TV, dataport, minibar, fridge, coffeemaker, hair dryer, iron.

INEXPENSIVE

Backpackers will find comfortable beds at **Tuatara Backpackers,** 30–32 Dee St. (© **0800/488-2827** in NZ, or 03/214-0954; tuataralodge@xtra.co.nz), in the heart of the city. Other reasonably priced inner city beds will be found at **Living Space** 👣👣, 15 Tay St. (© **0508/454-846** in NZ; www.livingspace.net), which has a colorful selection of studios and two- to three-bedroom apartments. You'll find good B&B beds at **Burtonwood,** 177 Gala St. (© **03/218-8884;** www.burtonwood.co.nz); and **Bella Retreat** 👣👣, 70 Retreat Rd., RD2, Invercargill (© **03/215-7688;** www.bella retreat.co.nz).

WHERE TO DINE

It's only been in recent years that Invercargill has come up to snuff on the dining scene. Restaurants are still few and far between given the size of the town, but there are some good eateries. **HMS Kings Restaurant,** 80 Tay St. (© **03/218-3433**), is consistently favored by locals for its seafood, although service can be erratic; and **148 on Elles,** 148 Elles St. (© **03/216-1000**), is recommended. **Global Byte Café** 👣👣, 150 Dee St. (© **03/214-4724**), has great breakfasts and Internet access. **Soprano's Pizzeria** 👣👣, 33 Tay St. (© **03/218-3464**), has a lively atmosphere and tasty pizzas if you just feel like a quick bite. And if good coffee is all you're after, try **Café 101** 👣👣, 35 Kelvin St. (© **03/218-3561**), which usually opens earlier than some of the others.

Tillermans 👣👣 WHOLE FOODS Tillermans has been serving exciting, healthy cuisine for 24 years and has the awards to prove it. Food here is simple, fresh, and delicious. Select sweet-and-sour tofu or pan-fried fish with capers and cream, and make a choice from the extensive salad bar to go with it. Tillermans transforms itself into a happening weekend night scene with two lively bars, DJs, and live bands (see "Invercargill After Dark," below).

16 Don St. © 03/218-9240. Reservations required. Main courses NZ$16–NZ$26 (US$11–US$18). AE, DC, MC, V. Mon–Fri 11:30am–2pm; Wed–Sat 6–10pm.

Zookeepers Café 👣👣 NEW ZEALAND/CAFE Look out for the large elephant on the roof and you won't miss Zookeepers. The interior is just as zany, and there's always a chummy atmosphere that makes it one of the most popular places in Invercargill. Crumbed Stewart Island blue cod with kumara fries, minced lamb kabobs, rib-eye steak, pastas, and salads are typical offerings. Come here for the mood more than the food. You'll find both young and old, locals and visitors.

50 Tay St. © 03/218-3373. Main courses NZ$12–NZ$25 (US$8.40–US$18). AE, DC, MC, V. Daily 10am–late.

INVERCARGILL AFTER DARK

Tillermans (see "Where to Dine," above) has two bars (one upstairs, one down), both with crazy interiors and filled with 20- and 30-somethings keen to move to DJs and live music. Lots of travelers head here as well as locals. **The Lone Star,** Dee and Leet streets (© **03/214-6225**), draws a crowd of mixed ages, and **Molly O'Grady's,** in the Kelvin Hotel, Kelvin and Esk streets (© **03/218-2829**), attracts Guinness fans and lovers of hearty Irish atmosphere. Sorry Invercargill, but it must be said—you could do with some classier options.

3 Stewart Island ★★

30km (19 miles) SW of Bluff, across the Foveaux Strait

Anyone who tries to visit Stewart Island in a day won't be giving this near-perfect place a chance. It is almost a cliché to call it one of New Zealand's best-kept secrets, but given that so few people are aware of its unspoiled tranquillity, it probably deserves this label more than any other place in the country.

New Zealand's third island is far bigger than most people imagine, and almost without exception, first-time visitors are surprised by its equitable climate and the range of activities it provides. Roughly triangular in shape, it is 65km (40 miles) long and 40km (25 miles) at its widest point, and with an area of 1,680 sq. km (655 sq. miles), it is about the size of Singapore or Fiji. Only 1% of the island is inhabited—the rest is given over to natural native bush, exquisite white-sand beaches, bird sanctuaries, and rugged mountains. All this makes it a naturalist's and tramper's paradise and the perfect place for a remote yet accessible holiday. You need to be here only a few hours before the rest of the world melts away and you find yourself adopting the unhurried, laid-back approach of the locals.

The main fishing village of Oban is your landing point, and this is where the population of approximately 360 bases itself. Most permanent residents are involved in the commercial fishing or tourism industries, and a surprisingly small number of other smart New Zealanders have invested in holiday homes, or cribs, here.

Originally called Te Punga o Te Waka a Maui by the Maori, which translates as "The Anchorstone of Maui's Canoe," it is more commonly known by the Maori name Rakiura, which means "Land of Glowing Skies," referring to the vivid colors of dawn and the twilight skies.

Today, the island community jealously guards the amazing natural heritage that surrounds it. This is natural New Zealand the way it used to be—truly picturesque and serene, a place where native birds will land within inches of your teacup, a place you should not overlook.

ESSENTIALS

GETTING THERE   By Plane   Air transport to Stewart Island is provided by **Stewart Island Flights** (© **03/218-9129;** www.stewartislandflights.com), which is based in Invercargill. You get breathtaking views of the island from the nine-seat Britten-Norman aircraft, which takes approximately 20 minutes to cross Foveaux Strait. Shuttle buses then deliver you to your accommodations in Oban. The adult fare is NZ$155 (US$109) round-trip. Stewart Island Flights can also help you plan and book your entire Stewart Island holiday.

By Boat   The passenger-only ferry, operated by **Stewart Island Experience,** will have you on Stewart Island in an hour. It departs Bluff ferry terminal September through April from 8:30am until 4pm and from May through August 9:30am to 5pm. There's connecting bus service from Invercargill to Bluff; secure car parking is available near the Bluff ferry terminal. The round-trip fare is NZ$98 (US$67) for adults and NZ$49 (US$34) for children ages 5 to 14. For inquiries and reservations, call © **0800/000-511** in NZ, or 03/212-7660; www.stewartislandexperience.co.nz.

GETTING AROUND   Most things on the island are within walking distance, although a number of the accommodations lie farther out. To reach them, and some of the divine beaches, means a good up- and downhill walk. You can rent cars (NZ$60/ US$42 for a half-day), mountain bikes (NZ$20/US$14 a day), and scooters (NZ$70/ US$49 per 2 hr.). A shuttle/minibus operates around the island like a taxi service. Both the **Stewart Island Visitor Terminal,** on the wharf (© **03/219-1134;** www.stewart islandexperience.co.nz), and the **visitor center** (see below) can provide details and rates on these options. Charter boats and water taxis can be arranged for sightseers, hunters, divers, trampers, and fishermen. Make reservations at the **Stewart Island Visitor Terminal** or with **Island Explorer,** Stewart Island Flights Depot (© **03/219-1090;** www. stewartislandflights.com). If you prefer, reservations can be made directly with the operators; go to the visitor center for information and brochures. Land transportation can also be arranged.

VISITOR INFORMATION   The ferry will deposit you on the wharf at Oban within a few hundred meters from the center of the village. The village itself consists of the **Ship to Shore General Store** (©/fax **03/219-1069**), which prides itself on sup- plying everything from a needle to an anchor; a hotel; a couple of restaurants; the Department of Conservation base; a small museum; a school and community hall; numerous homes; and various travel offices.

The **Stewart Island Visitor Information Centre** is in the Department of Conser- vation building on Main Road (© **03/219-0009** or 03/219-0002 [DOC]; fax 03/ 219-0003; www.doc.govt.nz or www.stewartisland.co.nz), just up from South Sea Hotel. All trampers must report here for walking-track and hut passes. The staff mem- bers here are extremely well informed about all aspects of tramping and exploring the island; since some of the tracks are challenging, it pays to ask their advice. Also take a look at the 4-minute tramping video, which gives you an idea of what you're in for. The center is open from December 26 to March 31, Monday through Friday from 8:30am to 7pm, Saturday and Sunday from 9am to 7pm; the rest of the year, Mon- day through Friday from 8:30am to 5pm, with reduced hours on weekends.

FAST FACTS   There is no full banking service available on the island. Credit cards are accepted by most businesses, but foreign traveler's checks and cash can be difficult to change, so it pays to arrive with New Zealand dollars.

EXPLORING THE ISLAND

Most visitors are drawn to Stewart Island's unspoiled beauty and unique lifestyle. Nowhere else in New Zealand will you find such ready access to fern-filled native forests and astonishing birdlife (see "Walking & Tramping," below).

Tips Rough Going

If you're taking the ferry, it is important to remember that Foveaux Strait is one of the most unpredictable passages in the world, and the water can be extremely rough. If you're prone to seasickness, come prepared. It may be a short trip (1 hr.), but can be notoriously uncomfortable. Many people like to fly one-way and take the ferry the other. This gives you two perspectives, and eliminates a difficult water crossing if the weather is not fine.

For those coming to simply unwind, there are lots of quirky activities that must be experienced. The **Rakiura Museum,** in Half Moon Bay (✆ **03/219-1049;** fax 03/219-1126), is worthwhile for those who want a glimpse at the island's past. It features photographs and exhibits tracing the island's history through sailing, whaling, tin mining, sawmilling, and fishing. It also has shell and Maori artifact displays. It's open Monday through Saturday from 10am to noon, Sunday from noon to 2pm, with extended hours during the summer holidays. Admission is around NZ$2 (US$1.40) for adults and NZ$1 (US70¢) for children.

Poke your nose into the **Empress Pearl Visitor Centre,** on Main Street (✆ **03/219-1123;** www.empress.co.nz), and talk to Joanne Leask about one of the island's latest ventures—cultured paua pearls. You'll see a range of exclusive jewelry featuring this lustrous treasure formed in New Zealand's famous abalone. It's open daily from 9:30am to 2:30pm. You might also be interested in the **Paua Abalone Farm,** Island Hatcheries, Horseshoe Bay Road (✆ **03/219-1226**), which cultivates paua for food. Daily half-hour tours are offered at 3pm for about NZ$8 (US$5.60) per adult, free for children.

The **Fernery,** on Golden Bay Road (✆/fax **03/219-1453**), is Stewart Island's crafts shop and gallery. It carries pottery, glassware, wood, silk, T-shirts, and souvenirs.

WALKING & TRAMPING

Stewart Island offers unparalleled walking and tramping opportunities. Trampers will go through undisturbed native vegetation and see hundreds of birds. It is important to remember that rain falls on Stewart Island about 275 days of the year, so bring good waterproof clothing. The weather is very changeable, often swinging from rain to warm sun in the space of an hour. Track surfaces are varied and include long sections of boardwalk, which protects the native vegetation. Some tracks also include long stretches of deep mud, so wear sturdy boots. You can get further information from the Department of Conservation.

Anyone staying in huts on Stewart Island must pay hut fees. You need to purchase a **Great Walks Pass,** hut tickets, or an annual hut pass from the Department of Conservation (see "Visitor Information," above). Comfortable huts are conveniently spaced along the tracks (ranging in size from 6 to 30 bunks), but they're packed in summer. There's a 2-night maximum stay in any one hut, and you can use tents as well. You will be fined a surcharge if you are found using the huts without a Great Walks Pass.

The **Rakiura Track** 🐦🐦🐦 is one of the Department of Conservation's eight identified Great Walks of New Zealand. The 36km (22-mile) track requires a moderate fitness level and can be comfortably hiked in 3 days, year-round. The circuit follows the open coast, climbs over a 300m (984-ft.) forested ridge, and traverses the sheltered shores of Paterson Inlet. Huts cost NZ$10 (US$7) per person per night, campsites NZ$6 (US$4.20) per person per night.

The **North West Circuit** 🐦🐦 requires a much greater level of fitness and is recommended for experienced trampers, who need to be completely self-sufficient and prepared for 7 hours of tramping a day for 10 days. This track has long stretches of mud and is dangerous once snow falls. It takes in the northern third of the island and the island's highest peak, Mount Anglem (980m/3,214 ft.). A North West Circuit Pass costs NZ$40 (US$28) and allows 1 night in each hut on the North West Circuit Track, including the Great Walks huts at Port William and North Arm. Back Country hut tickets (NZ$5/US$3.50 per night), or a Backcountry Pass (NZ$90/US$63), may be used on the North West and the Southern Circuit Tracks, but separate passes must be purchased for the Great Walks huts (NZ$10/US$7 per night).

The **Southern Circuit,** which can be added to the above or done separately, is more of a wilderness experience that requires 6 to 7 days of tramping.

Stewart Island Day Walks range from 15 minutes to 7 hours and spread out in a number of directions from Oban. They include comfortable walks to Observation Rock, Golden Bay, Lonneckers Bay, Lee Bay, and Ringaringa Beach (a great spot for shell hounds when the tide is right), and longer walks to Maori Beach (7 hr. round-trip) and Garden Mound (5 hr. round-trip).

Ulva Island 🐾🐾🐾 is one of the best soft-core walking experiences of all. The Department of Conservation recognizes Ulva Island as the "Showcase Project" for its Southland Conservancy, and you can see the results of successful pest-eradication and endangered-species enhancement projects at close quarters. Catch a water taxi to the island (NZ$20–NZ$25/US$14–US$18 per person round-trip for two or more people) from Golden Bay, which is a 20-minute walk over the hill from Oban. It's a short boat trip to somewhere close to paradise—a protected place where you can see rare birds and plants up close without harming them. The island has an 11km (6¾-mile) coastline, and there are walks from 20 minutes to 3 hours. You can spend several hours on the island—and if you're a keen photographer or naturalist, you'll want to—and arrange your return pickup with the water taxi when you land. The Department of Conservation has organized tours (from NZ$50/US$35 for adults, NZ$30/US$21 for school-age children), during January and February, four mornings a week, as well as a good brochure with map for the independent walker. For information on organized walking treks, see "Other Outdoor Pursuits" below.

OTHER OUTDOOR PURSUITS

GOLF   Don't miss New Zealand's only registered 6-hole golf course at **Ringaringa Heights,** overlooking Ringaringa Beach. Greens fees are NZ$5/US$3.50 for two people, which may well make it the cheapest golf course in the world. Club rentals are available at **Stewart Island Flight Depot** (✆ **03/219-1090**) for NZ$5/US$3.50.

HUNTING   The elusive American whitetail deer was liberated on Stewart Island in the early 1900s and now provides sport for the energetic hunter. Hunting parties may spend up to 2 weeks camped in isolated places during the winter "roar." **Southern Isle Charters** (✆ **03/219-1133;** lhhansen@xtra.co.nz) can arrange water transport and hunting parties.

KAYAKING   **Ruggedy Range™ Wilderness Experience** 🐾🐾 (✆ **03/219-1066;** www.ruggedyrange.com), offers six coastal and river kayaking adventures, including multi-activity options, priced from NZ$99 (US$69) per person to NZ$1,850 (US$1,295), around Stewart and Ulva Islands. **Rakiura Kayaks** 🐾 (✆ **03/219-1160;** www.rakiura.co.nz) has a range of trips in Paterson Inlet as well as overnight guided trips to Bravo Island.

SKIN DIVING & FISHING   You'll immediately notice how clear the seawater is around Stewart Island, making it ideal for diving. Both **Talisker Charters** (✆/fax **03/219-1151;** www.taliskercharter.co.nz) and **Takaroa II Adventure Cruises** (✆/fax **03/212-8170;** takaroa@ihug.co.nz) can arrange your diving expedition. **Thorfinn Charters** (✆/fax **03/219-1210;** www.thorfinn.co.nz) will organize personalized fishing charters. Fishermen should pick up the Department of Conservation leaflet called *New Regulations for Fishing in Paterson Inlet, Stewart Island.*

WALKING   Three companies offer excellent trekking options in various parts of Stewart Island. **Ruggedy Range™ Wilderness Experience** (✆ **03/219-1066;** www.ruggedyrange.com) has trips to Ulva Island (NZ$80–NZ$115/US$56–US$81), a kiwi-spotting adventure in Mason Bay (NZ$275–NZ$495/US$193–US$347), and

Moments **Making a Date with a Kiwi**

The nightlife on Stewart Island is a bit different from that on the mainland, and one of the strangest fellows you'll meet on your starlit adventures will be *Apteryx australis lawryi*, the Stewart Island brown kiwi. This bristly, brown flightless critter is a distinct subspecies of the brown kiwi found throughout New Zealand. It has larger legs and a longer beak, and females are generally bigger than males.

Everything you hear about this being the only place in New Zealand where you're likely to see a kiwi in the wild is true. They're often seen, day and night, foraging for sand hoppers among the kelp on the Stewart Island beaches. Just ask Phillip and Diane Smith—they're the experts at this kiwi-spotting game. Every second night, they gather up a bunch of curious, and hopefully fit, tourists and take them to the remote sandy beaches to find kiwis.

A shy creature at heart, the kiwi attracts a lot of attention, and in the interests of conservation, the Smiths limit their night tours to just 15 passengers (you'll have to book ahead). The evening starts with a twilight cruise on the 14m (48-ft.) MV *Volantis*, leaving from Half Moon Bay Wharf. After a 35-minute boat trip to Glory Bay, you'll make your way to the jetty (with a ladder, not steps!) and spend the evening, or 3 hours of it, prowling the length of Ocean Beach looking for the ungainly bird that has won the hearts of so many. If you're lucky, you'll see its plump, feathered backside plodding along the sand as it absent-mindedly looks for its evening meal.

You can expect some rare nights out in New Zealand, but this one is sure to surpass the lot. You may never have envisioned yourself as a bird-spotter, crouching in the darkness on some strange southern coastline, but when you see this rare bird playing hard to get—plodding, darting, hiding, reappearing—you'll know you have experienced something unique. It could well be the best date you have in New Zealand—and you'll pay around NZ$100 to NZ$150 (US$70–US$105) for the pleasure.

Gather up your sturdy footwear, warm clothing, and torch (flashlight) and contact Phillip and Diane Smith at **Bravo Adventure Cruises** (*, P.O. Box 104, Stewart Island (*/fax **03/219-1144**). The trip is subject to weather conditions and is not recommended for children under 10.

Rakiura Track walks from NZ$155 (US$109). **Ulva's Guided Walks** (*C* **03/219-1216;** www.ulva.co.nz) has half-day guided walks on Ulva Island for NZ$85 (US$60) per person, which includes the water-taxi fare. **Kiwi Wilderness Walks** (*C* **021/359-592;** www.nzwalk.com) has 5-day walks that depart from Riverton (near Invercargill) for Mason Bay on Stewart Island, including sea kayaking and kiwi spotting, priced from around NZ$1,500 (US$1,050) per person.

ORGANIZED TOURS

There are several options for organized sightseeing trips: water taxis, boat cruises, yacht charters, and scenic flights. Most of the following tours are subject to weather conditions and all have minimum-number requirements.

Stewart Island Experience ☆☆☆ (© **0800/000-511** in NZ, or 03/219-1134; www.stewartislandexperience.co.nz), has an excellent adventure in an underwater submersible that enables you to see diverse fish species, sponges, sea quirts, and shellfish as you drift through crystal-clear water and kelp forests. It departs from the Stewart Island Visitor Terminal at 11:15am and 3:15pm all year, with extra sailings at 10:15pm and 2:15pm from November through March. It costs NZ$37 (US$26) for adults and NZ$15 (US$11) for children. **Village & Bays Tours** (© **0800/000-511** in NZ, or 03/219-1134), gives a 1½-hour tour of Oban village and the surrounding bays, with a good commentary on local history. It allows for photo stops and short walks along the way and costs NZ$32 (US$22) for adults and NZ$15 (US$11) for children.

Bravo Adventure Cruises (©/fax **03/219-1144**; phildismith@xtra.co.nz), offers a guided evening walk on alternate nights for NZ$90 (US$63) per person. From Bluff, **Southern Isle Charters** (©/fax **03/219-1133**) is available for fishermen and deer-stalkers wanting to explore Stewart Island destinations. **Thorfinn Nature Trips** (©/fax **03/219-1210**) specializes in bird- and wildlife-viewing; and **Sails Scenic Tours,** 11 View St. (© **03/219-1151**; www.taliskercharter.co.nz), has very good sailing and walking tours.

One wonderful way to experience the island from several perspectives is to indulge in the **Coast to Coast** ☆☆ option with **Stewart Island Flights,** Invercargill (© **03/218-9129**), and **Seaview Water Taxis,** Stewart Island (© **03/219-1014**). This trip involves a flight to the magnificent **Mason's Bay** and a landing on its 13km (8-mile) stretch of unspoiled white-sand beach, a 4-hour bush walk to **Freshwater Landing,** and a return boat ride. The excursion is very dependent on tides, and you should be prepared for an unexpected night out if the weather gets rough. Stewart Island Flights also offers a short scenic flight for around NZ$75 (US$53) per person if its Cessna 172 happens to be based on the island at the time of inquiry.

WHERE TO STAY

If there is one negative thing to be said about Stewart Island, it must be about the overall standard of accommodations. There are numerous small backpacker operations, but they generally have a reputation for being pretty grim. Midrange lodgings are scattered, and upmarket choices are virtually nonexistent. On top of that, some of the better offerings have recently closed down, so I cannot promise anything startling in the way of a base. There is, however, a good range of holiday homes available for rent. Remember that summer accommodations are often booked months in advance. One new spot that has a lot more charm than many is **Greenvale Bed and Breakfast** ☆☆, P.O. Box 172 (© **03/219-1357**; www.greenvalestewartisland.co.nz), which has two very attractive rooms with en-suite bathrooms in a modern home, just a few minutes from Oban and just 50m (164 ft.) from the sea. **Bay Motel** ☆☆, 9 Dundee St., Half Moon Bay (© **03/219-1119**; www.baymotel.co.nz), is another new addition that I would happily recommend. It has 12 modern units priced from NZ$140 to NZ$160 (US$98–US$112).

Port of Call ☆☆ *Value* Arriving at Port of Call is like finding pearls in the middle of the desert! If you've managed to beat out other desperate tourists, you can put your feet up and relax—which is the way of things on Stewart Island. Hosts Ian and Philippa Wilson run a thriving tourism business on the island, and if you combine their local knowledge with the comfort of their modern guest rooms and their self-contained studio, you have a great little operation. There's outdoor charm in large decks, barbecue areas, and courtyards. They also have a self-contained cottage surrounded by native bush, 5 minutes from the waterfront.

Leask Bay Rd., Stewart Island. (℃ **03/219-1394.** Fax 03/219-1394. www.portofcall.co.nz. 3 units. NZ$285 (US$200) main house; NZ$220–NZ$285 (US$154–US$200) self-catering studio; NZ$150 (US$105) Turner Cottage. Long-stay and off-peak rates available. Rates include airport transfers; house rate includes breakfast. MC, V. No children under 12. **Amenities:** Nearby golf course; nonsmoking rooms. *In room:* Kitchen in studio and cottage, hair dryer, iron.

South Sea Hotel   This is the southernmost hotel in the world, the only one on Stewart Island, and about as far removed from most people's vision of the South Seas as you could imagine. The recently overhauled accommodations are comfortable and clean. Bathroom facilities are shared and close to most rooms. If you opt for a seaview unit, you may have to forgo a little sleep, as you'll be on top of the always-popular and generally rowdy bar, the hub of most things social on the island. A lovely balcony overlooks the beach. In 2000, new motel units opened at the rear of the existing hotel. If you want to experience a night in a real Kiwi country pub, this is as good a place as any.

Elgin Terrace, P.O. Box 25, Oban, Half Moon Bay, Stewart Island. (℃ **03/219-1059.** Fax 03/219-1120. www.stewart-island. co.nz. 17 hotel units (with shared bathrooms); 9 motel units. NZ$80 (US$56) double/twin, NZ$95 (US$67) seaview; NZ$135 (US$95) motel; NZ$10 (US$7) each extra person. AE, MC, V. **Amenities:** Restaurant; bar; nearby golf course; summer children's program; sauna; coin-op laundry; nonsmoking rooms. *In room:* Kitchen in motel units, fridge, coffeemaker, hair dryer, iron, no phone.

WHERE TO DINE

Dining out on Stewart Island barely warrants a separate section. **Church Hill Café & Restaurant,** 36 Kamahi Rd. (℃ **03/219-1323**), beside the Presbyterian Manse on the hill overlooking Oban, is not, according to local reports, quite as good as everyone had hoped, but I've heard others say it's surprisingly good and the seafood is to be highly recommended. It's open daily 10:30am to late. You might get cheaper food at the **Wharfside Cafe,** upstairs at the wharf (℃ **03/219-1470**). It's nothing fancy, but you'll be right in the island fishing atmosphere and you get good sea views. Another new feature is seasonal **KaiKart Takeaways,** a mobile caravan on Ayr Street, beside the museum and school (℃ **03/219-1225**). It's open daily from noon to 2pm and 5pm until late during summer, providing fish and chips, hamburgers, and assorted takeaways.

South Sea Hotel Dining Room *Overrated* SEAFOOD   Here you are on an island that boasts some of the best fish around—and the most established restaurant on the island doesn't really do it justice. On top of that, it charges city prices for meals that may be big, but just don't measure up in the flair department. If you like plain and hearty, though, you won't leave hungry. The scampi supreme, which includes local whole scampi and scampi tails, salmon terrine, and paua pickle, surrounded by green-lipped mussels and slipper lobsters, could be one offering to tempt the seafood connoisseur. I wasn't prepared to pay NZ$45 (US$32) for it, though. The atmosphere here is more colorful than the food: It's a social center for locals and travelers alike.

South Sea Hotel, Oban, Stewart Island. (℃ **03/219-1059.** Lunch NZ$12–NZ$20 (US$8.40–US$14); dinner NZ$22–NZ$45 (US$15–US$32). AE, MC, V. Daily noon–2pm and 6–8pm.

Appendix A: New Zealand in Depth

Many people think we live in remote, watery isolation down here in New Zealand, and that we're overrun by 60 million sheep and rugby players as big as kauri trees. Well, for a start, sheep numbers have dropped. Current estimates are closer to 44 million, and while there are some big boys out there, they're not all 7 feet tall, wearing rugby boots and All Blacks jerseys.

New Zealand is no longer the sleepy little backwater it was back in the 1950s, although lingering pockets do exist, and you'll still find that, as incomprehensible as it seems, thousands of North Islanders have never been to the South Island and vice versa. That aside, a lot has been achieved here in a few short decades. We share in the rapid changes of the big wide world and we celebrate the good things that progress has brought us. There have been downsides—like the brutal clearing of native forests and the lack of respect for a truly unique landscape—but we're wiser now, and we have 13 national parks protecting the most enviable slices of these little islands.

Although some still won't believe this, I'd like to clarify that New Zealand is not joined to the geographical hip of Australia. In fact, the 1,600km (992 miles) separating us account for some pretty significant differences. Australia, for instance, is vast; New Zealand is not. Australia has a very large red desert in its middle; New Zealand doesn't. And whereas Australia was settled by British convicts, we New Zealanders like to remind everyone that we started out as England's other pasture. The one irrefutable thing the two countries do share is a lively, generally good-spirited rivalry over just about everything, but especially sports.

1 The Natural Environment

THE LAND New Zealand is part of a fiery rim of volcanoes that encircle the Pacific Ocean. The last large eruption occurred in 1886—Mount Tarawera near Rotorua left an estimated 150 people dead. Our most recent show-off has been Mount Ruapehu, which has done its best to ruin the central North Island ski season in the past few years.

Today, New Zealand bears all the fascinating geographical hallmarks of a tumultuous geologic history. There are 500-million-year-old marble outcrops on the top of the Takaka Hills in Nelson, and volcanic ash and pumice have created a barren, desertlike landscape in the central North Island. Franz Josef is one of the fastest-moving glaciers in the world, and the Marlborough Sounds are a labyrinth of islands and waterways. Parched tussock country and strange rocky outcrops cover Central Otago, and the Canterbury Plains spread wide and flat as evidence of prehuman glacial erosion.

Despite all this earthly fury, the land has been blessed with an endless coastline of stunning beaches—white or golden sand on the east coasts, black or gray on the west coasts. Craters have filled to create jewel-like lakes, and rivers and streams are the endless arteries and veins that feed lush flora.

FLORA & FAUNA For 70 million years, New Zealand has been completely separate from all other landmasses. We've been left with some pretty strange creatures as a result: four flightless birds—the kiwi, weka, kakapo, and takahe—along with an ancient reptile directly descended from the dinosaurs. The **kiwi**, of course, has been embraced as a national symbol, so much so that many New Zealanders are quite happy to be called Kiwis themselves. And that odd spiky "lizard," the **tuatara,** is being encouraged to breed itself silly to ensure it'll be around for future generations to marvel at.

Our native birds are a rich lot. The **bellbird,** plain of feather and easily missed, is the songster supreme. The handsome inky **tui,** with his white-tufted neck, comes a close second. The flightless **weka** is rowdy rather than tuneful, and you'll see him in the bush or poking his nose into campsites. The green-and-orange **kea** is a cheeky mountain parrot with a reputation for mischief on the ski fields and in high-country camps. Attracted to anything shiny, he'll lift things if he can, but not before chewing the windshield wipers on your car. His big beak means business, so don't feed him. You'll be delighted by nesting **albatross** and **gannets,** elegant **white herons, penguins,** and many more.

New Zealand has no native mammals. It was the first Polynesian settlers who brought in both the dog and the rat.

Captain Cook then arrived with pigs, goats, fowl, and probably more rats. As more foreign animals were introduced, it became necessary to introduce other animals to control those that had become pests. We now have more than 33 introduced species of mammals, 34 species of birds, 14 species of freshwater fish, at least 1,000 species of introduced insects, plus an Australian lizard and frog or two. Unfortunately, a good many of the above are pests.

We have no nasties—no snakes, predatory animals, or deadly critters of any kind. The only one that comes close is the **poisonous katipo spider,** which you're unlikely to even see, unless you're on the western beaches of the North Island and spot a small black spider with a bright red stripe on its abdomen. There are sometimes **sharks** in the waters around New Zealand. Please ask the locals about this, even though shark attacks are rare.

When it comes to flora, we have diverse vegetation—moss-covered **rainforests** and dense **primeval forests** of ancient podocarp trees. Palms and Norfolk pines, bougainvillea, flame trees, and hibiscus are in the far north, tortured-looking alpine plants, brilliant lichens, and gigantic tree ferns in the south. It's outstanding: 84% of New Zealand's flowering plants are found nowhere else in the world.

Dateline

- **950** Estimated date of first New Zealand landfall by Maori.
- **Mid-1300s** First major influx of Maori settlers.
- **1642** Abel Tasman of the Dutch East India Company becomes first European to sight the South Island.
- **1769** Capt. James Cook begins 6-month mapping of North and South Islands.

- **1773** Cook's second visit to New Zealand.
- **1777** Cook's third and final visit to New Zealand.
- **1792** First sealers and whalers arrive in New Zealand waters.
- **1814** First Christian missionary, Rev. Samuel Marsden, arrives in Bay of Islands.
- **1833** James Busby is named as "British Resident" under jurisdiction of New South Wales.

- **1839–43** New Zealand Company sends out 57 ships out of England carrying 19,000 settlers.
- **1840** Treaty of Waitangi with Maori chiefs is signed in Bay of Islands.
- **1844** Maori Chief Hone Heke chops down British flagpole in Bay of Islands, beginning a 20-year revolt centered on land rights.

2 History 101

EARLY MAORI SETTLEMENT

There's more than one theory as to how New Zealand's first inhabitants settled here. The Maori legend tells of Kupe, who in A.D. 950 sailed from Hawaiiki, the traditional homeland of the Polynesians. The legend doesn't tell us exactly where Hawaiiki was located in the vast South Pacific, but present-day authorities believe it belonged to the Society Islands group that includes Tahiti.

It wasn't until the mid–14th century that Maori arrived in great numbers. These settlers found abundant supplies of seafood and berries, which they supplemented with tropical plants like taro, yams, and kumara (sweet potato) that they'd brought along from Hawaiiki. Dogs and rats also made the voyage, and they were added to the protein source. The cultivation of these imported vegetables and animals gradually led to an agricultural society in which Maori lived in permanent villages based on a central *marae* (village common or courtyard) and *whare runanga* (meetinghouse). This is where the distinctive Maori art forms of woodcarving and tattooing evolved.

ABEL TASMAN & DUTCH DISCOVERY

The first recorded sighting of New Zealand by Europeans occurred in December 1642. Abel Tasman, who was scouting territory for the Dutch East India Company, spied the west coast of the South Island, entered Golden Bay, and met the Maori before even reaching land. As his two ships anchored, several Maori war canoes entered the water and paddlers shouted hostile challenges. The next day, Maori attacked a cockboat, killing four sailors. Tasman fired at the retreating canoes and departed. Bad weather forced him to proceed up the west coast of the North Island. Failing to find a suitable landing spot, he sailed on to Tonga and Fiji, and Golden Bay was known as Murderer's Bay for many years to come.

CAPTAIN COOK

When Captain James Cook left England in 1768 on the *Endeavour*, he carried orders from King George III to sail south in search of the "continent" reported by Abel Tasman. If he found it uninhabited, he was to plant the English flag and claim it for the king; if not, he was to take possession of "convenient situations," but only with the consent of the indigenous people.

On October 7, 1769, Nicholas Young, son of the ship's surgeon, spotted New Zealand from his perch in the mast. Naming the headland (in the Gisborne area) Young Nick's Head, Cook sailed into a crescent-shaped bay and anchored.

- **1852** New Zealand Constitution Act is passed by British Parliament.
- **1860s** Discovery of gold on South Island's west coast and North Island's east coast, creating several boomtowns.
- **1860–81** Second Maori War over land rights.
- **1882** Refrigeration is introduced; first shipment of lamb to England.

- **1893** Voting rights are extended to women.
- **1914–18** 100,000 New Zealanders join Australia–New Zealand Army Corps to fight in World War I; New Zealand loses more soldiers per capita than any other nation.
- **1939** New Zealand enters World War II.

- **1947** Statute of Westminster is adopted by government; New Zealand gains full independence from Britain.
- **1951** New Zealand ratifies Australia–New Zealand–United States (ANZUS) mutual security pact.
- **1960s** New Zealand begins monitoring radioactivity in region as France accelerates

continues

With the help of a young Tahitian chief, Tupea, who had sailed with the crew as a guide and interpreter, Cook tried to make contact with the Maori, but to no avail. They remained hostile and would not accept Cook's gifts, nor let him take food and water to his men.

Disappointed, Cook claimed the country for King George, and named the bay Poverty Bay because, as he noted in his journal, "it afforded us not one thing we wanted." Sailing north, he rounded the tip of the North Island and went on to circumnavigate both islands. During the next 6 months, he accurately charted the country, and missed only the entrance to Milford Sound (which is virtually invisible from the open sea) and the fact that Stewart Island was not part of the mainland.

THE BRITISH ARRIVE Sealers began arriving in 1792 and essentially stripped the South Island waters of its seal colonies. Whalers, too, discovered rich hunting grounds in New Zealand waters. Oil vats soon dotted the Bay of Islands, which provided safe harbor.

Traders and merchants, attracted by the wealth of flax, the abundance of trees for shipbuilding, and the lucrative trading of muskets and other European goods with the Maori, were little better than the sealers and whalers in respecting the country's natural resources. Great forests were felled and luxuriant bushlands disappeared as land was cleared.

The immigration of Europeans, mostly from Great Britain, had a devastating impact on Maori culture. Most destructive was the introduction of liquor, muskets, and diseases against which the Maori had no immunity. Muskets intensified the fierce intertribal warfare, eventually becoming so common that no one tribe had superiority in terms of firepower. By 1830, Maori chiefs began to realize the weapon was destroying all their tribes.

Missionaries also began to come during this period. They were responsible for putting the Maori language in writing (largely for the purpose of translating and printing the Bible), establishing mission schools, and upgrading agricultural methods through the use of plows and windmills.

Lawlessness grew along with the number of British immigrants, and harm was inflicted on both Maori and the new settlers. The missionaries complained to the British government, which was by no means eager to recognize faraway New Zealand as a full-fledged colony, having already experienced problems with America and Canada. As an alternative, the Crown placed New Zealand under the jurisdiction of New South Wales in 1833, and dispatched James Busby as "British Resident" with full responsibilities to enforce law and order. Unfortunately, he was completely ineffective.

THE TREATY OF WAITANGI   Back in Britain, the newly formed New Zealand Company began sending ships to buy land from the Maori and establish permanent settlements. Their questionable methods caused increasing alarm in London. Between 1839 and 1843, the New Zealand Company sent out 57 ships carrying 19,000 settlers, the nucleus of the permanent British population.

In 1839, Captain William Hobson was sent by the government to sort out the concerns. By catering to the Maori sense of ceremony, he arranged an assembly of chiefs at the Busby residence in the Bay of Islands. There, on February 6, 1840, the Treaty of Waitangi was signed after lengthy debate. The treaty guaranteed Maori "all the rights and privileges of British subjects" in exchange for their acknowledgment of British sovereignty, while granting the Crown exclusive rights to buy land from the Maori. Many of the chiefs did not understand what they had signed. Nevertheless, 45 of them ultimately signed the treaty, and when it was circulated around the country, another 500 signed as well.

Instead of easing tensions, though, the Treaty of Waitangi ushered in one of the bloodiest periods in New Zealand's history. The British were eager to exercise their right to purchase Maori land, and while some chiefs were eager to sell, others were not. As pressures forced them to sell, the Maori revolted, and when Chief Hone Heke (the first to sign the treaty) hacked down the British flagpole at Kororareka (Russell) in 1844, it signaled the beginning of some 20 years of fierce battles. The British finally emerged the victors, but the seizure of that Maori land continues to be the subject of debate today.

3 New Zealand Today

Like any young country, New Zealand is growing rapidly and facing issues associated with progress. Urban drift accounts for 80% of the population living in towns and cities, most of which is north of Lake Taupo, with a full third of the population in the Auckland region alone. City infrastructures, transport systems, and housing developments are struggling in some cases to keep up with the pace.

Biculturalism has been the loudest catchphrase of the past decade. From the late 19th century until after World War II, there was a marked decline in the use of the Maori language because schools insisted that only English be taught.

the visit of Elizabeth II adds to the festivities commemorating the 150th anniversary of the Treaty of Waitangi.

- **1991** Relations between the United States and New Zealand, strained by the 1985 antinuclear ban, begin to thaw.
- **1993** New Zealand celebrates 100 years of female suffrage.

- **1994** The decade of belt-tightening starts to pay off, and New Zealand's economy is declared one of the world's most competitive; South African rugby team tours New Zealand without protest.
- **1995** Team New Zealand wins the America's Cup; Mount Ruapehu erupts for the first time in 8 years; New Zealand's population reaches 3.5 million; economic growth continues.
- **1996** Mount Ruapehu erupts again. Ash clouds disrupt air travel throughout much of the country.
- **1997** Maoris demand return of Crown lands; racial tensions increase. Maori activist damages the America's Cup.

continues

Since the 1960s, however, there has been a growing resurgence of interest in Maori identity, language, and tradition, and many Maori are now bilingual, thanks to extensive language programs in schools.

The Waitangi Tribunal, set up by the New Zealand government in 1987 to settle unresolved issues related to the Treaty of Waitangi, has brought Maori grievances to light. Many claim their ancestors were tricked out of much of their land. Today, much of that land has been returned to Maori ownership, including the Whanganui River in 1999.

The country's economy has traditionally depended on the success of wool, dairy, and meat exports with protected, unlimited access to British markets. This changed when Britain entered the European Common Market in the 1970s. New Zealand was then forced to diversify and do business with many other countries.

By the mid-1980s, meat, wool, and dairy products accounted for just under 50% of our export income.

The mid-1980s also heralded the complete deregulation of the domestic economy. It took a decade of struggle for many industries to come to terms with the changes. (This is the main reason our infamous sheep numbers dropped from 72 million in 1983 to the present low of 44 million.) The stern belt-tightening ultimately bore fruit, however, and by 1993, the economy was flourishing. Today, forestry, horticulture, fishing, tourism, and manufacturing are the leading industries. Tourism is the country's largest single source of foreign exchange. Overall standards and the level of professionalism have improved tenfold in recent years, making New Zealand one of the ripest countries in the world for visitors.

4 Maori Language & Culture

The Maori language is a Polynesian dialect. It was first given a written form in the early 19th century by missionaries and British linguists. In the latter part of the 19th century, Maori were forced to adopt the English language in schools, and it wasn't until the 1960s that a strong Maori resurgence began. The Maori Language Act of 1987 really changed things.

It made Maori an official New Zealand language along with English, and a Maori Language Commission was set up to create authentic Maori names for government departments and major organizations. Today, there are Maori radio stations and television channels, and Maori is taught in all levels of the education system.

- **1998** The first coalition government formed in 1996 between the National Party and New Zealand dissolves, but National maintains the balance of power.
- **1999** New Zealand hosts the first stages of the America's Cup Challenge and makes lavish preparations to celebrate the dawning of the new millennium on January

1, 2000. Parliamentary elections are held.
- **2000** Gisborne, New Zealand, is the first city in the world to see the rising sun of the new millennium. The final challenge of the America's Cup is held in Auckland; New Zealand wins again and the city goes on to host the World Power Boat Championships.

- **2001** The New Zealand Government gives the go-ahead for strictly controlled genetic modification research.
- **2001** Legendary sailor and environmentalist Peter Blake, who led New Zealand to the America's Cup championship in 1995 and 2000, is killed aboard his ship by pirates in the Amazon.

(Tips) **A Word on Cultural Protocol**

If you want to visit a Maori marae, always make sure you ask permission first. You must never eat, chew gum, or take food onto the premises. Some will also request that you take off your shoes, and some may have particular rules about visits by women during certain ceremonies. In short, behavior on the marae is governed by strict protocol. Please do not offend.

When you visit New Zealand, you will be surrounded by things Maori: Words, place names, and many tourist ventures are all indications of this revitalized culture. No one expects you to be able to pronounce many Maori names—it's hard enough for those who have spent all their lives here—but the following tips might make it easier for you. Some Maori words are both singular and plural and require no *s*. *Maori, Pakeha,* and *kea* are all good examples (like the English words deer and fish). There are only 15 letters in the Maori alphabet: A, E, H, I, K, M, N, O, P, R, T, U, W, NG, and WH, and every syllable in Maori ends in a vowel. The vowel sounds are of great importance and when two vowels come together, each is given its proper sound. WH is usually pronounced as an F.

5 A Taste of New Zealand

Surrounded by the azure Pacific, New Zealand floats in a gourmet paradise. Dozens of different fish and shellfish galore are gathered fresh. Rivers and streams yield endless numbers of trout and salmon, and the fields give us prime beef, lamb, venison, and even ostrich. Then there's the wine—but that's covered below in a section of its own.

For a country brought up on traditional English and Scottish fare like Yorkshire pudding, porridge, and scones, we haven't done too badly. Meals are much more adventurous than they used to be, and many young chefs have gone overseas for training. We can also thank an influx of immigrants for the diversification of New Zealand cuisine. Leading restaurants delight in playing with the flavors of Thailand, Japan, China, Vietnam, California, and Mexico. This is where you'll find Pacific Rim cuisine at its best, especially in Auckland.

- **2002** Auckland once again hosts the America's Cup Challenge.
- **2003** Homage is paid to Sir Edmund Hillary on the 50th anniversary of his ascent of Mount Everest.
- **2004** New Zealand film director Peter Jackson wins big at the Oscars for the third film of his trilogy, *The Lord of the Rings: The Return of the King.*
- **2005** New Zealand golfer Michael Campbell wins the U.S. Open Golf Championship.

Maori for Beginners

Here's a list of the most commonly used prefixes and suffixes for place names:

Ao   Cloud
Ika   Fish
Nui   Big, or plenty of
Roto   Lake
Rua   Cave, or hollow, or two (Rotorua's two lakes)
Tahi   One, single
Te   The
Wai   Water
Whanga   Bay, inlet, or stretch of water

These are other frequently used words:
Ariki   Chief or priest
Atua   Supernatural being, such as a god or demon
Haka   Dance (war, funeral, and so on)
Hangi   An oven made by filling a hole with heated stones, and the feast roasted in it
Karakia   Prayer or spell
Kaumatua   Elder
Kereru   Wood pigeon
Kumara   Sweet potato
Mana   Authority, prestige, psychic force
Marae   Courtyard, village common
Mere   War club made of greenstone (jade)
Pa   Stockade or fortified place
Pakeha   Caucasian person; primarily used to refer to those of European descent
Poi   Bulrush ball with string attached, twirled in action song
Tangi   Funeral mourning or lamentation
Taonga   Treasure
Tapu   Under religious or superstitious restriction (taboo)
Tiki   Human image, sometimes carved of greenstone
Whare   House

New Zealanders are among the world's top meat and butter eaters, and are some of the biggest egg and ice-cream eaters, making us, not surprisingly, the top protein consumers in the world. It must be said, though, that the fashionable trend toward European-style cooking, with lots of olive oil, has quickly caught on among the health-conscious. Immigrant cheese makers from Holland, Switzerland, and France produce European-style cheeses with distinctive New Zealand flavors. And you must try that traditional favorite dessert, the pavlova: crusty on the outside, soft on the inside, and oh-so-delicious!

Beer, introduced by Captain Cook, is almost a national pastime for some. In the 1990s, over 40 boutique breweries suddenly sprang to life. However, the country's huge beer consumption has

slowly been dropping as wine drinking increases.

6 Wine, Wine & More Wine

New Zealand wines continue to receive international acclaim. The chief areas are the Greater Auckland region and Waiheke Island, the Bay of Plenty and Gisborne, Martinborough, Marlborough, Nelson, Canterbury, and Otago. Auckland, North Auckland, and Hawkes Bay have the longest tradition of winemaking in New Zealand, but newcomers Martinborough and Marlborough have quickly established international award-winning reputations. The southern regions of Canterbury and Central Otago also have an enviable record for producing top vintages.

The *Cuisine Wine Annual,* by Bob Campbell, is the definitive guide to New Zealand classic wines and vineyards. This magazine is produced by Cuisine Publications Ltd. (© **09/307-0702;** www.cuisine.co.nz). Also check out *Michael Cooper's Buyer's Guide to New Zealand Wines,* which lists more than 1,500 rated wines, and *The Fine Wines of New Zealand,* by Keith Stewart.

To get you started, I've listed a few of New Zealand's top wines guaranteed to bring your taste buds to life. For **chardonnay,** uncork Cloudy Bay (Marlborough), Babich Irongate (Henderson), Neudorf Moutere (Nelson), and Kumeu River (Kumeu). For **sauvignon blanc,** go for Cloudy Bay (Marlborough), Hunter's Oak Aged (Marlborough), Grove Mill Marlborough (Marlborough), and Palliser (Martinborough). For **red wines,** make Atarangi pinot noir (Martinborough) your first choice, followed closely by Stonyridge Larose (Waiheke Island), Gibston Valley pinot noir (Central Otago), Te Mata Coleraine (Hawkes Bay), Brookfields Gold Label cabernet (Hawkes Bay), and, in fact, any pinot noir from Martinborough. If **methode traditionelle** is your thing, pop the cork on just about any of Daniel Le Brun's bottles in Marlborough, or Deutz Marlborough Cuvee or Pelorus Vintage (Marlborough). Botrytised **sweet wines** don't get much better than Villa Maria's Reserve Noble Riesling from Auckland.

Appendix B:
A Glossary of Useful Terms

Who would have thought the English language could be so confusing? New Zealand may seem like an easy place to negotiate, but it has developed some very distinctive language characteristics. Here's a guide to help you negotiate everyday colloquialisms.

1 Kiwi/Yankee Terms

Air-conditioning   Refers to both heating and cooling the air

All Blacks   New Zealand rugby team

Bach   North Island term for vacation house (plural: baches)

Bath   Bathtub

Bathroom   Where one bathes; bath

Biro   Ballpoint pen

Biscuits/bickies   Cookies

Bludge   Borrow

Bonnet   Hood of car

Boot   Trunk of car

Bush   Forest

Chemist shop   Drugstore

Chilly bin   Styrofoam cooler (U.S.), esky (Aus.)

Coach   Long-distance bus

Cocky   Farmer

College   High school

Cot   Crib (place where a baby or toddler sleeps)

Crib   South Island term for holiday house

Cuppa   Cup of tea

Cyclone   Hurricane

Dairy   Convenience store

Dinner   The main meal of the day; can be the meal eaten in the middle of the day

Doona   Comforter, quilt

En suite   In-room bathroom

Entree   Smallish first course, appetizer

Fanny   Female genitalia; you'll shock Kiwis if you call the thing you wear around your waist a "fanny pack"

Footpath   Sidewalk

Gallops   Thoroughbred horse racing

Get stuck in Get started

Grizzle Complain

Grog Booze

Gumboots Waterproof rubber boots (U.S.), wellingtons (Britain)

Hire Rent

Homely Homey

Hooker Front-row rugby player

Hotties Hot-water bottles

Housie Bingo

Jandals Thongs (Aus.), flip-flops (U.S./Britain)

Jersey Pullover sweater (U.S.), jumper (Aus.)

Judder bars Speed bumps (U.S.), sleeping policeman (Britain)

Jug Electric kettle or a pitcher

Kiwi Person from New Zealand; native bird of New Zealand

Knickers Underwear, undies

Knock up Wake up

LSZ Low-speed zone

Lift Elevator

Loo Toilet

Lounge Living room

Main course Entree

Mate Friend

Mossie Mosquito

Nappy Diaper

Pakeha Anyone of European descent

Private facilities Private bathroom

Pushchair Baby stroller

Queue Line, to wait in line

Rates Property taxes

Return ticket Round-trip ticket

Rug Blanket

Serviette Napkin

Shout Treat someone (usually refers to a meal or a drink), buy a round

Single bed Twin bed

Singlet Sleeveless undershirt

Sister Nurse

Smoko Morning or afternoon break

Strides Trousers

Ta Thank you

Tea Beverage; also a light evening meal, supper; see also "Dinner," above

To call   To visit
To ring   To phone
Togs   Swimsuit (U.S.), cozzie (Aus.)
Track   Trail
Trots   Harness racing
Uplift   Pick up
Varsity   University, college
Wop wops   Remote location, boondocks
Yank   American

2 Menu Terms

Afghans   Popular Kiwi cookies made with cornflakes and cocoa
ANZAC biscuits   Cookies named for the Australia New Zealand Army Corps; they contain rolled oats and golden syrup
Bangers   Sausages
Beetroot   Beets
Biscuits   Cookies
Blue vein   Bleu cheese
Capsicum   Green or red bell pepper
Chips   French-fried potatoes
Chook   Chicken
Courgette   Zucchini
Devonshire tea   Morning or afternoon tea, plus scones with cream and jam
Entree   Appetizer
Grilled   Broiled
Hogget   Year-old lamb
Jelly   Gelatin dessert
Kumara   Kiwi sweet potato
Lemonade   7-Up
Lollies   Candy
Main course   Entree
Milk shake   Flavored milk
Meat pie   A two-crust pie filled with stewed, cubed, or ground meat (usually beef) and gravy
Milo   A hot drink similar to Ovaltine
Pavlova   Popular meringue dessert named after prima ballerina Anna Pavlova, served with whipped cream and fruit
Pikelets   Small pancakes served at teatime
Pipis   Clams
Pudding   Dessert in general, not necessarily pudding

Roast dinner   Roast beef or leg of lamb served with potatoes and other vegetables that have been cooked with the meat

Rock melon   Cantaloupe

Saveloy   A type of wiener

Scone   A biscuit served at teatime

Silverbeet   Swiss chard

Silverside   A superior cut of corned beef

Takeaway   Takeout

Tamarillos   Tree tomatoes

Tea   The national beverage; also, colloquially, dinner

Thick shake   Milkshake

Tomato sauce   Ketchup

Water biscuit   Cracker

Weetbix   A breakfast cereal similar to shredded wheat

Whitebait   Very tiny fish, served whole without being cleaned

White tea   Tea with milk

Index

FROMMER'S® COMPLETE TRAVEL GUIDES

Alaska
Amalfi Coast
American Southwest
Amsterdam
Argentina & Chile
Arizona
Atlanta
Australia
Austria
Bahamas
Barcelona
Beijing
Belgium, Holland & Luxembourg
Belize
Bermuda
Boston
Brazil
British Columbia & the Canadian Rockies
Brussels & Bruges
Budapest & the Best of Hungary
Buenos Aires
Calgary
California
Canada
Cancún, Cozumel & the Yucatán
Cape Cod, Nantucket & Martha's Vineyard
Caribbean
Caribbean Ports of Call
Carolinas & Georgia
Chicago
China
Colorado
Costa Rica
Croatia
Cuba
Denmark
Denver, Boulder & Colorado Springs
Edinburgh & Glasgow
England
Europe
Europe by Rail

Florence, Tuscany & Umbria
Florida
France
Germany
Greece
Greek Islands
Hawaii
Hong Kong
Honolulu, Waikiki & Oahu
India
Ireland
Italy
Jamaica
Japan
Kauai
Las Vegas
London
Los Angeles
Los Cabos & Baja
Madrid
Maine Coast
Maryland & Delaware
Maui
Mexico
Montana & Wyoming
Montréal & Québec City
Moscow & St. Petersburg
Munich & the Bavarian Alps
Nashville & Memphis
New England
Newfoundland & Labrador
New Mexico
New Orleans
New York City
New York State
New Zealand
Northern Italy
Norway
Nova Scotia, New Brunswick & Prince Edward Island
Oregon
Paris
Peru

Philadelphia & the Amish Country
Portugal
Prague & the Best of the Czech Republic
Provence & the Riviera
Puerto Rico
Rome
San Antonio & Austin
San Diego
San Francisco
Santa Fe, Taos & Albuquerque
Scandinavia
Scotland
Seattle
Seville, Granada & the Best of Andalusia
Shanghai
Sicily
Singapore & Malaysia
South Africa
South America
South Florida
South Pacific
Southeast Asia
Spain
Sweden
Switzerland
Texas
Thailand
Tokyo
Toronto
Turkey
USA
Utah
Vancouver & Victoria
Vermont, New Hampshire & Maine
Vienna & the Danube Valley
Vietnam
Virgin Islands
Virginia
Walt Disney World® & Orlando
Washington, D.C.
Washington State

FROMMER'S® DOLLAR-A-DAY GUIDES

Australia from $60 a Day
California from $70 a Day
England from $75 a Day
Europe from $85 a Day
Florida from $70 a Day

Hawaii from $80 a Day
Ireland from $90 a Day
Italy from $90 a Day
London from $95 a Day

New York City from $90 a Day
Paris from $95 a Day
San Francisco from $70 a Day
Washington, D.C. from $80 a Day

FROMMER'S® PORTABLE GUIDES

Acapulco, Ixtapa & Zihuatanejo
Amsterdam
Aruba
Australia's Great Barrier Reef
Bahamas
Berlin
Big Island of Hawaii
Boston
California Wine Country
Cancún
Cayman Islands
Charleston
Chicago

Disneyland®
Dominican Republic
Dublin
Florence
Las Vegas
Las Vegas for Non-Gamblers
London
Los Angeles
Maui
Nantucket & Martha's Vineyard
New Orleans
New York City
Paris

Portland
Puerto Rico
Puerto Vallarta, Manzanillo & Guadalajara
Rio de Janeiro
San Diego
San Francisco
Savannah
Vancouver
Venice
Virgin Islands
Washington, D.C.
Whistler

FROMMER'S® CRUISE GUIDES

Alaska Cruises & Ports of Call

Cruises & Ports of Call

European Cruises & Ports of Call

FROMMER'S® DAY BY DAY GUIDES

Amsterdam
Chicago
Florence & Tuscany

London
New York City
Paris

Rome
San Francisco
Venice

FROMMER'S® NATIONAL PARK GUIDES

Algonquin Provincial Park
Banff & Jasper
Grand Canyon

National Parks of the American West
Rocky Mountain
Yellowstone & Grand Teton

Yosemite and Sequoia & Kings
 Canyon
Zion & Bryce Canyon

FROMMER'S® MEMORABLE WALKS

Chicago
London

New York
Paris

Rome
San Francisco

FROMMER'S® WITH KIDS GUIDES

Chicago
Hawaii
Las Vegas
London

National Parks
New York City
San Francisco

Toronto
Walt Disney World® & Orlando
Washington, D.C.

SUZY GERSHMAN'S BORN TO SHOP GUIDES

Born to Shop: France
Born to Shop: Hong Kong, Shanghai
 & Beijing

Born to Shop: Italy
Born to Shop: London

Born to Shop: New York
Born to Shop: Paris

FROMMER'S® IRREVERENT GUIDES

Amsterdam
Boston
Chicago
Las Vegas
London

Los Angeles
Manhattan
New Orleans
Paris

Rome
San Francisco
Walt Disney World®
Washington, D.C.

FROMMER'S® BEST-LOVED DRIVING TOURS

Austria
Britain
California
France

Germany
Ireland
Italy
New England

Northern Italy
Scotland
Spain
Tuscany & Umbria

THE UNOFFICIAL GUIDES®

Adventure Travel in Alaska
Beyond Disney
California with Kids
Central Italy
Chicago
Cruises
Disneyland®
England
Florida
Florida with Kids

Hawaii
Ireland
Las Vegas
London
Maui
Mexico's Best Beach Resorts
Mini Las Vegas
Mini Mickey
New Orleans
New York City

Paris
San Francisco
South Florida including Miami &
 the Keys
Walt Disney World®
Walt Disney World® for
 Grown-ups
Walt Disney World® with Kids
Washington, D.C.

SPECIAL-INTEREST TITLES

Athens Past & Present
Cities Ranked & Rated
Frommer's Best Day Trips from London
Frommer's Best RV & Tent Campgrounds
 in the U.S.A.

Frommer's Exploring America by RV
Frommer's NYC Free & Dirt Cheap
Frommer's Road Atlas Europe
Frommer's Road Atlas Ireland
Retirement Places Rated

FROMMER'S® PHRASEFINDER DICTIONARY GUIDES

French

Italian

Spanish

THE NEW TRAVELOCITY GUARANTEE

EVERYTHING YOU BOOK WILL BE RIGHT, OR WE'LL WORK WITH OUR TRAVEL PARTNERS TO MAKE IT RIGHT, RIGHT AWAY.

To drive home the point,
we're going to use the word "right" in every single sentence.

Let's get right to it. Right to the meat! Only Travelocity guarantees everything about your booking will be right, or we'll work with our travel partners to make it right, right away. Right on!

Here's a picture taken smack dab right in the middle of Antigua, where the guarantee also covers you.

The guarantee covers all but one of the items pictured to the right.

For example, what if the ocean view you booked actually looks out at a downright ugly parking lot? You'd be right to call – we're there for you. And no one in their right mind would be pleased to learn the rental car place has closed and left them stranded. Call Travelocity and we'll help get you back on the right track.

Now, you may be thinking, "Yeah, right, I'm so sure." That's OK; you have the right to remain skeptical. That is until we mention help is always right around the corner. Call us right off the bat, knowing that our customer service reps are there for you 24/7. Righting wrongs. Left and right.

Now if you're guessing there are some things we can't control, like the weather, well you're right. But we can help you with most things – to get all the details in righting,* visit **travelocity.com/guarantee**.

*Sorry, spelling things right is one of the few things not covered under the guarantee.

I'd give my right arm for a guarantee like this, although I'm glad I don't have to.

IF YOU BOOK IT, IT SHOULD BE THERE.

Only Travelocity guarantees it will be, or we'll work with our travel partners to make it right, right away. So if you're missing a balcony or anything else you booked, just call us 24/7. **1-888-TRAVELOCITY.**

travelocity
You'll never roam alone